Nineteenth-Century
Literature Criticism

Guide to Gale Literary Criticism Series

When you need to review criticism of literary works, these are the Gale series to use:

If the author's death date is: **You should turn to:**

After Dec. 31, 1959
(or author is still living)

CONTEMPORARY LITERARY CRITICISM

for example: Jorge Luis Borges, Anthony Burgess,
             William Faulkner, Mary Gordon,
             Ernest Hemingway, Iris Murdoch

1900 through 1959

TWENTIETH-CENTURY LITERARY CRITICISM

for example: Willa Cather, F. Scott Fitzgerald,
             Henry James, Mark Twain, Virginia Woolf

1800 through 1899

NINETEENTH-CENTURY LITERATURE CRITICISM

for example: Fedor Dostoevski, George Sand,
             Gerard Manley Hopkins, Emily Dickinson

1400 through 1799

LITERATURE CRITICISM FROM 1400 TO 1800
(excluding Shakespeare)

for example: Anne Bradstreet, Pierre Corneille,
             Daniel Defoe, Alexander Pope,
             Jonathan Swift, Phillis Wheatley

SHAKESPEAREAN CRITICISM

             Shakespeare's plays and poetry

Antiquity through 1399

CLASSICAL AND MEDIEVAL LITERATURE CRITICISM

for example: Dante, Plato, Homer, Sophocles, Vergil,
             the Beowulf poet

(Volume 1 forthcoming)

Gale also publishes related criticism series:

CHILDREN'S LITERATURE REVIEW

         This ongoing series covers authors of all eras.
         Presents criticism on authors and author/illustrators
         who write for the preschool to junior-high audience.

CONTEMPORARY ISSUES CRITICISM

         This two volume set presents criticism on
         contemporary authors writing on current issues.
         Topics covered include the social sciences,
         philosophy, economics, natural science, law, and
         related areas.

ISSN 0732-1864

Volume 11

Nineteenth-Century Literature Criticism

Excerpts from Criticism of the
Works of Novelists, Poets, Playwrights,
Short Story Writers, Philosophers, and Other
Creative Writers Who Died between 1800
and 1900, from the First Published Critical
Appraisals to Current Evaluations

Laurie Lanzen Harris
Cherie D. Abbey
Editors

Jelena Obradovic Kronick
Janet Mullane
Associate Editors

Gale Research Company
Book Tower
Detroit, Michigan 48226

STAFF

Laurie Lanzen Harris, Cherie D. Abbey, *Editors*

Jelena Obradovic Kronick, Janet Mullane, *Associate Editors*

Patricia Askie Mackmiller, Gail Ann Schulte, *Senior Assistant Editors*

Jeanne M. Lesinski, Robert Thomas Wilson, *Assistant Editors*

James E. Person, Jr., Mark W. Scott, Emily B. Tennyson,
Anna C. Wallbillich, *Contributing Editors*

Lizbeth A. Purdy, *Production Supervisor*
Denise Michlewicz Broderick, *Production Coordinator*
Eric Berger, *Assistant Production Coordinator*
Robin Du Blanc, Sheila J. Nasea, *Editorial Assistants*

Victoria B. Cariappa, *Research Coordinator*
Jeannine Schiffman Davidson, *Assistant Research Coordinator*
Vincenza G. DiNoto, Daniel Kurt Gilbert, Grace E. Gillis,
Maureen R. Richards, Keith E. Schooley, Filomena Sgambati,
Valerie J. Webster, Mary D. Wise, *Research Assistants*

Linda Marcella Pugliese, *Manuscript Coordinator*
Donna Craft, *Assistant Manuscript Coordinator*
Maureen A. Puhl, Rosetta Irene Simms, *Manuscript Assistants*

Jeanne A. Gough, *Permissions Supervisor*
Janice M. Mach, *Permissions Coordinator, Text*
Patricia A. Seefelt, *Permissions Coordinator, Illustrations*
Susan D. Battista, *Assistant Permissions Coordinator*
Margaret A. Chamberlain, Sandra C. Davis, Mary M. Matuz, *Senior Permissions Assistants*
Colleen M. Crane, Kathy Grell, Josephine M. Keene,
Mabel C. Schoening, *Permissions Assistants*
Margaret A. Carson, H. Diane Cooper, Dorothy J. Fowler, Anita Williams, *Permissions Clerks*
Margaret Mary Missar, *Photo Research*

Frederick G. Ruffner, *Publisher*
Dedria Bryfonski, *Editorial Director*
Christine Nasso, *Director, Literature Division*
Laurie Lanzen Harris, *Senior Editor, Literary Criticism Series*
Dennis Poupard, *Managing Editor, Literary Criticism Series*

Library of Congress Catalog Card Number 81-6943
ISBN 0-8103-5811-5
ISSN 0732-1864

Computerized photocomposition by
Typographics, Incorporated
Kansas City, Missouri

Printed in the United States

Contents

Preface

The nineteenth century was a time of tremendous growth in human endeavor: in science, in social history, and particularly in literature. The era saw the development of the novel, witnessed radical changes from classicism to romanticism to realism, and contained intellectual and artistic ideas that continue to inspire authors of our own century. The importance of the writers of the nineteenth century is twofold, for they provide insight into their own time as well as into the universal nature of human experience.

The literary criticism of an era can also give us insight into the moral and intellectual atmosphere of the past, because the criteria by which a work of art is judged reflect current philosophical and social attitudes. Literary criticism takes many forms: the traditional essay, the book or play review, even the parodic poem. Criticism can also be of several types: normative, descriptive, interpretive, textual, appreciative, generic. Collectively, the range of critical response helps us to understand a work of art, an author, an era.

The Scope of the Work

The success of two of Gale's current literary series, *Contemporary Literary Criticism (CLC)* and *Twentieth-Century Literary Criticism (TCLC),* which excerpt criticism of creative writing from the twentieth century, suggested an equivalent need among students and teachers of literature of the nineteenth century. Moreover, since the analysis of this literature spans almost two hundred years, a vast amount of critical material confronts the student.

Nineteenth-Century Literature Criticism (NCLC) presents significant passages from published criticism on authors who died between 1800 and 1900. The author list for each volume of *NCLC* is carefully compiled to represent a variety of genres and nationalities and to cover authors who are currently regarded as the most important writers of their era as well as those whose contribution to literature and literary history is significant. The truly great writers are rare, and in the intervals between them lesser but genuine artists, as well as writers who enjoyed immense popularity in their own time and in their own countries, are important to the study of nineteenth-century literature. The length of each author entry is intended to reflect the amount of attention the author has received from critics writing in English and from foreign critics in translation. Articles and books that have not been translated into English are excluded. However, since many of the major foreign studies have been translated into English and are excerpted in *NCLC,* author entries reflect the viewpoints of many nationalities. Each author entry represents a historical overview of critical reaction to the author's work: early criticism is presented to indicate initial responses and later selections represent any rise or decline in the author's literary reputation. We have also attempted to identify and include excerpts from the seminal essays on each author as well as modern perspectives. Thus, *NCLC* is designed to serve as an introduction for the student of nineteenth-century literature to the authors of that period and to the most significant commentators on these authors.

NCLC entries are intended to be definitive overviews. In order to devote more attention to each writer, approximately fifteen authors are included in each 600-page volume compared with about fifty authors in a *CLC* volume of similar size. Because of the great quantity of critical material available on many authors, and because of the resurgence of criticism generated by such events as an author's centennial or anniversary celebration, the republication of an author's works, or publication of a newly translated work or volume of letters, an author may appear more than once. In addition, *NCLC* now includes author entries on the important political, social, and economic philosophers of the nineteenth century. Recent volumes include entries on Alexis de Tocqueville, John Stuart Mill, and Thomas Jefferson—writers who are important to the study of the nineteenth century and who are frequently discussed in literature, philosophy, and history courses.

The Organization of the Book

An author section consists of the following elements: author heading, biographical and critical introduction, principal works, excerpts of criticism (each preceded by explanatory notes and followed by a bibliographical citation), and an additional bibliography.

- The *author heading* consists of the author's full name, followed by birth and death dates. The unbracketed portion of the name denotes the form under which the author most commonly wrote. If an author wrote consistently under a pseudonym, the pseudonym will be listed in the author heading and the real name given in parentheses on the first line of the biographical and critical introduction. Also located at the beginning of the introduction are any name variations under which an author wrote, including transliterated forms for authors whose languages use nonroman alphabets. Uncertainty as to a birth or death date is indicated by a question mark.

- A *portrait* of the author is included when available. Many entries also feature illustrations of materials pertinent to an author's career, including manuscript pages, letters, book illustrations, and representations of important people, places, and events in an author's life.

- The *biographical and critical introduction* contains background information that elucidates the author's creative output. When applicable, biographical and critical introductions are followed by references to additional entries on the author in past volumes of *NCLC* and in other literary reference series published by Gale Research Company. These include *Dictionary of Literary Biography, Children's Literature Review,* and *Something about the Author.*

- The list of *principal works* is chronological by date of first book publication and identifies genres. In those instances where the first publication was in other than the English language, the title and date of the first English-language edition are given in brackets. Unless otherwise indicated, dramas are dated by the first performance, rather than first publication.

- *Criticism* is arranged chronologically in each author section to provide a perspective on any changes in critical evaluation over the years. In the text of each author entry, titles by the author are printed in boldface type. This allows the reader to ascertain without difficulty the works being discussed. For purposes of easier identification, the critic's name and the publication date of the essay are given at the beginning of each piece of criticism. Unsigned criticism is preceded by the title of the journal in which it appeared. For an anonymous essay later attributed to a critic, the critic's name appears in brackets at the beginning of the excerpt and in the bibliographical citation.

- Essays are prefaced with *explanatory notes* as an additional aid to students using *NCLC.* The explanatory notes provide several types of useful information, including the reputation of the critic, the importance of a work of criticism, a synopsis of the essay, the specific approach of the critic (biographical, psychoanalytic, structuralist, etc.), and the growth of critical controversy or changes in critical trends regarding an author's work. In many cases, these notes include cross-references to related criticism in the author's entry or in the additional bibliography. Dates in parentheses within the explanatory notes refer to other essays in the author entry.

- A complete *bibliographical citation* designed to facilitate the location of the original essay or book follows each piece of criticism. An asterisk (*) at the end of the citation indicates that the essay is on more than one author.

- The *additional bibliography* appearing at the end of each author entry suggests further reading on the author. In some cases it includes essays for which the editors could not obtain reprint rights. An asterisk (*) at the end of a citation indicates that the essay is on more than one author.

An appendix lists the sources from which material in the volume is reprinted. It does not, however, list every book or periodical consulted for the volume.

Cumulative Indexes

Each volume of *NCLC* includes a cumulative index listing all the authors who have appeared in *Contemporary Literary Criticism, Twentieth-Century Literary Criticism, Nineteenth-Century Literature Criticism,* and *Literature Criticism from 1400 to 1800,* along with cross-references to the Gale series *Children's Literature Review, Authors in the News, Contemporary Authors, Contemporary Authors Autobiography Series, Dictionary of Literary Biography, Something about the Author,* and *Yesterday's Authors of Books for Children.* Users will welcome this cumulated author index as a useful tool for locating an author within the various series. The index, which lists birth and death dates when available, will be particularly valuable for those authors who are identified with a certain period but whose death date causes them to be placed in another, or for those authors whose careers span two periods. For example, Fedor Dostoevski is found in *NCLC,* yet Leo Tolstoy, another major nineteenth-century Russian novelist, is found in *TCLC.*

NCLC also includes a cumulative nationality index to authors. Authors are listed alphabetically by nationality, followed by the volume numbers in which they appear.

A cumulative index to critics is another useful feature of *NCLC*. Under each critic's name are listed the authors on whom the critic has written and the volume and page where the criticism appears.

Acknowledgments

No work of this scope can be accomplished without the cooperation of many people. The editors especially wish to thank the copyright holders of the excerpts included in this volume, the permissions managers of the book and magazine publishing companies for assisting us in securing reprint rights, and the staffs of the Detroit Public Library, University of Michigan Library, and Wayne State University Library for making their resources available to us. We are also grateful to Anthony J. Bogucki for his assistance with copyright research.

Suggestions Are Welcome

The editors welcome the comments and suggestions of readers to expand the coverage and enhance the usefulness of the series.

Authors to Appear in Future Volumes

About, Edmond Francois 1828-1885
Aguilo I. Fuster, Maria 1825-1897
Ainsworth, William Harrison 1805-1882
Aksakov, Konstantin 1817-1860
Aleardi, Aleadro 1812-1878
Alecsandri, Vasile 1821-1890
Alencar, Jose 1829-1877
Alfieri, Vittorio 1749-1803
Allingham, William 1824-1889
Almquist, Carl Jonas Love 1793-1866
Alorne, Leonor de Almeida 1750-1839
Alsop, Richard 1761-1815
Altimirano, Ignacio Manuel 1834-1893
Alvarenga, Manuel Inacio da Silva
  1749-1814
Alvares de Azevedo, Manuel Antonio
  1831-1852
Anzengruber, Ludwig 1839-1889
Arany, Janos 1817-1882
Arene, Paul 1843-1893
Aribau, Bonaventura Carlos 1798-1862
Arjona de Cubas, Manuel Maria de
  1771-1820
Arnault, Antoine Vincent 1766-1834
Arneth, Alfred von 1819-1897
Arnim, Bettina von 1785-1859
Arnold, Thomas 1795-1842
Arriaza y Superviela, Juan Bautista
  1770-1837
Asbjornsen, Peter Christian 1812-1885
Ascasubi, Hilario 1807-1875
Atterbom, Per Daniel Amadeus
  1790-1855
Aubanel, Theodore 1829-1886
Auerbach, Berthold 1812-1882
Augier, Guillaume V.E. 1820-1889
Azeglio, Massimo D' 1798-1866
Azevedo, Guilherme de 1839-1882
Bakin (pseud. of Takizawa Okikani)
  1767-1848
Bakunin, Mikhail Aleksandrovich
  1814-1876
Baratynski, Jewgenij Abramovich
  1800-1844
Barnes, William 1801-1886
Batyushkov, Konstantin 1778-1855
Beattie, James 1735-1803
Beckford, William 1760-1844
Becquer, Gustavo Adolfo 1836-1870
Bentham, Jeremy 1748-1832
Beranger, Jean-Pierre de 1780-1857
Berchet, Ciovanni 1783-1851
Berzsenyi, Daniel 1776-1836
Black, William 1841-1898
Blair, Hugh 1718-1800
Blake, William 1757-1827
Blicher, Steen Steensen 1782-1848

Bocage, Manuel Maria Barbosa du
  1765-1805
Boratynsky, Yevgeny 1800-1844
Borel, Petrus 1809-1859
Boreman, Yokutiel 1825-1890
Borne, Ludwig 1786-1837
Botev, Hristo 1778-1842
Brinckman, John 1814-1870
Bronte, Emily 1812-1848
Brown, Charles Brockden 1777-1810
Browning, Robert 1812-1889
Buchner, Georg 1813-1837
Burney, Fanny 1752-1840
Campbell, James Edwin 1867-1895
Campbell, Thomas 1777-1844
Carlyle, Thomas 1795-1881
Castelo Branco, Camilo 1825-1890
Castro Alves, Antonio de 1847-1871
Channing, William Ellery 1780-1842
Chatterje, Bankin Chanda 1838-1894
Chivers, Thomas Holly 1807?-1858
Claudius, Matthais 1740-1815
Clough, Arthur Hugh 1819-1861
Cobbett, William 1762-1835
Colenso, John William 1814-1883
Coleridge, Hartley 1796-1849
Collett, Camilla 1813-1895
Comte, Auguste 1798-1857
Conrad, Robert T. 1810-1858
Conscience, Hendrik 1812-1883
Cooke, Philip Pendleton 1816-1850
Corbiere, Edouard 1845-1875
Crabbe, George 1754-1832
Crawford, Isabella Valancy 1850-1886
Cruz E Sousa, Joao da 1861-1898
Desbordes-Valmore, Marceline
  1786-1859
Deschamps, Emile 1791-1871
Deus, Joao de 1830-1896
Dickinson, Emily 1830-1886
Dinis, Julio 1839-1871
Dinsmoor, Robert 1757-1836
Du Maurier, George 1834-1896
Dwight, Timothy 1752-1817
Echeverria, Esteban 1805-1851
Eminescy, Mihai 1850-1889
Engels, Friedrich 1820-1895
Espronceda, Jose 1808-1842
Ettinger, Solomon 1799-1855
Fuchel, Issac 1756-1804
Ferguson, Samuel 1810-1886
Fernandez de Lizardi, Jose Joaquin
  1776-1827
Fernandez de Moratin, Leandro
  1760-1828
Fet, Afanasy 1820-1892
Feuillet, Octave 1821-1890

Fontane, Theodor 1819-1898
Freiligrath, Hermann Ferdinand
  1810-1876
Freytag, Gustav 1816-1895
Gaboriau, Emile 1835-1873
Ganivet, Angel 1865-1898
Garrett, Almeida 1799-1854
Garshin, Vsevolod Mikhaylovich
  1855-1888
Gezelle, Guido 1830-1899
Ghalib, Asadullah Khan 1797-1869
Godwin, William 1756-1836
Goldschmidt, Meir Aron 1819-1887
Goncalves Dias, Antonio 1823-1864
Griboyedov, Aleksander Sergeyevich
  1795-1829
Grigor'yev, Appolon Aleksandrovich
  1822-1864
Groth, Klaus 1819-1899
Grun, Anastasius (pseud. of Anton
  Alexander Graf von Auersperg)
  1806-1876
Guerrazzi, Francesco Domenico
  1804-1873
Gutierrez Najera, Manuel 1859-1895
Gutzkow, Karl Ferdinand 1811-1878
Ha-Kohen, Shalom 1772-1845
Halleck, Fitz-Greene 1790-1867
Harris, George Washington 1814-1869
Hayne, Paul Hamilton 1830-1886
Hazlitt, William 1778-1830
Hebbel, Christian Friedrich 1813-1863
Hebel, Johann Peter 1760-1826
Hegel, Georg Wilhelm Friedrich
  1770-1831
Heiberg, Johann Ludvig 1813-1863
Herculano, Alexandre 1810-1866
Hernandez, Jose 1834-1886
Hertz, Henrik 1798-1870
Herwegh, Georg 1817-1875
Hoffman, Charles Fenno 1806-1884
Holderlin, Friedrich 1770-1843
Holmes, Oliver Wendell 1809-1894
Hood, Thomas 1799-1845
Hooper, Johnson Jones 1815-1863
Hopkins, Gerard Manley 1844-1889
Horton, George Moses 1798-1880
Howitt, William 1792-1879
Hughes, Thomas 1822-1896
Imlay, Gilbert 1754?-1828?
Irwin, Thomas Caulfield 1823-1892
Issacs, Jorge 1837-1895
Jacobsen, Jens Peter 1847-1885
Jippensha, Ikku 1765-1831
Kant, Immanuel 1724-1804
Karr, Jean Baptiste Alphonse 1808-1890
Keble, John 1792-1866

Khomyakov, Alexey S. 1804-1860
Kierkegaard, Soren 1813-1855
Kinglake, Alexander W. 1809-1891
Kingsley, Charles 1819-1875
Kivi, Alexis 1834-1872
Koltsov, Alexey Vasilyevich 1809-1842
Kotzebue, August von 1761-1819
Kraszewski, Josef Ignacy 1812-1887
Kreutzwald, Friedrich Reinhold
　1803-1882
Krochmal, Nahman 1785-1840
Krudener, Valeria Barbara Julia de
　Wietinghoff 1766-1824
Lampman, Archibald 1861-1899
Landon, Letitia Elizabeth 1802-1838
Landor, Walter Savage 1775-1864
Larra y Sanchez de Castro, Mariano
　1809-1837
Lautreamont (pseud. of Isidore Ducasse)
　1846-1870
Lebensohn, Micah Joseph 1828-1852
Leconte de Lisle, Charles-Marie-Rene
　1818-1894
Lenau, Nikolaus 1802-1850
Leontyev, Konstantin 1831-1891
Leopardi, Giacoma 1798-1837
Leskov, Nikolai 1831-1895
Lever, Charles James 1806-1872
Levisohn, Solomon 1789-1822
Lewes, George Henry 1817-1878
Leyden, John 1775-1811
Lobensohn, Micah Gregory 1775-1810
Longstreet, Augustus Baldwin 1790-1870
Lopez de Ayola y Herrera, Adelardo
　1819-1871
Lover, Samuel 1797-1868
Luzzato, Samuel David 1800-1865
Macedo, Joaquim Manuel de 1820-1882
Macha, Karel Hynek 1810-1836
Mackenzie, Henry 1745-1831
Malmon, Solomon 1754-1800
Mangan, James Clarence 1803-1849
Manzoni, Alessandro 1785-1873
Mapu, Abraham 1808-1868
Marii, Jose 1853-1895
Markovic, Svetozar 1846-1875
Martinez de La Rosa, Francisco
　1787-1862
Mathews, Cornelius 1817-1889
McCulloch, Thomas 1776-1843
Merriman, Brian 1747-1805
Meyer, Conrad Ferdinand 1825-1898
Montgomery, James 1771-1854
Moodie, Susanna 1803-1885
Morton, Sarah Wentworth 1759-1846

Muller, Friedrich 1749-1825
Murger, Henri 1822-1861
Neruda, Jan 1834-1891
Nestroy, Johann 1801-1862
Newman, John Henry 1801-1890
Niccolini, Giambattista 1782-1861
Nievo, Ippolito 1831-1861
Nodier, Charles 1780-1844
Novalis (pseud. of Friedrich von
　Hardenberg) 1772-1801
Obradovic, Dositej 1742-1811
Oehlenschlager, Adam 1779-1850
O'Neddy, Philothee (pseud. of
　Theophile Dondey) 1811-1875
O'Shaughnessy, Arthur William
　Edgar 1844-1881
Ostrovsky, Alexander 1823-1886
Paine, Thomas 1737-1809
Parkman, Francis 1823-1893
Peacock, Thomas Love 1785-1866
Perk, Jacques 1859-1881
Pisemsky, Alexey F. 1820-1881
Pompeia, Raul D'Avila 1863-1895
Popovic, Jovan Sterija 1806-1856
Praed, Winthrop Mackworth 1802-1839
Prati, Giovanni 1814-1884
Preseren, France 1800-1849
Pringle, Thomas 1789-1834
Procter, Adelaide Ann 1825-1864
Procter, Bryan Waller 1787-1874
Pye, Henry James 1745-1813
Quental, Antero Tarquinio de 1842-1891
Quinet, Edgar 1803-1875
Quintana, Manuel Jose 1772-1857
Radishchev, Aleksander 1749-1802
Raftery, Anthony 1784-1835
Raimund, Ferdinand 1790-1836
Reid, Mayne 1818-1883
Renan, Ernest 1823-1892
Reuter, Fritz 1810-1874
Rogers, Samuel 1763-1855
Ruckert, Friedrich 1788-1866
Runeberg, Johan 1804-1877
Rydberg, Viktor 1828-1895
Saavedra y Ramirez de Boquedano,
　Angel de 1791-1865
Sacher-Mosoch, Leopold von 1836-1895
Saltykov-Shchedrin, Mikhail 1826-1892
Satanov, Isaac 1732-1805
Schiller, Johann Friedrich 1759-1805
Schlegel, August 1767-1845
Schlegel, Karl 1772-1829
Scott, Sir Walter 1771-1832
Scribe, Augustin Eugene 1791-1861
Sedgwick, Catherine Maria 1789-1867

Senoa, August 1838-1881
Shelley, Mary W. 1797-1851
Shelley, Percy Bysshe 1792-1822
Shulman, Kalman 1819-1899
Sigourney, Lydia Howard Huntley
　1791-1856
Silva, Jose Asuncion 1865-1896
Slaveykov, Petko 1828-1895
Slowacki, Juliusz 1809-1848
Smith, Richard Penn 1799-1854
Smolenskin, Peretz 1842-1885
Stagnelius, Erik Johan 1793-1823
Staring, Antonie Christiaan
　Wynand 1767-1840
Stendhal (pseud. of Henri Beyle)
　1783-1842
Stifter, Adalbert 1805-1868
Stone, John Augustus 1801-1834
Taine, Hippolyte 1828-1893
Taunay, Alfredo d'Ecragnole 1843-1899
Taylor, Bayard 1825-1878
Tennyson, Alfred, Lord 1809-1892
Terry, Lucy (Lucy Terry Prince)
　1730-1821
Thompson, Daniel Pierce 1795-1868
Thompson, Samuel 1766-1816
Thomson, James 1834-1882
Tiedge, Christoph August 1752-1841
Timrod, Henry 1828-1867
Tommaseo, Nicolo 1802-1874
Tompa, Mihaly 1817-1888
Topelius, Zachris 1818-1898
Turgenev, Ivan 1818-1883
Tyutchev, Fedor I. 1803-1873
Uhland, Ludvig 1787-1862
Valaoritis, Aristotelis 1824-1879
Valles, Jules 1832-1885
Verde, Cesario 1855-1886
Vigny, Alfred Victor de 1797-1863
Villaverde, Cirilio 1812-1894
Vinje, Aasmund Olavsson 1818-1870
Vorosmarty, Mihaly 1800-1855
Warren, Mercy Otis 1728-1814
Weisse, Christian Felix 1726-1804
Welhaven, Johan S. 1807-1873
Werner, Zacharius 1768-1823
Wescott, Edward Noyes 1846-1898
Wessely, Nattali Herz 1725-1805
Whitman, Sarah Helen 1803-1878
Wieland, Christoph Martin 1733-1813
Woolson, Constance Fenimore
　1840-1894
Wordsworth, William 1770-1850
Zhukovsky, Vasily 1783-1852

Fredrika Bremer

1801-1865

Swedish novelist, letter, journal, short story, and sketch writer, poet, and autobiographer.

Considered the first Swedish novelist of manners, Bremer achieved popularity in her own day with her fictional accounts of upper-middle-class family life. Bremer's early fame was established by such novels as *Familjen H.* (*The H— Family*), *Presidentens döttrar* (*The President's Daughters: A Narrative of a Governess*), and *Grannarne* (*The Neighbours: A Story of Every-Day Life*), which were frequently praised by contemporary critics for their inspirational moral tone and realistic portrayal of Swedish customs. During the 1850s, Bremer became well known for her advocacy of female emancipation. Her later novels, particularly *Hertha,* contributed to the development of the women's rights movement in Sweden, though many early commentators regarded them as tendentious and artistically flawed. Bremer was also popular as a travel writer. Her *Hemmen i den nya verlden: En dagbok i bref, skrifna under tvenne års resor i Norra Amerika och på Cuba* (*The Homes of the New World: Impressions of America*), a collection of letters describing her two-year stay in the United States and Cuba, was widely read in both Sweden and America. Despite the popularity of Bremer's works with her contemporaries, today she is virtually unknown outside Sweden. Nevertheless, she is acclaimed by some modern scholars as a pioneering novelist and feminist.

The second child of a wealthy merchant and his wife, Bremer was born in Åbo, Finland. In 1804, when Bremer's father learned that Finland was soon to be annexed to Russia, the family moved to Stockholm, Sweden. A year later, they purchased a country estate in nearby Årsta, where Bremer spent most of her youth. An unhappy child, she led a solitary existence and received little attention from her parents, who nevertheless rigidly controlled her activities. Bremer received private tutoring in history, philosophy, literature, music, and art. In addition, she was expected to become proficient in a number of languages, including English, German, French, and Italian. Bremer displayed a talent for writing at an early age; she composed her first poems when she was eight and later wrote a number of short plays that she and her brothers and sisters performed for their family. As an adolescent, Bremer devoted what little spare time she had to reading the works of the English romantic novelist Fanny Burney, which intensified her desire to escape from the repressive atmosphere at Årsta.

To relieve the tedium of provincial life, Bremer became involved in a variety of charitable activities in the early 1820s. She resolved to become a nurse, but was dissuaded by her parents, who considered the occupation beneath her social status. However, they allowed Bremer to care for her bedridden younger sister at Årsta during the winters of 1826 and 1827 while the rest of the family stayed in Stockholm. Bremer spent much of this time writing short stories, sketches, and poems, which she anonymously published in *Teckningar utur hvardagslifvet* in order to raise money for her favorite charities. The positive popular and critical response to this work encouraged Bremer, and her father's death in 1830, which freed her from many domestic obligations, provided a further impetus to continue

writing. With the publication of *The H— Family*, Bremer's first signed work, her reputation as a skillful chronicler of Swedish life and manners was established. *The H— Family* was followed in the 1830s and 1840s by a number of enormously successful novels, all of which focus on family relationships among the people of Bremer's social class. Because she often drew upon her childhood experiences in composing these works, critics have frequently pointed out that several of Bremer's characters, including the intelligent but socially awkward Edla in *The President's Daughters* and *Nina*, are autobiographical.

During the 1840s, Bremer became increasingly convinced of the need for social and political reform in Sweden. Late in the decade, she made a long-anticipated trip to America for the express purpose of observing the influence of democratic government on "the home, the family, the position of women and . . . the development and the happiness of the individual." Her novels had become well known to American readers through English translations, and when Bremer arrived in the United States in October, 1849, she was welcomed into the intellectual circles of New York and Boston and befriended by many prominent Americans. Before returning to Sweden in 1851, Bremer toured twenty-seven of the thirty-one states in the Union and briefly traveled in Cuba. In addition to visiting prisons, schools, and factories in the United States, she witnessed slave auctions and attended sessions of the Senate and the House of Representatives. The special object of her attention, however, was the women's rights movement. Her conversations with such noted American feminists as Lucretia Mott and Dorothea Dix convinced her that Swedish women should no longer assume a subordinate position in society, and Bremer resolved to spend the rest of her life campaigning for the emancipation of her sex.

Bremer had not planned to write a book about her travel experiences, which she had described in dozens of letters to her sister in Sweden. Upon returning to her own country, however, she decided to publish these letters as a gesture of gratitude for her hospitable reception in the United States. *The Homes of the New World* is a detailed account of Bremer's travels containing observations on the political and social climate of America as well as her impressions of the many prominent literary figures she met there, including Henry Wadsworth Longfellow, Ralph Waldo Emerson, James Russell Lowell, and Catherine Sedgwick. The work was generally well received in both Sweden and America, although some reviewers condemned Bremer for her indiscretion in providing personal commentary on her new acquaintances.

After publishing *The Homes of the New World*, Bremer actively worked to improve women's rights in Sweden. She encouraged her compatriots to become involved in charitable activities because she believed that women's legal and social status would be improved if their contributions to society were recognized. Her writings served as the main vehicle for her feminist beliefs. In *Hertha* and, to a lesser extent, in *Fader och dotter: En skildring ur lifvet (Father and Daughter: A Portraiture from the Life)*, she championed legal, educational, and political rights for women. Of these two novels, *Hertha* was most influential in furthering these reforms. Although the work met with angry protests by Swedish critics who charged that Bremer had made the story subservient to her didactic purpose, it led to the founding of a Swedish women's rights journal and helped secure the passage of a law that granted unmarried women majority at the age of twenty-five. Stung by adverse criticism of *Hertha*, Bremer left for an extended tour of Switzerland, Italy, Palestine, and Greece late in 1856. She returned to Sweden in 1861 and died there of pneumonia four years later.

Although Bremer's novels were widely reviewed in both England and America during the 1840s, they have since received little critical attention outside Sweden. Early critics valued these works primarily for their realistic descriptions of Swedish life, and many commentators favorably likened them to Jane Austen's novels of manners. Reviewers also praised their wholesome moral tone. Walt Whitman, one of her most enthusiastic early critics, found her stories so spiritually inspiring that he placed them second only to the Bible among the books that children should read. Yet contemporary response was not wholly positive. Some critics faulted Bremer's novels for their sentimentalism and poor construction, flaws also cited by a few later commentators, most notably Alrik T. Gustafson. Today, Bremer's novels prompt little critical commentary.

Bremer's record of her travels has been largely overlooked by modern commentators. However, the 1924 publication of *America of the Fifties: Letters of Fredrika Bremer*, a condensed version of *The Homes of the New World*, briefly reawakened scholarly interest in the work. In contrast to some contemporary reviewers who faulted what they considered her indiscreet comments on the people she had met, early twentieth-century critics

appreciated her candor and praised the letters as an accurate representation of mid-nineteenth-century American life.

Despite the critical neglect of Bremer's works, she is remembered today as an early Swedish novelist of manners. In addition, because she ardently advocated the emancipation of women in both her fiction and personal life, she is recognized in Sweden for her contribution to the advancement of women's rights.

PRINCIPAL WORKS

Teckningar utur hvardagslifvet   (sketches, short stories, and
    poetry) 1828
Familjen H. (novel) 1831
    [*The H— Family*, 1843]
Presidentens döttrar (novel) 1834
    [*The President's Daughters: A Narrative of a Governess*,
    1843]
Nina (novel) 1835
    [*Nina*, 1843]
Grannarne (novel) 1837
    [*The Neighbours: A Story of Every-Day Life*, 1842]
Hemmet; eller, Familje-sorger och fröjder (novel) 1839
    [*The Home; or, Family Cares and Family Joys*, 1843]
Strid och frid; eller, Några soener i Norge (novel) 1840
    [*Strife and Peace; or, Scenes in Norway*, 1843]
En dagbok (novel) 1843
    [*A Diary* published in *New Sketches of Every-Day Life: A
    Diary, Together with Strife and Peace*, 1844]
Syskonlif (novel) 1848
    [*Brothers and Sisters: A Tale of Domestic Life*, 1848]
*Hemmen i den nya verlden: En dagbok i bref, skrifna under
    tvenne års resor i Norra Amerika och på Cuba*. 3 vols.
    (letters) 1853-54
    [*The Homes of the New World: Impressions of America*,
    1853; also published as *America of the Fifties: Letters
    of Fredrika Bremer* (partial translation), 1924]
Hertha (novel) 1856
    [*Hertha*, 1856]
Fader och dotter: En skildring ur lifvet (novel) 1858
    [*Father and Daughter: A Portraiture from the Life*, 1859]
*Lifvet i gamla verlden: Dagboks-anteckningar under resor i
    Söder- och Österland*. 3 vols. (journal) 1860-62
    [Published in three volumes: *Two Years in Switzerland
    and Italy*, 1861; *Travels in the Holy Land*, 1862;
    *Greece and the Greeks: The Narrative of a Winter
    Residence and Summer Travel in Greece and Its
    Islands*, 1863]
**Sjelfbiografiska anteckningar, bref och efterlemnade
    skrifter* (sketches, letters, autobiography, and poetry)
    1868
    [*Life, Letters, and Posthumous Works of Fredrika Bremer*,
    1868]
Fredrika Bremer brev. 4 vols. (letters) 1915-20

*This work also includes a biographical sketch of Bremer written by
her older sister, Charlotte Bremer.

MARY HOWITT (essay date 1842)

[*A British poet and novelist, Howitt provided the first English
translations of Bremer's novels. In the following excerpt from her*

preface to The Neighbours, *Howitt explains her reasons for introducing the British public to Bremer's works and favorably likens them to the domestic novels of Jane Austen.*]

Of the rich treasure of intellect and literature in Sweden, little or nothing is known in England. To give a specimen of what exists there, even in the department of living story and scenes of society, I have selected this work of Frederika Bremer, which is one of a series. **"The Neighbors"** has not been first chosen on the principle of presenting the best first in order to excite expectation, but as believing it a fair and average example. Some of the others possess unquestionably a stronger interest in the narrative, and perhaps more masterly exposition of character. They are, in my opinion, most admirable in their lessons of social wisdom; in their life of relation; in their playful humour; and in all those qualities which can make writings acceptable to the fireside circle of the good and refined. Frederika Bremer is, indeed, the MISS AUSTIN of Sweden. . . . [Frederika Bremer has] seen much of the society and scenery of her native land, and no one can sketch these with more graphic truth and vivacity. (pp. 3-4)

> Mary Howitt, in a preface to The Neighbours: A Story of Every-Day Life *by Frederika Bremer, translated by Mary Howitt, 1842. Reprint by George Bell & Sons, 1892, pp. 3-4.*

THE NORTH AMERICAN REVIEW (essay date 1843)

[*The following excerpt from an appreciative review of* The Neighbours *focuses on the novel's characterization. Arguing that* The Neighbours's *greatest merit is its "pure and healthy tone of moral feeling," the critic praises those characters who embody the simple virtues of Swedish domestic life, including Dr. Werner, his wife,* Ma chère mère, *and Serena.*]

[The great popularity which **"The Neighbours; a Story of Every-day Life"** has enjoyed] is a compliment alike to the good taste of our people and the merits of the book itself. For, although the favor with which it has been received is to be ascribed partly to the new scenes and forms of life which it delineates, and partly to the fact that it describes a state of society and manner of living not unlike those of New England, yet we think, that its success rests not so much upon these elements as upon its truth, its simplicity, its naturalness, and its pure moral feeling. . . . (p. 497)

The scene of this novel is laid in Sweden, in the country, in our own age, and among persons in the middle ranks of life; consequently, the author relies upon the fidelity of her pictures, and the accuracy of her sketches, to awaken and keep alive the interest of the reader, and derives no aid from either the softening haze of antiquity, or the dazzling atmosphere of high life. It was an experiment of some boldness, but one in which her success has been complete. Her work is a new proof of the power, with which genius is clothed, of finding the materials for poetry, and the elements of romantic fiction, in the life that lies around us, and in those joys and sorrows, hopes and fears, that bloom like wild flowers, along that common highway that leads from the cradle to the grave. She has taught us to apprehend the force of Goethe's remark, that "Life outweighs all things, if love lies within it."

It begins, where most novels end, with a marriage. A physician, in the autumn of his life, selects for his wife a lady no longer young; and the early chapters describe, with great simplicity and beauty, the journey of the new married couple to their home, and their first experiments in housekeeping. As is not unfrequently the case in the Old World, it is a union brought about more by mutual esteem and confidence than by love; and the gradual unfolding of a warmer feeling in the breast of the grateful and conscientious wife is very pleasingly and naturally traced. The writer has not taken any considerable pains with the construction of her story, and many of her incidents are mere episodes, contributing nothing to the *dénouement* of the plot. It is rather an imaginary journal than any thing else, kept by a clever, observant, and warm-hearted woman, in which she sketches, for the amusement of an absent friend, the characters of her neighbours, and relates the events of her own tranquil home, and the occurences that take place around her. The highest charm of the work, in our apprehension, dwells, from first to last, in the humble home of the hero and heroine, if we may so call them; a home dignified by tranquil virtue, blest with serene contentment, and bright with the sunshine of confiding love. Nor are we at all displeased with the occasional glimpses, which the young housekeeper gives us, into the flour-barrel and the store-closet, though, on one or two occasions, we confess, a fastidious taste might object that the principle of unreserve has been carried a little too far. The character of the husband, Dr. Werner, (we acknowledge that we grow a little weary of his *soubriquet* of "Bear"), is very happily conceived and executed; and, though perfectly natural, is by no means a commonplace one. His various excellences of mind and heart are gradually unfolded, and with no violations of probability; so that, though we begin with nothing more than respect, we end with reverence and admiration. And the artless simplicity and unaffected modesty with which the writer speaks of herself, her errors, her mistakes, her short-comings, her unreasonable fears, and her self-distrust, interest us also warmly in her, and give us assurance, that the good Doctor has chosen for his helpmate a loving and yet a strong nature, who will judge herself with more severity than any one else, who will bear cheerfully her part of the burdens of life, and is only in danger of carrying the principle of self-sacrifice too far. The simple, homely beauty, and perfect naturalness, of some of the passages in their domestic life, can hardly be surpassed, and they touch, at once, the source of smiles and tears.

The most elaborately drawn character, and, on the whole, a very successful one, is that of the widowed mother-in-law. The combination which she presents, of high and stern qualities of character and resolute strength of will, with the homely virtues of thrift, order, punctuality, and good housekeeping, though not very uncommon in real life, is yet a difficult one for a writer of fiction to manage. When the attempt is made, the result is apt to be a sort of hybrid monster, in which the blending of the two classes of qualities is as violent and unnatural as the union of the two parts of a centaur or a mermaid. But this is not the case with *"Ma chère mère,"* whose character is a harmonious whole, well proportioned and symmetrically developed. The conception is quite original, and it is very well executed and sustained. Her strong sense, her energy of will, her sternness, her fierce explosions of temper, her superficial harshness and real kindness of nature, her depth of feeling, and stoical power of suppressing all expressions of it, her excellent management of her household affairs, her economy, and practical knowledge of life, all conspire to produce a very impressive picture, which becomes more and more striking to the last. Her speeches and proverbs are rather too long and too frequent, and her severity of tongue seems sometimes carried too far. We confess, too, that we like her better in the quiet and every-day scenes, such as those in which she scolds and manages her froward daughters-in-law, than in those more impassioned ones, in which the deeper chords of her nature are struck, and which the author has most carefully elaborated. The scene immediately following the detection of her son's fault seems a little overdone, and the effects produced are rather disproportioned to the cause; but, on the other hand, the pathetic beauty of the reconciliation is of the highest order, and the heart of him is little to be envied who can read it unmoved. The incident, too, of her discovery of her own blindness, is strikingly and naturally told; and the softening influence of her revived affection for her son upon her stern nature is beautifully delineated. We feel that we owe an obligation to the writer, who has enriched the gallery of fiction with a portrait of a character at once so original and so natural, and which we may contemplate with the mind's eye with the highest satisifaction. . . . (pp. 497-99)

The writer has evidently labored the character of Bruno very much; but here her success has not been so great. She is not so much at home in the dark, the terrible, and the tragic, as in the gentle, the domestic, and the feminine. He does not seem to be in unison with the rest of the picture; and the tranquil landscape, into which he is thrown, forms hardly an appropriate background for the wild and stormy grandeur of a figure like his. The impression, which the character as a whole leaves upon us, is that it is not a perfectly natural one. There is too much of stage effect in him, and too many elements of the melo-dramatic hero, made up of starts and burnt cork. There is so much that is dangerous in his nature, that we cannot stifle a vague feeling of apprehension as to the happiness of the gentle and lovely being whose fate becomes linked with his. It seems like the lamb lying down with the lion, and we cannot but fear that his very caresses may draw blood. The incident of his killing the horse is a gratuitous piece of barbarity, for which we can hardly forgive him or the author. But we would not be understood by these criticisms as saying, that the character is a failure. Such is by no means the case, for it has great, though not unqualified, merit. We are provoked into making these unfavorable comparisons by the admirable skill with which the other characters are drawn; and what we say in disparagement of Bruno must be taken as a compliment to the rest of the book. We wish that Hagar had been entirely omitted. She seems, from first to last, an unseemly excrescence; and the tragedy with which she interrupts the "golden wedding" of the Dahls appears out of keeping and in bad taste. And, in spite of her death-bed confessions, we have some ugly misgivings on the subject of her relations with Bruno, and as to how far they may or may not have made him unworthy of Serena.

And Serena; how shall we adequately express our sense of her serene and tranquil beauty, of that water-lily grace and purity that float softly around her, of that mild lunar light that beams from her gentle brow and eyes? She recalls one of whom an English poet so beautifully sings;

> A perfect woman, nobly planned
> To warn, to comfort, and command;
> And yet a spirit still, and bright
> With something of an angel light.

Again do we thank the author for this fine picture of feminine excellence, in which we see so admirably harmonized and blended all the best attributes of a womanly nature; imagination, sensibility, taste, high sense of duty, religious faith, cultivation, united with warm affections, practical good sense, knowledge of common things, a cheerful temperament, and the daily, unrepining discharge of lowly duties. There is always danger that a character like hers, in the hands of a writer of

fiction, will degenerate into insipidity. But from that danger our author has most happily escaped, and she has made her as interesting as she is innocent and lovely; thanks to the touch of a pencil at once firm, delicate, and discriminating. She glides from house to house, and from scene to scene, like a sunbeam, making every one feel that they are nearer heaven, while she is with them. As we lay down the book, we feel as if she must be a person whom we had known and loved, who had given us a new sense of the capacities of humanity, and we involuntarily call down a benediction upon her head, and pray that her "life may be all poetry."

There are many other characters, drawn with more or less excellence, and all giving us that impression of reality, which is so sure a test of the creative hand of genius. There are also many lively and entertaining scenes, described with great spirit and truth, showing an uncommon power of observation, a strong, though well-regulated, perception of the ludicrous, and a marked talent for satirical painting. And on almost every page, we find a casual remark, a reflection, a little trait of human goodness or of human weakness, which fairly startles us by its truth, and by its reminding us of something in our own experience. What a touch of nature, for instance, there is in the self-distrust with which Madame Werner goes to visit the Dahls, . . . feeling that she will be no more welcome than a dun, and then, when she is so warmly and cordially received, saying to herself, with all the alacrity of self-disparagement, that it is all on her husband's account! How perfectly natural, too, is the breaking up of the party at the Dahls', . . . where "*Ma chère mère,*" after all the guests are shawled and cloaked for their departure, seizes her violin and plays a merry tune, and all the company begin dancing in their strange costume! Who has not marked the same reluctance to leave a pleasant party, when the spirits are all attuned to enjoyment, and a light form is seen to bound into the drawing-room to take a farewell whirl in her cloak and moccasins? These little touches, like Shakspeare's Caesar asking Antony to pass round and to speak to him in the other ear, because he was deaf on one side, mark, more than any thing else, the master hand.

The impression which the book, as a whole, leaves upon us, is one of great truth and fidelity to nature in all its essential elements. We have remarked, that it delineates a kind of life not unlike our own in New England, the resemblance being suggested by the long winters, the indoor occupations, the general cultivation, and the absence of any marked differences of rank and fortune. But in one respect, there is an emphatic distinction, and a similarity to the manners and social habits delineated in German works of fiction. There is a great deal more of the expression of feeling of all kinds. Emotions lie much nearer the surface than among us, where something of coldness and reserve characterizes the intercourse of friends and relatives. Tears, kisses, embraces, claspings of the hand, and enthusiastic speeches, are in much more common circulation than with us. There are many things described as taking place, which, judged by our standard, would seem extravagant and unnatural, not to say in bad taste or even ludicrous; and some of the communications which the new-married wife makes to her correspondent startle us as being very unreserved. But we must be careful not to judge of these things by our own standard, till we are assured that this is the true one, and that we do not err towards the other extreme of apathy, coldness, and reserve. We can have no question, that these things are perfectly natural to a Swede or a German, and that our habits would strike him as singular and repulsive.

But the highest charm of the book is its pure and healthy tone of moral feeling. The lessons which it teaches are weighty, and impressively conveyed. It shows us how much better a contented spirit is than houses and lands,—what pure and unfailing sources of happiness are to be found in that culture of the moral, intellectual, and social nature, from which no human being is excluded. It gives cheerful and animating views of human life and the Providence that governs it, and teaches us that no life can be unhappy, which is dedicated to duty and quickened by the affections. It proclaims the value of those simple and natural pleasures which lie scattered at our feet, and which may be freely enjoyed without wealth, or conspicuous station, or high endowments. The author's mind is an eminently healthy one, and such is the tone of her book. It breathes over the mind with a bracing and invigorating influence, akin to that of the mountain wind upon the bodily frame. She has looked at the world through no false and distorting medium of pride or gloom. We hear no voice of whining discontent, or sullen misanthropy, or querulous distress. And, above all, we recognize with peculiar pleasure her emphatic testimony against the pestilent doctrine, that great powers necessarily produce great misery, that susceptibility to beauty is only productive of keener pangs of disappointment, and that the more finely attuned souls must of necessity be jangled into harsher discord. High gifts, superior endowments, fine susceptibilities, are increased means of enjoyment; and it is only from the abuse and perversion of them, that misery and discontent arise. It is from the indulgence of the selfish passions, that most of the unhappiness of life springs. The first rule, to insure happiness, is, to forget one's self, and the second is, to remember others; and we honor and feel grateful to the author of **"The Neighbours,"** for the power and beauty with which she has enforced these truths. (pp. 500-03)

"Bremer's 'Neighbours'," in The North American Review, *Vol. LVI, No. CXIX, April, 1843, pp. 497-503.*

THE CHRISTIAN EXAMINER AND GENERAL REVIEW (essay date 1843)

[*In the following excerpt from a survey of Bremer's novels, the reviewer commends Bremer's faithful descriptions of Swedish life, but objects to certain scenes in* The Neighbors, The H—Family, *and* Hemmet; eller, Familje-sorger och fröjder (The Home; or, Family Cares and Family Joys) *on the grounds that they are immoral. Despite this reservation, the critic maintains that Bremer's novels inspire "wholesome" and "noble" feelings.*]

The decided favor, with which the productions of Frederika Bremer have been received among us, speaks well for the moral taste of the American community; and in saying this we have uttered one of the warmest commendations of the author. It is true that there are certain criticisms uttered as to the tendency of certain parts of these fascinating sketches. These criticisms seem to us just, and the very fact, that such are uttered, is a good symptom, and is an evidence that it is the general moral beauty of these sketches, which is giving them their strong hold upon all hearts, and that faults which incur such censure are the more obvious, because they are in such strange, glaring inconsistency with the grand tenor of the works, with what appears to us the healthy character of Miss Bremer's views of life.

It is amusing to remember the expressions of disgust with which many threw down **"The Neighbors,"** on its first appearance. Practised novel-readers found it so unlike their favorite works,

those unacquainted with foreign literature were so annoyed by its foreign peculiarities, those little accustomed to translations were so disturbed by what appeared to them oddities of style, and many applied to it so unintelligently the same rules by which they would judge a book written by an English or American lady, that they pronounced a hasty and unfavorable verdict, and were not a little amazed to find it set aside so unceremoniously by the public. It is a recommendation of [**"The Neighbors," "The H— Family," "The President's Daughters," "The Home,"** and **"Strife and Peace,"**] that they are not written by an author of one country, laying the scene in another, and attempting to paint it from description or cursory inspection. The circumstance, that they are written by a Swede, leads us to hope that they are correct as the Daguerreotype itself; that the pictures are the very transcripts of nature, engraved by the sunbeams of truth. So only can they have the high value of conveying to us fact, and giving us that for which all readers should thirst, knowledge.

In the same way we become reconciled to much that offends our attachment to our own conventionalisms, and notions of refinement. We meet here no more with heroines who live upon dewdrops, moonlight, and thin air, like the fair ones with whom we have long been familiar in our English poetry, and romance. The ladies to whom Miss Bremer introduces us do not even sustain life, from choice, upon the lightest farinaceous edibles and cold water, like many gentle creatures of flesh and blood around us. They not only fare sumptuously, but solidly, every day; and eating seems to social life in the North not only a thing of necessity, but of much pleasurable importance; and there is no hiding this attention to creature-comforts. Nobody has learned to be ashamed of eating, nor of what is eaten; and Miss Bremer is not ashamed to describe all this as it is, whoever may cry "out upon her want of taste!" or, "out upon the half civilized people!" She tells us, in evident unconsciousness of carelessness, of the impression of many a dish upon the table, and many a custom of the consumers, at which we stand amazed. And what sense is there in our doing so? Might not a tale be written among us, faithfully sketching our every-day life, and sent into Sweden, there to awaken wonder, and perhaps laughter, among the thoughtless or narrow-minded? It is not thus that national differences are to be regarded; they are fit subjects of intelligent curiosity, and the philanthropic philosopher may speculate upon them for good. And we hold that while Miss Bremer paints faithfully the customs of her brave, virtuous, and well instructed people, of whose history and position the world ought to know more than it does, we are not to come forward with a false refinement and illiberal fastidiousness, charging her with a coarse taste. Nor does it show cultivated, large minds, to suffer our contempt to be awakened by modes of living different from our own, even though we pronounce them behind the age. It may be that if the nations of the North retain an undue interest in the table, and, among their relics of primitive simplicity, use viands which we deem unpalatable, they also hold fast some other and better things, which we, to our wo [*sic*], have lost. It may be that Honesty, public and private, with ancient face and rude speech, yet lingers honored among her "Neighbours," and in her "Homes." (pp. 382-83)

What story is contained in **"The Neighbors,"** is conveyed in a series of letters from Franciska, a newly-married lady, whom most readers, we suspect, feel to be the real heroine of the book. Her husband, too, a personage as totally unlike an ordinary hero of romance, as a substantial silver teapot is unlike a graceful alabaster vase, is its real hero; he and his "little wife," so full of goodness and arch simplicity, take deep hold of all hearts. . . . There are three other characters of importance, according to the places assigned them by Miss Bremer. There is Serena, who would be very lovely in real life; but as we seek copies from nature in such fictions as these, we cannot help feeling all the while, ''there never was such a creature in real life; she is too shadowy, too angelic for anything but poetry. Tegner should have described her, not Miss Bremer.'' A little more of human imperfection would have made her more interesting to all but thorough-bred novel readers, who expect, as a matter of course, to pursue one such "faultless monster" through the mazes of a romance. Then there is Bruno, whose character does not seem to us either natural or edifying, and whose marriage with Serena makes us glad she is only a thing of the imagination; not a real woman, whose fate we should follow into such wedlock with aching hearts. Then there is 'ma chère mère,'' on whom Miss Bremer seems to have expended much effort; she too appears to us overdrawn and extravagant. There is wonderful power in the scenes of her struggles with her son, and of their parting; and a good lesson in the mutual suffering which follows her grand mistake in the education of this fiery being. So too there is power in some of the developments of Bruno's nature; but that power is apparently exercised in display of itself. There is an evident wish to produce effect in many interviews between mother and son; nor can we keep away the recollection of Byron and some of his heroes. The female companion of Bruno is altogether a painful superfluity.

Of 'The H— Family,'' we do not care to say much. With scarcely an exception its readers have pronounced it inferior to ''The Neighbors;'' and the love of the blind girl, still more, its acknowledged return by a virtuous married man, although the whole be conveyed with the greatest delicacy of expression, have been received with such an universal murmur of disapprobation, as to evince a hopeful quickness and purity of moral sense in our society. It is not enough to say that such attachments have actually taken place. It can do no human being any good to know that fact; they have not happened often enough to justify their being held up to our gaze in warning. The only cases in which it can profit man to look upon representations of evil in any shape, are as admonitions against besetting sins and probable temptations. Miss Bremer's singular gifts as a great moral teacher, who can win man to love goodness by the exercise of her powers in this simple mode, impose it upon her as a duty. Heaven itself has set her apart as a sort of missionary in the world of mind and heart; and henceforth, if conscious of her holy vocation, she will go on with a single purpose, to evoke and call into action the religious sentiment that lies deep in every soul, to purify the tastes of the young, to prepare for the conflict with temptations which *must* come. We hold, that writers labor not in such a province, when they drag from the recesses of human hearts, from the nooks of society, rare specimens of human frailty, and for the sake of a little novelty or spicy strangeness, show what certainly does not ''adorn a tale,'' and is not needed to ''point a moral.''

We believe that ''The President's Daughters'' is a greater favorite with the public than [''The H— Family,''] and it surely deserves to be. But after its perusal, we began to hear the complaint which is so common, when people read many books from the same pen, especially if they are read in rapid succession. They spoke of ''too strong family likenesses,'' of ''repetitions,'' of ''meeting the same characters with new names and in new positions.'' And some now find a difficulty in recalling separately and distinctly the various individuals of

the fine tales before us, and assigning each portrait to its own frame. . . . (pp. 383-85)

There is indeed much of the same material found in each of these sketches; and since they are so modest in profession, calling themselves sketches only, and the material is so good, we do not object to it. We think that Miss Bremer would have flourished well in the almost forgotten era of Richardson, when she could have thrown all her ideas into one voluminous production, the fruit of some years of labor; and have made one set of characters keep fast hold upon our heart-strings, through the beautiful follies of childhood, through courtship, through married life or a charming celibacy, the joys and sorrows of the parent, and a holy old age. We see the flighty readers of our day, who like to ''get through'' a book in twenty-four hours, holding up their deprecating hands at this suggestion; but there is something in Miss Bremer's peculiar capacities as a writer, which makes us feel that she could do this if any one could, in an age of steam vessels and rail-roads, of abridgments and pictorial histories, of physical, intellectual, and moral bustle.

Adelaide, the ''bright particular star'' among the President's daughters, is a beautiful and not unnatural creation of the author's fancy. We would have this character studied, yes, studied by the many lovely creatures whom God has sent into this world with that peculiar and fearful responsibility, of which they are so often sadly unconscious. We would have those who are always sure to know that Beauty has been given them,— beauty! which is power and therefore brings responsibility— we would have them here contemplate in Adelaide as we first see her, what is the true position of the Beauty, and in her growth and development of character, that which the most tempted may become. . . . We think Miss Bremer has been singularly skilful in giving this character a higher existence than that of ordinary novel heroines, by placing her among such temptations as meet fascinating girls often in real life, and amid them developing in her a practical goodness, and exquisite sweetness and principle. (pp. 386-87)

As in every family where there is a being somewhat like Adelaide, we not unfrequently find an Edla too, we think this whole character will awaken sympathy, and lift some tried spirits above circumstances.

''The Home!'' what an eloquent title! how it stirs every good heart and true heart! how much did we expect, when the cold North East winds brought us from the pen of Frederika Bremer a work bearing this name on its title page! It came over the bleak Atlantic, and its glowing pages have not been chilled on the voyage; it is full of love, warmth, peace, beauty. It meets the expectation and fulfils the hope. . . . We recognize all the characteristics of Miss Bremer's mind and heart in this volume, much longer than the others, and better . . . , we think, though many would except their first love, ''The Neighbors.'' The force of first impressions, and the sprightliness of the style have given to ''The Neighbors'' a charm which ''The Home'' must want; but we think that had it appeared first, it would have still remained without a rival. And if we judge it by the grand test, which is likely to *do most good*, its claim seems indisputable. It is full of practical wisdom, of naturally drawn characters, of touching incidents, of deep yet simple truths, of genuine, lovely religion.

All Miss Bremer's tales, in a quiet, unobtrusive manner, show us the actual operation of religion in life, and make the most careless feel both its reality and beauty. She does not delay her narrative that her characters may moralize or preach; there is not a line which the thought-hater can call mere cant. But she makes religion do the same work in her pages which it does wherever found; it strengthens the tempted, gives peace of mind under worldly trial, develops the higher nature, brings back the penitent, and blesses all; and this so naturally and exquisitely, that we forget the enchantress and her wand, look on the phantom scene as a reality, and feel its lessons sink deep into our souls. It does us more good than some graver books aiming at the same object, just as to live, day after day, in an interesting family, who are sincerely pious and benevolent, helps the soul's appreciation of goodness more than listening for years to eloquent sermons, without such illustrations. (pp. 387-88)

["**Strife and Peace**"] is a mere sketch, but it is worthy of Miss Bremer. There is, indeed, one of those hacknied recognitions in it with which novel readers are pretty familiar; but the descriptions of life and scenery, and the beautifully drawn character of Susanna redeem all. We feel at times that the author is indeed countrywoman of [Tegner] who poured forth the wild, stirring stanzas of Frithiof's Saga.

To us the picturesque scenery and dark romantic legends of the north have long appealed against the neglect with which the blooming world of civilization has treated them; and we are thankful, literally thankful, that the cloud of ignorance or prejudice, which has shut us out from so much knowledge and enjoyment, is likely to pass away under this Northern Light, this silver Aurora of female genius. (p. 388)

The most striking attributes of Miss Bremer's character, as a writer, are those grand ones, genius, and moral excellence. We see her genius as she brings scenes and human beings vividly before us, and throws herself into different characters with that instinctive adaptation of act and speech which is the power of genius alone. She, the single woman, gives us the joys, the anxieties, the hopes and fears, the almost unutterable sorrows of a parent's heart, with a thrilling fidelity. We can scarcely believe that she has not herself given her plighted hand at the altar, and watched by the cradle, and trained the young spirit with fear and trembling, and gloried in the opening promise of "her summer child," uttered heart-felt warnings against secret dangers, imprudent marriage, youthful rashness; and then sat down in joy by the matured fruit of her toil, or in humble resignation beside its premature grave.

Where these elements of genius and moral excellence are so beautifully combined, the author is a blessing. Criticism may indeed find something to say; there is no perfection in commonplace, certainly, and we have no more right to expect it in works of genuine talent. We are the more disposed to approach these works in a fault-seeking spirit, because we foresee that their extraordinary merit will produce a host of imitators, as likely to seize that which had better not be copied, as that which they cannot copy, for their lives. (p. 389)

Yet after criticism has done her utmost, works of genius still hold their places in the hearts of men, unless there be some element of moral evil within, which, to the credit of human nature be it spoken, is usually an element of decay. We do not think there is any such element in Miss Bremer's writings. It would be inconsistent with what we have said above of her two main characteristics as an author. Yet many of her warmest admirers cry out against certain strange blemishes in some of her tales; and these blemishes are of so serious a nature as to deserve examination. In "**The Neighbors**," a young man, whom

the author evidently intends that we shall like, becomes attached to a married woman. His love is rejected; but there it is; this love is one of the incidents of the work. In "**The H— Family**," a blind girl falls in love with her Uncle! This incident is painful enough to virtuous minds, though the girl is represented as one whose undisciplined feelings have brought upon her all wo, even to insanity. But how can we apologize for the introduction of another love? The Uncle is held up to us throughout the tale as an object of respect, the husband of an excellent wife, the good father of a family. Yet in one scene which we should call not merely highly wrought, but extravagant, he acknowledges that he has loved this niece,—acknowledges it to *her!* And then we have her ecstasy of joy. One familiar with the deeper wickedness of the world might say, "but there was no sin; he proved his virtue by ruling this love; once only was it ever breathed from his lips; he mastered it." For what good purpose can such a passion have been introduced at all? It is incredible that such a man can have had such a horrid temptation to resist. . . . [We] know that this sketch has been read to more than one American party, and this part of it received with a thrill of something sterner than disapprobation. It is vain to say that it is good to set forth the struggles and conquests of principle, though it be true as a general rule. Such struggles as this never occur where true principle reigns. . . . We wish that Miss Bremer had spared her readers this unnecessary shock to every better feeling; though we have a deep conviction that it was in her but an error of taste.

In "**The Home**," a work whose general tone is exquisitely lofty and pure, we are again confounded by the introduction of a conflict between goodness and sin, where we should have expected that the very atmosphere of the former would have kept the latter at an unapproachable distance. And it is the same form of sin, too, for the third time: it is love entertained unlawfully, for a being consecrated by marriage, and by one in whom the author evidently wishes to interest us. We wondered at first how Elsie could endure that Jacobi should remain under the same roof, after he had insulted her by seeking her heart; for that is what man never seeks without some hope of obtaining, and the faintest hope in this case was insult. But her noble speech of repulse, and her noble motive for permitting him to stay, plead in her defence. Still it seems to us, that the whole affair between Elise and Jacobi, with the suspicions of Louise afterwards, is improbable, too disagreeable for introduction, and of injurious tendency. As in the case of Judge H. [in "**The H— Family**"], it is not calculated to excite sufficient horror of a spiritual fall, an infidelity of the heart alone. It does not sufficiently impress upon us the solemn truth, that Christian obligation and God's judgment penetrate to the very innermost hiding-places of thought and feeling. Could we believe that such trials often entered the sanctuaries of virtuous homes, and tested the principles of good wives and mothers, we should still think Miss Bremer's management of this particular illustration injudicious. With regard to the character of Jacobi, we are perplexed not a little by the various aspects in which he appears from the beginning to the end of the book, and we can hardly think it sustained throughout with distinctness or consistency. (pp. 389-91)

And now comes up the question, how has such a writer as Miss Bremer, distinguished for knowledge of human nature and a high appreciation of moral excellence—an appreciation of which the pure-minded alone are capable—how has she fallen into such mistakes? Are they faults of taste early formed on some bad model? Or is it that, since the French have had so much influence in Sweden, French immorality has stolen into the holy places of the land, the virtuous homes, and Miss Bremer is bound to paint truly what she mournfully beholds, and warn loudly against insidious dangers? If so, God forbid that hers should be the fate of Cassandra! Or is it that she has been led astray by her desire to startle, to strike out something new, to produce strong emotion in her readers?

We cannot answer these questions. But it is this desire which has injured the efforts of many an able writer, and we have some evidence of its influence on Miss Bremer in nearly all her tales. There are extravagant and false conceptions of character in each; and marvellous, improbable adventures in each. Could she but throw away all this, and confine herself to the sphere in which she is so admirable, using her powers only to convey faithful pictures of life and human nature, as they move and change around her, pouring out the cheerful, benevolence, the deep spiritual wisdom, the hopeful piety of her nature over her witching pages, we should follow her without a murmur, with reverence, with much gain to our souls, all round and through the mountains and the valleys, the cities and plains of honest Sweden, and glorious old Norway. She could lead us silent and rapt to the eternal ice of the Pole; and even there, in the stillness and seeming death of creation, make us thrill with love to God and man, with eagerness for more of knowledge and goodness, with consciousness of our better nature and sure destiny. (pp. 391-92)

In spite of the blemishes which we have mentioned so freely above,—the author has merit and popularity enough to bear Freedom,—we consider [Miss Bremer's works] entitled to high estimation among philanthropists, because the spirit they breathe, the noble sentiments scattered throughout them, are likely to do good, to give wholesome views of life and duty, to awaken the thinking powers, and stir the nobler impulses of the soul. (p. 392)

> L. J. H., "Novels of Frederika Bremer," in The Christian Examiner and General Review, n.s. Vol. XVI, No. III, July, 1843, pp. 381-94.

FRASER'S MAGAZINE (essay date 1843)

[In the following excerpt from a review of The Neighbours, The Home, and The President's Daughters; including Nina, the critic praises Bremer's skillful delineations of Swedish life and manners, but contends that, with the exception of The President's Daughters, these novels lack dramatic power.]

[Miss Bremer's] skill as a story-teller is of the humblest order. She has no dramatic power about her, and her poetic enthusiasm, of which she seems to possess her share, hurries her at times into perfect drivelling. But, to counterbalance this, she has an eye for observing the peculiarities of social life, and she makes good use of it among her country-people. Neither must we stop here. Miss Bremer is no unsuccessful student of human nature. She understands character and describes it well; she is a capital delineator of habits of speaking, and acting, which she connects, by a subtle, yet an intimate chain, with the habits of thinking from which they arise. Moreover, Miss Bremer is, in the true sense of the term, a Christian moralist. Born in a land where the domestic virtues are more generally disregarded than, perhaps, any where else in Europe, Miss Bremer labours to bring about a better order of things; by exhibiting now the happy effects of keeping the feelings and passions under control, now by setting forth examples, more or less melancholy, of the evils that arise from their indulgence.

Her religious principles, likewise, are just and sound at the bottom, though she does clothe her ideas from time to time in a very equivocal dress. . . . [While] we admit that, as painters of manners, and, perhaps, as teachers of truth through the medium of fable, she and Miss Edgeworth may be classed together, the immeasurable superiority of the latter as a novelist places a wide gulf between them. Miss Bremer may follow her vocation for half a century to come, but she will never give us a Castle Rackrent or a Belinda. (pp. 505-06)

[We regard "The Neighbors"] as well deserving of a perusal. The story is, indeed, an absurdity, so are all the characters, especially such as the writer has evidently laboured with the greatest care, and on which we doubt not she mainly piques herself. But the pictures of domestic life are exquisite; the delineations of human motives, passions, and peculiarities, masterly, and the work on that account deserving of all the favour with which it has been received. . . .

We are inclined to think that The Home has been received in this country with a degree of favour to which [neither The Neighbors nor The President's Daughters; including Nina] lay claim, and we are by no means surprised at the circumstance. Of startling incident there is, indeed, a total absence, for the story is precisely such as the title of the book might lead us to anticipate; but the few events that do occur are admirably managed, and the delineation of character and feeling is perfect. We have besides much less of transcendentalism here than is offered to us in either of Miss Bremer's other performances. She may here and there put into the mouths of her interlocutors a fair proportion of nonsense, but whenever she delivers what we perceive to be her own opinions, her philosophy is Christian and sound. Nor let us omit to observe, that if genius be needed to weave a tale which shall take captive our imaginations and hurry us whithersover the writer may choose, a faculty scarcely more common is required to enlist our sympathies on the side of those many yet petty trials which make up the sum of domestic life. Of this faculty Miss Bremer shews herself to be largely possessed, and in the tale of The Home she has exercised it very freely. (p. 513)

To be understood and relished [The Home] must be read throughout. . . . For ourselves, we confess that many a day has gone from us since by any work of the kind we have been so deeply moved, not by the events of the tale, for they are meagre enough, but by the exquisite philosophy which adorns it. And yet it is full of imperfections too.

We have hitherto spoken of Miss Bremer rather as a depicter of manners than as a novelist. It is necessary, in considering [The President's Daughters; including Nina], . . . seriously to modify this judgment. The former of the two tales into which these volumes divide themselves is as perfect a drama of its kind as we remember any where to have met with. From first to last, it keeps in view the results which actually come to pass; and if there be a little overstraining in the means by which the catastrophe is effected, such overstraining is not greater than we meet with every where, perhaps except in the pages of Scott. Moreover, the character of Edla and Adelaide, the president's two daughters, are drawn with a masterly hand. (p. 520)

The story of Adelaide, as the first portion of the President's Daughters may be called, is excellent. Our interest never flags while we peruse it; and though the adventures be both few and small, they come in naturally, and therefore please us. We are sorry that we cannot say so much for Nina. As a tale, it is a sad mess of extravagances; and it falls infinitely short, in other respects, of what previous etchings by the same hand justified us in expecting. Its sketches of manners are rhapsodies,—its poetry dreamy,—its philosophy mere German transcendentalism. Of Nina herself we have little to say, except that she is a very poor edition of Adelaide, and deserves much of the evil which overtakes her, were it only because of her extreme inflammability. (p. 522)

[With] all their faults, and they abound, the Swedish novels, hitherto made familiar to us in an English dress, deserve the full meed of favour with which they have been received. . . . We are very much obliged to both [Miss Bremer and her translator Mrs. Howitt] for the intellectual treat which they have afforded us; and we sincerly hope that they will be no losers by their hospitality. (p. 525)

> *"The Swedish Romances,"* in Fraser's Magazine, *Vol. XXVIII, No. CLXVII, November, 1843, pp. 505-25.*

THE NORTH AMERICAN REVIEW   (essay date 1844)

[*The excerpt below was drawn from an unsigned review of* Trälinnan (The Bondmaid), En dagbok (A Diary), *and* Strid och frid; eller, Några soener i Norge (Strife and Peace; or, Scenes in Norway) *that is commonly attributed to the American critic and poet James Russell Lowell. Noting that Bremer's novels typify a salutary change in contemporary literature, the reviewer lauds her simple "fireside style," "universal" characters, and ability to recapture the innocence of youth through descriptions of Swedish domestic life.*]

If we needed any . . . proof, that a popular aristocracy, if we may give such a name to the middle class, is almost wholly wanting in Sweden, we might find it in the works of [Miss Bremer]. Had Miss Bremer been born in England, we doubt not that her nature would have led her to choose her characters chiefly from this class, who, by their industry, energy, and strong sense, have there raised the Saxon race again to a level with its Norman conquerors, if they have not given it even a preponderating weight. As it is, the sympathies of education and refinement have forced her to select from the highest order of her countrymen. Even where the manners are essentially those of the middle ranks of life, we must remember that the characters are nearly all chosen from the upper classes. Where the whole population is divided so strictly into two classes, where the dividing line is so absolute and well defined, and the mass of the people are in a state scarcely better than degraded, since it is one from which there is but a bare possibility of rising, it is not to be wondered at, that we look in vain through Miss Bremer's works for delineations of the nobility of humble life.

The novel of society must necessarily be confined within a conventional horizon, the boundaries of which are modified by the state of things in the country where it is produced, and, in judging it, the jury should be empanelled from the country where the *venue* is laid. That only necessity has stinted Miss Bremer in the choice of her characters is plain enough from the fact, that the interest always springs from the character itself, and not from any accidents of birth or station. Unless Bruno and St. Orme may be taken as exceptions, she gives us no gentlemen who possess a tragic interest merely from the fact that they have deep, dark eyes and noble foreheads, surmounted by curls of glossy blackness, and who have a purulent loquacity on the subject of destiny and kindred matters. We

have no maidens whom some knavish guardian has dispossessed of immense fortunes, to show us how much better off they are without them, but which they nevertheless miraculously recover. There is no smell of burnt cork and *rouge,* no melodramatic suggestion of buskined tyrants, oppressed maidens with unmanageable trains of white satin, and impregnable castles an inch thick, which excited ideas of the horrible and the marvellous in our childish imaginations. Hers are all tales of the present day. The purple, hazy distance of antiquity is not needed to give her characters their proper keeping in the mind's eye of the reader. Her novels show the healthier tone which is beginning to pervade the light literature of the day. (pp. 486-87)

Though sometimes a little ambitious, sometimes deficient in those nicer delicacies of taste which distinguish her sex, often confused in her metaphors, and occasionally too willing to say a profound thing to be able to do so, she generally writes in a sweet, domestic, fireside style of great simplicity, and which gives our hearts the most convincing proof of her being a woman of genius, by leaving them happier and kinder than she found them. In one respect, we think her superior to most of the contemporary novelists, her characters being universal, and not national. Whatever Swedish peculiarity there may be in their manners, there is none in their natures. They are not simply Swedes and Norwegians, but men and women. We recognize them, after a moment's thought, as old acquaintances. They are as much at home in Boston as in Stockholm. Her children, too, and especially her little girls, are hitherto unequalled. In spite of the obstinate assertion of spinsterhood in the prefix to her name, we can hardly help believing that she has a nursery of her own. We know the particular footsteps of each of the little ones, as they hop about overhead. We hear familiar voices from the high chairs at the breakfast-table. We know by rote the exact weight of every one of their heads, and, when we hear a thump upon the staircase or the floor, we are sure beforehand whose voice will be raised to expostulate against destiny and the laws of gravitation. When they ask questions, we remember with a thrill the unanswerable philosophical theories and inextricable syllogisms, that have been propounded to us by the unbreeched Newtons and Leibnitzes of the nursery. While they are in the parlour, we shudder for the vases and the teapoys. While they are out of it, we expect to hear crashes from the china-closet, or cries for assistance from *impromptu* difficulties, to get into which would seem to have demanded a week's forethought. When they levy a tribute of stories, we are reminded how often our stock of invention, and fairy-lore, and improvised doggerel, has been pumped dry by the little besieging army that scaled our knees. And Petrea's nose [in *The Home; or Family Cares and Family Joys*]! It is a character by itself,—a more distinct one than the indefatigable Mr. James has been able to *souvenir,* as the musicians say, out of Scott. Ovid's nose, or Herrick's, was not more individual. (pp. 490-91)

But it is not merely as a painter of character, though she does almost always give us the fresh flowers, and not a mere *hortus siccus,* with designating labels, that Miss Bremer claims our regard. To read them brings us out of the jostling world, and seems gently to lead us back again to the dear circle round the hearth of home; a circle the memory of which, be it bright or gloomy, accompanies the heart through life like a moving horizon, where the clouds still hang at a distance, as if they were made only to be turned into golden towers and pinnacles by the sun, and which keeps alive in us the purest and freshest of our inspirations, the yet dewy, half-opened blossoms of hope and morning. If dear Sancho Panza [a character in Cervantes's *Don Quixote*] blessed the man who invented sleep, so would we, with our whole hearts, bless those who invent thoughts and images for us, that make us children again, and set us chasing butterflies and binding weed nosegays again, in those old meadows, or listening to the history and the legend around the old woodfire, that flickered so pleasantly on the dear faces, which throng about us once more, as ruddy and as free from wrinkles, as they were then. And therefore bless Fredrika Bremer! And who more richly has earned a blessing, than she who can make bloom again those wilted roses of our spring,—who can make us feel that we have yet lost nothing, if we have not lost the angelic capability of being made children again? Those writers who teach us to trust in the buckler of the impenetrable sneer, may, for a while, win the praise of strength from our unsteady and anchorless minds; but in our time of trial, we learn that their strength is but weakness, and that they only are truly mighty who give us back our homely faith. (pp. 491-92)

> *"New Translations of the Writings of Miss Bremer,"* in The North American Review, *Vol. LVIII, No. CXXIII, April, 1844, pp. 480-508.*

JOHN GREENLEAF WHITTIER   (essay date 1844)

[*Whittier was a noted poet, abolitionist, journalist, and critic. His works, informed by his Quaker faith, are noted for their moral content, simple sentiment, and humanitarianism. As a critic, Whittier employed an approach to literature that praised the moralistic efforts of obscure writers and condemned sensational, "immoral" attempts by more well-known writers, such as Lord Byron. Most importantly, Whittier encouraged the idea of American literary nationalism. In the excerpt below, which begins with a quote from* Strife and Peace, *he commends Bremer for her spiritually inspiring works and humanitarian efforts. This essay was originally published in the Lowell, Massachusetts* Middlesex Standard *on August 1, 1844.*]

> AH! that I could be heard by all the oppressed, dejected souls! I would cry to them—"Lift up your head; and confide still in the future, and believe that it is never too late!"—See! I too was bowed down by long suffering, and old age had moreover overtaken me, and I believed that all my strength had vanished:—that my life and my sufferings were in vain—and behold! My head had again been lifted up, my heart appeased, my soul strengthened; and now, in my fiftieth year, I advance into a new future, attended by all that life has of beautiful and worthy of love. The change in my soul has enabled me better to comprehend life and suffering, and I am now firmly convinced that there is no fruitless suffering, and that no virtuous endeavor is in vain. Winter days and nights may bury beneath their pall of snow the sown corn; but when the spring arrives, it will be found equally true, that "there grows much bread in the winter night."
>
> (p. 117)

There are truth, and power, and beauty in the above extract from the writings of the gifted Frederika Bremer. It is worthy the attention of every one who feels the load of life growing heavy, and who is ready to cry out "my burden is greater than I can bear." The great secret of rising above sorrow, of conquering misfortune, of reconciling disappointments, is to be found in a resolution to do good to others—to make others happy. Once firmly entered upon, this resolution will save us. In the pure and healthful excitement of some great and good object of benevolence and duty, we forget ourselves, and our sufferings; the weary woe which has been settling around our hearts melts away like mist in the sunshine; the troubled and haunting thoughts which have maddened us give place to "the peace which passeth understanding."

Frederika Bremer has experienced all this—and hence her ability to "minister to minds diseased."—She has made herself happy while contributing to the intellectual enjoyment of others—and her writings, especially her admirable **"Strife and Peace"** are characterized by democratic sentiment, and a clear appreciation of the equal claims of humanity. She is a decided ABOLITIONIST; and, like her gifted English sister Harriet Martineau, evinces a deep interest in the progress of anti-slavery sentiment in America. (pp. 117-18)

> *John Greenleaf Whittier, "It Is Never Too Late (Frederika Bremer)," in his* Whittier on Writers and Writing: The Uncollected Critical Writings of John Greenleaf Whittier, *edited by Edwin Harrison Cady and Harry Hayden Clark, Syracuse University Press, 1950, pp. 117-18.*

WALT WHITMAN   (essay date 1846)

[*Whitman is regarded as one of America's finest nineteenth-century poets and a great literary innovator. His* Leaves of Grass, *in which he celebrated the common man, democracy, and sexuality, had a major influence on modern free verse. Here, Whitman recommends that children read Bremer's novels because of the useful moral lessons they impart. This essay first appeared in the Brooklyn* Daily Eagle *on August 18, 1846.*]

If we ever have children, the first book after the New Testament, (with reverence we say it) that shall be made their household companion—a book whose spirit shall be infused in them as sun-warmth is infused in the earth in spring—shall be Miss Bremer's novels. We know nothing more likely to melt and refine the human character—particularly the young character. In the study of the soul portraits therein delineated—in their motives, actions, and the results of those actions—every youth, of either sex, will be irresistibly impelled to draw some moral, and make some profitable application to his or her own case.

> *Walt Whitman, "Extracts from Whitman's Criticisms of Books and Authors: Frederika Bremer," in his* The Uncollected Poetry and Prose of Walt Whitman, *Vol. 1, edited by Emory Holloway, Peter Smith, 1972, p. 128.*

THE CHRISTIAN REMEMBRANCER   (essay date 1849)

[*This anonymous reviewer maintains that Bremer's "absolute want of settled principle and Christian faith" is revealed through her use of the themes of life and love.*]

[Frederika Bremer's] heart and imagination dwell more gladly, expatiate more freely, in scenes of innocent affection, harmless mirth, honest, pure, self-sacrifice, than in the workings of a dark misanthropic spirit. There is no *love* of evil in her mind; on the contrary, it warms to everything pure, generous, and noble. This all her works testify, especially (we are sorry to enforce the qualification) her earlier ones. But the persual of them all forces one painful conviction on the mind—that with all a certain constant, and we believe sincere profession of religious feeling, the series of her works betrays an absolute want of settled principle and Christian faith. She has a religion of her own, but it is not the Christian religion. There is no recognition even of the duty of casting down imaginations, no bringing into captivity *any* thought to the obedience of Christ. If her reason or fancy falls in with the revealed word, she makes much of it, and talks religiously; but where they diverge, she follows without scruple her own reason, as it would seem, not concealing from herself that she does so. Gifted with great natural endowments, with an intense love of nature and appreciation of art, with a heart and intellect apparently formed for enjoyment, and a power of entering into, realising, and almost prolonging the present; with an extraordinary knowledge of character, and insight into motives; an admiration for what is great and powerful, and a contempt for everything mean and unreal; and inspired by a genial expansive benevolence which feels as if it could embrace all mankind; she sets herself to study and comprehend this world which she so dearly loves, this life in which natures like hers find so much to satisfy and to enjoy, and yet where she sees so much evil and misery; and without looking for a guide, without depending on that which Providence gives her—as if indeed there were neither guide she must follow nor revelation to which she must bow,—she sets herself to reconcile difficulties, to make a world of her own, an image of this present one, where things can go as she chooses, where she may follow out her speculations, and set to right all that is wrong in her own way; where she may allay the doubts and answer the questions of a restless, undisciplined spirit. (pp. 19-20)

Miss Bremer's do not *aim* to be what in any strict sense may be called religious novels. She takes her own course, developing her own views, apparently not conscious of infringing any rule, or opposing any man's prejudices. She has one enigma which she seeks to solve, and one panacea for all evils moral and physical. The enigma—*the* question of questions, is, 'What is Life?'—the universal panacea is 'Love;' and these two watchwords pervade all her works.

And first, of 'Life.' Authors have, by prescriptive right, the privilege of representing the whole world, the entire human family, as exclusively occupied with their own peculiar speculations; and Miss Bremer gives up none of the advantages her position thus offers her. With her, the whole world—young or old, grave or gay, prosperous or unfortunate—is perplexed, overwhelmed, engrossed, by that problem called Life; what it is, in what it consists, who has it, and who has it not. Not very intelligible questions; and, as definite subjects of inquiry, we believe, absolutely unknown to the world at large; but apparently the first thought of the opening mind in Sweden. Life has many meanings, which adds greatly to the difficulties of the solution. With Miss Bremer it sometimes means thought, sometimes excitement, sometimes success and prosperity, sometimes sympathy, sometimes happiness—knowledge—acquaintance with self—the fulfilment of active duties—impulse—feeling—animation—enjoyment; anything and everything that is not dull, inanimate, sleepy, unreal; and the too frequent tendency of the discussions of these various aspects is to make this life all in all, to make the present everything, and in it practically to forget the future. There is permanency and sufficiency given to it; it is a palace, and not a caravansary. As the scene of our probation, it has a length and breadth and height given to it; not like 'the ship that passeth over the waves of the waters, and the trace thereof cannot be found;' nor 'the bird, which when it has flown through the air, no token of her way can be seen;' nor 'the arrow shot at a mark,' nor 'the life

that passeth away like a shadow.' There is no sympathy with such images of transitoriness as these. With her, life is real, not only as it affects our immortal interests, but it is something real, admirable, *sufficient* in itself. And if a sense of its insufficiency will creep in, it is only because men are yet ignorant of the glories to which mortal life can attain:—the period of universal enlightenment is to come; we may even live to see it; we may now realise it to ourselves if we will. Visions are opened out of what is to be; we are not always to be imperfect, not always shortcomers, beginners, in this world. 'Life' is to be something complete, with developed powers and capacities for happiness; with a beginning, a middle, and an end; with not only 'rich moments,' but rich periods; not mere foretastes of a future state of things, but a settled, present, blissful existence. This vision of life, it is no wonder, stands in some measure for heaven; it dazzles the eyes till they cannot see beyond. It is one of the forms of setting up the temporal against the eternal, which would seem to belong peculiarly to a self-indulgent, luxurious age; not denying the eternal and unseen, even in thought, but *looking* at the present, and teaching the heart to be satisfied with it,—as with health and spirits and active intellect men can readily be; and into Miss Bremer's earthly paradise they will admit no other. Those who, to use her fanciful language, at present 'creep mole-like round the roots of the tree of life'—those who are dull, unfortunate, sick, stupid, must look about them. She feels pity for them; she would willingly raise them to her level; she seeks to work a transformation in their 'inner life;' but if, in spite of these benevolent pains, dull and sick and sorrowful they still remain, there is no room for them in the terrestrial paradise—they must knock at another Door. (pp. 27-9)

In connexion with her adoration of . . . ['Life,'] is her evident shrinking from decay and death; not that death is absent from her thoughts, or that she does not sometimes avail herself very freely of its agency; but death, as absolutely irresistible, is a growing *crux*, and is becoming almost revolting to her feelings. She imagines human strength contending against it, and prevailing in the contest. She invokes unheard of powers of nature to her aid. In this spirit she delights in impossible, we may say, miraculous cures; in bringing people to the very jaws of death, the verge of the grave, when by all natural laws they must die, and then snatching them from it by some new discovery of science. In the case, for example, of Augustin, one of the 'Brothers,' in ['**Brothers and Sisters**']: he is sinking under a fatal disease, or what is expected to prove so; and is attended by a bevy of physicians, who are without hope: his sister, in despair, writes to her old lover in India, and conjures him to come and help her; he obeys the summons, brings a plant of unknown powers which he has discovered in the East, applies it, and effects a complete cure; a contemptible piece of *hocus pocus,* which no sensible mind, unwarped by fancy or theory, could have devised. Two other personages in the same book are restored to health, and live, in much the same impossible fashion. (p. 35)

From Life, the transition with Miss Bremer is inevitable to *Love,* holding, as it does, so leading a place in her list of remedies [for potentially fatal illnesses]. It is indeed more potent than all the herbs of the East, and perhaps with more reason. With her the *word* is everything, for in order to adapt it to the wants of all her characters in their different moral stages, she is obliged to allow great deviations in its meaning. She confounds heavenly and earthly love, pure and impure, lawful affection and idolatry. There is but one absolutely necessary quality; so it is but strong, an intense passion, it is the wonder-working, reforming power. She does not oppose mortal and divine love, but takes them for one and the same, and literally applies the words in Scripture which relate to the one, to the other. (p. 36)

[In] '**Brothers and Sisters,**' Engel, represented as peculiarly innocent and religious, speaks thus of her atheist lover:

> If above me there was a world full of light and beauty, with angels' songs, and all the glory of the world or of heaven, but *he* was not there— and if below me were another world, dark and desolate, cold and silent as the grave, but *he* was there; in which of the two would I be? In the grave! in the grave, in eternal darkness, with him!

At this profession, Hedvig, the elder, pattern sister, the idea of perfection, 'smiled; a gentle light was kindled in her eye through a swelling tear!'

How a writer of Miss Bremer's natural penetration should really be delighted with such proofs of affection as this, should attach any weight to them, even so far as they profess to go—that she should imagine any person nearer doing this, for saying it, supposing her brought to the proof, and the scene of eternal horror and darkness as visibly before her eyes, as this world and her lover now are—that she should believe there is anything in the nature of a sacrifice in the profession, is wonderful, and is a proof how stupifying and blinding such imaginations are. It simply proves that the speaker is engrossed with the present passion, to the utter disregard, that is, *disbelief,* for the time, of anything beyond. It shows that at the time Engel did not practically believe in either heaven or hell; she simply wished to indulge her present inclination. There is nothing finer in all this, than in giving way to *any* temptation. All who live in sin, simply prefer present gratification to future consequences. However, Miss Bremer evidently considers it a noble sentiment, a sort of desperate heroic generosity, to defy Heaven. (pp. 36-7)

We could multiply examples of love and love-making, in all their innumberable bearings and aspects, *ad infinitum,* but they are not wanted for any purpose of our own, and would not prove very edifying to our readers. None but a woman certainly could give this sentiment so commanding and abiding a control over all the concerns of life. We must however in justice to Miss Bremer say, that with so much for grave censure and reprobation on this topic, she is free from many of the commoner, vulgarer errors in its mode of treatment. We have no designing mothers or designing daughters; nor, in spite of all her preposterous expectations of 'life' and power from marriage, does she yet treat it as the sole object of woman's ambition. She does not forget respect to her sex; she has proper *esprit-de-corps*—almost too much so, we must think, for her ordinary mode of viewing the marriage tie is simply as instructing, reforming, edifying the men. The harsh nature is to be softened, the irreligious converted, the heedless sobered, the evil liver reformed, the bashful made self-possessed, the awkward refined; and all this without a corresponding class of advantages to the other side. The ladies are a sort of guardian angel, who sacrifice their own peace to us ruder mortals for our good. All that men can impart in return is *strength*—a quality of which indeed Miss Bremer makes a great point, but it is a severe and bitter tonic to most of the gentle beings who require the remedy, as in the pathetic case of poor Nina [in the novel of the same name] who has the austere and forbidding

Count Ludvig as it were forced down her throat, and literally dies of the bitter draught. (pp. 37-8)

[Each of Miss Bremer's novels] has its peculiar set of characters, which harmonize well together, and are remembered in connexion with each other; but all her stories are deficient in plot and arrangement, to a degree which prevents many readers from ever appreciating their otherwise great ability. They are in fact what she calls them, with some consciousness of her want of skill as a story-architect,—'Sketches,' groupings of characters and scenes, rather than well ordered fictions. And it is surprising how important a well managed, well arranged plot is to the interest. The scenes *tell* so much more when given in proper order, and leading up to a climax. But in Miss Bremer, the climax may be anywhere; sometimes in the beginning, as in '**The H— Family;**' sometimes in the middle, as in '**The Home;**' and then after this pleasant excitement, we have to wander off in the dark, as it were, not knowing what to expect, or why we wait any longer; while she introduces new characters and fresh incidents, which would have done excellently well to lead up to a grand climax, but seem poor or out of place, or long-drawn-out, after. And if her stories suffer so much at present from this defect, their continuance in general acceptance and popularity is likely to be still more affected. They stand a chance of being forgotten, like so many loose leaves. (pp. 38-9)

Those who made acquaintance with Miss Bremer first in '**Strife and Peace,**' would perhaps of all her readers be most favourably impressed—not that it equals some others in power, but—by a certain sweetness and rustic grace that characterize this little story especially, which is besides more a whole than her longer histories. It is indeed a very pretty and graceful pastoral; and the character of Susannah, with its ebullitions of temper, warm generosity, and affectionate heart, is quite one to dwell on the memory. The struggles she goes through in combating her disappointed feelings, the humble sense of her own deficiencies, the devoted love which outweighs them all, the practical good sense compensating for the want of intellectual cultivation, and the gradual influence all these qualities gain upon Harold, are detailed with great truth and delicacy. Nothing, too, can be more spirited than their 'Strifes,' carried on with such utter unreasonableness, and the disputes on the comparative merits of Sweden and Norway, from the magnitude of their mountains and waves down to their national dishes. The beautiful descriptions of wild Norwegian country—the sympathy, too, with the small domestic world of the poultry yard, showing such vivid enjoyment of every natural scene—all make this a most delightful little story. . . . (p. 45)

We now come to ['**Brothers and Sisters'**]—Miss Bremer's latest production, and, we are sorry to add, her worst. The weeds, which have shown themselves in all her writings, have here overpowered the flowers. It is rambling, flighty, unnatural. The watchwords 'Life,' 'Love,' and 'Beauty,' are more prominent, and play an overbearing part. The book is a sort of harmonizing of heathenism and Christianity, an attempt to construct a Valhalla, in which the Bible is allowed the first place, though it is but a nominal sovereignty. The golden age is certainly coming, and everything, even evil, is made to tend towards that blissful period. In this work, especially, we feel that in her idea of the Supreme Being, and the Christian's God, there is little in common but the name;—so much superstition is there, so many heathenish thoughts and images; such recklessness in the expression of profane thoughts; such a want of holy fear, true faith, or hatred of evil. And in this moral obscuration the intellect also has suffered. Some good scenes there are, but as a whole the falling off is melancholy. Instead of her characteristic faults being occasional clouds and mists, they form the atmosphere; and we are sometimes disposed to think that Nature is dead, as well as 'the good Balder,' the deity over whom she laments. And when we have a glimpse of the old manner, it is disfigured by something monstrous. Uncle Herkules, who is the advocate of common sense, and represents the wisdom of our forefathers, now and then reminding us of *ma chère mère* [in **'The Neighbours'**], swears horribly. His vocation, indeed, is alternately to swear and pray, which he does with so rapid a transition, that he has scarcely risen from the one exercise before he delivers himself to the other. His conscience, however, is entirely at rest on the question of this habit. But his easy apologies, and the mode in which he expresses his conviction that all is right in spite of this 'breath of the mouth,' as he designates his oaths, are, unfortunately, of too cool and irreverent a nature to be repeated. These constant allusions to the Evil One, the sort of familiarity with that awful power which the book implies, is something astonishing, when we know it to come from female hands, so familiar with the beautiful, the angelic—the 'rich,' the 'full,' in life. But from other sources we learn that swearing is a Swedish vice; and Miss Bremer apparently considers it her vocation to reconcile whatever is universally practised with her theory of good. So, if people will swear, she has, in her benevolence, to prove that at least it does no harm, and to resolve it into a sort of piquant characteristic seasoning.

Again, there is his pet niece, Gothilda, one of the 'sisters' not taken up by the philanthropic visions of the rest of the party, and whose part is to be lively and amusing. She shows real spirit and animation, but every now and then utters impieties enough to make the hair stand on end; indeed, such a little heathen was never before imagined at sixteen. (pp. 49-50)

There is one point, however, on which Miss Bremer knows still how to appeal to the sympathies of her readers, and which we really believe to have been one cause of her general popularity. It is the prominence, the interest she gives to those necessary duties and pleasures of life, eating and drinking. These she treats as a true woman of genius. She knows their power over the heart of man, and does not scruple to invest them with all their real importance. She knows as a fact, that they do act a part in every event and circumstance of life; that, in sorrow or joy, we must eat; and she is not afraid of investing them with their full consequence in the social drama. No grief is too poignant, no anxiety too engrossing, no joy too transcendant, for eating and drinking not to assert their influence in sustaining the mourner, encouraging the dejected, and helping the happy to realise their joy. And not only does this appeal to our appetite give a genuine, hearty, genial character to her writings; it has also assisted in establishing their moral reputation, in giving a general impression of soundness and domesticity: for if the gentlemen eat, the ladies cook; and what harm can we really suspect in spite of appearances, in a household where its mistress spends half her time in her store-room weighing out coffee and sugar, and where her daughters bake the patties, fry the pancakes, and whip the creams?—where a threatened *liaison* is interrupted by care for the preserves, and a wife's well-founded jealousies lost sight of in a misapprehension about the veal cutlets?

We can hardly lose the impression, that this homely simplicity of manners implies what it would do in our country. The perpetual discussion of dinners and suppers, the never-ending baskets of provisions, the share the ladies take in their preparation, the warm disputes on baking and brewing, quite carry our thoughts out of the region of unlawful speculation and low morality. With us, these evils are the fruit of idleness and nothing-to-do which must always be their more natural sphere. We cannot readily suppose them compatible with a social state, in which scepticism and infidelity are tolerated, and the most sacred domestic ties too often disregarded.

Of toleration and sympathy for unbelief, we have adduced proof enough in Miss Bremer's writings; and though we give her credit for sincere desire to raise the moral tone of her countrymen, there are yet too many indications of familiarity with a corrupt social state throughout her works, we find too confused an idea of what are the duties and callings of her own sex, too great an indulgence in what she thinks inevitable evils, to make her a safe guide even in those points where her naturally pure feeling and good sense might otherwise have qualified her to become one. (pp. 61-2)

> *"Miss Bremer's Novels," in* The Christian Remembrancer, *n.s. Vol. XVII, No. LXIII, January, 1849, pp. 18-62.*

J.G.W. [JOHN GREENLEAF WHITTIER]   (poem date 1849)

[*In the following poem, which was first published in the Washington, D.C.* National Era *on November 15, 1849, Whittier welcomes Bremer to the United States.*]

> Welcome from thy dusky Norland,
>   Daughter of the Vikings bold!
> Welcome to the sunny Vineland
>   Which they sought and found of old!
>
> Soft as lapse of Silga's waters
>   When the moon of summer shines,
> Strong as winter from his mountains
>   Roaring through the Northern pines,
>
> Swan of Abo! we have listened
>   To thy saga and thy song,
> Till a household joy and gladness
>   We have known and loved thee long.
>
> By the mansion's marble mantel,
>   By the log-warmed cabin's hearth,
> Thy sweet thoughts and Northern fancies,
>   Meet and mingle with our mirth;
>
> And o'er weary spirits keeping
>   Sorrow's night-watch, long and chill,
> Shine they like the sun of summer
>   Over midnight vale and hill.
>
> Sweet eyes smile for us in Norland,
>   Household forms we love are there;
> In their bitter grief of parting,
>   And their bridal joy, we share.
>
> We alone are strangers to thee,
>   Thou our friend and teacher art;
> Come and know us as we know thee,
>   Let us meet thee heart to heart!

To our household homes and altars,
    We, in turn, thy steps would lead,
As thy loving hand has led us
    O'er the threshold of the Swede.

> *J.G.W. [John Greenleaf Whittier], "To Frederika Bremer," in* Littell's Living Age, *Vol. XXIII, No. 291, December 15, 1849, p. 518.*

THE ATHENAEUM (essay date 1853)

[*This anonymous reviewer considers* The Homes of the New World *an inaccurate representation of American society and attacks Bremer for her indiscretion in publishing her personal impressions of the people she met in the United States. The critic concludes that* The Homes of the New World *"is not equal to [Bremer's] abilities or to her reputation."*]

[*The Homes of the New World: Impressions of America*] will not increase Miss Bremer's reputation. The topics of which it treats, and the manner of that treatment, are not suited to the habits and character of her mind. Nor were the circumstances under which Miss Bremer acquired her knowledge of America, and of what she calls the Homes of the New World, favourable to her object of writing a book. She seems to have been received almost everywhere in that country very much in the capacity of a public character,—certainly as one of those European celebrities to whom America was much indebted for the honour of a visit. Everywhere, therefore, she met with the urgent hospitality of persons whose resources enabled them to provide a distinguished entertainment. Miss Bremer, in truth, was the guest of the higher class of the American people; and it is greatly to the credit of that class, and greatly to the credit of literature, that so much zeal was displayed in behalf of the Swedish authoress. But to be the object of hospitality such as we have described implies duties and involves conditions. The stranger is in a great measure lost in the guest; and a freedom of observation and discussion which would be perfectly natural and proper on the part of a foreign traveller who entirely by his own contrivances and resources should make his way throughout the provinces and among the people of a country, would be altogether preposterous and unbearable on the part of a foreign guest enjoying the distinguished hospitality of the inhabitants and of the State to be criticized and dissected. It is almost a necessity that a book like the one before us, written in the midst of the "Homes" which it describes, should be essentially imperfect and partial. Personal names and allusions are altogether unavoidable:—individual places must be described, and described as being seen in company with certain companions. The real sentiments of the writer, therefore, can be expressed in writing only with considerable restraint,—and always, in the case of a generous mind, under the influence of a strong desire to avoid expressions and reflections distasteful to the circle which has done its best to remove sources of annoyance. The principal characteristic of Miss Bremer's book is, the manifest prevalence of this constraint,—and of this desire to convey her views of the truth, not unfairly, but as agreeably and softly as possible, and to leave a subject imperfect rather than venture upon doubtful ground. As a description, therefore, of America and American society, we regard these volumes as entitled to very little attention.—Nor can we praise Miss Bremer's work highly on the ground of its literary merits. It is certainly tedious. The subjects are overdone,—there is neither narrative nor adventure,—and there is a great deal too much of the author's own self. The first volume appears to us wholly superfluous. The second is rather better;—

and in the third, some of the chapters deserve our high commendation.

A considerable part, however, of each of the three volumes ought never to have been printed,—perhaps never to have been written. We allude to those numerous passages occupied wholly in dilating on the characters and capacities of the private persons with whom, as a guest principally, Miss Bremer became acquainted. We are fully sensible of Miss Bremer's delicacy in scrupulously refraining from all harsh reflections in these cases. But the course actually taken is only one degree less objectionable than it would have been to fill a book with severe criticisms on men and women from whom infinite kindness had been received. As the matter really stands, Miss Bremer has injured literature, that she might gratify her friends:—for, we cannot but regard as indefensible and injurious those constantly-recurring pages in which we find personal descriptions manifestly governed by a desire to see only the bright side of the picture. We admit the amiable nature of the motive,—but we object decidedly to literature being converted into a vehicle of private gratitude. Miss Bremer's acknowledgements, we make no doubt, were expressed personally with becoming warmth and dignity,—and there the matter should have had an end. It was unadvisable that any book which she might write on America should attempt to make public characters of the sensible Mr. A.; the amiable Mrs. B; the attractive Miss C; and so on to the end of a procession of alphabets, simply because she had received from them great civility. We desire to speak strongly on this point,—and on this occasion,—because the practice to which we refer is becoming prevalent and offensive; and if it is to continue, we cannot help saying that it would be a blessing to mankind if authors and authoresses as a visible race should become wholly extinct,—and literature, like the ancient Oracles, proceed entirely from unseen and thoroughly anonymous professors.

The manner in which Miss Bremer refers to most of the eminent Americans with whom she became acquainted is almost as open to remark as her mode of dealing with what may be called the publico-private portions of the book. It was natural and proper that she should record her meeting or her conversations with persons so distinguished as Mr. Emerson and Mr. Webster,—and for a statement of facts the world would have been thankful. But between a record of that nature, and the recurrence of page after page of admiring disquisition on a particular person, there is a broad difference:—at all events, when the disquistion is printed as part of a philosophical work on a grave subject. Miss Bremer has an undoubted right to admire Mr. Emerson, and to suppose that she is carried off her feet by the depth of his transcendental writings,—but the book which she now publishes is not the proper place for saying so with the emphasis she employs. Miss Bremer is, we fancy, capable of something much exceeding barren admiration of an eccentric philosopher;—and if Mr. Emerson and his views had been introduced at all, they should have been manfully and fairly discussed,—not employed as occasions for mere drawing-room rhetoric.

The successful portions of Miss Bremer's work are those which discuss questions more or less ethical:—as, for example, the principles and beliefs and practical effect of the various sects of America. Still better are those passages which describe natural objects,—and endeavour to convey general impressions of large regions:—as, for instance, such descriptions as those of Cuba and of the Western States. The descriptions also of the public proceedings of which Miss Bremer happened to be a witness—such as, the sittings of Congress, and public meetings in various towns,—are very vigorous. (p. 1153)

We have been particularly struck with the vigour and truthfulness of the general description given by Miss Bremer—in the admirable chapter addressed to the Queen Dowager of Denmark—of the origin and rise of an American settlement. The planting of the solitary log-house—its expansion into a hamlet, then into a village—the first imperfect provisions for religion and education—the casual visits of a vagrant steamboat, leading at last to the sailings of a fleet—finally, the growth of a large city distinguished, as is well said, by the School, the Church, the Printing Press, and the State's House, everywhere the ensign of the Anglo-American—these make a perfect and rapid picture.—Equally entitled to attention is an admirable outline of the resources and character of the Western States.—The capacity for generalization and the singular felicity of expression manifested in such passages excite regret that Miss Bremer has been led by her amiable temper to amplify into three volumes materials and reflections which if compressed into less space might have occupied a distinguished place in our libraries. . . . We are disposed to think that, if Miss Bremer had given herself time and fair play she would have produced a book on America which might have become an authority. As it is, truth compels us to say, that her eminent gifts have, unfortunately for herself and for others, not saved her from falling into serious errors in the publication of a work which as a whole is not equal to her abilities or to her reputation. (p. 1154)

A review of "The Homes of the New World: Impressions of America," in The Athenaeum, *No. 1353, October 1, 1853, pp. 1153-54.*

GRAHAM'S MAGAZINE (essay date 1853)

[*This anonymous critic dismisses* The Homes of the New World *as "kitchen gossip" and condemns Bremer for violating the confidences of the people she met in the United States by publishing commentary on their personal lives. The reviewer concedes that* The Homes of the New World *is entertaining, but labels the work "a ridiculous production" when viewed as a representation of American life.*]

It is impossible to read ["**The Homes of the New World; Impressions in America**"] without being impressed with the occasional injustice of literary fame. The article which Miss Bremer supplies is a poor one, but it is by the author of "**Home**" and "**The Neighbors**," and therefore will be sure to sell in the market. . . . Miss Bremer is a woman of a certain affectionateness of genius, who has written novels which have given her a worldwide celebrity, and which have converted her readers into personal friends. Their great merit is confined to the representation of domestic life, for when she aims at passion, she concocts out of impotent Byronics, and faded Weterisms, a broth of emotional forcible-feebleness, too vapid for any but the most jaded sentimentalist to relish. But she has an audience, and every thing she writes is read in Sweden, Germany, Great Britain, and the United States. Accordingly, her present book will be read by thousands who will never condescend to read a better one on the subject. It requires but very little information to decide that the work, considered as a representation of the United States, is a ridiculous production; and one is vexed at the thought of how much confident ignorance she will communicate to her army of readers. The book is lean in thought, loose in style, pert in judgment, deficient in almost every thing which makes a book valuable. It may entertain, but it cannot

inform. It is made up of personal gossip and grandmother chatter. Indeed, the authoress chatters about every thing, persons, principles, politics, religion, scenery, democracy, literature, art, slavery, her own aspirations, her dyspepsia, her sentiments, and about six hundred and forty-three other things—pleasant chatter enough, but hardly worthy of publication and translation. It is provoking to think that such confused talk, hardly up to the level of ordinary conversation among educated people, should be presented to so large a portion of the civilized world in the shape of a book, should be puffed by literary journals, and should be so extensively read as to make its flashy and superficial gossip exert a positive influence on opinion.

It must be admitted that, of the numerous varieties of chatter in which Miss Bremer indulges, her chatter about persons is the raciest and most entertaining. She saw a great many people, public and domestic, and she gives her impressions of all. But on what principle of propriety or even decency, she can justify the publication of much of her personal gossip, must be a mystery to everybody at all infected with English or American reserve. She was received with great hospitality into many private families. . . . But her hosts and hostesses, while they were thus opening their arms, hearts, and houses to welcome her, probably did not dream that she tripped up to her chamber to record all the opinions and confidences she had heard in the parlor—that she was dispatching to Sweden the gossip of Boston and New York—and, more than all, that she would publish to the world all the dear little secrets which had been lisped and whispered in her ear. Mr. A., a merchant, is introduced to three continents as a handsome man; Miss B., innocent even of an anonymous magazine article, is paraded before the same vast public as a heavenly soul; and Mrs. C, wife and mother, hears a thousand-fold reverberation of the merits of her pastry and her children. Miss Bremer contrives to hit upon those qualities of mind, or heart, or person, which throw their modest possessors into agonies to see in print. There can be no sanctity or privacy in life, if this fondling, and caressing, and pawing of private individuals, gets to be established in literature. Such things may harmonize with Swedish manners, and persons who are handsome and heavenly there, may desire to have all the world know it, but in sneering, reserved, ironical England and America, exhibitions of this kind are more apt to make people titter than to evoke their tearful sympathy. . . . It is bad enough when praise is heaped on a man's qualities of mind, but when it is lavished on his comeliness, or affectionateness, or morality, or religion, it becomes absolutely excruciating to the recipient, and wakes the hoarsest kind of horse-laughs from an unsympathizing public. Besides, Miss Bremer assumes very often a patronizing kindliness toward her entertainers, more provoking, perhaps, than her confectionery and sweetmeats of compliment. One lady is a dear, little, pleasant body; another is a dear, little, bustling body; another a dear, little, chatting, inquisitive, funny body; another, a dear, little charming nobody; and so on. The blessed recipients of these gracious condescensions must feel like assassinating her with their bodkins.

If private hospitality to public characters is to be chronicled in this way, the time will soon come when people will be compelled to put over their parlor-doors the sign—"No authors admitted here: inquire at the kitchen." And, indeed, the kind of gossip that Miss Bremer indulges in is admirably adapted for the latter locality. If what she publishes ought to be published at all, it certainly should not be obtained in the beaten way of friendship, but by questioning the domestics. If our readers can conceive of the cooks and chambermaids of a family prattling about their employers in a vast sounding gallery, by which their chat was heard all over the globe, they may appreciate the terrible effects of having at their houses a gossiping woman of genius.

We have likewise to notice the indelicacy which Miss Bremer exhibits in the freedom of her comments on persons whose invitations she accepted, but which she wished to decline. While staying with Mrs. A. she is tormented with the thought that, in a few days, she must fulfill an engagement to stay a week with Miss B.; and this reluctance to go she expresses in print. Now this may be very proper in private letter to her sister in Sweden, but it appears to us the height of conceit and impertinence to publish it. She finds, to be sure, that Miss B. is not half so much of a bore as she expected; is, indeed, a nice, dear, well-meaning, bustling, tidy little body, who loves her to distraction; and this discovery is so gratifying that she publishes it likewise. Can the impudence of condescension go further? We cannot believe the notions of propriety which ostracise such impertinences as these are confined to any nation. Politeness has been defined as "benevolence in small things;" and what benevolence can there be in first expressing contempt of an entertainer, and then modifying it into good-natured toleration? In private society such superciliousness acts like a fire poison, and it becomes a million times more insulting when published to the world. In a flash newspaper, of limited circulation, it would be disgraceful; and we cannot conceive of its being lifted into any dignity by its appearance in the pages of a tourist, whose reputation gives it an extensive circulation.

In passing from Miss Bremer's comments on private individuals to her descriptions of the persons, families, and houses of the authors and public men she visited in America, we can hardly decide whether or not she violates any principles of proper reserve. It seems to be now an understood maxim that eminent men can have no private life. Whom they married, when they married, why they married, how much they married, how many times they married, the number of their children, the intellectual or unintellectual character of their wives, their joys, sorrows, whims, crotchets, peculiarities—all are considered public property; and fortunate is the gossiping tourist who can give the world information respecting such important matters. It is doubtless unpleasant for a man who has, perhaps, committed no offense but that of publishing a book, to be trotted out before the public in this way; but then *his* feelings are not thought worthy of being considered where the public curiosity is roused. We suppose that Miss Bremer would expect the same treatment if an American tourist visited her in Sweden, and therefore does as she would be done by. But, it must be admitted, she has used her privileges in this respect to their full extent. Irving, Bryant, Longfellow, Emerson, Lowell, Parker, Alcott, Sumner, Downing, Miss Lynch, Channing, not to mention others, are the objects of her insatiable gossip. Undoubtedly many of her descriptions exhibit a shrewd insight of character, and, occasionally, a quality of mind, or disposition, or person, is happily caught and embodied. She, however, necessarily makes mistakes. Had she informed these persons that she intended to sketch their portraits for the public, they would have been on their guard. Those who did not escape from her altogether, would have appended to their conversation explanatory notes. They would have said, after hazarding a careless remark, "I beg you to consider this as not being my whole philosophy of life;" or, "Miss Bremer, you will have the kindness to consider this as a joke;" or, "Miss Bremer, as I shall probably forget the observation I am now going to make the moment after it has passed my lips, I beg you to consign it to a similar oblivion." As it is, however, they are held responsible before the world for trifles, chance sayings, capricious expressions, and all the little nothings which so readily escape from a man in conversation, but which appear ridiculous in print. Hawthorne, with his usual genius for dodging lion-hunters, succeeded in giving her the slip, though she was on his trail two or three times. She, however, saw Mrs Hawthorne, honors her with a good deal of pert, Bremer condescension, and unhesitatingly prints every thing about Hawthorne himself, which, in the simplicities of conversation, she obtains from his wife. This is almost the greatest outrage in a book full of outrages against common sense and common propriety. Yet a work, crammed with stuff of the kind we have described, has for its motto—"Sing unto the Lord a new song." If kitchen gossip is thus to be raised to the dignity of a solemn psalm, and prattle is to be substituted for prayer, we think that Miss Bremer can present strong claims to be the mouth-piece of the new religion.

The readers of these volumes will be amused, and the unfortunate victims correspondingly vexed, at the sentimentality of some of her friendships with authors. She desires, with true German ravenousness, to commune with the soul of each great person she meets, and, in one case, records what, in America, would be deemed quite an "affair of the heart." Two souls, of which hers is one, look through their visual organs at the stars—a pressure of the hand follows this terrestrial contemplation—and they are friends forever. There is nothing essentially ridiculous in this, except the publication of it to the world. Unutterable emotions should be unprinted emotions, especially when names are recorded at full length, and a man of fine genius and lofty character may be represented in a ludicrous light. But reserve is not Miss Bremer's forte. Again, she makes honorable mention of a cast of her hands being made at the request of two friends, who desired to possess the "counterfeit presentiment" of those little organs; and then she wonders, with exquisite simplicity, that people will insist upon it that her hand is beautiful, when, in fact, it is *only* small and delicate—a delicious bit of candor, which would be considered a subtle stroke of genius in a humorist. (pp. 645-46)

The charge that Miss Bremer brings against Lucretia Mott [in **"The Homes of the New World"**], of not listening to other people's thoughts and observations, is hardly a severe one, if the said thoughts and observations are of the character which Miss Bremer is accustomed to make. Indeed, she has too great a desire to hear herself talk. According to her own account she thought and observed a good deal to Mr. Emerson; and if that gentleman retains the errors of his metaphysical system, it will be from an utter incapacity to receive the light which the author of **"The Neighbors"** was kind enough to radiate upon him. The Rev. Theodore Parker also came in for a share of her bountiful intellectual wealth. It seems, from her account, that Mr. Parker, though he has spent his life in exploring theology, has only arrived at ethics; and, with the kindness of her nature, she informed him of that fact, and opened a controversy on the subject. She probably availed herself liberally of that logical resource known as "the lady's reason," and Mr. P., to his eternal honor, was too gallant to contradict a woman, and heard her with admirable "candor," and "conceded many thing." Mr. Parker is a master of irony, and we can conceive of his reading this account of his "giving in" with a peculiar sparkle about his lips and eyes. Mr. Alcott, a man unfortunate in some expressions of his opinions which have wandered abroad, but in the depth, delicacy, and largeness of his detached thoughts second to few transcendentalists in the United States, and an idealist who has really grappled with some of the problems of life, is dismissed as "the good Alcott," after his system has been overturned by the citation of a commonplace. Miss Bremer has complacently recorded the trashy truisms by which she obtained these triumphs over men who are at least thinkers; and she does not appear to be aware that they know that two and two make four as well as she. Indeed, the most edifying portions of her volumes are those which chronicle her victories in matters relating to metaphysics and theology, when metaphysicians and theologians "listened to her thoughts and observations." We trust that this beneficent result of her visit to the United States, will be felt in the conversion of all the heresiarchs she met to the true faith. If they persist now in holding their naughty opinions, charity will be thrown away upon them, for they sin against light, and error is transferred from their intellects to their wills. But we conclude that this last and worst consequence of their heresies will not occur, for Miss Bremer is careful to inform us that they are admirable and virtuous people, and that their defects are speculative and not moral.

In addition to her remarks on persons, Miss Bremer favors her readers with numerous "thoughts and observations" on American institutions, manners, and life, and some fine descriptions of scenery. She appears to have gleaned her information principally from conversation, and as she talked with a great variety of people, representing widely different views, her mind was pretty well filled with a disordered mass of facts, principles, and opinions, not likely to be systematized in an understanding, which Providence does not appear to have constructed with a view to its exercise on philosophical questions. The general representation of the United States is highly favorable, but the most superficial reader can perceive that this is owing to the pertinacious way in which she was petted by all classes. She judges from impressions not insight; and an American who should go to Austria and receive such universal attention as Miss Bremer met with here, would be strongly inclined, unless he had strong powers of philosophical abstraction, to diffuse his own complacent sensations over his description of the nation, and despotism itself would be "turned to favor and to prettiness," in the mild operation of his amiable feelings.

We have spoken harshly of Miss Bremer's book, because we think that its personalities are an offense to good taste, a violation of implied confidence, and a scandal to literature. If the private letters of which the volumes are made up, had fallen into the hands of some modern Curll or Osborn, and had been published without any consultation with their writer, the publisher would have been denounced as being concerned in a disreputable transaction. Miss Bremer, long after they were originally written, coolly publishes them herself, and does not deem herself called upon for apology or explanation. To her mind there is evidently nothing in the letters which the whole world should not read. She has, doubtless, a perfect right to make herself ridiculous, but we dispute her right to make capital out of the hospitality of well-meaning friends, and gossip them into uncomfortable notoriety. Besides, for the truth may as well be spoken, the thing is done to make money, and out of such trash and scandal, and vanity, and bad manners, it is for the interest of literature that money should not be made. There is undoubtedly a demand for the commodity, as there is a demand for many other commodities which it is considered disgraceful to supply. We hope to see the time come when a man can invite a literary person to dinner, with the blessed assurance on the part of the host, that his guest will not sell a description of his house, and a record of his conversation to a bookseller, until after the entertainer is in the grave. The suc-

cess of the opposite practice, sanctioned by the high reputation of Miss Bremer, proves that this time has not yet come. (p. 647)

A review of "The Homes of the New World: Impressions in America," in Graham's Magazine, *Vol. XLIII, No. 6, December, 1853, pp. 645-47.*

PUTNAM'S MONTHLY   (essay date 1853)

[*In the following excerpt from a positive review of* The Homes of the New World, *the critic defends Bremer against charges of imprudence in publishing personal comments on her American acquaintances.*]

No one can complain of a want of frankness and transparent thinking [in Miss Bremer's **"Homes of the New World"**]. To make use of a Westernism, she records her impressions "with a perfect looseness;" and apparently with a most amiable unconsciousness that there is any thing at all improper in her doing so. She is, in fact, the *enfant terrible* of travellers in the United States; and her sayings are all the more valuable and entertaining from their innocent freshness. They were made on the spot, and have none of the dubious indistinctness and hesitancy of second thoughts or remembered impressions. When she slept in a cold bedroom she notes it on the spot, if she was bored by a formal dinner down goes the fact, with the names of those who bored her, while they vainly imagined they were giving her an entertainment. We have no fault to find with her on this account. It is very well for people to see themselves as others see them. The motive of the borer might plead in extenuation of the offence, in some minds; but Miss Bremer only knew that she was bored, and didn't regard the homage to herself, which it implied, as a sufficient offset. She was a Sybarite in pursuit of comfort, and rebelled against being killed with kindness. Her aim was enjoyment and not sacrifice. And who shall condemn her for it? Must one be grateful for an unsought dinner that inflicts dyspepsia? The people who entertained Miss Bremer appear to have been like the good woman who thought too much couldn't be done for her minister, when she sweetened his tea with molasses. (p. 668)

[Our country men] imagine that the great aim of all authors is personal attentions, and not profit to themselves; hence [foreign authors] receive the most liberal attentions when they land among us, and are paid for the delight and the instruction which their works have afforded us, not in coin but in compliments. . . . In the case of Miss Bremer, there was the double desire to see a literary lioness, and an amiable anxiety to render her visit pleasing to herself; and, since she had shown herself so skilful an artist in painting . . . her own country, who could tell but she would do the same by . . . the New World, it would be worth while to see one's self mirrored in her quaint pages. Well, we are all there, and at once begin to find fault with the artist; which strikes us as being most absurdly captious. It would have been the easiest thing in the world to keep out of Miss Bremer's book; but we would rush in. She misspells our names, misquotes the titles of our books, and makes an astonishing jumble of our political distinctions and geographical lines. Something of this is owing, of course, to the unfamiliarity of her translator with the persons mentioned and the scenes described, and then it is not to be supposed that the authoress herself was very particular in making her notes; for whether it were Brown or Smith about whom she was writing, it would be all one to her friends in Stockholm, to whom her letters were addressed. It is neither a subject of wonder, nor of much consequence, when Mr. Wise figures in her pages as Mr. Weise,

Professor Hackley, as ''the respectable Mr. Hackett,'' when Senator Seward becomes a native of Boston, and Colonel Benton is transfigured into Davy Crockett. There are a good many people alluded to by their initals only, who might better have been designated by the letter X as representing an unknown person. But, in nearly every case, Miss Bremer's initial personages are readily enough recognized by the circumstances narrated in connection with them, and our Bully Bottoms are continually proclaiming themselves from under the asses' heads which this Swedish Titania places upon their shoulders. The ''good Marcuses,'' the ''good Rebeccas,'' and the ''Doctor O.'s,'' are well enough known to the readers of Miss Bremer. One of her novels is called the **''H. Family,''** so it appears to be a favorite mode with her of designating people. No one has a right to be disappointed in Miss Bremer's [**''Homes of the New World''**]; it is written in the vein of her other works, gossippy, tender, quaint, personal, and affectionate. But, if she were to revisit the United States, we fear there would be a wide difference between her second reception and her first, and even ''the good Marcus,'' we doubt, would not be so attentive as he was before, and ''Mrs. L.,'' whose romantic marriage Miss Bremer hints at, but, with singular forbearance, hesitates to reveal, might not be so anxious to entertain her at her ''Villa on the Hudson.'' It was Miss Bremer's mission to note the oddities and peculiarities of individuals; it was her doing such things that first endeared her to us, and made us so anxious to see the little lady who had given us such amusing portraits of her own neighbors and country people. What else could she do when she visited us? She came for no other purpose. . . . It is not agreeable to one's feelings to be a subject of ridicule, but, if we will invite a caricaturist into our houses we must expect to be caricatured. (pp. 668-69)

Many querulous remarks have been made by our contemporaries of the Press, about the imprudences of Miss Bremer, in her revelations of domestic society, but her amiability and overflowing love for every body with whom she came in contact, should be considered as a sufficient apology for her unreserve. As to the other complaint that she elevates into importance personages whom we had never before heard of, and makes heroes and heroines of quiet people who had never been suspected of heroic qualities by their acquaintances, it does not strike us as a very serious offence; if she sees a park in a little inclosure of two or three city lots, shadowed by one or two ailanthus trees, it does not follow that her other descriptions were all in her eye, for she seems to have been fully impressed by the grandeur of our river scenery, and she has given some very graphic sketches of the rural districts, both of the East and the West. It is inevitable that travellers should make mistakes in their description of foreign countries; but, when, as in the case of Miss Bremer, they are all in favor of the country visited, the people whom she describes should be the last to complain. We do not believe that her book will have a tendency to make us less respected in Europe, that it will cause Americans to be received with diminished consideration abroad, or that it will cause a single Scandinavian to change his purpose of emigrating with his family and household gods to the wilderness of the New World. From various little asides in her letters we are led to believe that Miss Bremer is not indifferent to the pleasures of the table, and she seems to have been most favorably impressed with the American *ménage*, except in the case of the hot breakfasts in winter, which appeared to her as contrasting too violently with the cold bedrooms. But the only purely American dish which she speaks of with enthusiasm is gumbo, a delicacy that can be eaten in perfection only in New Orleans. . . .

We fully ''indorse'' the eulogium of Miss Bremer on the gumbo of New Orleans. Nearly every thing American with which she becomes acquainted receives as warm and genial an approbation, and we would recommend all American readers of her book to bear in mind the generous sentiment of Sir Lucius O'Trigger [in Sheridan's ''The Rivals'']. ''When affection guides the pen he must be a brute who would find fault with the style.'' (p. 672)

> ''Miss Bremer's 'Homes of the New World','' in Putnam's Monthly, Vol. II, No. XII, December, 1853, pp. 668-72.

GEORGE ELIOT [PSEUDONYM OF MARY ANN EVANS] (essay date 1856)

[*Eliot is considered one of the foremost English novelists of the nineteenth century. Her novels, including* Middlemarch *and* The Mill on the Floss, *explore psychological and moral issues while providing intimate pictures of everyday life informed by profound insight into human character. Here, Eliot argues that Bremer's strengths as a novelist—her ''humourous realism'' and ''attention to detail''—are overshadowed in* Hertha *by two defects common to all her fictional writings: sentimentality and religious dogmatism. While Eliot admires Bremer's attention to feminist causes in* Hertha, *she laments that the author presented her ideas ''in the pink haze of visions and romance'' rather than ''in the 'light of common day'.'' This essay first appeared in the* Westminster Review *in October, 1856.*]

The appearance of a new novel [**'Hertha'**] by Miss Bremer, revives the impressions of ten years ago, when all the novel-reading world was discussing the merits of **'The Neighbours,' 'The President's Daughters,' 'The H— Family,'** and the rest of the 'Swedish novels,' which about that time were creating a strong current in the literary and bookselling world. The discussion soon died out; and perhaps there is hardly another instance of fictions so eagerly read in England which have left so little trace in English literature as Miss Bremer's. No one quotes them, no one alludes to them: and grave people who have entered on their fourth decade, remember their enthusiasm for the Swedish novels among those intellectual 'wild oats' to which their mature wisdom can afford to give a pitying smile. And yet, how is this? For Miss Bremer had not only the advantage of describing manners which were fresh to the English public; she also brought to the description unusual gifts—lively imagination, poetic feeling, wealth of language, a quick eye for details, and considerable humour, of that easy, domestic kind which throws a pleasant light on every-day things. The perusal of **'Hertha'** has confirmed in our minds the answer we should have previously given to our own question. One reason, we think, why Miss Bremer's novels have not kept a high position among us is, that her luxuriant faculties are all overrun by a rank growth of sentimentality, which, like some faint-smelling creeper on the boughs of an American forest, oppresses us with the sense that air is unhealthy. Nothing can be more curious than the combination in her novels of the vapourishly affected and unreal with the most solid Dutch sort of realism. In one page we have copious sausage sandwiches and beer posset, and on another rhapsodies or wildly improbable incidents that seem rather to belong to sylphs and salamanders, than to a race of creatures who are nourished by the very excellent provisions just mentioned. Another reason why Miss Bremer's novels are not likely to take rank among the permanent creations of art, is the too confident tone of the religious philosophy which runs through them. When a novelist is quite sure that she has a theory which suffices to illustrate all the difficulties of our earthly existence, her novels are too likely to illustrate little else than her own theory.

These two characteristics of sentimentality and dogmatic confidence are very strongly marked in **'Hertha'**, while it has less of the attention to detail, less of the humorous realism, which was the ballast of Miss Bremer's earlier novels. It has been written not simply from an artistic impulse, but with the object of advocating the liberation of woman from those legal and educational restrictions which limit her opportunities of a position and a sphere of usefulness to the chance of matrimony; and we think there are few well-judging persons who will not admire the generous energy with which Miss Bremer, having long ago won fame and independence for herself, devotes the activity of her latter years to the cause of women who are less capable of mastering circumstance. Many wise and noble things she says in **'Hertha,'** but we cannot help regretting that she has not presented her views on a difficult and practical question in the 'light of common day,' rather than in the pink haze of visions and romance. (pp. 331-32)

Our objection [to **'Hertha'**] is, that it surrounds questions, which can only be satisfactorily solved by the application of very definite ideas to specific facts, with a cloudy kind of eloquence and flighty romance. Take, for example, the question whether it will not be well for women to study and practise medicine. It can only tend to retard the admission that women may pursue such a career with success, for a distinguished authoress to imply that they may be suitably prepared for effective activity by lectures on such a very nebulous thesis as this—'The consciousness of thought ought to be a living observation and will,' or to associate the attendance of women by the sick bed, not with the hard drudgery of real practice, but with the vicissitudes of a love-story. Women have not to prove that they can be emotional, and rhapsodic, and spiritualistic; every one believes that already. They have to prove that they are capable of accurate thought, severe study, and continuous self-command. But we say all this with reluctance, and should prefer noticing the many just and pathetic observations that Miss Bremer puts into the mouth of her heroine.... [We offer as an example] a passage where Hertha complains of the ignorance in which women are left of natural Science. 'In my youth,' she concludes, 'I used to look at the rocks, the trees, the grass, and all objects of nature, with unspeakable longing, wishing to know something about their kinds, their life, and their purpose. But the want of knowledge, the want of opportunity to acquire it, has caused nature to be to me a sealed book, and still to this moment it is to me a tantalizing, enticing, and ever-retreating wave, rather than a life-giving fountain which I can enjoy, and enjoying, thank the Creator.' (p. 334)

> *George Eliot [pseudonym of Mary Ann Evans], "Three Novels," in her* Essays of George Eliot, *edited by Thomas Pinney, Routledge and Kegan Paul, 1963, pp. 325-34.**

G. BARNETT SMITH   (essay date 1893)

[*Smith compares Bremer's works to those of Henrik Ibsen and Jane Austen.*]

Between those two remarkable Scandinavian writers, Frederika Bremer and Henrik Ibsen, there is a great gulf fixed. The same northern latitude produced both, and yet it would be impossible to cite two writers of any nationality who differed so widely in their literary character and methods. In the pages of Frederika

Bremer we seem to see reflected, as in some translucent lake, the green pastures of a moral and intellectual calm, or the mountains of a pure and lofty aspiration. With Ibsen, on the contrary, we might be standing on the heights of the Brocken, where the midnight storm lashes itself into tempest, and the lightnings make visible the dark and sublime things of the world. The writings of the one are suffused and permeated by a loving faith and hope, and a complete reliance upon the Divine will; the writings of the other are full of struggle, of mental analysis, of passionate yearnings after individual freedom, of feverish revolt against social canons, of tragic incidents, and of mystic and inextinguishable desires. Bremer is the more reposeful; Ibsen the more powerful and original. Bremer's is the happier soul, Ibsen's the greater, yet withal the more unsatisfiable. (p. 2)

Frederika Bremer has been compared with Jane Austen; but the Swedish writer was the intellectual superior of the English. Though not so great as a novelist, her culture was wider, and her thought deeper; she had also a more vigorous imagination, and a greater command both of the springs of humour and of pathos. She had the delicacy of perception and love of quiet home life which distinguished Jane Austen; but she could not rival the style of the English novelist...; nor could she lay claim to Jane Austen's marvellous insight into character, with its thousand little shades and divergences. But Frederika Bremer was an authoress of whom any country or people might be proud. There are those who, with brilliant talents, nevertheless degrade their national literature; but it is her glory to have adorned and elevated the literature of Sweden. (pp. 40-1)

> *G. Barnett Smith, "Fredrika Bremer," in his* Women of Renown: Nineteenth Century Studies, *W. H. Allen & Co., Limited, 1893, pp. 1-41.*

ADOLPH B. BENSON   (essay date 1924)

[*In his laudatory introduction to* America of the Fifties, *Benson summarizes Bremer's achievements as a novelist and travel writer.*]

[To-day Miss Bremer's] novels, with their slow movement and minimum of action, their superabundance of dialogue and description, and their letter form, appear dull and antiquated. Obviously, the heroes and heroines can no longer make the impression that they did eighty years ago, and it may be difficult to understand the almost phenomenal favor which these household tales enjoyed when they were first published, and continued to enjoy for a long time; but nothing approximating their quality had appeared before, and the readers were familiar with the background. Fortunately, Miss Bremer never lost her mental balance because of either success or failure. She wisely discounted the eulogistic reviews of her inital efforts, strove constantly for improvement, and sought truth and wholesomeness. Her literary achievements were sensible and moral withal, sensationalism was absent, and they possess a marked historical value as pictures of Sweden in her day. (p. xv)

It is no exaggeration to say that Fredrika Bremer was one of the most celebrated and influential Swedish women that ever lived. Although as a novelist she had during her lifetime successful rivals among her own sex, none of these could even remotely equal her in creative, intellectual, and spiritual force. She introduced the middle class domestic novel into Swedish literature; she raised Swedish realism to a higher plane that it had previously occupied; she inspired effective, well-needed social reforms, and stimulated an active love for humanity. (p. xvii)

[We] may safely assert that Miss Bremer's greatest claim to immortality abroad is based on her letters of [American] travel. These are classics of their kind, as fresh and charming as on the day they were written, and the wealth of their information is enhanced by the sympathetic personality of the recorder as well as by their humorous, compelling style. Her accounts of what she saw have served as reliable guides in innumerable fields of effort, both in Europe and America, and particularly as a mirror of conditions and characters as they existed in 1850. Occasionally her kind heart, generosity, and optimism obscure her critical judgment, and in the United States the ardent welcome she received may well have colored her observations. But, after all, there was much sunshine and promise in the America of Emerson and Webster, and it is to Fredrika Bremer's credit that she emphasizes these features rather than finding fault with everything. On the whole, she is a keen student, ever sincere and courageous, and if justified, according to the best of her belief, never hesitates to criticise unfavorably, though always in a friendly spirit. (pp. xvii-xviii)

> *Adolph B. Benson, in an introduction to* America of the Fifties: Letters of Fredrika Bremer *by Fredrika Bremer, edited by Adolph B. Benson, the American-Scandinavian Foundation, 1924, pp. viii-xx.*

HENRY ADAMS BELLOWS   (essay date 1924)

[*Bellows uses* America of the Fifties *to illustrate his conception of successful historical writing.*]

It is the curse of history that it has to be written by historians. Here and there, to be sure, some giant, some poet, some dramatist has taken the thing in hand, and written history so as to make it live, but in the main the laudable desire of historians to achieve accuracy and to leave out no essential facts has squeezed their works dry of sap. (p. 671)

To bridge the gap between history and life, events need a sympathetic yet dispassionate observer, shrewd of insight, possessed of the power of accurate expression, free to mingle with all classes and conditions of people, yet never of them, a human being, as it were, from another planet. Such a combination of gifts and opportunities is of necessity very rare. It is found only when a trained, skillful writer visits a country other than his own, and for no purpose save to observe open-mindedly; even then his vision is often distorted by circumstance, so that what he sees bears little relation to the whole. But with fair chances, such a visitor is in a position to write real history; the facts, the men and women, the ideals come to him at first hand through his five senses, and not through the dusty medium of old paper, and yet he is able to exercise something of the power of detachment and selection which is the historian's bulwark against the overwhelming floods of actuality.

Such a historian, rarely gifted and with rare opportunities, came to the United States in 1849. (pp. 671-72)

[Fredrika Bremer's] journeyings—she stayed in the United States two years—took her from the Franconia Notch of New Hampshire to the everglades of Florida, from St. Paul to New Orleans. She visited Emerson at Concord, talked with Webster and Clay at Washington, traveled with James Russell Lowell and his wife, was present at Calhoun's funeral in Charleston, stayed at Governor Ramsay's house in St. Paul. Senator Hale personally presented her to President Taylor at the White House; George Washington's nephew and his wife, thanks to a letter of introduction given to her by Henry Clay, entertained her at Mount Vernon.

This extraordinary wealth of opportunity would of itself have meant little if Fredrika Bremer had not been so peculiarly well fitted to take advantage of it. To begin with, she was a Swede; in other words, she was sympathetic with the American people and yet not of them. She could observe their hopes and their passions without falling a prey to them; she could understand and yet remain aloof. Second, she was a trained, experienced novelist, but a novelist without violent prejudice; her stories were masterpieces of unimpassioned observation. Finally, and perhaps most important of all, she had a keen sense of humor which never resorted to unkindly caricature. Hawthorne characterized her perfectly when he said she was "worthy of being the maiden aunt of the whole human race."

Had Miss Bremer come to America for the express purpose of writing a book, or even in order to seek literary material for her novels, the chances are that her vision of what she saw would have been more or less distorted; she would have sought, not experience, but copy. But there was no such warping influence at work. Her letters to Sweden, for all they were written with the punctilious care of a professional author, were not intended for publication. Now, letters of this sort generally suffer from the emotional intimacy that makes them dear to their recipients, but there was no such quality in Fredrika Bremer. A maiden aunt is almost the only type of correspondent whose letters are fit to be revealed to the world. (pp. 672-73)

One serious objection may be alleged to her published collection of letters on America in its original form: it is too long. Thirteen hundred printed octavo pages bulk formidably, and inevitably include much that, with the lapse of time, can well be dispensed with. For this reason, the publication of a new edition of her **Hemmen i Nya Verlden** [edited and condensed into 350 pages], . . . represents a notable service both to the memory of the Swedish novelist and to the cause of American history. In [**America of the Fifties: Letters of Fredrika Bremer,**], America of 1850 comes startlingly to life, North and South, East and West, from the frigid respectablity of the summer colony at Nahant, "with Mr. Prescott, the excellent historian; Mrs. Bryant; the preacher Bellows, from New York; Mr. Longfellow, with several other interesting persons," to the slave markets of New Orleans and an Indian tepee in Minnesota. Henry Clay discusses politics with her in the midst of his speeches on the California Compromise; she sits next to Webster at dinner; President Fillmore drops in to call of an evening; Lowell shows her the wonders of Niagara. The great men and women of America in the fifties come and go familiarly, and she appraises them, admiringly and yet humorously, out of her shrewd little old maid's eyes. (pp. 673-74)

Miss Bremer went to Charleston, South Carolina, and here, of course, slavery became the great subject of conversation. "One thing which astonishes and annoys me here, and which I did not expect to find, is that I hardly ever meet a man, or woman either, who can openly and honestly look the thing in the face." Her own views on slavery were, of course, sharply defined, and they gathered strength as she went among the slaves themselves, but for all that she showed an extraordinary broadmindedness in her ability to understand the point of view of her slave-owning hosts and hostesses. The picturesqueness of the South, and above all of the negro life, appealed to her enormously, and her letters written from Charleston and Savannah are full of admirable bits of first-hand description. (pp. 675-76)

[*America of the Fifties*] is an extraordinary document, this record of America in 1850, making history alive and luminous. And because, in those days, visitors from abroad saw this country as a rule only as through a glass darkly, every American, whether or not of Scandinavian ancestry, owes a special debt of gratitude to this remarkable Swedish novelist who had the opportunity and the shrewdness to understand American life as it really was, the skill to set it forth with vitality, and above all that detached, humorous, kindly personality which won for her the title of "maiden aunt of all the world." (p. 677)

> Henry Adams Bellows, "Fredrika Bremer and America," in The American-Scandinavian Review, *Vol. XII, No. 11, November, 1924, pp. 671-77.*

CHARLES WHARTON STORK   (essay date 1924)

[*Stork attributes the accuracy of Bremer's observations in* America of the Fifties *to her sympathetic interest in the United States.*]

[We boldly venture the statement that the letters from America contained in *America of the Fifties: The Letters of Frederika Bremer*] are both literary and historical documents of unique value. Cool of judgment, conscientious of purpose, above all sympathetic, [Frederika Bremer] combined a splendid equipment with splendid opportunities. Free from the national prejudice which every English man or woman felt in those days, she had, as artists put it, the innocent eye, the vision uncolored by prejudice. That she expected much of America was a severe test of her experiences. . . .

[The] most remarkable thing about the book is the author. Reading today, we trust absolutely this record of America's faults and virtues because we believe in the accuracy and intelligence of the recorder. . . .

[The principal charm and value of *America of the Fifties,*] consist in the extraordinary directness with which a hundred and odd incidents of travel are presented and analyzed. The generalizations—pitfalls of the cocksure—are equally just and subtle. For example, we are told of the beauty and good taste of American women, but that "there is a deficiency of shadow, of repose, of the mystery of being . . . which attracts the mind with a silent power in the consciousness of hidden and noble treasure." This one observation is the text on which were to be founded half the novels of Henry James and Edith Wharton.

Very few first-hand documents on the mid-century in America deserve to be more widely known than Frederika Bremer's letters. Their presentation of the past points a clear line through the present into the future. . . . What this volume leaves with us above all is that to know a country one must love it. One of her Swedish correspondents wrote the author. "Through you America has come, nearer to us than through all the steamboats and telegraphs." Frederika Bremer's love, though never blind to faults, was one which fully identified itself with its object. If the social historians of America, domestic as well as foreign, could achieve a similar attitude, we might have less ugly circumstantiality and more constructive criticism.

> Charles Wharton Stork, "Letters of American Travel by Frederika Bremer," in The New York Times Book Review, *November 23, 1924, p. 6.*

ALRIK T. GUSTAFSON   (essay date 1933)

[*Between 1931 and 1933, Gustafson contributed a three-part essay on Bremer's novels to the* Journal of English and Germanic Philology. *In the first two parts (see* Additional Bibliography*), he identifies the English romantic novels that most interested Bremer as a youth and examines their influence upon her artistic growth. The excerpt below was drawn from the concluding part of Gustafson's essay. Here he notes that Bremer's early novels display elements characteristic of English romanticism, but he emphasizes that her conception of the novel was essentially an original one that developed out of her belief in literature as a valuable tool for moral instruction. This conviction, according to Gustafson, is most obvious in Bremer's later novels, which he terms* tendenzroman, *or "realistic novels of purpose." To Gustafson, Bremer's originality lay in her spontaneous approach to novel writing, and he analyzes this aspect of her art as it relates to her style, characterization, and handling of structure.*]

Any intelligent analysis of Fredrika Bremer's art must postulate the paradox that she was not an artist, by which one means, of course, that she was not primarily an artist. It is not without significance that her first little volume of *Teckningar* was written for the purpose of social amelioration, not merely to satisfy an inner urge to create; she needed funds to carry out certain humanitarian efforts on her father's estate, and she wrote in order to get a small capital to realize these plans. Her early, rather unexpected, literary success led to more ambitious efforts in the narrative art, led in fact, quite inevitably, to a new emphasis upon the more purely aesthetic aspects of fiction; but in all of these efforts, with the exception of *Grannarna*, the didactic element is always primary. Her art being at all times secondary to her moral purpose, and this moral purpose being so deeply an expression of her own essential personality, it would seem to follow that her art would be correspondingly little influenced by the aesthetics of fiction as developed in the hands of the great masters of the novel before her time. The fact is that Miss Bremer never seriously developed an aesthetics, except in the most general sense of the term, either with reference to her own work or that of others. Her voluminous correspondence reveals that she was seldom preoccupied with the more purely aesthetic aspects of the authors that she read. An author's handling of plot, his management of characterization, his use of scene, his style seldom interested Miss Bremer. (p. 373)

It cannot be too strongly insisted upon that [the] moral bias in Miss Bremer's conception of art is primarily a direct expression of her own inner nature. As she applied it in her criticism of the art of others, so she insisted upon it in her own art. Her novels, in consequence, are to be looked upon primarily as the spontaneous expression of her own feelings; as such they are really lyric sketches, at points pure lyric effusions, rather than novels in the ordinary sense of the word. . . . It would seem to follow from this that her development as an artist must proceed largely from native forces within her and correspondingly less through influences from without. (pp. 374-75)

She is not, however, completely the free agent in her art; her novels bear at points the marks of her reading, though these marks are for the most part superficial and incidental. The point at which she follows most closely traditional developments in the fictional art of her predecessors . . . is in her not so occasional inadvertencies, especially in her early novels, into the faults of romantic fiction. Inadvertencies, they must be called, because she is always half-conscious of their potential excesses even when she employs them, and her ultimate development in the art of fiction reveals her receding farther and farther from their seductive snares until in the *Tendenzroman* of her late years she rejects them entirely and writes realistic novels of purpose. . . . [*Nina*], serious though its argument be, is structurally a weird piece of romantic patchwork;

and even *Grannarna* . . . , certainly fresh and original in its main conception, does not avoid some of the most obvious machinery of the romantic. However, in *Hemmet* . . . and *Syskonlif* . . . she frees herself almost completely from the trailing garments of romance and develops a form of realism that forebodes *Hertha* . . . , the ultimate in *Tendenz*. By 1858 [in *Fader och Dotter*] she goes even a step farther in her reaction against the romantic; now not only the so-called "machinery of romance"—its stylistic tricks, its extravagance of episode, its mystery, its color, and its atmosphere—must go by the board, but even its central theme, youthful love, must be sacrificed. . . . The early reading in romantic fiction had left its mark, but Fredrika Bremer's native buoyancy of spirit, her optimism, her sense of humor, and, most important, her realistic practical mindedness gradually weaned her from these early, largely perverted tastes, and developed in her hands a technique in fiction that was essentially her own. (pp. 375-77)

In [her] conception of art, which employs reality as the point of departure, but in which the imaginative function is penetrative and interpretative, yielding in its creative moments the inner significance of outward reality, Miss Bremer comes very close to the philosophy of art and the imagination as developed in England in the hands of Wordsworth and Coleridge, Leigh Hunt and Shelley. . . . Miss Bremer's constant emphasis on moral values leads her, of course, to look upon the final end of art as idealistic. Art should function, she insists, to lift man, to show him the inner beauty and harmony of outward reality. (p. 377)

[She] seldom deals with "humble folk," in the sense of the poor of this world. Her own life, having been lived almost exclusively among the upper middle-class of society, she recognized that her knowledge of the life of the humbler classes, despite her unbounded sympathy for them, is hardly sufficient to enable her to give a true picture of their state. . . . She turns, therefore, to her own social class as the basis for her novels, and the aspect of this class that is the especial object of her attention is its life in the home. All of her novels are novels of life in the home; they not only centre on the home, nearly all of their action takes place within its actual physical confines. Even *Nina*, the most romantic of all her tales, one which is constantly flirting with the romantic's notorious weakness for the exotic and the erotic, finds its ultimate centre in the home; and as for the others all one needs to do is recall their titles, *Presidentens Döttrar, Grannarna, Hemmet, Syskonlif*, in order to see how completely they are engaged with the life within the home. This emphasis upon life within the home . . . led Miss Bremer to neglect the romantic love theme so characteristic of the average novel. (p. 378)

The most characteristic strain in Fredrika Bremer's genius is its basic human spontaneity, which finds aesthetic outlet in a variety of manners, now in a certain lyric effusiveness of style, then in a refreshing vein of humor or satire, and again in an ingratiating immediate directness of characterization. This basic spontaneity is the source also, however, of our author's most obvious fault as an artist, her constant weakness in the matter of structure. Her novels, especially the early ones, are very loose in construction; in fact they can hardly be said to have construction in the strict sense of the term. Critics who seek to explain this defect alone on the basis of her undisciplined early training are only partially right. A more important source, it seems to me, is to be found in Miss Bremer's own essential temperament, a temperament too often naively spontaneous, constantly impatient with any of the severer intellec-

tual disciplines. . . . [In] her study of German philosophy she preferred the romantic mazes of Schelling to the sternly disciplined thought of Hegel. She was temperamentally just as impatient with the severe demands of perfect construction in a work of art, though she recognized, at times, that this attitude, in her capacity as an artist, was not a commendable one.

In her earliest years as an author she is conscious of this failure to construct her stories with care. . . . In the years that followed she sought to deepen her knowledge and strengthen her art by means of extensive philosophical, religious, and historical studies. The immediate effect of these studies on her art, however, is to tend to dislocate rather than to harmonize, to confuse rather than to unify. (pp. 379-80)

This looseness of construction characteristic of Miss Bremer's art quite inevitably allows for a variety of technical method quite unthinkable in the more rigidly constructed novel. A lack of plot in the strict sense is very noticeable. Instead of concentrating on the development of one clearly defined intrigue, with everything else strictly subordinated to it, she often, to the general confusion of the reader, seeks to develop several simultaneously, with much consequent overlapping. At times she even wilfully drops one unfinished intrigue or episode and takes up another, the reader meantime being quite at his wit's end as to why. . . . Overdevelopment of relatively unimportant individual episodes is another inevitable fault of Miss Bremer's method. The Don Juan episode and that concerning Nybyggaren in *Nina*, certainly of incidental significance structurally considered in the novel, become the occasion for utterly disproportionate treatment. The Angelika episodes in the early pages of the same novel might to advantage have been omitted altogether. The potpourri effect becomes even more pronounced when one notices the variety of narrative method employed by our author. In a single novel, *Hemmet*, Miss Bremer employs the direct narrative method, the character sketch, in the essay sense of the term, the dialogue in the strictly dramatic manner (in one case she resorts to a dramatic sketch in five scenes!), the letter form so characteristic of the eighteenth century novel, and the author's aside or "chat with the reader." The narrative methods that she employs with the greatest success are undoubtedly the letter form (*Grannarna* is a real triumph in this manner) and the aside to the reader. These lend themselves, of course, with unique facility to the basic spontaneity of Miss Bremer's genius. The asides, it must be said, are of unequal quality. Those in which philosophical and religious speculation are the immediate object of the author's concern are almost without exception a dead weight on the narrative movement. This is one of the chief reasons for the failure of *Nina*. Those, however, in which the aside is composed of a direct reaction, usually humorous or satiric, to an immediate narrative situation are often happy in conception and refreshing in execution. . . . The vigor and spirit of many of Miss Bremer's asides to the reader, it might be noted, are rather reminiscent of Fielding, and it is not at all improbable that she became fully aware of their possibilities only after her reading in the genial English master of the art. She handles them, however, with a feminine geniality all her own, though occasionally they tend to deteriorate into the naïve, almost sophomoric. She lacked the complete sophistication of her English predecessor.

Nowhere, perhaps, is Frederika Bremer's originality more apparent than in the handling of character. A few of her characters, such as Bruno and Hagar in *Grannarna* and Sara in *Hemmet*, are obviously inspired rather directly through some of the *Sturm und Drang* literature in Germany and the general

Byronic tradition of a somewhat later date on the Continent; but with the exception of Bruno these are distinctly minor figures in the novels mentioned, and in no case are they especially convincing. Her triumphs of characterization, on the other hand, Fransiska and Ma chère mère in *Grannarna,* Edla in *Presidentens Döttrar* and *Nina,* Fröken Greta in *Nina,* Petrea in *Hemmet,* and General Herkules in *Syskonlif,* are, with certain reservations in regard to the last, thoroughly original in both conception and execution. General Herkules . . . is certainly to be considered as a Scandinavian modification of Uncle Toby [a character in Sterne's *Tristram Shandy*] and Commodore Trunnion [a character in Smollett's *The Adventures of Peregrine Pickle*]. Miss Bremer, however, has used these English worthies of comic characterization merely as the starting point of her Wolmar Otto Herkules . . .—one of the first full-length portraits in Swedish literature of what the Swede fondly refers to as *en gammal original.* (pp. 381-84)

In any general examination of the characterization in Miss Bremer's novels two things might to advantage be taken into account, first, the sources of her characterization, and secondly, the method she employs in developing it. . . . The native ebullience and intensity of her own temperament led her quite naturally in upon herself as she sought to depict character. As a consequence every stage of development in her own experience of life finds its reflection in the pages of her novels. Pullorna in *Presidentens Döttrar* is clearly reminiscence from her own early childhood. Petrea in *Hemmet* is replete with reminiscence from her girlhood and early womanhood. Elisabet in *Familjen H—* and Edla in *Presidentens Döttrar* and *Nina* are representative of some of the less fortunate aspects of Fredrika Bremer's experience of life, products of family and social inhibitions, as she began to mature into womanhood. The sinister fanaticism of Edla, which brings about the *dénouement fatal* in *Nina,* is hardly that of Frederika Bremer herself, it is true; but in all other important respects—in her intense inner nature, in the failure of her father to understand that nature, with consequent paternal restraint resulting in violent, at times morbid, psychological repercussions in Edla, and in her final victory over this self, realized through a study of books and mankind—she provides an almost exact reproduction of Miss Bremer's own saga. (pp. 384-85)

When we come to examine the manner in which Miss Bremer reveals character, the technique of her character portrayal, we find our author, as might be expected, relatively crude and obvious. Here, as in her handling of plot, she is impatient of the niceties of the great artist. Instead of allowing the character to reveal itself naturally in the course of the action, she almost invariably thrusts upon the reader, at some time early in the novel, a little character sketch in essay form. . . . Then she picks up the narrative thread where she had abandoned it, and goes on with the story. At times, as in the case of Petrea in *Hemmet,* she scatters through the novel a whole series of portraits representative of different stages in the development of a given character. Her initial treatment of the lovable old Fru Gunilla in *Hemmet* is typical of her general method. . . . Were it not for the undeniable spirit, almost verve at points, with which such passages are rendered, they would tend to unpardonably halt the progress of the narrative; but our author quite often moves into them with a spontaneous intrepidity that is (or at least must have been to the reader of her day) contagious; and once she has intrigued the reader into forgetting the original technical inadequacy, she usually manages, by apt choice of realistic character detail ably seconded by a sparkling play of humor, to retain the reader's attention.

No discussion of Fredrika Bremer's technique as a novelist would be complete without some words on her style, for it is here that her native spontaneity, her rich buoyancy of temperament found its most natural outlet. From the moment of the appearance of the first of the *Teckningar* critics were nearly unanimous in one regard, that, despite faults of general construction, obvious inadequacies in character portrayal, and a thinness in basic content, there was a certain freshness in stylistic handling, a certain spontaneous accumulation of phrasing, a certain neatness and despatch of word choice that gave real promise of new developments in prose style in Swedish letters. . . . In certain unguarded moments, particularly frequent in *Nina,* this style tends, rather inevitably, to deteriorate into the fulsomely effusive, almost feverish, prose lyricism reminiscent of certain German hyper-romantic stylists such as Jean Paul Richter. On the whole, however, and this is particularly true of the novels beginning with *Grannarna* . . . , Miss Bremer's healthy sense of the realistic and the humorous enable her to lift herself clear of the insidious entanglements of hyper-romanticism in prose style. Her romantic discipleship in prose style is short lived, and never very profound. In her best moments she is, with a rather strong admixture of pure lyricism, the counterpart in Swedish prose style of her great feminine predecessor in poetry, Anna Maria Lenngren. She has a similar deftness in turn of phrase, the same rapidity of movement, and the same flavor in satire . . . , human, sympathetic. It is not too much to say, I think, that in its more purely lyric moments, and they are not few, her style reminds one inevitably of Selma Lagerlöf in *Gösta Berlings Saga.* It has in these moments a richness of coloring, a rapidity of movement, an imaginative abandon that does not equal, it is obvious, the best in *Gösta Berlings Saga,* but it certainly suggests an inherent kinship and at least approximates the later triumphs of her much greater successor in the field of the Swedish novel. (pp. 388-91)

Alrik T. Gustafson, "English Influences in Fredrika Bremer, III," in The Journal of English and Germanic Philology, *Vol. XXXII, No. 3, July, 1933, pp. 373-91.*

CARL L. ANDERSON (essay date 1965)

[*Anderson argues that* Hertha *occupies a climactic position in Bremer's career because it incorporates all the principal themes of her earlier fiction. These themes, according to Anderson, are father-daughter relationships, marriage, women's rights, and theodicy.*]

Hertha has more than its share of the typical faults of the propaganda novel. It is episodic and highly discursive, its characters mostly go undeveloped, its structure rambles. Its language, to a greater degree than in any of Miss Bremer's previous novels, is the vocabulary of overwrought nineteenth-century sensibility and the rhetoric of liberalism which she had learned from the novels of Bulwer-Lytton and his Swedish imitators. Nevertheless, . . . in some respects it is her most important work, bringing to a climax principal themes of her fiction.

She announced its existence first in a letter to her friend Böklin, to whom she described it as "a little book—the first fruits of the spirit of the New World married to Swedish circumstances in my soul. A woman is at the center, and its theme is woman's rightful development. . . . I have never paid more serious homage to truth." Her previous fiction had in its time been dedicated to the "truth" no less than *Hertha,* but her thesis was more clearly defined and more outspoken than ever before.

The novel argues for radical improvements in the legal and social position of women. It rests this argument principally on the difficult situation which it depicts of a gifted woman repressed by despotic, man-made conventions. Hertha Falk's fictional situation corresponds to much of what is known of Fredrika Bremer's personal experiences; these had already found their way into her previous fiction, but the treatment given them in *Hertha* is the least disguised of many attempts to get at the root of conflicting feelings of love and hatred for a tyrannical father. The father's tyranny in *Hertha* is not merely exasperating but cruel, and the good-natured humor of characters in Miss Bremer's previous fiction who anticipate the central figure of the daughter is almost entirely missing in *Hertha*. The issues in *Hertha* had been joined by Fredrika Bremer in dead earnest.

When the novel opens, Hertha is a woman of twenty-seven. Appalled, she watches her sister Alma dying of heartbreak caused by their father's refusal to allow her to marry. His iron rule in the home, now that his wife is dead, is incontestable in law and custom. Nor will he give Hertha, in her turn, permission to marry, nor render an accounting to her of an inheritance from her mother which would give her some measure of freedom. Marriage being the only respectable "career" open to ladies, it is within his power, if he wishes, to force his daughter into total economic dependence on him and thus into spinsterhood and servitude to him. In her despair over her father's despotism, the serious-minded, dutiful Hertha, whose religious faith had formerly gone unquestioned, is led to doubt the justice and even the mercy of God. She considers life "a dark and joyless riddle," and in desperation she turns for relief and whatever self-justification she can find in works of charity—a typical Bremer solution to the problem of theodicy. Hertha helps found a Ladies Society for community welfare and becomes mistress of a school for girls—both daring enough ventures for a woman of her time and place. Her motives in this work are several: to discover what values may accrue to the individual in charitable works; to restore, if possible, her former faith in God and man; and finally, to try to reconcile her need for self-fulfillment with loyalty to a father who, like society as a whole, does not recognize that need.

These are Hertha's motives as they are developed in the novel; they form the substance of her protest against the tyranny of men and of her plea for women's rights. More than this, however, in them can be seen coming together all the important themes of Fredrika Bremer's fiction: *the father-daughter theme,* a complicated, harrowing conflict between love and independence, duty and rebellion; *the marriage theme,* another form of essentially the same conflict, the husband substituting for the father as the potentially tyrannous male; *the theme of women's rights,* an extension of the first two themes to general considerations of the position of women in the home and in society; and finally, *the theodicy theme,* especially as it explores the part that women can play in combatting evil and thus *morally* justify the rise that they seek in their legal and social status. The multiplicity of themes in *Hertha* presented virtually insoluble problems of structure to a writer whose first published work had been entitled "sketches of everyday life." But at the same time it explains the climactic position which the novel occupies in Fredrika Bremer's writing. (pp. 189-92)

Though tediously sentimental to the end, *Hertha* is not a silly novel. Our heroine does not exult in the victories which her patience and humanitarian zeal have brought her. She has learned to be forgiving of human frailty, even her father's, for she realizes that in opposing him, she has fought not merely cruel selfishness, but a whole way of life. Unthinking and selfish, he is yet as much a victim as his daughter. The rhythms of tragedy may be faint in *Hertha,* but they are there. Despite many faults, its "truth," to which Fredrika Bremer said she had never before paid such serious homage, emerged powerfully. . . . The novel must be described as a personal and a spiritual triumph for Fredrika Bremer. It combined the major themes of her life's work, and to it she had brought all the authority of her years and experience. (pp. 193-94)

> *Carl L. Anderson, "Fredrika Bremer's 'Spirit of the New World',"* in The New England Quarterly, *Vol. XXXVIII, No. 2, June, 1965, pp. 187-201.*

ADDITIONAL BIBLIOGRAPHY

Asmundsson, Doris R. "Fredrika Bremer and Her English Friends." *The American-Scandinavian Review* LVII, No. 2 (June 1969): 159-68.*
   Discusses Bremer's visit to England in 1851, focusing on the friendships she formed with such British authors as Elizabeth Gaskell, Charles Kingsley, and Anna Maria Hall.

Benson, Adolph B. "American Ideals among Women Writers of Sweden." *Scandinavian Studies and Notes* V, No. 5 (February 1919): 157-68.*
   Reprints selected passages from *The Homes of the New World* to illustrate Bremer's enthusiasm for American social and political institutions.

———. "American Appreciation of Fredrika Bremer." *Scandinavian Studies and Notes* VIII (1924-25): 14-33.
   Provides a "representative" selection of extracts from contemporary American and English criticism of Bremer's novels. In addition, Benson contends that scholars have erred in attributing an unsigned essay on Bremer's works that appeared in the *North American Review* in April, 1844 (see excerpt above) to James Russell Lowell. According to Benson, the essay was written by Henry Wadsworth Longfellow.

———. "The Essays on Fredrika Bremer in the *North American Review.*" *PMLA* XLI, No. 3 (September 1926): 747-55.
   Changes his former opinion (see annotation above, 1924-25) on the authorship of an unsigned essay on Bremer's works that appeared in the *North American Review* in April, 1844 (see excerpt above). Benson presents evidence that the essay was written by James Russell Lowell rather than Henry Wadsworth Longfellow.

Bremer, Charlotte. "Biography." In *Life, Letters, and Posthumous Works of Fredrika Bremer,* by Fredrika Bremer, edited by Charlotte Bremer, translated by Fredr. Milow, pp. 1-100. New York: Hurd and Houghton, 1869.
   A detailed biographical sketch, written by Bremer's older sister.

Dana, Henry Wadsworth Longfellow, and Hawthorne, Manning. "'The Maiden Aunt of the Whole Human Race': Fredrika Bremer's Friendship with Longfellow and Hawthorne." *The American-Scandinavian Review* XXXVII, No. 3 (September 1949): 217-29.*
   Describes Bremer's relationships with the American writers Henry Wadsworth Longfellow and Nathaniel Hawthorne, both of whom she met during her stay in the United States. The authors of this essay are, respectively, the grandson of Longfellow and the great-grandson of Hawthorne.

Duyckinck, Evert A. "Frederika Bremer." In his *Portrait Gallery of Eminent Men and Women of Europe and America,* Vol. II, pp. 145-49. New York: Johnson, Wilson and Co., 1873.
   A sympathetic biographical sketch.

Flanagan, John T. "Fredrika Bremer: Traveler and Prophet." *Minnesota History* XX (1939): 129-39.

Describes Bremer's travels in Minnesota during her tour of the United States.

Gustafson, Alrik T. "English Influences in Fredrika Bremer: Parts I and II." *Journal of English and Germanic Philology* XXX, No. 2 (April 1931): 223-35; XXXI, No. 1 (January 1932): 92-123.
The first two parts of a three-part essay in which Gustafson assesses Bremer's indebtedness to the English Romantic tradition. In the first part, Gustafson describes Bremer's early education, focusing on the English Romantic novels that she read as a youth. In the second part, Gustafson traces the influence of these novels on Bremer's artistic development. As in the concluding part of his essay (see excerpt above, 1933), Gustafson emphasizes that Bremer's conception of the novel was essentially an original one. However, he notes four elements characteristic of English Romanticism that appear in her early works: sentimentalism, Ossianism, Byronism, and Gothicism.

Hamilton, Catherine J. "Fredrika Bremer (1801-1865)." In her *Women Writers: Their Works and Ways, second series*, pp. 44-71. London: Ward, Lock, & Bowden, 1893.
A laudatory account of Bremer's life and career.

Howitt, Margaret. *Twelve Months with Fredrika Bremer in Sweden.* 2 vols. London: Jackson, Walford, and Hodder, 1866.
A journal describing Howitt's stay with Bremer in Sweden from October, 1863 to October, 1864. The critic's mother, Mary Howitt, provided the first English translations of Bremer's novels.

Larsen, Hanna Astrup. "Four Scandinavian Feminists." *The Yale Review* V, No. 2 (January 1916): 347-62.*

Contends that the works of four Scandinavian feminists—Bremer, Camilla Collett, Selma Lagerlöf, and Ellen Key—profoundly influenced the progress of women's rights movements in Sweden, Norway, and Denmark. Larsen's discussion of Bremer focuses on *Hertha* and its positive impact on the development of equal employment opportunities for women in Sweden.

"Fredrika Bremer." *The Monthly Religious Magazine* XXXV, No. 3 (March 1866): 187-94.
An obituary that concentrates on Bremer's interest in feminist causes in both the United States and Sweden.

Rooth, Signe Alice. *Seeress of the Northland: Fredrika Bremer's American Journey, 1849-1851.* Philadelphia: American Swedish Historical Foundation, 1955, 327 p.
Reconstructs Bremer's journey through America. Rooth relies heavily on newspaper articles describing Bremer's activities in the United States and quotes liberally from the journals and diaries of prominent Americans she visited, including Henry Wadsworth Longfellow, Lydia Maria Child, Catherine Sedgwick, James Russell Lowell, Nathaniel Hawthorne, and Ralph Waldo Emerson. This work contains previously unpublished letters that Bremer wrote to American friends between 1849 and 1865 and a comprehensive bibliography of commentary on her life and works.

Thompson, Lawrence. "Fredrika Bremer As a Critic of American Literature." *Edda* XLI, No. 28 (1941): 166-76.
Praises *The Homes of the New World* as the first "thorough" survey of American literature written by a European. Thompson summarizes Bremer's commentary on the works of such authors as Nathaniel Hawthorne, Ralph Waldo Emerson, Henry Wadsworth Longfellow, James Russell Lowell, and Margaret Fuller.

Alexandre (Davy de la Pailleterie) Dumas (*père*)
1802-1870

French novelist, dramatist, memoirist, historian, essayist, and short story and travel sketch writer.

Dumas is widely regarded as one of the world's premier storytellers. Enormously popular and prolific, he wrote two of the best-loved and most widely read novels in literary history, *Le comte de Monte-Cristo* (*The Count of Monte Cristo*) and *Les trois mousquetaires* (*The Three Musketeers; or, The Feats and Fortunes of a Gascon Adventurer*). He also helped to inaugurate and popularize Romantic drama on the French stage with his two plays *Henri III et sa cour* (*Henri III and His Court*) and *Antony*. In concert with his prodigious literary output and flamboyant personality, these accomplishments have ensured Dumas's renown as a prominent figure in nineteenth-century French letters.

Dumas was the child of Marie-Louise-Elisabeth Labouret, an innkeeper's daughter, and Thomas-Alexandre Dumas. The elder Dumas enjoyed a brilliant career as a general in the armies of the First Republic; but after repeatedly offending Napoleon Bonaparte with his outspoken criticism, he soon fell on hard times and, upon his death in 1806, left his family in dire financial circumstances. Dumas was subsequently raised by his mother in the town of Villers-Cotterêts and educated at a local parochial school. He worked as a clerk as a young man, but his growing interest in the theater brought him to Paris in 1822, where he was encouraged by the famous actor François Joseph Talma.

Dumas moved permanently to Paris in 1823. Soon after becoming a clerk for the duc d'Orléans, he collaborated with Adolphe de Leuven and Pierre-Joseph Rousseau on his first staged play, a one-act vaudeville entitled *La chasse et l'amour*. But it was not until 1827, after he attended a British performance of William Shakespeare's *Hamlet*, that he discovered a direction for his dramas. "The battlement scene, the scene of the two portraits, Ophelia's madness, the gravedigger's scene, these shook me to the core," he later stated. "From this time on, but only then, did I have an idea of what the theater could be, and out of all the broken fragments of the past I glimpsed the possibility of creating a world." Thus inspired, he wrote *Stockholm, Fontainebleau, et Rome*, a historical tragedy founded on Queen Christina of Sweden's assassination of the Italian marchese Giovanni Monaldeschi. This play was preceded on the stage, however, by *Henri III and His Court*, an innovative and influential work that is generally accepted as the first French Romantic drama. By investing his play with a semblance of historical verisimilitude and by skillfully showcasing his melodramatic material, Dumas broke with the stagnating precepts Neoclassicism had imposed on the French stage for well over a century. His efforts made him an instant celebrity, winning even the praise of such illustrious contemporaries as Victor Hugo and Alfred de Vigny.

Dumas continued to build on his dramatic reputation in the 1830s. Involved in peripheral action as a republican partisan in the July Revolution of 1830, he yielded to the political pressures of the period and, in the following year, produced *Napoléon Bonaparte; ou, Trente ans de l'histoire de France.*

The year 1831 also marked the first performance of three of his best-known plays: *Antony, Charles VII chez ses grands vassaux,* and *Richard Darlington. Antony* in particular was a triumph for Dumas; the first depiction of Romantic passion and defiance in a contemporary setting, the drama electrified audiences. Yet its notoriety was soon rivaled by his play *La tour de Nesle* (*The Tower of Nesle*), first produced in 1832. Dealing with orgies and homicide among the aristocracy during the reign of Louis X, this lurid work became one of the playwright's most popular dramas. Because of his republican affiliations and activities, which the new king Louis Philippe regarded with disfavor, Dumas was advised to leave France for a time. In 1832, he embarked on a tour of Switzerland, recording his impressions in *Impressions de voyage: Suisse* (*Travels in Switzerland*), a work that established his reputation as an innovative travel writer and anticipated a number of similar books covering his travels in Russia, Italy, and other lands. These works were later collected and published as "Impressions de voyage" in his *Oeuvres complètes*. Dumas also became involved with the actress Ida Ferrier at this time. Although the couple lived together for eight years before marrying in 1840, their marriage was unhappy and they separated in 1844. But Dumas was not long in seeking female companionship. Having had numerous affairs previous to his relationship with Ferrier and having fathered several illegitimate children (including the future playwright Alexandre Dumas, *fils*), he continued to lead an openly promiscuous life well into his old age.

Dumas achieved fame and fortune as a novelist in the 1840s. In collaboration with Auguste Maquet, he serialized *Le chevalier d'Harmental* in the periodical *Le siècle* in 1842. Compounded of history, intrigue, adventure, and romance, it is generally regarded as the first of Dumas's great historical novels. The years 1844 and 1845 were productive for the partners, distinguished by the serial and book publication of *The Three Musketeers* and *The Count of Monte Cristo*. Dumas subsequently collaborated with Maquet on a steady stream of historical romances, most of which were published serially in Parisian periodicals and eagerly consumed by the French public. Between 1840 and 1850, they produced two celebrated "series" of novels: the "D'Artagnan Romances," composed of *The Three Musketeers, Vingt ans après* (*Twenty Years After; or, The Further Feats and Fortunes of a Gascon Adventurer*), and *Le vicomte de Bragelonne; ou, Dix ans plus tard* (*The Vicomte de Bragelonne; or, Ten Years Later*); and the "Valois Romances," composed of *La reine Margot* (*Marguerite de Valois*), *La dame de Monsoreau* (*Chicot the Jester; or, The Lady of Monsoreau*), and *Les quarante-cinq* (*The Forty-Five Guardsmen*). Indeed, Dumas's productivity was so remarkable that the French journalist and writer Eugène de Mirecourt publicly accused him of operating a literary "factory" and exploiting the services of slave-like collaborators. Mirecourt was eventually convicted of slander, but doubts concerning the authorship of his works beleaguered Dumas throughout his career. The author was well compensated, however, using the income from his writings to support an extravagant lifestyle epitomized by his opulent residence at Marly-le-Roi. Dubbed the "Château de Monte-Cristo," it was home to a menagerie of Dumas's pets and a parade of hangers-on until 1850, when their patron's finances collapsed.

Dumas's insolvency was closely linked to the closing of the Théâtre Historique. Begun by Dumas in 1847 as a vehicle for staging dramatizations of his historical novels, the theater's failure in 1850 left him destitute and precipitated a two-year retreat to Brussels to avoid his creditors. In addition, Dumas's partnership with Maquet dissolved at this time. Although Maquet had collaborated with Dumas on two of the four novels in the "Memoirs of a Physician" series—*Mémoires d'un médecin: Joseph Balsamo* (*Memoirs of a Physician*) and *Le collier de la reine* (*The Queen's Necklace*)—he then withdrew his services and Dumas composed the succeeding romances, *Ange Pitou* and *La comtesse de Charny* (*The Countess de Charny*), by himself. With the help of his secretary in Brussels, who brought order to his financial affairs, Dumas returned to Paris in 1853. His voluminous memoirs had been published serially in his absence, and he subsequently devoted considerable energy to publishing and writing for a string of his own periodicals, including *Le mousquetaire* and *Le Monte-Cristo*. Dumas toured Russia in 1858-59 and lived in Italy from 1860 to 1864. Thereafter his life was relatively subdued. Although he enjoyed a flamboyant liaison with the young American actress Adah Isaacs Menken and published several collections of essays in the late 1860s, he was also beset by poverty and declining spirits. Dumas died in his sixty-eighth year at the home of Alexandre Dumas, *fils* in Puys.

As Victor Hugo is considered the chief theorist of French Romantic drama, so Dumas is regarded as its chief popularizer. Most critics attribute this achievement to Dumas's peculiar ability to exploit the sensational: by using his peerless management of stagecraft and dramatic effect to magnify the high passion of Romanticism, he created some of the most powerful and popular dramas of his era. *Antony* was one of his greatest successes in this manner. Described by *Le constitutionnel* as "the most daringly obscene piece that has appeared in even these days of obscenity," the play features a Byronic hero who seduces his married lover and then slays her in a defiant attempt to disguise their relationship and save her reputation. The fact that Dumas challenged tradition by placing his inflammatory drama in a contemporary setting undoubtedly contributed to the play's success. *The Tower of Nesle* stands out as the most potent of Dumas's numerous historical melodramas. Yet many critics have remarked that the play also epitomizes the weaknesses of Dumas's dramaturgy. As with many of his plays, *The Tower of Nesle* is often criticized for its indiscriminate presentation of vice and violence—frequently at the expense of morality, probability, profundity, and good taste—and for its appeal to the baser instincts of the crowd. This tendency toward "popularizing" his works offended the moral standards of contemporary critics, and it continues to detract from Dumas's reputation as a serious dramatic author.

George Bernard Shaw best reflected the consensus of critical opinion in his description of Dumas as "one of the best storytellers, narrative or dramatic, that ever lived." Although Dumas used his storytelling skills to great advantage in his memoirs and travel books, they are especially manifest in his novels. One of his ambitions as a novelist was to write a body of romances that would span French history from the Middle Ages to contemporary times. He nearly realized his goal, though more importantly his efforts established a unique brand of fiction that combines well-known events and historical personalities with characters and incidents of his own creation. Critics emphasize, however, that history is at the service of romance in these works. Likewise, stylistic and thematic concerns are largely subordinated to the demands of fast-paced adventure and intrigue. Dumas's skill in managing his racing plots is acknowledged by many commentators and may well represent his greatest technical asset as a novelist; indeed, G. K. Chesterton pointed to his "structural, systematic, almost numerical method" of planning an incident or series of incidents as the surest sign of Dumas's genius.

Critics regard *The Three Musketeers* as one of Dumas's greatest and most representative works. Like many of his romances, the story is partly based on a quasi-historical document, in this case Gatien de Courtilz de Sandras's *Mémoires de M. d'Artagnan*. Dumas drew the character of D'Artagnan and the names of the famous trio of Athos, Porthos, and Aramis from this source and embroidered their fictional adventures around actual or reputed intrigues involving Louis XIII, Anne of Austria, Cardinal Richelieu, and the duke of Buckingham. While critics generally acknowledge the zest and brio with which Dumas conducted his tale, they also focus on the factors that have contributed to the musketeers' continuing popularity. Most commentators praise the protagonists as well-wrought character types—D'Artagnan is commonly recognized as the type of the adventurous Gascon, Athos as the melancholic aristocrat, Porthos as the boastful strongman, and Aramis as the elegant schemer. They also acknowledge the musketeers' broad appeal as swashbuckling heroes endowed with rather pragmatic morals. More complex interpretations of these figures have been suggested as well: Hippolyte Parigot described the adventurers as representatives of the "four cardinal points of French civilization," which he defines as "fierce determination, aristocratic melancholy, a somewhat vainglorious strength, [and] an elegance, at once delicate and gay''; André Maurois has explained their popularity in terms of the hunger among all societies for ''action, strength, and generosity.'' Dumas's heroes also share the distinction of ranking among the favorite characters of William Makepeace Thackeray, Robert Louis Stevenson, and other eminent novelists.

The Count of Monte Cristo is an equally popular but somewhat more problematic work than *The Three Musketeers.* Inspired by Jacques Peuchet's account of François Picaud's search for vengeance in *Mémoires tirés des archives de la police de Paris,* Dumas devised the thrilling story of Edmond Dantès's unjust imprisonment in the Château d'If and his subsequent escape and search for revenge disguised as the mysterious and fabulously wealthy count of Monte-Cristo. Critics occasionally distinguish between the first and second ''parts'' of the novel, generally preferring the account of Dantès's victimization and captivity in the first part to the history of his revenge. Most troublesome to critics is the count's petty cruelty and the improbability of his escapades, which depend on his access to a hidden treasure on the island of Monte-Cristo. Yet commentators generally concede that the novel draws its power from these same sources. Critics agree that by exploiting Monte-Cristo's sudden wealth and lust for vengeance, Dumas evidently tapped potent, archetypal fantasies in the human psyche and thus created a story of near universal appeal.

Critical appreciation of Dumas's achievements has increased over time. During his lifetime, he was beset by accusations of plagiarism and outright fraud. He defended his practices, minimizing the contribution of his collaborators and arguing that he had reworked rather than copied the writings of others, but his reputation was severely damaged nonetheless. His tendency late in his career to pad his works for the sake of profit further jeopardized his fame. However, Dumas's literary stature rebounded shortly after his death, as critics showed a greater tolerance towards his authorial practices. Many of these commentators emphasized that Dumas was indeed responsible for the original quality of his works regardless of his borrowings and collaborations. Still, most critics grant that Dumas neither aspired to nor inspires profundity. Instead, he is usually discussed in terms of his unmatched storytelling ability and depicted as an entertainer *par excellence.* Recognition of this nature effectively excludes Dumas from the ranks of literary immortals, yet it has not prevented him from assuming an enviable position as one of the best-loved writers in world literature. The English novelist and critic Margaret Oliphant admirably summarized her French colleague's strengths, weaknesses, and literary standing in 1873, stating, ''Adventure, sensation, excitement, these were his honest objects; and when they are procured by honest means, does any one deny them a legitimate place among the wholesome pleasures of humanity? . . . He might not be either great or wise, no model for any one to follow; but yet there was a real place for him in the world, and he filled it with a certain fitness. Many men of his generation have moved us more deeply, more beneficially; but few have amused us in so primitive a way, or so much, or so long, or with so little harm.''

*PRINCIPAL WORKS

La chasse et l'amour   (drama)   1825
Henri III et sa cour   (drama)   1829
   [*Catherine of Cleves* published in *''Catherine of Cleves''
   and ''Hernani'': Tragedies,* 1832; also published as
   Henri III and His Court in *Nineteenth Century French
   Plays,* 1931]

Stockholm, Fontainebleau, et Rome   (drama)   1830; also
   published as *Christine; ou, Stockholm, Fontainebleau,
   et Rome,* 1841
Antony   (drama)   1831
   [*Antony,* 1880]
Charles VII chez ses grands vassaux   (drama)   1831
Napoléon Bonaparte; ou, Trente ans de l'histoire de France
   (drama)   1831
Richard Darlington   (drama)   1831
Térésa   (drama)   1832
La tour de Nesle   (drama)   1832
   [*The Tower of Nesle,* 1906]
Impressions de voyage. 5 vols.   (travel sketches)   1833-37;
   also published as *Impressions de voyage: Suisse,* 1851
   [*The Glacier Land,* 1848; also published as *Travels in
   Switzerland,* 1958]
Don Juan de Marana; ou, La chute d'un ange   (drama)
   1836
   [*Don Juan de Marana,* 1939]
Caligula   (drama)   1837
**Crimes célèbres.* 8 vols.   (essays)   1839-40
   [*Celebrated Crimes,* 1895]
Une année à Florence   (travel sketches)   1841
Excursions sur les bords du Rhin   (travel sketches)   1841
Nouvelles impressions de voyage: Midi de la France
   (travel sketches)   1841
   [*Pictures of Travel in the South of France,* 1852]
Le capitaine Aréna   (travel sketches)   1842
Le chevalier d'Harmental   (novel)   1842
   [*The Chevalier d'Harmental,* 1856]
Le spéronare   (travel sketches)   1842
   [*Journeys with Dumas: The Speronara* (partial
   translation), 1902]
Le corricolo   (travel sketches)   1843
La villa Palmieri   (travel sketches)   1843
Louis XIV et son siècle. 2 vols.   (history)   1844-45
Les trois mousquetaires   (novel)   1844
   [*The Three Musketeers; or, The Feats and Fortunes of a
   Gascon Adventurer,* 1846]
Le chevalier de Maison-Rouge. 6 vols.   (novel)   1845-46
   [*Marie Antoinette; or, The Chevalier of the Red House: A
   Tale of the French Revolution,* 1846; also published as
   *The Chevalier de Maison Rouge: A Tale of the Reign of
   Terror,* 1859]
Le comte de Monte-Cristo   (novel)   1845
   [*The Count of Monte Cristo,* 1846]
Une fille du Régent   (novel)   1845
   [*The Regent's Daughter,* 1845]
La reine Margot   (novel)   1845
   [*Margaret of Navarre; or, The Massacre of Saint
   Bartholomew's Eve,* 1845; also published as *Marguerite
   de Valois,* 1846]
Vingt ans après   (novel)   1845
   [*Twenty Years After; or, The Further Feats and Fortunes
   of a Gascon Adventurer,* 1846]
Le bâtard de Mauléon. 9 vols.   (novel)   1846-47
   [*The Half Brothers; or, The Head and the Hand,* 1858;
   also published as *The Bastard of Mauléon,* 1891]
La dame de Monsoreau   (novel)   1846
   [*Chicot the Jester; or, The Lady of Monsoreau,* 1857; also
   published as *Diana of Meridor; or, The Lady of
   Monsoreau,* 1860]
Mémoires d'un médecin: Joseph Balsamo. 19 vols.   (novel)
   1846-48
   [*Memoirs of a Physician,* 1850?]

Impressions de voyage: De Paris à Cadix. 5 vols. (travel sketches) 1847-48
[*From Paris to Cadiz,* 1958]

Les quarante-cinq (novel) 1847
[*The Forty-Five Guardsmen,* 1848; also published as *The Forty-Five,* 1889]

Oeuvres complètes. 286 vols. (novels, short stories, travel sketches, memoirs, histories, and essays) 1848-1900

Le véloce; ou, Tanger, Alger, et Tunis. 4 vols. (travel sketches) 1848-51
[*Tales of Algeria; or, Life among the Arabs* (partial translation), 1868]

Le vicomte de Bragelonne; ou, Dix ans plus tard. 26 vols. (novel) 1848-50
***[*The Vicomte de Bragelonne; or, Ten Years Later,* 1857]

Le collier de la reine. 11 vols. (novel) 1849-50
[*The Queen's Necklace,* 1855]

La tulipe noire (novel) 1850
[*Rosa; or, The Black Tulip,* 1854; also published as *The Black Tulip,* 1877]

Ange Pitou (novel) 1851
[*Taking the Bastille; or, Six Years Later,* 1859; also published as *Ange Pitou,* 1890]

La comtesse de Charny. 19 vols. (novel) 1852-55
[*The Countess de Charny,* 1894]

Mes mémoires. 22 vols. (memoirs) 1852-54
[*My Memoirs.* 6 vols., 1907-09]

Souvenirs de 1830 à 1842. 8 vols. (memoirs) 1854-55

De Paris à Astrakan: Nouvelles impressions de voyage (travel sketches) 1858-59; also published as *Impressions de voyage: En Russie* in *Oeuvres complètes,* 1865-66

Le Caucase: Voyage d'Alexandre Dumas (travel sketches) 1859
[*Adventures in the Caucasus,* 1962]

Théâtre complet d'Alexandre Dumas. 15 vols. (dramas) 1863-74

Histoire de mes bêtes (essays) 1867
[*My Pets,* 1909]

Souvenirs dramatiques. 2 vols. (essays) 1868

Les blancs et les bleus (drama) 1869

The Romances of Alexandre Dumas. 60 vols. (novels) 1893-97

Oeuvres d'Alexandre Dumas père. 38 vols. (novels) 1962-67

Théâtre complet (dramas) 1974-

*Most of Dumas's prose works were originally published serially in periodicals. In addition, due to the controversy surrounding the authorship of many of his works, Dumas's collaborators are not identified here.

**This work also includes essays written by Auguste Jean François Arnould, Narcisse Fournier, Pier Angelo Fiorentino, and Jean Pierre Félicien Mallefille.

***Portions of this work have frequently been translated and published as *Ten Years Later, The Vicomte de Bragelonne, Louise de La Vallière,* and *The Man in the Iron Mask.*

ALEXANDRE DUMAS *(père)* (essay date 1833)

[*In 1833, Dumas wrote an autobiographical account of the beginning of his dramatic career for* La revue des deux mondes; *this essay, excerpted in English translation below, includes his controversial response to charges that he was guilty of plagiarism. Dumas argues that complete originality in creative literature is impossible and cites the example of William Shakespeare and Molière in advancing the dictum that "genius does not plagiarize, it conquers." For Dumas's comments on the practice of collaboration, see the excerpt dated 1868.*]

[When I embarked on my career as a dramatist, I took,] one after the other, those men of genius called Shakespeare, Corneille, Molière, Calderon, Goethe and Schiller, analysed and studied and dissected their works as a doctor analyses and studies and dissects dead bodies on the operating table, and spent whole nights probing into the springs of life and the sources of the circulation of the blood. I tried to discover the means by which they put life into the nerves and muscles of their creations, and covered the identical bones with ever-differing flesh.

For it is men, and not man, that invent. To each one comes his time and hour; each in his turn uses the means known to his predecessors, but inventing ever-new combinations, and then passes on after adding his own tally to the sum of human knowledge, a star in the vast arena of a Constellation. As for complete and ready-made creation, I do not believe such a state possible. God himself, when he created man, either could not or dared not invent something completely new: he made him in his own image.

Thus it was that Shakespeare, when a carping critic accused him of lifting a whole scene from some contemporary writer, retorted:

"It is a child I have taken from bad company and put into good."

And Molière, still more bluntly, replied to the same charge:

"I take what I need wherever I find it."

And Shakespeare and Molière were right, for genius does not plagiarize, it conquers.

I am driven to speak strongly on this point because, the question of genius apart, the critics today accuse me of the same crimes as, in former times, they accused Shakespeare and Molière; they even go to the lengths of reproaching me for my long and laborious studies and, when I imitated or transcribed certain plays and scenes partly for my own benefit and partly to make them better known, of shouting "Plagiarist"! There is perhaps some slight consolation for me, however, in the fact that I resemble Shakespeare and Molière in that the critics who attacked them are so obscure that their very names are unknown to future generations. (pp. 255-56)

> Alexandre Dumas (père), "How I Became a Playwright ('Comment je devins auteur dramatique')," translated by A. Craig Bell, in Modern Drama, *Vol. 2, No. 3, December, 1959, pp. 251-62.*

THE KNICKERBOCKER (essay date 1834)

[*Noting Dumas's precocity as a dramatist, this anonymous critic briefly reviews some of the playwright's early works and comments on their reception.*]

[Alexander Dumas] is a wonderful example of almost precocious talents overcoming the rivalry of age and experience. . . . His passion for Dramatic writing exhibited itself at a very early age, and his success has been as great and sudden as it is richly merited. (pp. 200-01)

When only 23 he produced his Tragedy of **"Henri III,"** at the Theatre Français, where, with the talents of Mad'lle Mars as the Duchess De Guise and the assistance of the best artists in the capital, the piece was eminently successful. . . . [With] this broad foundation of his fame, Dumas applied himself diligently to the study of the new style in which he had adventured; and from that time to the present, a period of hardly seven years, he has attained for himself a place in the first rank of French Dramatists. . . .

Among the works of which he is the author, we have barely space to notice the following:—**"Antony,"** a Drama in 3 acts, produced at the Porte St. Martin. The subject of this piece is treated with remarkable talent; the prejudices of birth are held up in their truly ridiculous light, while in the vivid picture of Duty struggling with Love, the final triumph of the latter is managed in a style of infinite power, and evinces a profound knowledge of the human heart.

At a later date the tragedy of **"Fontainbleau"** was brought out at the Odeon. . . . Possessing neither the unities of place or time, this piece has yet passages of great beauty, and some scenes which even reach the sublime. Dumas is perhaps the only author who could succeed in this peculiar style of the Drama; which, while it possesses all the principal merits of tragedy, does not approach so near to it as to be trammelled by its rules or the strict principles of its constitution. **"Napoleon, ou 30 ans de l'histoire de France"** . . . is considered a chef d'oeuvre. Among the many pieces of this name produced at about the same time, our author bore the palm, and was honored with extraordinary notice at the Porte St. Martin. **"Charles VII. chez ses grands vassaux,"** a tragedy in 5 acts; one of his happiest efforts, which, together with the Dramas of **"Theresa,"** the **"Gambler's Fate"** and the **"Tower of Nesle,"** have definitely marked the high place of Mons. Dumas among the successful Dramatists of France. Many of these pieces have already taken their stand among the living plays of the English stage. The great success lately of the **"Tower of Nesle"** . . . has induced a gentleman of this city to translate a new Drama of sterling merit by this author [**"Richard Darlington."**] (p. 201)

[This work] combines many of the best attributes of [Dumas's] genius. It displays eminently his originality and truth in the conception of character; his numerous and happy touches of nature; and his admirable use of situations calculated to produce striking theatrical effect. (p. 211)

"The Dramatic Genius of Alexander Dumas," in The Knickerbocker, *Vol. III, No. 3, March, 1834, pp. 199-211.*

LE CONSTITUTIONNEL   (essay date 1834)

[*On April 28, 1834, under pressure from the politically influential journal* Le constitutionnel, *Minister of the Interior Louis Adolphe Thiers banned* Antony *from appearing at the state-supported Théâtre Français.* Le constitutionnel's *article urging Thiers to take this action, which was originally published on the day he banned the play, is excerpted in English translation below.*]

There are literally no bounds now to the excesses of the stage, to the absence of all decency. Adultery, murder, incest, rape, crime in its most revolting shapes, these are the elements of this boasted dramatic era which affects to despise the true masters of the art, and takes an infernal pleasure in poisoning every generous sentiment, and spreading corruption among the people. The great artists of this theatre [the Théâtre Française] should not be forced to lend the aid of their talents to these pernicious works, whose tendency is to degrade public morals, for which the state is responsible. Who would credit that at such a theatre the performance of '*Antony*' is announced, the most daringly obscene piece that has appeared in even these days of obscenity, a piece which made a decent father of a family declare, 'For some time we have not been able to bring our daughters to the theatre, now we cannot take our wives!' On a stage hallowed by the memory of Corneille, Racine, Molière, and Voltaire, we are now to see a woman dragged into an alcove with a handkerchief over her mouth. . . . Here is a proper spectacle with which to school our youth, who will presently acknowledge no restraint! There is no country in the world in which this deliberate corruption by the state would be tolerated.

All that we ask is, that in this universal decay of manners a single decent theatre be left to which we can take our families. To M. Thiers we make this appeal, in the hope that he will try and save youth from destruction, already greedy of all kinds of pleasure, soon satiated and weary of life. This appalling phenomenon is really owing to these shocking and exciting spectacles, when the wildest passions are shown in all their unbridled nakedness. (pp. 216-18)

An extract from a review of "Antony," translated by Percy Fitzgerald, in Life and Adventures of Alexander Dumas, Vol. I *by Percy Fitzgerald, Tinsley Brothers, 1873, pp. 216-18.*

HENRY LYTTON BULWER   (essay date 1834)

[*Bulwer, who regarded Dumas and Victor Marie Hugo as leaders of a new epoch in the French drama, compares the two authors and discusses their impact on the Gallic theater. Bulwer considers Dumas a "more natural" writer than Hugo, though not as profound or powerful a talent; however, the critic chastises both writers for the immoral and ignoble tendencies of their works.*]

I remember a story, told in some learned nursery book, of a contest between the archers of King Richard and those of Robin Hood. The archers of King Richard, rather too confident perhaps in their skill, preferred showing it by shooting at the moon, while the shrewder archers of Robin Hood shot at the target. It is hardly necessary to say that the archers of Robin Hood carried off all the prizes. This is just the difference between M. Victor Hugo and M. Dumas. The one aims at attainable, the other at unattainable objects. The one looks to the success he is to obtain, the other at the theory through which he is determined to obtain it. For strength and poesy of language, for force and magnificence of conception, there can be no comparison between M. V. Hugo and M. Dumas. The first has nobler and loftier elements for the composition of a dramatic poet, the second produces a more perfect effect from inferior materials. M. V. Hugo never steps out of the sublime without falling at once into the absurd—however triumphant the piece you are listening to may be in a particular passage, you never feel sure that it will succeed as a whole—some word, some phrase surprises and shocks you when you least expect it. From the moment that the curtain is lifted, until the moment it falls, the author is in a perpetual struggle with his audience— now you are inclined to smile, and he suddenly forces you to admire,—now you are inclined to admire, and again you are involuntarily compelled to laugh. (pp. 190-91)

[Hugo] despises and confounds, in the most painful manner, historical facts. In 'Marie Tudor,' Mary of England, whose chastity, poor woman, was her only virtue, is brought on the stage with an Italian musician for her lover, in the character of Mary Queen of Scots, with whom it is impossible to believe that M. Hugo really confounded her.

Monsieur Dumas is not quite so prodigal of these defects. The drama of **'Henry III.'** is almost perfect in its keeping with the times of that prince's court. The gallantry, the frivolity, the confusion, the superstition of that epoch, all find a place there. The character of Henry III., crafty, courageous, weak, enervated, effeminate, sunk in vice, pleasure, and devotion—the character of Catherine de Medicis, reading, perchance believing, the stars—but not trusting to them—man in her ambition, woman in her ways—daring every thing, and daring nothing openly—meeting the rebellious plans of the Duc de Guise by a counterplot against his marriage bed—advising her son to put down the League by declaring himself its head—these two characters of Henry and his mother are as perfect historical portraits, as the melancholy, interesting, and high and stern-minded St. Mégrim is a perfect imaginative picture.

Set **'Henry III.'** by the side of 'Lucrèce Borgia'—there is no one part in **'Henry III.'** to be compared with the last act—the supper in the Negroni Palace, in 'Lucrèce Borgia.' There is no one part in **'Henry III.'** in which such splendid and gay and dark images are so massed together—where such terror and such luxury, such gayety and such horror, are thrust in vivid contrast at once upon you. But the play of M. Dumas, though it does not strike you as the product of *so powerful a talent* as that of M. Hugo, satisfies you better as the work of *a more natural talent*. Its action seems to you more easily animated, more unaffectedly developed. It does not startle you so much at different passages, but it keeps your attention more continually alive—it does not agitate you at times so terribly during the performance, but it leaves a more full and complete impression upon your mind when the curtain drops.

Between **'Henry III.'** and the other pieces of M. A. Dumas, there appears to me, however, no comparison. There is in that piece a grace, a dignity, a truth, which one seeks in vain, as it appears to me, in the subsequent productions which crowded audiences have declared equally successful. (pp. 191-93)

M. Dumas has written **'Henry III.,' 'Antony,' 'Angèle,' 'Darlington,' 'Teresa,'** and also claims a share in the **'Tour de Nesle.'** The **'Tour de Nesle'** is the most powerful of these performances. . . . [Marguerite de Bourgoyne] furnishes the author of the piece with his heroine, and the plot turns on her intrigue with two brothers, whose parentage she was ignorant of, but who prove to be her own sons, by an adventurer "Buridan." One of these sons is murdered by the mother's order, another by the father's contrivance. . . . There is hardly any horrible or terrible position of which the stage affords an example, into which the author has not contrived to place his heroine or heroes—there are some events (the sudden nomination, for instance, of Buridan to be prime minister) too improbable for even the necessities of the scene to justify; but there are no flagrant violations of history such as those in 'Marie Tudor'—nor is there any wanton attempt to interest you in crime. You are not told that you should feel as M. V. Hugo would have told you that you should feel—the deepest interest for the lady who had been strangling her lovers all her life, because she felt some compunction at having accidentally strangled her son at last. Your feelings are allowed to run on in their ordinary course, and your breast is dark from every gleam

of pity when the guard leads off the queen and her paramour, caught in their own snares, to execution.

If you choose to judge the **'Tour de Nesle'** by the ordinary rules of criticism, it is a melo-dramatic monstrosity; but if you think that to seize, to excite, to suspend, to transport the feelings of an audience, to hush them into the deepest silence, to wring out from them the loudest applause—to keep them with an eye eager, an ear awake, an attention unflagged from the first scene to the last—if you think that to do this is to be a dramatist—that to have done this is to have written a drama—bow down to M. Dumas, or M. Gaillardet—to the author of the **'Tour de Nesle,'** whoever he be—that man is a dramatist, the piece he has written is a drama. And yet, powerful as this play is, it wants poesy; there are no glorious passages, no magnificent situations,—written in prose, its prose is strong, nervous, but strictly prosaic. I should find it impossible to sum up an opinion of this performance, by calling it bad or good—Go, reader, to see it! There is great art, great defects, great nature, great improbabilities, all massed and mingled up together in the rapid rush of terrible things, which pour upon you, press upon you, keep you fixed to your seat, breathless, motionless. And then a pause comes—the piece is over—you shake your head, you stretch your limbs, you still feel shocked, bewildered, and walk home as if awaked from a terrible nightmare. Such is the effect of the **'Tour de Nesle.'** (pp. 202-05)

[No] subject, as it appears to me, offends the rules of art which is in harmony with the character, or with our general ideas of the character, of the time in which it is introduced. The offence against the rules of art in bringing "bloody Queen Mary" on the stage is in not making "bloody Queen Mary" bloody enough. The offence against the rules of art in bringing Darlington on the stage is in making Darlington a much greater political profligate than he could possibly have been.

I do not, then, I confess, join in the usual cant which denounces as an abomination the mere bringing Lucrèce Borgia and Marguerite of Burgoyne on the stage. I see no reason, as a question of art, why any person, why any passion, why any subject should be prohibited the author that his audience does not forbid; but I do see every reason, as a question of art, why the persons he creates should be in the image of the times in which he creates them—why the persons, for whom he is indebted to history, should stand forth in their historical characters—why the countries of which he speaks should be spoken of with a knowledge of their manners—why the events that take place in the drama should not be wholly unnatural in their comparison with the events of real life.

It is in these, the finer parts of their pursuit, that the present dramatic writers of France are universally defective. If M. V. Hugo and M. Dumas were schoolboys, and told to write about English history in the time of Marie Tudor, or English manners and laws at the present time, they would have been whipped for the ridiculous faults that they have both committed. These are not faults of genius; they are purely and entirely faults of negligence or ignorance.

I turn, then, from this first inquiry to the second—viz. how far these subjects offend, what every dramatist is most bound to protect, the laws and the interest of morality. . . . It is of the rules of morality as of the rules of art: it is not the horrid nature of a subject that offends either the one or the other; it is in the manner in which that subject is treated that its beauty as a piece of composition, or its value as a lesson of virtue, depends. The immorality of M. V. Hugo and of M. Dumas is, not in having brought Marion de Lorme and Antony upon the stage, but in affecting to breathe a mawkish interest over th infamy of the prostitute, and attaching a romantic heroism to the adulterous seducer of female honour. The inverted philosophy of M. Hugo appears to me . . . a kind of unphilosophic madness, with which I have no sympathy, for which I think there is no excuse; and what I say of the intentional follies of M. V. Hugo, I say of the wild and whining vice of M. Dumas.

And why is this? Why, M. Dumas, instead of attempting to breathe a false poesy into the grovelling amours of a Parisian salon, or holding up for imitation a political profligacy—which, thank God, is yet untrue—in the public men, and the parliament of Great Britain,—why have you sought for no truer, no better, no brighter models for the emulation of those ardent youths who admire your talent and worship your career? . . . Have you had no men in France who have been disinterested and brave? Have you had no women in France who have been noble and virtuous? Must you fill your stage with sickly-faced apothecaries in the frontispiece attitude of Lord Byron, and fourth-rate fine ladies vulgarly imitating the vices and the ton of Mde. de Mirepoix? Why should you invent imaginary personages in the representation of your age who are exceptions to your age? Why should you make as the heroes and heroines of your drama the creatures whom it would sicken you to meet in the commerce of daily life?

And you, M. V. Hugo!—you, . . . who seemed by instinct to have caught the chivalry and the grace of the old knightly time, with the popular language that goes to the heart of the present day—have you no better mode of elevating your countrywomen than by teaching them to be good mothers by the example of

Dumas's birthplace at Villers-Cotterêts.

Lucrèce Borgia, or devoted mistresses by the example of Marion de Lorme? (pp. 210-12)

Is not this stuff! Is not this prostrate and dust-licking flattery! Can you talk of the ringing of a courtier to his monarch, when you bow thus slavishly before the meanest of your mob? Nor is my praise or censure indifferent to you—if I, a foreigner, far away from all your petty jealousies and rival cliques . . . have allowed words to be wrung out from me, words of reproach, strong words, words expressive of more than my regret at the manner in which you have allowed ignorance, and prejudice, and adulation, and negligence, and indifference, and immorality to obscure and to tarnish the lustre of talents for which such a country, and such a time, as that in which you live, opened so great, and so noble, and so heart-cheering a path to fame—if I have had language such as that which I have used, unwillingly, I declare, extorted from me—is it not possible, that far away from that feeble chorus of easily-enchanted friends, who, like the bird in the Arabian Nights, pass their lives in repeating "there is but one poesy, and Dumas and Victor Hugo are its true prophets!"—is it not possible, I say, that, far away from these sicklied sounds, there is an opinion rising, gathering, swelling—an opinion which shall be the opinion of Europe, the opinion of posterity—an opinion which might have raised you in a new time to such pedestals as those of the old time occupy—an opinion which shall break as busts of clay what you might have made statues of stone and of marble—an opinion which shall leave you the lions of a drawing-room, and which might have made you the landmarks of an epoch? (pp. 212-13)

> *Henry Lytton Bulwer, "Drama," in his* France: Social, Literary, Political, Vol. II, *Harper & Brothers, 1834, pp. 162-219.**

WILLIAM MAKEPEACE THACKERAY   (essay date 1840)

[*A famed Victorian author, Thackeray is best known for his satiric sketches and novels of upper- and middle-class English life. He is also credited with bringing a simpler style and greater realism to English fiction. In the following excerpt, he turns a jaundiced eye on Dumas's dramas, focusing on their excessive vice, violence, and specious morality. He particularly criticizes Dumas for debauching "sacred and sublime" aspects of Christianity, as he does in* Don Juan de Marana; ou, La chute d'un ange *and* Caligula. *Thackeray's remarks were originally published in the 1840 edition of his* Paris Sketch Book; *for his commentary on Dumas's novels, see the excerpt dated 1862.*]

Victor Hugo and Dumas are the well-known and respectable guardians [of the *drame* in France]. Every piece Victor Hugo has written, since "Hernani," has contained a monster—a delightful monster, saved by one virtue. There is Triboulet, a foolish monster; Lucrèce Borgia, a maternal monster; Mary Tudor, a religious monster; Monsieur Quasimodo, a humpback monster; and others, that might be named, whose monstrosities we are induced to pardon—nay, admiringly to witness—because they are agreeably mingled with some exquisite display of affection. And, as the great Hugo has one monster to each play, the great Dumas has, ordinarily, half a dozen, to whom murder is nothing; common intrigue, and simple breakage of the [seventh] commandment, nothing; but who live and move in a vast, delightful complication of crime, that cannot be easily conceived in England, much less described. (p. 359)

After having seen most of the grand dramas which have been produced at Paris for the last half-dozen years, and thinking over all that one has seen,—the fictitious murders, rapes, adulteries, and other crimes, by which one has been interested and exicted,—a man may take leave to be heartily ashamed of the manner in which he has spent his time; and of the hideous kind of mental intoxication in which he has permitted himself to indulge.

Nor are simple society outrages the only sort of crime in which the spectator of Paris plays has permitted himself to indulge; he has recreated himself with a deal of blasphemy besides, and has passed many pleasant evenings in beholding religion defiled and ridiculed. (pp. 360-61)

The great Dumas . . . has brought a vast quantity of religion before the foot-lights. There was his famous tragedy of **"Caligula,"** which, be it spoken to the shame of the Paris critics, was coldly-received; nay, actually hissed by them. And why? Because, says Dumas, it contained a great deal too much piety for the rogues. The public, he says, was much more religious, and understood him at once.

"As for the critics," says he, nobly, "let those who cried out against the immorality of Antony and Marguérite de Bourgogne, reproach me for *the chastity of Messalina.*" (This dear creature is the heroine of the play of **"Caligula."**) "It matters little to me. These people have but seen the form of my work: they have walked round the tent, but have not seen the arch which it covered; they have examined the vases and candles of the altar, but have not opened the tabernacle!

"The public alone has, instinctively, comprehended that there was, beneath this outward sign, an inward and mysterious grace: it followed the action of the piece in all its serpentine windings: it listened for four hours, with pious attention (*avec recueillement et religion*), to the sound of this rolling river of thoughts, which may have appeared to it new and bold, perhaps, but chaste and grave; and it retired, with its head on its breast, like a man who had just perceived, in a dream, the solution of a problem which he has long and vainly sought in his waking hours." (pp. 361-62)

We have people in England who write for bread, like Dumas . . . , and are paid so much for their line; but they don't set up for prophets. Mrs. Trollope has never declared that her novels are inspired by Heaven; Mr. Buckstone has written a great number of farces, and never talked about the altar and the tabernacle. Even Sir Edward Bulwer (who, on a similar occasion, when the critics found fault with a play of his, answered them by a pretty decent declaration of his own merits), never ventured to say that he had received a divine mission, and was uttering five-act revelations.

All things considered, the tragedy of **"Caligula"** is a decent tragedy; as decent as the decent characters of the hero and heroine can allow it to be; it may be almost said, provokingly decent: but this, it must be remembered, is the characteristic of the modern French school (nay, of the English school too); and if the writer take the character of a remarkable scoundrel, it is ten to one but he turns out an amiable fellow, in whom we have all the warmest sympathy. Caligula is killed at the end of the performance; Messalina is comparatively well-behaved; and the sacred part of the performance, the tabernacle characters apart from the mere "vase" and "candlestick" personages, may be said to be depicted in the person of a Christian convert, Stella, who has had the good fortune to be converted by no less a person than Mary Magdalene, when she, Stella, was staying on a visit to her aunt, near Narbonne. (pp. 362-63)

Something "tabernacular" may be found in Dumas's famous piece of **"Don Juan de Marana."** The poet has laid the scene of his play in a vast number of places: in heaven (where we have the Virgin Mary and little angels, in blue, swinging censers before her!)—on earth, under the earth, and in a place still lower, but not mentionable to ears polite; and the plot, as it appears from a dialogue between a good and a bad angel . . . , turns upon a contest between these two worthies for the possession of the soul of a member of the family of Marana.

Don Juan de Marana not only resembles his namesake, celebrated by Mozart and Molière, in his peculiar successes among the ladies, but possesses further qualities which render his character eminently fitting for stage representation: he unites the virtues of Lovelace and Lacenaire; he blasphemes upon all occasions; he murders at the slightest provocation, and without the most trifling remorse; he overcomes ladies of rigid virtue, ladies of easy virtue, and ladies of no virtue at all; and the poet, inspired by the contemplation of such a character, has depicted his hero's adventures and conversation with wonderful feeling and truth.

The first act of the play contains a half-dozen of murders and intrigues; which would have sufficed humbler genius than Monsieur Dumas's, for the completion of, at least, half a dozen tragedies. In the second act our hero flogs his elder brother, and runs away with his sister-in-law; in the third, he fights a duel with a rival, and kills him; whereupon the mistress of his victim takes poison, and dies, in great agonies, on the stage. In the fourth act, Don Juan, having entered a church for the purpose of carrying off a nun, with whom he is in love, is seized by the statue of one of the ladies whom he has previously victimized, and made to behold the ghosts of all those unfortunate persons whose deaths he has caused.

This is a most edifying spectacle. The ghosts rise solemnly, each in a white sheet, preceded by a wax-candle; and, having declared their names and qualities, call, in chorus, for vengeance upon Don Juan, as thus:—

> Don Sandoval *loquitur.*
> "I am Don Sandoval d'Ojedo. I played against
> Don Juan my fortune, the tomb of my fathers,
> and the heart of my mistress;—I lost all; I played
> against him my life, and I lost it. Vengeance
> against the murderer! vengeance!"—(*The candle goes out.*)

The candle goes out, and an angel descends—a flaming sword in his hand—and asks: "Is there no voice in favor of Don Juan?" when lo! Don Juan's father (like one of those ingenious toys called "Jack-in-the-box") jumps up from his coffin, and demands grace for his son.

When Martha the nun returns, having prepared all things for her elopement, she finds Don Juan fainting upon the ground.— "I am no longer your husband," says he, upon coming to himself; "I am no longer Don Juan; I am Brother Juan the Trappist. Sister Martha, recollect that you must die!"

This was a most cruel blow upon Sister Martha, who is no less a person than an angel, an angel in disguise—the good spirit of the house of Marana, who has gone to the length of losing her wings and forfeiting her place in heaven, in order to keep company with Don Juan on earth, and, if possible, to convert him. (pp. 366-68)

In spite, however, of the utter contempt with which Don Juan treats her, . . . the unfortunate angel feels a certain inclination for the Don, and actually flies up to heaven to ask permission to remain with him on earth. (p. 368)

[Her] request is granted, her star is *blown out* (O poetic allusion!) and she descends to earth to love, and to go mad, and to die for Don Juan!

The reader will require no further explanation, in order to be satisfied as to the moral of this play: but is it not a very bitter satire upon the country, which calls itself the politest nation in the world, that the incidents, the indecency, the coarse blasphemy, and the vulgar wit of this piece, should find admirers among the public, and procure reputation for the author? . . . The honest English reader, who has a faith in his clergyman, and is a regular attendant at Sunday worship, will not be a little surprised at the march of intellect among our neighbors across the Channel, and at the kind of consideration in which they hold their religion. Here is a man who seizes upon saints and angels, merely to put sentiments in their mouths which might suit a nymph of Drury Lane. He shows heaven, in order that he may carry debauch into it; and avails himself of the most sacred and sublime parts of our creed as a vehicle for a scene-painter's skill, or an occasion for a handsome actress to wear a new dress. (pp. 370-71)

> William Makepeace Thackeray, "French Dramas and Melodramas," in his The Paris Sketch Book of Mr. M. A. Titmarsh, *Estes & Lauriat, 1891, pp. 358-83.*

[T. A. TROLLOPE] (essay date 1842)

[*In reviewing* Crimes célèbres (Celebrated Crimes), *Trollope praises Dumas's skillful combination of history and romance, but takes him to task for heightening the violence of his material and for being "constantly anxious to produce an effect" in his works.*]

The most voluminous literary workman we know—out of our own happy country—is Monsieur Alexandre Dumas. . . . We cannot but grieve that it will occur to us, before even our present number closes, to throw some less flattering light on his remarkably prolific style: but we are all the more anxious just now to do full justice to a book, in which the writer seems to have taken greater pains than on any former occasion to do justice to himself.

M. Dumas has two elements in his nature—that of the dramatist, and that of the minute historian. By the union of these, in his more successful efforts, he has hoped to infuse a new spirit both into history and romance, vivifying the former, while he gives veracity to the latter. The union, however, has not been always complete: indeed he seems to assume either character alternately: and instead of being completely the historical romancist or the romantic historian, he exhibits himself by turns, as the thorough dramatic romancist and the thorough historian, not only in one and the same work, but in one and the same volume, in one and the same chapter. In spite of this peculiarity, or rather perhaps in consequence of this peculiarity, M. Dumas, when at his best, is capable of doing much in the way of rendering the general reader acquainted with a wide range of history. Not a mere artist, he has nevertheless in his historical tales been able at once to seize on those dramatic "effects" which have so much distinguished his theatrical career, and to give those sharp and distinct reproductions of character which alone can present to the reader the mind and spirit of an age:—not a mere historian, he has nevertheless carefully consulted the original sources of information, has weighed testimonies, elicited theories, and, at the risk of te-

diousness, has interpolated the poetry of history, with its most thorough prose. . . . Those who only know Dumas by his inaccuracies when treating of English subjects in a dramatic form, as for instance in his play of *Kean,* may smile incredulously at this mention of his carefulness; but let any impartial reader take his *Crimes Célèbres,* and observe his careful reference to authority, his skilful records of history, his scrupulous adherence to the chain of events, and it will be found that praise in this respect is not wrongly bestowed.

Under the head of *Crimes Célèbres,* M. Dumas has collected a remarkable race of heroes and heroines. He has not confined himself to age or country. It is enough for him that an individual has been criminal, and has been celebrated, to find a nook in his four volumes. The ambitious criminal of the middle ages, who sweeps away the human obstacles in his path by doses of mysterious poison; the profligate criminal of the time of Louis XIV., who stabs a lady that *will* be virtuous, or steals an heir to come into possession of an estate . . . ; and the cold-blooded Russian criminal, who sees her lover lifeless before her, yet refuses to utter a sound of grief aloud, lest it may compromise her honour—all these are the subjects of M. Dumas's very interesting work. . . . In all these narratives there is a similarity of form; in all of them the author darts at first *in medias res,* and forms a striking dramatical group: and in all of them likewise does he soon drop into the orderly narrator. It is a peculiarity of M. Dumas that his strongest "effect" is invariably at the opening of his story. (pp. 36-7)

[In this regard] we cannot help remarking on one fault of M. Dumas: a fault which he has in common with many of his brother writers of modern France, and which is a kind of reaction against the old delicacy, when a murder on the Parisian stage would have thrown an audience into convulsions. It runs riot through all his performances: and even in the clever book we have been noticing, there is hardly an effort to subdue it. He is constantly anxious to produce an effect; and often the talent which he displays in concentrating to this end the means that history affords him, is beyond praise; but he too frequently attempts to excite a powerful sensation by physical horror only, forgetting that it is one thing to touch the imagination of his readers, and another to attack the stomach. We are quite willing to learn that the different unfortunate people who figure in his book were tortured in various ways; but surely he need not tell us how every joint of Beatrice Cenci, of Madame Brinvilliers, of Urbain Grandier, cracked after its own peculiar fashion. . . . Having united the character of the artist with that of the historian, to give his narrative a more attractive form, M. Dumas might have softened the dry records of the chronicler, when they happened to be disgusting. But, on the contrary, he has used his art to heighten the horors which history has given him: dwelling with peculiar satisfaction on the limb that starts upon the rack, on the flesh that quivers in the pincers. In the same spirit we regret that he should needlessly have dwelled on the indecencies of history. There was no necessity to transcribe the beastly orgies of the Borgia family, especially when he assumed that he should have . . . lady-readers. (pp. 59-60)

[These] blemishes are the more to be regretted because the few disgusting pages will limit the circle of the readers of a book, which from the research to which it owes its origin, and the power with which it is written, well deserves to be generally known. For it is not a mere history of cut-throats and housebreakers; of the common criminals of their day, who were the mere excrescences of society; but of personages who forcibly reflect their period, and are connected with its leading features.

The same praise that was given by Hegel to Göthe for connecting his idyll of ''Hermann and Dorothea'' with the great events of the French revolution, is due to M. Dumas, who has invariably shown the link that binds his ''criminals'' to the fortunes of Europe. (p. 60)

[*T. A. Trollope*], *in a review of ''Celebrated Crimes,'' in* The Foreign Quarterly Review, *Vol. XXX, No. LIX, October, 1842, pp. 36-60.*

THE NORTH AMERICAN REVIEW   (essay date 1843)

[*This anonymous critic characterizes Dumas as a moderately gifted ''hack author'' whose popularity results from his willingness to cater to the popular demand for sensational literature. Superficiality, immorality, and improbability are among the many defects that the critic detects in Dumas's works.*]

Alexander Dumas, though at times a pleasing, and even a brilliant writer, and certainly a very acceptable one to his countrymen, is not the ablest or the most distinguished representative of the new school of prose fiction and the drama in France. He is too much of a hack author, adapting his works with great readiness and skill to the popular taste, but leaving upon them no strong and distinct image of his individual character. He is much inferior to Victor Hugo in invention, variety, picturesque description, and all the higher attributes of a poet and a dramatist; and to *George Sand* in the intense conception of passion and in eloquence of style. But he is very lively and graphic in manner, is often successful in the exhibition of character, and shows himself a thorough student of effect. His great aim apparently is to startle the reader, and his contrivances for this end are frequently happy, though sometimes they flash in the pan. But he is not capable of exciting the deeper passions, or of keeping up a strong emotion, while the effort to do so is very apparent. The influence of his dramatic experience is quite visible, even when he is occupied with prose fiction, history, or the medley which he calls *travels;* he is continually making points, that remind one strongly of the clap-traps of a third-rate tragedian. His figures are bold, and sometimes magnificent; but they are often marred by bad taste, and not unfrequently sink into bathos. The secret of his popularity is found in his spirited narration, in his heaping together incidents of a striking but very improbable character, and in his free use of the wildest speculations and the most atrocious sentiments, which a lively fancy and a bad heart can devise.

To say that he is perfectly lawless and unprincipled in all that relates to art, propriety, or morals, is only to remind one of the school to which he belongs. In these respects, he is neither better nor worse than Balzac, *George Sand,* and a crowd of coadjutors. His favorite characters are jailbirds and cut-throats, who sometimes affect to disguise their villany with a parade of sentiment, and, at others, brazen the matter out with a disgusting brutality; and his incidents are drawn from the darkest annals of crime. No regard is paid to poetical justice, nor is any respect shown for the sympathies of the reader, as they are drawn out by the course of events; but the action is carried on with a view only to excite and astonish, and all minor considerations are sacrificed to the desire of weaving a fearful and absorbing tale. Poverty of invention is betrayed by a frequent recourse to history for some wild scene or striking event, though the truth is then so disguised and mixed up with fictitious and extravagant adjuncts, that the reader feels mocked with the presence of familiar names in connexion with incidents which are no longer recognised. (pp. 113-14)

Though our author sometimes inveighs against existing institutions and the customs of society, we cannot find that he has any particular grievance to avenge, or any favorite theory to inculcate. The invective does not come from the heart, nor are the writer's peculiar views urged with that sincerity and warmth, which belong to the passionate pleadings of *George Sand* and other theorists and innovators. He has evidently not been led astray by fantastic speculations, and, provided his books sell, he probably cares little whether the public adopt or reject his opinions. In politics, he occasionally manifests more earnestness, for he is a furious republican; but, even here, we suspect there is a prudent reference to the wishes and prejudices of that part of the community, to whom his books are chiefly addressed, and no deeply grounded personal conviction. He seems to be more intent upon pleasing his readers, than upon altering the form of government. (pp. 114-15)

His writings for the stage may be divided into two classes, the first including four tragedies in verse, **''Christine,'' ''The Alchymist,'' ''Charles the Seventh,''** and **''Caligula,''** which in form, though not in substance, follow the classical models of Corneille and Racine. In two of them the unities are strictly preserved, and in all, the fetters of rhyme operating as a happy restraint on the extravagance of his conceptions, the more offensive peculiarities of the Romantic school are scarcely visible. The second class comprises **''Antony,'' ''Richard Darlington,'' ''Teresa,'' ''Catherine Howard,''** and several other dramas in prose, which are most characteristic of the man, and of the school to which he belongs. Some of these, such as **''Kean''** and **''Don Juan de Marana,''**—a bad copy and continuation of a bad original,—are as contemptible in point of execution, as they are execrable in design. The others show much talent, though polluted to the last degree by immorality, extravagance, and bad taste. They contain powerfully written scenes, affording admirable scope for the abilities of the performers, and have, consequently, been very successful upon the stage. . . . [**''La tour de Nesle''**] had a great run upon the stage; but it has subsequently appeared, that this play, although represented and printed as the production of Dumas, was actually written by another person [Frédéric Gaillardet], who has made good his title to the profits in a court of law. It is evident, however, from the style, that Dumas retouched and modelled the raw material; and the honor of originating such an extravagant picture of impurity and crime may be fairly divided between the two claimants. (pp. 116-17)

''Caligula'' contains some striking scenes, the action is carried on with much spirit, and the diction, though occasionally rough-hewn, is often rich and impressive. But . . . no one would suspect, except from reading the preface, that . . . [Dumas had] a lofty end in view, or that he designed any thing more than to represent with theatrical effect the frightful crimes and terrible death of the worst of the Roman emperors. The characters in general are feebly drawn, especially Stella, who was designed to be the impersonation of Christian faith and the martyr spirit. . . . [Though] increased interest might attach to her, in the present case, from the higher belief and noble sentiments which she professes, this is precisely the advantage which our poet is incapable of using. He is wholly incapable of portraying ideal purity, faith, and excellence, and the attempt to accomplish such an end produces nothing but mawkish sentiment, or extravagance and bathos. But he is quite at home in delineating such a monster as Caligula, to whom history attributes as much ferocity and madness as Dumas is fond of representing in his fictitious heroes. The most natural and striking personage in the tragedy . . . is Lepidus, a dissipated and reckless young patrician, but with some traces of high feeling, who, having been denounced to the emperor for using seditious language, opens his own veins in the bath, in order to escape a more ignominious death. The quickness and composure, with which the young trifler, when apprized of his danger, conceives his plan of forestalling the executioner, and goes jesting to his death, are brought out with great effect.

The union of strength and crime, the junction of a powerful intellect with violent passions and a bad heart, is the compound which our author loves to exhibit, both in his plays and in his prose fictions. With his usual exaggeration, he carries the first element so far that it appears superhuman, and he gives a degree of atrocity to the other, which augments the horror, as much as it lessens the credibility, of the tale. Alfred d'Alvimar, Richard Darlington, Marguerite, Antony, and Don Juan de Marana are all personations of unmitigated wickedness coupled with extraordinary power, and the course of events usually brings about the triumph of these demons, instead of their defeat and punishment. Dumas professes great admiration for Shakspeare, and seems to imagine that in this respect, as in many others, he is only following in the steps of the great dramatist. He forgets, that the "mighty master" always qualifies guilt with some marks of compunction or some touches of natural feeling; or he shows the magnitude of the temptation together with the atrocity of the crime, and paints the struggle of conflicting desires which is thus occasioned; or, at most, wickedness is used only as a foil to virtue, and appears only in a subordinate part. . . . Not so with the villains that our French dramatist is delighted to portray. He seeks only to startle the reader by the magnitude and gratuitous character of the crime, or by the atrocious motives which even heighten its guilt. And the effect is, when the interest is most absorbing, that we detest most heartily the writer and the book. (pp. 120-22)

["**Charles the Seventh**"] presents rather a vivid sketch of some peculiarities of the Feudal system, as exhibited in their influence on social life, and of the distracted state of France at the time when that system was rapidly crumbling to pieces, and the monarchy was gradually becoming consolidated in the hands of the king. . . . The chief interest [of the drama] attends the developement of the character of Yaqoub, a young Arab, whom the Count de Savoisy had brought home on his return from a warlike expedition to the East. . . . To borrow the pedantic style, in which our author speaks of his art, the several characters are presented rather as types of things, than as individuals. Yaquob represents the slavery of the East, Raymond the servitude of the West, the Count himself pictures forth the Feudal system, and the monarchy, of course, appears in the person of the King. The moral idea,—for Dumas fancies that the play contains one,—is, that nature has organized every individual in harmony with the place where he was born, and where he ought to live and die. To transplant him is to do more or less violence to his original constitution. The principles of good, which, in his natural climate, and on his maternal earth, might ripen into fruit, are turned to evil on a foreign soil. (pp. 126-27)

This "moral idea" is rather a striking one; the only difficulty is, that it is not true,—that it is contradicted by history and daily experience. Man is neither a polar bear, that can live only on the ice, nor a palm tree, that will grow only within the tropics. Early habits may make a change of country irksome for a time, and to an ardent temperament the new locality may produce serious evil; and this fact is enough for our author's present purpose. But human nature is especially distinguished from that of the brutes by its great power of adaptation to the most dissimilar circumstances. Yaqoub is irritated by the insults to which he is exposed as a captive and an unbeliever, and not merely by the change of air and the novel circumstances with which he is surrounded. The higher part of his nature is called out as readily by the affection which he conceives for Bérengère, the noble lady of a Frank, as it would have been by a passion for a daughter of the desert. If he had visited the country as a conqueror, instead of a slave, he would have found the soil as genial and the new home as pleasant, as that of Spain appeared to his Arab ancestors, who wrested it from the Goths. The contrasts that are presented by the characters grouped around him, and the scenes in which they are called to act, certainly present a fine scope for the powers of the dramatist, and, though the execution falls short of the design, the whole play is one of the most pleasing and effective of our author's performances.

We have purposely selected for particular comment the least exceptionable of the dramas of Dumas, since a full notice of the others would only create weariness and disgust. In "**Antony**," "**Richard Darlington**," and "**Angela**," the incidents are even more glaringly improbable than any which we have noticed; the plot turns generally upon adultery, murder, or incest, and the personages are worthy of the atrocious sentiments which they are made to express. As the writer has shown himself capable of better things, as he does not appear, like some of his contemporaries, to be a sincere and devoted advocate of anti-social theories and licentious speculations, we must attribute these lamentable perversions of talent rather to the taste of the audiences for whom he labors, than to the natural obliquity of his own disposition. (pp. 127-28)

[Dumas's other writings] are very miscellaneous in character, and certainly show a ready and versatile mind. The most considerable in dimensions and importance are the "**Impressions of Travel**," a medley of fancies, tales, and sketches, a large portion of which have but a slender connexion with a journey and residence of the author for a few months in Switzerland; and "**Fifteen Days of Sinai**," a work which has rather better founded pretensions than the other to be called a book of travels, though it also contains much extraneous matter. The artifices of the bookmaker are very apparent in these volumes, which are swelled to their present size for no other object that we can perceive, except to increase the profits of the author and publisher. Even as they are, from the liveliness of the style and the great variety of matter, they furnish very pleasant, though certainly very light reading. (pp. 128-29)

Dumas has an eye and a heart for the more striking aspects of outward nature; and though the wonders of Switzerland have already wellnigh exhausted the pen and the pencil of the tourist and the draughtsman, his descriptions are thrown off with such spirit and graphic power, that the reader willingly lingers over them, and even turns to them for a second time. Then the crowd of motley characters from all parts of the world, whom the attractions of this country bring together at its chief places of interest during the summer months, afford fine scope for his ready talent in sketching portraits and caricatures. As he has no scruple in inventing scenes and incidents for showing off their peculiarities to the best advantage, he forms a very amusing gallery of grotesque and life-like personages. (pp. 132-33)

[The novels of Dumas] evince less talent than his other productions, though they are equally characteristic of his school. . . .

One of them, **"Pauline,"** appeared recently from the American press. It is a strange tale, in which horrible incidents are accumulated, too improbable to create any illusion, and without sufficient force of coloring or style to become interesting as a work of art. **"Isabel of Bavaria"** and some others are historical romances, the story following at times very closely the course of real events, and not embellished with sufficient copiousness of invention or descriptive power to correspond with the dignity of the characters or the richness of the materials. It would be idle to compare them with the magic creations of Scott, as they are much inferior to works of the same class by the writer's countrymen. They belong to the mass of indifferent fictions, which the press of France, England, and America is now sending forth in vast profusion, adapted for a great multitude of uninstructed readers, who seem to find nothing better than the perusal of such trash for the amusement of their leisure hours. (p. 137)

> *"Works of Alexandre Dumas," in* The North American Review, *Vol. LVI, No. 118, January, 1843, pp. 109-37.*

[WILLIAM HENRY SMITH]   (essay date 1843)

> [*In reviewing* Souvenirs de voyage en Italie, *Smith lauds Dumas's practice of "uniting the two characters of tourist and novelist" as an innovative and highly entertaining approach to travel writing.*]

France has lately sent forth her poets in great force, to travel, and to write travels. Delamartine, Victor Hugo, Alexandre Dumas, and others, have been forth in the high-ways and the high-seas, observing, portraying, poetizing, romancing. The last-mentioned of these, M. Dumas, a dramatist very ingenious in the construction of plots, and one who tells a story admirably, has travelled quite in character. There is a dramatic air thrown over all his proceedings, things happen as pat as if they had been rehearsed, and he blends the novelist and tourist together after a very bold and original fashion. It is a new method of writing travels that he has hit upon, and we recommend it to the notice of our countrymen or countrywomen, who start from home with the fixed idea, happen what may, of inditing a book. He does not depend altogether upon the incidents of the road, or the raptures of sight-seeing, or any odd fantasy that buildings or scenery may be kind enough to suggest: he provides himself with full half of his materials before he starts, in the shape of historical anecdote and romantic story, which he distributes as he goes along. A better plan for an amusing book could not be devised. (p. 551)

M. Dumas has contrived, by uniting the two characters of tourist and novelist, to make them act as reliefs to each other. Whilst he shares with other travellers the daily adventures of the road—the journey, the sight, and the dinner—he is not compelled to be always moving; he can pause when he pleases, and, like the *fableur* of olden times, sitting down in the market place, in the public square, at the corner of some column or statue, he narrates his history or his romance. Then, the story told, up starts the busy and provident tourist; lo! the *voiture* is waiting for him at the hotel; in he leaps, and we with him, and off we rattle through other scenes, and to other cities. He has a track *in space* to which he is bound; we recognize the necessity that he should proceed thereon; but he can diverge at pleasure through all *time,* bear us off into what age he pleases, make us utterly oblivious of the present, and lap us in the Elysium of a good story.

With a book written palpably for the sole and most amiable purpose of amusement, and succeeding in this purpose, how should we deal? How but receive it with a passive acquiescence equally amiable, content solely to be amused, and giving all severer criticism—to him who to his other merits may add, if he pleases, that of being the first critic. Most especially let us not be carping and questioning as to the how far, or what precisely, we are to set down for *true.* . . . We are not poring through a microscope, or through a telescope, to discover new truths; we are looking at the old landscape through coloured glasses, blue, or black, or roseate, as the occasion may require. (pp. 551-52)

> [*William Henry Smith*], *"Dumas in Italy," in* Blackwood's Edinburgh Magazine, *Vol. LIII, No. CCCXXXI, May, 1843, pp. 551-67.*

THE WESTMINSTER AND FOREIGN QUARTERLY REVIEW (essay date 1847)

> [*This anonymous critic expresses a divided opinion concerning Dumas's travel sketch* Impressions de voyage: De Paris à Cadix (From Paris to Cadiz); *having lampooned the writer's vanity for consistently focusing on himself rather than his travels, the commentator grudgingly acknowledges the work's great appeal as a "book for mere amusement."*]

M. Alexandre Dumas, that awful man, whose literary fertility, as all the world knows, has in it something astounding, preternatural; whose most ordinary feats are only to be paralleled by those of his renowned countryman, Mons. Philippe, the magician, when, from a small hand-basket, he produces bouquets enough to fill Covent Garden Market; and whose performances can only be explained by the supposition of diabolical assistance;—this new Alexander the Great, in these two small volumes [**'De Paris à Cadix'**], presents to an admiring world—not as they might perhaps imagine any account of the regions lying between Paris and Cadiz, or the dwellers therein—but, what must be far more welcome, a series of studies of himself in different attitudes, with now and then a few features of local scenery or manners varying the backgrounds. If we might be permitted a suggestion, however, we should say that it would have been better to put more prominently forward in the title-page the chief attraction of the work, and call it, in the second, or fifty-second edition, 'Mons. Alexandre Dumas de Paris à Cadix.'

The adventures are given in a series of letters addressed to a lady; but M. Dumas tells her, or, rather, the public, that he does not mean to play the modest, or pretend to have any doubt that his letters will be printed. Nothing is more common than the opposite declaration, that letters "now published were never intended to meet the public eye"—were written for the amusement of a family circle, &c; and whereas, in this latter case, we often perceive the writer casting glances across the family group to the reviewers, and suspect that he has all along had some idea of the ultimate destination of his confidential epistles—in M. Dumas' case we might be tempted to the contrary supposition, and say that no man could write such letters under the idea of their meeting any other eye than those of an intimate friend. But then, to be sure, the whole reading public of Europe are M. Dumas' intimate friends, and before his mighty name all barriers fall down, and even the hearts of custom-house officers are melted within them. He adopts this epistolary form, he says, because he found pleasure in throwing his thoughts into a new mould, "passing my style through a new crucible, and making glitter in a new setting the stones which I draw from the mine of my own mind, be they diamond or paste; to which Time, that uncorruptible lapidary, will one day affix their true worth.'' He will address himself then to Madame; but he does not disguise from himself that the public will make a third party in the conversation. ''I have always remarked,'' he says, ''that I had more wit and talent than usual, when I guessed there was some indiscreet listener standing with his ear to the keyhole.'' Undoubtedly he has. What actor can play well to empty benches?—and M. Dumas, we suspect, is seldom off the stage.

Having made our protest, however, we must confess it is not easy to remain out of humour with a man who is so delighted with himself, and who presents himself with such an airy grace and sparkling vivacity, and has the art of keeping us always amused; and perhaps there is some ingratitude in finding fault with the harmless effervescence of vanity which certainly assists this effect. (pp. 210-11)

Our readers will . . . perceive, that if they take up M. Dumas' book for mere amusement, they will have no cause to repent doing so; and even such as are more critically inclined will probably be almost reconciled to its egotism and impertinence, by its frolicsome humour and exuberance of animal spirits. (p. 217)

> A review of *''Paris to Cadiz,''* in The Westminster and Foreign Quarterly Review, *Vol. XLVIII, No. 1, October, 1847, pp. 210-17.*

THE BRITISH QUARTERLY REVIEW   (essay date 1848)

[*The following excerpt, taken from a review of a multi-volume edition of Dumas's historical romances, represents a resounding condemnation of the author and his works. First, the reviewer comments upon Dumas's prodigality and flamboyance, but defends him against charges of plagiarism. The critic then inveighs against Dumas's historical inaccuracies and superficiality, declaring his works to be artistically worthless despite their tremendous popular appeal.*]

The objects of [Alexandre Dumas's] existence seem to be two: firstly, to make enormous sums of money to spend with princely prodigality; secondly, incessantly to astonish the world. Above all things, he courts notoriety, scandal, and the power to set men wondering. He began life as a daring innovator, as a romanticist. Racine, and the whole traditional style of French art, he attempted to replace by effective melodramas, which he audaciously asserted were modelled after Shakspeare—his audacity was crowned with a loud but fugitive success. Since then his restless activity has exhibited itself in many ways, and of late, the *author* has almost been eclipsed by the *éclat* attached to the *man.* (pp. 181-82)

[Let us give a specimen of the man's private activities and mode of life.] When his dramatic arrangement of his own novel, *Les Trois Mousquetaires,* was finished, he invited all the performers to his house near Versailles, which he has christened the Chateau de Monte Christo, and sent carriages to convey them. The proposed object was to read the play to the performers. Arrived, they were shown over the grounds, and then seated before a splendid *dejeuner.* Having done honour to it, they imagined the reading of the play was to commence; but no: time passed in gay conversation; a magnificent dinner followed; then came the reading; then a supper, and finally, the whole party was conducted back again to Paris. The expense of such a *fête* we leave others to estimate. No wonder that couriers, ready saddled, and express trains . . . [wait to trans-

port Dumas's manuscript], when 'copy' is to furnish the proceeds for such prodigality.

But now comes the mystery: how does any mortal's *pen* . . . traverse the vast regions of space—those reams, not realms, of fancy and invention which bear the signature of Alexandre Dumas? We have had rapid writers before now, and prodigies; but whose rapidity ever approached that of *Alexandre le Grand?* . . . His rapidity is something so fabulous, that all sorts of suppositions are put forward to explain it; and one virulent pamphlet undertakes to prove that he has a regular manufactory where numbers of young men work, he only putting his name to their productions.

There is, however, one very strong objection to the current theory that Dumas sells under his own name the works of others; and in justice to the literary curiosity of the case, we must adduce it. It is this: if a number of men were employed writing novels, which Dumas had only to retouch, or if he only gave them a plot which they had to work out, Dumas would never be at a loss for 'copy' to satisfy the demands of those journals to which he is engaged. But in [a recent trial], it came out that not only had the journals great difficulty in getting from him the promised 'copy,' but that having printed one or more volumes, they were, much to their disadvantage, compelled to publish volumes by other writers, because Dumas had not furnished them with the continuation. . . . [On] the supposition that he, in conjunction with Auguste Maquet, and, perhaps, also his son, really does write the works published under his name, the *delay* becomes intelligible. On the supposition of a manufactory, the delay is inexplicable. . . . On the whole, we believe this to be the truth: Dumas, in conjunction with Auguste Maquet, invents and dictates the novels, which young Dumas, whose handwriting is very like his father's, copies.

Should this be so, the fertility and rapidity of Dumas are really marvellous. Think of a man who binds himself, in consideration of a large retaining fee, not to publish *more* than five-and-thirty volumes in the course of the year—one more volume and it would be exactly three volumes a month! To accomplish such a feat for one month would be remarkable enough; but here is a man who is paid not to exceed that every month in the year! (pp. 183-85)

This, then, is the man who is the Historical Romancist of our times. Our rapid survey of his activity and his mode of life will have prepared the reader for the style of the novels which, under the pretence of being historical, and therefore 'instructive,' are read by those who could not otherwise read them. He is a man utterly without a literary conscience, so that conscientious works must not be expected from him. He chooses historical subjects, because it is the easiest style of fiction: in that department, a writer only requires a reasonable fund of historical ignorance, and, with a dashing pen, he is sure to succeed; if he unhappily knows anything about the period he has selected, he is in great danger of being troubled by misgivings, and his facile progress will be stopped.

But if we cannot accept Dumas as 'instructive,' we must, at least, do him the justice of saying that his writings, for the most part, are free from two of the vices which deform the generality of French novels: he does not often stain his works with disgusting subjects, nor with the modern cant of gilding rags and dirt. Curious it is to observe the modern Frenchmen, having escaped from their old servilities, and no longer proclaiming the divine right of kings and kingly virtues, rushing to the opposite extreme, and deifying the lowest classes. The Romanticists proclaim that *le vrai beau c'est le laid,* and the new school of novelists proclaim that the seat of kingly grandeur and sublime virtue is not on the throne, but in the kennel. . . . [According to them, the people] are great, moral, chivalric, disinterested, Christian—all by virtue of dirty hands and questionable linen. The People! Does not the very name exalt your soul? 'The People' is not only a name, it is an *Idea!*

Dumas indulges in no such rodomontade. He is not 'philosophical,' he is not 'earnest,' he has no 'theory of society,' he cares very little for the People, and still less for Ideas spelled with a capital *I.* He leaves to Eugène Sue and Company the whole realm of filth and rags, of sentiment and social regeneration. He loves to deal more with velvet doublets and slashed satins, with 'amiable' roués, and ladies who rouge and coquet. There is not much to be said for the moral worth of the persons whom he clothes in velvet and satin; but it is some comfort to find that he does not imitate his contemporaries, who treat the reader as Raleigh treated Queen Bess—throwing the rich velvet cloak upon the ground, that her feet might not be soiled by the mud. They take you into very bad company, but your pockets are in no danger; they take you into very dirty places, but you have no occasion to hold your nose: the morals of the library and the perfumes of fancy are provided for the occasion. (pp. 188-89)

Dumas has not this sort of vice to answer for, but we should, nevertheless, be sorry to be understood as defending him. The tone of his morals is decidedly low, if not worse. If he has no cant, on the other hand, he has no apparent respect for moral worth. His heroes and heroines are often more than questionable. He seems more at home in the atmosphere of *la Régence* than in any other: its gaiety, easy morals, and love of adventure quite charm him. (p. 189)

[We] are sorry to say, the gloss he gives to the vices of that epoch—the brilliant colours in which he paints it—the absence of anything like reprobation of its worthlessness and frivolity, have a very immoral tendency. The Regent, Philip of Orleans, himself—one of the most reprobate of rulers, in whom history can detect scarcely any good qualities beyond an easy temper—is painted by Dumas as a loving father, a careless, good-natured, easy sovereign, and an excellent companion.

This is among the objections reasonably raised against History perverted to the purposes of Fiction: the romance writer abuses the licence allowed him, and goes far to undo the very purposes of History. (p. 190)

[As a writer of historical romances,] Scott had at least abundant knowledge; but Dumas, who travels over the whole history of France from the thirteenth to the nineteenth century—not to mention Italy, Spain, and England—has, perhaps, less knowledge than even our lady novelists. His falsifications are perpetual, and of all kinds. He not only fails to present a picture of the epoch—its beliefs, its feelings, and its manners—he also carelessly misrepresents almost every personage. . . . If any persons ought to be accurately painted, surely Mademoiselle de Launay—the charming Madame de Staal—and Jean Jacques Rousseau, are the persons: they have left us minute and ample details of themselves, in works with which every one professing to know anything of French literature must be familiar; yet how has Dumas drawn them in *Le Chevalier d'Harmental* and in *Les Mémoires d'un Médecin*? The first named is an agreeable romance of the subject of the Cellamare conspiracy; the memoirs of that period are abundant and explicit in materials, and

give us full-length portraits of all the principal actors; but if any one has the curiosity to compare these portraits with those painted by Dumas, he will know what to think of the value of historical romance!

Then, again, such portraits as Dumas presents us with of Cardinal Dubois in *La Fille du Régent,* and of Catherine de Medicis in *La Reine Margot*! The Cardinal was a man of whom impartial history can say little that is good, either as to his aims or his means; but to make him the mere pimp and pander, the mere police spy of a Surrey melodrama, incarnate selfishness, pettiness, and intrigue, is to fix an idea in the reader's mind which will distort the whole career and character of the ambitious Abbé. Catherine de Medicis is, it is true, a traditional bugbear; but even she was not so black as she is painted. She was at any rate a woman, and Dumas has made her the fiend of a puppet-show. This is not historical, but hysterical romance!

The falsifications, of which these are only specimens, may be said to run through his works; in all we have read, we have met with no single historical character correctly drawn, with no single event accurately presented. As to blunders of detail, they are as thick as leaves in Vallambrosa. Here is a specimen: in *Le Batard de Mauléon,* he makes Blanche of Castile, the wife of Don Pedro, in love with Don Henri de Trastamarra. This is a double blunder: the innocence of Blanche is so well established, that only fabulists and scandalmongers pretend to doubt it; moreover, the person with whom she was suspected of having been guilty was not Don Henri at all, but a very different person, Don Fadrique. (pp. 192-93)

Perhaps it is unfair, pedantic, to allude thus to the inaccuracies of a writer whose existence, instead of being passed in the solitudes of spacious libraries, ransacking the treasures there contained, is passed in scampering over Europe, and writing 'impressions'—in lounging with princes—patronizing the Emperor of Morocco—saving the lives of *les braves des braves*—glittering at Spanish marriages—giving splendid fêtes—and keeping couriers, ready saddled, as well as express trains, to convey his manuscripts. To expect erudition from such a man is to expect a greater marvel than all the rest. We do not expect it; we will not harshly blame him for the deficiency; but we may be permitted to express a doubt whether the 'instruction' derivable from such works as he produces be really sufficient to give a taste for history. (pp. 193-94)

[Dumas's] faults are very striking; nay, we are inclined to assert that his worthlessness is complete, unless some value is to be attached to the power of producing a transitory amusement. No one ever re-reads him. No one ever ponders on what he has written. He has added nothing to our intellectual stores; he has hung no fresh pictures in our gallery of imaginative portraits. What, then, has he done? He has amused thousands. How has he done it? To answer this question, it is necessary to take a survey of his qualities.

Dumas has gained loud popularity in three distinct departments of literature, and gained it by the same merits. He began as a dramatist, attacking the traditional form of French art, and substituting for it that hybrid species called *le drame*: the great conquest of the Romanticists in their assaults against Racine. . . . Three *drames* were performed to furious acclamations. As works of art they were worthless, but they made an uproar: their novelty, audacity, and clever use of stage effect attracted attention. But the novelty wore off, and his succeeding efforts grew feebler and feebler, till they ended in the astounding dulness of *Caligula.*

He next succeeded as a traveller, and his *Impressions de Voyages* are certainly the most amusing, impudent, and reckless works ever published under the pretence of travels. His light, careless pen skims over the surface—his admirable power of telling a story is called into play, and with it his audacious disregard of truth or probability; you read with a smile, and close the volume without a yawn; but there can be no misgiving as to the value of what you have read.

Novels succeeded; at first they were poor enough, but by practice he learned the art of telling a story with such rapidity and precision, with such a complication of incidents, yet such clearness in their conduct, and with characters so clearly represented, that it is difficult to open a volume and not proceed with it to the end.... [There] is no disguising the fact that he possesses some of the qualities which command success, though none of those which render success enduring.

Style he has none; but he has an easy, agreeable, off-hand manner, destitute of pretension, and possessing in an extraordinary degree the excellent union of minute detail with rapidity. His dialogue, unless when the passions are called into play, or when the more ideal characteristics of man are touched on, is very life-like, gay, sparkling, and rapid. His characters are always happily presented, though never deeply conceived, or minutely analysed. They have somewhat the merit of Scott's portraits, only more superficial. Passion he has none; nor has he much humour; but considerable gaiety and a good eye for the picturesque. Such men as the Captain Roquefinette, in *Le Chevalier d' Harmental,* or the old copyist, in the same novel, who thinks it never too early to begin a child's education, and accordingly sets it a copy of *straight strokes* before it is a year old!—such men as Chicot and Gorenflot, in *La Dame de Monsoreau*; as Coconnas, in *La Reine Margot*; or as Porthos, in *Les Trois Mousquetaires,* are characters he draws with great felicity.... But his great art lies in the power of minutely yet vividly painting a long scene of adventure or of intrigue, so that it stands before you with almost unrivalled precision.

Probability is a thing he utterly sets at nought; and this is the great defect and drawback of *Monte Christo,* where the *incredulus odi* rises in the reader's mind at every chapter. This improbability is the more unpardonable as it is accompanied with great power of accurate delineation of the situations thus improbably brought about; but when we reflect upon the rapidity with which he writes, and on the gross indifference of his multitude of readers to anything beyond the sensation of the moment, we are not to wonder at this defect.... Dumas never ruffles [his readers'] repose. No reflection disturbs the even current of his narrative. No felicity of style causes them for an instant to pause and admire; no trait of human nature rouses a train of thought in their minds; no subtle glimpse into the complex world of character—no searching analysis of motive—no moral indignation bursting forth from the preacher drawing a lesson from the examples he has given—none of the *instruction* which it is in the novelist's power so felicitously to convey, ever retards the breath-suspended interest of his tale. The reader is hurried onwards to the end, impatient to see how the hero will extricate himself from the difficulties he is in. To express our condemnation, and to characterize his writings in one sentence, we should say: Dumas stimulates the vulgarest curiosity, but never stimulates the mind.

'Waste of time' the reading of his works assuredly is, except to those who want to fill the vacant hours of their worthless lives with a little amusement; or to those who after the fatigues of a laborious day are unable to bear any greater mental stim-

ulus; yet no one who knows the frivolous public will wonder at the enormous success of these works: written rapidly, read rapidly, and as rapidly forgotten. (pp. 194-96)

We are at no pains to conceal the contempt which we feel for Dumas, in spite of an undeniable cleverness and adroitness displayed in his works; but neither are we desirous of fulminating critical thunders against him for the absence of qualities to the possession of which he makes no pretence.... He is not an artist, and cannot be criticised as such. He has no literary conscience; little literary merit. He is not a teacher; has no moral influence for good or for bad; if he does not proclaim truths, he abstains from dressing up sophisms. Amusement, and that of the lowest kind—the mere stimulus of the curiosity—is his object and his only object; and regarded as a sort of literary pyrotechnist, he is the most remarkable man of his time. (pp. 196-97)

> *"Historical Romance—Alexandre Dumas," in* The British Quarterly Review, *Vol. VII, No. XIII, February, 1848, pp. 181-204.*

FRASER'S MAGAZINE   (essay date 1849)

[*This anonymous critic focuses primarily on Dumas's politics, challenging the author's assertion that he had championed the republican cause prior to the Revolution of 1848 and censuring his treatment of republicanism in the post-Revolutionary drama* Catilina. *Ultimately, the critic suggests that Dumas, through his drama, falsely sought to establish himself as a member of the vanguard of republicanism in France, though he in fact was not a staunch advocate of republican ideals.*]

Dumas as a young man.

[Alexandre Dumas's play] *Chevalier de Maison-Rouge,* taken from one of his own novels, had a long 'run' upon the boards of his theatre, but more because of the living pictures of the past that it presented, from its taking scenery, and the pomp of its show, than from any intrinsic merit. A chorus, sung by the Girondin party when, in the course of the piece (the scene of which is laid during the first Republic), they are taken to execution, was set to a new air, which became popular long before the outbreak of the Revolution. The words, written, seemingly, at haphazard, and not of the highest order, happened to suit the new ideas of frantic heads after the days of February: the chorus became more popular than ever in a new way; and those who were in Paris during the first four months of the Revolution can feelingly attest how often their ears were torn with the discordant howlings of the *Mourir pour la Patrie* of the Girondins. To this circumstance, then, Monsieur Alexandre Dumas clung when he issued bulletins to prove himself a Republican, and posted proclamations announcing himself a candidate for the national representation; he vaunted that he had not only fostered, but *produced* the revolutionary spirit by means of this popular air, and claimed on this account to be received as the very father of the Republic; and he ascribed 'the honour and glory of the people' to his own *hauts faits* in the production of the *Chevalier de Maison-Rouge.* Unfortunately for the claims of Monsieur Dumas . . . , the very words had come from the pen of his *collaborateur,* Monsieur Maquet. Poor Monsieur Dumas then appealed to the principles of the piece; but here, alas! again the interest chiefly turned upon the efforts made to rescue from the prison of the Temple the unhappy Marie Antoinette; the man who gave his name to the title was her champion and her hoped-for deliverer; the Republic was made odious in the person of one of its *sansculottes;* the scenes of the revolutionary tribunals were such as to excite horror instead of enthusiasm; and it was cast in Monsieur Dumas' teeth, that, when the frightful nature of the subject was made a matter of blame to him by the [French] princes, he had replied, that he had purposely shewed the horrors of revolution as a scarecrow to any lurking revolutionary or republican spirit. It was in vain, then, that Monsieur Alexandre Dumas contended in favour of his long-existing Republicanism; it was notorious that a marvellous transformation existed in his opinions *après,* compared with his opinions *avant.* But, once engaged in his career of currying republican favour *à tout prix,* Monsieur Dumas played another card, and staked upon the future, since the past had failed him; he produced his great republican tragedy of *Catilina,*—the first great republican theatrical production of the new republican era of France. He was again doomed to a semi-disappointment; he arrived rather too late in the market with his republican wares: men had already modified their opinions and veered round; they had already begun to flock to theatres where the smallest *jeu de mot* which could be regarded as a squib against the republic attracted nightly crowds; and *Catilina* found his rantings less enthusiastically applauded than his foster-papa had hoped. This drama, however, . . . has made itself too marked a place in the French modern drama, especially in its political tendencies, not to be worthy of remark.

The old republican tragedies of the first French Republic bore the impress of the strictly classical forms by which the dramatic school was then ruled in France, and scarcely ever departed from those subjects of Grecian and Roman history, which were held up to admiration and regarded as models to copy in those days, when men put off their old and anti-republican, good Christian names, to rebaptize themselves Aristides and Scaevola, Leonidas and Publicola, without much regard for the fitness of the typical name thus adopted. At all events, they did not go beyond those ordinary claptraps of so-called liberty, which consisted in tirades of some hundred lines against 'tyrants,' in the extolling of the virtues of a magnanimous emancipated people, or in certain vigorous declamations concerning the breaking of chains. . . . Monsieur Alexandre Dumas, however, as one of the great chiefs of the romantic school, has gone beyond his predecessors in attempting to open the new era of a modern Republican French drama, and amended what was wanting in the commonplaces of the old school, in his tragedy of *Catilina.* He has done more: he has taken upon himself a veritable *tour de force* in the choice of the hero of his drama. In the days of the former Republic the heroes, adopted for popular admiration, and in whose mouths were placed those fulminating tirades about liberty which brought down responsive thunders of applause from the republican spectators, were the Brutuses and similar classical defenders of liberty. . . . But Monsieur Alexandre Dumas has disdained such namby-pamby types of Republicanism, and although he has again sought his model in the annals of Rome, he has with his usual bold elevation of purpose, selected for his hero almost the only man who, among the many great Roman models set before us in our school-boy days, has been usually held up to execration. He does not, however, attempt to divest Catiline of the vices laid to his charge in the accusatory orations of Cicero, and which have been accepted by history as his avowed qualities. No! the *tour de force* would be a small one in his own eyes were he to slur over the evil deeds of his hero, in order thus weakly to enhance the interest to be bestowed upon his character. No! he loads him from the first with crimes; he exhibits him in the very beginning as a perpetrator of the atrocities of rape and assassination, without any reason or purpose, it would seem, but the mere impulse of an evil nature. . . . He never shews him afterwards as feeling repentance for his deeds, scarcely even a shade of remorse; he makes him corrupt, profligate, mean, and cynical in his vice; and yet with all this, the author's end and aim throughout the drama is to throw a veil of deep interest over his hero, to establish him as a noble revolutionary model, to excite the sympathies and applause of the public in his favour. Of course this *tour de force* has to be performed at the expense of those personages in the groups around him whom history has held up, more or less, to our admiration. Consequently, in order to enhance the interest in the hero, such men as Cicero and Cato have either to be humiliated before him, to be rendered in some respects odious (although, even then, not brought to the level of the hero in corruption of principle), or, at least, to be represented as ridiculous. (pp. 191-93)

How far the principal characters introduced into Monsieur Dumas's tragedy—and they amount to nearly thirty—may be interpreted as types of the leading personages of the day, or of the fermenting democratic opinions, such as they are, now more or less prevalent in France, is not very clear: it is difficult amidst the crude and confused mass of passions, principles, and ideas therein vaguely depicted, and constantly varying in the actions and words of the different persons, to assign to each his or her personal or philosophical type: but as Monsieur Dumas has expressly and avowedly brought forward his *Catilina* as a picture of modern French principles, parties, and opinions, it has to be judged as such, however confusedly the groupings of the different characters may be arranged in his picture. (p. 193)

[As] the character of Catiline, depicted by Monsieur Dumas, and the interest attached to him, evidently claim the first consideration, this personage may be, without hesitation, set down as the ennobled and ideal type of the Red Republicanism and Socialist ideas of the present day. In order fully to comprehend the true expression of the portrait painted by Monsieur Dumas, it would be necessary . . . to give an analysis, or programme, as it is called in theatrical language, of the plot. But to follow the author through the details of a plot, ill-constructed, melodramatic, and yet almost devoid of that interest of forced excitement which gives a spurious charm to the Parisian boulevard-school of the drama, would be to follow him through a path of mire and blood, frequently enveloped in the mistiest obscurity. Suffice it to say, that the interest is made to be attached to the sympathy and love of Catiline for an unknown son, born of a crime by which a Vestal was the unconscious victim of his lust, and to protect whom against the hatred of a certain Aurelia Orestilla—a woman whom Catiline is about to marry for the sake of her wealth, and who has accepted him on account of the position it will give to her after a degraded past—he goes through sundry adventures, and offers to make a variety of sacrifices. The feeling, however, upon which this mainspring of the action of the drama is based, remains wholly unexplained. The hatred of Aurelia to the youth Charinus is absurd, unnatural, and without foundation, and makes no pretext of any cause except in a sort of jealousy that Catiline should love him: Catiline's fear for the life of his son, and his endeavours to effect the escape of the boy from the persecution of Aurelia, which produce the chief *coups de théâtre* in the piece, are equally absurd and unfounded. In the midst of the more or less historical action of the drama, and even at the moment of the famous insurrection, Catiline is always represented as running after his boy, full of an overflowing paternal feeling: but, spite of all the melodramatic turns in the fate of the youth, Aurelia at last attains her incomprehensible ends by murdering him, and then appears disguised in the form of Nemesis,—in the name of common sense, what had she ever to avenge on Catiline?—in the midst of a last Red Republican banquet given by Catiline to his associates, when she dooms him to the infernal gods! The ghost of the murdered Charinus appears ascending to heaven in clouds; and the tragedy nominally ends. In a sort of epilogue-tableau, however, Catiline is shewn to the audience dying on his field of battle; and the victim Vestal mother throws her veil over his corpse with a sort of emblem of forgiveness of *errors*.

In the midst of all the absurdities and disgusting details of this main plot, . . . the historical action is constantly going on; and around these fantastic personages are grouped other characters, which are either persons of history, introduced as types of great political opinions and social questions, or other fictitious types of Republicans of the present time. Thus, in the prologue, we have Sylla, who seems to be introduced only as a figure of Napoleon, and to shew the influence of the warrior upon the further destinies of the country; we have Cato and Cicero as Conservatives or moderate Republicans; Julius Caesar, as the careless *élégant* and voluptuary of the day, sacrificing the dearest interests of his country, and wavering between the two great parties, whenever it may suit the purposes of his debaucheries; Lucullus, as the utterly selfish and apathetic placeman, or perhaps the egotistical and interested *bourgeois* of his day: and the fictitious characters, such as Storax, the cunning man of the people and acolyte of the Red Republicans; Volens, the old soldier of Sylla, discontented with his present lot; Cicada, the restless boy, putting his finger, from the mere spirit of mischief, into every brew concocted by the revolutionary spirit—in fact, the *gamin de Paris,* and others of the same stamp, with a few distinctive variations of character among the higher spirits of the Catiline or Red Republican conspiracy. (pp. 194-95)

With these elements the tragedy stumbles on its uncertain course: and, leaving them thus, we shall confine ourselves chiefly to the interest attached to the character of Catiline, as the main tendency of this new 'mirror held up to nature' before the French nation, and as demonstrative of the ill-concealed apology of the excesses of the ultra-Republican opinions in the capital, put forward by Monsieur Dumas for the purpose of courting popular favour and the applause of the 'sovereign people.' . . . [In all Catiline] does and says, 'noble ambition' is represented as the mainspring motive, which sways him; his evil nature is ennobled in his interview and compact with Aurelia, when she proposes to undertake any *crime* to make herself *worthy* of him: and his declamations in favour of the 'people,' and against the injustice done to them in revolutions, and his determination to render them their rights—evident claptraps to catch Republican applause—set him forward as a lover of his country and humanity at large. A disgusting apology of his deeds as a murderer and a felon runs through the whole of his unnatural interview, in the third act, with the Vestal Marcia, the victim of his lust in the prologue, at the expense of every received notion, not only of morality, but of the probabilities of nature: and his appeal to the mother to give him his son, with the words,—*Le monde m'attend. Eh bien! je perds le monde pour lui!* is evidently intended as the sublimity of true feeling and virtue. The equally improbable scene with Cicero in the same act, when Cicero offers to his political adversary his friendship and a division of the Roman empire between them—offers rejected by Catiline because Cicero has no real love for his country and the people's rights—attaches all the interest to Catiline, and shews Cicero in a base, disloyal, and mean light; and even the denouncer of the villanies of the conspirators is made, as if forced in spite of himself, to avow the grand and noble qualities of Catiline. . . . Up to the very last this system of captivating the sympathies of the public in favour of the revolutionary hero, by rendering him an object of interest, and even of pity, is sedulously pursued on every occasion. After his disappointment in losing the consulship . . . , and at the moment of the outbreak of his insurrection, when all depends upon his active energies, he is still represented as the virtuous father dreaming above all of his boy, weeping on his bosom, and offering an apology for his own conduct and his memory. . . . (p. 195)

Mixed with this general tendency to render interesting and an object of applause the Red Republican conspirator, and to defend the doctrine of the establishment of the most ultra-Socialist opinions by force, there are other minor tendencies equally prejudicial, or still more so, in a moral point of view. For instance (Act iii. scene vii.), virtue in general is denounced as hypocrisy, virtuous men as *intriguants*; and, in the following act, the virtuous Cato informs his confederate Cicero that he intends acting the part of 'Sir Pandarus of Troy,' and offering his sister to Caesar, as a means of ensuring the many votes for the consulship possessed by the voluptuary—a revolting proposal, which Cicero seems to consider as perfectly natural and acceptable.

It would be an almost endless task to follow the author through all his claptraps about 'fraternity,' *le partage des biens,* the right of the people to the soil of the country, equality, and humanity. With such the tragedy abounds, shewing thereby the intention of the author to curry favour with the extreme Republican party—whether with the hope of attaining by its means the post of national representative, or any other pinnacle of future power, it is not for us to determine, or even guess at. It may be added, that some of the most felicitous parts of the drama, as a typical picture of the present day, are to be found in the manner in which the conspirators proceed to divide power and place among them, after the fashion of the Provisional Government; and in the scenes of the elections for the consulship, where the most absurd and frantic promises are made to the people, and a perfect *cynisme* of corruption is displayed; and in the hurry and skirmish of the final outbreak of the Red Republican insurrection.

It is now long ago that Victor Hugo, in his preface to *Lucrèce Borgia,* boldly stated, in almost as many words, that crime rendered interesting by the exhibition of contrasting good feeling and virtuous passion in the bosom of the criminal, was one of the first elements of the drama; and this principle of making an appeal to the sympathies of the public has been often very exactly adopted by the romantic school. . . . But really Monsieur Alexandre Dumas has gone beyond all bounds in his gallop over this crooked path; and it is not in our English natures to understand how, after pandering, as he has done in his tragedy of **Catilina,** to the worst passions of the mob, and most perverted Socialist doctrines, which have already brought so much evil upon France, he can again make any pretensions to lead the taste or direct the spirit of the country, even in a purely literary point of view. We should be loath, in condemning the last dramatic production and first Republican work of Monsieur Dumas, to impute to him such detestable motives as the apparent aim of his work would suggest to men's minds. But there is one passage of his tragedy that ought to be noticed as suspicious. Monsieur Dumas has rested his chief claims to Republican distinction upon his false authorship of the famous *Hymne des Girondins,* and the enthusiastic popularity with which it was received in the first months of the Republic. In his tragedy of **Catilina** a similar chorus is introduced; but it is the hideous song of the Red Republican: its pictures are of *flamme, souffre,* and *sang:* its cry is for the burning of Rome, as that of the insurgents of June was for the burning of reactionary Paris: its burden is *pilons! frappons!* Should the Red Republicans ever triumph, and seize upon the destinies of Paris by a *coup de main,* may not Monsieur Alexandre Dumas point to his Red Republican chorus, as he has done to his Girondin death-song, and say once more,—'This led you on—this roused the spirit—it was I who paved the way for your triumph—honour to me!' (p. 196)

"A Modern Republican Tragedy," in Fraser's Magazine, *Vol. XXXIX, No. CCXXX, February, 1849, pp. 188-96.*

THE LIVING AGE (essay date 1852)

[*This anonymous commentator reviews the initial volumes of* Mes mémoires (My Memoirs), *emphasizing the truthfulness and simplicity of Dumas's depiction of life in his hometown of Villers-Cotterêts.*]

[Amidst] the ocean of French memoirs, how few are there that give a faithful and interesting sketch of private and domestic life! Marmontel is charming, but his autobiography savors of the pastoral. Rousseau is abominable. We have on record the life of a soldier, that of a courtier, of a lawyer, of the artist and goldsmith, as in Benvenuto, of a man of letters, of the actor. But a vivid representation of *bourgeois* life, that we have not.

Had we been told that Alexandre Dumas would have treated the world to such a picture, we should not have believed it. The dramatist, always seeking to surprise, the novelist ever

revelling in the fabulous, the portrayer of court and military adventurers and duellists, of all kinds of extraordinary and bustling scenes and character, to sit down and give us the picture of village life. George Sand may do that, we should say, but Dumas never. Yet it is this precisely that Dumas has done. He spent the first fifteen years of his life in a little town, Villers Coterets, about sixty miles north-east of Paris. And he has given a most detailed and pictorial history of this village, or rather town, during ten or twelve years, from the middle of Napoleon's reign to the middle of Louis the Eighteenth's. Dumas' memoirs are of course an *Olla Podrida,* a mixture of everything, politics, literature, courts and *coulisses,* dramas, and *coups d'état.* But amidst such a world of stirring scenes and personages there is nothing so charming or so interesting as the sketches from the life of the friends and acquaintances who illumined his young days, from the humble tradesman and smart *modisté,* to the lords and ladies of the *châteaus* in his vicinity.

In this minute picture of a French town, its habits, ways, troubles, prejudices, amusements, and opinions, there is nothing fabulous, improbable, exaggerated, or given for effect. It is the simple truth, told of himself and others, by one who artistically knows that in the representation of that section of life, truth, the simple truth, is the greatest of all charms. (p. 587)

The memoir contains some charming pictures of village *fêtes* and rustic festivities, with full-length portraits of the personages, so truly done as to interest the reader as much as if he had accompanied, and was destined to accompany them through sixteen volumes of a harrowing and diluted story. Another powerful portion of the volume consists of sporting stories— the description of the boar-hunts especially in the forest of Villers Coterets. Dumas gives minute portraits of every *garde chasse,* and does not spare us a dog, much less a boar, each of which is painted as Sneyders or Landseer might delight to do. These hunting expeditions are, indeed, *chefs-d'oeuvre* in their way. (p. 588)

Dumas is an excellent dramatist; at least, he possesses some of the highest qualities of the drama, and had he sobriety, patience, taste, would have left *chefs-d'oeuvre* for the stage. And yet, in our opinion at least, it is as a narrator, a *conteur,* that Dumas excels; that is, in the quality which is the reverse of the dramatic. There is no writer who can be so powerful or *entrainant* in narrating, as the readers of his interminable novels can tell. But there is no *corps* of novelists, no temple of mere letters; whereas there is a *corps* of dramatists, and they have not one temple, but a thousand. A dramatist or an actor is, therefore, in Dumas' eyes, the first character in existence, the first personage of his age. . . . The autobiography of Dumas is thus, in truth, a history of the drama in France, its writers, and its actors. And in this history of them is a great deal to interest; there is also much that is *seccatura.* We willingly read accounts and anecdotes of Talma, Georges, and Duchesnois, as well as of three or four of the first dramatists. But of the *hoc genus omne,* of whom Dumas speaks, and at considerable length, the English reader at least cares not one button. There will thus be much to skip for a reader, to shorten for a translator. . . .

The literary sketches are fewer than the dramatic, but some of them are characteristic. That in Madame Girardin's saloon, where Hugo suggests to Theophile Gautier his verses on Corneille, which Arsene Houssaye, the director, demands, and which the censor forbids, is a striking scene of yesterday life. The political anecdotes are neither good nor original. . . .

[This autobiography has] not as yet come down to 1830. The writer is still immersed in the theatrical and literary doings of Louis the Eighteenth's reign, including his own early dramas, and the struggle which he and Hugo undertook against the classics. . . . Dumas' career and successes as a dramatist deserve, however, to be treated specially and apart. He himself has as yet scarcely entered on the subject, and has but sketched the characters of his predecessors. (p. 590)

[Dumas is not always successful] on other topics. For example, when he sketches England, Dumas is rudely ignorant. He has three chapters on Byron full of nonsense and error. As many on the Emperor Alexander are mere book-making. And yet even in these there is that charm of vivacious and agreeable narrative, which compels the reader to continue. . . . The most interesting part of this autobiography will be, no doubt, where it begins to treat of his illustrious contemporaries, with some of whom he is on the worst, but, with others, on the best of terms. . . . [As] the "Presse" owes its great vogue and sale to these publications [in serial form], which are at the same time the main sheet of poor Dumas' resources in his present exile, we may expect even more life and interest from what is to come, than from the parts already written. (pp. 590-91)

> *"Autobiography of Alexandre Dumas," in* The Living Age, *Vol. XXXV, No. 449, December 25, 1852, pp. 587-91.*

[ALPHONSE DE] LAMARTINE   (letter date 1853)

[*Lamartine is considered one of the greatest French poets of the nineteenth century. A pioneer of the French Romantic movement, he is best known for his collection of verse* Méditations poétiques (The Poetical Meditations of M. Alphonse de La Martine), *in which he stressed emotion, mysticism, and his response to nature. Lamartine was also a prominent statesman and wrote a number of historical works, but his modern reputation rests on his poetry, which marked the transition from the restraint of the Neoclassical era to the passion and lyricism of Romanticism. In the letter to Dumas excerpted below, Lamartine marvels at Dumas's prodigious literary productivity. The immediate cause of his astonishment was the recent publication of* Le mousquetaire, *a daily journal boasting Dumas as its sole contributor.*]

You have been informed that I have become one of your subscribers (*abonnés*), and you ask my opinion of your journal [*Le mousquetaire*]. I have an opinion on things human: I have none on miracles: you are superhuman. My opinion of you! It is a note of exclamation! People have tried to discover perpetual motion. You have done better: you have created perpetual astonishment. Adieu; live; in other words, write: I am there to read.

> [*Alphonse de*] Lamartine, *in a letter to Alexandre Dumas on December 20, 1853, in* The Quarterly Review, *Vol. CXXXI, No. CCLXI, July, 1871, p. 190.*

THE NORTH AMERICAN REVIEW   (essay date 1854)

[*The following excerpt, taken from an article entitled "Literary Impostures: Alexandre Dumas," constitutes a resounding indictment of Dumas as a plagiarist. In addition to providing textual evidence of Dumas's plagiarisms, the critic scorns the author's assertion that he was merely following such prominent writers as William Shakespeare in the practice of "conquering" other authors' works (see excerpt dated 1833). The critic's evidence is mainly derived from Joseph Marie Quérard's* Les supercheries

littéraires dévoilées, *a study by a contemporary of Dumas in which he and other writers of the previous four centuries are discussed as literary frauds.*]

[What] shall we say of a man, who, in the space of about twenty years, had given to the public no less than one hundred and thirty separate works, a large proportion, if not the majority, of which he knew to be not of his own composition, and yet, so far from finding any cause for mortification or reproach in the discovery and proclamation of this fact, positively claims it as an additional merit, as another point in which the efforts of his Muse are assimilated to those of Shakespeare, Corneille, and Moliere? Nor is this the most singular part of the story; (for we can readily understand, that, after all, any thing may be looked for from the *cacoethes scribendi* of an author, and above all, of a French author;) but that so large a body of readers and admirers should not only remain his supporters, but become his partisans, and this too in the teeth of the most convincing and irrefragable evidence of his plagiarisms, is to us almost incomprehensible. (p. 306)

We cannot concede to this overweening aspirant a seat upon high Olympus; we cannot even place him among the demigods of literature; and with the convictions we entertain of his actual merits and of the means by which he has attained his present elevation, as well as of the extreme absurdity and dangerous tendency of the taste that has thus far caused his books to be received by so numerous a public as perfect masterpieces of genius, we deem it our bounden duty to lay before our readers some account of the history of the literary productions of M. Alexandre Dumas. (p. 307)

We beg to state here, once for all, that nothing is farther from our purpose than the idea of depriving M. Dumas of one tittle of the fame to which he is justly entitled, or of abating by a single grain the real merit that he undoubtedly possesses. So far as we may decide, from a general survey of his career, the mind of this author appears to be one of a rather singular description. To a decided tact in picturesque arrangement and grouping, he unites considerable ability and skill as to stage effect. But as regards knowledge of human nature, and power to fathom the deep-sunken wells of passion, or to reveal the hidden springs that govern conduct, he is very deficient. The instances in his books that may seem to refute this statement will be considered in due season: it is enough to mention here, that, not being the composition of M. Dumas, they in no wise affect our estimate of his genius. As to minuteness of detail,— that fine delicacy of finish which gives to some books the value of a Medicean gem or a goblet of Cellini,—nothing of the kind is to be looked for in his pages. It is foreign alike to his disposition and his manner. (pp. 317-18)

The first famously successful production of M. Dumas was . . . "**Henri III.**"; and it is also one of the very few of which he may in great part be called the author. The majority of his works of the better class are not written exclusively, many not at all, by their nominal creator; this is a fact to be dwelt upon hereafter. But "**Henri III.**" owes no "divided duty." Its plot and its dialogue, such as they are, belong to M. Dumas; its incidents, however, may be traced to other sources; and whether they are the fruit of his own mind, or borrowed without acknowledgment from others, the praise or the blame therefor must fall exclusively at his door. (pp. 323-24)

Perhaps those critics are not altogether wrong, who, admitting an author's privilege, to spare himself the trouble of invention, of using freely any romantic historical incident that falls in his way, yet protest against his distorting or falsifying it to suit his particular end, still retaining names, dates, and circumstances to a sufficient extent to render it difficult for a tyro to separate the true from the untrue. But whether on this question they are correct or not, there can be no doubt of the propriety of their charging the author of **"Henri III."** with paraphrasing the language and sentiments of other writers, provided they sustain their accusations with sufficient proof. How successfully they have done this, a few comparisons must show. (p. 324)

In **"Henri III."** (Act I. Sc. 7 and 8), the Duc de Guise gives vent to these reflections:—

> I ought to mistrust Saint-Mégrin: Mayenne thought he had perceived that he was in love with the Duchesse de Guise, and warned me of him by Bassompierre.—Tête Dieu! If I were not very confident of the virtue of my wife, M. de Saint-Mégrin should dearly pay for that suspicion!—What is that?—*Mille damnations!* this handkerchief belongs to the Duchesse de Guise,—she has been here!—Saint-Mégrin!—O Mayenne, Mayenne, you did not then deceive yourself! . . .

Now turn to Schiller's "Conspiracy of Fiesco" (Act II. Sc. 5):—

> Fiesco.—I pity you, Calcagno: but do you think I would risk a matter so delicate as conjugal honor, if the virtue of my wife were not a sufficient guaranty?—This handkerchief was upon the sofa.—My wife was here,—the kerchief is still moist, etc.

The Duc de Guise, convinced of his wife's infidelity, seizes her wrist in his steel gauntlet, and forces her to write the fatal note which is to lure her lover to his doom. It is impossible not to recognize in this scene a striking resemblance to a passage in Scott's novel of "The Abbot," where the ruffianly Lord Lindesay, in the eagerness of his passion to extort from the captive Queen of Scots a renunciation of her right to the throne, grasps the frail arm of the prisoner in his iron fingers so closely as to leave the purple marks of his gripe imprinted upon her wrist. (p. 325)

We will cite but one more unlucky likeness of expression between our author and one of his predecessors. . . . When the unsuspecting Saint-Mégrin has received the Duchess's letter, and has, according to its tenor, repaired stealthily at midnight to her chamber, the jealous husband, who is watching for this moment, knocks violently at the door. Then the wretched Duchess . . . resolutely passes her arm through the rings of iron that are placed upon the door and the posts on either side for the reception of bars, and by this feeble resistance seeks to prevent the entrance of her husband. This is again taken from "The Abbot," where the Lady of Lochleven, attempting to enter Queen Mary's apartments, is denied entrance by Catherine Seyton [in a similar manner]. (pp. 325-26)

We need not pursue this analysis; enough has been shown, we think, to warrant the idea that there is a similarity which could not have been the result of fortuitous accident between **"Henri III."** and the other works we have cited. (p. 326)

"Christine"—or **"Stockholm, Fontainebleau, and Rome,"** as it was at first called—did not meet with the same success as **"Henri III.,"** although like it the action and dialogue contain some of the prettiest bits from Hugo and Schiller. . . . And, besides the contributions exacted from these two authors, the reader will find that more than one scene . . . is taken bodily from "Love and Honor" by Lope de Vega.

"Napoleon Bonaparte," though bearing the sole name of M. Dumas on the title-page, is in reality almost entirely the composition of Cordellier-Delanoue. As may be guessed from its title, however, it is more of a spectacle-play than any thing else. In a very few months, it was succeeded at the Porte Saint-Martin by **"Antony,"** a piece of much greater pretensions. Emile Souvestre, a novelist who has, by a singular exhibition of good taste and propriety in his stories, risen of late years to an enviable distinction in France, was, if we are to believe M. de Mirecourt, the secret and the chief author of this work. If he is so, he must be also content to bear the brunt of the undeniable plagiarisms from Victor Hugo's "Marion de l'Orme" that it contains. The characters of Antony and of Jacques Didier are evidently formed in the same mould. . . . **"Charles VII.,"** the plot of which is taken from Chartier, and much of the treatment of it from the "Andromaque" of Racine, was far less popular upon the stage. Still, thanks to the generous springs from which it was fed, this play contains many fine passages. Compare for instance the following lines from the third scene with those from the "Feu du Ciel," which we place in connection with them:—

> Je vois se dérouler sur l'ardente savane
> Comme un serpent marbré la longue caravane.

Victor Hugo has it:—

> L'oeil au loin suit leur foule,
> Qui, sur l'ardente houle,
> Ondule et se deroule,
>   Comme un serpent marbré.

(pp. 326-27)

"La Tour de Nesle," a tragedy founded on the history of Margaret of Burgundy, was composed by Gaillardet and Dumas, and we must bear witness that, however historical truth is falsified in the plot, there was no disguisement of the double authorship upon the [original] title-page. The amazing success of this play was perhaps owing in part to the exaggerated immoralities and crimes that were portrayed in the character of the queen. History convicts her of simple adultery; she is here painted as living in incest with her own son. . . . But we must not blame M. Dumas for these distortions of facts: legal investigations have long since determined the question of the authorship of this drama, and have established that, with the exception of some scenes drawn from Goethe and Lope de Vega, its chief composition belongs to M. Gaillardet. Nevertheless, it is reprinted in the collected and authorized edition of the whole works of Dumas.

We cannot be expected in our present limits to recapitulate the scores of theatrical productions that have appeared under the name of this prolific author. Suffice it to say, that a very large proportion of them are either copied, to a greater or less extent, from other works, and without acknowledgment, or that they are not the unaided compositions of M. Dumas. In either case, there can be but one opinion as to the propriety of his presenting them to the world as his own. We could wish to pause upon such pieces as **"Angèle"** or **"Mademoiselle de Belle-Isle,"** and to expatiate upon the real merit of a certain style that they display, as well as upon the defects they exhibit. But how shall we apportion our praise or our censure? How shall we know when we are rewarding Dumas for the merits of Anicet-Bourgeois, or blaming him for the errors of the Comte de Walewsky? We know that no inconsiderable part of these pieces was written by these two authors, but we cannot point out what is theirs, what their coadjutor's. (pp. 327-28)

"La Salle d'Armes," "Isabel de Bavière," and **"Le Capitaine Paul,"** are three works which Dumas . . . wrote in the fresher part of his career as a novelist. If he had any assistants, we know not who they were, and therefore believe these to be all his own. With their flashy, meretricious style, they possess just that sort of merit that had distinguished their brethren upon the boards,—a skilful grouping, and artistic, but coarse, contrasts of light and shade. The last-named of the three is a modest attempt to supply the deficiencies of Fenimore Cooper's tale of "The Pilot." M. Dumas coolly takes up the thread of his brother novelist's story, and wherever he can find room, strings upon it the incidents of his own fiction. In 1839, however, our modern Alexander the Conqueror . . . gave to the public his **"Jacques Ortis,"** the examination of which has led us into a train of the oddest reflections into which we have ever been betrayed respecting the character and motives of a writer of eminence. (p. 331)

[Jacopo Ortis's] letters were published by Ugo Foscolo in 1802. There had been no less than four separate translations of these Letters into the French tongue, the last of which, by Gosselin, was published at Paris by Didot, in 1829. **"Jacques Ortis"** opens with a preface signed Pier-Angelo Fiorentino, . . . proclaiming that it is the great, the admirable Dumas that has done the Italian nation the honor of giving to one of its sons new claims to fame by immortalizing his work in another tongue.

> There was but one man in France . . . who could understand and translate Ortis: that man was the author of **"Antony."** . . . M. Dumas appreciates with such profound learning the hidden beauties of our most eminent Italian writers, that it was easy to see that this dramatic luminary would conqueringly bear away some of our most famous pieces, and that he would manage his seizure with so much address, that no one could compel him to restitution. The translation of the letters of Jacopo Ortis proves that my predictions were correct. M. Dumas has placed himself upon a level with Foscolo. In all justice, Ortis belongs to him: it is at once a conquest and a heritage.
>
> (pp. 331-32)

[A] glance at the opening pages will convert all Fiorentino's praise into the bitterest irony. Would it be credited that this "seizure, managed with so much address that no one could compel him to restitution,"—this "conquest and heritage" by the only man in France that could read and understand Ortis,—is the most glaring adaptation, conquest, annexation,—any thing, of course, but theft,—from the translation of Gosselin, that any one has ever seen? The charge is easily made; it is as easily substantiated. We print from Quérard citations, side by side, taken from the opening letters of either translation, and we put it to our readers, whether the resemblance between M. Dumas and Molière or Shakespeare, so far as they all are charged in common with appropriating the labors of others, goes any farther than that between the crow and the eagle? The one boldly seizes on his prey and devours it in mid-air: the other, ambitiously swooping at a prize which he lacks power to bear away, remains with his feet entangled in the wool of his intended victim, the inglorious spoil of the herdsman.

Translation of M. Gosselin.

Des Monts Euganéens,
11 Octobre, 1797.

Le sacrifice de notre patrie est consommé: tout est perdu; et la vie, si l'on daigne nous la laisser, ne nous servira plus qu'à deplorer nos malheurs et notre infamie. Mon nom est sur la liste de proscription, je la sais: mais veux-tu donc que, pour me soustraire à mes oppresseurs, je me livre à des traitres? Console ma mère: vaincu par ses larmes, je lui ai obéi, et j'ai quitté Venise pour éviter les premières persécutions, qui sont toujours les plus cruelles.

(pp. 332-33)

Translation of M. Dumas.

Des Collines Euganéennes,
ce 17 Octobre, 1797.

Le sacrifice de notre patrie est consommé; tout est perdu, et la vie, *si toutefois on nous l'accorde, ne nous restera plus que pour pleurer* nos malheurs et notre infamie. Mon nom est sur la liste des proscriptions, je le sais: mais veux-tu que, *pour fuir qui m'opprime, j'aille me livrer à qui m'a trahi?* Console ma mère; vaincu par ses larmes, je lui ai obéi, et j'ai quitté Venise, pour *me soustraire aux* premières persécutions, toujours plus *terribles*.

(p. 333)

That we may not deprive M. Dumas of any honor to which he is entitled, we have been careful to put in italics every phrase in the foregoing extract which differs from the language of M. Gosselin; and we freely tender our compliments upon the success of the conquests therein made, not only of foreign, but of native authors. . . . He levies with equal freedom upon the wealth of his own countrymen and upon that of strangers, and the ingenuity too with which an arm is substituted for a hand, a body for its bones, merits our special applause. (pp. 333-34)

[We] fancy that our readers would be surprised to learn how little the invention was tasked to furnish some of the most interesting details in **"Les Trois Mousquetaires."** The amours,—the duels of D'Artagnan with the three friends Athos, Perthos, and Aramis,—this precise nomenclature even,—are all to be found in [the "Mémoires d'Artagnan," written by Sandraz de Courtilz and published in 1701-02]. The author of the preface to the novel, it is true, points out, to those who desire to see a graphic picture of the times of Mazarin, the "Mémoires d'Artagnan," but he does it in a light, careless way, as though it were merely incidental to the more elaborate reference he makes to a certain manuscript volume of Memoirs of the Count de la Fère, naming even the particular shelf of the library in which it is to be found. The success of this effort to mislead his readers was so perfect, that the editor of the "Bibliographie de France" announced it as the publication of an ancient manuscript. Is it necessary to add, that no such Memoirs of the Count de la Fère ever existed?

"Les Trois Mousquetaires" was printed in eight volumes . . . : **"Twenty Years After,"** its sequel . . . , filled no less than ten volumes of the same size. Both works were written by M. Auguste Maquet. **"Le Viscount de Bragelonne,"** in six volumes, octavo, has since come out, a sequel to the sequel, and whether it is to be the ultimate, the penultimate, or the antepenultimate of the series, Heaven only knows. The posterity

Dumas's residence at Marly-le-Roi, known as the Château de Monte-Cristo.

of that adopted babe may yet survive to figure in another twenty-four-volume series. (pp. 335-36)

[The first part of **"The Count of Montechristo"**] was written by the same Fiorentino who had expressed such delight at the meeting of Dumas and Ugo Foscolo, and the second by M. Maquet. As a matter of historical interest, we may mention that, in two of its episodes, the facts, very much as they are told in the novel, are to be found in Peuchet's "Memoirs extracted from the Archives of the Parisian Police." . . . A novel of Arnould's, called "The Wheel of Fortune," is also liberally drawn upon in the narrative of Morel's career. Whether the rumors were correct which whispered that the rest of **"Montechristo"** was translated from some German novel or other, we do not possess the means of deciding, not being very well versed in the yearly efflux of the Leipzig fair. (p. 337)

Wherever patient research, analytical investigation, profound reflection, betrays itself in a passage [of Dumas's works], we may indeed be tolerably sure that he is not its writer. But for many exceedingly vivid sketches, more remarkable for stage effect than for an air of probability, for hastiness of execution than for accuracy of detail, for tasteful combination than for originality of conception, Dumas is entitled to ample credit. That he is not altogether fitted to shine as an historian, may well be inferred; how is it, then, that by his admirers—and not unfrequently by men of good judgment—he is placed in the same rank with Chateaubriand and with Thierry? We can answer this question but in part. That some portions of his his-

torical compositions should be esteemed as equal, if not superior, to the style of these great men, is a mere matter of taste; one critic thinks in one way, his neighbor in another. But that there are many passages in some of his volumes fully equal to corresponding passages in the works of his rivals, the incredulous may be convinced by the most cursory examination. It is a self-evident proposition, that Thierry is equal to Thierry, that Chateaubriand is equal to Chateaubriand,—that there can be no comparison instituted between a passage in a book of Dumas and a passage precisely identical in another book. Only, M. Dumas cannot be allowed any other praise than that of a faithful copyist,—than that of introducing to the admiration of the public the hidden beauties of those two obscure and unknown authors. (pp. 339-40)

[We] cannot but express our sincere regret that a man of such brilliant parts (albeit none of the most solid) as M. Dumas, should have fallen into the misfortune of so constantly thinking the same thoughts, and expressing them in the same language, with other and earlier men, less gifted doubtless, but more original. As to the books purchased by him in their unpublished state, they may perhaps be considered by himself and his booksellers as thoroughly and perfectly his own,—selected with his perspicacity, paid for with his money,—and therefore subject entirely to his control. And being his, what is there to prevent his writing his name upon the title-page? But the unfortunate Thierry and Chateaubriand, what is to be done with them? They are not in the market; Chateaubriand is not even in the world; the passages kidnapped from them are wrongfully held captive among strangers; how shall M. Dumas reconcile it to his conscience to send his body's guest into that spiritual world where it will be inevitably encountered by the angry ghosts of the plundered victims? With what energy will the offended birds attack the popinjay, radiant in borrowed plumes, when he obtrudes himself upon their society! Here, a feather will be plucked away by Schiller; there, a waving plume by Corneille; on the one hand, Lope de Vega is again restored to his own; on the other, Chateaubriand wrests away a perfect shower of downy plumage; till at last the bird that entered such a magnificent peacock will be contumeliously driven away, a very bare, beggarly, miserable little daw! (p. 344)

"Literary Impostures: Alexandre Dumas," in The North American Review, *Vol. LXXVIII, No. 163, April, 1854, pp. 305-45.*

WILLIAM MAKEPEACE THACKERAY (essay date 1862)

[*Thackeray identifies his favorite "heroic heroes" in fiction, placing the three musketeers Athos, Porthos, and Aramis in this select group. He also humorously addresses Dumas's alleged practice of using literary "assistants" in composing his novels, claiming that he, too, would like to employ some "smart professional hand" to take care of the "business" of his stories. Thackeray's remarks were originally published in the* Cornhill Magazine *in September, 1862. For his comments on Dumas's dramas, see the excerpt dated 1840.*]

Of your heroic heroes, I think our friend Monseigneur Athos, Count de la Fère, is my favorite. I have read about him from sunrise to sunset with the utmost contentment of mind. He has passed through how many volumes? Forty? Fifty? I wish for my part there were a hundred more, and would never tire of him rescuing prisoners, punishing ruffians, and running scoundrels through the midriff with his most graceful rapier. Ah, Athos, Porthos, and Aramis, you are a magnificent trio. I think I like d'Artagnan in his own memoirs best. . . . Dumas glorifies him and makes a Marshal of him; if I remember rightly, the original d'Artagnan was a needy adventurer, who died in exile very early in Louis XIV.'s reign. Did you ever read the **"Chevalier d'Harmenthal"**? Did you ever read the **"Tulipe Noire,"** as modest as a story by Miss Edgeworth? . . . They say that all the works bearing Dumas's name are not written by him. Well? Does not the chief cook have *aides* under him? Did not Rubens's pupils paint on his canvases? Had not Lawrence assistants for his backgrounds? For myself, being also *du métier,* I confess I would often like to have a competent, respectable, and rapid clerk for the business part of my novels; and on his arrival, at eleven o'clock, would say, "Mr. Jones, if you please, the archbishop must die this morning in about five pages. Turn to article 'Dropsy' (or what you will) in Encyclopaedia. Take care there are no medical blunders in his death. Group his daughters, physicians, and chaplains round him. In Wales's 'London,' letter B, third shelf, you will find an account of Lambeth, and some prints of the place. Color in with local coloring. The daughter will come down, and speak to her lover in his wherry at Lambeth Stairs," &c., &c. Jones (an intelligent young man) examines the medical, historical, topographical books necessary; his chief points out to him in Jeremy Taylor (fol., London, M.DCLV.) a few remarks, such as might befit a dear old archbishop departing this life. When I come back to dress for dinner, the archbishop is dead on my table in five pages; medicine, topography, theology, all right, and Jones has gone home to his family some hours. Sir Christopher is the architect of St. Paul's. He has not laid the stones or carried up the mortar. There is a great deal of carpenter's and joiner's work in novels which surely a smart professional hand might supply. A smart professional hand? I give you my word, there seem to me parts of novels—let us say the love-making, the "business," the villain in the cupboard, and so forth, which I should like to order John Footman to take in hand, as I desire him to bring the coals and polish the boots. (pp. 211-13)

William Makepeace Thackeray, "On a Peal of Bells,"
in his Roundabout Papers, *1863. Reprint by John W.*
*Lovell Company, 1883, pp. 205-13.**

ALEXANDRE DUMAS (*père*)　　(essay date 1868?)

[*In the following excerpt, included in an 1868 collection of previously published essays entitled* Souvenirs dramatiques, *Dumas describes the process and perils of collaboration. He states that had he never worked with a collaborator he would have written "ten plays and a hundred volumes less," but would have enjoyed "the sweetest life ever lived by a dramatist or a romance-writer." For Dumas's remarks on his alleged plagiarisms, see the excerpt dated 1833.*]

There is one object . . . which I regard with more suspicion than all others—the roll of paper my servant brings me with a card, or which I find on my desk when I return from walking out. A roll of paper is a manuscript. A manuscript is a romance or a drama. A romance or a drama means three months of squabbles and one more enemy. All the worry of my life has sprung from my collaborators in romances and dramas. If I had had no collaborators I should have written ten plays and a hundred volumes less than I have written; but then I should have lived the sweetest life ever lived by a dramatist or a romance-writer.

Collaboration in my dramas has cost me two duels; collaboration in my romances has embroiled me with a man whom I regarded as my best friend—the loss of whose friendship I shall regret all my life. It is vain to promise yourself that you will

never again work in collaboration: when once you have placed your name beside that of another, the thing becomes impossible. In collaboration, one of the two—the stronger—is always the dupe. He commences by inventing and mapping out the romance or the drama—has his own conception of it—and is naturally dissatisfied with the work when his feebler assistant brings him the manuscript. 'Well, leave it with me,' he says, 'I will revise it.' And, some day, he takes his pen to revise it. He begins by correcting words which seem to him improper, or out of place; then he strikes out whole sentences, replacing them with others; then he cancels an entire page; then he tears up the manuscript, and throws it into the fire, saying, 'I shall have to rewrite the whole of this.'

And he proceeds to do so, recomposing the entire work, with all the more fatigue that he works on a subject which is not his own, and which—though he has made it and then made it over again by himself—still remains eternally inferior to the book or the drama which it would have proved had the entire creation and execution been his own. And then for this toil— to him a double labor—he receives but half the reward, and the world cries out:

'You know this successful drama, or romance; it was taken to So-and-so by the real writer, and So-and-so only signed it! This is the way poor young writers are oppressed and forced to pass under the Caudine forks of the great authors before they can reach the public!'

And when a lady brings a tangle of romance or drama, the case is even worse. She is a young girl obliged to write to support her mother—a young widow compelled to provide bread for her children. At first you refuse—then come prayers: 'You will preserve a whole family—they will be eternally grateful.' You cannot utter a brutal *'No!'* to all this—you try to find excuses—they are all met with the logic of want—and you yield. You exact a promise that your name shall not appear in connection with the play or volume—you set to work, often against the grain, for the manuscript is bad, and it costs you all the trouble in the world to make a mediocre affair of it; and then, three weeks afterward, you read in the journals: 'Monsieur So-and-so has just finished a play, in collaboration with Madame So-and-so, which is destined for the Théâtre Français, or the Odéon, or Porte St.-Martin.' Then you find yourself compelled to contradict the statement—the lady continues, nevertheless, to maintain that you worked *in collaboration with her*—and you are dragged into an unending controversy.

Alexandre Dumas (père), in an extract, translated
by John Esten Cooke, in Appleton's Journal, *Vol.*
XV, No. 379, June 24, 1876, p. 815.

THE SPECTATOR　　(essay date 1870)

[*The following excerpt is taken from an essay written on the occasion of Dumas's death. In it, the critic links Dumas's literary abilities to his race, alluding to his black grandmother and maintaining that his works are marred by the undisciplined, "tropical" genius that one would expect in a black author. This "tropicality" exhibits itself, according to the commentator, in Dumas's extravagantly improbable plots, in his intense characters, and in his serene indifference to "immutable right and wrong." The critic also discusses at some length the appeal of Dumas's most popular work,* The Count of Monte Cristo, *claiming that it derives from the desire of all readers of fiction to give free reign to their "secret, disjointed, useless fancies."*]

The literary career of Alexander Dumas was specially interesting to Englishmen for two reasons. He was, so far as we know, the only true quadroon, the only grandchild of a negro, the only man with woolly hair, and deficient calves, and black pigment in the creases of the joints of his fingers, who ever gained a considerable place in the literature of the world. . . . We cannot say his genius was of the quadroon type, for there being so few examples of quadroon genius, we do not know precisely what that type would be; but we can say it was of the type observers like Mrs. Stowe have always expected the race to produce,—a type in which the predominating feature is the blaze of colour. It was not Oriental exactly—for though that convenient word covers most divergencies from European modes of thought and expression, we do not see why it should cover the specialties of the black as well as of the brown races— but it certainly was tropical. Its defect was rankness, over-luxuriance, splendour of colour without corresponding solidity or sweetness, a tendency to profusion without reference to the quality of the supply so abundantly poured out. Flowers or weeds, oaks or trees looking like oaks and rotten as touchwood, every product of Dumas' pen bewildered the spectator by the waste of power which it appeared only too truly to indicate. Dumas would crowd into a chapter incidents which might make a novel, and half of which had no bearing on the story; create characters by the dozen only to kill them off; exhaust patience in painting a hero, and still more a heroine, by an infinitude of touches, half of which were repetitions; while of the remainder many were rather poises with the brush, leaving the idea that he would touch, than actual touches. Without the faintest gleam of spiritual feeling, unless we seek it in the undertone of **"Monte Christo,"** that Providence is wiser than the wisest man, he had a passion for introducing the supernatural or quasi-supernatural, as a machinery which relieved him at once of the trouble of minutely painting character and of making his incidents reasonably probable. That he could create is undeniable,—most of his smaller figures are true creations; but just try to make out, apart from the machinery, what he took the Cagliostro to be, who under many names is the hero of so many of his tales; or what . . . he meant by his delineation of Monte Christo, or of Henry IV., the latter not a character at all, but a mixture of two almost incompatible natures, with no clue to their point of contact. He was tropical, too, in his atmosphere, with its bright lights, and clear outlines, and sense of heat *not* arising from strain, and gorgeousness which escapes analysis; tropical in the intensity he gives to his characters, intensity which is sometimes force, as in Noirtier, sometimes weakness, as in Edmond Dantes himself, and, as we think, in Joseph Balsamo; tropical in the scale of his conceptions; tropical, most of all, in the kind of immorality which pervades his books. They are not immoral often in the sense in which that word is usually applied to French novels. We do not pretend to have read all the forty novels he is said to have given to the world, or half of them; but in the nine or ten we have read Dumas is not so much immoral, or prurient, or unclean—the latter he did not, we conceive, intend to be,— as indifferent to immutable right and wrong, capable of accepting any kind of law which occurred to him as the one governing that series of situations. His history, for instance, for he meant it to be history, of the relation of Marguerite of Valois to Henry of Navarre is, if tried by any standard recognized in England, an evil, though not an unclean book. It would be impossible to give any description of the plot which would not leave an infinitely deeper impression of impurity than the novel itself does. Yet the probability is that Dumas thought he was rather carefully avoiding the impure, rejecting

strong temptations towards the sensational as France understands it; and it is possible to comprehend why he so imagined. He had caught the tone of the Valois Court, its fundamental idea that there was no law for princes other than to be princely; that in particular the Sixth and Seventh Commandments were rules highly expedient for the community, but of no meaning whatever for a "Child of France;" and wrote under those conditions as a historiographer of the Court might have done, with infinitely less intention to injure or debauch anybody than Margaret herself would have displayed. . . . That Margaret was an immoral character never struck him, any more than it would strike a negro, were negroes what we suppose them to be; she pursued her own way, and in that way met adventures, and he described them, and described them with such art that the reader feels that he is in an atmosphere in which somehow truth and falsehood, right and wrong, have scarcely a meaning,—is studying an author who, his atmosphere granted, is writing from a point of view decidedly higher than any his puppets would have accepted. A respectable Pagan is writing of Pagans who ought to have been disreputable, but being Princes, were not.

The other point of interest about M. Dumas is that he wrote a book which, with the exception of "Paul and Virginia," is probably the only French novel yet written which will live as an English one. Since the "Arabian Nights" there has been nothing like **"Monte Christo;"** no such revel of improbabilities, no such fandango of absurdities, and no book which, to those who can enjoy the "Arabian Nights," who can bear to be released from the laws of the universe, who care nothing about likelihood, and are incurious about character, loving to "see the people" as girls see a review or men a great spectacle, has been so enchanting as the history of the low Southern sailor who makes of himself gentleman, millionaire, earthly Providence, and goes through the world supporting the right and punishing the wrong by sheer volition; who, though intent for years on a black scheme of private revenge, is as gentle and holy as an apostle; who, living in unimaginable luxury, is a self-restrained anchoret; who, tropical to his toes in habits, beliefs, ways, is through it all the last highest product of the European cultivation. Dumas has taken little pains, or rather none, to make us understand Edmond Dantes in his second phase. He has not troubled himself to account for the middle passage of his career, the period between his rescue from prison and his appearance as the Count, though in the interim he had rescued Haidée and seen all the world. He has not even condescended to be consistent in his account of his machine for performing wonders, the Count's vast wealth, for while he gives him originally some £800,000, he allows him towards the end three letters of unlimited credit from houses like Rothschilds', and makes him perform extravagances to which his very moderate means for our modern society would be totally inadequate. And yet with what eagerness does one read of his rise, his grandeurs, his vengeance, and his repentance as he passes on his way through that ever-varying succession of incidents, and among that host of living people. The secret of the charm is not in the incidents, for apart from their gross improbability, Dumas has depicted many as lively in novels which will almost instantly be consigned to the butterman; nor in the characters, for men and women as real and as original overflow in his stories; nor in his style, for in many chapters of **"Monte Christo"** it is not at his best, is occasionally so far from it as to lend colour to the report that even in this, his most characteristic work, he was assisted by his pupils. It is not a story of passion, save so far as Dantes' hunger for revenge may be called passion, and the only love story it contains is idyllic in its purity, and when told scarcely amounts to more than an incident; and yet we should like to try with the book some grave hater of novels, or—a far harder trial—some lover of mental analysis. We believe the secret of its success is the deep, full gratification Dumas gives to one of the strongest weaknesses of human nature, the passion of Aladdinism, the desire to realize day-dreams by volition. Edmond Dantes acts as men might act were their secret, disjointed, useless fancies executive. He finds the royal road to knowledge for which we all sigh. He gains the social influence of all kinds for which we do not even hope. He acquires at a blow the wealth beyond the dreams of avarice which we all should think so pleasant. He finds the silent, devoted, yet willing agents of his will, who in the ordinary world can be secured only by Kings and leaders of men; and he, above all, secures to every incident of his career that dramatic completeness on which men ponder when they give the rein to reflection on the past. We enjoy that realization of day-dreaming, that world in which obstacles are not, or exist only to enhance the pleasure of their removal, in which there are many Genii of the Lamp, and one controls them all. Dumas himself, like every man of his race, had this imaginative dreaminess, this love for the concrete unreal in his blood; he revels and riots in his own imaginings, and it is a curious evidence of our view of his character, of the superficiality of the evil in it, that in this book, in which, of all others, he is least restrained by any ties, in which he gives freest rein to his inner self, he rises to his moral best, shakes himself totally free of uncleanness, conceives the character of the Abbé Faria, which is worthy to stand by that of Bishop Myriel, gives in the shipowner's family a fine picture of nobleness without ineptitude, and as it were unconsciously, or in his own despite, graves deep his ultimate moral,—that in seeking revenge, however terrible the provocation, however lawful the means in the spirit of revenge, man does throughout but strive to be wiser than his God. (pp. 1506-07)

"Alexander Dumas," in The Spectator, *Vol. 43, No. 2216, December 17, 1870, pp. 1506-07.*

[ABRAHAM HAYWARD]   (essay date 1871)

[*Hayward surveys Dumas's literary career and predicts that the author will eventually be regarded as "one of the three or four most popular, influential, and gifted writers that the France of the nineteenth century has produced." However, Hayward's opinion on major critical issues concerning Dumas is divided; while he parries criticism of Dumas's alleged plagiarisms by minimizing the contributions of other authors to his works, he joins Dumas's detractors in condemning the "immorality" of some of the writer's plays, specifically, those works—such as* Antony *and* Richard Darlington—*based on contemporary figures or events.*]

[The] most cursory glance at [Alexander Dumas'] career will show that its irregularities were indissolubly connected with its brilliancy. It was an adventurous one, in every sense of the term. From its commencement to its close he threw reflection overboard, and cast prudence to the winds. He is one of the most remarkable examples of fearless self-reliance, restless activity, and sustained exertion, we ever read or heard of. (p. 190)

[It] can no longer be denied in any quarter that Dumas' influence, whether for good or evil, has been immense on both sides of the Channel. Indeed, we are by no means sure that his romances have not been more read by the higher class in this country than in his own. Nor, in glancing over his multifarious claims to rank amongst the leading spirits of his age

must we forget his numerous '**Voyages**' and '**Impressions de Voyages.**' . . . [They] are wholly unlike what are commonly called Travels, and constitute an entirely new style of writing. He has a prodigious memory, filled to overflowing with the genuine romance of history; he lights instinctively upon every local tradition that is worth recording; he has a quick eye for the picturesque and (above all) an exquisite perception of the humorous. He is about the best possible storyteller in print, and he rarely dwells too long on a ludicrous incident, nor forces us to keep company with his laughable characters till they grow wearisome.

The wonder at his unprecedented fertility and versatility had led at one time to a very general belief that most of his publications were concocted by a set of 'prentice hands or journeymen, whom he paid at so much a sheet; and that the utmost he contributed to their handiwork was a masterly touch here and there and his name on the title-page. One of these, named Macquet, boldly laid claim to a lion's share in the composition of the best, and was strenuously supported by critics of authority. But Macquet was avowedly employed by Dumas for twenty years to hunt up subjects, supply accessories, or do for him what eminent portrait painters are wont to leave to pupils, namely, the preparation of the canvas, the mixing of the colours, the rough outline of the figures, or the drapery. That Macquet was capable of nothing better or higher, was proved by his utter failure as a novelist, whenever, both before and after the alleged partnership, he set up for himself. (p. 191)

The charge of plagiarism is one easily brought, and not easily parried except by showing that there is nothing new under the sun, and that the most inventive minds have not disdained to borrow from their predecessors. Virgil borrowed from Homer; Racine, from Euripides; Corneille (for his Cid), from a Spanish dramatist. '*Je prends mon bien ou je le trouve,*' was the unabashed avowal of Molière. (p. 193)

If we are to put faith in his assailants, [Dumas] has pushed to extravagance the appropriation doctrine of Moliére: he has rivalled not only the broom-maker who stole the materials, but the one who stole his brooms readymade: he has taken entire passages like Mr. Disraeli, complete stories like Voltaire and Lord Brougham; and as for plots, scenes, images, dialogues, if restitution to the original proprietors were enforced, he would be like the daw stripped of its borrowed plumes. . . . But somehow these charges, though pointedly urged, have utterly failed in their main object: there is no denying the real genius, the genuine originality, of the man after all: and the decisive test is that what he takes assimilates to what he creates, and helps to form an harmonious whole, instead of lying, 'like lumps of marl upon a barren moor, encumbering what they cannot fertilise.' (pp. 195-96)

It was as dramatist that he was resolved to make the desiderated name; and the time was singularly opportune, for the innovating and vivifying influences which had transformed and elevated the literature of the Restoration were on the point of extending to the stage,—that stage which had survived the monarchy, survived the republic, survived the first empire, and might have survived the second but for the united and co-operating energies of two master spirits, of whom Dumas took the lead. (p. 212)

It was a clear gain to the dramatist to be emancipated from the rigid observance of the unities, to be free to choose subjects from modern history or the ordinary walks of life, to drape them appropriately, and make them talk naturally, instead of being tied down to Greek and Roman models, or rather what passed for Greek and Roman amongst the courtiers of the Grand Monarque. But a revolution in literature and art is as difficult to moderate as a revolution in government: it is idle to play Canute, and say 'thus far shalt thou go and no farther' to the advancing waves of thought: we must take the evil with the good; and it was Victor Hugo himself who drew a parallel between the excesses of the Reign of Terror and what he called the nightmares of the new school, as the necessities or inevitable results of progress. The extravagance to which they pushed their doctrine may be collected from the fact that, on the night of their crowning triumph after the first representation of **'Henri Trois,'** a party of them formed a ring by joining hands in the *foyer* of the Theatre Français, and danced round the bust of Racine, shouting in chorus, *'Enfoncé, Racine! Enfoncé, Racine!'* Dumas, to do him justice, never lost his reverence for the best classic models, and in the first of his accepted dramas, **'Christine,'** he was obviously still trammelled by their rules. (pp. 213-14)

Although the accusation of immorality was unscrupulously brought against the chiefs of the romantic school, they were not more open to it than the classicists in regard to the choice of subjects, so long as these were taken from history. (p. 217)

It was when Dumas abandoned the past for the present, forsook romance for reality, chose his heroes and heroines from modern life, and bade us sympathise with their perverted notions of right and wrong, their systematic defiance of all social ties, their sensuality, and their selfishness,—when, in short, he 'dressed up the nineteenth century in a livery of heroism, turned up with assassination and incest,' that he justly fell within the critic's ban, and gave point to the most stinging epigram levelled at his school:—

> A croire ces Messieurs, on ne trouve dans les rues,
> Que des enfants trouvés et des femmes perdues.

In his drama of **'Antony'** he set all notions of morality at defiance; yet his bitterest opponents were obliged to confess that it bore the strongest impress of originality, and that its faults were quite as much those of the epoch, of the applauding public, as of the author. (p. 218)

[The] profound immorality, the ingrained corruption and perversion of principle, the mockery of sensibility, which pervade **'Antony,'** and struck a sympathetic chord in a highly cultivated audience . . . are positively startling. There is nothing to idealise; nothing to throw a delusive halo over vice; not a particle of ennobling passion. . . . What one redeeming quality had Adèle, who only shrinks from remaining under the conjugal roof, and affecting innocence, for fear of discovery? What one redeeming quality has Antony, if we except the nerve to perpetrate crime and the courage to face the criminal court? He is hard, selfish, material, brutal throughout; and the crowning atrocity is an absurdity. . . . [How] could Antony hope to silence a scandal, which was already the talk of Paris, by deepening it? What human being would believe that he had killed his known, almost avowed, mistress for resisting him! But the French mind, or rather the mind of the French play-going public, is so constituted that a moral paradox or sentimental extravagance fascinates them, and they will applaud impulsively whatever creates a sensation or excites, however false or foolish in conception or in act. And that public, when **'Antony'** was brought out, was still fevered and disordered, still seething and surging, from the Revolution of July. The subversive spirit was in the ascendant: established rules and principles had shared the fate of established institutions: the legit-

imate drama had fallen with the legitimate monarchy; and the Academy was at a discount like the throne. (p. 220)

[At the Porte St. Martin, Dumas] brought out a succession of pieces, which, thanks to his prodigality of resource and unrivalled knowledge of stage effect, secured and permanently retained an applauding public, although many of them seemed written to try to what extent the recognised rules of art might be set aside. To take **'La Tour de Nesle,'** for example, we agree with [Henry Lytton Bulwer (see excerpt dated 1834)], that judging by the ordinary rules of criticism, it is a melodramatic monstrosity; but if you think that to seize, to excite, to suspend, to transport the feelings of an audience, to keep them with an eye eager, an attention unflagged, from the first scene to the last—if you think that to do this is to be a dramatist, that to have done this is to have written a drama—bow down to M. Dumas or M. Gaillard, to the author of **'Tour de Nesle'** whoever he be, that man is a dramatist, the piece he has written is a drama. . . . (p. 223)

It was as a dramatist that Dumas became famous, although his world-wide renown is owing to his romances, which he composed at headlong speed, contemporaneously with his dramas, without much adding to his reputation until 1844-45, when he published **'Les Trois Mousquetaires,' 'Vingt ans Après,'** and **'Monte Christo,'** the most popular of his works. (p. 224)

In point of plot, they are on a par with 'Don Quixote' and 'Gil Blas:' in point of incident, situation, character, animated narrative, and dialogue, they will rarely lose by comparison with the author of 'Waverley.' Compare, for example, the scene in **'Les Trois Mousquetaires'** between Buckingham and Anne of Austria, with the strikingly analogous scene between Leicester and Elizabeth in 'Kenilworth.'

If Dumas occasionally spun out his romances till they grew wearisome, it was not because he was incapable of compressing them. His **'Chevalier d'Harmenthal,'** which we ourselves are inclined to consider one of his best novels, is contained in three volumes. His **'Impressions de Voyage'** abound in short novels and stories, which are quite incomparable in their way, like pictures by Meissonnier and Gerome. (p. 225)

Where Dumas erred and fell behind was in pushing to excess the failing with which Byron reproached Scott—

> Let others spin their meagre brains for hire,
> Enough for genius if itself inspire.

He could not resist the temptation of making hay whilst the sun shone—of using his popularity as if, like the purse of Fortunatus, it had been inexhaustible—of overtasking his powers till, like the overtasked elephant, they proved unequal to the call. (p. 226)

Take him for all in all, [Dumas] richly merits a niche in the Temple of Fame; and what writer does not who has been unceasingly before the public for nearly half a century without once forfeiting his popularity, whose multifarious productions have been equally and constantly in request in London, Paris, St. Petersburg, Vienna, Calcutta, Sydney, and New York? Think of the amount of amusement and information he has diffused, the weary hours he has helped to while away, the despondency he has lightened, the sick-beds he has relieved, the gay fancies, the humourous associations, the inspiriting thoughts, we owe to him. To lie on a sofa and read eternal new novels of Marivaux and Crebillon, was the *beau idéal*, the day dream, of Gray, one of the finest and most fastidious minds of the eighteenth century; and what is there of Marivaux or Crebillon to compete in attractiveness with the wondrous fortunes of a Monte Christo or the chivalrous adventures of a D'Artagnan?

A title to fame, like a chain of proofs, may be cumulative. It may rest on the multiplicity and universality of production and capacity. Voltaire, for example, who symbolizes an age, produced no one work in poetry or prose that approximates to first rate in its kind, if we except 'Candide' and 'Zadig;' and their kind is not the first. Dumas must be judged by the same standard; as one who was at everything in the ring, whose foot was ever in the stirrup, whose lance was ever in the rest, who infused new life into the acting drama, indefinitely extended the domain of fiction, and (in his **'Impressions de Voyage'**) invented a new literature of the road. So judged . . . he will certainly take rank as one of the three or four most popular, influential, and gifted writers that the France of the nineteenth century has produced. (pp. 228-29)

> [*Abraham Hayward*], "Alexander Dumas," in The Quarterly Review, *Vol. CXXXI, No. 261, July, 1871, pp. 189-229.*

[MARGARET OLIPHANT]   (essay date 1873)

[*Oliphant was a prolific nineteenth-century Scottish novelist, biographer, critic, and historian. A regular contributor to* Blackwood's Magazine, *she published nearly one hundred novels, many of them popular tales of English and Scottish provincial life similar to the* Chronicles of Carlingford, *her best-known work. Here, Oliphant discusses Dumas's accomplishments as a novelist largely in terms of his ability to satisfy the "primitive Curiosity and thirst for story without which man would scarcely be man." In particular, she cites such qualities as dramatic suspense, variety of incident, and narrative vivacity as compelling constants in Dumas's romances. Oliphant also praises* The Three Musketeers *as the novelist's greatest story, while characterizing* The Count of Monte Cristo *as something of a critical disappointment.*]

[We] owe more innocent amusement [to Alexandre Dumas] than to almost any other writer of his generation.

We would not, however, have it supposed that in saying this we are setting up Alexandre Dumas as a model writer, or recommending his works as a moral regimen for the young. Nothing could be further from our intention. All that we venture to assert is, that he is purity itself and good taste itself in comparison with the more recent and much more pretentious school of fiction which has openly dedicated itself to the study and elucidation of vice, and which is generally meant when the contemptuous phrase "French novel" drops from British lips. (p. 112)

It is not from the modern inspiration of fiction, but from [the] wild source of boundless adventure and incident, that [Dumas] draws his power. He appeals not to the deeper principles of nature in his hearers, nor to their sympathy with the struggles of heart and soul, the complications of will and passion, which are the true subjects of poetry; but to that which is most universal in us, the intellectual quality (if it can be justly called intellectual at all) which most entirely pervades humanity, which is common to the child and the sage, the simplest and the most educated—that primitive Curiosity and thirst for story without which man would scarcely be man. (p. 117)

His was not the art of reflection, of careful balance, and elaborate completeness. He produced his effects *sur-le-champ,* by chance, by the inspiration of the moment, without pausing to consider, or making any conscious selection of circumstances.

He began—but there never appeared to him any necessity to close. The story which he told was one long-continued tale, such as children and simple natures love—a story without an end. With a wild and gay and careless exuberance of strength and of material such as none of his contemporaries could equal, he rushed on from incident to incident, each new adventure leading to another, like the endless peaks of a mountain-range. From one day to another, from one year to another, what matter how far the story led him, he carried his audience on with unflagging interest and frequent excitement. . . . The charm of dramatic suspense, of uncertainty, and eager curiosity—those universal stimulants of the common mind—attended him wherever he moved. (pp. 118-19)

[In our opinion, Dumas's greatest work] was the **'Trois Mousquetaires.'** . . . It is the most spontaneous and dazzling, the most joyous, effortless, and endless of romances. . . . What gay vitality overflows in it, what bustling scenes open around its heroes!—scenes which are so real, so crowded, so full of incident, that we never dream of inquiring into their historical accuracy, nor of bringing them to that dull standard of fact which is alien to romance. Such scenes indeed do not belong to one historical period or another, nor can the bold and brilliant narrative be bound down to formal limits of costume, or the still harder bondage of actual events. They belong rather to that vague period "once upon a time," familiar to all primitive audiences, in which the action of all fairy tales is laid, and which is the age proper to the primary poet, vague in chronology but dauntless in invention, who is always the earliest chronicler. (p. 119)

[The] unbounded vivacity of the narrative, its endless variety, the delightful prodigality of movement and frolic-wealth, is to the *blasé* reader of more reasonable and profitable literature like a dip into some sunshiny sea with flashing waves and currents, with wild puffs of wind and dashes of spray, after the calm navigation of stately rivers. Athos, Porthos, and Aramis are as delightfully real as they are impossible. Does any one ask whether we believe in them? we laugh at the question, and at all the gravity and conformance to ordinary rule which it implies. Believe in them! we know that our four paladins are impossible—as impossible as the seven champions of Christendom, but equally delightful and true to the instincts which, once in a way, ask something more from imagination than sketches of recognisable men and comprehensible circumstances. They are possible as Puck and Ariel are possible, though they are not at all ethereal, but most vigorous and solid human beings, with swords of prodigious temper, and arms of iron, giving blows which no man would willingly encounter. Their combination of ancient knight-errantry with the rude and careless habits of a modern soldier of fortune, their delicate honour and indifferent morals, their mutual praise and honest adulation, combined with the perfect frankness of the author as to their faults, give a reality to these martial figures which no chronological deficiency can detract from, and which even their wonderful and unheard-of successes do not abate. (pp. 120-21)

[The] author never forgets the characteristic differences of his adventurers. The calm and somewhat sad indifferentism of Athos, the sentimentalism of Aramis, the sturdy conviviality of Porthos, are kept up throughout with unfailing consistency; and nothing can be more individual than the character of D'Artagnan, who is more distinctly the soldier of fortune than any of his friends, and who, . . . in the very heat of adventure keeps always a corner of his eye upon his own advantage, or rather the advantage of the brotherhood, which to each of the four is as his own. The perpetual contrast and variety thus kept up adds immensely to our interest in the Mousquetaires. It supplies the charm of character which is sometimes wanting to the rapid strain of the improvisatore, and adds what is in its way a distinct intellectual enjoyment to that pleasure which can scarcely be called intellectual—the delight of simple story, a primitive and savage joy.

The tragic thread which runs through this record of warlike exploits, and which brings in certain chapters which we would gladly get rid of, has on the whole but little to do with the adventures of our Mousquetaires. The portentous creation of Milady, the depraved and dishonoured woman whom we divine at once to have been the wife of the proud Athos and cause of his misfortunes, has little attraction to the wholesome imagination, though she has been the origin of a whole school of wicked heroines.... [We] cannot take upon us to say that any of the women who figure now and then in the story do any credit to Dumas. The best that can be said for him is, that he brings them in only when he cannot help it, and has himself no predilection for scenes of passion, or any intrigues except those which are political. Embarrassing situations and the "delicate" suggestions of vice in which some other French writers delight, are entirely out of the way of the honest *raconteur*. (pp. 122-23)

That Dumas should have been sorry to relinquish the four bold brethren whom he had made so famous is not wonderful; and there is a higher faculty, and a glimpse of more serious power in the *reprise* of the familiar strain than in its first fytte....

From the gay young gallants of twenty to the middle-aged heroes [in **'Vingt Ans après'**], worn with life, dispersed over the country, dropped almost into oblivion of their ancient friendship, and absorbed in new cares of their own, what a wonderful difference! When D'Artagnan sets out in pursuit of his separated companions, we feel the doubtfulness of the search all the more, from the less important but yet significant changes that have passed upon himself. Still as brave, as self-confident and ready to assert himself as ever, the Gascon is partially saddened and partially embittered by his long attendance in antechambers, and the dull blank of doing nothing and hoping nothing which has fallen upon his life.... Twenty years of waiting have calmed and curbed, at least externally, his fiery spirit. They have developed his acute perceptions of self-interest and determination to seize the first chance which can lead to fortune. We are allowed to perceive very plainly that whether it is the Fronde or the Court which offers highest, the Mousquetaire will take advantage of the best offer.... The other companions are not less effectively set before us. (p. 123)

The men thrust themselves through the fiery excitement of their adventures, their characters are given to us *par dessus le marché*. We bargained only for story, and we get these individual beings in addition—not framed, we allow, like ordinary men, but yet men—full of vitality and force, as not many men are in this washed-out and feeble world.

The narrative of **'Vingt Ans après'** keeps up much of the force of the first volumes. The second sequel with which Dumas was so daring as to present his readers, the **'Vicomte de Bragelonne, ou Dix Ans plus tard,'** finds them, perhaps, a little weakened, though the author has given with great feeling and power—qualities, again we say, which are *pas dessus le marché*, and which nobody expected from him—the gradual weakening of his heroes, the dropping aside into the background . . . and

elevation of the new generation to the central place in the picture.... It is mournful to assist at the very end of our heroes, but perhaps on the whole it is the most satisfactory thing to do; for had we not seen them securely buried, how could we ever have made sure that six volumes more, *encore plus tard*, might not have been poured upon us? ... The loss of the simple-hearted giant [Porthos] is grievous to us. He has never been better than in some of the last scenes. His matter-of-fact simplicity and downrightness—his faith in his comrades—the ease with which Porthos "s'est convaincu quoiqu'il ne comprend pas"—is always delightful. Athos has a grand end in the elevation and sublimity of grief, and dies of a broken heart when the news of his son's death reaches him. D'Artagnan receives his bullet of dismissal just as he has been presented with his *bâton* as Marshal of France. Only Aramis, the wily intriguer, sentimentalist, and false priest, the least attractive of the brotherhood, is allowed to live. "Athos, Porthos, au revoir—Aramis, adieu pour jamais!" cries D'Artagnan when he is dying. Thus Dumas points his robust moral. He has a charitable heaven for his rough soldier, his erring yet noble gentleman—but none for the gallant who masquerades in the sacred habit of bishop and confessor. This delightful bit of conventional poetic justice is our romancer's tribute to *les bons moeurs*. (pp. 124-25)

'Monte Christo' is, we believe, regarded, at least in England, much more entirely as the epitome of Dumas's productive power than is the history of our Mousquetaires; but we cannot think that, as a whole, this book is at all equal to the other. The first part of **'Monte Christo,'** however, is finer, purer, and more true to nature than anything in the **'Trois Mousquetaires;'** it stands alone among its author's productions, and promises an altogether higher strain of poetic romance than anything else he ever reached. Beside the wild and complicated tale of intrigue and vengeance, the horrible entanglements of fate, and still more horrible schemes of pitiless vindictive will, that opening story, so soft in tone, so vigorous in conception, so idyllic, pure, and reasonable, strikes the reader with a surprise which perhaps enhances the very different effect of all that follows. Up to the moment when Edmond Dantes is thrown into the sea, under the semblance of a corpse, there is scarcely anything in the story to which the most severe critic could take exception. That fine young sailor himself, his gentle, beautiful, and pensive bride, and the delightful sketch of the imprisoned Abbé Faria, so learned, so benevolent, and so forgiving even in his dungeon, have very seldom been surpassed. Nothing is forced in the tale—the despair and agony of the young bridegroom, snatched from everything he holds dear at the very moment when his hopes are about to be realised, is neither exaggerated nor unduly lengthened out. There is not only fine talent, but absolute good taste and perception, in the manner of the picture, which any girl may read and any man enjoy.

The Count de Monte Christo, however, is not so delightful as Edmond Dantes; and though there is the same wild charm of rapid incident and sensation, the same breathless brilliancy of dialogue and interest of situation, the narrative of Monte Christo's vengeance has nothing like the delightful novelty and wholesome stir and bustle of the **'Trois Mousquetaires.'** Dumas is not potent enough to impress upon us, as his contemporary Victor Hugo can do so well, the solemn gathering of those clouds of fate round the doomed and guilty beings whose evil deeds have to be expiated before they can escape their author's hands. The lurid lights and horrible creeping shadows which we see and feel in 'Notre Dame,' have no place at all in the slowly developing revenge of Monte Christo. We recognise from the beginning the transparent *tours de force* which bring all his enemies within reach of that revenge; and we feel that Monte Christo himself is very poor and petty in many of his expedients, cruel without dignity, and spiteful rather than terrible. There is an abstract character about him which detracts greatly from the effect of all his operations. He loses our sympathy, at first so powerfully excited. We find no feature in him of the Edmond Dantes whose wrongs we felt as if they were our own, and to whom we could accord the right of punishing his enemies. On the contrary, it is altogether a new being, a stranger to us, who steps on to the stage like a magician, and whom we cannot identify. This is the great mistake of the book, a greater mistake even than the fact that Monte Christo goes much too far, that his vengeance is diabolical, and his heart unnaturally hard, which was no doubt according to the author's intentions—who meant to show us not only the pleasure and satisfactoriness, but at the same time the unsuccess and evil tendencies of revenge. No doubt Dumas meant to transfer our sympathies to the other side, and to make us at last almost partisans of the hapless multitude who are driven to despair by his transformed hero; but he did not, we suppose, mean to transform that hero so that he should be unrecognisable; and in this he shows the weakness of his rapid work, and supreme regard for sensation. But this defect in art is more than counterbalanced by the skill with which he has seized upon two primary instincts of nature—the prejudice we all have in favour of what is called poetic justice, and the delight we all take in such complete transformations of fortune as place the injured poor on the pinnacle of wealth, and make them capable of showing their gratitude and their hate in the plainest way. (pp. 125-27)

The strength and the weakness of the book, its immense popularity with the common mass of readers, and its unsatisfactoriness to the critic, are all involved in these, its peculiar characteristics. More emphatically than any of Dumas's other works it is framed on the model of the Arabian Nights. The interest is deepened by the fact that it is a tale of retribution, and that the evil which has to be punished was done before our eyes, and excited us all to a fierce longing for poetic justice; and this interest is enough to carry on the primitive mind, especially when the new complications through which the Avenger moves are so exciting and so varied. But the abstractness of the story disappoints and throws out the closer critic. The thread of human sympathy is broken off short, at the moment when all the better laws of art are abandoned, and when Dantes sinks in the sea, to rise for us no more. Henceforward all is wild, fantastic, and of a primitive artificiality. The crowd applauds, the critic is silent. (p. 127)

Dumas's life was a succession of triumphs and distresses almost equal to those of his own adventurers. He was perfectly thriftless, extravagant, and foolish in his expenditure; his money was all consumed, sometimes twice over, before he had earned it; and he seems to have been somewhat shifty about his literary engagements, and, in the latter part of his life at least, not much to be depended upon. But he would seem to have possessed that liberality to others which is the redeeming feature of the prodigal. . . . And he worked hard, though waywardly and by fits and starts; and if he had no objection to introduce an equivocal adventure, or unequivocal intrigue, at any moment when it might happen to suit him, he is never the historian, never the philosopher of vice, and the tendency of his works is certainly not immoral. . . . Adventure, sensation, excitement, these were his honest objects; and when they are procured by honest means, does any one deny them a legitimate place

Edmond Dantès and the Abbé Faria held captive in the Château d'If. This illustration originally appeared in an early edition of The Count of Monte Cristo.

among the wholesome pleasures of humanity? Peace be to the memory of the old *Raconteur*! He might not be either great or wise, no model for any one to follow; but yet there was a real place for him in the world, and he filled it with a certain fitness. Many men of his generation have moved us more deeply, more beneficially; but few have amused us in so primitive a way, or so much, or so long, or with so little harm. (p. 130)

[*Margaret Oliphant*], "*Alexandre Dumas,*" in Blackwood's Edinburgh Magazine, *Vol. CXIV, No. DCXCIII, July, 1873, pp. 111-30.*

PERCY FITZGERALD   (essay date 1873)

[*Fitzgerald contends that Dumas's vice-laden plays of modern life violate some of the cardinal principles of drama. According to the critic, genuine drama pleases the audience by presenting unusual events or situations in a compelling manner while maintaining a clear distinction between actor and spectator. Dumas is said to flout these precepts by taking commonplace corruption as his subject and displaying it unrefined upon the stage, inviting the audience to associate themselves with his characters. Fitzgerald's remarks are taken from his* Life and Adventures of Alexander Dumas, *a biography noted primarily for its virulent attacks upon Dumas's alleged plagiarism.*]

"**Antony**" was, perhaps, the most conspicuous, if not the earliest, of the long line of [Dumas's] plays which . . . might be described, without exaggeration, as being "base, bloody, and brutal." The reproach of extravagant realism has been made against modern pieces—of placing on the stage ordinary material objects, such as carriages, and railway stations, and under such conditions might be considered to have reached the profoundest depth. But it was reserved for the French writer to find a depth yet deeper—the *realism* of brutal crime and passion. There is something far more gross and *material* in the exhibition of such phenomena than even in the cheap prodigies of scene painters and carpenters, that is in the naked spectacle of revolting crimes, and of gross human passions let loose. The mere display of a collection of murders, adulteries, rapes, ingeniously complicated, are wholly outside the domain of dramatic art and interest. To Dumas belongs the distinction of having boldly carried this revolting system as far as it could possibly go, and in a series of dramas that began with **"Antony,"** was followed by **"Richard Darlington," "Angéle," "Térésa,"** and others, he inaugurated that corruption, not only of the French stage, but of Parisian manners, which has since obtained. (pp. 206-07)

It is curious . . . to note what an advance this was on the character of pieces like **"Henry III.,"** which, though it contained the germ of the monstrosities that were to come later, was still redeemed by a certain romance and chivalry. Such elements as unlawful love, murder, combats, abductions, executions, jealousy, and hatred, by being placed in a remote age, were more or less in keeping with the historical instincts of the audience, and those whose taste was tolerably chastened might accept what they saw as an overdrawn picture of a scene from French history. But now they were plunged into a tide of atrocities, which were not merely false in their dramatic arrangement, but false as a picture of existing manners, or, at least, could only be accepted as *possibly* true by the more degraded classes, whose sympathies went with such horrors. From that time the French theatre was inundated with a bloody flood of slaughterings, stranglings, incests, adulteries, violations, secret accouchements, represented with literal accuracy. (pp. 208-09)

[In] justification of this offence against public decency, Dumas vehemently urged the classic precedents of the old Greek drama, where shocking and revolting excesses are made the subject of the play. It has been urged with plausibility that it is the age, not the writer, that is accountable. The age furnishes the materials, and if these be corrupt, the drama, to be faithful, must exhibit this corruption. . . . [An] answer to this view can be found in an illustration taken from the kindred art of painting, the same, in fact, that was given to the modern pre-Raphaelites, when these were setting forth for admiration elaborately wrought "patches of brick-wall," "satin dresses," "bits of carpet," and the like. The imitation of such objects is of no value, while, if there *be* any interest in such things, the originals are superior and sufficiently accessible. So with the incidents of "fast life." It should be remembered that the aim of painting is to supply what delights and enchants; those rare and poetical elements of expression, either in the countenance or in landscape, which escape ordinary observers, which persons search for eagerly and rarely find. Both in painting as well as in the drama, the source of *pleasure* and entertainment is found in this principle—viz., in something which we have not the instinct or skill of discovering for ourselves, and which the genius of painter or of the dramatist sets before us. In the case of ordinary events of life, or of ordinary objects transferred to the stage, the sensation is at best only that of curiosity or of mild surprise. The brutal results, therefore, of violent pas-

sions, or mere *crimes* brought forward on the stage, are only like the minute imitation of decayed vegetable matter which these modern pre-Raphaelites were so fond of presenting: they are pieces of morbid anatomy, professedly unpleasant dissections of human character. Such are merely things to look at, to appreciate with eyes and ears; but there is nothing *dramatic* about them. Again, there is no precedent to be drawn from the dreadful plots of Aeschylus, for here there is the awful presence of *Fate,* against which the victims struggle, and which furnishes the most impressively dramatic element conceivable. Finally, these grossly complicated scenes of guilt, as given by Dumas and his school, are undramatic, because improbable and false to nature. As one of his critics said justly of [**"Antony"**]:

> Such a conception no more bears the scrutiny of honest instinct than a crime tried at the assizes would the investigation of a jury. The author, in choosing to place himself within the range of frantic passions, which is purely exceptional, mad passions which are not to be meddled with but at the price of blood and tears, has withdrawn himself from all literary jurisdiction. The piece is simply a monstrosity.

There is here precisely the difference that we see in real life, when a corrupt man tells a story of guilt or wickedness, or a good man. By the former it is told with a certain *sympathy* which he can hardly avoid, and which will produce a corresponding sympathy in some of his hearers. In the case of a man who feels a repulsion to such things it will assume a different aspect, and he will inspire his hearers with a feeling as of something odious and revolting. When, therefore, Dumas and his followers try to justify themselves for exhibiting scenes of guilt and brutal passion by the example of Aeschylus and the monstrous crimes of Atreus, they wholly forget this distinction. *There* the result is not sympathy but awe, a sense of warning, and the workings of passion are not exhibited, but its evil results. In other words, in a play like **"Antony,"** the spectator himself is brought on the stage in the shape of the actor, who, he feels, is artfully put forward as a representative of the frail part of human nature; whereas, from guilt and passion, as put before him by the classical writer, he turns away with dread, thankful that there is a gulf between him and such a spectacle. (pp. 211-15)

Percy Fitzgerald, in his Life and Adventures of Alexander Dumas, Vol. I, *Tinsley Brothers, 1873, 302 p.*

GEORGE SAINTSBURY   (essay date 1878)

[*Saintsbury was an English literary historian and critic of the late nineteenth and early twentieth centuries. A prolific writer, he composed several histories of English and European literature as well as numerous critical works on individual authors, styles, and periods. In the following excerpt, Saintsbury assesses Dumas's handling of plot, description, characterization, and dialogue in his novels and comments extensively on* The Count of Monte Cristo. *Like Margaret Oliphant (1873), he contrasts the near perfection of the first volume of* The Count of Monte Cristo *with the patent imperfection of the remainder of the novel. Overall, Saintsbury characterizes Dumas as "one of the princes of all . . . improvising writers" who also possessed "something better than improvisation." In his excerpt dated 1894, Saintsbury compares Dumas and Walter Scott.*]

For a novelist who is so prodigal of incident, Dumas is remarkably indifferent to a regular or cunningly entangled plot.

In many of his works, indeed, there is really no particular reason why they should begin or end at the precise points of their beginning and ending. They are emphatically chronicles, slices from the history of the world or of certain individuals, the dimensions of which are determined merely by the arbitrary will of the carver. This is why they lend themselves so admirably to continuations, and why Dumas is one of the very few writers whose second parts do not disappoint us. It is true that in many of his books there is a central incident of some sort, but its development bears often no proportion to the extraneous matter introduced. What, for instance, is the central interest of *Les Trois Mousquetaires*? The quest for the diamonds? It finishes too soon. The wrath and discomfiture of Milady? It does not begin till too late. What is the central interest of *Vingt Ans Après*? The attempt to rescue Charles I. perhaps, but yet this occupies but a very small part of the book. In *Le Vicomte de Bragelonne* there are two distinct themes— the restoration of Charles II., and the winning of Belleisle for Louis XIV.—and the two might well have made two separate books. . . . The authorities at the disposal of the author or his own fertile imagination usually supply him with an inexhaustible store of moving incidents, and these he connects together as well as may be by the expedient of making the same personages figure in all or most of them. Nor is he any more to be called a novelist of description than a novelist of plot. Indeed he is less abundant and less successful in this respect than almost any other writer of great volume. Little bits of description of houses, dresses, and so forth are frequent enough, and the authorities are sometimes drawn upon largely for a festival or a battle. But Dumas seems to have felt that his readers did not want elaborate set-pieces from him, but plenty of "business" and lively speech. His characters, however, are a much more curious study. Those who call his general method scene-painting, of course, call his characters lay-figures. The appellation does not do their observation much credit. Dumas is nothing so little as an analyst, and he does not attempt to give us complicated or intricate studies of character, but his men and women are curiously adapted to their purpose and curiously lifelike of their kind. They are naturally types rather than individuals, and types of a somewhat loose and vague order, but still there is an amount of individuality about them which is very rarely found in novels of incident. No one will deny that the three, or rather four, musketeers are sustained in their contrast of dispositions throughout the score or so of volumes they occupy, with a good deal of skill. Nor are the repetitions of the types in different books merely *calqués* the one on the other. Chicot and D'Artagnan have remarkable points of contact, yet they are not mere duplicates. Ernauton de Carmainges is a clever variation of La Mole, rather than a mere reproduction of the character.

But it is in his dialogue that Dumas's real secret consists, and it is this which is the rosin that none of his imitators have ever succeeded in stealing, however confident they may be that they have got the fiddle. Its extraordinary volume would be the most remarkable point about it, if its goodness, considering its volume, were not equally remarkable. The rapidity of it deprives it necessarily of much literary grace, and prevents it from supplying any jewels five words long. Indeed Dumas . . . is one of the least quotable of writers. But still, if not quotable, his dialogue is extraordinarily readable, and carries the reader along with it in a manner hardly to be paralleled elsewhere. Dumas possesses fully the secret of making dialogue express action, and this is where he is supreme. His gift, however, in this respect is of the kind which is almost necessarily a snare. He abuses his dialogic facility constantly, and the result is the

exorbitant length of some of his books. It is absolutely impossible for him to be concise. He will make a single interview extend over half-a-dozen chapters, and give a volume to the talk of a single day. . . . [It is undeniable] that his situations have a tendency to repeat themselves, though, as in the case of his characters, the repetition is often very skilfully masked and coloured. But on the whole he succeeds not merely in rivetting the attention of the reader, but also in securing his affection for and interest in his characters. No one has ever managed the process called "working up" better than he has. In such scenes as that where the four princes wait at Marguerite's door, ready to assassinate La Mole, where the powder is found in the wine-casks, where D'Artagnan extracts the Queen and Mazarin from the clutches of the Parisians, and scores of others, it is impossible to avert the attention when once fairly engaged, and impossible to avoid identifying one's self with the characters. That is the triumph of this sort of novel-writing. (pp. 530-32)

[*La Reine Margot, La Dame de Monsoreau, Les Quarante-cinq,* and the D'Artagnan series] seem to me to be on the whole not merely the author's best [novels], but also the most characteristic of his genius. The period which they cover seems to have had a special faculty of inspiring him, or, perhaps, we may say that it was the only one with which he was sufficiently familiar to be able to employ his method with successful effect. In those of his historical novels which are earlier in date, the elements are less happily blended. . . . [In the *Bâtard de Mauléon,* for example,] the life is not in the characters in the same way as it is in Aramis and Porthos. One feels that the author is not so sure of his surroundings, and is chary of the little touches that make scenes and characters live. Nor do the novels whose scene is in more modern times please me much better. Almost all those of purely modern society may be swept away altogether. . . . They sink mostly to the level of mere recitals, interesting simply from the actual facts they contain. Nor, again, has he been happier than other novelists in treating the great revolution. Of the *Collier de la Reine* I shall speak presently. But the *Chevalier de Maisonrouge* adds, to my mind, only one more to the long list of failures which might be made up of French novels having '89 and its sequel for their subjects. . . . There are, however, two novels besides the *Collier de la Reine* and *Monte Cristo,* which lie outside the limits I have drawn, and which are usually ranked among the author's masterpieces. These are *La Tulipe Noire* and the *Chevalier d'Harmental.* With respect to *La Tulipe Noire,* I am inclined to think that, charming as it is in parts, it has been overpraised. . . . The tulip fancying and the loves of the excellent Cornelius Van Baerle make a perfect subject for a really short tale of a hundred pages or so. But Dumas's unfortunate prolixity is here especially unfortunate. The tale is choked up with irrelevant matter and spun out to an unconscionable length. . . . *Le Chevalier d'Harmental* contains detached passages of very striking merit. Le Capitaine Roquefinette, the last of the descendants of Dugald Dalgetty, is a great creation, though Dumas has been extremely hard on him. There is no reason whatever why the uninteresting chevalier should have been allowed to obtain such a victory, except the necessity, which Alexander the Great generally recognises, of making the end of his books melancholy. The caligraphist, Buvat, is another triumph; and his incarceration in the gilded captivity of the Palais Royal is most charmingly told. The Regent Philippe, again, is excellent; and the way in which Richelieu, Saint Simon, and other historical characters are made to play their part, is most artful. Lastly, it must be remembered, in favour of the *Chevalier d'Harmental,* that it is one of the very few books of its author that has a regular plot. The Cellamare conspiracy gives just enough framework for the book, and not too much, and the episodes and digressions are scarcely disproportionate in their extent. After allowing all these merits, which can certainly not be allowed in like measure to many others of Dumas's books, it might seem only reasonable to call it his masterpiece. Yet there is about it something wanting which is present elsewhere. The dialogue is not of the best, and the lack of interest which one feels in the hero is a serious drawback. For once, Dumas has let himself follow Scott in the mistake of making his hero too generally faultless and lucky, and this is the cause, I think, of failure, if failure there be, in the *Chevalier d'Harmental.* (pp. 532-34)

Le Collier de la Reine is one of Dumas's most popular works, but it seems to me to be very far from being one of his best. There is no single character in it of any particular excellence, and the endless scenes of intrigue between Jeanne de la Motte and the Cardinal de Rohan, between Oliva and Cagliostro, between the Queen and a half-a-dozen different personages, are altogether wearisome. The author has not succeeded in interesting us sufficiently to make his volume tolerable, and it is not tolerable in itself in virtue of any skill in handling the subject. This subject, moreover, is felt to be too much for Dumas. The stupendous interest of the French Revolution wants quite a different chronicler and quite other modes of treatment. The particular episode, too, of the diamond necklace is one of those which have, in virtue of their special interest and strangeness, passed out of the class of subjects which can be successfully treated by fiction. All those who have studied the philosophy of novel-writing at all closely know that great historical events are bad subjects, or are only good subjects on one condition—a condition the steady observance of which constitutes one of the great merits of Sir Walter Scott. The central interest in all such cases must be connected with a wholly fictitious personage, or one of whom sufficiently little is known to give the romancer free play. When this condition is complied with, the actual historical events may be, and constantly have been, used with effect as aids in developing the story and working out the fortunes of the characters. Dumas himself has observed this law in his more successful efforts; he has not observed it here. . . . The character of Cagliostro as here given, moreover, is one which no writer could manage. He is at once too supernatural and not supernatural enough. (pp. 534-35)

Monte Cristo is said to have been at its first appearance, and for some time subsequently, the most popular book in Europe. . . . [It] still remains the book with which, with the possible exception of the *Three Musketeers,* more people connect the name of Dumas than with any other of his works. How far does it deserve this popularity? The answer of most critical persons would probably be, without any intention of flippancy, as far as the end of the first volume. The Château d'If indeed, as this section has sometimes been called, is almost faultless, and few persons can have found anything to object to in it except the rather dubious omniscience of the Abbé Faria. The style and character of the book, moreover, is so far all the author's own, and deals only with subjects which he can well manage. From the time, however, that Dantès has discovered the treasure, the case is altered. The succeeding scenes give indeed an opportunity of portraying what Dumas has always endeavoured and loved to portray, the rise of an adventurer to supreme power and importance. Nor is there any taint of the supernatural as in the case of Cagliostro; but, on the other hand, the scenes described and the characters attempted are

scenes and characters in which the author is not himself at home, and which constantly recall to us scenes and characters in the work of other men who can manage them. Take, to begin with, Monte Cristo himself. Whether it is altogether fair for the generation which has come after him, and which he himself has helped to render *blasé* with persons of extraordinary attributes, may be answered in the negative by a fervent Alexandrian. But it cannot be denied that at the present day Edmond Dantès in his parts, of Lord Wilmore, or the Abbé Busoni, or the Count, appears to us a very tiresome and rather ludicrous player at providence. His use of his money seems ostentatious, and sometimes, as in the case of the horses bought from Danglars, intolerably vulgar. His mania for theatrical peripeteias—which might have resulted in the death both of Morrel and his son—is equally to be objected to, and the skimble-skamble stuff which so impresses his Parisian friends (for instance, in his first interview with Villefort) is pitiable enough. In few of the author's books, moreover, is the abuse of over-length greater, and the complicated series of intrigues, though managed with considerable skill, wearies the reader more than it interests him. But the involuntary comparisons that one makes in reading the book are the most unfortunate. No one, for instance, who knows Gautier's literary dealings with haschisch can avoid a sigh over the pages in which Franz d'Epinay's very commonplace experiences of the drug are described. I am not myself among those who consider Henri de Marsay, Bixiou, Blondel, and the rest as absolutely perfect creations beyond which the wit of man cannot go, but Châteaurenaud, Debray, the journalist Beauchamp, and others of De Morcerf's set, certainly remind one but unpleasantly of Balzac's favourite cliques. The viscount himself would have been more acceptable if he had not in his excessive hospitality displayed "all the tobaccos of the known world" when he was expecting his visitors. Another point in which Dumas here fails is his description. This is, as I already said, probably his weakest point, and it is particularly noticeable in a book where description, one would have thought, was particularly in place. But the prevailing want all through is the want of a sufficient grasp of character to make scenes so familiar and modern as those of Parisian life in the middle of the present century tolerable. The plan is the plan of Balzac, the hand is the hand of Dumas, and it is impossible that the inefficiency of the workmanship should not be felt. There is no attempt at an impression of growing horror culminating in the horrible death of Madame de Villefort and her child. The interest is frittered away in endless details and episodes. The narrow escape of Valentine, and the burglarious attempt of Caderousse, are treated at the same length and on the same scale; and, above all, the dangerous method of introducing long recitals by various characters in order to help on the movement and join the intrigue is unscrupulously resorted to. The first impulse of the reader is to wish that the five last volumes had been condensed to at most two; it is to be feared that his last is to regret that they were ever written at all. (pp. 535-36)

That much of [Dumas's work] will go the way of all but the best fictitious literature, cannot for a moment be doubted. Whether any will survive is a question less easy to answer. The danger to which writers like Dumas are exposed, as a rule, is that there is not enough idiosyncrasy in their work to keep it fresh in men's memory. Every age, or almost every age, produces for itself specimens of the talented improvisatore who has energy enough to produce enormously, and originality enough to launch his work in popular favour. Every age too naturally prefers its own practitioners in this manner, because they can hit its own tastes, and because the ephemeral adornments and fashion of their work are such as it understands and appreciates. The next age has no such inducements to read work of little permanent literary value. That Dumas is one of the princes of all such improvising writers I have no doubt whatever, and that he possesses the element of something better than improvisation must I think be evident to careful readers of him.

In order to estimate his deficiencies and at the same time the merits which accompany them, I do not know a more curious exercise than the comparison of one of these books, say *La Reine Margot* or the *Mousquetaires,* with Gautier's *Capitaine Fracasse*. They are in intention exactly similar. But Gautier had one thing which Dumas had not, an incomparable literary faculty, and Dumas had what Gautier had not, the knowledge how to *charpenter* a novel. The consequence is that, while *Le Capitaine Fracasse* is a magnificent piece of writing, it is only a second-rate story, and that *La Reine Margot,* though offering no special quotations or passages to the memory, is a book which it is impossible to put down till you have finished it. Such things as the Chateau de la Misère, as the description of the swordsman's garret and his tavern haunt, and above all as the wonderful duel between Lampourde and Sigognac, Dumas was utterly incapable of writing. He never wrote positively badly, but his writing never attracts admiration for itself. It is not negligent, but on the other hand it is not careful. The first word that comes into his head is used. Probably it is not a bad word, and serves very well to convey the impression intended. But of art, of careful choice, and laborious adaptation of words and phrases and paragraphs, there is none. It is even capable of being argued whether, consistently with his peculiar plan and object, there could have been or ought to have been any. The presence in a novel of incident of passages of the highest literary value may be plausibly contended to be a mistake, as well as an unnecessary extravagance. When the palate is tempted to linger over individual pages, to savour them slowly, and to dwell on the flavour, the continuity of interest of the story proper runs a danger of being broken. On the other hand, if the interest be strong enough to induce rapid reading, it is impossible to do justice to the vintage that it set before one. It is not, therefore, either accidental or from incapacity that the great masters of style in fictitious writing, like Merimée and Gautier, have usually preferred to write short stories. It is rather from a sense of incongruity. A story that takes at shortest half-an-hour to read may, without wearying the appetite for it as a story, have a couple of hours spent upon it. But supposing that the time necessary to read *Les Trois Mousquetaires* is half a day, no one who has this appetite at all will consent to spend three days over it. Nor again in such a story is it possible, as it is with one of the analytic kind, to read first for the story and afterwards for the style. A novel of incident that allows itself to be treated in this way is a bad novel of incident, and if it be good it must be read just as rapidly the seventh time as it is the first. (pp. 540-41)

Dumas has the faculty, as no other novelist has, of presenting rapid and brilliant dioramas of the picturesque aspects of history, animating them with really human if not very intricately analysed passion, and connecting them with dialogue matchless of its kind. He can do nothing more than this, and to ask him for anything more is a blunder. But he will pass time for you as hardly any other novelist will, and unlike most novelists of his class his pictures, at least the best of them, do not lose their virtue by rebeholding. I at least find the *Three Musketeers* as effectual for its purpose now as I found it nearly twenty years ago, and [contrary to common belief,] I think there must be something more in work of such a virtue than mere scene-painting for a background and mere lay figures for actors. (p. 542)

George Saintsbury, "Alexandre Dumas," in The Fortnightly Review, n.s. Vol. XXIV, No. XVII, October 1, 1878, pp. 527-42.

BRANDER MATTHEWS   (essay date 1881)

[*An American critic, playwright, and novelist, Matthews wrote extensively on world drama and served for a quarter-century at Columbia University as a professor of dramatic literature, the first person to hold that title at an American university. He was also a founding member and president of the National Institute of Arts and Letters. In the excerpt below, Matthews defends Dumas's authorial practices, stating that although he plagiarized freely and occasionally exploited his collaborators, it is inappropriate to characterize him as "a mere vulgar appropriator of the labors of other men." He suggests that Dumas is better understood as a prodigal man who took others' possessions as readily as he gave of his own and as a talented author who usually reworked and improved upon the materials that he borrowed. Matthews's comments were originally published in 1881 in the first edition of his* French Dramatists of the 19th Century.]

Ben Jonson, we are told, once dreamed that he saw the Romans and Carthaginians fighting on his big toe. No doubt Dumas had not dissimilar dreams; for his vanity was at least as stalwart and as frank as Ben Jonson's. To defend himself against all charges of plagiarism, the French dramatist echoed the magniloquent phrase of the English dramatist, and declared that he did not steal, he conquered [see excerpt dated 1833]. It is but justice to say that there was no mean and petty pilfering about Dumas. He annexed as openly as a statesman, and made no attempt at disguise. In his memoirs he is very frank about his sources of inspiration, and tells us at length where he found a certain situation, and what it suggested to him, and how he combined it with another effect which had struck him somewhere else. When one goes to the places thus pointed out, one finds something very different from what it became after it had passed through Dumas's hands, and, more often than not, far inferior to it. It can scarcely be said that Dumas touched nothing he did not adorn; for he once laid sacrilegious hands on Shakspere, and brought out a 'Hamlet' with a very French and epigrammatic last act. But whatever he took from other authors he made over into something very different, something truly his own, something that had *Dumas fecit* in the corner, even though the canvas and the colors were not his own. . . . In a word, all his plagiarisms, and they were not a few, are the veriest trifles when compared with his indisputable and extraordinary powers.

Besides plagiarism, Dumas has been accused of "devilling," as the English term it; that is to say, of putting his name to plays written either wholly or in part by others. There is no doubt that the accusation can be sustained, although many of the separate specifications are groundless. The habit of collaboration obtains widely in France; and collaboration runs easily into "devilling." When two men write a play together, and one of them is famous and the other unknown, there is a strong temptation to get the full benefit of celebrity, and to say nothing at all about the author whose name has no market-value. That Dumas yielded to it now and then is not to be wondered at. There was something imperious in his character, as there was something imperial in his power. He had dominion over so many departments of literature, that he had accustomed himself to be monarch of all he surveyed; and if a follower came with the germ of a plot, or a suggestion for a strong situation, Dumas took it as tribute due to his superior ability. In his hands the hint was worked out, and made to render all it had of effect. Even when he had avowed collaborators, as in **'Richard Darlington,'** he alone wrote the whole play. His partners got their share of the pecuniary profits, benefiting by his skill and his renown; and most of them did not care whether he who had done the best of the work should get all the glory or not. (pp. 66-8)

That Dumas plagiarized freely in his earliest plays, and had the aid of "devils" in the second stage of his career, is not to be denied, and neither proceeding is praiseworthy; but, although he is not blameless, it irks one to see him pilloried as a mere vulgar appropriator of the labors of other men. The exact fact is, that he had no strict regard for mine and thine. He took as freely as he gave. In literature, as in life, he was a spendthrift; and a prodigal is not always as scrupulous as he might be in replenishing his purse. Dumas's ethics deteriorated as he advanced. One may safely say, that there is none of the plays bearing his name which does not prove itself his by its workmanship. When, however, he began to write serial stories, and to publish a score of volumes a year, then he trafficked in his reputation, and signed his name to books which he had not even read. An effort has been made to show that even **'Monte Cristo'** and the **'Three Musketeers'** series were the work of M. Auguste Maquet, and that Dumas contributed to them only his name on the titlepage. . . . I must confess that I do not see how any one with any pretence to the critical faculty can doubt that **'Monte Cristo'** and the **'Three Musketeers'** are Dumas's own work. That M. Maquet made historical researches, accumulated notes, invented scenes even, is probable; but the mighty impress of Dumas's hand is too plainly visible in every important passage for us to believe that either series owes more to M. Maquet than the service a pupil might fairly render to a master. That these services were considerable is sufficiently obvious from the printing of M. Maquet's name by the side of Dumas's on the titlepages of the dramatizations from the stories. That it was Dumas's share of the work which was inconsiderable is as absurd as it is to scoff at his creative faculty because he was wont to borrow. Señor Castelar has said that all Dumas's collaborators together do not weigh half as much in the literary balance as Dumas alone; and this is true. I have no wish to reflect on the talents of Dinaux, the author of 'Thirty Years, or a Gambler's Life,' and of 'Louise de Lignerrolles,' or on the talents of M. Maquet himself, whose own novels and plays have succeeded, and who is so highly esteemed by his fellow-dramatists as to have been elected and re-elected the president of the Society of Dramatic Authors; yet I must say that the plays which either Dinaux or M. Maquet has written by himself do not show the possession of the secret which charmed us in the work in which they helped Dumas. It is to be said, too, that the later plays taken from his own novels, in which Dumas was assisted by M. Maquet, are very inferior to his earlier plays, written wholly by himself. They are mere dramatizations of romances, and not in a true sense dramas at all. The earlier plays, however extravagant they might be in individual details, had a distinct and essential unity not to be detected in the dramatizations, which were little more than sequences of scenes snipped with the scissors from the interminable series of tales of adventure. . . . Full as these pieces are of life and bustle and gayety, they are poor substitutes for plays, which depend for success on themselves, and not on the vague desire to see in action figures which the reader has learned to like in endless stories. These dramatizations were unduly long-drawn, naturally prolix, not to say garrulous.

When his tales were paid for by the word, when he was "writing on space," as they say in a newspaper office, Dumas let the vice of saying all there was to be said grow on him. On the stage, the half is more than the whole. (pp. 69-72)

Brander Matthews, "Alexandre Dumas," in his French Dramatists of the 19th Century, *third edition, Charles Scribner's Sons, 1901, pp. 46-77.*

GEORGE BRANDES   (essay date 1882)

[*Brandes, a Danish literary critic and biographer, was the principal leader of the intellectual movement which helped to bring an end to Scandinavian cultural isolation. He believed that literature reflects the spirit and problems of its time, and that it must be understood within its social and aesthetic context. Brandes's major critical work, first published in 1882 as* Hovedstrømninger i det 19de aarhundredes litteratur (Main Currents in Nineteenth-Century Literature), *won him admiration for his ability to view literary movements within the broader context of all of European literature. In the following excerpt from* Main Currents, *Brandes discusses the unequal merits of Dumas's historical plays and describes* Antony *as the quintessence of Romantic passion and defiance.*]

[A] man of brilliant, spontaneous talent and Titanic constitution, [Dumas] displayed the same aptitude for Herculean tasks in literature as his father had done in war. For forty years he continued without a pause to produce tragedies, comedies, novels, short stories, books of travel, and memoirs. It would be foolish to write contemptuously of such prodigious inventiveness, such incredible productivity. . . . Assisted by numerous collaborators, all much inferior to himself, Dumas peopled the stages, crowded the booksellers' shelves, filled the *feuilleton* columns of the newspapers with the creations of his brain; the printing-presses creaked and groaned in their efforts to keep pace with his incessant production. What one cannot but regret is the easy-going worldliness which prevented any real process of development taking place. Dumas was an artist only in his first period. Beginning in a romantic age, he began romantically; continuing in a commercial age, he continued commercially.

In *Henri III. et sa Cour* he . . . produced a spirited and playable drama; but it was a drama in which the defiance of classic theatrical convention was of the most superficial kind. He ventured to reproduce in externals the court customs of the period. On the boards where for a couple of centuries the hero and his confidant had conversed either with both arms hanging by their sides or with their left hands on their sword-hilts, a whole troop of King Henry's courtiers appeared with cups and balls (the game of cup-and-ball was an invention of that day); and in the pauses these same gentlemen amused themselves by blowing small darts out of blow-pipes. Nevertheless they felt and spoke like the young men of 1828.

The psychology of the other historical plays of Dumas' youth (*Napoléon Bonaparte, Charles VII. chez ses grands Vassaux,* &c.) is equally superficial. It was not until he lit upon an age the spirit of which he understood and could master, that he succeeded in giving such excellent representations of past days as we have in the interesting and effective dramas, *Un Mariage sous Louis XV.* and *Gabrielle de Belle Isle,* both of which (and especially the latter, with its slightly idealised picture of the manners and customs of the Regency) possess real literary value. But before this, in 1831, it had fallen to Dumas' lot to present the young Romantic generation with one of the typical figures which it recognised as representative of itself. He wrote *Antony*.

With all its faults, there is something in this play which makes it better than even the best of Dumas' other works. There is warmer blood, more human nature in it than in the others. And the reason why, with all its naïveté, it makes a really powerful impression on us is, that in it Dumas has flung his own ego, himself, with his wild passion, his youthful enthusiasm, and chivalrous instincts, on to the stage. Antony is an 1830 hero, of the same type as all of Hugo's—broad-shouldered, lion-maned, enthusiastic and despairing, capable of living without food or sleep, ready at any moment to blow out his own or any one else's brains. But the sensation produced by *Antony* was due to the fact that Dumas had done what Hugo never would or could do, namely, laid the action of his play in 1830, and put his hero on the stage dressed in the fashion of the day, in the very same black coat as the male members of the audience wore. Hitherto Romanticism had voluntarily restricted itself on the stage to the Middle Ages. Now it revealed itself in undisguised modernity.

We come upon a vindication of this step in the play itself. A conversation on the subject of the literary disputes of the day is introduced into the fourth act. During the course of it a poet, who is defending the Romanticists' practice of going back to the Middle Ages for their themes, says:

> The drama of passion must necessarily be historical drama. History bequeaths to us the passionate deeds which were really done. If in the midst of our modern society we were to attempt to lay bare the heart which beats under our ugly short black coats, the resemblance between the hero and the public would be too great; the spectator who was following the development of a passion would desire to have it arrested exactly where it would have stopped in his own case. He would cry: 'Stop! that is wrong; that is not how I feel. When the woman whom I love deceives me I suffer, certainly, but I neither kill her nor myself.' And the outcry against exaggeration and melodrama would drown the applause of the few who feel that the passions of the nineteenth century are the same as those of the sixteenth, and that the blood can course as hotly beneath a cloth coat as beneath a steel corselet.

We can imagine the applause which followed this speech. All wished to show that they belonged to these few. Passion was the order of the day, and they proved themselves to be passionate by applauding. And *Antony* truly is a symphony of raging passions, the like of which it would be difficult to find. (pp. 342-45)

What chiefly strikes us now on reading the play is its preposterous absurdity. We feel that if we were to see it acted, as a new play, we should not be able to refrain from smiling at the parts intended to touch us. We can hardly understand to-day how it happened that on the night of its first performance in 1831 a select audience were excited by it to the wildest enthusiasm. . . . The explanation is, that men never laugh at a work which gives expression to their own moods and feelings. Antony was not merely the impersonation of passion verging on savagery, in combination with a tenderness so great that it would rather take upon itself the responsibility of a murder

than expose the beloved one to insult and scorn; he was also the Byronic, mysterious young hero, who is predestined to struggle against the injustice of fate, and is greater than his fate. (p. 346)

Whilst **Antony** may be described as the Romantic fit of hysterics, [Alfred de Vigny's] *Chatterton* . . . may be designated the Romantic dirge. These two favourite dramas of the generation of 1830 complement each other; the one represents the cult of genius, the other the cult of passion; the one sympathy with the suffering, the other admiration for energetic action; or, to go deeper, the one the Teutonic, the other the Latin side of Romanticism. (p. 347)

> George Brandes, "The Drama: Vitet, Dumas, De Vigny, Hugo," in his Main Currents in Nineteenth Century Literature: The Romantic School in France, Vol. V, *translated by Diana White and Mary Morison, William Heinemann, 1904, pp. 339-56.**

ROBERT LOUIS STEVENSON   (essay date 1887)

[*Stevenson, a famed Scottish novelist and essayist, wrote some of the nineteenth century's most beloved novels, including* Treasure Island, Doctor Jekyll and Mr. Hyde, *and* Kidnapped. *His novels are considered classics for their fast-paced action, strong plots, and well-drawn characters. In the excerpt below, Stevenson discusses* The Vicomte de Bragelonne, *which he includes among his favorite novels. Extolling the merits of the work, he especially commends the "wholesome" spirit of morality informing the novel and its artful embodiment in the character of D'Artagnan. Stevenson's essay was originally published in 1887 in his* Memories and Portraits.]

I have now just risen from my last (let me call it my fifth) perusal [of the **Vicomte de Bragelonne**], having liked it better and admired it more seriously than ever. . . . I avow myself a partisan; and when I compare the popularity of the **Vicomte** with that of **Monte Cristo,** or its own elder brother, the **Trois Mousquetaires,** I confess I am both pained and puzzled. (p. 344)

[Perhaps] a proportion of readers stumble at the threshold. In so vast a mansion there were sure to be back stairs and kitchen offices where no one would delight to linger; but it was at least unhappy that the vestibule should be so badly lighted; and until, in the seventeenth chapter, d'Artagnan sets off to seek his friends, I must confess, the book goes heavily enough. But, from thenceforward, what a feast is spread! Monk kidnapped; d'Artagnan enriched; Mazarin's death; the ever delectable adventure of Belle Isle, wherein Aramis outwits d'Artagnan, with its epilogue . . . , where d'Artagnan regains the moral superiority; the love adventures at Fontainebleau, with St. Aignan's story of the dryad and the business of de Guiche, de Wardes, and Manicamp; Aramis made general of the Jesuits; Aramis at the bastille; the night talk in the forest of Sénart; Belle Isle again, with the death of Porthos; and last, but not least, the taming of d'Artagnan the untamable, under the lash of the young King. What other novel has such epic variety and nobility of incident? often, if you will, impossible; often of the order of an Arabian story; and yet all based in human nature. For if you come to that, what novel has more human nature? not studied with the microscope, but seen largely, in plain daylight, with the natural eye? What novel has more good sense, and gaiety, and wit, and unflagging, admirable literary skill? Good souls, I suppose, must sometimes read it in the blackguard travesty of a translation. But there is no style so untranslatable; light as a whipped trifle, strong as silk; wordly like a village tale; pat like a general's despatch; with every fault, yet never tedious; with no merit, yet inimitably right. And, once more, to make an end of commendations, what novel is inspired with a more unstrained or a more wholesome morality? (pp. 346-47)

I would scarce send to the *Vicomte* a reader who was in quest of what we may call puritan morality. . . . In a man who finds all things good, you will scarce expect much zeal for negative virtues: the active alone will have a charm for him; abstinence, however wise, however kind, will always seem to such a judge entirely mean and partly impious. So with Dumas. Chastity is not near his heart; nor yet, to his own sore cost, that virtue of frugality which is the armour of the artist. Now, in the *Vicomte,* he had much to do with the contest of Fouquet and Colbert. Historic justice should be all upon the side of Colbert, of official honesty, and fiscal competence. And Dumas knew it well: three times at least he shows his knowledge; once it is but flashed upon us and received with the laughter of Fouquet himself, in the jesting controversy in the gardens of Saint Mandé; once it is touched on by Aramis in the forest of Sénart; in the end, it is set before us clearly in one dignified speech of the triumphant Colbert. But in Fouquet, the waster, the lover of good cheer and wit and art, the swift transactor of much business, . . . Dumas saw something of himself and drew the figure the more tenderly. It is to me even touching to see how he insists on Fouquet's honour; not seeing, you might think, that unflawed honour is impossible to spendthrifts; but rather, perhaps, in the light of his own life, seeing it too well, and clinging the more to what was left. Honour can survive a wound; it can live and thrive without a member. The man rebounds from his disgrace; he begins fresh foundations on the ruins of the old; and when his sword is broken, he will do valiantly with his dagger. So it is with Fouquet in the book; so it was with Dumas on the battlefield of life.

To cling to what is left of any damaged quality is virtue in the man; but perhaps to sing its praises is scarcely to be called morality in the writer. And it is elsewhere, it is in the character of d'Artagnan, that we must look for that spirit of morality, which is one of the chief merits of the book, makes one of the main joys of its perusal, and sets it high above more popular rivals. Athos, with the coming of years, has declined too much into the preacher, and the preacher of a sapless creed; but d'Artagnan has mellowed into a man so witty, rough, kind and upright, that he takes the heart by storm. There is nothing of the copy-book about his virtues, nothing of the drawing-room in his fine, natural civility; he will sail near the wind; he is no district visitor—no Wesley or Robespierre; his conscience is void of all refinement whether for good or evil; but the whole man rings true like a good sovereign. Readers who have approached the *Vicomte,* not across country, but by the legitimate, five-volumed avenue of the *Mousquetaires* and *Vingt Ans Après,* will not have forgotten d'Artagnan's ungentlemanly and perfectly improbable trick upon Milady. What a pleasure it is, then, what a reward, and how agreeable a lesson, to see the old captain humble himself to the son of the man whom he had personated! Here, and throughout, if I am to choose virtues for myself or my friends, let me choose the virtues of d'Artagnan. I do not say there is no character as well drawn in Shakespeare; I do say there is none that I love so wholly. There are many spiritual eyes that seem to spy upon our actions—eyes of the dead and the absent, whom we imagine to behold us in our most private hours, and whom we fear and scruple to offend: our witnesses and judges. And among these, even if you should think me childish, I must count my d'Artagnan—not d'Artagnan of the memoirs whom Thackeray pretended to

prefer [see excerpt dated 1862]—a preference, I take the freedom of saying, in which he stands alone; not the d'Artagnan of flesh and blood, but him of the ink and paper; not Nature's, but Dumas's. And this is the particular crown and triumph of the artist—not to be true merely, but to be lovable; not simply to convince, but to enchant. (pp. 347-50)

I can recall no other work of the imagination in which the end of life is represented with so nice a tact. I was asked the other day if Dumas made me laugh or cry. Well, in this my late fifth reading of the *Vicomte,* I did laugh once at the small Coquelin de Volière business, and was perhaps a thought surprised at having done so: to make up for it, I smiled continually. But for tears, I do not know. If you put a pistol to my throat, I must own the tale trips upon a very airy foot—within a measurable distance of unreality; and for those who like the big guns to be discharged and the great passions to appear authentically, it may even seem inadequate from first to last. Not so to me; I cannot count that a poor dinner, or a poor book, where I meet with those I love; and, above all, in this last volume, I find a singular charm of spirit. It breathes a pleasant and a tonic sadness, always brave, never hysterical. Upon the crowded, noisy life of this long tale, evening gradually falls; and the lights are extinguished, and the heroes pass away one by one. One by one they go, and not a regret embitters their departure; the young succeed them in their places, Louis Quatorze is swelling larger and shining broader, another generation and another France dawn on the horizon; but for us and these old men whom we have loved so long, the inevitable end draws near and is welcome. To read this well is to anticipate experience. Ah, if only when these hours of the long shadows fall

for us in reality and not in figure, we may hope to face them with a mind as quiet!

But my paper is running out; the siege guns are firing on the Dutch frontier; and I must say adieu for the fifth time to my old comrade fallen on the field of glory. *Adieu*—rather *au revoir*! Yet a sixth time, dearest d'Artagnan, we shall kidnap Monk and take horse together for Belle Isle. (p. 350)

> Robert Louis Stevenson, "A Gossip on a Novel of Dumas's," in his The Essays of Robert Louis Stevenson: A Selection, *edited by Malcolm Elwin, Macdonald, 1950, pp. 342-50.*

ANDREW LANG   (essay date 1891)

[*Lang was one of England's most powerful men of letters during the closing decades of the nineteenth century. A proponent of the revival of Romantic fiction, Lang championed the works of H. Rider Haggard, Robert Louis Stevenson, and Rudyard Kipling and was harshly critical of the Naturalistic and Realistic techniques of such novelists as Émile Zola and Henry James. A nostalgic vision of the past colored his work as a translator, poet, and revisionist historian. While most of his writings are seldom read today, he is remembered as the editor of the "color fairy book" series, a twelve-volume collection of fairy tales considered a classic in the genre. In the following excerpt, Lang uses Fedor Mikhailovich Dostoevski, Émile Zola, and other authors as foils in emphasizing the attractions of Dumas's ingenuous approach to art and life. To quote Lang: "Let it be enough for these new authors to be industrious, keen, accurate,* précieux, *pitiful, charitable, veracious; but give us high spirits now and then, a light heart, a sharp sword, a fair wench, a good horse, or even that old Gascon rouncy of D'Artagnan's." For further commentary by Lang on Dumas's life and work, see Additional Bibliography.*]

[An anecdote is] told of Dumas' books . . . which [shows], in brief space, why this novelist is so beloved, and why he deserves our affection and esteem. M. Villaud, a railway engineer who had lived much in Italy, Russia, and Spain, was the person whose enthusiasm finally secured a statue for Dumas. He felt so much gratitude to the unknown friend of lonely nights in long exiles, that he could not be happy till his gratitude found a permanent expression. On returning to France he went to consult M. Victor Borie, who told him this tale about George Sand. M. Borie chanced to visit the famous novelist just before her death, and found Dumas' novel, **"Les Quarante Cinq"** (one of the cycle about the Valois kings) lying on her table. He expressed his wonder that she was reading it for the first time.

"For the first time!—why, this is the fifth or sixth time I have read **'Les Quarante Cinq,'** and the others. When I am ill, anxious, melancholy, tired, discouraged, nothing helps me against moral or physical troubles like a book of Dumas." (pp. 2-3)

Does any one suppose that when George Sand was old and tired, and near her death, she would have found this anodyne, and this stimulant, in the novels of M. Tolstoï, M. Dostoiefsky, M. Zola, or any of the "scientific" observers whom we are actually requested to hail as the masters of a new art, the art of the future? Would they make her laugh, as Chicot does? make her forget, as Porthos, Athos, and Aramis do? take her away from the heavy, familiar time, as the enchanter Dumas takes us? No; let it be enough for these new authors to be industrious, keen, accurate, *précieux*, pitiful, charitable, veracious; but give us high spirits now and then, a light heart, a sharp sword, a fair wench, a good horse, or even that old

Gascon rouncy of D'Artagnan's. Like the good Lord James Douglas, we had liefer hear the lark sing over moor and down, with Chicot, than listen to the starved-mouse squeak in the *bouge* of Thérèse Raquin, with M. Zola. Not that there is not a place and an hour for him, and others like him; but they are not, if you please, to have the whole world to themselves, and all the time, and all the praise; they are not to turn the world into a dissecting-room, time into tedium, and the laurels of Scott and Dumas into crowns of nettles. (p. 4)

In all [Dumas] does, at his best, as in the **"Chevalier d'Harmenthal,"** he has movement, kindness, courage, and gaiety. His philosophy of life is that old philosophy of the sagas and of Homer. Let us enjoy the movement of the fray, the faces of fair women, the taste of good wine; let us welcome life like a mistress, let us welcome death like a friend, and with a jest—if death comes with honour.

Dumas is no pessimist. "Heaven has made but one drama for man—the world," he writes, "and during these three thousand years mankind has been hissing it." . . . But Dumas, for one, will not hiss it, but applauds with all his might—a charmed spectator, a fortunate actor in the eternal piece, where all the men and women are only players. (pp. 18-19)

His may not be the best, nor the ultimate philosophy, but it *is* a philosophy, and one of which we may some day feel the want. I read the stilted criticisms, the pedantic carpings of some modern men who cannot write their own language, and I gather that Dumas is out of date. There is a new philosophy of doubts and delicacies, of dallyings and refinements, of half-hearted lookers-on, desiring and fearing some new order of the world. Dumas does not dally nor doubt: he takes his side, he rushes into the smoke, he strikes his foe; but there is never an unkind word on his lip, nor a grudging thought in his heart.

It may be said that Dumas is not a master of words and phrases, that he is not a *raffiné* of expression, nor a jeweller of style. When I read the maunderings, the stilted and staggering sentences, the hesitating phrases, the far-sought and dear-bought and worthless word-juggles; the sham scientific verbiage, the native pedantries of many modern so-called "stylists," I rejoice that Dumas was not one of these. He told a plain tale, in the language suited to a plain tale, with abundance of wit and gaiety, as in the reflections of his Chicot, as in all his dialogues. . . . Speed, directness, lucidity are the characteristics of Dumas' style, and they are exactly the characteristics which his novels required. Scott often failed, his most loyal admirers may admit, in these essentials; but it is rarely that Dumas fails, when he is himself and at his best. (pp. 19-20)

[Dumas'] faults are on the surface, visible to all men. He was not only rapid, he was hasty, he was inconsistent; his need of money as well as his love of work made him put his hand to dozens of perishable things. A beginner, entering the forest of Dumas' books, may fail to see the trees for the wood. He may be counselled to select first the cycle of d'Artagnan—the **"Musketeers," "Twenty Years After,"** and the **"Vicomte de Bragelonne."** Mr. Stevenson's delightful essay on the last may have sent many readers to it [see excerpt dated 1887]; I confess to preferring the youth of the **"Musketeers"** to their old age. Then there is the cycle of the Valois, whereof the **"Dame de Monsereau"** is the best—perhaps the best thing Dumas ever wrote. The **"Tulipe Noire"** is a novel girls may read, as Thackeray said, with confidence. The **"Chevalier d'Harmenthal"** is nearly (not quite) as good as "Quentin Durward." **"Monte Cristo"** has the best beginning—and loses itself in the sands.

The novels on the Revolution are not among the most alluring. . . . [But] the Revolution is in itself too terrible and pitiful, and too near us (on both sides!) for fiction.

On Dumas' faults it has been no pleasure to dwell. . . . He who had enriched so many died poor; he who had told of conquering France, died during the Terrible Year. But he could forgive, could appreciate, the valour of an enemy. Of the Scotch at Waterloo he writes: "It was not enough to kill them: we had to push them down." Dead, they still stood "shoulder to shoulder." In the same generous temper an English cavalry officer wrote home, after Waterloo, that he would gladly have given the rest of his life to have served, on that day, in our infantry or in the French cavalry. These are the spirits that warm the heart, that make us all friends; and to the great, the brave, the generous Dumas we cry, across the years and across the tomb, our *Ave alque vale!* (pp. 22-3)

> Andrew Lang, "Alexandre Dumas," in his Essays in Little, *Charles Scribner's Sons, 1891, pp. 1-23.*

THEODORE WATTS   (essay date 1894)

[*In discussing Dumas's literary development, Watts maintains that the writer never reached intellectual maturity, but relied instead on his juvenile charm. While Watts considers Dumas's lack of intellectual development a weakness, he also admits that it was this juvenility that supplied the "gusto" to his novels.*]

From the time when he produced **'Henri Trois et Sa Cour'** to the time when he produced **'La Tour de Nesle,'** Dumas' wealth of invention, imagination, and brilliant dialogue went on increasing, and afterwards became simply prodigious. As to mere stage-craft, there is, I will venture to say, nothing in drama to equal the famous prison scene where Buridan is released from his bonds in **'La Tour de Nesle,'** the crown of melodrama. Not even the ladder scene in Hugo's 'Le Roi s'amuse' can be compared with it. Had Dumas' intellect gone on growing from his thirtieth year, his place would have been not at the top of *raconteurs* and masters of stagecraft; it would have been almost in the front rank of the great artists of the world. The truth is, however, that when, after thirty, growth goes on as it did in the case of Shakespeare, it does so because the imagination of youth has become strengthened by the growing luminosity of the mere intelligence. But dazzling as is the work of the year 1844, there is apparent no growth of the intellect in Dumas.

In a certain sense, indeed, it may be said that Dumas never reached intellectual manhood at all; and hence his works are never novels in the true sense, but stories.

And if this juvenility is his weakness, it is also his charm—his unique, his ineffable charm. Splendid as were the animal spirits of Dickens when he wrote the 'Pickwick Papers,' they began even in 'Nicholas Nickleby' to wane; and afterwards, although his wit, humour, and wisdom went on growing, it was very rarely that he drew for his effects upon those animal spirits which made the fortune of 'Pickwick.' But **'Les Trois Mousquetaires'** was written when Dumas was forty-two, and the gusto of every page is that of a schoolboy. A boy he remained—indeed, a marvellous boy—down to his latest moment. (pp. 238-39)

> Theodore Watts, "'Edition de luxe' of Alexandre Dumas," *in* The Nineteenth Century, *Vol. XXXV, No. 204, February, 1894, pp. 237-40.*

GEORGE SAINTSBURY   (essay date 1894)

[*According to Saintsbury, Dumas ranks second only to the early-nineteenth-century Scottish novelist Walter Scott as a writer of historical novels. He contrasts the authors in the excerpt below, observing that, unlike Scott, Dumas generally sacrificed intellection, description, and character development in his attempt to absorb readers in his stories per se. Saintsbury commends this approach, asserting that "it was . . . this strengthening and extending of the absorbing and exciting quality which the Historical Novel chiefly owed to Dumas." For additional commentary by Saintsbury, see the excerpt dated 1878.*]

Although Alexandre Dumas had begun to write years before Sir Walter Scott's death, he had not at that time turned his attention to the novels which have ranked him as second only to Sir Walter himself in that department. . . . He was busy on dramatic composition, in which, though he never attained anything like Scott's excellence in his own kind of poetry, he was nearly as great an innovator in his own country and way. Nor can it be doubted that this practice helped him considerably in his later work, just as poetry had helped Scott; and in particular that it taught Dumas a more closely knit construction and a more constant "eye to the audience" than Scott had always shown. Not indeed that the plots of Dumas, as plots, are by any means of exceptional regularity. . . . But when they are looked at from the strictly dramatic side, all more or less are "chronicle-plays" in the form of novels, rather than novels; lengths of adventure prolonged or cut short at the pleasure or convenience of the writer, rather than definite evolutions of a certain definite scheme, which has got to come to an end when the ball is fully unrolled. The advantage of Dumas's dramatic practice shows itself most in the business-like way in which at his best he works by *tableaux*, connected, it may be, with each other rather by sequence and identity of personages than by strict causality, but each possessing a distinct dramatic and narrative interest of its own, and so enchaining the attention. (pp. 327-28)

Another point in which Dumas may be said to have improved, or at any rate alternated, upon Scott, and which also may, without impropriety, be connected with his practice for the stage, is the enormously increased part allotted to dialogue in his novels. . . . Take down at hazard three or four different volumes of Dumas from the shelf; open them, and run over the pages, noting of what stuff the letterpress is composed. Then do exactly the same with the same number of Scott. You will find that the number of whole pages, and still more the number of consecutive pages, entirely filled with dialogue, or variegated with other matter in hardly greater proportion than that of stage-directions, is far larger in the French than in the English master. . . . [At] his best Dumas delighted in telling his tale as much as possible through the mouths of his characters. In all his most famous passages . . . , the thing is always talked rather than narrated. It is hardly fanciful to trace Dumas's preference for heroes like D'Artagnan and Chicot to the fact that they had it by kind to talk.

I do not know whether it is worth while to lay much stress on another difference between Scott and Dumas,—the much greater length of the latter's novels, and his tendency to run them into series. . . . Even if we neglect the trilogy system of which the adventures of D'Artagnan and Chicot are the main specimens, the individual length of Dumas's books is much greater than that of Scott's. . . . But this increase in length was only a return to old practices; for Scott himself had been a great shortener of the novel. (pp. 328-29)

[Thus] the main points of strictly technical variation in Dumas as compared with Scott are the more important use made of dialogue, the greater length of the stories, and the tendency to run them on in series. In quality of enjoyment, also, the French master added something to his English model. If Scott is not deep . . . , Dumas is positively superficial. His rapid and absorbing current of narrative gives no time for any strictly intellectual exertion on the part either of writer or reader; the style as style is even less distinct and less distinguished than Scott's; we receive not only few ideas but even few images of anything but action—few pictures of scenery, no extraordinarily vivid touches of customs or manners. Dumas is an infinitely inferior master of character to Scott; he can make up a personage admirably, but seldom attains to a real character. Chicot himself and Porthos are the chief exceptions; for D'Artagnan is more a type than an individual, Athos is the incarnate gentleman chiefly, Aramis is incomplete and shadowy, and Monte Cristo is a mere creature of melodrama. But Dumas excels even Scott himself in the peculiar and sustained faculty of keeping hold on his reader by and for the story. With Sir Walter one is never quite unconscious, and one is delighted to be conscious, of the existence and individuality of the narrator. Of Dumas's personality (and no doubt this is in a way a triumph of his art) we never think at all. We think of nothing but of the story: whether D'Artagnan will ever bring the diamonds safe home; whether the compact between Richelieu and Milady can possibly be fulfilled; whether that most terrible of all "black strap", that flowed into the pewter pot when Grimaud tried the cask, will do its intended duty or not; whether Margaret will be able to divert the silk cord in Alençon's hand from its destination on La Môle's neck. No doubt Scott has moments of the same arresting excitement; but they are not so much his direct object, and from the difference of his method they are not so prominent or so numerous or engineered in such a manner as to take an equally complete hold of the reader. . . .

[In] the scenes where Scott as a rule excels [Dumas],—the scenes where the mere excitement of adventure is enhanced by nobility of sentiment—[Dumas] has a few, with the death of Porthos at the head of them, which are worthy of Scott himself; while of passages like the famous rescue of Henry Morton from the Cameronians he has literally hundreds.

It was . . . this strengthening and extending of the absorbing and exciting quality which the Historical Novel chiefly owed to Dumas, just as it owed its first just and true concoction and the indication of almost all the ways in which it could seek perfection to Scott. I shall not, I think, be charged with being unjust to the Pupil; but, wonderful as his work is, I think it not so much likely as certain that it never would have been done at all if it had not been for the Master. (pp. 329-30)

George Saintsbury, "The Historical Novel, II: Scott and Dumas," in Macmillan's Magazine, *Vol. LXX, No. 419, September, 1894, pp. 321-30.**

ARTHUR F. DAVIDSON (essay date 1899)

[*Davidson discusses the reasons for Dumas's enduring popularity, emphasizing his consistent appeal to basic human fantasies and emotions as well as his extraordinary gift for dramatic storytelling.*]

[On the whole, neither here in England] nor elsewhere, neither alive nor dead, has Dumas owed much to the higher criticism. On the other hand . . . he has had the more substantial advantage of being read in the four corners of the earth, and that not only spasmodically, as might happen at the present time, but with a steady persistence untouched by the changes of literary fashion. The reasons for this persistence of Dumas might fill a volume, but they must be reduced now to a few plain propositions.

In dealing with the primary emotions he worked on a material little affected by differences of position or education. Most people at some time crave for the wonderful and the sensational; *Monte Cristo* appeals both to the philosopher and the housemaid. It matters not how much their impressions of it diverge; they have both been touched at some common point, probably that need of occasional desipience which Horace long ago observed to be an instinct of human nature. The popular if vulgar ideas of Wealth, Power, Justice, or its "wilder kind" Revenge, have never had a more skilful manipulator than Dumas. One or other such abstractions may be noticed as the foundation of his most popular works. *Monte Cristo* stands for several, a human Providence operating by effective contrast amid ordinary circumstances; *Joseph Balsamo* represents Magic and Fate; *Le Chevalier de Maison Rouge,* Love and Loyalty; *Les Trois Mousquetaires,* Crime and Retribution, in the person of Milady; *Vingt Ans Après,* in the person of Mordaunt, Vengeance and Nemesis. The man who used these themes with no moral purpose in view, but for the simple sake of entertainment, offers us a perpetual refuge from the dulness or troubles of life in spheres where the improbable only just stops short of the impossible. With the exception of *Monte Cristo,*—one of the best-known, if not the best, of his novels and at any rate a marvellous *tour de force*—the chief romances of Dumas are set in a framework of history, an alliance the value of which Scott had first shown. But with Sir Walter Romance was the handmaid of History, with Dumas History existed for the benefit of Romance. The one was spiritual, the other ethereal; the one used his qualities of poet and student to enrich fiction, the other used his unrivalled dramatic instinct to enliven history. The admirable thing about Scott was that his seriousness never spoiled his imagination, about Dumas that his levity did so little harm to his facts. It is true that he treated history in a free and easy fashion, *les manches retroussées,* and that in details he assumed a licence of invention regulated only by his conception of the principal characters and their surroundings. Yet by intuition, it seems, he reproduced these surroundings,— the age of the last Valois sovereigns for example or that of Louis the Thirteenth—with rare felicity and with admitted fidelity. And as to his great personages it must be for experts to decide how far Henri Trois, Catherine de Médicis, Richelieu, Cromwell, Marie Antoinette have been distorted. . . . [But] it is pleasant to believe that our judgment has not been seriously perverted by certain early and ineffaceable impressions which we owe to the brilliant pages of Dumas.

His superficiality has often been remarked, but there is one point about it which should not be overlooked. No one has accused Dumas of profundity; width not depth was his characteristic. . . . In all respects the very antithesis of Balzac he is so especially in this, that, while the feeling left by any one volume of the *Comédie Humaine* is that of a subject completely exhausted, the effect of Dumas is rather to open out prospects by a suggestiveness which, if it disappoints our reason, attracts and stimulates our imagination. With imagination, that precious relic of a pre-scientific age, Dumas was richly endowed, but he had the equally valuable gift of telling a story. This is only to say that he was first and last a dramatist, and indeed his dramas are (as he himself considered) his best, certainly his most proper and distinctive work. Clever as he was in filling out, interweaving, and elaborating to any extent, we should not go for the best examples of his constructive skill to the long romances spun out for a special purpose, but rather to his plays and certain of his shorter novels. An amiable horticulturist, his jealous rival, a gruff gaoler, his charming daughter, and William of Orange,—these are the figures of one of the prettiest and most self-complete stories possible. Compare it with another delightful flower-story,—admirable too and full of poetry, philosophy, and botany—but compare them in the matter of workmanship, and *La Tulipe Noire* will appear far superior to *Picciola*. A similar conclusion might be drawn from a comparison on this point between *Le Chevalier de Maison Rouge* and *A Tale of Two Cities*. It is impossible indeed to emphasise too much the richness of Dumas's dramatic faculty as explaining the success with which he used . . . all the conventional effects of surprise, suspense, and contrast. And as the qualities of the good playwright also make the good story-teller, it follows that Dumas was . . . the one who could from the least make the most. We like him none the worse because he was only a story-teller,—an entertainer pure and simple, but a God-given entertainer . . . , spontaneous and unforced, always working and never labouring. "One of the forces of Nature," that happy phrase of Michelet, itself inexplicable, explains everything about Dumas,—his fertility, his inequality, his wastefulness. For the order of Nature (as a philosopher has remarked) though beneficent is not optimistic. And this man was like a tree bearing fruit abundantly in its kind, from which all men pluck at their will, keeping the choice and flinging away that which is over-ripe or under-ripe, but sometimes abusing what they have flung away and forgetting how good was what they kept.

Such was Alexandre Dumas. Take from him the elements, extravagant or grotesque as they may strike us, common to the ecstatic age into which he came; . . . take from him whatever attraction may accrue from a weariness of other writers and other aims,—take all this away as temporary and accidental, and there still remain imperishable qualities which belong not to the province of criticism or even of praise, but to that of admiration and perhaps reverence. (pp. 266-68)

Arthur F. Davidson, "The Author of 'The Three Musketeers'," in Macmillan's Magazine, *Vol. LXXIX, No. 472, February, 1899, pp. 257-68.*

G. K. CHESTERTON (essay date 1902)

[*Chesterton was one of England's most prominent and colorful men of letters during the early twentieth century. Although he is best known today as a detective novelist and essayist, he was also an eminent literary critic. Chesterton's works are characterized by their humor, frequent use of paradox, and chatty, rambling style. In the excerpt below, Chesterton argues that the uncertainties and odium surrounding Dumas's authorial practices cannot gainsay the greatness of his achievement. The key to this greatness, suggests Chesterton, resided in Dumas's ability to logically assemble a dramatic sequence of events and adventures and move this mass towards that expected, or at least "half-expected," conclusion necessary to all good romance.*]

Dumas's fame is wrapped in similar clouds to those which wrap the fame of about half of the great Elizabethans. Nobody is quite certain that any idea which Dumas presented was invented by him. Nobody is quite certain that any line which Dumas published was written by him. But for all that, we know that Dumas was, and must have been, a great man. There are some people who think this kind of doubt clinging to every

specific detail does really invalidate the intellectual certainty of the whole. They think that when we are in the presence of a mass that is confessedly solid and inimitable, we must refrain from admiring that mass until we have decided what parts of it are authentic; where the fictitious begins and where the genuine leaves off. Thus, they say that because the books of the New Testament may have been tampered with, we know not to what extent, we must, therefore, surrender altogether a series of utterances which every rational person has admitted to strike the deepest note of the human spirit. They might as well say that because Vesuvius is surrounded by sloping meadows, and because no one can say exactly where the plain leaves off and the mountain begins, therefore there is no mountain of Vesuvius at all, but a beautiful, uninterrupted plain on the spot where it is popularly supposed to stand. Most reasonable people agree that it is possible to see, through whatever mists of misrepresentations, that an intellectual marvel has occurred. Most people agree that, whatever may be the interpolations, an intellectual marvel occurred which produced the Gospels. To descend to smaller things, most people agree that whatever lending and stealing confused the Elizabethan Age, an intellectual marvel occurred which produced the Elizabethan drama. And to descend to things yet smaller again, most people agree that whatever have been the sins, the evasions, the thefts, the plagiarism, the hackwork, the brazen idleness of the author, an intellectual miracle occurred which produced the novels of Dumas.

In novels of this kind, novels produced in such immeasurable quantities, of such prodigious length, and marked throughout with its haste of production and dubiety of authorship, it is, indeed, impossible that we should find that particular order of literary merit which marks so much of the work that is now produced and is so much demanded by modern critics; the merit of exact verbal finish and the precision of the *mot juste*. Stevenson would have lain awake at night wondering whether, in describing the death of a marquis in a duel he should describe a sword as glittering or gleaming, or speak of the stricken man staggering back or reeling back. Dumas could not, in the nature of things, have troubled his head about such points as that, so long as somebody killed the marquis for him at a moderate figure. All technical gusto, the whole of that abstract lust for words which separates the literary man from the mere thinker, were certain, through the facts of the case, to fade more or less out of Dumas. The supreme element of greatness in him . . . [may be described as] the power of massing a building. He was a great architect, and stands among his hired scribblers like Sir Christopher Wren among the masons at work upon St. Paul's. The idea that he did actually publish books written in detail by others is very much borne out by the fact that nothing is more noticeable in his work than that its talent is chiefly shown in the planning of an incident or a series of incidents. Without going into any of the actual examples, we can ourselves imagine the class of eventualities which are the glory of Dumas's romances; and we can imagine Dumas planning them out as a general plans a campaign. We can imagine him telling a secretary, as he went out for the day, that the two cavaliers were to go to six inns, one after another, and find in each a huge banquet prepared for them by an unknown benefactor, or a man in a mask seeking to fix a quarrel upon them. We can imagine him scribbling on a loose piece of paper a list of six Royal Princes, each of whom in succession was to be summoned by the King to assist him against an assassin, and each of whom in turn was to turn his sword against the King. It was in this dramatic sequence that Dumas was greatest and most readable; he excelled in a kind of systematic disaster and a kind of orderly crime. He was, after all, a Frenchman in more ways than one, and with all his violence, worldliness and appetite there remains in his work something fundamentally logical. The man who made the finest scenes in his romantic writings turn on tangles of relationship, like the triple duel which opens *The Three Musketeers,* had almost the mind of a mathematician.

This structural, systematic, almost numerical method of Dumas's is really important as throwing some light on the conditions which produce romance so popular and so great as his. There is a very general notion in existence that romance depends upon the unexpected. This is altogether an error: romance depends upon the expected. Unless the elements already existing in the story point to and hint at more or less darkly, but more or less inevitably, the thing that is to follow, the mere brute occurrence of that thing, without rhyme or reason, does not either excite or entertain us.... Anybody could make a mad bull enter the drawing-room in the middle of one of Miss Fowler's epigrammatic conversations, or make one of Mr. W. W. Jacobs's stories end abruptly with the blowing of the trump of the Resurrection. Nothing could be more unexpected than these things would be; but they would not excite us; they would bore us like the conversational rambling of an idiot in a cell. Romance depends, if not absolutely upon the expected, at least upon something that may be called the half-expected. The true romantic ending is something that has been prophesied by our sub-consciousness. We feel the spirit of romance when Ulysses springs upon the table, his rags falling from him, and shoots Antinous in the throat. It would be much more unexpected, if that were all, if he turned three somersaults in the air and announced that he was only Ulysses's ship's carpenter playing a practical joke. Similarly, we feel the spirit of romance when D'Artagnan joins his three adversaries in turning their swords against the musketeers of the Cardinal. It is not unexpected that the four should thus get into a fight together. The most unexpected thing one can imagine in Dumas would be that they should not get into one. (pp. 448-50)

[Dumas's large scheme of orderly and successive adventures] is his great merit as an artist. He had the power of making us feel that his heroes were moving parts of a great scheme of adventures, a scheme as wide, as politic, as universal and sagacious as one of the plots of his own Cardinal Richelieu. And it is in this that almost all his imitators fail; they imagine that his triumph consisted in the swaggering inconsequence of his events, in innumerable drawn swords; in ceaseless torrents of blood; in the mere multiplication of cloaks, and feathers, and halberds, and rope ladders. These things are not romance: here, as everywhere, materials and materialism mislead us. Dumas was a great romanticist, because he had the sense of something solid and eternal in old valour, in old manners, in old friends. But a mere drawn sword is no more poetical than a pocket-knife. A mere dead man is not in any sense so dramatic as a living one. Men who find no romance in life will certainly find none in death. (p. 450)

G. K. Chesterton, "Alexandre Dumas," *in* The Bookman, *New York, Vol. XV, No. 5, July, 1902, pp. 446-50.*

HIPPOLYTE PARIGOT   (essay date 1902)

[*In a translated excerpt from his 1902 study* Alexandre Dumas père, *included in André Maurois's biography of the Dumas family, Parigot hails D'Artagnan, Athos, Porthos, and Aramis as embodiments of "the four cardinal points of French civilization":*

"*fierce determination, aristocratic melancholy, a somewhat vainglorious strength,* [*and*] *an elegance, at once delicate and gay.*"]

A living *sense* of France—in that lies the secret charm of the four heroes: d'Artagnan, Athos, Porthos and Aramis. Fierce determination, aristocratic melancholy, a somewhat vainglorious strength, an elegance, at once delicate and gay—it is these qualities that make of them, as it were, an epitome of that gracious, courageous, light-hearted France which we still like to recover through the imagination. It contained, to be sure, in addition to the restless world in which amorous intrigue went hand in hand with political plotting, men like Descartes and Pascal, though even they were not without experience, in the course of their lives, of the ways of soldiers and men of the court. But what grace, elegance, decision, vigour and intelligence there is in those young men who meet as comrades in arms before being reunited in the garb of religion! There is no one ... who does not rank courage above virtue.

D'Artagnan, the dexterous Gascon, twirling his moustache; the boisterous Porthos with the frame of a giant; Athos, the slightly romantic grand seigneur; Aramis, the discreet Aramis, the dashing pupil of the good fathers (*non inutile est desiderium in oblatione*), who conceals both his religion and his love-affairs: these four friends ... stand for the four cardinal points of French civilization. What torrential perseverance and vigour they exhibit! How simply they carry through their deeds of prowess! They ride hell-for-leather, they overcome difficulties with those high spirits which, in France, raise courage to a higher level. The ride to Calais, merely indicated in [Courtilz's] *Mémoires,* can rank in rapidity of execution with the campaigns of Italy: and when we see Athos sitting in judgment on his abominable wife, let us not forget the courts-marital and the tribunals of the Revolution. If Danton and Napoleon were exemplars of Gallic energy, Dumas, in *The Three Musketeers* is the national novelist who puts it into words.

Hippolyte Parigot, in an extract in The Titans: A Three-generation Biography of the Dumas *by André Maurois, translated by Gerard Hopkins, Harper & Brothers Publishers, 1957, p. 179.*

HUGH ALLISON SMITH   (essay date 1925)

[*In his* Main Currents of Modern French Drama, *from which the following excerpt is taken, Smith identifies Dumas as a central figure in the "development of popular and, strictly speaking, unliterary elements in the legitimate French theatre." It is in light of this that he discusses* Henri III and His Court, The Tower of Nesle, *and* Antony, *asserting that these plays introduced to the French theatre three elements: "historic melodrama, the psychology of popular imagination and the brutal drama of guilty passion.*"]

The first development of popular and, strictly speaking, unliterary elements in the legitimate French theatre [began] ... with Alexandre Dumas, that robust Napoleonic quadroon who elbowed his way so unceremoniously into literature, and who, the year before the appearance of *Hernani,* broke down the doors of the *Comédie* [*Française*] and brought in his melodramatic *Henri III,* followed by the crowd. (p. 36)

As a historic drama, *Henri III* is typical of Dumas. Its local color and history are laid on with a lavish but not discriminating hand. We find a little of everything of the times: facts, follies and fashions. We learn the cost of theatre tickets, the latest games and oaths, and the recent style of turn-down collars.

History is not separated from legend, and even magic and superstition seem accepted. Catherine de Medeci lays bare her most secret schemes for dominating the young King, schemes which, if ever formulated, were certainly never put into words. Dumas's history, then, is usually trivial and gossipy, the sort . . . that is recounted of the great by valets and chambermaids.

Nevertheless there is underneath all this a plot full of invention and of sustained power and interest, which is conducted with great rapidity and skill, and which progresses with exciting interest to a breathless finish. Dumas is, in plot at least, a born playwright, and this quality explains largely his success. It is he, and not Hugo, who really popularized Romantic drama. Moreover, the subject of this play, illicit or immoral love treated with unconscious approval, is significant of Romantic philosophy and practice, although the real vogue and power of this theme were much more strikingly established in one of Dumas's subsequent pieces.

Henri III, despite its historic pretensions, is at heart popular melodrama, a little on its good behavior in its first appearance in polite society, and somewhat cramped in the severe confines of the *Comédie.* But, once introduced it quickly becomes familiar. A little later Dumas allows it to run riot in that stupendous play, *La Tour de Nesle.* . . . *La Tour de Nesle* is the father of all melodrama. Nothing has ever equalled it in pure melodramatic power, nor in success. (pp. 38-9)

Despite the non-literary quality of *La Tour de Nesle,* it is a significant play of Dumas, since we see here without disguise one of the important elements that he introduced into legitimate drama. This element, which is one of the secrets of Dumas's genius, is the strikingly popular character of his imagination, of his character creations, and of his whole conception of life. It is, as we shall see, the very essence of melodrama.

Historically, melodrama is the theatre of the common people, of those not trained to think, preferably of the credulous and ignorant. It portrays life fashioned to their tastes—life as they imagine it, and not at all as they have lived it or seen it. Its most fundamental characteristics are: first, a lack of literary or artistic merit; second, a desire to arouse or shock, to thrill with joy or to move to tears; and third a capricious imagination without the restraint of experience and judgment, giving unexpected or improbable incidents rather than logical development of action. (pp. 39-40)

Dumas's type of drama is based on a conception of life formed not by observation and experience but by imagination. Surely no thoughtful person ought to be mistaken as to the identity or reality of his character creations. These startling figures whom he launches into his breathless plots simply throw all probabilities to the winds, and, clothed with the merest fig leaf of possibility, depend on their speed to run the gauntlet of the realistic observer—and they usually get through. They are not true to real life and are even absurd, but they are remarkably typical of popular fancy in its mood of relaxation.

Dumas's manner of conceiving life was much dependent on exaggeration and antithesis, as it was in Hugo. Most often it rested on the assumption that all the vices belonged to the great and noble, in appearance, and all the virtues to the poor and humble. One example in many of this amusing type of logic is the speech of Buridan in *La Tour de Nesle,* where he proves to the companion of his strange adventure that the masked women who had invited them so mysteriously to this orgy belong to the highest society. After each recital of the effrontery, perversion, and unrestrained debauchery of these women,

he draws the conclusion: "*Ce sont de grandes dames.*" A few lines at the end will give an idea of his style: "You see well then that these are noble ladies. At the table they abandoned themselves to all that love and intoxication can have of impulse and unrestraint; they spoke blasphemies; they pronounced perverse speeches and vile words; they forgot all restraint, all modesty, forgot heaven and earth. They are noble ladies, the most noble of ladies, I assure you."

Such characterizations undoubtedly flatter popular imagination. (pp. 40-1)

Dumas, then, as well as Hugo, and much more than Hugo in style, imagination and character conception, introduced popular psychology into literature and posed as a champion of the common people. (p. 41)

But Dumas was not only a popularizer of melodrama in the Romantic theatre, he was also the most powerful and influential creator of the contemporary drama of passion, a form that has long outlived the Romantic movement proper. The play which above all others popularized the drama of passion is *Antony;* . . . it occupies a place in the drama of passion similar to that of *La Tour de Nesle* in melodrama. . . .

This play is a breathless drama of guilty love, and is particularly remarkable for the audacity of its situations and of the character of its chief figure. (p. 42)

As a type or a general conception Antony is Byronic, and Dumas's motto beneath the title of this play, taken from Byron, is doubly significant as we shall see: "They have said that *Childe Harold* was I, what do I care!" Antony is also the proud illegitimate outcast, the Didier of *Marion Delorme.* But in one quality, and that is the backbone of his creation, he is Dumas himself. The usual Romantic hero had been an irresolute creature, exhaling his violence in words and led by fate to a pathetic death or suicide. But Antony is not a suicide; he does not kill himself because he can not win an impossible love; he takes love by brute force and kills his mistress to protect her reputation and honor!

The audacity of this dramatic character is precisely the most prominent quality of Dumas himself; as suggested by the quotation from Byron, he has created Antony in his own image. The character is not an agreeable one here, but as an instrument of drama, a will in action, it is much superior to that of a Hernani or a Ruy Blas, and when properly civilized later and divested of its Romantic nimbus, it is a most popular conception. (pp. 42-3)

Dumas's plays were of a short-lived race, and most of them died of old age while still young in years. The three we have mentioned, *Henri III, La Tour de Nesle,* and *Antony,* typify perfectly the chief contributions of Dumas to the development of the theatre, namely historic melodrama, the psychology of popular imagination and the brutal drama of guilty passion. (p. 43)

He was not a theorist as Hugo was, and his robust good sense turned naturally to the chief possibility of popular success in Romantic drama, an exciting story or plot which would exploit the emotional character of Romantic literature. Had he lived in the Naturalistic period and had he been a realist—which he was not—he would doubtless have been one of the first to fling to the public that "bleeding slice of life" of which so much has been said; placed as he was, he could only offer them a "bleeding slice of imagination." This served very well until they had tasted real blood. (p. 44)

Hugh Allison Smith, "Other Romantic Dramatists (Dumas—Delavigne—Vigny—Musset)," in his Main Currents of Modern French Drama, *Henry Holt and Company, 1925, pp. 36-58.**

JOHN GALSWORTHY (essay date 1928)

[*Galsworthy was an early-twentieth-century English novelist, dramatist, and short story writer. Best known as the author of the popular "Forsyte Saga" novel sequence, he was regarded as a literary giant in the 1920s and received the Nobel Prize for literature in 1932. In the excerpt below, originally published in 1928, Galsworthy focuses on the excellences of Dumas's narration and characterization. He identifies D'Artagnan as the greatest of Dumas's creations, stating that "few, if any, characters in fiction inspire one with such belief in their individual existences, or their importance as types."*]

It has been the mode of late for writers to take some historical personage and make him or her the centre of a biographical play or novel: if you desire to measure Dumas' genius, line these modern recreations up beside the Frenchman's historical figures, and you will find the moderns pale and thin, lacking in flavour and fascination. And then make another comparison: line up Dumas' historical characters with the figures of his fancy, such as D'Artagnan, Aramis, Porthos, Athos, Coconnas, Chicot, Bussy (who though they had their living prototypes never paid any attention to them) and his genius will be still more apparent, for these figures of his unfettered imagination are even more vigorous and alive than his historical characters. Dumas excelled with men rather than with women. Anne of Austria, Margot, Louise, la dame de Monsoreau, and la Duchesse de Chévreuse, are good but not great creations; Miladi is a mere monstress, and no other of his women are terribly exciting. But his male figures ruffle it with the very best; they simply strut through Time—'rich,' our fathers would have called them! While for zest in narrative Dumas is the equal of Dickens, and more than that one cannot say. Sniff if you like at his "panache," as at the extravagance of the English master, but that which offends in lesser writers seems natural to the make-up of these great showmen.

I must apologize for mentioning narrative in days when so many regard it as a dead and buried form and are engaged in trying to express the human story by a series of hyphenated detonations; but really one cannot leave it out in speaking of Dumas. At his best he had no peer at sustaining the interest of a tale. He generally had a number of plots, and drove them four-in-hand at a sharp and steady pace and with a fine evenness of motion. **"Le Vicomte de Bragelonne"** is, perhaps, for wealth of incident and character intricately interwoven, his greatest effort. Oh! Undoubtedly a great raconteur! And with something of the magician about him, but a magician who used the pigments and potions of actual life and feeling. Highly-coloured and strongly-flavoured Dumas was, but he was never windy and just fanciful.

Fiction from the days of Homer on has been devised to satisfy two demands—for narrative and for character. Human nature changes so slowly that a thousand years are but as yesterday; and the reader requires narrative and character to-day just as much as he did in the time of Chaucer. Dumas, though he may be scouted by the eclectic, is still read eagerly, and will be read a hundred, nay, three hundred years on. While nothing, I think, is more certain than that no single work of what one may call protoplasmic fiction—spineless, all jelly and wrig-

gles—will be remembered even by name thirty years hence. (pp. 251-52)

[Dumas] must be accounted a romanticist, for he is bent primarily on entertaining. His work gives practically no indication that he had predilections, prejudices, passions or philosophy. His tales offer no criticism of life, are written from no temperamental angle. Of English writers perhaps only Shakespeare is so completely impersonal. But though he was a romanticist, he never got into the air. Romantic in mood, he was realistic in method, and he had his absorptions in character.

His greatest creation is undoubtedly D'Artagnan, that backbone of eleven volumes, type at once of the fighting adventurer and of the trusty servant, whose wily blade is ever at the back of those whose hearts have neither his magnanimity nor his courage, but whose heads have a cold concentration that his head lacks. Few, if any, characters in fiction inspire one with such belief in their individual existences, or their importance as types. D'Artagnan is the world's 'lieutenant'—the man who does the job that others profit by; and he is none the less fascinating because he is always "going to make his fortune" out of it, and never does anything but make someone else's. So very like such a lot of people! To one who made D'Artagnan all shall be forgiven. (p. 253)

John Galsworthy, "Four More Novelists in Profile: An Address," in his Candelabra: Selected Essays and Addresses, *Charles Scribner's Sons, 1933, pp. 249-69.**

ANDRÉ MAUROIS (essay date 1957)

[*Maurois, an extremely versatile French writer, made his most significant contribution to literature as a biographer. Following in the tradition of Lytton Strachey's "new" biography, Maurois believed that a biography should adhere to facts without regard for the subject's reputation. He also espoused the view that a biographer should explore the psychological aspects of personality and that a biographical work should be an interpretive expression of the author. The following excerpt is taken from an English translation of Maurois's* Les trois Dumas (The Titans: A Three-generation Biography of the Dumas); *in it, Maurois commends Dumas's technique of intercalating fictional characters in historical events and offers a brief autobiographical interpretation of such characters as Porthos and Aramis.*]

One generation may be deceived about the value of a work of art: four or five generations rarely are. The lasting and universal popularity of **The Three Musketeers** shows that Dumas, by artlessly expressing his own nature in the persons of his heroes, was responding to that craving for action, strength and generosity which is a fact in all periods and all places. So well adapted is his technique to this type of novel that it has remained a model for all who have since tried their hands at the same form of composition. Dumas, or Dumas-Maquet, based many stories on sources already known, sometimes apocryphal like the *Mémoires* of d'Artagnan, sometimes authentic, like those of Madame de la Fayette, from which the **Vicomte de Bragelonne** was drawn. Madame de la Fayette narrates, without dialogue, the tale of the early loves of Louis XIV, the rupture with Marie Mancini, the meeting with Louise de la Valière, the death of Mazarin and the disgrace of Fouquet. It is all told briefly, soberly, perfectly. The drama is implied rather than expressed. Madame de la Fayette carefully refrains from giving imaginative versions of scenes at which she was not present as an eye-witness.

Caricature of Dumas by Etienne Carjat. The Granger Collection, New York.

Dumas, on the other hand, seizes hold of the characters, of the general framework, and uses everything as grist for his mill. Whenever he comes upon the hint of a scene, he writes it, treating it as he would do on the stage, with calculated effects of surprise, violence or comedy. Madame de la Fayette's delicate line-drawing becomes a collection of coloured, dressed-up figures, faintly caricatured, maybe, but creating the illusion of life. The personages of history are painted without any pretence of detachment. Dumas either loves or hates his people. *His* Mazarin is as antipathetic as the Mazarin presented by the Cardinal de Retz. Dumas takes up the cudgels for Fouquet against Colbert. History demands more subtle treatment. The reader of serials likes his characters to be either black or white.

Above all, and therein lies his secret, Dumas introduces secondary figures into his stories, who are entirely of his own imagining, and through the actions of these unknown persons explains the great events of the past. Sometimes they have actually existed. There is a vicomte de Bragelonne, a shadowy and barely glimpsed presence, in Madame de la Fayette: sometimes they are sheer inventions. The miracle is that the imagined heroes always happen to be on the spot at every crucial moment of genuine history. Athos, standing under the scaffold at the execution of Charles I, treasures his last words. It is to his ears that the famous 'Remember!' is addressed. Athos and

d'Artagnan between them re-establish Charles II on the throne of England. Aramis tries to substitute for Louis XIV the twin brother who later becomes the Man in the Iron Mask. History is brought down to the level of loved and familiar characters and, at the same time, to that of the ordinary reader.

The method is infallible, always on condition that the author has as much temperament as Dumas had. No writer can create heroes who produce the illusion of reality without putting a great deal of himself into them. Molière found within himself both Alceste *and* Philinte; Musset both Octave *and* Coelio. So it was that Dumas divided himself in order to give birth to both Porthos *and* Aramis. Porthos is the incarnation of all that he had inherited from his father, while Aramis embodies the elegance which father and son owed to Davy de la Pailleterie. 'Strong muscles, and finely articulated joints'—there we have Dumas.

Nor must it be forgotten that his moral standards and his philosophy were those, not of the better educated and more thoughtful members of French society, but of the mass of his readers. Sir Walter, that sound and solid Scot, was kept supplied by a moral and artistic providence with virtuous epilogues. Dumas's moral code may be summed up as a love of glory combined with a considerable dose of 'good sense' not entirely free from cynicism. He combined in his own person the Frenchman of the *chansons de geste* and that other of the *fabliaux,* a mixture which, though it does not account for the whole of France, certainly represents a large part of it. Like Rabelais, Dumas loved eating, drinking and irresponsible love-making. If d'Artagnan were not a hero he would be singularly amoral. The Musketeers resembled their creator in this, that they saw no harm in changing mistresses, in having more than one at a time, or in asking them for money. This apart, Dumas's novels were neither indecent nor aggressively immoral. His work, taken as a whole, was in brilliant contrast to that storehouse of macabre accessories which furnished the stock-in-trade of his friends, the romantics. It gave pleasure. (pp. 179-81)

> *André Maurois, "In Which the Man of the Theatre Turns Novelist," in his* The Titans: A Three-generation Biography of the Dumas, *translated by Gerard Hopkins, Harper & Brothers Publishers, 1957, pp. 171-81.*

A. W. RAITT (essay date 1965)

[*Act IV, scene 6 of* Antony *includes a conversation in which the fictive historical dramatist Eugène anticipates the difficulties of employing contemporary settings and themes in the theater. Raitt argues that, through Eugène and his interlocutors, Dumas effectively enunciates the conditions that led to the development of realistic, post-Romantic dramas in France in the 1850s.*]

LA VICOMTESSE

Est-ce que vous faites une préface?

LE BARON DE MARSANNE

Les romantiques font tous des préfaces . . . *Le Constitutionnel* les plaisantait l'autre jour là-dessus avec une grâce . . .

ADÈLE

Vous le voyez, monsieur, vous avez usé, à vous défendre, un temps qui aurait suffi à développer tout un système.

EUGÈNE

Et vous aussi, madame, faites-y attention . . . Vous l'exigez, je ne suis plus responsable de l'ennui . . . Voici mes motifs: la comédie est la peinture des moeurs; le drame, celle des passions. La Révolution, en passant sur notre France, a rendu les hommes égaux, confondu les rangs, généralisé les costumes. Rien n'indique la profession, nul cercle ne renferme telles moeurs ou telles habitudes; tout est fondu ensemble, les nuances ont remplacé les couleurs, et il faut des couleurs et non des nuances au peintre qui veut faire un tableau.

ADÈLE

C'est juste.

LE BARON DE MARSANNE

Cependant, monsieur, *le Constitutionnel*. . .

EUGÉNE, *sans écouter*

Je disais donc que la comédie de moeurs devenait, de cette manière, sinon impossible, du moins très difficile à exécuter. Reste le drame de passion, et ici une autre difficulté se présente. L'histoire nous lègue des faits, ils nous appartiennent par droit d'héritage, ils sont incontestables, ils sont au poète: il exhume les hommes d'autrefois, les revêt de leurs costumes, les agite de leurs passions, qu'il augmente ou diminue selon le point où il veut porter le dramatique. Mais, que nous essayions, nous, au milieu de notre société moderne, sous notre frac gauche et écourté, de montrer à nu le coeur de l'homme, on ne le reconnaîtra pas . . . La ressemblance entre le héros et le parterre sera trop grande, l'analogie trop intime; le spectateur qui suivra chez l'acteur le développement de la passion voudra l'arrêter là où elle se serait arrêtée chez lui; si elle dépasse sa faculté de sentir ou d'exprimer à lui, il ne la comprendra plus, il dira: ''C'est faux; moi, je n'éprouve pas ainsi; quand la femme que j'aime me trompe, je souffre sans doute . . . oui . . . quelque temps . . . mais je ne la poignarde ni ne meurs, et la preuve, c'est que me voilà.'' Puis les cris à l'exagération, au mélodrame, couvrant les applaudissements de ces quelques hommes qui, plus heureusement ou plus malheureusement organisés que les autres, sentent que les passions sont les mêmes au XVᶜ qu'au XIXᶜ siècle, et que le coeur bat d'un sang aussi chaud sous un frac de drap que sous un corselet d'acier. . .

ADÈLE

Eh bien, monsieur, l'approbation de ces quelques hommes vous dédommagerait amplement de la froideur des autres.

ALEXANDRE DUMAS *père*, *Antony*, act IV, sc. 6
(pp. 36-7)

[*Antony* was produced] at the height of the great flowering of Romantic drama. . . . Its frantic emotionalism, its theatrical gestures, its exalted volubility make it a typical example of the dramatic literature of the time, with the important exception that, instead of a historical setting, it has a contemporary one. Dumas, no great theorist but well aware of the interest of this innovation, had the ingenious idea of drawing attention to his audacity and at the same time justifying it by inserting [a] conversation in the fourth act, during a party given by the Vicomtesse de Lacy. Adèle, the heroine, asks Eugène, a dramatist, if he is still writing plays about the Middle Ages, and when he replies that he is, she inquires: 'Mais pourquoi ne pas attaquer un sujet au milieu de notre société moderne?' The Vicomtesse agrees:

C'est ce que je lui répète à chaque instant: ''Faites de l'actualité.'' N'est-ce pas que l'on s'intéresse bien plus à des personnages de notre époque, habillés comme nous, parlant comme nous?

Eugène is persuaded to explain his reasons, after which the discussion moves on and the plot resumes its headlong course. (pp. 37-8)

[One] is conscious of a faint self-irony when Dumas, hitherto a specialist in historical drama, makes Eugène admit that what he writes about is 'toujours du moyen âge'. Dumas seems to have realised sooner than most of his fellow-playwrights that the logical conclusion of the Romantic view of art was complete modernity, and that it was something of an accident that the return to modern times had become bogged down half-way through past history. And so, with commendable forthrightness, he set about writing a play with a wholly contemporary theme and setting. . . . (pp. 38-9)

It is true that Dumas was not the first dramatist to deal with modern themes, nor even the only one of his time. There was the precedent of Diderot's *drame bourgeois* in the eighteenth century, and numerous minor authors were busily scribbling mediocre plays on contemporary subjects in the 1830s and 1840s. Even the Romantics introduced topics of the same kind into their plays, albeit in disguised form. *Chatterton,* though set in eighteenth-century England, contains some pertinent observations on industrial relations; *Ruy Blas* is, among other things, an impassioned plea for the emancipation of the lower classes; and *Angélo,* another costume drama by Hugo, . . . incriminates 'le fait social' for the injustices done to women in society. But Dumas is the only major dramatist among the Romantics to have faced the problem of the social responsibility of the theatre in the modern world by bringing the action of his play right up to the time at which he was writing. (p. 39)

[If] Dumas did not persuade the other Romantics to take to contemporary settings, he did foresee the course which the drama would be forced to follow, though not in the form which he expected. It was true that the spectator at a 'drame de passion' would soon complain that in real life people behaved more calmly and talked less poetically. . . . Eugène's argument that such an objection could be met if the actors were decked out in medieval costume failed to hold good for long. Ten years after *Antony*, the public was coming to think that at no time had anyone lived as depicted in *Hernani* or *Ruy Blas,* and was beginning to hanker after something closer to its own experience both in setting and in emotion. Even in *Antony,* Dumas has not solved that particular problem. The high-flown tirades jar with the modern costume and contrive to suggest that reality is still several removes away. Instead of people realising, as Dumas had hoped, that 'le coeur bat d'un sang aussi chaud sous un frac de drap que sous un corselet d'acier', they became sceptical about the possibility of its ever having beaten as hectically as the Romantic dramatists would have had them believe.

The result of this change in taste was the formation, by about 1850, of a realistic theatre in France, which depended for its effect on what Dumas aptly terms 'la ressemblance entre le héros et le parterre', and which dominated the stage until the last decade of the century. The leading writers of this school—Dumas *fils*, Augier, Labiche—not only brought their characters and settings up to date, but treated subjects which they knew to be close to the hearts of their audiences, and with a mentality which was also that of their audiences. So one finds the theatre transformed both into a mirror for the spectators and into a debating society where the topical talking-points of the day were aired—money in Dumas's *La Question d'argent* and Augier's *La Ceinture dorée*, difficulties of married life in Dumas's *L'Ami des femmes* and Meilhac and Halévy's *Froufrou*, questions of class prejudice in Augier's *Le Gendre de M. Poirier*, the social relations between the sexes in Dumas's *La Dame aux camélias* and *Monsieur Alphonse,* and so on. In so doing, they were fulfilling the programme sketched out for them in *Antony,* for though Dumas does not say so specifically here, the rest of the play makes it clear that he too envisages modern-dress drama as a suitable place for raising controversial issues. Indeed, the problems on which *Antony* centres—the status of illegitimate children, the position of women in marriage, the social consequences of adultery—are precisely those which were to attract the writers of social plays thirty years later. (pp. 40-1)

[Dumas] was well aware of the dangers involved in adopting a combative position on current affairs. *Antony,* for all its contemporary trappings, is scarcely a committed play as we would understand the term nowadays. Yet even the relatively innocuous piece of dialogue [mentioned above] had awkward repercussions for the author. The Baron de Marsanne (a very minor figure in the play) is ridiculed by the fact that he never opens his mouth without making some absurdly flattering reference to *Le Constitutionnel*, the newspaper of the liberal middle classes, which, after having at one time lent lukewarm support to the Romantics, had since 1830 been among their sternest critics. But *Le Constitutionnel* took its revenge on Dumas in 1834, when *Antony* was due to be revived. It claimed that the play was immoral and succeeded in blackmailing Thiers, then Minister of the Interior, into banning it [see the excerpt dated 1834]. Dumas went to law and won his case, but even this trifling incident illustrates the fact that the more authors take it upon themselves to comment on personalities and events of the day, the more they are liable to find their freedom interfered with. (pp. 41-2)

Dumas *père,* unlike his son, was not cut out to be a polemist, either in politics or in literature, and when the Baron de Marsanne says that 'les romantiques font tous des préfaces', Dumas is one of the few who could plead innocent. But he nevertheless had ideas of his own about the theatre, and what he used to call 'le feuilleton', that is to say, this page of dramatic criticism, 'l'apologie du drame moderne', is 'la vraie préface d'*Antony*'. For all its uncertain arguments, its over-simplifications and its fallacies, it might also be called the real preface to the post-Romantic theatre in France. (p. 42)

A. W. Raitt, "Alexandre Dumas père: 'Antony',' in his The Nineteenth Century. Life and Letters in France, Vol. 3, Charles Scribner's Sons, 1965, pp. 36-42.

AMELITA MARINETTI (essay date 1976)

[*Marinetti discerns two mythic cycles of fall and resurrection at the structural and thematic core of* The Count of Monte Cristo.

According to her, these cycles serve as vehicles for reflection on the theme of human competence and independence as arbiters of justice, a concern that Marinetti traces to social and political upheavals in Dumas's France.]

Le Comte de Monte-Cristo contains two mythic cycles, similar in pattern yet different in development and emphasis. The first begins with the hero in a state of relative innocence, followed by a fall which if far more terrible than a modicum of guilt would seem to justify (and therefore resembles the catastrophe of death in the life of man), which in turn leads to a hard-won but spectacular resurrection into a position of power far beyond any known by ordinary mortals. This cycle, covering Dantès' imprisonment, escape, and discovery of the treasure willed to him by Father Faria, is contained within the first twenty-four chapters of the book, less than a fourth of the whole. The remainder of the novel recounts another cycle, carrying the hero from a position of noble but contaminated omniscience to a second fall, this time clearly justified, and at last to an ambiguous second resurrection. This is the story of Monte-Cristo's revenge on those who put him in prison, his recompense to his loyal employer, his increasing loss of faith in the rightness of his mission, and his return to the world of death through the two young lovers he has chosen as his spiritual descendants, followed by their rebirth and his own disappearance from the known world.

The essential idea of the fall, at least until its reinterpretation in Camus' work, has been that of a basically innocent man or lesser god, of great stature and good intentions, who oversteps the bounds permitted to aspiring humanity, falls into error, and is severely punished. The basic innocence of Dantès is more evident than in most other versions of the myth. Capable sailor, devoted son, faithful lover, totally honest in his relations with the world, he is not without a certain lack of foresight and a too-easy unawareness of the misery and evil lurking in the hearts of his associates. Owing money to the untrustworthy Caderousse, he departed on a long voyage leaving his old father with barely enough money to last until his return. Once back, with the promise of promotion to captain and marriage to the girl he loves, he is oblivious to the enraged jealousy of Fernand and Danglars who covet, respectively, the woman and the job.

Of deeper interest, however, than these slight implications of neglect or indifference on the part of the young hero is the suggestion made by Dantès himself at the height of happiness in his forthcoming marriage and position that innocence alone cannot merit happiness: "Il me semble," he reflects to Danglars, "que l'homme n'est pas fait pour être si facilement heureux! Le bonheur est comme ces palais des îles enchantées dont les dragons gardent les portes. Il faut combattre pour le conquérir." . . . (pp. 261-62)

The form of Dantès' fall is a solitary and interminable confinement which is as close to death as a living man can get. The fallen hero disappears at this point and is transformed into the dead hero who will eventually be resurrected. According to Joseph Campbell, the myth of the resurrected hero is universal in scope, originally concerning a god or the incarnation of one in a human being. When the hero is not divine in nature, the story concerns his leaving the world of everyday existence and going into a strange region where fabulous forces are at work; there a decisive victory is won, and he returns with the power to grant favors to his fellow men. His adventures usually involve instruction, testing, and transmission of power by a father figure of godlike character. Everywhere in mythical thought truly creative acts have their origin in some sort of dying to the world, after which the hero "comes back as one reborn, made great and filled with creative power."

The analogy which Dumas intended between his hero and the Christian version of the resurrection myth is apparent in the title itself, and it is interesting to recall that the element of the novel which first occurred to its author was its title, the island of that name which he happened upon while on a hunting expedition with Prince Napoleon in 1841. Moreover, in describing the coat of arms adopted by the Count to go with his new fortune and title (both derived from the island), the narrator says that it is a gold-colored mountain on a blue sea, with a red cross at the summit, "ce qui pouvait aussi bien être une allusion à son nom rappelant le Calvaire, que la passion de Notre-Seigneur a fait une montagne plus précieuse que l'or, et la croix infâme que son sang divin a faite sainte, qu'à quelque souvenir personnel de souffrance et de régénération enseveli dans la nuit du passé de cet homme mystérieux." . . . (pp. 262-63)

Dumas reiterates throughout the story that Dantès' imprisonment . . . was a death for him, and that the Count of Monte-Cristo was a man who had returned from the grave. Dantès' entry into the town jail (even before going to the omnious Château d'If) is rendered fateful by the three resounding knocks on the heavy door, by the young man's fearful hesitation on the threshold, and by a reference to the air on the other side as "other," noxious and heavy. . . . Dantès soon comes to look upon himself as dead and to think of the world outside as that of the living. The spiritual equivalent of physical death comes progressively with his loss of pride (he comes to long to be with other prisoners, even the dregs of humanity), his loss of all sense of time, and finally his loss of identity, becoming merely "Number 34." (p. 263)

As was the case in Greek mythology, a journey into the realm of death must involve a descent into an underground place. Dantès' cell is below ground, with only a small shaft of light coming from above, and the place he constructs on the Island of Monte-Cristo after his escape is set deep in an underground cavern. . . . [For] the resurrection of Valentine the Count chooses this same underground cavern, into which her lover Maximilien must descend as did Orpheus in search of his lost love.

The process of Dantès' resurrection begins in prison, long before the possibility of actual escape presents itself. As is often the case in myth, it is brought about through the agency of a semidivine creature who comes to the aid of the hero, here the all-wise Faria. It is only at the very threshold of real, physical death . . . that Dantès first hears the scratching of this other prisoner and finds in the hope of a companion something to live for. But the rebirth that is Faria's gift to Dantès involves far more than release from prison. Through Faria Dantès is completely regenerated into a new man, with all the wisdom, knowledge, wealth, and strength of character to make it possible for him to play the role of a god in the eyes of others. . . . It is he who is able to penetrate the mystery of why Dantès was accused and locked up indefinitely without ever being brought to trial, thus bringing the innocent young man to his first confrontation with real evil. In this way, although Faria is himself angelic in nature, he plays the mythic role of serpent who presents to the hero the knowledge of good and evil. Finally, Faria provides Dantès with the means of using all his acquired knowledge and strength to real advantage by giving him the secret of an immense hidden fortune. Even more important to the mythic aspects of the story is the fact that the escape plans of the two men end in frustration and failure, and

that it is ultimately only through Faria's death, and Dantès' sewing himself into the shroud, that the latter is able to escape.

At this point the story incorporates another widespread myth, that of the father-seeker and the father-slayer. (p. 264)

There is no doubt that Faria is a father figure for Dantès. The latter calls upon Faria long after his death as his "second père . . . toi qui m'as donné la liberté, la science, la richesse." . . . Dantès' natural father is seen from the beginning as a helpless old man, incapable of doing anything to aid his son in his hour of need, or even of preventing himself from dying of starvation once deprived of his son's support. Dantès is in desperate need of another father, if he is to be reborn as another man, one capable of rising above and triumphing over the weight of evil which threatens to crush him. Mythic thought requires that a price be paid for such a miracle. The life of the father must be sacrificed, symbolically if not actually. Birth symbolism is very strong in this episode of the novel: the birth canal is represented by the narrow passage dug between the two cells, the womb by the shroud in which Dantès substitutes himself for Faria, the birth cries by the terrible shout uttered by Dantès just before he hits the surface of the sea (of life) when the guards whom he expected to dig him a grave throw him into the ocean instead.

Another theme which is widespread in mythology and closely connected to primitive ritual is that of the testing of the hero. In ritual this involves severe exercises of severance whereby the mind is radically cut away from attitudes appropriate to the old life patterns, in order to prepare the individual for a new state in life, such as puberty or marriage. After the tests there follows an interval of more or less extended retirement, from which the person returns to ordinary life as a new man, as though reborn. In myth, the hero must pass through a series of trials aimed at rendering him worthy of the favor he asks of the gods or the exalted position he is to fill (i.e., the ordeal of Psyche and the labors of Hercules). . . .

The theme of testing plays an important part in the novel of Dumas, both in the prison episode and in the subsequent ten years during which the Count prepares for his revenge. It is repeated at the end of the story as an epilogue. The first test of Dantès' moral fiber comes when Faria is half paralyzed by an attack of apoplexy which puts an end to the two prisoners' hope of escaping together. Although Faria urges his young friend to escape alone, Dantès refuses to leave and vows to stay with him to the end of his life. The reward for this act of loyalty and sacrifice is the secret of Faria's treasure, in the reality of which Dantès refuses for a long time to believe. The crux of the testing within the Château d'If is the withstanding of pain while maintaining hope and moral values. The self-testing to which Monte-Cristo submits after his escape from prison is for the purpose of hardening him to the pain and death of others, essential to one embarked on a spectacular and merciless revenge. (p. 265)

When the resurrected hero reappears, as though from nowhere, it is to rescue the older Morrel from bankruptcy and suicide, to save Albert from Roman bandits, to bedazzle all Paris by his fabulous wealth and apparent omniscience. More than this, the reader sees Dantès as a Protean figure who is able to appear as entirely different people in different places, and within minutes of a prior appearance. Thus, like his mythic predecessors, he is not only reborn, but comes back to the world a totally different person from the Dantès who had entered prison twenty-four years earlier. (p. 266)

Monte-Cristo's identity, unknown to all but Mercédès, is revealed to each enemy in turn, but only when the latter is on the brink of death, madness, or utter ruin, and is no longer in a position to retaliate. Each revelation of the name of Dantès is a moment of such intense drama, is so devastating to the enemy who learns it, and so exhilarating to Monte-Cristo, that one is reminded of the importance in myth and religion of the very name of the deity. . . . In a rapidly shifting social and political environment, the status and role of the individual, therefore his identity, are a matter of doubt for him. Small wonder that for Dumas and his contemporaries who had grown up in the post-Revolutionary era, there was untold satisfaction in the fact that the pronouncing of one's name alone could produce utter despair in one's enemies, and hope out of despair in those who merited one's gratitude.

Unfortunately, Monte-Cristo's apotheosis, splendid as it is, contains within it the seeds of a new fall. Dantès' state of relative innocence had lasted only until the gift of power and knowledge bestowed on him by Faria offered the possibility of taking action to free himself. It appears that when man defends himself against evil he inevitably becomes to some extent corrupted by it. A basic implication of the myth of the fall is that perfect happiness is necessarily accompanied by perfect innocence and trust, i.e., man before the fall. Knowledge is equated with the temptation to evil. Ambition and inventiveness, which demonstrate an aggressive and analytic attitude toward the universe, are associated with rebellion against God. The children of Cain were both wicked and inventive (inventing the harp, the organ, metal work, planning cities) as was Prometheus (who brought not only fire and light, but the sciences, city building, agriculture, transportation, and music, to man). Thus competence is idealized, but it is also suspect. . . . (pp. 266-67)

Monte-Cristo was warned very early, at the brink of his discovery of Faria's treasure, that evil lurks in this new power. A poisonous snake lay coiled at the entrance of the cave like a guardian of the treasure. Yet he clings to the belief that he has been chosen as an agent of Providence for the punishment of the wicked: "Je me sentais poussé comme le nuage de feu passant dans le ciel pour aller brûler les villes maudites." . . . He receives each of his early successes as confirmations of his calling. His pride goes to greater extremes when he boasts of finding pleasure unknown to other men in struggling "contre la nature qui est Dieu, et contre le monde qui peut bien passer pour le diable" (II, 341). Nowhere is the exaggerated pride of Monte-Cristo more evident than in the scene following his promise to Mercédès to spare her son in the duel between them, a forbearance which must necessarily entail his own death. More unbearable to him than the idea of death or of giving up his great project is the fear of being thought defeated, the victim rather than the agent of Providence. Above all else, he is anxious to let the world know in some way that he has stopped the course of Providence *by his own will alone*. (p. 267)

This immoderate pride is vanquished when the Count perceives that the pursuit of his revenge entails harming the innocent. The discovery that Villefort's daughter Valentine, about to be poisoned by her stepmother, is loved by his beloved protégé Maximilien, and even more the discovery of the death of Villefort's son, only a child, both of which situations he brought about himself, are the events that truly shake his faith in his mission. He can no longer number himself among the gods because they have the power to limit the results of their actions—chance is not stronger than they. Symbolic of this prob-

lem is the red elixir, the recipe for which Monte-Cristo gives to the ambitious poisoner, Mme de Villefort. On the exact dosage depends whether it cures, injures, or kills. Man can control the dosage of a drug, but once he has attained supreme knowledge and power he cannot control the dosage so as to do only justice and no evil.

This impasse which Monte-Cristo must confront between the legitimate aspirations of man for a social order closer to his conception of justice, and his inability to control the power unleashed by his new freedom to act, is an echo of the central ambivalence of the age. Men of all shades of political opinion were convinced that the forces released by the two revolutions, the French and the industrial, would inevitably bring tremendous changes. But some felt that these changes would be in the direction of greater social justice through scientific rationality, while others were filled with dread of coming chaos and horror. As Jacob Talman has expressed it: "The progressives of all hues spoke of the rights of man: the reactionaries countered with the malignant fickleness of man and the omnipotent, benevolent wisdom of God." Dumas himself was basically republican and liberal in spirit. But he felt horror for the excesses of the Revolution, and he blamed Napoleon for what he had cost in the blood of Frenchmen.

The last chapters of the novel are devoted to Monte-Cristo's attempt to resolve this problem. The resolution involves, on the one hand, his own efforts to do good deeds in order to add to the "poids jeté dans la balance en regard du plateau ou j'ai laissé tomber le mal" . . . , and on the other hand, an attempt to relive, through the agency of Maximilien, who is as a son to him, the whole experience of death and rebirth through testing and the sacrifice of the father. This time the goal is not revenge or even justice, but love alone, and Maximilien is reborn not as a monster of power and knowledge but as a purely good man. (p. 268)

[Monte-Cristo] has already saved Valentine from death by poison. But it is not enough simply to reunite the young lovers. Maximilien must believe Valentine dead, must be ready to die himself, not just immediately in the first throes of grief, but after a period of time which would dull the pain of a less devoted lover and give him hope of finding solace elsewhere. Like Dantès many years earlier, he must go to the very door of death in order to be born again into the perfect bliss of love. Only thus will he become worthy of possessing Valentine, "un bonheur infini, immense, inconnu, un bonheur trop grand, trop complet, trop divin pour ce monde." . . .

The temptation motif . . . is very clearly analogous to that of Christ when it is Morrel's turn to be tested. Monte-Cristo offers him his entire fortune, reminding him of all the power and pleasure it provides, if only he consent to go on living without Valentine. When Maximilien withstands this temptation, Monte-Cristo chooses for the scene of resurrection (of both Morrel and Valentine) the underground cavern that is his palace and has Morrel enter the realm of death through taking hashish, which the latter thinks is a fatal drug. As Morrel is recovering consciousness Monte-Cristo says to Valentine: "Désormais vous ne devez plus vous séparer sur la terre; car pour vous retrouver il se précipitait dans la tombe." . . . Even the theme of the sacrifice of the father reappears, for Monte-Cristo, after leaving them wealth in the form of all his European property, disappears into some mysterious realm, probably never to be seen again. His final message to Morrel is, "Attendre et espérer!" This is the essence of faith and trust in God, and the opposite of the implacable force and omniscient wisdom of the self he had spent most of his adult life to construct and unleash upon the world.

The overall theme of *Le Comte de Monte-Cristo* is a deeply ambivalent one. Although human independence and competence, in the person of Monte-Cristo, have been shown imperfect and even dangerous, they have brought about a much closer approximation of justice than this particular society offered before his coming. Therefore, despite the shedding of a little innocent (though shown to be potentially guilty) blood in the death of Villefort's young son, it cannot be said that Dantès would have done better to wait and hope. On the contrary, only because a Monte-Cristo has taken on man's guilt, can a Morrel live in innocence and follow his admonition to "attendre et espérer." (p. 269)

Amelita Marinetti, "Death, Resurrection, and Fall in Dumas' 'Comte de Monte-Cristo'," in The French Review, *Vol. L, No. 2, December, 1976, pp. 260-69.*

RICHARD S. STOWE   (essay date 1976)

[*Stowe elaborates on Dumas's methods and achievement in* The Three Musketeers, *providing interesting insights into his skillful use of historical events, his emphasis on situation and episode, and his delineation of character through dialogue and action, rather than description and narration.*]

If Dumas had written nothing but *The Three Musketeers* his fame would have been assured. Certainly no other work of his is better known and certainly none has surpassed it in consistent and widespread popularity. It remains also, as a total achievement, Dumas's finest novel. For this last reason, especially, it is almost an inevitable choice for the reader who wishes not only to sample Dumas's storytelling at its best but to examine the way he uses historical materials and builds a novel. (p. 66)

Far from being a mere backdrop, [history] forms the very fabric of the tale. Widely known historical events provide the basis for important actions in the novel just as history supplies its major characters. But secondary episodes and less prominent characters are also grounded in fact. The siege of La Rochelle and the assassination of the Duke of Buckingham, for example, are immediately recognizable historical realities. But the story of the queen's diamonds which dominates the first half of the book, though seeming too fantastic to be real, can also be documented. The same is true of the hints of Richelieu's romantic interest in the queen and even of such a detail as Buckingham's order to close the English ports while the duplicate studs are being made. . . .

Besides the obviously historical figures in the novel—Louis XIII, Anne d'Autriche, Richelieu, and Buckingham—the large majority of other characters too have counterparts in history. D'Artagnan, Athos, Porthos, and Aramis were all real people. Milady, Constance Bonacieux, and de Wardes have all been identified, or at least plausibly associated, with known individuals. A host of characters mentioned in passing bear historical names. Even John Felton, Milady's young English "jailer," was in fact, as in the book, the assassin of the Duke of Buckingham. But in *Les Trois Mousquetaires* Dumas was writing a novel, not history. If a knowledge of history is unnecessary in order to enjoy it—indeed, too thorough a knowledge may be a distraction—a glance at the principal changes Dumas made and his probable reasons for them can most effectively illuminate his methods and his conception of the historical romance. (p. 68)

Dumas drew the character of d'Artagnan and the names of Athos, Porthos, and Aramis [from Gatien Courtilz de Sandras's *Mémoirs de Monsieur d'Artagnan*]. . . . The opening episodes—d'Artagnan's departure from home, the encounter at Meung (including the characters of Rochefort and Milady), d'Artagnan's settling in Paris, his meeting with M. de Tréville and his three future friends, his first duels and the fight with Richelieu's guards, the characters (but not the names) of M. and Mme Bonacieux—also come from Courtilz, though incidents and characters all undergo development at Dumas's hands. Much of this development comes from Dumas's rich imagination and love of concrete detail; much comes also from his knowledge of the period absorbed from his extensive reading of other . . . memoirs. But the direction that the development takes is to a large degee determined by one significant change that Dumas made in his hero: he made him ten years older than he was in history.

Thus lifted from his proper historical context and placed in another one, d'Artagnan becomes a fictional creation. The events in which this fictional d'Artagnan participates were real ones, as he was a real person, but because his role in them is an imagined one both characters and events now partake of a new reality, that of the novel. It is in terms of this new reality and its exigencies that d'Artagnan develops and acts. Dumas takes such liberties as he needs to with fact; where facts are unavailable or unusable he has a framework for invention.

Pure invention plays a greater part in the creation of Athos, Porthos, and Aramis simply because Dumas had less to work with. Less was known of their historical models and their role in [the *Mémoires de Monsieur d'Artagnan*] is more episodic than the one Dumas chose to give them. At the same time, as in the case of d'Artagnan, Dumas strengthens the sense of their historical validity by having them perform, whenever possible, deeds that though not performed by them were nonetheless really executed by someone.

The character of Milady reveals further aspects of Dumasian inventiveness. Again Dumas starts with a character he found in the *Mémoires de M. d'Artagnan*. As enigmatic and mysterious there as in *Les Trois Mousquetaires*, she is much less than the pervasive nemesis of d'Artagnan and his companions that she becomes in Dumas's hands. He develops her as a character and expands her role by both appropriation and invention. He borrows from history, giving her in the affair of the diamond studs the role that had actually been played by a former mistress of Buckingham, Lady Carlisle. He borrows from another book of spurious memoirs attributed to Courtilz de Sandras the important episode in which d'Artagnan, replacing de Wardes in Milady's chamber for a night, discovers the fleur-de-lis branded on her shoulder. And he enriches her characterization from his own imagination by such devices as the past he attributes to her—former *galérienne* and repudiated wife of Athos—and by having her. . . . motivate John Felton to kill Buckingham. (pp. 69-70)

Only a word needs to be said about Louis XIII, Anne d'Autriche, Richelieu, and Buckingham. Though none of them . . . would have had contact with d'Artagnan, each of them otherwise plays substantially his authentic role. In his depiction of them Dumas follows contemporary sources faithfully, simplifying and dramatizing more than he changes. If he invents dialogue for them and puts them in imaginary situations with more-or-less fictitious characters, he always does so with skill and versimilitude. For these reasons the characterizations remain, in their broad lines, consistent with history. Such consistency also fits Dumas's aims as a novelist. It was manifestly because he wanted to evoke these particular personages and their period that he transported his musketeer heroes back in time. His task then was to portray them and their drama as convincingly as he could. (p. 70)

[The] action of *Les Trois Mousquetaires,* like its characters, is drawn substantially from historical sources, or at least from what Dumas believed to be such. As he did with characters, Dumas adapts and alters events; his version of the siege of La Rochelle is typical of his procedure.

Since the siege in reality was long, he compresses the action. Selecting key episodes to develop, he skips over others and over long periods of time in between, while still observing chronological sequence. He makes the historical siege more integral to the action by making it a confrontation between his characters as well as a military action directed by Richelieu against a Protestant stronghold:

> Richelieu, as everyone knows, had been in love with the queen. . . .
>
> For Richelieu, then, it was a question not only of ridding France of an enemy but of avenging himself on a rival. . . .
>
> Richelieu knew that in fighting England he was fighting Buckingham . . . that in humiliating England in the eyes of Europe he was humiliating Buckingham in the eyes of the queen.
>
> For his part, Buckingham, while defending the honor of England, was moved by concerns exactly comparable to those of the cardinal; Buckingham also was pursuing a personal vengeance. . . .
>
> Consequently the true stake in this match, engaged in by the two most powerful kingdoms at the whim of two men in love, was a simple glance from Anne of Austria.
>
> (Chapter XLI, ''Le Siège de La Rochelle'')

Dumas obviously knew his public well enough to recognize that passion would have broader appeal than politics. But however far-fetched and melodramatic this interpretation of the issues at stake at La Rochelle may be, it could be admitted without necessarily doing violence to recorded events. In the case of the musketeers Dumas handled matters somewhat differently. Though d'Artagnan, Athos, Porthos, and Aramis did not participate in the siege, the known presence there of the King's Musketeers lends plausibility to their activities. Yet Dumas does not hesitate to introduce a completely fictional incident—the taking of the Bastion Saint-Gervais—to give them the kind of adventure he wants them to have just then and to provide a transition he deems necessary between other episodes.

In and around such inventions, as well as in the web of real events, Dumas incorporates countless little touches—details of manners and dress, passing incidents and allusions, familiar or unusual names—which all contribute concretely to the "feel" of the period. When a real name or a genuine incident can be used to heighten the sense of historical authenticity, Dumas rarely fails to do so, be it a signature on an order or a ballet for Louis XIII to dance.

But Dumas can and does slip on occasion. Wrong and inconsistent spelling abounds in his novels, especially in the case of foreign names. His classic and most frequently cited historical error occurs in the d'Artagnan trilogy: he several times uses house numbers, which were not introduced in Paris until 150 years after the era in which he set these novels. More than once, too, he innocently refers to streets by their nineteenth century names rather than by those they bore two centuries earlier. . . . He assigns a different date to Milady's safe-conduct pass from Richelieu each of the three times he quotes it, though this may be a discreet attempt at masking a potentially more obvious error in chronology. Such slips, though numerous, are rarely significant and they commonly escape all but the most attentive reader. They certainly do not constitute a real deformation of history—least of all by a writer who, even in his most serious moments, could lay no claim to being either a precise or a scientific historian.

But if Dumas was never a scientific historian, he was first, last, and always a dramatist. Both in their conception and their execution his novels, no less surely than his plays, reveal his essentially dramatic vision of the world. This vision is reflected in Dumas's incomparable sense of situation, his instinctive reduction of complex or abstract issues to concrete human conflicts, his awareness of the roles—often multiple—that individuals play in their constantly varying confrontations. It is expressed through all the devices, if not all the dimensions, of drama, but most tellingly in the primary importance he attaches to action and episode as opposed to narrative and description.

In *Les Trois Mousquetaires* we are plunged immediately into the action: ''The first Monday of April, 1625, the town of Meung, where the author of the *Roman de la Rose* was born, seemed to be in the throes of as total a revolution as if the Huguenots had come to make of it a second La Rochelle.'' In this setting—evoked in terms of movement and mood, not physical description—Dumas's ''Don Quixote at eighteen,'' riding his yellow *bidet de Béarn*, makes his entrance. When the reader needs to know what brings him there a flashback permits the exposition to be accomplished by equally concrete, dramatic means, and the reader is quickly transported again into the midst of the crowd watching d'Artagnan's arrival. A moment later the insult occurs, d'Artagnan's antagonists are introduced, and the plot is engaged in a flurry of verbal exchanges and swordplay. Four short paragraphs at the end of the chapter carry d'Artagnan from Meung to Paris, establish him there, and leave him ready to call on M. de Tréville. In contrast with the full development of the events at Meung, the very conciseness of these paragraphs emphasizes Dumas's approach to his story as a series of episodes connected only by as much narrative transition as is absolutely necessary. The prologue over, the curtain is now ready to rise on Act I.

Dominance of dialogue and action, thus apparent from the opening pages, is a constant in *Les Trois Mousquetaires* as it is in virtually all of Dumas's novels. There is narration, of course, and explanation, wherever they are essential (for example, in the passage cited from Chapter XLI). . . . But chapter after chapter filled with rapid dialogue speeds the tale along and lets the characters act it out. The sense of speed is underscored by the terseness of the narration, the series of short paragraphs—often single sentences—that ordinarily comprise it. It is often observed that Dumas's paragraphing and extended dialogues reflect his desire to capitalize on being paid by the line of printed text. This may be true, and seems especially so in some of the more sprawling novels, but the stylistic effect remains. It too often calls to mind the crackling dialogue and rush of events in the plays to be entirely accidental. And the devices of melodrama—surprise, coincidence, terror—which are exploited here as in the plays are all dependent on the maintenance of pace, a fact of which Dumas would be the last to be unaware.

Les Trois Mousquetaires is built around three principal historical actions—the queen's diamonds, the siege of La Rochelle, and the assassination of Buckingham—which are like the acts in a drama on a grand scalé. Against and within this framework Dumas's characters work out their destinies. This underlying structural simplicity in a plot rich in surface complications and unexpected twists further reminds us that Dumas was also a playwright. Characters are painted in broad strokes and elaborated cumulatively rather than analytically, through their deeds and words rather than reflection about them. Suspense and comic relief are manipulated with skill and faultless timing— witness the juxtaposition of Porthos's amusing courtship of Mme Coquenard and d'Artagnan's melodramatic "wooing" of Milady, or d'Artagnan's return home wearing the clothes of Milady's maid after the violent scene in her chamber and his hairbreadth escape. Perhaps the most masterly—and in a sense most subtly theatrical—episode in the book is the taking of the Bastion Saint-Gervais, with its superb mixture of high comedy and genuine suspense, real heroism and burlesque. And if other proof is needed of the justness of the term *"roman-drame"* ("novel-drama") that Sigaux applies to Dumas's historical romances, one need look no farther than the chapter endings. Designed to whet the appetite of the *feuilleton* reader for the next installment, they slice through the book like so many breathtaking "curtains," compelling the reader to turn the page and let the next act commence. (pp. 70-4)

As in his plays, Dumas used tried and true methods in his novels as long as they worked. Technical innovations held little interest for him as such; style was something he admired in other writers but was too busy to concern himself with in his own writing beyond saying what he wanted to say simply, directly, and entertainingly.

But, having examined his methods, we have still said little about Dumas's real achievement in *Les Trois Mousquetaires*. Whatever liberties and mistakes may be ascribed to him, in this novel he has produced a convincing illusion of historical reality, bringing a remote period to life with exceptional immediacy and concreteness. He has told a rich and absorbing tale of adventure with matchless verve, humor, and inventiveness. And he has created memorable characters, at once types and artfully individualized, simple but always believable. To a degree he did all these things in his plays also, but even his greatest theatrical triumphs neither penetrated far beyond the borders of France nor outlived his century. The enduring international popularity of *Les Trois Mousquetaires* is ample demonstration that here Dumas has transcended limits of country and time to attain universality.

Universality in characters: Milady—evil personified, the classic *femme fatale;* Athos, Porthos, Aramis—together symbols of daring and fraternal loyalty; separately noble, pompous and devious, mysterious, engaging and secretive; d'Artagnan—the most complex and greatest creation of them all—archetypal Gascon, rash yet prudent, courageous and sentimental, idealistic yet shrewdly ambitious. Like these characters, a gallery of others, great and small, live both in and beyond the pages of history and romance.

Universality in vision: D'Artagnan arriving in Meung is every cowboy arriving, ready for adventure, in a little western town, as he is also every young hero of a *Bildungsroman* embarking on his education in the ways of the world. Conflicts assume

Dumas with the American actress Adah Isaacs Menken.

the dimensions of struggles between right and wrong, good and evil, while conversely nations go to war because their leaders, for all their rank and power, are no less subject to the very human failings of jealousy and vengefulness.

Universality in theme: The idealism of youth, the thirst for glory, the thrill of worlds to conquer and the urgency of noble causes to defend, readiness to risk all for the sake of friendship or love—such are the themes and values embodied in the world of d'Artagnan and the musketeers as conceived by Dumas. But if they reflect first of all his own Romantic outlook, they also speak to a deeper Romanticism, inherent perhaps in human nature, that knows no limits of time or place. In this appeal to universal feelings and strivings lies the secret of the fascination of this perennially youthful work. (pp. 74-5)

Richard S. Stowe, in his Alexandre Dumas père, *Twayne Publishers, 1976, 164 p.*

F.W.J. HEMMINGS (essay date 1979)

[*As part of his biography* Alexandre Dumas: The King of Romance, *Hemmings explores the underlying appeal of several of Dumas's most popular works:* Antony, The Tower of Nesle, Travels in Switzerland, *and* The Three Musketeers. *According to Hemmings,* Antony *achieved "universal appeal" by courting social revolutionaries and conservatives alike, while* The Tower of Nesle *fascinated audiences with its reversal of traditional social and sexual roles. In addition, Hemmings focuses on the attractions of Dumas's narrative style in* Travels in Switzerland *and discusses the escapist and sexual aspects of* The Three Musketeers.]

[*Antony* is] best described as a modern tragedy, that is to say, a play set in contemporary society but ending with a catastrophe. Previously, all plays with contemporary settings, from Molière down to Eugène Scribe, had been as a matter of course comedies, with the exception of a few experimental imitations of the German *bürgerliches Trauerspiel;* and conversely, any play written in the tragic mode, whether classical or romantic, was almost invariably set in the distant past. But with *Antony,* Dumas did away with this convention, and inaugurated the tradition that was to culminate, in the latter part of the century, in the dramatic masterpieces of Ibsen, Strindberg, and Chekhov.

His theme—adultery—was a peculiarly modern one too, at least in the way he treated it. Phèdre is no more than a would-be adulteress; Desdemona, an unjustly suspected one. In Adèle d'Hervey, however, Dumas created a heroine who is an unfaithful wife and yet an object more of pity than of reprobation. Here he may be said to have founded a different kind of dynasty, since Adèle is in some important sense the prototype of both Anna Karenina and Fontane's Effi Briest. (p. 72)

The first night of *Antony* . . . was one of the most memorable premières in the annals of romantic drama. As had happened with *Henri III et sa cour,* it was the curtain lines that whipped up the fever; there was a particularly effective one at the end of the first act when Antony, in order to make it impossible for Adèle d'Hervey to have him moved out of her house to more suitable quarters (he had been brought in badly injured after a street accident) tears away his bandages, crying before he faints from renewed loss of blood: 'And now, I may stay, may I not?' But Dumas knew it was the third act that would make or break the play; the last scene came nearer to an enactment of rape than anything previously attempted on the stage. . . . The act ended with a vivid piece of dumb show. Antony appears on the balcony behind the window, breaks a pane of glass, climbs in, walks over to the door and bolts it; as Adèle, startled at the sound, emerges from her bedroom, he thrusts a handkerchief over her mouth and draws her back through the bedroom door. As the curtain fell, there was a brief moment of absolute silence in the theatre, and then a great roar followed by the sound of frantic clapping which went on for a full five minutes. Dumas's audacity had paid off once more. (p. 74)

Even when due allowance is made for Dumas's consummate stagecraft and for the excitement generated, in this post-revolutionary period of ideological effervescence, by the audacity of certain tirades he put in the mouth of his hero, the spectacular success of *Antony* in 1831 is not easily explained if one confines oneself to an examination of the bare bones of the text. How was it that Dumas managed to arouse in his whole audience, irrespective of differences of age and sex—and not just on this first occasion but whenever and wherever the play was put on in France during the July Monarchy—such a universally responsive reaction, so that young girls dissolved into tears, young men shouted themselves hoarse, and even the respectable middle-aged burgher took off his gloves and clap and went home feeling something akin to the cathartic purification of the mind that great tragedy is supposed to produce?

The answer appears to be that Dumas had, by sleight-of-hand that almost amounts to a stroke of genius, succeeded in pro-

viding his play with an ambiguous message which satisfied the rebels and yet did not offend the conservatives. Antony, with his brandished dagger, had the air of threatening all the sacrosanct institutions of the time, and like a new Samson to be blindly shaking to pieces the two central pillars of bourgeois society, the sanctity of marriage and the inviolability of the home. This adulterer, this blasphemer against the holy of holies, was the undoubted hero of the play; every word, every act of his, from beginning to end, was calculated to arouse a thrill of sympathetic emotion among the younger members of the audience. Conversely, the wronged husband is given no say; he is not even in court, he remains an absent figure throughout, never appearing until the last scene. He returns in the guise of an avenging angel to purge his dishonour; but our sympathies, by this time, are entirely on the side of the guilty pair whom public opinion would expect him to punish. The question is, how shall Adèle be saved, not from his violence but, what is far worse, from the blighting contumely that was the lot of the woman taken in adultery? In the few moments that precede his expected irruption, as the locked door rattles and the angry man's shouts can be clearly heard, Antony asks Adèle whether she would prefer death to loss of reputation. 'I would beg for it on bended knees,' she replies. 'With my dying breath I would bless my murderer.' So he stabs her as he holds her in his arms, a second before the outraged Colonel d'Hervey bursts into the room.

But this is not all. The romantic hero, having committed the ultimate crime of murder, proceeds in effect to pay supreme tribute to established social values. The adulteress dies, her death being midway between suicide and execution; but, more fortunate than her successor Anna Karenina, she is spared the worse torture of public humiliation, and is even granted a complete posthumous rehabilitation. Antony, turning to the horrified husband and pointing to the butchered body of his wife, utters the sublime lie that will still all slanderous tongues: 'Aye, she is dead. She was resisting me, so I killed her.' In these two brief sentences, Antony transforms Adèle, in the eyes of the world, from a weak-willed wanton into a chaste martyr, more unsullied even than Lucretia, since Lucretia was at least raped before she fell on the sword.

Antony, as socially disruptive a play as had been seen in the nineteenth century, thus ends in a superb gesture of reconciliation, and the values that had been so eloquently assailed from the start are finally seen to be implicitly accepted even by the rebel who had denounced and discarded them. It was not, after all, a revolutionary play, but one that played at being revolutionary; the last line put everything right. (pp. 75-6)

Too little systematic investigation has been undertaken of the factors that give certain works of dubious literary merit lasting popularity on the stage for one to do more than speculate on the cause of the perennial fascination that *La Tour de Nesle* exerted over its audiences in the nineteenth century. In a Europe where monarchy as yet retained . . . much of its ancient aura and prestige, the average man could still experience a delicious thrill at the spectacle of a solitary individual, without rights or privileges, defying, and successfully defying for a while, the limitless power of the wearer of the crown. This theme, which Schiller was probably the first to exploit in *Wilhelm Tell,* gave Dumas the inspiration for the climactic prison scene in his third act, where Buridan, bound hand and foot, lying in a dungeon, facing the prospect of execution without trial on the morrow, is visited by the Queen, come to gloat sadistically over her captive. By revealing to her his knowledge of the guilty secrets of her past and by threatening to have the documentary proof placed in the King's hands unless she not only releases him but has him appointed first minister, he turns the tables on her; it is the Queen now who meekly obeys the dictates of her transfigured subject. Such a sudden reversal of fortunes derives, no doubt, from the stock-in-trade of the traditional melodrama, but the fact that the tiger, in this instance, is a woman and the tamer a man introduces an element of paradox into the situation, for in terms of the conventional scenario, it is always a male potentate, in one guise or another, who is shown lording it over the quailing girl martyr.

As one examines more closely the problematic mechanics of the spell cast by *La Tour de Nesle* over several generations of playgoers, the core image demanding evaluation reveals itself as this sinister 'dark tower' . . . , which on certain nights blazes with lights, while in the grey dawns that follow, the sluggish currents of the Seine regularly cast up on to its banks the blood-boltered corpses of handsome young men, always strangers to the city and, to judge by their apparel, of no mean birth. The nymphomaniac queen and her accomplices have no trouble in attracting, on tempting assignations, young blades always ready for an intrigue spiced with mystery. Having spent the night in their arms, these Messalinas leave them to hired ruffians to despatch; the lifeless bodies are then thrown into the river and the great ladies' bouts of debauchery remain a well-guarded secret. The myth this story incarnates reaches beyond the fairly hackneyed correlation between love and death or, more properly, between carnality and mortality; it connects with the creepy horror aroused in most men by accounts of female spiders devouring their diminutive mates after copulation, or worker-bees stinging to death the males of their species once the queen of the hive has been fertilized. Queens, as Simone de Beauvoir has pointed out, are exceptional and in a way sacred in a male-dominated society, for they alone among women are invested with the power of life and death. Probably Dumas was playing unwittingly, in his drama of the duel between Buridan and Marguerite, on the deep-seated psychic fear from which few men have been exempt, at least down to the present century, of losing their overlordship; the symbol of such deposition being woman's successful establishment of her claim to the same right to indiscriminate sexual adventure, unattended by remorse or dread of consequences, as man has traditionally enjoyed. (pp. 85-6)

The romantic period in France witnessed the appearance of a number of travel-books of outstanding literary merit; Dumas was competing in this field with some of the best writers of the age, Chateaubriand, Stendhal, Gautier, among others. If his books proved more popular than any of theirs, this was due in the first instance to his skill in conveying the raw excitement of travel, the thrill of seeing with one's own eyes all the wonders of the wide world, glaciers and volcanoes, old battlefields and ruined monuments, fierce nomadic tribes and exotic birds and animals. As he expressed it himself, 'to travel is to live in the full meaning of the word; the past and the future are swallowed up in the present; one fills one's lungs, takes pleasure in everything, holds all creation in the hollow of one's hand.' But in addition, he was able to bring a personal touch to everything he wrote. . . . The *Impressions de voyage* are packed with accounts of the strange and sometimes uncomfortable adventures that befell him and of his encounters with odd, or occasionally famous people on his way. Lastly, Dumas used the framework of the travel-book to engage in a form of literary activity which was eventually to give him a far wider

and more lasting reputation than the stage plays which had been his staple until then; that is, story-telling. The *Impressions de voyage en Suisse* include fewer descriptive passages than passages of narrative; whole chapters are given over to the retelling of local legends which Dumas set down—or so he assures us—as he heard them from the lips of the mountain-dwellers in the remote fastnesses of the Alps. Some of these are pure fairy-stories, involving magical animals or encounters with the Devil, others represent popular versions of historical events, which Dumas noted down even though he was well aware they were in part apocryphal. . . . Whether all the tales Dumas consigned to the pages of his book represent a living oral tradition is something that perhaps only a Swiss folklorist could tell us; occasionally, no doubt, he cheated, using an earlier printed source and pretending to have heard the story from some garrulous herdsman. But whether the legends he narrates were really related to him or whether they were picked up in the course of his desultory reading, he retells them with an inimitable mixture of simplicity and gusto which stamps them as his own. His journey through Switzerland had the unforeseen result of revealing to his public, and to Dumas himself, a rare talent as a teller of tales, justifying Heine's tribute: 'Assuredly, after Don Miguel de Cervantes and Madame Scheriar, better known as Queen Scheherezade, you are the most amusing spinner of yarns I know. (pp. 90-1)

It is curious that Dumas should have been so successful in reviving the vogue for the historical novel in France, long after the original interest aroused by the translations of Scott's novels had faded. But his treatment of the form was in one essential respect different from Scott's and from the way Scott's principal French imitators, Vigny, Hugo, and Mérimée, handled it. For them, what counted was 'local colour': the reconstitution of what they took to be the flavour of the period their novels were set in. For Dumas, however, this kind of conscientious authenticity was of minor importance. In a moment of candour, he once admitted that his way of dealing with history was 'strange'.

> I start by devising a story. I try to make it romantic, moving, dramatic, and when scope has been found for the emotions and the imagination, I search through the annals of the past to find a frame in which to set it; and it has never happened that history has failed to provide this frame, so exactly adjusted to the subject that it seemed it was not a case of the frame being made for the picture, but that the picture had been made to fit into the frame.

History, in short, was used by Dumas in much the same way as science was used by Zola: to confer a semblance of veracity on his fiction. . . . But for Dumas, as presumably for Maquet, any detail found in print in a roughly contemporaneous record could be assumed to be 'true history'; they did not trouble themselves with the finer distinctions between memoirs and 'pseudo-memoirs'.

In *Les Trois Mousquetaires* we are given a peculiarly rose-tinted, partial, not so much distorted as disinfected view of the past, as anyone can see who compares the book with, say, Manzoni's *The Betrothed*, another historical novel of which the definitive edition came out just a couple of years before *Les Trois Mousquetaires*. Dumas's picture of the seventeenth century omits everything that would have made it a most uncomfortable age for any of his nineteenth-century readers were they to have been magically transported back into it. The epidemics, the famines, the injustices, the barbarous superstitions of the period have no place in his account. Even war is reduced to a gay picnic beneath the fortifications of La Rochelle.

This is no criticism. Only a pedant would cavil at the anachronisms, the historical implausibilities, the glaring omissions, for in the final analysis history is for Dumas, paradoxically, a means of projecting his novel out of real time completely, and this is precisely what gives his fiction its perennial and endearing freshness. Athos, Porthos, and Aramis, like D'Artagnan himself, exist on a plane where none of the usual dull concerns of adult humanity have any hold. Money and possessions are not merely of no account, they are things one does not need to trouble one's head about, for in the last resort God will provide—God taking the form sometimes of their captain M. de Tréville, sometimes of the women they serve or love. . . . (pp. 122-24)

Although the book is one that, ideally should be read for the first time in one's boyhood, it is not, like other boys' classics—*Martin Rattler, Tom Sawyer, Treasure Island*—a story of pre-adult adventure. The heroes are brave, loyal, energetic and enterprising, but also strongly susceptible to sexual temptation. Each of the three musketeers is characterized by the special quality of his relations with women—tragic in the case of Athos, light-hearted in the case of Porthos, mysterious in the case of Aramis. D'Artagnan's attitude to the opposite sex is a somewhat ambiguous one, idealistic and materialistic in turn. Perhaps, like his creator, he is simply greedy. There is in the first place the romantic affair, never consummated, with Constance Bonacieux; but in addition he engages in a very unplatonic relationship with the charming Ketty, Milady's waiting-woman. The episode of his impersonating, with Ketty's help, Milady's lover the Comte de Wardes, to the point of finally substituting himself for the Count in Milady's bed—. . . all this is not boy's stuff at all. However carefully the book is written so as not to offend the susceptibilities of the delicately minded, it is impossible to overlook a certain obsession with the various forms taken by the war between the sexes, which comes to the surface particularly in those parts of the book where the blonde siren Milady is in the foreground. There is one scene, in chapter LVI, which can only be described as sadistic; what makes it acceptable none the less is that it is related as a story within a story, and a palpably false one at that which the reader is not asked to imagine as having actually happened. Milady has been taken prisoner and is being kept under close guard in a castle near Portsmouth. She can escape, and carry out the mission entrusted to her by Richelieu, only if she can seduce the puritan officer Felton who has been detailed to guard her. She begins by pretending to be one of the elect herself; then, having won his interest by posing as a co-religionary, tells him the story of the violence done her by Buckingham when, as an innocent girl, she was abducted by that licentious nobleman and raped by him repeatedly after he had added a powerful narcotic to her drinking water. The whole salacious episode is related in a suitably chaste manner though in most convincing detail; and although a fabrication, it has the intended effect not only of winning Felton over, but of making him the blind instrument of Milady's political purpose under the illusion that he is avenging her lost honour. (pp. 124-25)

> *F. W. J. Hemmings, in his* Alexandre Dumas: The King of Romance, *Charles Scribner's Sons, 1979, 231 p.*

ADDITIONAL BIBLIOGRAPHY

Aldridge, A. Owen. "The Vampire Theme: Dumas Pere and the English Stage." *Revue des langues vivantes* 39, No. 4 (1973): 312-24.*
  Discusses the sources of Dumas's treatment of vampirism in his play *Le vampire*. Aldridge also describes the influence of Dumas's handling of the vampire theme on the writers Dion Boucicault and Augustus G. Harris.

Brogan, D. W. "Alexander the Great." In his *French Personalities and Problems*, pp. 3-7. New York: Alfred A. Knopf, 1947.
  Depicts Dumas as an author who championed French courage and heroism in a country traditionally given to debunking its heroes.

The Dumasian. Keighley, England: Dumas Association, 1956-60.
  A triannual journal devoted to Dumas criticism.

"Monte Cristo and Alexandre Dumas." *The Eclectic Magazine* XXXIX, No. I (September 1856): 33-6.
  A contemporary recounts a tour through Dumas's Monte-Cristo estate.

Garnett, R. S. "The Genius and the Ghost: or, 'Athos, Porthos, and Aramis'." *Blackwood's Edinburgh Magazine* CCXXVI, No. MCCCLXV (July 1929): 129-42.
  Rebuts the contention that Auguste Maquet wrote *The Three Musketeers*.

George, Albert J. "The Major Romantics: Dumas, père." In his *Short Fiction in France: 1800-1850*, pp. 153-57. Syracuse, N.Y.: Syracuse University Press, 1964.
  Comments on Dumas's treatment of form and theme in his short fiction. George observes that while he employed a fair variety of themes in his shorter works, Dumas consistently used "the form time had proved most successful: a simple tale told in a straightforward manner."

Gorman, Herbert. *The Incredible Marquis*. New York: Farrar & Rinehart, 1929, 466 p.
  A reliable popular biography.

Gribble, Francis. *Dumas: Father and Son*. New York: E. P. Dutton & Co., 1930, 280 p.*
  Chronicles the lives of Dumas *(père)* and Dumas *(fils)*. Gribble describes his biography of the elder Dumas as primarily an attempt to "depict the man—to consider how success affected him and what was his outlook on life, when, having money in his pocket, he was able to indulge his tastes and amuse himself as he chose."

Kroff, Alexander Yale. "The Critics, the Public and the *Tour de Nesle*." *Romanic Review* XXXIV, No. 4 (December 1943): 346-64.
  Reviews and analyzes the history of the critical and popular response to *The Tower of Nesle* and assesses the importance of the drama in the history of the French theater.

Lang, Andrew. "To Alexandre Dumas." In his *Letters to Dead Authors*, pp. 100-08. London: Longmans, Green, & Co., 1892.
  A literary eulogy.

Luciani, Vincent. "The Genesis of *Lorenzino*: A Study in Dumas Pere's Method of Composition." *Philological Quarterly* XXXV, No. 2 (April 1956): 175-85.
  Examines Dumas's use of historical and literary sources in the play *Lorenzine*, purposing thereby to "cast some light upon [his] method of composition."

Matlaw, Myron. "English and American Dramatizations of *Le Comte de Monte-Cristo*." *Nineteenth Century Theatre Research* 7, No. 1 (Spring 1979): 39-53.
  A study of the English-language dramatizations of *The Count of Monte Cristo*, particularly those versions connected with the career of James O'Neill, who starred in the role of Edmond Dantès from 1883 to 1912.

Maurois, André. *Alexandre Dumas: A Great Life in Brief*. Translated by Jack Palmer White. Great Lives in Brief. New York: Alfred A. Knopf, 1955, 198 p.

> A well-researched, readable short biography. Maurois incorporated revised portions of this work in his *The Titans: A Three-generation Biography of the Dumas* (see excerpt dated 1957).

Moraud, Marcel. "The French Romantic Drama: The Evolution of the Romantic Drama in the Plays of Alexandre Dumas and Victor Hugo." *The Rice Institute Pamphlet* XV, No. 2 (April 1928): 95-111.*

> Traces the first flowerings of French Romantic drama in the plays of Dumas and Victor Marie Hugo. Moraud suggests that Dumas introduced popular, novelistic elements into his dramas at the expense of "nobility and inspiration."

Reed, F. W. *A Bibliography of Alexandre Dumas Père*. Pinner Hill, England: J. A. Neuhuys, 1933, 467 p.

> A comprehensive bibliography of Dumas's writings. Reed provides information concerning the composition, publication, staging, and translation into English of individual works.

S[haw], G[eorge] B[ernard]. "Mr. Grundy's Improvements on Dumas." *The Saturday Review*, London 84, No. 2177 (17 July 1897): 59-61.*

> A review of *The Silver Key*, Sydney Grundy's version of Dumas's play *Mademoiselle de Belle-Isle*. Shaw describes Dumas as a "summit in art" and recognizes in him "one of the best story-tellers, narrative or dramatic, that ever lived."

Spurr, Harry A. *The Life and Writings of Alexandre Dumas (1802-1870)*. New York: Frederick A. Stokes, Co., 1902, 382 p.

> A biographical and critical study. In assessing Dumas's works, Spurr relies extensively on quotations from Robert Louis Stevenson, Brander Matthews, and other prominent commentators.

Swinburne, Algernon Charles. "The Centenary of Alexandre Dumas." *The Nineteenth Century and After* LII, No. CCCVI (August 1902): 177-78.

> A commemorative poem. Swinburne characterizes Dumas as France's "deathless boy."

Thibaudet, Albert. "The Generation of 1820: The Romantic Theater." In his *French Literature from 1795 to Our Era*, translated by Charles Lam Markmann, pp. 165-75. New York: Funk & Wagnalls, 1967.*

> An outspoken account of the genesis and demise of Romantic drama in France. In discussing Dumas, Thibaudet comments on the significance of *Antony* and *The Tower of Nesle*.

Thompson, John A. *Alexandre Dumas Pere and Spanish Romantic Drama*. Louisiana State University Studies, no. 37. University: Louisiana State University Press, 1938, 229 p.

> A detailed examination of Dumas's influence on Spanish Romantic drama. Thompson focuses on Spanish translations, criticism, and utilization of Dumas's plays during the years 1834-50.

Van Maanen, W. "Kean: From Dumas to Sartre." *Neophilologus* LVI, No. 2 (April 1972): 221-30.*

> Provides background information concerning Edmund Kean and two plays in which the English actor figures as the principal character: *Kean; ou, Désordre et génie*, by Dumas, and *Kean*, an adaptation of Dumas's work by Jean-Paul Sartre.

Wenger, Jared. "Violence as a Technique in the Dramas and Dramatizations of Dumas *Père*." *Romanic Review* XXXI, No. 3 (October 1940): 265-79.

> A qualitative evaluation of violence in Dumas's dramas.

John Forster

1812-1876

English biographer, historian, critic, and journalist.

Forster's *The Life of Charles Dickens* is considered one of the finest biographies of a literary figure in the English language. Because of his lifelong friendship with Dickens, Forster brought a unique perspective to the novelist's life, one combining the thorough approach, broad scope, and firsthand knowledge characteristic of such highly regarded biographies as James Boswell's *The Life of Samuel Johnson, LL.D.* and John Gibson Lockhart's *Memoirs of the Life of Sir Walter Scott, Bart*. While Forster also assisted, advised, and provided support to many prominent English authors of his day, his reputation rests primarily upon his association with Dickens. Though various aspects of *The Life of Charles Dickens* have been controversial since it first appeared, it remains significant in the history of biography as an essential study of a major nineteenth-century author.

Forster was born in Newcastle, England, where he attended the Royal Grammar School. In 1828, he enrolled at Cambridge University, but spent only a month there before deciding to study law at New University College, London. He soon abandoned his legal studies for literary pursuits, however, and by 1831 was regularly contributing essays and reviews to periodicals. In 1834, he became principal drama and literary critic and subeditor of the *Examiner*. Throughout his life, Forster cultivated close relationships with a wide range of notable literary figures, including Thomas Carlyle, Edward Bulwer-Lytton, Robert Browning, Leigh Hunt, Charles Lamb, and Walter Savage Landor. He acted as proofreader, advisor, and literary agent and exercised considerable influence over nearly every major English author of his day. After meeting Dickens in 1836, he quickly became the novelist's closest friend and most trusted advisor. Though the two men grew apart in the decade before Dickens's death, their personal and working relationship evolved over a period of nearly thirty-five years into one of the more memorable and productive in English literary history.

In 1847, Forster became chief editor of the *Examiner*, and then the following year published his first major biography, *The Life and Adventures of Oliver Goldsmith*. In this work, Forster sought both to enlarge and correct the contemporary conception of Goldsmith, and to depict the author more positively than had previous commentators. He therefore emphasized the purity of Goldsmith's "true" character as revealed in his works and tended to ignore or explain away the author's personal shortcomings. His contention that Goldsmith had been undervalued by society reflected his concern with a contemporary debate over what became known as the "dignity of literature issue." With other writers, including Dickens, Forster campaigned in the press for greater public recognition and monetary support for authors. He thus presented Goldsmith's life of hardship as an example of the consequences of society's lack of respect and encouragement for the literary profession. The biography was a popular as well as a critical success, though some reviewers complained that Forster had idealized his subject.

In 1855, Forster became secretary to the Lunacy Commission overseeing the administration of British asylums. The following year, he resigned as editor of the *Examiner* and married Eliza Ann Colburn, the widow of a noted publisher. His health was poor, but his new position, obtained through the influence of friends, provided him with a steady income and time for his scholarly studies. Forster's interest in history, particularly the conflict between Charles I and Parliament that led to the English Civil War, had borne fruit as early as 1836, when he began publishing a series of biographies in *Lardner's Cabinet Encyclopaedia*. Following his appointment to the commission, he expanded the scope of his historical studies through several new books and enlarged editions of his previously published works, including *Historical and Biographical Essays* and *Arrest of the Five Members by Charles the First: A Chapter of English History Rewritten*. With the death of Walter Savage Landor in 1864, however, Forster ceased writing historical works. He had been closely involved with Landor's personal and literary affairs since the 1830s and had promised the poet that he would write his biography.

Walter Savage Landor was published in 1869 to mixed reviews. Forster had faced several problems in writing about the poet's sometimes scandalous life, and for the first time he was writing about a close friend. The idealized approach Forster had used in his life of Goldsmith was totally unsuited to Landor's character; the result was a more objective work, but one limited both by the libel laws which made it impossible to discuss several controversial episodes in Landor's life and by Forster's strong sense of propriety. Contemporary criticism of *Walter Savage Landor* centered on Forster's handling of the controversial aspects of the poet's life and on what many writers felt was the work's unnecessary length and ponderous style. A number of critics asserted that the biography possessed little artistic value, but would serve as a useful reference tool.

In 1870, shortly after the publication of *Walter Savage Landor,* Dickens's death prompted Forster to embark upon the major task of his career. Despite its flaws, *The Life of Charles Dickens* is considered a monumental work and a successful one within the guidelines Forster set for himself. His survey of Dickens's career and writings was comprehensive, and his revelations about the novelist's early life and humble origins came as a complete surprise to readers who had conceived of Dickens as the product of a middle-class background and led to a new approach in interpreting Dickens's work. The biography was also remarkable for the sheer mass of information Forster had assembled. While his sense of discretion and the dictates of Victorian morality meant that he could not deal in depth with Dickens's separation from his wife or discuss the author's relationship with the actress Ellen Ternan, he did not refrain from pointing out what he felt were flaws in his friend's character.

In *The Life of Charles Dickens,* Forster largely relied on letters from the novelist to himself, and criticism of the biography through the years has centered around the accusation that Forster himself occupies too prominent a place in the narrative to the exclusion of Dickens's other friends and correspondents. Evidence uncovered over the last century shows that Forster did indeed distort many aspects of his relationship with Dickens and that he even altered the novelist's letters to make his own role more significant. A number of scholars, however, have pointed out that the subsequent publication of many of Dickens's letters to other correspondents has revealed little about the author beyond what his letters to Forster already suggest. Early critics also charged Forster with misrepresenting Dickens's character, but recent commentators have maintained that the biographer's factual omissions and suspect editorial practices were made in pursuit of an overall portrait that remains remarkably accurate.

Following the completion of *The Life of Charles Dickens* in 1873, Forster turned to writing a biography of Jonathan Swift, for which he had collected materials throughout his life. His health continued to decline, and despite his resignation from the Lunacy Commission in 1871, writing was a severe strain. He managed to finish only the first volume of *The Life of Jonathan Swift* before his death. Reviews of this volume focus on Forster's avowed purpose of altering common misconceptions about Swift's character. Most critics agree that the completed *Life* would have been one of his most respected works.

Forster is best known today as the friend and biographer of Charles Dickens. His historical works, though praised by his contemporaries for their scholarship, are marred by his partisan approach to politics and by his tendency to idealize historical figures he admired. His lives of Goldsmith, Landor, and Swift are now notable chiefly as sources for later studies, and his literary reputation seems likely to remain vested in a single work. The objectivity of *The Life of Charles Dickens* has been regularly debated since its publication, but modern commentators suggest that many of its limitations were the result of conscious decisions by Forster made in the interest of coherence

and unity. While subsequent biographers have filled in the missing details of Dickens's life, their overall approach has been similar to Forster's, supplementing his work, but rarely disputing it. *The Life of Charles Dickens* endures over one hundred years after its publication as a fascinating and insightful account of the life of one of the nineteenth century's greatest literary figures.

PRINCIPAL WORKS

*The Statesmen of the Commonwealth of England: With a Treatise on the Popular Progress in English History (biographies and essay) 1840
The Life and Adventures of Oliver Goldsmith (biography) 1848; also published in revised form as *The Life and Times of Oliver Goldsmith,* 1854
Historical and Biographical Essays (essays) 1858
Arrest of the Five Members by Charles the First: A Chapter of English History Rewritten (history) 1860
The Debates on the Grand Remonstrance, November and December, 1641: With an Introductory Essay on English Freedom under the Plantagenet and Tudor Sovereigns (history and essay) 1860
Sir John Eliot (biography) 1864
Walter Savage Landor (biography) 1869
The Life of Charles Dickens. 3 vols. (biography) 1872-74
The Life of Jonathan Swift (unfinished biography) 1875

*This work includes biographies originally published in *Lardner's Cabinet Encyclopaedia,* vols. 44-46 and 48-49, 1836-39.

WALTER SAVAGE LANDOR (poem date 1846)

[*Landor was an English poet, critic, and essayist. Though seldom read today, he is remembered for his* Imaginary Conversations— *a series of fictionalized dialogues between historical characters— and for his poetry written in imitation of classical Greek and Roman authors. In the following poem, which originally appeared in an 1846 edition of Landor's works jointly edited by the poet and Forster, Landor expresses his gratitude for Forster's advice and assistance and indicates his desire for critical respect.*]

FORSTER! whose zeal hath seiz'd each written page
That fell from me, and over many lands
Hath clear'd for me a broad and solid way,
Whence one more age, ay, haply more than one,
May be arrived at (all through thee), accept
No false or faint or perishable thanks.
From better men, and greater, friendship turn'd
Thy willing steps to me. From ELIOT's cell
Death-dark; from HAMPDEN's sadder battle-field;
From steadfast CROMWELL's tribunitian throne,
Loftier than king's supported knees could mount;
Hast thou departed with me, and hast climbed
Cecropian heights, and ploughed Aegean waves.
Therefore it never grieved me when I saw
That she who guards those regions and those seas
Hath lookt with eyes more gracious upon thee.
There are no few like that conspirator
Who, under prétext of power-worship, fell
At CAESAR's feet, only to hold him down
While others stabb'd him with repeated blows:

And there are more who fling light jibes, immerst
In gutter-filth, against the car that mounts
Weighty with triumph up the Sacred Way.
Protect in every place my stranger guests,
Born in the lucid land of free pure song,
Now first appearing on repulsive shores,
Bleak, and where safely none but natives move,
Red-poll'd, red-handed, siller-grasping men.
Ah! lead them far away, for they are used
To genial climes and gentle speech; but most
CYMODAMEIA: warn the Tritons off
While she ascends, while through the opening plain
Of the green sea (brighten'd by bearing it)
Gushes redundantly her golden hair.

> *Walter Savage Landor, "To John Forster," in* Wal-
> ter Savage Landor, a Biography: 1821-1864, *Vol. II
> by John Forster, Chapman & Hall, 1869, p. 449.*

T[HOMAS] CARLYLE (letter date 1847)

[*A noted nineteenth-century essayist, historian, critic, and social
commentator, Carlyle was a central figure of the Victorian age
in England and Scotland. In his writings, Carlyle advocated a
Christian work ethic and stressed the importance of order, piety,
and spiritual fulfillment. Known to his contemporaries as the
"Sage of Chelsea," Carlyle exerted a powerful moral influence
in an era of rapidly shifting values. In the following excerpt from
a letter to Forster, he questions Forster's selection of Oliver
Goldsmith for a biographical study. Carlyle's comments reflect
his conviction that the study of history is the study of the heroic
figures who shape it; he contends that Goldsmith is undeserving
of such attention. Despite his criticisms, however, Carlyle praises
Forster's achievement within the limitations of his subject matter.*]

The essential objection . . . [to the Life of *Goldsmith*], I fancy
is, that you had not a better hero than poor Goldy; that you
had not a higher virtue than good-nature, good-humour, and a
certain Irish "keep never minding," to celebrate and deify!
Certainly poor Goldy is but a weak wire to string his century
upon,—poor fellow, his contribution to it, that of painting one
or two small Pictures *de genre* in a happy manner, which still
hang pleasantly on our walls, was essentially not a great one.
He built nothing, pulled down nothing; changed nothing in any
way for the better; merely painted his dainty little *tableaux de
genre*, under thriftless, imprudent insolvent circumstances; and
generously left them to us, and went his unknown way. Poor
Goldy—and yet you may say justly, what help? I could get no
better hero in that century; no other that would suit my purpose!
True enough, the blame is not essentially yours;—and it is
beautiful withal to see, as you show us, how one of Nature's
own Gentlemen may live, and do some kind of work that is
worthy of him, under the husk of a poor ragged Irish slave
(for such poor Goldy was); which also is a kind of Gospel!
(pp. 51-2)

> *T[homas] Carlyle, in a letter to John Forster on
> November 18, 1847, in his* New Letters of Thomas
> Carlyle, *Vol. II, edited by Alexander Carlyle, John
> Lane/The Bodley Head, 1904, pp. 51-2.*

CHARLES DICKENS (letter date 1848)

[*In the following excerpt from a letter to Forster, Dickens offers
high praise for* The Life and Adventures of Oliver Goldsmith,
which he considers superior in certain respects to James Boswell's
Life of Johnson. *Dickens also comments on Forster's contribution
to the dignity of literature as a profession in his portrayal of*

*Goldsmith. The novelist concludes with the prophetic declaration:
"I desire no better for my fame, when my personal dustiness shall
be past my control of my love of order, than such a biographer
and such a critic."*]

I finished ["**The Life and Adventures of Oliver Goldsmith**"]
yesterday, after dinner, having read it from the first page to
the last with the greatest care and attention.

As a picture of the time, I really think it impossible to give it
too much praise. It seems to me to be the very essence of all
about the time that I have ever seen in biography or fiction,
presented in most wise and humane lights, and in a thousand
new and just aspects. . . . I should point to that, if I didn't
know the author, as being done by somebody with a remarkably
vivid conception of what he narrated, and a most admirable
and fanciful power of communicating it to another. All about
Reynolds is charming; and the first account of the Literary
Club and of Beauclerc as excellent a piece of description as
ever I read in my life. But to read the book is to be in the
time. It lives again in as fresh and lively a manner as if it were
presented on an impossibly good stage by the very best actors
that ever lived, or by the real actors come out of their graves
on purpose.

And as to Goldsmith himself, and *his* life, and the tracing of
it out in his own writings, and the manful and dignified assertion of him without any sobs, whines, or convulsions of any
sort, it is throughout a noble achievement, of which, apart from
any private and personal affection for you, I think (and really
believe) I should feel proud, as one who had no indifferent
perception of these books of his—to the best of my remembrance—when little more than a child. I was a little afraid in
the beginning, when he committed those very discouraging
imprudences, that you were going to champion him somewhat
indiscriminately; but I very soon got over that fear, and found
reason in every page to admire the sense, calmness, and moderation with which you make the love and admiration of the
reader cluster about him from his youth, and strengthen with
his strength—and weakness too, which is better still.

I don't quite agree with you in two small respects. First, I
question very much whether it would have been a good thing
for every great man to have had his Boswell, inasmuch as I
think that two Boswells, or three at most, would have made
great men extraordinarily false, and would have set them on
always playing a part, and would have made distinguished
people about them for ever restless and distrustful. I can imagine a succession of Boswells bringing about a tremendous state
of falsehood in society, and playing the very devil with confidence and friendship. Secondly, I cannot help objecting to
that practice (begun, I think, or greatly enlarged by Hunt) of
italicising lines and words and whole passages in extracts,
without some very special reason indeed. (pp. 217-20)

I have reserved for a closing word—though I *don't* mean to
be eloquent about it, being far too much in earnest—the admirable manner in which the case of the literary man is stated
throughout this book. It is splendid. I don't believe that any
book was ever written, or anything every done or said, half so
conducive to the dignity and honour of literature as "**The Life
and Adventures of Oliver Goldsmith,**" by J. F., of the Inner
Temple. The gratitude of every man who is content to rest his
station and claims quietly on literature, and to make no feint
of living by anything else, is your due for evermore. I have
often said, here and there, when you have been at work upon
the book, that I was sure it would be; and I shall insist on that
debt being due to you (though there will be no need for insisting

about it) as long as I have any tediousness and obstinacy to bestow on anybody. Lastly, I never will hear the biography compared with Boswell's except under vigorous protest. For I do say that it is mere folly to put into opposite scales a book, however amusing and curious, written by an unconscious coxcomb like that, and one which surveys and grandly understands the characters of all the illustrious company that move in it.

My dear Forster, I cannot sufficiently say how proud I am of what you have done, or how sensible I am of being so tenderly connected with it. When I look over this note, I feel as if I had said no part of what I think; and yet if I were to write another I should say no more, for I can't get it out. I desire no better for my fame, when my personal dustiness shall be past my control of my love of order, than such a biographer and such a critic. And again I say, most solemnly, that literature in England has never had, and probably never will have, such a champion as you are, in right of this book. (pp. 220-21)

Charles Dickens, in a letter to John Forster on April 22, 1848, in his The Letters of Charles Dickens: 1833 to 1856, Vol. I, *edited by Mamie Dickens and Georgina Hogarth, Charles Scribner's Sons, 1879, pp. 217-21.*

[THOMAS De QUINCEY] (essay date 1848)

[*An English critic and essayist, De Quincey used his own life as the subject of his best-known work,* Confessions of an English Opium Eater, *in which he chronicled his addiction to opium. In addition, De Quincey contributed reviews to a number of London journals and earned a reputation as an insightful if occasionally long-winded literary critic. At the time of De Quincey's death, his critical expertise was underestimated, though his prose talent had long been acknowledged. In the twentieth century, some critics still disdain the digressive qualities of De Quincey's writing, yet others find that his essays display an acute psychological awareness. In the excerpt below, De Quincey argues that the circumstances under which Goldsmith lived and wrote were not as unfavorable as Forster depicts them in* The Life and Adventures of Oliver Goldsmith. *The critic also faults Forster's denunciation of the ill treatment afforded literary men in Goldsmith's time, and, in a comparison of Forster with Thomas Carlyle, insists that the biographer ought to provide solutions if he is going to point out injustices. In conclusion, however, De Quincey applauds Forster's vindication of Goldsmith's character and offers thanks for "this successful labour of love in restoring a half-subverted statue to its upright position."*]

[*The Life and Adventures of Oliver Goldsmith*] accomplishes a retribution which the world has waited for through seventy and odd years. Welcome at any rate by its purpose, it is trebly welcome by its execution, to all hearts that linger indulgently over the frailties of a national favourite once wickedly exaggerated—to all hearts that brood indignantly over the powers of that favourite once maliciously undervalued.

A man of original genius, shewn to us as revolving through the leisurely stages of a biographical memoir, lays open, to readers prepared for sympathy, two separate theatres of interest: one in his personal career; the other in his works and his intellectual development. Both unfold together; and each borrows a secondary interest from the other: the life from the recollection of the works—the works from the joy and sorrow of the life. There have, indeed, been authors whose great creations, severely preconceived in a region of thought transcendent to all impulses of earth, would have been pretty nearly what they are under any possible changes in the dramatic arrangement of their lives. Happy or not happy—gay or sad—

these authors would equally have fulfilled a mission too solemn and too stern in its obligations to suffer any warping from chance, or to bend before the accidents of life, whether dressed in sunshine or in wintry gloom. But generally this is otherwise. Children of Paradise, like the Miltons of our planet, have the privilege of stars—to "dwell apart." But the children of flesh, whose pulses beat too sympathetically with the agitations of mother-earth, cannot sequester themselves in that way. They walk in no such altitudes, but at elevations easily reached by ground-winds of humble calamity. And from that cup of sorrow, which upon all lips is pressed in some proportion, they must submit, by the very tenure on which they hold their gifts, to drink, if not more profoundly than others, yet always with more peril to the accomplishment of their earthly mission.

Amongst this household of children too tremulously associated to the fluctuations of earth, stands forward conspicuously Oliver Goldsmith. And there is a belief current—that he was conspicuous, not only in the sense of being constitutionally flexible to the impressions of sorrow and adversity, in case they had happened to occur, but also that he really *had* more than his share of those afflictions. We are disposed to think that this was not so. Our trust is, that Goldsmith lived upon the whole a life which, though troubled, was one of average enjoyment. . . . Goldsmith enjoyed the two privileges, one subjective—the other objective—which, when uniting in the same man, would prove more than a match for all difficulties that *could* arise in a literary career to him who was at once a man of genius so popular, of talents so versatile, of reading so various, and of opportunities so large for still more extended reading. The subjective privilege lay in his buoyancy of animal spirits; the objective in his freedom from responsibilities. Goldsmith wanted very little more than Diogenes: now Diogenes *could* only have been robbed of his tub: which perhaps was about as big as most of poor Goldsmith's sitting-rooms, and far better ventilated. So that the liability of these two men, cynic and non-cynic, to the kicks of fortune, was pretty much on a par; whilst Goldsmith had the advantage of a better temper for bearing them, though certainly Diogenes had the better climate for soothing his temper.

But it may be imagined, that if Goldsmith were thus fortunately equipped for authorship, on the other hand the position of literature, as a money-making resource, was in Goldsmith's days less advantageous than in ours. We are not of that opinion; and the representation by which Mr. Forster endeavours to sustain it seems to us a showy but untenable refinement. The outline of his argument is, that the aristocratic patron had, in Goldsmith's day, by the progress of society, disappeared; he belonged to the past—that the mercenary publisher had taken his place—he represented the ugly present—but that the great reading public (that true and equitable patron, as some fancy) had not yet matured its means of effectual action upon literature: this reading public virtually, perhaps, belonged to the future. All this we steadfastly resist. No doubt the old full-blown patron, *en grand costume*, with his heraldic bearings emblazoned at the head of the Dedication, was dying out, like the golden pippin. But he still lingered in sheltered situations. And part of the machinery by which patronage had ever moved, viz., using influence for obtaining subscriptions, was still in capital working order—a fact which we know from Goldsmith himself. . . . As to the public, *that* respectable character must always have presided over the true and final court of appeal, silently defying alike the *prestige* of patronage and the intriguing mysteries of publishing. Lordly patronage might fill the sails of one edition, and masterly publishing of three. But the books that ran contagiously through the educated circles, or that lingered amongst them for a generation, must have owed their success to the unbiassed feelings of the reader—not over-awed by authority, not mystified by artifice. Varying, however, in whatever proportion as to power, the three possible parties to an act of publication will always be seen intermittingly at work—the voluptuous self-indulging public, and the insidious publisher, of course; but even the brow-beating patron still exists in a new *avatar*. (pp. 187-92)

We are not therefore of Mr. Forster's opinion, that Goldsmith fell upon an age less favourable to the expansion of literary powers, or to the attainment of literary distinction, than any other. The patron might be a tradition—but the public was not therefore a prophecy. My lord's trumpets had ceased to sound, but the *vox populi* was not therefore muffled. (p. 193)

Goldsmith, . . . as regards the political aspects of his own times, was fortunately placed; a thrush or a nightingale is hushed by the thunderings which are awakening to Jove's eagle. But an author stands in relation to other influences than political; and some of these are described by Mr. Forster as peculiarly unfavourable to comfort and respectability at the era of Gold-smith's novitiate in literature. Will Mr. Forster excuse us for quarrelling with his whole doctrine upon this subject—a subject and a doctrine continually forced upon our attention in these days, by the extending lines of our own literary order, and continually refreshed in warmth of colouring by the contrast as regards *social* consideration, between our literary body and the corresponding order in France. (pp. 195-96)

Mr. Forster, in his views upon the *social* rights of literature, is rowing pretty nearly in the same boat as Mr. Carlyle in *his* views upon the rights of labour. Each denounces, or by im-plication denounces, as an oppression and a nuisance, what *we* believe to be a necessity inalienable from the economy and structure of our society. Some years ago Mr. Carlyle offended us all (or all of us that were interested in social philosophy) by enlarging on a social affliction, which few indeed needed to see exposed, but most men would have rejoiced to see remedied, if it were but on paper, and by way of tentative suggestion. Precisely at that point, however, where his aid was invoked, Mr. Carlyle halted. So does Mr. Forster with regard to *his* grievance; he states it, and we partly understand him—as ancient Pistol says—"we hear him with ears;" and when we wait for him to go on, saying—"well, here's a sort of evil in life, how would you redress it? you've shewn, or you've made another hole in the tin-kettle of society; how do you propose to tinker it?"—behold! he is suddenly almost silent. But this cannot be allowed. The right to insist upon a well known grievance cannot be granted to that man (Mr. Carlyle, for instance, or Mr. Forster) who uses it as matter of blame and denunciation, unless at the same time he points out the methods by which it could have been prevented. He that simply bemoans an evil has a right to his moan, though he should make no pretensions to a remedy; but he that criminates—that imputes the evil as a fault—that charges the evil upon selfish-ness or neglect lurking in some alterable arrangements of so-ciety, has no right to do so, unless he can instantly sketch the remedy; for the very first step by which he could have learned that the evil involved a blame, the first step that could have entitled him to denounce it as a wrong, must have been that step which brought him within the knowledge (wanting to ev-erybody else) that it admitted of a cure. A wrong it could not have been even in *his* eyes, so long as it was a necessity, nor a ground of complaint until the cure appeared to him a pos-

sibility. And the over-riding motto for these parallel specula-tions of Messrs. Carlyle and Forster, in relation to the frailties of our social system, ought to have been—"*Sanabilibus ae-grotamus malis.*" Unless with this watchword they had no right to commence their crusading march. *Curable* evils justify clamorous complaints; the incurable justify only prayers. (pp. 196-97)

[We] perceive on looking round, that we have actually been skirmishing with Mr. Forster, . . . and thus we have left our-selves but a corner for the main purpose (to which our other purpose of "arglebargling" was altogether subordinate) of ex-pressing emphatically our thanks to him for this successful labour of love in restoring a half-subverted statue to its upright position. We are satisfied that many thousands of readers will utter the same thanks to him, with equal fervour and with the same sincerity. Admiration for the versatile ability with which he has pursued his object is swallowed up for the moment in gratitude for his perfect success. It might have been imagined, that exquisite truth of household pathos, and of humour, with happy graces of style plastic as the air or the surface of a lake to the pure impulses of nature sweeping them by the motions of her eternal breath, were qualities authorized to justify them-selves before the hearts of men, in defiance of all that sickly scorn or the condescension of masquerading envy could avail for their disturbance. And so they are: and left to plead for themselves at such a bar as unbiassed human hearts, they could not have their natural influences intercepted. But in the case of Goldsmith, literary traditions have *not* left these qualities to their natural influences. It is a fact that up to this hour the contemporary falsehoods at Goldsmith's expense, and (worse perhaps than those falsehoods,) the malicious constructions of incidents partly true, having wings lent to them by the levity and amusing gossip of Boswell, continue to obstruct the full ratification of Goldsmith's pretensions. To this hour the scorn from many of his own age, runs side by side with the misgiving sense of his real native power. A feeling still survives, origi-nally derived from his own age, that the "inspired idiot," wherever he succeeded, ought *not* to have succeeded—having owed his success to accident, or even to some inexplicable perverseness in running counter to his own nature. It was by shooting awry that he had hit the mark; and, when most he came near to the bull's eye, most of all "by rights" he ought to have missed it. (pp. 209-10)

In this condition of Goldsmith's traditionary character, so in-juriously disturbing to the natural effect of his inimitable works, (for in its own class each of his best works *is* inimitable,) Mr. Forster steps forward with a three-fold exposure of the false-hood inherent in the anecdotes upon which this traditional char-acter has arisen. Some of these anecdotes he challenges as *literally* false; others as virtually so; they are true perhaps, but under such a version of their circumstances as would altogether take out the sting of their offensive interpretation. For others again, and this is a profounder service, he furnishes a most just and philosophic explanation, that brings them at once within the reader's toleration, nay, sometimes within a deep reaction of pity. (p. 210)

[In cases] where there really *may* have been some fretful ex-pression of self-esteem, Mr. Forster's explanation transfers the foible to a truer and a more pathetic station. Goldsmith's own precipitancy, his overmastering defect in proper reserve, in self-control, and in presence of mind, falling in with the ha-bitual undervaluation of many amongst his associates, placed him at a great disadvantage in animated conversation. His very truthfulness, his simplicity, his frankness, his hurry of feeling, all told against him. They betrayed him into inconsiderate expressions that lent a colour of plausibility to the malicious ridicule of those who disliked him the more, from being compelled, after all, to respect him. . . .

But a day of accounting comes at last—a day of rehearing for the cause, and of revision for the judgment. The longer this review has been delayed, the more impressive it becomes in the changes which it works. (p. 211)

[In] the particular case now before the public, we shall all be ready to agree that this reconciling friend, who might have entitled his work *Vindiciae Oliverianae*, has, by the piety of his service to a man of exquisite genius, so long and so foully misrepresented, earned a right to interweave for ever his own cipher and cognizance in filial union with those of OLIVER GOLDSMITH. (p. 212)

> [*Thomas De Quincey*], *"Forster's 'Life of Gold-smith',"* in The North British Review, *Vol. IX, No. XVII, May, 1848, pp. 187-212.*

[EDWARD BULWER-LYTTON]   (essay date 1848)

[*An English novelist, dramatist, poet, and essayist, Bulwer was one of the most versatile and popular writers of the nineteenth century. Though his works are rarely read today, his success once rivaled that of Charles Dickens and his novels were considered the epitome of fashionable style. In the excerpt below, Bulwer outlines some of the salient characteristics of Forster's approach to biography in* The Life and Adventures of Oliver Goldsmith. *While he praises Forster's thoroughness, he finds his style occasionally awkward and his treatment of many of the events in Goldsmith's life partisan. He concludes that the work is "a gentle but a manly apology for the life" of its subject.*]

We know of no man more fit for the task he has undertaken than Mr. Forster. He brings to it a mind habitually critical, subtle, and inquiring; that strong sympathy with men of letters which the life of Goldsmith especially demands; a large practical knowledge of the infirmities and misfortunes, as well as the virtues and solaces of the class, with which kindred pursuits must have made him familiar; an extensive store of general information; a style, not always equal it is true, and occasionally injured by mannerisms not visible in his former writings, but never bald or insipid; often weighty with earnest thought, often coloured with eloquence, animated or touching. . . .

It is no ordinary talent that can make a biography of this kind both interesting and important; give not only a seeming but a genuine originality to materials with which we had thought ourselves familiar; and supply a gap in previous researches of which we were scarcely aware, till the ingenuity which detected the gap had durably repaired it. Mr. Forster has treated the subject before us, on the whole, with a judgment correspondent to the ability. That he is more lenient to his hero than we always are, is natural. The duties of a reviewer are sterner than those of a biographer. (p. 221)

The subdivisions of Mr. Forster's work are philosophical and effective. In the first, he presents to us the childhood, the youth, the desultory adventures, which prepare us for the second—Authorship by compulsion; he leads us on through the Authorship by choice, to the time when labour and inclination, both combined, place his hero where we now behold him, amongst the constellation of imperishable names—'the novelist, the dramatist, the poet.'

Without that eternal attempt at stage grouping and stage effect, by which some of the French writers have distorted the even course of history, our pleasant biographer has quietly contrived to render picturesque and touching all the more interesting positions of the poet. Nothing can be more artful than the pause from ungenial and dreary studies, which invites us to contemplate the poor sizar listening to his own ballads;—or, before we see in full length the snubbed and derided butt of the London coteries, bids us halt to greet Nature, smiling on her darling in the garret of 'Garden Court;'—nothing more impressive for Goldsmith's vindication, than the steady enforcement of those scenes in which, what elsewhere might be warning, assumes the nobler lesson of example—scenes in which distress is met with sunny spirit, poverty endured with manly courage, and labours that startle us to contemplate, cheerfully undertaken by one constitutionally indolent, in the double aim (both noble) of independence and renown.

In the multiform groups, which, at different stages of Goldsmith's life, Mr. Forster presents to our view, we have some reproach to make perhaps, especially in the later portions of the work, that he deals too summarily with certain of the great shapes he invokes, and occasionally treats, with an air too 'eager and nipping,' some of the political and incidental events he rather decides than discusses. But a portrait-painter assumes a kind of prescriptive right to use the background as may best set off the figure; and we readily confess the skill with which Mr. Forster has placed his hero in the midst of every circle, in that position he really occupied, while suggesting temperately that which was more his due. (pp. 223-24)

In the criticisms which Mr. Forster introduces, he betrays the subtlety of an accomplished intellect, and the sympathy of a kindred taste. And it is not a little to his praise that he has contrived to say much that is new upon 'The Vicar of Wakefield,' and to point out the graver benefits to society, the moral effect on later authors, which that delight of all ages has indirectly bequeathed. When, after quoting Dr. Primrose's unpretending boast, 'that in less than a fortnight he had formed them (the felons of the gaol) into something social and humane,' Mr. Forster adds, 'In how many hearts may this have planted a desire which as yet had become no man's care?' we instinctively turned to the distinguished writer [Charles Dickens] to whom Mr. Forster has appropriately dedicated his book, and asked ourselves what Oliver Twist may have owed to Oliver Goldsmith.

Here, then, for all else, whether in praise or in qualification, we dismiss Mr. Forster's book to the judgment of the public—a fitting, and, we think, a permanent companion to the works of the author whose career it commemorates:—a gentle but a manly apology for the life, which it tracks through each pathetic transition of light and shadow: written in that spirit of which Goldsmith himself would have approved—pleasing while it instructs us, mild without tameness, earnest without acerbity. (pp. 224-25)

> [*Edward Bulwer-Lytton*], *"'Goldsmith',"* in The Edinburgh Review, *Vol. LXXXVIII, July, 1848, pp. 193-225.*

[GEORGE HENRY LEWES]   (essay date 1848)

[*Lewes was one of the most versatile men of letters in the Victorian era. A prominent English journalist, he was the founder, with Leigh Hunt, of the* Leader, *a radical political journal which he also edited from 1851 to 1854. He served as the first editor of the* Fortnightly Review *from 1865 to 1866, a journal which he also helped to establish. Critics often cite Lewes's influence on the novelist George Eliot, to whom he was companion and mentor, as his principal contribution to English letters, but they also credit him with critical acumen in his literary commentary, most notably in his dramatic criticism. In the following excerpt, Lewes presents a highly favorable assessment of* The Life and Adventures of Oliver Goldsmith. *Dividing his discussion into two parts, the critic explores both the artistic value of Forster's achievement and his contribution to the history of literature.*]

There are few biographies in any language to be compared with this minute, extensive, well-conceived, and entertaining work. [*'The Life and Adventures of Oliver Goldsmith'*] has been a labour of love; and, as the product of searching industry and generous enthusiasm, it will not only throw fresh light upon Goldsmith and upon Goldsmith's age, but will go far towards raising biography into something like the position due to it as an Art. Johnson said of some one, that he was 'a dead hand at a biography.' He might have extended the remark to biographers in general, who certainly have handled their subject with as little reference to its being the *life* of a man, as if they had the 'subject' on the dissecting table, and had to demonstrate the muscles of the back rather than the complicated mystery of vital existence. With such 'dead hands,' such droning 'demonstrators,' Mr. Forster has nothing in common. He holds biography to be the art of setting forth, in some imperfect representation, the life of a man; how he looked, spoke, acted, lived; what were his hopes, his aims, his follies, his virtues, his shortcomings; in what element of circumstance he lived, and how that element was not the one in which we now live. The work is not mainly critical, not philosophical, not eulogistic,—although criticism, philosophy, and eulogy enter into its composition,—but *pictorial*. He does not attempt to dissect the man, but to represent him. He does not dissertate; he narrates. He does not eulogize; he loves. (p. 1)

As a contribution to the art of biography, we welcome this **'Life and Adventures'**; as a picture of Goldsmith's life and times it is still more welcome. Our review of it will divide itself into two sections: the one considering it as a work of art; the other, as a bit of literary history.

As a work of art, with many fine qualities, it has defects, upon which we may be permitted to enlarge, warranted as we are by our hearty admiration of its beauties. Minor faults it has, of course: *aliter non fit, Avite, liber!* But these we may pass over. Let us rather confine ourselves to matters of importance. And to begin: it is surely a fault of design that the picture should be so crowded as to obscure the principal figure? In Mr. Forster's picture of Goldsmith's times, he has, unhappily too often, and for too long, forgotten Goldsmith. Page after page (very amusing, it is true) may you read, without the slightest reference to the hero. Sketches of politicians and political movements are introduced by the author's discursive abundance, without a shadow of pretence. . . . He was not a politician—not a place-hunter—not even a political hack. He lived not in the troubled element of politics; rather kept himself sedulously aloof from it. A few lines might have conveyed all the information necessary; but where the artist should have thrown in a few potent touches, he has 'made out' elaborate figures. Observe, however, that it is only as a fault in art we object to these discursive passages; in themselves they are excellent, and add to the entertainment of the book. One only asks, might they not have been elsewhere, and better elsewhere?

Is there a fatality of insignificance attached to Goldsmith the man? During his life, at the height of his celebrity, he was lost amidst the crowd of lesser men who jostled him; and here, in these pages, where he lives again, he is overshadowed by his contemporaries—lost amidst the Johnsons, Burkes, Reynoldses, Garricks, Hawkesworths, Hawkinses, Davises, Topham Beauclercs, Bennet Langtons, and Boswells. As Goldy had to be silenced by the ingenuous German, because 'Toctor Shonson' was going to say something; so he is now huddled into a corner, or altogether withdrawn from our sight by his affectionate biographer, who wants to let 'Toctor Shonson,' or Burke, or Garrick, or Walpole, or Reynolds, speak.

Another defect is the imitation of Carlyle. Mr. Forster writes so well when he writes like himself, that every one must regret the presence of a certain tone, which sounds like an echo of another's voice. The imitation is never glaring; never reflecting the grotesqueness of the original; but is, nevertheless, too like to be pleasing. Carlyle has evidently had a great influence on Mr. Forster, who reproduces here some of his favourite ideas; and we all know how difficult it is to escape unconscious imitation of any style which powerfully affects us. Few things are rarer than an original, *personal* style. Carlyle himself is an imitator. (pp. 2-3)

[Let] us note in Mr. Forster's book the absence of any serious attempt to analyze Goldsmith's character. We speak not of failure, for he has not attempted. It came not within his mode of treating the subject. He has attempted to paint, and only to paint. So far he has succeeded. But in giving us this portrait, he would have added another charm if he could have let us

A silhouette of Forster as a boy.

see the workings of the poet's soul; in presenting this figure on the stage, it was in his power to have admitted us behind the scenes. We *see* the man, we do not *know* him yet. To know him we must ponder long upon his life and works; we must interpret the riddle for ourselves, with scanty aid from his biographer. Yet what a tempting subject for the psychologist! What strange apparent contradictions for the observer of moral phenomena to reconcile! In revising this book for a second edition, how gladly should we find Mr. Forster cutting away several repetitions—some pointless anecdotes—and some pages of mere digression, to substitute in their place some thoughtful pages of analytical exposition, in which Goldsmith's *mind* might be depicted as vividly as his appearance and ways are now presented to us.

As a fault against the truth and integrity of art must be noted Mr. Forster's *indulgence* towards his hero. True it is that he is less bitten by the *furor biographicus* than most writers; and we shall perhaps be accused of severity in noticing so modified a form of the malady, but the malady is there, and demands recognition. He does not exalt his hero into a demi-god; does not discover that his ugliness was beauty; his foibles, graces; his vices, virtues. There is no spurious enthusiasm, no 'got up' sensibility, no raving of any kind. The tone is manly and moderate; but it has not the severe beauty of truth. We do not object to his love for Goldsmith: let the biographer's love be as hearty as possible for his hero, but let his love rise superior to defects, not blind itself to them. Love the scarred face, if you will, and paint it; but do not make it smooth. The man in his truth is lovelier than in any colours of falsehood with which the adroitest artist can disguise him. Mr. Forster's sins on this head are comparatively small; but they are, nevertheless, great enough to warrant notice, because great enough to interfere with the perfect truth of the delineation. Goldsmith had, perhaps, all the excellence which his biographer ascribes to him; but with it there was a large amount of human infirmity and moral deficiency, and this Mr. Forster does not so much deny, as slur over. (pp. 3-4)

Having thus set down what appear to us the points which, judging the work by its own high standard, criticism may reasonably object to, let us not forget to add those which claim our hearty applause. First, the unflagging spirit of the whole book; next, the true and novel light in which Goldsmith is placed. . . . Anecdotes of his absurdities were staple commodities in all literary *ana.* His conceit became a proverb; his envy of the most trivial success has been a stereotyped phrase. Much of this Mr. Forster has set right. He has clearly seen that a great deal of what stupid people have taken for conceit and jealousy, was nothing more than playfulness and exuberant animal spirits. (pp. 4-5)

Worthy of remark, also, is the deeply interesting picture here drawn of the life of a man of letters in that eighteenth century, and the earnest, manly tone, in which Mr. Forster throughout asserts the dignity of letters. There is no wailing here over the 'miseries of genius,' no drivelling cant about 'neglected genius,' no arrogant assumption of superiority claiming its immunity from all moral and social restraints. In a wise and earnest moderation men are reminded of the importance of letters to a civilized state, and authors are reminded of the dignity they too often forget.

In touching upon the merits of this biography as a work of art, we must not omit to mention how admirably the eighteenth century is sketched in its pages. By the adroit union of pictorial

power with pleasant gossip, we are introduced to this busy world, and made familiar at once with it. . . .

We have now to consider this work as a contribution to literary history in general, and to the history of Goldsmith in particular.

As so much of the work relates to the position of literature in respect to society, we shall begin with that topic. What Mr. Forster says on it, is for the most part excellent. . . . (p. 6)

It is, indeed, desirable that society should more distinctly recognise the importance of literature. One cannot but deplore a state of things which tolerates hall porters to government houses being paid higher than astronomers royal. One cannot but deplore the indifference of governments to literature—an indifference shown in the scanty encouragement given to men of letters, and their exclusion from all official situations. (p. 10)

But Mr. Forster has forgotten to add one essential condition— viz., that if society has its part to play, no less have authors theirs. Before society can truly award literature that respect which is due to it, authors must learn to *respect themselves.* That men of letters are all, or even the majority of them, disreputable, no one will perhaps maintain; yet the idea of literature, as a profession, is too distinctly associated in the public mind with sordid poverty, with reckless improvidence, and with disreputable conduct, not to have ample cause in general experience. (p. 11)

Again we say, authors must respect themselves, must respect their calling, must stand by it through good and ill report, refusing to acknowledge scamps as its true representatives, disdaining to follow the 'tricks of the trade,' bringing their *consciences* into their task, and judging their literary acts by the same severe standard of morality as that by which they judge the rest of their lives. Then will society respect them; then will all the world see that literature is not like rope-dancing, is not a craft, not an amusement, but the written thought of earnest men, and as such worthy of all honour.

Quitting this inexhaustible subject, we turn to Mr. Forster's vindication of the character of Goldsmith—a vindication rather latent and implied than distinctly expressed, and which, while quite successful on some points, has by no means satisfied us on the whole. . . . He has satisfactorily shown Goldsmith's exuberant animal spirits to have been the real prompter of much that has hitherto been taken for stupidity, envy, and intolerable conceit; he has satisfactorily shown that Goldsmith was a man more loveable and loved than people asserted—a man by no means so ridiculous and contemptible as he appears in Boswell and Hawkins; but while he has shown all this, and more, he has not rescued Goldsmith's moral character; he has not firmly grasped it, and held it up to our gaze. . . . He has an evident partiality for his hero, and his pity for failings takes sometimes the form of tender sympathy. He does not excuse him; he does not argue the point; he contrives to represent the failings in such a pleasant light and under such mild aspects, that what was really morally reprehensible, appears at the worst a sort of amiable weakness. (pp. 11-12)

Mr. Forster . . . is not the dupe of Goldsmith's showy qualities, and not to him are these observations addressed; but we doubt whether his readers will not carry away a false *impression* of Goldsmith's moral character, owing to the tone in which it is generally spoken of by his biographer. There is no suppression, but the whole is narrated with a delusive tenderness. With regard to the literary character, on the other hand, there is positive suppression. (p. 16)

On closing this book, no man will easily banish from his mind the crowding reflections it suggests. Such a picture of such a life is to be contemplated long and steadily 'in the still air of delightful studies,' to be recurred to, and re-read with minute care and ever new instruction. Considering the vitality of the subject—considering Goldsmith's imperishable fame—we may safely pronounce of this picture of his career, that as a work long matured it will not pass away. . . . (p. 23)

The question respecting an author's happiness and success, which this painful history will raise, Mr. Forster has well answered, both in his preface and in the book itself. He has clearly kept in view the fact, that inasmuch as an author's aims, an author's means, and an author's enjoyments, are not those dependent on merely worldly success, they should not be tested by that standard. (pp. 23-4)

Mr. Forster's argument is strengthened by the very unpromising appearance of his illustration. Goldsmith certainly was not a type of literary prosperity. He suffered all the ills which genius complainingly declares to be the 'badge of all its tribe;' but above and around all these ills Mr. Forster has shown us the bright halo which no suffering can dim. He has taken a notoriously unsuccessful case, to point out how, even there, genius achieved true success. Goldsmith was unhappy, it is true; but he was not unhappy *through literature;* it was not his genius which caused his sufferings. In any sphere of life he would have been as unsuccessful, as unhappy, if not incomparably more so. The sufferings he endured were the penalties paid by his weaknesses, they were not caused by his strength!

From this **'Life and Adventures of Oliver Goldsmith'** we not only carry away with us much valuable information, but we also carry with us the conviction that literature is a great and sacred thing, and that men of letters have a calling in this world which nothing but the want of proper dignity in themselves can prevent the world from acknowledging. This is no small gain. If, as we said, the great and perhaps only practical remedy for the ills now affecting literature is to spring from respect, such books as this now before us are the heralds of a new era. (p. 25)

> [*George Henry Lewes*], "*Forster's Life of Goldsmith*," *in* The British Quarterly Review, *Vol. VIII, No. XV, August 1, 1848, pp. 1-25.*

JOHN FORSTER   (essay date 1854)

[*In the following excerpt from his preface to* The Life and Times of Oliver Goldsmith, *Forster discusses the irony in the fact that the good nature and wisdom expressed in Goldsmith's works benefitted him so little. Further, Forster suggests that Goldsmith's simplicity and sincerity worked against him in social and literary circles, but adds that these qualities were inseparable from his personality and were inevitably reflected in his art.*]

Oliver Goldsmith, whose life and adventures should be known to all who know his writings, must be held to have succeeded in nothing that his friends would have had him succeed in. He was intended for a clergyman, and was rejected when he applied for orders; he practised as a physician, and never made what would have paid for a degree; what he was not asked or expected to do, was to write, but he wrote and paid the penalty. His existence was a continued privation. The days were few, in which he had resources for the night, or dared to look forward

to the morrow. There was not any miserable want, in the long and sordid catalogue, which in its turn and in all its bitterness he did not feel. He had shared the experience of those to whom he makes affecting reference in his *Animated Nature,* "people who die really of hunger, in common language of a broken heart;" and when he succeeded at the last, success was but a feeble sunshine on a rapidly approaching decay, which was to lead him, by its flickering and uncertain light, to an early grave.

Self-benefit seems out of the question here, and the way to happiness is indeed distant from this. But if we look a little closer, we shall see that he has passed through it all with a childlike purity of heart unsullied. Much of the misery vanishes when that is known; and when it is remembered, too, that in spite of it the *Vicar of Wakefield* was written, nay, that without it, in all human probability, a book so delightful and wise could not have been written. Fifty-six years after its author's death, the greatest of Germans recounted to a friend how much he had been indebted to the celebrated Irishman. "It is not to be described," wrote Goethe to Zelter, in 1830, "the effect that Goldsmith's *Vicar* had upon me, just at the critical moment of mental development. That lofty and benevolent irony, that fair and indulgent view of all infirmities and faults, that meekness under all calamities, that equanimity under all changes and chances, and the whole train of kindred virtues, whatever names they bear, proved my best education; and in the end," he added with sound philosophy, "these are the thoughts and feelings which have reclaimed us from all the errors of life."

And why were they so enforced in that charming book, but because the writer had undergone them all; because they had reclaimed himself, not from the world's errors only, but also from its suffering and care; and because his own life and adventures had been the same chequered and beautiful romance of the triumph of good over evil.

Though what is called worldly success, then, was not attained by Goldsmith, it may be that the way to happiness was yet not missed altogether. . . . His own benefit he had not successfully "endeavoured," when the gloom of his early life embittered life to the last, and the trouble he had endured was made excuse for a sorrowful philosophy, and for manners that were an outrage to the kindness of his heart. What had fallen to Johnson's lot, fell not less heavily to Goldsmith's; of the calamities to which the literary life is subject,

> Toil, envy, want, the patron, and the gaol,

none were spared to him: but they found, and left him, gentle and unspoiled; and though the discipline that thus taught him charity entailed some social disadvantage, by unfeigned sincerity and simplicity of heart he diffused every social enjoyment. When his conduct least agreed with his writings, these characteristics did not fail him. What he gained, was others' gain; what he lost, concerned himself only; he suffered pain, but never inflicted it; and it is amazing to think how small an amount of mere insensibility to other people's opinions would have exalted Doctor Goldsmith's position in the literary circles of his day. He lost caste because he could not acquire it, and could as little assume the habit of indifference, as trade upon the gravity of the repute he had won. . . . Few cared to think or speak of him but as little Goldy, honest Goldy; and every one laughed at him for the oddity of his blunders, and the awkwardness of his manners.

But I invite the reader to his life and adventures, and the times wherein they were cast. No uninstructive explanation of all this may possibly await us there, if together we review the scene, and move among its actors as they play their parts. (pp. 1-4)

> John Forster, "The Author to the Reader," in his
> The Life and Times of Oliver Goldsmith, Vol. I,
> *second edition, Bradbury and Evans, 1854, pp. 1-4.*

THE ATHENAEUM (essay date 1864)

[*The anonymous critic of the following excerpt considers* Sir John Eliot *a definitive biography and praises Forster for having chosen to write a thorough and scholarly work rather than a popular one.*]

A good deal of honest and fruitful labour has been given to **'Sir John Eliot.'** Nearly thirty years ago Mr. Forster, who had then undertaken to write a series of Lives of our eminent Statesmen of the Commonwealth for Lardner's 'Cabinet Cyclopaedia,' selected Eliot from the great list of English patriots who had found no biographers. On Eliot he bestowed the virgin freshness of his pen. The volume which he produced supplied a distinct need of the student of our Stuart history; and, indeed, it has never failed to receive from scholars and historians a due measure of respect and quotation. Beyond all comparison it was the best of Mr. Forster's early works; for the ground on which the writer trod was fresh, the materials were gathered by himself, and the picture presented had an unstudied vigour and animation all its own. . . .

The book is a big book. It is, indeed, curious to consider that here was an Orator of whom up to 1836 no one had thought it worth while to write a separate life. When the idea dawned on Mr. Forster, the materials for a picture of the man appeared to be scanty, and had to be sought for in many quarters. Now, his biography fills two stout volumes, numbering in the twain about 1,300 pages; and not one page too much. The general reader will, of course, think differently from ourselves on such a point. The interest of a general reader lies, as it should do, mainly in his own time, and in things which connect themselves with the sympathies of his own time. Yet a leader satisfies him about Mr. Gladstone or Lord Palmerston. If a great prince departs from among us, he expects to be told everything about him in one article. In that which is remote, either as to space or time, his interest must be roused by subtle art, by brilliant pictures, and a dramatic march of events. This is a kind of demand which the writer of this Life of Eliot has not had much in his thoughts. Mr. Forster aims at the philosophical rather than the picturesque: at being useful and complete rather than showy and popular. . . . Idlers may therefore be warned off. Let those who find a big book a great evil leave **'Sir John Eliot'** to more earnest men. To real students its fullness will be found to be its principal charm. On three or four important points, our public history is here treated with a degree of detail not to be found elsewhere. In fact, Mr. Forster's book, though unlikely to be much in vogue at the circulating libraries during the dining and dancing months, will have its place on the study-table, and will lie on the shelf for consultation and reference long after the book of the season has been given up to the chandler's man. (p. 363)

> *A review of "Sir John Eliot: A Biography,
> 1590-1632," in* The Athenaeum, *No. 1898, March
> 12, 1864, pp. 363-65.*

[R. MONCKTON MILNES] (essay date 1869)

[*Milnes, who later became Lord Houghton, was an English politician, poet, critic, and essayist. In the following excerpt, Milnes praises Forster's discretion in dealing with the controversial aspects of Landor's life in* Walter Savage Landor. *He also suggests that the biography holds more of a scholarly than a popular appeal.*]

[In **'Walter Savage Landor,'**] Mr. Forster has added to the tragic biographies of men of genius—of Otway and of Savage, of Byron and of Keats. He has performed a task, which his reverent friendship of many years made most difficult and delicate, with dignity and affection. Nothing is concealed that is worth revealing, nothing is lauded which is unjust, and nothing is left unreproved and unregretted which is wrong in moral conception or unbecoming in the action of life. In this conduct of his subject he has followed the dictates of the highest prudence; he has shown that if the temperament of his friend made him most troublesome to the societies in which he lived, made his acquaintance uneasy and his friendship perilous, it was he himself who was the foremost sufferer; that neither honourable birth, nor independent fortune, nor sturdy health, nor a marriage of free choice, nor a goodly family, nor rare talents, nor fine tastes, nor appropriate culture, nor sufficient fame, could ensure him a life of even moderate happiness, while the events of the day depended on the wild instincts of the moment, while the undisciplined and thoughtless will over-ruled all capacity of reflection and all suggestions of experience. (p. 219)

Though Mr. Forster's personal intimacy with Mr. Landor was limited to his mature and later life, the details of earlier years, supplied to him by Mr. Robert Landor—the last of the brothers— . . . and the abundant collection of letters from distinguished men which has fallen into his hands in his capacity of literary executor, have supplied him with a mass of material from which it has clearly been no easy labour to select what is most interesting and characteristic. Like all self-absorbed men, Landor had no repugnance to repetition of matter in which he himself was interested, and the same thought and mode of expression serve for many uses. There is, besides, a certain monotony in the very entirety of the character, the same susceptibility of offence, the same exaggeration of trivial circumstance, the same inability to understand and appreciate other men, which requires all the management of a skilful and practised biographer not to become tiresome to the reader who approaches the subject with no previous interest or favourable inclination. Mr. Forster found not here the genial varieties, the sweet and generous humours, of dear old 'Goldy,' which he has embodied in an English classic, and the audience of the 'Imaginary Conversations' will never be that which, all the world over, listens to the exhortations of Dr. Primrose in prison, or the story of the Irish Village Deserted long before the days of famine or emigration. In a certain sense, the enjoyment of this biography will belong to a scholarly circle, to men who value culture for its own sake, who care for the appropriate quotation and love the ring of the epigram, who take a pleasure in style analogous to that derived from a musical perception, to whom beautiful thoughts come with tenfold meaning when beautifully said; a class visibly narrowing about us, but to whom, nevertheless, this country has owed a large amount of rational happiness, and whom the aspirants after a more rugged and sincere intellectual life may themselves not be the last to regret. (p. 220)

> [*R. Monckton Milnes*], *"Forster's 'Life of Landor',"
> in* The Edinburgh Review, *Vol. CXXX, No. CCLXV,
> July, 1869, pp. 217-54.*

THE SATURDAY REVIEW, LONDON   (essay date 1869)

[*The anonymous critic of the following excerpt terms* Walter Savage Landor *an overly long and ponderous work, declaring that "Mr. Forster has decidedly overdone the business."*]

Some one, in reference to writers who, like Landor, have failed to obtain a public recognition such as their genius entitled them to expect, says of Posterity that she has no doubt many virtues, but accessibility is not one of them. Mr. Forster, in [*Walter Savage Landor*]. . . , has recourse to sheer weight of metal, with the hope of breaking down her barriers, and forcing an entrance into her presence-chamber for his friend. The book is an enormously big one, and very trying to a conscientious reviewer. It may be pleaded that the great powers of Mr. Landor, coupled as they were with one of the strangest of characters, constitute an apology, perhaps a sufficient one, for this [work] . . . , which we hope will find, as it deserves to find, readers in spite of its bulk. Nevertheless we will say at once, speaking for ourselves, that although the comparative want of popularity which always disappointed Mr. Landor and Mr. Landor's friends may have forced his biographer into quoting largely, Mr. Forster has decidedly overdone the business. Those interminable abstracts which "lie floating many a rood" on his oceanlike expanse of print weary the reader, and produce no effect which might not have been equally well accomplished by a less unrelenting use of the scissors. (p. 92)

Mr. Forster has recorded all his actions and analysed all his works. That it was unnecessary to quote quite so much, and to make abstracts quite so numerous, we have said before. But Landor is one of the few men who deserve an elaborate biography, and he certainly has got one. (p. 93)

> *"Forster's Life of Landor," in* The Saturday Review, *London, Vol. 28, No. 716, July 17, 1869, pp. 92-3.*

[WHITWELL ELWIN]   (essay date 1872)

[*Elwin, a close friend of Forster who served as executor of his estate, edited the* Quarterly Review *from 1853 to 1860. In the following excerpt, he offers a highly complimentary view of the first volume of* The Life of Charles Dickens, *citing the completeness and accuracy of Forster's portrait.*]

To us it appears that a more faithful biography [than **'The Life of Charles Dickens'**] could not be written. The testimony which Sir Joshua Reynolds bore to 'Boswell's Life of Johnson,' 'that every word of it might be depended upon as if given on oath,' is true of Mr. Forster's work. Dickens is seen in his pages precisely as he showed in his ordinary intercourse, with the accession of honour which accrues to him from the story of his boyhood and youth. It was always supposed that he had told much of his early history in 'David Copperfield.' Mr. Forster has separated the facts from the fiction, and completely as the two coincide for a while the real life had a sequel to which there is nothing comparable in the tale. (p. 125)

The life of a literary man should be the history both of the author and his works. Mr. Forster has been attentive to his double function. Dickens was accustomed to talk over with him every story while it was in conception or in progress, and submitted every proof sheet to his judgment, from 'Pickwick' to 'Edwin Drood.' His intimate knowledge of his friend's design in the scope and purpose of each tale gives an importance beyond mere opinion to the critical expositions of Mr. Forster. He has shown that there was always some grave central purpose

in the mind of Dickens which was as the axis upon which the amusement revolved, and, without dwelling upon the obvious qualities that are recognised by all the world, he has pointed out the wealth of subtler excellencies that are likely to be overlooked. His view of the man is marked by the same perspicacity in exhibiting delicate lights and shadows. The biography, in its incipient stage, takes its place already among the very few lives which bring before us a figure of pre-eminent individuality in its native distinctness. The service is especially important because there has rarely been a genius whose life was a more essential supplement to his works, for the works grew out of the life, and until we know from his biography how he got at his characters, our comprehension of them is incomplete. The story is elevating. Few persons could follow, without surprise and admiration, the silent, secret growth of a genius, which shaped itself unaided in the midst of an unintellectual, depressing atmosphere, assimilated to itself all kinds of common materials, and moulded them into rich immortal forms. . . . People have sometimes fabricated from parts of [Dickens's] writings an imaginary likeness of him, which had not the faintest resemblance to the original. Except in fragments, such as passages in the adventures of Copperfield, the characters he describes are no more his own character than a landscape painter is the prospect he paints. The real man is the Charles Dickens of Mr. Forster's biography, and the singular history, which is the apology for his faults, is most of all conspicuous for the ennobling qualities that heighten the lustre of his genius. (pp. 146-47)

> [Whitwell Elwin], *"Forster's 'Life of Dickens'," in* The Quarterly Review, *Vol. 132, No. 263, January, 1872, pp. 125-47.*

THOMAS CARLYLE   (letter date 1872)

[*In the following letter to Forster, Carlyle applauds the biographer's restraint and painstaking approach to detail in the first volume of* The Life of Charles Dickens. *Carlyle also offers his hope that Forster will adopt a broader perspective in the third volume of the work.*]

Like all mankind, I have been reading your *Life of Dickens*. . . . It is a work of wonderful diligence, friendliness and clearness of detail; gives us as it were, a complete Photograph of Dickens's existence, literary and other; everything is said too with perfect neatness graceful precision and propriety: some complain that there is an *over*-minuteness of detail. . . . Perhaps in the third Vol. you will gather yourself more into epochs, and direct your chief force of detail in making visual the *last* American voyage, which has to me always so tragical a character; and stands in such strange and mournful contrast to the First, and to its own external splendour of colouring, Ah me, Ah me! (pp. 222-23)

> *Thomas Carlyle, in a letter to John Forster on November 22, 1872, in* Bulletin of The John Rylands Library, *Vol. 38, No. 1, September, 1955, pp. 222-23.*

[WILLIAM DEAN HOWELLS]   (essay date 1873)

[*Howells was the chief progenitor of American realism and an influential American literary critic during the late nineteenth and early twentieth centuries. Although he wrote nearly three dozen novels, few of them are read today. Despite his eclipse, however, he stands as one of the major literary figures of the late nineteenth century; having successfully weaned American literature from the sentimental romanticism of its infancy, he earned the popular* sobriquet *"the Dean of American Letters." In the following excerpt from his negative assessment of the second volume of* The Life of Charles Dickens, *Howells criticizes Forster's use of Dickens's letters to himself to the near exclusion of those written to the novelist's other correspondents. Howells declares Forster's biography misleading and states that "there could be no greater misfortune to Charles Dickens's memory than that it should be permanently accepted as his history."*]

The second volume of Mr. Forster's *Life of Dickens* is not so interesting as the first. It does not reach the period of Dickens's separation from his wife, and it gives no facts of his *vie intime* to compare in effect with those already related of his childhood. On the other hand, it has all the disagreeable qualities of the first volume: it is even more bragging in tone, feeble and wandering in analysis, and comical in criticism. (p. 237)

The letters throughout the book are nearly always to Mr. Forster; as if Mr. Forster did not like to connect any other name with Dickens's. It is true that he quotes some passages of the letters to President Felton from Mr. Fields's *Yesterdays with Authors,* and these are so much better than any written to himself that one wishes his biographer had cast about him a little to see if he could not discover some other correspondent of Dickens. Though the letters given are not easy reading, though their fun seems often pitilessly forced, and their seriousness of the blackest midnight hue, and their fervor of the very red hottest, they are extremely useful in possessing us fully with an idea of the pressure under which Dickens felt, joked, wept, wrote, lived. (p. 238)

[Graciousness] is not a characteristic of this odd biography, in which the unamiable traits of the biographer combine with the unamiable traits of his subject to give the book as disagreeable a tone as a book ever had. We behold in one case a high-pressure egotist, living in a world pervaded by himself, eager for gain, and dismayed by smaller profits than he expected, suspicious of those whom he dealt with in business, relentless in his own interests, a dreadful machine capable of walking ten miles every day and writing a chapter of fiction, quoting himself continually, and behaving himself generally in a manner to be wearisome to the flesh and spirit of all other men; and, on the other hand, we have a jealous and greedy intimate of his who insists upon representing him solely from his own personal and epistolary knowledge. But we feel sure that this is a false view of Charles Dickens. The letters to Mr. Forster are of less value than his other letters, because they have the stamp of an exaggerated and exacting friendship on them; they are all of the operatic pitch; and latterly they appear to have been written with a consciousness that they were some day to be used as literary material. It is not credible that these letters alone were accessible to the biographer, and it is strange that he seldom or never gives any reminiscences of Dickens besides his own. The closest friend cannot see the whole character of any man; but this biography seems to be written upon the contrary theory, and it renders another life of Dickens necessary. It must always remain as a most entertaining mass of material, but there could be no greater misfortune to Charles Dickens's memory than that it should be permanently accepted as his history. (p. 239)

[William Dean Howells], in a review of "The Life of Charles Dickens, Vol. II," in The Atlantic Monthly, *Vol. XXXI, No. 184, February, 1873, pp. 237-39.*

[FRANCES CASHEL HOEY] (essay date 1873)

[In the following excerpt, Hoey censures various aspects of the second volume of The Life of Charles Dickens. *The critic maintains that Forster's handling of Dickens's relationship with his mother is an insult to the latter, that the biographer's place in his work is too prominent, and that his overall portrait of Dickens's character is inaccurate.]*

Without impeaching Mr. Forster's sincerity in any respect or degree—without imputing to him a particle of the treacherous ingratitude and deadly damaging cunning which made Leigh Hunt's 'Life of Byron' notorious—it may be gravely doubted whether the little poet dealt the great one's memory a more cruel blow than Mr. Forster, in the character of a mourning Mentor out of work, has dealt the memory of Telemachus Dickens. To all unprejudiced persons, with just notions of the relations of men with their fellows, he presents the object of his preposterously inflated praise in an aspect both painful and surprising. Who is to correct this impression? We are forced to believe that Mr. Forster, from his long and close association with him, is the person who can best paint Mr. Dickens as he was in reality; we are forced to accept the man whose writings so charmed and delighted us on the evidence of a close and long-sustained correspondence with Mr. Forster, to whom he apparently assigned the foremost place in his literary and private life as guide, friend, companion, and critic. Mr. Dickens might have had no other intimate associate than his future biographer throughout the long term of years during which he was constantly appealing to his judgment, adopting his corrections, yielding to his advice, and gushing about walks, rides, dinners, and drinks in his company. There are no people in the book but these two; the rest are merely names, to which casual reference is made in records of jovial dinners and meetings for purposes of unlimited flattery. . . . By every device of omission, as well as by open assertion, Mr. Forster claims to represent Mr. Dickens as he was—to be the only licensed interpreter of the great novelist to the world. The world grants his claim, and, judging his book by it, is surprised by the nature of the information which is the outcome of so many years of close and unreserved intercourse. Not only is the one-sidedness common to biographies conspicuous in this one, but the two large volumes published up to the present time are as scanty in one sense as they are diffuse in another. Did Mr. Dickens correspond with no one but Mr. Forster? Has no one preserved letters from him to which his biographer might have procured access? Were there no side-lights to be had? The most fantastic of his own creations is hardly less like a living responsible man than the excited, restless, hysterical, self-engrossed, quarrelsome, unreasonable egotist shown to the world as the real Charles Dickens throughout at least three-fourths of these two volumes; shown, it is true, upon the evidence of his own letters—perhaps the most wonderful records of human vanity which have ever seen the light of print—but shown also, through the fault of his biographer, in appalling nakedness, by his strict limitation of Mr. Dickens's "life" to the chronicle of his relations with Mr. Forster. (pp. 170-71)

Was it . . . characteristic of Mr. Dickens to act, in all the grave circumstances of life, with a hard self-assertion, an utter ignoring of everybody's rights, feelings, and interests except his own—an assumption of the holy and infallible supremacy of his own views and his own claims which are direct contradictions of all his finest and most effusive sentiments? If not, then his biographer has to answer for producing the impression upon the mind of the reader, who looks in vain throughout these volumes for any indication that Mr. Dickens's fine writing about human relations has any but a Pecksniffian sense. In every reference to Mr. Dickens in his filial capacity there is evident a repulsive hardness, a contemptuous want of feeling.

His parents were poor, in constant difficulties, and their son made capital of the fact for some of his cleverest and some of his least pleasing fictions; the Micawbers among the former, the Dorrits among the latter. Every allusion to his father grates upon the reader's feelings. (pp. 172-73)

In another instance the biographer shocks yet more profoundly the moral sense of persons who believe that genius is not less, but more, bound by the common law of duty in feeling and in action. There is a vast amount of sentiment, there are numerous prettinesses about mothers and babies, and about motherhood and sonhood in the abstract, in Mr. Dickens's works; and in this case also, he, for whom it is so persistently claimed that he lived *in* and *with* his books that he must needs incur the penalty of this praise, is made by Mr. Forster to produce the effect of falseness and inconsistency. The slight mention made of Mr. Dickens's mother by the biographer is contemptuous, and his own solitary direct allusion to her is unjust and unfilial. Could not Mr. Forster recall anything, ever so slight, in all that long intimacy, so close and constant that it seems to have left no room and no time in the novelist's life for any other, to counterbalance that impression? The temptation, which no doubt strongly beset the *littérateur*, to colour as highly as possible the picture of the "blacking-bottle period," has been too strong for the biographer, who has failed to perceive that in making the episode exceedingly interesting, very alluring to public curiosity, he has made the subject of it contemptible. The picture is a painful one, not altogether and only from the side on which alone it is contemplated by Mr. Dickens and Mr. Forster; it is pervaded by the characteristics of all the pictures of Mr. Dickens's earlier years, and of all dealings with everybody on occasions when they did not turn out to his entire satisfaction. Neither Mr. Dickens nor his biographer regard this period of the celebrated novelist's life justly; they both look at it from the standpoint of accomplished facts, of mature life, developed genius, and achieved fame. (pp. 174-75)

Mr. Forster looks upon the childhood and youth of Mr. Dickens with the eyes of his fame and maturity, and cries out against the ignoring of a prodigy before there had been anything prodigious about him, just as Mr. Dickens himself complains of the publishers, to whom he owed the opportunity of making a reputation, for ill-treating *a famous author*, and fattening on his brains. Mr. Forster is emphatic in his blame of every one who was concerned in the matter—or indeed who was not, for "friends" are taken to task—that Charles Dickens was not given a good education, and eloquent about the education which he afterwards gave himself. Here, again, the besetting temptation of the biographer to invest his subject with attributes which do not belong to him, as well as to exaggerate those which do, assails Mr. Forster. There are no facts in his narrative to prove that Mr. Dickens ever was an educated man, and all the testimony of his works is against the supposition. No trait of his genius is more salient than its entire self-dependence; no defects of it are more marked than his intolerance of subjects which he did not understand, and his high-handed dogmatic treatment of matters which he regarded with the facile contempt of ignorance. This unfortunate tendency was fostered by the atmosphere of flattery in which he lived; a life which, in the truly educational sense, was singularly narrow; and though he was not entirely to blame for the extent, it affected his later works very much to their disadvantage. As a novelist he is distinguished, as a humourist he is unrivalled in this age; but when he deals with the larger spheres of morals, with politics, and with the mechanism of state and official life, he is absurd. He announces truisms and tritenesses with an air of discovery

impossible to a well-read man, and he propounds with an air of conviction, hardly provoking, it is so simply foolish, flourishing solutions of problems, which have long perplexed the gravest and ablest minds in the higher ranges of thought.

We hear of his extensive and varied reading. Where is the evidence that he ever read anything beyond fiction, and some of the essayists? Certainly not in his books, which might be the only books in the world, for any indication of study or book-knowledge in them. Not a little of their charm, not a little of their wide-spread miscellaneous popularity, is referable to that very thing. Every one can understand them; they are not for educated people only; they do not suggest comparisons, or require explanations, or imply associations; they stand alone, self-existent, delightful facts. A slight reference to Fielding and Smollett, a fine rendering of one chapter in English history—the Gordon riots—very finely done, and a clever adaptation of Mr. Carlyle's 'Scarecrows' to his own stage, in 'A Tale of Two Cities,' are positively the only traces of books to be found in the long series of his works. (pp. 176-77)

It is not only in the education of books that we perceive Mr. Dickens to have been defective. Mr. Forster's account of him makes it evident that he was deficient in that higher education of the mind, by which men attain to an habitually nice adjustment of the rights of others in all mutual dealings, and to that strictly-regulated consideration which is a large component of self-respect. If this biography is true and trustworthy; if the public, to whom the author of books which supplied them with a whole circle of personal friends was an abstraction, are to accept this portrait of Mr. Dickens as a living verity, then they are forced to believe that, though a spasmodically generous, he was not a just man. According to the narrative before the world, he had a most exacting, even a grinding estimate, of the sacredness and inviolability of his own rights. To underestimate *his* claims was the unpardonable stupidity; to stand against *his* interests was the inexpiable sin. This deplorable tendency was lamentably encouraged by Mr. Forster—who in 1837 made his appearance on the scene which thenceforward he occupied so very conspicuously as a party to Mr. Dickens's second quarrel in the course of a literary career then recently commenced. (pp. 178-79)

Even the humour of the great humourist suffers by the handling of his ardent but undiscriminating worshipper. The rubbish by which the tradition of Mrs. Gamp is continued, the silly letters in dubious French, which exhibit Mr. Dickens's absolute incapacity to comprehend any foreign country, and the unpardonable nonsense, in which he was encouraged by wiser men, of his pretended admiration for the Queen, are flagrant examples of injudiciousness, which heavily punishes the folly it parades. Mr. Dickens's letter about her Majesty, written thirty years' ago, was a sorry jest. Mr. Forster's publication of it now is supreme bad taste.

Mr. Dickens's sentimentalism, always exaggerated and frequently false, suffers at the hands of his biographer even more severely than his humour. Mr. Forster as confidant, and Mr. Dickens as Tilburina, in intercommunicated hysterics over the 'Christmas Stories,' 'Dombey and Son,' and 'David Copperfield,' become so very wearisome, especially when Mr. Forster solemnly declares his belief that the 'Christmas Carol' "for some may have realised the philosopher's famous experience, and by a single fortunate thought revised the whole manner of a life," that it is a positive relief when they are parted. (pp. 184-85)

It must be acknowledged that Mr. Forster's advice was very sound and valuable in many instances. Perhaps his consciousness of that fact has blinded him to the extent to which his exposure of his friend's weaknesses has gone. . . .

In one more volume this warmly-welcomed, eagerly-read biography is to be completed. That volume must necessarily be a more difficult and responsible task than its predecessors. It is to be hoped that it will fulfil the expectations of the public more satisfactorily, and that it will do more justice to Mr. Dickens by doing less injustice to all with whom he was concerned. It is to be hoped that it will put before the world a more substantial representation of the great novelist who was so variously gifted; that it will leave its readers able in some measure to respect and esteem its subject as a man, for real qualities, while ceasing to urge an imaginary claim to misplaced consideration, and especially that it will be free from the faint suggestion which pervades the present volumes, that, essentially, "Codlin was the friend, not Short." (p. 185)

> *[Frances Cashel Hoey], in a review of "The Life of Charles Dickens," in* Temple Bar, *Vol. XXXVIII, May, 1873, pp. 169-85.*

JOHN FORSTER (essay date 1874)

[*In the following excerpt from volume three of* The Life of Charles Dickens, *Forster discusses critical objections to the biography's first two volumes. Specifically, he replies to charges that he failed to include letters by Dickens to correspondents other than himself, that he figured too prominently in the narrative, and that he did not make his readers "talk to Dickens as Boswell makes them talk to Johnson."*]

Objection has been taken to this biography as likely to disappoint its readers in not making them "talk to Dickens as Boswell makes them talk to Johnson." But where will the blame lie if a man takes up *Pickwick* and is disappointed to find that he is not reading *Rasselas?* A book must be judged for what it aims to be, and not for what it cannot by possibility be. I suppose so remarkable an author as Dickens hardly ever lived who carried so little of authorship into ordinary social intercourse. Potent as the sway of his writings was over him, it expressed itself in other ways. Traces or triumphs of literary labour, displays of conversational or other personal predominance, were no part of the influence he exerted over friends. To them he was only the pleasantest of companions, with whom they forgot that he had ever written anything, and felt only the charm which a nature of such capacity for supreme enjoyment causes every one around it to enjoy. (pp. 478-79)

Of course a book must stand or fall by its contents. Macaulay said very truly that the place of books in the public estimation is fixed, not by what is written about them, but by what is written in them. I offer no complaint of any remark made upon these volumes, but there have been some misapprehensions. Though Dickens bore outwardly so little of the impress of his writings, they formed the whole of that inner life which essentially constituted the man; and as in this respect he was actually, I have thought that his biography should endeavour to present him. The story of his books, therefore, at all stages of their progress, and of the hopes or designs connected with them, was my first care. With that view, and to give also to the memoir what was attainable of the value of autobiography, letters to myself, such as were never addressed to any other of his correspondents, and covering all the important incidents in the life to be retraced, were used with few exceptions ex-

clusively; and though the exceptions are much more numerous in the present volume, this general plan has guided me to the end. Such were my limits indeed, that half even of those letters had to be put aside; and to have added all such others as were open to me would have doubled the size of my book, not contributed to it a new fact of life or character, and altered materially its design. It would have been so much lively illustration added to the subject, but out of place here. The purpose here was to make Dickens the sole central figure in the scenes revived, narrator as well as principal actor; and only by the means employed could consistency or unity be given to the self-revelation, and the picture made definite and clear. It is the peculiarity of few men to be to their most intimate friend neither more nor less than they are to themselves, but this was true of Dickens; and what kind or quality of nature such intercourse expressed in him, of what strength, tenderness, and delicacy susceptible, of what steady level warmth, of what daily unresting activity of intellect, of what unbroken continuity of kindly impulse through the change and vicissitude of three-and-thirty years, the letters to myself given in these volumes could alone express. Gathered from various and differing sources, their interest could not have been as the interest of these; in which everything comprised in the successive stages of a most attractive career is written with unexampled candour and truthfulness, and set forth in definite pictures of what he saw and stood in the midst of, unblurred by vagueness or reserve. Of the charge of obtruding myself to which their publication has exposed me, I can only say that I studied nothing so hard as to suppress my own personality, and have to regret my ill success where I supposed I had even too perfectly succeeded. But we have all of us frequent occasion to say, parodying Mrs. Peachem's remark, that we are bitter bad judges of ourselves. (pp. 479-81)

> *John Forster, in his* The Life of Charles Dickens: 1852-1870, *Vol. III, J. B. Lippincott & Co., 1874, 600 p.*

THE SATURDAY REVIEW, LONDON (essay date 1874)

[*The following anonymous excerpt offers a predominantly negative perspective on the third volume of* The Life of Charles Dickens. *In a reply to Forster's comments in the third volume on criticism of the first two volumes, the critic asserts that the biographer does not entirely explain his failure to suppress his own personality. The critic also argues that the "real" Dickens is missing from the biography and terms the work as a whole "very incomplete and unsatisfactory." For Forster's comments on criticism of the first two volumes, see excerpt dated 1874.*]

In one of the last chapters of this, the concluding, volume of Mr. Forster's . . . [*The Life of Charles Dickens*], the author makes a few remarks in answer to criticisms upon the earlier parts of his work. He was charged with making himself too conspicuous. He replies that he "studied nothing so hard as to suppress his own personality, and has to regret his ill success where he supposed that he had only too perfectly succeeded." We cannot withdraw our opinion as to Mr. Forster's success in self-suppression; but, after such an apology, we shall not press the charge any further; and we are the more ready to withdraw from the question because the present volume is not open in anything like the same degree to our former criticism. Mr. Forster is here a much less conspicuous figure, and has published some letters which were not addressed to himself. Of another charge which he endeavours equally to repel we must say a little more. People, he says, have complained not

A portrait of Forster at eighteen by Daniel Maclise and Thomas Warrington.

only of Mr. Forster's presence, but of Dickens's absence. They have been disappointed because Mr. Forster does not make them talk to Dickens as Boswell made them talk to Johnson. Mr. Forster's reply is remarkable. He says that the book could not have resembled Boswell, because Dickens carried nothing of his authorship into social intercourse. "His talk was unaffected and natural, never bookish in the smallest degree." Just the same remark might have been made of Johnson. The charm of Boswell is precisely that he shows us the man Johnson whom we should never have inferred from Johnson the author. The reason for Mr. Forster's incapacity to rival Boswell is a simpler one. It is that Dickens was not a Johnson, and that Mr. Forster is not a Boswell. The biographer has not the power of dramatic representation, and the subject of the biography did not, it may be presumed, present such good materials for the art of conversational reporting. Yet Dickens's mode of uttering himself was characteristic in its way, and perhaps a writer of the necessary qualifications might have succeeded in setting the man before us more vividly than Mr. Forster has done. To compare any book with the most successful work of its own kind ever produced is necessarily unfair; and we have no right to measure Mr. Forster's merits by the degree in which he has fallen short of Boswell. Such a felicitous combination has only happened once in the whole course of English literary history, and may never happen again. We do say, however, that a biographer of so much experience as Mr. Forster, and with such opportunities of knowledge, might have been expected to give us a really vivid account of a friend known so long and so intimately, and so well deserving a skilful portraiture. And we must express our conviction that, judged by a very moderate standard, the book is on the whole disappointing.

What, we naturally ask, was the real Dickens? What was his domestic and social character? What view did he take of his own calling, and how far did he act up to his beliefs? The curtain cannot be altogether drawn aside; but we may expect to learn something of that inner life which can never be completely recorded in a man's own writings. The answer which Mr. Forster gives us is very inadequate. We are indeed rather grateful than otherwise for certain omissions. Mr. Forster touches very lightly indeed upon that passage in the life of Dickens which chiefly determined the course of his later years, and which, in consequence of some unfortunate revelations, has left a rather disagreeable impression upon the minds of many of us. It is plain, however, that the whole truth cannot be told, if any one is competent to tell it, with due regard to the rights of social privacy and to the feelings of survivors. Under these circumstances we unreservedly approve of Mr. Forster's reticence, though we must add that the reticence necessarily deprives us of the means of judging of Dickens's behaviour under the most critical circumstances. Leaving this question, however, we proceed to ask what kind of impression Mr. Forster gives us in this volume of the last twenty years of Dickens's life? The first answer must be that it is on the whole a melancholy one. The book consists chiefly of letters in which Dickens describes some of the scenes in which he was placed; of other letters giving the account of his success in public readings; and, finally, of criticisms upon his later books and his general merits as a writer. The first of these divisions is agreeable enough. The letters in which Dickens gives his impressions of French life and manners are admirable in their way. They are in much the same vein as his charming *Uncommercial Traveller;* and perhaps even pleasanter, because less marked by his peculiar mannerism. . . .

We pass, however, to the more personal part of the narrative; and here we become sensible of that melancholy impression which we have noticed. The story of Dickens's last years, as here set before us, is indeed as sad as it is simple. We see a man of genius killing himself by inches in the effort to make money. The strong man breaks down by constantly straining his powers a little too far; the work which was once done spontaneously without a conscious effort has to be performed at high pressure, and with an ever-increasing sense of its painfulness; and, moreover, as Mr. Forster says himself, the task under which Dickens ultimately broke down was one which, if not below his dignity, was at least not the highest to which he might have devoted himself. (p. 182)

Mr. Forster takes occasion in this volume to attack M. Taine, for whose estimate of Dickens we have little sympathy; having settled M. Taine, he proceeds to make a rather angry reply to a paper contributed by Mr. Lewes to the *Fortnightly Review.* Mr. Forster hints his opinion that the article was biassed by some personal feeling. We do not think that Mr. Forster's answer is calculated to persuade anybody who does not already agree with him, or that he even seizes very distinctly the force of Mr. Lewes's remarks. But such questions as these are not strictly relevant to the biography. The readers of Dickens may doubtless find many things in Mr. Forster's three volumes which will throw more light upon the novels than any direct criticism. The portrait of Dickens is, indeed, very incomplete and unsatisfactory; but it would be unfair to deny that it puts us in possession of many facts which render both the merits and the defects of the novels more intelligible. That will be its principal merit, for its independent interest is certainly less than might have been expected from the subject. (p. 183)

"Forster's Life of Dickens," in The Saturday Review, *London, Vol. 37, No. 954, February 7, 1874, pp. 182-83.*

[R. H. HUTTON]   (essay date 1874)

[*Hutton expresses qualified praise for* The Life of Charles Dickens *in the following excerpt from a review of volume three. The critic argues that the biography lowers Dickens's moral stature in the eyes of the reader because of its emphasis on the unhappy circumstances of the last two decades of his life. However, Hutton asserts that the book is likely to endure as an important and popular study of Dickens.*]

[The third volume of *The Life of Charles Dickens*] is a melancholy close to a book which, in spite of the many traits of astonishing perceptive power, and prodigal generosity, and unbounded humour, contained in it, will certainly not add to the personal fascination with which Dickens is regarded by so many of his countrymen. The closing volume naturally contains more evidence than any of the others of the very great defect of character which seems to have grown from the very roots of Dickens's genius. Mr. Forster himself admits it fully enough, though he hardly seems to be aware what an admission it is. "There was for him," says his biographer, "no 'city of the mind' against outward ills for inner consolation and shelter." In other words, Dickens depended more than most men on the stimulus which outer things provided for him; first, on the excitement caused by the popularity of his books, and on that which he drew from his own personal friends' private appreciation; then on the applause which attended his actings and readings, the intensity of the eagerness to hear him and the emotion he excited; and lastly, on the triumph excited by the counting-up of the almost fabulous sums which the readings produced. . . . The painful story of his estrangement from his wife, which Mr. Forster has told at once with judicious candour and equally judicious reticence, is evidently closely connected with this dependence of his on the stimulus of external excitement. There would indeed have been no reason for any public reference to that story at all, but for the inexcusable intolerance of public censure which made Dickens, when he was contemplating his first course of public readings, insist on publishing a defence of himself against the false and slanderous rumours which were abroad. (pp. 174-75)

The volume before us, so far as it illustrates Dickens's moral qualities at all, may be said to be one long chronicle of his craving for these delights of popular applause,—sometimes outweighing, as in the case to which we have alluded, what the least modicum of magnanimity would have enforced upon him,—at other times, extinguishing all the sense of personal dignity which might have been expected in an author of so much genius,—and finally overpowering the commonest prudence, and leading directly, no doubt, to his premature death. Mr. Forster, by giving so much prominence to the certainly extraordinary and marvellous popularity of the public readings, and recording, at excessive length, Dickens's unbounded triumph in the enthusiasm and numbers and reckless prodigality of his audiences, has given to this craving of his hero's a somewhat needless emphasis, and has, moreover, extended his already very big book beyond reasonable limits. Nobody wants to hear how the people at Tynemouth did exactly what the people at Dover did; how Cambridge and Edinburgh behaved in exactly the same manner as Dublin and Manchester, and so forth. . . . It would have added to the literary worth of the book, and certainly not have diminished the reader's admiration, if Mr. Forster had curtailed greatly the tiresome redundancy of Dickens's own gratitude for the popular enthusiasm with which he was received.

Mr. Forster notes another quality besides this absence in Dickens of any inner life in which he could take refuge from the craving for external excitement,—a quality which, while it very much increased the danger of this dependence on the stimulus of bursts of popular favour, was also inseparable from his greatest qualities. There was "something of the despot, seldom separable from genius," says Mr. Forster, in Dickens. No doubt there was, but we should say that genius is quite as often found without it as with it; that it was the peculiarity of Dickens's own genius, and closely connected with his highly-strung nerves, rather than the token of genius in general. (p. 175)

On the whole, we cannot deny either that Mr. Forster's biography was a very difficult book indeed to write, or that it has been well done. It has painted to us a picture morally much more disappointing than we expected, and it has perhaps dwelt on some of the most disappointing features at unnecessary length, and with a certain awkward air of half-admission, half-deprecation. There is far too much criticism on individual works of Dickens, to some of which Mr. Forster recurs repeatedly; and it does not appear to us that the criticism is always sound. His attack on Mr. Lewes in the present volume is very fierce, but by no means as effective as it is fierce, and though we cannot pretend to accept Mr. Lewes's judgment,—we believe Dickens to be certainly the greatest humourist of his nation, and Mr. Lewes appears to give him credit only for fun,—Mr. Forster quite fails to make good against Mr. Lewes the largeness and wholeness of the humanity in Dickens's creations. But with all these faults and short-comings, Mr. Forster's life of Dickens will always be as eagerly read as long as Dickens himself is eagerly read; and that will be as long as Englishmen retain their delight in English literature. (p. 176)

> [R. H. Hutton], "Charles Dickens," in The Spectator, *Vol. 47, No. 2380, February 7, 1874, pp. 174-76.*

THOMAS CARLYLE   (letter date 1874)

[*In the following excerpt from a letter to Forster, Carlyle praises the third volume of* The Life of Charles Dickens, *declaring the biography as a whole to be the equal of James Boswell's* Life of Johnson. *For Carlyle's assessment of the first volume, see excerpt dated 1872.*]

I am happy to say, as I can with perfect sincerity, that I have read your third volume of *Dickens* with continued interest and pleasure—and with a glad surprise, moreover, which heightens all these feelings. Surprise I say, for the narrative flows with limpid clearness, soft harmony, perfection of phrase and idea; not a trace in it anywhere of the horrid state of pain in which I too well know you to have been all the while.

This Third Volume throws a new light and character to me over the Work at large. I incline to consider this Biography as taking rank, in essential respects, parallel to Boswell himself, though on widely different grounds. Boswell, by those genial abridgments and vivid face to face pictures of Johnson's thoughts, conversational ways and modes of appearance among his fellow-creatures, has given, as you often hear me say, such a delineation of a man's existence as was never given by another man. By quite different resources, by those sparkling, clear and sunny utterances of Dickens's own (bits of *auto*-biography unrivalled in clearness and credibility) which were at your disposal and have been intercalated every now and then, you have given to every intelligent eye the power of looking down to the very bottom of Dickens's mode of existing in this world; and I say have performed a feat which, except in Boswell, the unique, I know not where to parallel. So long as Dickens is interesting to his fellow-men, here will be seen, face to face, what Dickens's manner of existing was; his steady practicality, withal; the singularly solid business talent he continually had; and deeper than all, if one had the eye to see deep enough, dark, fateful silent elements, tragical to look upon, and hiding amid dazzling radiances as of the sun, the elements of death itself. Those two American Journies especially transcend in tragic interest to a thinking reader most things one has seen in writing.

On the whole, therefore, I declare you to have done right well, my Friend. . . .

Thomas Carlyle, in a letter to John Forster on February 16, 1874, in Bulletin of The John Rylands Library, *Vol. 38, No. 1, September, 1955, p. 223.*

A[NDREW] LANG   (essay date 1874)

[*Lang was one of England's most powerful men of letters during the closing decades of the nineteenth century. A proponent of the revival of Romantic fiction, Lang championed the works of H. Rider Haggard, Robert Louis Stevenson, and Rudyard Kipling and was harshly critical of the Naturalistic and Realistic techniques of such novelists as Émile Zola and Henry James. A nostalgic vision of the past colored his work as a translator, poet, and revisionist historian. While most of his writings are seldom read today, he is remembered as the editor of the "color fairy book" series, a twelve-volume collection of fairy tales considered a classic in the genre. In the excerpt below, Lang argues that* The Life of Charles Dickens *"is a thoroughly successful picture of the life of the great humourist" and defends Forster from the charge that he intruded himself too much into the book. For Forster's comments on his role in the biography, see excerpt dated 1874.*]

Mr. Forster's *Life of Dickens,* now completed in the third volume, is a thoroughly successful picture of the life of the great humourist, and an invaluable aid to the attempt to estimate his genius. It was objected to Mr. Forster's earlier volumes, that he himself occupied too prominent a place in the narrative, and that he did not represent his friend in the most amiable and pleasing light. But it is not easy to see how the biographer could have obtruded himself less. An attachment so close, so long, and so unbroken, is perhaps unparalleled in the annals of literary friendships. There was no moment in the life of Dickens in which he did not appeal to Mr. Forster as to another self. Whether it was a question of putting off a dinner-party, or of going to America, of changing the name of a character, or of changing his domestic relations, or of giving public readings—these two last steps Mr. Dickens spoke of as the Plunge and the Dash—his constant cry to Mr. Forster was "advise, advise!" It was not possible to tell the story of the one life without admitting something of the other. Then as to the keenness, the hardness, the masterful side of Mr. Dickens' character, his restlessness, his uneasy endurance of society, his too lofty estimate of the importance of himself and his affairs, all these are easily accounted for by the story of a life which made such blemishes almost fatal. Thus Mr. Forster's book is an *apologia* for the life, and for the genius, with its defects. For the genius of Dickens, immense as it was, cannot be absolved from criticism, as Mr. Forster almost seems to wish. It is true that since Shakespeare there has lived no writer with such a power of comic invention, or gifted with such swift and sure observation; no one who has given us all so many new friends—and so many new butts—no one whose words have become so much a part of the language, and whose works have been so universally "a truce with sorrows, and forgetfulness of

evils." . . . "Who can listen," as Thackeray said, "to objections to such books as these? They seem to me a national benefit, and to every man or woman who reads them, a personal kindness."

Yet objections there were—"critical cant," Mr. Forster would say—but not wanting in truth. Mr. Forster is very angry with these criticisms, and seems to attribute Mr. Lewes' rather lumbering review to personal feeling. If he happens to remember the advice which the author of *Ranthorpe* dealt so freely to the author of *Jane Eyre,* he will find that Mr. Lewes could be very candid, without being at all unfriendly. Yet it cannot be denied that some of the detractors of Mr. Dickens were moved by his extraordinary popularity. (pp. 190-91)

[His] cheerfulness gave pain to many cultivated minds. And so out of reaction, envy if you please, against this wonderful popularity of Dickens, out of annoyance at his tricks and affectations, at his worshippers and his imitators, there arose objections enough to furnish weapons to a school of hostile critics. The first volume of the *Life of Dickens* seemed to increase this hostility. There were people who failed to see that the keenness, the vanity, the defects in culture of Mr. Dickens, were only the scanty results for evil of so bitter a youth, so hard a training, acting on the most delicately sensitive organisation and character.

We speak of the limitations of Mr. Dickens, of his want of connection with the literary and social forces of the world. We contrast this with the culture of Goethe, the wonderful goodness and humanity of Scott, the urbane art of Thackeray. And then Mr. Forster's first two volumes explain these limitations, and leave the stranger marvel that Dickens still could deserve these words of Mr. Carlyle, "a most cordial, sincere, clearsighted, quietly-decisive, just, and loving man." (p. 191)

Mr. Forster's earlier volumes explained much of the defects in Mr. Dickens' genius by the misfortunes of his youth. The misfortune of his later age, the constant excitement which that intense life of eternal watchfulness of men and things produced, goes far to account for his later strained and "tormented" style. Beside this restless excitability, there were domestic troubles of which he let the world hear too much, and of which Mr. Forster tells no more. The interest of the volume is a melancholy one. . . . His American experiences only add to the melancholy interest of the book—the spectacle of a man of the greatest genius so bereft of any "city of the mind" that he is driven to seek excitement and even repose in constant change of work, change of scene, and of applauding crowds. . . . No man, as Mr. Forster says, cared less for money; and it cannot be doubted that his real motive for these exertions was the search for repose in counter-excitement, and something of the feeling that there was a match between the strength of his will and the strength of his constitution. The latter gave him many warnings before it broke down, but most happily when it did give way, it was decisively. . . . It is good to know what we do of Dickens. The keen student of human nature wished that his own story should be told in full. (pp. 191-92)

A[ndrew] Lang, in a review of "The Life of Charles Dickens, Vol. III," in The Academy, *Vol. V, February 21, 1874, pp. 190-92.*

THE SATURDAY REVIEW, LONDON   (essay date 1875)

[*This anonymous critic applauds Forster for dispelling many of the common misconceptions about Swift's life in his biography of the author. Critical of repetition within* The Life of Jonathan Swift, *the reviewer nevertheless terms Forster's use of factual detail "always indisputably lucid."*]

A long-expected book, like a long-expected friend, must on appearing at last be prepared to answer a great many questions, and perhaps to meet a few demands and disappoint a few hopes of a not altogether reasonable description. Mr. Forster's *Life of Swift,* of which the present generation has after all lived to have at least the first volume in its hands, is not likely to prove an exception to the rule. In the world of letters, as elsewhere, many reputations are, temporarily if not permanently, sustained by a judicious display of the power of seeing mysteries, which is by no means invariably tantamount to that of seeing into them. But those who do not themselves "list to speak" are naturally all the more anxious to have their tongues untied by the revelations of those who can speak with knowledge. Swift, by his own confession, loved above most other things "a life by stealth"; and unhappily the efforts of many who have written and talked about him, when not concerned with obscuring the ascertainable facts of his career, have been frequently directed to vague suggestions of secrets beneath the surface. "Few men," says Mr. Forster of the subject of his biography, "who have been talked about so much are known so little." Yet the existence of a dark mystery in Swift's personal life has been frequently assumed with the most determined persistency, and to this mystery Mr. Forster, who has long been known to be collecting materials for a biography of Swift, has doubtless often been credited with possessing the key. So far, however, as the volume before us goes, the lovers of secrets—and of the scandal which secrets are fondly supposed to conceal—are likely to be grievously disappointed. With the conscientiousness and thoroughness to which his previous works have accustomed us, Mr. Forster has gathered, sifted, and interpreted the materials within his reach; there is in his book much that is new by the side of what is old, but more that is true in the place of what is false. In the way of positive discoveries of fresh facts of importance there is, as yet at all events, little to announce; but the biography is not the less welcome in consequence. We hope it may be the signal for the casting aside by even the most inveterate of literary *quidtunes* (if we may take leave to coin the word) of groundless inventions, which have sufficiently long been allowed to

wane and wax alternate like the moon.

It is at the same time, we confess, rather hard upon readers, of whatever kind, that Mr. Forster should not have found himself able to publish his biography of Swift as a completed whole. For our part—and we hope it may not savour of thanklessness to say so—we own that, having waited so long, we would even have waited a little longer if we could thus have obtained the entire narrative at once. For we can call to mind no other instance in which the interest excited by a biography has been so cruelly suspended by this method of publication. May the day never come when our best biographers shall imitate our most popular authors of fiction, and publish their masterpieces in numbers.

The value of this volume is, however, intrinsically very great. Whether Mr. Forster blends his facts into a connected narrative, or otherwise marshals them in carefully tabulated groups, their arrangement is always indisputably lucid; Swift himself cannot have prized order more highly than it is esteemed by his biographer. When Mr. Forster destroys fictions, he annihilates them with the most satisfactory completeness, and "smiling eddies" are alone left to "dimple on the main." Finally, while

he strictly confines himself to his subject, and avoids the temptation to digressions in which no one could have had a better excuse for indulging, his narrative is thoroughly consistent with itself and solid without the least approach to heaviness. We only regret that he should not have preferred to interweave the biographical notes from the letters to Esther Johnson contained in the first section of his Sixth Book with the general course of his narrative, and to relegate the section on the unprinted and misprinted Journals into an appendix pure and simple, while incidentally using so much of them as was suitable for the purpose of occasional illustration. It was Boswell who taught English biography the charm which a copiously illustrated but consecutive narrative possesses; and who is willing to turn from Boswell to the supplementary anecdotes accumulated in the last volumes of Croker's edition? Mr. Forster, to be sure, merely supplements his review of one side of Swift's life in a particular period by illustrations of its other sides drawn from Swift's own letters. But the disadvantages of the parallel system remain; and from this or other causes Mr. Forster is in his present work not altogether free from repetitions, though, if we remember right, he only on a single occasion confesses to repeating himself. Thus this *Life of Swift,* while surpassing in interest, as it does in elaboration, all the earlier works by which its author has established his claim to rank as the foremost of living English biographers, is not, if we may judge from the present volume, certain to prove the most perfect in form among them. (p. 714)

> *A review of "Forster's Life of Swift—Vol. I," in* The Saturday Review, *London, Vol. 40, No. 1049, December 4, 1875, pp. 714-16.*

STEWART MARSH ELLIS (essay date 1912)

[*In the excerpt below, Ellis asserts that* The Life of Charles Dickens *is one of the finest biographies in the English language. Yet he also examines various shortcomings of the work, including Forster's prominent place in the narrative, his cursory treatment of the early years of Dickens's literary success, and the one-sided nature of his account of the novelist's quarrel with publisher Richard Bentley. Nevertheless, Ellis believes the faults of the biography are outweighed by Forster's extensive knowledge of and admiration for Dickens. The following excerpt was drawn from an essay that originally appeared in* Chambers's Journal, *January 20, 1912.*]

Forster's *Life of Dickens* is now generally acknowledged to be one of the few great biographies in the English language, and has a place in the select group which includes Boswell's *Johnson,* Lockhart's *Scott,* Morley's *Gladstone,* and Mrs. Gaskell's *Charlotte Brontë.* And yet no biography has ever been more adversely criticised. Personal friends of Dickens, who had known him intimately, were dissatisfied with it. James Crossley, the famous bibliophile, speaking of Forster, said: "I cannot call him the successful biographer of Dickens." And Ainsworth observed: "I see he only tells half the story."

No doubt the views of Dickens's friends were biased by annoyance at the scant notice they received in the authoritative biography; and this lapse, of course, *is* where the book is most open to effective attack. Forster himself is unduly prominent; but other intimates of Dickens, who very strongly influenced his career and literary work, are relegated to an obscure position, and often their share in the life-story is entirely ignored and omitted. It is the same with the correspondence; the letters quoted are practically all addressed to Forster, and no attempt is made to utilise the many valuable letters written by Dickens to other correspondents. Further, the documents Forster did use in his narrative are inartistically introduced and cruelly mutilated. (p. 80)

It will ever be matter for regret that Forster, with his unique opportunities for a detailed and intimate picture, has given but an incomplete record of perhaps the most interesting period of Dickens's life, the years 1836-1839, the outset of his literary career, when the early books were written with all the young, fresh brilliancy of their author. The biographer gives an unsatisfactory version of Dickens's relations and quarrels with his first publisher, Macrone; in fact, he suppresses all mention of the important point that the author had signed an agreement to write, for two hundred pounds, a novel—probably *Oliver Twist*—to be published by Macrone; but that, owing to the dispute and ill-feeling which had arisen between Dickens and Macrone concerning the copyright and reissue of *Sketches by Boz*, Dickens absolutely declined to carry out the contract, and disposed of his proposed novel to Richard Bentley for five hundred pounds, thus risking a legal action, which, however, was rendered inoperative by Macrone's sudden death. These events occurred in the late autumn of 1836.

Forster's account of Dickens's quarrel, some two years later, with Bentley is also open to criticism. There were two sides to this historic separation, as in every other dispute, and both Dickens and Bentley were justified in fighting for what they considered their rights. Judging by the expressed views of his contemporaries, Bentley was certainly a hard man to deal with; but it does not follow that he was quite the rapacious taskmaster depicted by Forster in his earlier pages. Here we must make allowance for the biographer's affectionate bias towards his friend-hero. (p. 81)

Before dismissing the limitations in Forster's otherwise great biography, one may perhaps express a personal regret that the biographer devotes but a few words to the social or convivial phase of Dickens in these first glorious years of youth and fame. He barely mentions the frequent rides through the lovely country then surrounding the surburbs of London, which Dickens delighted to take in company with his two intimates, Forster and Ainsworth; and the even more frequent dinings and festivities the trio enjoyed go almost unrecorded. (p. 83)

Granting . . . that Forster's book has faults both of omission and commission, that it is egotistical and at times prejudiced, that its arrangement is bad and its chronology chaotic, yet, owing to the biographer's whole-hearted admiration and enthusiasm for his subject, and by his sympathetic and vivid presentment of his hero's character and achievements, the final result is a great biography, the greatest, it is safe to say, of its great subject, and one that will never be superseded. Many reasons support this conclusion. Dickens himself wished Forster to be his biographer; and the novelist's near relatives, those best qualified to judge of its claims and merits, have always given their *cachet* of approval to this particular work. Dickens's most trusted friend and the executrix of his last wishes, Miss Georgina Hogarth, has stated to me:—

> Mr. Forster was the only person with the material and authority to write the biography. But it was written very soon after Mr. Dickens's death, and a great deal could not be said *then* which becomes possible as years go on. I always feel that Mr. Forster's book will be more appreciated in years to come than it is now.

The truth of Miss Hogarth's belief (expressed eight years ago) is already becoming justified as the Dickens centenary approaches. (pp. 85-6)

Stewart Marsh Ellis, "Dickens and Forster," in his Mainly Victorian, *Books for Libraries Press, 1969; distributed by Arno Press, Inc., pp. 80-7.**

JOHN B. CASTIEAU (lecture date 1916)

[*In the following excerpt, drawn from a lecture delivered on June 5, 1916, Castieau presents a highly negative appraisal of* The Life of Charles Dickens, *declaring it "a long tedious avenue of adulations through a desert of dates." Castieau's objections to the biography center around his conviction that Forster's portrait of Dickens is one-dimensional, highly idealized, and lacking in personal detail. For a discussion of Castieau's argument, see the excerpt by Sylvère Monod dated 1965.*]

My subject deals with John Forster's **"Life of Charles Dickens,"** a book which holds pride of place, wrongly I think, as the leading authority on the author. The fictions of which I complain are sins of omission. The biography fails in nearly all of the elements which are essential to the true record of a man's life. It lacks the personal note; it conveys no adequate idea of character; and throughout, it portrays Dickens the author rather than Dickens the man. And it is the man who is the most interesting, for the works themselves are amply informative regarding the author. (p. 264)

My chief complaint about Forster's **"Life"** is that it has hardly any atmosphere or light and shade. It is a long tedious avenue of adulations through a desert of dates. Various persons of no importance say how they met Dickens at school; shook hands with him; saw him buy a penny paper, etc. Then there is a plethora of letters written by Dickens, in which the personal pronoun I stands out, as Mr. Kipling once put it, "like the telegraph poles along a railway line." As for dates, they are the boresome basis of the book. There are dates of births, deaths and marriages; dates when novels were begun and when they were ended; dates when travels commenced and when they finished, and so on, until one becomes as weary of dates as a schoolboy. To anybody who has read the works of Dickens and their prefaces, Forster's **"Life"** is a mere excrescence. It simply puts a halo around Dickens's head, a harp in his hand, and makes wings sprout from his shoulders. We develop love for a man who is presented to us as being humanly imperfect; but we grow hatred for a pedestalled person who is always presented as being a paragon. . . . Forster, "the infallible Forster," as he was known, wrote the life too soon after Dickens's death. He put too much halo around his hero, and not enough battered tall-hat.

Carlyle, in that high-falutin' style of his, which now only deceives the very young, compared Forster's **"Life of Dickens"** with Boswell's "Life of Johnson" [see excerpt dated 1874]. . . . This judgment has always surprised me. Of course, Carlyle could not discuss a flea on a dog's back without enlarging upon the crimes and enormities of the insect world, and the long-suffering of the canine community. We must always discount his statements. But this comparison of Forster's with Boswell's "Life" is so absurd that it deserves to be discounted to the disappearing point. It is palpably ridiculous.

Boswell certainly panegyrised his hero to the point of worship; but, at the same time, he just as certainly painted him with all his warts. Forster did not paint Dickens with even a freckle. Boswell sometimes bores you with Johnson's conversation.

Forster was candid enough to say that Dickens had no conversation, and so he escaped the responsibility of recording any at all. That is, he avoided writing anything of Dickens which was not good. (pp. 264-65)

[Certain of Forster's omissions] are only trifles, but I . . . propose to deal with a very grave omission in Forster's life, which does a great injustice to a good woman, wife and mother— Mrs. Charles Dickens. Forster refers to her just about a dozen times, and then in so cursory and almost apologetic fashion as to be very nearly contemptous. They are nearly all remarks made by Dickens in his letters such as "Kate cries dismally if I mention the subject of going to America"; "Kate has a horribly bad face-ache"; "Kate has so bad a sore throat that she is obliged to keep to her bed"; "I have still a horrible cold and so has Kate." (p. 266)

But Forster did not adequately describe Charles Dickens himself. His references to his personal appearance,—references which should not only have been interesting, but of historical value,—are flimsy and unsatisfactory. Just as deficient are the details given of disposition, deportment, and dress. Even the daily habits of Dickens are slurred over. Indeed, Forster practically only tells us what Dickens had already told us himself in his letters and minor works. (pp. 266-67)

While the temperament of Dickens appears to have been naturally buoyant and vivacious, there is no doubt that in later years, it became soured by sickness and depressed by domestic worry. But making all this allowance, there remains much evidence, that Dickens was by no means that genial and generous débonair Bohemian suggested by his own writings and emphasised by Forster. (pp. 267-68)

The silences of John Forster are really appalling. . . . One letter to Dean Hole from Dickens should have been known to Forster. In it, the novelist said "Shocked by the misuse of the private letters of public men . . . I destroyed a very large and very rare mass of correspondence." Surely a very commendable act! But that is Forster. He omits the good *and* the bad. There is no reference to Dickens's quarrel with John Leech; hardly any to his generosity to Leigh Hunt. In short, Forster's **"Life"** is a lamentable failure as a biography of a truly great man.

I have not used half of my material. The work of gathering it has been a pleasure. It has shown me that there is a quite different Dickens from the prig portrayed in Forster's pages, a more human, a more lovable Dickens! It has proved to me that the material exists for the preparation of quite a different Life altogether. But great as the material is, there is more to be had. The contemporaries of Dickens are, however, passing away and the new biographer should lose no time.

Charles Dickens cannot be handed down to history as a man unless his Life is written by a man. It is all very well to tell us that Dickens was always full of rollicking fun, exuberance and animal spirits. But no man can go through life all the time like a clown in a circus or a pantomine. There must be some occasions when he disappears behind the scenes. Forster seldom relates them. He tells us that Dickens was brilliant, affectionate, indignant at the wrongs of the workers and the poor, intolerant of sham and cant, a redresser of grievances and a reformer in every sense; in short, that Charles Dickens was a saint. What we want is a biographer who will come along and candidly admit that Charles Dickens once in a while said, "damn!" (pp. 268-69)

John B. Castieau, "The Fictions of Forster," in The Dickensian, *Vol. XII, No. 10, October, 1916, pp. 264-69.*

G. K. CHESTERTON (essay date 1927)

[*Remembered primarily for his detective stories, Chesterton was also an eminent biographer, essayist, novelist, poet, journalist, dramatist, and critic of the early twentieth century. His essays are characterized by their humor, frequent use of paradox, and rambling style. His* The Victorian Age in Literature *is considered a standard source. The following excerpt was drawn from an essay that originally appeared as the introduction to a 1927 edition of* The Life of Charles Dickens. *Chesterton here explores the strengths of Forster's approach and contests inappropriate criticisms of the work by writers who fail to consider the era and spirit of its composition. Chesterton also discusses Forster's comments on Dickens's unfinished novel,* The Mystery of Edwin Drood, *suggesting that the biographer's interpretation of how the book was to have been completed has been widely misunderstood by readers and critics.*]

A good book of biography is one in which the book vanishes and the man remains; not the man who wrote the book but the man about whom it was written. At the end of Forster's *Life of Dickens* we are admiring Dickens and not admiring Forster; and that alone is a good reason for Forster being admired. Most reasonable readers will agree that Forster does achieve this essential purpose of making Dickens visible and himself invisible; though in the real friendship of the two men the less famous man bulked large and was sometimes, it is said, even a shade too positive. It is this which makes Dickens's biography in some sense a fitting sequel to Dickens's books. The genius of Dickens has been very variously estimated and defined; but perhaps the best rough summary of it is this. He was a man whose imagination could draw other men out, in the sense of developing some germ of fun or folly in them which mere life was not warm enough to germinate. He exaggerated them because they could not exaggerate themselves. (pp. 238-39)

If it was the genius of Dickens to draw everybody out, it is only justice to say that it was the talent of Forster to draw Dickens out. He could not always draw him; even when as in the case of *Edwin Drood* (of which a word may be said presently) it is possible that he imagined that he had. Nor was the drawing out of that triumphant and almost faultless kind which exists in the great model of biography. He could not draw Dickens out as Boswell could draw Johnson out. He did not even attempt to do so in anything like the same series of ingenious interviews. But his own success was of the same essential sort; though he generally achieved it more by reporting correspondence than conversation. He understood that he had to deal with an individuality that was interesting not only in public but in private; though he observed a Victorian restraint (for which some will think none the worse of him) concerning the private things that can be public and the private things that had better be private. But the essentials of such a biographical success remain the same. In dealing with Dickens he was dealing not only with a creator but with a character; we might almost say with a Dickens character. Dickens must be encouraged to give himself away; as it is the essence of every Dickens character to give itself away. And in the case of Dickens, as of the Dickens characters, it is the very best of gifts. There was indeed a certain real reserve behind the external exuberance of Dickens's correspondence and conversation; but that is concerned with other private problems; and I am only speaking of the spontaneous effect of being introduced to a character, as in a club or an evening party. And this sense of a personality, or what is commonly called a portrait, does certainly emerge from the letters and memories preserved by Forster. Anybody who will try to make such a literary portrait of any one of his personal friends will soon find out how difficult is the achievement and how high is the praise. The life of Dickens is not like the life of the Victorian poet or politician; which was often not so much a matter of painting a portrait as of white-washing a portrait. We do receive a very vivid impression of a very vivacious person; we do feel that he is walking briskly about the street and not that he is lying in a coffin helpless under funeral orations; and that is victory in the arduous art of biography.

A biographical success of that sort must be judged as a whole. It is not reasonable to argue about every opinion of the biographer, so long as he has given us the material for forming our own opinion. It is not a question of everything that he thinks about Dickens; but of the fact that he has given us a Dickens to think about. We cannot even think about the whited sepulchre of the purely official biography. In the great model already mentioned, James Boswell as an individual utters many opinions that seem almost meant to make him look silly; and a few that seem almost meant to make his friend look silly. He was not perhaps competent to be the critic of Dr. Johnson. And yet he was competent to be the creator of Dr. Johnson. He made him over again as a great character in fiction is made; and that impression is a general impression, that has nothing to do with the accuracy of his own detached individual thoughts. But this principle of common sense, which has been commonly conceded in the case of Boswell, has occasionally been rather neglected in the case of Forster. A lady whose opinion has the highest authority in the matter has hinted that Forster as a friend took himself a little too seriously. Curiously enough, she seemed to give this as a reason for herself taking him almost equally seriously. She suggested that he was a little touchy and exacting in the matter of secrets being kept from him, and no doubt she was right; but it seems doubtful whether we can draw the inference that none were kept. And indeed, in the particular case at issue, it seems to me much more probable that the secrets were sometimes all the more carefully kept.

It is in the affair of *The Mystery of Edwin Drood* that this problem principally arises; and it may well serve as an example. Forster himself reports Dickens as saying that he had conceived a new and original idea for that story, an idea very difficult to work and one which must not be revealed beforehand, or the interest of the story would be gone. And yet, strangely enough, this is the very passage upon which many Dickensians base their insistence that the idea *was* revealed beforehand; so that the interest of the story presumably *was* gone, even before the story was begun. They base this inference on the fact that Forster, a few lines lower down, proceeds to say that the point of this crime story was to be the peculiar form taken by the confession of the criminal; that he was to tell his own story as if it were the story of another. Now it seems quite obvious to me that this is merely an example of one of those accidental confusions which may occur easily when a man does not very strictly connect the sentence he is writing with a sentence he wrote recently in another connexion. Forster does not mean that the mode of confession constituted the revelation of the great idea which Dickens admittedly refused to reveal. Obviously it could not be, the autobiographical antic of John Jasper could not *be* the mystery of Edwin Drood. He only means that this was to be the point of the confession scene, which Dickens had described as distinct from the main mystery which he had

refused to describe. Forster only means that this was a very interesting feature of the scheme; and he leaves this slight ambiguity because he was a human being who had no call to be a faultless logician or a radiantly lucid literary man; but was simply a good biographer writing about a man he knew in a natural and ordinary way. But in this case critics have refused to allow poor Forster to write in a natural and ordinary way. They have not allowed him to have any accidental ambiguities. They have treated every line of a long and variegated biography as if it were a sworn affidavit examined by lawyers and corrected by logicians. . . . He must be not only logically but literally exact. He must be literally exact not only in what he says, but in what can be indirectly and rather doubtfully inferred from what he says. Above all, he must be exact not only about what he says that he knows, but about what he distinctly says that he does not know. Assuredly it was not only John Forster who took John Forster too seriously.

As a matter of fact, his merits as much as his limitations make him the very last man in the world to be treated in this strict and stringent fashion. It is not the least virtue in the biography of the great Victorian novelist that it is itself a very Victorian book; full of that delightful air of ease and sanity and social comfort which is the lost secret of that historical interlude. In this sense the life of Dickens is less like a book of Dickens than like a book of Trollope. Forster gives us a hundred opportunities of getting to know the man; he is not intensely interested in intellectual things except as they affect a man. This is the last sort of spirit and atmosphere in which we should look for this sort of mathematical precision, or litigious vigilance. His chief charm is the air of amplitude and largesse with which he scatters before us the scraps and scribbles of a man of genius, the admirable letters of Dickens; and shows how much true creative literature there was in his post-bag and even his wastepaper basket. (pp. 239-46)

G. K. Chesterton, "Dickens's Forster," in his G.K.C. As M.C.: Being a Collection of Thirty-Seven Introductions, edited by J. P. de Fonseka, Methuen & Co. Ltd., 1929, pp. 238-46.

Forster as sketched by Daniel Maclise in 1840.

J.W.T. LEY (essay date 1928)

[*In the excerpt below, Ley outlines three episodes in Dickens's life that presented a challenge to Forster as he wrote* The Life of Charles Dickens. *These include the novelist's youthful love affair with Maria Beadnell, his separation from his wife, and his lengthy dispute with his publishers Bradbury and Evans. In addition, Ley contests various criticisms of the biography, arguing that despite its faults, it will remain the definitive study of Dickens's life.*]

There are three phases of Dickens's life which call for thoughtful treatment. Two of them were undoubtedly intermingled in a way which only the novelist himself could have understood. That is to say, there can be no doubt but that the early love affair with Maria Beadnell had definite reactions upon his later relations with his wife, and thus upon his whole life. Forster either knew very little about that early incident, or he felt some diffidence in dealing with it in the lifetime of his friend's widow, and so he leaves us under the impression that it was just a calf-love which burned strongly while it lasted, but died right out and left only the tenderly-whimsical memories that calf-love generally does leave behind it. He speaks of Maria Beadnell as Dickens's Dora, certainly, but he does not suggest that the experience was as deep and intense as David's love for his child-wife, and that the memory of it was with the novelist all the days of his life, never ceasing to influence him. The later knowledge of that brief early love passage has thrown new light on Dickens's life and work.

Forster had no option but to tell something of his friend's domestic trouble, but he touched upon it as lightly as he could. Yet it was a tremendously important influence in Dickens's life. One is familiar with the argument that the domestic affairs of a great novelist are no concern of his readers; but we accept biography as an important branch of literature, and it can have no purpose save the revealing of the motives and influences which urge men to achievement or beckon them to failure. . . . The truth is that Forster was too close to his subject, and that he worked under a consciousness of that handicap. We are bound to miss much in the assessing of Dickens's character and work if we know practically nothing of the two great emotional and most intimate experiences of his life. Forster knew little of one; he knew too much of the other. This book has been spoken of in the same breath with Boswell's—by Carlyle [see excerpt dated 1874], for instance—but they have little in common. They could not have much in common. Apart from the wide differences between the two subjects, Boswell worked under none of Forster's restraints. He knew Johnson, when all is said and done, only in the social circle. No biographer ever knew his subject more intimately than Forster knew Dickens. Johnson left no widow, no children. Somebody once complained that Forster does not record that Mrs. Dickens was "a large woman with a great deal of colour, and rather coarse." Boswell describes Mrs. Johnson in very similar terms, but she had been dead nearly forty years. Mrs. Dickens and all her children save two were alive when Forster wrote. Such a description of her—even if it had been accurate, which it was not; and even if it had been in any degree a matter of public interest, which it was not—would have been an outrage. (pp. xiv-xv)

Then, again, his attitude—for the purpose of this book—towards Dickens's domestic affairs made it impossible for him to tell another important story. He tells us all about the disputes with Macrone, Bentley, and Chapman and Hall; but of that with Bradbury and Evans, which went further than any of these, in that it led to the law courts, he tells us practically nothing. That was because it arose out of the domestic trouble, and he could not have told the one story without telling the other. There was a second reason for not reopening the story, and that was that Dickens's eldest son was married to the daughter of one of the partners in the firm of Bradbury and Evans, and, with the family supervising the book, it was natural they should prefer, for the sake of Charles the Younger and his wife, that the affair should be dismissed as briefly as possible. (p. xvi)

Of Forster's book, as a whole, this may be said: That few books of first-class importance have been more criticised, and yet it remains, and must remain, the final authority on Dickens's life and work. It remains, as Mr. J. B. Priestley has said, "a very big book on a very great writer." Mr. J. C. Squire is more emphatic. "It remains a great book," he says, and when all the criticisms are considered, when all Forster's limitations are admitted, and when these are all considered in the light of the difficulties under which he worked, and of the fact that he wrote when his health was completely broken—that indeed, it is almost true to say he staved off his own end that he might complete this, the greatest task of his life—when all these things are weighed up, we have to admit that Mr. Squire's estimate of the book is not an exaggerated one. When all is said and done, how many "full-dress" English biographies shall we place before it? Boswell's of course; Lockhart's no doubt; and when those have been named, which biography will this not challenge for third place? (p. xvii)

The most vital criticism of this book is that it does not present to us the "inner Dickens." I wonder if Forster is wholly to blame for that?—putting aside the handicap under which, as we have seen, he was working. It is worth while reflecting that no English man of letters has been more written about by all sorts of people who knew him well; yet where do we find the picture of that inner Dickens which Forster fails to give us? It is a rather surprising reflection, is it not? For what man of genius has more frankly worn his heart on his sleeve? The truth is that, for all his "plebeian frankness," as somebody has called it; for all that he lived so much in the glare of the limelight; for all that he was continually the leader in the social circle; for all that he seemed so demonstrative in his joys and his sorrows, the sordid experiences of his boyhood, and the bitterness of his early disappointment in love had permanent, ever-present effects. But he kept them hidden in his heart. With them, of course, were the effects of that domestic infelicity, which naturally he tried to hide. Here was the secret of that restlessness, which, allowing for the fact that he was a man of genius, was fundamentally the outcome of an ever-present desire to escape from himself—a manifestation of that morbidity with which it cannot be denied that his nature was tinged. In other words, there was an "inner Dickens" of whom none but Forster ever saw anything, and even he only caught an occasional fleeting glimpse. Be it remembered that the blacking warehouse experience remained unknown to his wife and children until they read of it in this book. Surely the fact is significant?

On the other hand, it is true that Forster never once gives us an intimate domestic picture—never once shows us this man who wrote so glowingly of home felicity in his own home circle. There must have been a time when the clouds had not lowered, there must have been bright intervals later on—the sun must have broken through the clouds sometimes. Yet we hear nothing of Mrs. Dickens beyond bare references, which are sometimes almost of a patronising character; and all that we are told about the children is facts—just facts. (pp. xviii-xix)

So with Dickens's friendships. We are told really nothing about many intimacies. There was much uproarious laughter during [his] trip to Cornwall; there was much good fellowship generally, but there is not one intimate touch. . . . There must have been much more than good fellowship in these friendships. It was something more than good fellowship that won the affection of Carlyle, Landor, Jeffrey; the utter devotion of Chauncey Hare Townshend and H. F. Chorley; the grudging esteem of Samuel Carter Hall.

But, while all this is true, we must be just to Forster and admit the surprising fact—and first realisation of it is startling—that though many of these friends have written of Dickens, not one of them has given us anything more intimate than is to be found here. . . .

For certain other criticisms of this book there is less justification. Some of Dickens's friends complained that Forster had denied a place in the sun to everybody but himself. . . . The answer to this criticism is: "More than fifty years have passed. Many scores of books about Dickens have been published in that time. A selection from his letters, made by his sister-in-law and his daughter, has been published; a selection from his letters to Wilkie Collins has been published; all existing letters to Mark Lemon has been published. Do they tell us anything more than his letters to Forster tell us?" The answer to that question is an unhesitating "No." If Forster had accepted all the material offered to him he would have increased the difficulty of his task a hundredfold, and, as we know quite certainly to-day, he would have gained nothing at all. (p. xx)

When we have considered Forster's task from every point of view, could he have adopted a better course than to allow Dickens, always vivid and virile, to express himself through his letters? That was his deliberate purpose. He departed from it only to record facts which he regarded as essential, and to offer us criticisms of his friend's books, which are the best that have been written. The Dickensian's shelves contain many volumes of criticism. In which of those volumes is a higher, saner level reached than in this one? Of course, Forster is sympathetic, yet he is always balanced, and he is always detached—a very high tribute in view of his peculiar position. It is rather surprising that the critical chapters in this biography have never been published as a separate volume. If that were done, I am certain the book would be acclaimed as the best of its kind. (pp. xxi-xxii)

> *J.W.T. Ley, in an introduction to* The Life of Charles Dickens *by John Forster, edited by J.W.T. Ley, Cecil Palmer, 1928, pp. xiii-xxvii.*

MALCOLM ELWIN   (essay date 1934)

[*In the excerpt below, Elwin maintains that previous critics of Forster's biographies have neglected to take into account the circumstances under which he was forced to write. Pointing out that friends and relatives of both Landor and Dickens were still alive at the time Forster wrote* Walter Savage Landor *and* The Life of Charles Dickens, *Elwin asserts that given such constraints, the biographer's achievement was considerable. Elwin also declares that while Forster's reputation as a writer rests more on his biographies than his histories, his importance to literary history rests on his influential personality rather than his writings.*]

In estimating [Forster's] work as a biographer, critics have too often inclined to take the books at their face value, regardless of the circumstances in which they were written. Writing the biography of a man recently deceased is a very different busi-

ness from working on one who lived a century or more ago. In the latter case, no personal prejudice, unless scholarly bias, can interfere with an attitude of detached impartiality, and the biographer usually profits from the errors of predecessors, the unreserved use of family papers, and the published biographies, letters and diaries of persons contemporary with his subject. In the case of a man recently dead, there are living relatives and friends demanding the suppression of this and that, and often, secretly or admittedly, withholding for personal reasons collections of letters or particular details, which they only could supply. (pp. 199-200)

There have been few satisfactory biographies by surviving friends of the subjects, but, of these, Forster's lives of Landor and Dickens, despite their obvious limitations, are eminently successful examples. In both cases, he was faced with the prospect of offending relatives and friends, he was unaware of what letters or other material remained in the secret possession of other surviving contemporaries, and he ran the risk of embroiling himself with them by the revelation of the part played by himself in affairs between them and his subject. He had one peculiar advantage—of having been, in both cases, the intimate friend of his subject—and on this he rightly decided to base his manner of treatment, relying upon his own personal impressions and, as far as possible, upon facts for the authenticity of which he could personally vouch. . . . It is the only satisfactory method for the contemporary biographer; the biography of detached impartiality can only be written at a distance of decades from the death of the subject.

Of the latter kind, Forster achieved an example in his *Life of Goldsmith.* As Henry Reeve told de Tocqueville, 'Forster has a very exact knowledge of English society at that period'. . . . Obsessed by the biographer's inevitable bogey of missing some essential detail, he was tireless in the accumulation of material. . . . As conscientious as a scholar as he was painstaking and diligent in research, he regarded, as Percy Fitzgerald remarked, the giving of the results to the press as 'a sort of solemn, responsible thing, not to be lightly attempted'. He developed a skilled faculty for selection and rejection, sifting the ore from the dross of his massed materials, avoiding the temptation to include interesting letters and documents for their own sake, and using them only to illustrate the argument of his narrative and his construction of character. Being equally careful in composition, his finished work is as remarkable for its fluent and finely tempered style as for conciseness and relevance.

His reputation as a writer rests for posterity upon his work as a biographer—on his lives of Landor and Goldsmith, the unfinished *Life of Swift,* which, though incomplete, comprises his crowning achievement as a scholar, and, principally, the *Life of Dickens.* His historical works—*The Statesmen of the Commonwealth,* a monumental work in seven volumes, the two-volume *Life of Sir John Eliot,* and the *Arrest of the Five Members*—are out of fashion even with historical students, to whom, from their specialized nature, they make their sole appeal. His articles for the *Edinburgh* and the *Quarterly* have never been collected, even in selection, though their value is equal to those of Bagehot, while those in the *Examiner,* by the most 'slashing' of which he made his contemporary reputation as a critic, are hopelessly lost in the files of ephemeral journalism.

But on neither the permanent value of his biographies nor the eminence of his contemporary reputation rests his interest and importance in literary history; his claim to remembrance is his

personality, which influenced the greatest writers of a generation and registered an indelible impression upon an entire
epoch. . . . [His biography] remains unwritten, though offering
unique opportunities for exposition of character combined with
variety of interest, and meanwhile literary history records the
ironical anomaly of the most Johnsonian figure of the nineteenth century being remembered only as a Boswell. (pp. 200-02)

> *Malcolm Elwin, "Wallflower the Fifth: John Fors-
> ter," in his* Victorian Wallflowers: A Panoramic Sur-
> vey of the Popular Literary Periodicals, *Jonathan
> Cape, 1934, pp. 177-202.*

ALBERT BRITT   (essay date 1936)

[*Britt's discussion of* The Life of Charles Dickens *in the excerpt
below emphasizes the difficulties faced by Forster in writing about
a close friend. Britt asserts that though Forster excelled in arranging the factual details of Dickens's life, his relationship with
the author distorted his critical perspective.*]

A student of different Victorian periods of biography is constantly tempted to over-criticism, perhaps to the setting of
standards that can not fairly be applied to contemporary writing. One man who invites such treatment is John Forster, whose
"Life of Charles Dickens" is standard for the time and is also
a favorite source for those who wish to know something of the
great caricaturist. Here again, as in the case of Mrs. Gaskell,
the accident of friendship, of close association, of sympathetic
relationship, has operated against rather than in favor of that
comprehensive understanding and historical accuracy that are
necessary to proper biographical treatment.

John Forster was a professional writer. In fact he might be
called the first professional biographer in that he was the first
man to make in any sense a profession of the study of other
men's lives. . . . As a writer he was competent, industrious,
and in obvious matters of dates, places, actions, and the external world generally, scrupulously exact. His **"Life of Charles
Dickens"** is a model of what might be called internal docu-
mentation. He knew his subject thoroughly and could cite chapter and verse not only from the records of letters, diaries,
contracts, records of conversation, but from his knowledge of
his subject's inner processes. For the last reason he betrays
himself into assumptions or conclusions that are unnecessary,
and deductions from the facts which might better be left to the
reader. He relies overmuch on his own high opinion of Dickens,
which often leads him to the citing of such incidents as would,
if given in proper detail, in themselves illustrate Dickens's
methods and problems far more vividly than do Forster's generalizations.

It is perhaps not quite fair to criticize Mr. Forster for his lack
of perspective. It is impossible for a contemporary to see his
subject down a lengthening avenue of time and correspondingly
difficult for him to realize that it is down precisely such an
avenue that his book will be read if it has the good fortune to
live more than half a score of years. Mr. Forster quite fails to
realize that certain of his casual references are today lacking
in importance or reality for the modern reader. (pp. 128-30)

Another fault is a too high emphasis on his own part in the
Dickens's panorama. To be sure it was to his role of friend,
adviser, and guide that he owed his extremely intimate knowledge of the novelist's life. But while the reader is prepared to
admit that Mr. Forster played as large a part as he implies, it
is a little wearisome to find one's self passing over a constant
succession of such phrases as "we both laughed," "who shared

with us," "whom we visited," "that dear friend of his and
mine." His sense of kinship leads him at times to intrude
himself with no obvious reason for the intrusion. (p. 130)

Forster's failure to recognize the inadequacy of his allusions
and references leaves the reader speculating on several points.
There are many references, for example, to arguments with
publishers over contracts, casual allusions to unsatisfactory
terms, but little enlargement and no indication of an understanding that in half a century or less the conditions of publishing would be so altered that most of his references would
be blind and unilluminating.

There are other instances, for example, in the infrequent and
usually tantalizing intimations of the manner in which ideas
came to Dickens and of the formation and direction of their
growth. Almost without exception such references are too vague
for us to reach a more definite conclusion than that the novelist
in most cases began his writing with a rather loose group of
characters or a general situation in mind, the situation being
an involved one or the implied character being of a quaint or
whimsical or unpleasant sort, and that the plot developed out
of character and situation as he wrote. This is at least a conclusion which is commonly held. So far as Mr. Forster is
concerned, however, it seems not to have occurred to him that
a generation might appear which would appreciate a more definite and detailed description of the novelist's method and we
are left largely to hypothesis and inference.

Throughout the book there is abundant evidence of a desire on
the part of Forster to monopolize Dickens. . . . The Dickens
letters quoted are almost without exception addressed to Forster, although there is no reason to complain of a lack of letters.
The point of view is that of an unflinching advocate prepared
to defend the novelist not only against attack but even the
possibility of mild criticism. Forster makes much of the letters
which Dickens wrote him from America and particularly of
the fact that he told in those letters much more than he later
confided to the public in his "American Notes." Fortunately
for us of today Forster was too blinded by affection to realize
that the feeling which Dickens revealed was largely his own
childish joy over the reception which those queer Americans
gave him. It was his first taste of the sweets of fame and the
fact that they were tendered him in cloying kind and quantity
without much intelligence or discrimination did not affect the
pleasure with which he received them. Aside from this, the
information conveyed to Forster in his letters from America
makes their exclusion from the "American Notes" of small
importance.

It is impossible to avoid the conclusion that there should be
another life of Dickens, not for the sake of refuting Forster so
much as to do for him what Benson has done for Mrs. Gaskell,
and incidentally to save Dickens from the smothering clutch
of overrighteous affection. It is interesting, however, that in
spite of a steady avoidance of even a mildly critical view of
Dickens, the net result of the book is an emphasis of the naïve
surprise and joy the novelist felt over his own success. (pp.
131-33)

> *Albert Britt, "The Professional Appears," in his* The
> Great Biographers, *McGraw-Hill Book Company, Inc.,
> 1936, pp. 128-33.*

GEORGE H. FORD   (essay date 1955)

[*In the following excerpt, Ford argues that the defects of Forster's*
The Life of Charles Dickens *were inevitable given "the difficulties*

of writing about a contemporary to whom he had been too closely attached." Despite this assertion, however, Ford acknowledges both the mass of important information contained in Forster's account and the enduring value of many of his conclusions about Dickens's character.]

Forster was faced with the difficult task of trying to keep before the public their idealized conception of Dickens' character and, at the same time, to paint an accurate portrait of one of his closest friends. That he failed to satisfy either his contemporaries or posterity was almost inevitable. Swinburne considered it extraordinary that when Forster wrote biographies of men he had never seen, such as Goldsmith, his work was of high quality, but that when he wrote of Landor and Dickens, his work was "execrable." There was nothing extraordinary about the difference; Forster was simply overwhelmed by the difficulties of writing about a contemporary to whom he had been too closely attached. In his role as a critic, his attachments were likewise too close. Lewes once described Forster as "Pungent, the editor of the 'Exterminator,'" and complained that his literary criticism was always marred by asperity. But because Forster had acted as Dickens' constant sounding-board, there is not much pungency in his discussion of novels which had been partly shaped by his own editorial advice. Hence his discussions are packed with valuable information, but as criticism they are not distinguished.

In most twentieth-century studies of Dickens, Forster is used as a mere butt. The absurd pomposity of his character, his elephantine manner of managing his protégés, his insularity and egotism were sometimes oppressively evident to Dickens in his later years. In the biography itself, it is the egotism which is especially evident. One wit described it as "The Autobiography of John Forster with Recollections of Charles Dickens." Another reviewer protested that the theme of the book suggested that "Codlin was the friend, not Short" [see excerpt by Frances Cashel Hoey dated 1873]. Subsequently, it has often been pointed out that Forster's obtrusiveness is marked not only by the large role he assigns to himself in the story of Dickens' life, but in his omission of the importance of other friends, in particular his petulant overlooking of Wilkie Collins. Like all subsequent biographers (with the exception of Edgar Johnson), Forster was at his weakest in describing the last dozen years of Dickens' life, the period during which Collins was most closely associated with the Inimitable. (pp. 160-61)

Despite these important omissions and shortcomings, the surprising quality of Forster's work is its permanence. If his sprawling volumes are studied with care, one often encounters evidence of his awareness of aspects of Dickens' character which have later been hailed as discoveries. The hearty and cheerful extrovert aspects of Dickens are, of course, predominant, and they established the tone of Dickensian biography for sixty years. But Forster knew his subject well enough to perceive many of the conflicts which had obsessed him even though he did not underline them. Oddly enough, it was this redeeming quality of awareness that displeased Forster's early readers. . . .

The first volume, unlike the later two, was well received on the whole, especially because of its revelation of the blacking-warehouse incident. It was the dramatic story of the self-made man. . . . To most readers, such a story was moving; to others, it was primarily a confirmation of their suspicions that Dickens' irregularities as a writer were the fruits of a lack of education and suitable social background. (p. 162)

A second aspect of Forster's biography which lowered Dickens' reputation in other quarters was his emphasis, in the later volumes, upon pounds, shillings, and pence. Inevitably, much of the correspondence between Dickens and his financial advisor was concerned with profit and loss—horrifying to aesthetes. . . . Most offensively, Forster's final volume gave the impression that Dickens drove himself to death in a greedy effort to make an ample fortune more ample. That Forster failed to perceive Dickens' more complex motives in this final phase is understandable. Dickens took great pains to screen them not only from his old friend but from himself. The total effect of these impressions and disclosures was summed up by an essayist of 1880 who commented upon the undeniable irony of Forster's efforts. "The popular estimate of Dickens was distinctly lowered by a work, every line of which was inspired by an almost infatuated admiration for him." (p. 163)

> *George H. Ford, "Biography," in his* Dickens and His Readers: Aspects of Novel-Criticism Since 1836, *Princeton University Press, 1955, pp. 159-69.**

GERALD G. GRUBB (essay date 1956)

[*In the following excerpt, Grubb reassesses some of Forster's editorial practices and factual omissions in* The Life of Charles Dickens. *The critic's findings are based on the contents of newly discovered letters from Dickens to Forster. Grubb compares these letters with Forster's edited versions of them in* The Life of Charles Dickens *and comments on his motivations and methods as a biographer.*]

One cannot escape the conclusion that almost every thing of any consequence which Forster omitted [from *The Life of Charles Dickens*] was the result of deliberate design, not of ignorance.

It is true that Wilkie Collins is said to have thought that the Dickens letters which he held should have been utilized by Forster; but that was, perhaps, only a pretext, a rationalization, which he put forward as a justification for withholding his letters from the edition which was published by Mamie Dickens and Georgina Hogarth, and for publishing them himself. (pp. 152-53)

What were Forster's motives as a biographer. . .? In passing judgment upon Forster's motives, one must remember that he was a Victorian who was writing about a Victorian for a Victorian reading public, and that he proposed to write about the *public* life, not the *private* life of an idol of the Victorian people. Forster belonged to a generation of writers who looked upon a man's private life as his own private affair and no more the property of the public than was his private bank account. Forster was no better and no worse than his generation. The twentieth-century biographer, with the instincts, training, and methods of an objective research scientist, had not yet appeared, and would not appear for almost another half century. Prince Albert was still looked upon as the ideal gentleman, the Queen's private household was still the universal model, and the public had not yet learned to divorce the private life of a great man from the artistic genius of that man. Therefore, Forster proposed to do two things: keep alive the public idolatry of Dickens, and to please, insofar as possible, the conflicting elements of Dickens' own family (considering Georgina Hogarth as one of them) on the one hand, and the Hogarth family (considering Mrs. Dickens as one of them) on the other. A comparison of [newly discovered letters from Dickens to Forster with Forster's edited versions of them in *The Life of Charles Dickens*] shows these motives in operation. (p. 153)

What were Forster's methods of incorporating Dickens' letters in his biography, and how are those methods revealed in a study of these letters in comparison with his text? It is precisely on this important point that these unpublished letters prove most valuable; for they furnish a significant segment of the whole, one extensive enough to be useful as an index to the whole. In them the student of Forster gets more than a glimpse of the biographer at work. In fact, these letters tell us more about Forster than they tell us about Dickens.

For one to understand Forster's narrative methods, one must first understand the nature of the materials he had in hand to work with. These letters are, almost without exception, mere jottings, with here and there an inspired phrase or clause of the type which characterizes most of Dickens' correspondence with such friends as Macready, Bulwer-Lytton, Angela Burdett-Coutts, Mary Boyle, Thomas Carlyle, and scores of others. They are even below the literary level of the routine letters Dickens wrote to William Henry Wills on the weekly business of editing *Household Words* and *All the Year Round*. They resemble, in a sense, the heads of topics which he had expected to expand later. No other batch of his letters is so obscure in meaning to a third party. Such perfect rapport existed between Dickens and Forster that only a word, a phrase, an obscure hint was sufficient to convey the burden of the message. The letters were generally dashed off in great haste, with little attention to finish, sentence structure, or punctuation. Indeed, they were intended as nothing more than reminders of appointments, cancellation of appointments, and such everyday living concerns of two busy friends who knew each other's minds to an uncanny degree. They have no more literary significance than hastily written notes which pass daily between executives in large business firms. These letters will not add to Dickens' literary fame or to his reputation as a great letter writer. But they do show Forster's literary qualities in two ways: first, they demonstrate his ability to polish rough diamonds, to tighten up the style, to omit words, phrases, and even whole paragraphs, without violating Dickens' original meaning; and second, they enhance one's opinion of Forster's critical judgment and somewhat justify, from an artistic point of view, Forster's determination to destroy most of Dickens' letters used in the biography, knowing full well that their preservation would add nothing to his friend's reputation. Our great loss is in a wealth of biographical and bibliographical details rather than in literary output.

Perhaps the most striking revelation is that Dickens' letters are but the framework upon which Forster stretched his memory. Actually, the great force at work in the biography is Forster's memory. These letters show conclusively that Forster was not a documentary biographer. He never maintained a great card file of facts, clippings, mementos, and such other secondary aids as modern biographers are accustomed to use. These letters show why Forster's life of Dickens is unsystematic in organization and uneven in literary excellence, as illogical as life itself. His memory hovered around certain events, and his method of selection was eclectic, centering his memories and his uses of the letters around the events he loved to recall, while shunning, insofar as possible, those scenes and events that were painful. His book may not be a definitive biography in the modern sense of serving as an omnium-gatherum of dull details; but it is a living biography which refuses to be relegated to the dusty shelves of forgotten archives. In it Forster's spirit walks again through the years with his beloved friend. (pp. 153-55)

Gerald G. Grubb, "The Significance of the Letters," in Boston University Studies in English, *Vol. II, No. 3, Autumn, 1956, pp. 150-56.**

SYLVÈRE MONOD   (lecture date 1965)

[*Monod's analysis of Forster's literary criticism in* The Life of Charles Dickens *takes as its starting point the statement by critic John B. Castieau (1916) that the biography is "a long tedious avenue of adulations through a desert of dates." Monod uses various passages from* The Life of Charles Dickens *to show that Forster's critical commentary is in fact much more discriminating and impartial than Castieau and others have allowed. The following excerpt was drawn from a lecture delivered in August, 1965.*]

Whoever has had occasion to study the literary history of the Victorian era must have come across the figure of John Forster and realized that he knew everybody, that he was useful to a great many important people, and that he was heartily disliked by nearly everybody. In short, the position occupied by Forster in Victorian letters can be summed up with tolerable fairness by saying that he was both an indispensable figure and an immensely unpopular one. (p. 357)

I have often wondered whether the same two epithets, indispensable and unpopular, might not, in the opinion of its average reader (that is, if the book still finds readers nowadays), be applied to John Forster's masterpiece, *The Life of Charles Dickens*, just as fitly as to the author himself. Is not the *Life of Dickens* widely regarded as both indispensable (because it is a storehouse of valuable documents put together by a privileged witness of the novelist's life and career) and unpopular (because it seems to be on the whole an uninspired performance)? I have further wondered whether one of the main objections to the *Life* is not founded on its sections of literary criticism; and finally I have wondered also whether such a view of Forster's book is not after all unfair. Such, at any rate, is the origin of the present paper, and such are the questions I propose to examine, or glance at, in the time at my disposal.

Few serious opinions have been expressed about John Forster's merits as a literary critic in the *Life of Dickens*, possibly because few detailed examinations of the relevant material—which is both abundant and fragmentary—have been thought worth making. (pp. 357-58)

[The] most startling attack ever launched against Forster's biography of Dickens is to be found, surprisingly enough, in *The Dickensian*, and, no less surprisingly, it was published in 1916, i.e., in the days when *The Dickensian* and the Dickens Fellowship were at their most Forsterian in spirit. The author of the article, one John B. Castieau, gave the following memorable definition of the *Life of Dickens*: "a long tedious avenue of adulation through a desert of dates". This terse phrase combines a number of charges, some of which it would be hard to disprove: Forster's book *is* long, and there *are* tedious parts in it. As to its being a "desert of dates", this is already a more controversial point: dates there are in the *Life*, and some are erroneous, others hopelessly tangled, while too many are omitted or too vaguely referred to; yet on the whole the complaint that a *biography* should make use of *dates* is not seriously to be entertained. Let us therefore concentrate on the formula "an avenue of adulation" and attempt to show that a close examination of Forster's book by no means bears out John B. Castieau's view of it. (p. 359)

[Let] us turn now to Forster's criticism of Dickens's fiction. Is it equivalent to an avenue of adulation? It may appear such only to the hurried reader of the early chapters, which are indeed filled with high praise, sometimes indiscriminate or injudicious. (p. 360)

Yet it should be observed—but this can be observed only by the conscientious reader who stays with Forster to the end— *a)* that the apparent avenue of adulation stops rather abruptly after the time of *David Copperfield; b)* that it is composed of well chosen trees, the praise being based on serious arguments and supported by precise illustration; *c)* that it is by no means uniform even while it lasts.

Certainly Forster has his favourites among Dickens's books, and no less certainly he admires Dickens very much; as to the second point, I for one sympathize with him, and rejoice in the possibility of doing so less militantly, less combatively in 1965 than might have been necessary in 1880 or in 1920; yet my criticism of Forster's criticism of Dickens is inevitably influenced by the secret failing I share with Forster, and to which I cannot but plead guilty, since I have failed to keep it entirely secret, namely, that I admire and enjoy Dickens; as to Forster's individual preferences, should we not recognize his right to have them? They may not coincide with ours; but does that deprive them of any value? Are we always right? And is an honest liking for *Pickwick, Chuzzlewit, Copperfield, Great Expectations,* and *Mrs. Lirriper,* scandalous, or shameful, or even inconsistent? I do not think so; or that when Forster more or less turns his criticism into an endeavour to find some rational theoretical basis for his instinctive preferences, his procedure is any more wrongheaded or any less legitimate than the reverse procedure so often adopted by later critics, that of founding one's preferences on some preconceived critical position. In other words, Forster's "adulation" of *Copperfield* shocks me neither more nor less than the stimulating essays in which minds as diverse as John Ruskin, G. B. Shaw and Dr. Leavis have chosen to single out *Hard Times* for praise.

In any case, Forster's literary criticism of Dickens's writings does not even need that form of defence. It is only the superficial view of it that might seem to require apology. But there is no reason for remaining at that superficial level any longer. And if we delve somewhat deeper, we shall soon find that not only has Forster established a hierarchy of praise, he has also introduced reservations among his most laudatory paragraphs; he has made a judicious use of criticism by implication and indirection; and he has uttered pronouncements which are the exact opposite of adulation, or even of praise; in fact he has been on more than one occasion excessively severe.

Sometimes, indeed, the severity is involuntary, as when Forster writes ... that in *Nickleby* "when good is going on, we are sure to see all the beauty of it; and when there is evil, we are in no danger of mistaking it for good", thus clumsily implying that Dickens, through lack of subtlety, was creating a Manichean kind of universe.

But, far more often, the reservations are inspired by critical conscientiousness. On the same page of comment on *Nickleby,* we find for example such a phrase as "always thoroughly intelligible and for the most part thoroughly natural". (pp. 361-62)

Another technique frequently used by Forster in the first half of his book consists in praising some specific progress, some specific quality appearing for the first time in Dickens's fiction, and thereby implying that it had not been there before. Thus

we find that in *Nickleby* Dickens had paid "more attention to the important requisite of a story" ... and that there was therefore "a better-laid design, more connected incidents, and a greater precision of character".... (p. 362)

I hope I have already made it clear that Forster's praise is not uniform. But we must now come to the cases where there is no praise at all. Indeed, the reader who has remained under the impression that he was walking along an avenue of adulation must have missed statements like the following: about *Oliver Twist* ... "Rose and her lover are trivial enough beside Bill and his mistress, being indeed the weak part of the story"; about *Barnaby Rudge* ... "the feeblest parts of the book are those in which Lord George and his secretary appear"; about *The Chimes* "It was a large theme for so small an instrument ... the little book ... was not one of his greater successes".... (pp. 362-63)

So far, I have merely attempted to defend Forster's criticism against a specific charge made against it. It would not be difficult to show that it has some positive virtues; this, however, is not easy to illustrate by means of brief quotations; let me therefore merely refer to the passages in which Forster's critical gifts and acumen are best displayed: they are, in my opinion, his comments on Pecksniff ..., on Dickens's imagination ..., on Micawber and Skimpole ..., on Dickens's humour in general (to which a considerable part of chapter I, Book IX, is devoted); his discussions of Taine's and G. H. Lewes's criticism of Dickens are lively and interesting.... (p. 363)

Of course I have no intention to claim that Forster's criticism is perfect. He missed the point of such a creation as Mrs. Harris in *Chuzzlewit* and the purpose of Miss Wade in *Dorrit.* He sometimes takes to task the reader or other critics, as when he complains that there have been "grave underestimates" of *Dombey....* His own estimate of Rosa Dartle and a few other characters in *Copperfield* is very disappointing. In addition, his criticism has been unduly influenced by the waning of his intimacy with Dickens after 1854, and perhaps his attitude is rather too egotistic. (p. 364)

Yet, on the whole, in spite of its many shortcomings, Forster's contribution to literary criticism in **The Life of Dickens** is far from negligible; it is competent and sound, and no one will question the rather obvious—but often disregarded—commonsense of the principle he expresses and by which he abides: "a book must be judged for what it aims to be, and not for what it cannot by possibility be ... A book must stand or fall by its contents".... Nor is there any reason to doubt the sincerity of some conscientious misgivings entertained and voiced by Forster about the value of his own judgment: "this", he writes, "is entitled to no weight other than as an individual opinion"...; or "here meanwhile may close my criticism— itself a fragment left for worthier completion by a stronger hand than mine". (pp. 364-65)

There remain, however, at least two major problems: on the one hand, why is it that Forster as critic in the *Life of Dickens* has had such scant recognition, while the text is there for everyone to see? And, on the other, however good or bad the criticism may be, should it be in the biography at all? It is by addressing myself to these two problems successively that I propose to bring this paper to its close.

Forster's criticism has suffered, in the judgment of many readers and even of expert Dickensians, from several deficiencies

Forster in mid-life.

of examples, but they are so disagreeable that I cannot find courage to quote more than a few representative specimens: "Reserving for mention in its place what was written after his return, it will be proper here to interpose, before the closing word of my criticism, some account of the manuscript volume" . . . ; (of two chapters dealing with the same period) "Another chapter will be given to Paris; this deals only with Boulogne" . . . ; in the account of Dickens's longest visit to Italy, we come across one of the least felicitous comments: "Of incidents during these remaining weeks there were few, but such as he mentioned had in them points of humour or character still worth remembering. Two men were hanged in the city" . . . : whether being hanged is a point of humour or of character, Forster wisely refrains from telling us. (pp. 366-67)

The method used in criticism of the novels is not of a high order; it consists chiefly of: *a)* lists of Forster's favourite passages or characters; *b)* enumeration of the leading incidents, or *c)* more systematic summaries of a whole story, sometimes degenerating into paraphrase or making unnecessary use of longish quotations; *d)* efforts to bring out the moral lesson or significance of a work. . . . Occasionally also, the biographer as critic will take refuge behind the authority of distinguished admirers of his friend, like Bulwer Lytton (about whom Forster and Dickens shared the delusion that he was a great writer), or Lord Jeffrey, whose unfailing, though senile, enthusiasm, earned him the self-chosen title of Dickens's "critic-Laureate".

All of this is presented in Forster's somewhat peculiar English, although, admittedly, the *Life of Dickens* is far better written than his previous books. This part of my discussion I now come to with due trepidation, since I must appear, before such an audience as the present, in the guise of a foreign critic of a born English writer's use of his own native language. One thing I must say against him at the outset: Forster does not conform to the rules of the best, if not the only respectable, variety of English. . . . (p. 367)

Forster was not style-conscious. The only two manuscripts of his books to have survived are those of biographies which were left unfinished at his death: the *Life of Swift* and the enlarged *Life of Strafford*. They afford no evidence of a desire on his part to refine the expression of his thought, either while writing or at proof-stage. His English has some pronounced features. His fondness for the adverb *hardly,* and for the mitigated assertiveness of the double negative *(not infrequent* instead of *frequent)* is obvious, as is his love of the adjective *characteristic;* but, as this is used chiefly as a justification for including anecdotes, sayings, and the like, it can be regarded as a mannerism of method rather than of style.

Most of the damage done to Forster's style is a consequence of his inordinate addiction to the use of adverbs. In his early works, and even in the uninspired *Life of Landor*, one often finds as many as three lumped together. . . . The effect of this passion for adverbs and adverbial clauses is that Forster's sentences often become disrupted and involved. (p. 368)

In all this there is much to account for the average reader's unfavourable impression of Forster's writing. Yet it would be grievously unfair not to add at once that his style has many positive qualities also. He is not devoid of humour, for instance. How, indeed, could any man have remained Dickens's intimate friend and earnest supporter otherwise? . . .

And when he writes about a subject that he knows well and feels strongly about, his style can become vivid and efficient.

that it shares with the bulk of the book. They are mainly its tone, its method (or lack of method), and its style.

The tone of the *Life* is often marred by the kind of preoccupations with propriety, dignity and gentlemanliness, which, until recently, one would readily associate with Victorianism. (p. 365)

As to the method of the *Life* generally, and of its critical sections in particular, it is clearly unsatisfactory. To a certain extent, this can be ascribed to Dickens's own influence. The *Life* was published, not of course in weekly instalments or in monthly parts, but in yearly volumes, each of which had been read and criticized before its successor appeared, so that Forster more than once felt called upon to turn aside from his main chronological narrative, in order to reply to specific objections by making use of further arguments or newly discovered documents. Obviously, he did not, and could not because he was old and ill, apply to his *Life of Dickens* the scrupulous care which one finds in his historical biographies.

Yet, the major unpleasantness of Forster's method lies in his constant self-justification, in his need to explain to the reader what he is doing, and why. His departures from chronology, his digressions, his abrupt changes of subject, his many inconsistencies, would be sufficiently irritating in themselves, as illustrations of mistaken organizational ambitions, or of congenital inability to cope with a large mass of variegated material. But where he fails, Forster can never leave well, or rather ill, alone; he must flaunt his very errors and defeats. I suppose this habit has alienated more readers from him than any other aspect of his work, with the possible exception of his style, to which I shall come in a moment. There are scores

The whole satire against G. H. Lewes's criticism of Dickens is pungent and telling; it is in the course of it that he calls Lewes and his followers "the criticisers of Dickens" . . . to distinguish them by this felicitous coinage from more honest critics. And Forster can even write a few superb phrases here and there. Isn't there a great deal of sad beauty in what he says of one of Dickens's deficiencies: "There was for him no 'city of the mind' against outward ills, for inner consolation and shelter" . . .? Isn't there a quasi Churchillian ring about his analysis of Charles Collins's character and fate: "no man disappointed so many reasonable hopes with so little fault or failure of his own" . . .? (p. 370)

To sum up this analysis of the unappetizing aspects of the *Life of Dickens* both as biography and as criticism, it seems to me that Forster had quaint and unsatisfactory views about method, and lacked the will-power necessary to adhere even to such plans as he had formed; and it seems to me that although he could and occasionally did write almost supremely well, he did not often care to do so, and when he did not care, he could and did write, as he would have put it, "nearly supremely badly". This considerably lessened his readers' pleasure.

There remains only one point: is the presence of literary criticism in the *Life of Dickens* legitimate? This has a twofold aspect; there is the general question of literary biography and biographical criticism and there is the personal situation of Forster. (p. 371)

[Forster's] was indeed a unique position, in that the biographer had been his subject's literary adviser and collaborator. So the kind of first-hand knowledge Forster brought to his task is what the modern Dickensian must labour hard in order to acquire even an infinitesimal part of. Forster gives us, as no one else could, not merely the biography of a writer, but also the biography of each of his works. The task is made immensely complex as well as urgently necessary by Dickens's methods of serial publication. Our sense of its value is bound to depend on the importance we are ready to attach to the study of the relationship between a writer's purpose and his achievement. But no one can deny that Forster's criticism, before it came to be reflected in the biography, and incorporated into it, had been exerted on each novel in the making and had even materially influenced some of them at that early stage. His criticism has the further interest of embodying a truly contemporary and sympathetic reaction to Dickens, of presenting to us a vivid picture of the kind of public Dickens was writing for. We may, or indeed we can, no longer share that reaction, but it remains illuminating from a historical point of view. (p. 372)

Of course, Forster's book owes a great deal of its value to its being above all a moving record of an exceptional friendship, which elicited from the French critic Louis Dépret in 1879 this lyrical outburst: "Throughout the XIXth century, I know of no such delightful example of that heavenly thing, friendship, than Dickens and Forster". And Forster would have rested satisfied with that view, for he probably agreed with Dickens, who once wrote to him: "Friendship is better than criticism". . . .

Finally, Forster was probably not a really great biographer, because he was neither a powerful thinker, nor an evenly gifted writer. Yet he did not lack insight and competence, and his *Life of Dickens* contributes to literary history and literary criticism an original document: the inside view of literary creation. (p. 373)

Sylvère Monod, "John Forster's 'Life of Dickens' and Literary Criticism," in English Studies Today, fourth series, edited by Ilva Cellini and Giorgio Melchiori, Edizioni di Storia e Letteratura, 1966, pp. 357-73.

K. J. FIELDING   (essay date 1974)

[*Fielding maintains that Forster's critical commentary in* The Life of Charles Dickens *is valuable primarily as a guide to the contemporary standards by which Dickens's works were judged. According to Fielding, Forster "can still give us the sense better than anyone else of what it was like to read Dickens in his time."*]

[There] *is* a shape to Forster's criticism. First, as a biographer he is concerned to show how Dickens (as he believes) rapidly develops from the wonderful opening with *Pickwick,* to the major triumphs of *Chuzzlewit, Dombey* and *Copperfield;* then *Bleak House* begins a series which he likes less because of its bitterness of tone and, dating from *Little Dorrit,* a decline in spontaneity. He has no reservations in admiring *Great Expectations,* but finds *Our Mutual Friend* lacking in 'freshness and natural development'. Such is not the customary critical view today. Yet it was inevitable that, knowing Dickens personally and in looking at his career as a writer while giving his biography, Forster should comment on the novels in the light of his experience of Dicken's life; and these critical opinions may well come from the personal changes he saw in Dickens.

Secondly, he does make room for some critical free play in the course of the biography and in the two chapters in the last volume entitled 'Dickens as a Novelist' and 'Personal Characteristics'. It may be a pity that in the former he entangles himself with Taine and G. H. Lewes who had both criticised his friend, but again he was writing for his time and felt they had to be answered. What they had in common was the belief that Dickens's imagination, according to Taine, was 'simply monomaniacal' and according to Lewes 'merely hallucinatory'. Forster's reply is perfectly sound in rejecting what they say and in demanding recognition for Dickens as an artist. This he is able to give, though more concerned to stress Dickens's achievement than analyse it. He has sensible comments to make, such as that Dickens's 'leading quality was Humour' which 'accounts for his magnificent successes, as well as for his not infrequent failures'. He has praise for his pathos, his dialogue, his growing seriousness and his imagination. Where he takes issue with Taine and Lewes, once again, is that (as he says throughout the *Life*) Dickens is at his greatest as a creator of characters. He is, of course, right to claim that if Dickens's characters are memorable and seem alive it is because of the quality of their dialogue and the insight and vigour with which they are shown. He also returns to the moral question, since he notes that Taine had not only deplored Dickens's inability to be 'like Balzac' and 'leave morality out of account', but made this a grievance against Henry Fielding that he was such a moralist 'he wants us to take sides'. We must surely sympathise with Forster; for Dickens, as Taine very well knew, could never be 'like Balzac'. The consequences for a novelist in the English tradition, as we see by the end of the century, would have been to have to re-shape the form of his novels and to use 'point of view' or multiple narration; not merely to take on an easy new aesthetic or set of beliefs. Simply to have removed the moral frame of reference would have led to disintegration.

Yet the main problem Forster sets us is that he interprets the last fifteen years of Dickens's life as a kind of decline, partly because their views diverged. Most of us, on the other hand, see the last three monthly-serials as possibly his greatest achievement, and some would put this more strongly.

Even so his arguments deserve respect, though my own opinion does not go altogether with them. In the first place, his criticism of the later novels is partly in regret for what they might have been as well as for what they are. We should also see that he is perfectly clear that, 'as to the matter' of Dickens's 'writings, the actual truth was that his creative genius' never left him. . . . After this, there may be said to be three reasons for his lack of appreciation for the later work. First, a personal one, in that there were aspects of Dickens he disliked; then he fails to appreciate their general tendency; and, finally, he has some sound points to make.

His chief discontent seems to lie in his dislike for the very sharpness in Dickens's satire which we now admire not only for the manner of writing but for what he says. For readers sometimes believe that Dickens's views somehow agree with their own, when in fact that is unlikely but they are carried away by his writing. Forster, of course, could not help seeing Dickens's opinions in his fiction, and he knew how in later years Dickens could often be very impatient and intolerant. No doubt, for example, he and Forster shared an admiration for what Dickens calls, 'that great seventeenth-century time' of the Commonwealth period, but he does not seem to have agreed with Dickens's impatient wish to give Parliament up completely. If Forster, perhaps, could never have coined Dickens's remarks about distrust of the 'people governing' and 'illimitable' faith in the 'People Governed', it may be better for the constitutionally liberal Forster. He loved Dickens, but when he says that he could sometimes be a 'despot' we may well feel some sympathy for him, and even recognise that these personal qualities sometimes entered into his conception of society and humanity. Forster is clear that Dickens's faults were almost inseparable from his achievements as an artist— yet not quite; and his regret that what is best in the tone and outlook of *Dombey* and *David Copperfield* was followed by the darkness of some of the later novels is surely understandable. That he misses what lies below the surface of these later novels, is what even Dickens himself may have done. It is possible that neither would have explained them as anything but the satiric exposure of isolated abuses rather than as searching attempts to find a common root in humanity or society to 'Chancery abuses, administrative incompetence, politico-economic shortcomings and social flunkeyism'. . . . (There is an unwillingness on Forster's part to investigate the kind of social criticism he touches on in connection with *Oliver Twist*. . . .) Yet if we were to see this from the later Forster's point of view, he was not unreasonable even in suggesting that they might have been satirized in the 'cheerier tone that had struck with much sharper effect' in the earlier novels. It remains a curious fact of Dickens's later biography that there is little in the life rather than the work to indicate his radicalism, and a good deal to show that he was puzzled and impatient.

Forster's weakness is that he shies away from this. Critically he might have presented his own views more forcefully. Yet since it would have made a case against his friend, he was unable to do it and he falls back on making a few 'points' for and against each novel. Yet this appears to be at the heart of his objection, and where he is still valuable is in reminding us how it was possible for someone apparently so close to Dickens to hold this view.

We have to select if we are to examine some of the critical points in the *Life*. To take, as an example, his criticism of *Nicholas Nickleby* and the *Old Curiosity Shop*, we find that he says of the earlier novels, that though 'inferior in imagination and fancy to some of the later works . . . there was increasing and steady growth in them on the side of humour, observation and character'. . . . He is rather severe on *Nickleby*, in fact, but is interesting in what he has to say about the 'reality' of Dickens's characters. It lies in 'the secret and form of his art. There never was any one who had less need to talk about his characters, because never were characters so surely revealed by themselves; and it was thus their reality made itself felt at once.' This he says (perhaps unexpectedly) was the art that Jane Austen had perfected, and 'under widely different conditions both of art and work, it was pre-eminently that of Dickens'. . . . Forster was known to his friends for his admiration of Jane Austen, much to Bulwer's disgust, and it is further evidence for the discriminating breadth of his enjoyment of fiction.

On the *Old Curiosity Shop* he is indispensable for the account he gives of the genesis of *Master Humphrey's Clock,* when he worked extremely closely with Dickens. (pp. 165-67)

The fairest way of summing up Forster as a critic of fiction is to say that it cannot be done. There is not only so much of him, but the issues he raises cannot be discussed without putting them back into the context of the time. Essentially he was a reviewer; and, except in his last years when he was struggling with Dickens's *Life,* he must have positively enjoyed working under pressure. . . . The biographer who, it is more generously said, is the only one who leaves us with the sense of [being in Dickens's presence], can recapture past events; but as a critic we have to co-operate with him. We have to allow for the way in which Forster's views were affected by the conventions of the mid-Victorian novel. If we do so, he can still give us the sense better than anyone else of what it was like to read Dickens in his time. (p. 169)

K. J. Fielding, "Forster: Critic of Fiction," in The Dickensian, *Vol. 70, No. 374, September, 1974, pp. 159-70.*

ALEC W. BRICE (essay date 1974)

[*In the following excerpt, Brice suggests that a "Romantic theory of biography," one emphasizing the biographer's intuitive understanding and conscious manipulation of source materials, influenced Forster's use of critical commentary in* The Life of Charles Dickens.]

We now know . . . that Forster could be pretty ruthless in his manipulation of Dickens's correspondence when using it in the *Life.* We also know, from subsequent discoveries about Dickens's private life, that Forster left out a great deal of important biographical material. We may therefore suspect that even his critical commentary in the *Life* is not entirely straightforward. In fact it now appears that it was subjected to at least as much manipulation as were other aspects of the biographical material, and that this makes it advisable to re-examine some standard assumptions about the *Life.*

Forster's method in compiling the critical commentary *seems* to have been relatively straightforward. Before he began writing, he had a complete file of the notices of Dickens's works from the *Examiner* in front of him. From a comparison of the *Examiner* and the *Life,* it is clear that he made a generous use of these notices dating from 1836 right up to 1870. He also had in front of him a large number of letters to which he occasionally referred, as well as some miscellaneous essays, such as those by Taine, Lewes, and Ruskin. But by far the greater bulk of his critical commentary originated from the notices from the *Examiner*.

There were clearly advantages for Forster in using these notices throughout the *Life*. In the first place, he had been (at first) literary and dramatic editor, then editor of the journal (1834-55), and was no doubt familiar and in general agreement with most of the reviews that had appeared during those years. Secondly, since they had appeared in a journal with a fairly consistent political bias, and usually reflected this bias, it must have been easier for Forster to see them as a complete body of criticism than if he had compiled a dossier or scrapbook of miscellaneous criticism. Again, they were apparently ready to hand—an important consideration for a very sick man, as Forster then was. Finally, and perhaps most important, they lent themselves most fittingly to his biographical intent. For, by referring to such notices from the *Examiner*, he was usually able to reconstruct, in a concise manner, what amounts to a fairly representative account of the contemporary critical reception of each of Dickens's works as it appeared. He makes this intention clear when he says of the critical remarks about *Pickwick* and *Nickleby*, that such comments were meant to be 'biographical rather than critical'.

His use of the notices from the *Examiner*, moreover, was particularly appropriate in another biographical sense, since they were written by men who were also a part of Dickens's circle of friendship and influence. Thus, there was not only a sense of coherence about the notices as a collection, but also a feeling—from Forster's point of view, at least—that they were actually a part of Dickens's biography, especially since they (the early ones particularly) must often have been shaped partly through informal conversations with Dickens himself, as well as having been discussed with him *after* their publication in the journal.

Forster reinforces the biographical intention of the critical commentary time and time again in the *Life*, and it is important to take this into consideration when evaluating him as a critic of Dickens. Perhaps the most noticeable way that he reinforces his biographical purpose is in the way that he usually opens the critical commentary on each novel with a recollection of the novel's reception by himself or others and then continues with critical comments largely compiled (except in the last volume of the *Life*) from relatively unchanged extracts from the contemporary notices in the *Examiner*. The resulting sense of contemporaneousness in the critical commentary in the *Life* is further heightened by his frequent use of letters contemporary with the work under consideration, as well as by a contrast with his occasional and pointed references to more recent reviews by such critics as Taine and Lewes. All this, as well as the fact that his 'critiques' are in any case embedded in a biographical narrative, leaves little doubt about his chief intention in using the notices from the *Examiner*. (pp. 185-87)

My suggestion that Forster had a biographical intention in the way that he used the notices from the *Examiner*, is a constructive way of viewing what can be seen today as 'plagiarisms' of others' works, for nowhere does Forster give any indication that he was using their material in the *Life*. The bulk of the account of *Oliver Twist*, for example, was compiled from notices by Leigh Hunt, while its concluding paragraphs make a generous use of another notice that was most likely partly written by Dickens himself. Yet nowhere are these debts even hinted at by Forster.

The least satisfying way of viewing Forster's 'borrowings', would be to see him as a blatant plagiarist. (pp. 187-88)

It is also possible that Forster considered contributions published anonymously in his own columns as partly his own, or common property, since he usually had to accept the full liability for them. Also rationalising his sense of possession is the way that leaders and reviews were often contributed jointly, and were frequently vetted by Forster himself. After a period of time, in the absence of any record, it must have been difficult to sort out exactly who wrote what.

Yet there is another more generous way of seeing Forster's free-handed approach in compiling the critical commentary in the *Life*. In his recent book [*Lockhart As Romantic Biographer*], Professor R. Hart talks about a 'Romantic theory' of biography which was the inspiration for the great biographies of Boswell and Lockhart.

He suggests that we should recognise in the Romantic biographer (among other things) a reverence for his subject based on 'a religious awe at the mystery of the true self, and a cultural view of art and creativity'. . . . Hart goes on to argue—quoting from Stanfield—that this biographer enters 'intimately into the character he would exhibit', endeavouring for the time 'to see things in the same point of view', and conceiving 'sentiments of the same nature and feelings'. 'The Romantic biographer', Hart continues . . .

> would not work without voluminous original materials merely narrating and summarising. Nor could he work with them, extracting, excerpting, destroying their personal integrity. The solution, then, was to work *through* them, selecting, manipulating, even 'contaminating', to make them accord more closely with his intuitive grasp of his subject. The solution was to Boswellise or Scottise his originals, and having by selection or revision made the self-revaluation more true to the essential character than it always seemed in the originals, to arrange his materials, to cause them to evolve in an organic form which would reveal the life as the reticent biographer had conceived and experienced it.

In fact, at this point, it would probably be quite safe to place Forster's major biographies in this tradition. For without going into detail it is clear that like Lockhart and Boswell, Forster did not just write Dickens's biography without thought; as a reviewer, biographer, and critic, he had theories of biography which he shared with others, and although their theory may have been invoked to excuse the way in which they borrowed and manipulated material, there was a Romantic theory of biography. (pp. 188-89)

An essential question remaining, therefore, is how all of this should affect our attitude towards the *Life* and its author. Clearly this is a question that can only be fully answered after this study has been taken further. Yet, as far as it has gone, there are a number of general observations worth making.

In the first place it is important to appreciate Forster's biographical purpose (apparently based on a 'Romantic theory' of biography) in compiling the critical commentary in the way that he did. Secondly, it is important to take into account the journalistic background of its author. Finally, it is essential to recognise that regardless of—or more likely, because of—Forster's free-handed methods with his materials, the *Life* still remains probably the closest that we can get to Dickens, outside his own writings. For, it should be becoming clear now, that Forster took pains to create what he saw as the true picture of Dickens, and of the contemporary reception of his works. (pp. 189-90)

> Alec W. Brice, "The Compilation of the Critical Commentary in Forster's 'Life of Charles Dickens'," in The Dickensian, Vol. 70, No. 374, September, 1974, pp. 185-90.

JAMES A. DAVIES   (essay date 1983)

[*In the following excerpt, Davies explores the process by which Forster's approach to biography gradually evolved from one of "judicious slanting" in his eighteenth-century studies to a more objective and honest treatment of his subject in his lives of Walter Savage Landor, Charles Dickens, and Jonathan Swift. The critic compares Forster's candid discussion of sensitive subjects in* The Life of Charles Dickens *with the relatively superficial treatment of the same by Dickens's other early biographers to show that it was not, as previous critics have often maintained, his intention merely to idealize the novelist. Davies also discusses the influence of various contemporaries, including Thomas Carlyle, on Forster as well as the difficulties he faced in writing about close friends.*]

As a group [Forster's literary biographies and essays] reveal a consistent approach shaped by several basic and familiar influences. Those of Charles Lamb, Leigh Hunt and Bulwer Lytton partly explain Forster's choice of subjects whilst associating them (and here Carlyle also played his part) with the idealization of writers and a concern for the dignity of literature. Further, the eighteenth-century studies reflect Forster's legal training and experience of the press: the lawyer-turned-journalist was skilled at undermining opposing points of view and presenting partial impressions. The tenor of the times, the numerous pressures on biographical truth, was the strongest force of all.

Thus, Forster's work is both aggressively polemical and judiciously slanted, the former quality seen at its most extreme in the essay on Churchill. This opens with a full-blooded attack on Churchill's editor, William Tooke: 'It would be difficult to imagine a worse biographer than Mr. Tooke . . . But though Mr. Tooke is a bad biographer and a bad annotator, he is a worse critic. . . . Whether he praises or blames, he has the rare felicity of never making a criticism that is not a mistake.' Damning evidence is supplied and the attack extended to expose Tooke's factual and grammatical errors. Other targets are Boswell on Goldsmith; Scott and Hazlitt on Defoe; Macaulay on Foote, Steele, and Swift; Cooke on Foote; and Jeffrey and Johnson on Swift. Frequently Forster's work seems that of a biographically inclined Tom Cribb.

As for judicious slanting: this involves suppression, distortion, and—for us—revealing comparisons with modern authorities. Many things are silently omitted from Forster's pages: Goldsmith's envy, coarseness in company, extravagant gambling, and failure to honour contracts; Churchill's hatred and harrying of Smollett and vindictive satirical attacks on the man who thwarted him of his father's living, his participation in the rites at Medmenham Abbey, the hedonism of his epitaph; Defoe's uncontrollable anger; Foote, fat and flabby, leaving his estate to his illegitimate sons; Steele's heavy drinking, homicidal duelling, mercenary marriage, illegitimate children, and fla-

grant dishonesty; Swift as absentee parish priest and congenital misanthrope. (pp. 243-44)

[Such] faults, argued Forster, resulted either from spontaneity—Churchill and Swift splendidly carried away in the heat of literary and political battle, Foote enraptured by his own creativity, Steele and Goldsmith tempted by the good things of life or into ill-afforded kindness—or from unpropitious circumstances, the latter clearly seen in Forster's comment on Churchill: 'The stars do not more surely keep their courses, than an ill-regulated manhood will follow a misdirected youth.' Churchill's riotous life was the consequence of 'a marriage most imprudent—most unhappy,' contracted too early in life as a reaction to parental pressure to enter the Church. Similarly, Defoe's limitations were linked to his 'Presbyterian breeding', and Goldsmith's faults further explained by reference to his unhappy childhood, the boy persecuted because of his ugliness and seeming stupidity: 'It was early to trample fun out of a child; and he bore marks of it to his dying day.' The insults and brutality of college life also cast a 'shadow . . . over his spirit, the uneasy sense of disadvantage which obscured his manners in later years.' In contrast, faults that were both socially dishonourable and indicative of basic personal deficiencies, faults hard to excuse or condone and too often occurring when the spontaneous became the uncontrolled, were silently suppressed.

Forster's *selection* of material is also governed by recognizable principles. His eighteenth-century studies illustrate the Romantic fallacy that the nature of the work reflects the author's character: for example, Steele's *Tatler* 'could have arisen only to a fancy as pure as the heart that prompted it was loving and true.' . . . But though he considered that his subjects produced idealistic and morally sound literature, they were generally regarded as an unlikely band of paragons, the main biographical problem being clearly put in a letter from Procter: 'You must be so tired and perplexed with your labour, in trying to make out a good character for Mr. Jonathan Swift.' The solution involved a concept of 'essential character,' an inviolate core of innate goodness expressed by the author's works. Hence Forster's description of Goldsmith: 'His existence was a continued privation. . . . But . . . he passes through it all without one enduring stain upon the childlike purity of his heart,' and frequent assertions that Goldsmith 'looked into his heart and wrote.'

Closely allied to 'essential character' is Forster's idea of genius: 'to charming issues did the providence of Goldsmith's genius shape these rough-hewn times. It was not alone that it made him wise enough to know what infirmities he had, but it gave him the rarer wisdom of turning them to entertainment and to profit. . . . it lighted him to those last uses of experience and suffering which have given him an immortal name.' (pp. 244-45)

Inviolate itself, literary genius transforms circumstances and reassures its possessor. Such ideas partly reflect the influence of Carlyle's lectures on 'The Hero as Man of Letters,' which Forster, of course, attended and from which he quoted in the life of Goldsmith; Carlyle, like Forster, insists on the writer's 'inward sphere' of superior moral qualities expressed by his literary work. But there is one important difference: Carlyle's mystical rhetoric is absent from Forster's work. Whereas, for example, Carlyle envisages literary genius as 'continually unfolding the Godlike to men,' in Forster's scheme, to use only the quotations immediately above, it 'shaped' and 'overflowed.' Such words are more matter-of-fact than transcendental, for Forster's literary-biographical method associates the

Romantic with, if not the ordinary, at least the socially desirable.

This latter is heavily stressed. Above all, Forster's writers are indomitable: Goldsmith 'shows to the last a bright and cordial happiness of soul, unconquered and unconquerable,' Foote has 'a fulness and invincibility of *courage* . . . which unfailingly warded off humiliation,' Churchill a compelling fearlessness. They are men of integrity: what Forster wrote of Swift ('He had nothing in him of the hired scribe, and was never at any time in any one's pay') applies to all his subjects. Despite intolerable financial pressures they wage ceaseless war against hypocrisy and corruption. . . . His writers *strive* and even though general recognition, let alone monetary reward, is rarely gained, yet such massive perseverance *forces* praise from the discerning contemporary and from posterity. . . . [Forster] endows them with his own qualities of courage, integrity, and fierce determination to pursue literary fame and power. And whereas his contemporary relationships could become strained when he sought to transform friends into self-portraits, he was more successful with the dead.

The influence of Forster's mentors shows itself mainly in his stress on the socially commendable: his eighteenth-century studies present literary history from Dryden onwards in terms of the desire of writers for social acceptance and just rewards. (pp. 245-47)

Goldsmith's life of poverty and misery, chronologically the last of Forster's eighteenth-century studies, is offered as an example of how not to treat literary genius; here Forster departs from his biographical brief to argue that mid-Victorian England needed to recognize such genius without patronage or other degradation. . . . The theme of 'dignity' unifies all Forster's literary-historical work. (pp. 247-48)

[Much] of *Walter Savage Landor* is very dull, and consists of arid summaries of Landor's works, long illustrative quotations, and extracts from correspondence offered without comment. But it is of interest for two reasons. Firstly, and for the first time, we see Forster applying his biographical principles to the life of a close friend. Polemical attacks on Landor's critics, suppression and falsification of material, some attempt to explain Landor's faults in terms of his undisciplined childhood and early freedom from monetary cares, the basic pattern of struggle and worldly failure, part of Landor's works offered as evidence of 'the nobler part of his character,' the attempt to stress socially acceptable qualities, all remind us of Forster's earlier studies—as does, also, the language of undaunted striving: 'To the end we see him as it were unconquerable. He keeps an unquailing aspect to the very close, has yielded nothing in the duel he has been fighting so long single-handed with the world, and dies at last with harness on his back.'

But despite these similarities, there are crucial differences in Forster's approach. Even though he indicates Landor's good qualities, such as his ability to inspire affection and his 'pervading passion for liberty,' Forster is now openly critical of the essential character both of his subject and his subject's literary works. Landor's failure properly to educate his children ('such nonsense . . . Such a fool's paradise'), and his desertion of his family ('more for his own sake than for theirs') are condemned unequivocally as expressions of an extreme and damaging egotism and, even though libel laws prevented explicit mention of Landor's improprieties, such as the seduction of Nancy Jones and the old man's scandalous relationship with 16-year-old Geraldine Hooper, Forster does hint strongly at

these. And in Landor's work he detects basic flaws, writing, for example, of *Gebir* that 'Impetuosity, want of patience, is as bad in literature as in life.'

Further, and not only because of personal faults and literary defects, Landor was hard to associate with the 'dignity of literature' theme; 'Landor wrote without any other aim than to please himself,' knew nothing of the hardships of the author by profession, and refused to write for pay. The biography's real hero is Southey, 'the representative man of letters of his day'; Forster prints his correspondence and eulogizes his character. The 'dignity' theme is thus carried into the nineteenth century but at the expense of Landor's reputation. Forster preserved his own by presenting himself, in *Walter Savage Landor,* as the man who furthered Landor's literary career and sought to keep his friend out of trouble; Landor was grateful but not always obedient; he begged Forster to be his biographer. Such treatment of himself is the predictable (because partial) reaction of Forster-as-Podsnap, a contrast to the treatment of Landor and to the more insistent fact that at that point in his life when Forster seemed more likely to purvey whitewashed distortion he began to incline towards honesty.

Walter Savage Landor appeared in 1869; in 1870 Dickens's death forced Forster to shoulder another massive biographical burden. His appalling health, the constant harassment of Lunacy business, his grief as friends died, made him despair of the new task before him. 'This book hangs over me now like a nightmare,' he wrote desperately to Carlyle. Certainly the state of Forster's 'Now' must have tempted him to sentimentalize the biographical 'Then.' The tendency to idealization of Forster's approach to literary subjects, the constraints of libel laws with many principals still alive, the wishes of Georgina Hogarth and Dickens's daughter Mamie, the early appearance of significant studies of Dickens by Hotten (blandly uncritical) and Sala (adulatory), together with Forster's own affection for and admiration of his dead friend, and his own enhanced social position—all these seemed to make such temptation irresistible.

Most modern critics agree that Forster succumbed. Notable exceptions are the Leavises, who appear to assert the straightforward and candid nature of Forster's presentation. . . . But other commentators divide into two groups. The first considers that Forster made an effort to tell the truth and achieved a certain truthfulness before idealizing pressures prevailed. (pp. 248-50)

The second group is less inclined to stress Forster's good intentions, and views him, more simply, as a successful idealizer. (p. 250)

This present account seeks to relate to other modern critics. Like them, it accepts that Forster idealizes; unlike them, it does not believe that this was his main aim. And whereas the most favourable commentators treat Forster as truthful and perceptive only up to a point, this account emphasizes that Forster does face the consequences of his perceptivity. . . . Or, to put matters in yet another way: modern critics, with their stress on Forster's 'deliberate design' in the interests of idealization, implicitly support a view of the *Life* as illustrative of the principles that govern Forster's eighteenth-century literary studies; but it is suggested here that the study of those latter, and of *Landor,* in relation to the *Life,* is the best way of demonstrating that, in the *Life,* Forster's biographical approach has changed.

The change is not absolute, however, for to an extent the *Life* is another work by a slanting polemicist and partial advocate. As is well known, Forster edited and falsified documents to stress the lively, sparkling side of Dickens, removed vulgarisms or the cutting response, and suppressed socially damaging facts such as Dickens's dandyism, the extent to which his family sponged on him, his antagonism towards the established church, and the depth of his pessimism about the condition of England. Forster is again able to assert, more plausibly because of such suppressions, the Romantic relationship between author and work: much of the latter taught 'the invaluable lesson of what men ought to be from what they are' and reflected 'that inner life which essentially constituted the man.' The associated concept of inviolate genius is, here, socialized by Forster to stress both Dickens's indomitable spirit and integrity, and those of his qualities attractive to hearth and home: Dickens the family man, the lover of regularity and order, and Dickens the hearty extrovert, never bookish, never highbrow, fond of riding and walking and amateur dramatics, irrepressible companion, good friend, philanthropist. To this extent Dickens is assimilated into Forster's 'composite literary man.'

But the *Life* reveals what *Landor* revealed, that whereas, when writing of the long-dead, Forster could impose ideas (about biography, literary men, personality) upon all his material, when writing of his friends the immediacy of their lives' truth drew him towards honest revelation, to a fundamental change of emphasis apparent in *Landor* and intensified in the *Life*. In the former Forster faced facts but had to draw back from complete disclosure; in the latter, despite some local bias and falsification, so far as the key incidents are concerned Forster not only faces facts but also seeks ways round obstacles to explicitness.

The contrast between the *Life* and Forster's earlier works shows the change in his principles. Such change is underlined when Forster's treatment of key topics is contrasted with the work of Hotten and Sala, the most important earlier biographers of Dickens. Thus, Hotten's treatment of Dickens's childhood and youth simply refers to his 'education at a good school' and his boyhood reading of 'the standard works of the best authors'; Sala is more certain but equally inaccurate: 'He had not been born in poverty, but in a respectable middle-class family. He had never known—save, perhaps, in early youth, the occasional "harduppishness" of a young man striving to attain a position—actual poverty. . . . He had no terrible experiences to tell. . . . From youth to age he lived in honour, and affluence, and splendour.' Only Forster knew the truth, and Engel has skilfully shown, with special reference to Dickens's childhood and youth, that 'one way of understanding the value of Forster's work is to discover how much information about Dickens it revealed which was completely new to the Victorian reader.' Even more impressive is the use Forster makes of this unique material. Dickens's autobiographical account is linked to the rags-to-riches theme of the *Life,* as the source of 'the fixed and eager determination, the restless and resistless energy, which opened to him opportunities of escape from many mean environments, not by turning off from any path of duty, but by resolutely rising to such excellence of distinction as might be attainable in it,' it is also the beginning of a counter-theme, the relationship between early humiliations and Dickens's persisting and ultimately self-destructive faults of character: 'A too great confidence in himself, a sense that everything was possible to the will that would make it so, laid occasionally upon him self-imposed burdens greater than might be borne by any one with safety.' The purely pathetic and sentimental potential of the account is manfully resisted.

This presence of theme and counter-theme supports . . . [the] assertion that Forster's approach is not simply uncritical. But the consequences of such explicit statements, in particular the rigorous tracing of character flaws, are also faced with some frankness. And when sufficient frankness is not possible Forster resorts to a kind of fearless implication: documents are printed and arranged so that they seem to speak for themselves. We can see this in a minor way in, for example, Forster's treatment of Dickens's relations with Richard Bentley. Though Forster refrains from explicit condemnation of Dickens's lack of moral awareness in his disputes with the publisher, he does print the letter in which Dickens admits to having foolishly agreed the poor terms to which he was now objecting, refers to his (Forster's) 'no small difficulty in restraining him from throwing up the agreement altogether,' thus implying where at least some right lay, before appealing, with slight ambiguity, for a 'considerate construction to be placed on every effort made by [Dickens] to escape from obligations incurred in ignorance of the sacrifices implied by them.'

Again, without comment, Forster offers much quite startling evidence of the morbid side of Dickens's imagination: for example, he does not delete Dickens's thoughts of the drowned, in *The Old Curiosity Shop,* with 'the stars shining down upon their drowned eyes,' or Dickens's description of his eagerness, when in America, to 'see the exact localities where Professor Webster did that amazing murder.' Forster retains Dickens's thoughts of Mary Hogarth, including his friend's reaction to Mrs Hogarth's death that meant he could no longer be buried next to her daughter Mary ('I cannot bear the thought of being excluded from her dust,') and Dickens's strange and emotional dream of Mary Hogarth's apparition urging Roman Catholicism upon him. The last incident draws from Forster direct reference to 'trying regions of reflection' that trouble men of genius, and to Dickens's 'disturbing fancies.'

Forster allows such incidents to offer evidence of Dickens's obsessive and insensitive singlemindedness. This use of the frank and the implicit in developing the counter-theme is most clearly and importantly seen in his handling of two major topics, Dickens's marital troubles and the reading tours. Once more, we are helped to see the changed emphasis in Forster's work by contrasting it with Hotten and Sala. Hotten attempts to whitewash Dickens's marital troubles: brief references to the *Household Words* 'manifesto' and to 'a misunderstanding . . . betwixt Mr. and Mrs. Dickens, of a purely domestic character—so domestic—almost trivial, indeed—that neither law nor friendly arbitration could define or fix the difficulty sufficiently clear to adjudicate upon it. . . . we trust the reader will think we act wisely in dropping any further mention of it.' Sala is pompously vague. . . . (pp. 250-53)

Forster is more candid. He illustrates Dickens's developing unhappiness, analyses his state of mind in 1858, and sees Dickens's inability properly to consider others and his impulsive and restless behaviour as manifestations of the too-great concern for self and the fierce determination to get what he wanted that were legacies of the early hardship: Forster criticizes the 'manifesto' and the writing of the 'violated letter,' and states: 'Thenceforward he and his wife lived apart. The eldest son went with his mother, Dickens at once giving effect to her expressed wish in this respect; and the other children remained with himself, their intercourse with Mrs. Dickens being left entirely to themselves.' Forster writes with impressive compassion and events force from him the haunting phrase and some fine sentences: 'There was for him no "city of the mind" against outward ills, for inner consolation and shelter. It was in and from the actual he still stretched forward to find the freedom and satisfactions of an ideal, and by his very attempts to escape the world he was driven back into the thick of it.' The moving imagery and rhythms appropriate in their anguished awkwardness suggest both Dickens's predicament and his biographer's sincere sadness. Nonetheless, Forster goes as far as the libel laws allowed *and* at the end of 'Volume the Third' he prints Dickens's will.

Hotten had remarked that 'After his [Dickens's] wishes had been put into legal form by his solicitors, he copied out the entire document in his own handwriting,' and then quotes Dickens's description of Georgina Hogarth as 'the best friend I ever had,' his instructions for a quiet burial, and his expressions of religious faith. Forster, however, prints the will in its entirety, an inclusion almost certainly unique in Victorian biography. In doing so he is able to give Ellen Ternan due prominence as first legatee and recipient of a generous bequest, and is able to remind his readers of his own role as Dickens's 'dear and trusty friend' and an executor of the will. Further, the will provides a penetrating insight into Dickens's thinking and into his household arrangements by contrasting Georgina Hogarth, his children's 'ever useful self-denying and devoted friend,' with Mrs Dickens, the unhelpful beneficiary of Dickens's post-marital financial generosity. It is a cruel and bitter document, final suggestive testimony of those faults of character that aggravated the separation. Its inclusion circumvents libel laws and other pressures to demonstrate the strength of Forster's desire to tell the whole truth. . . . (pp. 253-54)

Finally, the reading tours: Hotten records without comment that, in 1858, Dickens began to read 'professionally, and as an avowed source of income,' and cites dates and subjects during his narrative. Sala's main concern is with the 'Sikes and Nancy' reading, questioning the 'taste and the usefulness of the display,' criticizing Dickens for some overacting, and summing up: '[Dickens gained] by these performances many thousands of pounds, but losing, I am afraid, many years of the life which he might have reasonably hoped to attain.' Forster begins with Dickens's request for his opinion, restates his opposition to the readings ('It was a substitution of lower for higher aims; a change to commonplace from more elevated pursuits; and it had so much of the character of a public exhibition for money as to raise, in the question of respect for his calling as a writer, a question also of respect for himself as a gentleman,') and then, once again, ascribes Dickens's disregard of all arguments against the tours to the defects of character consequent upon his traumatic upbringing by repeating his earlier comments about Dickens's hard and aggressive confidence and fierce determination. Having expressed his disapproval, Forster then devotes over a quarter of 'Volume the Third' to descriptions of the tours, mainly in Dickens's own words, that exhibit significant changes of emphasis. (pp. 254-55)

In *The Life of Charles Dickens* Forster is no longer the restorer of wronged reputations but the Carlylean biographer valuing integrity in the face of mealy-mouthed pressures.

This last is underlined as we recall Forster's own abiding obsession with the 'dignity of literature,' and the unifying progress from Dryden through the essays to Goldsmith and on to Southey that seems, in the early stages of the *Life,* to be completed by Dickens:

> He would have laughed if, at this outset of his wonderful fortunes in literature, his genius acknowledged by all without misgiving, young,

popular, and prosperous, any one had compared him to the luckless men of letters of former days, whose common fate was to be sold into a slavery which their later lives were passed in vain endeavours to escape from. Not so was his fate to be, yet, something of it he was doomed to experience.

But the shining jewel of the literary profession, the man who, through the good influence of his books and the example of his life, seemed to be forcing 'writer' and 'gentleman' into permanent juxtaposition, not only began writing books that attacked the very foundations of the society whose acclaim Forster wished literary men to receive, but also took up with an actress half his age, separated from his wife, and made much money through non-literary, ungentlemanly, and obsessively self-destructive activities. Forster's chagrin must have been intense, yet, amidst disappointed hopes and crumbling theories, he sought valiantly and ingeniously to be truthful to life.

A final consequence of such seeking is Forster's treatment of his own role in Dickens's life. As is well known, he manipulated and falsified documents to emphasize Dickens's reliance upon him and to counter the fact that the two had been less close in later years. There is . . . a long tradition of regarding the biography as an expression of Forster's egotism: 'The Autobiography of John Forster with Recollections of Charles Dickens'. . . . Forster could have said very much more about the overall effect he had on Dickens's work, and he says little or nothing about, for example, the platform and support he provided for Dickens in the *Examiner,* and the way he brought Dickens into London literary life. Self-aggrandizement is thus an inadequate description of his approach. We see further that Forster's treatment of himself is consistent with his treatment of Dickens: whereas, in treating his friend, a more localized idealizing is countered by a general emphasis on frankness and implicit revelation, so, in treating himself, a carefully controlled stress on his own importance is at least balanced by what can, perhaps, be called a policy of dissociation. . . . Forster advised against Dickens taking the editorship of the *Daily News,* against his separation from his wife, against making a public statement about the separation, against giving paid public readings, against the tour of America, against the inclusion of the Sikes/Nancy reading. We are allowed to see only too clearly that he might as well have kept silent. The resemblance to his role in *Walter Savage Landor* is considerable, but with this difference, again marking the changing emphasis, that Forster's treatment of himself in the *Life* is of a piece with the treatment of his subject.

In one sense Forster paid the price of his honesty, for contemporary reviewers were shrewd and accurate in their reading. They were almost unanimous in praising the biography of Goldsmith for its advocacy of the worth of its central figure and of the wider claims of literature. . . . Few thought Forster's Landor to have advanced literary men in the public's estimation. As for *The Life of Charles Dickens,* there was much agreement that Forster had harmed his friend's reputation by stressing his lowly background and lust for lucre. (pp. 256-58)

Though Carlyle may well have influenced Forster against the popular literary world, as he had into franker biography, there can be no doubt that Forster still found the pursuit of truth to be a wretched one. It was, he told Longfellow, a task 'more painful and heavy to me than I could ever hope to convey to you.' Nonetheless the aging, sick, and saddened man sought to reject all applicable biographical precedents, to tell much and when unable to tell more to imply much more. In this there was the kind of heroism, the undaunted attempts at obstacles, the striving towards commendable goals, that Forster had so often portrayed in his subjects. (p. 258)

James A. Davies, in his John Forster: A Literary Life, *Barnes & Noble Books, 1983, 318 p.*

JOHN J. FENSTERMAKER (essay date 1984)

[*The following excerpt provides an overview of Forster's biographical works, including a summary of his achievements as a writer and a detailed analysis of his methods and aims in* The Life and Times of Oliver Goldsmith, Walter Savage Landor, *and* The Life of Charles Dickens. *In his discussion, Fenstermaker examines the motives that shaped Forster's early biographical works and the trend away from idealization of his subjects in the later biographies.*]

Forster's literary biographies . . . fall into two categories—those of eighteenth-century writers and those of his contemporaries, Landor and Dickens. The eighteenth-century studies include sketches of Churchill, Defoe, Foote, and Steele, and a single full portrait, that of Goldsmith. The sketches provide an excellent opportunity for describing Forster's theory of biography. Not surprisingly, we can see in these studies attitudes and techniques that we have found elsewhere in his works.

The lives he records were of men whose writings he admired because their subjects and attitudes seemed to him to be "right." He painted idealized portraits, having found, through a sensitive reading of each author's best work, that his essential character was moral and optimistic, as Forster's aesthetics required. Like Carlyle, Ruskin, and Browning, Forster believed that great literature portrayed a moral world and did so because its author was at heart moral. The man might have weaknesses in his character, but they were important only insofar as they revealed what he had had to overcome. For Forster, the primary function of biographical detail was to reveal this essential moral bent. He did not believe that the biographer should report all of the evil a man might have done or that he should attempt to balance evenly the good with the bad, but rather that he should discover what best indicated the man's true nature as revealed in his works, and seeing that, insure that it would receive its due emphasis. . . . (pp. 77-8)

In a sense, then, Forster the advocate is guilty of arranging the biographical facts of his authors (as distinct from his critical judgment of individual works) in a selective manner, involving suppression and even distortion. (p. 78)

And it is true . . . that Forster would slant his studies in order to make his authors more acceptable to middle-class Victorians who might be unable otherwise accurately to gauge the man's true spirit in his works. To Forster, one could convey the essential truth, but one would have to know how one's readers would respond to individual details, and so know what to include and exclude, if one were to succeed. Forster's idealized portraits are meant to do just that. He would not have considered himself misleading the public with his methods; rather, he would have argued, he was leading them more truthfully than otherwise might be the case. Like the artist in Pater's essay on "Style," Forster thought it not enough to ask if something were a fact, but whether that fact, that action, that word, would do the true thing to the reader, convey the true idea. Forster had his own unified vision of the man to convey—a vision he found corroborated in the author's best literary

work—and, Victorian artist that Forster was, he would use only those details that would convey his vision into the reader's mind.

On the other hand, he does not altogether fail to note character weaknesses in his authors or flaws in their works. His studies are not "lives of saints." (p. 79)

Forster divided [*The Life and Adventures of Oliver Goldsmith*] into four books. In each we witness Goldsmith's weaknesses and mistakes spread upon a broad canvas, but also in each we come to share Forster's mitigating assessment of these flaws as he emphasizes Goldsmith's good heart, explains away his painful social ineptness, and chastises those who knew and appreciated him best—Johnson, Reynolds, Burke—for the lack of feeling they too often demonstrated toward him. And, as always, problematic biographical details are put into perspective by the reader's never being long away from discussion of Goldsmith's literary genius as revealed in the major works he created.

Goldsmith's first thirty years constituted a virtually unbroken series of misadventures. He drifted aimlessly, suffering through young childhood—where he was considered "impenetrably stupid" . . .—desultory schooling, physical abuse from his tutor at college, and failure to find a suitable profession despite efforts toward religion, education, law, and medicine. But, constant in all of the aimlessness, idleness, and eternal indebtedness, Goldsmith maintained a gentle cheerfulness, an unstinting charity toward those with less than he, and a sometimes very touching humanity, such as in the scenes of his playing the flute for his keep as he wandered across Europe. Speaking of these times, especially of two years of almost total idleness, Forster urged that the reader not judge negatively—as the world too quickly does—this soon to be hero-as-man-of-letters, for he will turn to good account even his genuine frailties:

> . . . if these irregular early years unsettled him for the pursuits his friends would have had him follow, and sent him wandering, with no pursuit, to mix among the poor and happy of other lands, he assuredly brought back some secrets both of poverty and happiness which were worth the finding, and, having paid for his errors by infinite personal privation, turned all the rest to the comfort and instruction of the world. There is a Providence that shapes our ends, rough-hew them how we will; and to charming issues did the providence of Goldsmith's genius shape these rough-hewn times. . . . Through the pains and obstructions of his childhood, through the uneasy failures of his youth, through the desperate struggles of his manhood, it lighted him to those last uses of experience and suffering which have given him an immortal name. . . .

These lines offer a schema for the entire volume: Forster detailed Goldsmith's "pains," "obstructions," "desperate struggles," and "suffering"; he then discussed their meanings by showing them transmogrified into various of Goldsmith's works. . . . [Such] works reveal the artist's moral nature and show the value for mankind of what that moral nature communicated in the author's best writing. At the same time, we witness an heroic spirit in its struggle to create in the grossly unfavorable Grub Street world of the mid-eighteenth century.

Book Two, "Authorship by Compulsion," and Book Three, "Authorship by Choice," are more similar in the events they relate than their titles suggest. In the first, we see clearly and painfully life as a Grub Street drudge; paid little for their efforts, authors must produce reams of work just to scrape by. To make matters worse, many hacks prostituted their pens for corrupt politicians, thereby giving all men of letters, by simple association, a disreputable social position: "To become author, was to be treated as adventurer: a man had only to write, to be classed with what Johnson calls the lowest of all human beings, the scribbler for party." . . . In Book Two, Goldsmith is shown busy at his new literary trade: writing reviews for the *Monthly Review,* where the publisher, Griffiths, added insult to low pay by allowing his wife to alter Goldsmith's copy; translating under a pseudonym; trying to write his own first work, "An Enquiry into the Present State of Polite Learning in Europe," also to be published without his name; and suffering incredible deprivation: "Oh Gods! Gods! HERE IN A GARRET,WRITING FOR BREAD, AND EXPECTING TO BE DUNNED FOR A MILK SCORE!" . . . (pp. 89-91)

Book Three reveals Goldsmith finally achieving success through *The Vicar of Wakefield* and *Letters from a Citizen of the World.* But the real change came in his growing relationship with Johnson, Reynolds, and Burke, who became Goldsmith's friends, particularly Johnson, who became a mentor of sorts. In Books Three and Four, the scenes among these men account for much of the volume's charm. They include, for example, the wonderful description of Boswell when Goldsmith first met him: "But little does Goldsmith or any other man suspect as yet, that within this wine-bibbing, tavern babbler, this meddling, conceited, inquisitive, loquacious lion hunter, this bloated and vain young Scot, lie qualities of reverence, real insight, quick observation, and marvelous memory, which, strangely assorted as they are with those other meaner habits, and parasitical, self-complacent absurdities, will one day connect his name eternally with the men of genius of his time, and enable him to influence posterity in its judgments on them." . . . But despite Goldsmith's fame and his friendships with many of the major figures of his age, life was filled with the old frustrations, interminable drudge labor for booksellers merely to keep himself out of debt, and the new frustration of struggling with Garrick in a first attempt to write and stage a comedy.

Also in Books Three and Four, Forster most directly confronted the common charges, both of Goldsmith's contemporaries and of posterity, that he was envious or jealous of the success of others and that he was so socially inept that he was a constant target for jokes and, occasionally, for more serious ridicule even among his friends and close acquaintants. Forster's rhetorical strategy for dealing with such allegations conformed to that pattern seen before in his literary biographies: he explained how these weaknesses occurred, making them appear at least understandable and, more often, entirely forgivable; he reduced their biographical significance by showing how they were apotheosized as exampla in Goldsmith's writings or were unimportant when juxtaposed with the author's essential character as revealed in his best works. For example, in one of the many instances where Forster asked the reader "charitably [to] judge" Goldsmith, he exhorted: "Nor let us omit from . . . consideration the nature to which he was born, the land in which he was raised, his tender temperament neglected in early youth, the brogue and the blunders he described as his only inheritance. . . . Manful, in spite of all, was Goldsmith's endeavor and noble its result." . . . (pp. 91-2)

Such judgmental summaries of biographical facts are sprinkled heavily throughout this study. "Conversation is a game," Forster reminded his reader, referring to the numerous anecdotes describing Goldsmith's failures in polite gatherings, "where the wise do not always win. When men talk together, the acute man will count higher than the subtle man." . . . And of his envy or jealousy: "No one who thus examines the whole case can doubt, I think, that Goldsmith had never cause to be really content with his position among the men of his time. . . . even the booksellers who crowded round the author of *The Vicar of Wakefield* and the *Traveller,* came to talk but of booksellers' drudgery and catchpenny compilations. . . . May it not be forgiven him if, in galling moments of slighting disregard, he made occasional silent comparisons of *Rasselas* with the *Vicar,* of the *Rambler* with the *Citizen of the World.* . . .''

Hence in both his personal and his professional endeavors, Goldsmith suffered calamities: "But they found him, and left him, gentle; and though the discipline that taught him charity had little contributed to his social ease, by unfeigned sincerity and unaffected simplicity of heart he diffused every social enjoyment. When his conduct least agreed with his writings, these characteristics failed him not.'' . . . The *Goldsmith* volumes constitute Forster's last completed biography of eighteenth-century writers. The lives of Landor and Dickens presented their biographer very different problems, and despite obvious similarities, very different kinds of biographies resulted. (p. 92)

Many features of [*Walter Savage Landor*] are praiseworthy. The volumes contain upward of four hundred letters, most new to print. The single greatest treasure is the correspondence between Landor and Robert Southey, which records in detail a friendship of more than three decades between these two literary figures. Appearing, too, are certain of Landor's works never before published, including the last five scenes of his *Imaginary Conversations.* Generous extracts of Landor's writing abound, underpinned by equally generous portions of Forster's critical commentary, frequently lifted whole from the many reviews of Landor he had published in the *Examiner* and the quarterlies. One of the most serious weaknesses in the study, however, is that this material is inadequately assimilated, marring the coherence of the story. . . .

Forster wished to avoid suggesting too intimate a personal relationship with Landor. By far the most important contemporary praise for the volumes shows that this "distancing" was judged generally to have been effective and is precisely the praise that must at first strike a modern reader as most surprising: that the volumes are "frank," "candid," and "fair" in assessing Landor's character. (p. 94)

Forster's sense of integrity as a biographer led him to a more absolute "truth" than he had accomplished earlier. Not that he completely abandoned all idealizing, for without doubt Forster felt compelled to make the best case he could for his longtime friend and unquestionably he genuinely believed that much in Landor's writings was worthy and reflected a unique genius, which the world had consistently and unfairly neglected. Here, of course, was precisely the difficulty: how to give Landor his due and remain truthful. One response to this problem was Forster's abandoning of the idea of "hero" when describing Landor. That word has little place in these volumes and is supplanted by "genius," "original," and "special" as positive terms. Further, Forster did not argue that Landor's character was essentially moral or that the excesses in his personal life were rendered unimportant by the value of his works.

Indeed, he believed that Landor's self-centered and undisciplined life, often expressing itself in the lack of restraint in his writing, substantially reduced the stature of the man and of the writer. Recording this "truth" in the *Landor,* Forster remained consistent with his primary aesthetic principle—that the quality of the artistic vision is determined by the quality of the writer's essential character. The earlier writers whose lives he recorded appear as greater artists because the flaws in their personal lives were superficial, not fundamental aspects of their characters. Forster may have made errors in judgment about one or more of these earlier figures, but his firsthand knowledge of Landor's life precluded such errors in his case. Following out the truth of this principle in the *Landor,* Forster created a biography quite different from his earlier ones.

No single biographical fact, by itself, whether included, suppressed, or distorted in the *Landor,* reveals the difference: for example, Forster suppressed most of the details about Landor's early love affairs and his later scandal and court case—though that both occurred is indicated—in much the same way that earlier he suppressed details about the drunkenness, uncontrollable anger, and illegitimate children in [earlier biographical studies].... But in the *Landor,* the biographer's candor, obvious from the outset, and the tone of his introductory remarks make clear that the negative judgments forthcoming about the writer's personal life possess greater importance than in the former studies:

> It is not my intention to speak otherwise than frankly of his character and his books. Though I place him in the first rank as a writer of English prose; though he was also a genuine poet.... It was unfortunate for him in his early years that self-control was not necessarily forced upon a temperament which had peculiar need of it; and its absence in later time affected both his books and his life disastrously. Even the ordinary influences and restraints of a professional writer were not known to him. Literature was to him neither a spiritual calling, as Wordsworth regarded it; nor the lucrative employment for which Scott valued it. Landor wrote without any other aim than to please himself, or satisfy the impulse as it rose. Writing was in that sense an indulgence to which no limits were put, and wherein no laws of government were admitted.
>
> (pp. 96-7)

These lines, virtually the first set down, represent an almost exact reversal of Forster's usual emphases: heretofore the permanent value of the works—positive, instructive, and entertaining while reflecting the author's essentially moral character—has reduced the import of any personal failings noted. These opening lines do show, however, Forster's adherence to his most important critical principle: that the greatness of the art will correspond to the greatness of the artist's nature. Lack of restraint in the one, for example, should manifest itself in the other. In this sense, Landor provides an exact test of this principle. Had such an undisciplined nature produced works of ordered clarity, Forster would have been hard pressed to hold to his critical imperatives. But Landor's writing does lack discipline; the art and the man are of a piece. The difficulty came in saying so without seeming to betray a friend. Regardless, Forster meant every word of this initial judgment. Nearly eleven-hundred pages later, he wrote:

> What was wanting most, in his books and his life alike, was the submission to some kind of law. To this effect a remark was made at the opening of this biography, which has had confirmation in almost every page of it written since.... I am not going now to preach any homily over my old friend. Whatever there was to say has been said already with as much completeness as I found to be open to me. Attempt has been honestly made in this book to estimate with fairness and candour Landor's several writings ... and judgment has been passed, with an equal desire to be only just, on all the qualities of his temperament which affected necessarily not his own life only.... what was really imperishable in Landor's genius will not be treasured less, or less understood, for the more perfect knowledge of his character.
>
> (pp. 97-8)

The emphasis in the present discussion upon the character of Landor fairly represents Forster's own proportioning. Although he offered critical analysis of Landor's writings, especially *Gebir, Count Julian,* and the *Imaginary Conversations,* through borrowings from his own critical reviews and especially from the letters of Southey, when he is speaking in his own voice of the late 1860s he usually hangs biographical detail upon his discussion of the literary works, frequently in the role of albatross. An example is Forster's assertion that the dialogue format is that most suited to Landor's talents and character: "When a man writes a dialogue he has it all to himself, the pro and the con, the argument and the reply.... In no other style of composition is a writer so free from orderly restraints upon opinion, or so absolved from self-control.... How far such a style or method would be found suitable to the weakness as well as the strength of the character depicted in these pages, the reader has the means of judging. By many it may be thought that I have supplied such means too amply." ...

Yet he ends his study with a fitting tribute to his friend wherein the life of this old firebrand political radical and the literary works he produced are seen in a worthy and admirable meld:

> There is hardly a conceivable subject, in life or literature, which they [Landor's works] do not illustrate by striking aphorisms, by concise and profound observations, by wisdom ever applicable to the needs of men, and by wit as available for their enjoyment. Nor, above all, will there anywhere be found a more pervading passion for liberty, a fiercer hatred of the base, a wider sympathy with the wronged and the oppressed, or help more ready at all times for those who fight at odds and disadvantage against the powerful and the fortunate, than in the writings of WALTER SAVAGE LANDOR.
>
> (p. 98)

Forster did believe this judgment; yet much in the biography seriously erodes this positive final assessment. Without doubt the man Landor and Forster's *Landor* stand apart from the other writers and biographies Forster wrote. Landor is alone on a side track—"original," "individual," "unique" in his "genius"—but not a hero-as-man-of-letters in the line of writers from Defoe to Dickens whose "lives" constitute Forster's best and most coherent biographical writing. (pp. 98-9)

Dickens's willingness to share his most private thoughts is obvious in many of the nearly one thousand letters spanning an intimate relationship of thirty-three years that Forster quoted in *The Life of Charles Dickens*; indeed, it was to Forster that Dickens revealed his experience as a young boy in a blacking warehouse and the devastating effect it had on his self-image, the attendant relationship with his parents and others around him, and his childhood resolve for his future life. Dickens shared these details with no other person in his lifetime.

Whereas the biography of Landor presented Forster with serious problems, the greater part of Dickens's personal life and especially his works were excellent subjects for Forster, the advocate of the dignity of authorship as a profession. Dickens's works were universally acknowledged for their positive moral and social content; his own life, even apart from its Horatio Alger dimension, was full of public acts of charity that frequently included well-publicized efforts in company with Forster, Bulwer, and others to assist struggling authors. The weaknesses in Dickens's private life and character, such as his handling of the breakup of his marriage, could be seen simply as human failings, bringing Dickens the hero more properly into perspective as Dickens the human being, and not in any way genuinely contradictory to the positive moral bent of his essential character so well defined by his greatest works. (p. 99)

[*The Life of Charles Dickens*] was Forster's last completed work and clearly his crowning achievement. The format is similar to the *Landor*: much of the text is composed of Dickens's letters; a complete history of the writing and publishing details of each work is included with analyses of each novel, drawn in many cases from reviews published earlier. Unlike the *Landor*, the various biographical and critical details are handled in a unified and coherent style supporting Forster's opening descriptive judgment of Dickens, "the most popular novelist of the century, and one of the greatest humourists that England has produced." ... The emphasis suggested in this opening is crucial: we have returned to a biography that describes the hero-as-man-of-letters. (p. 100)

Forster accepted as the essential Dickens the Dickens of the letters. In this way, his defense of using the letters also refutes the charge that his study idealizes Dickens. The issue of idealization is, of course, pertinent to all of Forster's biographies. And it is with the "dignity of literature" question that the idealizing tendency is most demonstrable. Focusing upon it, we may consider how Forster manipulated his materials in portraying Dickens in these volumes.

Modern scholarship has gone far in examining Forster's various uses of documentary material in the *Life*. The editors of the Pilgrim Edition of *The Letters of Charles Dickens* have discovered that Forster occasionally altered letters by rephrasing or rearranging to emphasize his own importance in a particular decision or event, by changing dates, by "improving" style, usually to the end of making Dickens more appealing, by implying that letters written to others were, in fact, written to him. The editors' conclusion, however, is precisely what we have found in the other biographies: Forster "had his subject remarkably in perspective. He was, moreover, concerned not simply with public image ... but with the truth, as he conceived it. The *Life* contains numerous small distortions of fact; but paradoxically these distortions were in the interest of a larger, or ideal, truth."

Working with the critical commentary on Dickens's works included in the biography, Alec Brice [see excerpt dated 1974]

has found that these analyses, largely from the pages of the *Examiner,* include, without identification, some critiques not written by Forster but by other critics, for example, Hunt and Fonblanque. Forster's motivation was to recapture for his reader as closely as possible the contemporary reaction to each work by using reviews and letters to re-create these moments: his success at producing a single style and nearly faultless coherence is genuinely remarkable. This technique, as Brice points out, is similar to that of Boswell with Johnson and Lockhart with Scott: the biographer manipulates primary materials to create a portrait of the man true to his experience of him. As was the case with the letters: "it should be becoming clear now, that Forster took pains to create what he saw as the true picture of Dickens, and of the contemporary reception of his works."

How, then, does Dickens, hero-as-man-of-letters, appear in these volumes? He emerges as no simple character but a complicated literary man whose life became more and more tragic and limited as he grew older. In the period from the 1830s to the mid-1850s, Dickens the man and author is unmatched in sheer physical energy and popularity. Forster shows him outmaneuvering fellow reporters, inventing a shorthand system he put to good use, and creating moral and positive novels and stories peopled by hundreds of memorable characters; his private life is a blur of travel (the letters from America are wonderful in their details), charitable works, and enormous social gatherings. Experimentation leads generally to success in the Christmas books but failure in establishing a weekly journal, *Master Humphrey's Clock,* and in editing a daily newspaper, the *Daily News.* The 1850s open optimistically: after repeated failures to find a journalistic outlet for his energies and social concerns, he succeeds in finding the proper vehicle with the founding of *Household Words,* his popularity rises with *David Copperfield* and *Bleak House,* and amateur theatricals and the Guild of Literature and Art provide him a means for aiding struggling authors. Typical of this early period is Dickens's energy and excitement over the writing of *A Christmas Carol.* ... (pp. 101-03)

Typical, too, of these good times, as Forster viewed them, was the expression of Dickens's just and noble heart in the great social themes of his fiction. (p. 103)

But behind the buoyant optimism, intense dedication to improved social justice, and extraordinary success of these years were darker intimations, which Forster also recorded. These judgments first appear in the assessment of Dickens's blacking warehouse experience—where the young boy was humiliated by being taken from school and forced to do drudge work pasting labels on jars of boot-black while his family was for a brief period resident in the Marshalsea debtor's prison. As a result of this trial, Dickens determined never again to face poverty and social degradation. His success in avoiding any similar experience when in control of his own fate prompted, Forster believed, a "too great confidence in himself, a sense that everything was possible to the will that would make it so," and produced in him "something that had almost the tone of fierceness; something in his nature that made his resolves insuperable, however hasty the opinions on which they had been formed." ... This assessment rendered very early in the first volume contains Forster's explanation for the harmful decisions, both large (separation from his wife, his public readings) and small (squabbles with publishers, using real people as models for negative characters), that Dickens made throughout his life. The tragic mistakes this character flaw produced came in the later years of Dickens's life, 1858-1870.

Over the separation from his wife, Forster struggled to accord Dickens justice. He quoted the author's letter on the incompatibility of his and Catherine's personalities and particularly of his own restlessness: "I have now no relief but in action. I am become incapable of rest. . . . Why is it, that as with poor David, a sense comes always crushing on me now, when I fall into low spirits, as of one happiness I have missed in life, and one friend and companion I have never made?" . . . Forster could accept no excuse. He explained that Dickens had learned the value of a "determined resolve" from his early sufferings but nothing of "renunciation and self-sacrifice"; more than that, his early rise to fame made him "master of everything that might seem to be attainable in life, before he had mastered what a man must undergo to be equal to its hardest trials." . . . He concluded his brief discussion of the breakup—one that never hinted of Dickens's affair with Ellen Ternan, an eighteen-year-old actress—with unequivocal condemnation couched in the language of fairness: "Such illustration of grave defects in Dickens's character as the passage in his life affords, I have not shrunk from placing side by side with such excuses in regard to it as he had unquestionable right to claim should be put forward also." . . . (pp. 103-04)

The public readings, unlike Dickens's relationship with his wife, touched directly on the literary side of his life, specifically for Forster, on the dignity-of-literature issue. For that reason he dealt with them prominently—nearly a fourth of the third volume is devoted to the readings. Forster's position was consistent and unequivocal: "It was a substitution of lower for higher aims; a change to commonplace from more elevated pursuits; and it had so much of the character of a public exhibition for money as to raise, in the question of respect for his calling as a writer, a question also of respect for himself as a gentleman." . . . The "dignity" issue so defined soon ceases to be the problem in that more serious consequences result from the readings than questions of social prestige. Forster links Dickens's desire to escape into the readings and into the applause of the crowd with Dickens's desire to escape the dissolution of his marriage, and Dickens's remarks about his motivations at this time—"Much better to die, doing" . . .—echoes ominously in the reader's mind as Forster piles up the correspondence from a Dickens exultant in the enormous amounts of money he is making and the effects he is creating on his tours both at home and in America. (p. 105)

The greatest single accomplishment of these volumes, beyond their giving to the world this unflinchingly three-dimensional portrait of Dickens, involves the dignity-of-literature issue and Forster's own place in the *Life*. It is Forster himself who carries the torch of hero-as-man-of-letters unremittingly throughout. This fact is not readily apparent and hence not intrusive for two reasons: in the years from 1837-1857, Forster and Dickens share the limelight: Forster as advisor, confidant, and companion assists Dickens in all his literary enterprises but in a dutifully subordinate role, always helping in very tangible ways but always willingly subordinate to the literary genius. After 1857-58, with Dickens's separation from his wife and the inception of the first reading tours, Forster was not much directly on the stage, but his judgments, particularly about the readings, hang over all of Dickens's obsessive concerns for money and approval as he quite literally drives himself to self-destruction, vindicating terribly Forster's original disapproval. In these two major crises, but also in a host of smaller ones—in disputes with his publishers; in opposing Dickens's decision to edit the *Daily News*, to publish a letter justifying his separation, to include the "Nancy-Sikes" reading; and by publishing Dick-

ens's will wherein Ellen Ternan received the first bequest, £1,000—Forster upheld dignity in his own person and judged Dickens severly for its lack in him.

We see, then, that Forster captured the complexity of Dickens's character even as he affirmed characteristic moral judgments, particularly as they affect the dignity of literature as a profession. But while Forster saw Dickens as a complicated man, he also held a consistent vision of Dickens's essential self. Forster was grieved by what he described as the tragedy of Dickens's later years, but his tone is never harsh, only sad. Forster himself never lost sight of what was noble in Dickens's character; the closing scenes and the reaction of the world after his death are genuinely affecting. Forster revered Charles Dickens, and the greatness bodied forth in his best works, forming "the whole of that inner life which essentially constituted the man," went far in Forster's vision of this literary genius to mitigate the sad confusions evident in certain of his actions in the later years. (pp. 105-06)

According Forster the just appraisal attendant to a reading of his best works is difficult: his critical reviews are buried in the files of the *Examiner* and other now-rare newspapers, and in the only slightly more often consulted quarterlies; his historical writings and, too, his biographies of eighteenth-century literary figures have been largely superseded; and his only widely known work, *The Life of Charles Dickens*, serves primarily as a reference tool for persons studying Dickens. Due, therefore, to Forster's too perfect, and frequently too voluble, embodiment of Victorian middle-class respectability in his personal life, the relative inaccessibility of some of his best writing (his criticism), the datedness of much of the rest, and an interest focused almost exclusively upon the subject and not upon the author in his single work still well known today, his reputation as one of the premier men of letters of his time is largely eclipsed. (pp. 107-08)

Some of his finest work, if not always his most elegant prose, considering the time constraints involved, is his criticism. His complete mastery of the tastes of his age, expanded and liberalized by his own vast reading in classical literature and the English masters of the sixteenth, seventeenth, and eighteenth centuries, allowed him to note and record praise for virtually every contemporary writer and dramatist we now consider worthy. . . . The assistance he gave to men such as Browning, Bulwer, Tennyson, Landor, Dickens, and Carlyle is incalculable because our only records are letters and his formal critiques; the informal, oral advice and criticism are, of course, lost, though obvious from the recorded comments of these famous men themselves. Each privately acknowledged the value to him personally of Forster's advice, and all but Tennyson in this grouping did so publicly either by dedicating to him individual works or collected editions or by naming him literary executor. More important than any assistance Forster's reviews may have produced for individual works or reputations is the extent to which his published criticism provides a comprehensive gloss on the moral aesthetics of the cultivated, middle-class reader of the early and high Victorian age regarding literary, political, and religious ideas.

The histories and historical biographies offer essentially the same value, however much they may present a picture of the Commonwealth period now known to be partial. In them we find eloquently and forcefully expressed a Whig view centered to a large extent upon a Carlylean conception of the hero in history. (pp. 108-09)

Seeing in the figures of his literary biographies the same un-compromised integrity, the same indomitable commitment to their work, and the same moral center to their character that he saw in the patriots of the Commonwealth, Forster argued unequivocally for the dignity of the profession of authorship by underscoring the importance to posterity of justly appre-ciating the moral, positive, and entertaining works of writers he considered worthy of the highest public esteem. Throughout all of his writings and in his private life, he urged a more just evaluation of the profession of letters, believing it to be more valuable to the nation than those of business, law, or the mil-itary. In dedicating himself and his works to this struggle for a just recognition, respect, and reward for men of letters, he saw himself as a critic in company with Hazlitt, Lamb, and Hunt—and truly he was their heir. . . .

In his honest striving to recognize, encourage, and publicize both the best and the most promising writers of his own time and to record as exemplars the lives of particular literary ge-niuses, he assisted many to the reputations and rewards they deserved. Judged by his best writings, any negative personal characteristics are reduced to insignificance, and John Forster emerges as one with the writers he most cherished: a hero-as-man-of-letters. (p. 109)

> *John J. Fenstermaker, in his* John Forster, *Twayne Publishers, 1984, 132 p.*

ADDITIONAL BIBLIOGRAPHY

Collins, Philip, ed. *Dickens: The Critical Heritage*. The Critical Her-itage Series, edited by B. C. Southam. New York: Barnes & Noble, 1971, 641 p.
  Reprints extracts from contemporary reviews of *The Life of Charles Dickens* and Forster's reviews of Dickens's works.

Davies, James Atterbury. "Leigh Hunt and John Forster." *The Review of English Studies* n.s. XIX, No. 73 (1968): 25-40.*
  Explores the influence of Leigh Hunt on Forster's critical meth-odology as well as Forster's role as Hunt's financial and literary adviser.

———. "Forster and Dickens: The Making of Podsnap." *The Dick-ensian* 70, No. 374 (September 1974): 145-58.*
  Discusses the close if occasionally strained relationship between Charles Dickens and Forster, focusing on the novelist's caricature of Forster's less desirable traits in his character Podsnap in *Our Mutual Friend*.

———. "Charles Lamb, John Forster, and a Victorian Shakespeare." *The Review of English Studies* n.s. XXVI, No. 104 (November 1975): 442-50.*
  Examines Charles Lamb's role in shaping Forster's literary tastes in general and his approach to Shakespeare in particular.

Dickens, Charles. *The Letters of Charles Dickens*. 3 vols. Edited by Walter Dexter. London: Nonesuch Press, 1938.
  A primary source documenting the relationship between Charles Dickens and Forster. This collection contains letters not yet in-cluded in the ongoing Pilgrim edition (see annotation below) of the author's correspondence.

———. *The Letters of Charles Dickens*. 5 vols. to date. Edited by Madeline House and Graham Storey. Oxford: Clarendon Press, 1965.
  With the Nonesuch edition of Charles Dickens's letters (see an-notation above), an essential source of information about the re-lationship between Dickens and Forster.

Fitzgerald, Percy. *John Forster by One of His Friends*. London: Chap-man & Hall, 1903, 79 p.
  An anecdotal reminiscence by a younger member of the "Dickens Circle." Fitzgerald focuses his recollections on the colorful as-pects of Forster's often idiosyncratic personality.

Johnson, Edgar. *Charles Dickens: His Tragedy and Triumph*. 2 vols. New York: Simon and Schuster, 1952.
  The definitive modern biography of Charles Dickens. Johnson thoroughly explores the relationship between the novelist and Forster.

Renton, Richard. *John Forster and His Friendships*. London: Chap-man and Hall, 1912, 279 p.*
  Outlines Forster's relationships with many prominent writers, art-ists, and public figures of his day, including Thomas Carlyle, Robert Browning, Charles Dickens, and William Charles Ma-cready.

Tillotson, Kathleen, and Burgis, Nina. "Forster's Reviews in the *Ex-aminer*, 1840-1841." *The Dickensian* 68, No. 367 (May 1972): 105-08.
  Identifies Forster as the author of several essays that were pub-lished anonymously in the *Examiner* between 1841 and 1842. Tillotson and Burgis briefly study these essays for the light they shed on Forster's literary tastes and critical methods.

Vallance, Rosalind. "Forster's *Goldsmith*." *The Dickensian* 71, No. 375 (January 1975): 21-9.
  Touches upon a range of issues relevant to Forster's biography of Oliver Goldsmith, including its dedication to Charles Dickens, Forster's conception of Goldsmith's character and achievement, and the differences between the several editions of the book.

Woolley, David. "Forster's *Swift*." *The Dickensian* 70, No. 374 (Sep-tember 1974): 191-204.
  Describes the circumstances surrounding the composition of *The Life of Jonathan Swift*. Woolley also discusses the large quantity of Swift materials included in the collection of books, manu-scripts, and artworks Forster bequeathed to the South Kensington Museum upon his death.

Thomas Jefferson
1743-1826

American statesman, philosopher, and essayist.

The third president of the United States, Jefferson is best known as a revered statesman whose belief in natural rights, equality, individual liberties, and self-government found its fullest expression in the Declaration of Independence. As the Declaration demonstrates, Jefferson was also a skilled writer noted for his simple yet elegant prose. Through the clear and persuasive articulation of the revolutionary political philosophy of an emerging nation, Jefferson profoundly influenced the direction of American politics, inspiring generations of Americans. Yet his stature as a writer has often been overshadowed by the variety of his accomplishments: in addition to his pivotal political role, he was an educator, architect, philosopher, scientist, linguist, and inventor.

Jefferson's youth was typical of a Virginia planter's son. He was born at Shadwell, in Goochland (now Albemarle) County, Virginia. His mother was a member of a prominent Colonial family, the Randolphs, and his father was a self-made man and an early settler of what was then wilderness country. After attending private schools, Jefferson enrolled in 1760 at the College of William and Mary. His studies there reflect his lifelong interests: he read widely in law, science, literature, and ancient and modern philosophy. While at college, Jefferson studied under two teachers whose pervasive influence he later acknowledged: William Small, a professor of mathematics and philosophy, who aroused Jefferson's interest in science, and George Wyeth, the most respected Virginia law scholar of his day. In 1767, Jefferson was admitted to the bar and practiced law for two years; he was then elected to the Virginia House of Burgesses, which marked the debut of his political career. During the same year, Jefferson designed and began building Monticello, his family home, on a mountaintop in the Blue Ridge Mountains.

In 1774, while a member of the House of Burgesses, Jefferson wrote his first important political treatise. *A Summary View of the Rights of British America* is a major presentation of the concept of natural rights: that people have certain inalienable rights superior to civil law. As such, it contains what are considered the philosophical antecedents of the ideas that Jefferson fully articulated in the Declaration. In *A Summary View of the Rights of British America,* Jefferson forcefully denied that the British Parliament held any political authority over the colonists, and demanded free trade and an end to British taxation. The essay's considerable influence during pre-revolutionary debates brought Jefferson wide attention and contributed to his selection by the Second Continental Congress to write the Declaration.

In 1775, Jefferson joined the Continental Congress in Philadelphia with what John Adams described as "a reputation for literature, science and a happy talent for composition." One year later, Congress appointed him to a committee of five charged with drafting a declaration of independence. Although debate continues to this day over the exact circumstances of its composition, most historians agree that Jefferson wrote the original draft of the Declaration of Independence during June,

1776; that he then submitted it to two committee members, Adams and Benjamin Franklin; and that they suggested minor changes before sending it to Congress. The delegates debated its text line by line for two and a half days and adopted it on July 4, 1776. Despite changes made by members of Congress, Jefferson is generally credited with authorship of the Declaration.

The Declaration of Independence, according to Robert Ginsberg, "is the most widely known and influential secular document in the history of the world." Its philosophy, according to most critics, is derived from several sources, including John Locke's *Two Treatises on Civil Government*, George Mason's Virginia Declaration of Rights, and Jefferson's own *A Summary View of the Rights of British America* as well as his proposed constitution for the state of Virginia. Because of the Declaration's similarity to these works and to debates in the Continental Congress, many critics charged that the Declaration lacked originality. However, originality was not Jefferson's intent, as he indicated in a letter to Henry Lee: "Not to find out new principles, or new arguments, never before thought of, not merely to say things which had never been said before; but to place before mankind the common sense of the subject, in terms so plain and firm as to command their assent. . . . Neither aiming at originality of principle or sentiment, nor yet copied from any particular and previous writing, it was intended to be an expression of the American mind." Despite Jefferson's claim, the Declaration is considered at once a recital of commonly held beliefs and a summary of his own political credo: that the universe is governed by natural law; that all men are created equal; that they possess inalienable rights, granted by their creator; that governments exist to secure these rights; that governments derive their authority from the consent of the governed; and that when governments destroy these rights, they forfeit their claim to obedience, and the people have the right to rebel.

In addition to its significance as a political manifesto, the Declaration is an important literary text, and Jefferson employed various structural and stylistic elements to enhance his political message. The Declaration consists of four parts: the opening paragraph, which introduces the purpose of the document; the second paragraph, perhaps the best-known segment, which outlines the political philosophy of the American Revolution; the third part, which lists the twenty-eight grievances against King George III and enumerates the specific causes for rebellion; and the closing paragraph, which declares independence from Great Britain. Despite its diversity of subject and style, the Declaration is said to possess a high degree of structural unity. All its parts contribute to a single idea: that the colonists were not rebelling against an established authority, but were instead maintaining their rights against a usurping king. Among other literary devices, Jefferson used sharply contrasting styles to further his purpose. The opening and closing paragraphs are marked by a cadenced, majestic style depicting the colonists as passively and submissively awaiting their fate, while the grievances are characterized by a crisp, incisive style describing the king as an aggressive force over the colonists. Many critics have recognized the influence of the Enlightenment writers on Jefferson's prose, praising its clarity, subtlety, persuasiveness, eloquence, and above all, its distinctiveness. Thus, Jefferson is revered for creating the foremost literary work of the American Revolution and the single most important political document in American history.

After the Continental Congress adopted the Declaration, Jefferson's political career continued with his term in the Virginia House of Delegates, from 1776 to 1779, and his election as governor in 1779. In these positions, he attempted to translate the ideas of the Declaration into reality by developing legislation that would reform the penal code and abolish primogeniture and entail. In 1778, he outlined his educational philosophy in his Bill for the More General Diffusion of Knowledge, which was not approved by the legislature. The bill proposed a complete system of public education, from elementary school through college, and is now considered a landmark in the development of public education. At this time, Jefferson also wrote *An Act for Establishing Religious Freedom, Passed in the Assembly of Virginia in the Beginning of the Year 1786*. Like the Declaration of Independence, this bill is based on the concept of natural rights, the assumption that each individual's conscience, rather than any secular institution, should dictate in religious matters, and the contention that civil liberties should be independent from religious beliefs. While Jefferson's bill was originally intended only for Virginia, it is now considered a central document of the American experiment in the separation of church and state.

While governor, Jefferson also composed the first version of *Notes on the State of Virginia*, his only full-length book. Written in response to a series of queries on the natural history and society of Virginia posed by the Marquis François de Barbé-

Marbois, the secretary of the French legation in Philadelphia, the work contains two sections that outline first the geography, flora, and fauna of Virginia, followed by a description of its social, economic, and political structure. Using statistics to support his patriotic intent, Jefferson disputed the theories of the French naturalists and philosophers Georges Louis Leclerc de Buffon and Guillaume Thomas François Raynal, who argued that the intellectual standards and animal life of the New World were inferior to those of Europe. In *Notes on the State of Virginia*, Jefferson also explains his racial philosophy: he believed that blacks were intellectually inferior to whites. Indeed, Jefferson's racial philosophy appears rife with contradictions. Although he wrote the famous line "all men are created equal," he owned slaves. And while his private correspondence often includes abolitionist sentiments, as a plantation owner he refrained from freeing his slaves, and as a political leader he did not support abolition. Jefferson's controversial views on race, presented in this work and others, greatly affected his public image during the Civil War and, more recently, in the 1960s. Although many modern critics consider the work flawed, *Notes on the State of Virginia* established Jefferson's reputation as a scholar and a pioneer American scientist.

In 1782, Jefferson briefly retired from politics following several unhappy public and personal experiences. The previous year, as Jefferson's gubernatorial term expired, British troops reached Virginia and drove him from Monticello. In addition, his wife of ten years, Martha Wayles Skelton, had died shortly after the birth of their sixth child. Jefferson returned to politics in 1784, and Congress appointed him envoy to France to assist Franklin in negotiating commercial treaties. Jefferson succeeded Franklin as minister to France one year later. Although he resided primarily in Paris, Jefferson traveled throughout Europe during his five-year stay and developed a keen interest in Classical architecture. This influence is evident in his architectural masterpieces, Monticello, the Virginia state capital building at Richmond, and the University of Virginia at Charlottesville. Indeed, Jefferson is credited with initiating the Classical revival in American architecture. Jefferson left Paris in 1789 at the start of the French Revolution and returned home at a time of great political upheaval.

During the 1790s, the American political scene was dominated by the debate between the Federalist and Republican factions, which resulted in the formation of the two-party system. Jefferson was a prominent participant in the proceedings. Although he served in Federalist administrations in several capacities—he was secretary of state under George Washington from 1790 through 1793 and was later elected vice president in 1796 under Adams—he was bitterly at odds with the Federalists and particularly with their chief spokesman, Alexander Hamilton. Jefferson's and Hamilton's conflicting philosophies on political and economic issues symbolized the two opposing views of society and government that continue to dominate the Democratic and Republican parties in American politics. Hamilton, who was secretary of the treasury under Washington, advocated a strong, centralized government controlled by the elite and economic policies favoring industrialism, commercialism, and banking. Jefferson, in sharp contrast, founded his vision of government on individual liberties, majority rule, states' rights, and self-reliant agrarianism. He feared that under Hamilton's plan, the federal government would be tied to the moneyed interests, creating, in effect, an aristocracy. By his outspoken opposition to Federalist policies, Jefferson became the leader of the Republican (now Democratic) party.

In 1800, Jefferson was elected president in the first contest between two organized political parties, and he served for two terms, until 1809. His first inaugural address, delivered on March 4, 1801, presaged the style of his presidency: characterized by restraint, it sought reconciliation and compromise between Republicans and Federalists. As president, in domestic affairs he combined reform of fiscal policy with a reduction of government while maintaining economic and political stability. In foreign affairs, Jefferson experienced both his greatest triumph and defeat. The Louisiana Purchase, which doubled the territory of the United States and provided complete control of the Mississippi River, is considered his finest achievement as president. Yet during the Napoleonic Wars, difficulties with Great Britain and France threatened American maritime neutrality, and his Embargo Act of 1807, which prohibited trade with both countries, resulted in protest and economic hardship. Refusing to run for a third term, Jefferson retired in 1809 after forty years of public service.

Jefferson's last years at Monticello were active despite ongoing financial difficulties. He entertained a steady stream of visitors, advised a new generation of public figures, composed the *Autobiography of Thomas Jefferson,* carried on an extensive correspondence, engaged in philosophical pursuits, developed educational programs, and drafted architectural plans. These latter two activities culminated in one of his greatest achievements, the creation of the University of Virginia. Although the Virginia legislature consistently rejected his comprehensive educational proposals, they eventually allocated funds for the creation of the first state-supported university, which was chartered in 1817. Jefferson was involved in every aspect of its development: he drafted many of the architectural plans for the "academical village," supervised the construction and landscaping, planned the curriculum, and recruited the faculty. In the University of Virginia, opened just one year before his death, Jefferson created a modern, public, secular university of high academic standards. Jefferson died on July 4, 1826, exactly fifty years after the adoption of the Declaration of Independence. On his tombstone, he summarized what he considered his finest accomplishments: "Here lies Thomas Jefferson, Author of the Declaration of American Independence, of the Statute of Virginia for Religious Freedom and Father of the University of Virginia."

Jefferson wrote no single, comprehensive treatise outlining his philosophy. In an effort to reconstruct his thought, scholars have pieced together his ideas from essays, letters, legislative bills, state papers, and the Declaration and many have noted the contradictory nature of his ideas. However, his fundamental principles of natural rights, individual liberties, and self-government inform all his political works. He envisioned an economically self-reliant agrarian society. Unlike many of his contemporaries, Jefferson had a profound faith in the innate goodness of human nature and in the people's ability to govern themselves. Because of this belief, he contended that the best government is that which governs least. According to Jefferson, the purpose of government is to protect the rights of the individual, and the form of government best suited to achieve this purpose is majority rule, or democracy. Recognizing that an informed citizenry is essential to self-government, Jefferson supported public education and freedom of the press. He also advocated the separation of church and state to ensure religious freedom for the individual. For his articulation of a new vision of society and government, Jefferson is today considered one of the central figures in the development of American democracy.

Jefferson's posthumous reputation is a complex amalgam of his historical, political, and public images. Because of the variety of his activities and the contradictions in his writings, many of Jefferson's supporters and detractors have selectively interpreted his policies to reflect their own beliefs. American politicians, in particular, have consistently used Jefferson as a symbol to support their positions on contemporary issues. In addition, Jefferson was a profoundly private man, as the factual nature of his *Autobiography* indicates. He divulged very little information about his personal life, and this elusiveness of the historical figure has allowed great freedom of biographical interpretation.

As Merrill D. Peterson argues in his influential study *The Jefferson Image in the American Mind,* Jefferson's public image can be read as a shifting index to American political thought. Jefferson was revered in the early nineteenth century. Immediately after his death, he became known as an apostle of liberty, an image which prevailed until the onset of the Civil War. The Democratic Party championed him as a symbol of its origins, and Andrew Jackson was lauded as the inheritor of Jeffersonian principles. As slavery became an increasingly important issue in American politics, Jefferson's name was invoked by both pro- and anti-slavery groups to vindicate their positions, as demonstrated in the debates between Abraham Lincoln and Stephen Arnold Douglas. The Civil War, which shattered the national image of a unified republic, was also interpreted as the failure of Jeffersonian government, and his reputation declined dramatically. Jefferson did not regain his influential political stature until the 1880s.

Jefferson's public image in the first half of the twentieth century mirrored the fortunes of the Democratic party: as its popularity increased, so did Jefferson's. Yet politicians had difficulty applying Jeffersonian principles to modern problems. Jefferson's reputation collapsed after World War I and continued to suffer during the Republican ascendence of the 1920s. His name became embroiled in the controversy over American expansionism, as his followers attempted to reconcile his idealistic beliefs as outlined in the Declaration with his pragmatic policies as represented by the Louisiana Purchase. With the publication of Claude Bowers's study on Jefferson and Hamilton, the election of Franklin Delano Roosevelt, and the rise of the New Deal, Jefferson's name was again invoked, although with a twist: Democrats now emphasized his pragmatism instead of his idealism, subordinating doctrine to a modern interpretation of the spirit of Jefferson. Scholarly interest in Jefferson during this period generally can be divided into four categories: studies of his political administrations, notably that of Henry Adams which, though published earlier, received significant attention at this time; a renewed interest in his writings, including several new editions of his works as well as Carl Becker's seminal study of the Declaration; histories of American political parties, as evidenced in Bowers's treatise and Charles A. Beard's economic interpretation; and surveys of the Jeffersonian tradition, including Vernon Louis Parrington's important analysis of Jeffersonian democracy that depicts him as an agrarian.

The year 1943 marked the bicentennial of Jefferson's birth, the dedication of the Jefferson Monument in Washington, D.C., and the apotheosis of his reputation as what Peterson calls the "Culture Hero": "the man glorified in the monument had transcended politics to become the hero of civilization." Although critics continued to analyze Jefferson's political philosophy, they increasingly turned to his accomplishments as an architect, scientist, educator, administrator, and man of letters. This investigation has been greatly aided by the appearance of a comprehensive collection of his writings compiled by Julian Boyd. Interest in Jefferson as an author has increased significantly, as evidenced by the Library of America publication of his *Writings* and numerous literary analyses of the Declaration and the *Notes on the State of Virginia*. In addition, Dumas Malone closely examined Jefferson as a historical figure in his monumental biography. Only Jefferson's comments on race, which have received widespread attention since the 1960s, have tarnished the modern image of Jefferson as a heroic figure. Critics have found it increasingly difficult to reconcile his ownership of slaves and his philosophy of racial inequality with his reputation as the apostle of freedom and equality. While modern scholars have continued to stress the diversity of Jefferson's achievements, most would still agree with Abraham Lincoln's estimate of the man and his accomplishments, written over one hundred years ago: "All honor to Jefferson—to the man, who in the concrete pressure of a struggle for national independence by a single people, had the coolness, forecaste, and sagacity to introduce into a merely revolutionary document an abstract truth, applicable to all men and all times, and so embalm it there that to-day and in all coming days it shall be a rebuke and a stumbling-block to the very harbingers of reappearing tyranny and oppression."

(See also *Dictionary of Literary Biography*, Vol. 31: *American Colonial Writers, 1735-1781*.)

PRINCIPAL WORKS

A Summary View of the Rights of British America   (essay)
   1774
*In Congress, July 4, 1776: A Declaration by the
   Representatives of the United States of America, in
   General Congress Assembled*   (state paper)   1776
Notes on the State of Virginia   (essay)   1785
*An Act for Establishing Religious Freedom, Passed in the
   Assembly of Virginia in the Beginning of the Year 1786*
   (statute)   1786
*The Address of Thomas Jefferson, to the Senate, the
   Members of the House of Representatives, the Public
   Officers, and a Large Concourse of Citizens*
   (inaugural address)   1801
A Manual of Parliamentary Practice   (manual)   1801
**Memoir, Correspondence, and Miscellanies, from the
   Papers of Thomas Jefferson*. 4 vols.   (autobiography
   and letters)   1829
The Writings of Thomas Jefferson. 9 vols.   (autobiography,
   letters, essays, state papers, and biographical sketches)
   1853-54
*Correspondence of John Adams and Thomas Jefferson,
   1812-1826*   (letters)   1925
*The Commonplace Book of Thomas Jefferson: A Repertory
   of His Ideas on Government*   (notebook)   1926
*The Literary Bible of Thomas Jefferson: His Commonplace
   Book of Philosophers and Poets*   (notebook)   1928
*Correspondence between Thomas Jefferson and Pierre
   Samuel du Pont de Nemours, 1798-1817*   (letters)
   1930
*My Head and My Heart: A Little History of Thomas
   Jefferson and Maria Cosway*   (letters)   1945
The Papers of Thomas Jefferson. 20 vols. to date.   (letters,
   addresses, state papers, and journals)   1950-
The Family Letters of Thomas Jefferson   (letters)   1966

Writings   (autobiography, essays, state papers, addresses,
   journals, and letters)   1984

**This work includes the *Autobiography of Thomas Jefferson*.

AN ENGLISHMAN   (letter date 1776)

[*These anonymous comments were submitted to the editor of the* Scots Magazine *and reprinted in that journal with the text of the Declaration of Independence. The author examines the meaning of several of its propositions, denouncing them as either meaningless or untrue. With regard to the members of the American Congress, he states that the Declaration "reflects no honour upon either their erudition or honesty."*]

So many pamphlets having been published on the subject of the American rebellion, any farther publications of that kind might be surfeiting; I shall therefore address myself to you in this manner, and desire you to communicate to the public in your paper, some thoughts on the late **Declaration** of the American Congress.—The **Declaration** is without doubt of the most extraordinary nature both with regard to sentiment and language; and considering that the motive of it is to assign some justifiable reasons of their separating themselves from G. Britain, unless it had been fraught with more truth and sense, might well have been spared, as it reflects no honour upon either their erudition or honesty.

[We hold these truths to be self-evident: That
   all men are created equal. . . .]

In what are they created equal? Is it in size, strength, understanding, figure, moral or civil accomplishments, or situation of life? Every ploughman knows that they are not created equal in any of these. All men, it is true, are equally created: but what is this to the purpose? It certainly is no reason why the Americans should turn rebels, because the people of G. Britain are their fellow-creatures, *i.e.* are created as well as themselves. It may be a reason why they should not rebel, but most indisputably is none why they should. They therefore have introduced their self-evident truth, either through ignorance, or by design, with a self-evident falsehood; since I will defy any American rebel, or any of their patriotic retainers here in England, to point out to me any two men throughout the whole world of whom it may with truth be said, that they are created equal.

[That they are endowed by their Creator with
   certain unalienable rights; That among these are
   life, liberty, and the pursuit of happiness. . . .]

The meaning of these words the Congress appear not at all to understand; among which are life, liberty, and the pursuit of happiness. Let us put some of these words together.—All men are endowed by their Creator with the unalienable right of life. How far they may be endowed with this unalienable right I do not yet say, but, sure I am, these gentry assume to themselves an unalienable right of talking nonsense. Was it ever heard since the introduction of blunders into the world, that life was a man's right? Life or animation is of the essence of human nature, and is that without which one is not a man; and therefore to call life a right, is to betray a total ignorance of the meaning of words. A living man, *i.e.* a man with life, hath a right to a great many things; but to say that a man with life hath a right to be a man with life, is so purely American, that I believe the texture of no other brain upon the face of the earth will admit the idea. Whatever it may be, I have tried to make an idea out of it, but own I am unable. Prior to my having any right at all as a man, it is certain *I* must be a man, and such a man *I* certainly cannot be if I have no life; and therefore if it be said that *I* have a right to life, then the word *I* must signify something without life; and, consequently, something without life must be supposed to have a property, which without life it is not possible it can have.

Well, but they say, all men have not only a right to life, but an unalienable right. The word *unalienable* signifies that which is not alienable, and that which is not alienable is what cannot be transferred so as to become another's; so that their unalienable right is a right which they cannot transfer to a broomstick or a cabbage-stalk; and because they cannot transfer their own lives from themselves to a cabbage-stalk, therefore they think it absolutely necessary that they should rebel; and, out of a decent respect to the opinions of mankind, alleged this as one of the causes which impels them to separate themselves from those to whom they owe obedience.

The next assigned cause and ground of their rebellion is, that every man hath an unalienable right to liberty: and here the words, as it happens, are not nonsense; but then they are not true: slaves there are in America; and where there are slaves, their liberty is alienated.

If the Creator hath endowed man with an unalienable right to liberty, no reason in the world will justify the abridgement of that liberty, and a man hath a right to do every thing that he thinks proper without controul or restraint; and upon the same principle, there can be no such things as servants, subjects, or government of any kind whatsoever. In a word, every law that hath been in the world since the formation of Adam, gives the lie to this self-evident truth, (as they are pleased to term it); because every law, divine or human, that is or hath been in the world, is an abridgement of man's liberty.

Their next self-evident truth and ground of rebellion is, that they have an unalienable right to the pursuit of happiness. The pursuit of happiness an unalienable right! This surely is outdoing every thing that went before. Put it into English: The pursuit of happiness is a right with which the Creator hath endowed me, and which can neither be taken from me, nor can I transfer it to another. Did ever any mortal alive hear of taking a pursuit of happiness from a man? What they possibly can mean by these words, I own, is beyond my comprehension. A man may take from me a horse or a cow, or I may alienate either of them from myself, as I may likewise any thing that I have; but how that can be taken from me, or alienated, which I have not, must be left for the solution of some unborn Oedipus. (pp. 433-34)

An Englishman, in an extract from a letter to the editor of The Scots Magazine, *Vol. XXXVIII, August, 1776, pp. 433-36.*

[JOHN LIND] (essay date 1776)

[*Lind, an English barrister, responds to the assertions in the Declaration of Independence, condemning its theory of government, political maxims, and charges against the British king and Parliament. He first discusses the opening paragraphs and attacks the concept of the right to life, liberty, and the pursuit of happiness, suggesting that it would prohibit legislation that would govern society: "Thieves are not to be restrained from theft, murderers from murder, rebels from rebellion." Lind then divides the grievances into several groups, or heads, including acts that concern Great Britain's right to govern the colonies, acts that affect the maintenance or amendment of the Constitution, and acts that the British termed self-defense and the Americans deemed oppression. Lind's remarks were first published in 1776 in* An Answer to the Declaration of the American Congress.]

The opinions of the modern Americans on Government, like those of their good ancestors on witchcraft, would be too ridiculous to deserve any notice, if like them too, contemptible and extravagant as they be, they had not led to the most serious evils.

In [the] preamble however it is, that they attempt to establish a *theory of Government;* a theory, as absurd and visionary, as the system of conduct in defence of which it is established, is nefarious. Here it is, that maxims are advanced in justification of their enterprises against the British Government. To these maxims, adduced for *this purpose,* it would be sufficient to say, that they are *repugnant to the British Constitution.* But beyond this they are subversive of every actual or imaginable kind of Government.

They are about *"to assume,"* as they tell us, *"among the powers of the earth, that equal and separate station to which"*— they have lately discovered—*"the laws of Nature, and of Nature's God entitle them."* What difference these acute legislators suppose between the laws of *Nature,* and of *Nature's God,* is more than I can take upon me to determine, or even to guess. If to what they now demand they were entitled by any law of God, they had only to produce that law, and all controversy was at an end. Instead of this, what do they produce? What they call self-evident truths. *"All men,"* they tell us, "are created equal." This surely is a new discovery; now, for the first time, we learn, that a child, at the moment of his birth, has the same quantity of *natural* power as the parent, the same quantity of *political* power as the magistrate.

The rights of *"life, liberty,* and *the pursuit of happiness"*— by which, if they mean any thing, they must mean the right to *enjoy* life, to *enjoy* liberty, and to *pursue* happiness—they *"hold to be unalienable."* This they *"hold to be among truths self-evident."* At the same time, to secure these rights, they are content that Governments should be instituted. They perceive not, or will not seem to perceive, that nothing which can be called Government ever was, or ever could be, in any instance, exercised, but at the expence of one or other of those rights.—That, consequently, in as many instances as Government is ever exercised, some one or other of these rights, pretended to be unalienable, is actually alienated.

That men who are engaged in the design of subverting a lawful Government, should endeavour by a cloud of words, to throw a veil over their design; that they should endeavour to beat down the criteria between tyranny and lawful government, is not at all surprising. But rather surprising it must certainly appear, that they should advance maxims so incompatible with their own present conduct. If the right of enjoying life be unalienable, whence came their invasion of his Majesty's province of Canada? Whence the unprovoked destruction of so many lives of the inhabitants of that province? If the right of enjoying liberty be unalienable, whence came so many of his Majesty's peaceable subjects among them, without any offence, without so much as a pretended offence, merely for being suspected not to wish well to their enormities, to be held by them in durance? If the right of pursuing happiness be unalienable, how is it that so many others of their fellow-citizens are by the same injustice and violence made miserable, their fortunes ruined, their persons banished and driven from their friends and families? Or would they have it believed, that there is in their selves some superior sanctity, some peculiar privilege, by which those things are lawful to them, which are unlawful to all the world besides? Or is it, that among acts of coercion, acts by which life or liberty are taken away, and the pursuit of happiness restrained, those only are unlawful, which their delinquency has brought upon them, and which are exercised by regular, long established, accustomed governments?

In these tenets they have outdone the utmost extravagance of all former fanatics. The German Anabaptists indeed went so far as to speak of the right of enjoying life as a right unalienable. To take away life, even in the Magistrate, they held to be unlawful. But they went no farther, it was reserved for an American Congress, to add to the number of unalienable rights, that of enjoying liberty, and pursuing happiness;—that is,—if they mean any thing,—pursuing it wherever a man thinks he can see it, and by whatever means he thinks he can attain it:— That is, that all *penal* laws—those made by their selves among others—which affect life or liberty, are contrary to the law of God, and the unalienable rights of mankind:—That is, that thieves are not to be restrained from theft, murderers from murder, rebels from rebellion.

Here then they have put the axe to the root of all Government; and yet, in the same breath, they talk of "Governments," of Governments "long established." To these last, they attribute some kind of respect; they vouchsafe even to go so far as to admit, that *"Governments, long established, should not be changed for light or transient reasons."*

Yet they are about to *change* a Government, a Government whose establishment is coeval with their own existence as a Community. What causes do they assign? Circumstances which have always subsisted, which must continue to subsist, wherever Government has subsisted, or can subsist.

For what, according to their own shewing, what was their original, their *only original grievance*? That they were actually taxed more than they could bear? No; but that they were *liable* to be so taxed. What is the amount of all the *subsequent* grievances they allege? That they were *actually* oppressed by Government? That Government had *actually* misused its power? No; but that it was *possible* they might be oppressed; *possible* that Government might misuse its powers. Is there any where, can there be imagined any where, *that* Government, where subjects are not liable to be taxed more than they can bear? where it is not possible that subjects may be oppressed, not possible that Government may misuse its powers?

This, I say, is the amount, the *whole sum and substance of all* their grievances. For in taking a general review of the charges brought against his Majesty, and his Parliament, we may observe that there is a studied confusion in the arrangement of them. It may therefore be worth while to reduce them to the several distinct heads, under which I should have classed them at the first, had not the order of the Answer been necessarily prescribed by the order—or rather the disorder—of the **Declaration**.

The first head consists of Acts of *Government,* charged as so many acts of *incroachment,* so many *usurpations* upon the present King and his Parliaments exclusively, which had been constantly exercised by his Predecessors and their Parliaments.

In all the articles comprised in this head, is there a single power alleged to have been exercised during the present reign, which had not been constantly exercised by preceding Kings, and preceding Parliaments? Read only the commission and instruction for the Council of Trade, drawn up in the 9th of King William III. addressed to Mr. *Locke,* and others. See there what powers were exercised by the King and Parliament over the Colonies. (pp. 9-12)

The powers then, of which the several articles now before us complain, are supported by usage; were conceived to be so supported *then,* just after the Revolution, at the time these instructions were given; and were they to be supported *only* upon this foot of usage, still that usage being coeval with the Colonies, their tacit consent and approbation, through all the successive periods in which that usage has prevailed, would be implied;—even then the legality of those powers would stand upon the same foot as most of the prerogatives of the Crown, most of the rights of the people;—even then the exercise of those powers could in no wise be deemed usurpations or encroachments.

But the truth is, to the exercise of these powers, the Colonies have not tacitly, but *expressly,* consented; as expressly as any subject of Great Britain ever consented to Acts of the British Parliament. Consult the Journals of either House of Parliament; consult the proceedings of their own Assemblies; and innumerable will be the occasions, on which the legality of these powers will be found to be expressly recognised by Acts of the Colonial Assemblies. For in preceding reigns, the petitions from these Assemblies were couched in a language, very different from that which they have assumed under the present reign. In praying for the non-exercise of these powers, in particular instances, they acknowledged their legality; the right in general was recognised; the exercise of it, in particular instances, was prayed to be suspended on the sole ground of *inexpedience.*

The less reason can the Americans have to complain against the exercise of these powers, as it was under the constant exercise of the self-same powers, that they have grown up with a vigour and rapidity unexampled: That within a period, in which other communities have scarcely had time to take root, they have shot forth exuberant branches. So flourishing is their agriculture, that—we are told—"besides feeding plentifully their own growing multitudes, their annual exports have exceeded a *million.*" So flourishing is their trade, that—we are told—"it has increased far beyond the speculations of the most sanguine imagination." So powerful are they in arms, that we see them defy the united force of that nation, which, but a little century ago, called them into being; which, but a few years ago, in their defence, encountered and subdued almost the united force of Europe.

If the exercise of powers, thus established by usage, thus recognised by express declarations, thus sanctified by their beneficial effects, can justify rebellion, there is not that subject in the world, but who has, ever has had, and ever must have, reason sufficient to rebel: There never was, never can be, established, any government upon earth.

The second head consists of Acts, whose professed object was either the maintenance, or the amendment of their Constitution. These Acts were passed with the view either of freeing from impediments the course of their *commercial* transactions, or of facilitating the administration of justice, or of poising more equally the different powers in their Constitution; or of preventing the establishment of Courts, inconsistent with the spirit of the Constitution.

To state the object of these Acts, is to justify them. Acts of *tyranny* they cannot be: Acts of *usurpation* they *are not;* because no new power is assumed. (pp. 13-14)

The third head consists of temporary Acts, passed *pro re natâ,* the object of each of which was to remedy some temporary evil, and the duration of which was restrained to the duration of the evil itself.

Neither in these Acts was any new power assumed; in some instances only, the objects upon which that power was exercised, were new. Nothing was done but what former Kings and former Parliaments have shewn their selves ready to do, had the same circumstances subsisted. The same circumstances never did subsist before, because, till the present reign, the Colonies never dared to call in question the supreme authority of Parliament.

No charge, classed under this head, can be called a *grievance.* Then only is the subject aggrieved, when, paying *due obedience* to the established Laws of his country, he is not protected in his established rights. From the moment he withholds *obedience,* he forfeits his right to *protection.* Nor can the means, employed to bring him back to obedience, however severe, be called grievances; especially if those means be to cease the very moment that the end is obtained.

The last head consists of Acts of self-defence, exercised in *consequence* of resistance already shewn, but represented in the Declaration as Acts of oppression, tending to provoke resistance. Has his Majesty cut off their trade with all parts of the world? They first attempted to cut off the trade of Great Britain. Has his Majesty ordered their vessels to be seized? They first burnt the vessels of the King. Has his Majesty sent troops to chastise them? They first took up arms against the authority of the King. Has his Majesty engaged the Indians against them? They first engaged Indians against the troops of the King. Has his Majesty commanded their captives to serve on board his fleet? He has only saved them from the gallows.

By some, these acts have been improperly called *"Acts of punishment."* And we are then asked, with an air of insult, "What! will you punish without a trial, without a hearing?" And no doubt punishment, whether ordinary or extraordinary; whether by *indictment, impeachment,* or bill of *attainder,* should be preceded by judicial examination. But, the acts comprised under this head are not acts of *punishment;* they are, as we have called them, acts of *self-defence.* And these are not, cannot be, preceded by any judicial examination. (pp. 14-16)

These are the Acts—these exertions of constitutional, and hitherto, *undisputed* powers, for which, in this audacious paper, a patriot King is traduced—as "a Prince, whose character is marked by every Act which may define a tyrant;" as "unfit to be the ruler of a free people." These are the Acts, these exertions of constitutional, and, hitherto, undisputed powers, by which the Members of the Congress declare their selves and their constituents to be "absolved from all allegiance to the British Crown;" pronounce "all political connection between Great Britain and America to be totally dissolved." With that hypocrisy which pervades the whole of the **Declaration,** they pretend indeed, that this event is not of their seeking; that it is forced upon them; that they only *"acquiesce in the necessity which denounces their separation from us:"* which compels them hereafter to hold us, as they "hold the rest of mankind; *enemies in war; in peace, friends."*

How this **Declaration** may strike others, I know not. To me, I own, it appears that it cannot fail—to use the words of a great Orator [Edmund Burke]—"of doing us *Knight's* service." The mouth of faction, we may reasonably presume, will be closed; the eyes of those who saw not, or would not see, that the Americans were long since aspiring at independence, will be opened; the nation will unite as one man, and teach this rebellious people, that it is one thing for them to *say,* the connection, which bound them to us, is *dissolved,* another to *dissolve* it; that to *accomplish* their *independence* is not quite so easy as to *declare* it: *that there is no peace with them, but the peace of the King: no war with them, but that war, which offended justice wages against criminals.*—We too, I hope, shall *acquiesce in the necessity* of submitting to whatever burdens, of making whatever efforts may be necessary, to bring this ungrateful and rebellious people back to that allegiance they have long had it in contemplation to renounce, and have now at last so daringly renounced. (p. 17)

> [*John Lind], "An Answer to the Declaration," in* A Casebook on The Declaration of Independence, *edited by Robert Ginsberg, Thomas Y. Crowell Company, 1967, pp. 9-17.*

[THOMAS HUTCHINSON]   (letter date 1776)

[*Hutchinson was the last civil governor of the colony of Massachusetts. His first-hand knowledge of the causes that led up to the Declaration of Independence informs this excerpt from a letter to an unidentified English lord. In addition to the following disparaging critique of the beginning and ending sections of the Declaration of Independence, Hutchinson also analyzes many of the specific charges against the king.*]

The last time I had the honour of being in your Lordships company, you observed that you was utterly at a loss to what facts many parts of the **Declaration of Independence** published by the Philadelphia Congress referred, and that you wished they had been more particularly mentioned, that you might better judge of the grievances, alledged as special causes of the separation of the Colonies from the other parts of the Empire. This hint from your Lordship induced me to attempt a few Strictures upon the **Declaration.** Upon my first reading it, I thought there would have been more policy in leaving the World altogether ignorant of the motives to this Rebellion, than in offering such false and frivolous reasons in support of it; and I flatter myself, that before I have finished this letter, your Lordship will be of the same mind. But I beg leave, first to make a few remarks upon its rise and progress.

I have often heard men, (who I believe were free from party influence) express their wishes, that the claims of the Colonies to an exemption from the authority of Parliament in imposing Taxes had been conceded; because they had no doubts that America would have submitted in all other cases; and so this unhappy Rebellion, which has already proved fatal to many hundreds of the Subjects of the Empire, and probably will to many thousands more, might have been prevented.

The Acts for imposing Duties and Taxes may have accelerated the Rebellion, and if this could have been foreseen, perhaps, it might have been good policy to have omitted or deferred them; but I am of opinion, that if no Taxes or Duties had been laid upon the Colonies, other pretences would have been found for exception to the authority of Parliament. The body of the people in the Colonies, I know, were easy and quiet. They felt no burdens. They were attached, indeed, in every Colony to their own particular Constitutions, but the Supremacy of Parliament over the whole gave them no concern. They had been happy under it for an hundred years past: They feared no imaginary evils for an hundred years to come. But there were men in each of the principal Colonies, who had Independence in view, before any of those Taxes were laid, or proposed, which have since been the ostensible cause of resisting the execution of Acts of Parliament. Those men have conducted the Rebellion in the several stages of it, until they have removed the constitutional powers of Government in each Colony, and have assumed to themselves, with others, a supreme authority over the whole.

Their designs of Independence began soon after the reduction of Canada, relying upon the future cession of it by treaty. They could have no other pretence to a claim of Independence, and they made no other at first, than what they called the natural rights of mankind, to chuse their own forms of Government, and to change them when they please. This, they were soon convinced, would not be sufficient to draw the people from their attachment to constitutions under which they had so long been easy and happy: Some grievances, real or imaginary, were therefore necessary. (pp. 3-4)

[It does not] appear that there was any regular plan formed for attaining to Independence, any further than that every fresh incident which could be made to serve the purpose, by alienating the affections of the Colonies from the Kingdom, should be improved accordingly. (p. 5)

It will cause greater prolixity to analize the various parts of this **Declaration**, than to recite the whole. I will therefore present it to your Lordship's view in distinct paragraphs, with my remarks, in order as the paragraphs are published:

> In Congress, July 4, 1776.

> A Declaration by the Representatives of the United States of America in General Congress assembled.

> When in the course of human events it becomes necessary for one People to dissolve the political bands which have connected them with another, and to assume among the Powers of the earth, the separate and equal station to which the laws of nature and of nature's God entitle them, a decent respect to the opinions of mankind requires that they should declare the causes which impel them to the separation.

> We hold these truths to be self-evident—That all men are created equal, that they are endowed by their Creator with certain unalienable rights, that among these are life, liberty and the pursuit of happiness, that to secure these rights, governments are instituted among men, deriving their just powers from the consent of the governed; and whenever any form of government becomes destructive of these ends, it is the right of the people to alter or abolish it, and to institute new government, laying its foundation on such principles, and organizing its powers in such form as to them shall seem most likely to effect their safety and happiness. Prudence indeed will dictate that governments long established, should not be changed for light and

transient causes; and accordingly all experience hath shewn that mankind are more disposed to suffer while evils are sufferable, than to right themselves by abolishing the forms to which they are accustomed. But when a long train of abuses and usurpations pursuing invariably the same object, evinces a design to reduce them under absolute despotism, it is their right, it is their duty to throw off such government, and to provide new guards for their future security. Such has been the patient sufferance of these Colonies, and such is now the necessity which constrains them to alter their former systems of Government. The history of the present King of Great Britain is a history of repeated injuries and usurpations, and having its direct object, the establishment of an absolute tyranny over these States. To prove this, let facts be submitted to a candid world.

They begin, my Lord, with a false hypothesis. That the Colonies are one *distinct people,* and the kingdom another, connected by *political* bands. The Colonies, *politically* considered, never were a *distinct* people from the kingdom. There never has been but one *political* band, and that was just the same before the first Colonists emigrated as it has been ever since, the Supreme Legislative Authority, which hath essential right, and is indispensably bound to keep all parts of the Empire entire, until there may be a separation consistent with the general good of the Empire, of which good, from the nature of government, this authority must be the sole judge. I should therefore be impertinent, if I attemped to shew in what case a *whole people* may be justified in rising up in oppugnation to the powers of government, altering or abolishing them, and substituting, in whole or in part, new powers in their stead; or in what sense all men are created equal; or how far life, liberty, and the *pursuit of happiness* may be said to be unalienable; only I could wish to ask the Delegates of Maryland, Virginia, and the Carolinas, how their Constituents justify the depriving more than an hundred thousand Africans of their rights to liberty, and *the pursuit of happiness,* and in some degree to their lives, if these rights are so absolutely unalienable; nor shall I attempt to confute the absurd notions of government, or to expose the equivocal or inconclusive expressions contained in this **Declaration**; but rather to shew the false representation made of the facts which are alledged to be the evidence of injuries and usurpations, and the special motives to Rebellion. There are many of them, with design, left obscure; for as soon as they are developed, instead of justifying, they rather aggravate the criminality of this Revolt. (pp. 8-10)

> Nor have we been wanting in attention to our British Brethren. We have warned them from time to time of attempts by their legislature, to extend an unwarrantable jurisdiction over us. We have reminded them of the circumstances of our emigration and settlement here. We have appealed to their native justice and magnanimity, and we have conjured them by the ties of our common kindred to disavow those usurpations which would inevitably interrupt our connections and correspondence. They too have been deaf to the voice of justice and corsanguinity. We must therefore acquiesce in the necessity which denounces our separation and

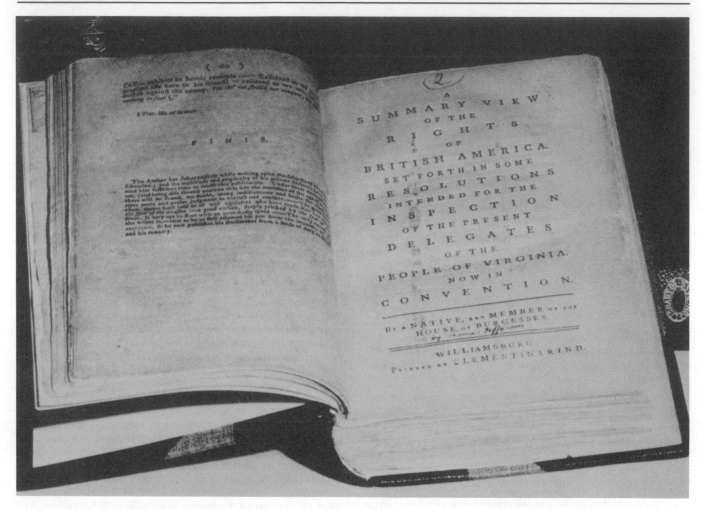

Jefferson's copy of A Summary View of the Rights of British America. *Photograph by Joseph C. Farber from* Thomas Jefferson Redivivus. *Reprinted by permission of Georges Borchardt, Inc., as agents for the photographer.*

hold them as we hold the rest of mankind, Enemies in War, in Peace, Friends.

We therefore, the Representatives of the United States of America, in General Congress assembled, appealing to the Supreme Judge of the World, for the rectitude of our intentions, do in the name and by the authority of the good People of these Colonies, solemnly publish and declare, That these United Colonies, are, and ought to be, Free and Independent States, and that they are absolved from all allegiance to the British Crown, and that all political connection between them and the State of Great Britain, is and ought to be totally dissolved, and that as free and Independent States they have full power to levy War, conclude Peace, contract Alliances, establish Commerce, and to do all other Acts and things which Independent States may of right do. And for the support of this Declaration, with a firm reliance on the protection of Divine Providence, we mutually pledge to each other, our Lives, our Fortunes and our Sacred Honour. Signed by order and in behalf of the Congress.

JOHN HANCOCK, President.

They have, my Lord, in their late address to the people of Great Britain, fully avowed these principles of Independence, by declaring they will pay no obedience to the laws of the Supreme Legislature; they have also pretended, that these laws were the mandates or edicts of the Ministers, not the acts of a constitutional legislative power, and have endeavoured to persuade such as they called their British Brethren, to justify the Rebellion begun in America; and from thence they expected a general convulsion in the Kingdom, and that measures to compel a submission would in this way be obstructed. These expectations failing, after they had gone too far in acts of Rebellion to hope for impunity, they were under the *necessity* of a separation, and of involving themselves, and all over whom they had usurped authority, in the distresses and horrors of war against that power from which they revolted, and against all who continued in their subjection and fidelity to it.

Gratitude, I am sensible, is seldom to be found in a community, but so sudden a revolt from the rest of the Empire, which had incurred so immense a debt, and with which it remains burdened, for the protection and defence of the Colonies, and at their most importunate request, is an instance of ingratitude no where to be parallelled.

Suffer me, my Lord, before I close this Letter, to observe, that though the professed reason for publishing the **Declaration** was a decent respect to the opinions of mankind, yet the real design was to reconcile the people of America to that Independence, which always before, they had been made to believe was not intended. This design has too well succeeded. The people have not observed the fallacy in reasoning from the *whole* to *part*; nor the absurdity of making the *governed* to be *governors*. From a disposition to receive willingly complaints against Rulers, facts misrepresented have passed without examining. Discerning men have concealed their sentiments, because under the present *free* government in America, no man may, by writing or speaking, contradict any part of this **Declaration**, without being deemed an enemy to his country, and exposed to the rage and fury of the populace. (pp. 30-2)

> *[Thomas Hutchinson], in his* Strictures upon the Declaration of the Congress at Philadelphia: In a Letter to a Noble Lord, &c., *n.p., 1776, 32 p.*

COMTE DE MIRABEAU   (essay date 1782)

[*Mirabeau was a leader of the French Revolution who advocated a limited or constitutional monarchy. He was repeatedly imprisoned for his political activities immediately before and during the Revolution. Here, he praises the Declaration of Independence yet questions how many national leaders would live up to its standards. This excerpt was originally published in 1782 in French in* Des lettres de cachet et des prison d'état, Oeuvres, Vol. VII.*]*

The sublime manifesto of the United States of America has been very generally applauded. God forbid that I protest against public opinion in this respect, I, who if not in irons would seek instruction among them and fight for them, but I ask if the powers who have contracted alliances with them have dared to read this manifesto or to examine their conscience after having read it. I ask if there is today any government in Europe, the Swiss and Batavian confederations and the British Isles alone excepted, which judged according to the principles proclaimed by Congress in the **Declaration** of July 4, 1776, would not have lost its titles. I ask if, of the thirty-two princes of the third race of our kings, there are not more than two-thirds of them who have rendered themselves much more guilty towards their subjects than the kings of Great Britain towards the English colonies.

> *Comte de Mirabeau, "The Declaration in France: Mirabeau," translated by Robert Ginsberg, in* A Casebook on The Declaration of Independence, *edited by Robert Ginsberg, Thomas Y. Crowell Company, 1967, p. 20.*

THOMAS JEFFERSON   (lecture date 1801)

[*Jefferson's first inaugural address, from which the following excerpt is drawn, was delivered on March 4, 1801. Here, he begins with a call for national reconciliation after a divisive political contest, proclaiming that "we are all republicans—we are federalists." Jefferson then presents what is considered the most concise statement of his political principles. For additional commentary by Jefferson, see excerpts dated 1823 and 1825.*]

During the contest of opinion through which we have passed, the animation of discussion and of exertions has sometimes worn an aspect which might impose on strangers unused to think freely and to speak and to write what they think; but this being now decided by the voice of the nation, announced according to the rules of the constitution, all will, of course, arrange themselves under the will of the law, and unite in common efforts for the common good. All, too, will bear in mind this sacred principle, that though the will of the majority is in all cases to prevail, that will, to be rightful, must be reasonable; that the minority possess their equal rights, which equal laws must protect, and to violate which would be oppression. Let us, then, fellow-citizens, unite with one heart and one mind. Let us restore to social intercourse that harmony and affection without which liberty and even life itself are but dreary things. And let us reflect that having banished from our land that religious intolerance under which mankind so long bled and suffered, we have yet gained little if we countenance a political intolerance as despotic, as wicked, and capable of as bitter and bloody persecutions. During the throes and convulsions of the ancient world, during the agonizing spasms of infuriated man, seeking through blood and slaughter his long-lost liberty, it was not wonderful that the agitation of the billows should reach even this distant and peaceful shore; that this should be more felt and feared by some and less by others; that this should divide opinions as to measures of safety. But every difference of opinion is not a difference of principle. We have called by different names brethren of the same principle. We are all republicans—we are federalists. If there be any among us who would wish to dissolve this Union or to change its republican form, let them stand undisturbed as monuments of the safety with which error of opinion may be tolerated where reason is left free to combat it. I know, indeed, that some honest men fear that a republican government cannot be strong; that this government is not strong enough. But would the honest patriot, in the full tide of successful experiment, abandon a government which has so far kept us free and firm, on the theoretic and visionary fear that this government, the world's best hope, may by possibility want energy to preserve itself? I trust not. I believe this, on the contrary, the strongest government on earth. I believe it is the only one where every man, at the call of the laws, would fly to the standard of the law, and would meet invasions of the public order as his own personal concern. Sometimes it is said that man cannot be trusted with the government of himself. Can he, then, be trusted with the government of others? Or have we found angels in the forms of kings to govern him? Let history answer this question.

Let us, then, with courage and confidence pursue our own federal and republican principles, our attachment to our union and representative government. Kindly separated by nature and a wide ocean from the exterminating havoc of one quarter of the globe; too high-minded to endure the degradations of the others; possessing a chosen country, with room enough for our descendants to the hundredth and thousandth generation; entertaining a due sense of our equal right to the use of our own faculties, to the acquisitions of our industry, to honor and confidence from our fellow citizens, resulting not from birth but from our actions and their sense of them; enlightened by a benign religion, professed, indeed, and practiced in various forms, yet all of them including honesty, truth, temperance, gratitude, and the love of man; acknowledging and adoring an overruling Providence, which by all its dispensations proves that it delights in the happiness of man here and his greater happiness hereafter; with all these blessings, what more is necessary to make us a happy and prosperous people? Still one thing more, fellow citizens—a wise and frugal government, which shall restrain men from injuring one another, which shall leave them otherwise free to regulate their own pursuits of industry and improvement, and shall not take from the mouth of labor the bread it has earned. This is the sum of good government, and this is necessary to close the circle of our felicities.

About to enter, fellow citizens, on the exercise of duties which comprehend everything dear and valuable to you, it is proper that you should understand what I deem the essential principles of our government, and consequently those which ought to shape its administration. I will compress them within the narrowest compass they will bear, stating the general principle, but not all its limitations. Equal and exact justice to all men, of whatever state or persuasion, religious or political; peace, commerce, and honest friendship with all nations—entangling alliances with none; the support of the State governments in all their rights, as the most competent administrations for our domestic concerns and the surest bulwarks against anti-republican tendencies; the preservation of the general government in its whole constitutional vigor, as the sheet anchor of our peace at home and safety abroad; a jealous care of the right of election by the people—a mild and safe corrective of abuses which are lopped by the sword of the revolution where peaceable remedies are unprovided; absolute acquiescence in the decisions of the majority—the vital principle of republics, from which there is no appeal but to force, the vital principle and immediate parent of despotism; a well-disciplined militia—our best reliance in peace and for the first moments of war, till regulars may relieve them; the supremacy of the civil over the military authority; economy in the public expense, that labor may be lightly burdened; the honest payment of our debts and sacred preservation of the public faith; encouragement of agriculture, and of commerce as its handmaid; the diffusion of information and the arraignment of all abuses at the bar of public reason; freedom of religion; freedom of the press; freedom of person under the protection of the *habeas corpus;* and trial by juries impartially selected—these principles form the bright constellation which has gone before us, and guided our steps through an age of revolution and reformation. The wisdom of our sages and the blood of our heroes have been devoted to their attainment. They should be the creed of our political faith—the text of civil instruction—the touchstone by which to try the services of those we trust; and should we wander from them in moments of error or alarm, let us hasten to retrace our steps and to regain the road which alone leads to peace, liberty, and safety. (pp. 2-5)

> *Thomas Jefferson, in an inaugural address given on March 4, 1801, in his* The Writings of Thomas Jefferson: Being His Autobiography, Correspondence, Reports, Messages, Addresses, and Other Writings, Official and Private, Vol. VIII, *edited by H. A. Washington, J. C. Riker, 1856, pp. 1-5.*

JOHN ADAMS   (letter date 1822)

[*Adams was the second president of the United States. Though friends, he and Jefferson were estranged throughout much of their political careers because of differences in their political views; their eventual reconciliation after both had retired from public life produced a wide-ranging correspondence in which they continued to express their differences over contemporary issues. In the following letter to Timothy Pickering, Adams comments on Jefferson's first draft of the Declaration of Independence and recounts what he remembers as the circumstances in which Jefferson was selected to write it. Jefferson provides an alternate version of this story in his letter to James Madison (1823).*]

You inquire why so young a man as Mr. Jefferson was placed at the head of the Committee for preparing a **Declaration of Independence**? I answer; It was the Frankfort advice, to place Virginia at the head of every thing. Mr. Richard Henry Lee might be gone to Virginia, to his sick family, for aught I know, but that was not the reason of Mr. Jefferson's appointment. There were three committees appointed at the same time. One for the **Declaration of Independence**, another for preparing articles of Confederation, and another for preparing a treaty to be proposed to France. Mr. Lee was chosen for the Committee of Confederation, and it was not thought convenient that the same person should be upon both. Mr. Jefferson came into Congress, in June, 1775, and brought with him a reputation for literature, science, and a happy talent of composition. Writings of his were handed about, remarkable for the peculiar felicity of expression. Though a silent member in Congress, he was so prompt, frank, explicit, and decisive upon committees and in conversation, not even Samuel Adams was more so, that he soon seized upon my heart; and upon this occasion I gave him my vote, and did all in my power to procure the votes of others. I think he had one more vote than any other, and that placed him at the head of the committee. I had the next highest number, and that placed me the second. The committee met, discussed the subject, and then appointed Mr. Jefferson and me to make the draught, I suppose because we were the two first on the list.

The sub-committee met. Jefferson proposed to me to make the draught. I said, "I will not." "You should do it." "Oh! no." "Why will you not? You ought to do it." "I will not." "Why?" "Reasons enough." "What can be your reasons?" "Reason first—You are a Virginian, and a Virginian ought to appear at the head of this business. Reason second—I am obnoxious, suspected, and unpopular. You are very much otherwise. Reason third—You can write ten times better than I can." "Well," said Jefferson, "if you are decided, I will do as well as I can." "Very well. When you have drawn it up, we will have a meeting."

The last page of Jefferson's first inaugural address.

A meeting we accordingly had, and conned the paper over. I was delighted with its high tone and the flights of oratory with which it abounded, especially that concerning negro slavery, which, though I knew his Southern brethren would never suffer to pass in Congress, I certainly never would oppose. There were other expressions which I would not have inserted, if I had drawn it up, particularly that which called the King tyrant. I thought this too personal; for I never believed George to be a tyrant in disposition and in nature; I always believed him to be deceived by his courtiers on both sides of the Atlantic, and in his official capacity only, cruel. I thought the expression too passionate, and too much like scolding, for so grave and solemn a document; but as Franklin and Sherman were to inspect it afterwards, I thought it would not become me to strike it out. I consented to report it, and do not now remember that I made or suggested a single alteration.

We reported it to the committee of five. It was read, and I do not remember that Franklin or Sherman criticized any thing. We were all in haste. Congress was impatient, and the instrument was reported, as I believe, in Jefferson's handwriting, as he first drew it. Congress cut off about a quarter of it, as I expected they would; but they obliterated some of the best of it, and left all that was exceptionable, if any thing in it was. I have long wondered that the original draught has not been published. I suppose the reason is, the vehement philippic against negro slavery.

As you justly observe, there is not an idea in it but what had been hackneyed in Congress for two years before. The substance of it is contained in the declaration of rights and the violation of those rights, in the Journals of Congress, in 1774. Indeed, the essence of it is contained in a pamphlet, voted and printed by the town of Boston, before the first Congress met, composed by James Otis, as I suppose, in one of his lucid intervals, and pruned and polished by Samuel Adams. (pp. 26-7)

> *John Adams, in an extract from a letter to Timothy Pickering on August 6, 1822, in* A Casebook on The Declaration of Independence, *edited by Robert Ginsberg, Thomas Y. Crowell Company, 1967, pp. 26-7.*

TIMOTHY PICKERING (lecture date 1823)

[*Pickering was a general during the Revolutionary War and an early American statesman and political leader. The following address was delivered on July 4, 1823. In portions of the text not excerpted below, Pickering relates the events leading up to the composition of the Declaration of Independence, relying heavily on John Adams's account and quoting extensively from his letter of August 6, 1822 (see excerpt above). Pickering echoes Adams's opinion that the ideas expressed in the Declaration were not original and adds that the substantial alterations made by Congress greatly improved it. Jefferson responds to the comments of both Adams and Pickering in the excerpt below.*]

Having been unexpectedly requested to read, to my fellow-citizens who should assemble here this day, that great act of the people of the Thirteen United Colonies, by which their Representatives in Congress declared them to be free and independent States,—I assented to the request, on the ground of its presenting a convenient opportunity to give a concise history of that transaction, with a few remarks on the character of the **Declaration** itself, and on the spirit and temper which should ever accompany its public repetition. (p. 463)

[It] appears that this celebrated paper was (as in its nature it must in substance have been) a compilation of facts and sentiments stated and expressed, in some preceding years, by those who wrote and vindicated the rights of the Colonies. A compilation, however, may have great merit by its lucid and forcible arrangement of the matter. But a great national act particularly demanded *precision,* which should exclude every minor idea and comparatively feeble expression. Whether this, among other considerations in Congress, caused a reduction of the reported draught to three-fourths of its original size, cannot now be known. In my humble opinion (having had an opportunity of examining and comparing), by the parts expunged, and by the few passages introduced and others altered in Congress, the instrument was manifestly improved. The **Declaration**, in the form in which it was finally adopted and proclaimed, has ever been received, not only as a most important, but a dignified, State Paper. (p. 468)

The 'high tone' of the **Declaration**, then so pleasing to Mr. Adams, was in unison with the warm feelings of the time, when ardent patriots were engaged in resisting oppression. The inspiring language of Liberty is congenial to the heart of man. But, on that great occasion, public policy doubtless united with a strong sense of real injuries in describing these in the most forcible and glowing style of excitement, to animate the citizens to a zealous and invincible perseverance in the cause. The effect was such as was desired and expected. The **Declaration of Independence** was received in all the States with demonstrations of joy; and all good citizens considered themselves bound by the solemn pledge which their representatives in Congress had mutually given to maintain it.

Having succeeded in the great and arduous enterprise, every heart bounded with joy at the annunciation of peace, after suffering the privations and calamities of eight years of war. In the definitive treaty of peace with Great Britain, the contending parties acknowledge the hand of Divine Providence in disposing the hearts of both 'to forget all past misunderstandings and differences that have unhappily interrupted the good correspondence and friendship which they mutually wish to restore; and to establish such a beneficial and satisfactory intercourse between the two countries, upon the ground of reciprocal advantages and mutual convenience, as may promote and secure to both perpetual peace and harmony.' The solemn profession here recited regards our best interests as well as our moral obligations; and is in exact correspondence with the fine sentiment happily expressed by Mr. Jefferson in the **Declaration of Independence**, concerning our then British brethren, 'to hold them, as we hold the rest of mankind, enemies in war, in peace friends.' This sentiment you will hear near the close of the **Declaration**, which, as an eminent historical document, I am now to read,—a sentiment which should never be forgotten; and the duties it enjoins should especially be borne in mind on every celebration of this anniversary,—duties of which our national interests, our character as an enlightened people, and our moral and religious obligations, alike require the observance. (pp. 468-69)

> *Timothy Pickering, "Colonel Pickering's Observations," in* The Life of Timothy Pickering, *Vol. IV by Charles W. Upham, Little, Brown, and Company, 1873, pp. 463-69.*

THOMAS JEFFERSON (letter date 1823)

[*Here Jefferson responds to John Adams's and Timothy Pickering's accounts of the circumstances in which Jefferson was chosen to write the Declaration of Independence. His version of the story differs markedly from that of Adams. Jefferson then explains his conception of his role as author of the Declaration: to be "a passive auditor of the opinions of others." For further commentary by Jefferson, see excerpts dated 1801 and 1825; see also excerpts by Adams (1822), Pickering (1823), and James Madison (1823).]*

You have doubtless seen Timothy Pickering's fourth of July observations on the **Declaration of Independence**. If his principles and prejudices, personal and political, gave us no reason to doubt whether he had truly quoted the information he alleges to have received from Mr. Adams, I should then say, that in some of the particulars, Mr. Adams' memory has led him into unquestionable error. At the age of eighty-eight, and forty-seven years after the transactions of Independence, this is not wonderful. Nor should I, at the age of eighty, on the small advantage of that difference only, venture to oppose my memory to his, were it not supported by written notes, taken by myself at the moment and on the spot. He says, "the committee of five, to wit, Dr. Franklin, Sherman, Livingston, and ourselves, met, discussed the subject, and then appointed him and myself to make the draught; that we, as a sub-committee, met, and after the urgencies of each on the other, I consented to undertake the task; that the draught being made, we, the sub-committee, met, and conned the paper over, and he does not remember that he made or suggested a single alteration." Now these details are quite incorrect. The committee of five met; no such thing as a sub-committee was proposed, but they unanimously pressed on myself alone to undertake the draught. I consented; I drew it; but before I reported it to the committee, I communicated it *separately* to Dr. Franklin and Mr. Adams, requesting their corrections, because they were the two members of whose judgments and amendments I wished most to have the benefit, before presenting it to the committee; and you have seen the original paper now in my hands, with the corrections of Dr. Franklin and Mr. Adams interlined in their own hand writings. Their alterations were two or three only, and merely verbal. I then wrote a fair copy, reported it to the committee, and from them, unaltered, to Congress. This personal communication and consultation with Mr. Adams, he has misremembered into the actings of a sub-committee. Pickering's observations, and Mr. Adams' in addition, "that it contained no new ideas, that it is a common-place compilation, its sentiments hacknied in Congress for two years before, and its essence contained in Otis' pamphlet," may all be true. Of that I am not to be the judge. Richard Henry Lee charged it as copied from Locke's treatise on government. Otis' pamphlet I never saw, and whether I had gathered my ideas from reading or reflection I do not know. I know only that I turned to neither book nor pamphlet while writing it. I did not consider it as any part of my charge to invent new ideas altogether, and to offer no sentiment which had ever been expressed before. Had Mr. Adams been so restrained, Congress would have lost the benefit of his bold and impressive advocations of the rights of Revolution. For no man's confident and fervid addresses, more than Mr. Adams', encouraged and supported us through the difficulties surrounding us, which, like the ceaseless action of gravity weighed on us by night and by day. Yet, on the same ground, we may ask what of these elevated thoughts was new, or can be affirmed never before to have entered the conceptions of man?

Whether, also, the sentiments of Independence, and the reasons for declaring it, which make so great a portion of the instrument, had been hackneyed in Congress for two years before

the 4th of July, '76, or this dictum also of Mr. Adams be another slip of memory, let history say. This, however, I will say for Mr. Adams, that he supported the Declaration with zeal and ability, fighting fearlessly for every word of it. As to myself, I thought it a duty to be, on that occasion, a passive auditor of the opinions of others, more impartial judges than I could be, of its merits or demerits. (pp. 267-68)

Timothy thinks the instrument the better for having a fourth of it expunged. He would have thought it still better, had the other three-fourths gone out also, all but the single sentiment (the only one he approves), which recommends friendship to his dear England, whenever she is willing to be at peace with us. His insinuations are, that although "the high tone of the instrument was in unison with the warm feelings of the times, this sentiment of habitual friendship to England should never be forgotten, and that the duties it enjoins should *especially* be borne in mind on every celebration of this anniversary." In other words, that the **Declaration**, as being a libel on the government of England, composed in times of passion, should now be buried in utter oblivion, to spare the feelings of our English friends and Angloman fellow-citizens. But it is not to wound them that we wish to keep it in mind; but to cherish the principles of the instrument in the bosoms of our own citizens: and it is a heavenly comfort to see that these principles are yet so strongly felt, as to render a circumstance so trifling as this little lapse of memory of Mr. Adams, worthy of being solemnly announced and supported at an anniversary assemblage of the nation on its birthday. In opposition, however, to Mr. Pickering, I pray God that these principles may be eternal, and close the prayer with my affectionate wishes for yourself of long life, health and happiness. (pp. 268-69)

> *Thomas Jefferson, in a letter to James Madison on August 30, 1823, in his* The Writings of Thomas Jefferson: 1816-1826, Vol. X, *edited by Paul Leicester Ford, G. P. Putnam's Sons, 1899, pp. 266-69.*

JAMES MADISON   (letter date 1823)

[Madison was the fourth president of the United States. Here, he responds to Jefferson's letter excerpted above and discusses the charges made by Timothy Pickering in his Fourth of July oration. In that speech, Pickering, like John Adams before him, acknowledges Jefferson's lack of originality in the Declaration. Madison sides with Jefferson, agreeing that the object of the Declaration was to declare and defend the Revolution, not to discover new truths. For further commentary on this issue, see excerpts by Adams (1822), Pickering (1823), and Jefferson (1823 and 1825).]

I am glad you have put on paper a correction of the apocryphal tradition, furnished by Pickering, of the Draught of the **Declaration of Independence**. If he derived it from the misrecollections of Mr. Adams, it is well that the alterations of the original paper proposed by the latter, in his own handwriting, attest the fallibility of his aged memory. Nothing can be more absurd than the cavil that the **Declaration** contains known and not new truths. The object was to assert, not to discover truths, and to make them the basis of the Revolutionary act. The merit of the Draught, therefore, could only consist in a lucid communication of human rights, in a condensed enumeration of the reasons for such an exercise of them, and in a style and tone appropriate to the great occasion, and to the spirit of the American people. (pp. 336-37)

> *James Madison, in a letter to Thomas Jefferson on September 6, 1823, in his* Letters and Other Writings of James Madison, Fourth President of the United

States: 1816-1828, Vol. III, *J. B. Lippincott & Co.,
1865, pp. 336-37.*

THOMAS JEFFERSON   (letter date 1825)

[*Here, Jefferson elaborates on his conception of the Declaration
of Independence. He explains that his goal was not to discover
new principles, but instead to reflect the common sentiment of
the people and to provide "an expression of the American mind."
For further commentary by Jefferson, see excerpts dated 1801
and 1823.*]

[With] respect to our rights, and the acts of the British government contravening those rights, there was but one opinion
on this side of the water. All American whigs thought alike
on these subjects. When forced, therefore, to resort to arms
for redress, an appeal to the tribunal of the world was deemed
proper for our justification. This was the object of the **Declaration of Independence**. Not to find out new principles, or
new arguments, never before thought of, not merely to say
things which had never been said before; but to place before
mankind the common sense of the subject, in terms so plain
and firm as to command their assent, and to justify ourselves
in the independent stand we are compelled to take. Neither
aiming at originality of principle or sentiment, nor yet copied
from any particular and previous writing, it was intended to
be an expression of the American mind, and to give to that
expression the proper tone and spirit called for by the occasion.
All its authority rests then on the harmonizing sentiments of
the day, whether expressed in conversation, in letters, printed
essays, or in the elementary books of public right, as Aristotle,
Cicero, Locke, Sidney, &c. (p. 343)

> *Thomas Jefferson, in a letter to Henry Lee on May
> 8, 1825, in his* The Writings of Thomas Jefferson:
> 1816-1826, Vol. X, *edited by Paul Leicester Ford,
> G. P. Putnam's Sons, 1899, pp. 342-43.*

DANIEL WEBSTER   (lecture date 1826)

[*Webster was an early American political leader famed for his
oratorical skills. The following excerpt is from his tribute to Jefferson and John Adams delivered in Boston on August 2, 1826,
on the fiftieth anniversary of the signing of the Declaration of
Independence. Included in Webster's review of Jefferson's life are
comments on his authorship of the Declaration. Webster also
examines the reasons for the dispute between England and the
American colonies and defends Jefferson against charges that he
had inappropriately attacked the king.*]

Mr. Jefferson appears to have been imbued with an early love
of letters and science, and to have cherished a strong disposition
to pursue these objects. To the physical sciences, especially,
and to ancient classic literature, he is understood to have had
a warm attachment, and never entirely to have lost sight of
them in the midst of the busiest occupations. But the times
were times of action, rather than for contemplation. The country was to be defended, and to be saved, before it could be
enjoyed. Philosophic leisure and literary pursuits, and even the
objects of professional attention, were all necessarily postponed
to the urgent calls of the public service. The exigency of the
country made the same demand on Mr. Jefferson that it made
on others who had the ability and the disposition to serve it;
and he obeyed the call. . . . (p. 124)

Entering with all his heart into the cause of liberty, his ability,
patriotism, and power with the pen naturally drew upon him

a large participation in the most important concerns. Wherever
he was, there was found a soul devoted to the cause, power
to defend and maintain it, and willingness to incur all its hazards. (p. 125)

[Although Mr. Jefferson was appointed by a congressional
committee to write the first draft of the **Declaration of Independence**, some] changes were made in it at the suggestion of
other members of the committee, and others by Congress while
it was under discussion. But none of them altered the tone, the
frame, the arrangement, or the general character of the instrument. As a composition, the **Declaration** is Mr. Jefferson's.
It is the production of his mind, and the high honor of it belongs
to him, clearly and absolutely.

It has sometimes been said, as if it were a derogation from the
merits of this paper, that it contains nothing new; that it only
states grounds of proceeding, and presses topics of argument,
which had often been stated and pressed before. But it was not
the object of the **Declaration** to produce any thing new. It was
not to invent reasons for independence, but to state those which
governed the Congress. For great and sufficient causes, it was
proposed to declare independence; and the proper business of
the paper to be drawn was to set forth those causes, and justify
the authors of the measure, in any event of fortune, to the
country and to posterity. The cause of American independence,
moreover, was now to be presented to the world in such manner, if it might so be, as to engage its sympathy, to command
its respect, to attract its admiration; and in an assembly of most
able and distinguished men, THOMAS JEFFERSON had the high
honor of being the selected advocate of this cause. To say that
he performed his great work well, would be doing him injustice. To say that he did excellently well, admirably well, would
be inadequate and halting praise. Let us rather say, that he so
discharged the duty assigned him, that all Americans may well
rejoice that the work of drawing the title-deed of their liberties
devolved upon him.

With all its merits, there are those who have thought that there
was one thing in the **Declaration** to be regretted; and that is,
the asperity and apparent anger with which it speaks of the
person of the king; the industrious ability with which it ac-
cumulates and charges upon him all the injuries which the
Colonies had suffered from the mother country. Possibly some
degree of injustice, now or hereafter, at home or abroad, may
be done to the character of Mr. Jefferson, if this part of the
Declaration be not placed in its proper light. Anger or resentment, certainly much less personal reproach and invective,
could not properly find place in a composition of such high
dignity, and of such lofty and permanent character.

A single reflection on the original ground of dispute between
England and the Colonies is sufficient to remove any unfavorable impression in this respect.

The inhabitants of all the Colonies, while Colonies, admitted
themselves bound by their allegiance to the king; but they
disclaimed altogether the authority of Parliament; holding
themselves, in this respect, to resemble the condition of Scotland and Ireland before the respective unions of those kingdoms
with England, when they acknowledged allegiance to the same
king, but had each its separate legislature. The tie, therefore,
which our Revolution was to break did not subsist between us
and the British Parliament, or between us and the British government in the aggregate, but directly between us and the king
himself. The Colonies had never admitted themselves subject
to Parliament. That was precisely the point of the original

controversy. They had uniformly denied that Parliament had authority to make laws for them. There was, therefore, no subjection to Parliament to be thrown off. But allegiance to the king did exist, and had been uniformly acknowledged; and down to 1775 the most solemn assurances had been given that it was not intended to break that allegiance, or to throw it off. Therefore, as the direct object and only effect of the **Declaration**, according to the principles on which the controversy had been maintained on our part, were to sever the tie of allegiance which bound us to the king, it was properly and necessarily founded on acts of the crown itself, as its justifying causes. Parliament is not so much as mentioned in the whole instrument. When odious and oppressive acts are referred to, it is done by charging the king with confederating with others "in pretended acts of legislation"; the object being constantly to hold the king himself directly responsible for those measures which were the grounds of separation. Even the precedent of the English Revolution was not overlooked, and in this case, as well as in that, occasion was found to say that the king had *abdicated* the government. Consistency with the principles upon which resistance began, and with all the previous state papers issued by Congress, required that the **Declaration** should be bottomed on the misgovernment of the king; and therefore it was properly framed with that aim and to that end. The king was known, indeed, to have acted, as in other cases, by his ministers, and with his Parliament; but as our ancestors had never admitted themselves subject either to ministers or to Parliament, there were no reasons to be given for now refusing obedience to their authority. This clear and obvious necessity of founding the **Declaration** on the misconduct of the king himself, gives to that instrument its personal application, and its character of direct and pointed accusation. (pp. 126-28)

> *Daniel Webster, "Adams and Jefferson," in his* The Works of Daniel Webster, Vol. I, *Charles C. Little and James Brown, 1851, pp. 109-50.**

GEORGE TUCKER   (essay date 1837)

[*The following excerpt is from the conclusion to the first book-length biography of Jefferson. Here, Tucker appraises Jefferson's achievements, concluding that he will be remembered "as a lawgiver and political philosopher" rather than as an author.*]

If we estimate [Mr. Jefferson's] intellect by its great results rather than by its particular efforts, we must place it in the highest rank. He was able to keep together, to animate, and guide the republican party, from the time that he became secretary of state in 1790, to 1809, when he retired to private life; during the whole of which period he had undisputed precedence in the love, esteem, and deference of that party, and in the hatred of their opponents. In effecting a revolution of parties, he had to contend against no ordinary men; and if he was aided by fortuitous circumstances, especially by the French revolution, it was only a master spirit that could have so profited by them.

Of the peculiar character of his mind it may be said that it was, perhaps, yet more distinguished for justness than quickness; for comprehension than invention; and though not wanting in originality, still more remarkable for boldness. Over that field of political speculation to which his mind was habitually turned, he seems to have been the most far-sighted of his countrymen in his estimate of the practicability of popular government; and the civilized world is every day approximating to opinions which he had deliberately formed fifty years ago.

He was thus subjected to the reproach of being visionary from many of his countrymen, because he had the sagacity to see farther than their obtuser vision could reach; and while Mr. Hamilton, Mr. Adams, Mr. Jay, and the politicians of that school drew their fundamental principles of government from examples afforded by the history of Great Britain and other European nations, he saw that these principles must change, because time was washing away the foundations on which they rested. They looked to the accidents of history, and assumed that the future would be like the past: he to the principles of human action, modified as they are by the progressive changes of civil society. But he looked to the changing character of the soil itself. He saw too, more distinctly than any of his contemporaries, the effects of the rapidly increasing population of these states. He anticipated the melancholy destiny of the Indian race, and cherished the only system which could have averted it, consistently with the safety and honour of the whites. His views of the future difficulties arising from domestic slavery, are yet in a state of probation, and are to be verified or contradicted by time. But on all these great questions there are more and more converts to his opinions, among intelligent minds; and maxims which were once adopted by his adherents with the blind deference formerly paid to the *dicta* of Pythagoras, are now embraced by speculative minds as the discoveries of political sagacity, or the logical deductions of political wisdom. (pp. 503-04)

Mr. Jefferson's acquirements were extensive, and generally accurate. There was no branch of human knowledge in which he had not made more or less proficiency. Mathematics, astronomy, physics—in all its departments, law—municipal and national, language, philosophy, history, all the liberal, and most of the mechanical arts. His knowledge of architecture extended to its minutest details. In such a multiplicity of subjects, his acquaintance with some was of course slight, especially with chemistry and metaphysics. But his knowledge of mankind—of the diversities of human character, and the motives of human action—was consummate. He made a just estimate of every man, whether a friend or foe, whom he judged worthy of serious attention. He was indeed often deceived in his stewards and overseers; but that was partly because, beyond the reach of his supervision, they yielded to the temptations of negligence, and waste, or fraud; and partly because he was all his life too much engrossed by the public affairs to give due attention to his own. When acting for the public, no one ever made choice of fitter agents.

As an author, he has left no memorial that is worthy of his genius; for the public papers drawn by him are admired rather for the patriotic spirit which dictated them than for the intellectual power they exhibit. They presented no occasion for novelty of thought, or argument, or diction. His purpose was only to make a judicious and felicitous use of that which every body knew and would assent to; and this object he has eminently fulfilled. His **"Notes on Virginia,"** though stamped with his characteristic independence of mind, are rather remarkable for the extent of his statistical knowledge, in a country and at a period when knowledge of that kind was so difficult of attainment; and his **"Manual"** of parliamentary practice required nothing more than care and discrimination. His diplomatic correspondence throughout, shows that he possessed logical powers of the highest order; and his letters, especially those of his latter years, are written with great elegance and felicity. They have all the ease of Addison, with far greater precision. His style is always natural, flowing, and perspicuous; rarely imaginative, and never declamatory. It was occasionally marked by neologisms, where he thought there were no apt words already in use. It was neither diffuse nor concise, but more inclined to the former. (pp. 504-05)

But it is on his merits as a lawgiver and political philosopher, that his claims to greatness chiefly rest: it is for these that he is to be praised or condemned by posterity; for, beyond all his contemporaries has he impressed his opinions of government on the minds of the great mass of his countrymen. He thought he saw the sources of misgovernment in the conflict of interests and of passions between the rulers and the people; and that the only effectual way of avoiding this conflict was, by placing the government in the hands of a majority of the nation. All his political schemes and institutions were framed with a view to this object. Such were his opposition to the funding system, to banks, to court ceremonies, to the Cincinnati, to the independence of the judiciary, to the county courts of Virginia. His zeal in behalf of a general system of popular instruction; of his ward system; of the extension of the right of suffrage, all aimed at the same object of placing the power of the state in the hands of the greater number. It was these objects of his untiring zeal which won for him the title he most prized, "THE MAN OF THE PEOPLE." How future ages will regard this character it is perhaps not given to the present generation to anticipate; but from pregnant signs of the times, his friends have reason to believe that posterity is quite as likely to exceed as to fall short of their own veneration for the political character of THOMAS JEFFERSON. (pp. 507-08)

> *George Tucker, in his* The Life of Thomas Jefferson, Third President of the United States, Vol. II, *Carey, Lea & Blanchard, 1837, 525 p.*

MON DROIT [PSEUDONYM OF RICHARD ELY SELDEN] (essay date 1846)

[Selden assesses the Declaration of Independence as a literary work. He condemns much of the wording and the logic of the first two and the last paragraphs, criticizing especially their poor grammar and awkward construction. Yet Selden praises the middle section that enumerates the charges against the king. To explain this dichotomy, he contends that the Declaration "is evidently the production of two minds": one clear and honest, the other mystifying and vain. Selden's essay was originally published as Criticism on the Declaration of Independence as a Literary Document *in 1846.]*

[The **Declaration of Independence**] has every where and at all times received the plaudits and huzzas of the multitude. The question comes now to be considered, whether upon a careful review, it deserves the approbation of the scholar. Whether we ought to have a more exalted idea of some of the actors in the drama of the revolution, in consequence of this production, or a less one, is certainly a legitimate subject of inquiry. But that matter can only be settled by a close inspection of the document itself. I understand to be sure, that great men will not always bear close inspection; but who ever claims to be a great writer, or for whomsoever that reputation is claimed, their works must abide that test, or their claims must fall.

These brief preliminaries being all I deem clearly necessary upon commencing the subject, I invite the examination of my readers to the first paragraph. . . .

> [When in the course of human events, it becomes necessary for one people to dissolve the political bands which have connected them with another, and to assume, among the powers of

the earth, the separate and equal station *to* which the laws of nature and of nature's God entitle them, a decent respect to the opinions of mankind requires, that they should declare the causes, which impel them to the separation.]

(p. 38)

"When in the course of human events" it appears *expedient* "for one people to dissolve the political bands which have connected them with an other," I admit it would not be improper for that people to declare the causes which made that expediency apparent to them. But I entirely deny the propriety of a similar declaration "when in the course of human events it becomes *necessary* for one people to dissolve the political bands" that have connected them with an other. That necessity knows no law, is a thoroughly established maxim—that it knows no apologies—can neither make them or receive them, is as evident as the maxim of which it is but another version. More strenuously should I deny the propriety of a declaration of causes, when a necessity (necessity is obligatory if it is any thing) obliges them "to *assume* among the powers of the earth, the separate and equal station *to* which the laws of nature and of nature's God entitle them."

A mere philological criticism was no part of my design; perhaps then I ought to apologise for noticing the queer position of the preposition "*to*," in the lines last quoted. To assume a station, which the laws of nature entitled them to occupy; would have been *natural*, and perhaps easy: but "to assume a station *to* which the laws of nature and of nature's God entitle them," it occurs to me, would have been an exploit as awkward in the performance as it is in the grammar. (pp. 38-9)

The distinction we ought to make, between the "laws of nature" and the "laws of nature's God," the writer, doubtless, were he living, would be able to explain. But being dead, we are left to conjecture what the difference is. I will put the best construction upon it, and suppose, by "the laws of nature" the writer meant that physical arrangement of the globe, by which an ocean separated us from the ruling power, making the propriety of an independent government, more obvious on that account. And by the expression "laws of nature's God" he contemplated those ever springing aspirations in the heart of man, to possess all the liberty he could get, and power too. If this was the meaning, it suffers only for the want of an interpretation. If it was not, the latter clause is merely an useless expansion of the first—a mode of expression admissible in the paroxysms of frantic eloquence on a fourth of July; but entirely out of place in a grave piece of writing. (p. 40)

My remarks upon the first paragraph, having been protracted far beyond any expectation or previous design; it may be proper to state here, that I do not meditate a querulous critic upon the whole piece. So far from that, I look upon the **Declaration** as possessing literary merit of a high order. It is too late to deny it, if one had the disposition. A composition that for seventy years can carry such a burthen of defects as this has, must possess great strength somewhere. I had rather carry the gates of Gaza than such a load. And since it was once discovered, that the great strength of a giant lay in his hair, let no neophite suppose, as a corresponding paradox, that the vigor of the composition under review, lies concealed in the unintelligible generalities at the beginning, or the sounding nonsense at the end. Whoever possesses sufficient acumen to distinguish flourishes of rhetoric from facts, will perceive (as he reads the passages that follow the one commencing thus—"The history of the present king of Great Britain, is a history of repeated injuries and usurpations'') that the bold, honest, straightforward recital of facts that follow, is a different affair altogether, both in style and sentiment from the verbiage that precedes it. But more of this in its appropriate place.

The second paragraph of the **Declaration,** is the one on which I purpose to extend my reflections; both because it is oftenest quoted, and as I think, most unhappily calculated to create the same confusion of ideas in the reader, that the mind of its writer unquestionably was troubled with. If I am charged with microscopic views, I shall treat the charge as captious, unless its author is able to show, that a different lens would lead to different conclusions.

We will quote so much of it here as I purpose to comment upon; that the reader of these pages may refer to it as often as occasion requires.

> We hold these truths to be self-evident—that all men are created equal; that they are endowed by their Creator with certain unalienable rights; that among these are life, liberty, and the pursuit of happiness; that to secure these rights governments are instituted among men, &c.

It is to be observed that the preceding paragraph had closed with the sentiment, ''that a decent respect to the opinions of mankind required that they should declare the causes which impelled them'' to certain acts. Now it occurs to me, that a decent respect to the hearers or readers of the document would have impelled its author immediately to declare those ''causes.'' So far however from such a sequence, the author drops the subject of ''causes'' and goes into a statement of views, having not the least relation to what had preceded, nor any necessary connection with what was to follow. While the mind of the reader is occupied in vigorous efforts to discover the verity of the author's self-evident truths, he can hardly fail to forget that there was any necessity for a declaration of causes, or in fact any causes to declare. But this defect in the composition is doubtless pardonable, it is so common, and known to arise from the juvenile desire on the part of an author, to exhibit himself instead of his subject.

Let us see what the author holds to. Says he ''we hold these truths to be self-evident,'' &c.—going on to make a statement of them. Is it not obvious to remark, that what is self-evident, needs no attestation? Is it not a needless piece of supererogation to declare, what in the same breath is affirmed to be evident without a declaration? What is self-evident, is, what is known. To inform men of what they knew before, seems but a slow way of increasing knowledge: nevertheless, the author of this part of the **Declaration of Independence** thought proper to undertake it. The measure of his success in this peculiar method of instruction, is a matter yet to be determined. (pp. 41-3)

A self-evident *truth,* is what no man can avoid knowing. If a knowledge of it can be avoided, it ceases to be self-evident. A self-evident proposition, is one that invariably carries conviction with the mere statement. In mathematics, propositions of this nature, are not necessarily ludicrous. But in ethics, this mirth moving quality is unalterably connected with every statement.

• • • • •

Leaving for the present the absurdity of stating, what in the same breath, it is conceded no man can avoid knowing, to the consolations of its own company; let us see what is the first famous truth the author of the **Declaration** affirms to be self-

evident. Why! ''that all men are created equal!!'' If the professor of mathematics in Yale College, should gravely announce to his pupils, the following theorem—''I hold this truth to be self-evident—that all geometrical figures are exactly similar,'' he would place his reputation for veracity and acumen, in the same position I conceive the author of the **Declaration** to occupy. And if his pupils should give a gaping credence to his asseverations, I should look also upon them, as entitled to the same degree of respect, which the applauders of these passages in the **Declaration** deserve.

Would it be disrespectful to inquire of the author, if living, by what authority he made this statement? For how are we to believe him possessed of this extraordinary piece of knowledge, when no other man does or can know it without a special revelation? If the author had prepared our minds for his marvellous statement, by informing us that he held the truth he was about to utter, as *revealed,* then no doubt, we should all be willing to concede to him, the same measure of respect we invariably pay to a Mormon; but since he entirely neglected so to prepare our minds, we cannot think him entitled to that measure of respect. (pp. 43-4)

If the statement ''all men are created equal,'' had been found among the passages of scripture, which reveal to us the information, ''that the day is set when God will judge the world in righteousness,''—had the statement been invested with the sanctity such company would give it; then indeed should I have yielded my assent to its truth, not as a matter of reason, but of faith: and not then without the reflection that my faith in that particular, was indeed a virtue, as difficult to practise as any other connected with self-denial.

But the passage under consideration is invested with no sanctity commending it to our faith; neither does it possess a speciousness that commends it to our reason. It is neither more nor less than an uninspired and presumptous asseveration, upon a subject that no man can possibly know any thing about.

We draw our inferences from facts as they exist, or from facts as they are presented to us. And what are those facts? Under every conceivable contingency—under circumstances unlimited in their dissimilitude and inequality, are men born; under all these do they continue to live; and under them also they die. Whether all men are *created* equal (using the verb in its true and literal sense) can be known only to their Creator. And since there is no revelation on that point, it is as impossible for man to know any thing about it, as it is to beget himself.

But admitting the word to be used in an expanded or figurative sense; and that the creation alluded to, is to man as he is, or as he appears. How are the facts more applicable then? Still, from forms of surpassing beauty, through a long series of gradations to the most offensive deformity—from minds of the purest radiance, through like gradations, to those of the obscurity, fog and confusion of his, whose profitless aphorisms are under review—from the extremest verge of what is lovely and desirable, to the limit of all that is odious in complexion, condition or circumstance are men created. These are facts, as palpable as the continent on which we stand. No reasoning, no study, faith or patience can make them or unmake them. These are the facts, and there are no other. One might as soon reason the Andes from their foundations, as reason us out of knowledge we cannot avoid possessing.

What apology then, is there to be found for the man, who, in the face of all these facts, and against the convictions of a conscience, if he had one, took occasion upon the going forth of a solemn public document, to parade the absurd crudity of his own "that he held it to be a self-evident truth, that all men were created equal?" What national dignity have we gained for our consolation, or what national honor for our comfort, for thus publishing to the world in our first and gravest document, this swelling axiom, as contemptible for its inapplicability, as for its falsehood? Neither the Divine government, nor any human government, with which history or experience have made us acquainted, have treated men as created equal, or as being equal; and for the best of all reasons. It is an impossibility. The attempt would confound all distinctions between right and wrong, good and bad, useful and useless. The human government that should attempt it, would attempt its own nullification. It might as well attempt the task of singing the dirge at its own funeral. (pp. 44-5)

[There is one point of negative testimony which] favors the supposition, that the declaration under review is self-evident. It is this. What is self-evident, cannot be shown to be true, by demonstration clearer than itself. I allow therefore, the expression "all men are created equal," to be self-evident, if evident at all; for it is clearly incapable of any proof whatever.

The second truth affirmed to be self-evident is expressed thus— "that they (i.e. all men) are endowed by their Creator with certain unalienable rights; that among these are life, liberty and the pursuit of happiness."

To *alien*, is to dispose of, part with, put away. What is *unalienable*, is what cannot be disposed of, parted with, or put away, either by the possessor, or by any one else: for if it can, it ceases to be *unalienable*. Life is affirmed to be one of these possessions. If it were true that no man could alienate (dispose of) his own life or any one's else, it would prove an immense comfort to braggarts. They could parade their patriotism and bravery without serious risk. Wars too, would cease to be attended with those losses, which have hitherto been accounted their chief terror. For myself I had supposed that life was alienable: and I apprehend the author of the very sentence under remark, thought so; for before he closes this famous declaration, he pledges his "life," among other things. To pledge what one cannot dispose of, amounts to no higher virtue, than to give away what one does not own. If life were unalienable, the pledge so sonorously paraded at the close of the **Declaration**, would be as worthless as a Virginia abstraction, or an abstract Virginian.

Moreover, if life is unalienable, there can be no more evidence of true patriotism. No man can part with his, for the good of his country. The **Declaration** that contains the self-evident truth that life was unalienable, was published the 4th July, 1776. The battle of Bunker Hill, where Warren, and many brave warriors had alienated their lives for the benefit of their country, had taken place in June, of the previous year. Montgomery also, with his companions in glory, had the same year alienated their lives under the ramparts of Quebec, for the same purpose. The patriots, likewise, who were slain at Lexington, had done the same thing. They sleep in their graves, each one with the sweet hope of immortal joy for his bed-fellow; and when they awake, they will find that their smiling companion had awoke before them.

It seems fortunate for the posthumous fame of these glorious old warriors, that they effected this impossible *alienation*, and secured their renown, a little before the *self-evident truth* made it evident they could do no such thing. (pp. 46-7)

If the author of the **Declaration** had asserted, that all men were endowed by their Creator with an unalienable right to die, he would have come as much nearer the fact, than he has, by all the distance there is between falsehood and truth.

• • • • •

To be endowed with a right to live, and yet at the same time can not live—that is to say, a right to life, and yet not in possession—is not an endowment of any practical value. An abstract right to life, which some one has taken away from us is worth less than the carcass of a dead cat. The Creator, I apprehend, has higher occupation than making such endowments. (p. 48)

We come now to an examination of the expression "right to liberty." It is true in this case, the right, under certain circumstances, may be worth something without the possession: and in that particular the word as applicable to "liberty," has some meaning, but as applicable to "life" none; and herein in part consists the cheat of the sophistry under review. The right to liberty, in a given case, may be valuable just in proportion to the chances of obtaining actual possession. But an abstract right to what one has not got, and what there is no probability of his getting, seems worth no more than a *right* to be disappointed. To suppose our Creator makes endowments of that sort, is a presumption I would not like to answer for. "All men" includes black men!! Perhaps the reader ought to be informed that the above, is a self-evident truth; otherwise he might possibly doubt its verity. . . . The truth is, the *value* of the right, without the possession, exists only in theory, not in fact. To be endowed with a right to think, without being endowed with any mind to think with, would be just such another endowment—just such an one as the author of the **Declaration** must have contemplated, if he had any distinct idea of the subject. To this complexion it must come at last.

The point to be proved then was this, that the *right* to liberty, though nominally appreciable as a thing separate from the possession, is not in ninety-nine cases in a hundred, worth more than the *right* to life without the possession. To all practical intents and useful purposes, the word "rights" as connected with liberty, may be dropped from the text, and the idea will in fact be as little impaired, as I have shown it would be by omitting it before the word "life." The whole idea there was to be communicated, so far as life and liberty are concerned, might have been expressed without the word "rights" and would have stood thus—"endowed by their Creator with unalienable life, liberty," &c. If my reasoning on this subject has not been fair, I should not know how to appreciate that which was.

• • • • •

The third item with which we are endowed, and which is affirmed to possess the same fixed attributes as the others, is the "*right* to the pursuit of happiness!!" The idea, if there was one attached to this expression, is too remote and vague for criticism. The attempt to weigh an abstraction in scales, or moonshine in a balance, would require the same manipulations as an attempt to calculate the value of an idea which its author could not express. The most favorable construction I can put upon it is, that no idea was meant to be communicated. The passage was particularly designed for southern ears; therefore sound, not sense, was required. It was more euphonious to terminate the clause with these sounds, than to stop where the idea stopped; hence they were added. (pp. 49-50)

The first page of Jefferson's draft of the Declaration of Independence, written in June, 1776. The Granger Collection, New York.

Some men's pursuit of happiness consists in picking our pockets; others in taking our lives; a third makes his pursuit of happiness consist in getting the two first convicted of their pursuits; and in getting them alienated of their unalienable rights to liberty and life. Success in the latter pursuit is quite after my notion of what ought to take place. But these antagonist and ever conflicting rights!! Are they divine endowments? Rights! nullifying and devouring each other!!! The rights of the Kilkenny cats to fight till there was nothing left but their tails, were just such rights.

Such, Oh Progressive Democracy! is the length and the breadth, the weight, the superfices, substance and sum-total of the sounding sophistry in this part of the **Declaration of Independence**. If in our first and most solemn public document we parade such stuff as this—if we quote it, utter it, laud it, is it to be wondered at, that other nations should scoff at our pretensions, and mock when our vain-glory cometh? . . . [What] views of our sense or sanity, is all this ostentatious setting forth of unintelligible aphorisms and inappreciable generalities, calculated to create in our contemporaries? Oh that we were endowed with an unalienable disposition to divest ourselves of vanity and lies. I would give more for such an endowment, than for all the abstract rights this side of the moon.

The third self-evident truth asserted, is expressed thus—"that to secure these rights" (meaning those we have just been contemplating) "governments are instituted among men, deriving their just powers from the consent of the governed," &c. Rights! with which we are endowed by our Creator, and in a manner withal, that makes them self-evidently unalienable, a sane man would suppose, were about as secure as any thing could well be made on this side of the grave. Who would want a human government, to secure, what in the same breath is alledged, a Divine one had secured, so as make the loss of it self-evidently impossible? (pp. 50-1)

The most astonishing thing about these passages of the **Declaration** is, that such an immense quantity of nonsense could be got into so small a compass. . . . (p. 52)

The first and most fatal mistake of its author, as I conceive, lay in his attempt to *make* truths. As if the truth was something that could be made. The first prerequisite and vital quality of truth, is, that it is something which *exists*. Men may tell it, or neglect to tell it. But the attempt to make it, is evidence, that what they purposed to make, did not exist; consequently it could not be the truth. Visionaries like the author under review, and most persons of some learning without any thorough discipline of mind, are very fond of these attempts to *make* important truths. They succeed in making a statement. Afterwards on looking round for facts in its support, finding none, nevertheless its author never seems to alter his opinions of its value. (Let them find the facts, or make them, who are interested in having it true.) The value of a statement consists in its truth: unless the design was to deceive. In that case its value is a minus quantity to all who are deceived. (pp. 52-3)

The composition is evidently the production of two minds. Upon a close and critical examination of this instrument—the style of its ideas and expressions, I have come to a settled conviction on that point. The same amount of testimony necessary to convince me, that the whitest children of our country are the offspring of the blackest inhabitants, would be required to prove to my satisfaction, that the clear straight forward statements in the body of the document, were the production of the same mind as the verbiage that precedes them. The difference in solidity between ramparts of stone, and the mists of the morning, is but a trifle more conspicuous, than the difference between the thoughts to be expressed and the mode of expressing them, observable in the two parts of this production. The clear, strong-minded and honest man, when he has any thing to declare, takes the method which becomes conspicuous in the document, where it says "The history of the present King of Great Britain, is a history of repeated injuries and usurpations," &c.—the man whose mind is forty-nine parts fog, and fifty-one self-conceit will invariably employ the style, mystification and pompous nonsense of the passages we have been reviewing.

Moreover, from many analogies I am inclined to the opinion, that one of these minds had been invigorated by the discipline of a higher latitude; the other enervated by the lassitude of a lower—one from the land of facts and truth, the other from the land of abstractions and vain philosophy. The mind of the higher latitude begins to manifest itself in the **Declaration**, as soon as we begin to find any truth in it, or any appreciable idea. The sentences in the second paragraph, following those I have commented on, are intelligible. I think it reasonable to suppose therefore, that no southern mind produced them. This intelligibility increases apace till the composition comes to the recital of facts, when that intelligibility is complete. We come now to statements that carry conviction with them—to ideas that cannot be misunderstood and facts that no man can dispute. Not only what truth or honesty there is in its **Declaration**; but all the strength, beauty and value lie in this plain, unambitious narrative. (pp. 53-4)

On reading the **Declaration**, my interest continues unabated from the beginning of the recital of facts, through all that part of it which was evidently the production of a northern mind. At the last paragraph but one, that interest rises to excitement. I venture the opinion, that a specimen of more touching pathos than is there set forth, is not to be found in any State paper, of this country or of any other. That, is the way in which a strongminded man speaks, when he feels himself wronged, and his purpose has become fixed to redress that wrong.

We see no more of the soft latitude in this production until we come to the concluding clause of the last sentence: there it bursts forth again with its "peculiar" rhetoric and unmistakable characteristics.

As the passage is often quoted—as it is more frequently in the mouths of the mock orators and quack patriots than any other, we will subject it to the same considerate and fair criticism, we have applied to its cognate and fellow passages in the first part of the document. I will quote so much of it here as I purpose to inspect.—"We mutually pledge to each other our lives, our fortunes, and our sacred honor."!! If this is not bathos, what is? If here is not a specimen of anti-climax, in the place of a supposed sublime asseveration—laughable but from our respect to the circumstances, where can we find one? If after a man had pledged his fortune, he should propose to increase the security by pledging his movable estate, we should hardly think him sane enough to make any pledge at all. "All that a man hath will he give for his life" saith a far wiser writer than the one we are reviewing. Life is by so much the most valuable of all our possessions, that in its common meaning, it is used as comprehending every thing else that belongs to us. Life, in the sense in which it is used in the passage before us, is not confined to mere animal vitality; it comprehends all that goes to make up the man. It includes his qualities of soul, as much as it does the blood in his veins. But if we take the passage as it stands, we must conclude that when they pledged their lives, they made a reservation of honor; as if that attribute was something which did not necessarily belong to *their* lives: for afterwards, as if upon second thought, they pledge that too.

• • • • •

The expression "our lives, our fortunes and our sacred honor," I cannot but contemplate as verbiage of the poorest sort. Nothing is added to the idea after the word "lives." Had the sentence of which we have quoted a part, been written thus— "and for the support of this **Declaration**, with a firm reliance on the protection of Divine providence, we mutually pledge to each other our lives" it would have expressed all the meaning it does as it stands. But sound!! sound!! the Jupiter-tonans and the ding-dong it would not have had. These, to chivalric ears, are of more consequence than sense; therefore those insipid and profitless appendages are affixed to a sentence, which but for them would have been sublime.

Men in the strong agonies of death, make no parade of rhetoric, and in the trying emergencies of life, public or private, when the strain of rigorous necessity brings us to as straight a condition; a brevity as rigid as the condition we are in, is the first, last, and sole characteristic of our speech. In the emergency which constrained our leading men at the time of the **Declaration**, we should suppose they would have pledged all they had to pledge at once; and so they would undoubtedly have done, if left to the promptings of their own good sense; but the document makes them dribble out the items they propose to pledge one by one; and the mind in contemplating the worth of the separate parts, loses sight of the value of the whole. (pp. 54-6)

> *Mon Droit [pseudonym of Richard Ely Selden], "Criticism on the Declaration of Independence as a Literary Document," in* A Casebook on The Declaration of Independence, *edited by Robert Ginsberg, Thomas Y. Crowell Company, 1967, pp. 37-56.*

JOHN C. CALHOUN   (speech date 1848)

[*Calhoun was an American political leader who served as representative, senator, secretary of state, and vice-president of the United States. A noted orator, Calhoun championed states' rights, slavery, and other southern causes in congressional debates. Here, he quarrels with the language and logic of the Declaration. Calhoun's comments were originally part of a speech on the Oregon Bill delivered on June 27, 1848, and published in the* Appendix to the Congressional Globe.]

Taking the proposition ["all men are born free and equal"] literally, (it is in that sense it is understood,) there is not a word of truth in it. It begins with "all men are born," which is utterly untrue. Men are not born. Infants are born. They grow to be men. And concludes with asserting that they are born "free and equal," which is not less false. They are not born free. While infants they are incapable of freedom, being destitute alike of the capacity of thinking and acting, without which there can be no freedom. Besides, they are necessarily born subject to their parents, and remain so among all people, savage and civilized, until the development of their intellect and physical capacity enables them to take care of themselves. They grow to all the freedom, of which the condition in which they were born permits, by growing to be men. Nor is it less false that they are born "equal." They are not so in any sense in which it can be regarded; and thus, as I have asserted, there

is not a word of truth in the whole proposition, as expressed and generally understood.

If we trace it back, we shall find the proposition differently expressed in the **Declaration of Independence.** That asserts that "all men are created equal." The form of expression, though less dangerous, is not less erroneous. All men are not created. According to the Bible, only two, a man and a woman, ever were, and of these one was pronounced subordinate to the other. All others have come into the world by being born, and in no sense, as I have shown, either free or equal. But this form of expression being less striking and popular, has given way to the present, and under the authority of a document put forth on so great an occasion, and leading to such important consequences, has spread far and wide, and fixed itself deeply in the public mind. It was inserted in our **Declaration of Independence** without any necessity. It made no necessary part of our justification in separating from the parent country, and declaring ourselves independent. Breach of our chartered privileges, and lawless encroachment on our acknowledged and well-established rights by the parent country, were the real causes, and of themselves sufficient, without resorting to any other, to justify the step. Nor had it any weight in constructing the governments which were substituted in the place of the colonial. They were formed of the old materials and on practical and well-established principles, borrowed for the most part from our own experience and that of the country from which we sprang. (pp. 57-8)

> *John C. Calhoun, "The Most False and Dangerous of All Political Errors," in* A Casebook on The Declaration of Independence, *edited by Robert Ginsberg, Thomas Y. Crowell Company, 1967, pp. 57-8.*

RUFUS WILMOT GRISWOLD   (essay date 1852)

[*Griswold was a nineteenth-century American anthologist, literary critic, and magazine editor. His works on American writers, including* Prose Writers of America, *feature brief biographical sketches along with critical commentary. While his critical judgment is considered limited by personal prejudice, he did leave a valuable store of factual material on the writers of his era. Despite this contribution, his editorial deceit and indiscretion have secured his reputation as a villain of nineteenth-century American letters. In this excerpt from his essay on Jefferson, Griswold demonstrates his low estimate of the former president's achievements. Griswold questions Jefferson's literary and intellectual abilities and concludes by doubting that he "possessed any inherent greatness."*]

[Coincidences] of expression, which could hardly have been accidental, have been pointed out in the **Declaration** and documents previously written by other men. The instances are rare in which the committees of public bodies are in any just sense the authors of its reports, which are commonly but embodiments of the spirit of its discussions. While the Congress was in a state of intense excitement, on the seventh of June, 1776, Richard Henry Lee moved that the country be declared independent, and soon after the committee to prepare the declaration was appointed. For twenty days the subject was discussed in fervid and powerful speeches by the ablest men in the assembly: Mr. Jefferson being present all the while, taking notes of the heads of the arguments, and treasuring in his mind every striking expression of fact or opinion. It is reasonable to suppose that no important statement or suggestion is contained in the **Declaration** which had not been uttered in the debates. Its literary merits are not remarkable, and they were less as it came from the hands of Mr. Jefferson. Mr. Adams and Dr. Franklin suggested some improvements in the committee, and others were made in the House, which struck out or amended the style of several passages.

As a cultivator of elegant literature, under favourable circumstances, Mr. Jefferson would have attained to considerable excellence. His appropriate field perhaps would have been the essay on manners. He was wanting in power, assiduity and integrity for moral speculations, but had the ready penetration and vivacity necessary to a painter of society. His style was flexible, easy, and familiar, and had considerable variety, but was diffuse. He cannot with propriety be said to have been a student, yet he read much, especially in his old age. His reading, however, was one-sided, though discursive, and seldom brought him into contact with the master minds. In his elevation, the air, to his bewildered eyes, was filled with storms of stars, and he mistook the disorder for the perfection of vision. The light which comes from the past to him was darkness. He tells us that "Plato's brain was foggy," and that "a child should be ashamed of his whimsies and peurilities;" that the sweet singer of Israel, and wisest of kings, gave us but "fumes of disordered imaginations," and that the holy company of the apostles was a "band of dupes and impostors." Christ himself he regarded for his wit, and was kindly incredulous of the "dishonesty" of which he was "reasonably suspected." It was one of his political doctrines that one generation is not bound by the acts of another. Struck with its brevity and point, which would have given it currency, and finally authority, if more plausible, he was ready to publish it with all the circumstance of a new revelation; but Madison saw its absurdity, and persuaded him not to give it to the world. Many of his views, in religion, morals, and politics, were but reflexes of the radicalism of the French revolution, of which he had been a sympathizing spectator. (pp. 72-3)

A want of steadiness, comprehensiveness, and foresight is apparent in all Mr. Jefferson's controversies and speculations, and we are left in doubt, after the most careful study of his life and works, whether he possessed any inherent greatness, or in any pursuit or condition would have entitled himself to a higher reputation than is awarded to him at the close of the first quarter of a century after his death. (p. 73)

> *Rufus Wilmot Griswold, "Thomas Jefferson," in his*
> The Prose Writers of America, *revised edition, 1852.*
> *Reprint by Garrett Press, Inc., 1969, pp. 71-8.*

ABRAHAM LINCOLN AND STEPHEN ARNOLD DOUGLAS
(speech dates 1858)

[*Lincoln was president of the United States from 1861 until his assassination in 1865; Douglas was a political leader and prominent figure in the nation-wide controversy about slavery that led to the Civil War. The following excerpt is drawn from the transcriptions of the famous series of debates between Lincoln and Douglas held between August 21 and October 15, 1858, during their contest for a seat in the United States Senate. Much of the debate focuses on the question of slavery and the meaning of the proposition in the Declaration of Independence that "all men are created equal." Both Lincoln and Douglas use that proposition to uphold their views regarding slavery: Lincoln argues that the principles of the Declaration apply equally to slaves, while Douglas counters that only white men of European heritage were guaranteed equal rights. Lincoln's comments were drawn from the* Chicago Press and Tribune, *while Douglas's remarks originally appeared in the* Chicago Times. *Parenthetical and bracketed comments are audience reactions.*]

[*Lincoln at Chicago, June 10, 1858*]

We hold this annual celebration to remind ourselves of all the good done in this process of time of how it was done and who did it, and how we are historically connected with it; and we go from these meetings in better humor with ourselves—we feel more attached the one to the other, and more firmly bound to the country we inhabit. In every way we are better men in the age, and race, and country in which we live for these celebrations. But after we have done all this we have not yet reached the whole. There is something else connected with it. We have besides these men—descended by blood from our ancestors—among us perhaps half our people who are not descendants at all of these men, they are men who have come from Europe—German, Irish, French and Scandinavian—men that have come from Europe themselves, or whose ancestors have come hither and settled here, finding themselves our equals in all things. If they look back through this history to trace their connection with those days by blood, they find they have none, they cannot carry themselves back into that glorious epoch and make themselves feel that they are part of us, but when they look through that old **Declaration of Independence** they find that those old men say that "We hold these truths to be self-evident, that all men are created equal," and then they feel that that moral sentiment taught in that day evidences their relation to those men, that it is the father of all moral principle in them, and that they have a right to claim it as though they were blood of the blood, and flesh of the flesh of the men who wrote that **Declaration**, (loud and long continued applause) and so they are. That is the electric cord in that **Declaration** that links the hearts of patriotic and liberty-loving men together, that will link those patriotic hearts as long as the love of freedom exists in the minds of men throughout the world. (Applause.)

Now, sirs, for the purpose of squaring things with this idea of "don't care if slavery is voted up or voted down," for sustaining the Dred Scott decision [A voice—"Hit him again"], for holding that the **Declaration of Independence** did not mean anything at all, we have Judge Douglas giving his exposition of what the **Declaration of Independence** means, and we have him saying that the people of America are equal to the people of England. According to his construction, you Germans are not connected with it. Now I ask you in all soberness, if all these things, if indulged in, if ratified, if confirmed and endorsed, if taught to our children, and repeated to them, do not tend to rub out the sentiment of liberty in the country, and to transform this Government into a government of some other form. Those arguments that are made, that the inferior race are to be treated with as much allowance as they are capable of enjoying; that as much is to be done for them as their condition will allow. What are these arguments? They are the arguments that kings have made for enslaving the people in all ages of the world. You will find that all the arguments in favor of king-craft were of this class; they always bestrode the necks of the people, not that they wanted to do it, but because the people were better off for being ridden. That is their argument, and this argument of the Judge is the same old serpent that says you work and I eat, you toil and I will enjoy the fruits of it. Turn in whatever way you will—whether it come from the mouth of a King, an excuse for enslaving the people of his country, or from the mouth of men of one race as a reason for enslaving the men of another race, it is all the same old serpent, and I hold if that course of argumentation that is made for the purpose of convincing the public mind that we should not care about this, should be granted, it does not stop with the negro.

I should like to know if taking this old **Declaration of Independence**, which declares that all men are equal upon principle and making exceptions to it where will it stop. If one man says it does not mean a negro, why not another say it does not mean some other man? If that declaration is not the truth, let us get the Statute book, in which we find it and tear it out! Who is so bold as to do it! [Voices—"me," "no one," &c.] If it is not true let us tear it out! [cries of "no, no,"] let us stick to it then, [cheers] let us stand firmly by it then. [Applause.] (pp. 45-7)

• • • • •

[*Douglas at Springfield, July 17, 1858*]

Mr. Lincoln and myself come to a direct issue on this whole doctrine of slavery. He is going to wage a war against it everywhere, not only in Illinois but in his native State of Kentucky. And why? Because he says that the **Declaration of Independence** contains this language: "We hold these truths to be self-evident, that all men are created equal; that they are endowed by their Creator with certain inalienable rights: that among these are life, liberty and the pursuit of happiness," and he asks whether that instrument does not declare that all men are created equal. ["Not niggers."] Mr. Lincoln then goes on to say that that clause of the **Declaration of Independence** includes negroes. ["I say not."] Well, if you say not I do not think you will vote for Mr. Lincoln. [Laughter, and the same voice, "I'll be d——d if I do."] Mr. Lincoln goes on to argue that the language "all men" included the negroes, Indians and all inferior races.

In his Chicago speech he says in so many words that it includes the negroes, that they were endowed by the Almighty with the right of equality with the white man, and therefore that that right is divine—a right under the higher law: that the law of God makes them equal to the white man, and therefore that the law of the white man cannot deprive them of that right. This is Mr. Lincoln's argument. He is conscientious in his belief. I do not question his sincerity, I do not doubt that he, in his conscience, believes that the Almighty made the negro equal to the white man. He thinks that the negro is his brother. [Laughter.] I do not think that the negro is any kin of mine at all. [Laughter and cheers.] And here is the difference between us. I believe that the **Declaration of Independence**, in the words "all men are created equal," was intended to allude only to the people of the United States, to men of European birth or descent, being white men, that they were created equal, and hence that Great Britain had no right to deprive them of their political and religious privileges; but the signers of that paper did not intend to include the Indian or the negro in that declaration, ["never," &c.] for if they had would they not have been bound to abolish slavery in every state and colony from that day. ["Certainly," and cheers.] Remember, too, that at the time the **Declaration** was put forth every one of the thirteen colonies were slaveholding colonies; every man who signed that **Declaration** represented slave-holding constituents. ["Hurrah for Douglas."] Did those signers mean by that act to charge themselves and all their constituents with having violated the law of God, in holding the negro in an inferior condition to the white man? ["No, certainly not."] And yet, if they included negroes in that term they were bound, as conscientious men, that day and that hour, not only to have abolished slavery throughout the land, but to have conferred political rights and privileges on the negro, and elevated him to an equality with the white man. ["They did not do it."] I know they did not do it, and the very fact that they did not shows that they did

not understand the language they used to include any but the white race. Did they mean to say that the Indian, on this continent, was created equal to the white man, and that he was endowed by the Almighty with inalienable rights—rights so sacred that they could not be taken away by any constitution or law that man could pass? Why, their whole action towards the Indian showed that they never dreamed that they were bound to put him on an equality. I am not only opposed to negro equality, but I am opposed to Indian equality. I am opposed to putting the coolies, now importing into this country, on an equality with us, or putting the Chinese or any inferior race on an equality with us. I hold that the white race, the European race, I care not whether Irish, German, French, Scotch, English, or to what nation they belong, so they are the white race to be our equals, ["Good, that's the doctrine," and cheers.] and I am for placing them, as our fathers did, on an equality with us. [Cheers.] Emigrants from Europe and their descendants constitute the people of the U.S. [Renewed applause.] The [**Declaration of Independence**] only included the white people of the U.S. ["Not the negro."] (pp. 77-9)

• • • • •

[*Lincoln at Springfield, July 17, 1858*]

Last night Judge Douglas tormented himself with horrors about my disposition to make negros perfectly equal with white men in social and political relations. He did not stop to show that I have said any such thing, or that it legitimately follows from any thing I have said, but he rushes on with his assertions. I adhere to the **Declaration of Independence**. If Judge Douglas and his friends are not willing to stand by it, let them come up and amend it. Let them make it read that all men are created equal except negroes. Let us have it decided, whether the **Declaration of Independence**, in this blessed year of 1858, shall be thus amended. In his construction of the **Declaration** last year he said it only meant that Americans in America were equal to Englishmen in England. Then, when I pointed out to him that by that rule he excludes the Germans, the Irish, the Portuguese, and all the other people who have come amongst us since the Revolution, he reconstructs his construction. In his last speech he tells us it meant Europeans.

I press him a little further, and ask if it meant to include the Russians in Asia? or does he mean to exclude that vast population from the principles of our **Declaration of Independence**? I expect ere long he will introduce another amendment to his definition. He is not at all particular. He is satisfied with any thing which does not endanger the nationalizing of negro slavery. It may draw white men down, but it must not lift negroes up. Who shall say, "I am the superior, and you are the inferior?"

My declarations upon this subject of negro slavery may be misrepresented, but can not be misunderstood. I have said that I do not understand the **Declaration** to mean that all men were created equal in all respects. They are not our equal in color; but I suppose that it does mean to declare that all men are equal in some respects; they are equal in their right to "life, liberty, and the pursuit of happiness." Certainly the negro is not our equal in color—perhaps not in many other respects; still, in the right to put into his mouth the bread that his own hands have earned, he is the equal of every other man, white or black. In pointing out that more has been given you, you can not be justified in taking away the little which has been given him. All I ask for the negro is that if you do not like him, let him alone. If God gave him but little, that little let him enjoy. (p. 89)

・ ・ ・ ・ ・

[Douglas at Galesburg, October 7, 1858]

I tell you that this Chicago doctrine of Lincoln's—declaring that the negro and the white man are made equal by the **Declaration of Independence** and by Divine Providence—is a monstrous heresy. (That's so, and terrific applause.) The signers of the **Declaration of Independence** never dreamed of the negro when they were writing that document. They referred to white men, to men of European birth and European descent, when they declared the equality of all men. I see a gentleman there in the crowd shaking his head. Let me remind him that when Thomas Jefferson wrote that document he was the owner, and so continued until his death, of a large number of slaves. Did he intend to say in that **Declaration** that his negro slaves, which he held and treated as property, were created his equals by Divine law, and that he was violating the law of God every day of his life by holding them as slaves? (''No, no.'') It must be borne in mind that when that **Declaration** was put forth every one of the thirteen colonies were slaveholding colonies, and every man who signed that instrument represented a slaveholding constituency. Recollect, also, that no one of them

The portable desk on which Jefferson wrote the Declaration. University of Virginia Library.

emancipated his slaves, much less put them on an equality with himself, after he signed the **Declaration**. On the contrary, they all continued to hold their negroes as slaves during the revolutionary war. Now, do you believe—are you willing to have it said—that every man who signed the **Declaration of Independence** declared the negro his equal, and then was hypocrite enough to continue to hold him as a slave, in violation of what he believed to be the divine law. (''No, no.'') And yet when you say that the **Declaration of Independence** includes the negro, you charge the signers of it with hypocrisy.

I say to you, frankly, that in my opinion this government was made by our fathers on the white basis. It was made by white men for the benefit of white men and their posterity forever, and was intended to be administered by white men in all time to come. (That's so, and cheers.) (p. 165)

・ ・ ・ ・ ・

[Lincoln at Galesburg, October 7, 1858]

The Judge has alluded to the **Declaration of Independence**, and insisted that negroes are not included in that **Declaration**; and that it is a slander upon the framers of that instrument, to suppose that negroes were meant therein; and he asks you: Is it possible to believe that Mr. Jefferson, who penned the immortal paper, could have supposed himself applying the language of that instrument to the negro race, and yet held a portion of that race in slavery? Would he not at once have freed them? I only have to remark upon this part of the Judge's speech, (and that, too, very briefly, for I shall not detain myself, or you, upon that point for any great length of time,) that I believe the entire records of the world, from the date of the **Declaration of Independence** up to within three years ago, may be searched in vain for one single affirmation, from one single man, that the negro was not included in the **Declaration of Independence**. I think I may defy Judge Douglas to show that he ever said so, that Washington ever said so, that any President ever said so, that any member of Congress ever said so, or that any living man upon the whole earth ever said so, until the necessities of the present policy of the Democratic party, in regard to slavery, had to invent that affirmation. [Tremendous applause.] And I will remind Judge Douglas and this audience, that while Mr. Jefferson was the owner of slaves, as undoubtedly he was, in speaking upon this very subject, he used the strong language that ''he trembled for his country when he remembered that God was just;'' and I will offer the highest premium in my power to Judge Douglas if he will show that he, in all his life, ever uttered a sentiment at all akin to that of Jefferson. [Great applause and cries of ''Hit him again,'' ''good,'' ''good.''] (p. 167)

> *Abraham Lincoln and Stephen Arnold Douglas, in speeches delivered from June 10, 1858 through October 7, 1858, in* The Illinois Political Campaign of 1858: A Facsimile of the Printer's Copy of His Debates with Senator Stephen Arnold Douglas as Edited and Prepared for Press by Abraham Lincoln, *The Library of Congress, 1958, pp. 45-167.*

A[BRAHAM] LINCOLN   (letter date 1859)

[The following excerpt is from Lincoln's reply to an invitation from H. L. Pierce to attend a Republican festival in Boston in honor of Jefferson's birthday. Lincoln compares the two political parties of his era with their eighteenth-century counterparts, contending that Jefferson's principles are better served by Lincoln's fellow Republicans than by the Democratic party which Jefferson

helped form. In conclusion, Lincoln provides a glowing tribute to Jefferson as the champion of individual freedom. This letter, which circulated freely during the 1860 presidential campaign, was widely denounced by Democrats.]

Bearing in mind that about seventy years ago two great political parties were first formed in this country, that Thomas Jefferson was the head of one of them and Boston the headquarters of the other, it is both curious and interesting that those supposed to descend politically from the party opposed to Jefferson should now be celebrating his birthday in their own original seat and empire, while those claiming political descent from him have nearly ceased to breathe his name everywhere.

Remembering, too, that the Jefferson party formed upon the supposed superior devotion to the personal rights of men, holding the rights of property to be secondary only and greatly inferior, and assuming that the so called Democracy of to-day are the Jefferson, and their opponents the anti-Jefferson party, it will be equally interesting to note how completely the two have changed hands as to the principle upon which they were originally supposed to be divided. The Democracy of to-day hold the liberty of one man to be absolutely nothing, when in conflict with another man's right of property; Republicans, on the contrary, are for both the man and the dollar, but in case of conflict the man before the dollar.

I remember being very much amused at seeing two partially intoxicated men engaged in a fight with their great-coats on, which fight, after a long and rather harmless contest, ended in each having fought himself out of his own coat and into that of the other. If the two leading parties of this day are really identical with the two in the days of Jefferson and Adams they have performed the same feat as the two drunken men.

But soberly, it is now no child's play to save the principles of Jefferson from total overthrow in this nation. One would state with great confidence that he could convince any sane child that the simpler propositions of Euclid are true, but nevertheless he would fail, utterly, with one who should deny the definitions and axioms.

The principles of Jefferson are the definitions and axioms of free society and yet they are denied and evaded, with no small show of success. One dashingly calls them "glittering generalities." Another bluntly calls them "self-evident lies" and others insidiously argue that they apply to "superior races." These expressions, differing in form, are identical in object and effect—the supplanting the principles of free government, and restoring those of classification, caste, and legitimacy. They would delight a convocation of crowned heads plotting against the people. They are the vanguard, the miners and sappers of returning despotism. We must repulse them, or they will subjugate us. This is a world of compensation; and he who would be no slave must consent to have no slave. Those who deny freedom to others deserve it not for themselves, and, under a just God, cannot long retain it. *All honor to Jefferson— to the man, who in the concrete pressure of a struggle for national independence by a single people, had the coolness, forecaste, and sagacity to introduce into a merely revolutionary document an abstract truth, applicable to all men and all times, and so embalm it there that to-day and in all coming days it shall be a rebuke and a stumbling-block to the very harbingers of reappearing tyranny and oppression.* (pp. xv-xvii)

A[braham] Lincoln, in a letter to H. L. Pierce and others on April 6, 1859, in The Writings of Thomas Jefferson, Vol. I *by Thomas Jefferson, edited by An-*

drew A. Lipscomb, The Thomas Jefferson Memorial Association of the United States, 1903, pp. xv-xvii.

[ANDREW D. WHITE]   (essay date 1862)

[*In the following excerpt, White defines Jefferson's contribution to the development of democratic government. He identifies the three qualities that made Jefferson a great statesman as insight, foresight, and faith in democracy. In portions of the essay not excerpted below, White examines Jefferson's views on slavery and the social and intellectual influences that formed them.*]

Any one who feels deeply the truths in which our great men of old founded this Democracy, and who sees clearly the great lines of political architecture by which alone it shall stand firm or rise high, finds in the direct plan and work the agency mainly of six men.

These may be set in three groups.

First, three men, who, through a series of earnest thoughts, taking shape sometimes in apt words, sometimes in bold acts, did most to *found* the Republic: and these three are Washington, Adams, and Jefferson.

Secondly, two men, who, as statesmen, by a healthful division between the two great natural policies, and, as politicians, by a healthful antagonism between the two great natural parties, did most to *build* the Republic: and these two are Jefferson and Hamilton.

Thirdly, three men, who, having a clear theory in their heads, and a deep conviction in their hearts, working on the nation by sermons, epistles, programmes, hints, quips, innuendoes, by every form of winged word, have done most to get this people into simple trains of humanitarian thought, and have therefore done most to *brace* the Republic: and these three men are Franklin, Jefferson, and Channing.

So, rising above the dust raised in our old quarrels, and taking a broad view over this Democracy, we see Jefferson firmly placed in each of these groups.

If we search in Jefferson's writings and in the contemporary records to ascertain what that power was which won him these positions, we find that it was no personal skill in cajoling friends or scaring enemies. No sound-hearted man ever rose from talk with him with a tithe of the veneration felt by those who sat at the feet of Washington or Hamilton or Channing. Neither was his position due to oratory: he could deal neither in sweet words nor in lofty words. Yet, in spite of these wants, he wrought on the nation with immense power.

The real secret of this power was, first of all, that Jefferson saw infinitely deeper into the principles of the rising Democracy, and infinitely farther into its future working, than any other man of his time. Those who earnestly read him will often halt astounded at proofs of a foresight in him almost miraculous. (p. 29)

[In addition to insight and foresight,] there was yet a greater quality which gave him a place in each of these three great groups,—his faith in Democracy.

At a time when the French Revolution had scared even Burke, and when the British Constitution was thought by many to have seduced even Washington, Jefferson held fast to his great faith in the rights and capacities of the people. The only effect on him of the shocks and failures of that period was to make his anxiety sometimes morbid, and his action sometimes spasmodic. Hence much that to many men has seemed unjust suspicion of Adams, and persecution of Hamilton, and disrespect for Washington. Yet all this was but the jarring of that strong mind in the struggle and crash of his times,—mere spasms of bigotry which prove the vigor of his faith in Democracy. (p. 30)

[*Andrew D. White*], *"Jefferson and Slavery," in* The Atlantic Monthly, *Vol. IX, No. LI, January, 1862, pp. 29-40.*

JOHN MORLEY (essay date 1867)

[*Morley defends the Declaration of Independence, praising it as a moral work because of its assertion that all men are equally entitled to the pursuit of happiness and are hence obligated to promote the happiness of others.*]

Much ridicule, a little of it not altogether undeserved, has been thrown upon the opening clause of the **Declaration of Independence**, which asserts the inherent natural right of man to enjoy life and liberty, with the means of acquiring and possessing property, and pursuing and obtaining happiness and safety. Yet there is an implied corollary in this which enjoins the highest morality that in our present state we are able to think of as possible. If happiness is the right of our neighbour, then not to hinder him, but to help him in its pursuit, must plainly be our duty. If all men have a claim, then each man is under an obligation. The corollary thus involved is the corner-stone of morality. It was an act of good augury thus to inscribe happiness as entering at once into the right of all, and into the duty of all, in the very head and front of the new charter, as the base of a national existence, and the first principle of a national government. The omen has not been falsified. The Americans have been true to their first doctrine. They have never swerved aside to set up caste and privilege, to lay down the doctrine that one man's happiness ought to be an object of greater solicitude to society than any other man's, or that one order should be encouraged to seek its prosperity through the depression of any other order. Their example proved infectious. The assertion in the New World, that men have a right to happiness and an obligation to promote the happiness of one another, struck a spark in the Old World. Political construction in America immediately preceded the last violent stage of demolition in Europe. (pp. 161-62)

John Morley, "American Independence," in his Edmund Burke: A Historical Study, *Macmillan and Co., 1867, pp. 125-64.**

WILHELM ONCKEN (essay date 1882)

[*Oncken views the Declaration of Independence as a "calculated" piece of writing designed to win the approval of other governments as well as of the American people. According to Oncken, the appeal for human rights was intentionally used as a weapon against England and as a means of gaining the support of other nations, particularly France. This essay was originally published in 1882 in German as* Das Zeitalter Friedrichs des Grossen, Allgemeine Geschichte.]

In declaring themselves free and independent states, the rebellious Colonies claimed the rights of a belligerent power capable of making alliances, and in designating their renunciation of England as irrevocable, they meant to give a pledge to the French and Spanish Crowns which was the necessary prerequisite to any open alliance with them. . . .

The **Declaration**—never would America again become a province of the King of England—was intended for the *governments* plagued with fear that the reunited power of England and America could one day snatch away their last colonies in the new world. The further content of the **Declaration** was meant for the *peoples,* and it struck quite happily the tone that promised the greatest effect upon their collaborators, namely *the French.*

Here right at the beginning they speak in solemn priestly tones:

When, in the course of human events, it becomes necessary for one people to dissolve the political bands which have connected them with another, and to assume among the powers of the earth the separate and equal station to which the laws of nature and of nature's God entitle them, a decent respect to the opinions of mankind requires that they should declare the causes which impel them to the separation.

We hold these truths to be self evident: that all men are created equal; that they are endowed by their creator with [certain] inalienable rights; that among these are life, liberty, and the pursuit of happiness; that to secure these rights, governments are instituted among men, deriving their just powers from the consent of the governed; that whenever any form of government becomes destructive of these ends, it is the right of the people to alter or to abolish it, and to institute new government, laying its foundation on such principles, and organizing its powers in such form, as to them shall seem most likely to effect their safety and happiness.

The natural right of men to equality, the natural right of nations to liberty, the dream of Rousseau, the intellectual yearning of the entire young generation that inflamed its pathos: here it was publicly claimed for the first time in a great controversy between nations and formulated with the certainty of a universally valid law. It was not the audible soliloquy of enthusiastic visionaries; it was the will, the solemn vow of a contending nation, enunciated by simple colonists who knew nothing of the heartaches that oppressed the peoples of old Europe. The effect was indescribable; in seething France it worked with volcanic might. (p. 73)

Following the appeal to human rights in the text, is evidence of frequent encroachments upon these rights of the Americans. If this had actually happened, the fault, as we have seen, was not that of any individual will but of the active *national will of England* in Parliament, the world then first learning to what extent it had become subservient to the *commercial interests* of the merchants and manufacturers. (p. 74)

[Despite the King's despotic temper], it was the grossest misconception, or rather disavowal, first of English constitutional law and then of the most well-known facts of contemporary history, when in the **Declaration of Independence** King George III was uniquely and exclusively accused as originator and executor of the 28 diverse species of genocidal crime. Only once, quite incidentally, was he thought of as doing this in conjunction "with others," i.e., Parliament, but never was there a thought of the whole duly-resolved *Law* in accordance with which his Ministers and Governors acted, and whose execution was, indeed, thoroughly frustrated by the opposition and defensiveness of the Americans. Here liberty makes a stand against despotism, the despot being not a king but an entire people, the people of England who outside of Parliament had no constitutional will, but who had sanctioned as explicitly as possible through their elections the avowed will of the country on this question in Parliament. . . . This obscuring of the accused party was an artifice of demagogy, above all splendidly calculated for the hatred of despots in a France fresh from the school of Rousseau and Montesquieu. It would have been considerably more effective if under the alleged offenses of King George a very special one, treated by Jefferson with extremely forceful language, had met with good reception:

> He has waged cruel war against human nature itself, violating its most sacred rights of life and liberty in the persons of a distant people who never offended him, captivating and carrying them into slavery in another hemisphere, or to incur miserable death in their transportation thither. This piratical warfare, the opprobrium of INFIDEL powers, is the warfare of the CHRISTIAN king of Great Britain. Determined to keep open a market where MEN should be bought and sold, he has prostituted his negative for suppressing every legislative attempt to prohibit or to restrain this execrable commerce. And that this assemblage of horrors might want no fact of distinguished die, he is now exciting those very people to rise in arms among us, and to purchase that liberty of which he has deprived them, by murdering the people on whom he also obtruded them: thus paying off former crimes committed against the LIBERTIES of one people, with crimes he urges them to commit against the LIVES of another.

A scorching critique of *negro slavery,* a solemn proscription of the *slave trade* in its first manifesto, would not merely have done honor to the United States, it was really quite indispensable in a document which began with expression of the "self-evident truth" that "all men are created equal" and their right to life, liberty, and the pursuit of happiness is "inalienable," especially if one was warranted, as Jefferson at least assumed, in allowing all the crimes in the list of wicked acts of the King of England to culminate in this one. We know, unfortunately, how little the royalty of England was an accomplice in the genesis and growth of this affliction. . . . (pp. 75-6)

The appeal to human rights was thus only a weapon against England and a means to win over the opinion of nations, but it certainly was not itself meant to furnish the legal basis for the constitutional life of America. Since the Americans could not appeal to written law, they referred to the unwritten natural law of the philosophers; to this artifice they appended the other that all their grievances and accusations were erected exclusively against that personage of England who according to the plainest doctrines of English constitutional law could not at all be accused and also was no more guilty in this affair than the Ministers and both Houses of Parliament. Both were calculated to the mental state of France, where two strong feelings prevailed: one was enthusiasm for human rights, the other hatred of despots and love of liberty. The calculated effect was not wanting, but that it was calculated and how very much so, people in France did not suspect. . . . (pp. 76-7)

> *Wilhelm Oncken, "The Strategy of Composition," translated by Robert Ginsberg, in* A Casebook on The Declaration of Independence, *edited by Robert Ginsberg, Thomas Y. Crowell Company, 1967, pp. 71-7.*

PAUL LEICESTER FORD (essay date 1892)

[*Ford's essay was originally published in 1892 as an introduction to the first volume of* The Writings of Thomas Jefferson. *In the following excerpt, Ford enumerates the many inconsistencies between Jefferson's stated political beliefs and his actions, yet contends that his concern for and advocacy of democracy overrides these inequities. In portions of the essay not excerpted below, Ford reviews Jefferson's career and describes the many official documents he wrote.*]

The political theories and usages originated or adopted by Thomas Jefferson have shown such persistence and permanence in their value to our people and government as to demonstrate a far deeper and broader principle underlying them than is always recognized. In popular estimation, Jefferson stands as the founder of the Democratic party, and the developer of the theory of State Rights; and on these foundations are based the so called "Jeffersonian principles," and the respect and acceptance, as well as the criticism and contravention, accorded to them. That this basis was deemed sufficient during his life, is natural, for judgment of a living man must always be partial and superficial. That this limited view should during that time acquire prestige and momentum enough to project it into history, is not strange, the more that the logical conclusions of certain theories advanced by him suited the policy of one of our political parties. The acceptance of this limited view has enabled his antagonists and critics to charge him with hypocrisy, opportunism, and even lack of any political principles; and the contradictions and instability they have cited in his opinions and conduct have embarrassed even his most devoted adherents. If this limited view is still to be accepted as sufficient and final, these criticisms must stand:—His advocacy of a weak national government; with his complaints that it was "a rope of sand," and his far-reaching augmentations to its power. His advocacy of a strict construing of our constitution; and yet his so exceeding the implied powers granted by it, as to make it, in his own words, "waste paper." His support of the State governments as "sovereign"; and his dislike and attempted changes in and over-riding of their constitutions. His arguments in favor of an absolutely independent jury and judiciary; and his attacks on both. His desire for a national navy; and his later opposition. His demands that the executive and legislative departments should be beyond reciprocal influence; yet, when president, his interference in the latter to an extent which led to a stinging rebuke on the floor of Congress in open debate. His dread of a partizan civil service as a means of influencing and defeating free elections, and his oft repeated claim that public officers should be selected only on their merit; while himself inaugurating the spoils system, sending his political friends commissions in blank, and retaining a federalist official "because of his connections." His disapproval of the re-eligibility of the president, and advocacy of rotation in office to prevent the creation of a bureaucracy; with his subsequent willingness that the former should serve more than two terms, and his writing to a superannuated appointee, "would it be a relief to transfer the office to your son, for your use, with the understanding that it should be afterwards continued with him for the benefit of the family?" His opposition to the alien act; and his framing of a bill directed against foreigners of far greater injustice than that enactment. His support of the passage of the funding and assumption act; and his unending opposition to its execution. His condemnation of the national bank, not merely on constitutional grounds, but because he believed it to be unduly influencing the national government; yet when himself at the head of that government advocating "a judicious distribution" of favors to that and other banks "to engage the individuals who belong to them in support" of his administration. His early opposition to national internal improvements, his later recommendation of this policy to Congress, and his final resolutions declaring it unconstitutional. His arguments and labors in opposition to slavery; while owning many negroes, and refusing to act as executor of a will because the testator freed his slaves—And many other actions apparently implying so little principle, or views so shifting, as superficially to reduce them to nothing else than a mass of inconsistencies, each one notable only for its immediate results. Judged by these standards, the marvel of the Federalists and his later critics, that he should have been the chosen instrument of American democracy, is proper. The scholarly and reclusive nature of his tastes and studies; the retiring and limited character of his intercourse with the world; the influence of his social equals; his dislike of party and personal antagonism; and his sensitiveness to abuse and criticism, make his acceptance of that leadership, as strange a problem, as that the people should have chosen for their representative a man lacking nearly all of the personal qualities which are presumed to win popularity with the masses. And only explicable from the narrow view of his critics as the success of an ambitious and unprincipled self-seeking man, attained by astuteness and chicane so great as to deceive the masses.

But if the people embody the total of human thought and experience, as our political theories maintain, there are better reasons than these for his elevation, and for the political influence his name has carried for over one hundred years— better reasons than the leadership of a party, or a fine-spun theory of the respective powers of the state and national governments. The explanation of these apparent anomalies lies deeper than any mere matter of individuality, party success, or rigid political platform. (pp. ix-xii)

To understand why Jefferson was one of the few men of intellect of his time able to appreciate, sympathize with, and aid this popular movement [toward democracy], a retrospect of certain factors in his life and times is necessary. Inheriting unsettling tendencies of mind, he was from an early age a thorough skeptic of tradition and precedent. In his own words, he never "feared to follow truth and reason to whatever results they led, and bearding every authority which stood in their way." Almost alone of the revolutionary leaders, he was born on the frontier, which, as already stated, was the ultimate of local self-government. Among those conditions he passed the formative period of his life, and as representative of this district he made his first essay in politics, naturally as an advocate and defender of the democratic mountaineers. In the Virginia Assembly, in which his earliest battles were fought, the strongest line of party division was between the aristocratic "planter" interest—great landed and slave-holding proprietors, with the prestige and inertia of favorable laws and offices—and the "settler" interest—inhabiting the frontier, far from the law or protection of government, but strong in numbers, independence, and necessities;—and in these conflicts he learned how absolutely selfish and grasping all class legislation is. Then came the Revolution, and Jefferson saw governments, deriving their authority from laws innumerable, and their force from the strongest nation of Europe, utterly destroyed, with hardly a blow, merely through their non-recognition by the masses. . . . Had he been in America between 1784 and 1788, he . . . might have become doubtful as to how far the masses could control themselves, for the reaction of the revolutionary struggle was severe, and strained democratic institutions almost to anarchy.

But at this time he was in France, witnessing another great struggle between the privileged and unprivileged. So he returned to America, true to the influences and lessons of his life, to find his theories in disfavor with the conservative, and government slipping more and more from the control of the governed. And because he believed that only the people truly knew what the people needed; that those who could take care of themselves were wise and practical enough to help care for the nation; and that the only way of enforcing laws was that they should be made by those who are to obey them, he undertook, with reluctance and self-sacrifice, to be the instrument of popular action. That he was the founder of the Democratic party is a claim little less than absurd, for there always has been, and always will be, such a party. But he united the democratic elements on certain principles and objects, and proved himself such a leader as the party has seldom been able to obtain.

Recognition of what he endeavored to accomplish explains many of his apparent inconsistencies. The dominant principle of his creed was that all powers belonged to the people, and that governments, constitutions, laws, precedent, and all other artificial clogs and "protections," are entitled to respect and obedience only as they fulfilled their limited function of aiding—not curtailing—the greatest freedom to the individual. For this reason, he held that no power existed to bind the people or posterity, except by their own acts. For this reason, he was the strict construer of the national constitution, where he believed it destructive of personal freedom; and construed it liberally where it threatened to limit the development of the people. He was the defender of the State governments; for he regarded them as a necessary division for local self-government and as natural checks on the national power, and so a safe-guard to the people. That he appealed to them in his resolutions of 1798, was because he believed the people for once unable to act for their own interest, and the theories of that paper are a radical and short-lived contradiction of his true beliefs. Because he believed the national judiciary and the national bank to be opposed to the will of the people, he attacked them. Because he believed he was furthering the popular will, he interfered in the legislative department and changed office-holders. Because he wished them free to think and act, he favored separation from England, abolition of slavery, free lands, free education, freedom of religion, and the largest degree of local self-government. His methods and results were not always good. His character and conduct had many serious flaws. Yet in some subtle way the people understood him, and forgave in him weaknesses and defects they have seldom condoned. And eventually this judgment will universally obtain, as the fact becomes clearer and clearer, that neither national independence, nor state sovereignty, with the national and party rancors that attach to them, were the controlling aim and attempt of his life; that no party or temporary advantage was the object of his endeavors, but that he fought for the ever enduring privilege of personal freedom. (pp. xv-xviii)

Paul Leicester Ford, in an introduction to Autobiography of Thomas Jefferson, 1743-1790 *by Thomas Jefferson, G. P. Putnam's Sons, 1914, pp. ix-xxxi.*

WOODROW WILSON   (essay date 1894)

[*Wilson was president of the United States from 1913 to 1921. In the following excerpt, he defines the qualities that he believes make a great American. He considers Jefferson a man of "mixed breed" because he adopted the political philosophies of other nations. Wilson contends that the influence of the French made Jefferson's philosophy "abstract, sentimental, rationalistic, rather than practical"; thus, while he conceded that Jefferson was a great man, Wilson does not consider him a great American. As this excerpt attests, in his early writings Wilson characterized Jefferson as an aristocrat; yet Wilson's opinion gradually changed, and in his later writings and political speeches he praised Jefferson for his frontier background, belief in the common man, and idealism tempered by practicality.]*

Jefferson was not a thorough American because of the strain of French philosophy that permeated and weakened all his thought. . . . He brought a foreign product of thought to a market where no natural or wholesome demand for it could exist. There were not two incompatible parts to him. . . : he was a philosophical radical by nature as well as by acquirement; his reading and his temperament went suitably together. The man is homogeneous throughout. The American shows in him very plainly, too, notwithstanding the strong and inherent dash of what was foreign in his make-up. He was a natural leader and manager of men, not because he was imperative or masterful, but because of a native shrewdness, tact, and sagacity, an inborn art and aptness for combination, such as no Frenchman ever displayed in the management of common men. Jefferson had just a touch of rusticity about him, besides; and it was not pretence on his part or merely a love of power that made him democratic. His indiscriminate hospitality, his almost passionate love for the simple equality of country life, his steady devotion to what he deemed to be the cause of the people, all mark him a genuine democrat, a nature native to America. It is his speculative philosophy that is exotic, and that runs like a false and artificial note through all his thought. It was un-American in being abstract, sentimental, rationalistic, rather than practical. That he held it sincerely need not be doubted; but the more sincerely he accepted it so much the more thoroughly was he un-American. His writings lack hard and practical sense. Liberty, among us, is not a sentiment, indeed, but a product of experience; its derivation is not rationalistic, but practical. It is a hard-headed spirit of independence, not the conclusion of a syllogism. The very aërated quality of Jefferson's principles gives them an air of insincerity, which attaches to them rather because they do not suit the climate of the country and the practical aspect of affairs than because they do not suit the character of Jefferson's mind and the atmosphere of abstract philosophy. It is because both they and the philosophical system of which they form a part do seem suitable to his mind and character, that we must pronounce him, though a great man, not a great American. (pp. 720-21)

Woodrow Wilson, "A Calendar of Great Americans," in Forum, *Vol. XVI, February, 1894, pp. 715-27.**

MOSES COIT TYLER (essay date 1897)

[*An American teacher, minister, and literary historian, Tyler was one of the first critics to examine American literature. His* History of American Literature During the Colonial Time: 1607-1765 *and* The Literary History of the American Revolution: 1763-1783 *are examples of his methodical research, authoritative style, and keen insight. While Tyler's* History of American Literature During the Colonial Time *is now considered dated, his study of the American Revolution remains a valuable sourcebook for modern scholars. The following excerpt was drawn from Tyler's* The Literary History of the American Revolution. *In portions of the essay not included below, Tyler recounts the events leading up to the selection of Jefferson to write the Declaration of Independence, his qualifications for that task, and the reactions of both English and*

American political leaders. Here, Tyler discusses its value as a political and historical document. After responding to the claims of John Adams (1822) and others that the Declaration lacks originality, Tyler evaluates the veracity of the document's two central charges: that the acts imposed by the British government exposed its desire to tyrannize the American colonists and that the king was chiefly responsible for these tyrannical acts. In addition, Tyler contends that the Declaration's continued importance as a political treatise is evident in its influence on later generations of Americans and readers abroad. Tyler concludes with a brief appreciation of the Declaration as a literary work, citing its perfect form, incisive thought, exquisite diction, moral earnestness, and emotional fervor.]

It can hardly be doubted that some hindrance to a right estimate of the **Declaration of Independence** is occasioned by either of two opposite conditions of mind, both of which are often to be met with among us: on the one hand, a condition of hereditary, uncritical awe and worship of the American Revolution and of this state paper as its absolutely perfect and glorious expression; on the other hand, a later condition of cultivated distrust of the **Declaration,** as a piece of writing lifted up into inordinate renown by the passionate and heroic circumstances of its origin, and ever since then extolled beyond reason by the blind energy of patriotic enthusiasm. Turning from the former state of mind,—which obviously calls for no further comment,—we may note, as a partial illustration of the latter, that American confidence in the supreme intellectual merit of this all-famous document received a serious wound, some forty years ago, from the hand of Rufus Choate, when, with a courage greater than would now be required for such an act, he characterized it as made up of "glittering and sounding generalities of natural right" [see Additional Bibliography]. What the great advocate then so unhesitantly suggested, many a thoughtful American since then has at least suspected,—that this famous proclamation, as a piece of political literature, cannot stand the test of modern analysis; that it belongs to the immense class of over-praised productions; that it is, in fact, a stately patchwork of sweeping propositions of somewhat doubtful validity; that it has long imposed upon mankind by the well-known effectiveness of verbal glitter and sound; that, at the best, it is an example of florid political declamation belonging to the sophomoric period of our national life—a period which, as we flatter ourselves, we have now outgrown.

Nevertheless, it is to be noted that, whatever authority the **Declaration of Independence** has acquired in the world, has been due to no lack of criticism, either at the time of its first appearance or since then,—a fact which seems to tell in favor of its essential worth and strength. From the date of its original publication down to the present moment, it has been attacked again and again, either in anger or in contempt, by friends as well as by enemies of the American Revolution, by liberals in politics as well as by conservatives. It has been censured for its substance, it has been censured for its form: for its misstatements of fact, for its fallacies in reasoning; for its audacious novelties and paradoxes, for its total lack of all novelty, for its repetition of old and threadbare statements, even for its downright plagiarisms; finally, for its grandiose and vaporing style. (pp. 498-99)

Perhaps nowhere in our literature would it be possible to find a criticism brought forward by a really able man against any piece of writing, less applicable to the case, and of less force or value, than is this particular criticism by John Adams and others, as to the lack of originality in the **Declaration of Independence.** Indeed, for such a paper as Jefferson was commissioned to write, the one quality which it could not properly have had—the one quality which would have been fatal to its acceptance either by the American Congress or by the American people—is originality. They were then at the culmination of a tremendous controversy over alleged grievances of the most serious kind—a controversy that had been fiercely raging for at least twelve years. In the course of that long dispute, every phase of it, whether as to abstract right or constitutional privilege or personal procedure, had been presented in almost every conceivable form of speech. At last, they had resolved, in view of all this experience, no longer to prosecute the controversy as members of the empire: they had resolved to revolt, and casting off forever their ancient fealty to the British crown, to separate from the empire, and to establish themselves as a new nation among the nations of the earth. In this emergency, as it happened, Jefferson was called upon to put into form a suitable statement of the chief considerations which prompted them to this great act of revolution, and which, as they believed, justified it. What, then, was Jefferson to do? Was he to regard himself as a mere literary essayist, set to produce before the world a sort of prize dissertation,—a calm, analytic, judicial treatise on history and politics with a particular application to Anglo-American affairs,—one essential merit of which would be its originality as a contribution to historical and political literature? Was he not, rather, to regard himself as, for the time being, the very mouthpiece and prophet of the people whom he represented, and as such required to bring together and to set in order, in their name, not what was new, but what was old; to gather up into his own soul, as much as possible, whatever was then also in their souls—their very thoughts and passions, their ideas of constitutional law, their interpretations of fact, their opinions as to men and as to events in all that ugly quarrel; their notions of justice, of civic dignity, of human rights; finally, their memories of wrongs which seemed to them intolerable, especially of wrongs inflicted upon them during those twelve years by the hands of insolent and brutal men, in the name of the king, and by his apparent command?

Moreover, as the nature of the task laid upon him made it necessary that he should thus state, as the reasons for their intended act, those very considerations both as to fact and as to opinion which had actually operated upon their minds, so did it require him to do so, to some extent, in the very language which the people themselves, in their more formal and deliberate utterances, had all along been using. In the development of political life in England and America, there had already been created a vast literature of constitutional progress,—a literature common to both portions of the English race, pervaded by its own stately traditions, and reverberating certain great phrases which formed, as one may say, almost the vernacular of English justice, and of English aspiration for a free, manly, and orderly political life. In this vernacular the **Declaration of Independence** was written. The phraseology thus characteristic of it, is the very phraseology of the champions of constitutional expansion, of civic dignity and of progress, within the English race ever since Magna Charta; of the great state papers of English freedom in the seventeenth century, particularly the Petition of Right in 1629, and the Bill of Rights in 1689; of the great English charters for colonization in America; of the great English exponents of legal and political progress,—Sir Edward Coke, John Milton, Algernon Sidney, John Locke; finally, of the great American exponents of political liberty and of the chief representative bodies, whether local or general, which had convened in America from the time of the Stamp Act Congress until that of the Congress which resolved upon our Independence. To say, therefore, that the official **Declaration** of that resolve is a paper made up of the very opinions,

beliefs, unbeliefs, the very sentiments, prejudices, passions, even the errors in judgment and the personal misconstructions—if they were such—which then actually impelled the American people to that mighty act, and that all these are expressed in the very phrases which they had been accustomed to use, is to pay to that state paper the highest tribute as to its fitness for the purpose for which it was framed. (pp. 505-07)

Before passing from this phase of the subject, however, it should be added that, while the **Declaration of Independence** lacks originality in the sense just indicated, in another and perhaps in a higher sense, it possesses originality—it is individualized by the character and the genius of its author. Jefferson gathered up the thoughts and emotions and even the characteristic phrases of the people for whom he wrote, and these he perfectly incorporated with what was already in his own mind, and then to the music of his own keen, rich, passionate, and enkindling style, he mustered them into that stately and triumphant procession wherein, as some of us still think, they will go marching on to the world's end.

There were then in Congress several other men who could have written the **Declaration of Independence,** and written it well—notably, Franklin, either of the two Adamses, Richard Henry Lee, William Livingston, and, best of all—but for his own opposition to the measure—John Dickinson; but had any one of these other men written the **Declaration of Independence,** while it would have contained, doubtless, nearly the same topics and nearly the same great formulas of political statement, it would yet have been a wholly different composition from this of Jefferson's. No one at all familiar with his other writings as well as with the writings of his chief contemporaries, could ever have a moment's doubt, even if the fact were not already notorious, that this document was by Jefferson. He put into it something that was his own, and that no one else could have put there. He put himself into it,—his own genius, his own moral force, his faith in God, his faith in ideas, his love of innovation, his passion for progress, his invincible enthusiasm, his intolerance of prescription, of injustice, of cruelty, his sympathy, his clarity of vision, his affluence of diction, his power to fling out great phrases which will long fire and cheer the souls of men struggling against political unrighteousness. And herein lies its essential originality, perhaps the most precious, and indeed almost the only, originality ever attaching to any great literary product that is representative of its time. He made for himself no improper claim, therefore, when he directed that upon the granite obelisk at his grave should be carved the words,—"Here was buried Thomas Jefferson, author of the **Declaration of Independence.**"

If the **Declaration of Independence** is now to be fairly judged by us, it must be judged with reference to what it was intended to be—namely, an impassioned manifesto of one party, and that the weaker party, in a violent race quarrel; of a party resolved, at last, upon the extremity of revolution, and already menaced by the inconceivable disaster of being defeated in the very act of armed rebellion against the mightiest military power on earth. This manifesto, then, is not to be censured because, being avowedly a statement of its own side of the quarrel, it does not also contain a moderate and judicial statement of the opposite side; or because, being necessarily partisan in method, it is likewise both partisan and vehement in tone; or because it bristles with accusations against the enemy so fierce and so unqualified as now to seem in some respects overdrawn; or because it resounds with certain great aphorisms about the natural rights of man, at which, indeed, political science cannot

"The Declaration of Independence" by John Trumbull. This painting depicts the presentation of the Declaration to Congress. Jefferson is the tallest of the five committee members standing in the center. Copyright Yale University Art Gallery.

now smile except to its own discomfiture and shame—aphorisms which are likely to abide in this world as the chief source and inspiration of heroic enterprises among men for self-deliverance from oppression.

Taking into account, therefore, as we are bound to do, the circumstances of its origin, and especially its purpose as a solemn and piercing appeal to mankind, on behalf of a small and weak nation against the alleged injustice and cruelty of a great and powerful one, it still remains our duty to enquire whether, as has been asserted in our time, history must set aside either of the two central charges embodied in the **Declaration of Independence.**

The first of these charges affirms that the several acts complained of by the colonists, evinced "a design to reduce them under absolute despotism," and had as their "direct object the establishment of an absolute tyranny" over the American people. Was this, indeed, a groundless charge, in the sense intended by the words "despotism" and "tyranny,"—that is, in the sense commonly given to those words in the usage of the English-speaking race? (pp. 508-10)

Accordingly, the meaning which the English race on both sides of the Atlantic were accustomed to attach to the words "tyranny" and "despotism," was a meaning to some degree ideal: it was a meaning drawn from the extraordinary political sa-

gacity with which that race is endowed, from their extraordinary sensitiveness as to the use of the taxing-power in government, from their instinctive perception of the commanding place of the taxing-power among all the other forms of power in the state, from their perfect assurance that he who holds the purse with the power to fill it and to empty it, holds the key of the situation,—can maintain an army of his own, can rule without consulting parliament, can silence criticism, can crush opposition, can strip his subjects of every vestige of political life; in other words, he can make slaves of them, he can make a despot and a tyrant of himself. Therefore, the system which in the end might develop into results so palpably tyrannic and despotic, they bluntly called a tyranny and a despotism in the beginning. To say, therefore, that the **Declaration of Independence** did the same, is to say that it spoke good English. Of course, history will be ready to set aside the charge thus made in language not at all liable to be misunderstood, just so soon as history is ready to set aside the common opinion that the several acts of the British government, from 1763 to 1776, for laying and enforcing taxation in America, did evince a somewhat particular and systematic design to take away some portion of the property of the American people without their consent.

The second of the two great charges contained in the **Declaration of Independence,** while intimating that some share in the blame is due to the British parliament and to the British people, yet fastens upon the king himself as the one person chiefly responsible for the scheme of American tyranny therein set forth, and culminates in the frank description of him as "a prince whose character is thus marked by every act which may define a tyrant." Is this accusation of George the Third now to be set aside as unhistoric? Was that king, or was he not, chiefly responsible for the American policy of the British government between the years 1763 and 1776? If he was so, then the historic soundness of the most important portion of the **Declaration of Independence** is vindicated.

Fortunately, this question can be answered without hesitation, and in few words; and for these few words, an American writer of to-day, conscious of his own bias of nationality, will rightly prefer to cite such as have been uttered by the ablest English historians of our time, who have dealt with the subject. Upon their statements alone it must be concluded, that George the Third ascended his throne with the fixed purpose of resuming to the crown many of those powers which by the constitution of England did not then belong to it, and that in this purpose, at least during the first twenty-five years of his reign, he substantially succeeded,—himself determining what opinions his ministers should advocate in parliament, and what measures parliament itself should adopt. (pp. 511-13)

[There] need be no anxiety in any quarter as to the historic soundness of the two great accusations which together make up the principal portion of the **Declaration of Independence.** In the presence of these verdicts, also, even the passion, the intensity of language, in which those accusations are uttered, seem to find a perfect justification. Indeed, in the light of the most recent and most unprejudiced expert testimony, the whole document, both in its substance and in its form, seems to have been the logical response of a nation of brave men. . . . (pp. 514-15)

It is proper for us to remember that what we call criticism, is not the only valid test of the genuineness and worth of any piece of writing of great practical interest to mankind: there is, also, the test of actual use and service in the world, in direct contact with the common sense and the moral sense of large masses of men, under various conditions, and for a long period. Probably no writing which is not essentially sound and true has ever survived this test.

Neither from this test has the great **Declaration** any need to shrink. Probably no public paper ever more perfectly satisfied the immediate purposes for which it was sent forth. From one end of the country to the other, and as fast as it could be spread among the people, it was greeted in public and in private with every demonstration of approval and delight. To a marvelous degree, it quickened the friends of the Revolution for their great task. (p. 515)

Moreover, during the century and a quarter since the close of the Revolution, the influence of this state paper on the political character and the political conduct of the American people has been great beyond all calculation. For example, after we had achieved our own national deliverance, and had advanced into that enormous and somewhat corrupting material prosperity which followed the adoption of the constitution, the development of the cotton interest, and the expansion of the republic into a trans-continental power, we fell, as is now most apparent, under an appalling national temptation,—the temptation to forget, or to repudiate, or to refuse to apply to the case of our human brethren in bondage, the very principles which we ourselves had once proclaimed as the basis of every rightful gov-

ernment, and as the ultimate source of our own claim to an untrammeled national life. The prodigious service rendered to us in this awful moral emergency by the **Declaration of Independence** was, that its public repetition, at least once every year, in the hearing of vast throngs of the American people, in every portion of the republic, kept constantly before our minds, in a form of almost religious sanctity, those few great ideas as to the dignity of human nature, and the sacredness of personality, and the indestructible rights of man as mere man, with which we had so gloriously identified the beginnings of our national existence, and upon which we had proceeded to erect all our political institutions both for the nation and for the States. It did, indeed, at last become very hard for us to listen each year to the preamble of the **Declaration of Independence,** and still to remain the owners and users and catchers of slaves; still harder, to accept the doctrine that the righteousness and prosperity of slavery was to be taken as the dominant policy of the nation. The logic of Calhoun was as flawless as usual, when he concluded that the chief obstruction in the way of his system, was the preamble of the **Declaration of Independence.** Had it not been for the inviolable sacredness given by it to those sweeping aphorisms about the natural rights of man, it may be doubted whether, under the vast practical inducements involved, Calhoun might not have succeeded in winning over an immense majority of the American people to the support of his compact and plausible scheme for making slavery the basis of the republic. It was the preamble of the **Declaration of Independence** which elected Lincoln, which sent forth the Emancipation Proclamation, which gave victory to Grant, which ratified the Thirteenth Amendment.

Moreover, we cannot doubt that the permanent effects of the great **Declaration** on the political and even the ethical ideals of the American people are wider and deeper than can be measured by our experience in grappling with any single political problem; for they touch all the spiritual springs of American national character, and they create, for us and for all human beings, a new standard of political justice and a new principle in the science of government. (pp. 516-17)

We shall not here attempt to delineate the influence of this state paper upon mankind in general. Of course, the emergence of the American Republic as an imposing world-power is a phenomenon which has now for many years attracted the attention of the human race. Surely, no slight effect must have resulted from the fact that, among all civilized peoples, the one American document best known, is the **Declaration of Independence** and that thus the spectacle of so vast and beneficent a political success has been everywhere associated with the assertion of the natural rights of man. . . . [In] many lands, among many peoples, it has been appealed to again and again as an inspiration for political courage, as a model for political conduct; and if, as the brilliant English historian . . . has affirmed, "that noble **Declaration** . . . ought to be hung up in the nursery of every king, and blazoned on the porch of every royal palace," it is because it has become the classic statement of political truths which must at last abolish kings altogether, or else teach them to identify their existence with the dignity and happiness of human nature.

It would be unfitting, in a work like the present, to treat of the **Declaration of Independence** without making more than an incidental reference to its purely literary character.

Very likely, most writings—even most writings of genuine and high quality—have had the misfortune of being read too little. There is, however, a misfortune—perhaps, a greater misfortune—which has overtaken some literary compositions, and these not necessarily the noblest and the best,—the misfortune of being read too much. At any rate, the writer of a piece of literature which has been neglected, need not be refused the consolation he may get from reflecting that he is, at least, not the writer of a piece of literature which has become hackneyed. Just this is the sort of calamity which seems to have befallen the **Declaration of Independence.** Is it, indeed, possible for us Americans, near the close of the nineteenth century, to be entirely just to the literary quality of this most monumental document—this much belauded, much bespouted, much beflouted document?—since, in order to be so, we need to rid ourselves, if we can, of the obstreperous memories of a lifetime of Independence Days, and to unlink and disperse the associations which have somehow confounded Jefferson's masterpiece with the rattle of fire-crackers, with the flash and the splutter of burning tar-barrels, and with that unreserved, that gyratory and perspiratory, eloquence now for more than a hundred years consecrated to the return of our fateful Fourth of July.

Had the **Declaration of Independence** been, what many a revolutionary state paper is, a clumsy, verbose, and vaporing production, not even the robust literary taste and the all-forgiving patriotism of the American people could have endured the weariness, the nausea, of hearing its repetition, in ten thousand different places, at least once every year, for so long a period. Nothing which has not supreme literary merit has ever triumphantly endured such an ordeal, or ever been subjected to it. No man can adequately explain the persistent fascination which this state-paper has had, and which it still has, for the American people, or for its undiminished power over them, without taking into account its extraordinary literary merits— its possession of the witchery of true substance wedded to perfect form:—its massiveness and incisiveness of thought, its art in the marshaling of the topics with which it deals, its symmetry, its energy, the definiteness and limpidity of its statements, its exquisite diction—at once terse, musical, and electrical; and, as an essential part of his literary outfit, many of those spiritual notes which can attract and enthrall our hearts,— veneration for God, veneration for man, veneration for principle, respect for public opinion, moral earnestness, moral courage, optimism, a stately and noble pathos, finally, self-sacrificing devotion to a cause so great as to be herein identified with the happiness, not of one people only, or of one race only, but of human nature itself.

Upon the whole, this is the most commanding and the most pathetic utterance, in any age, in any language, of national grievances and of national purposes; having a Demosthenic momentum of thought, and a fervor of emotional appeal such as Tyrtaeus might have put into his war-songs. Indeed, the **Declaration of Independence** is a kind of war-song; it is a stately and a passionate chant of human freedom; it is a prose lyric of civil military heroism. We may be altogether sure that no genuine development of literary taste among the American people in any period of our future history can result in serious misfortune to this particular specimen of American literature. (pp. 518-21)

> *Moses Coit Tyler, "Thomas Jefferson and the Great Declaration," in his* The Literary History of the American Revolution, 1763-1783: 1763-1776, Vol. I, *G. P. Putnam's Sons, 1897, pp. 494-521.*

CHARLES EDWARD MERRIAM (essay date 1903)

[*Merriam examines Jefferson's official papers and correspondence to reconstruct and explicate his political theories. The critic includes discussions of Jefferson's views on natural rights, alternate means of perpetuating the social contract, and several forms of government, including monarchy, aristocracy, and democracy. Merriam contends that Jefferson's correspondence with John Adams contains the essence of his views on democracy. While Adams doubted the people's ability to govern themselves and sought legal recognition of the aristocracy, Jefferson trusted the people's rationality, sense of justice, and judgment; thus, "the essence, then, of Jefferson's democracy was confidence in the self-governing capacity of the great mass of the people."*]

No name is more often or more intimately associated with American democracy than that of Thomas Jefferson. During his lifetime he was the American democrat *par excellence;* on his death he was politically canonized, and his words are still quoted with confidence and received with respect in the consideration of almost all political questions. Brought into prominence as the author of the **Declaration of Independence,** identified with the growth and triumph of the Republican party, inaugurated as its first President, framing its policies and providing its philosophy, Jefferson was undoubtedly the central figure in the early development of American democracy.

Though regarded as the great advocate of democracy, Jefferson bequeathed to posterity no systematic treatise on the principles of politics. His *Summary View . . .* and *Notes on Virginia . . .* are the nearest approach to his, and they can scarcely be considered an approximation. Moreover, he was not a great orator, and there is no collection of addresses in which his ideas are embodied. He was, however, a great correspondent, and we have a large collection of his letters, written to such persons as Madison, John Adams, Lafayette, Dupont de Nemours, Taylor, Kercheval, Johnston, and others. From this extensive correspondence, in which topics of political theory frequently appear, together with some of his official papers, it is possible to reconstruct the theory of Jefferson, if not in minute detail, at least in general outline.

The first important statement of Jefferson's political theory is contained in the **Declaration of Independence.** Here are eloquently expressed the now familiar doctrines of human equality, of the natural and inalienable rights of man, of the guaranty of these rights as the first cause of government, and of the right and duty of revolution when they are subverted. These doctrines, it is perhaps needless to say, were not original with the writer of the **Declaration.** They were the common property of his time, were on the lips of every patriot orator, and found copious expression in resolutions throughout the colonies. It was later charged that the substance of the **Declaration** had been "hackneyed in Congress for two years before" [see excerpt by John Adams dated 1822]. Jefferson himself was fully conscious that the originality of the statements lay in their form, rather than in their content, and his own explanation of his work is excellent: "Neither aiming at originality of principle or sentiment, nor yet copied from any particular or previous writings, it was intended to be an expression of the American mind, and to give to that expression the proper tone and spirit called for by the occasion" [see excerpt dated 1825]. Jefferson crystallized the common sentiment into a very effective form, but he could not and did not claim for himself the merit of presenting to the world a series of new or hitherto undiscovered truths. This is not to say, however, that the authorship of the **Declaration** was not a signal distinction; it merely changes the category in which the distinction lay.

Inquiring more closely into Jefferson's theory of inalienable rights, we find him protesting against the idea that we surrender any of our natural rights on entering into society. Jefferson argues that these rights are not given up, but, on the contrary, are rendered more secure. He holds that the state should declare and enforce our rights, but should take none of them from us. Reasoning in this way, it is possible, he thinks, to mark out the proper sphere of state activity. Thus, as no man has a natural right to interfere with the rights of others, it is the duty of the law to restrain every one from such interference. Every man should contribute to the necessities of society; therefore the law should see that he does so. No man has a natural right to judge in his own cause; therefore the law must judge. Thus it appears that one does not lose his natural rights under government, but obtains a better guaranty of them.

Government is established, however, by the "consent of the governed," or at least a just government is so supported. What, then, is the nature of this consent, and how is it to be made effective amid constantly changing conditions? Jefferson was not satisfied with a contract made once and for all, like that of Hobbes, or with a merely hypothetical contract or even with a presumption of tacit consent from the fact of residence. He looked upon the government, and he considered that the agreement should have historical as well as logical validity. The principle of the social contract must be sacredly preserved in the life of the people, and Jefferson proposed two ways of insuring this end: first, by revolution; second, by periodical renewal of the agreement.

Revolution, Jefferson did not regard with great horror, if principle were involved in the process. He did not believe in government as something so sacred in nature as to be above human criticism. He did not "look at constitutions with sanctimonious reverence and deem them like the ark of the covenant, too sacred to be touched." Government appeared to him as an institution existing for the governed; and if it failed to serve this purpose, then it might be overthrown and another erected on its ruins. So far did he go in this direction that the beneficent elements in government were at times almost lost to view. He declared his dislike of energetic government because it is always oppressive. He was on one occasion doubtful whether the first state of man, without government, as he says, would not be the most desirable, if the society were not too large. He thought that republics should not be too severe in their treatment of rebellions, lest the free spirit of the people be suppressed. (pp. 145-49)

The idea of adherence to the principle of the social contract finds a less violent expression in Jefferson's argument for periodical renewals of the agreement. Rebellion or revolution serves to keep alive the public spirit; but it acts through irregular and illegal channels, and hence is best adapted to countries where the government is tyrannically inclined. For a free state, however, there are other plans that may be followed, without passing outside the boundaries of the law. A convention, reconsidering the organic law of the land and submitting the result of its deliberations to the people, really constitutes, he maintains, a renewal of the fundamental agreement. In this way the "consent of the governed" may be again invoked and the government reëstablished on a just foundation. Each generation, such is the argument, has a right to establish its own law. "The earth belongs in usufruct to the living; the dead have neither powers nor rights over it." It follows, then, that no generation of men can pass any law binding for a period longer than the lifetime of that generation, because their lawmaking power ceases with their existence. If one generation could bind another, the dead and not the living would rule. Since conditions change and men change, there must be op-

portunity for corresponding change in political institutions, and also for a renewal of the principle of government by consent of the governed. (pp. 150-51)

Having considered Jefferson's theory as to the basis of the government, it is now in order to examine his position as to the various classes of government. What, then, was his opinion of monarchy? The government of a king Jefferson regarded, at least in the earlier part of his life, with utter abhorrence. Though not the equal of Paine in the vigor of his invective against kings, he was but little inferior. He declared that "no race of kings has ever presented above one man of common sense in twenty generations." . . . Jefferson's favorite and perhaps most effective form of attack upon his opponents was to arouse the suspicion that they were at heart monarchists, longing for the restoration of royalty. In later years, however, after the failure of the European revolutions to establish democracy, he was inclined to concede that under certain conditions a monarchy might really be the most desirable form of government.

The next point of inquiry is Jefferson's opinion of aristocracy. Judging from his famous utterance, "All men are created equal," he is generally regarded as the great champion of human equality. Against this is sometimes urged the fact that the ownership of slaves is hardly in keeping with ideas of universal equality. It should not be forgotten, however, that Jefferson was really opposed to the institution of negro slavery and more than once went on record against it. . . . (pp. 153-55)

Aside from this point, however, it is easy to show that Jefferson was not at all a believer in the absolute equality of men. In this connection it is interesting to examine his correspondence with John Adams upon this very question of aristocracy. Adams denounces in set terms the theory of the equality of all men, declares that society is divided into two classes, "gentlemen" and "simplemen," and demands the legal recognition of this difference in ability. Jefferson does not deny the existence of an aristocracy among men, but distinguishes between the *natural* aristocracy and the *artificial* aristocracy. One is based upon virtue and talent, the other upon wealth and birth. The "natural aristocracy" appears to him as the "most precious gift of nature," and highly useful for the purpose of instructing and governing society. He even goes so far as to say, "That form of government is the best which provides the most effectively for a pure selection of these natural *aristoi* into the offices of government." The "artificial aristocracy," based on wealth and birth, is mischievous, even dangerous, and should not receive legal recognition. In reply to Adams's proposition that the aristocracy should be represented in one legislative chamber and the people in the other, he urges that the separation of the pseudo-aristocracy from the genuine should be left to the people themselves. Some mistakes will doubtless be made, but the really good and wise will generally be selected. Jefferson, it may be said, believed in an aristocracy, but only in the sense that the best fitted for governing should rule, and that the selection of the *aristoi* should rule, and that the selection of the *aristoi* should be made by popular election rather than on a basis of birth or wealth. He wanted aristocratic rulers democratically chosen. (pp. 155-56)

Having reviewed his ideas on monarchy and aristocracy, it remains to consider Jefferson's doctrine of democracy. What was the theory of "Jeffersonian democracy"? The doctrines of natural rights and the "consent of the governed" have already been examined; but, more specifically, what was his idea as to the characteristic features of a democratic government?

This is not easy to determine; for, in the first place, his notions were never systematically and not always clearly expressed; and, in the second place, there are contradictions between his political theory and his practical politics. The theory of Jefferson, the political scientist, and the practice of Jefferson, the man of affairs, are not always free from inconsistency. An effort will be made there, however, to show as clearly as possible from the scattered sources at command what Jefferson's theory of democracy really was.

Jefferson defines a republic as "a government by the [its] citizens in mass, acting directly and personally, according to rules established by the majority." Governments are republican in proportion to the degree of direct action on the part of the citizens, and there are of course many varying degrees. This is, however, only a very general statement and lacks definiteness of outline. One of the best supplementary explanations is that found in Jefferson's first inaugural address [see excerpt dated 1801]. Here are laid down the main principles which should obtain within a democracy. They include, among others, the following propositions: equal and exact justice; jealous care of the right of election by the people; the rule of the majority; the preservation of the guaranties of civil liberty, such as freedom of religion, freedom of the press, the habeas corpus and jury trial; the subordination of the military to the civil authority; and economical administration. In these phrases are summed up his democratic program, and under his type of government they would all be found in operation.

Further evidence as to Jefferson's notion of democracy is given by examination of what he once termed the "two hooks" upon which republican government depends. These were an educational system and a scheme of local government. Keenly appreciating the necessity of popular intelligence as a basis for successful popular government, Jefferson was a constant advocate of all measures for the diffusion of knowledge among the masses. If government rests upon public opinion, he said, then our first and foremost care is to see that this opinion is kept right. Opinion that is unenlightened and unsound would be the death of free government. He once said that, if forced to choose between a government without newspapers and newspapers without a government, he would not hesitate to choose the latter alternative, assuming that every man received the papers and were capable of understanding them. Jefferson exerted himself in behalf of educational institutions in his own state, and to his earnest efforts was largely due the establishment of the University of Virginia.

The second "hook" was local government. Referring to his experience at the time of the Embargo Act, Jefferson said: "I felt the foundations of the government shaken under my feet by the New England townships." He recommended for Virginia a system of local government modelled quite closely after the New England type, to take the place of the "large and lubberly divisions into counties." "Wards" were to take charge of the elementary schools, to care for the poor and the roads, and to have a system of justices, constables, and police. But the "ward" was merely one step in the scheme of governmental gradation which Jefferson had in mind. He conceived that liberty should be secured, not only by a tripartite division of governmental powers, but also by a further distribution among a series of organizations extending from ward to nation. First should come the elementary republics or wards, then the country republics, then the states, and finally the nation. Governmental powers should be delegated "by a synthetical process to higher and higher orders of functionaries, so as to trust fewer

and fewer powers in proportion as the trustees become more and more oligarchical." Local government would thus be made a part of the complicated "check and balance" system in the intricacies of which despotism would be entangled and rendered powerless.

Another feature in the Jeffersonian program should perhaps receive mention at this point; namely, the plea for the subordination of the military to the civil authority. He argued against a large standing army as a likely instrument of oppression. Absolute governments must depend upon force, but a free state, he held, should place its confidence in the good-will of its citizens. So far as military power is necessary for purposes of defence, the need should be supplied by a well-disciplined militia. A standing army was associated with monarchical power, and it was, therefore, a part of the republican policy to reduce the army and the navy to as low a footing as possible. Under Jefferson this was the line of conduct followed by the administration. . . . The suppression of the military power was undoubtedly one of the features in the Republican plan for governmental regeneration—indeed, it has been urged that this was the real significance of the transition in 1801; but Jefferson did not present any very elaborate arguments upon the question, and it did not occupy a very prominent place in his political theory.

Thus far this inquiry has extended into Jefferson's definition of a republic and an examination of various features included in the program of such a government. Yet all these considerations fail to show what was the real essence of Jeffersonian democracy. They reveal in part his policy, but his policy was never complete either in theory or in actual practice. That which gave life and color to all these measures for democratic reform was the article in the Jeffersonian political creed which must now be considered. The distinctive and characteristic feature of his doctrine is most clearly expressed in his correspondence with John Adams; here may be seen the real difference that divided these two great leaders, one the advocate of the "well-born," the other the apostle of democracy—their opinions characteristic of two great parties and of two great schools of political thought. (pp. 157-62)

Adams was anxious for a balanced government of the most complex nature, including, as one of its elements, a legal recognition of the aristocracy, and . . . he appeared to doubt and distrust the capacity of the people for any high degree of self-government.

Against such a theory, Jefferson maintained that men are naturally divided into two classes: (1) those who fear and distrust the people; (2) those who identify themselves with the people, have confidence in them, consider them as the most honest and safe, although not always the most wise, depositories of public interests.

In the opinion of the first class, the masses must be held in check by physical and moral force, and can be restrained in no other way; men are essentially incapable of ruling themselves, and must be governed by authorities independent of their will and not subject to their judgment. But the second class, on the other hand, argues Jefferson, place their trust in popular capacity for self-government, maintaining that man is a rational animal, possessing a natural and innate sense of justice, and that for the preservation of peace and order he does not require restraint from above or outside, but is competent to choose his own rulers and hold them dependent on his will. The same idea as to the two classes of opinions is expressed in a letter to Dupont de Nemours, in which Jefferson says: "We both love the people, but you love them as infants whom you are afraid to trust without nurses, and I as adults whom I freely leave to self-government."

The essence, then, of Jefferson's democracy was confidence in the self-governing capacity of the great mass of the people— a belief in the ability of the average man or of average men to select rulers who will conduct the administration in general accord with the interests of the society. The divergence of opinion just here made Adams an aristocrat and Jefferson a democrat—not that Adams had no confidence, or that Jefferson had all confidence, in the people, but the degrees of confidence differed widely. We might say that one looked with suspicion on the people first of all, the other distrusted first the government and after that the people. Both favored a balanced government; but Adams desired primarily to prevent violent action on the part of the people, whereas Jefferson's first aim was to prevent oppression by the government; one reasoned that the people should be watched, the other that the government should be kept in constant view. Confidence in the people was, therefore, the distinguishing characteristic in the *theory* of Jeffersonian democracy. (pp. 162-64)

[What] should be said of Jefferson's rank as a political theorist? The important service rendered by the Sage of Monticello was not the scientific elucidation of theory. The doctrines he advocated had all been discussed and developed long before his time, and he did not improve much on the classic analysis of Aristotle, the reasoning of Locke, or the brilliant logic of Rousseau. He cannot be classed as one of the great political thinkers. He did not inquire deeply into the nature of the state, its forms of organization, or any of the numerous problems arising out of the complex relations of political association. He did not write systematically at all, and what he did write was notable rather because of its rhetoric than because of its scientific depth or clearness. Tested by the canons of the schools, Jefferson falls far short of the stature of a great political philosopher.

What, then, shall be said of this personality so preëminent in the annals of American democracy? What was the source of his power, and what the significance of his career? One great cause of his power was the unusual sagacity and astuteness that made him a great party leader. With a "machine" that was ill organized, if organized at all, and with little patronage, Jefferson's political genius guided the Republicans on to the destruction of their rivals. Another cause was his singular gift for vivid statement of popular ideas. He crystallized the common democratic sentiment, giving it form and power. He was great in his ability to interpret and express popular feeling. And finally, he had great confidence in the people. He believed in their capacity for self-government, had confidence in the soundness of their judgment, and was hopeful of the future of democratic institutions. In spite of the many inconsistencies in his conduct, Jefferson stands out as the great apostle of the democratic faith in his day. He appeared as the advocate of the "people" against the claims of "monarchists" and "aristocrats." He not only defended the people on theoretical grounds, but he was identified with a fairly definite program of democratic reform, a part of which he was successful in carrying out, and much of which was realized later under the Jacksonian democracy. He stood for the extension of the suffrage, periodical revision of the Constitution, religious liberty, subordination of military to civil authority, the maintenance of local governments as a barrier against excessive centralization, and for a certain democratic simplicity in place of the elaborate ceremony of kings and courts. This was the framework of his political system, while the life and spirit of it was faith in the self-governing capacity of the people. (pp. 171-73)

Charles Edward Merriam, "The Jeffersonian Democracy," in his A History of American Political Theories, *The Macmillan Company, 1903, pp. 143-75.*

CHARLES EMORY SMITH   (essay date 1903)

[*Smith explains the importance of the Louisiana Purchase to the growth of the nation and to Jefferson's political stature. While noting that the act was inconsistent with the principles espoused in the Declaration of Independence and the Constitution, Smith describes the Louisiana Purchase as "an act of transcendent statesmanship."*]

The Louisiana Purchase was, by common consent, the supreme act of the administration of Thomas Jefferson as President, though he makes no reference to it in citing the features of his career which he chose to have perpetuated in his epitaph. For that commemoration he chose principles rather than acts. There have been others who have framed or founded universities. There have been others who have framed statutes of religious liberty. But there was only one Louisiana Purchase.

I venture to think that there are three great master facts upon which the enduring fame of Jefferson will rest: First, he was the author of the **Declaration of Independence**; second, he was the founder and leader of a great party, of a school of political thought which, under varying names, has divided the republic from the beginning to the present time; third, he made the Louisiana Purchase. In its historical importance this great act ranks with half a dozen of the most momentous and epochal events in our national annals, with his own **Declaration of Independence,** with the adoption of the Constitution, with the molding of national power through constitutional construction by Chief Justice Marshall, with the abolition of slavery, with the overthrow of secession and the complete triumph of an indissoluble union, and with the Spanish war and all its far-reaching consequences. The Louisiana Purchase nearly doubled the boundaries of the republic. It added to her territory a little less than a million square miles of territory. It broadened the domain of our country by an extension which was larger in itself than Great Britain, France, Germany, Spain, Portugal and Italy combined. It gave us what has become one of the most fertile and opulent sections of the nation and the home of nearly fifteen millions of happy and contented Americans. It was an indispensable preliminary to the later acquisition of that vast domain which extends from the Gulf to Vancouver, embracing Texas, California, Oregon and Washington, and which added more than a million square miles to our territory, now the home of six millions more of thrifty and happy Americans who live and move and have their being within its domain. It was the first great expansion of the republic, and the manifesto of its continued extension with the advance of the world. (pp. i-ii)

It has often been urged that in this great act, the greatest act of our history between the adoption of the Constitution and the Civil War, Jefferson was inconsistent with his principles and his professions. He was the leader of the strict constructionists and this act was outside of the strict letter of the Constitution. But that charge of inconsistency can be made with equal force against every great party and almost every conspicuous statesman in our history. (p. iv)

It would be, indeed, easy to find inconsistencies between the principles of the **Declaration of Independence** and the practice of the Louisiana Purchase. What of it? When it comes to an issue between an abstract doctrine and vital practical statesmanship what masterful man, with great destinies in his hand, does not turn from the theoretical dogma to the living and commanding act? What true statesman permits a general and vague conception to paralyze a distinct, definite and unmistakable good? As a political philosopher Jefferson taught great doctrines. As President of the United States he met the direct and immediate responsibilities. He did not violate the Constitution—whatever was said at the time, we know it now; but in a great public emergency he departed from his general theory of interpretation, and in doing so he did an act of transcendent statesmanship and he achieved an incalculable advantage for the republic. (pp. v-vi)

> Charles Emory Smith, "The Louisiana Purchase,"
> in The Writings of Thomas Jefferson, Vol. III by
> Thomas Jefferson, edited by Andrew A. Lipscomb,
> The Thomas Jefferson Memorial Association of the
> United States, 1903, pp. i-vi.

W[ILLIAM] J[ENNINGS] BRYAN (essay date 1903)

[*Bryan was an American political leader and lawyer who is perhaps best remembered for his role as one of the prosecuting attorneys in the Scopes trial, which contested the right of John Scopes to teach the principles of Darwinian evolution in the public schools. Bryan greatly admired Jefferson. Here, he extols the Statute for Establishing Religious Freedom, which Jefferson wrote and Virginia adopted in 1786, for the clarity of its language and the truth of its arguments. According to Bryan, Jefferson's claim to greatness rests on his love of humankind and his ability to embody political principles in legislation, thus ensuring their continued acceptance.*]

Jefferson was a political philosopher, and thought far in advance of his time. And yet he differed in one essential particular from the philosophers who do not live to see the triumph of their ideas. He proclaimed great living truths, and then he applied those truths to the questions with which he had to deal. Some have contented themselves with laying down abstract principles, and have not sought to give them vitality in the present day; but Jefferson not only saw the future but he saw the present, and we have this great advantage in the study of the principles of Jefferson, that he gave us those principles embodied in legislation. I have been more and more surprised as I have studied the questions with which we have to deal, to find that there is no subject with which our people grapple to-day that he did not consider in principle. Take the questions that are subjects of controversy and you will find that he stated principles and applied principles at that time that apply to the questions at this time; and to-day we do not have to go beyond his writings to find principles that will solve aright the problems of to-day. He saw great fundamental truths, self-evident truths, if you please; and I am coming to believe that there are not only self-evident truths but that all truth is self-evident—that the best service that a man can render to a truth is to state it so that it can be understood. Jefferson had the power of statement, and he stated the truths so that they could be understood. I do not mean to speak lightly of the work of Jefferson in purchasing the Louisiana territory, but if that territory had not been bought then it would have been bought afterward, for it was there, and it was necessary that it should become United States territory. I cannot believe that the purchase of that land—dull, inanimate matter—can be compared with the proclama-

tion of immortal truth. I place far above any purchase of acres or square miles, the utterance of those truths upon which human liberty must rest. Philosophy is above geography. (pp. i-ii)

I have been asked to write about the **Statute for Establishing Religious Freedom,** prepared by Thomas Jefferson, and enacted by the State of Virginia in 1786, about eight years after it was drafted. Let me quote you the statute:

> That the General Assembly do enact that no man shall be compelled to frequent, or support, any religious worship, place or ministry whatsoever, nor shall be enforced, restrained, molested, or burthened in his body or goods, nor shall otherwise suffer, on account of his religious opinions or belief; but that all men shall be free to profess, and by argument to maintain, their opinions in matters of religion and that the same shall in no wise diminish, enlarge, or affect the civil capacities.

The conciseness of Jefferson's style is well illustrated in this statute. Read it over. There is not a superfluous word, and yet there is enough to guard religious liberty. It is not strange that this doctrine, so well set forth by Jefferson more than a century ago, is now a part of the Constitution and Bill of Rights of every State of this Union. Not only is that to-day the law of this land, but it is spreading throughout the world. . . . I believe that when we come to measure the relative importance of things, the importance of an act like that, the very foundation upon which we build religious liberty—the importance of an act like that which, gradually spreading, has become the creed of eighty millions of people, and is ultimately to become the creed of all the world—when we come to consider the vast importance of a thing like that, how can we compare lands or earthly possessions with it?

In the preamble to this statute Jefferson set forth the main reasons urged by those who believed in religious freedom. Let me call attention to some of the more important ones. He said, in the first place, that to attempt to compel people to accept a religious doctrine, by act of law, was to make, not Christians but hypocrites. That was one of the reasons, and it was a strong one. He said, too, that there was no earthly judge who was competent to sit in a case and try a man for his religious opinions, for the judgment of the court, he said, would not be a judgment of law, but would be the personal opinion of the judge. What could be more true? No man who has religious convictions himself bears them so lightly that he can lay them aside and act as a judge when another man's religious convictions are involved. Then he suggested—and I think that I am justified in elaborating upon this suggestion a moment—that religion does not need the support of government to enable it to overcome error. Let me give the exact words of his report, for I cannot change them without doing injury to them:

> And finally that truth is great and will prevail if left to herself; that she is the proper and sufficient antagonist of error, and has nothing to fear from the conflict unless, by human interposition, disarmed of her natural weapons—free argument and debate; errors ceasing to be dangerous when it is permitted freely to contradict them.

Tell me that Jefferson lacked reverence for religion! He rather lacks reverence who believes that religion is unable to defend herself in a contest with error. He places a low estimate upon

A portrait of Jefferson painted by Charles Willson Peale in 1791, while Jefferson was secretary of state. Courtesy of Independence National Historical Park Collections, Philadelphia, PA.

the strength of religion, who thinks that the wisdom of God must be supplemented by the force of man's puny arm. (pp. iii-v)

In the preamble to the **Statute for Religious Freedom** Jefferson put first that which I want to speak of last. It was that the regulation of the opinions of men on religious questions by law was contrary to the laws of God and to the plans of God. He pointed out that God had it in His power to control man's mind and body, but that He did not see fit to coerce the mind or the body into obedience to even the divine will; and that if God Himself was not willing to use coercion to force man to accept certain religious views, man uninspired and liable to error ought not to use the means that Jehovah would not employ. Jefferson realized that our religion was a religion of love and not a religion of force. (p. vii)

It has been said that it marks an epoch in history when God lets loose a thinker in the world. God let loose a thinker when Jefferson was born. Carlyle says that thought is stronger than artillery parks; that thought moulds the world like soft clay; that it writes and unwrites laws, makes and unmakes parliaments—and that back of every great thought is love; that love is the ruling force in the world. I believe it is true. I believe that Jefferson's greatness rests more upon his love of human kind than upon his intellect—great as was his intellect, and that he was great because his heart was big enough to embrace the world. And the people loved him "because he first loved them." He wanted our religion to rest on the basis of love and not on the basis of force; and when we get down to the foundation of our government, and the foundation of our religion,

we find that they alike rest on the doctrine of human brotherhood—on the doctrine "that all men are created equal," "that they are endowed by their creator with certain inalienable rights,"—rights that government did not give, rights that government cannot take away; that the object of government is to secure to the individual the enjoyment of his inalienable rights, and that governments derive their just powers from the consent of the governed. But all of these things rest upon that conception of human brotherhood which one cannot have unless he has the love that is back of every great thought. I believe that, when Jefferson assisted in establishing religious freedom, he assisted in giving to our government its strongest support. Chain the conscience, bind the heart, and you cannot have for the support of our form of government the strength and the enthusiasm it deserves. But let conscience be free to commune with its God, let the heart be free to send forth its love, and the conscience and the heart will be the best defenders of a government resting upon the consent of the governed. (pp. viii-ix)

> W[illiam] J[ennings] Bryan, "The Statute for Establishing Religious Freedom," in The Writings of Thomas Jefferson, Vol. VIII, by Thomas Jefferson, edited by Andrew A. Lipscomb, The Thomas Jefferson Memorial Association of the United States, 1903, pp. i-xi.

MAX J. HERZBERG   (essay date 1914)

[*Herzberg assesses Jefferson as a writer. He begins by investigating Jefferson's relation to his age, contending that he can best be understood as a product of his era. Jefferson lived in a time of transition between the rational and practical spirit of the Neoclassical era and the idealistic and sentimental spirit of the developing Romantic movement, and Herzberg traces evidence of the conflict between the idealist and the practical man of affairs in Jefferson's works. After briefly surveying his writings, Herzberg attests that the state papers, and most notably the Declaration of Independence, are his greatest achievement. Although Jefferson is remembered for his political rather than literary accomplishments, Herzberg concludes, the Declaration "will remain an eternal literary monument to his fame, a monument secure from the mutations of politics and the change of issues."*]

To a great extent the career of Jefferson can be explained only by the fact that he lived at a certain period of the eighteenth century. That he was a man of his age in certain prominent characteristics is evident at a glance. Thus, for example, we trace the influence of the century upon his development as it is evident in his general skepticism; in the broad field of his knowledge and activities; in the hold of the "esprit gaulois" upon him as upon most of Europe at the time; in his interest in "Man" and his humanitarianism; in the obviously prosaic qualities of his personality; in his humdrum and rhetorical style; and finally in that bad taste that led him to write and publish the **"Anas"**, just as, for example, it led Pope to write, and as we suspect, cause to be published certain nasty letters. But Jefferson is at one with his contemporaries in a more important respect.

As the great neo-classic era in literature was drawing to a close, it is well known that a strong reaction set in to the clearly defined characteristics that had marked European civilization, and particularly letters, for so many decades. The utilitarian, practical spirit was still predominant, but everywhere was stirring obscurely new life: The leaders of the new movement groped blindly in the dark, struggled vainly with the spirit of the age, and often were obliged to take refuge in a weak negation rather than in any positive doing. Men like Kant in Germany, it is true, were laying the strong foundations of a new idealism; but mainly the reaction to the rationality of the period found vent in a weak sentimentality and vaporous dreaming. Ossian in England, Rousseau in France, Goethe with his "Sorrows of Werther" and the *Sturm and Drang* in Germany, Chateaubriand in France again, Byron and Shelley in England again, the Romantic School in Germany again,—these were the gradually cumulative product of the new spirit. (p. 311)

Jefferson is a curious example of those in whom the new life and spirit stirred with sufficient vigor to make possible an occasional conflict with the old, and yet in whom the conflict was fraught with more good than evil. Jefferson had in him two powerful tendencies: one that of the idealist and dreamer, one that of the practical man of affairs. He has been aptly called a "transcendentalist in politics." At any other era there would have been no conflict between the two: in fact, the greatest men in all times have been the idealists in action. But in the late eighteenth century there was necessarily a conflict. Shrewdness, hardheadedness, cool reason, these were the qualities respected and admired. They were the qualities respected and admired in literature as in life: this century is remarkable for the large number of men of affairs who find mention in histories of literature, and this should be ascribed to the fact that the characteristics required for success in literature were the same as those required for success in life. Nor can it be denied that the idealists of the time, daunted by such an environment, were not able to put forward much of a case before the world. We have little respect even today for a weak-kneed sentimentalist like Rousseau, who spoke with the lips of an angel, and whose life arouses disgust and contempt; and little real respect for a Coleridge, later and better born, who spun beautiful cobwebs of metaphysics, and left Southey to support his wife and children. But Jefferson to a great extent escaped the unsubstantiality and the contempt justly earned by many of the eighteenth and early nineteenth century idealists. And he escaped them mainly because of the very conflict that has been mentioned. He was practical enough to win the respect of his contemporaries, and idealist enough to influence posterity. He wrought great deeds in his own time, and he left great ideas to the future. Yet there was a conflict in him, with certain practical consequences, which may be illustrated from various phases of his activities.

Thus, for example, the first consequence of this conflict is a certain timidity that marked Jefferson's character throughout his life. He evolved many schemes of political philosophy, but when it came to putting them into practice, the cautious spirit of the age overcame him, and he was afraid. Jefferson rarely acknowledged directly that he was the author of any scheme or undertaking—even a literary undertaking. He was not merely no maker of books, but he even kept most of his productions current only among his friends. His most important literary work, the **"Notes on Virginia,"** was published against his will and anonymously. There exists moreover no definite system of Jeffersonian philosophy, excepting possibly in the first inaugural address. This philosophy can only be pieced together from innumerable letters, pamphlets, declarations, and the like. Jefferson worked like a mole, underground: as Mr. Ford points out, he suggested to Madison that he do or write this, to Monroe that he do or write that; he revised one man's book and outlined another's; he labored indefatigably in committee or delegation to impress his ideas on his colleagues. But always he is the man behind the scenes that pulls the wires; never, if it can be helped, does he himself come forward as an actor. (pp. 312-13)

A second consequence of this conflict is apparent in almost all the literary productions of Jefferson. Taking the **Declaration of Independence** as an example, we notice that it begins with certain general statements of abstract rights, and proceeds then to enumerate the particular grievances of the colonies against the king. Here your philosopher has held the field for a while till the practical politician returned. Jefferson has soared in great exaltation and lofty imagination: then he descends to walk soberly on the common earth. In Jefferson's other writings the same characteristics may be observed. In them also we find good hard facts liberally interspersed with broad generalizations and philosophical reflections. Nowhere in Jefferson are the philosophical and the practical far apart.

A third consequence of the conflict was [Jefferson's inconsistency]. . . . Regarded from this standpoint, it is on his very inconsistency that Jefferson's best claims to be considered a great statesman are founded. For had he, on the one hand, been a mere politician, as some claim, he would undoubtedly have had no principles to be inconsistent to; and had he, on the other hand, been a mere dreamer and philosopher, as some claim, he would undoubtedly have allowed that "hobgoblin of little minds", a weak desire for consistency, to defeat his largest ends and prevent the accomplishment of his greatest hopes. Jefferson, the man of affairs, was keenly sensible that the attempt to put his theories into practice must certainly reveal many defects of details, and he was prepared to alter these details in accordance with experience: he was ready to give up his pet schemes, if the sacrifice would redound to the benefit of his greater ideals. Jefferson's little foibles were not with him, as with many men, the means of destroying any more important good, and he was true to his larger principles if not always to his innumerable notions. Jefferson often made mistakes, but he "erred in integrity," and—always with the most intense longing for the good of the masses of mankind—he strove to repair his errors. . . . Jefferson was a dreamer, but a dreamer who in reducing his dreams to realities did not fail to avoid the insubstantiality and gray mistiness of ghostland: therefore his dreams often came true.

Thus, all in all, in the sphere of action as in the sphere of thought, Jefferson was a typical product of his age. His timidity, his practicality, his inconsistency, the conflict in him of idealism and expediency, his cosmopolitanism, his polish, his fluctuant morality, his humanitarianism, his skepticism: all alike are qualities that mark the epoch. Keeping these general characteristics in mind, it will be easier to consider Jefferson more particularly in his literary relations.

It would be a mistake to imagine for a moment that the author of the **Declaration of Independence,** was, in any sense of the word, a great man of letters; or that if his reputation depended on the work of his pen, his name would find more than incidental mention in any history of literature. It needs but a glance at the list of his writings to establish at once the fact that Jefferson is not on the roll of great writers. All is discursive and brief; and one famous document and one published book constitute the greater part of the literary baggage of Jefferson. In considering the literary work of men like Washington or John Adams or Madison or Jefferson, it must constantly be remembered that they were all of them employed in the active duties of public service, and that, as Edward Everett has remarked, "the fruits of their intellect are not to be sought in the systematic volumes of learned leisure, but in the files of office, in the archives of state, and in a most extensive public and private correspondence." But these are not the staple of literature. . . . In the case of Jefferson, moreover, who during a long and active life was lawyer, statesman, governor, diplomat, cabinet minister, vice-president, and president, to say nothing of his other functions as pamphleteer, letter-writer, and author of many small treatises in the interests of science, education, and the like, the mass of purely unliterary documents is necessarily more than usually large. Yet to a certain extent the amount of formal work in his writings is greater than in those of any other man of his time, and rewards systematic investigation.

Leaving for the moment his state papers, and particularly the **Declaration of Independence,** out of account, the writings of Jefferson may be considered under three heads: (1) the *Notes on Virginia*; (2) the *Letters*; (3) the miscellaneous writings. With regard to the first . . . , it has been said that "as a whole, perhaps no book of information was ever more pleasantly and vigorously written." . . . Jefferson lavished upon [the *Notes on Virginia*] all the wealth of information he had gathered in many years, and mingled with this are vivid descriptions and profound reflections. (pp. 313-16)

Jefferson has been called "probably the greatest letter-writer that has ever lived." . . . [His] correspondence possesses great historical value, and has a remarkable significance as embodying Jefferson's doctrines. To a certain extent, also, the letters are of a literary character in that they reveal personality—in this respect reminding us somewhat of Pepys' diary. Beginning with a very early period they carry us from Jefferson's first love disappointment and his ensuing cynicism down to the last years of his life, when Monticello had become a political and intellectual Mecca. Despite some elegance and polish, however, they lack charm when read for themselves, and not for a moment can Jefferson be compared with men like Chesterfield and Cowper. Yet for their historical interest letters must always continue to be read, more so perhaps than those of either Chesterfield or Cowper.

The miscellaneous writings of Jefferson are less important. The *Autobiography,* written in his usual flowing style, deals largely with his public career and lacks the personal interest of Franklin's similar work. The *Anas* mentioned above, will probably always attract readers for its scandalous and mean-minded details, and reveals the weakness of the man rather than his greatness. Most students will prefer to ignore it entirely, just as the evidences of Carlyle's similar pettiness towards Leigh Hunt and Charles Lamb are wisely ignored. Such collections of shady anecdotes are essentially Gallic and eighteenth century in nature: that Jefferson should have been guilty of a breach of good taste in this matter must be attributed to the influence of the older epoch on his character. In the realm of eloquence Jefferson need not be considered. Though he is supposed to have indited speeches occasionally for others, he rarely spoke in the assemblies to which he was elected—he was no orator as Brutus is. As a pamphleteer Jefferson's most important service was in *The Summary View of the Rights of British America*. . . . Considering the time, this was a remarkably bold and firm expression of opinion, wherein he anticipated many of the arguments and doctrines later laid down in the **Declaration of Independence.** Jefferson wrote many other pamphlets of one kind and another during the course of his life, but utterly fails to stand any comparison with the great English pamphleteers, with the grandeur and large utterance of Burke, the savage irony and sustained strength of Swift, or the ingenuity and effectiveness of Arbuthnot. Nor do Jefferson's pamphlets at all compare with the remarkably influential papers of the "Fed-eralist." Finally, such compositions as his commercial reports for 1793 and his diplomatic papers, well written in their way, again cannot claim to stand beside Hamilton's masterly work in this line. Thus in almost every sphere we find that Jefferson's work, excellent of its kind, is surpassed by that of many other men.

It is on his state papers, and especially on one famous document, that Jefferson's chief claim to literary power must rest. He excelled all his colleagues in the Virginia House of Burgesses as a drafter of state papers; and when he entered Congress, he brought with him, as John Adams expressed it, "a reputation for literature, science, and a happy talent of composition. Writings of his were handed about, remarkable for the peculiar felicity of expression," a quality they retained to the last. . . . He wrote memorably and forcibly: his tone was lofty and dignified; and finally, after serving on many important committees, he was elected, early in June 1776, chairman of an illustrious committee to draft a **Declaration of Independence.** (pp. 316-18)

Its immediate and permanent influence was tremendous. The people and army received it with enthusiasm; it enabled the colonies to present a united front to England; it was the justification of America in the eyes of the world. France was deeply impressed by it, and it had its share in precipitating the crisis of the French Revolution. It was written for thirteen colonies and three million people: now a century has barely revealed the possibilities of American development and American influence in a land that stretches unbrokenly over three million square miles of territory, and that has attracted to its shores enough old-world pioneers to swell its population to a ninety millions that will soon be a hundred millions—and yet no end. Like a banner in this march onward of American ideals and of courageous conquest of the wilderness has been the **Declaration of Independence,** and long ago it began to react further on Europe and European institutions. (p. 319)

It may be objected that so much force should not be attached to mere words; that all the ideas expressed in the **Declaration** were by no means novel; that to the expansion of human conceptions should be ascribed the important changes of the nineteenth century, and not to a few ringing phrases. No doubt this is true, and yet after all the danger is greater of minimizing the importance of just such a crystallization of ideas as the **Declaration of Independence** affords. It is not to be forgotten that for the commonalty of mankind thinking is vague, and watchwords necessary: men somehow feel that their cause is right, and yet are unable so to formulate their rights in words as to form a good defense of their cause before the bar of public opinion. Give them, however, a document in black and white, wherein are phrased memorably all their thoughts and ideals, and the words will burn themselves into the hearts.

Nor is it to be forgotten in this connection how insistently, for example, the refrain of those few simple words, "all men are created equal," rang in the ears of the American nation in the years before the Civil War. They flamed as if in fire before all eyes, North and South. Calhoun admitted that the chief obstacle to the adoption of his plausible scheme for a state founded on negro slavery was the preamble of the **Declaration of Independence.** If ever a history of the Civil War be written from a psychological standpoint, assuredly to those words, "All men are created equal," should be ascribed no mean portion of the credit for awakening the dormant conscience of the North. Such was the power of one phrase of what was called an obsolescent and antiquated document. (pp. 319-20)

[Despite] occasional bombast and despite occasional inaccuracy it is a tremendous document. It is surely not accidental that this is the only document in American annals that has won for itself a place in the hearts of the people. The fact that it has so long and so successfully withstood the test of time and of constant reiteration should be sufficient proof of the essential literary power and soundness of the **Declaration.** American hearts in all times have thrilled to its majestic and resonant words: American liberties, and in part the liberties of the world, are founded upon it as upon a rock. It is more than a piece of literature: it is the soul of a people. It is more than an assertion of grievances; it is a charter of manhood. The particular form of emotionalism that rings in the **Declaration** is today perhaps a little quaint, but it should nevertheless be clear that America stands or falls with the **Declaration of Independence.** If ever a time shall come when Americans deny the full cogency of the Preamble, the time will have come when America in her turn shall give way to a new evangel of humanity. Jefferson may therefore be said in this document to express a nation and a civilization—a remarkable literary feat. (pp. 323-24)

[Apart] from their historical and literary value Jefferson's writings are vitally important today. They will continue to exert more direct influence on American life than the works of any other of America's greatest men. . . .

To some [Jefferson] is still far in advance of modern thought: to others he represents a dangerous heresy that has unfortunately proved highly attractive. In either case his writings are the subject of deep study and close attention. This is much more true, indeed, than is the fortune of many professed writers of literature with established reputations.

In a certain sense, then, the time has hardly come to judge of Jefferson from the literary point of view. Because of their intellectual value, we may be inclined to exaggerate the literary significance of views that are still so much a subject of controversy. But so long as the States endure, one of the writings of Jefferson, the **Declaration of Independence,** will remain an eternal literary monument to his fame, a monument secure from the mutations of politics and the changes of issues. Its words will take on inspiration with the ages; it will seem the great bulwark of the oppressed. To be the author of this document, to hear one's words on the reverend lips of mankind forever, is not this more honorable than all honor? No mere piece of literature, we are assured, has ever had or ever will have the vogue of Thomas Jefferson's **Declaration of Independence**. (pp. 326-27)

Max J. Herzberg, "Thomas Jefferson as a Man of Letters," in South Atlantic Quarterly, *Vol. XIII, No. 4, October, 1914, pp. 310-27.*

CARL BECKER (essay date 1922)

[*In his authoritative and influential study* The Declaration of Independence, *Becker analyzes its historical antecedents, composition, deductive logic, legal principles, and reception. Becker, who provides what is considered a seminal interpretation of the political philosophy of the Declaration, is also noted for his multiple lines of inquiry: he is equally interested in the sources of Jefferson's ideas as in the evolution of the text. In the following excerpt, Becker focuses on the Declaration as a literary work. He begins by praising Jefferson's distinctive style, noting its concise and graceful phrasing—or, as John Adams described it, "the peculiar felicity of expression" (see excerpt dated 1822). Becker then explains the work's logical sequence and structural unity. According to this critic, Jefferson's purpose in the Declaration*

was to convince the world that the colonists had a moral and legal right to rebel. Becker notes that all parts of the Declaration—the opening and closing paragraphs as well as the individual grievances—contribute to this governing idea: that the colonists were not rebels, but were instead a free people with long-established rights to form their own government, and that the king had usurped these rights. Becker then evaluates the changes that Congress made in the Declaration and focuses on the deletion of the anti-slavery passage, which he condemns because of its abstract and unemotional tone. This passage, according to Becker, reveals much of what is wrong with Jefferson's writing: despite its "felicity of expression," the Declaration lacks "the grand manner—that passion under control which lifts prose to the level of true poetry." For additional criticism by Becker, see excerpt dated 1943.]

[As] the original drafts of his papers show, [Jefferson] revised and corrected his writings with care, seeking, yet without wearing his soul threadbare in the search, for the better word, the happier phrase, the smoother transition. His style has not indeed the achieved perfection, the impeccable surface, of that of a master-craftsman like Flaubert, or Walter Pater; but neither has it the objectivity, the impersonal frigidity of writing that is perhaps too curiously and deliberately integrated, too consciously made. Having something to say, he says it, with as much art as may be, yet not solely for the art's sake, aiming rather at the ease, the simplicity, the genial urbanity of cultivated conversation. The grace and felicity of his style have a distinctly personal flavor, something Jeffersonian in the implication of the idea, or in the beat and measure of the words. Franklin had equal ease, simplicity, felicity; but no one who knows the writings of Franklin could attribute the **Declaration** to him. Jefferson communicated an undefinable yet distinctive quality to the **Declaration** which makes it his.

The **Declaration** is filled with these felicities of phrase which bear the stamp of Jefferson's mind and temperament: *a decent respect to the opinions of mankind; more disposed to suffer, while evils are sufferable, than to right themselves by abolishing the forms to which they are accustomed; for the sole purpose of fatiguing them into compliance with his measures; sent hither swarms of officers to harrass our people and eat out their substance; hold them as we hold the rest of mankind, enemies in war, in peace friends.* There are some sentences in the **Declaration** which are more than felicitous. The closing sentence, for example, is perfection itself. Congress amended the sentence by including the phrase, "with a firm reliance upon the protection of divine Providence." It may be that Providence always welcomes the responsibilities thrust upon it in times of war and revolution; but personally, I like the sentence better as Jefferson wrote it. "And for the support of this **Declaration** we mutually pledge to each other our lives, our fortunes, and our sacred honor." It is true (assuming that men value life more than property, which is doubtful) that the statement violates the rhetorical rule of climax; but it was a sure sense that made Jefferson place 'lives' first and 'fortunes' second. How much weaker if he had written 'our fortunes, our lives, and our sacred honor"! Or suppose him to have used the word 'property' instead of 'fortunes!' Or suppose him to have omitted 'sacred!' Consider the effect of omitting any of the words, such as the last two 'ours'—"our lives, fortunes, and sacred honor." No, the sentence can hardly be improved.

There are probably more of these Jeffersonian felicities in the **Declaration** than in any other writing by him of equal length. Jefferson realized that, if the colonies won their independence, this would prove to be a public document of supreme importance; and the Rough Draft (which may not be the first one) bears ample evidence of his search for the right word, the right phrasing. (pp. 195-98)

Apart from the peculiar felicities of phrasing, what strikes one particularly in reading the **Declaration** as a whole is the absence of declamation. Everything considered, the **Declaration** is brief, free of verbiage, a model of clear, concise, and simple statement. In 1856 Rufus Choate referred to it as "that passionate and eloquent manifesto," made up of "glittering and sounding generalities of natural right" [see Additional Bibliography]. Eloquent the **Declaration** frequently is, in virtue of a certain high seriousness with which Jefferson contrived to invest what was ostensibly a direct and simple statement of fact. Of all words in the language, 'passionate' is the one which is least applicable to Jefferson or to his writings. As to 'generalities,' the **Declaration** contains relatively few; and if those few are 'glittering and sounding' it is in their substance and not in their form that they are so. You may not believe

> that all men are created equal; that they are endowed by their creator with certain unalienable rights; that among these are life, liberty, and the pursuit of happiness; that to secure these rights governments are instituted among men, deriving their just powers from the consent of the governed; that whenever any form of government becomes destructive of these ends, it is the right of the people to alter or to abolish it, and to institute new government, laying its foundations on such principles, and organizing its powers in such form, as to them shall seem most likely to effect their safety and happiness.

You may not believe this; but if you do believe it, as Jefferson and his contemporaries did, you would find it difficult to say it more concisely; in words more direct, simple, precise, and appropriate; with less of passionate declamation, of rhetorical magniloquence, or of verbal ornament. The second paragraph of the **Declaration of Independence** reminds one of Lincoln's Gettysburg Address in its unimpassioned simplicity of statement. It glitters as much, or as little, as that famous document.

Logical sequence and structural unity are not always essential to good writing; but the rambling and discursive method would scarcely be appropriate to a declaration of independence. Jefferson's declaration, read casually, seems not to possess a high degree of unity. Superficially considered, it might easily strike one as the result of an uneasy marriage of convenience between an abstract philosophy of government and certain concrete political grievances. But in truth the **Declaration** is built up around a single idea, and its various parts are admirably chosen and skilfully disposed for the production of a particular effect. The grievances against the king occupy so much space that one is apt to think of them as the main theme. Such is not the case. The primary purpose of the **Declaration** was to convince a candid world that the colonies had a moral and legal right to separate from Great Britain. This would be difficult to do, however many and serious their grievances might be, if the candid world was to suppose that the colonies were politically subordinate to the British government in the ordinary sense. It is difficult to justify rebellion against established political authority. Accordingly, the idea around which Jefferson built the **Declaration** was that the colonists were not rebels against established political authority, but a free people maintaining long established and imprescriptible rights against a usurping king. The effect which he wished to produce was to leave a candid

world wondering why the colonies had so long submitted to the oppressions of this king.

The major premise from which this conclusion is derived is that every 'people' has a natural right to make and unmake its own government; the minor premise is that the Americans are a 'people' in this sense. In establishing themselves in America, the people of the colonies exercised their natural rights to frame governments suited to their ideas and conditions; but at the same time they voluntarily retained a union with the people of Great Britain by professing allegiance to the same king. From this allegiance they might at any time have withdrawn; if they had not so withdrawn it was because of the advantages of being associated with the people of Great Britain; if they now proposed to withdraw, it was not because they now any less than formerly desired to maintain the ancient association, but because the king by repeated and deliberate actions had endeavored to usurp an absolute authority over them contrary to every natural right and to long established custom. The minor premise of the argument is easily overlooked because it is not explicitly stated in the **Declaration**—at least not in its final form. To have stated it explicitly would perhaps have been to bring into too glaring a light certain incongruities between the assumed premise and known historical facts. The rôle of the list of grievances against the king is to make the assumed premise emerge, of its own accord as it were, from a carefully formulated but apparently straightforward statement of concrete historical events. From the point of view of structural unity, the rôle which the list of grievances plays in the **Declaration** is a subordinate one; its part is to exhibit the historical circumstances under which the colonists, as a 'free people,' had thrust upon them the high obligation of defending the imprescriptible rights of all men.

Although occupying a subordinate place in the logical structure, the list of grievances is of the highest importance in respect to the total effect which the **Declaration** aims to produce. From this point of view, the form and substance of these paragraphs constitute not the least masterly part of the **Declaration.** It is true, books upon rhetoric warn the candidate for literary honors at all hazards to avoid monotony; he ought, they say, to seek a pleasing variety by alternating long and short sentences; and while they consider it correct to develop a single idea in each paragraph, they consider it inadvisable to make more than one paragraph out of a single sentence. These are no doubt good rules, for writing in general; but Jefferson violated them all, perhaps because he was writing something in particular. Of set purpose, throughout this part of the **Declaration,** he began each charge against the king with 'he has': 'he has refused his assent'; 'he has forbidden his governors'; 'he has refused to pass laws'; 'he has called together legislative bodies'; 'he has refused for a long time.' As if fearing that the reader might not after all notice this oft-repeated 'he has,' Jefferson made it still more conspicuous by beginning a new paragraph with each 'he has.' To perform thus is not to be 'literary' in a genteel sense; but for the particular purpose of drawing an indictment against the king it served very well indeed. Nothing could be more effective than these brief, crisp sentences, each one the bare affirmation of a malevolent act. Keep your mind on the king, Jefferson seems to say; he is the man: *'he has refused'; 'he has forbidden'; 'he has combined'; 'he has incited'; 'he has plundered'; 'he has abdicated.'* I will say he has.

These hard, incisive sentences are all the more effective as an indictment of the king because of the sharp contrast between them and the paragraphs, immediately preceding and follow-

ing, in which Jefferson touches upon the sad state of the colonists. In these paragraphs there is something in the carefully
chosen words, something in the falling cadence of the sentences, that conveys a mournful, almost a funereal, sense of
evils apprehended and long forefended but now unhappily realized. Consider the phrases which give tone and pitch to the
first two paragraphs: 'when in the course of human events';
'decent respect to the opinions of mankind'; 'all experience
hath shewn'; 'suffer while evils are sufferable'; 'forms to which
they are accustomed'; 'patient sufferance of these colonies';
'no solitary fact to contradict the uniform tenor of the rest.'
Such phrases skilfully disposed have this result, that the opening passages of the **Declaration** give one the sense of fateful
things impending, of hopes defeated and injuries sustained with
unavailing fortitude. The contrast in manner is accentuated by
the fact that whereas the king is represented as exclusively
aggressive, the colonists are represented as essentially submissive. In this drama the king alone acts—he conspires, in-
cites, plunders; the colonists have the passive part, never lifting
a hand to burn stamps or destroy tea; they suffer while evils
are sufferable. It is a high literary merit of the **Declaration** that
by subtle contrasts Jefferson contrives to conjure up for us a
vision of the virtuous and long-suffering colonists standing like
martyrs to receive on their defenseless heads the ceaseless
blows of the tyrant's hand.

Like many men with a sense of style, Jefferson, although much
given to polishing and correcting his own manuscripts, did not
always welcome changes which others might make. Congress
discussed his draft for three successive days. What uncompli-
mentary remarks the members may have made is not known;
but it is known that in the end certain paragraphs were greatly
changed and others omitted altogether. (pp. 201-08)

[On] the whole it must be said that Congress left the **Declaration**
better than it found it. The few verbal changes that were made
improved the phraseology, I am inclined to think, in every
case. Where Jefferson wrote: "He has erected a multitude of
new offices by a self-assumed power, and sent hither swarms
of officers to harrass our people and eat out their substance,"
Congress cut out the phrase, "by a self-assumed power." Again,
Jefferson's sentence, "He has abdicated government here,
withdrawing his governors, and declaring us out of his allegiance and protection," Congress changed to read, "he has
abdicated government here by declaring us out of his protection
and waging war against us." Is not the phraseology of Congress, in both cases, more incisive, and does it not thus add
something to that very effect which Jefferson himself wished
to produce?

Aside from merely verbal changes, Congress rewrote the final
paragraph, cut out the greater part of the paragraph next to the
last, and omitted altogether the last of Jefferson's charges against
the king. The final paragraph as it stands is certainly much
stronger than in its original form. The **Declaration** was greatly
strengthened by using, for the renunciation of allegiance, the
very phraseology of the resolution of July 2, by which Congress
had officially decreed that independence which it was the function of the **Declaration** to justify. It was no doubt for this reason
mainly that Congress rewrote the paragraph; but the revision
had in addition the merit of giving to the final paragraph, what
such a paragraph especially needed, greater directness and assurance. In its final form, the **Declaration** closes with the air
of accepting the issue with confident decision.

In cutting out the greater part of the next to the last paragraph,
Congress omitted, among other things, the sentence in which

*A marble bust of Jefferson sculpted by Jean-Antoine Houdon
in Paris in 1789. This is considered a superb likeness of
Jefferson. Courtesy of Museum of Fine Arts, Boston.*

Jefferson formulated, not directly indeed but by allusion, that
theory of the constitutional relation of the colonies to Great
Britain which is elsewhere taken for granted: "We have reminded them [our British brethren] . . . that in constituting
indeed our several forms of government, we had adopted one
common king; thereby laying a foundation for perpetual league
and amity with them; but that submission to their parliament
was no part of our constitution, nor ever in idea, if history
may be credited." Perhaps the **Declaration** would have been
strengthened by including an explicit formulation of this theory.
But if the theory was to be expressly formulated at all, Jefferson
was unfortunate both in the form and in the order of the statement. Unfortunate in the form, which is allusive, and in the
last phrase ambiguous—"Nor ever in idea, if history may be
credited." Unfortunate in the order, because, if the theory was
to be expressly formulated at all, its formulation should manifestly have preceded the list of charges against the king. In
general, this paragraph, as originally written, leaves one with
the feeling that the author, not quite aware that he is done, is
beginning over again. In the form adopted, it is an admirable
brief prelude to the closing paragraph.

The last of Jefferson's charges against the king was what John
Adams called the "vehement philippic against negro slavery"
[see excerpt dated 1822].

> He has waged cruel war against human nature
> itself, violating its most sacred rights of life
> and liberty in the persons of a distant people

who never offended him, captivating and carrying them into slavery in another hemisphere, or to incur miserable death in their transportation thither. This piratical warfare, the opprobrium of *infidel* powers, is the warfare of the *Christian* king of Great Britain. Determined to keep open a market where MEN should be bought and sold, he has prostituted his negative for suppressing every legislative attempt to prohibit or to restrain this execrable commerce; and that this assemblage of horrors might want no fact of distinguished die, he is now exciting these very people to rise in arms among us, and to purchase that liberty of which *he* deprived them, by murdering the people upon whom *he* also obtruded them; thus paying off former crimes committed against the *liberties* of one people, with crimes which he urges them to commit against the *lives* of another.

Congress omitted this passage altogether. I am glad it did. One does not expect a declaration of independence to represent historical events with the objectivity and exactitude of a scientific treatise; but here the discrepancy between the fact and the representation is too flagrant. Expecially, in view of the subsequent history of the slave trade, and of slavery itself, without which there would have been no slave trade, these charges against the king lose whatever plausibility, slight enough at best, they may have had at the time. But I have quoted this passage in full . . . , not on account of its substance but on account of its form, which is interesting, and peculiarly significant in its bearing upon Jefferson's qualities and limitations as a writer. John Adams thought it one of the best parts of the **Declaration.** It is possible that Jefferson thought so too. He evidently gave much attention to the wording of it. But to me, even assuming the charges against the king to be true, it is the part of the **Declaration** in which Jefferson conspicuously failed to achieve literary excellence.

The reason is, I think, that in this passage Jefferson attempted something which he was temperamentally unfitted to achieve. The passage was to have been the climax of the charges against the king; on its own showing of facts it imputes to him the most inhuman acts, the basest motives; its purpose, one supposes, is to stir the reader's emotions, to make him feel a righteous indignation at the king's acts, a profound contempt for the man and his motives. Well, the passage is clear, precise, carefully balanced. It employs the most tremendous words— "murder," "piratical warfare," "prostituted," "miserable death." But in spite of every effort, the passage somehow leaves us cold; it remains, like all of Jefferson's writing, calm and quiescent; it lacks warmth; it fails to lift us out of our equanimity. There is in it even (something rare indeed in Jefferson's writings) a sense of labored effort, of deliberate striving for an effect that does not come.

This curious effect, or lack of effect, is partly due to the fact that the king's base actions are presented to us in abstract terms. We are not permitted to see George III. George III does not repeal a statute of South Carolina in order that Sambo may be sold at the port of Charleston. No, the Christian king wages "cruel war against human nature," he prostitutes "his negative for the suppression of every legislative attempt to prohibit or to restrain this execrable commerce." We have never a glimpse of poor dumb negroes gasping for breath in the foul hold of a transport ship, or driven with whips like cattle to labor in a fetid rice swamp; what we see is human nature, and the "violation of its most sacred rights in the persons of a distant people." The thin vision of things in the abstract rarely reaches the sympathies. Few things are less moving than to gaze upon the concept of miserable death, and it is possible to contemplate "an assemblage of horrors that wants no act of distinguished die" without much righteous indignation.

Yet the real reason lies deeper. It is of course quite possible to invest a generalized statement with an emotional quality. Consider the famous passage from Lincoln's second Inaugural:

> Fondly do we hope—fervently do we pray— that this mighty scourge of war may speedily pass away. Yet, if God wills that it continue until all the wealth piled by the bondman's two hundred and fifty years of unrequited toil shall be sunk, and until every drop of blood drawn with the lash shall be paid by another drawn by the sword, as was said three thousand years ago, so still it must be said, "the judgments of the Lord are true and righteous altogether."

Compare this with Jefferson's

> And that this assemblage of horrors might want no fact of distinguished die, he is now exciting these very people to rise in arms against us, and to purchase that liberty of which *he* deprived them, by murdering the people upon whom *he* also obtruded them; thus paying off former crimes committed against the *liberties* of one people, with crimes which he urges them to commit against the *lives* of another.

Making every allowance for difference in subject and in occasion, these passages differ as light differs from darkness. There is a quality of deep feeling about the first, an indefinable something which is profoundly moving; and this something, which informs and enriches much of Lincoln's writing, is rarely, almost never present in the writing of Jefferson.

This something, which Jefferson lacked but which Lincoln possessed in full measure, may perhaps for want of a better term be called a profoundly emotional apprehension of experience. One might say that Jefferson felt with the mind, as some people think with the heart. He had enthusiasm, but it was enthusiasm engendered by an irrepressible intellectual curiosity. He was ardent, but his ardors were cool, giving forth light without heat. One never feels with Jefferson, as one does with Washington, that his restraint is the effect of a powerful will persistently holding down a profoundly passionate nature. One has every confidence that Jefferson will never lose control of himself, will never give way to purifying rage, relieving his overwrought feelings by an outburst of divine swearing. All his ideas and sentiments seem of easy birth, flowing felicitously from an alert and expeditious brain rather than slowly and painfully welling up from the obscure depths of his nature. "I looked for gravity," says Maclay, giving his first impressions of Jefferson, "but a laxity of manner seemed shed about him. He spoke almost without ceasing; but even his discourse partook of his personal demeanor. It was loose and rambling; and yet he scattered information wherever he went, and some even brilliant sentiments sparkled from him."

Jefferson's writing is much like that—a ceaseless flow, sparkling, often brilliant, a kind of easy improvisation. There are in his writings few of those ominous overtones charged with emotion, and implying more than is expressed. Sometimes, indeed, by virtue of a certain facility, a certain complacent optimism, by virtue of saying disputed things in such a pleasant way, his words imply even less than they mean. When, for example, Jefferson says "the tree of liberty must be refreshed from time to time with the blood of patriots and tyrants," so far from making us shudder, he contrives to throw about this unlovely picture a kind of arcadian charm. You will hardly think of Jefferson, with lifted hand and vibrant voice, in the heat of emotion striking off the tremendous sentence, "Give me liberty or give me death!" I can imagine him saying, "Manly spirit bids us choose to die freemen rather than to live slaves." The words would scarcely lift us out of our seats, however we might applaud the orator for his peculiar felicity of expression.

Felicity of expression—certainly Jefferson had that; but one wonders whether he did not perhaps have too much of it. This sustained felicity gives one at times a certain feeling of insecurity, as of resting one's weight on something fragile. Jefferson's placidity, the complacent optimism of his sentiments and ideas, carry him at times perilously near the fatuous. One would like more evidence that the iron had some time or other entered his soul, more evidence of his having profoundly reflected upon the enigma of existence, of having more deeply felt its tragic import, of having won his convictions and his optimisms and his felicities at the expense of some painful travail of the spirit. What saved Jefferson from futility was of course his clear, alert intelligence, his insatiable curiosity, his rarely failing candor, his loyalty to ideas, his humane sympathies. Yet we feel that his convictions, his sympathies, his ideas are essentially of the intellect, somehow curiously abstracted from reality, a consciously woven drapery laid over the surface of a nature essentially aristocratic, essentially fastidious, instinctively shrinking from close contact with men and things as they are.

Not without reason was Jefferson most at home in Paris. By the qualities of his mind and temperament he really belonged to the philosophical school, to the Encyclopaedists, those generous souls who loved mankind by virtue of not knowing too much about men, who worshipped reason with unreasoning faith, who made a religion of Nature while cultivating a studied aversion for 'enthusiasm,' and strong religious emotion. Like them, Jefferson, in his earlier years especially, impresses one as being a radical by profession. We often feel that he defends certain practices and ideas, that he denounces certain customs or institutions, not so much from independent reflection or deep-seated conviction on the particular matter in hand as because in general these are the things that a philosopher and a man of virtue ought naturally to defend or denounce. It belonged to the eighteenth-century philosopher, as a matter of course, to apostrophize Nature, to defend Liberty, to denounce Tyranny, perchance to shed tears at the thought of a virtuous action. It was always in character for him to feel the degradation of Human nature when confronted with the idea of Negro Slavery.

This academic accent, as of ideas and sentiments belonging to a system, of ideas uncriticized and sentiments no more than conventionally felt, is what gives a labored and perfunctory effect to Jefferson's famous 'philippic against Negro slavery.' Adams described it better than he knew. It is indeed a philippic; it is indeed vehement; but it is not moving. It is such a piece as would be expected of a *'philosopher'* on such an occasion. We remain calm in reading it because Jefferson, one cannot but think, remained calm in writing it. For want of phrases

charged with deep feeling, he resorts to italics, vainly endeavoring to stir the reader by capitalizing and underlining the words that need to be stressed—a futile device, which serves only to accentuate the sense of artifice and effort, and, in the case of 'the *Christian* king of Great Britain,' introduces the wholly incongruous note of snarling sarcasm, reminding us for all the world of Shylock's 'these be the *Christian* husbands.' Jefferson apprehended the injustice of slavery; but one is inclined to ask how deeply he felt it.

It may be said that Jefferson touches the emotion as little in other parts of the **Declaration** as in the philippic on slavery. That is in great measure true; but in the other parts of the **Declaration,** which have to do for the most part with an exposition of the constitutional rights of the colonies, or with a categorical statement of the king's violations of these rights, the appeal is more properly to the mind than to the heart; and it was in appealing to the reader's mind, of course, that Jefferson was at his best. Taking the **Declaration** as a whole, this is indeed its conspicuous quality: it states clearly, reasons lucidly, exposes felicitously; its high virtue is in this, that it makes a strong bid for the reader's assent. But it was beyond the power of Jefferson to impregnate the **Declaration** with qualities that would give to the reader's assent the moving force of profound conviction. With all its precision, its concise rapidity, its clarity, its subtle implications and engaging felicities, one misses a certain unsophisticated directness, a certain sense of impregnable solidity and massive strength, a certain effect of passion restrained and deep convictions held in reserve, which would have given to it that accent of perfect sincerity and that emotional content which belong to the grand manner.

The **Declaration** has not the grand manner—that passion under control which lifts prose to the level of true poetry. Yet it has, what is the next best thing, a quality which saves it from falling to the prosaic. It has elevation. I have said that Franklin had, equally with Jefferson, clarity, simplicity, precision, felicity. If Franklin had written the **Declaration** it would have had all of these qualities; but Franklin would have communicated to it something homely and intimate and confidential, some smell of homespun, some air of the tavern or the print shop. Franklin could not, I think, have written this sentence:

> When in the course of human events it becomes necessary for one people to dissolve the political bands which have connected them with another, and to assume among the powers of the earth the separate and equal station to which the laws of nature and of nature's god entitle them, a decent respect to the opinions of mankind requires that they should declare the causes which impel them to the separation.

Or this one:

> Prudence indeed will dictate that governments long established should not be changed for light and transient causes; and accordingly all experience hath shewn that mankind are more disposed to suffer, while evils are sufferable, than to right themselves by abolishing the forms to which they are accustomed.

Or this:

> And for the support of this declaration we mutually pledge to each other our lives, our fortunes, and our sacred honor.

These sentences may not be quite in the grand manner; but they have a high seriousness, a kind of lofty pathos which at least lift the **Declaration** to the level of a great occasion. These qualities Jefferson was able to communicate to his writing by virtue of possessing a nature exquisitely sensitive, and a mind finely tempered; they illustrate, in its subtler forms, what John Adams called his 'peculiar felicity of expression.' (pp. 209-23)

> *Carl Becker, in his* The Declaration of Independence: A Study in the History of Political Ideas, *1922. Reprint by Peter Smith, 1933, 286 p.*

VERNON LOUIS PARRINGTON   (essay date 1927)

[*An American historian, biographer, and critic, Parrington is best known for his unfinished literary history of the United States,* Main Currents in American Thought. *Though modern scholars now disagree with many of his conclusions, they view Parrington's work as a significant first attempt at fashioning an intellectual history of America based on a broad interpretive thesis. Written from the point of view of a Jeffersonian liberal,* Main Currents in American Thought *has proven a widely influential work in American criticism. Here, Parrington explicates Jefferson's political philosophy, writing much of the essay as a paraphrase of his thought processes. Parrington focuses on Jefferson as an agrarian and Physiocrat. Although Jefferson eventually grudgingly accepted the need for industrial development, his conception of society focused on self-reliance, humanitarianism, decentralized government, local home rule, economic individualism, and an agricultural economy. According to Parrington, Jefferson believed that an agrarian society would encourage the development of democratic government. Parrington compares Jefferson's views to those of Alexander Hamilton and the Federalists, who advocated centralized government, the modification of individual and states' rights, and an industrial and capitalistic economy. Parrington's essay is considered one of the most important interpretations of Jefferson's political philosophy.*]

Thomas Jefferson devoted himself with immense tact and untiring patience [to efforts to oust Hamilton's Federalist party from power]. A master of political strategy, he spun his webs far and wide, quietly awaiting the time when the bumbling Federalist bees should range too carelessly in search of their honey. Accepted at once as the leader of agrarian America, he was to prove in the course of a long life the most original and native of the political leaders of the time.

Despite the mass of comment that has gathered about Jefferson, the full reach and significance of his political philosophy remains too little understood. Uncritical praise and censure have obscured or distorted his purpose, and allied his principles with narrow and temporary ends. Detraction will not let him alone. The hostility of his enemies, as a recent biographer [Francis W. Hirst] has remarked, has frequently taken "the peculiar form of editing his works or writing his life." For this distortion there is, perhaps, more than usual excuse. Certainly Jefferson is the most elusive of our great political leaders. Apparently inconsistent, changing his program with the changing times, he seemed to his enemies devoid of principle, a shallow demagogue who incited the mob in order to dupe the people. One of the most bitterly hated and greatly loved men in the day when love and hate were intense, he was the spokesman of the new order at a time of transition from a dependent monarchical state, to an independent republican state. Back of the figure of Jefferson, with his aristocratic head set on a plebeian frame, was the philosophy of a new age and a new people—an age and a people not yet come to the consistency of maturity, but feeling a way through experiment to solid achievement. Far

more completely than any other American of his generation he embodied the idealisms of the great revolution—its faith in human nature, its economic individualism, its conviction that here in America, through the instrumentality of political democracy, the lot of the common man should somehow be made better.

From the distinguished group of contemporary political thinkers Jefferson emerges as the preëminent intellectual, widely read, familiar with ideas, at home in the field of speculation, a critical observer of men and manners. . . . [Early] in life he began a wide reading in the political classics that far outweighed Coke and Blackstone in creative influence on his mind. He was equally at home with the English liberals of the seventeenth century and the French liberals of the eighteenth; and if he came eventually to set the French school above the English, it was because he found in the back-to-nature philosophy, with its corollary of an agrarian economics and its emphasis on social well-being, a philosophy more consonant with Virginian experience and his own temperament than Locke's philosophy of property. But he was very far from being a narrow French partisan, as has been often charged; rather he judged old-world theory in the light of its applicability to existing American conditions, and restrained his love of speculation by immediate practical considerations. The man of affairs kept a watchful eye on the philosopher in his study.

In the major doctrines of his political philosophy Jefferson was an amalgam of English and French liberalisms, supplemented by the conscious influence of the American frontier. That fusion early took place in his mind. The first bill that he introduced into the Virginia Assembly, at the age of twenty-six, was a bill to permit slave-owners to manumit their slaves; and his first published pamphlet [*A Summary View of the Rights of British America*] . . . rejected the legal reasoning of John Dickinson and Daniel Dulaney—supporting the parliamentary right to impose external taxation—and took its stand on the doctrine of natural right to local self-government and freedom of trade. When two years later he drafted the **Declaration of Independence** the fusion was complete. The strong influence of French humanitarianism is revealed in the passage on slavery that was stricken out on the floor of Congress, and more significantly in the change in the familiar phrasing of the several natural rights. Samuel Adams and other followers of Locke had been content with the classical enumeration of life, liberty, and property; but in Jefferson's hands the English doctrine was given a revolutionary shift. The substitution of "pursuit of happiness" for "property" marks a complete break with the Whiggish doctrine of property rights that Locke had bequeathed to the English middle class, and the substitution of a broader sociological conception; and it was this substitution that gave to the document the note of idealism which was to make its appeal so perennially human and vital. The words were far more than a political gesture to draw popular support; they were an embodiment of Jefferson's deepest convictions, and his total life thenceforward was given over to the work of providing such political machinery for America as should guarantee for all the enjoyment of these inalienable rights. If the fact that he set the pursuit of happiness above abstract property rights is to be taken as proof that Jefferson was an impractical French theorist, the critic may take what comfort he can from his deduction.

That Jefferson was an idealist was singularly fortunate for America; there was need of idealism to leaven the materialistic realism of the times. It was a critical period and he came at the turn of a long running tide. He watched the beginnings of the political shift in America from isolated colonial commonwealths to a unitary sovereign state; and his wide reading and close observation had convinced him that the impending change was fraught with momentous issues for the common man. He had mediated much on the social results of the slow oscillations in western civilization between social decentralization and centralization, with their contrasting political and economic structures; and he understood how the movement from simplicity to complexity—from freedom to regimentation—creates a psychology and an institutionalism that conducts straight to the leviathan state, controlled by a ruling cast, serving the demands of exploitation, heedless of the well-being of the regimented mass. This great lesson in social drifts he brought home to America. There had been created here the psychology and institutions of a decentralized society, with a corresponding exaltation of the individual and the breakdown of caste. In the broad spaces of America the old-world coercive state had dwindled to a mere police arrangement for parochial duties; the free citizen refused to be regimented; the several communities insisted on managing their affairs by their own agents. Such was the natural consequence of free economics; but with the turning of the tide would not the drift towards centralization nullify the results of earlier American experience and repeat here the unhappy history of European peoples?

To the philosophic mind of Jefferson, such a question was not academic, but urgent and vital. He had been bred in that older world, he believed passionately in the excellence of its virtues, and his political and social philosophy was determined by that experience. He sprang from a society deep-rooted in an agrarian economy, and he wished to preserve that society. . . . [His] neighbors and associates were capable and vigorous frontier democrats, who managed the affairs of local government with the same homespun skill that went to their farming. . . . [His] early conviction of the excellence of a freehold order was confirmed by later experience; wide observation and much travel convinced him that no other people was so favored by circumstance as the American, or so vigorously self-reliant. That such well-being resulted from a plastic economics, he regarded as self-evident; and from this economic freedom came political freedom. In his European travels he saw everywhere want and wretchedness dwelling in the shadow of the aristocratic state, and he could not dissociate the two. Political tyranny was the outward and visible sign of greater tyrannies that ran down to the very roots of society; the leviathan state was the convenient instrument through which those tyrannies took their heavy toll of the common well-being. America was a land of free men; it was exploited neither by an aristocracy nor a plutocracy. Surely there could be no greater or nobler ambition for an American than to assist in preserving his country from the misery that must attend a change from the present happy condition of democratic industry, to the serfdom of the European wage-taker and peasant.

To a mind imbued with such conceptions the appeal of the Physiocratic theory of social economics would be irresistible. The ground was prepared for the sowing of the seeds of the liberal French thought. With its emphasis laid upon agriculture, its doctrine of the *produit net,* its principle of *laissez faire,* and its social concern, the Physiocratic theory accorded exactly with his familiar experience, and it must have seemed to Jefferson that it was little other than a deduction from the open facts of American life. He had read much in the works of the Physiocratic group, and was intimately acquainted with DuPont de Nemours; and the major principles of the school sank deep

into his mind and creatively determined his thinking, with the result that Jeffersonian democracy as it spread through Virginia and west along the frontier assumed a pronounced Physiocratic bias. The sharp struggle between Jefferson and Hamilton must be reckoned, in part at least, a conflict between the rival principles of Quesnay and Adam Smith, between an agrarian and a capitalistic economy. Much as Jefferson feared the ambitions of an aristocracy, he feared quite as much the creation of a proletariat. As he looked into the future he saw great cities rising to breed their Roman mobs, duped and exploited by demagogues, the convenient tools of autocracy; and counting the cost in social well-being, he set his face like flint against the rising capitalism. A free yeomanry he regarded as the backbone of every great people, the producers of the real wealth, the guardians of manly independence; and the number of factory workers measured for him the extent of social disease. It is this Physiocratic conception that explains his bitter hostility to protective tariffs, national banks, funding manipulations, the machinery of credit, and all the agencies of capitalism which Hamilton was skillfully erecting in America. Not to have hated such things Jefferson must first have emptied his mind of the teachings of experience and the lessons of the social philosophers. (pp. 348-52)

[He eventually] modified his views of industrialism. The bitter experience of the Napoleonic wars, with the hardships and losses visited upon neutral shipping, had convinced him of the need of domestic manufactures, and he was then deeply interested in improved machinery, new methods, original ventures. "We must now place the manufacturer by the side of the agriculturist," he conceded, or remain in economic dependence. But how much further the country should be industrialized, whether it "shall be proposed to go beyond our own supply" to compete in foreign markets, was not yet clear to him; the problem remained still to be determined whether "the *surplus* labor" would be "most beneficially employed in the culture of the earth, or in the fabrications of art." In such commentary Jefferson failed to measure the thrust of economic determinism that drives every people to go through with the industrial revolution, once it is begun; but if we recall the primary principle of his political philosophy, that the "care of human life and happiness, and not their destruction, is the first and only legitimate object of good government," we may perhaps judge what would have been his attitude towards a centralized industrialism. He would have judged its desirability, not by the balance sheet of corporate business, but by the social ledger. As a social economist he could not think in terms of the economic man, nor simplify human beings to labor commodity, nor reduce the social tie to the cash nexus. It is inconceivable that he should have shared Hamilton's satisfaction at the contemplation of women and children—and many of the latter "of tender age"—wasting away in the mills; he was too social-minded for that, too much an idealist, too human in short. Though necessity might force him away from a simple agrarian economy, it does not follow that he would become partisan to a centralizing industrialism, with control vested in banking credit.

It is a common charge that Jefferson was consumed with suspicion, and it is set down against him as the mark of a mean and ungenerous nature. That in later years he was suspicious of fair-spoken advocates and plausible programs was as true of Jefferson as of Sam Adams; . . . with so much at stake he would practice caution. He feared many things, for he was acutely aware of the incapacity of the heedless majority to defend itself against an able and instructed minority. As a child of an aristocratic age he fell into the mistake of visualizing that minority in the guise of a landed gentry, rather than in the guise of plutocracy; but in his quick fear of a minority he had all history as counselor. When he took his seat in Washington's cabinet his suspicions of the Hamiltonian program were quickly aroused. He believed that a monarchy was aimed at, and if that proved unattainable, then a highly centralized state designed to hold in check the democratic tendencies. His line of reasoning may be summarized thus: In consequence of the republican enthusiasm of the early years of the Revolution, democratic reorganization of the several state governments had been successfully achieved. Very great progress towards democracy had been made. Certain legislative acts of agrarian assemblies were now being turned against democracy, to invalidate it as a working system of government. But if agrarian majorities had used their power to enact laws beneficial to their interests, they were only applying a lesson learned from long experience with aristocratic legislatures. Such acts were no serious indictment of the democratic principle, and to make partisan use of them to justify curtailing the powers of the majority, was a betrayal of popular rights. And this, Jefferson believed, was the deliberate purpose of the Federalist leaders. Unable to stem the popular tide in the several commonwealths, the wealthy minority had devised a plan to superimpose upon the sovereign commonwealths a centralized federal government, so hedged about as to lie beyond the reach of local majorities, and hence able to override and nullify the democratic will. Once safely established, this federal government would gather fresh powers into its hands, until there emerged a rigorous machine, modeled after the British system, and as little regardful of the common interests. If this were not the Federalist purpose, why all the praise of the British system as the ripe product of experience, exactly adapted to the political genius of the English race?

In the matter of appeal to past experience, which provided the stable of Federalist argument, Jefferson discovered fresh grounds of fear. The past he looked upon as evil, and the record of experience was a tale of injustice and bitter wrong. He would not have America follow the trodden paths, for whither they led he knew too well. He would countenance no entangling alliances with old-world upper-class systems of statecraft, for such systems would reproduce in America the evils it should be the chief business of America to prevent. There must be erected here no counterpart of the European state; there must be no king, no aristocracy, no plutocracy; but a new democratic organization of government, in which the welfare of the whole people should be the sole concern. (pp. 353-55)

Not past experience but present need should instruct America in drawing the plans of a new system of government and a new code of law. In analyzing the evils of European systems Jefferson came to certain conclusions that dominated all his later thinking, and that may be phrased thus: The political state tends inevitably to self-aggrandizement, the logical outcome of which is a political leviathan, too big and too complex for popular control. With sovereign powers vested in the hands of governmental agents, those agents lie under a constant temptation to corruption and tyranny, and in the end they align the powers of the state on the side of the most ambitious and capable. The greater the power of government, the ampler its revenues, the more energetic its administration, the more dangerous it may become to the rights of men; for where the prize is greatest, men struggle most ruthlessly, and what prize could be greater than the privilege of exploiting society in the name of the state? History knows no objective more tempting to the

will to power, than the control of the absolute state. A government adequately socialized, intent solely upon furthering the common well-being, Jefferson would have been unanxious about. But such governments existed only in the dreams of Sir Thomas More and the Utopians; he could discover none such either in the past or present. Everywhere strong governments were little more than efficient tax-machines to support armies and provide subsidies and places for the minority. Against such forces of corruption the people struggle in vain.

If such was the common testimony of old-world experience— and no man who knew the inner workings of government there would deny it—what reason was there to expect that like causes would work unlike results in America? To what purpose was the talk of strong government encouraged amongst the holders of the public debt? To what end had lobbyists for the funding bill invaded the floor of Congress? It was idle to expect in America a nullification of the law, that where power sits within, corruption waits without. The love of power is universal. Most men are potential autocrats, the strong and capable may become actual autocrats. No man is good enough, no group of men, to be trusted with unrestrained powers—in America any more than in Europe. A centralized government in control of the tax-machine, and secure from popular restraint, would undo the results of the Revolutionary War. The movement to consolidate power, Jefferson asserted, was "but Toryism in disguise." (pp. 356-57)

The practice of local home rule had grown up in America in response to native conditions; it had resulted from democratic needs; and Jefferson was too throughly American, too instinctively democratic, to overlook the significance of local sovereignties in a democratic philosophy. From the sharp contrast between American and European practice he deduced a cardinal principle, namely, that good government springs from a common interest in public affairs, and that such common interest is possible only when the field of activities is circumscribed. Set government apart from the people, or above them, and public interest is lost in a sense of futility. The danger of an encroaching tyranny by a superimposed sovereignty is made easy by the public lethargy in respect to distant and unfamiliar things, and establishes itself through the psychology of custom. Jefferson was never greatly concerned about stable government; he was very much more concerned about responsive government—that it should faithfully serve the majority will. He made no god of the political state. He had no conventional reverence for established law and order; he inquired rather what sort of law and order he was asked to accept, was it just or unjust. Changing conditions make ancient good uncouth, and established institutions tend to fall into dry-rot, or to become tyrannical. Men are more important than constitutions, and the public well-being is more sacred than statutes. An occasional revolution, he commented grimly apropos of the hue and cry over Shays's Rebellion, is salutary; if it does not come of itself it might well be brought about. Progress in government results from experiment; and it is easier and safer to experiment on a small scale than on a great. Inertia increases with size, and the more consolidated the government, the more unyielding it becomes. The longest delayed revolutions are the gravest.

In asserting the principle of the majority will, Jefferson like other democratic thinkers of the time, found himself countered by the argument of abstract justice. Vehement denunciation had greeted Paine's doctrine that what a nation chooses to do, it has a right to do. There can be no rights, it was confidently asserted, superior to the right. The people may legislate, but

The 1800 portrait of Jefferson by Rembrandt Peale. This portrait, which hangs in the White House, was perhaps the best known likeness of Jefferson during his lifetime. The White House Collection.

It is a very dangerous doctrine to consider the judges as the ultimate arbiters of all constitutional questions. It is one which would place us under the despotism of an oligarchy. . . . The Constitution has erected no such single tribunal, knowing that to whatever hands confided, with the corruptions of time and party, its members would become despots.

As Jefferson watched Chief Justice John Marshall gathering all things within the purview of the Federal judiciary, preparing future strongholds by the skillful use of *obiter dicta,* legislating by means of judicial interpretation, nullifying the will of the majority, and with the power of repeal made nugatory by the complexity of the process, he saw clearly what the outcome would be. Surely that was no democracy where judge-made laws were enforced by bench warrants, and where the sovereign power lay beyond the immediate reach of the popular will. The government that he desired would not rest on the legal fiction of an abstract justice above statutes and constitutions, whereof a group of judicial gentlemen were the repositories and guardians. (p. 359)

Granted the truth of Jefferson's premises that power tends to contract to the hands of a few, and that all government of the few is vicious, then democracy is the only form of government under which an approximation to justice can be realized. A class will serve class interests. Government by an aristocracy is government in the interest of the aristocracy. For the staple argument of the Federalists, that gentlemen of principle and property alone may be intrusted with affairs of state, Jefferson had a quiet contempt. "I have never observed men's honesty to increase with their riches," he remarked. On the contrary, he regarded the "better sort of people" as a chief hindrance to the spread of social justice. The past had been evil because the past had been exploited by gentlemen of principle and property. They had kept government away from the people, and with their secret councils and secret diplomacy they had plundered the taxpayers and drenched nations in blood. Their selfish rivalries everywhere exacted a heavy toll of society and left behind a trail of poverty and wretchedness. The future would be better in the degree that mastery passed into common hands.

From the conclusions of his democratic premise he did not shrink. If it were indeed true that the people were beasts, then the democratic government of the future would be bestial government—and even that might be better than the old arrangement of masters and slaves. But the American people whom Jefferson trusted were very far from beasts; he was convinced that they were honest and well-meaning; and if government were brought close to them, kept responsive to their will, a new and beneficent chapter in human history would open. The populistic laws passed by the legislatures of Rhode Island and New Hampshire, about which such an uproar was raised by fearful creditors, and which were urged as an argument against popular government, gave him no concern. He understood the ways of propaganda, and he never accepted judgment of the American people from the mouths of their enemies. The cure for the evils of democracy, he believed, was more democracy. The whole are far less likely to be unjust than the few; and if sovereignty does not rest in the majority will, where shall it lodge? (pp. 359-60)

The America of Jefferson's day was a simple world, with a simple domestic economy. More than ninety per cent were plain country folk, farmers and villagers, largely freeholders,

it remains to determine the validity of statutes in the light of justice; that which is unjust is *ipso facto* null and void. It was Coke's doctrine judicial review, set up in America after its repudiation in England, and Jefferson's hostility to it was bitter. As an intellectual he had none of the lawyer's complacency with legal principles, or conceit of the law's sufficiency; and as a democrat he would not yield sovereignty into the hands of the judiciary. He had no veneration for the Common Law of England: it had grown up by slow accretions during centuries of absolutism; how should it be expected to answer the needs of a freer age? It must be purged of outworn elements, imbued with democratic sympathies. The Revolution had been fought in defense of rights that are broader and more human than legal principles; and to hand over those rights to be interpreted away by lawyers, seemed to him moonstruck madness. (pp. 357-58)

As Jefferson grew older his fear of judicial encroachment on the popular will became acute, but it shifted from distrust of the Common Law to concern over the Supreme Court. A strong and outspoken hatred of the Federal judiciary runs through all his later writings, and he lost no opportunity to popularize the thesis—"It is a misnomer to call a government republican, in which a branch of the supreme power is independent of the nation."

> The great object of my fear is the Federal Judiciary. That body, like gravity, ever acting, with noiseless foot, and unalarming advance, gaining ground step by step, and holding what it gains, is engulfing insidiously the special governments into the jaws of that which feeds them.

managing their local affairs in the traditional way. There were no great extremes of poverty and wealth, no closely organized class groups. With its sharp restrictions on suffrage and the prestige accorded the gentry, it was still far from a political democracy; but it was hastening towards a more democratic order. Remote from the cesspools of European diplomacy, and not yet acquainted with the imperialism, it had no need for a leviathan state. Economic conditions sanctioned a *laissez-faire* government, simple and unambitious. In such a world the well-known words of Jefferson's first inaugural address [see excerpt dated 1801], justified themselves to all who did not seek to use the state for personal advantage. . . . In one significant direction he would extend the scope of government—the encouragement of education. An intelligent people is necessary to a democracy; free schools are a sign of a free society. Tyranny thrives on ignorance and superstition, and every exploiting group fears popular education. Free himself in thought and action, believing in the unshackled commerce of ideas, hating all censorships, Jefferson accounted the founding of the University of Virginia his largest contribution to the well-being of his native commonwealth.

To all who profess faith in the democratic ideal Jefferson is a perennial inspiration. A free soul, he loved freedom enough to deny it to none; an idealist, he believed that the welfare of the whole, and not the prosperity of any group, is the single end of government. He was our first great leader to erect a political philosophy native to the economics and experience of America, as he was the first to break consciously with the past. His life was dedicated to the service of freedom, and later generations may well recall his words, "I have sworn upon the altar of God eternal hostility against every form of tyranny over the mind of man." Europe made Jefferson wholly American. From his studies in France he came to see that where men enjoy free access to the sources of subsistence, government is likely to be simple and honest, and society free and content; but where a policy of preëmption has run its course, the function of government is seduced from its social purpose to perpetuate the inequalities which spring from the progressive monopolization of natural resources, with augmenting corruption and injustice. To preserve government in America from such degradation, to keep the natural resources open to all, were the prime desire and object of his life. That such an effort was foredoomed to failure, in presence of imperious forces that shape society beyond the capacity of political means to change or prevent, cannot detract from the nobility of his ideal, or the inspiration of his life. Among the greater thinkers of the constitutional period Jefferson remains by far the most vital and suggestive, the one to whom later generations may return most hopefully. (pp. 361-62)

> *Vernon Louis Parrington, "Political Thinkers—The French Group," in his* Main Currents in American Thought: The Colonial Mind, 1620-1800, Vol. 1, *1927. Reprint by Harcourt Brace Jovanovich, 1954, pp. 333-62.**

FRANKLIN D. ROOSEVELT (essay date 1933)

[*Roosevelt was the thirty-second president of the United States, serving from 1933 to 1945. In this essay, written during the Depression, he exhorts Americans to accept his leadership and to participate in rebuilding the country's economic health. Roosevelt cites the continuity in American thought from the principles of Jefferson to the political realities of the 1930s and calls for national unity.*]

Federalism, as Woodrow Wilson so wisely put it, was a group "possessed of unity and informed by a conscious solidarity of interest." It was Jefferson's purpose to teach the country that the solidarity of Federalism was only a partial one, that it represented only a minority of the people and that to build a great nation the interests of all groups in every part must be considered. He has been called a politician because he devoted years to the building of a political party. But his labor was in itself a definite and practical contribution to the unification of all parts of the country in support of common principles. When people carelessly or snobbishly deride political parties, they overlook the fact that the party system of government is one of the greatest methods of unification and of teaching people to think in common terms of our civilization.

We have in our own history three men who chiefly stand out for the universality of their interest and of their knowledge—Benjamin Franklin, Thomas Jefferson and Theodore Roosevelt. All three knew at first hand every cross current of national and of international life. All three were possessed of a profound culture in the best sense of the word, and yet all three understood the yearnings and the lack of opportunity—the hopes and fears of millions of their fellow beings. All true culture finally comes down to an appreciation of just that.

And of the three, I think that Jefferson was in many ways the deepest student—the one with the most inquiring and diversified intellect and, above all, the one who at all times looked the farthest into the future, examining the ultimate effects on humanity of the actions of the present.

Jefferson's methods were usually illustrative of government based upon a universality of interest. I can picture the weeks on horseback when he was travelling into the different states of the union, slowly and laboriously accumulating an understanding of the people of his country. He was not only drinking in the needs of the people in every walk of life, but he was also giving to them an understanding of the essential principles of self-government. (pp. 11-12)

If Jefferson could return to our councils he would find that while economic changes of a century have changed the necessary methods of government action, the principles of that action are still wholly his own. He labored for a widespread concert of thought, capable of concert of action, based on a fair and just concert of interests. He labored to bring the scattered farmers, the workers, the business men into a participation in national affairs. This was his purpose and this is the principle upon which the party he founded was based. It should now present itself as an agency of national unity.

Faith in America, faith in our tradition of our personal responsibility, faith in our institutions, faith in ourselves, demands that we recognize the new terms of the old social contract. In this comment I outline my basic conception of these terms, with the confidence that you will follow the action of your new national administration, understanding that its aims and objects are yours and that our responsibility is mutual. (pp. 13-14)

> *Franklin D. Roosevelt, in an introduction to his* Looking Forward, *The John Day Company, 1933, pp. 7-14.*

EZRA POUND (essay date 1937-38)

[*An American poet, translator, essayist, and critic, Pound was "the principal inventor of modern poetry," according to Archi-*

bald MacLeish. His importance rests in part on his encouragement and editorial and financial support of such other artists as William Butler Yeats, T. S. Eliot, James Joyce, and William Carlos Williams; but he is chiefly renowned for his poetic masterpiece, the Cantos, *which he revised and enlarged throughout much of his life. These poems are noted for their lyrical intensity, metrical experimentation, literary allusions, varied subject matter and verse forms, and incorporation of phrases from foreign languages, including Chinese ideographs and Egyptian hieroglyphs. History and politics also greatly interested Pound, and many of his poems and critical writings reflect his attempt to synthesize his aesthetic vision with his political, economic, and cultural ideals. His pro-Fascist activities during World War II led to his indictment for treason and for a time diminished his reputation as one of the most innovative and creative artists of the twentieth century. Here, Pound examines the correspondence between Jefferson and John Adams. In portions of the essay not excerpted below, Pound identifies two systems of European philosophy: the Mediterranean (Greek and Roman) system, which produced the Italian theologian Thomas Aquinas; and the Teutonic system, which produced the philosophers of the Renaissance, Reformation, and the Encyclopedist movements. He then briefly traces the development of these two philosophic systems throughout history, their influence on Jefferson, and their evidence in his correspondence with Adams. According to Pound, these letters, which he praises for "their sanity and civilization, their varied culture and omnivorous curiosity," highlight Jefferson's ability to synthesize the knowledge and curiosity of the Encyclopedists with the orderly universe of Aquinas. For further commentary by Pound, see Additional Bibliography.]*

Between 1760 and 1826 two civilized men lived and to a considerable extent reigned in America. They did not feel themselves isolated phenomena. They were not by any means shrunk into a clique or dependent on mutual admiration, or on a clique estimation. They both wrote an excellent prose which has not, so far as I know, been surpassed in our fatherland, though Henry James had a style of his own, narrative, which was fit for a different purpose.

The correspondence between Thomas Jefferson and John Adams, following their reconciliation, is a landmark of American culture. It should be for literate Americans both a shrine and a monument. The fact that it is not, that these letters are not part of the regular curricula in American colleges, that the works of both founders are so difficult to obtain, is a damning commentary on American historians and educators. Nothing surpasses the Jefferson-Adams correspondence as evidence of what civilization was in early America. Jefferson and Adams were *civilized* men as well as patriots. Their culture, and that of men like them, was the link between the minds of the old and new worlds; a study of their exchange of ideas illumines both. (p. 314)

Our national culture can perhaps be better defined from the Jefferson letters than from any other three sources, and mainly to its advantage. I do not think that they have ever been analyzed very clearly in themselves, and I am not sure that anyone has tried very coherently to relate them to anything else. Such a treatment might here seem indicated, but I do not wish, by giving a résumé of the correspondence, to keep anyone who might profit by it from going directly to the letters themselves. Let them serve rather as axes of reference to related ideas, for a yardstick to be applied to other cultural values. Let this essay have no point in the sense that it would *prove* anything about the Jefferson-Adams correspondence. It is rather an attempt to show how it might serve as a point of departure, a workable dynamo, for a revalorization of our cultural heritage. (p. 315)

[I wish] to set up, as a background for Jefferson's thinking, two poles of reference: one, a graduated system in which all actions were relatively good or evil according to almost millimetric measurement, but in the absolute; two, a system in which everything was good or bad without any such graduation, but as taboo, though the system itself was continually modified in action by contingencies. (p. 318)

Jefferson, in his range of knowledge and empirical curiosity, was the heir of the encyclopedists, but he was Aquinian in his tendency to fit everything observable into an orderly system. He had the totalitarian view, seeing forces not in isolation but as interactive. (p. 319)

One of the main implications to be gathered from the letters is that they stand for a life not split into bits. They tell of a kind of life that had wholeness and mental order. Their sanity and civilization, their varied culture and omnivorous curiosity stem from the encyclopedists, but they are not accompanied by the thinning, the impoverishment of mental life, which lack of structural order was to produce in a few decades. (p. 320)

Adams and Jefferson existed in a full world. They were not English provincials, though grounded in the European cultural heritage. It was their fresh Americanism which liberated them from the sterility which followed the encyclopedists. Their letters abound in consciousness of Europe, and the truly appalling suburbanism that set in after the Civil War, our relapse into cerebral tutelage, did not afflict Adams and Jefferson. Not only were they level and contemporary with the best minds of Europe, but they entered into the making of that mind itself. (p. 323)

> Ezra Pound, "The Jefferson-Adams Correspondence," in The North American Review, Vol. 244, No. 2, Winter, 1937-38, pp. 314-24.*

CARL BECKER (lecture date 1943)

[In the following excerpt, written on the bicentennial of Jefferson's birth, Becker provides a comprehensive discussion of his political philosophy. He begins by examining the Declaration to uncover Jefferson's fundamental principles, which Becker summarizes as "(1) that the universe and man in it is governed by natural law; (2) that all men have certain inherent natural rights; (3) that governments exist to secure these rights; and (4) that all just governments derive their authority from the consent of the governed." Becker then explicates these principles, concluding with an estimate of their current relevance. In light of the policies of Nazi Germany, according to Becker, Jefferson's advocacy of the rights of the individual and of representative government based on majority vote are still vitally important. For additional commentary by Becker, see excerpt dated 1922.]

[Jefferson's] name is for us inevitably associated with a certain general idea, a certain way of regarding man and the life of man, a certain political philosophy. The word that best denotes this political philosophy is democracy. More than any other man we think of Jefferson as having formulated the fundamental principles of American democracy, of what we now like to call the American way of life. (p. 201)

The political philosophy of Thomas Jefferson was not in its fundamental principles original with him. It was his only in the sense that he gave to ideas widely current, and genuinely entertained by him, a Jeffersonian form and flavor. Nowhere is this peculiarity of form and flavor so evident as in the famous **Declaration of Independence,** but Jefferson did not claim that the ideas themselves were in any way novel. . . . [The] high value of the **Declaration** for his own time [was] that it expressed in lucid and persuasive form ideas then widely accepted, and thereby provided a reasoned justification for renouncing the authority of the British government. But the **Declaration** purports to have a higher value than that; for in providing reasons for renouncing the authority of a particular government at a particular time, Jefferson took occasion to formulate the universal principles that, as he believed, could alone justify the authority of any government at any time.

These principles are formulated in a single paragraph. We are all familiar with it, having read it or heard it read many times. But it will always, and certainly at no time more than now, bear repeating; and I will therefore repeat it once more, not precisely as it appears in the **Declaration,** but as Jefferson first wrote it in the original draft.

> We hold these truths to be sacred and undeniable; that all men are created equal and independent; that from that equal creation they derive rights inherent and inalienable, among which are the preservation of life, and liberty, and the pursuit of happiness; that to secure these rights governments are instituted among men, deriving their just powers from the consent of the governed; that whenever any form of government shall become destructive of these ends, it is the right of the people to alter or to abolish it, and to institute new government, laying its foundation on such principles and organizing its powers in such form, as to them shall seem most likely to effect their safety and happiness.

This statement contains the sum and substance of Jefferson's political philosophy, which may be reduced to four fundamental principles: (1) that the universe and man in it is governed by natural law; (2) that all men have certain inherent natural rights; (3) that governments exist to secure these rights; and (4) that all just governments derive their authority from the consent of the governed. These principles, made explicit in our federal and state constitutions, are still the fundamental principles of our political system; and on this anniversary occasion, when we are fighting a desperate war to safeguard the political system that Jefferson did so much to establish, it is indeed appropriate for us to ask: What is still living in this political philosophy? In order to answer this question, I will break it down into two more specific questions. First, what did Jefferson understand by natural law and natural rights, and what form of government did he think best suited to secure these rights? Second, to what extent is his conception of rights and government still valid for us?

The doctrine of natural law and natural rights, as Jefferson understood it, was revolutionary only in the sense that it was a reinterpretation, in secular and liberal terms, of the Christian theory of the origin, nature, and destiny of man. As commonly understood in the eighteenth century, it was perhaps never better stated than by the French writer, Volney.

> Natural law is the regular and constant order of facts by which God rules the universe; the order which his wisdom presents to the sense and reason of men, to serve them as an equal and common rule of conduct, and to guide them, without distinction of race or sect, towards perfection and happiness.

For Jefferson as for Volney, God still existed. But for them God the Father of Christian tradition had become attenuated into God the Creator, or First Cause. Having originally created the world for a beneficent purpose and according to a rational plan, the Creator had withdrawn from immediate and arbitrary control of human affairs to the dim recesses where absolute being dwells, leaving men to work out their own salvation as best they could. But they could work out their salvation very well because the Creator had revealed his beneficent purpose, not in Holy Writ, but in the open Book of Nature, which all men by the light of reason could read and interpret. "Is it simple," exclaimed Rousseau, "is it natural, that God should have gone in search of Moses in order to speak to Jean Jacques Rousseau?" To Rousseau, to Jefferson and Volney, it seemed more natural that God should have revealed his beneficent purpose through his works; from which it seemed self-evident that the whole duty of man was to discover progressively, by studying his created works, the invariable laws of nature and of nature's god, and to bring their ideas, their conduct, and their social and political institutions into harmony with them.

From this conception of natural law Jefferson and his fellows derived the doctrine that all men are created equal and are endowed by their creator with certain natural and imprescriptible rights. Many otherwise intelligent persons have thought to refute Jefferson by pointing out that all men are in fact not equal. With the same ingenuity and poverty of imagination one might refute St. Augustine's doctrine of the brotherhood of man by pointing out that all men are in fact not brothers. All men, St. Augustine would have replied, are brothers in the sight of God; and Jefferson's doctrine of equality comes to the same thing—that all men are equal in the possession of a common humanity, and if they are not in fact equal, and have not in fact the same rights and privileges, the highest morality, both for the individual and for society, is to act always on the assumption that all men should be accorded, so far as is humanly possible, the same opportunities and consideration. To act on this assumption would be, both for individuals and for society, to do the will of God and to live the good life. (pp. 201-03)

[Jefferson's natural rights philosophy] affirmed that men are endowed by their Creator with reason in order that they may progressively discover what is true, and with conscience in order that they may be disposed, in the measure of their enlightenment, to follow that which is good. It was perhaps the dominant quality of Jefferson's mind and temperament, as it was of so many men of his time, to have faith in the worth and dignity, the rational intelligence and good will, of the individual man; and it was for this reason that, in considering the means for achieving the good life, they relied so confidently upon the negative principle of freedom of the individual from social constraint—freedom of opinion, in order that the truth might prevail; freedom of occupation and of enterprise, in order that careers might be open to talent; and freedom from arbitrary political control, in order that no man might be compelled against his will.

These freedoms were precisely what Jefferson meant by "liberty" as one of the inalienable rights of man, and it was through the fullest enjoyment of these freedoms that the "pursuit of happiness" would be most likely to end in happiness for the greatest number of men. And so we arrive at the central idea of the natural rights philosophy in respect to the proper function of government—the happy idea that the best way to secure the inalienable rights of man is just to leave the individual as free as possible to enjoy them, and that accordingly no form of government can secure them so well as the one that governs least. This idea was so engaging that any one with an unbounded faith in the natural goodness of men, and an equal faith in the validity of formal logic, might easily push straight on to the conclusion reached by Proudhon—the conclusion, namely, that "property is theft," that all governments exist to condone it, and that men will never be free and happy until all governments are abolished.

Jefferson had not sufficient faith either in the native goodness of men or in formal logic ever to reach that conclusion. . . . History and political experience, rather than the logic of political theory, convinced Jefferson that men had been governed too much, and above all too arbitrarily, by kings claiming divine right, and that among the institutions that obscured the native goodness of men by depriving them of equal rights none was less defensible than a hereditary aristocracy enjoying privileges that were unearned and exacting a deference that was unmerited. It seemed to him self-evident, therefore, that the people could govern themselves better than kings and aristocrats, whose powers and privileges rested upon the accident of birth, could do it for them. Not that the people could govern themselves with perfection, or without difficulty. All forms of government, he was aware, had their evils, and of popular government the principal evil, he said, was "turbulence; but weigh this against the oppressions of monarchy, and it becomes nothing."

The evils of government by the people were even less than nothing when compared with its virtues, its chief virtue being that "it is the only form of government that is not eternally at open or secret war with the rights of mankind." But what, in concrete instances, did Jefferson mean by "the people" who have a right to govern themselves? The people, in this sense, might mean all the people in the world, or all the people in Virginia, or all the people composing a particular race or sect. Practical statesman that he was, Jefferson took the world, politically speaking, as he found it, divided into groups that by tradition and community of interest regarded themselves, and were commonly regarded, as "nations." For purposes of government, all such nations might at any time "assume, among the powers of the earth, the separate and equal station, to which the laws of nature and of nature's God entitle them." Thus nations as well as individuals had their natural rights—the right of political self-determination. But how was this self-determination to be effected, how was the consent of the governed to be obtained? Any nation is composed of individuals, and individuals necessarily differ in their opinions and their interests; and it seemed to Jefferson self-evident that the only practicable way of reconciling these differences was by majority vote. Even a monarchy with all of its trappings, or an aristocracy with all of its privileges, if really supported by a majority vote, would be a "just government" because it would rest on the "consent of the governed." (pp. 203-04)

There is, of course, no more fundamental or obdurate problem in political philosophy than that of the conflicting interests of the one and the many—the difficulty being to reconcile the desirable liberties of the individual with the necessary powers of society; and Jefferson was not more successful than other philosophers in providing a satisfactory solution of it. His solution, such as it was, is presented in a letter to Dupont de Nemours, some portions of which I venture to quote, because in it he states briefly and categorically, and better perhaps than anywhere else, the chief tenets of his political faith.

I believe with you that morality, compassion, generosity, are innate elements of the human constitution; that there exists a right independent of force; that the right to property is founded on our natural wants, in the measure with which we are endowed to satisfy these wants, and the right to what we acquire by those means without violating the similar rights of other sensible beings; that no one has a right to obstruct another exercising his faculty innocently for the relief of sensibilities made a part of his nature; that justice is the fundamental law of society; that the majority, oppressing an individual, is guilty of a crime, abuses its strength, and by acting on the law of the strongest breaks up the foundations of society; that action by the citizens in person, in affairs within their reach and competence, and in all others by representatives, chosen immediately, and removable by themselves, constitutes the essence of a republic; that all governments are more or less republican in proportion as this principle enters more or less into their composition; and that government by a republic is capable of extension over a greater surface of country than any other form.

The right of national self-determination, and republican government based upon popular suffrage and majority vote—these were Jefferson's fundamental ideas as to the form of government to secure the natural rights of man. Turning then from the proper form of government to its function, we find that Jefferson would confine its activities within narrow limits. In the passage just quoted, and in Jefferson's writings generally, we can note his disposition to believe that man is naturally good but that men are prone to evil; or, translating it into political terms, that citizens in the mass are to be trusted but that citizens elected to office need to be carefully watched. I have quoted Jefferson as saying that the chief evil of republican government is "turbulence"; but he did not really think so. Indeed, he said that a little turbulence on the part of the people now and then would do no harm, since it would serve to remind elected officials that their authority was after all only a delegated and limited franchise from the people. What Jefferson really believed is that political power is inherently dangerous, and that accordingly the chief evil in any form of government is that there may be too much of it. From this it followed that in devising a republican government the chief aim should be to avoid that danger by dispersing power among individual magistrates, separating it in respect to function, and otherwise limiting it by applying the grand negative principle of checks and balances. Fundamentally, Jefferson agreed with Thomas Paine, that whereas society is the result of men's virtues, government is the result of their vices, and therefore a necessary evil; necessary in order to preserve order, protect property, and guarantee contracts; evil because inherently prone to magnify its authority and thereby impair the liberties of the individual. (pp. 204-05)

Closely associated with Jefferson's fear of the open usurpation of political power, was his fear of the secret and more insidious influences by which men become debased and corrupted. Republican government, he was aware, could not well succeed unless the majority of citizens were independent, honest, and reasonably intelligent. Intelligence could be sufficiently trained and directed by education—schools for the people and colleges for the leaders. But honesty and independence depended far less upon precept than upon the conditions in which men lived. The best conditions were those of country life. "Cultivators of the earth," Jefferson said, "are the most virtuous and independent citizens." Vice and political corruption flourished, as he thought, chiefly in cities. In cities, where people were mostly unknown to each other, unscrupulous individuals could push their selfish interests under cover of the general indifference; and industrial communities, making so much of impalpable and evanescent forms of wealth, opened the door to speculation for unearned profit, stimulated greed, and rewarded conspicuous but useless luxury: provided all the conditions, in short, for the rise of a corrupt and politically influential "money power." Jefferson regarded a limited commerce and industry as necessary adjuncts of agriculture, but he had the farmer's settled antipathy to banks and their dubious financial manipulations. . . . Capital invested in agriculture and useful manufactures was productively employed; but "all of the capital employed in paper speculation is barren and useless, producing, like that on a gaming table, no accession to itself"; and as for banks they are "a blot left in all our constitutions, which, if not covered, will end in their destruction." Jefferson was never weary of pointing to England as the most ominous example of a nation rapidly losing its freedom by the unchecked multiplication of such evils; and he was convinced that the United States would suffer the same loss if it did not profit in time by that example.

Such in brief was Thomas Jefferson's political philosophy—his conception of human rights, and of the particular form of government best suited to secure those rights. What then is still living in this philosophy? To what extent is Jefferson's conception of rights still valid for us? To what extent is the form of government recommended by him well adapted for securing the rights, whatever they are, that need to be secured in our time?

Any careful study of Jefferson and his ideas is apt, sooner or later, to leave one with the general impression that he was more at home in the world of ideas than in the world of men and affairs. He had little of Franklin's salty zest for life in the rough, little of his genial, tolerant acceptance of men as they are, and none of his talent for being comfortable in crowds and hobnobbing with persons of every station. . . . One may say that he felt with the mind as some people think with the heart. John Adams said that his writings were characterized by "a peculiar felicity of expression" [see excerpt dated 1822]. They were indeed—perhaps a little too much so. In reading Jefferson one feels that it would be a relief to come, now and then, upon a hard, uncompromising, passionate sentence, such as: "As for me, give me liberty or give me death." What one expects to find is rather: "Manly sentiment bids us to die freemen rather than to live as slaves." Jefferson's ideas had also this felicity, and also perhaps a little too much of it. They come to birth a little too easily, and rest a little precariously on the aspirations and ideals of good men, and not sufficiently on the brute concrete facts of the world as it is. . . . One suspects that with a little more humane feeling and a great deal more passion in his make-up, Jefferson would have been an out-and-out non-resistance pacifist; as it is he presents us with the anomaly of a revolutionist who hated violence, and a President of the United States who was disconcerted by the possession of political power.

If Jefferson was more at home in the world of ideas than in the world of men and affairs, it follows, more or less as a

A photograph of the Rotunda at the University of Virginia, which Jefferson designed. Photograph by Joseph C. Farber from Thomas Jefferson Redivivus. *Reprinted by permission of Georges Borchardt, Inc., as agents for the photographer.*

consequence, that, as a political philosopher, he was a better judge of ends than of means. In all that relates to the fundamental values of life, both for the individual and for society, in all that relates to the ideal aims that democratic government professes to realize, his understanding was profound. But in respect to the means, the particular institutional forms through which these values and ideal aims were to be realized, he was often at fault, if not for his own time at least for the future. And when he was at fault, he was so partly because he conceived of society as more static than it really is; partly because he conceived of American society in his time as something that could, by relatively simple political devices, be kept relatively isolated and with slight changes be preserved in its relatively Arcadian simplicity. But his chief limitation as a political philosopher (and one should in fairness remember that it was the chief limitation of most political thinkers of his time) was that he was unduly influenced by the idea that the only thing to do with political power, since it is inherently dangerous, is to abate it. Jefferson did not sufficiently recognize the harsh fact that political power, whether dangerous or not, always exists in the world and will be used by those who possess it; and as a consequence of this failure he was too much concerned with negative devices for obstructing the use of political power for bad ends, and too little concerned with positive devices for making use of it for good ends. (pp. 205-07)

That the republican form of government—that is to say, government by elected representatives and magistrates—is the best form Jefferson was convinced because, as he said, it "is the only form of government that is not eternally at open or secret war with the rights of mankind.'' The republican form of government, which Jefferson helped to organize under the Constitution of 1787, still exists essentially unchanged; and today we accept it with even less qualification and divided loyalty than obtained in Jefferson's time. We accept it for many reasons, no doubt—because we have become habituated to it, and because there is nothing in our political traditions to provide us with a model of any other form. But we also accept it for the same fundamental reason that Jefferson accepted it—from the profound conviction that it is the only form of government that is not at war with the natural rights of mankind, or at all events with those familiar rights and privileges which we regard as in some sense natural because from long habituation they seem to us so imprescriptibly American.

Recent events have greatly strengthened this conviction. Some twenty years ago we were in a mood to ask whether the representative system of government might not be, if not at open, at least too often at secret war with the rights of mankind. That was a mood induced by comparing the democratic practice with the democratic ideal, with the inevitable if perhaps salutary result of magnifying the defects and minimizing the virtues of the democratic system as a going concern. But for ten years past we have been permitted, have indeed been compelled, to reappraise the democratic system with all of its defects in the light, not of the democratic ideal, but of the practical alternative as exhibited for our admiration in Germany and elsewhere; and the result of this reappraisal has been to make it clear that the defects of our system of government are after all, in comparison, trivial, while its virtues are substantial. Indeed, the incredible cynicism and brutality of Adolf Hitler's way of regarding man and the life of man, made real by the servile and remorseless activities of his bleak-faced, humorless Nazi supporters, has forced men everywhere to reexamine the validity of half-forgotten ideas, and to entertain once more half-discarded convictions as to the substance of things not seen. One of these convictions is that ''liberty, equality, fraternity,'' and ''the inalienable rights of man'' are generalities, whether glittering or not, that denote realities—the fundamental realities that men will always fight and die for rather than surrender.

It is in defense of these rights, and of the democratic or republican form of government that we are now fighting a desperate war; and we justify our action by the very reasons advanced by Jefferson—that the democratic form of government is the form best suited to secure the inalienable rights of man. We may be less sure than Jefferson was that a beneficent intelligence created the world on a rational plan for man's special convenience. We may think that the laws of nature, and especially the laws of human nature, are less easily discovered and applied than he supposed. We may have found it more difficult to define the rights of man and to secure them by simple institutional forms than he anticipated. Above all, we have learned that human reason is not quite so infallible an instrument for recording truth as he believed it to be, and that men themselves are less amenable to rational persuasion. Nevertheless, in essentials the political philosophy of Jefferson is our political philosophy; in essentials democracy means for us what it meant for him.

Democracy is for us, as it was for him, primarily a set of values, a way of regarding man and the life of man. It is also for us, as it was for him, a set of concrete institutions devised for the purpose of realizing those values. We understand, as

he did, but rather more clearly than he did, that the concrete institutions are bound to change: they have changed in many ways since Jefferson's time, they are changing now, and they will change even more in time to come. But we may believe, as Jefferson did, that the essential values of life are enduring; and one reason for believing so is that the values which we cherish are those which Jefferson proclaimed, and which for more than two thousand years the saints and sages of the world have commonly regarded as the ideal end and ultimate test of civilized living. If we were to write a modern declaration of the democratic faith, it might run somewhat as follows:

> We hold these truths to be self-evident: that the individual man has dignity and worth in his own right; that it is better to be governed by persuasion than by force; that fraternal good will is more worthy than a selfish and contentious spirit; that in the long run all values, both for the individual and for society, are inseparable from the love of truth and the disinterested search for it; that the truth can be discovered only in so far as the mind of man is free; that knowledge and the power it confers should be used for promoting the welfare and happiness of all men rather than for serving the selfish interests of those individuals and classes whom fortune and intelligence have endowed with a temporary advantage; and that to secure these high aims in the life of man no form of government yet devised is so well adapted as one which is designed to be a government of the people, by the people, and for the people.

To this declaration of the modern democratic faith Thomas Jefferson would, I feel sure, have subscribed without qualification. And it is in this sense, the most important sense of all, that his political philosophy, and still more the humane and liberal spirit of the man himself, abides with us, as a living force, to clarify our aims, to strengthen our faith, and to fortify our courage. (pp. 209-10)

> *Carl Becker, ''What Is Still Living in the Political Philosophy of Thomas Jefferson?'' in* Proceedings of the American Philosophical Society, *Vol. 87, No. 3, July, 1943, pp. 201-10.*

HARRY TRUMAN   (speech date 1948)

[*Truman was president of the United States from Franklin Delano Roosevelt's death in 1945 until 1953. The following excerpt was drawn from a transcription of a speech given by Truman during his successful campaign for a second term. In this speech, presented at a dinner given by the Democratic party commemorating Jefferson and Andrew Jackson, Truman lauds these two great Americans as the forerunners of the modern Democratic party. He also compares Jefferson with Alexander Hamilton, contending that the influence of their disparate philosophies continues to be felt in the progressive liberalism of the Democrats and the reactionary conservatism of their opponents.*]

We meet tonight, on the occasion of the 100th anniversary of the Democratic National Committee to honor two great Americans. These men early in our history inspired the people of this country to assert their rights against privilege.

They endowed the United States with a liberal philosophy and tradition. At the same time they were practical men, able to translate liberal philosophy into law and political fact.

I speak of the father of American liberalism—Thomas Jefferson.

I speak also of the man who later gave American liberalism a new and even richer meaning—Andrew Jackson. . . .

Alexander Hamilton, the first Secretary of the Treasury, frankly affirmed his belief that government should be controlled by the rich and the well-born. He believed that Government should be aristocratic and that it should operate primarily in the interest of wealth and privilege.

Fortunately for the people, there was also in Washington's Administration a powerful man, Thomas Jefferson, who believed just as strongly that government should be by the whole people and for the whole people. He was convinced that true democratic progress could be attained only by extending political and economic liberty, religious freedom, and educational opportunity.

Jefferson passionately believed that the genius of America rested in the ranks of ordinary men, and that they must control the Government.

There could hardly have been a sharper cleavage than that between Hamilton and Jefferson.

The supporters of Jefferson organized a political party of progressive liberalism that has continued in American political life down to the present day. That party is today known as the Democratic party.

The followers of Alexander Hamilton also banded themselves together as a political party. This, the party of conservatism, the party of rule by, and for the privileged few, has its counterpart in our national life today.

I have long been impressed by the continuity of these two political philosophies throughout American history.

I have been impressed because the policies of their disciples are such faithful images of the philosophies themselves. The parcel of reactionary conservatism may be wrapped in bright colors and gay tinsel, but when you open it, you always find party rule for the benefit of the privileged few. Inside the parcel of progressive liberalism, however, you always find government for the benefit of all the people—true democratic government.

The forces that fought Jefferson, the forces that Jackson fought—and that progressive liberals have had to fight throughout our history have been the forces of selfish wealth and privilege.

The party of progressive liberalism—the Democratic party—believes today, as it has always believed, that it is the duty of popular Government to protect and promote the interests, not of just the privileged few, but of all the groups and individuals in our nation.

> *Harry Truman, in an address delivered at the Jefferson-Jackson Day dinner of Washington, in* The New York Times, *February 20, 1948, p. 2.*

EDD WINFIELD PARKS (essay date 1952)

[*Parks surveys Jefferson's achievements as a man of letters, focusing on his style, opinions of the classical writers, literary aesthetic, and views on prosody in English and American poetry.*]

When George Washington was questioned about the relative advantages of knowing Greek and French, he answered that he could not pretend to judge of Greek but that French was useful to a traveler. This practical response was probably typical of Virginian thought of his day, or of thought anywhere, at any time. Usually, philosophical and literary values are casually disregarded. A wide-ranging curiosity, an instinctive desire to judge facts and values, an almost tireless mental and physical energy, a quick interest in any matter that might extend the boundaries of man's knowledge—these are traits rarely possessed. Thomas Jefferson had them in abundance, and this quality gives importance to his work in fields where he remained a gifted amateur. He could get excited over measuring the fall of rain, over a new type of seed or plow, over the rights of man and the principles of government, and over the correct scansion of a poem. Although his statements and ideas have, naturally, a varying value on the subjects he touched upon, his first-hand observation and reasoned, independent thought give to most of his reflections a personal validity and a wide interest.

If he took many fields of knowledge as proper for his own inquiries, he was never satisfied with merely idle speculation. It was not enough that a thing be good; it should serve a tangible and preferably an immediate end. He did not ask that profit or credit accrue to him: if he could add to the knowledge of French scientists by sending them strange bones, increase the yield of rice on Carolina farms, or inculcate the ideas of democratic freedom by encouraging the study of Anglo-Saxon, he had helped somewhat in the slow, continuous battle against ignorance, against poverty, against injustice. . . . [His] concept of tangible good went beyond the needs and comforts of the body. A man's mind and soul were to be reckoned with as living entities which must be nourished in their own right. He desired to systematize and order the knowledge available to man, but he desired with equal fervor to expand the realm of man's knowledge.

These efforts were not, in his estimation, a part of his professional life. He was a farmer. . . . Except for the seven years that he worked as a practising lawyer, until Governor Dunmore closed the Virginia courts, he had no other profession. His terms as Governor of Virginia, Ambassador to France, Secretary of State, Vice-President and President of the United States filled many years of his life, and he was beyond question proud of his work. Yet he regarded these periods of service as, in a way, interludes; a man had to assume those public responsibilities for which he was fitted, and a man had to do all that was in his power to put into practical operation the ideals of living which he advocated. Jefferson was an expert politician, but one ingredient in his proficiency was this: in his own mind and in the estimation of most Americans, he remained an amateur. He could maintain a moral position because with him it was not a pose. (pp. 450-51)

Although his collected works will run, according to the latest estimate, to fifty-odd stout volumes, [Jefferson] was never in the professional sense a man of letters. . . . He was proud of his style, but it was not pride in writing which caused him to reckon among his finest achievements the authorship of the **Declaration of Independence** and religious freedom ["**An Act for Establishing Religious Freedom**"]: they were symbols rather than personal achievements; they illustrated certain principles, and they helped to extend the freedom of mankind. His writing had a definite object; it was strictly occasional, and was meant to serve an immediate purpose. He was master of a clear, dry, classic style, which could occasionally take on emotion and color; he sought hard for the precise word, and generally he found it; he could adjust and sharpen and heighten his style until it said admirably what he wanted to say and what the occasion demanded. But interest in good prose writing was a personal, almost an aristocratic, interest. His felicity of expression appears in public documents, state papers, and private letters. (pp. 451-52)

To him, Homer was always "the first of poets." The work of Homer was a criterion of poetic judgment and a guide to conduct. In Gilbert Chinard's phrase, he "evidently saw in Homer a repository of the wisdoms of an ancient civilization." There is evidence in Jefferson's literary commonplace book that he was interested in a poet's philosophy, and in those descriptions which were as applicable to Virginia as to ancient Greece and Italy. . . . [His] knowledge of the *Iliad* and the *Odyssey* was thorough enough that, in a commentary on slavery, he remembered Homer's statement that slavery takes away half of a man's worth; when he read the account of a new wheel, he could turn instantly to a similar description. After his wife's death he chose for her epitaph two lines from the *Iliad*.

If his quotations are an index, Jefferson got from Homer primarily a sense of man's weakness, his faith, his moral strength, and his capacity for stoic endurance. No poet could lessen the chances of adversity or the certainty of death, but poetry wisely read could strengthen the mind to endure them. As he grew older, Jefferson's taste constricted. It became more austere, until he was satisfied only with the highest and deepest of poetry. The small doses of sense, imagination, and rhythm were no longer enough, and he wrote, in **"Thoughts on English Prosody"**: "I suspect we are left at last only with Homer and Virgil, perhaps with Homer alone." (pp. 453-54)

[Early] in life Jefferson developed a tenable if limited aesthetic, which mainly guided his appreciation of creative writing. Using the term *fiction* in the broadest sense, he wrote in 1771 that "the entertainments of fiction are useful as well as pleasant . . . everything is useful which contributes to fix in the principles and practices of virtue." For this purpose, it did not matter whether the work were truth or fiction. From Laurence Sterne we can gain much by viewing "with emulation a soul candidly acknowledging its fault and making a just reparation"—a judgment that, sixteen years later, he stated even more forcibly: "read good books, because they will encourage, as well as direct your feelings. The writings of Sterne, particularly, form the best course of morality that ever was written." After praising Shakespeare in general and *Macbeth* in particular, Jefferson adds that "a living and lasting sense of filial duty is more effectually impressed on the mind of a son or daughter by reading *King Lear* than by all the dry volumes of ethics and divinity that ever were written."

Books were to be read for a purpose. But Jefferson's aesthetic seems at once to broaden and deepen when we realize that among the useful values to be gained were generosity, charitableness, humaneness, warmth of thought and sentiment—that they were to help make a man true, just, firm, orderly, courageous, and steadfast. Here is no narrow didacticism, no doctrine of immediate utility, but a firm belief that books existed to illuminate life. He did not ask for a complete illumination. It was sufficient if the hand of make-believe adumbrated the world of reality, but the cross-reference must be implicit in the work. He wanted to yoke together the practical and the imaginative. Reading is at once an "innocent and elegant luxury," a source of taste, and a source of information—all good things. (pp. 454-55)

Jefferson's approach to English and American literature was that of a classicist. It is all the more remarkable, therefore, that he wrote one of the first technical essays on English prosody ever produced in this country.

The manner of its writing was typical of his attitude toward literature. At Monticello and in France he had discussed versification with a French friend, F. J. de Chastellaux. Jefferson started with the assumption that English prosody depended, like Greek and Roman verse, "on long and short syllables arranged into regular feet. You were of a different opinion." He set out to convert a foreigner. In leisure hours while serving under great pressure as Ambassador to France and perhaps later as Secretary of State (for the letter to his friend is not dated), he relaxed by walking and at the same time "turning this subject in my mind."

He knew little about prosody, and contented himself with noting that of those who "have mounted the English poetry on Greek and Latin feet," the commentaries of Samuel Johnson are the best. But he did not turn back to the scholars and critics for guidance; he went directly to the poets. Reading and reflection convinced him that he had been wrong, and somewhat ruefully he confesses to de Chastellaux that it was a Frenchman who "recalled me from an error in my native tongue, and that, too, in a point the most difficult of all others to a foreigner, the law of its poetical numbers."

His method was simple. He tested lines and verses by pronouncing the words aloud, drawing upon the works of minor as well as of major poets. This simple and practical test soon convinced him that English prosody had an accentual, not a quantitative, basis. Essentially an amateur, he was alert, independent—and little concerned with precedent. (pp. 456-57)

No poet himself, Jefferson arrived at conclusions that are almost startling in their rigidity. The fundamental law of English verse, he decided, was that "the accent shall never be displaced from the syllable whereon usage hath established it." He tried to reduce the kind of feet to three (the equivalent of trochaic, iambic, and anapaestic), but in those to allow for a certain amount of elision: "There are but three arrangements into which these accents can be thrown in the English language which entitle the composition to be distinguished by the name of verse. That is. 1. Where the accent falls on all the odd syllables; 2. Where it falls on all the even syllables; 3. Where it falls on every third syllable. If the reason of this be asked, no other can be assigned but that it results from the nature of the sounds which compose the English language and from the construction of the human ear."

On this basis he tests many lines of poetry, working out for himself a method of indicating the relative strength of accents. But technical rules for reading are not enough. The gradations of sound and tone and accent are intimately connected with usage, and with the sense of the poem. If a man has "a well-organized ear," he will be conscious of the verse: to prove this, Jefferson prints as prose a passage from the Greek of Homer and proclaims that the man who can read it without pausing at every sixth foot "is an unfavored son of nature." For such persons little could be done, but for those who had a natural ear some knowledge of the technical rules would improve their art.

In one respect he was before and after his period, in preferring blank verse to rhyme. In every form of literature he demanded the condensed, the well-digested, and the reasonable. Rhyme had a jingly quality but, even worse, it forced the poet into padding his lines with "feeble nothings necessary to introtrude the rhyming word. With no other trammel than that of measure he is able to condense his thoughts and images and to leave nothing but what is truly poetical."

The time spent on a technical study of prosody, if only as a relaxation from political work and worries, seems to contradict Jefferson's demand that literature be useful. He saw no contradiction. His definition of use was so wide-ranging that it provided for spiritual as well as material good. He advocated the study of a simplified form of Anglo-Saxon because it would enable us better to use and understand modern English, but also because it would enable people to "read Shakespeare and Milton with a superior degree of intelligence and delight." There was a second, perhaps more potent, reason: from the Anglo-Saxons we had inherited our love of freedom, and students would "imbibe with the language their free principles of government." (pp. 457-58)

A good book or a sound piece of knowledge enlarged the domain of man's mind. This was the most important field of all—more important to him than wealth or success or personal well-being. In many ways a practical man, Jefferson spent most of his life in the hurly-burly of politics, and he climaxed a distinguished career with eight years in the presidency. Yet he was always willing to steal time from the immediately practical to give it to the long-range intellectual concept. What one did was no more important to him than how one thought.

Always his knowledge was at the service of others. But he never forced it upon them, or desired personal credit. It was important that a job be well done, but not important that he do it. That was his feeling about architecture as well as about writing. He preferred to share with friends rather than to expose his work for judgment before the world. When the occasion demanded, he did not hesitate; but he preferred when possible to limit his remarks to private letters.

This was his attitude toward literature. He never looked upon himself as a writer, but always as a discriminating reader who was sometimes forced into writing for the public. Yet out of his books and his literary speculations he evolved a clean, distinguished style—a distinction of thought that found expression in words. His taste was sound, if a bit austere, and his standards high, for himself as well as for the books he read. In this field, as in many others, he remained in his own mind an amateur. But the independent-minded amateur can contribute something that the professional might overlook. Jefferson does this. Whether he felt himself qualified to write on the subject or not, his scattered remarks on literature have a two-fold value: what he says about literature reveals much about Jefferson, but his critical insights help also to reveal much about literature, and even a bit about ourselves. Jefferson would have liked this double-barreled usefulness. (pp. 458-59)

Edd Winfield Parks, "Jefferson as a Man of Letters," in The Georgia Review, *Vol. VI, No. 4, Winter, 1952, pp. 450-59.*

ELISHA P. DOUGLASS   (essay date 1955)

[*Douglass counters the interpretation of Jefferson posited by Vernon Louis Parrington (1927) and others and anticipates later revisionist views of Jefferson's democratic theories. Differentiating between Revolutionary democrats and liberals, Douglass assigns Jefferson to the latter category. According to Douglass, Jefferson differed substantially from the true democrats: he was of aristocratic birth; he accepted British legal tradition as the basis for United States law; and he defined the ideal government as one controlled by the natural aristocracy, or those who were morally, spiritually, and intellectually superior. In a portion of his commentary not excerpted below, Douglass offers a detailed examination of Jefferson's 1776 draft of a constitution for the state of Virginia and his reform bills presented in the House of Delegates between 1776 and 1780.*]

Jefferson has displayed himself for posterity in voluminous literary remains as a friend of the common man and the champion of democratic principles in government. He is revered as the founder of the Democratic party and the philosopher whose ideals of freedom have played a tremendously important part in the shaping of the American tradition. Splendid personal qualities, such as humanitarianism, lack of prejudice, candor, generosity, and versatility, have accorded him a host of admirers down through the years. It is no exaggeration to say that today no other figure in American history—with the possible exception of Lincoln—enjoys such affectionate regard.

On the basis of personal writings Jefferson would certainly qualify as a democrat by eighteenth-century standards. He repeatedly testified to the conviction that all men should be equal in political rights and that the ideal republic was a representative government in which the will of the majority of citizens constituted the ultimate authority for legislative decision. Yet it is just as apparent that Jefferson was a different type of person than the equalitarian democrats . . . , and a closer study of his career reveals many points of affinity with the conservative Whigs of his day which set him apart from the democrats of the Revolutionary period.

Thomas Jefferson was by tastes, education, and inheritance an aristocrat, far removed from the yeoman farmers, so often nameless, who demanded reform of the state governments. Even though he could write to DuPont de Nemours that he loved the people "as adults whom I freely leave to self government," he tacitly regarded them as an objective entity apart from himself, as did other Revolutionary leaders. Although an informal manner led some of his more rigidly class-conscious colleagues to consider him something of a leveller, he never quarrelled with the social distinctions maintained in the eighteenth-century American republic. Democracy to him was more an enlightened philosophy than a program of action against a political system characterized by privilege, as was the case with the lower-class Revolutionary democrats. Nowhere in Jefferson's writings do we find the sense of injury and urgency and the dominant note of protest which characterized the emanations from the democrats with whom this book is concerned. He usually held himself aloof from the bitter political controversies of the day, seldom levelling charges at enemies and never indulging in billingsgate. He preferred to leave this phase of political operations to others while pursuing his objectives by quiet and effective back-stage maneuvering and persuasion.

Perhaps the most striking difference between Jefferson and the Revolutionary democrats lay in his acceptance of the basic political relationships established by eighteenth-century American constitutions and in the strain of conservative thinking which appears in his constitutional and legislative proposals. Jefferson never evinced much interest in altering the institutions of Whig government in such a way as to realize equalitarian and majoritarian ideals. Instead he appeared to accept without serious reservation a political science which in many respects made impossible the realization of his political philosophy. To some degree this may be explained as the unavoidable concession of a practical politician compelled to work in a milieu completely dominated by a ruling class drawn from the upper strata of society, but when he actually went out of his way on occasion to endorse institutional arrangements specially designed to qualify political equality and erect barriers against majority will, then his attitude shows undoubted inconsistencies which are difficult to explain. (pp. 287-89)

In addition to his acceptance of conventional political science, there was a strain of traditionalism in Jefferson's thinking—particularly during his early years—which set him apart from lower-class democrats. He fully shared the Whig conviction that the purpose of opposing British imperial legislation was to rescue traditional British rights from the attacks undertaken by an omnipotent, and therefore revolutionary Parliament. Study of history and philosophy had given him a sense of the growth and continuity of institutions and an admiration for many of those which had developed in the motherland over the centuries. Therefore, unlike the more unsophisticated democrats of the day, he attached great value to precedent and did not expect that freedom could be secured or maintained without utilizing accumulated experience. In his early plans for the American future Jefferson was looking backward to the English past for guidance; only later, after contacts with contemporary French thinkers, did his horizons widen to include more cosmopolitan sources of inspiration.

Reliance on the English tradition first appears in one of his earliest writings, the *Summary View of the Rights of British America*. . . . The object here was to find an ethical and legal basis for the autonomy which the Whigs desired after 1773. . . . [Some] way had to be found to reconcile colonial self-government and the British constitution.

This was the problem to which Jefferson addressed himself. His solution was to demonstrate historically and legally that the "true" British constitution rested on a compact between the colonists, acting through their legislatures, and the king. He asserted that the first settlers, like the ancient Saxons who left Germany for Britain in the sixth century, had expatriated themselves when they left the homeland, bringing with them their own laws, customs, and rights. Once established in America—entirely at their own expense—amity and consanguinity induced them to re-establish relations with England by voluntarily acknowledging the sovereignty of their former king. Parliament was not included in this reunion for the colonists owed allegiance only to the king, and only to the extent of the implied compact freely entered into after settlement.

Jefferson's theory of the process of colonization and the relationship between the colonies and the mother country is certainly ingenious, but it is, of course, quite unhistorical. Yet it would be unfair to condemn him for his lack of critical and impartial analysis. Like most of his contemporaries, he used history as a means of demonstrating the truth of certain generally accepted philosophical propositions. As Bolingbroke expressed it, history was philosophy teaching by example. Therefore, if the Whig conception of the constitution was "true" (and who in their party could doubt it?) the facts of settlement must demonstrate this truth. Jefferson's philosophy was therefore the determinant of his historical analysis. The distortion of the *Summary View* illustrates the intellectual processes of the age.

But the importance of the *Summary View,* for our purposes, lies not in its illustration of Jefferson the historian, but in its description and analysis of the traditional rights of British subjects. The most important of these, which Jefferson resurrected

from the dim past of Saxon England, were the rights to establish legislative bodies, to hold lands in allodial ownership, and to be free from the arbitrary exercise of the royal prerogative. These rights were part of the true heritage of Englishmen which had been obscured from view by the dark cloud of feudalism which had settled over England after the Norman conquest. The object of Americans should be to purge the dross of this unenlightened age and return to the pristine purity of original English institutions. (pp. 290-92)

[From a] brief survey of Jefferson's activities in the field of reform during the Revolutionary period it would appear that on the whole he leaned more toward eighteenth-century Whiggism than toward eighteenth-century democracy. In common with democrats he held no palpable fear of the people and was optimistic for the future of free government. In criticising the constitutions established by legislative enactment and in advocating easy amendment processes he joined with democrats in attempting to institutionalize the constituent power in the people. His disregard of property qualifications (he never specifically attacked them, however, until well into the nineteenth century) and his provision for proportionate representation in his constitutional drafts amounted to an endorsement of political equality. Yet, even after these factors have been taken into consideration, his personal tastes and manner of living, his failure to make political issues of his more radical proposals, his traditionalism and his acceptance of the Whig political science all combined to set him apart from the yeoman farmers who strove for democratic government in the Revolutionary period. Although in his constitutions of 1776 he would give the people political equality, they could exercise their equal rights only under the paternalism of an "independent," non-representative legislative house whose members held their positions for long terms of years. In the *Notes on Virginia* Jefferson voiced the fear that rule by the people's representatives alone would become "an elective despotism" as oppressive as the tyranny of a dictator.

The celebrated Virginia reforms, while ostensibly undertaken as a means of diminishing the privileges of aristocracy, broadening economic and political opportunity, reforming the criminal law, and safeguarding the rights of conscience either failed to achieve the decisive results Jefferson later claimed for them or lack the particular importance he attached to them. The abolition of entail placed no obstacle to the accumulation of wealth on the part of the great planters nor diminished their political power. The Bill Concerning Slaves, as it stood, offered freedom under harsh terms and appeared to be motivated more by a desire to rid Virginia of the blacks than to rid the blacks of their chains. The Bill for Proportioning Crimes and Punishments was in some respects a legal retrogression. The Bill for Establishing Religious Freedom by contrast was indeed a vital measure in the main stream of democratic reform, but its importance lies in separating church and state rather than in guarding the rights of conscience. Paradoxically, however, the measure actually ran counter to the desires of most yeoman farmers who desired majoritarian and equalitarian constitutions during the Revolution because it would have prevented the imposition of religious tests for office.

In the last analysis, Jefferson's ideal government was aristocracy in the sense of government by the best—the best morally, spiritually, and intellectually. He felt those in authority should be checked by the people, it is true, but only because all humans needed checks. Lord Acton's famous phrase, "All power corrupts and absolute power corrupts absolutely" might well have come from Jefferson's lips. To keep the natural aristocracy pure and capable he thought that it must be continually revitalized by new recruits from the mass of the people, geniuses "raked from the rubbish" of the untalented.

The rule of virtue meant rule by the virtuous, and these would always be in a minority. Jefferson's optimism for the future of society rested as much on a faith in those who had the capacity to rise above the people as on the people themselves. It was the duty of government to keep the channels of advancement clear. Every opportunity must be allowed for the individual to develop himself according to his own particular capacities. Jefferson's individualism was inherently rugged.

His philosophy, therefore, was liberal rather than democratic. Although liberalism has wider connotations today, in the eighteenth century it could be defined as acknowledgment and respect for reasonable diversities in human affairs, and could be found in different political systems. If a democratic state protected and maintained these diversities, it could be called liberal; if it allowed majority will to enforce conformity it would be obviously authoritarian, but at the same time, no less democratic. In the eighteenth century, democracy designated who should exercise political power and liberalism prescribed the manner of its exercise.

As previously indicated, the Whigs believed that the primary purpose of government was to maintain the natural rights without which free society could not exist. The liberals among them, like Jefferson, felt that this would not be a difficult task, for mankind was naturally good and disposed to be cooperative. Therefore government could afford to be lenient and restrict the sphere of its operations as much as possible. Conservatives like Adams who took a dimmer view of mankind felt that stricter controls were necessary. In order to protect society against the centrifugal forces set loose by the inherent selfishness in human nature, they asserted that government must adhere rigidly to the principle of separation of powers. Both liberals and conservatives were agreed, however, that rights must be guarded against any manifestation of will, whether majority or minority. (pp. 311-14)

Revolutionary liberalism as opposed to Revolutionary democracy was conservative on two counts: first, because it elevated rights above will, and second, because these rights were largely traditional. Liberals like Jefferson of course believed that there were some natural rights not yet translated into the statutes and political usages of England and the colonies, but for the most part the freedom they wished could be obtained without an appeal to philosophy. They preferred to rest their case against Britain on the solid ground of the rights of Englishmen, which embodied the most important of natural rights. This explains in part why three-fourths of the **Declaration of Independence** is devoted to the enumeration of specific violations of English rights by the sovereign. The famous preamble, which we value so highly today, may have been in 1776 the least important part of the document. Its primary purpose was to inform the world that the rights of Englishmen had a universal quality which made them indispensable for freedom everywhere.

If "Jeffersonian democracy," considered both in theory and practice, contains more of the elements of liberalism than democracy, why is the term still common currency today? Possibly one reason is a propensity on the part of biographers to make Jefferson the standard for democracy rather than the reverse. But even more important is the fact that democracy today is primarily concerned with the same values which Jef-

ferson so strikingly exemplified. In combatting fascism and communism we are fighting on a different field the same battles which he carried on against the authoritarianism of his own day. Similar enemies promote similar ideologies of defense; since we are upholding Jefferson's rights it is inevitable that his philosophy should provide tremendous inspiration. (pp. 314-15)

Today, primarily concerned with the protection of human rights, democracy bears the coloration of eighteenth-century liberalism, the essence of which was the acknowledgment and protection of reasonable diversities. Hence, paradoxically, Jefferson, as the greatest eighteenth-century exponent of liberalism, becomes more democratic by contemporary standards than by eighteenth-century standards. The problem of "Jeffersonian democracy" is therefore primarily one of definition. When democracy is construed as political processes establishing political equality and majority rule, Jefferson cannot be considered a democrat to the same extent as the dissident groups in the Revolutionary era. But when democracy is considered to be a symbol of the values of human freedom about which world controversy rages today, then Jefferson emerges as a democratic philosopher and statesman of primary importance. (pp. 315-16)

Elisha P. Douglass, "Thomas Jefferson and Revolutionary Democracy," in his Rebels and Democrats: The Struggle for Equal Political Rights and Majority Rule during the American Revolution, *1955. Reprint by Quadrangle Books, 1965, pp. 287-316.*

HERBERT APTHEKER   (essay date 1960)

[*Aptheker provides a Marxist interpretation of the Declaration of Independence. He begins by explicating several passages and then explains their philosophical underpinnings, notably the importance of the phrase "the pursuit of happiness" and Jefferson's concept of property. Aptheker's essay was originally published in 1960 in his* The American Revolution, 1763-1783: A History of the American People.]

In June 1776 a 33-year-old Virginian, working in a room rented from a bricklayer, wrote—in the words of Moses Coit Taylor—a "passionate chant of human freedom" whose influence has been as momentous as that of any other single human creation.

He made no claim to originality; on the contrary he strove to present the "common sense of the matter"; to convey, as he said, the "American mind"; to put into a brief declaration the essential facts driving the colonists to separation, and the theory of government which, to those colonists, was so universally held as to appear "self-evident." (p. 184)

Most of the **Declaration,** as adopted, consists of an enumeration of the "repeated injuries and usurpations, all having in direct object the establishment of an absolute Tyranny over these states." . . . Its philosophic, and immortal, pronouncements consist of less than 300 words.

The Americans in their manifesto of revolution begin by declaring that "a decent respect to the opinion of mankind requires that they should declare the causes which impel" them to their momentous step. This itself is new and reflects the essence of the **Declaration**'s political philosophy—the sovereignty of the people. Believing in this sovereignty and staking their lives on an attempt to establish it, they naturally are impelled to explain their cause and their motivation to the peoples of the world. If the people's will is to be supreme, then their good will is omnipotent.

Then comes the enunciation of that cause. It consists of three basic ideas: (1) human beings—essentially equal in attributes, needs, obligations and desires—possess basic rights to life, liberty and the pursuit of happiness; (2) to obtain these rights men create governments; (3) governments destructive of these rights are tyrannical; such governments may be, and indeed, should be, altered or abolished by the people who then have the right and the duty to create the kind of government which "to them shall seem most likely to effect their safety and Happiness."

These ideas were of international origin. Directly, in terms of the 18th century Americans who approved them, they were derived from the humanist and libertarian arguments of ancient Greece and Rome. They were derived from the whole magnificent Age of Reason with its titans who struggled against dogma and authoritarianism—Bacon, Grotius, Vesalius, Copernicus, Spinoza. More immediately the sources were the writings of the Irish revolutionist, Charles Lucas, the Italian economist, Beccaria, the Swiss philosopher, Vattel, and his compatriot, Burlamaqui, the German jurist, Pufendorf, from the Frenchmen, Montesquieu, Voltaire, Diderot, from the Englishmen, Milton, Sidney, Harrington, Priestley, and Locke, particularly, and from the Americans, Roger Williams, Jonathan Mayhew and John Wise.

All of these were products, as they were voices, of the central fact in human history—the struggle against oppression, and the dynamic, ever-advancing nature of that struggle. The international sources of the **Declaration** in no way, of course, contradict its national essence. It remains American, or better, therefore, it is American.

The political theory of the **Declaration** is intensely democratic and profoundly revolutionary. When Copernicus discarded the medieval concept of the qualitative inferiority of the earth's movements as compared with those of heavenly bodies, he helped revolutionize astronomy. So Jefferson's pronouncement signalized the revolutionizing of political science by discarding the medieval concept of the qualitative inferiority of earthly life as compared with heavenly bliss.

Life on earth, Jefferson held, was not supposed to be a vale of tears and suffering. The meaning of life was not unending pain to be endured meekly in order to get into heaven; and man's travail was not his cross to be borne because of original sin—because man was naturally evil. Moreover, governments were not the secular arm of the Lord, as priests were not his ecclesiastical arm.

No; this entire elaborate machine for the justification and perpetuation of the hierarchical, non-dynamic, burdensome feudal order is denied. Men are good, not evil; men are capable of governing themselves well; governments are man-made; the purpose of life is its ennoblement here on earth. The "freedom and happiness of man," Jefferson wrote to Kosciusko in 1810, must be the objects of political organization and, indeed, "the end of all science, of all human endeavor."

Hierarchy is, then, rejected and with it aristocracy and monarchy and the divine right of ruler or rulers. Equality of man replaces it and therefore sovereignty lies with these equals, and it is their will which is divine, if anything is; at any rate, it is their will which must be decisive where government seeks

their welfare. And this is dynamic, not static. The (then new) idea of progress permeates the whole argument. . . . (pp. 185-87)

If to the above is added its logical corollary—that government must rest on "the consent of the governed," as the **Declaration** says—then the right of revolution is indubitable. It is a right not to be lightly exercised, as the **Declaration** also declares, but, nevertheless, an inalienable right, which exists so long as government exists. . . . The **Declaration of Independence** admits of no exceptions to the right of revolution; it only warns against hastiness and adventurism.

Where governments oppress, where they stifle and are engines of exploitation, where they do not serve to further happiness (and clearly the majority of the people living under such governments are the authority as to whether or not they so act), they have then become tyrannical and acquiescence in tyranny is treason to man.

Certain rights are fundamental, in the **Declaration**'s view. These are the people's "unalienable rights," expressed in that magnificent phrase, crashing through the corridors of history— "arousing men to burst the chains," as Jefferson himself wrote in his last letter—"Life, Liberty and the Pursuit of Happiness."

It is the idea of man's right to the pursuit of happiness which is the heart of the document's revolutionary enunciation and one which, by its magnificent, timeless generalization makes the document meaningful and stirring for all time.

That Jefferson chose this expression rather than the more usual Whig-Lockeian one of "life, liberty and property" was deliberate and reflects the advanced position of Jefferson personally and of the revolutionary coalition which adopted it. (pp. 187-88)

Also, in order not to exaggerate the significance of Jefferson's change of the Lockeian phrase, it is important to note that Locke viewed property in a sense much broader than mere material possession. Typically, in his *Two Treatises on Government*, Locke wrote that "every man has a property in his own person" and also referred to "that property which men have in their persons as well as goods." (p. 188)

[When] Jefferson stated he had tried to say nothing novel in the **Declaration,** but rather to offer in summary fashion the generally accepted view of things to most Americans, he did not mean to exclude the idea of the pursuit of happiness. Indeed this idea, expressed in identical language, recurs in Locke himself and appears in the writings of such influential contemporaries of Jefferson as Oliver Goldsmith, Joseph Priestley and Adam Smith.

Nevertheless, Jefferson's choice of words to omit and words to include is indicative of the intensely democratic content of the American Revolution, especially at its high point. Jefferson did conceive of liberty, as had the Levellers in the 17th century, in the sense of freedom of speech and press and person, and of the pursuit of happiness, as more elemental, more profound than property rights.

Relevant, too, is it that Jefferson—while, of course, in no way conceiving of, let alone favoring, Socialism, but, on the contrary, assuming private ownership of means of production— was very sensitive to the concentration of property-holding and felt it to be the central threat to democratic rights. He saw "enormous inequality" of property ownership, especially in land, as the cause of "so much misery to the bulk of mankind" that he insisted, in 1785, that "legislators cannot invent too many devices for subdividing property."

Basic to the **Declaration** also, of course, is its affirmation of a nation's right to self-determination. This clearly is the meaning of the first sentence in the **Declaration,** affirming the right of "one people to dissolve the political bands which have connected them with another, and to assume among the powers of the earth, the separate and equal station to which the Laws of Nature and of Nature's God entitle them." This right is also derived from popular sovereignty, but it is simultaneously expressive of another central force in modern history—the sense of nationality. (pp. 188-89)

The limitations of the **Declaration of Independence** are the limitations of the century and the class which produced it. The **Declaration** presents the State in an idealist fashion; it sees man in an abstract manner, not men and women in a class society, with the state as a reflection and a bulwark of the dominant class.

The revolutionary bourgeoisie sees the state, which it is capturing and remolding, as an object in itself, standing above classes, or as some sort of an arbiter between conflicting classes within society. While its insistence that men create the state for their own purposes is a leap beyond the feudal concept, it is perhaps an even greater distance short of the historical-materialist class concept of the state.

This supra-class view limits, too, the **Declaration**'s theory of equality, for while that theory is revolutionary *vis-à-vis* feudal hierarchical notions, it is largely illusory in terms of the material base of bourgeois society, in terms of property and class relationship, in terms of effective power—considerations of vital importance for a full understanding of equality.

The relationship between property ownership and inequality was, of course, axiomatic to the Revolutionary Fathers. Said Alexander Hamilton, for example (in the 79th number of *The Federalist*): "In the general course of human nature, *a power over a man's subsistence amounts to a power over his will*" (italics in original). But they generally saw the State in abstracted political terms and so expressed a theory of equality, which while of the highest consequence in the whole democratic struggle of mankind, was itself largely confined to the political and even there, in practice, was highly partial.

As a result, property limitations on the political power of adult white males are not per se condemned in the **Declaration** and existed in the rebellious colonies while their delegates signed the document. Other limitations, as religious tests for the enjoyment of political power, were viewed by many as not incongruous or inconsistent.

As the disabilities become even more complete, the incongruity becomes less apparent to the **Declaration**'s signers. Thus, the full, if temporary, disability of the several hundred thousand indentured servants was quite compatible, to the signers, with the **Declaration.**

Jefferson's study at Monticello. Photograph by John Grant.

Especially striking is the fact that while the **Declaration** spoke of equality, liberty, and the pursuit of happiness, 600,000 American slaves—slaves for life, who transmitted their status to all offspring, through the maternal line—were held to labor under the lash. It is indeed one of the most painful and yet most revealing facts in American history that the author of the **Declaration of Independence** was himself a slave-owner.

This central failing of the **Declaration,** and of the American Revolution, reflects the organic connection between the rise of capitalism and the ideology and practice of racism. . . . It is certainly racism which helps account for the revolutionists going into battle with the slogan, "Liberty or Death" on their banners, and over half a million slaves on their fields. (pp. 191-92)

Also reflective of the limitations of the **Declaration** is the fact that when it said, "All men are created equal," it did not mean all men and women; had this been offered for ratification the document would not have been signed. This limitation did not go unremarked at the time, for both in England and in the colonies there were rudimentary stirrings of what, in three generations, was to become a major social movement.

Thus it is that John Adams' wife, Abigail, wrote him: "I cannot say that I think you are very generous to the ladies; for, whilst you are proclaiming peace and good-will to men, emancipating all nations, you insist upon retaining an absolute power over wives." Somewhat later, in 1778, this splendid woman declared: "I regret the trifling, narrow, contracted education of the females of my own country." Rare were the men in America who agreed. . . . (p. 192)

But, of course, it is not the limitations of the **Declaration of Independence** which define its historic impact. Those limitations, of time and place and class, are omissions; the actual words of the document, having universality and humanity, remain fresh and inspiring. . . .

[For generations] the **Declaration** was abhorred as seditious by the earth's rulers; its distribution or possession in many places was a capital crime. Professors in Italy, France, Denmark, Austria, and Prussia, well into the 19th century, were fired, and even imprisoned, for insisting on teaching their students its challenging ideas.

Butt of cynics, yet scourge of tyrants, the birth certificate of the American Republic stands today as Lincoln said in 1859—when a slave-holding class jeered at it as pernicious and false—"a rebuke and a stumbling block to the very harbingers of reappearing tyranny and oppression." (p. 193)

> *Herbert Aptheker, "A Marxist Interpretation," in* A Casebook on The Declaration of Independence, *edited by Robert Ginsberg, Thomas Y. Crowell Company, 1967, pp. 184-93.*

LEONARD W. LEVY (essay date 1963)

[*Levy analyzes Jefferson's reputation as a civil libertarian, challenging the popular view that Jefferson was an unceasing defender of individual rights. Instead, according to Levy, Jefferson had a "darker" side that resulted from several causes: his fear of any threats to the new government and his accompanying desire to protect that government; his lack of a "systematic and consistent philosophy of freedom"; and his era's standards, which differed markedly from the modern conception of civil liberties.*]

A few years after Jefferson's death, John Quincy Adams, upon reading Jefferson's **Autobiography,** yielded to his censorious and cantankerous nature. Jefferson, confided Adams to his diary, told nothing that was not creditable to him, as if he had always been right. Yet he had an "infidel philosophy," "pliability of principle," a "treacherous" memory, a "double dealing character," and was so filled with "deep duplicity" and "insincerity" that in deceiving others, "he seems to have begun by deceiving himself." The curious thing about this massive indictment, which was founded on just enough shreds of truth not to be utterly ridiculous, was that Adams spiced it with a dash of credit and a pinch of praise. Even from his jaundiced view, Jefferson was a great patriot with an "ardent passion for liberty and the rights of man." Thus the image of Jefferson as the apostle of freedom had formed even in his own time.

Unlike the Liberty Bell, that image never tarnished or cracked in any serious way. After all, nations live by symbols and have a need for vital illusions. Thomas Jefferson was by no means ill-suited for the symbolic role in which he has been cast by American history. It was a role that he had cast for himself when he left instructions for the epitaph bearing testimony to the three achievements by which he wished "most to be remembered":

> Here was buried
> Thomas Jefferson
> Author of the Declaration of American Independence
> of the Statute of Virginia for religious freedom
> & Father of the University of Virginia

The words chosen for inscription on the Jefferson Memorial— "I have sworn upon the altar of God, eternal hostility against every form of tyranny over the mind of man"—reflect his enduring spirit and will speak to mankind as long as liberty is cherished on earth. At the dedication of the shrine built by a grateful nation, President Franklin Roosevelt in 1943 quite naturally discoursed on "Thomas Jefferson, Apostle of Freedom." "We judge him," declared Roosevelt, "by the application of his philosophy to the circumstances of his life. But in such applying we come to understand that his life was given for those deeper values that persist throughout all time." The sentiment was a noble one, poetically true. But it was not the whole historical truth.

When judged by his application of "his philosophy to the circumstances of his life," a fair enough test, the saintly vapors that veil the real Jefferson clear away. He himself hated hagiolatry. Posterity, about which he cared so much, had a greater need for a realistic understanding of their heritage than for historical fictions paraded as "images." Jefferson was not larger than life; he was human and held great power. His mistaken judgments were many, his failings plentiful. Much of Jefferson that passed for wisdom has passed out of date. He was, to be sure, a libertarian, and American civil liberties were deeply in his debt. But he was scarcely the constantly faithful libertarian and rarely, if ever, the courageous one.

The finest moments of American liberty occurred when men defied popular prejudices and defended right and justice at the risk of destroying their own careers. Thus John Adams, at a peak of passionate opposition to the British, defended the hated redcoats against a charge of murder growing out of the Boston Massacre. By contrast Thomas Jefferson never once risked career or reputation to champion free speech, fair trial, or any other libertarian value. On many occasions he was on the wrong side. On others he trimmed his sails and remained silent.

As Secretary of State Jefferson signed the proclamation against the Whiskey Rebels; as Vice President and presiding officer of the Senate, he signed the warrant of arrest for William Duane for a seditious contempt of that august body. Jefferson chose the easy path of lawful performance of his duties instead of conscientious opposition on the ground that liberty and justice were being victimized. In neither case did he speak out *publicly*. He signed in silence and characteristically complained in his private correspondence about the government's abridgments of freedom. His opposition to the Alien and Sedition Acts is famous: what is not so well known is that he never publicly declared his opposition during the period of hysteria. He kept his participation in the Kentucky Resolutions of 1798-99 a secret. In the winter of liberty's danger there was the greatest need for the heated and undisguised voice of dissent to be heard in the land.

Any depiction of Jefferson as the nearly faultless civil libertarian, the oracle of freedom's encyclicals and model of its virtues, should provoke a critical reader who is reasonably aware of human frailties—from which political figures are not notably exempt—to react like [Bret] Harte's M'liss. Upon being told that the sun had obeyed Joshua's command to stand still in the heavens, she slammed her astronomy book shut with the defiant assertion, "It's a damned lie. I don't believe it." Jefferson was no demigod. That he was party to many abridgments of personal and public liberty should neither shock nor surprise. It would have been surprising had he not on occasion during his long career taken his hatchet in hand and cut down a few libertarian cherry trees. He said himself that he had been bent like a long bow by irresistible circumstances, his public life being a war against his natural feelings and desires. The compulsions of politics, the exigencies of office, and the responsibilities of leadership sometimes conspired to anesthetize his sensitivity to libertarian values. Nor did his own drives have an opposite effect. He yearned for the contemplative intellectual life but he could not resist the temptations of power. He had as great a need for the means of carrying out policies in the national interest, as he understood it, as he did for the quiet life of scholarship.

He was capable of ruthlessness in the exercise of power. As President he behaved as if compensating for his notorious weakness as wartime governor of Virginia, when constitutional scruples and an inclination to shrink from the harsher aspects of politics had made him incapable of bold leadership. Thereafter he acted as if he had disciplined himself to serve in office with energy and decisiveness, at whatever cost. A hard resolution to lead and triumph certainly characterized his presidency.

Often the master politician, he was not averse to the most devious and harsh tactics to achieve his ends. Usually gentle and amiable in his personal relationships, he possessed a streak of wilfulness that sometimes expressed itself in flaring temper, violence, and toughness. His grandson portrayed him as a "bold and fearless" horseman who loved to ride booted with whip in hand. "The only impatience of temper he ever exhibited," recalled Thomas Jefferson Randolph, "was with his horse, which he subdued to his will by a fearless application of the whip, on the slightest manifestation of restiveness." He rode the nation in the same way, booted and spurred during the embargo days, notwithstanding the fact that one of his most memorable utterances announced his belief that mankind had

not been born with saddles on their backs to be ridden booted and spurred by those in power over them. (pp. 158-62)

Practices once reprehended by Jefferson as shocking betrayals of natural and constitutional rights suddenly seemed innocent, even necessary and salutary, when the government was in his hands. His accession to power seemed to stimulate a fresh understanding of the existence of public dangers requiring forceful measures that often did not result in a union of principle and practice.... Jefferson's presidency, particularly the second term which witnessed the federal sedition prosecutions in Connecticut, the Wilkinson-Burr imbroglio and trials, and the five embargo acts, was an obligato on the arts of political manipulation and severity.

Some of his antilibertarianism can be explained by the ironic fact that he was, in the words of a clear-eyed admirer, a "terrifying idealist, tinged with fanaticism." What other sort of man would impersonally applaud a little bloodletting now and then to fertilize the tree of liberty? Jefferson held his convictions with a fierceness that admitted little room for compromise—if he was in a position of power to deny it—and no room for self-doubt. Unduly sensitive to criticism by others, he wore a hair shirt—often a dangerous attire for a politician—which covered a spirit rarely capable of objective disinterestedness.

Jefferson had the mentality and passion of a true believer, certain that he was absolutely right, a marked contrast to the skepticism of modern libertarians such as Justice Oliver Wendell Holmes or Judge Learned Hand. Holmes believed that the first mark of a civilized man was the capacity to doubt his own first principles, while Hand remarked that the spirit of liberty was the spirit which was not too sure that it was right. Jefferson was a product of the eighteenth century which regarded truths as immutable and self-evident. Yet philosophic truths concerning the nature of man or the first principles of government were not on a footing with practical legislation or executive policies. Jefferson had read Locke and the British empiricists as well as the Deists, scientists, and French *philosophes*. He might reasonably have been somewhat more skeptical of the rightness of his own favorite theories that he translated into national policy; he might have been less cocksure, less ready to subscribe to the proposition that certitude was the test of certainty. (pp. 162-64)

Jefferson's only constitutional qualms during his presidency concerned what he believed to be his questionable authority to purchase Louisiana. He never doubted for a moment the rightness of his behavior during the Burr and embargo episodes. The intensity of his convictions and his incapacity for self-criticism propelled him onward, more resolute than ever in the face of outside criticism. The certainty that he was right, combined with his terrifying idealism, led him to risk the fate of the nation on the chance that an experiment in commercial sanctions might prove a substitute for war. Opposition only goaded him to redouble his efforts to prove himself right. He behaved as if a prisoner of his ideas, or, to put the thought less charitably, as a doctrinaire "tinged with fanaticism."

The self-skeptic, the practical politician, and the democrat conduct themselves otherwise. Any one of them in a position of power tends to operate with an understanding of the necessity of compromise and the obnoxiousness, not to mention the immorality or political stupidity, of cramming legislation "down the throats of dissenting brethren." ... Exhilarated by the experience of putting an idea in motion and backing it by force, he could not back down or admit that he had been wrong. What counted most was the attainment of his objective, the validation of his conviction, not its impact on those who, failing to appreciate his idealism or personal stake, hollered long and loud. He reacted not by relieving their hollering but by a stretch of the rack that increased their protests and his own power to override them.

Jefferson tended to stretch his political powers as he stretched his mind in intellectual matters, leaving his conscience behind—and sometimes his good sense. His voluminous correspondence showed no hint that he suffered from uncertainty or was tormented by his conscience when he so readily used the army to enforce the embargo and recklessly disregarded the injunctions of the Fourth Amendment. Lincoln in the greatest of all crises in American history had a supreme moral objective as well as a political one to sustain him; but he was constantly racked by self-doubt. The exercise of power, not always constitutionally justifiable, exacted of him a price that included melancholy and an agonized soul. In moments of despair he could doubt that Providence was with him and even that his position was indeed the morally superior one.

The contrast with Jefferson was towering. Thwarted by the courts in Burr's case, Jefferson doubted not himself but the loyalty of the judges. Evasions of the embargo filled him with astonishment not that his policy could have such a result but that the people could be so rankly fraudulent and corrupt. Rumors of resistance were matched by his impulse to crush it by force. There was no inner struggle in Jefferson; the tragedy of his antilibertarianism lacked poignancy. He was oblivious of the tragedy itself, symbolized by that moment of enormity when he approved of the use of any means, even if odious and arbitrary, to achieve his end.

Vanity, the enemy of self-doubt, also played its role in fashioning his darker side. His *amour-propre* prevented him from checking an illiberal act once begun or from admitting his error after the event. Witness his conduct of the Burr prosecutions and the way in which he was driven to defend Wilkinson. His persistent defense of his role in the case of Josiah Philips bears testimony to the same trait. When caught in a flagrancy . . . , he denied the truth. In deceiving others, as John Quincy Adams said, he deceived himself. In deceiving himself he denied himself insight into his abridgments of liberty, though he was acutely perceptive of abridgments by others.

Perhaps the chief explanation of his darker side was his conviction that the great American experiment in self-government and liberty was in nearly constant danger. He completely identified with that experiment, to the point that an attack on him or on the wisdom of his policies quickly became transmuted in his mind as a threat to the security of the tender democratic plant. (pp. 165-67)

Over the years he constantly sensed a conspiracy against republicanism. He had a feeling of being besieged by the enemies of freedom who would use it to subvert it. The face of the enemy changed—now that of a Tory; later that of a monarchist, a political priest, an Essex Juntoman, a Quid, or a Burrite; still later that of a judicial sapper-and-miner, an American-system consolidationist, or a Richmond lawyer. The face of the enemy or his name might change, but not his tory principles nor his subversive goal.

To the experiment of democracy in America, as Jefferson called it, he was committed heart, mind, and soul. Believing that experiment to be in grave jeopardy throughout most of his public life, he was capable of ruthlessness in defeating its enemies. His own goal was free men in a free society, but he did not always use freedom's instruments to attain it. He sometimes confused the goal with self-vindication or the triumph of his party. On other occasions instability and a lack of faith were revealed by his doubts of the opposition's loyalty. They were prone, he believed, to betray the principles of the Revolution as expressed in the **Declaration of Independence.** On still other occasions his eagerness to make America safe for democracy made him forgetful of Franklin's wise aphorism that they who seek safety at the expense of liberty deserve neither liberty nor safety.

The terrible complexities of any major issue, such as Burr's conspiracy or the embargo, particularly as seen from the White House, also help to explain Jefferson's conduct. The strain and responsibilities of the highest office did not stimulate the taking of bold risks on the side of liberty when it seemed to be pitted against national security. Moreover, problems had a way of presenting themselves in a form that mixed conflicting political considerations and obscured clear-cut decisions on libertarian merits. To a mind that was keenly alerted against the conspiracies of Federalist boogeymen and sensed a union between self, party, and nation, the virtue of an independent judiciary became the vice of judicial interference with majority rule; fair trial and a strict interpretation of treason became obstacles to the preservation of the Union; academic freedom became a guise for the dissemination of pernicious doctrines.

Jefferson's darker side derived in part, too, from the fact he had no systematic and consistent philosophy of freedom. He was neither a seminal nor a profound thinker. Part of his genius consisted of his ability to give imperishable expression to old principles and to the deepest yearnings of his fellow citizens. Style, as much as substance, accounted for his staying power. . . . [He] had the superlative talent of organizing a party that might realize his ideals by infusing the new nation with a sense of its special democratic destiny. But his failure to develop a theory of liberty existed and more than likely influenced his antilibertarian thought and action.

In the thousands of pages of his published works there is a notable scarcity of extended treatments on a single subject. Insatiably curious, he knew a little about nearly everything under the sun and a great deal more about law and politics than any man of his time. But in all his writings, over a period of fifty years of high productivity, there is not a single sustained analysis of liberty. He was pithy, felicitous, repetitive, and ever absorbed by the subject, but never wrote a book or even a tract on the meaning of liberty, its dimensions, limitations, and history.

That he made no contribution of this kind is not per se a criticism, for the brief preambles to the **Declaration of Independence** and the **Virginia Statute of Religious Freedom** are worth all the books that have been written on liberty. He had not, however, thought through the tough and perplexing problems posed by liberty: the conditions for its survival and promotion; the types of liberty and conflicts between them; the validity of various legal tests for measuring the scope of liberty or its permissible area of operation; and the competing claims of other values.

Jefferson contented himself with a dedication to the general principle, apparently without realizing that general principles do not satisfactorily decide hard, concrete cases. Only in the area of religious liberty did he have a well-developed philosophy, replete with a usable and rationalized test for application to specific cases. There his contribution was pre-eminent, even if derived from English sources. (pp. 168-71)

A philosopher of freedom without a philosophy of freedom, Jefferson was ill-equipped, by his ritualistic affirmations of nebulous and transcendental truths, to confront the problem posed by General Wilkinson's conduct in New Orleans, or the circulation of Hume's history of England in the colleges, or the savage distortions of the opposition press. He reacted expediently on an *ad hoc* basis and too often hastily. Then his *amour-propre* prevented his candid acknowledgment of a mistaken judgment that demeaned the libertarian values he symbolized to the nation. (p. 172)

Maxims of liberty—"glittering generalities" [as Rufus Choate described the **Declaration of Independence** (see Additional Bibliography)]—were frail props for a sound, realistic libertarianism. A mind filled with maxims will falter when put to the test of experience. A mind filled with maxims contents itself with the resonant quality of a noble utterance. Such a mind, although libertarian, cannot produce a libertarian analysis like Madison's *Report* of 1799-1800 on the Alien and Sedition Acts, or Wortman's *Treatise Concerning Political Enquiry.* Jefferson's only tracts and books were *A Summary View of the Rights of British America,* which was a protest against British encroachments on colonial freedom at the eve of the Revolution; *Notes on the State of Virginia,* a guidebook and utilitarian history; the **Manual of Parliamentary Practice**; his *Autobiography* and *The Anas,* which comprise his memoirs; *The Life and Morals of Jesus of Nazareth*; and the philological work, *Essay on Anglo-Saxon.* Despite his interest in freedom, its meaning did not interest him as a subject for even an essay.

A plausible but not wholly convincing explanation of Jefferson's darker side may be founded on the argument that he lived at a time when the understanding of civil liberties was quite different from that of our own. Libertarian standards were also quite new and inchoate, making modern yardsticks of judgment anachronistic as well as unfair and ununderstanding. The first bills of rights did not come into existence until 1776; the national Bill of Rights, not until 1791. The meanings of their provisions were not always clear; their restraints in that formative era constituted an experiment in government. Deviations, inconsistencies, and even gross abridgments were not to be unexpected when experience provided few guides. It was a time of testing, of groping and growth, of trial and error, out of which issued the improvised wisdom of subsequent generations. In any case, counsels of perfection and hindsight come rather cheap when aimed by those not on the firing line or of a later time.

This explanation is certainly a plausible one. Yet it is like the theory that was spoiled by the facts. During the Revolutionary War, only Tory voices—and they were not necessarily wrong—could be found in opposition to loyalty tests, bills of attainder, and suppression of "traitorous" speech. Thereafter there were always respectable, instructive voices, even if heard only in dissent, to sound the alarm against abridgments of liberty. Jefferson needed only to hear or read in order to know that a particular measure could be seriously construed as a threat to the Bill of Rights or the undermining of a libertarian value. For every example of his darker side . . . , a congressional speech, a popular tract, a letter, a newspaper editorial, a judicial opinion, or, more likely than not, a pronouncement by Jefferson himself can be adduced to show a judgment of his own time placing his action in an antilibertarian light. By 1800 or thereabouts the standards of his own time did not noticeably differ from those of ours on the kind of civil-liberty questions that he confronted.

Though contributing little to any breakthroughs in libertarian thought, except in the important realm of freedom of religion, Jefferson more than any was responsible for the public sensitivity to libertarian considerations. If the quality of the new nation was measured by the ideals and aspirations that animated it, Jefferson had erred only slightly in confusing his own reputation with that of the democratic experiment. Notwithstanding the reciprocal scurrilities and suspicions of the opposed parties, or more importantly their conflicting interests, Americans were indeed all Federalists, all Republicans. They were equally attached to the "experiment in freedom" and the "empire of liberty." Anyone who depreciates the national commitment to libertarian values, which were bottomed on an extraordinary legal and political sophistication, deprives himself of an understanding of the times—and of the impact of Thomas Jefferson upon it. Jefferson cannot lightly be excused because he lived in an earlier time.

That Jefferson's libertarianism was considerably less than perfect or that his practice flagged behind his faith does not one whit diminish the achievements by which he is best remembered and should be. That he did not always adhere to his libertarian principles does not erode their enduring rightness. It proves only that Jefferson often set the highest standard of freedom for himself and posterity to be measured against. His legacy was the idea that as an indispensable condition for the development of free men in a free society, the state must be bitted and bridled by a Bill of Rights which should be construed in the most generous terms, its protections not to be the playthings of momentary majorities or of those in power. (pp. 173-76)

> *Leonard W. Levy, in his* Jefferson & Civil Liberties: The Darker Side, *Cambridge, Mass.: Belknap Press, 1963, 225 p.*

ROBERT GINSBERG　(essay date 1967)

[*Ginsberg evaluates the rhetoric of the Declaration of Independence. After identifying the components of a rhetorical work as audience, speaker, argument, and style, he begins by pointing out elements in the text that indicate to whom the document is addressed and the character of the speaker. The excerpt continues with an analysis of the persuasive character of its style. The success of the Declaration of Independence, according to Ginsberg, rests on its power to inspire individuals to take action. In a portion of the essay not excerpted below, Ginsberg also details the presentation of the argument.*]

The **Declaration of Independence** is primarily an effort made by certain men at a given moment to persuade other men to adopt special attitudes and courses of action. Three questions arise in dealing with a work of persuasion: (1) Who is it that is to be persuaded and how is he treated by the persuader? (2) Who is the persuader that undertakes by his character and statements to influence his audience? (3) What reasoning is offered to the listener for the action or the placing of approval and blame that he is urged to? Persuasion presupposes a relationship between what is spoken and to whom and by whom it is spoken, and this relationship may be discovered in the work itself. Determining who the audience was, insofar as it is indicated by the strategy of the speech, and how the speaker represented himself to his audience are different issues than determining the nature of the historical character of the British, Americans, and other parties involved. If the art of rhetoric consists in discovering the best means of persuasion available in a specific case, then the analysis of the **Declaration** should subordinate the knowledge of the origin of any feature in the text to an appreciation of how it functions in the text. The rhetorical "source" of a device or claim in the **Declaration** is the requirements of one or more of the powers of persuasion: the appeal to a specific audience, the use of one's specific character to gain goodwill and assent, and the offering of the appearance of a good argument. The rhetorician, having discovered the means of persuasion through these powers, seeks the appropriate language for expression and the effective order for presentation. These too, then, should fall within the scope of our analysis.

Let us take up the question of the audience first since it is the reference point to which the character of the speaker and the shape of his argument must be adjusted. Who is the **Declaration** made to? The first sentence tells us that *a decent Respect to the Opinions of Mankind* requires the **Declaration.** More specifically, the Americans aspire to a position *among the Powers of the Earth.* The powers are separate and equal, there is a basis in natural law for them, and they are sanctioned by divine arrangement. There is little that is revolutionary here. The audience as a community of nations is assured that the American uprising is not the beginning of world upheaval. Having offered a characterization of world politics that could hardly be rejected by their audience as seditious or disrespectful, the Americans may then move themselves up into the world to play a role alongside of the audience. (pp. 220-22)

To prove its contentions against the King, the **Declaration** submits facts to the *candid World.* The making public of one's grievances to an impartial judge is an assurance that the speaker has his head about him and that being engaged in a controversy does not weaken his proper attitude towards the rest of the world. A certain weight is also given to what are called "facts," which are then enumerated. (p. 222)

The King is made out to be a warlord dangerous to nations, while the colonists, who are in rebellion, take on the guise of peacelovers posing no threat to the world. The King, apparently without any need for it, has kept *Standing Armies* in the Colonies (*& ships of war* unfortunately omitted by Congress) (accusation xi). He is depicted as warring on sea, coast, and town, and *transporting large Armies of foreign Mercenaries* (accusations xxiv, xxv). He has turned prisoners against their countrymen, incited insurrections against the citizenry of the Colonies, and made use of wild savages, encouraging them to uncivilized acts of war (accusations xxvi, xxvii). If the King acts thus with his innocent subjects, then he is no friend of the audience. Indeed, he is not to be counted among the company of civilized rulers, having done things *totally unworthy the Head of a civilized Nation* (accusation xxv) and being *unfit to be the Ruler of a free People* . . .—which refers to the Americans as well as to others in the British Empire.

By making the King guilty of all the offenses, the **Declaration** does not respect the truth, but there is something other than proof to be achieved in so formulating these "facts" for third parties. What is a war between peoples, or a war between segments of one people, takes on the appearance of the mistreatment of one people by one man. The plausibility of that man mistreating other peoples is established; therefore it is in the interests of others to aid the Americans in frustrating the aggressive King. Even if one knew the truth, it would be easier

to work against England . . . , given this public portrayal of the King as an enemy of mankind. The appeal to the audience, then, is made in an opposition of attitudes—the King malevolent, the Americans civil and proper—and in the suggestion of political and commercial advantages that follow from acting in accordance with such attitudes.

Although a number of things are declared in the **Declaration of Independence,** there is a purpose that distinguishes this work from other declarations and deeds. Independence itself may have been announced by such acts as the nullification of the British governorships, the rejection of Parliamentary supremacy, the institution of a revolutionary Congress, the taking up of arms, and the issuance of numerous pamphlets and resolutions. John Adams was particularly fond of arguing that independence had been declared before the **Declaration** penned by his rival Jefferson. But these prior steps had not openly called for the participation of the outside world. The declaration of war had been made in the state paper on taking up arms, yet this document stressed the defensive nature of the insurrection and called for reconciliation. War was resorted to as a last avenue to obtain redress without extinction. A pertinent distinction was drawn by James Macpherson, in his reply to the Declaration of Taking up Arms, between warring independent states that "endeavour to impress the World with a favourable opinion of their own cause" and those people who are in rebellion within a state to whom the "opinions of mankind" are invariably opposed. What was necessary in facing the world's greatest military power in 1776 was, precisely, the outside help that would follow from the goodwill of mankind. Aware of the distinction that Macpherson drew, Congress exercised this reasoning in its deliberations in early June, 1776, as recorded by Jefferson: The irreconcilable conflict with England cannot be successfully concluded without foreign aid; foreign aid depends upon re-opening trade; trade with nations cannot be opened, due to "European delicacy," except as an independent power; hence, a **Declaration of Independence** is necessary. What the text of the **Declaration of Independence** distinctively declares, in accordance with this historical situation, is the appropriateness of foreign aid to the American revolution. (pp. 222-24)

Are the neutral nations of the world the only audience addressed by the **Declaration**? The historical situation provides other possibilities for persuasion: one may speak to the enemy, warning that the fight is in earnest; one may speak to sympathetic elements among the enemy to gain them over to the rebellion's cause; one may address the people in one's own ranks hesitant to fight against the mother country. But each address must be made with an eye to the primary audience: vituperation against the enemy is to be avoided, as is the suggestion of disunity among the Americans, while brotherly sentiments for the British people will be appreciated.

The long series of grievances, by being formulated in terms of the King, avoids fraternal insult and points out a common enemy to proper British ways of life. Instead of monarchy it is the present *King of Great-Britain* (Adams introduced this phrase in place of the reference to *his majesty*) that is vilified. What he is doing in America, he may try elsewhere in the Empire. He is already responsible for *abolishing the free System of English Laws in a neighbouring Province* (accusation xx). What some people took to be the forethought and generosity of the British in the Canadian question is here treated as the despotic destruction of the rights of British subjects. After all, if Britain had recently been magnanimous and just in Canada, a conquered province, then there would be reason to believe she would behave the same towards the neighboring Americans after their rebellion is crushed. The charge of establishing an *arbitrary Government* in Canada is deftly accompanied by another claim that would draw sympathy from the British people and from anyone generally: the boundaries of Canada have been enlarged to the detriment of the bordering Colonies. . . . There is the germ here of the principle that a revolution must liberate those suppressed by the evil power even if they are reluctant to contribute to their own liberation. (pp. 224-25)

[The] appeal in the **Declaration** is not phrased directly to the British nor is it in the present tense. The explanation is still made to a third party, recounting a series of *We have dones*. One continues to pay respect to mankind by setting all grievances before it rather than lashing out at one's opponent or pleading with him. The question, If you have had trouble with the King, why have you not appealed to the people? is thus answered without tarnishing the speaker's character. (p. 226)

The colonists themselves are given a view of their present struggles. The **Declaration** stimulates solidarity among the Americans. In its title the official name UNITED STATES OF AMERICA is established. The Americans are *one People* distinguishable and separable from others. They have suffered together at the hands of the King. He has invaded their rights; endangered their state; harassed them with officers; subverted their civil authority; exposed them to murder; deprived them of trial; threatened their boundaries; wrecked their charters, laws, and forms of government; and waged war against them. Common sufferance invites mutual identification and joint action. The charges advance from interference with legislation (the first 13 accusations) to deeds of extreme violence. The natural response to the upsetting of law is to set up one's own legislative and representative bodies. The answer to deeds of war is to wage war.

The Americans have done their duty towards the British people. If anyone is guilty of turning brother against brother, it is the King (accusation xxvi). One may rebel against a king if he himself has *abdicated Government* (accusation xxiii) and is unfit to rule *a free People*. The American people are an important, if secondary, audience who cannot be alienated by the terms of the appeal made in their name to the foreigners. The American image will be embellished both for American and foreign eyes by the characterization the speaker presents of himself.

Who is the *speaker*, that is, the one making the **Declaration**? It is not Thomas Jefferson, nor the people of the United States, but, as the title informs, the *Representatives of the UNITED STATES*. One wonders about the motives, character, and capacities of such men, for these will influence one's acceptance of the import and validity of what they say. In the first sentence a third-person reference to the collective speaker, *they should declare*, identifies him as spokesman for the American people. Again, in the final paragraph the speaker claims his official capacity as *the Representatives of the UNITED STATES OF AMERICA, in GENERAL CONGRESS, Assembled*, acting *in the Name, and by Authority of the good People of these Colonies*. But how can one pretend to represent both state and people when assemblies and legislative bodies are subject to the King's will? The people have a fundamental right to representation (accusation vi).

The famous self-evident truths are not presented as self-evident truths. To do such would obviate the necessity of saying one

believes in them. The approach used reflects favorably on the speaker: *We hold these* truths to be self-evident. Modesty rather than dogmatism is suggested, because one is stating what one believes rather than making a categorically true statement, though it enhances one's character to believe something that others too must believe as self-evident. (pp. 226-27)

In the first sentence [of the second paragraph] the speaker shows that he has a *decent* respect for mankind. He reserves *prudence* for himself and his countrymen in the craftily arranged sentence that opens with that word:

> Prudence, indeed, will dictate that Governments long established should not be changed for light and transient Causes; and accordingly all Experience hath shewn, that Mankind are more disposed to suffer, while Evils are sufferable, than to right themselves by abolishing the Forms to which they are accustomed. . . .

In the second half of the sentence he shows his understanding of human nature and experience, an understanding reflected in the first sentence of the **Declaration** and whenever events in human history are mentioned. The arrangement of these universal pronouncements accrues authority and dignity to the speaker.

There is a certain care in keeping the attention of the audience away from the speaker in the first part of the text and instead onto his noble words. A dispassionate tone of explanation is the beguiling fruit of that care. Even when the bill of charges is raised, there is no direct self-reference, only *these States* (accusation vii), until accusation x where the compounding of sufferings initiates a flood of first-person plural references to call forth the sympathy of the audience. . . . The presence of the speaker progressively gains power, culminating in the heroic pledge of the closing words. (p. 228)

The persuasive artist like the poetic artist imagines, discovers, invents, fuses, and expresses. Knowing what the persuasive situation is does not produce the result. Rhetoric is a practical art; its aim is to affect men through language, and not merely to please them as do the poetic arts. Hence the verbalization of the persuasive appeals and their presentation in the speech are important.

The variety of style in the **Declaration** is striking—by turns abstract, dispassionate, passionate, and officious. This matches the rich content which includes a miniature history, an outline of political theory, a mass of grievances, and a juridical act. These variations upon reiterated themes—*injury, usurpation, tyranny, rights, people, power*—hold the attention of the reader while his mind and heart are worked upon. He is engaged from the first sentence, itself a paragraph, with its interwoven strands of persuasiveness: respect for the audience, dignity of the speaker, necessity of the action. The second paragraph disinterestedly commences, treading cautiously with philosophic gravity into the issue at hand. Then come the facts in bold and massive accusation. Thirteen sentences are lined up beginning *He has*. A variation is achieved in the nine clauses beginning *For*. Two miscellaneous claims have been slipped in here, that is, they are not principally matters of law and justice or of military activity. These acts of pretended legislation are couched in economic terms, treating of trade and taxes (accusations xvi, xvii). The former is pertinent to foreign eyes, while the latter is of local interest, since, as Lind suggested [see excerpt dated 1776], men generally do not like to pay taxes. The *Fors* are looser in organization than the *Hes*, and vaguer in causation.

Actually they are a subclass of accusation xiii. That one accusation can be expanded into subcharges suggests the same may be done elsewhere in the list. The return to five *He* sentences, one of which—it may go unnoticed—is not in the past tense (accusation xxv), attaches the greatest onus to the King.

The techniques by which the facts are presented were exposed by John Lind who sought to refute them. He showed how acts of omission are phrased as acts of commission, how temporary measures are spoken of as permanent, how specialized cases are set in general terms, how violent means are portrayed as ends, how future and present acts are treated in the same language as past cases. The aim, he claims, is "to *confuse* where they could not hope to *convince.*" The logician will find that the eighteen *He* accusations are not simple singular propositions; there are at least sixty accusations entailed. Combination of charges, as in the Canadian question, served to conceal weaknesses of individual claims.

The dry statement of the early legalistic facts gives way to swelling passion expressed in vivid language. There is revulsion in *Swarms* of officers that *eat out* the substance of the people. A string of verbs of violence—*plundered, ravaged, burnt, destroyed*—is impressively spread in one sentence to catch the pity of the reader. So too, *Works of Death, Desolation, and Tyranny* chill the bones and call for protest, especially since they are accompanied by *circumstances of Cruelty and Perfidy, scarcely paralleled in the most barbarous Ages* (the last seven words added by Congress). Congressional editing brought to the fore as the last accusation an evocation

Jefferson's notes for his tombstone and epitaph, which summarizes what he considered his greatest achievements. Library of Congress.

of the wildest desolation accessible to the European imagination: the *merciless Indian Savages* have been brought on, *whose known Rule of Warfare, is an undistinguished Destruction, of all Ages, Sexes and Conditions.*

The grotesque is left aside for the sentimental as in paragraph IV the colonists dilate on their fraternal feeling. The solemnity of the final paragraph keeps before us the fact that the government of a new state is speaking. (pp. 238-40)

Commentators have taken much trouble to indicate the debt owed by the wording of the **Declaration** to other works, generally proceeding on the assumption that the meaning of the words remained the same. In the **Declaration** there is no citation of any treatise or bill. That its terms should be the current and reiterated ones Jefferson recognized. It is expressed in the American political language. This language also was part of the fundamental British tradition. It is wise to justify oneself in terms taken over from or shared with the other party in a dispute. The American ways are more properly British in the final analysis, it is implied, than those of the British. But if the persuasive work makes use of a tradition of thought in order to command assent and of a manner of phrasing things appropriate to the occasion, it does not follow that in this case it accepts the full tradition, that it is a recognizable, consistent affirmation of natural rights philosophy. It sounds like Locke, but it isn't. (p. 240)

The charge will be made that an analysis of this kind reduces to propaganda what is a noble document replete with the courageous expression of ideals that serve as a foundation stone of the American way of life and a landmark for all men, free or otherwise.... [Parts] of the **Declaration** have been tossed off by critics as "mere" rhetoric, or "pure" rhetoric, or "only" rhetoric, implying that such parts cannot be taken seriously as offering arguments, as shaping facts, or as expressing genuine feelings. But rhetoric is essential in the affairs of men, so long as action and judgment are amenable to discussion. The crucial movements of war and peace demand that men take a part. The path to be chosen is often open to debate. Political rhetoric does not aim at the truth, which may be objective and abstract, but at that which is more urgent and important in politics, decision and action in particular circumstances. The problem in 1776 for America, Britain, Europe was one of *doing;* and the significance of the **Declaration** is in its contrivance as persuasion to commitment.

The criterion of excellence of a persuasive work is not whether you are convinced by it or agree with what it claims, for the work was not addressed to you, nor whether it achieved its purposes upon its intended audience; for in the responses to the work it is difficult to tell if the persuasive powers have been operative rather than something fortuitous. The compilation of the reactions of those to whom the rhetoric has been applied is never the test of persuasion. The judgment of whether the action urged was a good one, whether effectuated or not, belongs to ethics and politics rather than to rhetorical critique. The utility that can be found for the persuasive work is an index not of its rhetorical worth but of the imagination and purposes of those who use it. Re-creation of the **Declaration** or borrowing from it has long been a convenience in gaining authority for the credo of individuals or groups. Despite the reputation of the **Declaration** and the uses we make of it, what we can judge as rhetoric is whether the work made use in the best way of what was available to it in order to achieve its goals.

Could the **Declaration** have been still more persuasive if it had been given another form, that is, another exercise of the appeal to the audience conjoined with a representation of the speaker's character and method of argument? Given its form, could any alteration in its presentation, that is, the ordering, combining, and verbal expression of its materials, have increased its persuasiveness? To answer these questions is to see how good the **Declaration** is and *what* it is as an encounter of creativity with the pressures of actions, ideals, and feelings. Its genius, though directed uniquely to July 4, 1776, is accessible to the appreciation of men aware of the perpetual play of circumstance and aspiration in the course of human events. (pp. 243-44)

> Robert Ginsberg, *"The Declaration as Rhetoric,"*
> in A Casebook on The Declaration of Independence,
> *edited by Robert Ginsberg, Thomas Y. Crowell Company, 1967, pp. 219-44.*

WILLIAM COHEN (essay date 1969)

[*Cohen analyzes Jefferson's views on race. In this excerpt, he summarizes the contradictions between Jefferson's support of abolition and his ownership of slaves, focusing on his belief in the inferiority of blacks.*]

[There] was a significant gap between [Jefferson's] thought and action with regard to the abolition question. He fully believed that it was morally and politically evil to hold another man in slavery, but he continued to do so. Believing that bondage should be abolished, he wrote an amendment which would have accomplished this gradually. But he kept it a secret for fear the public was not ready. Meanwhile, he codified Virginia's slave law and added to it harsh provisions aimed against free Negroes. He agreed to the desirability of keeping slavery out of the western territory, but his proposal would have allowed the disease a sixteen-year incubation period.

The contradiction in Jefferson's intellectual position stemmed in large part from his equivocal stance on the question of racial equality. Jefferson's only systematic account of his views on race is to be found in *Notes on the State of Virginia*. Even here, the ambiguity of his position is pointed up by his attempts to prevent the work from being made public because he feared that the terms in which he spoke of slavery and the constitution of Virginia might "produce an irritation which will revolt the minds of our countrymen against reformation in these two articles and thus do more harm than good." Moreover, Jefferson must have been aware that such statements might harm his political career by provoking the ire of his fellow southerners.

Despite his attempt to prevent the publication of the book, Jefferson's remarks were generally moderate. In discussing the "revisal" of Virginia's laws, he described his proposed amendment to "emancipate all slaves born after the passing [of] the act" and then explained why wholesale manumissions would have to be accompanied by the expatriation of the freed Negroes. It would be impossible "to retain and incorporate the blacks into the State," he argued, because white prejudice and black memories of past wrongs would lead to disorders. Jefferson also discussed the physical and moral barriers which he believed would prevent the two races from living together harmoniously in a condition of freedom.

He made a series of observations about the physical and behavioral differences between the races which suggested that Negroes were cruder and more animalistic than whites. He found greater beauty in the flowing hair and variable coloration of the Caucasians than in the "immovable veil of black" which covered the emotions of the Negroes, and noted that they themselves seemed to prefer the whites. Since the factor of superior beauty was considered to be worthy of attention in the propagation of domestic animals, he asked, "why not in that of man." He observed that Negroes sweat more and urinate less than whites, which results in their having a "strong and disagreeable odor." They seemed to need less sleep and to have griefs that were "merely transient." Furthermore, they were "more ardent after their female; but love seems with them to be more an eager desire, than a tender delicate mixture of sentiment and sensation."

Jefferson found that the blacks were equal in memory to the whites, but far inferior in their ability to reason. In imagination they were "dull, tasteless and anomalous." He saw little to praise by objective standards in the works of the Negro writers which had come to his attention. Referring to the Negro poetess, Phillis Wheatley, he lauded the effect of religion upon her sentiments, but held that her compositions were "beneath the dignity of criticism." In 1791, Jefferson expressed high regard for the elegant geometrical solutions of Benjamin Banneker, a free Negro mathematician. In 1809, however, he voiced the suspicion that Banneker's attainments had been made with white assistance. He went on to add that a letter from the mathematician showed him to have "a mind of very common stature indeed."

In *Notes on the State of Virginia,* and elsewhere as well, Jefferson's remarks were usually conveyed in the dispassionate tones of the scientific investigator. Clearly aware of the environmentalist argument, he earnestly expressed the wish that future evidence might prove that the Negroes' inferiority was the result of their condition rather than their nature. Nevertheless, he did not seem to have much hope that this would be the case; and his appeal to science may, as Jordan points out (see Additional Bibliography), have been a veneer which covered the already formed conclusion that "it is not their condition then, but nature which has produced the distinction" between the intellectual attainments of blacks and whites. But he finally contented himself with a more tentative statement: "I advance it, therefore, as a suspicion only that the blacks, whether originally a distinct race, or made distinct by time and circumstances, are inferior to the whites in the endowments both of body and mind."

There was, however, one highly significant area in which Jefferson held that Negroes were every bit the equal of the whites: they possessed a "moral sense." As Jordan points out, for Jefferson to deny this would have been tantamount to excluding Negroes from membership in the human species; it was this faculty which, the Virginian believed, separated man from the animals. Although Jefferson may have doubted that all men were created equal, he did not deny that the blacks were men. Curiously, Jefferson, who was unable to view environment as responsible for the differences he observed between the intellectual abilities of the races, turned to this interpretation to explain the Negroes' lapses from white standards of morality. (pp. 512-14)

Jefferson's views on slavery and race suggest that his libertarian sentiments were more than counterbalanced by his conviction that Negroes were members of a race so alien and inferior that there was no hope that whites and blacks could coexist side by side on terms of equality. Jefferson's libertarian views, however, had virtually no impact upon his actions after 1784, and his belief in the inferiority of the slaves was completely congruent with his behavior as both a planter and a politician.

In his daily life there were few differences between Jefferson's behavior as an owner of men and that of Virginia plantation masters who opposed his antislavery speculations. His bondsmen were well fed and clothed, and their work load was comparable to that of white freemen. In this regard their lot may have been easier than that of many other slaves in the state. Nevertheless, when he dealt with runaways, sales of slaves, breeding, flogging, and manumissions, his behavior did not differ appreciably from that of other enlightened slaveholders who deplored needless cruelty, but would use whatever means they felt necessary to protect their peculiar form of property. (pp. 514-15)

In the abstract Jefferson did not believe one man had a right to own another, and, hence, no man had a right to sell another. He repeatedly expressed his dislike for this commerce, and he tried to avoid selling his human property except for misbehavior or at their own request. Nevertheless, slaves were sold when he was pressed for cash, regardless of their wishes in the matter. (p. 516)

If self-interest played a major role in determining Jefferson's behavior as a plantation owner, it was equally important in shaping his stance as a national leader on questions involving slavery. After 1784, he refrained from discussing the issue publicly for political reasons, but the matter came up occasionally in the course of his official duties. (p. 520)

[The] dominant theme of Jefferson's [presidential] administration on the subject of slavery was discreet silence. When citizens in the Indiana Territory were demanding that slavery be permitted throughout the Northwest Territory, the President made no comment. Although Jefferson privately continued to represent himself as a foe of human bondage and on rare occasions during his presidency voiced such sentiments in letters to men who shared his views, he was exceedingly careful to keep these thoughts from reaching the public. (p. 522)

Ten years after he left office, as the Missouri issue was dividing the nation, Jefferson . . . demonstrated his ability to mix vague abolition sentiments with a position that worked to the advantage of the slave states. Recognizing that the dispute over the admission of Missouri heralded an era of increasing national division over the slavery issue, he likened the controversy to a "fire bell in the night" and warned of impending disaster for the Union. Speaking of slavery, he implicitly endorsed the moral position of the North when he described the dilemma of the South: "We have the wolf by the ears and can neither hold him, nor safely let him go. Justice is in the one scale, and self-preservation in the other." He indicated his willingness to give up his bondsmen if any *"practicable"* way of achieving their "emancipation and *expatriation*" could be found.

Nevertheless, he endorsed the southern position and charged the Federalists with creating a geographical division based on an ostensibly moral question as a means of regaining their influence. He then denied that morality was involved because the limitation of the area of bondage would free no one. He also denied that the federal government could regulate the "condition of different descriptions of men composing a State," and he ruled out the only practical means by which emancipation might eventually have been brought about.

It may be argued that Jefferson's position on the Missouri issue and also his inactivity as President may have been dictated by his strict construction of the Constitution. When the object was large enough, however, Jefferson could be quite flexible; and he did not allow such scruples to prevent the acquisition of the Louisiana Territory. Moreover, he believed that the expatriation of America's blacks was a subject which merited a similar elasticity.

Despite his support for the southern position on the issue of Missouri, in 1821 Jefferson could still write: "Nothing is more certainly written in the book of fate than that these people are to be free, Nor is it less certain that the two races, equally free, cannot live in the same government." (pp. 522-23)

Jefferson was a man of many dimensions, and any explanation of his behavior must contain a myriad of seeming contradictions. He was a sincere and dedicated foe of the slave trade who bought and sold men whenever he found it personally necessary. He believed that all men were entitled to life and liberty regardless of their abilities, yet he tracked down those slaves who had the courage to take their rights by running away. He believed that slavery was morally and politically wrong, but still he wrote a slave code for his state and opposed a national attempt in 1819 to limit the further expansion of the institution. He believed that one hour of slavery was worse than ages of British oppression, yet he was able to discuss the matter of slave breeding in much the same terms that one would use when speaking of the propagation of dogs and horses.

From an intellectual point of view, his strong "suspicion" that the Negroes were innately inferior is probably of great significance in explaining his ability to ignore his own strictures about their rights. Thinking of them as lesser men, he was able to convince himself that his behavior toward them was benevolent and humane; and indeed it was, when judged by the traditional assumptions of the slaveholders. It is a mistake, however, to treat Jefferson's relationship to slavery in intellectual or psychological terms alone, for the institution shaped the warp and woof of life at Monticello and his abstract speculations about human freedom carried little weight when balanced against the whole pattern of his existence there.

Interacting with one another as both cause and effect to produce Jefferson's proslavery behavior was a complex set of factors which included his belief in Negro inferiority, a societal environment which took for granted the enslavement of one race by another, and the fact that he owned 10,000 acres of land and over 200 slaves. His wealth, his status, and his political position were tied to the system of slavery, and never once did he *actively* propose a plan that would have jeopardized all this. More often than not, the actions he took with regard to slavery actually strengthened the institution. (p. 525)

Monticello was the workshop of the maker of the "agrarian dream." It was here that Jefferson conducted his agricultural and scientific experiments and offered a generous hospitality to visitors. It was here that he lived a bustling, but gracious life far from the money changers in the cities of the North. This was the life that he sought to preserve against the incursions of the forces of commerce and industry. But it should not be forgotten that Jefferson's world depended upon forced labor for its very existence. (pp. 525-26)

William Cohen, "Thomas Jefferson and the Problem of Slavery," in The Journal of American History, *Vol. LVI, December, 1969, pp. 503-26.*

STEPHEN D. COX   (essay date 1977)

[*Cox attempts to define Jefferson's literary aesthetic. In portions of the essay not excerpted below, Cox reviews Jefferson's com-*

mentary on various authors to identify which qualities form the basis of his critical judgments; he asserts that Jefferson had difficulty resolving his conflicting expectations that a literary work should include exalted, sublime sentiment, rationality, moral utility, and a lucid style. In the following excerpt, Cox examines the extent to which Jefferson incorporated these aesthetic principles into his own writings. According to Cox, in parts of several works, including the Declaration, Notes on the State of Virginia, *and the* Autobiography, *Jefferson demonstrates his conscious artistry by creating narratives that ably combine rational intent with emotional effect.*]

Jefferson's concern for a rationalistic sublimity achieves some interesting expressions in his own literary works about the history and politics of his time. Sometimes, it must be admitted, his prose is merely routine—correct, but unexciting. Yet often it is exalted by his aspiration for the sublime. Jefferson's descriptions of nature in *Notes on Virginia* are probably his best-known attempts at lyric emotionality. In one instance, delighting in the "wild and tremendous" mountain scenery which he describes at some length, and speculating on its geologic origins, he offers the following reflection: "This scene is worth a voyage across the Atlantic. Yet here, as in the neighbourhood of the natural bridge, are people who have passed their lives within half a dozen miles, and have never been to survey these monuments of a war between rivers and mountains, which must have shaken the earth itself to its center." . . . A curious but, I think, significant analogy exists between this passage and certain others in Jefferson's works. Just as he here discovers the sublime in geological forces, so at other times he evokes the sublimity of tumultuous historical processes, particularly of revolutionary struggles for reason and liberty.

One would expect to find emotional effect in his writings on the American Revolution, especially the **Declaration of Independence.** In writing the **Declaration,** Jefferson acted somewhat like a lawyer preparing a brief, justifying action taken against the offending monarch by citing a series of particular violations of fundamental law. Yet he was successful in placing rational proof in an emotive context. He deeply regretted the editing that Congress performed on his original draft, and a glance at the portions removed shows that they contained some of his most emotional passages. In summarizing the grievances of America against the English nation, Jefferson becomes almost maudlin:

> These facts have given the last stab to agonizing affection, and manly spirit bids us to renounce for ever these unfeeling brethren. we must endeavor to forget our former love for them, and to [hold them as we hold the rest of mankind enemies in war, in peace friends]. we might have been a free and a great people together; but a communication of grandeur & of freedom it seems is below their dignity. be it so, since they will have it. the road to happiness & to glory is open to us too.

Jefferson would have concluded this sententiously emotional passage with a declaration not only of "separation," but of "eternal separation." In another passage ultimately deleted, he challenges the reader's imagination to conceive the British monarch's villainy: "Future ages will scarcely believe that the hardiness of one man adventured, within the short compass of twelve years only, to lay a foundation so broad & so undisguised for tyranny over a people fostered & fixed in principles of freedom." . . . If, according to late eighteenth-century ideas, the sublime can be suggested by depicting extreme actions,

states, or qualities, then this polemic clearly aspires to a type of sublimity.

Jefferson's other works also frequently contain highly-wrought passages; and, although hè is seldom very original in creating them, he at least employs them forcefully. He often represents revolutionary progress by vivid images of fire and light, as when, writing to Adams on July 9, 1819, he recalls Henry's resolutions of 1775 as "lightning" that "kindled both sides of the Atlantic." . . . Sometimes he images the drama of progress as a battle between the natural, freely-spreading fire of liberty and the tightly-controlled, artificial "engines" of tyranny. (pp. 246-47)

In his desire to find the proper emotional pitch, Jefferson sometimes produces rather ambitious arrays of imagery. In another letter written to Adams (January 11, 1816), a characteristic assertion that the "light from our West seems to have spread and illuminated the very engines employed to extinguish it" is one of a variety of exclamatory images representing scenes in the battle for liberty in Europe. In Jefferson's imagination, "rivers of blood" gush forth; "oppressors . . . cut off heads after heads, but like those of the Hydra, they multiply at every stroke"; captive peoples rise in insurrection; armies march back and forth across Europe; and the continent degenerates into "an Arena of gladiators." . . . Jefferson leaves no device untried in depicting the arduous ascent toward rational liberty as a drama of sublime violence. (p. 248)

[Jefferson often uses] images of terror to heighten the emotional tone of his descriptions of political and historical events. He typically employs hyperbolic expressions in reference to reactionary forces, denouncing them as "Incendiaries," or noting with disgust that "the Cannibals of Europe are going to eating [sic] one another again." . . . Through the years, Jefferson poured a torrent of transcendent abuse on his great enemy Napoleon. He represented the dictator as "the Attila of the age . . . the ruthless destroyer of 10. millions of the human race"; as "a moral monster" possessed of "a ravenous thirst for human blood"; and, after the Emperor's final defeat, as an "exorcised demon." Jefferson's ability to magnify the wickedness of his adversaries significantly aids his attempt to portray contemporary history as a tale fraught with sublime importance.

But although Jefferson's flashes of invective are entertaining, he shows his skill as a writer to greater advantage when he develops more extended literary effects. The latter part of his *Autobiography* in particular, shows Jefferson at his best at integrating "sublime" effects into a narrative structure. . . . The *Autobiography* is almost entirely occupied with his public life, and makes only passing references to his marriage and the deaths of his wife and one of his daughters. Unfortunately, its first sections, which recount Jefferson's role in Congress and in the Virginia legislature, can hardly be considered as emotive, or even very well-structured narrative. With a lawyerly interest in detail, Jefferson descends to minute descriptions of the legislative procedures he witnessed and the documents he wrote or reviewed; in this case, the fact that these proceedings were revolutionary and that one of these documents was the **Declaration of Independence** seldom awakens his eloquence. Although he includes several lively descriptions of men and events, he generally limits himself in these early sections to fulfilling the pragmatic intention he states at the beginning: "At the age of 77, I begin to make some memoranda, and state some recollections of dates and facts concerning myself, for my own more ready reference, and for the information of my family."

. . . But Jefferson's description of the opening days of the French Revolution, which fills most of the second half of his *Autobiography,* shows much more conscious art. Following his characteristic method of drawing extreme contrasts between progressive and reactionary forces, Jefferson repeatedly strives to reveal sublimity in the events he describes.

Beginning his account with a discussion of the "remote causes" of the Revolution . . . , he distinguishes the rational and libertarian proceedings of American statesmen from the degraded maneuvers of European courts. He describes the farcical politics surrounding France's abortive intervention in Holland in 1786 and 1787, revealing the feeble stupidity of almost all the European leaders involved. . . . Beside these emblems of wretched failure Jefferson tellingly inserts a discussion of the successful formation of the American Constitution. He emphasizes the fact that American "good sense" has avoided the irrational violence to which France was destined, and represents the success of rational politics as "a happy augury of the future march of our Confederacy." . . . Jefferson later uses this metaphor of orderly progression—the "march" of free men—to great effect. When he describes the beginning of the French Assembly's deliberations on the Declaration of the Rights of Man, he states that "the quiet of their march was soon disturbed by information that troops, and particularly the foreign troops, were advancing on Paris from various quarters. The King had probably been advised to this, on the pretext of preserving peace in Paris." . . . By repeating his metaphor, Jefferson thus establishes a poignant contrast between the rational advance of freedom and the false order which the marching troops of tyranny would impose upon society.

Yet before he depicts the actual outbreak of violent revolution, Jefferson's imagery effectively expresses the violent political polarization that caused it. He sharply contrasts the French people's growing pressure against a multitude of lurid abuses with the cool indolence of the French ministry in enacting reforms, and he invokes his characteristic imagery of inhumanly savage oppression by declaring that "this people were ground to powder" by "monstrous abuses of power." . . . This image is particularly apt, because it suggests not merely the atomized subjection of the French people, but also the fact that they were numerous and therefore potentially dangerous.

Having indicated the people's condition, Jefferson gradually describes the other leading forces involved in the Revolution, sometimes succinctly characterizing them by forceful images of weakness or strength, artifice or candor. . . . Jefferson draws an emblem of deceptive beauty in his character of Marie Antoinette. Though she is adorned by Burke's false eloquence, her decadence and irrationality belie her pretensions to grandeur and fix on her the responsibility for the greatest crimes. . . . On the other hand, Jefferson invariably represents the friends of liberty as rational, strong in moral force, and candid. They are "of honest but differing opinions, sensible of the necessity of effecting a coalition by mutual sacrifices, knowing each other, and not afraid, therefore, to unbosom themselves mutually." Their leader, La Fayette, is strength incarnate, an "Atlas, who had no secrets from me." . . . (pp. 248-51)

Having drawn two highly opposed sets of characters, Jefferson does not merely summarize the effects of their actions, but strives for dramatic impact by allowing them to display their natures in a number of vividly realized scenes. He shows a considerable ability to isolate salient details in the events he describes. (p. 251)

Jefferson does not, however, confine himself to vivid descriptions of revolutionary events; he also explicitly tries to exalt their importance. In order to do so, he surrounds the contrasting extremes of "monstrous" oppression and calmly rational liberation with highly emotive imagery. He speaks of the desired success of the Revolution under the metaphor of rebirth: "I considered a successful reformation of government in France, as insuring a general reformation through Europe, and the resurrection, to a new life, of their people, now ground to dust by the abuses of governing powers." . . . Having secularized this leading metaphor of religion to express the sublimity of the universal struggle for liberty, he later employs contrasting extremes of negative imagery to depict the Satanic results of that struggle's temporary failure. . . . [The] *Autobiography* as a whole patently constitutes a recommendation of rationalistic progress; yet it gains its considerable emotive force from Jefferson's contrastive method, his ability to portray contemporary events as part of a crucial struggle between two transcendent principles—the heroic desire to recreate the world, and the demonic impulse to tyrannize over its ruins. This work can therefore be viewed as a notable attempt on Jefferson's part to realize his critical insistence on both rationalism and sublimity. (pp. 252-53)

Jefferson's enthusiastic critical judgments may frequently sound simplistic or naive. Had he analyzed literature more systematically, he might have refined his ideas on the connection between reason and artistic excellence into more incisive observations. His criticism suffers from his tendency casually to suggest, from time to time, some new and rather imperfect relation between rational philosophy and effective art. Yet the same tendency likely helped him to enliven his own writing by converting political ideas into strongly emotional effects. Whether he is depicting the sublimity of revolutionary history or describing the libertarian genesis of artistic creation, he struggles to exalt his subject to a level of transcendent importance. No account of his critical ideas should neglect the fact that for Jefferson the act of reason can be the ally, rather than the enemy, of the aesthetic impulse. (p. 254)

Stephen D. Cox, "The Literary Aesthetic of Thomas Jefferson," in Essays in Early Virginia Literature Honoring Richard Beale Davis, *edited by J. A. Leo Lemay, Burt Franklin & Company, Inc., 1977, pp. 235-56.*

CLAYTON W. LEWIS   (essay date 1978)

[*Lewis analyzes the style, structure, and influences on* Notes on the State of Virginia *to argue that despite its diverse subject matter and arbitrary organization, it "achieves the imaginative unity and force of literature." Unity in the* Notes *is accomplished, according to Lewis, through a "complex, reflexive style" that brings together the author, reader, and content. Lewis concludes with a detailed discussion of Jefferson's account of the passage of the rivers through the Blue Ridge Mountains at Harpers Ferry. In his conclusion, Lewis mentions Jefferson's "disastrous personal and public experiences" in 1781; he is referring to the British invasion of Virginia, Jefferson's flight from Monticello during the revolutionary war, and also to the poor health of several family members.*]

Thomas Jefferson's only published book, *Notes on the State of Virginia,* occupies a curious position in American letters. While it has been called philosophy, natural history, and a guidebook to Virginia in the 1780s, it has also frequently been regarded as literature. . . . While *Notes* is certainly a repository of Jefferson's ideas, a guidebook to Virginia in the 1780s, and a document which may tell us a lot about Jefferson's psyche (and the psyche of the South, of America), it is also a text with literary effect. In the following essay I would like to attempt to identify how the text of *Notes* achieves the imaginative unity and force of literature.

Notes appears, on first reading, to lack the qualities we expect of literature. Its title suggests a collection of fragments. Its organization seems arbitrary—that is, to be Jefferson's answers to a series of queries posed by François Marbois, who was then secretary of the French legation in Philadelphia. The text contains extensive description, maps, passages of scientific disputation, tables of various kinds, arguments on some of Jefferson's deepest concerns, sublime recollections, agonizing explorations of race questions, and several passages of passionate exhortation. All this is interesting because it reveals an interesting mind, but at the same time the book seems to lack the coherence of imaginative literature. What principles of literary art shape this collection of information and reflection?

Jefferson was not a naïve stylist. Like other educated men of the eighteenth century, he knew the Greeks and Romans who had discussed style—Aristotle and Cicero, among others. In 1771 he was at least familiar with contemporary discussions of style in Burke's *On the Sublime and the Beautiful* and Kame's *Elements of Criticism*. Such reading evidently helped cultivate his taste in style. He admired Demosthenes, the "pith and brevity" of Tacitus, the Sallust, and Livy, and the "eloquence of pen" of Robertson, Sterne, Addison, and Hume. And his taste was discriminating, for he could admire a style like Hume's while disagreeing with the ideas presented by that style, and he could admire one element of a style while disliking others, which he did with Cicero, who was "diffuse, rapid, rhetorical, but enchanting."

Moreover, Jefferson articulated his own view of style. When he justifies the study of Latin and Greek he says these languages are "models of pure taste in writing. To these we are certainly indebted for the rational and chaste style of modern composition which so much distinguishes the nations to whom these styles are familiar. Without these models we should probably have continued to use the inflated style of our northern ancestors, or the hyperbolical and vague one of the east." The view of style he expresses here values the classical tradition, but elsewhere he equally values nature, place, one's native language. "I would observe to you," he writes to a young man, "that what is called style in writing or speaking is formed very early in life . . . I am of the opinion, that there never was an instance of a man's writing or speaking his native language with elegance, who passed from fifteen to twenty years of age out of the country where it was spoken." Jefferson's articulated view of style is, like many of his other views, a vital drawing together of the arts of civilization and the immediacy of experience in a particular place, in nature.

Finally, Jefferson was aware of having a style of his own; he was a self-conscious stylist. This awareness is apparent when he says "I am [no] friend to a scrupulous purism of style. I readily sacrifice the niceties of syntax to euphony and strength." His model for this vital style is Tacitus: "It is by neglecting the rigorisms of grammar, that Tacitus has made himself the strongest writer in the world." Jefferson sees in Tacitus what he is surely aware of practicing himself. As he makes this observation about Tacitus, he coins "rigorisms," which enact in style precisely what he is observing in Tacitus. Thus Jefferson is not simply learned in matters of style, a man of taste,

a theoretician; in his own style he enacts his views of style. His awareness of himself as a stylist is seen again in his remarks on writing the **Declaration of Independence**: ". . . it was intended to be an expression of the American mind, and to give to that expression the proper tone and spirit called for by the occasion." I suggest that *Notes on the State of Virginia* gains literary effect through Jefferson's use of a complex, reflexive style which unites Jefferson's sensibility, the content, the reader, and the act of writing itself.

The style of the language of *Notes* is, on first reading, remarkable for its control of large amounts of information. Rarely does the density of information overwhelm the reader's ability to comprehend; where it would overwhelm the reader, the presentation is tabular, thereby allowing the reader to use selectively only what he wishes to comprehend. In this way the style does not separate information from the qualities of mind necessary to comprehend that information. A typical descriptive passage will illustrate: "*Gold*. I know a single instance of gold found in this state. It was interspersed in small specks through a lump of ore, of about four pounds weight, which yielded seventeen penny-weight of gold, of extraordinary ductility. This ore was found on the North side of Rappahanoc, about four miles below the falls. I have never heard of any other indication of gold in its neighborhood." The passage presents highly specific information which could become tedious. Such a difficulty is avoided by placing an observing sensibility within the description. We have presented to us both the comprehending sensibility and the specifics of an empirical world. The sensibility is aware of its detailed subject matter and of its relationship to an implied reader. Put another way, the sensibility keeps in balance the need for descriptive precision and the need to convey comprehensible information to the reader.

There are other balances in the passage. It gives us an impression of contingency, of information which is relative to an observer, and at the same time an almost opposite sense of the very definite and specific. The passage avoids absolute statements by making the information relative to the experience of the observing sensibility. "I knew" and "I have never heard" are contingent, experience-relative statements. Balanced against this contingent language is the very definite and precise language used to describe the physical phenomena: ". . . yielded seventeen penny-weight of gold . . . the North side of Rappahanoc." The sensibility is placing, then, the definite phenomena of the ore and its discovery into a context which is contingent and relative to experience. In doing so the sensibility holds in balance apparently opposite attitudes. Thus in the relation to content, there is a sense of balance and a tone of calm, just as there is in the relationship to the implied reader. The balanced and reflexive relationships embodied in the style give the passage literary effect.

The same principal of literary art shapes the larger structures of *Notes*. Each of the book's twenty-three sections begins with a numbered query (Query I), title ("Boundaries of Virginia") and the query as Jefferson received it from Marbois ("An exact description of the limits and boundaries of the state of Virginia?"). If Jefferson had narrowly and simply answered these queries, *Notes* would be scientific discourse. But Jefferson has not construed his task in this way. Within the context provided by each query, Jefferson digresses—so much so that the digressions cease to be digressions as the queries become less and less the principle organizing structure. Fairly quickly we see that our experience of this text is primarily controlled by the sensibility, and that the queries have been subordinated to that sensibility—more particularly, to the processes of that sensibility's response in the broadest human and natural terms to the queries. It is the terms of these processes which shape our experience of the text. (pp. 668-71)

[The] reader is not receiving a simple answer to the query; he is instead participating in the process of Jefferson's thought. The reader feels the potential which Jefferson has to shift focus at any moment, to bring up tangential matters, to follow the living flow of thought, and it is this sense of open possibility which gives *Notes* its remarkable lightness and freshness. The operative notion of description is not, then, what we find in contemporary encyclopedias—that is, it is not a fixed viewpoint rendering empirical fact. Jefferson instead locates the describing sensibility within the world being described, so that the sensibility in the act of description manifests what it is describing. Man and his activities were to Jefferson part of nature. The natural processes which occur in Virginia—processes in the world of man's culture as well as in nature itself—are described by a sensibility which manifests those same processes.

Thus when Jefferson leaves his account of "Productions Mineral, Vegetable and Animal" for an extended refutation of Buffon's views on the size of animals in America and, later, disputes with Abbé Raynal's remarks about America's lack of geniuses, he is not abandoning his descriptive intention as much as he is modulating it, and thereby manifesting the existence of the sensibility *within* the processes of the natural and human world it is describing. In the act of writing, he is dismantling the abstractions which hinder perceptions of nature and the natural facts of man's existence. He is actively participating in the human and natural worlds as he describes these worlds. This is equally true when he leaves his account of "Laws" and "Manners" to agonize over slavery and the equality of the black and white races and, in the midst of discussing "Manufactures," breaks into an impassioned plea for "those who labor in the earth." In its style the text embodies a natural, moving, self-balancing process, which, in being so, manifests the processes of the natural and human worlds it is describing.

The content of *Notes* is thus not fixed. It is not the State of Virginia in a purely empirical sense, as much as it is the *process of Jefferson's experience of the human and natural condition in Virginia*. It is scientific in the best sense, and its central locus is the process of observation and evolving hypothesis. This sense of knowledge as process, as contingent and experience-relative, is embodied in the language and the responses to the queries. Furthermore, Jefferson's hesitant publication of the book . . . and his subsequent revisions and appendices show that he viewed the book as a continuing process—as a glimpse of that process at a particular moment, but no more than that—with himself and his evolving knowledge as the central locus. In language, content, style, and organization, *Notes* takes its form from reflexively related processes, and these in turn are reflexes of the activity and processes of nature itself. (pp. 671-73)

My view of *Notes* may be summarized by a look at Jefferson's well-known account of the passage of the rivers through the mountains at Harpers Ferry: "The passage of the Patowmac through the Blue Ridge is perhaps one of the most stupendous scenes in nature. You stand on a very high point of land. On your right comes up the Shenandoah, having ranged along the foot of the mountain an hundred miles to seek a vent. On your left approaches the Patowmac, in quest of a passage also."

Jefferson has placed himself within the scene he describes and, by doing so, makes his experience of the scene central. Here as elsewhere it is not just *what* is seen, but *how* one sees it that is important. This strategy makes the experience of the sensibility relative, not absolute. If, for example, he stood on the Potomac's south bank, the experience would be different. By placing himself within the scene, Jefferson involves us in his experience of the place. His use of the collective "you" adds to this involvement.

> In the moment of their junction they rush together against the mountain, rend it asunder and pass off to the sea. The first glance of this scene hurries our senses into the opinion, that this earth has been created in time, that the mountains were formed first, that the rivers began to flow afterwards, that in this place particularly they have been dammed up by the Blue ridge mountains, and have formed an ocean which filled the whole valley; that continuing to rise they have at length broken over at this spot, and have torn the mountain down from its summit to its base.

We experience four reflexively related processes in this passage. Two are set in the scene itself. The first is the passage of the river through the mountain in the immediately visible scene; the second is the geological process which has created this scene. Though vastly different in scale, each of these is a natural process of building tension, climax, and release.

The same is true of the style of the language. In its building constructions ("that . . . that . . . that . . . that . . . that") and release ("have at length broken . . . have torn") the language is an exact analog of the processes it is describing. And behind the language the process of perception moves in a similar way. The first of the sentences renders gross perceptions and feelings on first encountering the sight. Then in the long and finally climactic sentence we have the process of the sensibility's full perception of and response to the scene before him. (pp. 673-74)

The style of the passage thus forges a single, complex, rich experience out of four related processes, two in nature and two in the human world of the sensibility. Indeed the four can be viewed as manifestations of a single process. Here Jefferson enacts his belief that there is no *fundamental* difference between human and natural processes, no separation of subject from object, observer from observed. Jefferson is observing nature and at the same time participating in its active processes. He manifests nature in the act of writing about it. (p. 674)

This passage concerning the Potomac's breech of the Blue Ridge has "broken into" a description of mountain ridges, and occurs under the mountain query instead of the river query where it might more appropriately be included. Indeed the passage is in the middle of a long paragraph. It is incorrect to see it as a digression. To do so would imply the operation of a stationary pattern as the central structuring element in the book, and we have already seen that such structure comes, instead, from our sense of participation in reflexively related processes. Thus these passages "break into" the description of the mountains just as the dammed up sea had broken down the mountain, and the rivers here in "riot and tumult" pass through the breach. The action of the writing is, in a very fundamental sense, the action of the phenomena being described. (p. 675)

In writing *Notes,* Jefferson is observing and participating in [the processes of the natural and human world], which, it seems to me, are conceived by him to be fundamentally one process. By writing of the Potomac's break through the Blue Ridge, he makes known (to both American and European audiences) the marvelous workings of nature and thereby serves to break down in other men the artificiality and ignorance which keep them from being fully participant in these vitalizing processes. At the same time, Jefferson's writing itself, the action of his language, manifests these processes while it is describing their working in nature. There is evidence to suggest that the writing of *Notes* was for Jefferson an attempt to restore himself to these vital processes after disastrous personal and public experiences suffered in early 1781. I believe the reader experiences the same action as he reads *Notes*—the sense of being restored to the vitalizing processes in himself and in the larger world. Focused through the style, these varied and reflexively related processes largely transform ordinary discourse into forceful and coherent imagination. (pp. 675-76)

> Clayton W. Lewis, "Style in Jefferson's 'Notes on the State of Virginia'," in The Southern Review, Vol. XIV, No. 4, October, 1978, pp. 668-76.

JUDITH N. SHKLAR   (essay date 1984)

[*The following excerpt from a review of the Library of America edition of Jefferson's writings is representative of modern critical opinion of Jefferson. Shklar provides a wide-ranging assessment of Jefferson's beliefs and accomplishments, surveying his interest in and writings about politics, religion, morality, education, war, and slavery. Only in his observations on race and class relations, according to Shklar, did Jefferson fail to live up to his public image as a champion of human rights.*]

How are we to understand Thomas Jefferson? The epitaph he composed for himself at the end of his life tells us what he wanted us to think about him, and that is why it is as good a place as any to begin looking for the mind of this very reserved and elusive public man. "Here was buried Thomas Jefferson. Author of the American Declaration of Independence, of the Statute of Virginia for religious freedom. Father of the University of Virginia, because by these as testimonials that I have lived, I wish most to be remembered."

He was first of all a Virginian, deeply loyal to his native state and his neighbors. Only the **Declaration,** his masterpiece, spoke for all the colonies and to the world at large. Proud as he was of it, he did not regard it as an original production. Almost fifty years after it was written he recalled that he had not meant to "find out new principles or arguments never before thought of, but to place before mankind the common sense of the subject to command their assent, and to justify ourselves. It was intended to be an expression of the American mind. All its authority rests then on the harmonizing sentiments of the day." It was drawn from conversations, shared reading, and the current pamphlet literature. In Jefferson's view the **Declaration** was not only his, but all of America's collective self-understanding. The enduring intensity of his democratic convictions was such that he considered his entire political career not as a personal activity, but as a wholly representative one. Even of his Presidency he said that many others could have done it just as well as he had.

To express "the American mind" is no small achievement, but the **Declaration** is also Jefferson's work, not least in its austere and dignified rhetoric. Part of it is meant to read like a legal brief, declaring a just war under prevailing rules of international law, and to show "a decent regard for the opinion of mankind," as well as to convince the French of America's determination. Its accusations against Great Britain are the sum of a decade's complaints. But the call for "the inalienable rights" of men created equal, and for a government "deriving its just power from the consent of the governed," was not meant for the statesmen of Europe. It was for Americans; it gave them a cause to fight for; and it was radical by any standards. For not all Americans thought of Great Britain as an "absolute tyranny," and unlike Jefferson many did feel a "last stab of agonized affection."

As a "hail and farewell," the **Declaration** is a perfectly stunning classical oration. It also has some of Jefferson's own most cherished beliefs in it. "Nature" or "nature's God" is a very cool deity—"The Creator," who is known only by his works. These show us that "life, liberty, and the pursuit of happiness" are rights derived from the necessities to which God's nature impels us. Self-preservation is possible only if we are free to protect the integrity of our lives, and as each one of us is created uniquely different, we must seek in our own way the happiness to which our nature also drives us. Freedom is a right because "the opinions and beliefs of men depend not on their own will," as Jefferson was to say over and over again for the rest of his life. It was standard Lockean moral psychology, and it has never been really dislodged from our public ethos.

The Bill for the separation of state and church in Virginia [*An Act for Establishing Religious Freedom*], which Jefferson introduced and Madison saw through to enactment, expressed the same beliefs. Religious freedom was more than mere toleration. It meant the complete exclusion of religion from public life. Radical Protestantism had proposed such an arrangement to protect "the garden of the Lord" from the pollutions of the world, but Jefferson had other reasons for it. He really disliked the clergy and all organized religions. Priestcraft was responsible for our ignorance, superstition, and persecution. (pp. 29-30)

The famous "wall between church and state" was, Jefferson hoped, to protect the public against the "Gothic," backward-looking and inherently illiberal forces of revealed religion. In this, and his own natural religion, he was fortified by the thought that most southerners were as indifferent to religion as he was, and that only New England remained blighted by zealots. Evidently he misread the temper of his countrymen. . . .

[Behind Jefferson's] honorably held principles there was no deep moral philosophy. Jefferson had no interest in metaphysics or ethics, and he was bored even by political theory. . . .

His ideas on morality appear in only fragmentary form in letters, often to young people for whose education he felt responsible. We all have a "moral sense," he believed, or a conscience which the Creator gave us when he made us sociable. It amounts to the golden rule and requires neither intelligence nor education. Its rules are not uniform, being guided by utility, which depends on time and place. This relativism did not imply, however, that right and wrong were matters of self-interest, or selfish satisfactions; they are decidedly other-directed. Still, at times he thought that Epicureanism was as close to moral truth as one could ever get. At other times he admired the Stoics. This sort of eclectic practical moralizing was not unusual in the eighteenth century, especially among those who, like Jefferson, named Bacon, Locke, and Newton as their true heroes.

The only cure for mankind's self-inflicted ills was education. The rock upon which democracy would be built was elementary education for all citizens and the best of university educations for its "natural aristocrats," that is, for intellectually gifted men. From the *Notes on Virginia* of 1782 to the end of his days, Jefferson urged a comprehensive system of education upon his state. It was to begin with three years of free elementary schooling at the "ward" level, which was also to serve as the basic unit of local government, like the New England town meeting. Primary schools were to give every citizen the skills required for productive work and active political participation. Next there was to be an eight-year course of secondary education for which the rich would pay, while the gifted poor would attend at public expense.

The curriculum was vague, but it seemed to involve nothing less than a complete set of college-level courses in all literary, scientific, and historical subjects, as well as Greek, Latin, and several modern languages. Jefferson spent little time thinking through this part of his scheme. It was meant to prepare students at the district level for the university. . . . It was in each secondary school that, after two years of trials, twenty of "the best geniuses will be raked from the rubbish annually," and educated for six more years. As these awful words show, there is a war between egalitarian and meritocratic impulses even in dreams. For neither one of these schemes came to anything more.

Jefferson's only educational success was the University of Virginia, which he planned and whose buildings reveal his enormous gifts as an architect no less than Monticello does. His hope was that the university would train future Virginians for the professions, and for political leadership. The faculty were not to be disciplinarians, but fathers to the students, which the arrangement of the buildings encouraged. There was to be a lot of student self-government, which would "be more likely to nourish in the minds of our youth the combined spirit of order and self-respect, so congenial with our political institutions and so important to be woven into the American character." (p. 30)

It is not surprising that Jefferson was proud of the university he had founded, especially when one considers what its education was meant to accomplish. It was to create leaders, to train scientists and professional men, to be the source of unabating progress—and finally to replace politics. For an enlightened citizenry would freely entrust offices to its natural aristocrats. Knowledge, especially scientific knowledge, would make Americans open-minded, free, and responsible. If he did not believe in human perfection, then, Jefferson certainly did expect constant improvement, a word he loved; and schools were to be the temples and workshops in which improvement would be received and created. How else were ordinary men to become fit for free democratic republican government? "The principal foundations of future order are laid here," he wrote of the public school. (p. 31)

A Democratic natural aristocracy could not be educated in Europe. . . . The word was not yet in use, but what Jefferson already knew was that a European education created American snobs. He also thought that it ruined their health and sexual morals.

In fact, he detested England and its ways, and he hated Hamilton and his followers for their admiration of our former rulers. . . . [Lack of manners and] good music were the only defects that Jefferson was ready to recognize in America compared to Europe.

Jefferson's patriotism was intense, both in a cultural and a martial sense. Most of his writings on natural history were designed to refute Buffon's and Raynal's charges that the flora, fauna, and human population of the Americas were inferior to those of Europe. He was also entirely in favor of expansion, so that the United States would control the northern part of the hemisphere and keep European influence out of the South. The purchase of Louisiana was something he had long hoped for; only the absence of constitutional provisions for such an act bothered him. But he was so pleased with the result that he regarded that aspect of the matter as a mere "scrape." In fact he was hawkish generally, especially when American shipping was endangered on the Barbary Coast or by Britain. Unlike Adams, he thought that it would be best "to effect peace through the medium of war" rather than by negotiations. (pp. 31-2)

Moreover, foreign war was not the only occasion for a useful show of force. A little rebellion every so often would prevent any budding despotic tendencies in American government as well. For more than anything else Jefferson cherished the novelty and the democracy of America's political institutions. Only representative democracy is self-correcting, and only the people learn from their mistakes. "Calamity was our best physician," when we erred politically, and it was the people who responded by redressing the faults of state governments. In youth and in old age he was equally convinced "that the people are the only safe depositories of their own liberty." That made their enlightenment, however, all the more important.

Political leadership could not seem very significant to a man who put so much weight on education. And Jefferson was a dismal failure as the wartime governor of Virginia, and (apart from the Louisiana Purchase) was not a particularly successful President. Nor did he enjoy office. As a young man the "spice of ambition" and the desire for fame drove him on, but throughout he longed for another sort of life. Even before composing the **Declaration** he wrote to a Virginia friend that "my first wish is a restoration of our just rights; my second, a return to the happy period when consistently with duty, I may withdraw myself totally from a public stage, and pass the rest of my days in domestic ease and tranquility." At last, thirty-four years later, he could really become "the hermit of Monticello," which he never left again. (pp. 32-3)

As a scientist he was an inventor rather than a researcher. Usefulness was never far from his mind. With that pragmatism, moreover, came a great personal flexibility. He was quite capable of admitting mistakes. . . . He also accepted the necessity of commerce and manufacturing, because they secured America's independence from Europe, and because most of his countrymen wanted them, even though he was firmly convinced that the self-sufficient farmer was the best and most upright of citizens, the bearer of republican rectitude. He really thought that a central bank and stock-jobbers were the greatest danger to republican government.

At no time did Jefferson seem to realize that slavery, not Anglophilia, banking, or religious enthusiasm, was the real cancer eating away the very heart of American democracy. He knew that it was unjust to blacks, and a menace to the morals and the temper of the white slave owners. But he was so conveniently convinced of black inferiority that he could come up with nothing better than a wholly fantastic colonization scheme. And having condemned the institution, he felt absolved from further action; instead he indulged in speculation and blamed others for the predicament of the South.

And if his response to black slavery was completely inadequate, his dealing with Indians was even more lamentable. On one hand he ascribed all sorts of heroic characteristics to them, in order to parade before European eyes a distinguished American pre-history like that which Greece and Rome had once provided. But when he dealt with Indian chiefs directly he addressed them as "my children," and spoke to them in a revolting baby talk of his own invention. His avowed policy was "to bribe them into peace and to retain them in peace by eternal bribes." This was both economical and humane, he claimed. In fact he could see neither Indians nor blacks as anything but part of the flora and fauna of America, and his only regret toward them was that "they have never been viewed by us as subjects of natural history."

When a black writer sent Jefferson an almanac, he wrote him back to say that it proved that the black race was not altogether beneath the white. It never occurred to him to treat this man, or anyone else who was not white, as an individual. They were just instances of a species to be looked at and classified. This is a view of mankind that has nothing to recommend it under any circumstances, but it is utterly intolerable when it is proposed by someone who valued individuality as much as Jefferson did. . . . In principle he was quite ready to admit that the presumed intellectual failings of black people did not justify the deprivation of their rights, just as Newton's genius did not entitle him to political privilege; but in practice he found it impossible to see them as human beings at all. His genial optimism, his self-confidence no less than his faith in improvement, made him blind to the situation of those who had no part in, or were even obstacles to, America's expansive future, its geographic, scientific, and political pre-eminence.

Now that Jefferson's world is "lost" forever, what does he say to us? His hatreds can still inspire us. Intolerance, ignorance, persecution, despotism, and the suffering they bring— all are still here. But a liberal patriotism that is racist and has no room for anyone except the intelligent and the self-sufficient will not do. We cannot speak decently of the uneducated as "rubbish," nor shun the physical and spiritual needs of those who depend on others, or whose will to believe remains untouched by science or skepticism. It is not even democratic. For all Jefferson's talk about "the people," he seems to have had no very clear idea of what they were like. He knew only that the white male American farmer was superior to the *"canaille"* of European cities. And yet, for all that, he remains an icon. This is the man who put human rights on the map forever. If he had no sense of tragedy, no real idea of history, and no profound understanding of the human heart, he was still a great man, and for the very reasons for which he wanted us to honor him. He was also, as his letters show, affectionate, charming, clever, alert, curious and good-humored: the best American character. (pp. 33-5)

> *Judith N. Shklar, "The Renaissance American," in* The New Republic, *Vol. 191, No. 19, November 5, 1984, pp. 29-35.*

ADDITIONAL BIBLIOGRAPHY

Adams, Henry. *History of the United States of America during the First Administration of Thomas Jefferson.* 2 vols. New York: Charles Scribner's Sons, 1921.

————. *History of the United States of America during the Second Administration of Thomas Jefferson.* 2 vols. New York: Charles Scribner's Sons, 1921.
> A definitive yet controversial study of American history during Jefferson's terms as president. The work focuses on the conflict between ideals and realities in the conduct of government, often detailing policies in which, according to Adams, Jefferson betrayed his principles. In Adams's view, Jefferson's commitment to peace provides the explanation for his seeming inconsistencies.

Adams, Herbert B. *Thomas Jefferson and the University of Virginia.* Contributions to American Educational History, edited by Herbert B. Adams, no. 2. Washington: Government Printing Office, 1888, 308 p.
> A history of Jefferson's role as founder of the University of Virginia. Adams thoroughly documents Jefferson's innovative program planning and his influence on American higher education.

Adler, Mortimer J., and Gorman, William. "The Declaration of Independence." In their *The American Testament*, pp. 17-62. New York: Praeger Publishers, 1975.
> A lengthy and comprehensive line-by-line explication of the Declaration.

Baugh, A. C. "Thomas Jefferson, Linguistic Liberal." In *Studies for William A. Read: A Miscellany Presented by Some of His Colleagues and Friends*, edited by Nathaniel M. Caffee and Thomas A. Kirby, pp. 88-108. University: Louisiana State University Press, 1940.
> Assesses Jefferson's contributions to the study of language.

Beard, Charles A. *Economic Origins of Jeffersonian Democracy.* New York: Free Press, 1915, 474 p.
> An influential interpretation of the principles of Jeffersonian democracy. Beard applies the thesis that economic forces control political events to the history of the two-party system in America. According to Beard, the political struggle between the Republican and Federalist parties was, in reality, a conflict between the economic policies of the Jeffersonian agrarians and Federalist capitalists.

Beloff, Max. *Thomas Jefferson and American Democracy.* New York: Collier Books, 1962, 220 p.
> A biography that focuses on Jefferson's political ideology and accomplishments.

Berman, Eleanor Davidson. *Thomas Jefferson among the Arts: An Essay in Early American Esthetics.* New York: Philosophical Library, 1947, 305 p.
> Explores the sources of Jefferson's aesthetics, focusing especially on his ideas about painting, sculpture, architecture, gardening, music, rhetoric, and literature. Berman's study is considered one of the standard works on Jefferson's aesthetics.

Boorstin, Daniel J. *The Lost World of Thomas Jefferson.* New York: Henry Holt and Co., 1948, 306 p.*
> Examines the beliefs of a group of eighteenth-century political philosophers that Boorstin calls the Jeffersonians; this group includes Jefferson, Benjamin Franklin, David Rittenhouse, Benjamin Rush, Benjamin Smith Barton, Joseph Priestley, Charles Wilson Peale, and Thomas Paine. Boorstin attempts to "recapture the Jeffersonian world of ideas" by presenting their views on such topics as education, nature, religion, equality, and government.

————. "The American Revolution: Revolution without Dogma." In his *The Genius of American Politics*, pp. 66-98. Chicago: University of Chicago Press, 1953.
> A study of the development of political theory in America that attempts to define the character of the American Revolution. Unlike such historians as Carl Becker (see excerpts dated 1922 and

1943) and Charles A. Beard (see annotation above), Boorstin describes the political philosophy of the leaders of the Revolution as conservative and legalistic, and he supports this claim by comparing the Declaration of Independence with the French "Declaration of the Rights of Man and the Citizen." According to Boorstin, Jefferson based the reforms outlined in the Declaration on legal history rather than revolutionary dogma.

Bowers, Claude G. *Jefferson and Hamilton: The Struggle for Democracy in America*. Boston: Houghton Mifflin Co., 1925, 531 p.

————. *Jefferson in Power: The Death Struggle of the Federalists*. Boston: Houghton Mifflin Co., 1936, 538 p.

————. *The Young Jefferson: 1743-1789*. Boston: Houghton Mifflin Co., 1945, 544 p.
    A three-part biography. Bowers's study, which is noted for its imaginative and dramatic style, covers Jefferson's early life, his struggle with Hamilton during the 1790s, and his years as president. The publication of *Jefferson and Hamilton* was a major event in Jeffersonian historiography: it contributed to a shift in American political sympathies away from Hamilton and toward Jefferson and the Democratic party.

Boyd, Julian P. *The Declaration of Independence: The Evolution of the Text as Shown in Facsimiles of Various Drafts by Its Author, Thomas Jefferson*. Princeton: Princeton University Press, 1945, 46 p.
    A seminal study of the history of the Declaration of Independence. Boyd traces the evolution of the text from the first draft by Jefferson to its final form. In addition, he examines various facsimiles in an attempt to identify Jefferson's original version and the author of each of the subsequent alterations in the text. Boyd also edited the first twenty volumes of *The Papers of Thomas Jefferson*, which is highly respected by other historians for its thorough scholarly approach and definitive commentary.

Brodie, Fawn. *Thomas Jefferson: An Intimate History*. New York: W. W. Norton & Co., 1974, 594 p.
    A biography based primarily on Jefferson's letters and other writings. Unlike other biographers who focus on his intellect and achievements, Brodie attempts to illuminate his inner life, "the life of the heart." In addition to investigating Jefferson's relationship with Maria Cosway, Brodie establishes the controversial thesis that he carried on a lengthy clandestine affair with a slave, Sally Hemings.

Brown, Stuart Gerry. "The Mind of Thomas Jefferson." *Ethics: An International Journal of Social, Political, and Legal Philosophy* LXXIII, No. 2 (January 1963): 79-99.
    Traces the influence of Francis Bacon, Isaac Newton, John Locke, and Epicurus on Jefferson's political and personal philosophy.

Bush, Clive. "Origins of Natural History in America and First Syntheses." In his *The Dream of Reason: American Consciousness and Cultural Achievement from Independence to the Civil War*, pp. 191-209. New York: St. Martin's Press, 1977.
    Examines *Notes on the State of Virginia* as a work of geography and natural history.

Carter, Everett. "The Making of the Idea." In his *The American Idea: The Literary Response to American Optimism*, pp. 11-36. Chapel Hill: University of North Carolina Press, 1977.*
    Analyzes the relationship between literary form and the American idea in the Declaration of Independence.

Chinard, Gilbert. *Thomas Jefferson: The Apostle of Americanism*. Boston: Little, Brown, and Co., 1929, 548 p.
    A history of Jefferson's intellectual development written by a French scholar. In this work, which is considered one of the classic studies of Jefferson's philosophy, Chinard downplays the contribution of French theorists to Jefferson's political philosophy. Instead, according to this critic, his ideas were derived from and designed for his compatriots: "Jefferson did more than any other man of his generation to formulate the creed of Americanism."

Choate, Rufus. "Letter to the Whigs of Maine." In *The Works of Rufus Choate with a Memoir of His Life*, by Rufus Choate and Samuel Gilman Brown, pp. 212-16. Boston: Little, Brown and Co., 1862.
    A letter that outlines political strategy for the Whig party during the 1856 election. Choate uses the Declaration to support the view that civil war can be prevented only if the Whigs prevail. His description of the Declaration as a "passionate and eloquent manifesto" composed of "glittering and sounding generalities of natural right" is widely quoted by critics.

Cox, J. M. "Jefferson's *Autobiography:* Recovering Literature's Lost Ground." *The Southern Review* XIV, No. 4 (Autumn 1978): 633-52.
    Contends that Jefferson's *Autobiography* merits analysis as a literary work.

Dana, William F. "The Declaration of Independence." *Harvard Law Review* XIII, No. 5 (January 1900): 319-43.
    Questions the originality of the Declaration and compares it to the Virginia Bill of Rights, written by George Mason, and to Jefferson's *A Summary View of the Rights of British America*.

Dewey, John. "Presenting Thomas Jefferson." In *The Living Thoughts of Thomas Jefferson*, by Thomas Jefferson, edited by John Dewey, pp. 1-30. New York: Longmans, Green and Co., 1940.
    Analyzes Jefferson's writings in relation to the principle of moral idealism.

De Witt, Cornélis. *Jefferson and the American Democracy: An Historical Study*. Translated by R.S.H. Church. London: Longman, Green, Longman, Roberts, & Green, 1862, 448 p.
    A historical and biographical study of Jefferson written from an anti-democratic viewpoint.

Dos Passos, John. *The Head and Heart of Thomas Jefferson*. Garden City, N.Y.: Doubleday & Co., 1954, 442 p.
    A sympathetic biography covering Jefferson's life from his birth to his resignation from George Washington's cabinet in 1793.

————. *The Shackles of Power: Three Jeffersonian Decades*. Garden City, N.Y.: Doubleday & Co., 1966, 426 p.
    Covers from 1807 through Jefferson's death.

Dumbauld, Edward. *The Declaration of Independence and What It Means Today*. Norman: University of Oklahoma Press, 1950, 194 p.
    Presents a brief history of the background and composition of the Declaration followed by a line-by-line analysis and interpretation.

Erikson, Erik H. "The Founders: Jeffersonian Action and Faith." In his *Dimensions of a New Identity: The 1973 Jefferson Lectures in the Humanities*, pp. 9-60. New York: W. W. Norton & Co., 1974.
    A psychohistory of Jefferson. According to Erikson, this approach combines the methods of psychoanalysis and history to provide an appreciation of the subject's life, personality, and place in history. In his study of Jefferson, Erikson devotes particular attention to *Notes on the State of Virginia* and *Life and Morals of Jesus of Nazareth*.

Ethics: An International Journal of Social, Political, and Legal Philosophy LIII, No. 4 (July 1943): 237-310.
    A special issue devoted to Jefferson, published during the bicentennial of his birth, that includes essays by Claude G. Bowers, Gilbert Chinard, H. M. Kallen, and T. V. Smith.

Fisher, Sydney George. "The Twenty-Eight Charges against the King in the Declaration of Independence." *The Pennsylvania Magazine of History and Biography* XXXI, No. 3 (1907): 257-303.
    Examines the circumstances that led to the twenty-eight charges against King George III and analyzes each.

Foner, Philip S. *We, the Other People: Alternative Declarations of Independence by Labor Groups, Farmers, Women's Rights Advocates, Socialists, and Blacks, 1829-1975*. Urbana: University of Chicago Press, 1976, 205 p.
    A collection of alternative declarations of independence dating from the early nineteenth century to the present.

Franklin, Wayne. "Discovery Narrative: An Adventure of the Eye Alone." In his *Discoverers, Explorers, Settlers: The Diligent Writers*

of Early America, pp. 21-68. Chicago: University of Chicago Press, 1979.*
> Discusses *Notes on the State of Virginia* as a scientific treatise and a travel narrative.

Freehling, William W. "The Founding Fathers and Slavery." *The American Historical Review* 77, Vol. 1 (February 1972): 81-93.
> Examines the ambivalent views on slavery held by Jefferson and the other Founding Fathers.

Friedenwald, Herbert. *The Declaration of Independence: An Interpretation and an Analysis.* New York: Macmillan Co., 1904, 299 p.
> Provides a history of the events leading up to the Declaration and an analysis of its philosophical tenets.

Friedman, Milton, and Friedman, Rose. "Created Equal." In their *Free to Choose: A Personal Statement,* pp. 128-49. New York: Harcourt Brace Jovanovich, 1980.
> Attempts to define the terms "equality" and "liberty" as used in the Declaration of Independence. The Friedmans identify three meanings for the term equality: equality before God, which they posit was Jefferson's meaning; equality of opportunity, which emerged with the abolition of slavery; and equality of outcome, which emphasizes "fairness." While the critics consider the final definition the one most familiar and widespread today, they argue against this interpretation, contending that its implementation leads to the loss of both freedom and equality.

Ginsberg, Robert, ed. *A Casebook on the Declaration of Independence.* New York: Thomas Y. Crowell Co., 1967, 289 p.
> Reprints twenty-six important critical essays on the Declaration, including several critiques from the eighteenth and nineteenth centuries. Ginsberg also provides an extensive annotated bibliography.

Gittleman, Edwin. "Jefferson's 'Slave Narrative': The Declaration of Independence as a Literary Text." *Early American Literature* VIII, No. 3 (Winter 1974): 239-56.
> Treats the Declaration as a self-conscious slave narrative that uses such literary devices as syntax, diction, and form to depict the enslavement of the colonists by King George III.

Griswold, A. Whitney. "The Jeffersonian Ideal." In his *Farming and Democracy,* pp. 18-46. New York: Harcourt, Brace and Co., 1948.
> A classic analysis of Jefferson as an agrarian democrat.

Hartz, Louis. "The American Democrat: Hercules and Hamlet." In his *The Liberal Tradition in America: An Interpretation of American Political Thought since the Revolution,* pp. 114-42. New York: Harcourt, Brace & World, 1955.
> Charts Jefferson's role in the growth of democratic thought in America, with particular attention to his agrarian and anti-aristocratic belief.

Hauer, Stanley R. "Thomas Jefferson and the Anglo-Saxon Language." *PMLA* 98, No. 5 (October 1983): 879-98.
> A study of Jefferson as a linguist that explains his interest in the Anglo-Saxon language, analyzes his major works, and assesses the importance of his ideas.

Hazelton, John H. *The Declaration of Independence: Its History.* New York: Dodd, Mead and Co., 1906, 628 p.
> An authoritative study of the history of the Declaration. Hazelton recounts the events leading up to the Declaration, including its composition, revision by Congress, reception by contemporary politicians, and a history of its drafts.

Healey, Robert M. *Jefferson on Religion in Public Education.* New Haven: Yale University Press, 1962, 294 p.
> The definitive account of Jefferson's views on religion in public education.

Heslep, Robert D. "Thomas Jefferson's Major Philosophical Principles." *Educational Theory* 16, No. 2 (April 1966): 151-62.
> Interprets Jefferson's major philosophical principles in relation to his ideas on education.

Hofstadter, Richard. "Parrington and the Jeffersonian Tradition." *Journal of the History of Ideas* II, No. 4 (October 1941): 391-400.
> Counters Vernon Louis Parrington's contention that Jefferson founded his economic and democratic beliefs on the principles of agrarianism (see excerpt dated 1927). Hofstadter argues that "a survey of the Jeffersonian and Jacksonian movements shows that at no time did they ever produce, even in theory, a design for American agrarianism."

———. "The Founding Fathers: An Age of Realism" and "Thomas Jefferson: The Aristocrat as Democrat." In his *The American Political Tradition and the Men Who Made It,* pp. 3-17, pp. 18-43. New York: Alfred A. Knopf, 1948.*
> Characterizes Jefferson as both an aristocrat and a democrat. Hofstadter's work is said to embody the mid-twentieth century revisionist view of Jefferson, in which he emphasizes the unity of shared convictions between Jefferson and the Federalists.

Honeywell, Roy J. *The Educational Work of Thomas Jefferson.* Cambridge: Harvard University Press, 1931, 295 p.
> Examines Jefferson's efforts to establish an educational system. Honeywell thoroughly documents Jefferson's practical proposals regarding primary and secondary education and focuses on the University of Virginia.

Howell, Wilbur Samuel. "The Declaration of Independence and Eighteenth-Century Logic." *The William and Mary Quarterly* 3d series XVIII, No. 4 (October 1961): 463-84.
> Demonstrates the similarity between the argumentative structure of the Declaration and the theory set forth by the principal rhetoricians of Jefferson's era, notably William Duncan and John Locke.

Huddleston, Eugene L. *Thomas Jefferson: A Reference Guide.* Boston: G. K. Hall & Co., 1982, 374 p.
> An extensive annotated bibliography of writings about Jefferson through 1980. This work also includes an introduction that outlines the fluctuations in Jefferson's reputation and indicates the major essays dealing with each of his many different areas of accomplishment.

Jones, Howard Mumford. *The Pursuit of Happiness.* Cambridge: Harvard University Press, 1953, 168 p.
> Defines the phrase "the pursuit of happiness," outlining what it meant to Jefferson and to succeeding generations of Americans and how it has been interpreted by the judicial system.

———. *Jeffersonianism and the American Novel.* New York: Teachers College Press, 1966, 77 p.
> Attempts to define the philosophical basis of Jeffersonian democracy and determine whether the American novel has supported or rejected its goals.

———. "The Declaration of Independence: A Critique." *Proceedings of the American Antiquarian Society* 85 (1976): 55-72.
> A brief history of the Declaration that questions the validity of its logic and its modern relevance.

Jordan, Winthrop D. "Thomas Jefferson: Self and Society." In his *White over Black: American Attitudes toward the Negro, 1550-1812,* pp. 429-81. Chapel Hill: University of North Carolina Press, 1968.
> An influential analysis of Jefferson's views on slavery. Jordan examines what he describes as "Jefferson's central dilemma: he hated slavery but thought Negroes inferior to white men."

Kimball, Marie. *Jefferson: The Road to Glory, 1743 to 1776.* New York: Coward-McCann, 1943, 358 p.

———. *Jefferson: War and Peace, 1776 to 1784.* New York: Coward-McCann, 1947, 398 p.

———. *Jefferson: The Scene of Europe, 1784 to 1789.* New York: Coward McCann, 1950, 357 p.
> A three-part biography, left unfinished at the historian's death, that focuses on the external detail of Jefferson's life. Kimball also challenges the mid-twentieth-century view of Jefferson as a backwoods democrat, emphasizing instead his aristocratic heritage.

Kimball, S. Fiske, ed. *Thomas Jefferson, Architect: Original Designs in the Coolidge Collection of the Massachusetts Historical Society.* New York: Da Capo Press, 1968, 250 p.
 The definitive study of Jefferson's architectural work, with copious illustrations.

Koch, Adrienne. *The Philosophy of Thomas Jefferson.* Columbia Studies in American Culture, no. 14. Gloucester, Mass.: Peter Smith, 1943, 208 p.
 A respected study of Jefferson's personal beliefs that describes him as a positivist. Koch also traces the ideological antecedents and development of his ethics, political and educational philosophies, and theory of society.

Lee, Gordon C., ed. "Learning and Liberty: The Jeffersonian Tradition in Education." In *Crusade against Ignorance: Thomas Jefferson on Education,* pp. 1-26. Classics in Education, no. 6. New York: Bureau of Publications, Columbia University, 1961.
 Discusses Jefferson's importance to the American educational system. Lee emphasizes Jefferson's belief in the value of education in a democratic society.

Lehmann, Karl. *Thomas Jefferson: American Humanist.* New York: Macmillan Co., 1947, 273 p.
 Interprets modern scholarship to establish Jefferson as an heir to the humanistic tradition of the Renaissance. According to Lehmann, Jefferson's study of the classics taught him the balance between reason and imagination that inspired his actions.

Malone, Dumas. *Jefferson and His Time.* 6 vols. Boston: Little, Brown and Co., 1948-81.
 The definitive biography. Malone, one of the leading authorities on Jefferson, documents all aspects of Jefferson's life and personality. The work evidences Malone's great concern for accuracy and profound respect for the former president. Though most scholars praise Malone's thoroughness and objectivity, some have faulted his method for minimizing the controversial and paradoxical elements of Jefferson's life and thought.

Martin, Edwin T. *Thomas Jefferson: Scientist.* New York: Henry Schuman, 1952, 289 p.
 A wide-ranging survey of Jefferson's scientific pursuits.

Martin, John S. "Rhetoric, Society, and Literature in the Age of Jefferson." *Midcontinent American Studies Journal* IX, No. 1 (Spring 1968): 77-90.
 A study of the use of rhetoric during the Revolutionary era that focuses on Jefferson's First Inaugural Address (see excerpt dated 1801) and his *Notes on the State of Virginia.*

Marx, Leo. "The Garden." In his *The Machine in the Garden: Technology and the Pastoral Ideal in America,* pp. 73-144. New York: Oxford University Press, 1964.
 Analyzes *Notes on the State of Virginia* in relation to the pastoral ideal.

Mayo, Bernard. "The Strange Case of Thomas Jefferson." In his *Myths and Men: Patrick Henry, George Washington, Thomas Jefferson,* pp. 49-71. Athens: University of Georgia Press, 1959.
 A study of Jefferson's fluctuating reputation as an American hero.

McColley, Robert. "Gentlemen's Opinions on Race and Freedom." In his *Slavery and Jeffersonian Virginia,* pp. 114-40. Urbana: University of Illinois Press, 1978.
 An early reappraisal of Jefferson's views on slavery, first published in 1964. McColley argues that although Jefferson opposed slavery in principle, he did not seek to abolish it for political reasons. According to McColley, Jefferson's views on race were similar to those of other Virginia planters of his day: he believed that blacks were inferior to whites and that the two races could not live peacefully together.

Mencken, H. L. "Appendices: Specimens of the American Vulgate." In his *The American Language: An Inquiry into the Development of English in the United States,* rev. ed., pp. 388-96. New York: Alfred A. Knopf, 1921.*

Translates the Declaration of Independence into a modern American idiom.

Mirkin, Harris G. "Rebellion, Revolution, and the Constitution: Thomas Jefferson's Theory of Civil Disobedience." *American Studies* XIII, No. 2 (Fall 1972): 61-74.
 Examines Jefferson's contradictory views on revolution and civil disobedience. According to Mirkin, Jefferson both defended the people's right to revolution and tried to prevent upheaval of the constitutional government. Mirkin contends that much of Jefferson's political theory derives from the tension between these conflicting beliefs.

Moore, Frank, and Scott, John Anthony, eds. *The Diary of the American Revolution: 1775-1781.* New York: Washington Square Press, 1967, 605 p.
 A compendium of original source material from the Revolutionary era. This book, first published in 1860, reprints articles from Whig and Tory newspapers, entries from private diaries, and songs published as broadsides to portray the reception of the Declaration of Independence and chart the progress of the Revolutionary War.

Mumford, Lewis. "The Universalism of Thomas Jefferson." In his *The South in Architecture,* pp. 43-78. New York: Harcourt, Brace and Co., 1941.
 A detailed discussion of Jefferson's architectural education, abilities, and aesthetics. Mumford describes Jefferson's role as an architect as that of a "gifted amateur."

Nock, Albert Jay. *Jefferson.* New York: Harcourt, Brace and Co., 1926, 548 p.
 A history of Jefferson's life that Nock describes as "a study in conduct and character." Characterizing Jefferson as elusive and subtle, Nock argues that Jefferson was naive about economics and was therefore not a great political leader; instead, his greatness rests on his civilized and wide-ranging world view.

Nye, Russel B. "Jeffersonian Democracy." In *Main Problems in American History,* Vol. 1, edited by Howard H. Quint, Dean Albertson, and Milton Cantor, pp. 126-56. Homewood, Ill.: Dorsey Press, 1964.
 Studies the tenets of Jefferson's philosophy of democracy. Nye argues that Jefferson believed that the source of political power rests on the will of the people, who are rational and moral and can be educated; the aim of government is to protect the rights of the individual; and the means to achieve this are majority decision and representative government.

Ogburn, Floyd, Jr. "Structure and Meaning in Thomas Jefferson's *Notes on the State of Virginia.*" *Early American Literature* XV, No. 2 (Fall 1980): 141-50.
 A structuralist analysis of the *Notes on the State of Virginia.* Ogburn applies the linguistic tools of foregrounding and collocation to describe "the intricate manner in which words, images, and concepts work in *Notes.*"

Padover, Saul K. "Jefferson's Prose Poem: The Declaration of Independence." *The American Mercury* LIV, No. 218 (February 1942): 165-71.
 A brief history of the composition of the Declaration that treats it as a prose poem.

———. *Jefferson.* New York: Harcourt, Brace and Co., 1942, 459 p.
 A biography by a noted Jefferson scholar. Padover examines Jefferson's youth, its influence on his character, and his many accomplishments as an adult.

———, ed. *Thomas Jefferson and the Foundations of American Freedom.* Princeton: Van Nostrand Co., 1965, 192 p.
 A collection of Jefferson's writings prefaced with a lengthy essay that describes his life, accomplishments, and beliefs.

Pearce, Roy Harvey. "Character and Circumstance: The Idea of Savagism." In his *The Savages of America: A Study of the Indian and the Idea of Civilization,* pp. 76-104. Baltimore: Johns Hopkins Press, 1953.*

Discusses Jefferson's description of the nature of the American Indian in *Notes on the State of Virginia*.

Perry, Ralph Barton. "The Declaration of Independence." In his *Puritanism and Democracy*, pp. 117-46. New York: Vanguard Press, 1944.
Examines the philosophy and sources of the Declaration in relation to two American philosophical ideals: Puritanism and Democracy.

Peterson, Merrill D. *The Jefferson Image in the American Mind.* New York: Oxford University Press, 1970, 548 p.
A respected study of Jefferson's public image in America, first published in 1960. Peterson describes in great detail how Jefferson has been interpreted throughout history, claiming that his name has been invoked in support of almost every American political platform since his death. In addition, Peterson identifies the most important commentators on Jefferson, explains their interpretation of his significance, and documents the fluctuating trends in his reputation. This study is followed by a lengthy bibliographical essay.

————. *Thomas Jefferson and the New Nation: A Biography.* New York: Oxford University Press, 1970, 1072 p.
A biography that emphasizes Jefferson's public career, describing his life in relation to the history of the new nation. As such, the work is intended as a companion volume to *The Jefferson Image in the American Mind* (see entry above), in which Peterson documents the changes in Jefferson's reputation.

Pound, Ezra. *Jefferson and/or Mussolini; L'Idea Statale: Fascism as I Have Seen It.* New York: Liveright Publishing Corp., 1935, 128 p.*
Compares Jefferson and Benito Mussolini, who share, according to Pound, a dislike of bankers, industrialism, and the two-party system. In his controversial comparison of the two figures, Pound argues that "the heritage of Jefferson, Quincy Adams, old John Adams, Jackson, Van Buren is HERE, NOW *in the Italian Peninsula* at the beginning of fascist second decennio, not in Massachusetts or Delaware." For additional criticism by Pound, see excerpt dated 1937-38.

Randall, Henry S. *The Life of Thomas Jefferson.* 3 vols. New York: Derby & Jackson, 1858.
An early appreciative biography based largely on the previously unpublished private papers of Jefferson. By incorporating much of this material into the text, Randall illuminates two sides of Jefferson: his private domestic life and public image as a national hero.

Randolph, Sarah N. *The Domestic Life of Thomas Jefferson: Compiled from Family Letters and Reminiscences.* Charlottesville, Va.: The University Press of Virginia, 1978, 452 p.
A family portrait of Jefferson, written by his great-granddaughter in 1871. Randolph draws from his private papers to emphasize Jefferson's charming, warm, and faithful character.

Riley, I. Woodbridge. "Virginia and Jefferson." In his *American Philosophy: The Early Schools*, pp. 266-95. New York: Russell & Russell, 1907.
Describes Jefferson's Deistic beliefs.

Rosenberger, Francis Coleman, ed. *Jefferson Reader: A Treasury of Writings about Thomas Jefferson.* New York: E. P. Dutton, 1953, 345 p.
A collection of writings about Jefferson, including essays, biographical sketches, personal reminiscences, and poems.

Schachner, Nathan. *Thomas Jefferson: A Biography.* 2 vols. New York: Appleton-Century-Crofts, 1951.
A biography. Schachner avoids the reverential tone common to many studies of Jefferson; instead, his work is sympathetic, but critical.

Scheick, William J. "Chaos and Imaginative Order in Thomas Jefferson's *Notes on the State of Virginia.*" In *Essays in Early Virginia Literature Honoring Richard Beale Davis*, edited by J. A. Leo Lemay, pp. 221-35. New York: Burt Franklin & Co., 1977.
Contends that *Notes on the State of Virginia* demonstrates Jefferson's belief that chaos and order were among the most important issues facing the new republic. By considering *Notes* in relation to the other writings, Scheick argues that Jefferson recommended "temperate liberty," which this critic defines as "a delicate balance between stringent order and unrestricted freedom."

Sears, Louis Martin. *Jefferson and the Embargo.* Durham: Duke University Press, 1927, 340 p.
A complete history of Jefferson's role in the Embargo Act of 1807. Sears argues that the embargo represented a logical outgrowth of Jefferson's political philosophy and demonstrated his considerable administrative abilities.

Shibata, Shingo. "Fundamental Human Rights and Problems of Freedom: Marxism and the Contemporary Significance of the U.S. Declaration of Independence." *Social Praxis* 3, Nos. 3-4 (1975): 157-85.
A Marxist interpretation of the Declaration. Shibata identifies the Declaration's basic principles, notably the rights it guarantees, and demonstrates its contemporary significance.

Simpson, Lewis P. "The Symbolism of Literary Alienation in the Revolutionary Age." *The Journal of Politics* 38, No. 3 (August 1976): 79-100.*
Analyzes several representative works of the Revolutionary age, including the Declaration of Independence, as symbols of "cultural and literary displacement and alienation." Simpson also labels Jefferson the personification of the estranged American man-of-letters.

Smith, T. V. "Thomas Jefferson and the Perfectibility of Mankind." *Ethics: An International Journal of Social, Political, and Legal Philosophy* LIII, No. 4 (July 1943): 293-310.
Explicates Jefferson's political philosophy, focusing particularly on his credo that individuals in a democratic society may disagree about specific means and ends, but can still work together despite their differences.

The Virginia Quarterly Review: Jefferson Bicentennial Number 19, No. 2 (Spring 1943): 161-320.
A collection of essays by several noted Jefferson scholars, published in honor of the bicentennial of his birth.

Warren, Robert Penn. *Brothers to Dragons: A Tale in Verse and Voices.* New York: Random House, 1953, 230 p.
A novel in verse that features Jefferson in a central role. According to some critics, Warren uses Jefferson as a symbol for his hopes and fears for America.

————. *Democracy and Poetry.* Cambridge: Harvard University Press, 1975, 102 p.
A study of the relationship between democracy and literature that draws upon Jefferson's political views. The Jeffersonian ideal, according to Warren, is responsible for the American dream of fulfillment through democracy.

Weymouth, Lally, ed. *Thomas Jefferson: The Man ... His World ... His Influence.* London: Weidenfeld and Nicolson, 1973, 254 p.
A collection of essays by such commentators as Merrill Peterson, Garry Wills, Henry Steele Commager, Leonard Levy, and Christopher Lasch.

Wicks, Elliot K. "Thomas Jefferson—A Religious Man with a Passion for Religious Freedom." *Historical Magazine of the Protestant Episcopal Church* XXXVI, No. 3 (September 1967): 271-83.
Examines Jefferson's personal views on religion and his emphasis on religious freedom.

Wills, Garry. *Inventing America: Jefferson's Declaration of Independence.* Garden City, N.Y.: Doubleday & Co., 1978, 398 p.
A historical and textual analysis of the Declaration. Wills distinguishes three versions of the document: the Jeffersonian, or sci-

entific version; the Congressional, or political version; and the modern, or symbolic version. Wills's purpose is to determine what Jefferson intended the Declaration to mean and how it has been misinterpreted by generations of historians and politicians.

Wiltse, Charles Maurice. *The Jeffersonian Tradition in American Democracy*. Chapel Hill: University of North Carolina Press, 1935, 273 p.
Assumes that Jefferson's political ideas form a coherent system and attempts to reconstruct those ideas from his later writings. Wiltse also identifies Jefferson's legacy to the American political tradition, citing particularly his influence on the New Deal.

Wise, W. Harvey, Jr., and Cronin, John W. *A Bibliography of Thomas Jefferson*. Washington, D.C.: Riverford Publishing Co., 1935, 72 p.
A comprehensive bibliography of writings by and about Jefferson through 1935.

Yellin, Jean Fagan. "Jefferson's *Notes*." In *The Intricate Knot: Black Figures in American Literature, 1776-1863*, pp. 3-14. New York: New York University Press, 1972.
An examination of Jefferson's views on race and on slavery as presented in *Notes on the State of Virginia*.

Friedrich Gottlieb Klopstock

1724-1803

German poet, essayist, dramatist, and hymn writer.

One of the foremost lyric poets of the eighteenth century, Klopstock is remembered today for his innovative contributions to German poetic language, which include the adaptation of the Greek hexameter, the development of free verse, and the use of patriotic and religious themes. In composing his many odes and his masterpiece, the epic poem *Der Messias: Ein Heldengedicht (The Messiah),* Klopstock rejected the Neoclassical French style advocated by his contemporaries and promoted instead an emotive mode of expression. He is considered a precursor of the German *Sturm und Drang* (Storm and Stress), Romantic, and Classical movements, and several critics believe that he influenced such important writers as Johann Wolfgang von Goethe, Friedrich Hölderlin, Johann Christoph Friedrich von Schiller, and Richard Wagner. Despite the great fame Klopstock enjoyed during his lifetime, his reputation has waned substantially. Many modern critics now consider his poetic style dated and suggest that his initial importance was due in large measure to his emergence as a new voice in the eighteenth century.

Klopstock was born in Quendlinburg, Lower Saxony (now West Germany). As a boy he attended the *Schulpforte,* a Protestant academy, where he received a strict Christian education. At school he read John Milton's epic poem *Paradise Lost,* which inspired him to begin composing *The Messiah,* which he would not complete for many years. In 1745, Klopstock enrolled as a theology student at Jena University, but soon left to study law in Leipzig. There he met a group of young writers, the *Bremer Beiträger,* who were united in their rejection of the stylistic hegemony of the French in German letters. The first three cantos of *The Messiah,* published in the *Bremer Beiträge,* this group's journal, in 1748, quickly brought fame to Klopstock and established his importance as a poet. He soon secured the lifelong patronage of Denmark's King Frederik. During a journey to Copenhagen to receive his pension, Klopstock met Margareta Moller, whom he eventually wed. Happily married and freed from financial strictures, Klopstock settled in Denmark, where he devoted himself to literature, publishing odes, hymns, a drama, and several more cantos of *The Messiah.* When his wife died in 1758, Klopstock's productivity decreased markedly; several years later, he met the German poet and dramatist Heinrich Wilhelm von Gerstenberg, whose interest in Teutonic legends inspired Klopstock to compose a series of patriotic poems, *Vaterländische Oden.* He also composed essays on German prosody and philology and began a dramatic trilogy, which he referred to as the "Bardiete," based on the legendary German figure Hermann, or Arminius. In 1770, Klopstock left Denmark to settle in Hamburg, where he published *Oden,* a collection of odes that had previously appeared in periodicals, and several years later completed *The Messiah.* His masterpiece finished, Klopstock continued to compose short verse works until his death.

Klopstock's odes, collected in *Vaterländische Oden* and *Oden,* helped establish his reputation as a prominent German lyricist. Addressing a variety of topics, including friendship, religion, immortality, love, and politics, the odes embody the poetic

style for which he is famous. Klopstock composed the odes in free verse and rejected classical restraint in favor of lyricism, innovations which many critics praise, maintaining that Klopstock rejuvenated German poetic language. Among other forms, he employed the classical Greek hexameter, and although he was not the first German poet to use this verse form, he is considered the first to have successfully adapted it to the German language. Many of the odes were great popular successes, and the German critic Johann Gottfried von Herder proclaimed that "a single ode of Klopstock outweighs the whole lyric literature of Britain." Other early commentators, less enthusiastic in their appraisals, contended that despite their lyric appeal, the odes were seriously flawed by repetition and stilted diction.

Klopstock's dream of a united Germany informs his odes, essays on language and literature, and the "Bardiete." He coined the term "Bardiet" to designate his historical plays which include *Hermanns Schlacht, Hermann und die Fürsten,* and *Hermanns Tod.* Although they are generally discounted as undramatic, implausible, and monotonous, these plays are also remembered for helping to popularize nationalistic literature in Germany. Similarly, his essays on poetics and German culture, *Die deutsche Gelehrtenrepublik, Über Sprache und Dichtkunst,* and *Grammatische Gespräche von Klopstock,* treat national concerns. In *Die deutsche Gelehrtenrepublik,* Klopstock discusses poetics and his vision of a utopia ruled by an intellectual elite. *Grammatische Gespräche* contains his opinions on German grammar and stylistics. These works, though largely forgotten today, are considered noteworthy contributions to the development of German prosody and cultural awareness.

While Klopstock composed works in several genres and on a variety of topics, he is best known as the author of *The Messiah,* a twenty-canto narrative poem. His goal in composing this work was to create an epic that would rival those of the ancient Greeks, but instead of depicting a national hero, he retold the crucifixion and resurrection of Jesus Christ. *The Messiah* is written in lyrical hexameter, and the first three cantos were applauded enthusiastically by opponents of the Francophile literary school. Public interest waned markedly before the poem's completion, however, and critical opinion continues to vary. Several commentators praise its emotional tone and well-developed characters; yet its detractors contend that the work is marred by stilted diction, implausible characters, redundancy, and excessive length. Other critics assert that *The Messiah* is not an epic, likening it instead to the religious oratorios of Johann Sebastian Bach and George Frederick Handel. Though its length and archaic style render *The Messiah* largely inaccessible to the modern reader, it is recognized as one of the most important poems of eighteenth-century German literature.

Klopstock remains important as a transitional figure in German literature whose works embody both eighteenth- and nineteenth-century styles and concerns. On the basis of the emotive nature of his work, and his conceptions of the poet as prophet and Germany as a united country, Klopstock is labeled a spiritual forebear of the *Sturm und Drang* movement.

PRINCIPAL WORKS

An meine Freunde (poetry) 1747; also published as *Wingolf* [enlarged edition], 1767
Der Messias: Ein Heldengedicht (poetry) 1748-73; also published in revised form as *Der Messias* in *Klopstocks Werke,* 1798-1819
[*The Messiah,* 1814]
Der Tod Adams [first publication] (drama) 1757
[*The Death of Adam,* 1763]
Geistliche Lieder. 2 vols. (hymns) 1758-69
Vaterländische Oden. 3 vols. (poetry) 1764-68
Hermanns Schlacht [first publication] (drama) 1769
Oden (poetry) 1771
Die deutsche Gelehrtenrepublik (essay) 1774
Über Sprache und Dichtkunst (essays) 1779
Hermann und die Fürsten [first publication] (drama) 1784
Hermanns Tod [first publication] (drama) 1787
Grammatische Gespräche von Klopstock (essays) 1794
Klopstocks Werke. 12 vols. (poetry, hymns, dramas, and essays) 1798-1819
Memoirs of Frederick and Margaret Klopstock (letters) 1808
Klopstock and His Friends (letters) 1814
Odes of Klopstock from 1747 to 1780 (poetry) 1848
Werke. 9 vols. (poetry, hymns, dramas, essays, and epigrams) 1974

*These works are collectively referred to as the "Bardiete."

JOSEPH COLLYER (essay date 1763)

[*In his preface to one of the many nineteenth-century partial translations of* The Messiah, *Collyer indicates his preference for Klopstock's epic over John Milton's* Paradise Regained. *He praises many aspects of* The Messiah, *particularly its "important and extensive plan."*]

Mr. Klopstock has receiv'd from his *Messiah* the honour of being esteem'd the Milton of Germany, and is consider'd as having completed what that favourite son of the British muse had left unfinish'd. (p. x)

Mr. Klopstock's *Messiah* is form'd upon a more important and extensive plan [than Milton's *Paradise Regained*], and includes the sufferings and death of Christ; and as that gentleman may probably continue the work till after the resurrection of the Messiah, and his visible ascent into Heaven, it will then, in the original, be consider'd as a complete Epic poem: for it abounds in strength of invention, in grand imagery, and in a great variety of characters; some of which are entirely new, and all of them appear well supported. He particularly shines in his descriptions and speeches, in which there is sometimes an amazing sublimity, that seems almost impossible to be transfus'd, with all its force and energy, into another language. (p. xii)

> *Joseph Collyer, in a preface to* The Messiah, Vol. 1 *by Friedrich Gottlieb Klopstock, translated by Joseph Collyer, R. and J. Dodsley, 1763, pp. ix-xiv.*

THE CRITICAL REVIEW (essay date 1763)

[*The following is a laudatory assessment of Klopstock's drama* The Death of Adam.]

The Death of Adam, by Mr. Klopstock, is, in our opinion, a work of great merit; and . . . shews the author's intimate acquaintance with the Greek stage, that he has improved upon his masters, and written this piece, not according to the letter, but the spirit, of those great originals. . . .

The same uniform simplicity which directs the conduct of this dramatic poem, animates the style, sentiments, and language. . . .

The first speech of Selima has a kind of pastoral ease and simplicity, which will sufficiently recommend it to the lovers of pure and unadorned nature. (p. 38)

The grief, tenderness, and affection of Adam's children are pathetically described by our ingenious author, and the horror of Adam, on his approaching dissolution, finely expressed. (p. 39)

Adam's reflections on death, in the second act, are extremely pathetic. (p. 40)

Adam's conference with Cain, his parting with Eve, his address to the three mothers, and several other scenes, have great merit in them. . . . (p. 41)

> *A review of "The Death of Adam: A Tragedy," in* The Critical Review, *Vol. XVI, July, 1763, pp. 38-41.*

THE CRITICAL REVIEW (essay date 1771)

[*Here, the reviewer criticizes* The Messiah's *"improbable actions, affected sentiments and . . . turgid style." Partial translations of the work were available in English shortly after its publication in Germany.*]

We are sorry that [*The Messiah*], and other productions of the same species, have been introduced into the English language. They are by no means calculated to improve and reform the public taste, but rather to pervert and corrupt it.

In this performance we have improbable fictions, affected sentiments and a turgid style; sentences loaded with epithets, a false glare and pomp of words, a redundancy of unnatural, and frequently inconsistent images. The author never condescends to speak in plain and familiar language; he seems to have no idea of dignity united with ease, or that noble and majestic simplicity, for which almost all the classic writers are universally admired. We cannot say of his Muse, as Milton says of Eve, that

> Grace is in all her steps.

On the contrary, she moves with a stiff and formal air; her attitudes are awkward, and her ornaments fantastic. She is like a lubbard in armour, decorated with garlands, plumes, and tinsel. (p. 393)

There are, we confess, undoubted marks of a strong and lively imagination in this performance; but, in our opinion, not the least traces of judgment or taste. (p. 395)

A review of "The Messiah," in The Critical Review, *Vol. XXXII, November, 1771, pp. 393-95.*

JOHANN GOTTFRIED VON HERDER   (essay date 1773)

[*Herder is one of the most prominent and influential critics in literary history and a primary theoretician of the* Sturm und Drang *and Romantic movements. His essays on various topics, including religion, history, and the development of language and literature, are considered important to later studies on evolution and the development of the social sciences. In the following excerpt from a 1773 essay, Herder praises the diction and meter of* The Messiah *and asserts that it is less a national epic than a work universal in scope. For additional commentary by Herder, see the excerpts dated 1796 and 1803.*]

[The "**Messiah**"] is a "monument of German poetry and language", full of the purest emotions and an imagination which often approaches inspiration. Klopstock describes the most hidden complex feelings of the human soul, and pours them out into words. Not the least of the merits of the poem is that it is full of religion and song,—song like the echo of departed spirits out of a valley of innocence and love. The language almost ceases to be language and becomes music (Ton)! a resounding of golden strings, which sounds forth religion. . . . Klopstock's soul soared too high above the earth into realms beyond human ken; his hero is not national like Homer's Achilles and Ossian's Fingal. The German nation has not yet reached that point in its development in religion and general human sympathies to embrace such a work, great for all time and place, and to look upon it as its most precious possession. In its plan the poem is more a work of youth than of manhood; according to its first outline more an emulation of Milton than an immediate revelation. Christ, especially regarding his non-epic character, is more a Christ of the Halle school than the great Christ of religion. The last portion of the poem does not compare favorably with the first; the poet has grown older, and despite his endeavor to remain true to his early simplicity his work has become a more conscious product. Time has overtaken the poet; the German character and ideas have changed

in the twenty-five years which passed since the first appearance of the "**Messiah**". The views of religion have changed; and neither the most orthodox, nor the most pious reader would be satisfied with the poem. The times demand "a muse of more masculine, of firmer, and more philosophical form." "The worthiest poem of Germany" is not a national poem, (a "Volksgedicht"), like Homer and Ariosto. It is the most beautiful marionette of the world, of which whatever regards Biblical history and true folklore (Volksglaube) is but the wooden stick which the poet could not conceal carefully enough, as if he were ashamed of it. The diction and meter are entirely Klopstock's own; that is, poetic, bold, delicate, learned, and classic; never, however, or only rarely, language and song for the people, no matter how high the people might climb in culture. (pp. 34-5)

Johann Gottfried von Herder, in an extract from Herder and Klopstock: A Comparative Study *by Frederick Henry Adler, G. E. Stechert and Company, Publishers, 1914, pp. 34-7.*

FRIEDRICH SCHILLER   (essay date 1795-96)

[*A principal figure in German Classicism, Schiller was a dramatist, critic, and poet. He earned international acclaim for his historical dramas, among them* Die Räuber (The Robbers) *and* Wilhelm Tell *and published a number of essays on dramaturgy and aesthetics. In the most important of his theoretical essays,* Über naive und sentimentalische Dichtung (On Naive and Sentimental Poetry), *Schiller divided poetry into two categories— naive and sentimental. Naive verse is realistic, objective, and plastic; sentimental poetry is subjective, self-conscious, and lyrical. While the naive poet is one who, objectively observing reality and experiencing nature, depicts cosmic forces in concrete terms, the sentimental poet, experiencing self-conflict and at odds with a complex society, attempts to represent the infinite. In the following excerpt from this work, Schiller faults* The Messiah's *poorly developed characters and lack of action, yet praises Klopstock's mastery of the elegy, labeling him one of Germany's foremost sentimental poets. Schiller also comments on the musical qualities of Klopstock's verse. The essay was originally published in three parts in the German periodical* Die Horen *in November and December, 1795, and January, 1796.*]

In the sentimental genre and especially in the elegiac section of it there are few from the modern poets and still fewer from the ancients to compare with *Klopstock*. Whatever is to be achieved outside the boundaries of living form and outside the area of individuality in the field of the ideal has been achieved by this musical poet. . . . One would do him a great wrong if one were to deny him completely that individual truth and liveliness with which the naive poet depicts his subject. Many of his odes, several individual details in his plays and in his '**Messiah**' represent the subject with striking truth and excellent definition; especially where the subject is his own heart, he has often shown a great naturalness, a charming naiveté. It is just that *his* strength does not lie in this, this characteristic cannot be followed throughout the entire extent of his poetry. As wonderful a creation as the '**Messiah**' is in a *musical* and poetic way . . . , it yet leaves much to be desired in a *three-dimensional* and poetic sense, where one expects *definite* forms *created for contemplation.* The figures in this poem may be definite enough perhaps but not to be contemplated; only abstraction has created them, only abstraction can distinguish them one from another. They are good examples of concepts but they are not individuals or living figures. Much too much freedom has been given to the imagination, to which the poet must turn and which he should dominate by the consistent definition of his forms, as to the way in which it wants to render perceptible to the senses these men and angels, these gods and devils, this heaven and hell. An outline has been given within which the understanding must of necessity think of them, but no firm boundary has been laid down within which the imagination must of necessity portray them. What I am saying here of the characters is true of everything in this poem which is or is meant to be life and action, and not merely in this epic but also in the dramatic works of our author. Everything has been excellently ordered and defined for the understanding (I want here only to remind you of his Judas, his Pilate, his Philo, his Solomon in the tragedy of that name) but it is much too formless for the imagination and here, I admit it freely, I find this poet completely outside of his sphere.

His sphere is always the realm of ideas and he knows how to transpose everything which he is working on into the infinite. One might say that he strips everything which he treats of its body in order to make it into a spirit, just as other poets dress everything spiritual with a body. Almost every pleasure which his works afford us must be won by an exercise of the power of thought; all the emotions which he is able to excite in us, and so deeply and so powerfully too, flow from supra-sensual sources. From this stem the seriousness, the power, the verve, the profundity which characterise everything which comes from him; from this comes, too, the continuous tension of the emotions in which we are held when reading it. No poet . . . would be less suited to be a favourite and companion through life than Klopstock, who always only leads us away from life, always only calls the spirit to arms without enlivening the senses with the calm presence of his subject. His poetic muse is chaste, supernatural, uncorporeal, holy as his religion and one must admit with admiration that, although he has at times gone astray on these heights, he has never sunk from them; I admit therefore openly that I am a little uneasy about the wits of one who truly and without affectation can make this poet into his favourite reading, that is, can use him as a book to which one can attune oneself in every situation, to which one can return from every situation; also, I should think, we have seen enough fruits in Germany of his dangerous rule. Only in certain exalted moods of the spirit can he be sought out and experienced; for this reason too he is the idol of youth, although not the happiest choice for them by far. Youth, which always strives to go beyond life, which flees all form and finds any boundary too narrow, indulges itself with love and desire in the endless spaces which are opened for it by this poet. When the youth becomes a man and returns from the realm of ideas into the boundaries of experience, then he loses a deal, a great deal of that enthusiastic love, but nothing of the respect which is due to such a unique phenomenon, such an extraordinary genius, such an ennobled feeling, and which Germans especially owe to such high merit.

I called this poet great pre-eminently in the elegiac genre and it will scarcely be necessary to justify this judgment more particularly. Capable of every energy and a master in the whole field of sentimental poetry, he can at times shatter us by means of the highest pathos, at times cradle us in heavenly sweet sensations; but his heart does incline above all to a high, thoughtful sadness; and no matter how nobly his harp, his lyre sound, the melting tones of his lute will yet always ring deeper and truer and more stirring. I appeal to each feeling which rings true whether it would not give all that is daring and strong, all the fictions, all the magnificent descriptions, all the examples of rhetorical eloquence in the '**Messiah'**, all the shimmering metaphors in which our poet is so exceptionally suc-

cessful, for the tender emotions which breathe from the elegy '**To Ebert'**, from the wonderful poem '**Bardale'**, from '**Early Graves'**, from '**Summer Night'**, from '**Lake Zurich'** and many others of this genre. Thus the '**Messiah'** is dear to me as a treasure-house of elegiac feelings and ideal depictions, however little it satisfies me as the representation of an action and as an epic work. (pp. 53-6)

> *Friedrich Schiller, in his* On the Naive and Sentimental in Literature, *translated by Helen Watanabe-O'Kelly, Carcanet New Press, 1981, 107 p.**

JOHANN GOTTFRIED von HERDER   (essay date 1796)

[*Herder compares the works of Klopstock with those of John Milton and indicates his overwhelming preference for Klopstock's verse. For additional commentary by Herder, see the excerpts dated 1773 and 1803. This essay was originally published in* Herders sämmtliche Werke *in 1796.*]

We are accustomed to call *Klopstock* the German *Milton;* I wish they were never named together, and that Klopstock had never known Milton. Both have written sacred poesy, but they were not inspired by the same Urania. They bear to each other that relation that Moses bears to Christ, or the old to the new covenant. The edifice of Milton is a steadfast and well-planned building, resting on ancient columns; Klopstock's is an enchanted dome, echoing with the softest and purest tones of human feeling, hovering between heaven and earth, borne on angels' shoulders. Milton's muse is masculine, and harsh as his iambics; Klopstock's is a tender woman, dissolving in pious ecstasies, warbling elegies and hymns. Klopstock had studied deeply the language of his country, and won for it more powers than the Briton ever suspected his to possess. A single ode of Klopstock outweighs the whole lyric literature of Britain. The *Herman* of this writer awaked a spirit of simple nervous song, far loftier than that which animates the chorus-drama of antiquity. The *Sampson* of Milton attains not these models. When music shall acquire among us the highest powers of her art, whose words will she select to utter but those of Klopstock?

> *Johann Gottfried von Herder, in an extract from "Herders sämmtliche Werke," translated by J. A. Heraud, in* Fraser's Magazine, *Vol. IV, No. XXIII, December, 1831, p. 544.*

[WILLIAM TAYLOR]   (essay dates 1800 and 1801)

[*While acknowledging Klopstock's command of language in* The Messiah, *Taylor finds the work dull and uncohesive, faulting its superfluous details and implausible characters.*]

When Klopstock published the first five books of his *Messiah*, hexameter was assailed by the critics as a most unnatural costume for the German Muse: the poet persevered, and the nation is converted. Why should not his future translator anticipate a similar success?

It may be doubted however if the most fortunate englisher of Klopstock would obtain that national popularity and gratitude, that recognition of his work as a perpetual classic, which Mickle, beyond our other epic translators, seems to have attained. Klopstock's *Messiah*, why should it not be owned? will appear dull in English; because it is really so in German. . . . It wants distinctness, proportion, cohesion. The fable is consequently deficient in interest. Where there is no wholeness, there can be no care for the one great end. Nor does all the topical application of the poet overcome this constitutional imperfection of his work. The crucifixion and the resurrection ought to have been the focuses of expectation, the centres of attraction along the whole orbit of his cometary course: they are lost sight of in favor of a galaxy of minute anecdotes, and a zodiac of mythological apparitions. What the action wants of extent as to time, the poet has endeavoured to supply by extent as to space, and beckons spectators from every cranny of the universe. He seems aloof and adrift in a crowded atmosphere of spirits and angels, where every little groupe is gibbering, and occasionally veers to look at the execution that is going on: but his mortal astonishment, instead of selecting the mightier business for record, thinks every character in the throng worth describing, and gets bewildered in the infinitude of his task. No epopoea exists, out of which so many passages and personages could be cut without mutilation. Distracted by the multiplicity of subordinate objects, the curiosity excited concerning each is inconsiderable. That headlong participation in the pursuits of the heroes, which bawls aloud along with Hector for fire, is no where felt in the *Messiah*. Every secondary incident should have found a place only in as much as it tended to advance or retard, or influence, the grand catastrophe. An anxiety about the chief business of the poem might thus have been inspired. Now, the parts withdraw attention from the whole: one sees not the forest for the trees. Instead of bearing down on the point for which he is bound, and sailing with full canvas toward his main destination, Klopstock is continually laveering: beautiful or sublime as the islands and rocks may be which he thus brings into view, they indemnify not for his forgetting the voyage. One as willingly begins with the second book as with the first: one as willingly stops after the eighth canto as after the tenth. The thousand and one episodes of the second half of the poem have interrupted many a reader, and one translator, in his determination to travel to the end. The multiplicity of the pietistical rhapsodies would weary even Saint Theresa.

Another fault, or misfortune, of Klopstock, is his hyperorthodoxy. Those doctrines of the theologists, which wander farthest from common and natural sense, are precisely the ideas which he most delights to embody, and officiously to present in all the palpability of his poetic sculpture. The identity of different persons of the godhead, the pre-existence of the unborn, the migrations of Omnipresence are scarcely marvellous enough for his transubstantiating fancy. . . . By endeavouring to sublimate his Jesus into a Jehovah, he unhumanizes the most lovely of characters, and greatly lessens the sympathy, the personal attachment, the impassioned adherence, which a being more like ourselves might have inspired. The God-man, as Klopstock calls him, is by all his godship, in point of pity, a loser; the temptation, the agony, the crucifixion, are no burdens for the shoulders of Omnipotence: the resurrection—no miracle, no triumph, no recompense. The attempt to elevate other characters into fit companions for the Omniscient produces on all the Disciples a similar disinteresting effect: screwed up above the pitch of human nature, they insensibly become aliens to our regard. They act and speak rather as the puppets of cherubim and seraphim, than as living feeling irritable sons of clay. . . . More of those affectionate traits, which the original records have preserved, might have been interwoven with advantage in the character of Klopstock's prophet: they are well adapted to endear the memory of his love; and to impress lastingly on our recollection the most beneficial idea of human excellence, and the immortal model of the most usefully virtuous. Klopstock has been more successful in delineating the manners of Philo, Caiphas, Pilate, and the other enemies of

Jesus, than in portraying those of the Disciples. His fancy tends exclusively to the heroic: and heroic manners are better suited to the pharisee, the high-priest, and the governor, than to the honest Galilaean fishermen. But if from such wholesale animadversion on the plan and manners, one turns to a retail examination of the perpetual beauties of style and composition, to whom may not Klopstock confidently be compared? There is usually a wide wing'd colossal sublimity in his imagery, which outsoars all precedent. . . . There is often a tenderness yet a probingness in the pathos, which reminds of Euripides and recalls Tacitus. There is at times a completeness of expression, a polish, and a force of diction, as if obtained by the joint use of Tasso's file and Milton's hammer. But short efforts suit Klopstock best. He darts too high to fly long. His lyric therefore surpass his epic undertakings. In the perfection of minute parts he especially excels. (pp. 318-20)

•　•　•　•　•

From the twenty thousand lines of which the *Messiah* consists, a prudent author would have expunged about one-half, for feebleness, tautology, or irrelevance: so that the mass of excellent composition, which is chiefly to be sought between the second and eighth cantos, does not exceed that of the *Paradise Lost,* supposing it curtailed, in like manner, of what the critics censure for extravagance, ignobleness, or pedantry; such as Satan's journey, the Angelic war, Michael's narrative, and other thinly scattered passages, which may collectively amount to one-sixth of the whole. Poetry, like ore, is estimated not by the coarseness, but by the proportion, of its alloy; and is never valued for its bulk, but for its richness: if Milton therefore contains about one-sixth, and Klopstock one-half, of dross, the latter is the inferior specimen. (pp. 503-04)

Poets draw from nature, from art, and from idea. They may owe their materials chiefly to observation, chiefly to reading, or chiefly to reflection. They may delight in describing the phenomena of their experience; in compiling the treasures of their study; or, in exhibiting those substitutions of the fancy, which the senses sometimes, and sometimes books, suggest. Homer is surely of the first, Milton and Virgil of the second, but Klopstock of the third of these classes. He is the poet of *reflection*, in the strictest sense of the word: he always draws from the picture in his own imagination, even when he derives the hint of it from a preceding writer. His plagiarism is never occupied, like Milton's, in mending the passage which he means to borrow, but the scene which he means again to copy. In whatever he transfers therefore, the point of view, the colouring, the locality, the distribution changes; circumstances vary, and personages thicken on his canvas. But he is too apt to loiter over his amendments, until he forgets the motive for undertaking them, and, in completing a picture for a simile, to overshade the point of comparison. . . . [His] practice of second-hand painting is unwise: such sketches are apt, as artists would say, to want *the solid*. And in fact the scenery of Klopstock is illuminated by a certain gloomy twilight, a misty glory, an intangible rainbowy lustre, which disfavours an impression of reality. The vivid hues of his decorations, (in the simile of the pestilence, for instance,) on returning to the narrative, melt into thin air: spectres cluster about his fact, and dissolve it into phantasm. His mountains seem as it were clouds; his groves, of empyreal palm; his cities, suburbs of some new Jerusalem; his gorgeous palaces, his solemn temples, all appear to partake the fabric of a vision. To *dream* sights is the felicity of poets; it is remarkably that of Klopstock; he oftener looks within and seldomer without for objects than any other son of fancy.

Klopstock frequently deserts the epic for the dramatic form, and instead of introducing his speeches narratively, prefixes initials merely to the alternations of the dialogue. Indeed those short speeches which abound in the *Messiah*, could not have been employed at all, if always ushered in with a whole hexameter like Homer's. . . . Yet this licence has not conferred vivacity, because the speeches are mostly contemplative, not active; the effusions of bystanders, not the declarations of agents. One learns every body's opinion of what is going on, but that of the concerned. The sentiments of the personages, although often superfluous and unmotivated, are however strictly appropriate: they have moral and local aptness; they wear the livery of the person and the country. No flower of Hebrew origin escapes the preserving care of Klopstock; but he never offends by a misplaced paganism of imagery and illustration. Whatever he transplants loses wholly its raciness. Yet this very precaution excludes some sources of variety, which were all wanted in a poem, where the matter is too uniformly lofty, and wearies, by always keeping on the stretch, the reader's imagination. With a background more modest the radiant passages would have acquired a bolder relievo. In the art of wording, Klopstock is no mean proficient. His epithets are chosen judiciously: they are often new, always impressive, not idle or over frequent, and usually adapted, not merely to the substantive in general, but to the peculiar point of view in which it then attracts notice; so that they are what the Germans call *hitting* epithets, in contradistinction to such as miss their aim—to use an analogous idiom, they all *tell*. Nor is his command and selection of phrase inferior to that of single words; but he often misapplies his opulence, and prodigally squanders an exquisite passage on the adornment of an insignificant episode. Superfluity is indeed the leading character of Klopstock's style; but it is not a redundance of terms, so much as of accessary and subordinate ideas; a fibrous branchiness of thought, rather than parallel pullulations of phrase; amplification, not tautology. He appears to consider a liberal prolixity as the most radiant proof of genius, and to disdain any of the self-denying calculated retrenchments of taste. What Jeremy Taylor was in homiletic eloquence, Klopstock is in epic poetry. Both have expanded into a great book the life of Christ. Both delight alike in the extacies of piety and the marvels of mysticism; they are continually ascending from the ground of fact into the pleroma of hypothesis, extolling the simplest sentiments to rhapsodies of inspiration, and consecrating the veriest accidents into primordial dispensations and mysteries of Providence. Both indulge a fickle, abrupt, interstitial style, which betrays every repose of the pen. Layers of affecting plainness, and affected sonorosity, of scholastic jargon, and oriental sensualization, succeed each other without blending. . . . Religious zealotry, and German nationality, have occasionally bestowed on the author of the *Messiah* excessive applause; yet, when every allowance is made for what is temporary and local in opinion, enough of merit no doubt remains to place his work among the lasting monuments of mighty minds. Probably posterity will station him nearer to Macpherson in rank and quality, than to any other of the more distinguished epic poets: both err by a too frequent recurrence of analogous imagery, and by an unvarying long-drawn plaintiveness of tone: both delight by a perpetual majesty of style, and by the heroic elevation and purity of the manners of their personages. (pp. 504-05)

[*William Taylor*], "Klopstock's 'Messiah'," *in* The Monthly Magazine, *London, Vol. 10, Nos. 65 and 67, November 1, 1800 and January 1, 1801, pp. 317-20; 501-05.*

JOHANN GOTTFRIED von HERDER   (essay date 1803?)

[*Although Herder cites several flaws of* The Messiah, *including unrealistic characters and a lack of national sentiment, he nevertheless maintains that "the beauties of the poem . . . far outshine the faults." Since the composition date of this essay is unknown, Herder's remarks have been dated 1803, the year of his death. For further commentary by Herder, see the excerpts dated 1773 and 1796.*]

Klopstock has composed an original work [the "**Messiah**"] in spite of certain Miltonic features; he shows his great genius in having been able to produce a poem, an epic, and a Christian epic, out of a short historical account. . . . [However, the] poem lacks national spirit. If it was intended to be a Biblical epic, an epic of the Orient, Klopstock should have made more use of Biblical history; he should have introduced some features of the Old Testament. The scene of his epic is not really Jewish; the whole work should breath more of the national spirit and temper of the Jews. Klopstock should have concerned himself more with the national opinions of the Jews, the poetic import of the Old Testament, and with the taste of those times. The "**Messiah**" is not a Biblical epic; it is not a full, objective expression of the national life of the times of Christ. If Klopstock intended his poem to be a song of the origin of the Christian religion, it would have been necessary for him to emphasize the founding of the Church with all its vicissitudes; he would have had to bear in mind the historical events which took place at that time. The poem lacks historical background.

Nor has Klopstock succeeded . . . in making his hero the real subject of a tragic epic. His crucifixion is not sufficiently motivated. The Messiah possesses too much of the sublime, prophetic spirit and does not appear human enough; he does not accomplish enough through the ordinary course of human strife and endeavor. If he had wandered about in all the splendor which Klopstock gives him, he could not have aroused the bitter hatred of his enemies. Inasmuch as whatever Jesus has done to stir up their hatred is related and is not a natural result of something we see him do, we have effect without cause. There is too much frame-work, and too little structure; too much is related, and too little acted out. As creator of his own work, Klopstock should have made the Messiah more vividly real; in failing to do this he has fallen short of the Bible, for the Biblical Messiah is more human. Klopstock depicts him either as superhuman, or with a gentle, yielding heart, one which speaks and suffers but does not act. Unless one had read the Gospels first, a perusal of the poem would leave one wholly ignorant of the genuine grandeur of Christ. The prophets, too, Klopstock should not have represented as gentle, loving youths, but he should have given them human weaknesses, and at the same time have shown through their actions the possibility for future greatness in them as pillars of the Church.

In presenting superhuman beings, . . . Klopstock again fails to make them live, active beings with human qualities. The angels are not made an integral part of the poem; they are machines which their poetic creator does not know how to use. They possess little of the greatness (das Hohe) of those in the Old Testament; Klopstock forgets the external in his emphasis upon the internal. The poet's devils, also, lack the really human element; they are pure spirits whose malicious deeds against a God, whom they know too well, and against a Messiah, whom they know too little, are not fully motivated. They act out of a principle of envy, rather than from an inner impulse. Everything for which the poet uses the devils he could have developed out of the human soul. The devil ought to be more a devil of this world, the lord of the elements, with power over death and misfortune; he would then be a worthy adversary for Jesus to overthrow in the end.

But the beauties of the poem . . . far outshine the faults and even cause them to disappear. When one reads the work one very rarely finds anything to criticize adversely; one enjoys it; one enters intensely into its essence and meaning. The poet is best in the subjective, lyrical parts. . . . Nowhere is Klopstock greater than when he, as one who knows the human heart, succeeds in bringing up out of the depths of the soul a storm of thoughts and emotions, and permits this storm "to roar up to heaven"; when he stirs up an eddy of doubts, griefs, and fears, as in his Philo, his despairing Ischariot, his Peter, and especially in that great creation of his imagination, Abbadonna. In the tender scenes one always sees Klopstock describing his own heart—in Benoni and Lazarus, in Cidli and Maria, in Portia, Mirjam, and Debora.

Klopstock often emphasizes the sublime and the moral . . . at the expense of the epic; insofar he is the son of his time. (pp. 27-30)

> *Johann Gottfried von Herder, in an extract from* Herder and Klopstock: A Comparative Study *by Frederick Henry Adler, G. E. Stechert and Company, Publishers, 1914, pp. 27-30.*

SATYRANE [PSEUDONYM OF SAMUEL TAYLOR COLERIDGE] (essay date 1809)

[*An English poet and critic, Coleridge was central to the English Romantic movement and is considered one of the greatest literary critics in the English language. Besides his poetry, his most important contributions include his formulation of Romantic theory, his introduction of the ideas of the German Romantics to England, and his Shakespearean criticism, which overthrew the last remnants of the Neoclassical approach to William Shakespeare and focused on Shakespeare as a portrayer of human character. In the following excerpt, taken from an essay originally published in the weekly paper* The Friend *on December 21, 1809, Coleridge tersely expresses his opinion of Klopstock's reputation as the "German Milton."*]

You ask me, whether I have read the *Messiah,* and what I think of it? I answer—as yet the first four books only: and as to my opinion (the reasons of which hereafter) you may guess it from what I could not help muttering to myself, when the good Pastor this morning told me, that Klopstock was the German Milton——"a very *German* Milton indeed!!!" (p. 288)

> *Satyrane [pseudonym of Samuel Taylor Coleridge], "Satyrane's Letters: Letter III," in his* The Friend: A Series of Essays, *Gale and Curtis, 1812, pp. 276-88.**

MISS [ELIZABETH OGILVIE] BENGER (essay date 1814)

[*Benger briefly discusses the stylistic limitations of* The Messiah *and its source of emotional inspiration.*]

The *Messiah* has been happily compared to a Gothic church, and surely ought not to be judged by the rules of Grecian composition. The defects in the plan, the confusion produced by the fatiguing number of characters, who are rather names than personages, must be obvious to the most superficial glance, whilst the grandeur in the conceptions, the elevation and dignity of the sentiments, can, perhaps, be fully tasted only by a few poetical *ruminators.* (pp. xxv-xxvi)

The real power of Klopstock resides in the enthusiasm with which he yields to his own impressions, forgetting all but an ideal world. He was no master of the passions; he understood not their language. He had only studied man in the abstract, and was unacquainted with the artificial idioms acquired in society. He had no eloquence but for those domestic affections which form the primitive voice of nature; his imagination was conversant with beings of a higher order, yet in his wildest flights, he reminds the reader, by some native touches of pathos, that he is a man, and a brother.

Whatever he wrote is so perfectly in harmony with his own character, that his true source of inspiration should seem to have been the heart. In all his writings, he is animated either by friendship, or filial piety; by patriotism or devotion. Though decidedly of the English school, it cannot be said he proposed to himself any model of imitation. In exploring the same region as Milton, he deviates into an original track, and in adopting the same subjects as Young, he imparts to them his own amiable and almost feminine tenderness. His images of death have nothing to revolt the mind; he finds a sacred joy in grief; he delights in cherishing the images of departed friends, and anticipating their reunion in the realms of immortality. (pp. xxvi-xxvii)

> *Miss [Elizabeth Ogilvie] Benger, in an introduction to* Klopstock and His Friends: A Series of Familiar Letters Written between the Years 1750 and 1803, *translated by Elizabeth Ogilvie Benger, Henry Colburn, 1814, pp. i-xxxiii.*

[JOHN ABRAHAM HERAUD] (essay date 1830)

[*In this largely positive assessment of Klopstock's short verse, Heraud considers the odes "original and almost faultless productions."*]

["**The Contemplation of God,**" if an ode] of considerable piety, and enthusiastic in a high degree, is, nevertheless, difficult of apprehension to the ordinary reader. Its beauties are recondite, and to be sought for, as the ideal is in nature, but not in vain: they will surely be found by those capable of such investigation. In a word, it is completely Klopstockian. The Odes of Klopstock, to a careless reader, or one unacquainted with his peculiar genius and characteristic style in these singular productions, are apt to appear like compositions elaborated with much effort. In fact, not long ago, it was stated by an English critic, deceived by the deserved popularity of the *Messiah,* that this epic was the fruit of the poet's immediate inspirations, and that his Odes were mere hot-house plants and artificial products. The contrary, however, is the fact.

The *Messiah* was written slowly, and with difficulty; and its plan and execution are both very defective. His Odes, on the contrary, are *classics* in their way—original and almost faultless productions. They have, however, from their peculiar style and unique construction, been hitherto considered as untranslatable. Into French, they certainly may be; but assuredly they might be made to slide pretty easily into English verse, and hitch with comparative facility even into rhyme. Klopstock's fame, indeed, in his own country, celebrated as he is as the author of the *Messiah,* is principally grounded on his Odes; and it may be truly said, that in lyric composition he is unsurpassed. He strains too much, certainly, after new ideas; his conceptions are too frequently abstruse, and his illustrations far too far-fetched. The catachresis is his favourite figure of speech—indeed, almost his only figure; for, with this exception, he appears to have despised every thing resembling a tropical style. There is a bareness of diction and a barrenness of imagery . . . which the vulgar can make nothing of, because they find nothing of what they have been accustomed to consider as poetry, and which abounds so much in his *Messiah*. But if there is bareness of diction and barrenness of imagery, there is, instead,—what very seldom is found in union with that florid impertinence which is so very popular, because it is addressed to those who are capable of the *sensation* only, and not the *sense*, of what *is* truly poetical,—there is thought. Klopstock's Odes are not compact of the poetry of words— they are the finest exemplifications of the poetry of thought ever excogitated from an elevated mind. Depth, power, sublimity,—these are their attributes. Yet, let it not be rashly deemed that they are wanting in the requisites of language— God forbid! They manifest a mastery over his native tongue, and an abundance of language, such as no poet, in any country, ever exhibited more of, except, perhaps, our own Milton. Like Milton, Klopstock created a style of his own—collocations of phrase, and a march of verse, to which the phraseology and the versification of other poets is mere prose in loose metre. But this mastery and abundance of language was not displayed in wrapping round and round and round about, with gorgeous drapery, a mean and inane conception; but in always being ready with the only appropriate expression for the idea which was sought to be embodied. Embodied it was: it started forth abruptly in its gigantic proportions; but it was not draperied— nay, it was scarcely apparelled. Magnificent beyond example as were his ideas in these sublime effusions, they startle from their nakedness, and overwhelm with their impetuosity of movement. Were these Odes properly translated into English, we feel certain that they would give a new character to much of our national poetry, and influence beneficially its spirit and form. They would turn the attention of the poetical student to the matter, rather than the manner, of poesy;—they would shew him how to compose with thoughts rather than words, with ideas rather than images—how to *create*, in the true sense of the word, rather than to *combine*;—in a word, they would teach him to avoid commonplaces, and to ascend, with a bold eagle-wing, into the region of originality, sublimity, and power! (pp. 272-73)

[*John Abraham Heraud*], *"Odes from the German of Klopstock," in* Fraser's Magazine, *Vol. I, No. III, April, 1830, pp. 271-75.*

WOLFGANG MENZEL (essay date 1836)

[*A prominent German journalist of pronounced nationalistic and conservative literary opinions, Menzel fiercely opposed those German writers whose works embodied the philosophies of Romanticism, particularly Heinrich Heine, Johann Wolfgang von Goethe, and the members of the Junge Deutschland movement. For his influential history of German literature,* Die deutsche Literatur *(1836), Menzel earned the reputation of a savage and unscrupulous critic. In an excerpt from this work, he discusses Klopstock's contribution to German poetic language and praises the nationalistic and religious nature of his poetry.*]

[Above all the] German Horaces, Anacreons, Pindars, and Æsops, stands the German Homer Klopstock. He it was properly, who, by the mighty influence of his '**Messiah**' and his '**Odes**' brought the antique taste into vogue; and this not in defiance of German and Christian sentiment, but in friendly alliance with them. Religion and Fatherland were his main mark; but in regard to the outward form of poetry he looked

on that of the ancient Greeks as the most perfect, and conceived that he had united the most beautiful matter with the most beautiful form by singing the praises of Christianity in a Greek form. A strange error, no doubt, but an error which arose most naturally out of the strange character of the age in which he lived. 'Tis true, indeed, that the English literature was not without influence upon Klopstock, for his '**Messiah**' is only a pendant to Milton's 'Paradise Lost'; but Klopstock was nevertheless any thing but a mere imitator of the English; his merits in respect of German poetry are as peculiar as they are great. He expelled the French Alexandrine and the short light rhyming verse which had prevailed universally before him; and in their stead introduced the Greek hexameter, Sapphic, Alcaic, Iambic, and other verses of the ancients. By this means not only was the French bombast and the art of rhyming without sense laid aside, and the poet moreover forced to think more of the sense than of the sound of his verses, but the German language in respect of rhythmical harmony received a wonderful improvement, and attained to a compass and a flexibility which were even then of service to it, when succeeding poets rejected the Greek form as an exercise merely preparatory and prelusive. Besides this, Klopstock, though in form a Greek, was always in soul a German; and he it was who infused into our literature that spirit of patriotic enthusiasm and deification of Teutonism, which, since then, in spite of all foreign fashions, has never been extinguished. . . . [With] this man begins that healthy boldness of German poetry, which, at length, ventured to cast off the chains of foreign servitude, and to renounce for ever that humiliating air of submission which had marked it since the ill-omened peace of Westphalia. It was, indeed, high time for a man to come who should strike freely his breast and say, I am a GERMAN!

Lastly, this highest praise is not to be passed over in silence, that Klopstock's poetry and his patriotism were both deeply rooted in that sublime ethico-religious faith which his '**Messiah**' celebrates. And he it was who, next to Gellert, lent to modern German poetry that dignified, earnest, reverential character, which, in spite of all extravagances of fancy and of wit, it has never since lost, and which foreign nations have ever chiefly admired in our literature, or at least looked upon with awe. When we consider the influence of the frivolous French philosophy of the last century, and the fashion of sneering introduced by Voltaire, we can then only perfectly understand how strong the reacting influence of Klopstock was, to stem so overflowing a tide.

More powerfully, therefore, than even the thorough drilling to which he subjected the German language, have his patriotism and his noble spirit of piety tended to place his name in that position of respect and reverence which it will always maintain. These qualities of heart have always secured for him admiration even then, when no one was inclined to read him: according to the old saying of Lessing, 'Klopstock is very sublime certainly, but I shall be content to be more moderately admired, so that I be more diligently read.' It is true Klopstock loses every thing when one contemplates him at a nearer view and in detail. We must look at him from a certain distance, and be content with a general impression. When we read him he seems pedantic and long-winded: when we *have* read him, and look back upon him, he appears great and majestic. Then his two ideas, Fatherland and Religion, shine forth in their simple dignity, and impress the mind with a feeling of the sublime. We seem to behold a gigantic Ossianic ghost, a monstrous harp playing amid the clouds. When you come nearer him he dissolves in a thin, broad, misty cloud. But that first impression has mightily worked upon our soul, and tuned us to the permanent feeling of something great. Though a little metaphysical and cold at times, yet, in the two highest ideas of his poetry, he has given us two great doctrines: the one, that true poetry, if it would grow to a mighty tree, must ever strike its roots in the soil of fatherland; the other, that all higher literature must find both its humblest beginning and its highest culmination in religion. (pp. 461-63)

> *Wolfgang Menzel, in an extract from "Die deutsche Literatur," translated by J. S. Blackie, in* The Foreign Quarterly Review, *Vol. XXX, No. LX, January, 1843, pp. 461-63.*

[JOHN STUART BLACKIE]   (essay date 1843)

[*Focusing on* The Messiah, *Blackie contends that Klopstock's verse is overrated. He charges that Klopstock's verse is marred by such stylistic immaturities as "overflowing emotion, sentimental tenderness, [and] boisterous and extravagant passion." Blackie asserts that Klopstock's intensely lyric poetry exemplifies "*GERMAN EXTRAVAGANCE*."*]

For any full-grown British man at the present day to read the **'Messiah'** of Klopstock, and practically to feel even in the smallest degree that peculiar enthusiasm with which it was received by the Kleists and the Gleims, and even the Wielands and the Lessings, of the last century in Germany, is a moral impossibility. We can imagine an English young lady of piety and sentiment on a fine Sunday evening reading it rapturously enough even now; but further than this our English admiration of Klopstock in the nineteenth century is not likely to go. . . . [Before] there was a Göthe, a Schiller, a Herder, a Richter in Germany, amid a people of pigmies, it was easy for a man of ordinary dimensions to appear a giant. To the men of his time and place, Klopstock in fact was a giant; and herein lies his merit. So also let him be judged. We all read and relished authors at fourteen, or even at four-and-twenty, that pall upon us sadly now at forty. The literature of a people, like the life of an individual, has its youth, its manhood, and its old age. Klopstock is the representative of the youthful period of German literature. His writings will be fully relished only by the young, and by young women more than by young men. . . . (pp. 440-41)

Out from the flats of Northern Saxony . . . , [Klopstock] suddenly shot up, where there were no mountains before, a moving hill of emotion; glowing with the noblest fire, and mantled in the most magnificent smoke; beneath a sky also dewy with the brightest tears of tender sentiment, and arched with the most delicate lunar rainbows: a phenomenon that men in those arid regions had not been accustomed to, and well worthy to be gazed at. Then he had another advantage. He not only appeared where there was no great name to compete with, but he appeared like Minerva, starting out of Jove's cloven skull: a notable poet (in a certain emotional region), ready made, and in full panoply at his first appearance. He appeared as the poet of overflowing, unbounded emotion; as the young man, and the young man's poet; as good, ay, and perhaps better at four-and-twenty, than he ever could be at forty! This the character of his compositions, and the facts of his life, equally testify. The **'Messiah'** is essentially, from beginning to end, a young man's poem: overflowing emotion, sentimental tenderness, boisterous and extravagant passion, are its main characteristics. . . . [It] is not in the nature of things that the **'Messiah'** should bear in its front that stamp of manhood, and those lines of vigour, which so decidedly characterize Dante's 'Comedy,'

and Milton's 'Paradise Lost.' It is a vast idea, no doubt, and the offspring of a noble ambition; but it is the creation of a mere boy; and as was the conception, so is the execution. (pp. 442-43)

With a warm heart and a fine flow of sounding words, he had made his literary fortune at an age when common bards are but beginning it: he was the Pindar and the Homer of his fatherland in one: already publicly acknowledged—a Jupiter circumgyrated by a million of satellites—what more could he become? He had only to continue giving forth a solemn voice, from time to time, to keep the public in mind of his existence; and his canonization after death, having been worshipped already during his life, was secure.

In judging of the poetical reputation of Klopstock, we must never forget that he acquired it principally by his *sacred* poetry; and in all cases where the religious element enters into a purely critical question the judgment is innocently enough liable to be sadly confounded in more ways than one. Klopstock enjoyed, for half a century almost, not merely a German, but a European reputation, to an extent such as no modern author can boast of, with perhaps the single exception of Walter Scott. But how many persons ever gave themselves the trouble curiously to analyze the elements of this reputation, and to inquire minutely how much of this reputation was to be attributed to the Christian, and how much to the Poet, Klopstock? People admired, reverenced, yea, even worshipped the great Klopstock, the immortal author of the **'Messiah,'** the sublime epos of the New Testament; nor inquired further. The writer who edified them so much more than the common run of writers on religious subjects, claimed to be a poet; appeared in the fashion of a poet; invented, indeed, a new form of poetical rhythm to clothe the vastness of his conceptions (or his sentences), for which no channel in which poetical emotion had hitherto flowed seemed sufficiently broad. People were good enough, as the public is not an illnatured animal always, to take him on his word. But it was possible all the while, nay, very natural, that the man whom they were so zealously belauding as a poet, might be substantially only a preacher in a poet's dress; a sounding paraphraser of the three last chapters of the gospel; a florid and tawdry decorator of the walls of a pantheon whose gods the chisel of a Phidias (the evangelist) had sculptured. (pp. 444-45)

[The] first thing that strikes us [about the **'Messiah'**] is its monstrous bulk: twenty cantos of hexameters, some of them containing 1500 lines! With the rich materials of chivalry and romance, a luxuriant Ariosto might run on, like an arabesque decoration along a portico, to an immeasurable length without offence; but Klopstock, whose materials were of the scantiest, had he only possessed half as much sense as he had sound, could never have hesitated for a moment to confine himself within the bounds which Virgil and Milton had found too spacious rather than too narrow for a just epic effect. Klopstock, however, was and remained a BOY, in the whole style of his poetry; but as young preachers, partly from an overboiling of zeal in the heart, and partly from a defect of dexterous management in the head, are apt to make long sermons, so it is a marked characteristic of Klopstock, not in his **'Messiah'** only, but also in his Odes, that he never knows how to observe any bounds. (pp. 450-51)

[Even] in the structure and architecture of his poem, [Klopstock] aspired to produce an effect by the material sublime of mass and multitudinosity merely. Nothing is cheaper than this; by mere piling of quantity without quality, by telling of hundreds upon hundreds, and thousands upon thousands, to overpower the imagination of the vulgar. . . . Klopstock has no way of expressing the sublime on the most solemn occasions that seems to him so effectual, as a huge-gaping *tausend und aber tausend!* Thus in the description of the Creation . . . :

> God moved full of a thousand times a thousand thoughts, holding in his right hand a thousand times a thousand lives!

And in a like barrenness of moral and fruitfulness of arithmetical sublimity, our German Milton has no more ingenious method of conveying to our mind the extraordinary grandeur or excellence of any object, than by simply saying that it was the grandest and most excellent thing of the kind that ever had been in creation, or ever should be again. In this style Mary, the sister of Lazarus . . . is described as 'in her eye, full of melancholy repressing the most moving tear that ever was wept.' The writer of Klopstock's life in Chalmers's 'Biographical Dictionary,' though no great admirer of the poet, remarks, innocently enough, that there are many and great beauties in Klopstock's writings which it is impossible to transfer into another tongue. Now, so far from this being true, the fact is, that in the passage which we have just quoted, and others of the same shallow extravagancy, the German poet is indebted to his English translator for an air of chasteness and propriety that does in no wise belong to him. Thus, instead of

> In dem Auge voll Wehmuth hielt Sie die rührendste Thräne zurück die Jemals geweint war.

The English translator gives

> In her calm eye
> She checked the liquid sorrow, whose mute woe
> Touched every heart.

And so in other places. No man who has not read Klopstock in the original, and read a good deal of him, can be fully aware of this material grossness of his sublime. With a similar big-mouthed nothingness the German Milton describes the remorse of Iscariot after having betrayed his Master thus: "Terrible even as a wide-opened grave the thought spreads itself out before me; it is the most torturing of torturing thoughts that a dying man ever felt: the thought that I have betrayed him!" which in like manner the Englishman, with an instinctive good taste, has improved into

> Before me, like a yawning grave, the black,
> The hideous thought ingulfs my soul,
> I have betrayed him.

Klopstock is, perhaps, a solitary instance of a writer of reputation in a superior language whom it is impossible for a translator using an inferior language not to improve, and that without meaning to do so. Our English language has no conception of the immensity of sounding breadth with which he rolls himself along. With what proclamations, invocations, and adjurations does he not begin! How ominously does he not stalk from star to star upon his seven-league-boots, and ride upon a whirlwind of words furiously! When he stands he is a whole mountain! when he moves he is a thousand-voiced cataract, whose strength has been gathered from the torrents of a thousand hills! . . . His voice is thunder, and his look is lightning; the earth trembles where he treads, and the rocks fall in! Then when he is wrathful, how his eyes glare with red fire, and roll infuriate! how his hair floats like the trailing comet in the sky, how him mouth foams, his teeth gnash, and his feet stamp! Tender again or timid, how he starts, turns pale, stag-

gers, trembles, and melts away into darkness! Joyful, how he quakes all over with ecstasy, and weeps him out into a glorious rainbow of sentiment! Literally, and without exaggeration, we must say, 'unbecoming as it may be to speak disrespectfully of works that have enjoyed for a length of time a widely-spread reputation,' still we must say, that if any actor of broad farce should inquire of us where he might find the richest selection of extravagant words, extravagant descriptions, and extravagant speeches, wherewith to put together a master specimen of the mock sublime, we could direct him nowhere with so much propriety as to Klopstock's '**Messiah.**' It is by studying this man, much more than Kotzebue or any play-writer, that the Englishman can form to himself a perfect idea of what has long been known in England by the peculiar designation of GERMAN EXTRAVAGANCE.

As for the other works of Klopstock, dividing themselves as they naturally do into three departments; the lyric, the dramatic, and the critical; the first department only can claim a passing glance from the student. Unquestionably, Klopstock, if he is a poet at all, is a lyric poet, and nothing but a lyric poet. When not in a full flow of emotion, he is a very stiff formal personage indeed, and not at all engaging. He is all flame, all cloud, all billow, or all tears: solidity, stability, tangibility, reality, he has none. . . . (pp. 454-56)

But one may weep with Klopstock, though one cannot look at him; and this, after all, is his best point. A most invincible passion . . . he assuredly had for love: he was the warmest of friends and the most ardent of lovers. Therefore he could not understand Petrarch. That sort of calm, contemplative love, that could turn itself with leisurely elegance into all manner of sonnets, he could not comprehend. . . . Petrarch, he said, celebrated Laura in verses which the man of taste will admire, but which the lover will think cold. Not so are his own verses: whether friend or fatherland, love or religion, inspire the theme, he is never cold. He never forgets the man in the artist. His great fault rather is that he has too little art; that he pours himself out with too great impetuosity to carry the common reader along with him; with too much of sweeping vastitude to please any reader. But he is a true, sincere, and earnest man, 'writing always with tears in his eyes,' says [his wife] Meta; and if the Horatian *si vis me flere*, were the only, as it certainly is the main rule for pathetic composition, Klopstock in elegy certainly would never fail. Weeping, however, as well as shouting, requires a certain moderation and tempering, in order to produce what the Germans call an aesthetical effect. Now this moderation it is precisely that Klopstock can in no wise attain to; and the consequence is, that as his sublime always fumes into bombast, so his pathetic is seldom free from [Göthe's] Wertherism. (pp. 456-57)

Of Klopstock's dramatical and critical works the less that is said the better. He wrote his tragedies on the barren Greek model, because he wanted luxuriance and variety to write them on the English. Some of them, as '**The Battle of Herman'** ['**Hermanns Schlacht'**], are as much lyric as dramatic; their dialogue is prose in a passion; and their druidical hymns are the same sort of high-flown, exclamatory, violent-plunging, and abrupt-striding compositions with which we are familiar in the odes. Others, like '**Solomon,'** are purely dialogical, and written in the common ten-syllabled Iambic verse. This subject of Solomon, his apostacy from and return to Jehovah, has some fine dramatic materials. But to turn these to advantage, wit and grace and ease, and a nice perception of character, were necessary; all which Klopstock wanted. The same may be said

Klopstock's wife, Margareta Moller, who inspired many of his odes. The Granger Collection, New York.

of his great critical work, **'Die Deutsche Gelehrten Republik'**—**'The Literary Republic of the Germans';**—a dogmatico-satirico-historical scheme of what that German literature was in the year of grace 1772, and what it ought to be. But Klopstock had neither compass of intellect nor catholicity of heart to set himself up in the face of Germany as a literary dictator; and he was altogether destitute of that fine playful perception of the ridiculous, and that nice and delicate handling of what is foolish, without which the most gigantic Aristarchus is but a heavy giant dealing clumsy blows to make wicked boys laugh, and tailors boast of their muscle. Klopstock's prose is altogether something very peculiar. The author of the **'Messiah'** seems to have considered himself too great and almost sacred a person to be a man with other men; therefore, when he puts off his wings, he puts on stilts. It is but doing him justice, however, to state, that he strides more properly at this artificial elevation than many a notable German philosopher on his natural legs can walk. (p. 460)

> [*John Stuart Blackie*], *in a review of "Sämmtliche Werke," in* The Foreign Quarterly Review, *Vol. XXX, No. LX, January, 1843, pp. 439-65.*

TAIT'S EDINBURGH MAGAZINE (essay date 1846)

[*In this unsigned review, the critic attributes Klopstock's impressive reputation to his use of religious and patriotic subjects and the lack of serious artistic competition during his lifetime, rather than to artistic merit.*]

[Klopstock] is the much-echoed name that first taught Europe to suspect that such a thing as a German literature existed at all, or at least was attempting to exist. Klopstock is unquestionably a famous name in German literature; he at one time enjoyed a reputation as wide as Goethe's, a popularity almost as extensive as Schiller's: What is his true value?

One thing we hold to be certain: **"The Messiah"** was a failure, a decided failure. Klopstock has no claim to rank with Virgil and Milton; his character as a poet must stand on his lyric pieces: **"The Messiah,"** when it is read—which is seldom now—is read only because it is Klopstock's, and for a few isolated lyrical beauties. Neither can we say, much as we should wish to say it, that Klopstock's lyrics are of the highest order. They are not, indeed, without the essential element of all true lyric poetry, strong feeling: they are in no sense lukewarm, much less cold; nay, they are glowing hot, most outrageously hot, spitting out lightnings and rolling thunders on all occasions, and creating much smoke: there is no measure, no moderation, in their excitement; therein precisely lies their fault. To be enjoyed, in fact, perfectly, they must be read, as the host of them were written, by a young man; one in whose brain the evolution of purely internal impulses is yet so eager and so imperious, so overpowering and so monopolizing, that the external world possesses neither clearness nor interest. There is also, as must ever be in this sort of juvenile poetry, an utter want of concentration; that quality which, when combined with good sense and a happy tone, (as in the case of Horace,) compensates so often for the lack of what is magnificently called genius. But Klopstock is not merely an unripe and an unchastened lyrist. Our own Shelley also wrote poetry, which, in respect of what in more mature years he might have written, may well be called juvenile and unripe; but the calm blue expanse of his heaven is spangled with a thousand purest lights, altogether of a different temper from those feverish sparks that shoot forth from the rolling pomp of rhetorical vapour in Klopstock. In the "very German Milton" of **"The Messiah,"** the sublime is vast even to inanity, and its terror has a constant tendency to become insane. Shelley wants substance; so also does Klopstock: but the flimsiness of the one is never without a certain fairy delicacy which delights, while that of the other is ever apt to degenerate into a gigantic confusion which repels. But Klopstock is not merely unsubstantial and vapoury in his matter; he is harsh and stiff, stilted and affected in his manner. He fell, indeed, at an early age, into the very obvious and shallow mistake, that, to contend successfully with the great ancients, it was necessary for a modern poet to adopt the identical outward form and vesture in which it had pleased them to embody their noble and manly thoughts. He must needs imitate the Romans, as the Romans imitated the Greeks, to the exclusion of those forms of poetic embodiment which were traditionary in his own country. He nourished a pedantic pride in the rejection of rhyme from his lyric measures, as a barbarous modern innovation; whereas it is merely a pretty ornament, and perfectly inoffensive, except for a few special purposes; and in the attempt to re-create, for the edification of the modern ear, the lost rhythm of Pindaric strophes and Horatian stanzas, he twisted, and wrenched, and dislocated his good mother Deutsch in such an ungracious fashion, that, in reading some of his sublime strivings, we feel for all the world . . . as if we were "eating stones." In no respect, therefore, neither in respect of shape nor of substance, is Klopstock to be accounted a great lyric poet; not the true German oak certainly, but a gigantic mushroom of tropical breadth and magnificence, and, in a land where there were as yet no green trees, worthy to be looked on not without veneration. (pp. 94-5)

[The] bard of "**The Messiah**" owes his great reputation to three circumstances, none of which have any thing essential to do with first rate poetic excellence. *First*, He was a religious poet; *Second*, He was a patriotic poet; and, *Thirdly*, He appeared in an age when there were no great German poets from whom to take his measure. There was no strong pressure from without to keep him in his proper place; and thus, as, in a pretty experiment of the mechanical philosophers, we see a flaccid bladder in the receiver of an air-pump, on the removal of the circumambient aerial pressure, suddenly swell up into a full distended globe; so Klopstock, before Goethe and Schiller had created a healthy literary atmosphere in Germany, with his windy inanity occupied a great space. (p. 95)

> *"The Lyric Poetry of Germany," in* Tait's Edinburgh Magazine, *n.s. Vol. XIII, No. CXLVI, February, 1846, pp. 94-103.**

BAYARD TAYLOR   (lecture date 1879)

[*Taylor was a minor American poet, novelist, and travel writer. In the following commentary, originally prepared as a lecture to be delivered at Cornell University, he surveys Klopstock's writings and discusses their impact on eighteenth- and nineteenth-century German literature.*]

[The *Sturm und Drang* period of German literature] was partly a natural and inevitable phase of development; but in so far as it was brought about by the influence of living authors, Klopstock must be looked upon as one of the chief agencies. When we hear of the boy Goethe and his sister Cornelia declaiming passages from the "**Messiah**," with such energy that the frightened barber dropped his basin, and came near gashing the throat of Goethe the father, we may guess the power of the impression which Klopstock made. It is not sufficient, therefore, that we read the "**Messiah**" as if it had been written yesterday. We may smile at its over-laden passion and its diffusive sentiment, but when we come to it from the literature which preceded it, we feel, by contrast, that a pure and refreshing stream of poetry has at last burst forth from the barren soil. The number of those who in Germany, at present, read the whole of the "**Messiah**," is larger than the number of those who in England now read the whole of Spenser's "Faery Queene;" but it is yet very small. (pp. 238-39)

The "**Messiah**" is only indirectly didactic and doctrinal. On account of the multitude of characters, there is a great deal of action, and the narrative continually breaks into dialogue. It is pervaded throughout by the tender humanity of the Christian religion, and has many passages of genuine sublimity. But it is pitched altogether upon too lofty and ambitious a key, and the mind of the reader, at last, becomes very weary of hanging suspended between heaven and earth. (p. 240)

Klopstock's friends claim that he was the first to introduce the classic hexameter into the language. He was certainly the first who did so successfully; but Lessing shows that both the hexameter and the elegiac measure were used by Fischart, in the seventeenth century. Klopstock's hexameters, moreover, are by no means above criticism; many of his lines try both the ear and the tongue, while now and then we find one which is melody itself. . . . Klopstock did not perceive the truth, which Goethe afterward discovered, that the hexameter, to be agreeable, must put off its Greek or Latin habits, and adapt itself to the spirit and manner of the German language; but his labor was both honest and fruitful. The "**Messiah**" was the result of a deliberate purpose to produce an epic; the subject, we might almost say, was mechanically chosen, and we can only wonder that a work produced under such conditions had so much positive success in its day.

His "**Odes**," which also attained a great popularity, were formed upon classical models. He endeavored, in them, to make eloquence and sentiment supply the place of rhyme. To me they seem like a series of gymnastic exercises, whereby the muscles of the language became stronger and its joints more flexible, although the finer essence of poetry disappears in the process. Klopstock hoped, and his admirers believed, that he was creating a classic German literature, by adopting the forms which had become classic in other languages. All we can now admit is that he substituted the influence of Greek literature for that of the French: and this, at the time, was no slight service. His "**Odes**" were the earliest inspiration of Schiller, and he had also a crowd of imitators who have left no names behind them.

None of his dramatic poems can be called successful. His "**Herman's Fight**" ["**Hermanns Schlacht**"] was written, like his "**Messiah**," for a deliberate purpose—to counteract the French influence which was still upheld in Germany, not only by Gottsched and his school, but also by the Court of Frederick the Great. It was dedicated to Joseph II. of Austria, who was looked upon as the representative of the German spirit. But Klopstock, faithful to his idea of transplanting classic forms, revived the old Teutonic gods, and endeavored to construct a new German Olympus. The result is very much like a masquerade. We see the faces and beards of the old Teutonic tribes, their shields and war-clubs, but we hear would-be Grecian voices when they speak. His attempts in this direction, however, led him to a deeper study of the growth and development of the German language, and determined, for many years, the character of his literary activity. . . . [His] "**Fragments Relating to Language and Poetry**" ["**Über Sprache und Dichtkunst**"], and his "**Grammatical Conversations**" ["**Grammatische Gespräche von Klopstock**" are] both sound and valuable works. Yet in them, as in his dramatic poems, the effect was greater than its cause. Probably no author of the last century did so much toward creating a national sentiment, toward checking the impressibility of the race to foreign influences, arousing native pride and stimulating native ambition. This was his greatest service, especially since the German people saw in him the evidence of what he taught. Where Lessing cut his way by destructive criticism, Klopstock worked more slowly by example. In force and scope and originality of intellect there can be no comparison between the two men: Klopstock must always be ranked among minds of the second class: but when we estimate what they achieved during their lives, there is less difference. (pp. 241-44)

> *Bayard Taylor, "Klopstock, Wieland and Herder," in his* Studies in German Literature, *G. P. Putnam's Sons, 1879, pp. 234-65.**

[MUNGO W. MᴀᴄCALLUM]   (essay date 1880)

[*MacCallum cites numerous flaws in the odes and* The Messiah *which mar their lyric beauty. However, like some later critics of Klopstock's verse, MacCallum regards* The Messiah *as an oratorio rather than an epic. Unlike several of his predecessors, MacCallum discerns no similarities between Klopstock and John Milton.*]

[Klopstock's] gifts are chiefly lyric. There is no trace with him of the measured, stately self-control that we associate with great epic poets, with Virgil and Dante and Milton. And still less does he possess that quick, wide sympathy with all types of character, all shades of opinion which the dramatist requires. He once pronounced it sin to love a freethinker. But his continual enthusiasm, his raptures of despair and delight, would all find their vent in the intenser kinds of lyrical composition.

It is noteworthy that Horace and Pindar were his early favourites and inspired his first poetical attempts. With them he cultivated his sense of form. As soon as he tried odes in German he found that he must have a perfect control over his language, a thorough insight into its spirit, a complete mastery of its materials. He studied it in the light of his Greek and Roman masters; he plunged into it and it bore him up; he felt he could compete with the ancients in their own measures, and contemptuously rejected what he called "the modern click-clack of rhyme." He strove with might and main to reach the old classical perfection of form, and not without success. . . . It is unfortunate, but it is characteristic of the man, that this formal perfection means nothing more to him than mastery in speech, metres, and the arrangement of sounds. But in these he almost always succeeds, at least where they are the vehicle of exalted feeling. No doubt he takes liberties in his treatment of German, he forces it to be sublime, in spite of itself; what it gains in majesty, it loses in simplicity. A friend once told him that people did not understand his language: "Then they may learn it," was Klopstock's reply. In this he was too proud and uncompromising, he would not take a telling. He persevered in classical constructions, involved sentences, obscure allusions, which it requires some erudition to explain. To illustrate this it is usual to quote his verse—

> The pious monk's invention now resounds.

Perhaps few readers guess at once that he means *the gun is fired*, and that "the pious monk's invention" is the powder. A smart but somewhat flippant critic greatly annoyed Klopstock by proposing to translate his odes into *German*. Often he seems to have constructed his periods like Chinese puzzles, that his reader may have the pleasure of taking them to pieces again. But, after condemning all these faults, we must remember that they are by no means universal with Klopstock, and that it is very easy to make too much of them. Take him at his best and he is the unsurpassed ode-writer of the modern world (perhaps Dryden equals him in his one great effort). "Hence it comes that he has the ease and confidence of a master in all the primitive and original kinds of poetry. He seizes in its very essence the stormy ecstasy of the bards, the religious majesty of Psalms, and once or twice the more human beauty of the Greek lyrics." It has been said that in his youthful odes we hear again Pindar and David and the Edda. These names suggest a rough threefold division, not only of those, but of all his poems, according to three principles, which exercised a powerful influence on his life and development. Some of the odes are simple and severe, and have a faint breath of Greek beauty. Others are abrupt, difficult, involved and obscure, composed after Northern models and intended to express the *Urdeutsch*, the original native German. A third class are dithyrambic hymns of religious content, steeped in the spirit of David and Isaiah and St. John.

The Grecian inspiration . . . was his first. In the classical world he learned the significance of form: Pindar and Horace taught him their measures and their style. All his odes may be considered as the direct or indirect outcome of these influences. (pp. 535-36)

In his choice of a subject [for the *Messiah*] we must admit that Klopstock was wrong. When a poet treats a larger theme he is generally exposed to a twofold danger. On the one hand his tastes may be a little recondite, he may select what is neither well known nor popular. In this case he will fail to excite catholic sympathy, his work will not be national nor ever become household property. Or, again, he may choose what is too familiar, what is already sacred and hallowed in the minds of the people, so that no further artistic development is possible, and all change is regarded with suspicion. No one out of France is rash enough to write a new *Hamlet,* and Klopstock was guilty of almost as much foolhardiness when he undertook to work up the simple stories of the Gospel into an elaborate epic poem.

And the very conditions which determined his choice made it impossible for him fully to succeed. It was his orthodoxy dashed with pietism that drew him to the subject. Now while his pietism filled him with devout brooding reverence for the figure of Christ, his orthodoxy forced him to view it only through the old dogmas. These prescribed a certain treatment and forbade a certain treatment. He could not piece together, reject, remodel, and humanise. We have seen this done in the prose of Renan and others with at least far more artistic results than came within the range of Klopstock's verse. Even the Evangelical theologian, Dr. Dorner, says of him, "He failed to perceive that the divine, save when human, remains unrevealed, and hovers in a sublime haziness, which may inspire aspiration and ecstasy, but never keen plastic contemplation." Klopstock conceives the divine in what Dr. Dorner would call its unrevealed state. He seeks its expression not in the workings of man's spirit, but in signs and wonders. So, instead of bringing his theme more fully and clearly within our consciousness, he shifts it further away. To this result his artistic concurred with his religious orthodoxy. He held the baleful tenet that an epic poem demands supernatural machinery. All of it, therefore, which he found ready to his hand seemed to require enlargement rather than dismantling. So he introduces a multitude of marvels, a crowd of persons, an enormous daemonic apparatus, of which the Evangelists know nothing, and which every judicious reader must feel to be out of place. Samma, a convert, Philo, a Pharisee, play important parts, and Pilate's wife, Portia, with her dreams and presentiments, has nearly a whole canto to herself. Nicodemus, Joseph, Lazarus, are made the heroes of imaginary occurrences. Indeed all the minor characters of the Gospel, who are introduced casually, whose names are hardly mentioned, or are left unmentioned, become the centre of detailed and fantastical romances. Perhaps the most ridiculous example is the little love story of Semida and Cidli, the young man of Nain and the daughter of Jairus. Since both died and both were raised from the dead, Klopstock discovers that they were evidently intended for each other. Their connection is not indeed mentioned in Holy Writ, but, thank heaven! Herr Klopstock is at hand to remedy such omissions! So he conducts them through a long and tearful courtship, and at length unites them amid a company of glorified saints and prophets who visit the earth after the Crucifixion. Most of Klopstock's admirers would think this blasphemy, did it not occur in a religious poem.

Perhaps even more superfluous are the hosts of angels, demons, and genii who are intended to help on the action, but who really impede it. Nothing happens save through their agency. Herder condemns this with rather an amusing illustration. The Evangelist in his story of the Crucifixion says, "Now it was about the sixth hour, and there was darkness over all the earth until the ninth hour." These simple words are intended to bring out the solemnity of the time, and do so completely. But in Klopstock, the seraph Uriel has been waiting for the proper moment, and then punctually signals to a star to place itself before the sun. In the same way no one can talk or think but it is by the prompting of an angel or a devil. "We get to know not men, but their guardian spirits." This fashion of supernatural poetry became the bane of Germany, and Lessing proposed to write a satire upon it in which old Gottsched should ride out "to hunt the seraphim." Klopstock only once attempts to portray character, and that is in the case of the fallen angel Abadonna. . . . [Abadonna] alone of all the spirits has definite features. The others are a shadowy host, distinguishable only by their names. Schiller says truly, "From all that he touches Klopstock withdraws the body" [see excerpt above, 1795-96]. And yet despite that, he is grossly materialistic. He places the infernal regions in the centre of the earth, lighted by a sun of their own. He describes God as a visible figure in space. He conceives spirit as body that has somehow ceased to be solid. Coleridge rather unkindly translates his name "Clubstick," and certainly he has no great subtlety of discernment or fineness of thought.

This defect shows itself in the whole plan of the poem, or rather in its absence of plan. When the early cantos appeared, and every one was raving about the new epic, Lessing cautioned the people that their applause was premature. "You can't judge a work of art from the parts," he said, "but only as a whole." This warning was disregarded at the time, but every new canto proved more and more conclusively that Lessing's fears had been well founded. What an epic imperatively demands is unity of action, but the *Messiah* had in the first place no unity, and in the second no action. Christ is nailed on the Cross at the beginning of the eighth book; angels, mortals, saints, and devils gather round, sing and declaim during his dying agonies; and at last he gives up the ghost at the end of the tenth book. Now, one would think the story must draw to a close, the catastrophe is passed, the goal is reached. But in ten other cantos, quite as long as the first ten, Klopstock, with choruses, colloquies, and hymns, by a lavish use of celestial armies and the spirits of just men made perfect, fills up the interval between the Crucifixion and the Ascension. If this betrays a want of epical power, there is much else that absolutely contradicts the idea of a narrative poem. Instead of deeds, we have long debates; instead of acting, people talk. If before we were offended by Klopstock's interpolations, now we must marvel at his omissions. The procession to the Cross, the threefold denial of Peter, the end of Judas, should have been godsends to the poet; already there are touches about them hardly to be found out of our best old ballads. But Klopstock does not know when he is well off. We see the spectacle on the Cross; of the Via Dolorosa we hear no word. Peter's treason takes place in the background, and when all is over he comes forward and "weeps himself" (*erweint sich*) the martyr's crown. At Judas' suicide, first the culprit makes a long speech, then his genius and a bad angel discourse together, and finally the departed spirit joins in the talk with a fatal fluency that death has not impaired. Not only does everybody speak, but their words are broken with passion: they foam at the mouth, or if they do not lose their self-control, it is because they are sublime. Everything is at the highest possible pitch. "For very feeling," says Lessing, "we feel nothing." Klopstock exasperates his reader with continual interjections; he had to be reminded, "Not every one that crieth Lord! Lord! shall enter into the kingdom of poetry." The same phrases occur in wearisome iteration. Everybody wonders and weeps and swoons and smiles and embraces everybody else, and dissolves in tears scalding or holy as the case may be. This last performance is especially Klopstockian. In almost every page one finds the expression "weeping eyes."

All these criticisms we must make if we take Klopstock at his word and regard the *Messiah* as an epic poem. But if we do this we are less than just. We shall gain a truer point of view if for a moment we contrast the *Messiah* and the *Paradise Lost*. We will not echo Coleridge's biting answer to those who called Klopstock a German Milton. "Yes, a very German one!" Rather we must decide that the two poets have as little as possible in common. With Milton everything has distinctness, firm outline, definite shape. Even his more hideous images have been compared by Winckelmann to beautifully painted gorgons. But no one in his senses would think of naming painting in the same breath with Klopstock. With him there is nothing fixed, nothing plastic. . . .

> Again to bloom the seed the sower sows,
> The Lord of Harvest goes
> Gathering the sheaves,
> Death's sickle reaps and leaves;
>   Praise ye the Lord.

It is not too much to say that no pictorial thinker could have written this, for it labours under a radical confusion; sowing and reaping, seed time and harvest, are both employed as types of death. It certainly is no picture, but does it not suggest another art? Take now this poem, which he calls the *Rose Wreath:*—

> I found her by a shady rill,
>   I bound her with a wreath of rose,
> She felt it not, but slumbered still.
> I looked on her, and on the spot
>   My life with hers did blend and close.
> I felt it, but I knew it not.
> Some lisping broken words I spoke,
>   And rustled light the wreath of rose,
> Then from her slumber she awoke;
> She looked on me and from that hour
>   Her life with mine did blend and close,
> And round us it was Eden's bower.

The presentiment, the dreaminess, the hush of feeling that mark these lines at least in the original, do they not come over the soul like a breath of melody? All poetry contains ideally the arts of painting and music. It is word-painting and word-music, though it is something more than their union. Klopstock's peculiarity lies in this, that with him the first element is more nearly wanting, and the second more fully present than with almost any other poet. . . . Herder said that his odes must be read aloud; "then," he proceeds, "they rise from the page and become a dance of syllables." This is quite true, and Klopstock too often prefers the syllable to the word, the music to the meaning; he tickles our ears with pages of "sound and fury, signifying nothing." . . . [The twentieth canto of the *Messiah*] contains little more than shouts of Hosannah, choruses of Hallelujah , wavings of triumphal palms. Clearly the relation here is not with the painter, but with the musician. (pp. 539-44)

[The *Messiah*] is much liker an oratorio than an epic. It is one great ode, or rather a great collection of great odes. Klopstock is always a lyrical poet, and he is never more lyrical than in the *Messiah*. If we look at it in this light we shall like it better. Indeed, much that was repugnant to the idea of an epic we may now find to be powerful and impressive. We can now understand why the fragments were so popular while the whole failed to tell; for the parts must be read as lyrics. From this point of view some of the individual passages are in their way unsurpassed. (pp. 544-45)

Even the debates, if we regard them as splendid pieces of lyrical invective, may obtain their meed of approbation. The best of them is the dispute in the Sanhedri[n], when the perturbation of Caiaphas, the caution of Gamaliel, the charity of Nicodemus, and especially the ruthless hatred of Philo, would make a really powerful impression, were their harangues not quite so lengthy.

Many, too, of the phrases and similes have a true poetic ring. When Satan *pours* the evil dream into Judas' open ear, does it not suggest old Hamlet's tale how his brother "into the porches of his ear did pour the leperous distilment?" And the whole episode of this dream is one of Klopstock's triumphs. (p. 545)

[It is in passages] that afford scope for musical rhetoric, that Klopstock is at his best. It is a pity they are so scarce. They occur once or twice in the *Messiah*, in the dramas hardly ever. These last effusions are indeed hopelessly dull. . . . His sacred dramas are even poorer [than his "Bardiete"], and may be dismissed with a sentence: they are merely over-grown lyrics. The first and best of them, *Adam's Death*, deals with the mystery of death as it is first seen to approach, not at the beck of a murderer, but in the common course of things, and though monotonous, does not fail to impress. These dramas, however, are chiefly famous because of the evil fashion they introduced among the poetasters of Germany. For a few years every man who could versify, Wieland among them, and many who could not, seemed to study the genealogical chapters of Scripture for the purpose of weaving tragedies about the obscurest names. In the same way, the *Messiah* called forth a swarm of epics that were no more epical and far less lyrical than itself.

Klopstock's prevailing character then is vehement, high-strung enthusiasm. And it was well for reviving German literature that its first flight should be so bold and lofty. It soared at once beyond the "arrows, views, and shouts" of the profane Philistines. In his poem of the *Two Muses*, Klopstock proclaims at once that no cheap triumph will suffice him. The young untried Muse of Germany disdains contest save with her victorious sister of Britain. They prepare for the race—

> The herald sounds; they sped with eagle flight,
> Behind them into clouds the dust was tossed:
> I looked; but when the oaks were passed, my sight
> In dimness of the dust was lost.

Whatever we may think of the contest, we must grant that Klopstock restored German art to life and liberty. He himself revelled in this strange freedom, and abandoned himself to the guidance of his feelings. Probably this was necessary for the reformation of poetry, but it had its dangers. Klopstock's warmth of emotional raptures was wholly religious, but there were not wanting prophets of woe who foretold its issue in something very different. And they were right. It is proverbial that extremes meet. The excess of pietism swings round into an excess of frivolity. Both are the outcome of feeling and sensibility rather than of character, both look more to personal enjoyment than to a practical end. Klopstock himself was preserved from this transition by his priest-like purity and narrowness. But the logic of history made it necessary, nor is it to be considered merely a relapse. His overcharged religion and stilted diction need their supplement in an elegant style, and a gay graceful wisdom of the world. So in the fulness of days the spirit of Klopstock, who has been called the German Milton, moved and fulfilled itself, and assumed a new form in Wieland, who has been called the German Voltaire. (pp. 545-46)

[*Mungo W. MacCallum*], "Klopstock," in The Cornhill Magazine, Vol. XLI, No. 245, May, 1880, pp. 532-46.

KUNO FRANCKE (essay date 1896)

[*Francke discusses Klopstock's place in German literary history, characterizing him as an inspirational figure and comparing* The Messiah *to the oratorios of George Friedrich Handel and Johann Sebastian Bach. This essay was originally published in the first (1896) edition of Francke's study, then titled* Social Forces in German Literature: A Study in the History of Civilization.]

Klopstock led German literature from the narrow circle of private emotions and purposes to which the absolutism of the seventeenth century had come near confining it, into the broad realm of universal sympathy. He was the first great freeman since the days of Luther. . . . He addressed himself to the whole nation, nay, to all mankind. And by appealing to all that is grand and noble; by calling forth those passions and emotions which link the human to the divine; by awakening the poor down-trodden souls of men who thus far had known themselves only as the subjects of princes to the consciousness of their moral and spiritual citizenship, he became the prophet of that invisible republic which now for nearly a century and a half has been the ideal counterpart in German life of a stern monarchical reality. (p. 234)

[It was precisely through an] exaggerated and overstrained spirituality that Klopstock achieved the greatest of his work. He would never have produced the marvellous impression upon his contemporaries which he did produce, had he attempted to represent life as it is. . . . What was needed now was a higher view of human existence, the kindling of larger emotions, the pointing out of loftier aims. A man was needed who should give utterance to that religious idealism which, though buried under the ruins of popular independence, was nevertheless the one vital principle of Protestantism not yet extinct; a man who, through an exalted conception of nationality, should inspire his generation with a new faith in Germany's political future; a man who, by virtue of his own genuine sympathy with all that is human in the noblest sense, and through his unwavering belief in the high destiny of mankind, should usher in a new era of enlightened cosmopolitanism. It was Klopstock's spirituality which enabled him to assume this threefold leadership, and the immeasurable services rendered by him in this capacity to the cause of religion, fatherland, and humanity may well make us forget the artistic shortcomings by which they were accompanied.

None of Klopstock's works has been so much subjected to misleading and unappreciative criticism as his greatest religious poem, the *Messias*. Let us admit at the outset that in this seeming epic nearly all the most essential epic qualities are lacking. Reality in events, clearness of motive, naturalness of character, directness of style, all these are things for which, in most parts of the poem, we look in vain. Throughout its twenty cantos we constantly circle between heaven, hell, and earth, without at any given moment seeming to know where we are. Christ's passion and death, the central action of the work, is robbed of its human interest through the over-anxious desire of the poet to exalt the divine nature of the Saviour, and to represent the atonement as predetermined in the original plan of creation. The countless hosts of angelic and satanic spirits which hover before us in endless space are for the most part without individual features. Even the human sympathizers and adversaries of the Son of God play their parts more by portentous looks, unutterable thoughts, effusive prayer, or mysterious silence, than by straightforward action.

But what do all these criticisms mean? They simply mean that it was a mistake in Klopstock's admirers to call him a German Milton, and that the *Messias* ought not to be looked upon as an epic poem at all. Not Milton, but the great German composers of church music were Klopstock's spiritual predecessors; his place is by the side of Bach and Händel as the third great master of the oratorio. (pp. 235-36)

Klopstock's *Messias*, like the oratorio, consists of epic, lyric and dramatic elements. Of these, the epic element corresponds to what the recitative is in the oratorio. It is the background of the whole, it forms a connecting link between the other parts, but in itself it would be incomplete. Only in the lyric and dramatic passages, those passages which correspond to the arias and choruses of the oratorio, does the poem rise to its height; only here is the full splendour of Klopstock's musical genius revealed.

The time will certainly come when even the narrative part of the *Messias* will again, as in Goethe's youth, find readers willing to let themselves be carried along by its powerful and sonorous, though sometimes monotonous, flow of oratory. Nothing could be grander and, at the same time, simpler than the general outline of the poem. How, from the scene in the first canto, where Christ on the Mount of Olives consecrates himself to the work of redemption, we are led through the councils of heaven and hell, through Gethsemane and Golgotha, to the Resurrection and Ascension, until at last "the living heavens rejoice and sing about the throne, and a gleam of love irradiates the whole universe,"—all this is nobly planned.

Nor is there a lack of individual scenes full of inner life and divine fire. What an air of sublime mystery and awe lingers over the lonely night spent by Jesus on the Mount of Olives at the beginning of the poem. (pp. 237-38)

What a brilliancy of oratorical diction and invention there is in the scene where Christ, after his resurrection, holds judgment on Mount Tabor over the souls of those who have recently died! Among them the souls of warriors and those of infants are contrasted. (p. 239)

Or, to select a passage of less fanciful imagery, what could surpass in graceful delineation and true poetic feeling the description of the beautiful morning on lake Tiberias when the risen Christ appears to his disciples! (pp. 239-40)

[Even] that part of the *Messias* which is closest to the narrative of the gospels is by no means the dreary and tiresome waste which popular prejudice and pragmatic criticism have made it out to be. Looked upon as the recitative element of a musical composition, it appears to fulfil a perfectly legitimate function, that of transporting the hearer into the loftier realm of supernatural experiences, and of forming with its vague, shadowy sounds a background for the richer notes of the lyric and dramatic passages of the poem.

For the most part, these passages are so closely interwoven with the narrative itself that it is impossible to consider them separately. This is, for instance, the case with the poetic images and comparisons. Klopstock's most impressive comparisons are not epic, they do not serve to make a certain part of the narrative, by which they were suggested, more graphic and

tangible; they are lyrical, they lead out of the reality of the narrative into a realm of deeper emotions and higher experiences; they can be fully appreciated only when conceived of as uttered in song.... The same must be said of the many digressions and episodes. They also do not to any considerable extent heighten the reality of events, but they do heighten, perhaps more than anything else, the effect of the poem as a lyrical expression of a fervent and exalted spirituality. (pp. 240-41)

[Klopstock's lyrico-dramatic fervor, from the first canto to the last,] forces its way, as it were, with elemental power through the epic narrative, and assumes a form of its own. Sometimes it is the poet himself who in rapturous song gives vent to his religious enthusiasm, as at the beginning of the poem, where he calls upon his immortal soul to sing the redemption of mankind.... (p. 244)

In the later portions of the poem, finally, it is the choral element which carries everything before it. In fact, the whole of the last canto is a succession of jubilant choruses, thronging about the Redeemer, as he slowly pursues his triumphal path through the heavens until at last he ascends the throne and sits at the right hand of the Father. It would be hard to imagine a more impressive *finale* than this bursting of the universe into a mighty hymn of praise echoing from star to star, and embracing the voices of all zones and ages; and it is indeed strange that a poet who was capable of such visions as these should have been taken to task by modern critics for not having confined himself more closely to the representation of actual conditions. (p. 246)

Klopstock was a true liberator. He was the first among modern German poets who drew his inspiration from the depth of a heart beating for all humanity. He was the first among them, greater than his works. By putting the stamp of his own wonderful personality upon everything that he wrote or did, by lifting himself, his friends, the objects of his love and veneration into the sphere of extraordinary spiritual experiences, he raised the ideals of his age to a higher pitch; and although his memory has been dimmed through the greater men who came after him, the note struck by him still vibrates in the finest chords of the life of to-day. (p. 250)

Kuno Francke, "The Age of Frederick the Great and the Height of Enlightenment," in his A History of German Literature As Determined by Social Forces, *fourth edition, Henry Holt and Company, 1901, pp. 228-300.**

CALVIN THOMAS   (essay date 1909)

[*Thomas describes the aspects of* The Messiah *that make it "an intolerable monotony."*]

To-day it is almost impossible to read [the *Messiah*] at all as a whole. There are noble passages that fascinate in their own way—not at all the way of Virgil or Milton—but they are not numerous enough to sustain one through the twenty thousand lines of a narrative which in the main lacks objective human interest. Klopstock's hero is not the Jesus of the synoptic gospels, but the Messiah of theological tradition—a conception with which poets have always found it difficult to operate. The attempt to blend the anthropomorphism of the primitive church with metaphysic and spiritual religion results in baffling the reason without satisfying the imagination. Klopstock's vague and vasty heaven is quite unthinkable, while his angels and seraphs and thrones and choiring cherubim, who have nothing to do but express ecstatic emotions, soon become wearisome. The devils in hell are somewhat more interesting, but they, too, are only conduits of emotion, for one knows that their rage against Omnipotence is foredoomed to futility. As for the legion of human or quasi-human beings that are introduced, they feel intensely and express themselves in noble language, but they are mere voices; they have no individuality, they do nothing of importance, and their feelings reduce to a few simple types. The consequence is an intolerable monotony. Withal the *Messiah* is very prolix. The narrative begins just before the arrest and betrayal of Jesus, and ends with the ascension. The crucifixion is over in the tenth canto. Such a scheme involved the overloading of the poem with a great mass of details which are not vitally related to the main argument, and tend rather to obscure and confuse it. The simple pathos of the laconic gospel story makes a much more powerful appeal to the devout imagination. (pp. 210-11)

> Calvin Thomas, "Klopstock and Wieland," in his A History of German Literature, *1909. Reprint by Kennikat Press, 1970, pp. 206-25.**

A. CLOSS   (essay date 1938)

[*In this excerpt from* The Genius of the German Lyric: An Historical Survey of Its Formal and Metaphysical Values, *Closs discusses Klopstock's contributions to German lyric poetry. He, like many others, contends that although Klopstock was not the first German poet to compose lyric poetry, utilize classical meters, or write in free verse, he was the first to succeed in these areas. For the emotionalism of his verse, Closs considers Klopstock "first and foremost the prophet of the irrational and the emotional language of the heart" and terms him a precursor of the* Sturm and Drang *and the naturalistic movements.*]

[It] is wrong to suppose that Klopstock was the first to introduce a passionately lyric note and a lofty religious attitude towards nature into German poetry. But in one sense Klopstock may certainly be considered the victorious champion of a new epoch. He is the spiritual descendant of Pindar, the poet of the sublime style, and as such he foreshadows Hölderlin and Stefan George. Until Klopstock's day the New High German poet had enjoyed neither rank nor dignity, and could practise his art only as a side-line. The poet who was not blessed with worldly possessions suffered utter destitution. But Klopstock in all the proud surety of his genius held his own against the ruling forces of society. Never since the days of Wolfram von Eschenbach and Walther von der Vogelweide had a German poet (with the exception of Christian Günther) felt so strongly the ennobling glory of creative power. Never before, not even at the time of the minnesong, had a member of bourgeois society felt his poetic talent as a divine mission. Never before had a sublime subject like the '*Messias*' been treated with such poetic fire. Even seen against the horizon of the future, Klopstock's fame remains inviolable, though his epic is to the modern generation little more than a landmark in literary history. Nevertheless, with his birth the hour of Germany's entry into literary glory had struck. Klopstock freed poetry from the straitjacket of convention, from the limitations of the accidental, and endowed it with the sincerity of profound personal experience. (pp. 212-13)

The author of the '*Messias*' and the so-called *enthusiastic odes* was the first to give German poetry, which had already attained a certain freedom from the emotional point of view, true grandeur and power. His poetry was passionately religious. The eruptive force of its emotion was bound to have a violent effect on the reader. Klopstock became the prophet of the divinely fervent heart.

The verse-form he chose was essentially German in its tense vitality which followed the bounding curve of Klopstock's fervour in phrases now long, now short, now wide, now narrow. Even the hexameter takes on a German guise, as Klopstock explains in his fragment, '*Über Sprache und Dichtkunst.*' His hexameter has often something rugged and sharp, the sublime standing in immediate juxtaposition to the sweetly gentle. This type of metre thus appears by no means alien to the German genius. Many a poet had tried his hand at it already at the close of the Middle Ages, particularly, however, in the sixteenth (Fischart) and in the seventeenth centuries. The results had, however, sounded so unnatural that Schottelius and others opposed such experiments. Gottsched once more took up the dactylic six-beat metre. Thus Klopstock cannot be said to have inaugurated the adoption of the antique heroic verse, but he was the first to reconcile it with the spirit of the German language. But for him Goethe's '*Hermann und Dorothea*,' '*Reinecke Fuchs*,' or Schiller's six-foot dactyls, or ultimately Platen's verse, could never have been composed. . . . Klopstock's German hexameter is not based on quantitative metre, but adapts itself to the nature of German verse, and thus at times completely ignores the difference between dactylic and free rhythm. As the founder of German free verse Klopstock soon won many an imitator. . . . (pp. 213-14)

[Klopstock] was not exactly the originator of German free verse, but he was the first true genius to adopt the form. In contrast to Lange, Klopstock favours the falling rhythm; he uses enjambement, and thus is not so much influenced by classic literature but gathers inspiration rather from the Psalms. His ambition was to become not a German Horace, but a German David. Herein he far excels Pyra, though he did not, like Herder, possess a historic attitude towards literature. He thus failed to realize immediately the fruitlessness of such imitations, which could have no other advantage than that of providing a means of developing originality of style. The perfection of the natural German idiom was not achieved till Goethe, and his immediate source was not Klopstock but Herder, who recommended him Klopstock's free verse as a model. (p. 215)

We should already at this juncture point to an essential difference between Goethe and Klopstock, namely the former's emotional language and the latter's imagination. Klopstock's frequent conditional phrases and phantastic imagery afford a pronounced antithesis to the work of Goethe whose '*Künstlers Morgenlied*' must rank as an exception amongst his works. Whereas Goethe strives towards greater reality Klopstock forsakes the earth for the realm of the abstract. His is the language of profound religious emotion uttered in praise of God. Even in moments of bounding earthly vitality, as in his poem on skating ('*Eislauf*') he touches the sublime. He cares little for colour and palpable illusion and seeks to render the ecstasy of the soul. His passion for the mysteries of the spirit also provides the keynote of the '*Messias*,' lending it as we must admit something of monotony.

It is customary but hardly accurate to think that the '*Messias*' had an *immediate* effect on German literature. Only Klopstock's nearest friends and above all the poets of the *Bremer Beiträge*, in which the first three cantos appeared in 1748, realized that the sublime spirit of this poetry heralded a new springtide for German literature. . . . Yet at the time of his death Klopstock's fame was already a thing of the past. (pp. 216-17)

Klopstock suffered the tragedy of surviving his own downfall. He had remained to the last the "immortal German youth." Even his work underwent no momentous change in the course of his life. The frequent obscurity of his idiom was certainly a stumbling-block to popularity, for few could follow him in his ecstatic flights. It was his yearning, as we read in the *'Zürchersee'* ode, to conceive the Creation anew. The world was to him the revelation of the Almighty in its heroic as in its pettiest aspects. Even the glow-worm (cf. the *'Frühlings-feier'*) is no less than the planets, the work of God. He sees everything through the light of salvation, and the vagueness of his images is not born of poetic inability but of his own irrational nature; and he does not, in the manner of Brockes, allow theological proofs of divinity to intrude into his descriptions of nature. In spite of this characteristic trait, many a critic (even to some extent Paustian) numbers Klopstock among the enlightened poets.... Above all in the *'Gelehrtenrepublik'* we may admit the influence of enlightenment which had reached Germany from England by way of France ... and Lord Bolingbroke.... (pp. 217-18)

To us Klopstock, for all his emotional poetic constructions, is first and foremost the prophet of the irrational and the emotional language of the heart. Thus he has the elemental force of the *Stürmer und Dränger,* particularly in his odes. The lack of any really worthy selection of the odes and hymns may in some measure be responsible for the fact that Klopstock's mighty rhythms seem to attract so few readers today.

Heavenly and profane elements intermingle in his works. The boldness of his images, his words and syntax in which terseness alternates with lengthy cadences reveal his irrational concepts. God, freedom, the fatherland, friendship, his love for his cousin Fanny and for Meta ..., of whom death robbed him so soon, prove the varying burden of his lofty song. Klopstock frequently indulges in eulogies on his friends in his poems. Many of them ... died before him. He even sings the praise of his favourite sport, skating. Klopstock betrays a decided partiality for noble thoughts which find utterance already in his early ode *'Die Stunden der Weihe,'* a characteristic example of Klopstock's love of conciseness and pathos—an antithesis resulting here in a lack of formal unity. The opening lines of the ode are charged with a dynamic rhythm, but its keynote of holy solemnity appears sadly incompatible with the almost frivolous end, which is suggested by an accidental personal experience and is not worked out to form an organic part of the poem.

Nature became a ruling passion in Klopstock's life. He transfuses it with his burning zest for love, fame, friendship, though its outlines remain vague. External action only appears in transient, intangible images, as though magically suspended between the landscape and the poet's emotion. In his best passages the poet avoids mere description no less than abstract analysis of emotion.... (pp. 218-19)

The fatherland and heroism also play an important part in Klopstock's odes. Nevertheless, for all his praise of the great Prussian king [Frederick the Great], he could not forgive the latter's scorn of the German muse. The dream of liberty kindled a transient enthusiasm for France in Klopstock's heart until the horrors of the revolution brought bitter disillusionment. He dedicated his song to the fatherland, the great age of the Staufen, the fiery spirit of Arminius and the simple German maiden.... (p. 220)

Just at Opitz's star had once shed its light over the whole German realm, so Klopstock's earlier works exerted direct and indirect influence on his contemporaries, and if only for a short period, at any rate decisively. We need not emphasize here that not only the correct Ramler but even Herder and Goethe were acutely aware of the baroque flavour of Klopstock's free rhythms.... Klopstock also influenced the church hymnal; though the latter could never have become his true province, for his vital genius urged him to a personal emotional form of expression which was to find its consummation in Goethe.... Klopstock may in a certain sense, namely in regard to his metric idiom and his innovations in prosody, be called a forerunner of naturalism. In opposition to Opitz he championed the cause of natural German verse, and in his fragment *'Über Sprache und Dichtkunst'* laid the foundations of modern prosody, thereby actually striving towards the goal which the naturalistic movement before the Great War radically demanded both in poetry and theory, upholding that content and formal expression should be inseparable and that the verbal medium should reduce the boundary between object and word to a minimum. Klopstock did not yet draw such extreme conclusions from similar ideas, but in the last pages of the abovementioned treatise he clearly states that vital expression must on the whole fit the content. (p. 222)

The title page of the first separately published edition of cantos one through three of The Messiah. *The Granger Collection, New York.*

A. Closs, ''Klopstock,'' in his The Genius of the German Lyric: An Historic Survey of Its Formal and Metaphysical Values, *George Allen & Unwin Ltd, 1938, pp. 212-22.**

WALTER SILZ (essay date 1952)

[*Silz assesses Klopstock's various contributions to German literature and discusses him as a precursor of both the* Sturm und Drang *and Romantic movements.*]

[It] was Klopstock's special tragedy to have attained fame too early, and in the wrong genre. For he was no epic poet, any more than he was a dramatic one. Before he had left school, before he had discovered his real forte as a lyric poet, he committed himself to a life-program, burdened himself with a vast epic enterprise to which he was to cling, composing and revising, for virtually the rest of his many days: an edifice of eighteen and one-half thousand verses (as long as the *Iliad* and *Odyssey* together), a monument of admirable but misdirected devotion. He would have done better to leave the *Messias* a torso, or cast it into religious odes, which is what its grandest parts really are. He himself called it ''eine lyrische Erzählung''—which is half right, at least. (pp. 745-46)

We can see now, much more clearly than could Klopstock's time, what an unhappy error was his adoption of the so-called Germanic-Nordic mythology. What should have popularized his poetry, an indigenous ''Göttersage,'' made it more bookish instead, for the northern deities and heroes were much less definite and colorful concepts to the German mind of the eighteenth century than the ''foreign'' ones of Greece and Rome, and he had to resort to footnotes to explain Gna, Tialf, and Braga to the amazed reader. His innovation pointed new paths for German writers adventuring into Germanic origins and ''Volksdichtung'' and ''Sprachforschung''—all of which flowered abundantly in the Romantic period a generation or more later—but it would have been better for Klopstock's poetry if the order of things had been reversed and he had benefited by the scholarship he stimulated. He was especially wrong when he undertook to cast his misty notions of Germanic antiquity into dramatic form—he, the most undramatic of great German authors! This double error even the noble passages in his ''Bardiete'' could not go far to redeem. (p. 746)

But, granted these monumental aberrations—to which we can add that bizarre brainchild the *Gelehrtenrepublik*—what monumental achievements! Achievements that are so essential and fundamental to the structure of modern German poetry that we no longer think of them as the comparatively recent contributions of one man. Klopstock is the first German poet in whom life and poetry are deeply one, whose poetry is the expression of personal experience, feeling, and conviction. . . . One needs only to compare Klopstock's work with that of the nine rimesters whom he celebrates with uncritical friendship in *Wingolf,* all of them—and one could add Brockes and Hagedorn, Pyra and Lange, and many others—all of them highly esteemed as ''Dichter'' in their time, to measure the eminence of the new ideal of poet and poetry that came in with Klopstock. He demonstrated the essential importance of genius and inspiration as the source of great literature. The poet is no longer a scholar, or a cunning craftsman fabricating according to rules in which he is adept; he is the mouthpiece of an inner necessity and an inner voice, even the voice of God. He is a figure of great dignity, a seer, a *vates,* a symbol of national culture.

With Klopstock, modern German literature comes of age. In him Germany has, for the first time since Luther, a native-grown writer whom she can set beside the great of other European countries, no longer their echo but their peer. He is the first ''professional'' among German poets, the first who was purely a poet and nothing else. The poet's calling was for him a lifework, indeed a religious mission. He never took office, he never let anything interfere with his literary activity. He accepted revenues from a Danish king and a German margrave, but he dealt with them and with other crowned heads of Europe as their equal, even—in the case of Frederick of Prussia and the anti-revolutionary coalition—as their moral superior, appointed to show them the error of their ways. The attitude of ''Dichterstolz vor Königsthronen'' which we see later in Schiller, in Schubart and Voss, in Goethe, and in Richard Wagner, owes much to Klopstock.

Together with Luther and Goethe, Klopstock stands as one of the three great masters and shapers of the German language, exemplifying, like them, the power of the living speech as against the contrived diction of books and rules. He conceived of language as not merely conceptual and designatory, but symbolical and evocative. He rejuvenated in particular the language of poetry, giving it a new solemnity and tenderness, tuning withal the instrument from which Goethe and the Romantic lyricists were to call forth even grander and sweeter strains.

Klopstock was the first who felt, and at his best productively embodied the feeling, that the verbal and verse form of a poem is not a prefabricated shell imposed from without and interchangeable, but organically one with the ''content.'' . . . The expression of a thought or feeling, he once wrote, is like the shadow that moves with the tree. This view has been, since Goethe's time, so natural to us that we fail to remember that before Klopstock, in fact since Opitz, a radically different view of form had prevailed. So it is with rime. If we put ourselves at the point of view of, say, 1748, before Goethe was born, and consider what rime meant in the hands of the ''poets'' then reigning, we can understand Klopstock's disdain for its external jingle and his, on the whole regrettable, decision to abjure it, a decision strengthened, of course, by his ill-starred addiction to Teutonic antiquities. But the music which rime attained in the hands of Goethe and the Romanticists would in turn have been impossible without Klopstock's preparatory work in the German poetic language.

Klopstock first successfully championed—most clearly in his ''freie Rhythmen''—the validity of ''Rhythmik'' over ''Metrik.'' In place of syllable-counting metrics, he is guided, in his best poems, by his fine musical sense of the rhythm inherent in his matter and vibrating in his own soul. Here verse-form for the first time appears as cognate and coterminous with content.

Klopstock's influence is writ large on the German poets who succeeded him. . . . The poets of the Göttingen ''Hain'' stood closest to the master, linked even closer through the person of Fritz von Stolberg, his ''poetical son.'' In their ''Bardentum,'' their contempt for Wieland and the French, their patriotic ardor and ''Tyrannenhaβ''—both rather vague and rhetorical—their fervid cult of friendship, they were true liegemen of Klopstock. They constituted what one may call the lyrical wing of the ''Sturm und Drang,'' and Klopstock was, in a larger sense, the ideological father of that movement. (pp. 746-49)

Klopstock was the first German poet since Ulrich von Hutten to think of his ''country'' not as a particular small state or section or mere town, but as a unity of all German, in fact all Germanic, stocks. And, in turn, Klopstock is the first German poet whom we think of as simply German, not the representative of a particular locality.

His notions of Germanic antiquity were unscientific and mistaken, yet they were productive of genuine national feeling and national pride in the generation that followed him.... Klopstock's Germany, ancient and present, was a creation of pure idealism: he postulated a nation where there was none, and he wrote inspiring patriotic songs to it, which echo in Stolberg and Hölderlin and Kleist and Arndt and the poets of the "Freiheitskriege," as his ideas about the German language echo in Fichte's *Reden an die deutsche Nation.* If Freiherr vom Stein was justified in saying that the fire which consumed Napoleon was kindled at Heidelberg, one should remember that the Romantic glorification of the native past was but a fuller and better-equipped exploration of a region into which Klopstock had cut the first path.

Because of the patriotic naïvetés of his "Bardiete" and *Gelehrtenrepublik,* Klopstock has by some been regarded as a "nationalist" and tarred with the same clumsy brush as Herder. Both, to be sure, wrote things that a later, militant nationalism could readily exploit, and certain passages in the Hermann-dramas cannot be dismissed simply with a smile at their childishness. But there is a considerable, if commonly overlooked, difference between "Nationalgefühl" and "Nationalismus," and Klopstock, on the whole, represents only the former—at times, indeed, with a naïve insularity that is as akin to the British as is his Nether-Saxon race, but never with the remotest thought of military aggression. Though he admitted the necessity of wars of national self-preservation, and glorified that of his ancient forebears against the Romans; though he applauded wars for freedom like the American and French Revolutions, he was passionately opposed to all wars of conquest and his hatred of them is voiced, even intemperately at times, in many of his odes. (pp. 752-53)

That the charge of "nationalism," ... so little founded in the case of Klopstock, should also have been brought—usually with no greater perspicacity—against German Romanticism, is at least a superficial indication of the deeper kinship of the two. Klopstock in truth deserves to be ranked with Herder as a spiritual forebear of Romanticism. To be sure, neither was fitly acknowledged by his offspring.... Klopstock's is a basically Romantic mind: idealistic, imaginative, lyrical in its apperception and utterance. What some interpreters have termed "Barock" in Klopstock, his spacious imagination, his "Raumphantasie," is really an anticipation of the Romantic "Unendlichkeitsgefühl." Out of this sense of immeasurable Infinity, which never ceased to thrill him, Klopstock created the language of sublimity, with its great words ... , with its imagery of stars and interstellar distances that Hölderlin and Novalis were to use after him.

The antithesis between Man's insignificance before the divine Infinite and his indestructible value as a particle of the Infinite, is basic in Klopstock's thought and poetry; it is likewise basic in the Romantic "Lebensgefühl" and Romantic religiousness, for instance in Novalis and Schleiermacher. The Klopstockian antinomy of Man's glory and misery is of the essence of Romanticism.... The Romantic "Andacht zum Kleinen" is found already in Klopstock. For him, too, the flower in the crannied wall is a symbol of the Infinite.... In *Die Frühlingsfeier* ... the earth is conceived as but a "Tropfen am Eimer" of endless

Creation, yet on it in turn the tiniest of creatures, a "Frühlingswürmchen," may be a vessel of Immortality.

In his aversion to the ties of office, his desire to live for poetry alone, Klopstock is at variance with the usage of poets of his time and anticipates the "Amtsscheu" of the Romanticists. In his conviction of the inadequacy of words, in his instinctive reaching toward music to enlarge the range of utterance, he anticipates Hölderlin and Kleist and the Romantic lyricists. (pp. 755-57)

Klopstock oscillates between past and future. His heart even goes out to *future* friends, to a *future* beloved (in the fourth Song of *Wingolf;* in *Die künftiege Geliebte....* On the other hand, *Kaiser Heinrich* ... is a precursor of Romantic enthusiasm for the "Mittelalter," Romantic "Wehmut" over its lost treasures of native song, Romantic admiration of its brilliant Hohenstaufen dynasty. If Heine was right in seeing the heart and soul of German Romanticism in its medievalism, then Klopstock is, here at least, one of its progenitors.

One can single out other poems of his that are full of Romantic qualities, for example *Die frühen Gräber* ... , with its "Stimmung" of moonlit summer night and wistful retrospect, especially upon irretrievable youth; or *Die Sommernacht* ... , with a similar setting and mood, a blossoming linden, and sensuous appeal. Klopstock, like Hölderlin, lived always with an awareness of his past. The sense of spiritual continuities that adds pathos and depth to many a Romantic poem is found in various odes of Klopstock's, for instance, *Weihtrunk an die toten Freunde....* (pp. 757-58)

The deepest vista of Romantic retrospect is opened by death, and this rich and exalting theme is shared by Klopstock and his Romantic successors. It is found in dozens of his poems, and of course it occurs abundantly in the *Messias....* He did not, to be sure, court death, and the thought of suicide would have been repugnant to his orthodox conscience. Indeed, his consistently Christian attitude toward death, like that of a number of Romanticists, robbed it of its most tragic possibilities as a poetic theme; but the thought of it always served to open the floodgates of his feeling and imagination; it was a threshold from which his spirit soared into the empyrean spaces of that "Jenseits" to which the German Romanticists, first and last, were irresistibly drawn.

For Klopstock, however, as for Novalis, "Jenseitigkeit" is by no means "Weltverneinung": it does not exclude love of life and of mankind. The yearning for release into Infinity is balanced by an attachment to "motherly" Earth that is movingly voiced in more than one passage of the *Messias.* Klopstock, like Novalis, is a citizen of two worlds, an earthly and a heavenly fatherland (*Mein Vaterland* ...). Each tendency is strengthened by the "rebound" from the other; it is like the swing of a pendulum, or the interaction of opposite poles. In fact, this interplay of antitheses, this polarity, is so frequent in Klopstock's poetry that one is tempted to see in it the basic law or rhythm of his thought and personality. He is continually swinging: from present to past, from present to future, from the primal Eden to the final paradise, from dejection at the thought of death to exultation at the thought of immortality. In his happiest hours he thinks of death, amid jollity with present friends he invokes distant or deceased ones, in the moment of bereavement he visions the moment of reunion in Heaven. In his youth he sings of a future love (*Die künftige Geliebte* ...), in his old age he recalls a childhood love (*Aus der Vorzeit* ...), and he is even ready, like Novalis, to fuse a dead and a living love (*An Done* . . .). He generates his lyrical energy, as it were, by setting up opposite poles—Man and God, Soul and Body, Time and Eternity, reality and dream, the solar system and the caterpillar—within a single poem. It is not surprising, in view of these prodigious "Spannungen," that Klopstock has been more than once claimed for the Barock.

For him, life would be insignificant without the thought of death, and death unbearable without the assurance of resurrection, of life renewed; each is a foil to the other and lends it lustre. One of his favorite antitheses is that between the mouldering body and the immortal soul, . . . as in *Weihtrunk an die toten Freunde* . . ., where joyful conviviality contrasts with remembrance of departed friends. One of his favorite metaphors for man's mortality is the Biblical "Staub," and this contrasts sharply with God's glory as revealed by the starry heavens. . . . (pp. 758-59)

In *Die Königin Luise* . . . there is a monumental confrontation of earthly death (in realistic detail) with heavenly transfiguration. In *Dem Erlöser* . . . jubilation over the Creation contrasts with longing for death and resurrection. . . . Christ himself, celebrated in this ode, personifies the polarity of divine and human, infinite and finite, immortality and mortality, which never failed to fascinate Klopstock's imagination. That the Infinite deigned to take on finite form, the Divine to become human, the Deathless to submit to death, is for Klopstock the supreme wonder, and in the *Messias* too the central glory. The structure of the whole epic is fundamentally antithetical: two great principles, Good and Evil, God and Satan, are pitted against each other, and the action (more spiritual than real) surges forever upward and downward, from Earth to Heaven, from Heaven to Hell, in ample oscillations.

In contrast to Goethe and the younger generation (Sturm und Drang as well as Romantic), Klopstock did not as yet draw from the deep well of German folksong. But he knew the pathos of one of its favorite themes: separation. For him, however, separation is always balanced by reunion. A love frustrated on earth is realized in Heaven [*An Gott* and *An Fanny*]. . . . The tragedy of "Trennung" as a general human lot is lost in the rapture of "Wiedersehen" with a cherished friend (*An Giseke* . . .).

In the presence of his comrades, Klopstock thinks of their absence or death; when they are distant, they become vividly present to him. His supreme expressions of love are called forth by a sense of the unattainableness or loss of the beloved [*An Fanny* and *Der Abschied*]. . . . This too, perhaps, may be claimed as a Romantic trait in Klopstock. . . . Klopstock's art seemed to require, like the Romantic, a certain distancing from actuality.

The little ode *Weihtrunk an die toten Freunde* . . . illustrates his tendency and need to set up an opposite pole: the past against the present, the dead against the living, corruptible flesh against imperishable soul. At the time he wrote this poem he was barely twenty-seven, and had not yet lost any of the friends whose spirits he summons with such stately solemnity; but he instinctively " posits" them as dead, in order to express his love for them, in order to gain scope for his lyric emotion. Even three years earlier, in *An Ebert* . . ., he wrings real pathos from the mere *thought* that he and Ebert might live to be the last survivors of their little band; he even invents a woman who in the future will have loved him, and died. Almost a half-century later, *Die Erinnerung* . . . still shows the same basic "pattern"—now, of course, justified by the years: the

poet knows no reason for sadness, "dennoch" his soul is solemn, lovely breezes blow, flowers and trees still flourish in summer lushness, "aber" his soul is solemn; memory compels him to think of graves and hail departed friends.

At the end of the *Wingolf*-cycle . . ., Klopstock visions the poets of remote antiquity and those of the remote future; the present is for him a transient moment between that which was and that which is to be. In *An Bodmer* . . . he laments not meeting kindred souls of the past, nor the most kindred spirit of future time when he, the author, will be long dead. Thus Klopstock's thought flies backward and forward, from the first of all created men to the last whom Resurrection's trumpet shall transform (*Dem Allgegenwärtigen* . . .). In *Das Gegenwärtige* . . . he confesses that in his youth he lived forwards toward the future, in old age backwards toward the past, though he has always admonished himself to live in the present. . . . The very verbs in this poem . . ., in contradiction to its title, are in the past or future tense, and even the few present-tense ones deal with hope or remembrance and in effect still further attenuate "das Gegenwärtige." Thus Klopstock's mind habitually o'ervaults the present and many of his odes are really dream-visions or elegies. This is the habit of the Romantic mind in all ages, the source of its biologic weakness and of its poetic splendor.

Some of Klopstock's most famous poems can be almost "graphed" to show this dominant pattern of polarity. At the beginning of *Der Zürchersee* . . ., the poet first records—in just one line and a half—the beauty of the external scene; then he turns inward to the spiritual world as he sees the "great idea" of Creation reflected in a human face. Thus he erects at once the two poles between which the rest of the poem is suspended: the world of Nature and the world of the Soul. To use a somewhat irreverent figure, Klopstock is like a tightrope-walker, who cannot perform until he has found an anchorage for the other end of his rope. Or, to speak more poetically, he is like Antaeus or Euphorion, deriving strength from the rebound between earth and air. The entire ode is ribbed with antitheses: Nature is fair, but fairer is a happy human rejoicing in God. Sweet is the spring, winsome is wine, mighty the lure of deathless fame—but sweeter is friendship, which makes (another antithesis) this life worthy of Eternity. At the end of the poem, in the midst of admiring friends, on perhaps the merriest day of his life, Klopstock invokes the distant and the dead, and with characteristic flight from the present, looks toward an imaginary Elysian future for the realization of ideal Friendship—even the syntax here is, fitly, the "future subjunctive."

The relation of thought and feeling in this ode exemplifies the essential polarity of Klopstock's mind. For these two are not bare antitheses, but joined as poles; not excluding, but conditioning each other, productive opposites: feeling stimulates reflection, "grosse Gedanken" call forth emotional responses. The re-thinking of God's "great thought" of Creation brings radiant joy to a human face . . ., and this in turn will doubtless engender other great thoughts. The case of Klopstock reminds us that thought and feeling are not so distinct as we ordinarily assume. (pp. 759-62)

[A] dualistic "Lebensgefühl," which in a complex and dramatic nature like Kleist's becomes tragic, and in a philosophical mind like Hebbel's grows into a system of "Pantragismus," remains in Klopstock's simple and faith-full Christian soul untragic—pathetic at most, and above all, productive of that emotional-intellectual tension which he requires for lyric utterance.

While the learned but unpoetic critics of Leipzig and Zürich were still arguing, in the 1740's, over the theoretical ingredients of poetry, a new type of poet had entered the lists: no longer an "imitator" of Nature, a cataloguer of its features, like Brockes or Haller, but one who swings to a personal rhythm, who sings the inner music of his soul in language that seeks not to designate merely, but to weave a musical spell, evoking in the listener a kindred emotion. . . . (p. 763)

I say "listener," not "reader," designedly, for Klopstock's best poetry is eminently a matter not for the eye but for the ear, not of the printed page but of ever-new rendition. He doubtless had his own verse in mind when, in various epigrams, he stated his belief that poetry should not be merely seen, but should be heard. To *read* a poem without speaking it is like looking at a painting through a veil. . . . Klopstock's orthography and punctuation were determined by considerations of oral delivery; he even marked "longs" and "shorts" in the print of a number of his poems. Some things, like his hymns and psalms, he wrote directly for choral singing; many others, like *Morgengesang am Schöpfungsfeste* . . . with its duets and choruses, are musical in structure and call for musical setting; others, again, seem to demand something between reading aloud and singing.

Klopstock, in other words, as Schiller already discerned [see excerpt dated 1795-96], is a musical poet, and it is not without importance that he lived in a period when German music was reaching the heights of its development. It has become almost a truism that his *Messias* should not be measured as an epic against Homer, but compared with the great Biblical oratorios of Händel and Bach. Schiller noted its deficiency in "für die Anschauung bestimmte Formen" and in general Klopstock's tendency to divest things of their body in order to make them spirit. . . . The incorporeality of Klopstock's poetry—which is not so complete as Schiller's often-echoed remark implies—is due to its inherently musical nature. It is far less concerned with body in the static, plastic sense than with body as movement, rhythm, evocative symbol. Klopstock is more intent on the conceptions and feelings which things arouse in him than on the things themselves. His attitude is idealistic, transcendental, like that of the Romanticists. . . . In his lyrical and musical temper, Klopstock is an older brother of the Romanticists. It is significant that he was greatly interested in Greek poetry, in its bodiless verbal music, while Greek (and Roman) sculpture meant nothing to him.

The celebrated *Zürchersee* ode of 1750 is a case in point. . . . [Very] little of the real situation went into the poem. By actual count only twelve of its seventy-six lines allude—in an oblique way—to reality. The rest is a soaring paean on Joy and Friendship, musical in its "inner form": in its generality, its modulation of mood, its emotional movement; and one could readily imagine it set to music or reproduced in music.

The *Frühlingsfeier* . . . is an even grander example of musical composition. Repetitions, echoings, solos and orchestral interweaving of notes and motifs, changes of key and tempo, Jehovah's crashing thunders answered by the jubilant trumpet-calls of the soul, trembling but triumphant, as it utters His holy name; the mighty crescendos, and the soft diminuendo of the close—all this is a brilliant demonstration of the musicalization of language. (pp. 763-65)

Dem Unendlichen . . . suggests the picture of the poet as conductor of a vast universal orchestra, calling on various solo instruments: the things of earth, like trees and streams; the things of cosmic space: constellations, suns of the Milky Way; and finally sweeping them all together to a thundering climax of choral voices in never-ending and never-sufficing praise of the Lord. . . . In such odes, we see Klopstock striving to express what had never before been expressed by mere language, giving to words, above and beyond their thought-conveying function, a new value as musical notes; we see him, at the utter boundaries of "Wortkunst," reaching over into the domain of "Tonkunst."

There is, one may say, a musical value in the device of invocation, . . . of which Klopstock was perhaps the greatest master, followed by Hölderlin and Mörike and others. The ode, Klopstock's chosen form, of course invites this usage, but it is characteristic of his "rhythm" that he chose the ode. The "O" and the exclamation-point are as typical features of his page as the comma is of Kleist's. Klopstock's invocations have a musical "aura"; they are like the sounding of a solemn note that reverberates with rich overtones; they, too, seem to give his language an extra "reach" into the ultra-verbal. Goethe, in *Werther,* gives an excellent example of the magic of invocation, when he has Lotte speak Klopstock's own name in a climactic situation where no amount of other words would have sufficed.

Klopstock is usually thought of as limited to "sublime" or "sentimental" themes. If people really *read* his poems, beyond the hackneyed few of the anthologies, they would find that he deals with a great variety of subjects: God, the fatherland, love, Nature, friendship, fame, and immortality; philosophy, language and the arts, and the practical techniques of prosody; virtue, honor, Nordic antiquities, physical culture, and domestic animals. He ranges in time from ancient Germany to European politics of the early nineteenth century. When he was sixty-five, he launched out with youthful zest into political poetry occasioned by the French Revolution. At seventy-five, he was still voicing his opinions on public events with an almost journalistic immediacy. From the lofty ethereality of his early odes, from the cosmic spaciousness of the *Messias*, he could descend to the homeliest concerns of daily life: the cleverness of his saddle-horse Iduna (*Unterricht,* and *Mehr Unterricht* . . .), or the threatened blindness of his little dog (*Der Schoßhund* . . .), or the thoughts of two glow-worms (*Zwei Johanneswürmchen* . . .). He could write not only solemn hymns but rollicking songs in praise of wine (*Der Kapwein und der Johannesberger* . . .). Nor should we forget his poems that celebrate skating, riding, swimming, and other delights of bodily exercise. Here, too, he was a pioneer, preparing the way for Goethe and Mörike. In his purposeful physical culture, Goethe was the faithful follower of Klopstock, who has been called Germany's earliest sportsman.

In *Die Rache* . . . , directed against the great Frederick, Klopstock shows himself a master of withering, contemptuous satire, and indeed there is much satire, of a fantastic sort, in the *Gelehrtenrepublik.* At seventy, Klopstock enters a new field, the satirical treatment of the ugly and revolting: *Die Mutter und die Tochter* . . . is a grim lullaby sung by the Paris Reign of Terror to her newly-born daughter, the Geneva régime. In *Die Vergeltung* . . . , the poet vies with Dante in grandiose and gloomy imagination. For the cruel Carrier of the Nantes "noyades" he invents in hell torments that outdo in diabolical finesse the atrocities of the living fiend. The cold epic objectivity of this ode is a noteworthy departure from his usual style. In the macabre *Das Grab* . . . , the poet, with the same eye that beholds Sirius' remote glitter and the "white path" of the Milky Way, discerns swarms of microscopic bees and birds, including a chorus of the minutest nightingales, which die by being inhaled by him. In this weird and dreamlike poem, Klopstock appears to discover new forms of life and of death.

In his very last ode, *Die höheren Stufen* . . . , his poetic imagination seems still to be seeking new horizons. One can picture him sitting in the winter twilight, gazing at Jupiter, low on the horizon, and thinking his favorite thought of an afterlife on another star. He dozes off briefly, in the manner of old age, and is translated in spirit to realms such as he has never seen nor conceived. Everything is different here, not merely an extension of terrestrial existence (as most imaginings of "life on Mars" and the like are). Time and space seem to have vanished; a new landscape, fair beyond anything on earth, opens before him as the clouds roll away. Fire wells down from the mountains, like auroral red, but it is a mild fire, in which the denizens of this world bathe to refresh themselves. These are living beings, but of extraordinary shape; in fact, they frequently change shape, becoming more beautiful with each transformation. Their bodies are like pleasant fragrances or haze, out of which a mild radiance is diffused. Sometimes, when they change shape, they mimic the blissful beauty of the landscape, or subside into the rivers of fire. These immortal beings communicate, it seems, not through speech but through such transformations, which permit them to express feelings more fully and intensely than language could. The old poet gazes long in wonderment upon them as they throng about him. Suddenly there is beside him a Spirit, arrayed in splendor, but of human form and speaking the human tongue, albeit with a music such as he has never before heard, saying: these thou seest are inhabitants of Jupiter, but three of them will soon depart for the Sun, rising, as all of us do, to ever higher, happier spheres. And even as he speaks, the poet sees the departing ones joyfully drifting off between Jupiter's circling moons; his interlocutor follows—"und ich / Sah erwachend den Abendstern." He is back again in his chair by the western window, contemplating wistfully that beloved evening star to which his spirit has gone and returned on the wings of his poetic imagination, still swift and strong. (pp. 765-68)

Walter Silz, "On Rereading Klopstock," in PMLA, *67, Vol. LXVII, No. 5, September, 1952, pp. 744-68.*

SVEN V. LANGSJOEN (essay date 1960)

[*Langsjoen discusses how Klopstock's moral intent informs the characterization and tone of* The Messiah.]

The absence of concrete outline and detail from [Klopstock's] works is so nearly absolute that one may read the entire *Messias* without being able to imagine the distinctive appearance of any of the countless characters.

A common but erroneous reaction is to conclude . . . that Klopstock was incapable of representing the visual. The absence of this or that from a poet's works can never prove an incapacity on the part of the poet. Patently unsuccessful attempts may justify such a conclusion; but Klopstock never attempts to satisfy the eye.

What we are faced, or not faced, with here is the result of conscious purpose. . . . But what is the basic reason underlying this intent? It is not . . . a desire to preserve the sanctity of the

Messias. . . . Rather, the basic reason lies in Klopstock's pronounced and ever abiding *moral* purposiveness, a phenomenon unrecognized by the majority of critics. . . . Further, the oversight is not confined to Klopstock's works; it extends to eighteenth century German Sentimental literature in general. Apparently endorsing a far too rigid conception of the "feeling-reason" dichotomy applied to outstanding features of Sentimental and Rationalistic literature respectively, most scholars fail to see the moral purpose permeating the former. (p. 159)

Klopstock's "intentional intangibility" [a term used by Albert Köster in his *Die deutsche Literatur der Aufklärungszeit*] is seen to be a manifestation of his desire to present in unobscured form his Sentimental ethos—which derives its essence from the conscious association of virtue and vice with feelings. In other words, the absence of concrete outline and detail can be attributed to the exclusive nature of his moral purposiveness.

Dualistic in structure, Klopstock's ethical thinking . . . considers virtue to consist basically in spiritual love and all related tender emotions: friendship (identical to spiritual love), sympathy, melancholy longing, loneliness, elegiac distress, loving anticipation, and reminiscent nostalgia. If Klopstock had formulated his conception of virtue as explicitly as the young Lessing . . . , he might well have said: the best human being is the one with the greatest capacity for love and all tender affections emanating from a heart filled with love, the difference being that love is the central emotion in Klopstock's conception of virtue whereas sympathy constitutes the root of all virtue for the young Lessing. On the other hand, Klopstock consciously associates evil with the so-called violent emotions . . . of hate, jealousy, wrath, vengeance, greed, and the concomitant absence of their counterparts in virtue.

It is true that one does not encounter a direct expression of this dualism in Klopstock's subjective odes. With extremely few exceptions, they quite naturally dwell upon the good, the virtuous emotions. His moralistic intent, however, is clearly evident in his exaltation of love-friendship and in the very texture of his hymnic praise, which parades in unweakening review the German equivalents of love, friendship, loneliness, longing, melancholy, sympathy; all of these and related words are able to serve as the highest epithets of praise; because all of them attest to a heart with a capacity for love.

In the *Messias* (also in the Biblical dramas), on the other hand, the dualistic, black-white scheme of Klopstock's ethical disposition is clearly manifested through the juxtaposed characterization of Satanic forces and those which reflect the features of the "noble few." (p. 160)

To turn to a related phenomenon, Klopstock's works as a body are further characterized by the virtually complete exclusion of problematics. The few exceptions one might wish to cite are either unreal or minor in the sense that they do not assume a central position in the works concerned. (p. 161)

Since the concept of love is central in Klopstock's thinking, one might expect to find some variation of the potential spiritual versus sensual love problem. But Klopstock does not reward such a quest either. As a person, he did not share the Pietists' derogatory view of sensual love; he experienced no tension between Eros and Agape. And his essential poetic nature precluded the literary representation of even this problem. . . . For Klopstock was an *Erlebnisdichter* at least to the extent that he could not write what he did not feel; least of all could he proceed from an abstract idea with no deep roots in his own experience.

Klopstock's great *Erlebnis* was rethinking the great thought of creation: love. . . . He was always guided by his experience that love is the essence of the Godhead, that love is the spring of all virtue; and this combined with a second constant, the moral purposiveness of his poetic mission, to form the immovable foundation of his Sentimental orientation. (pp. 161-62)

Sven V. Langsjoen, "Moral Purpose in Klopstock,"
in Monatshefte, *Vol. LII, No. 4, April-May, 1960,*
pp. 158-62.

ALAN MENHENNET (essay date 1973)

[*In this excerpt from his socio-literary study of eighteenth-century German literature, Menhennet focuses on the balance between thought and feeling in Klopstock's verse. For further commentary by Menhennet, see Additional Bibliography.*]

It took a man of very considerable sensitivity and creative poetic ability to realize the positive contribution which, for all its limitations, Sentimentalism was capable of making, especially to poetry. The only writer of such calibre to appear was Klopstock.

We shall find in Klopstock the balance of two sides [evident] . . . in Gellert, Sophie von Laroche and others, but with a relatively strong bias towards freedom. Feeling . . . meets thought on more or less equal terms: at times, indeed, it can be described as 'victorious'. . . . But it is never uncontrolled. Certainly, it does not usurp the role of thought; rather, in the highest (i.e. religious) forms of thinking, it becomes the crown of the whole process. It must be made clear that in all things, the religious plane took precedence for Klopstock, and was always the ultimate goal of his thought and effort. The highest level of literary activity demanded a specially exalted quality of feeling and language. The poet must dedicate all his faculties to it, and the intellectual ones have their part to play. But without feeling, nothing can be achieved. He has to feel himself into the proper state of mind before he can have thoughts of God. Klopstock's first wife, Meta, describes him at work on his *Messias*: 'with the most nobly dignified . . . expression of devotion, pale with emotion and with tears in his eyes.'' The intellect alone cannot give man the knowledge he needs in this sphere. (pp. 108-09)

[The poem **'Die tote Clarissa'**] might appear at first glance to be all mood and feeling. It is indeed a very delicately felt piece and a fine example of Klopstock's earlier lyric manner, yet there is a perceptible intellectual strand in it, not only in the carefully worked-out metaphor of the flower cut off by the storm—a favourite of Klopstock's—but also in smaller details which have their origin in 'wit', for example the idea that those left behind will still admire the beautiful girl, 'but through our tears' or that, with the cypress-branches which Cidli has gathered, the poet will weave 'wreaths of the leaves of mourning' ('des Trauerlaubes Kränz': stanza eight). This blend of intellect and emotion recalls the way in which, in **'Die frühen Gräber'**, the moon functions at the same time as a creator of atmosphere, and as a stimulant to thought (as a 'Gedankenfreund'). The feeling is the stronger element, but it is coloured, and to some extent controlled, by thought. The poem aims to 'set the soul in motion', but assuredly not to free it from all rational controls. (pp. 109-10)

Klopstock's emotionalism is never free from rational consciousness and control. One of the most deliberately and intensively 'sentimental' episodes in Klopstock's whole *oeuvre*, that concerning the tender, yet hopeless love between Cidli and Semida, the 'youth of Nain' in Canto Four of *Der Messias*, is presented with analytical self-consciousness, even a certain pious *galanterie*. . . . The poet, as it were, feels his *thoughts about* feeling. The effect is considerably more emotive than any to be found in other 'Aufklärer': Klopstock has greater poetic power, of course; he can find more effective combinations of words and handle the hexameter with a sureness and flexibility unparalleled in German poetry before Goethe. But in view of the degree of calculation in [his] presentation of his young lover one cannot say that he looks likely to break the moulds of order and set passion truly free. (pp. 110-11)

It was probably as a poet of the cosmic and spectacular that Klopstock had most appeal for the 'Stürmer und Dränger'. Here, the thrill of freedom, of one's own independent strength and vigour, could most easily be felt. It is a thunderstorm and its aftermath, we remember, which calls Klopstock to mind in Goethe's *Werther*, the exact reference being to the fine hymn **'Die Frühlingsfeier'**. Greatness—especially the greatness of God—was not in itself an uncongenial theme of the 'Aufklärer'. But there is a limit beyond which he will not allow himself to be overwhelmed and beyond which he must not overwhelm his readers if the rational taste is not to be offended. Whether Klopstock actually infringed this limit was a matter of dispute at the time. Certainly, if he in fact probably remained within it, he went closer to overstepping the mark than any other 'Aufklärer'. . . . (p. 111)

[While Klopstock] writes with more daring and energy than any other author before the 'Sturm und Drang', the situation in this sphere is similar to that discussed in connection with the more personal lyrics. In the *Messias,* for example, there are many passages of rhetoric, sweeping gestures and inventions, passages in which a spirit of dynamism seems to be beginning to make itself felt. But while the element of movement on the whole outweighs the purely static, one would be hard put to it to find evidence of positive irrationalism, and in fact, much of the movement and emotional language is contained in passages of reflection and contemplation, considerably reducing the impact. This epic is indeed one of contemplation rather than action and it is noteworthy, from the point of view of the tenor of its emotion, how much of the feeling is generated by passive, martyr-like suffering, even apart from the central event itself. References to other martyrs and to martyrdom in general are frequent. . . . (pp. 111-12)

In many of his odes and hymns Klopstock sets out to scale the heights, and his concept of poetry demands that his spectacular object should be described in terms which are themselves spectacular. God, who is the ultimate goal of all these contemplations, cannot be 'thought', except through the emotions. The distinction between subject and object is not removed, and the object is still thought, but the thinker himself is inwardly in a state of motion. Thus, mere powerful rhetoric is not enough. . . . Klopstock allows the dynamic elements more scope. From his earliest attempts, he broke away from the strict form of the so-called alexandrine line, indeed from Germanic prosody as a whole as practised at that time, which relied on the repetition of simple, unvarying patterns of stressed and unstressed syllables, with no hint of the rich variety and subtlety which was later to be achieved by Goethe. Klopstock's handling of the ancient classical lyric and epic metres shows progressively more freedom and sensitivity to shifts of mood as he goes forward, and eventually he takes the further step to free rhythms. Structurally too, he moves away from the ultra-clear planning of most of his contemporaries to a form in which the element of planning subsists, but is more strongly influenced by feeling.

This picture of statics and dynamics holds good also of Klopstock's thought, a subject which can be studied best in those poems where he attempts to scale the metaphysical and cosmic heights. Dizziness is often expressed, indeed it is deliberately sought. The fact that these great themes transcend the powers of the mind is itself a stock theme with Klopstock. The solution to this problematic situation is a religious and emotional one, expressed in great bursts of exaltation (as in **'Die Glückseligkeit Aller'**) or of powerful imagery (e.g. the thunderstorm-passage in **'Die Frühlingsfeier'** or the cosmic review of **'Die Gestirne'**). The approach to the dilemma, however, is intellectual and philosophical: Klopstock makes no attempt to dethrone the reason and substitute emotion. He does not reject thought as a form for contemplation of these high themes, but rather attempts to retain its basic pattern and expand it so as to contain the emotional element which, to him, is essential if certain subjects are to be grasped at all. . . . Klopstock, in thought as in poetry in general, assigns . . . a high place to feeling, but does not free it from discipline. He wants greater freedom within a disciplined form rather than [vague meandering.] . . . (pp. 112-13)

[Interaction] between feeling and intellect is apparent in all Klopstock's presentation of thought—and a large proportion of his poetry is in fact presentation of thought. Klopstock treats ideas, not usually very intricate ones, but often quite profound in their implications, and makes coherent statements. Sometimes his technique obscures these a little, but it is rarely difficult to see what he means. The statement gives a clear and rationally appreciable framework. Within this, the handling of language, images and rhythm often gives considerable scope to feeling and there can be a kind of tension between the two sides. This is well contained and certainly not disruptive of order, though it does give the whole that dynamic and not exclusively rationalistic flavour which is Klopstock's most striking trademark. (p. 114)

> *Alan Menhennet, "Sentimentalism: F. G. Klopstock," in his* Order and Freedom: Literature and Society in Germany from 1720 to 1805, *Weidenfeld and Nicolson, 1973, pp. 102-15.*

ADDITIONAL BIBLIOGRAPHY

Batt, Max. "Friedrich Gottlieb Klopstock (1724-1803)." In his *The Treatment of Nature in German Literature from Günther to the Appearance of Goethe's "Werther,"* pp. 43-8. Chicago: University of Chicago Press, 1902.
　　Discusses Klopstock's use of nature imagery.

Betteridge, H. T. "Young Klopstock: A Psycho-Literary Study." *Orbis Litterarum* XV, No. 1 (1960): 3-35.
　　An examination of the sociological and psychological factors that influenced Klopstock's writings.

———. "An Early Poem by Klopstock." *The Modern Language Review* LVIII, No. 1 (January 1963): 29-32.
　　Presents several versions of "Verhängnisse," an ode attributed to Klopstock.

Bjorklund, Beth. "Klopstock's Poetic Innovations: The Emergence of German As a Prosodic Language." *The Germanic Review* LVI, No. 1 (Winter 1981): 20-7.

Outlines Klopstock's contributions to eighteenth-century German prosody.

Blackall, Eric A. "The Grand Manner." In his *The Emergence of German As a Literary Language: 1770-1775*, 2d ed., pp. 314-50. Ithaca, N.Y.: Cornell University Press, 1978.
　　Defines Klopstock's aesthetic theories as evidenced in his verse and essays.

Blume, Bernhard. "Orpheus and Messiah: The Mythology of Immortality in Klopstock's Poetry." *The German Quarterly* XXXIV, No. 3 (May 1961): 218-24.
　　Discusses the theme of the poet as immortal in Klopstock's verse.

Briggs, Fletcher. "Notes on Glover's Influence on Klopstock." *Philological Quarterly* I, No. 4 (October 1922): 290-300.*
　　A detailed comparison of *The Messiah* and Richard Glover's poem *Leonidas*.

Browning, Robert M. "The Cult of Feeling: Klopstock." In his *German Poetry in the Age of the Enlightenment: From Brockes to Klopstock*, pp. 196-295. University Park: Pennsylvania State University Press, 1978.
　　A discussion of Klopstock's odes focusing on their emotionalism and versification.

De Quincey, Thomas. "Klopstock, from the Danish." In his *New Essays by De Quincey: His Contributions to the "Edinburgh Saturday Post" and the "Edinburgh Evening Post,"* 1827-1828, edited by Stuart M. Tave, pp. 60-74. Princeton: Princeton University Press, 1966.
　　A biographical sketch of Klopstock based on the memoirs of Jens Baggesen.

King, Robert D. "In Defense of Klopstock As Spelling Reformer: A Linguistic Appraisal." *Journal of English and Germanic Philology* LXVI, No. 3 (July 1967): 369-82.
　　A positive evaluation of Klopstock as a reformer of German spelling. King discusses such topics as vowel length, unrepresented sounds, and inconsistent, foreign, and morphological spellings.

Kuehnemund, Richard. "Towards a National Drama: Culture-Nation, the Era of J. E. Schlegel and Klopstock." In his *Arminius or the Rise of a National Symbol in Literature (From Hutten to Grabbe)*, pp. 54-86. Studies in the Germanic Languages and Literatures. Chapel Hill: University of North Carolina Press, 1953.*
　　Traces and evaluates the ideological significance of the Arminius and Varus battle themes in patriotic German literature. Kuehnemund also comments on Klopstock's use of the Arminius legend in the "Bardiete."

Menhennet, A. "The 'Baroque' Element in Klopstock's Figurative Style." *Forum for Modern Language Studies* VI, No. 2 (April 1970): 140-48.
　　Points out the Baroque characteristics of Klopstock's verse as well as elements of the Enlightenment and the *Sturm und Drang* movements.

Paulin, Roger. "Six Sapphic Odes, 1753-1934: A Study in Literary Reception." *Seminar: A Journal of Germanic Studies* X, No. 3 (September 1974): 181-98.*
　　A historical survey of the ode in Germany. Paulin uses poems by Klopstock, August Platen, Rudolf Schröder, and Josef Weinheber to illustrate how German-speaking poets adapted classical stanza forms.

Prawer, S. S. "Klopstock and the 'Göttinger Hain': Klopstock, 'Der Zürcher See'." In his *German Lyric Poetry: A Critical Analysis of Selected Poems from Klopstock to Rilke*, pp. 36-43. London: Routledge & Kegan Paul, 1952.
　　A close analysis of "Der Zürcher See" from *Oden*.

Purdie, Edna. "Some Descriptive Compounds in Klopstock's Poetic Vocabulary." *The Germanic Review* XXXI, No. 2 (April 1956): 88-96.
　　An investigation of Klopstock's use of compound words in his verse.

Radandt, Friedhelm. "New Standards: Klopstock and the Development of Lyric Poetry." In his *From Baroque to Storm and Stress:*

1720-1775, pp. 88-96. London: Croom Helm; New York: Harper & Row Publishers, Barnes & Noble Books, 1977.

Briefly assesses Klopstock's contributions to German lyric poetry and outlines criticism of his works by his contemporaries, particularly Johann Gottfried von Herder and Gotthold Ephraim Lessing.

Ryder, Frank G. "Vowels and Consonants As Features of Style: Some Poems of Goethe and Klopstock." *Linguistics: An International Review*, No. 37 (1967): 89-110.*

Close analysis of "Wanderers Nachlied" by Johann Wolfgang von Goethe and "Wissbegierde" by Klopstock. The critic explores in each poem the particular pattern of sound employed by the poet.

Stewart, Morton C. "Traces of Thomson's *Seasons* in Klopstock's Earlier Works." *The Journal of English and Germanic Philology* VI, No. 3 (April 1907): 395-411.*

Compares Klopstock's verse, particularly *The Messiah* and the odes, to the poem *The Seasons* by the eighteenth-century Scottish poet James Thomson.

Thayer, Terence K. "Klopstock and the Literary Afterlife." In *Literaturwissenschaftliches Jahrbuch* , edited by Hermann Kunisch, pp. 183-208. Berlin: Duncker & Humblot, 1975.

A discussion of Klopstock's desire for literary immortality. Thayer maintains that although he sought fame, Klopstock "subsumed his humanistic ambition under Christian devotion."

————. "Rhetoric and the Rhetorical in Klopstock's Odes." *Euphorion* 74, No. 4 (1980): 335-59.

Describes the rhetorical framework and components of Klopstock's poetic theory and discusses the rhetorical nature of his odes.

————. "From *Topos* to *Mythos*: The Poet As Immortalizer in Klopstock's Works." *Journal of English and Germanic Philology* LXXX, No. 2 (April 1981): 157-75.

Examines the theme of the poet as immortalizer in Klopstock's verse.

————. "Intimations of Immortality: Klopstock's Ode 'Der Eislauf'." In *Goethezeit, Studien zur Erkenntnis und Rezeption Goethes und seiner Zeitgenossen: Festschrift für Stuart Atkins,* edited by Gerhart Hoffmeister, pp. 31-43. Bern: Francke Verlag, 1981.

A detailed analysis of the ode "Der Eislauf."

Tombo, Rudolf, Jr. "Ossian's Influence upon Klopstock and the Bards: Klopstock." In his *Ossian in Germany: Bibliography, General Survey, Ossian's Influence upon Klopstock and the Bards*, pp. 82-102. Columbia University Germanic Studies, vol. I, no. II. New York: Columbia University Press, 1901.

Studies the influence of Ossianic poems by the Scottish poet James Macpherson on Klopstock's poetry and dramas.

Alphonse (Marie Louis Prat) de Lamartine

1790-1869

French poet, novelist, and essayist.

Lamartine, a pioneer of the French Romantic movement, is considered one of the greatest French poets of the nineteenth century. He is best known for his collection of verse entitled *Méditations poétiques* (*The Poetical Meditations of M. Alphonse de La Martine*), in which he stressed emotion, mysticism, and nature. Lamartine was also a prominent statesman who wrote a number of historical works, including *Histoire des girondins* (*History of the Girondists; or, Personal Memoirs of the Patriots of the French Revolution*). Though popular during his life, Lamartine's histories are largely overlooked today. He is now remembered as a significant figure in the history of French literature whose poetry marked the transition from the restraints of the Neoclassical era to the passion and lyricism of the Romantics.

Descended from the minor French nobility, Lamartine was born in Mâcon, France. He was raised on his family's country estate in nearby Milly, where he devoted himself to the study of Greek and Roman classics as well as contemporary French works. In 1811, he visited Italy, where he fell in love with a young Neapolitan woman who eventually became the subject of *Graziella* (*Graziella; or, My First Sorrow*), an idyl included in his novel *Les confidences* (*Les confidences: Confidential Disclosures*); several years later, his passion for Julie Charles, the wife of the famous French physicist Jacques Charles, inspired many of the poems comprising *The Poetical Meditations*. This collection of twenty-four poems became an astounding critical and popular success when it was published in 1820. In two sets of poems in this work—those inspired by Julie Charles and those addressed to Elvire, his evocation of the universal woman—Lamartine wrote of ideal love and the grief experienced at its loss. In other poems, he described his religious beliefs and emotional reaction to nature. Lamartine viewed nature as a manifestation of divine grandeur and believed that its contemplation could inspire religious faith. At this time, Lamartine's religious views were those of an orthodox Catholic: he affirmed the existence of an afterlife and exhorted his readers to accept divine will. *The Poetical Meditations* includes Lamartine's most famous single work, "Le lac." In this poem, based on a boat ride with Julie Charles, Lamartine treats the ephemeral nature of life and love. Written in highly melodious and emotional verse, "Le lac" epitomizes the lyrical qualities of Lamartine's poetry.

The Poetical Meditations is considered a transitional work that helped pave the way for the French Romantic movement, and critics have pointed out both Neoclassical and Romantic elements. Adopting forms common to eighteenth-century poetry, Lamartine made use of the elegy and ode; reflecting the new spirit of nineteenth-century verse, he used the themes of love and death. *The Poetical Meditations* differs markedly from the emotionally restrained verse of the Neoclassical era in its sincere tone, lyric effusiveness, emotionality, and religious content. Now regarded as the first document of French Romanticism, *The Poetical Meditations* firmly established Lamartine's reputation as both a Romantic and Catholic poet.

In 1815, Lamartine served for several months as a personal guard to King Charles X. However, he found the life of a soldier dull and aspired to a diplomatic career. After his marriage in 1820 to Marianne Eliza Birch, an Englishwoman, he obtained an appointment to a French embassy in Italy, where he spent the next ten years. This proved to be a period of sustained creative activity, for Lamartine's minor diplomatic duties afforded him ample time to write. In addition to several lesser-known works, Lamartine published *Nouvelles méditations poétiques,* a collection of verse that enhanced his already substantial reputation as a poet. Similar in subject and tone to *The Poetical Meditations*, this work includes poems that combine religious topics and idyllic natural settings.

Soon after his return to France in 1828, Lamartine was defeated in his bid for a seat in the national parliament. He then toured the Middle East. His recollections of this journey are preserved in *Souvenirs, impressions, pensées, et paysages pendant un voyage en Orient, 1832-1833; ou, Notes d'un voyageur (A Pilgrimage to the Holy Land)*, a collection of travel sketches that was moderately successful. After leaving the Middle East in 1833, Lamartine moved to Paris, where he served as a member of the Chamber of Deputies until 1851.

In 1836, Lamartine published his next work, *Jocelyn: Épisode; Journal trouvé chez un curé de village*. He had long envisioned an *épopée humanitaire,* or universal epic, in which he would express his religious and social views. *Jocelyn* forms the first segment of *Les visions,* the title of his projected epic. In *Jocelyn,* Lamartine depicted a young priest's struggle with temptation and ultimate renunciation of forbidden love. While popular for its sensational subject, critical estimates of the work varied. Many reviewers faulted what they considered its implausible plot, laborious descriptions, and sentimentalism, though others praised its mellifluous verse and psychological insight. *La chute d'un ange,* the only other completed segment of the projected epic, appeared in 1838. This portion, which describes the earthly trials of a fallen angel in his quest for redemption, was not as popular as *Jocelyn* and received mixed reviews. While some commentators praised the work for its lucid, lyrical language, its detractors criticized its historical inaccuracies and unorthodox religious content. During his travels in the Middle East Lamartine had become interested in Eastern religions, and *La chute d'un ange* reflects his fascination with reincarnation and pantheism. Although he had been regarded previously as a deeply religious poet, both *Jocelyn* and *La chute d'un ange* were banned by the Catholic church, who considered them a refutation of traditional faith in favor of rationalism and deism.

Beginning in 1839, Lamartine abandoned poetry for prose writing. By 1847, he had completed his multi-volume interpretation of the French Revolution, *History of the Girondists.* Though critics have faulted its lack of objectivity and unscholarly approach, *History of the Girondists* was popular with his contemporaries and increased Lamartine's political following by presenting him as a moderate in a time of extremism. Lamartine's career as a statesman reached its apex in 1848 when Louis-Philippe was ousted in the Revolution and Lamartine became the president of the Second Republic's provisional government. He proved an ineffective leader during this volatile time, and his popularity diminished to such an extent that he was soundly defeated by Napoléon III in the presidential election held later that year.

Lamartine retired from politics in 1851 and wrote prolifically until his death in 1869 to support himself and his family. He composed a large body of prose writings, including historical works, novels, biographical sketches, and a monthly journal of literary essays. Lamartine's interest in social change, first evidenced in his political activities and in *Jocelyn* and *La chute d'un ange,* also informs the works of this period. Concerned with the French workers' quality of life, Lamartine argued for an improved standard of living and promoted honest labor, strict morality, and a return to a rural way of life. He also provided examples of exemplary historical characters in numerous biographical sketches that were later collected and published as *Le civilisateur: Histoire de l'humanité par les grands hommes (Memoirs of Celebrated Characters).* Although his prose works were widely read by his contemporaries, their popularity waned rapidly after Lamartine's death. Critics agree that his prose writings, unlike his poetry, were marred by hasty composition, and today they are considered of little artistic value.

During his lifetime, Lamartine achieved a substantial reputation as a poet and prose writer. By his death, his reputation had waned significantly: his prose works were seldom read, and his verse lost favor with an audience that preferred the more passionate lyrics of the late Romantics. Lamartine's work has received consistent notice in France, but little twentieth-century commentary in English. Modern scholars have focused their attention on the two completed parts of Lamartine's epic, *Jocelyn* and *La chute d'un ange,* and many individual poems, particularly "Le lac," have been the subject of close textual analyses. Critics have also demonstrated an increasing interest in Lamartine's role as a social reformer and his importance to the history of French literature. Today, Lamartine is renowned for his emotionally evocative verse that contributed to the development of the French Romantic movement.

PRINCIPAL WORKS

Méditations poétiques (poetry) 1820
  [*The Poetical Meditations of M. Alphonse de La Martine,* 1839]
Nouvelles méditations poétiques (poetry) 1823
Harmonies poétiques et religieuses (poetry) 1830
Souvenirs, impressions, pensées, et paysages pendant un voyage en Orient, 1832-1833; ou, Notes d'un voyageur (travel sketches) 1835
  [*A Pilgrimage to the Holy Land,* 1835]
Jocelyn: Épisode; Journal trouvé chez un curé de village (poetry) 1836
  [*Jocelyn,* 1837]
La chute d'un ange (poetry) 1838
Histoire des girondins (history) 1847
  [*History of the Girondists; or, Personal Memoirs of the Patriots of the French Revolution.* 3 vols., 1847-48]
Les confidences (novel) 1849
  [*Les confidences: Confidential Disclosures,* 1849]
Le conseiller du peuple. 2 vols. (essays) 1849-50
Histoire de la révolution de 1848 (history) 1849
  [*History of the French Revolution of 1848,* 1849]
Raphaël: Pages de la vingtième année (novel) 1849
  [*Raphael; or, Pages of the Book of Life at Twenty,* 1849]
Le civilisateur: Histoire de l'humanité par les grands hommes. 3 vols. (biographical sketches) 1852-54; also published as *Vie des grands hommes* (enlarged edition), 1855-56
  [*Memoirs of Celebrated Characters.* 3 vols., 1854-56]
Cours familier de littérature: Un entretien par mois. 28 vols. (essays) 1856-59
Oeuvres complètes de Lamartine publiées et inédites. 41 vols. (poetry, histories, biographical sketches, travel sketches, memoirs, and novels) 1860-66
Les foyers du peuple. 2 vols. (essays) 1866
Correspondance de Lamartine. 6 vols. (letters) 1873-74
Oeuvres poétiques (poetry and dramas) 1873-74

*These works were published in monthly installments previous to their publication in book form.

THE LONDON MAGAZINE (essay date 1821)

[*In the following excerpt from a review of* The Poetical Meditations, *the critic praises the "spontaneous feelings" that characterize Lamartine's finest poems.*]

[Whenever, in the] **"Poetical Meditations,"** as he calls them, the writer expresses what appear to be his own *unpremeditated* thoughts, and spontaneous feelings, without forcing himself into a state of excitement for the occasion, he is, for the most part, very pleasing. In some of his altitudes, it must be owned, we have followed him with much less satisfaction. Thus, in the first poem ["L'Isolement"], where he describes himself seated on an eminence, at the foot of an old oak, "watching with wistful gaze the setting sun." . . . (p. 277)

[M. de Lamartine] is placed, and employed exactly as a young poet of his disposition ought to be. But when in . . . ["**L'Homme**"], addressed to Lord Byron, he compares his Lordship to an eagle launching forth from the horrible summit of Mount Athos, and suspending his aerie over the abyss that yawns at its side; where, surrounded with palpitating limbs, and with rocks incessantly dripping with black gore, delighted with the shrieks of his prey, and, cradled by the tempest, he falls to sleep in his joy, . . . and when, not contented with this, and a good deal "of the like stuff," he perseveres in his compliment to the noble bard so far as to put him on a par with his Satanic majesty himself, . . . we begin to lose all sympathy with the poet, and most heartily wish ourselves away from such perilous company, and safe back again under the old oak, ready to forswear all illusions of the imagination for the future. . . . (pp. 277-78)

In the third Meditation ["**Le Soir**"] we are, therefore, well satisfied to find ourselves at the side of M. de Lamartine once more, in the silence of an evening landscape . . . and so far forget our late resolution as to fall into a *douce rêverie,* and believe that something in the shape of a gentle spirit is, indeed, gliding to us on a beam of the evening star. But we will not pursue the Meditator through all his moods and musings; but content ourselves with observing, that the sixth, entitled "**Le Désespoir**," is the least to our taste, as the tenth, called "**La Retraite**," is the most so. (p. 278)

> *"'Méditations Poétiques,' par M. Alphonse De Lamartine," in* The London Magazine, *Vol. IV, No. XXI, September, 1821, pp. 277-78.*

[RICHARD CHENEVIX AND FRANCIS JEFFREY]　(essay date 1822)

> [*Chenevix was a contributor to the* Edinburgh Review, *one of the most influential magazines in early nineteenth-century England, and Jeffrey was its founder and editor from 1803 to 1829. In the following positive evaluation of* The Poetical Meditations, *Chenevix and Jeffrey call Lamartine* "unquestionably the best of living French poets."]

The '**Méditations poétiques**' consist of about twenty short pieces, the reflections of the poet on various subjects of metaphysical discussion. The general character of these effusions is a pious melancholy; and they are evidently emanations from a mind deeply imbued with religious enthusiasm, the most elevated and overflowing fount of poetry. But his enthusiasm, though often running into excess, is always free from violence or fury. . . . But the leading distinction of M. De Lamartine's poetry in France is the boldness of its versification, which has not a little startled the worshippers of the old school, and has never before been tolerated to so great an extent. There is a frequent and happy incorrectness in the arrangement of his rhymes; and in place of the lucid insipidity, which characterizes the poetry of his country, that which he has given us, is tinged with the vague intensity, so effective in this kind of composition, when . . . it makes itself felt as the soul, and not as the body, of the verse.

We place high also on the list of M. De Lamartine's merits, what his countrymen would certainly call a fault, if they had sufficient candour to acknowledge it at all—his ample borrowings from English writers. We have no objection to see the poetry of France enriched by imitations of British writers, nor even by the occasional naturalization of their thoughts. . . . [M. De Lamartine may] draw as freely upon our poets, as both he

and all the writers of his country have done upon those of antiquity, without any risk of a protest, on our parts at least. . . . All good poets we hold to have been great imitators; and their practice is sufficient to excuse the little and the indifferent also. To the latter classes, M. De Lamartine does not certainly belong; and we hope to see him arrive to such a station, as will entitle him to be ranked among the first. We think him unquestionably the best of living French poets. . . . (pp. 420-21)

[We point out a few] of the '**Méditations**' which we approve the most. These are, '**La Foi**,' '**La Prière**,' and '**La Semaine Sainte**,' for their pious solemnity of feeling and expression; and '**Le Golfe de Baya**,' and '**Le lac de B******,' for their harmonious tone. The Ninth Méditation, called '**L'Enthousiasme**,' is forcible and good, but an evident imitation of Rousseau's Ode to the Comte de Luc—and '**Le Chretien Mourant**' and '**L'Homme**' are, as their titles betray, borrowed, both in name and matter, from Pope. The latter of these pieces, being addressed to Lord Byron, has acquired an extraordinary celebrity in France. We have seen a translation of it published in Paris; and it is certainly a production of very great power. We think it, however, a striking instance of that excess which we stated as the occasional consequence of M. de Lamartine's *enthousiasme.* (pp. 424-25)

> [*Richard Chenevix and Francis Jeffrey*], "*French Poetry," in* The Edinburgh Review, *Vol. XXXVII, No. LXXIV, November, 1822, pp. 407-32.**

THE MONTHLY REVIEW, LONDON　(essay date 1824)

> [*In this largely positive assessment of* Nouvelles méditations poétiques, *the reviewer compares the work favorably with* The Poetical Meditations *and maintains that negative criticism of Lamartine's verse is the result of jealousy.*]

[The poetry of M. de Lamartine] is in itself of so various a character, as to be almost equally admired by all ranks and all parties, and not less by the sentimentalist and the lover than by people of fashion and by devotees. Not obtrusively marked by either political or party feeling, it is deeply embued with passionate and devotional sentiments, such as are well calculated to excite the sympathy of Parisian readers; and with bursts of true poetry, not less suited to the taste of every other people. Such is more particularly the character of the '**New Poetical Meditations**' ['**Nouvelles méditations poétiques**'] now on our table, which are fully equal to the best in the former series;— even to *La Foi, La Prière,* and a few others that have been distinguished for their power and pathos.

Among the most touching and animated pieces . . . are those intitled *Bonaparte, Les Étoiles, La Solitude, Ischia, Le Poëte Mourant,* and *Les Préludes;*—many of which, however, are of very unequal merit. (pp. 506-07)

[We] are aware that both French and English critics have maintained that plagiarism and repetition may alike be detected in the sentiments of M. de Lamartine: that many of his later productions are inferior to his former; and that he has even been guilty of writing bad French grammar. We are conscious, at the same time, that similar accusations have also been brought against our Byrons and our Scotts, and that they have originated among those who have the most reason to envy their genius. One French critic, however, (M. de Stendhal,) who is fully equal to the appreciation of M. de Lamartine's merits, in some points at least, is inclined to run as much into the opposite extreme, when he compares the French stanzas on Napoleon to those of Lord Byron; and when he asserts that the present writer's contemplative enthusiasm is perfectly unequalled. . . . In spite of the cavillings of his enemies . . . [and] of his own faults, we consider M. de Lamartine in the light of a true poet; and, while we would direct his attention to the correction of some errors of style and manner, which might be amended, we at the same time encourage him to proceed. (pp. 512-13)

> *"De Lamartine's 'Meditations,' and 'Death of Socrates',"* in The Monthly Review, *London, Vol. CIII, April, 1824, pp. 504-13.*

GRIMM'S GRANDSON [PSEUDONYM OF HENRI BEYLE] (essay date 1825)

[*Most commonly known by the pseudonym Stendhal, Beyle is considered one of the greatest French novelists, and his masterpiece,* The Red and the Black, *is regarded as a significant contribution to the modern psychological novel. In the following excerpt, Beyle censures* La mort de Socrate (The Death of Socrates) *and* Le dernier chant du pèlerinage d'Harold (The Last Canto of Childe Harold's Pilgrimage), *stating that Lamartine "has an empty and sterile brain." For further commentary by Beyle, see excerpt dated 1825.*]

[The fame of M. de la Martine] would be much more brilliant, if he had published nothing since his first volume of **Meditations**. They were, like De Béranger's best songs, the *voice of his soul.* From that time, elated by the reputation which the ultra party conferred upon him, M. de la Martine has *chosen to write.* He has thus revealed the fact that, combined with great sensibility and the talent of describing objects in humorous verse, he has an empty and sterile brain. The total absence of the faculty of thought is incredibly felt in the poem of the **Death of Socrates**. . . . (p. 135)

I have heard a few pages of a new poem, by M. de la Martine, called the **Last Canto of Childe Harold**. . . .

Many of the lines I heard appeared to me negligently written. The same word is frequently repeated in two following lines, or even in the same line; faults of this kind, however, are not faults to me. The construction of French verse is become so mere a mechanical art, that M. de la Martine has very likely left these marks of negligence in order to distinguish himself from the two or three hundred poets who swarm in the drawing-rooms of Paris;—all perfectly correct and perfectly dull. (p. 136)

> Grimm's Grandson [*pseudonym of Henri Beyle*], *"Letters from Paris,"* in The London Magazine, *n.s. Vol. II, No. V, May, 1825, pp. 131-41.**

GRIMM'S GRANDSON [PSEUDONYM OF HENRI BEYLE] (essay date 1825)

[*Although Beyle acknowledges Lamartine's talent, labeling him "the second of living French poets," he faults the lack of common sense and frequent immaturity of thought in* The Last Canto of Childe Harold's Pilgrimage *and* Le chant du sacre. *For additional commentary by Beyle, see previous excerpt dated 1825.*]

The past month has produced four very remarkable works. The **Dernier Chant de Childe Harold,** and the **Chant du Sacre,** by M. de la Martine; the *Théâtre Espagnol* of Clara Gazul [by M. Mérimée], and the *Prisonniers du Caucase,* by the Count Xavier de Maistre. The two latter works will most probably be translated into English. As for M. de la Martine's poems, it appears to me almost impossible that a foreigner should be able to appreciate their merits. M. de la Martine is, in my

opinion, the second of living French poets, but he is utterly destitute of common sense. This is true to the letter.

In the **Dernier Chant de Childe Harold,** for instance, he makes the vessel set sail without weighing anchor. (p. 458)

The pleasant part of the story is, that M. de la Martine has frequently been at sea. But, instead of thinking of what was doing in the ship, instead of seeing the operations going on around him, he was absorbed in some waking dream. If M. de la Martine is incapable of acquiring a truth so simple as the necessity of weighing anchor before setting sail, what on earth will he make of all those moral and political truths, which are, as it were, the every-day current coin of conversation; the materials out of which the national stock of good sense is composed?

M. de la Martine has not so much as a suspicion of their existence. The thoughts which form the basis of the two poems in question have, consequently, an air of perfect childishness. You must know, such at least is the received report, that M. de la Martine was educated in an ultra family not less remarkable for the narrowness of its ideas than for its nobility. The young poet is hemmed in by obsolete, narrow, and paltry opinions. From the time of the publication of his **Méditations Poétiques** (which hold their rank as a master-piece) he has been taken under the protection of a powerful and artful party, the Jesuits. A certain M. de Genoude, the editor of the *Etoile,* the Blackwood of this country, is also a patron of M. de la Martine. Every thing thus aspires to keep the poor young man in perpetual ignorance of the first elements of real life. It may thus be said with truth that he is deficient in understanding, though a man of genius, that in spite of the upright character of his mind, he lends himself to acts which in any other person would be accounted meannesses. If I were to read you his poem on the Coronation [**Chant du Sacre**], you would blush with indignation at eight or ten different passages, and I should be obliged to explain to you that M. de la Martine is perhaps the only individual who does not comprehend the drift of what he has written. I am perfectly aware that a poet is permitted to be ignorant of the realities of life. I will go farther, it is necessary to his success as a poet that he should be so. If a man of honour and sensibility like M. de la Martine knew as much about mankind as a Sir Robert Walpole or a Villèle, his imagination, his sensibility, would become arid. (pp. 458-59)

[M. de la Martine] has always lived in the country, buried in some ultra château, surrounded by narrow prejudices. No stupidity at present existing in France can equal the stupidity of the provincial noble, who has lived for the last five and thirty years in a state of continual anger against every thing passing around him, and who really knows nothing whatever. . . . Among such people has it been the misfortune of M. de la Martine to pass his life. He has never seen society, its heartlessness disgusts and repels him.

Whence then did he derive his genius? From his heart alone. He never rises to the highest order of poetry of which this age has given example, but when he expresses in simple language some sentiment which has struck upon his soul. After one of these felicitous passages, you cannot read twenty lines without coming to some puerility, so extraordinary that your pleasure is utterly destroyed. (p. 459)

No French poet, not even Racine, Voltaire, Lafontaine, has ever produced any thing equal to the **Dedication** of the [**Last Canto of Childe Harold**]. There are three or four marks of negligence to be found in the two pages of which it consists.

The exaggerated praises of the Ultra party have rendered M. de la Martine conceited, and have had a very injurious effect upon his poetry. . . . [M. de la Martine] owes this breadth of touch to the good fortune of coming after the talent of the Abbé Delille, and the genius of Lord Byron. (p. 460)

M. de la Martine describes the last year of the life of the English poet [Lord Byron]; but his story wants clearness. It is sometimes impossible to discover who is speaking—and the poet—is he Lord Byron himself? This cannot be, since Lord Byron is the person described. It is evident that M. de la Martine has not condescended to read over his poem—he has even left defective lines. The quality of his poem, which unfortunately will be most obvious to foreigners, is the incoherence, and often the absurdity of its plan. (p. 461)

> *Grimm's Grandson* [*pseudonym of Henri Beyle*], *"Letters from Paris," in* The London Magazine, *n.s. Vol. II, No. VII, July, 1825, pp. 457-64.*

THE MONTHLY REVIEW, LONDON (essay date 1825)

[*In this excerpt from an unsigned review of* The Last Canto of Childe Harold's Pilgrimage, *the critic accuses Lamartine of blatantly imitating Lord Byron's* Childe Harold's Pilgrimage.]

["Le Dernier Chant du Pèlerinage d'Harold"] seems to have acquired some degree of popularity in France. . . . The title might possibly have induced many persons at first to believe, that the work was a translation from the fourth canto of [Lord Byron's] "Childe Harold." . . . It cannot be presumed, that [M. de Lamartine] could have entertained the design of attracting attention by hoisting a false flag. But he may not be so easily acquitted from the charge of temerity to which he has rendered himself liable, by attempting to trace the last footsteps of a being, whose strains are among the most sublime, varied, and peculiar, which are known to our language.

Strange to say, it is upon the hope of identifying himself with "Childe Harold" that M. de Lamartine founds his vindication, and even seriously prefers his claims to an unusual portion of modesty. He wishes us to believe, that nothing but his deference for the superior genius of Lord Byron induced him to adopt this theme and title, in order that he might record the premature fate of that distinguished poet. 'Imitation,' he adds, 'is not rivalry, it is homage!' Such an apology might, perhaps, extenuate the imputation of audacity, if the French bard did not follow it up with a very singular exposition of the extent of his 'imitation.' 'This phrase,' he observes, 'does not exactly convey my idea; the form alone of "Childe Harold" is imitated; the thoughts, the sentiments, the images, are not so. I have sedulously avoided every imitation of this kind. There is not in this fifth canto a single idea, or simile, of all those which the English poet has scattered through the four first cantos of his poem.'

It is not necessary to observe on the complacency with which M. de Lamartine speaks of his "Fifth Canto," or of the facility with which he places it in juxta-position with the "Four First Cantos" of the English poet. But we do admire the sophistry, by which he endeavors to delude his readers into a belief of the pure originality, which marks the "Dernier Chant." He confines his assertion to the "Pilgrimage," and observes a cautious silence as to his coquetry with Lord Byron's other poems, from which, however, he has borrowed almost every 'idea' and 'simile' that deserves the name in his production. Nor has he been so very abstemious with respect to the "Four

First Cantos," as he would wish his readers to imagine. (pp. 453-54)

We shall not fatigue the reader by following M. de Lamartine, through his reflections on the storied scenery of Greece. They are copied without any restraint from one or other of Lord Byron's poems. . . . It is the more surprizing that M. de Lamartine should have had the vanity to think that he could impose the "Dernier Chant" as an original poem on his French readers, when he must be aware, that Lord Byron's poetry is better known in France than his own. (p. 459)

It has been no pleasure to us to expose the pretensions of M. de Lamartine in this his latest work. We respected his talents, and his character, and were disposed to augur auspiciously of his career. But when a poet in the flower of his age, and the maturity of his genius, stoops to servile imitation, he must not be surprized if he be condemned to the dull oblivion which he courts. The author, who would attempt to persuade the world that his parodies are original poems, must either inflict a deep wound on his moral character, or obtain refuge for it in the delusions of inordinate vanity. (pp. 459-60)

> *"Lamartine's 'Pilgrimage of Harold'," in* The Monthly Review, *London, Vol. CVII, August, 1825, pp. 453-60.*

THE WESTERN MONTHLY REVIEW (essay date 1829)

[*In this excerpt from a laudatory review of* The Poetical Meditations, *the critic favorably compares Lamartine's poetic style to that of Lord Byron.*]

[Byron is clearly La Martine's] *beau ideal*, never in the light of a servile imitator, but as one, into whose deep spirit, whose profound melancholy, whose grand and original energy and compactness, he has drunk with effect. The one is the melancholy poet of skepticism; and his creed is, 'let us eat and drink, for to morrow we die;' and from the very gloom, despair and annihilation of the tomb, as they appear to his mind, he finds a terrible and affecting inspiration. The French poet draws from dark, troubled, and fathomless waters, also; but he is

Lamartine in 1825, in a lithograph by Ratier.

always the poet of religion. Death, to him, . . . is the source of conceptions of inexpressible grandeur; but he always sees a God through the gloom, the necessity of submission to his will, and he enters into the sweet, sublime and soothing sentiments of a joyous meeting of friends beyond the tomb. We have no where met with images more beautifully poetic, with more frequent recurrence of the most finished grandeur of sentiment, and nobler samples of moral sublime, than in [*Méditations Poétiques*]. There is the pathos, the melancholy, the striking originality, the novel images and diction, the dim and shadowy vastness of Byron, without any of his skeptical, misanthropic and revolting epicurism. We know few poets, living or dead, who, according to our estimate, ought to take place of La Martine. He is one of those rare, rich and endowed minds, that spring up from age to age, standing alone, while they live, and slowly, and reluctantly, and with all the withering abatements of envy, allowed to be what they are, until they are gone. (pp. 26-7)

"Literature of France," in The Western Monthly Review, *Vol. III, No. 1, July, 1829, pp. 25-32.*

[ELIZABETH FRIES ELLET]   (essay date 1835)

[*A minor American poet, Ellet was, according to C. M. Lombard (see Additional Bibliography, 1963), one of the first American critics to publish significant analyses of foreign literature. In the following excerpt, Ellet praises the imagery and religious tone of Lamartine's verse in* The Poetical Meditations, Nouvelles méditations poétiques, *and* Harmonies poétiques et religieuses. *For further commentary by Ellet, see excerpts dated 1835 and 1839.*]

The poetry of Lamartine differs from that of the rest of his countrymen in many respects. The points of contrast between him and Béranger are striking; and we have often heard the genius of the two poets compared, though not altogether with justice when the palm of superiority has been awarded to the gay *chansonnier* [Béranger], on account of the greater fancied utility of his productions. If whatever tends to elevate the imagination and correct the heart be pre-eminently useful, then is Lamartine especially entitled to the praise, such being the scope and the tendency of every thing he has written. We must notice one remarkable and characteristic difference between him and his great contemporary. In the words of Béranger, we forget the author, who seems frequently to forget himself in his stirring themes. This is more particularly the case in his loftier political odes, and in those effusions of pensive tenderness which describe so touchingly scenes of distress witnessed or conceived by the bard. Carried away by enthusiasm in the subject awakened by the most glowing language, we see or hear nothing of the writer himself. But the enthusiasm we feel in the poems of Lamartine has a source less external. The heart, the living heart of the poet is laid open to us; fraught with its warm feelings, its brilliant and fervid fancies, its treasures of rich and deep thought. The same spirit constantly exhibits itself, under every different form; we trace the same leading features in every picture, whether gorgeous or gloomy, adorned or undisguised. Nor is the likeness productive of monotony; they are features on which we love to gaze, and the spirit is one to whose sweet and solemn promptings we can never be weary of listening. It elevates us to the sublimer realities, perceived and appreciated only by those to whom some portion of the same influence has been imparted. Lamartine has drawn largely upon nature for his stores of imagery, and from the abundance she offers has selected with a graceful and discriminating hand. With the tumults and passions of men he has

little to do; the home of his muse is in the magnificence of woods and rivers and mountains, where she communes with ideal beings, and revels in a world of her own creation. To him every object in the natural, bears its relation to some sentiment in the moral world. . . . (p. 33)

The author has given the names of *Poetical Meditations* to about fifty-six poems, which seem each to have been inspired by some passing event, or to be the offspring of his own mind under the influence of temporary feeling. (pp. 33-4)

The first peculiarity that strikes us in these, and indeed in all the poems of Lamartine, is his power of conveying graphic images to the mind. Each line, almost each word, is a picture. The scenes he paints almost live before our eyes; in a few words, brief and forcible, he expresses vividly what others would have taken pages to describe. There is scarcely a sentence which would not serve as a text for eloquent discussion; the ideas suggested by a single phrase, could be readily expanded into a poem. This concentration we cannot help regarding as the test of poetry; he who is rich in the treasures of true genius, will study not to amplify, but to condense. The power of description belonging to our author, is displayed in all his poems, but particularly in those in which he paints some portion of natural scenery endeared by youthful recollections. Of this kind are *Milly, ou la terre natale, Le Lac,* and numerous others. (p. 34)

Lamartine, more frequently than any other poet, employs some striking or sublime object in external nature, to illustrate things or operations in the mental or moral world. His metaphors of this kind are always forcible and beautiful in a high degree. These gems abound in his productions, sparkling every where; and the very frequency of their recurrence renders it difficult to offer them in a detached form. He seems to revel in a luxuriance of splendid imagery; changing often, as if in caprice, his figures in every successive line, till the brilliant chain is terminated by some link more magnificent than the rest. This aptness for comparison between moral and external objects, we may pronounce the distinguishing characteristic of his poetry; one we confess peculiarly to our taste, especially as his comparisons are always new and striking. *Le Poète mourant* [from *Nouvelles méditations poétiques*], one of the finest lyrics ever composed, is an appropriate example of his propensity for bold and beautiful similes. (p. 37)

The sacred hymns of Lamartine [in *Harmonies poétiques et religieuses*] have a beauty unsurpassed by those of any other modern writer. The deep spirit of piety that pervades them, their majesty and sweetness, as well as the splendour of imagery with which they are adorned, place them in the first rank among lyrics. Their author has borrowed the solemn language of nature to adore the supreme Creator; to him, seas, forests, streams, and shores, with harmonious accord, seem to unite in praise; while he, joining the chaunt of universal love, becomes the inspired interpreter of voices "uttered in silence." His temple of worship is the solitary wood, the mountain, or the ocean side; where the rushing of rivers, or the sighing of winds, or the myriad tones of insect life, make vocal the solitude with the music sweetest to the poet's ear. It is impossible to listen to his devotional effusions without feeling a portion of the same enthusiasm which has filled the breast of the writer, inspiring sentiments so lofty. The *Hymn of the Morning, Hymn of Evening in the Temples,* and *Hymn of Death*, are each magnificent in their kind. (p. 39)

The Preludes [from *Nouvelles méditations poétiques*], for the sweetness and melody of verse, and the facility with which the metre is changed with the theme, is unrivalled, unless by the celebrated lyrics in Alfieri's tragedy of Saul. The very nature of language seems to be altered, to express various emotion; from the soft melancholy breathed in the first stanzas, to the full burst of enthusiasm in the ensuing description of a battle. (p. 41)

The dramatic fragments in these volumes, [*The Apparition of the Shade of Samuel* and *The Death of Jonathan* in *Poetical Meditations*], display the ability of our author for greater efforts; but we prefer his lyric productions. There is much energy and passion, and exquisite poetry, in the lamentations of the doomed monarch of Israel; but they fail to awaken that thrilling emotion, that *désordre sympathique*, by which elsewhere he sways the heart. In dramatic efforts most of the peculiar beauties of Lamartine's poetry must of necessity be sacrificed; and for their loss not even the force of passion can compensate us. In the *Death of Socrates*, the poet has gifted the philosopher on the threshold of death, with a vision which penetrates through the shades of mythological superstition, into the sublimest mysteries of revelation. (pp. 42-3)

[*Elizabeth Fries Ellet*], "Poems of Lamartine," in American Quarterly Review, Vol. XVII, No. XXXIII, March, 1835, pp. 32-52.

[ELIZABETH FRIES ELLET] (essay date 1835)

[*In the following excerpt, Ellet praises the descriptions and religious tone of* A Pilgrimage to the Holy Land, *though she acknowledges that its declamatory style may be unappealing to some readers. For additional commentary by Ellet, see excerpts dated 1835 and 1839.*]

Besides the expectation of superior elegance of style and beauty of description, justified by the previously high character of the writer, [*Souvenirs, Impressions, Pensées, et Paysages, pendant un Voyage en Orient (1832-1833); ou, Notes d'un Voyageur*] has another source of interest, beyond that which usually belongs to books of travels, or sketches of scenery. He has surveyed the scenes he depicts with the eye of a poet, a philosopher, and a Christian; their impression upon his fancy, and the results of reflection awakened by them, are conveyed to us in their first warmth and vigour; hallowed by the deep devotion with which he refers to the great events whose occurrence has made the East a land of wonders. His descriptions are pictures, brilliant in their colouring, and perfect in their outline, whose rich and glowing tints are softened and harmonized by the mellow and delicious sunshine of religious feeling. It is true, they transcend life; his ardent imagination invests whatever he looks upon with hues which may be deemed exaggerated; but this is a necessary consequence of his temperament; he could not think and write like ordinary men; and the peculiar charm of his language would be lost, should we attempt to set bounds to his expression of sentiment or emotion. (pp. 270-71)

We cordially recommend these charming volumes to the attentive perusal of our readers; the declamatory style, and somewhat overwrought pictures, may be unpleasing to some, but will, we hope, deter none from the enjoyment of the author's magnificent descriptions, or prevent them from following him in the frequent poetical trains of thought growing out of his contemplation of the scenes he witnessed. His religion is strongly tinctured with the imaginative character of his mind; but is undoubtedly not, on that account, less heartfelt than with those who deem it sacreligious to blend the visions of fancy with the feelings of devotion. (p. 289)

[*Elizabeth Fries Ellet*], "Lamartine's Travels in the East," in American Quarterly Review, Vol. XVIII, No. XXXVI, December, 1835, pp. 270-89.

ALFRED DE MUSSET (poem date 1836)

[*Musset was one of the leading figures of the French Romantic movement. Although his best dramas are often regarded as more original than his poetry, he distinguished himself in both genres. In the following portions of "Lettre à Lamartine," originally published in February, 1836, Musset praises "L'homme" and "Le lac" from* The Poetical Meditations.]

When the great Byron was about to leave
Ravenna's shores, and thence would seek reprieve
From ennui and unrest in other climes,
Having in mind toward Greece he'd go betimes,
Thus sitting at the feet of mistress pale,
His Guiccioli, waiting favoring gale,
She had a book about her lord of song,
And read your praise that bore his fame along.

You must have kept the memory of that time,
Those lines to Byron in his splendid prime;
You were their author, who wrote void of fear,
Lamartine, who became our glory dear,
'Twas your first essay on your tender lyre,
All sad and beautiful, yet full of fire.
Your heaven-born Muse inspires you nobly now,
While thought's enthroned upon your dreamy brow.

(p. 164)

. . . . .

Poet, now that thy faithful Muse and pure,
Of immortality by chaste love sure,
When bloom of vervain has once crowned thy head,
In turn, like Byron, be thou comforted.
I do not hope to ever be thy peer;
What Heaven has giv'n thee, no one brings me near.
Comparing fates, however great distance,
God will encompass it, and not blind chance.
I send thee homage, O soul greatly praised,
And ask no answer from a soul more raised.
For such exchanges, to be valued, must
Be signed by names which are not writ in dust.
Your name on glory's standard is unfurled;
Mine, I fear, counts but little in the world.
I've often thought I'm weary of my life,
And fain would end what seems a restless strife.
My shadow passed before me in dim light,
Which, full of vanity, I thought deep night.
Poet, I write to tell thee that I love;
A ray of sunshine smote me from above,
And in one day of mourning, when joy slept,
The tears that made me think of thee, I wept.
Which of us, Lamartine, knows not by heart
That song adored by lovers whose souls smart?
'Twas by a lake, one evening, thou didst sigh;
Who has not read a thousand times again
Those lines wherein thy mistress speaks betimes?

Who has not sobbed over those griefs divine,
Deep as the sky and pure as the sunshine?
Alas! those long regrets of love's deceit,
Those ruins everywhere which one may meet,
Those flashes infinite of fleeting light,
What man is he that does not know their sight?

(pp. 166-67)

. . . . .

Oh, lover of Elvire, whose love is strong,
You understand one saying fond adieu;
You understand when hand writes, ''I'll be
    true,''
And the heart signs it, and the lips are given,
The lips whose kiss unites us before heaven;
You understand the deep, unknown resolve
On which our inmost souls each day revolve;
The love that tears aside rebellious will,
And to another heart attaches still,
A powerful tie whose tissue, warp, and woof,
Firm as the solid rock, and diamond-proof;
Which has no fear of time, nor sword, nor flame,
Nor death itself, that which makes lovers game;
They fear no calumny, bear blows of stones,
And in the tomb will love each other's bones.
You understand, ten years such tie was spun,
And of two beings it made only one;
Then, broken suddenly and lost in space,
And we who love, feel terror and disgrace.

(p. 171)

. . . . .

Well, good or bad, inflexible or frail,
Humble or haughty, sad or gay, we sail
Forever moaning o'er life's troubled sea.
This being made of clay, oh, such is he,
Thou seest him, Lamartine; his blood thy blood,
His happiness is thine, thus understood,
Of all the ills on earth we must endure,
Not one but touches thee, pure or impure;
Thou knowest how to sing, O poet, weep;
Tell me, in sadness how your soul you keep?
What has misfortune whispered in thine ear?
What is thy balm to soothe the bitter tear?
Received by friends, and by thy mistress too,
Of heaven, and self, hast thou had doubts anew?

(p. 173)

Alfred de Musset, "Letter to Lamartine," in his The
Complete Writings of Alfred de Musset: Poems, *Vol.
II, translated by Marie Agathe Clarke, Edwin C. Hill
Company, 1905, pp. 164-75.*

THE LONDON AND WESTMINSTER REVIEW   (essay date 1836)

[*Focusing on the esoteric nature of* Harmonies poétiques et religieuses, *the reviewer asserts that Lamartine's highly idealized
and ornamental images obscure the reader's comprehension of
his verse.*]

[The **'Harmonies'**] present more fine verses, perhaps, but fewer
fine poems than the collection of the **'Meditations'**; and they
are more marked with the faults of readiness and facility, which
was destined to be the besetting sin of M. de Lamartine's
talent. . . .

[In the **'Harmonies,'** we] lose almost every trace of practical
life. In the **'Meditations'** the most humble reader might sometimes recognise his own feelings in the poet's reveries, in his
sorrows, in his pleasures; but in the **'Harmonies'** the poet
isolated himself more and more, withdrew himself from the
observation of men, and made himself visible but to God, in
a cloud of vapoury poetry. He was no longer the poet of the
epoch, of which a great prose writer, M. de Chateaubriand,
had observed with accuracy and characterised with precision
the more serious instincts, and all those of its uneasinesses
which were the least remote from the general constitution of
man. M. de Lamartine had transported thought into the realms
of vague and recondite speculations; into regions whither we
could no longer follow him, for want of wings; into a world
where there was not the smallest corner for us. (p. 520)

The title of these poems indicates their leading idea; which is,
or at least seems to be, that of displaying all the physical and
moral harmonies which connect the world with God. The poet
continually ascends from the visible to the invisible, and in-
terrogates all creation on the subject of its relations with the
Creator. (p. 521)

Sometimes he loses himself in sublime extacies: he mounts
from thought to thought up to the throne of God: and there his
voice has no longer anything human in it; his song is a mystical
and inarticulate hymn, into which the souls who are prepared
by meditations of a similar character can alone follow the poet;
we seem to hear the distant echo of a chorus of angels, in
which we join without understanding it. The soul of the poet
seems to melt away in the light of the divine presence, and he
can no longer utter anything but confused and harmonious
sighs. At other times he renews his flight towards the empyrean, still burning to see and to know; but this time, his faith
being less abundant, the Deity eludes his sight; he still tries to
soar, but with a wing weakened by doubt, until, exhausted by
his efforts, he falls from weariness upon the earth, and bruises
his wings against the rocks.

All creation is ennobled by the pen of the poet, to be worthy
of this direct communion with God. His descriptions are those
of a world of which ours is only a rude sketch. There exists
not a country so favoured of heaven that M. de Lamartine does
not embellish and idealize. . . . The poet of the **'Harmonies'**
is endowed with senses which we have not: what is to us silence
is to him a concert of unutterable melody; in the flowers which
we trample under our feet he finds intoxicating perfume. In
his first poems we could follow him into a world of thoughts,
superior, but still analogous to ours; we were below him, but
we beheld him beckoning to us from on high. But in the **'Harmonies'** we have lost sight of him; he has veiled himself from
us; he has soared beyond the reach of our vision; and those
who profess that theirs has followed him to the footstool of
the throne of God, have seen him, we fear, only with the eyes
of faith. (pp. 521-22)

D. N., "Lamartine," in The London and Westminster Review, *Vol. XXVI, No. II, October, 1836,
pp. 501-41.*

THE NEW YORK REVIEW   (essay date 1838)

[*In this excerpt from a negative assessment of* A Pilgrimage to
the Holy Land *and* Jocelyn, *the reviewer criticizes the works'
excessive emotionalism and disproportionate amount of detail.*]

250

An engraving by Tony Johannot depicting a scene from Jocelyn. *Laurence, wounded, faints in Jocelyn's arms.*

[Lamartine's **"Travels in the East,"** also known as **"A Pilgrimage to the Holy Land,"**] disenchanted us. We did not, it is true, expect it to be the work of an ordinary writer. We expected his pictures to transcend life; for his ardent temperament precludes the possibility of his thinking and painting like others. But we expected to discern the natural features of the landscape amidst the rich and glowing tints shed over them by his poetic and religious feeling. We expected to breathe an atmosphere of excitement, but not of strained and turgid sensibility. We did not expect to have the ideal forced upon us at every step—impeding our progress, obscuring our vision—actually *crammed into us*—amplified as it was beyond all bounds by its thick vestment of metaphor and simile. We did not expect the laborious expansion of every object, however insignificant, into romantic proportions; nor the envelopement of solemn realities in a misty haze; nor the ostentatious display of private feelings or of devotional ecstacies; nor the perpetual effort to find resemblances between things which of themselves certainly suggest no comparison. (pp. 342-43)

[**"Jocelyn"**] exhibits yet more strikingly the blemishes we have noticed. Here, a romantic story, which the author gives us to understand is a true one, is exalted out of all resemblance to truth or life. The poet has laid the bridle on the neck of his propensities, and takes leave of moderation altogether. Not content with a few bold touches, that might suffice to place the picture before us, he magnifies the minutest object into a

glaring grandeur. He puts forth the utmost powers of his imagination in every description he attempts; and thus falls into inevitable monotony. Every idea stands out prominently, decked in gorgeous phrase; there is a painful want of relief in the poem. (pp. 343-44)

[Lamartine] has all kind of suns and moons for the same limited spot of earth; his sunshine is brighter and more genial than belongs to this world; his lakes are more limpid, his lawns greener, his foliage fresher, and his shade more cooling. We are surrounded by a perpetual profusion of flowers and sweets, of diamond dews, of pearly networks covering the turf, of rainbows and purple clouds—of rich waving herbage, and foliage wreathing in every direction, of swarms of insects, "like winged clouds in the living air;"—till we are wearied, absolutely wearied, with the luxury of description and the continual stretch of the fancy. This passion for amplifying and decorating all things, destroys the definiteness of the picture; where all is prominent, there can be nothing in relief. It loses the semblance of truth. Thus, in describing Laurence, after enumerating beauties enough to have satisfied any painter, the poet tells us there was a brightness emanating from her figure and reflected on surrounding objects. His religious feelings are strongly tinctured with this imaginative character; he compares the aspirations of his soul to the doings of every animate or inanimate object in nature. (p. 349)

[We maintain that his] perpetual dilating upon blighted hopes, and disappointments, and sorrows—the constant burthens of the poet's song, is at variance with the true spirit of religion, whose tendency is to promote serenity and cheerfulness. Lamartine scorns to paint the natural world in the sombre colours employed by many of his brother bards; we wish he were more indulgent in his representations of the moral world; he should not let Religion wear a brow of gloom. . . .

To conclude: **"Jocelyn"** may prove popular as a romance; but, except in detached passages, will hardly gain many new admirers for the author's poetry. (p. 351)

> *"Lamartine's 'Jocelyn',"* in The New York Review, *Vol. II, No. IV, April, 1838, pp. 341-51.*

[ELIZABETH FRIES ELLET]   (essay date 1839)

[*Ellet maintains that Lamartine, though talented, did not develop artistically because he lacked poetic competition. She discusses several defects in* Jocelyn *and* La chute d'un ange, *including implausible plots, excessive emotionalism, and imprecise descriptions. For additional commentary by Ellet, see excerpts dated 1835.*]

The lyrics of M. de Lamartine commanded attention and admiration both in his own and other countries. The vigor and purity of thought and feeling, the richness and graphic beauty of imagery, and the mastery of versification, they displayed, secured at once for the author the first place among the living poets of France. He embodied the highest, the most serious, feelings of his age, and every cultivated mind acknowledged the truth of his sentiments. Unfortunate enough, however, to have few worthy rivals, the adulation lavished upon him, if it did not wholly blind him to his faults, incapacitated him for that high perception of excellence in his art, so indispensable to improvement. Nor was this all. He was essentially deficient in the loftiest attributes of genius. He possessed a pure heart, an active fancy, a ready apprehension of the beautiful, and an almost unbounded command of language. But not to him belonged the original faculty, that "bodies forth the forms of things unknown"; that penetrates the hidden recesses of nature, and brings us thence new objects of delight, new themes for meditation. Nor had he the overwhelming passion, that leads the soul captive, and is inferior only to the inventive power. His genius was imitative. It received its impulse, perhaps unconsciously, from the writers of other countries, though the novelty of his sentiments and his style gave him an ascendency over those of his own.

His latest productions exhibit, in a higher degree, the defects, both of conception and manner, growing out of his poetical self-complacency. **"Jocelyn,"** the first of his *scenes,* given to the world "to interrogate its judgment respecting a species of poetry never yet submitted by the author to criticism," possessed an unusual degree of local interest. It is a fragment of the history of the heart. . . . Its hero is a character familiar to us all; the village *curé,* the gospel priest. The details of the story are touching and true. But it creates no favorable opinion of the genius or taste of the author, to see how this simple and affecting tale has been transformed by his idealizing process into something that has no trace of probability; how the traits of humanity have faded into vague and mystic images; how sentiment is elaborated till it loses all its effect; how our sympathies are strewed about and evaporated. . . . (pp. 448-49)

The story of **"Jocelyn"** is beautiful, and we feel that we ought to be affected by it. That we are not, is the writer's fault. The scenery is magnificent, but the descriptions leave only a vague and confused impression of loveliness and grandeur. The thoughts are noble, but clad in phrase so gorgeous and amplified, that they astonish instead of elevating. It is as if we stood before a picture, where was exhibited every variety of color and figure to charm the sense, but where there was no shading or relief; the mental eye aches with the accumulation of objects and their confused brilliancy. The language is one glowing mass of illustration; it loses effect from its want of adaptation to the subjects presented. In feeling our author is not less elaborate and exaggerated than in description. His love is not like the love of ordinary mortals; even his religion is etherealized beyond the limits of reason and nature. (p. 449)

[**"The Fall of an Angel"** (**"La chute d'un ange"**)] has the advantage of all the embellishments of gorgeous imagery, and the rich flow of verse for which M. de Lamartine is distinguished. The interest is charmingly sustained. We know of no modern romance that can more pleasingly beguile a few hours; and this, notwithstanding grievous errors in taste, that sometimes interrupt the enchantment of the fiction. The episode of Isnel and Ichme, for example, is merely horrible, as are many of the pictures of the impious orgies of the giant gods. (pp. 459-60)

Our author's passion for illustrating things in the moral, by things in the natural world, is indulged throughout these volumes. Sometimes his similes are extremely happy; but that he often repeats himself, he would be in this particular the most ingenious of poets. (p. 460)

Graphic and glowing as are his descriptions, we have often . . . an impression of feebleness, occasioned by his assiduous accumulation of minute objects, and his habits of idealizing every thing, and of magnifying the smallest into the same proportions with the grandest. His torch-light is ever in danger of extinguishing his starlight. He seems wholly ignorant of the art of producing *effect* in a picture by a few vigorous touches. His landscapes are overladen with coloring and laborious ornament.

Nature is not good enough for him. His earth is not the same earth we inhabit. His suns shine with a purer and more golden light. So his men are moral monsters, colossal in good or evil. He has not the despairing, philosophical misanthropy of Lord Byron; his views do not shut out the better things of humanity; his heart apprehends them; but his fancy colors them with strange hues. He will not paint nature as she is, in the mind of man, any more than in the external world. In short, he lacks simplicity, which he sacrifices in his morbid desire to elevate the ideal. This is the reason why his creations fail to command universal interest, to touch the soul. They are not beings of our own brotherhood; they are creatures elaborated and refined in the furnace of M. de Lamartine's imagination, and then dressed for exhibition in his stiff vesture of embellishment. (pp. 460-61)

[Elizabeth Fries Ellet], "Lamartine's 'Chute d'un Ange'," in The North American Review, *Vol. XLVIII, No. CIII, April, 1839, pp. 447-61.*

[JOSEPH MAZZINI] (essay date 1839)

[*Focusing on the spiritual nature of Lamartine's verse, Mazzini maintains that Lamartine was not a true religious poet because he misrepresented Christian dogma and could not solve the problems of the human condition. Mazzini faults in particular the style of* La chute d'un ange, *which he considers a failure as a religious poem and a general indication of Lamartine's decline as a poet.*]

We had felt a sort of terror, when we heard the poet of vague aspirings, of soft regrets, of the soul's fugitive thoughts, announce his purpose of giving us an *epopoeia,* the Epopoeia of Humanity, of which *Jocelyn* (some ten or twelve thousand lines) was but an episode; we knew that M. de Lamartine must break down in the trial. The poetic talent of the author of the *Méditations,* brilliant undoubtedly, but somewhat of the improvisatore character, fruitful, but in a confined sphere, did not appear to us adequate to the vast proportions of the epic. His creeds, philosophic and religious, were not, in our opinion, sufficiently determinate or sufficiently complete for what he was undertaking. . . . [We] listen with deep attention to his confidential revelations; the fifth of his *Harmonies (La Source dans le Bois),* although sad and depressing, we think admirable, as we do many of the *Méditations.* But when he assumes the position of the religious poet,—when he says to us, "I know the malady of mankind, it is my own, and I come to cure it,"—when he talks to us of faith, of knowledge of the destinies of humanity,—if, after listening to him, we feel our wounds festering, and consciousness of our own impotence stealing into our soul with his lays, and scepticism, with the icy wind from his wings, driving away hope;—we feel ourselves entitled to say to him, "You are mistaken; the secret of cure lies not there." Now this is precisely our position relatively to M. de Lamartine. He has professed himself a religious poet, and been generally accepted as such. . . . Is this well or ill? Does his poetry contain the aliment required by the epoch? To us the inquiry appears important.

In a literary point of view, one fact is henceforward established which deserves attention;—this is a decline, a decline decided and striking as that of M. Victor Hugo, which has been pretty generally felt and recorded by the French press, and which would have met with still less leniency, if, like M. Victor Hugo, M. de Lamartine had preached a theory, founded a literary sect, and warred against criticism. There is a decline in M. de Lamartine's [*La Chute d'un Ange*] in respect of the form and the poetic accessories, a decline in respect of the substance of that which constitutes the life and essence of poetry. The first is serious, but may with ease be subsequently repaired; the second is much more so, and what is worse, from it there is far less chance of the poet's recovering himself. Faults of style that must be owned striking, images spoiled or repeated even to monotony, incorrectness of language and rhythm carried to a pitch that it were difficult to believe [are evident]. . . . A want of artistic conscientiousness and of respect for the public is evinced in the attempt to write an *epopoeia* extempore; but a hope may be entertained that the severity of the judgments pronounced upon his composition may recall M. de Lamartine to himself; and we know that in order to be a pure and elegant writer, he need only resolve to be so. Can we say as much of those faults which affect the very essence of the poetry, and, as it were, establish the fact of a second manner in the author? Can we, when, in *The Angel's Fall* [*La Chute d'un Ange*], we find the worship of the form substituted for the adoration of the idea, matter predominant over mind, and the colouring of the Venetian painters supplanting the spirituality of the school of Umbria, suppose all this a mere digression of the poet? (pp. 208-11)

La Chute d'un Ange has nothing in common with those compositions which the first verses of the sixth chapter of Genesis suggested to Byron and Moore; nor yet with that delicious little poem of Alfred de Vigny, *Eloa*. . . . M. de Lamartine's angel likewise falls through love; but that is the only point of contact. The idea of the poem is more comprehensive, more philosophic. The angel is here the personification of the human soul. The human soul, and the successive phases through which God has decreed that it must achieve its perfectible destinies—that is the subject of the grand *epopoeia* of which the poem here noticed is but a part, the second, perhaps, of the twelve or fourteen that, as is reported, are to compose the work. This is, then, one of the first pages of the history of moral man, written from the point of view of the Christian dogma of the Fall. (pp. 212-13)

[We] cannot, even while confining ourselves within the limits of art, forbear asking of the poet some account of his subject, of the primary idea of his poem. This idea, which ought to gleam through all the parts of the composition, which ought, in a word, to constitute its artistic unity, where is it, if not in what serves as a sort of prologue to the poem? Take away this prologue, begin with Cedar's conflict with the robbers of Doïdha . . . , and say where is the Fall, where the Angel. Say whether you can even guess that a great expiation is in question, that through all these events a religious mystery, an immense and holy rehabilitation is in progress. We find nothing but human concerns, the vicissitudes and miseries of men, without law, without bearing, without relation to the designs of Providence; there is no *fallen angel* here. Lamartine, in one of his first *Méditations,* said, "Man's a fallen God, who recollects the skies"; and we expected that the whole poem would be a commentary upon this line. Nothing of the kind; Cedar does not *recollect.* Never does his soul soar towards heaven on the wings of aspiration, never does it recognise heaven's presence by resignation. Cedar enjoys and suffers, struggles and yields to force, seeing only the material, immediate causes of his sufferings, and protesting against them with all his might. He drags himself through the tossings of a life incessantly crushed and dominated by crises altogether casual, and in which nothing, it must be said, could lead him back, by thought, *to his native heaven;* whilst not a single flash of the past, not a single presentiment of the future, crosses the darkness of his night. (pp. 217-18)

Now we say that there is not in his book any moral *measure* of the *fall.* It is not, it cannot be, with *remorse* that Cedar prepares to die; the words of the Spirit are there inapplicable, and can only serve as a text to the condemnation of the poem. If it is not by a certain measure of suffering alone that the soul may redeem its immortality, but, as it is to be believed, by a deep sense of the justice of the punishment, and of its value as an expiation, then *The Fall of an Angel* is and will remain completely null with regard to the religious and philosophic thought: in it Conscience has no representative.

We can therefore see in this work of M. de Lamartine only a series of fanciful pictures, containing the history of a man named Cedar and of a woman named Doïdha, and possessing simply an artistic value, which we have to appreciate. This value is unfortunately too slight to yield us any compensation for the deficiency in the thought, of which we have just complained.

There are, indeed, here and there poetic beauties, graceful images, descriptions brilliantly executed, pages which recall M. Lamartine and his best manner; but their number is very small, and there is not one that the poet has not surpassed in his preceding compositions. The hymn of the Cedars of Lebanon . . . has been cited as a magnificent passage; to us it appears only fine, and, even independently of the blemishes that disfigure it,—such as the comparison of the thrillings of prayer communicated to the cedars by the instinct of the divine virtue, to the undulations impressed upon the lion's mane by the wind of wrath, that reddens his nostril and growls in his breast,—we should not be at a loss to find in the *Harmonies* analogous and considerably superior passages. Some landscapes are well given, but never, in *La Chute d'un Ange,* does nature appear to us reproduced and felt as in *Jocelyn.* Doïdha's sleep . . . is a study by a master's hand; but it stands alone, or nearly so. The vision that comprises Cedar's captivity amidst the tribe of Phayz, the budding love of Doïdha, and the sort of education that she gives her lover, is beautiful from one end to the other: admirably in it do the graceful, the chaste and the sweet harmonize: one might say a group of children by Correggio, in a landscape of Claude Lorraine's. But this is all; and are *episodic* beauties sufficient for a poem? (pp. 218-19)

We may be interested, as we run it over, in the vicissitudes of its personages, as one is interested, through curiosity, in every action that develops itself before us; but when the book is closed, all is over. Neither the sphere nor the energy of our thought is aggrandized; no bewitching form has joined the group of ideal forms, our companions for life, created for us by Dante, Shakspeare and Goethe, under the names of Francesca, Ophelia, Clara, Margaret, and so many more. We need not, perhaps, speak of Cedar; but Doïdha herself, Doïdha, upon whom the poet has lavished, as upon a favourite child, all the treasures of his imagination, what is she to us? After perusing and reperusing those long, and often repeated, minutely-detailed descriptions of her person, we have closed our eyes to see if she would not appear to our soul, and we have seen nothing; vainly did we strive to evoke her image. The poet has only known how to paint to us every part of this being, he has not known how to transmit to us that which constitutes unity,— its individuality. He has killed life by analysis. (pp. 219-20)

We need not concern ourselves with the incorrectnesses of language, the violations of the laws of rhythm, the distortions of grammar itself; upon these French critics have long since done justice. But what they have overlooked, and what appears to us a far more important matter for animadversion, as affecting the very nature of the style, is a real poetic materialism, which, in an inconceivable and systematic manner, predominates throughout the whole poem,—a materialism always, to our mind, the fatal symptom of fall, but which, on the present occasion, strikes us the more, because it displays itself in two-thirds of the poem, in the representation of a *horrible* not possessing even the merit of M. Victor Hugo's *grotesque*, that of contrast. (pp. 220-21)

[There is] nothing vague or ideal, nothing of that intangible indefinite which abounded in M. Lamartine's first manner; everything is positive, palpable, massive; everywhere the appropriate word, the picturesque word, has dethroned the abstract or metaphysical word; everywhere, in the representation of objects, analysis and material detail have supplanted the synthetical expression, defining an object by that which constitutes its life and unity. No more of those figures, with lightly traced outlines, a little indeterminate and hovering, like the visions of thought, but of which the expression, caught in its prominent and characteristic feature, remains so thoroughly imprinted on our souls. No more of those pictures of nature, painted by masses, and of which some principal features, some deep lines, drawn after the manner of great artists, suffice to give us so just a conception of the whole. Doïdha is described, as by inventory, ten times in the poem; the first time in seventy-five lines: the giant who surprises her in her sleep requires forty. The landscapes are counterdrawn, represented in their smallest accessories, then inundated with light, shed equally upon all points, without contrasts, without shade. Does the poet seek images, similes, or analogies for anything? He quits not his sphere: one material object awakens in him no other idea than that of another material object; and that whole source of poetry, so difficult but so potent, which incessantly passes from the physical to the moral, seeking the harmonies of the two worlds, is for him dried up. He can, indeed, still descend from the world of spirit to the world of matter, and translate to the senses what should be addressed only to the soul, but he can no longer reascend. (pp. 221-22)

Nothing can be more monotonous, more wearisome, more opposite to the nature of poetry, which should lend the reader wings, than . . . [a luxuriance of materialization]. One rises sated, heavy, oppressed, as from sensual orgies. We say this, speaking only of the better parts of the poem, of those in which the worship of Form is kept within the limits of the Beautiful; for, what shall be said of those, much more numerous, in which this power of poetic materialism is employed in the service of the Ugly, the Horrible, the Disgusting? (p. 223)

Heaven be thanked, we have done! The reader has seen enough to understand M. de Lamartine's fall, and the nature of that fall. He must already, like us, have put the question to himself, how the author of the *Méditations,* the poet of the deepest emotions, of the most spiritual aspirations, can have come to delight in this gross and carnal poetry, in the manner of the Rubens'-school, without the genius of Rubens, or his worship of material *beauty*? This *how,* we will endeavour to explain to him, as it appears to us to follow necessarily from a comprehensive retrospect of Lamartine's whole poetic career.

When the first *Méditations* appeared in 1820, they made a sensation in France such as few books can make. It was poetry of a perfectly new species, raising its voice at the very moment when a generation, sick of the cold and measured versification of the Empire, was asserting that all poetry was dead, and that henceforward to prose, a lofty and poetic prose, appertained the expression of the thoughts of the epoch. This poetry looked

to the future by the nature of the ideas, or more properly of the sentiments, and by its aim; whilst by a certain chastity of form, by respect for the language, and even by some few old classical reminiscences, although proclaiming the independence of Art as a right, it preserved a connecting link with national literary traditions. It satisfied all demands, and was entitled to find favour with all schools. The author's poetic talent was, moreover, truly and incontestably powerful. Never had France known such elegy. Never had hope breathed amidst ruins hymns so sweetly melancholy. (pp. 224-25)

[M. de Lamartine] painted himself in his verses as suffering from the disease of the age, and labouring to cure both himself and it. In a word he assumed the attitude of the religious poet. . . .

Was he really a religious poet? No, he was not.

The malady of the age he indeed had; and never perhaps, at least in France, had it been so well expressed; but the remedy he had not. It might even be said that the poet sometimes detects himself doubting whether any exists. In the first, and in the new *Méditations* there is religious feeling, the disposition to which somebody has given the name of *religionism,*—but no religion: the yearning for a belief is not belief. In order to be a religious poet, it is not enough, in our eyes at least, to cry Lord! Lord! to lie prostrate before God, and, with the head in the dust, to confess his infinite power: it is necessary to *feel* his holy law, and to make others *feel* it, in such sort as that they shall constantly and calmly act in obedience to its precepts. (p. 226)

[The] author of the *Méditations,* what is his God? whom does he adore?

He adores Fear. The God whom he adores is the God of the East, before whose omnipotence he perceives but two possible parts for man—blasphemy or annihilation. Betwixt these two states the poet, as he himself tells us, long oscillated. He strove, by the solitary potency of his soul, to scale heaven like the Titans, to wrest his secret from the Everlasting, and seat himself by his side. . . . Like Victor Hugo, he has condemned man, science, the whole world, to annihilation; like him, perhaps even more than him, he plunged into that permanent contradiction which blasphemes the creation whilst blessing the Creator. (p. 227)

The expression of [his] struggle is found in many of the *Méditations,* sometimes even too vividly, and so as to hurry away unconsciously young, inexperienced minds. See, *Méditations,* II. *à Lord Byron,* VII. *Le Désespoir,* &c. . . . Nothingness, disenchantment, despondency, this is the eternal theme of the *Méditations,* it is only thus that the poet rises towards God. Hence that feeling of a struggle betwixt faith and reason which recurs at every step. . . . Hence,—whenever the poet, led away by his original instincts, returns to the search of happiness on earth,—that longing to find in it, not a renewal of energy to fulfil his mission, but forgetfulness, inaction, a sort of annihilation of his individuality, which, in the *Nouvelles Méditations,* dictated the Fourth (*La Sagesse*), the Eleventh (*Elégie*), the Twelfth (*Tristesse*), the Thirteenth—(*La Branche d'Amandier*), inspirations now Tibullian, now Horatian, in a word, Pagan, disguised under Christian forms; hence, in fine, that gloomy and unfruitful sorrow, that wind of sadness drying up the spirit, that sense of moral depression, of languor, piercing through his poetry, and which is likewise, as we firmly believe, its definitive result, the only effect remaining in the soul after its perusal. And, whilst thus writing, it is not of the avowedly melancholy *Méditations,* of those in which lamentation predominates, that we are thinking: far from it. . . . It is of the collective bearing that we speak. It is after the pieces strongest in Godward bursts, that we feel this something resembling exhaustion. It is on the wings of imagination, rather than on those of the heart, that we have been compelled to follow the poet in his flight: the heart has remained sunk in bitterness, *weary of all things, even of hope,* and repeating in whispers to itself, the *what can be done with life?* of the Nineteenth *Méditation.*

And men, his *brothers* in *sorrow,* what has he to say to them? What has he to give them for their support and guidance in their pilgrimage? Nothing. One consolation on their death-bed, in the Twenty-second *Méditation (Le Crucifix),* an admirable piece, the only one of the Meditations, perhaps, in which religious inspiration really touched M. de Lamartine. (pp. 228-29)

[The *Harmonies'* lack of success was not due] to a very decided poetic inferiority; the author's point of view once admitted, poetry flows in them often in brimming measure. Even independently of those which are confined to the sphere of personal emotions and affections, such as *Le Souvenir d'Enfance, Le Rossignol, Le Premier Regret,* &c., all very beautiful; and as such received;—the religious *Harmonies* bear traces of great power; but the predominant thought was not that which the times were then evolving. The *Harmonies* proclaimed that, for the poet, the struggle was over. They professed to give the solution of the problem; and this solution was nothing more than that of which some misgivings might have been felt from the *Méditations,* a moral suicide completed—an absolute obliteration of individuality—an overwhelming of all the active faculties, of moral power, of the mission undertaken, of liberty, under the sense of the Infinite. With the exception of *Le Chêne,* in which the poet admirably well rises from "nature up to nature's God"—of *L'Humanité,* in which, by the way, the portraiture of woman appears to us superior to that, so highly extolled, of Doïdha—of . . . *Pensées des Morts,* which . . . contains real poetic intuitions,—the four books of the *Harmonies* confirm our assertions. Orientalism in thought, orientalism in form! God burthens man with his whole immensity. . . . Accordingly, the poetic form shows the baneful influence: the attributes of power are employed, almost alone, to paint the Divine Nature; the same images momentarily recur; epithets multiply; the pompous, the sonorous, abound; everything, even the rhythmic cadence, assumes a monotony, the more important to observe, because the endeavour to avoid it is the motive that has since driven the poet to plunge into the faults that signalize the *Chute d'un Ange.* With regard to life, the same contempt, the same disenchantment, the same thirst for repose, for inaction. Man's divorce from the world is there distinctly pronounced (XI. *L'Abbaye de Vallombreuse*). Man, *praying remote from mortals,* is there presented as the ideal type of religious feeling (VIII. liv. 4., *Le Solitaire*). The opposition between reason and conscience is here (XI. liv. 4.) yet more loudly proclaimed than in the *Méditations.* . . . (pp. 232-33)

[In *Jocelyn,* contemplation and inaction predominate,] as in M. Lamartine's other poetic labours. But as the author has in some sort exempted himself from criticism with respect to the ideas, by presenting himself, upon this occasion, only as the historian,—as he tells us, even in his preface, "*Jocelyn* is the Christian type of our epoch; the reader who should see in this subject anything but its poetic part; there is here no concealed purpose, no system, no controversy for or against such or such a religious creed''; we need not seek

here for the development of the poet's thought; we accept it as a halt; and if we cite it here, it is only to mark therein the poet's last effort to maintain himself, at least as to poetic expression, in the right road, upon the ground of spirituality. In fact, the image here very seldom crushes the thought; and, at the beginning of the second *epoch,* there are passages in which reverie, the God-ward bursts of the soul, everything most difficult to catch and to express, is painted with the subtlety, purity and delicacy of the spider's web suspended betwixt two trees, and giving free passage to the sunbeams. The solitude of the grotto of the eagles on the summit of the Dauphiny Alps, and the gradations by which the yearning for love arises in the heart of the young priest who inhabits there . . . are equally well described; and, notwithstanding some faulty similes, and the inaccuracies inherent in rapid versification, *Jocelyn* has fine pages of poetry. It was a bold effort, but it exhausted the poet. *La Chute d'un Ange* followed *Jocelyn.* Depression and sterility of thought in the substance—adoration of form and materialism in the poetic expression,—it is the poet's last word, and does not in the least astonish us. (pp. 235-36)

[Like Victor Hugo, M. de Lamartine], influenced by the instincts of the age and of his own talent, proposed to himself, as his object, human rehabilitation from the religious point of view; like him, he has proved short-sighted, and incompetent to perceive that the only possible rehabilitation for the *individual* is through the *species.* He has proved incompetent to rise to a just conception of the whole. . . . He, for his part, saw only the individual, and has never overstepped that sphere. Thus he has been without a basis by which to appreciate value, by which to understand the sense, the object, the importance of actions: he has judged them all absolutely, and in their tangible, immediate results; not relatively and in their remote consequences, often impalpable, but always certain, as regards the great and combined work. . . . Concentrated in the narrow sphere of individuality—consequently having but an incomplete, mutilated conception of life,—contemplating it but partially, and at a given moment,—it was certain that he must, in a very short time, find himself drained of representations, of images, of combinations. More a poet than aught else, and unable to resign himself to remaining silent, he has endeavoured to substitute to the infinity of ideas that was denied him, the innumerability of forms—to the monotony of *Les Harmonies,* the delusive and material variety of *La Chute d'un Ange.* This experiment is not, however, in our opinion, natural to the poet, and we believe that it will be monotony, not variety of detail, that will dig the grave of his poetry.

This is the actual position of Lamartine at present; this is pretty nearly the actual position, though reached by somewhat divergent paths, of Victor Hugo;—Hugo and Lamartine—that is to say, the two most powerful poets of France of the nineteenth century, the two heads of the romantic school,—the only difference between whom is caused by the peculiar temper of the talent of each. . . . Neither the one nor the other is, as a religious educator-poet, the poet of the future. (pp. 236-38)

> [*Joseph Mazzini*], ''Lamartine's Poems,'' in The
> British and Foreign Review, *Vol. IX, No. XVII, July,*
> *1839, pp. 208-46.*

[CHARLES BULLER] (essay date 1848)

[*Buller praises* History of the Girondists *for its vivid descriptions and sketches of famous figures, but he faults the work's frequent exaggerations. Buller asserts that although* History of the Girondists *is "imperfect as a history, it is a striking and instructive historical study."*]

[Independently of the] adventitious causes of a momentary notoriety, the **'History of the Girondins'** [**'Histoire des Girondins'**] is a work that possesses solid claims to a more durable and extensive reputation. We cannot receive it as a satisfactory history of the period of which it treats. In fact the author, though he has given it the name of a 'history,' is content that it should be classed in a humbler category. 'As for the title of this book,' he says in his preface

> we have only adopted it for want of any other word to designate a narrative. This book has none of the pretensions of history, and must not assume its dignity. It is an intermediate work between history and memoirs. Events occupy in it a subordinate place to men and ideas. It is full of personal details. These details are the physiognomy of characters: it is through them that the latter impress themselves on the imagination. Great writers have already written the chronicles of this memorable epoch. Others will ere long write them. It will be doing us injustice to compare us with them. They have produced or will produce, the history of an age: we have produced nothing but a *study* of a group of men, and of some months of the Revolution.

With the scheme of his work before him, M. de Lamartine has not thought it necessary to give a detailed record of all the events of the period. He assumes that his reader has already acquired this knowledge from other sources. Relying on this he has not, as he tells us, scrupled in some instances to heighten the effect by neglecting the exact order of time. It is much to be regretted, however, that such omissions and inversions are accompanied by more serious defects, which impair our confidence in the accuracy of the narrative, and consequently in the justice of the views based upon it. The intermediate position between history and memoirs which the author would assume for his work is one which, unfortunately, possesses the claims of neither, as an authority concerning matters of fact. Its statements are not given, as in memoirs, on the author's personal knowledge; nor are they drawn, as in a trustworthy history, from original accounts of a known and authentic character. Incidents, which give an entirely new aspect to some of the principal persons, and to some even of the most important events of the period, are stated on the authority of no published work, or accessible record (in which case the authenticity or value of the statement could have been tested), but simply on that of private documents, which the reader has no means of examining for himself,—of conversations with unnamed individuals, the trustworthiness as well as the effect of whose evidence we are obliged to take entirely on credit from our author. . . . [The consequence of his] indisposition to encumber the story with the ordinary proofs of historical accuracy is, that when we get beyond the most familiar incidents, we never know the value of a single statement that is made: for instance, whether it is derived from most intelligent and impartial witnesses, or from the most discredited and heated partisans; whether it is capable of being supported by a reference to some indisputable and acknowledged authority, or rests entirely on the private conversation or letter of some survivor of the Revolution, whose good faith or judgment it is possible that particular circumstances may have led M. de Lamartine to overestimate. This is a fault peculiarly to be regretted in an author,

whose poetical reputation lays him open to the imputation of not being much in the habit of investigating closely, or weighing accurately, the evidences of historical facts: and the very character of whose work suggests the suspicion that he may have been ready to take on insufficient evidence any striking statement that would heighten the effect of his narrative, or bear out the view which he has formed of the character of some remarkable individual. M. de Lamartine promises that, after a while, in case any of his statements should be assailed, he will support them by a mass of proof. We would impress on him that this is a duty, which, even without any call of self-defence, it is incumbent on him to discharge, in order to stamp on the very face of his history those outward and visible signs of conscientious and laborious truthfulness, which can alone invest it with permanent utility and reputation.

But accuracy, unfortunately, is not one of M. de Lamartine's qualifications for writing history. Those who are most conversant with the events of the Revolution accuse him of frequent exaggeration. Imitating a habit of the ancient historians, which is not permitted by the present canons of historical propriety, he does not scruple to embody his own conception of the feelings of the various personages of his narrative in imaginary speeches, which he puts into their mouths. In some instances an ordinary acquaintance with the history of the Revolution exposes inaccuracies which are not to be attributed to any bias or misconception, but to sheer carelessness. But even with these very serious defects, this work remains a most valuable contribution to our knowledge of the Revolution. Imperfect as a history, it is a striking and instructive historical study. It brings before us that most stirring and important period with a clearness and vividness that all previous descriptions, except some of Carlyle's, have failed to realise: it presents us on the same page with distinct, highly-finished sketches of the principal actors, and with a careful and deliberate judgment on the causes, the nature, and consequences of the events. These are the objects at which the author has evidently aimed; and he has, in our opinion, attained them with greater success than any other writer on the Revolution. Skill and power in the representation of remarkable scenes and incidents was an excellence which M. de Lamartine's descriptive powers gave us reason to anticipate: and, he has combined this excellence with more discrimination and justice in his estimate of characters and events than we were prepared for. Though occasionally too apt to judge one man somewhat too harshly, or to elevate another into a species of imaginary hero—though often bewildered by the vastness of the subject, or misled by his own ardent temperament—M. de Lamartine seems to us on the whole to have brought to the consideration of the Revolution a more candid spirit and more wholesome sympathies, than any preceding writer. (pp. 3-6)

He who would give the world its historical beliefs, must bring to the task the gifts of the poet as well as of the philosopher; must be able to depict incidents as in an epic, and make each character appear and act with dramatic distinctness and effect. No historian of the Revolution has done this so strikingly as M. de Lamartine; and none, therefore, will in all probability exercise so extensive an influence on the popular views which will be generally entertained of it.

That influence, no question, will be very much diminished by the want, in M. de Lamartine, of other qualities which are required to complete the character of a historian. His work is wanting, not merely in accuracy and research, but in the indications of large, calm, and solid thought. While we think

A portrait of Graziella, adapted from a painting by Charles Lefebvre.

that the author does more than any preceding historian towards giving a reasonable explanation of the events of the Revolution, and while we generally agree in the justice of M. de Lamartine's conclusions and sympathise with his feelings; we feel that he does not express those conclusions in the tone of a philosopher, who has deeply meditated and thoroughly mastered his subject. His narrative exhibits constant marks of exaggeration. (pp. 44-5)

We should be happy to think that what we have taken for indications of a want of sound and sober thought, may be only the consequence of the excessive rapidity, with which the **'History of the Girondins'** has been written. It betokens, however, little wisdom in an author, who writes for fame and not for bread, to have composed a great work on a great subject without giving himself sufficient time for thought. Let us hope that M. de Lamartine will avoid this most deplorable fault in the **'History of the Constituent Assembly,'** which he promises us. (pp. 45-6)

> [*Charles Buller*], "Lamartine: 'History of the Girondins'," in The Edinburgh Review, *Vol. LXXXVII, No. CLXXV, January, 1848, pp. 1-46.*

[A. V. KIRWAN]   (essay date 1849)

[*While Kirwan commends the rich, melodious verse of* Raphaël: Pages de la vingtième année (Raphael; or, Pages of the Book of Life at Twenty), *he maintains that it is too ethereal to appeal to English readers.*]

[***Raphael***] exhibits a great deal of the genius and most of the faults of Lamartine. His style is always charming, and full of life and colour. It partakes of the eloquence and tenderness of Rousseau, of the grace and ease of Bernardin de St. Pierre, and of the magic wildness, fancy, and enthusiastic glow and warmth of Chateaubriand. It is at once limpid, facile, melodious. The images are rich and abundant: all nature,—the winds and the waves, the earth and sky, the flowers of the field and of the mountain, of the river's brink, and of the dark, unfathomed caves of ocean, are all familiar and tributary to him. The cadences and falls of his prose are melodious as his poetry, the phrases are as balanced and rhythmical as his best verses, the language is at once magnificent, picturesque, and enchanting. You feel that you have before you the prose of the most lyrical and flowery of orators, of the most melodious of poets, not even excepting Racine. But with all this, and though you feel in ***Raphael*** that the writer is painter, musician, and narrator, . . .—though you also feel that there is about him a melancholy which is interesting, and a tenderness that is winning and seductive, yet the book fails to satisfy in this,—that it is destitute of human frailty, of human weakness, and human interest. There is apparent in every line a sense of the beautiful in nature and in art, an exquisite sensibility, but a sensibility too sublimated, too unearthly, too remote for human passion,— in a word, too Platonic for English taste. (pp. 215-16)

As we said before, this is a remarkable work, reminding one of Fénélon, Bernardin de St. Pierre, Jean Jacques, and Chateaubriand. It exhibits grace, eloquence, poetry, and exquisite sensibility; but its great defect is the absence of human passion and human frailty. It is, indeed, a history of love, but of love disengaged and dissociated from the senses,—a spiritual love of two persons of different sexes, who love each other in visions and raptures of eternal and celestial beauty. This *quid divinum*, this ethereal essence of love, exists not in the present 'work-a-day' world, but only in the pages of the divine Plato, the learned St. Augustine, the tender Fénélon, the devout Madame Guyon, and in the exquisite and rhythmical phrase of Alphonse de Lamartine.

Had the author thrown more of real nature and of the hard realities of life into his tale, it would have been better relished and applauded in England. (p. 220)

> [*A. V. Kirwan*], "Lamartine's 'Raphael'," in Fraser's Magazine, *Vol. XXXIX, No. CCXXX, February, 1849, pp. 212-20.*

[N. W. SENIOR]   (essay date 1850)

[*Senior discusses the style of* Histoire de la révolution de 1848 (History of the French Revolution of 1848), *which he regards as an autobiography rather than a history. Though he considers the narrative vivid and interesting, he faults its exaggerations and poorly employed metaphors.*]

The most valuable materials for the history of great events are undoubtedly afforded by the autobiographies of those who took a distinguished part in them. . . . Such narratives, however, are comparatively rare: And those which we possess have generally been *written* long after the events—when the recollections of the narrator had lost their first vividness; while their *publication* is often delayed still longer, until the contemporaries of the writer have passed away,—perhaps until he has passed away himself,—so that much of the restraint, which the liability to denial and exposure would have imposed on his inventions or on his suppressions, has been removed. . . . [One] of the great merits of M. de Lamartine's [*Histoire de la Révolution de 1848*] is its freedom from these objections. It must have been written within a few months of the events which it relates; and it is published while almost every other actor in that great drama can protest against its statements or supply its omissions. On the other hand, of course, this proximity has its inconveniences. M. de Lamartine cannot feel as impartially as if his work had treated of times long since passed; or speak as boldly as if it had been intended to be posthumous. In following the course of this narrative, we accordingly often wish for names where we find mere designations, and for details where we find only general statements. Much is obviously concealed from us which it would have been useful to know, but dangerous to tell. Undeserved praise, too, appears to be frequently awarded; and deserved blame to be still more frequently withheld. These objections, however, are far more than counterbalanced by the freshness and vivacity of the narrative: a freshness and vivacity which even as great a poet as M. de Lamartine could not have given to it, if he had written it ten years later. But it is not what it calls itself. It is not a History of the Revolution of 1848. It is an account of what M. de Lamartine said and did from the 24th of February to the 24th of June in that year. But, as he took a great share during that period in the creation, organisation, and direction of the Republic, he cannot tell his own story without interweaving that of the Revolution. The accessory, however, is always kept in proper subordination to the principal. What we are told of the fortunes of France is always subservient to the real subject of the work—the fortunes of M. de Lamartine. We shall treat the work therefore, not as a history, but as an autobiography. As the former it would be meagre and unsatisfactory; as the latter it is as copious as we could wish it to be. (pp.228-29)

As a literary work it has striking merits, and glaring defects. The narrative is clear and interesting, and is interspersed with scenes full of picturesque details: often, however, so minute and so highly coloured, that the reader is inclined to suspect that they are the result rather of fancy than of recollection. Many of them look like pieces of a poem inserted by mistake in a history. (p. 296)

The style is vivid and forcible; but . . . often vague and forced, and deformed by broken metaphors and by almost ludicrous exaggerations. Exaggeration, indeed, is the prevailing fault both of his thoughts and of the language in which he clothes them. All those with whom he comes in contact are angels or demons. They are either endowed with perfect beauty, eloquence, and virtue, or are deformed by 'le vertige du désordre, la volupté du chaos, la 'soif du sang.' Under his pencil a riot becomes an insurrection, a street row a battle. A great source of the defects of the book probably is, that it was composed far too rapidly. M. de Lamartine has lately been writing at the rate of more than half a dozen octavos per year. It is impossible that works so hastily put together can do justice to their author. A man with powers like his ought to write for posterity. (p. 297)

> [*N. W. Senior*], ''*Lamartine's 'Historie de la Révolution de 1848','' in* The Edinburgh Review, *Vol. XCI, No. CLXXXIII, January, 1850, pp. 228-97.*

THE WESTMINSTER AND FOREIGN QUARTERLY REVIEW
(essay date 1850)

[*In the following excerpt from a negative review of* Toussaint L'ouverture, *the critic focuses on the drama's historical inaccuracies.*]

[M. de Lamartine's] fame will not be increased by his appearance as a dramatic author. We cannot but find him guilty of having produced a bad play; but it is guilty, with extenuating circumstances. In the first place, he did not, he says, intend [''**Toussaint l'Ouverture**''] for a play at all; it was not even *une oeuvre literaire*—it was merely ''a cry of humanity in five acts.'' For many years M. de Lamartine had been, as our readers know, a zealous and persevering advocate of negro emancipation. . . . At length he determined to address himself to another auditory, and to endeavour to awaken a feeling for the cause in the hearts of the people. With this view he wrote, during a few weeks of leisure, ''not a tragedy or a drama, but the dramatic and popular poem of **'Toussaint l'Ouverture'**,'' designing it, at most, for some melo-dramatic theatre of the Boulevards, and being conscious that it was better adapted to please the eyes of the million, than the ears and tastes of the more refined. (p. 236)

There are two points of view in which we may regard this production. We may consider it either as a ''*pièce de circonstance*,'' intended to serve a special purpose, according to the author's declared intention, or as a work of art; for, notwithstanding M. de Lamartine's disclaimer, its representation and subsequent publication must bring it within this category. (pp. 236-37)

On the first count, then, a simple historical narrative would, we conceive, have answered better the purpose of popularizing the subject; for the story of Toussaint l'Ouverture is one that may well afford to dispense with extraneous help. The character of the sable hero, as here presented, is by no means calculated to awaken the interest and admiration which the driest narrative of facts might have done. The feeble and lachrymose personage who weeps for the responsibility imposed upon him, and in the most important and decisive moments moves but at the prompting of another's will, bears but little resemblance to the extraordinary man whose fierce and fiery energy, promptitude, and decision, even more than his superior intelligence, raised him among his countrymen to an authority that has been compared to that of the most despotic sovereigns of Asia. . . . The kindlier side of his character, too; his grateful remembrance of his former master, to whom during his day of greatness Toussaint never neglected to transmit the produce, or more than the produce, of his former estate; his affectionate respect for his godfather, who could never be induced to change his humble abode, but whom the Dictator constantly visited,—these, and many similar features of character exhibited in his early life, as well as the pathos of its tragic catastrophe, are entirely lost in the unavoidable subjection to dramatic laws. . . .

Tried, either by what he professed to have in view, or by what might have been the object of a dramatic poet in taking up the subject, the author must, it appears to us, be found wanting. (p. 237)

> *A review of ''Toussaint L'ouverture,'' in* The Westminster and Foreign Quarterly Review, *Vol. LIV, No. I, October, 1850, pp. 236-45.*

BENTLEY'S MISCELLANY   (essay date 1854)

[*In the following excerpt from a positive review of* History of the Girondists *and* Memoirs of Celebrated Characters, *the critic praises these works for their poetic prose and historical authenticity.*]

The character of Lamartine's mind, and the direction of his occupations and studies during the last seven or eight years, are peculiarly calculated to impress a special value upon his literary labours. Few living writers possess in so high a degree the power of investing historical subjects with that dramatic and picturesque interest which distinguish the modern authorship of France. In all those qualities of vivid colouring, artistic grouping, and striking characterisation, which are estimated by French critics amongst the highest merits of the historian, Lamartine's wonderful narrative of the Girondists [in *History of the Girondins*] leaves all competition at an immeasurable distance behind. Combining force and perspicuity of statement with brilliancy of style, and a striking disposition and development of incidents, there was thrown over the whole a certain charm of sentiment which is always attractive in France, and which, incompatible as it appears to us, with the graver and more responsible claims of history, exercises, nevertheless, a secret influence over our judgment. The sentiment of Lamartine is not to be confounded with that vanity of phrase and finesse of expression which are so curiously assisted by the genius of the language, and which the popular taste has erected into a kind of established mode. In him it is the wild flower that springs up out of a rich poetical soil; while the sentiment of most other French writers may be compared, by way of completing the analogy, to the artificial flowers of a fashionable *magazin*. The union of the poet and the politician has seldom been productive of satisfactory results; yet there seems to be a special propriety in their combination in the historical works of Lamartine. It enables him to bring his full powers into play upon subjects that admit of animated treatment; and he has seldom chosen any other. His instinct carries him safely through the perils that beset him on both sides; he rarely overlays his descriptions with extraneous embellishments, or sacrifices facts to the suggestions of fancy; there is always a distinct purpose kept in view; there is matter as well as beauty in his most gorgeous passages; and if he sometimes converts history into romance, it is in the form rather than the substance. (pp. 163-64)

Macaulay in England, and Lamartine in France may be regarded as the pioneers upon the new track of [historical] enquiry, which, instead of stopping short in archives and palaces, conducts us out into the open air, and introduces us to the homes and haunts of the people. There is a marked difference between them, but it is a difference of climate, and not of aims. Their means are similar, and their object is identical. The whole philosophy of the question is admirably expressed by Lamartine, in his eloquent introduction to [*Memoirs of Celebrated Characters*].

> What is it in history . . . that moves or excites the masses? It is men—men only. You cannot excite yourself over a chart, or be moved by a chronology. These abridged and analytic processes are the algebra of history, freezing while they instruct. This algebra of memory must be left to the learned; who, amidst their dusty books, after reading all their lives, and crowding their repertories with millions of facts, names, and dates, desire to make a synoptical table of their science, in order to be able at any moment to lay their fingers on the date of a year, or the name of a dynasty. Popular reading is not like this; it is not erudite, but impassioned. . . .

[Lamartine's] is an argument on behalf of that method of dealing with historical materials which endows them with living, human interest; and is specially intended to point out the advantages of biography as a key to historical knowledge.

The biographies he has selected for the purpose of exhibiting practically what may be done in this way, for the instruction of the million, by a writer who is conversant with their wants, and who knows how to awaken their sympathies, embrace a wide range of time and character, and are designedly disconnected and independent of each other, but so comprehensive upon the whole as to leave a clear impression of isolated facts, which, in the end, will drop into their right places, and assume something of a continuous relation to each other in the mind of the reader. The reason assigned for scattering a collection of historical portraits up and down, with a premeditated disregard of chronological order, throws a light upon the plan of cheap popular literature M. de Lamartine is endeavouring, with indefatigable industry, to establish in France. Had he been delivering a series of lectures, he tells us, he would have proceeded systematically in the order of time; but he was writing a book, and the first condition of a book designed for popular circulation is variety. Attention must be stimulated; the feelings must be excited; the scene of the drama must be shifted; monotony and the appearance of study, must, above all things, be avoided. (pp. 164-65)

That Lamartine thoroughly understands the conditions upon which popular literature should be formed, is evinced in every page of [*Memoirs of Celebrated Characters*]. . . . Lamartine's mode of treating his topics throws a glow over them, which renders them additionally fascinating, without interfering with their symmetry, or reducing their value. His style is fervid and imagerial, and carries prosaic things into the region of imagination, where he bathes them in rich and vivid colours. But the responsibility of the prosaic fact is never lost sight of. His poetical tendency, although it pervades the work, is everywhere subservient to accuracy of statement. He sacrifices no truth, no principle, no necessary detail to the exuberance of his fancy. The biographies are comprehensive and luminous—the salient points of history are seized with precision, and displayed in a focal light—there is not a line of superfluous authorship—no exhibition of literary vanity—the whole is compact yet full, profound yet obvious, clear, animated and brilliant. The work will be read with profit by the most educated readers, and there is nothing in it that the least educated cannot at once understand.

The plan upon which it is constructed affords abundant scope for embracing a considerable extent of information, without making excursions in search of it beyond the strict boundary of the immediate subject. Each character illustrates an era or an art—an historical, moral, or a social problem. Thus, in the biography of Guttenberg, we have a history of the discovery of printing, introducing a masterly view of the previously existing means of "transposing speech from the ear to the eye," which passage occupies only a page or two; but it contains in that brief compass all that is necessary to impress upon the mind of the reader the nature of the change introduced into the world by the invention of types. How finely, too, is all this expressed; how pure and elevating the religious sentiment it awakens! . . . The subject is strikingly developed by the happy disposition and contrast of the materials, and while the reason is occupied upon the facts, the imagination is captivated by the manner in which they are presented. (pp. 168-69)

It may be easily anticipated, remembering the antecedents of the writer, that those historical portraits have a bearing, more or less, upon recent and present occurrences in France, and that M. de Lamartine, in drawing pictures of former celebrities, has not failed to give them an indirect application to his contemporaries. This is the feature which, beyond all others, has excited most curiosity in France; and it will, probably, attract hardly less notice in England. The allusions are masked with consummate skill and adroitness; and the reader should not suffer them to escape him. (p. 170)

> "Lamartine's Historical Characters," in Bentley's Miscellany, *Vol. XXXVI, 1854, pp. 163-70.*

THE CHRISTIAN OBSERVER   (essay date 1855)

[*This reviewer praises the narrative style of* Memoirs of Celebrated Characters, *but asserts that Lamartine fails as a moralist despite his intention of creating an inspirational historical work.*]

M. De Lamartine has always held a foremost place in the literature of his country. As a poet, and as an historian, he has sought and earned his laurels. We will venture to say, that [**Memoirs of Celebrated Characters**] will greatly enhance his former reputation, not perhaps so much as an historian as a picturesque writer. There is a sort of enchantment about his style. He waves his wand, and subjects, which in the hands of ordinary authors would be of the driest possible character, are by him invested with such an air of romance and poetry, that the reader is unconsciously carried on, and speeds almost breathless to the *denouement* of plots which have been familiar to him from his nursery days.

Such is the power of true genius. Such new light and beauty are shed over old faces, that we scarcely recognise them. Characters which we had looked upon as mere uninteresting puppets of the historical drama, are presented to us clothed in life and dignity—real beings of passions, sentiments, feelings, similar to our own. We are gradually drawn into a personal interest for them. We rejoice with them in success; we sympathize with them in sorrow. They seem, by some preternatural process, to pass before our eyes. We gaze on their forms; we unite with them in their actions; we are made one with them by the mere power of eloquence.

The celebrated characters whom Lamartine regards as worthy of a place in his work are, Nelson, Heloise, Christopher Columbus, Bernard de Palissy the potter, Roostam, Marcus Tullius Cicero, Socrates, Jacquard, Joan of Arc, Cromwell, Homer, Guttenberg, and Fenelon. It will be seen by this list, that our author has not been unmindful of the charms of variety. There is no sameness in the successive lives. (p. 197)

[In the histories of Cromwell and Joan of Arc], Lamartine's power of writing exceeds itself. We have seldom read anything more interesting than the life of Cromwell, seldom anything more affecting than that of Joan of Arc. Our author's great forte seems to be, in investing the death of his heroes with an halo of most romantic interest. (p. 200)

On his offences, as a moral writer, we must add a few words. His notions are certainly a little loose on this point. We are constantly hoping, as page follows page, he will rise to something of a higher level, and prove himself an eloquent moralist, as well as an eloquent historian. But such hopes are constantly disappointed. It is curious to be told by the author himself, in his "Introduction," that his highest literary ambition, in connection with the publication of this work, is "that it shall be carried about as a sort of devotional friend, and recited by fragments *on Sunday,* in the walks which the family and the neighbours may take amongst their corn or their blooming grapes." . . . Even those the least rigid in this opinion, as to the observance of the Lord's-day, will scarcely respond to his wish that the present work should be regarded as a Sunday

Vade Mecum, and that only such emotions should be awakened in the mind as these thoroughly earthly, secular, and far from devout narratives are calculated to inspire. (pp. 201-02)

> "Lamartine's 'Memoirs of Celebrated Characters'," in The Christian Observer, *n.s. Vol. 55, No. 207, March, 1855, pp. 196-207.*

THE CHRISTIAN EXAMINER AND RELIGIOUS MISCELLANY (essay date 1855)

[*The following excerpt is from a positive review of* Histoire de la Turquie (History of Turkey).]

[**History of Turkey**] is a history of Turkey and more, for, besides a very full Preface upon the Eastern Question, we have quite an elaborate account of the rise and progress of Islamism, the wonderful story of Mahomet, which, as it seems to us, has never been told so well as in this volume. . . . The book is exceedingly opportune, and cannot fail to interest a large circle of readers. . . . [The story of the progress of the Mussulmans] would of itself fasten the attention of the reader like the most highly wrought romance; and when such marvels are set forth by a writer so brilliant as Lamartine, our interest scarcely flags for a moment, unless perhaps we grow a little weary of the very brilliancy, and long for some prose, as one who had been fed for days upon confectionary might long for a little dry bread. For we will not deny that Lamartine is too rhetorical, too *French,* to please us altogether, and we never feel quite safe with a writer who will not in any circumstances be dull. Wondrous events are constantly coming into the light of the world, and yet some events are not wondrous, and if they are to be narrated at all, very plain words will suffice.

> A review of "History of Turkey," in The Christian Examiner and Religious Miscellany, *n.s. Vol. XXIV, No. II, September, 1855, p. 304.*

THE DUBLIN UNIVERSITY MAGAZINE   (essay date 1856)

[*This anonymous critic praises Lamartine's portraits of historical figures in* History of the Girondists, History of the French Revolution of 1848, *and* Histoire des constituents, *suggesting that his purpose in these works was to vindicate the revolutionaries.*]

[The] **History of the Girondists,** written under no spur of necessity, but composed in the undisturbed liberty of a matured mind, affords the most copious proof of [M. de Lamartine's] benevolence of feeling, in association with unrestrained imagination. The person, and we believe it was Chateaubriand, who, on reading that history, declared that the author had sprinkled the guillotine with rose water, and hung it round with flowers, used no extravagant hyperbole. The book would seem to have been written for the express purpose of vindicating the Dantons and the Robespierres. In the long picture gallery of those eight volumes, the worst actors of these times appear with aureoles round their brows, emanations of attributed good intention. That history produced an effect on the public mind so great as to have kindled an ardent desire for the revival of the Revolution, and the continuation of the work of its martyrs. Indeed by the ardor of sentiment and the kindling of imagination it awakened it did hasten the overthrow of a dynasty too prosaic to satisfy the political poetry with which readers,—and their name was legion—felt inspired. The same characteristic qualities mark the **History of the Revolution of 1848**. In that history, Blanqui, Sobrier, and Barbes figure as types of patriotism, religious exaltation, and chivalry. In personal contact with men,

M. de Lamartine sees as he reads, taking for granted the most favourable explanation of motives, and the most specious apology for acts. An exception to this disposition to paint all revolutionary heroes in bright colors, would seem to have occurred with respect to Mirabeau, the great preponderating figure in the *Histoire des Constituents,* intended as a sequel to that of the Girondists, so as that both might form a full view of the great Revolution. By the way in which Lamartine introduces Mirabeau, he throws new light on the history of the time, and imparts an original aspect to circumstances on which it was supposed no more remained to be said. The part played by Mirabeau was that of traitor in the darkest and most odious sense of the word. . . . For the political villain M. de Lamartine might have found a suggestion of mercy, were there any thing in the private conduct of the man sufficiently good to raise the possibility of doubt whether his public policy might not have been dictated by certain cold calculations, held unfortunately to be excusable in particular schools of statesmanship. But Mirabeau was throughout all the relations of life a bold, bad man. . . . And yet there is something so ennobling in the grand style and large manner of treatment of the author, that, while retaining his repulsiveness, Mirabeau loses nothing of his colossal stature. Out of that great fermenting mountain comes at one time mud and at another lava; but whatever does come bears with it the indication of mighty phenomena. The domestic virtues have evidently great redeeming charms for Lamartine. (pp. 415-16)

All M. de Lamartine's prose works, whether historical, biographical, or narratives of personal experience, are marked by one striking characteristic, which we may call a love of portrait painting. Take any volume, for instance, of the *Histoire des Girondins,* and wherever you see a man of note in the table of contents, the next item of the bill of fare will be "his portrait." The portrait, too, will represent the external features to a degree of minuteness, recalling more the mechanical wonders of the photograph than the bold generalisation of the artist, who seeks to show forth rather some quality of the mind or soul, according to his own ideal, than to paint correct familiar outline. Such a charge as this seems hardly consistent with the general notion that has been formed of the writer's genius, and yet that it is true must be evident to the most cursory reader. The vagueness of Lamartine's poetry, derived, as he tells us, from his early admiration of Ossian, and the similar sort of cloudy splendor which marked his descriptive impressions of oriental scenery, served perhaps to create this popular notion of his mode of thinking and manner of expression. . . . The quality to which we allude is, nevertheless, consistent with the peculiar nature of Lamartine's imagination. So quick is the imaginative faculty with him, that every object stirs it, and sets it to decorate the attraction of the moment with analogies and metaphors of richest variety. (pp. 416-17)

Whether the history be of ancient or modern times, or float in the dim haze of the middle ages, of the Caesars of Rome or of France, of the Maid of Orleans or the great Bishop of Meaux, of his own family friends or favorite authors, the portrait exhibits the finest finish of the miniature with the florid colours of the pastel. Nothing is left for the reader to fill up. The picture is held up in every light, and looked at from all points of view. Each trait is, as it were, repeated in a simile, and we see the whole as between a pair of mirrors, showing an endless perspective of repetition. One would think that no illustrative aid were needed to understand a pock-marked face; yet, speaking of Vergniaud's pitted cheeks, the description is helped out with a simile drawn from the slab of granite dressed with a

An illustration for "Le lac" from the 1855 edition of The Poetical Meditations.

hammer. When M. de Lamartine describes the magnificent person of his father, the majestic grace of his admirable mother, his beautiful sisters, and those with whom his earliest recollections are entwined, his canvas glows with the freshest and purest colours. Nor has the painter failed to imitate a habit authorised by most of the great masters, who in their historical pictures have found a modest place for themselves. Lamartine's life is in his own works. No writer recurs more frequently to his own experience. Not only all that he ever saw worth noting, and its effect on his mind at the time, is recorded, but his voice, look, personal appearance, and manners are minutely told, with the changes and modifications worked by the hand of time. There is an unsuspicious candor in these self references which shows that he is not prompted by motives of vulgar vanity, but that he obeys a law of his own nature. He looks at himself as he would at any other object of observation, and if he prefers the most favorable point of view, it is not from any narrow exception in his own favor. (p. 418)

"Lamartine, 'Homme de Lettres'," in The Dublin University Magazine, *Vol. XLVIII, No. CCLXXXVI, October, 1856, pp. 408-23.*

THE ECLECTIC MAGAZINE   (essay date 1856)

[*Citing in particular* Memoirs of Celebrated Characters, *the critic maintains that Lamartine's works, despite their elegant style, are frivolous, ephemeral, and historically inaccurate.*]

Criticism has long ceased to apply historical tests to the pictorial paradoxes of M. de Lamartine. He is a light and graphic narrator, a painter of elegant portraits; he has a subtle fancy; as a speculatist he is ingenious, but he violates all the laws of art to produce verbal and metaphorical effects, and he violates the integrity of history because he will write with passion and without study. The result has been that his first and best works have fallen into disrepute; that in England, he is held to be a poet who disdains the use of rhythm, and that in France, he is patronized as the most graceful of compilers. This, surely, has not been the object of an ambitious life spent in the gardens of poetry and knowledge; but M. de Lamartine, as he watches the daily withering of his deciduous fame, will learn that a warm and tinted style is not all that is essential to the elaboration of a high historical argument; that flowers of rhetoric, fragrant of an oriental fancy, and bold images suddenly struck upon the paper will not save the false story of great events and achievements from perishing with the works of far less prominent and less attractive writers. The lesson is severe; but it is due to justice. M. de Lamartine has been, in the world of letters, an idolator and a slave; in this [*Memoirs of Celebrated Characters*], his latest labor, he is more than ever the devotee of rhetoric; he spurns all the obligations of research and criticism, and he deserves the penalty he has paid. His books are read for their flippant audacity and for their glittering color, but they are counted among ephemerals, and die with the season that produced them.

To justify the rigors of criticism it is only necessary to examine M. de Lamartine's *Memoirs* in a literary as well as in an historical sense. Does his originality consist in grace, or in extravaganza? Is it power, or eccentricity? Is it purity, or is it not an abandonment of the imagination to eccentric postures, to attitudes that startle, not by their beauty, but by their fantastic defiance of all the laws of art and nature. M. de Lamartine, writing of Madame de Sévigné, carves a figure in marble, faultless and stainless, idealizes it into life, and buries its feet in flowers; he apostrophizes William Tell until he is an immortal genius of the mountains; he sings of Antar until the mythical Arab becomes a Hercules of the desert softened into an Apollo; he degrades Milton into a venal and malignant pamphleteer; and he exalts Bossuet until prophets and apostles grow pale by the side of the rival of Bourdalone. As, in the instance of Milton, M. de Lamartine proves that he can write in malice as well as in ignorance, so in the instance of Bossuet, his sounding analogies swell until we know not whether they are the symptoms of a bewildered enthusiasm or the excesses of a profane frivolity. (pp. 205-06)

> "Lamartine's Characters," *in* The Eclectic Magazine, *Vol. XXXIX, No. II, October, 1856, pp. 205-11.*

THE NORTH AMERICAN REVIEW (essay date 1856)

[*In the following excerpt, the critic praises the first volume of Lamartine's* Cours familier de littérature: Un entretien par mois, *stating that "nothing he ever wrote was finer, more poetical, or more touching."*]

It is more than probable, that, of all the succeeding numbers of the *Cours Familier de Littérature,* none will escape oblivion save the first; and it may also be predicted, that nothing Lamartine ever wrote will endure longer than that first number, for nothing he ever wrote was finer, more poetical, or more touching, because nothing was ever more intensely alive, more real. It lives, painfully if you will, but it lives; and the beat

of the pulse, the vibration of the heart, the strong, unmistakable evidences of individuality, meet you on every page. It is *self-inspired*. With nearly all true poets, this would be sufficient; with Lamartine it is pre-eminently so. Five numbers of the *Cours Familier* have already appeared.... (p. 480)

[The first number of the *Cours Familier*] is more than a mere return, it is a *rebound*, towards poetry; and it is so because, *full of self*, he has felt acutely, intensely, excruciatingly, that which he had to communicate to the world. The agony of despair has roused him to the passion inseparable from truth.

Lamartine's literary efforts may be regarded as uninfluenced directly by the state of politics in France, inasmuch as he never allows an acrimonious expression against that which is to escape him, and in no way draws his inspiration from the defence or attack of any political system. Indirectly, the present intellectual condition of his own country may, however, be said to bear upon him, because, in an organization of things where it is impossible for him to act or speak or take part in the government or administration, he can only write; all other activity being denied him, he perforce has resort to the activity of the pen. (p. 483)

> "Literature in France under the Empire," *in* The North American Review, *Vol. LXXXIII, No. CLXXIII, October, 1856, pp. 476-503.*

HENRI FRÉDÉRIC AMIEL (journal date 1862)

[*A nineteenth-century Swiss diarist, critic, and poet, Amiel is best known for his diary,* Journal intime, *which is considered an outstanding example of introspective literature. In the following excerpt, Amiel expresses his strong admiration for the "true poetry" of* Jocelyn.]

Read over a few songs from *Jocelyn*. They brought tears to my eyes (the dog, the death of the mother, the separation from Laurence, the meeting in Paris, the death of Laurence). It is admirable! (p. 164)

This is true poetry, that which lifts one up towards heaven and pervades one with the feeling of the divine, that sings of love and death, hope and sacrifice, and makes one feel the infinite. *Jocelyn* always stirs me with thrills of tenderness, which it would be odious to me to see profaned by irony. This tragedy of the heart has no parallel in French, for purity, except *Paul et Virginie* [by Jacques Henri Bernardin de Saint-Pierre], and I am not sure that I do not prefer *Jocelyn*. To be just, one would have to read them over together. (pp. 164-65)

> Henri Frédéric Amiel, *in a journal entry of April 25, 1862, in his* The Private Journal of Henri Frédéric Amiel, *translated by Van Wyck Brooks and Charles Van Wyck Brooks, revised edition, The Macmillan Company, 1935, pp. 163-65.*

THÉOPHILE GAUTIER (essay date 1874)

[*Gautier holds an important place in French letters as a transitional figure in the movement from Romanticism to Realism and as the originator of the concept of art for art's sake, which formed the basis of Parnassian aesthetics. The following extract was drawn from* Portraits of the Day, *a posthumous collection of essays that originally appeared in French in 1874 as* Portraits contemporains. *Here, Gautier praises Lamartine's effusive poetic style, stating that "Lamartine is probably the greatest magician in poetry."*]

["**Meditations**"] was an event infrequent in the course of ages. It contained a whole new world, a world of poetry, more difficult perhaps to discover than America or the Atlantides. While he seemed to be coming and going with indifference among other men, Lamartine was travelling over unknown seas, his eye fixed upon his star, drawn towards a shore on which no one had yet stepped, and had returned victorious like Columbus,—he had discovered the soul. (p. 158)

Lamartine was not merely a poet, he was poetry itself. His chaste, elegant, noble language seemed to ignore wholly the ugly and mean side of life. As the book was, so was the author, and the best frontispiece which could have been selected for the volume of verse was the poet's own portrait; a lyre in his hands and on his shoulders a cloak blown about by the storm were in no wise ridiculous.

What deep, new accents, what ethereal aspirations, what up-springing towards the ideal, what effusions of love, what tender and melancholy notes, what sighs and questionings of the soul which no poet had yet caused to sound! In the pictures drawn by Lamartine, the heavens always occupy much space. He needs that space to move about easily, and to draw broad circles around his thoughts. He floats, he flies, he soars; like the swan resting on its great, white wings, sometimes in the light, sometimes in a light haze, sometimes, too, in storm clouds, he rarely settles on the earth, and soon resumes his flight with the first breeze that ruffles his plumes. That fluid, transparent, aerial element which opens before him and closes behind him, is his natural road; he maintains himself in it without difficulty for many hours, and from his lofty heights he sees the landscape turn faint and blue, the waters shimmer and the buildings rise in vaporous effacement.

Lamartine is not one of those marvellous artist poets who hammer verse as if it were a blade of gold upon a steel anvil, making closer the grain of the metal and shaping it to sharp, accurate outlines. He ignores or disdains every excess of form, and with the negligence of the nobleman, who rimes only when minded, without restricting himself to technical matters, he writes admirable poems as he rides through the woods, as he floats in his boat along some shady bank, or leans on the window of one of his castles. His verse rolls on with harmonious murmur, like the waves of Italian or Greek waters, which bear on their transparent crests branches of laurel, golden fruits fallen from the shore, and reflect the sky, the birds or the sails, or break on the strand in brilliant, silvery foam. Its full, sweeping, successive undulating forms, impossible to fix as water, reach their aim, and, fluid as they are, bear thoughts as the sea bears vessels, whether a frail skiff or a ship of the line.

There is a magic charm in that breathing verse, which swells and sinks like the breast of ocean; one is carried away by the melody, by the chorus of rimes, as by the distant song of sailors or sirens. Lamartine is probably the greatest magician in poetry.

His broad, vague manner of writing suits the exalted spirituality of his nature. The soul does not need to be carved like Greek marble. Lights and sounds, breathings, opaline tints, rainbow colours, blue moonlight-beams, diaphanous gauze, aerial draperies swelling and rising in the breeze, suffice to depict and envelop it. The Latin expression, *musae ales,* seems to have been invented for Lamartine.

In that immortal poem, "**The Lake,**" in which passion speaks a tongue which the finest music has never equalled, vaporous nature appears as through a silver gauze, distant, afar, painted with a few touches so it shall serve as a framework and a background to that unforgettable remembrance; and yet everything is seen, the light in the heavens, the water and the rocks, the trees on the shore and the mountains on the horizon, and every wave that casts its foam upon the adored feet of Elvira.

And yet, because in Lamartine there is always a mist and a sound of the aeolian harp, it is not to be taken for granted that he is merely a melodious lake poet, and can only sigh softly of melancholy and love. If he sighs, he can also speak and shout; he rules as easily as he charms; his angelic voice, which seems to issue from the depths of the heavens, can assume at need a virile accent. (pp. 159-62)

> *Théophile Gautier, "Alphonse de Lamartine," in his* The Complete Works of Théophile Gautier: The Romance of a Mummy, Portraits of the Day, Vol. III, *edited and translated by F. C. De Sumichrast, Bigelow, Smith & Co., 1910, pp. 156-70.*

GEORGE BRANDES (essay date 1874)

[*Brandes, a Danish literary critic and biographer, was the principal leader of the intellectual movement that helped to bring an end to Scandinavian cultural isolation. He believed that literature reflects the spirit and problems of its time, and that it must be understood within its social and aesthetic context. Brandes's major critical work,* Main Currents in Nineteenth Century Literature, *won him admiration for his ability to view literary movements within the broader context of all of European literature. In the following excerpt from this work, originally published in Danish in 1874, Brandes describes Lamartine's early verse and discusses how his poetry reflects the age in which he lived. While faulting the repetitiveness and excessive length of many of Lamartine's poems and labeling the early religious verse "almost unreadable," Brandes asserts that the poems based on human emotion have lasting appeal. He concludes that Lamartine was "a true poet—in spite of his artistic defects one of the most genuine whom France has produced."*]

[The] Restoration period found in Lamartine's poetry an interpretation of its feelings and of all that moved its inmost heart— a picture of its ideal longings, painted in the clearest, loveliest dream-colours. It was poetry that resembled the music of an Aeolian harp, but the wind that played upon the strings was the spirit of the age. The poems were not so much songs as reflections, not so much heart as spirit harmonies; but in real life there had for long been enough, and more than enough, of the positive—definite forms, decided characters, solid substance, silent acceptance of the strokes of fate. It was by no means considered a fault that there was no strong passion in the poems, no tendency to see the dark and dreadful sides of life, or, in fact, life as it is. There had been enough of all this in reality. After a period during which so many instincts had been forcibly suppressed, men rejoiced in this purely poetic instinct, in this most melodious poet, who had, as he himself said, a chord for every feeling and mood. They longed for just such lyric restfulness after philosophy, revolution, and wars without end. The poem *Le Lac* was read with delight by the whole French-speaking world, just because it was so long since men had felt in sympathy with nature, so long since they had looked at the face of the earth from any point of view but the tactical one. It was not only, however, as the poet of feeling that Lamartine represented the spirit of the day; he also represented it in his character of orthodox Christian. The leading note in his poetry was the note of Christian royalism, and devotion to the Bourbon family in particular. (p. 200)

Lamartine's influence was due to the fact that he uttered, now the sad, now the comforting, now the inspiring words which thousands craved to hear. They did not feel the want of new thoughts in his utterances; they were moved by the sound of his sympathetic voice. They felt once more vibrating within them fibres which, during the period of universal depression, had been completely benumbed; he conjured tones from strings which had long given forth no sound; and men delighted in the novelty which consisted in a revival of old memories. But, besides all this, there was one really new element. For Lamartine the ugly and the bad, nay, even the petty and the mean, did not exist. He clothed everything in a garment of shining light. There was a heavenly radiance over his poetry. For the first time for long years, a wealth of beautiful feeling found expression in melodious verse. (pp. 205-06)

It was natural that the contemporaries of the youthful Lamartine should see in him first and foremost the poet of the throne and the altar. His earliest published poem was a heart-felt expression of gratitude to the Jesuit school which had sheltered him in his boyhood. Such a poem as his *Ode* was simply the essence of Chateaubriand's *Genie du Christianisme* versified. His lines on the birth of the Duke of Bordeaux (Comte de Chambord), after the death of his father, the Duc de Berry, with their refrain: "He is born, the miraculous child!" expressed the feelings of the most loyal Catholics. And on every occasion, in almost all of the poems, he lauds and magnifies, justifies and adores God, Providence. At times, as for instance in the poem *La Semaine Sainte,* written during a visit to the young Duc de Rohan, who later in life became an archbishop and a cardinal, his verse is almost like a fervently devotional burning of incense. If he is to be taken at his word when he asserts, in writing of this poem many years afterwards, that he alone, among the young men who gathered round the Duke, had no relish whatever for the church's mystic joys, all we can conclude is that his poetic talent was carried away by the current of the tendency of the day.

Most of the purely religious poetry of Lamartine's youthful period is, from its want of simplicity and real feeling, almost unreadable nowadays. It is not lyric; it is not concise; it is reflection without matter, meditation without thoughts, breadth without depth. A good example is the poem dedicated to Byron, entitled *L'Homme.* The French poet's conception of his English contemporary is the traditional, stereotyped, inexpressibly silly one of the day, namely, that he touches only the chords of despair, that his eye, like Satan's, fathoms abysses, &c. To show Byron how the true poet ought to sing, Lamartine strikes up the most servile hymn of praise to a God who, he himself tells us, plagues, tortures, plunders, overwhelms with misfortune and misery. . . . The notes appended at a later period to this poem betray an astonishing ignorance of Lord Byron's history; almost everything affirmed of him is incorrect. Though Lamartine wrote a poem to Childe-Harold, he never so much as learned to spell the name correctly. (pp. 208-09)

In only one of the poems which invoke the Deity is Lamartine really the lyric poet and not merely the fluent verse-writer, namely in *Le Désespoir,* a Meditation which expresses revolt against our idea of God. In this poem we have rhythmic flow, passion, and two qualities rarely found in Lamartine's productions—vigour and conciseness. (p. 209)

[All] the theological trappings were, as one might say, only glued on to Lamartine's poetry. Or one might perhaps with more propriety liken them to a carelessly constructed raft, which for a time floats upon the bosom of the stream and then breaks up into its component parts and disappears. All this pious dogmatism soon resolved itself into love of nature, worship of nature, a sincerely religious philosophy of nature.

What really lived and breathed in those early poems was something independent of their religious dogmatism, namely, the whole emotional life of a gentle, yet dignified soul. The soul which found expression in them had this characteristic of the new century, that it loved solitude, and only in solitude found itself and felt itself rich. It was an unsociable soul, only disposed to vibrate in harmony with nature. It was sad and pathetically earnest; under no circumstances whatever cheerful or gay. And, finally, it was never erotic; one only of the poems was an expression of the happiness of satisfied love; the feeling pervading all the rest was sorrow over the loss of the loved one, whom death had claimed as his prey. The poetry of the eighteenth century had resolved love into gallantry, had taken neither it nor woman seriously, but in this new poetry love was the silent worship of a memory, and woman was adored and glorified as she had been in the days of Minnesingers; only now it was woman as the departed one, as the spirit.

Never did Lamartine depict the wild grief of loss at the moment of the loss; in his poems grief has become a condition, a silent despair which blunts, stiffens, tortures, and at a rare time dissolves into tears.

This new song was song which flowed naturally from its fountain, plentiful and pure; it was music like harp-strains blended with the tones of celestial violins. And, borne on these tones, simple, familiar emotions communicated themselves to the reader's mind, such thoughts as that of the poem *La Retraite*—happiness awaits me nowhere; or of *L'Automne*—nature's autumnal mourning garb harmonises with my sorrow and is pleasant to my eyes. . . . (pp. 210-11)

There was never any systematic description of nature, or any attempt at painting; the momentary impression of nature was caught, even as it passed, by genius, and preserved for all time.

The poet is sitting at evening on the bare mountain side. Venus rises above the horizon (*Le Soir*). A ray from the star seems to glide across his brow and touch his eyes, and he feels as if the departed one, in whose companionship he had lived here, were hovering near him. (p. 211)

Or, sitting on a rock by the lake (*Le Bourget*), where in bygone happy days he had sat by her side, he is painfully affected by the feeling of the mutability of everything human as compared with the unchangeableness of inanimate nature. This is the emotion to which he gives expression in his poem *Le Lac,* which, in spite of its extraordinary popularity, is probably the best he ever wrote. It is an excellent type of his poetry; flowing gently, with no exertion perceptible, not even that exertion which we call art, it is as naturally melodious as the rippling of the lake. (pp. 211-12)

Of Lamartine's youthful verse [his] purely human poems are all that we really care for nowadays. We are terribly bored by the vapid compositions which, following the prescribed rule for religious poetry, consist of nothing but adoration of the Deity as he reveals himself in his works.

The poet whose acquaintance we make in the human poems is unmistakably very vain, much engrossed with himself and his own lovableness, and at times too honeyed in his language. But his vanity is so childlike and innocent that it does not affect us unpleasantly; and we are favourably impressed by the fact that it is not literary vanity. Lamartine rejoices that he is good-looking, a favourite with distinguished women, a good horse-man, in course of time an eloquent orator; but he is not conceited about his poetical gifts, not even proud of them. The man whose talent was that of the true improvisatore with proud humility describes himself in his prefaces and memoirs as one who cultivates art for his pleasure, and who does not belong to the number of the specially initiated. And he really is the dilettante in so far as he is too careless to be called a true artist. He has unconscious technique, he has flexibility and ease, but along with these an inclination to long-windedness and repetition which at times spoils his effects, and a want of the power of self-criticism which makes it difficult, nay, almost impossible, for him to correct and improve. Nevertheless, all his life long he was a poet, a true poet—in spite of his artistic defects one of the most genuine whom France has produced. (pp. 212-13)

> *George Brandes, "Lyric Poetry: Lamartine and Hugo," in his* Main Currents in Nineteenth Century Literature: The Reaction in France, Vol. III, *translated by Mary Morison, Boni & Liveright, Inc., 1923, pp. 198-221.**

[MARGARET OLIPHANT]　(essay date 1876)

[*Oliphant was a prolific nineteenth-century Scottish novelist, critic, biographer, and historian. A regular contributor to* Blackwood's Magazine, *she published nearly one hundred novels, many of them popular tales of English and Scottish provincial life, including her best-known work, the series of novels known as the* Chronicles of Carlingford. *In the following excerpt, Oliphant focuses on the autobiographical nature of Lamartine's work. She faults the monotony and sentimentality of much of his verse and considers his best works those in which he describes the countryside surrounding his family's estate.*]

There is nothing more attractive in all that Lamartine has left behind him than [**'Confidences,'** a] record of the ancient world as it appeared across his own cradle. In no way could the curious difference between the old time and the new appear more distinctly. The poet makes himself a link between the generations by this perhaps too often repeated but always delightful story. His many autobiographical self-revelations—revelations which became not only tiresome but pitiful when they treated of the man in the midst of his career and afforded a medium for the pouring forth of much egotism and vanity—do not affect us at all in the same way when they concern the parents, the uncles and aunts, who formed a kind of family council over all the acts of the one male descendant who was to be their heir. The after-life of the poet contains nothing half so touching or so charming as those pictures of his early days which he delighted to make, and in which he is always so happy. We know no poetical biography more perfect than the chapters which describe his childhood at Milly, the little dreary French country-house, where the family established themselves after the terrors of the Revolution were over. (p. 214)

The reader who has followed Lamartine through the **'Confidences'** and **'Nouvelles Confidences,'** out of which, unfortunately, he was always attempting to make more books and more money, may perhaps tire of the often-repeated description, the details so often begun *da capo*, the minute but always most loving touches by which he renews the portraiture of his home. For ourselves, we avow we can swallow a great deal of this without murmur or objection; and we could scarcely suggest a more perfect if tranquil pleasure to those unacquainted with or forgetful of Lamartine's history, than may be found in the handsome and not too long volume—a mere piece of bookmaking, the harsh critic may say, the old recollections served up again—which, under the title of **'Mémoires Inédites,'** has been published since his death;—or the companion book which he called **'Le Manuscrit de ma Mère,'** and himself published not long before the end of his life. The critic and the social philosopher may judge hardly such revelations to the public of the secrets of family life, but we doubt whether the profanation is in any way sufficient to counterbalance the advantages of so true and close and intimate a history. Whatever degree of genius may be allowed to him in his own field of poetry, no admirer will ever claim for Lamartine the glory of dramatic power. He is religious, descriptive, sentimental, tender, with a fine if vague sense of natural beauty; but he is never in the smallest degree dramatic. What nature, however, has not given him, memory and love have almost supplied; and the picture of Milly, and of the beautiful and tender woman who forms its centre, is such as few poets have been able to invent for us. We speak sometimes with a suppressed sneer of the Frenchman's ideal, the *ma mère* of a sentiment which it is so easy to stigmatise as sentimentality. But such a figure as that of Madame de Lamartine, as exhibited to us in her own journal, as well as through her son's half-adoring sketches, is one which no lover of humanity would be content to let go. (pp. 215-16)

[The characters of] **'Meditations,' 'Harmonies,' 'Recueillements,'** the appropriate names which he gives to his various collections of poems, may be gleaned at once by their titles. It is somewhat difficult to follow through many editions which have changed the arrangement and succession of the different poems, the actual verses which first saw the day; but they are all so similar in character that we cannot do the poet wrong by instancing at hazard the first that catch the eye. "**Benediction de Dieu dans la Solitude,**" "**Hymne du Soir dans les Temples,**" "**Pensée des Morts,**" "**L'Infini dans les Cieux,**" "**Hymne de la Douleur,**" "**Jehovah; ou l'idée de Dieu,**"—so run the strains. Vague piety of an elevated but very general kind, vague sentiment, melancholy, and sadness; vague descriptions of landscape, of rivers, of the sun, the sky, and the mountains,—are to be found in all, always gracefully, often melodiously expressed—sometimes resounding with the accumulation of epithets which suits declamation better than poetry; sometimes dropping into a murmurous sweet monotony, which, barring that the effort is produced by words instead of notes, resembles more . . . a song without words than a succession of articulate verses. It is impossible to discover in them much thought; but they are profoundly and tenderly reflective, and express what is recognised as thought by the majority of ordinary readers. Reflective, retrospective, full of the gentle sadness which is produced by recollections which are melancholy without being bitter—by the memory of the distant dead, whose loss has ceased to be a weighty and present grief—and by that consciousness of the transitory character of life, and peace, and happiness, and everything that man esteems, which is not pressed close by immediate neglect or dismay. They are of the class of poetry which delights youth at that stage when it loves to be made sad, and which affords to women and lonely persons a means of expressing the vague and causeless despondencies of a silent existence.

This is not the highest aim of poetry, but we are not sure that it is not one of its most beneficial uses. The active mind and passionate soul have need of stronger fare; but so long as human nature is framed as it is, the majority must always be subject to the languors and undefined dissatisfactions which result from nothing tangible in our lives, but are the very breath of a higher being. . . . (pp. 219-20)

In all these volumes, however, full as they are of the personality of the writer, and of his private recollections and moods of mind, there is no attempt to embody in any living type of character his theories of existence, or such counsel as he had to bestow upon his poetical audience. So far as he had a hero at all, Lamartine was his own hero. The dramatic faculty is almost altogether wanting to him. (p. 221)

It is only just to Lamartine . . . to say that his graceful but languishing and sentimental tales are more prepossessing to the reader, and call forth in a much lesser degree the natural opposition which is roused in everybody's mind by highly-pitched egotism and vanity, than those of Goethe. 'Graziella,' in particular, is a beautiful little idyl, perfectly pure, picturesque, and touching. The Italian girl herself has something of the charm which we have already remarked in Lamartine's early sketches of his own childhood. She is represented in all the homely circumstances of her lot, without any attempt to make an impossible young lady out of the humble Procitana. This error, which is one into which English romancers continually fall, does not seem to affect the Frenchman. . . . Altogether this poetic little tale is, we think, the finest thing Lamartine has done. It is a portion of his 'Confidences;' he is the hero, the god of the little southern world, into which he threw himself with all the enthusiasm of youth. Of all his landscapes, except the home scenery of Milly, there is none of which he has so taken in the peculiar and pervading charm. The sunny yet dangerous sea, the lovely isles, the hill terraces, with their wonderful Elysian points of vision, the subtle sweetness of the air, the mingling of sky and water, with all their ineffable tones of light and colour, have been nowhere more perfectly represented; and if the passion and despair of the young Neapolitan may be excessive, they are made possible by her country, by the softening effects of that seductive air, and by the extreme youth of the heroine. Very different is the sickly and unnatural effect of the companion story 'Raphael,' the scene of which is laid in the town, and on the lake, of Aix in Savoy, and in which the sentimental passion of the two lovers becomes nauseous to the reader in its very commencement, and is infinitely more objectionable in its ostentatious purity than any ordinary tale of passion. The hero of 'Graziella' is young and guileless, half unaware of, and more than half partaking, the innocent frenzy he awakens; but Raphael is a miserable poor creature, good for nothing but to lie at his mistress's feet, to listen to her movements through the door that divides them, to rave about her perfections and his love. The sickly caresses—the long silent raptures in which the two gaze into each other's eyes—the still more sickly ravings of their love, which has no pleasant beginning, no dramatic working up towards a climax, but jumps into languishing completeness at once,—all breathe an unhealthy, artificial, enervating atmosphere, pernicious to the last degree for any young mind which could be charmed by it, and not far from disgusting to the maturer reader. In both these productions, the poet, as we have said, is his own hero. The incidents are professedly true; and the author gives himself credit throughout his autobiographical works for having passed through all the tumults and agitations of these exhibitions of would-be passion. We say would-be, for there is not in reality any passion in them. Nothing of the fiery directness of overwhelming emotion is in either narrative. Raphael, in particular, is slowly piled up with a leisurely gloating over the mental fondnesses and fine sentiments of the languishing pair, which stops all feeling of in-

dulgence; and when the sentimental lover, wrapped up in thoughts of his Julia, accepts from his mother the price of her trees, and hurries away, under pretence of sickness, to Aix, to indulge his maudlin passion by another meeting, the reader loses all patience with so miserable a hero. But to the poet it seems quite reasonable and natural, not to say angelic, of the mother, to make any sacrifice to satisfy the necessities of her son's heart, and quite consistent with the son's honour and poetic nobility of soul to leave all the duties of life behind him, and moon his life away dancing attendance upon his sickly love. . . . (pp. 222-23)

In the other narratives of the 'Confidences,' such, for instance, as the tale called "Fior d'Aliza," the poet is not the hero but the sympathising friend of the chief sufferers, with some gain in point of modesty, but not much in point of art. All for love, in a sense which goes altogether beyond our robuster meaning, is his perpetual motto. The world appears to him only as a place in which two young persons may bill and coo, turning all its beautiful and noble scenery into a succession of nests for the inevitable turtle-doves. In all this, let us do him justice, there is nothing licentious or immoral. When there may happen to occur a love which cannot end in marriage, it is almost ostentatiously demonstrated to be a union of the heart only; and it is on the whole a pure idyl which Lamartine loves. The most that can be said of him is, that he indulges freely in the amiable indecency, chiefly concerned with babies and their mothers, which Continental manners permit and authorise. He is fond of nursery exhibitions, of sucklings and their play; but only the prudish English taste perhaps will object to this, such improprieties being considered in other regions virtuous, nay, religious. This defect, and an undue exhibition of the delights of wedded and lawful love, are almost all the moral sins of which we can accuse him; and there are even among ourselves, no doubt, a host of virtuous critics to whom the fact of wedlock makes everything correct and legitimate. This is not the kind of weakness, however, which we naturally expect from a Frenchman. (pp. 223-24)

When all other inspiration fails, the inspiration of home never fails [Lamartine]. Whatever he may be elsewhere, at Milly he is ever a true poet. This is the highest praise we can give to Lamartine. His longer poems are monotonous and cloying; his poetical romances of a mawkish and unwholesome sweetness. But on his native soil, in the homely house of his mother, all objectionable qualities disappear. He loves the skies which overarch that dear bit of country; he loves the hills and the fields because they surround that centre of all associations; and in his companionship with nature he is always tender and natural, seldom exaggerated, and scarcely ever morbid. His shorter strains are full of the fresh atmosphere of the country he loved; and the sentiment of pensive evenings and still nights, soft-breathing, full of stars and darkness, is to be found everywhere in the gentle melodious verse; not lofty or all absorbing like the Nature-worship of Wordsworth, but more within the range of the ordinary mind, and quite as genuine and true. Had he been content with this, and not aspired to represent passion of which he knew nothing, his fame would have been more real and more lasting. He was such a poet as the quieter intellectualist, the pensive thinker loves. He could not touch the greater springs of human feeling; but he could so play upon the milder stops of that great instinct as to fill his audience with a soft enthusiasm. Some of his prose works reach to a profounder influence; and those readers who remember, when it came out, the 'History of the Girondists,' will not refuse to the poet a certain power of moving and exciting the mind: but this work

Lamartine at his home in 1847.

and the many others which preceded and followed it, have little to do with our argument. They are poetical and exaggerated prose, and have no claim to the higher title of poetry. (p. 230)

[*Margaret Oliphant*], *"A Century of Great Poets, from 1759 Downwards,"* in Blackwood's Edinburgh Magazine, *Vol. CXIX, No. DCCXXIV, February, 1876, pp. 207-31.*

F. V. PAGET   (essay date 1883)

[*In the following excerpt, Paget focuses on Lamartine's poetic ability. He first discusses* A Pilgrimage to the Holy Land *and* History of the Girondists, *which he considers valuable for their poetic prose. The critic then examines Lamartine's major poetic works and concludes that he ceased writing verse when he had exhausted his poetic subjects.*]

If a critical sketch of Lamartine does not commence with the commonplace phrase, "we shall consider Lamartine as a man and a poet," it is because he was really only a poet. Poesy had so transported him into the imaginary kingdom of the ideal that, at least as long as he was a poet, he had no eye, no thought, no desire for anything here below. In him there was nothing like duality. I even wonder if he should be called a poet; for, on hearing such a word, people commonly see a contemplative being whose eye, continually gazing upon hu-

man nature and upon the external world, searches into their deepest mysteries, from which his creating imagination brings out pictures bearing the double stamp of their own objectivity and their author's subjectivity. (p. 361)

[Lamartine] neither searches nor labors. At his first flight he reaches the upper air. On one side at his feet lie immense plains, bounded far away by mountains lost in a luminous mist; on the other side, the blue waves of the Mediterranean; above his head, the beautiful southern skies display unlimited space, illuminated in turn by sparkling sun-fires or smooth silver moon radiance. Under the breathings of the Infinite, the soul of the poet vibrates and pours forth waves of floating harmony.

Lamartine's characteristics are nowhere marked with more clearness, I think, than in *Voyages en Orient* [*Souvenirs, impressions, pensées, et paysages pendant un voyage en Orient (1832-33); ou, Notes d'un voyageur*], though this book must be considered as one of his inferior works. If an accurate and scientific description of these singular lands is not expected from such a title—if not a real East—we look for an imaginary one, with here and there touches of reality. But this book is neither the one nor the other; there is no reality in it. Lamartine traveled all over the East without really seeing it. Yet the *Voyages en Orient* is worth reading, not for the love of the East, but for poetry's sake. By the Orient is here to be understood Greece, Constantinople, Syria, Asia Minor, and Palestine. But names are of no importance to Lamartine. All these countries, in reality so different, appear the same when described by him; what he says of one might as justly be applied to another. Under the overpowering control of his own sensations, he thinks and dreams and sings, and never in the least distinguishes between the real and the unreal. As successive landscapes pass before his eyes, as he stands in the presence of many departed civilizations, Greek, Roman, Christian, and Arabian, he pours forth exhaustless streams of enchanting melody. It is, however, only music. The characteristics which stamp the individuality of each country and nation are unperceived by him. To such a heavenly poet, what are Greeks or Turks or Jews—any or all of his Oriental fellow-creatures? He neither esteems nor despises them, neither praises nor disparages them; they are but mere incidents of the landscape—mere imperceptible specks here and there on the immense surface of imaginary skies and seas and lands, over which he is carried under the fallacious pretense of visiting eastern countries. Unfortunately, objects seen from such a height and from such a distance lose their relief, and Lamartine, in spite of the richness of his style, is often monotonous; his palette has but one tint for the severe lines of the Parthenon, the wooded slopes of Lebanon, the scorching plains of Palestine, and the splendid amphitheater of Constantinople. If he speaks of history, manners, philosophy, or religion, which he should never venture to do, he displays the most superb disdain for facts, though he is always sincere and always in earnest. With a brilliant metaphor he decides religious, political, or military questions that might occupy for years ecumenical councils, parliaments, or councils of war. (pp. 361-62)

[In *Histoire des Girondins,* Lamartine] was always moved by the deepest feeling while accomplishing his task, and so we became possessed of this magnificent poem about the French Revolution. It cannot be said that he comprehended and explained this wonderful soul-movement of a people. Lamartine was not an Edgar Quinet, capable of analyzing the soul of a nation as others analyze the soul of an individual. But he felt it, and so found himself in unison with all the patriotic and liberal instincts of France—a phenomenon so much the more to be wondered at, because he was a nobleman by birth, and was consequently expected to belong to the royalist reactionary party. This book is not to be counted among those grave compositions that throw light upon the past by a wise grouping of facts and a clear simplicity of style. It is not, properly speaking, a history, but a most lively and affecting poem. (p. 362)

[Lamartine] played his part, and he disappeared forever from the political stage. Was it a misfortune? No. Was it a misfortune that he ever appeared there; that in 1839 he abandoned poesy forever? Many people have thought so, and regretted that from that time he occupied himself with history, literary criticism, politics, and journalism—everything except poetry. For my part, I dare to say that these people are wrong. If Lamartine had been unfaithful to the muse only for the pleasure of playing at politics, or of writing edulcorated prose, it would assuredly be a matter for regret, since his verses are worth infinitely more than such politics and such prose. But this was not the case. He ceased to sing simply because he had nothing more to sing. Since he never went outside of his own impressions, which were necessarily limited, and since to enlarge their circle he never had recourse to the study of books, of nature, or of the human mind, it would have been easy to foresee that his *repertoire* would be exhausted. When that day came, there were but two things for him to do—remain silent or recommence. He chose to remain silent, and he was right. (p. 363)

Lamartine, a child of this faithless age, thirsting for hope, had been touched by this universal doubt, but he had too much youth, too much poetry to yield to it. "There is something beyond"; this is the whole of the **"Meditations"**; this explains how their appearance was such an event, how so many followers arose at the voice of this harmonious revealer of the Infinite. In opposition to Lord Byron and the Satanic school, to that bitter and sarcastic doubt which ended by cursing life, another flag was raised, under which were enrolled all those who believed because they had need to believe; all those who hoped because they required an eternity for a fruition. To all these the **"Meditations"** were an evangel. In this collection, which some call the *chef d'oeuvre* of the author, and which was, at least, the most talked of, Lamartine touched the whole key-board of poetical emotions; in *L'Isolement,* "that undefinable melancholy which pervades us at the close of day"; in the *Epitre à Lord Byron,* the most profound sentiments concerning life and the infinite; in the *Lac,* the sadness of the love which believes itself, and which has need to be eternal, but which scarcely lasted for an hour; and in the *Crucifix,* the sobbing of the lover at the death-bed of his beloved. In the *Ode à Bonaparte* he rose to the highest lyric conceptions; and in *Les Etoiles* he was able to idealize human love with a superabundance of images such as no poet before him had ever found. A great many more of these poems, and among them some of Lamartine's gems, might be cited. To be just, there should be mentioned almost all of the two series of the **"Meditations,"** the second of which, though published twelve years later, must not be separated from the first, because both are one and the same book, born of the same inspiration. This species of poetry was the true form for the genius of Lamartine. When he came to more definite subjects, such as *La Morte de Socrate* or *Le dernier Chant du Pélérinage de Childe Harold,* which imprisoned him within certain limits, he lost a great deal of his power. Yet there are some beautiful passages. . . . (pp. 364-65)

After the **"Meditations"** came the **"Harmonies."** Though still meditations, they reveal a new phase in the natural development of the genius of the poet. There are no more to be found such morning flowers as adorn his early works; but he appears to have greater power, more grandeur and loftiness of conception. If the style is less graceful, it has more force, amplitude, and magnificence. His inspiration is always the same; yet, and with more intensity, that sense of the infinite which may be given as the characteristic of the poetry of Lamartine. Less and less does he care for minute beauties; his poetry is now a grand whole, flowing with full banks and with a majestic current. (p. 365)

All of Lamartine's works might be represented in this trilogy: the **"Meditations,"** the **"Harmonies,"** *La Chute d'un Ange.* Many critics put the first of these above the rest; others—and they seem to be right—maintain that the **"Harmonies"** show an advancement; but almost all seem to think that the *Fall of an Angel* was also the fall of Lamartine. . . . It is true, there are grave faults in this poem; even some which are enormous: but it is also true that an unexpected quality here reveals itself, a startling energy appears, where sweetness, harmony, and a kind of vague grandeur have been the marked attributes. . . .

Strictly speaking, there is in this poem no commencement, no middle, no end; it is merely a series of episodes, of visions without connection; not the evolution of a progressive thought, but the irregular bounds of the most colossal and most wandering imagination. The sentiments are heaped up, the events crowd upon each other, the ideas and the impressions are massed in a most extraordinary manner. Here is excess—an abundance and an overflowing of poetry that bewilders. Therefore the critics, usually so lavish in their praise of Lamartine, were very severe upon *La Chute d'un Ange,* and the literary public hardly read it—which, however, did not prevent their condemning it. Let it be read first and condemned afterwards, if it must be condemned; but let it be read carefully, once, twice, six times; then perhaps, it will be found that the critics and the public have not been wise judges. In fact, in spite of so much well-deserved blame, nobody can deny that here are the boldest conceptions, the most brilliant metaphors, the most manly thoughts; real personages of flesh and bones, with hearts that beat and eyes that shed tears; the largest sympathy with the exterior world; a something that brings back the first ages—in short, all the intellectual riches of Lamartine are contained in this book, the last of his long poetical career. Whatever judgment is passed upon this work, whether or not it exhibits the fall of the angel of the **"Meditations,"** there is one thing which seems certain: it is that Lamartine exhausted himself here; after this his muse was voiceless. (p. 367)

> *F. V. Paget, "The Genius of Lamartine," in* Overland Monthly, *n.s. Vol. I, No. 4, April, 1883, pp. 361-68.*

ALBERT THIBAUDET (essay date 1936)

[*Thibaudet was an early twentieth-century French literary critic and follower of the French philosopher Henri Bergson. His work is considered versatile, well informed, and original, and critics cite his unfinished* Histoire de la littérature française de 1789 à nos jours, *first published in 1936, as his major critical treatise. In this work, Thibaudet classified authors by the generations of 1789, 1820, 1850, 1885, and 1914-1918, rather than by literary movements. In the following excerpt from* Histoire de la littérature française de 1789 à nos jours, *Thibaudet discusses Lamartine's role in the development of French poetry while examining in detail his poetic works.*]

Lamartine did not publish *Les Méditations poétiques* until he was thirty years old. But their very weight and quality are composed of an authentic, slow, regular continuity of the seasons that lie behind them. Or, better, of two continuities that meet and harmonize.

The first is the continuity of a poetry. Lamartine began with the poetry of the eighteenth century, and he never wholly abandoned it. His ears would always echo with the verse of Voltaire and Parny. His own poetry would fall back into that form at those times when he was merely facile. Lamartine's elegy was a continuation of the plaintive elegy in long mourning garments. . . . [The] readers of 1820 were still in a family and a climate that they knew. And yet, in the face of *Les Méditations,* these overtures no longer count. A long-drawn-out poetic chrysalis became a winged poetry. That very thing that the genius of the Restoration aroused in society, that flower of endowed youth, that first poetry of the tradition that the July sun would vulgarize as it dried it out, was set down, idealized into the pure state by *Les Méditations.*

The other continuity was that of a poet, of a poet in his domain—that is, in the world of continuity. Schools, longings—and, too, exalted sentiments, principles, a whole "what a young man should be" for the ladies—and a great love, which, at the appointed time, worked this soil and sowed in it the supernatural teeth of the dragon, caused the miraculous harvest to rise out of the hereditary furrow. *Les Méditations* truly brought to French poetry a discovery of love that resembled the discovery revealed to a young man and a young girl, for the only beautiful verses of love lyrics, those of Ronsard or François de Maynard, which were three centuries old, had been forgotten.

Has there existed since a protracted continuity that exactly corresponds to that continuity of 1820? Can *Les Méditations* still be for us what they were for their contemporaries? Let us point out first of all that *Méditations* must be understood to mean, not the arbitrarily confused collection, padded with mediocrities and desk-drawer fragments, that Lamartine later provided for the booksellers and that is always reprinted in its final form, but the twenty-four poems of the original volume. (pp. 110-11)

Let us acknowledge first that, of the twenty-four poems, there are only four that still bring to life for us, in intact purity, that note of pure poetry, that sound, as Lamartine himself wrote in a letter, "as pure as art, as sad as death, as soft as velvet," that connects the Lamartinian meaning of *Méditations* to a musical meaning (as the word is used in the program notes at concerts), and that, as soon as it is spoken, is evoked in everyone's memory by the famous title: these are *L'Isolement, Le Vallon, Le Lac de B* . . . (which later became simply *Le Lac*), and *L'Automne,* four themes in stanzas for love and loneliness. It is the fine point beneath which a less pure poetry has body and harmony. Lamartine, who as a judge of his own poetry was usually prejudiced against himself, always distinguished between the exquisite quality and the necessary quantity in his work. He always regarded true poetry, "poetry itself," as a precarious state of grace that it would be rash to consolidate into a habit.

From the opposite point of view, let us discard the insignificant pieces . . .—*Le Soir, Le Souvenir, La Gloire, La Prière, L'Invocation, Le Golfe de Baïa, Les Chants lyriques de Saül, L'Hymne au soleil.* This still leaves a dozen important poems that might be called the average *Méditations,* which are still far superior to any poetry published since 1700, which transport us into unquestionably the best atmosphere of 1820, and which were the major factors in Lamartine's success.

These are religious discourses, and precisely those religious discourses that had been waited for, those of a *Génie du christianisme* [by François René de Chateaubriand] in the language of beautiful verse. On the one hand, the Voltairean form of the epistle and the discourse in verse; on the other, the sentimental and spiritual poetry of *Le Génie*—both brought together into a transfiguring fusion, the poetry of a restoration, the restoration of a poetry, in the dual historical dawn of the Restoration and of romanticism. . . . The unexpected poetry of *Les Méditations,* without effort and in a single movement, put the seal to a great hope. (pp. 111-12)

The voice of the time, the voice of the women, the voice of the *salons* said: "We need a *Génie du christianisme* in poetry." Those voices said too: "If only Byron were a Christian! Then we should have a Christian Byron." The arrangement of *Les Méditations* was very painstakingly planned: it was not by accident that *L'Homme*—that is, the epistle to Lord Byron—immediately followed *L'Isolement,* with its sweeping solitary view of the horizon. In *L'Homme* Lamartine imagined that repentant, Christian, French Byron that the *salons* demanded. It is no secret that it amused the real Byron.

Quite as aptly as the later *Harmonies, Les Méditations poétiques* could have included *et religieuses* in its title. It went to a religious public, and it contained all the religious turns of Lamartine's lyrics and epics. The theme of the fallen angel animated the whole poem *A Byron.* In the great treatises of *L'Immortalité, La Foi, La Prière, Le Temple, Dieu,* Lamartine (who had long since lost any positive faith) seemed to be writing for an audience as much as for himself, and no one will be astonished to find that *Poésie sacrée,* a dithyramb to M. Eugène Genoude [the publisher] that is the last of *Les Méditations,* is all formality, a chore. The true, alive religious tone of *Les Méditations* is nowhere better struck than in the fine poem, *Semaine sainte,* in which there is nothing of the ritual Christian emotion of a Holy Week, but rather an exquisite and very faithful picture of those retreats to which Edouard de Rohan, the future cardinal, invited the young conservatives of his generation in his chateau of La Roche-Guyon, where the exquisite chapel in the grotto seemed the perfectly designed oratory for *Le Génie du christianisme* and the ladies devoted to M. de Chateaubriand.

It might be said that with *La Mort de Socrate* Lamartine had set up in the philosopher's prison a chapel like that of La Roche-Guyon, or wound the swaddling of the Jesuit style around an Italian tenor Socrates. Let us view it as the first example of those poems in groups of lines set off by suspension points, in which Lamartine imitated (as the preface attributed to his publisher says) the clipped lyric tale of Byron. *La Mort de Socrate* is a very strange poem, first of all in that it shows us to the full the extent to which Lamartine . . . was alien to Greek art; then because, inspired by the translation of the *Phaido* that Cousin had just made, it joined that spiritual movement that excited Restoration society; and finally because its oratorical vigor is often magnificent. . . . A forceful, rich, harmonious and mellow Italianism was to run through his lyrics until 1830.

It is manifest first in *Les Nouvelles Méditations,* which appeared at the same time as *La Mort de Socrate.* Obviously less original than their predecessors, they were more rich. The poet had gained and grown. *Le Lac* of *Les Nouvelles Méditations* was the bay of Naples: *Ischia,* the hazy softness of a Mediterranean evening, some hints of mandolin and water ice, but also the divine strophe and pure music. *Le Poète mourant* soars high above its old-fashioned, tearful title. *Bonaparte* is the first of those great solid odes whose every strophe, like a victory, marches with the ring of bronze sandals and that would constitute the finest chorus of Lamartine's lyricism after 1830. But *Les Etoiles* was already a *Harmonie,* a harmony of night. This nocturne of Lamartine's has the softness of the Milky Way above land and water, it is a vision taking place in a tender Elysian dew, the feeling of the cosmic dust in which we float, of the living space through which the planet whirls. As for *Les Préludes,* it is a shower of sparks, a triumph of pure virtuosity. Here the muse is naked under the Tuscan sun, in all the proud glow of her beauty: "a sonata in poetry," Lamartine called it; written in Florence, of course. The poet sings for the sake of singing. An inexhaustible nature at his side provides him with themes and pictures. He crystallizes one of those hours of well-being, of opulence, when life fills the poet to overflowing and makes him seethe with the intoxication of giving. It is not so much the sound of his lyre, it is the lyre itself that is offered to us to be touched and caressed. The opposite extreme is the masterpiece of *Les Nouvelles Méditations—Le Crucifix.* Much more vaguely religious than precisely Christian, Lamartine nevertheless reached the high point of Christian poetry here, he reached it before the Cross and by means of the Cross. This goes very far beyond *L'Immortalité* and *La Mort de Socrate.* The crucifix that is passed from one dying man to the next, handed down from Christ to humanity, the crucifix of Elvire's death, the future crucifix of the poet's own death, the fusion of heart with heart that is the life of the spirit as the fusion of seed with seed is the life of the body—*Le Crucifix* rises in a perfection of pure music; made of nothing, it encompasses everything.

Le Crucifix, a Christian counterpart to *Le Lac,* is an evocation of the original *Méditations.* But the Italian climate of Lamartine's poetry, which luxuriates through *Les Préludes,* includes in general a strength, a vitality, a thirst for active life in which there naturally continued to be a place for that Byronian destiny that haunted Lamartine (one of his last works, in his old age, was a *Vie de Byron*) and that this poet of the same breed always envisaged as remotely possible for himself. On vacation at Saint-Point, before he went back to Tuscany, he wrote *Le Dernier Chant du pélérinage d'Harold,* a tribute to Byron from a candidate to succeed him in art and history. . . . *Le Dernier Chant* was in a way to be his *Henriade* [by François René de Chateaubriand], eloquent and artificial. But these poems assume a peculiar worth as direction signs along his road: *Le Dernier Chant* already revealed his idea of a European career as a poet-prophet and a commanding muse, and *Le Chant du sacre* made an enemy of the future Louis-Philippe, whose family he insulted in this official poem with a frivolity as reckless as that with which, in *Le Dernier Chant,* he insulted the Italy whose king he portrayed. (pp. 112-15)

Lamartine's great book of those years, *Les Harmonies poétiques et religieuses* . . . was at the same time the peak of his Italian inspiration and of the religious poetry peculiar to the Restoration.

Lamartine admitted in a letter to Virieu that of the fifty poems there were only fifteen worth reading. But here even the padding helps to give us the feeling of the aura of poetry, the diffuse and divine presence to which he alluded when he said of *Les Harmonies:* "I wrote some of them in verse, some in prose; thousands of others I heard only in my heart." Those that were written in the four books of 1829 are islands, islands in an Italian abundance and liquidity and light. *L'Invocation* at the beginning, written at Santa Croce, stamps this seal of an Italian church on the whole volume. *L'Hymne de la nuit, L'Hymne du matin* seem Guido Reni's *Night,* Francesco Albani's *Dawn.* With *La Hymne du soir dans les temples,* dedicated to the Princess Borghese, the poet takes the keyboard of a vast organ and makes the vaults ring with a song that is rich and empty. . . . *Le Paysage dans le Golfe de Gênes, L'Infini dans les cieux, Désir, Le Premier Regret* display the flow and the light of nature in Italy with an exalted voluptuousness or a melodious melancholy. But the islands are indeed those fifteen poems whose number Lamartine established and that we can find without trouble.

La Bénédiction de Dieu dans la solitude, written at Saint-Point, is perhaps the fullest, the most exuberant of the poetry of Lamartine, of the landowner, the clan chief, and the poet, revealing his depths of salubrity and tradition: thick human roots under a cover of leaves that vibrates with the presence of centuries, the simple picture of a patriarchal day in the country, the act of living solemnized at length by a music without end, and the clearly perceived essence of the thousands of unwritten *Harmonies* beneath the *Harmonie* sung here. *L'Occident*—strophes of bronze and gold, the peace of the day over the earth and the spirit. *L'Hymne à la douleur*—a masterpiece of moral poetry and beautiful gnomic lines. *Jéhovah ou L'Idée de Dieu*—an oratorio that mounts slowly into the brilliance of a splendid ending. *Le Chêne*—in which the poetry follows the hidden, slow, long, vegetal life of the oak tree. *L'Humanité*—out of the great paintings of Bologna, with its marvelous portrait of the Virgin, its soft, stroked verses, the hymn to the Virgin Mother of whom spiritual man was born. *L'Idée de Dieu* and its ending of light and faith; *Le Souvenir d'enfance ou La Vie cachée*—faith full and abounding as a running stream, the height of the familiar epistle in the whole of French poetry. . . . *Milly ou La Terre natale*—another of those epistles of which Lamartine was the master, the only master . . . , an expanse of fertile land that naturally, with its many verses, took on the appearance of shaped parallel furrows. *Le Cri de l'âme*—genuine and vehement, it fulfills its title: it seems that in the sensuality of the Tuscan summer (almost all the *Harmonies* were written in the summer or the autumn) a love without women mounts in a mystic intoxication, burgeons in the vision of God and fuses in a pillar of light. *Le Tombeau d'une mère,* as poignant as *Le Crucifix. Pourquoi mon âme est-elle triste?*—a lyric meditation whose strength is given it not by its subject, which is poor, barren in language and poetry, but by its oratorical movement, its commonplace spirit having encountered one of the great tides of the human soul and ridden it with all sails spread. *Novissima Verba,* written at Montculot, Bossuet's sermon transposed into the lyric mode, a consideration of man by man, grave, cadenced, flowing like a river swollen and unleashed in a winter night, no rare or novel sentiments, but the royal road of the human heart. The cry to *L'Esprit saint,* the breathless conclusion of which is weak but in which it seems that, completing *Les Harmonies* and publishing them in the summer of 1830, the poet is demanding investiture and sanctification for the political prophet of tomorrow.

The two volumes of *Harmonies* are to Lamartine's work what the two volumes of *Contemplations* are to Hugo's—his summer, his poetic testament, his long, full dialogue with life, men, and God, and also a lyric accounting by which the poet dispenses with a part of himself in order to ascend to the full peak of maturity, to mount to the Homeric Acropolis, to fulfill himself in the epic, in an *Odyssey* of the soul and human destinies. (pp. 115-17)

With *Jocelyn* Lamartine repeated the triumph of *Les Médita- tions,* a success of sentiment and tears that recalled (and perhaps aimed for) that of *Paul et Virginie* [by Jacques Henri Bernardin de Saint-Pierre]. Later *Jocelyn* went out of fashion—like all narratives in verse, and also because of the speed and the carelessness of the writing, especially in the second part, writ- ten after 1834. Its idealism seemed mawkish. And yet it was enough to save it that it unflaggingly hewed to the key word in the epigraph that Lamartine gave it: . . . [Psyche]. It had soul. It was soul. Fulfilling every individual and social meaning of the word, it remains the poem of the soul.

However Lamartine strove to relocate it and idealize it in the Alps . . . , *Jocelyn,* which owed its origin to a revolutionary incident in the history of Milly, and whose hero was Dumont, M. de Lamartine's curate . . . , remains the poem of that same earthy substance of local Christian tradition on which Lamar- tine's genius was borne (and into which he plunged huge roots). The poem of the soul becomes poetically human because it is also the poem of the man of soul in his most elementary, ordinary, and simple form, the guardian of souls in every vil- lage, the country priest as he exists ideally—and soul in action consists in the belief in an ideal existence. But soul is not given, or easily borne. Soul is created by sacrifice, by effort that toils again up a height, the same height from which one has fallen. Lamartine's epic takes as its theme the struggle against that very facility with which Lamartine had passed for hero and victim. In so far as it remembers heaven, the soul— the divine spark that returns to the flame—is Jocelyn the priest, not so much through his vocation of faith as through his vo- cation of sacrifice, sacrifice and expiation for Laurence, a mil- itant love that sacrifices for the happiness of his sister, then an existence endured through suffering love to win to trium- phant love. But the soul has a double meaning and it lives on a double level. There is the individual soul of man and there is the collective soul of humanity, and for the Christian that collective soul of humanity is called the Church. From this point of view the central scene of *Jocelyn* is that of the prison, the spark from cleric to cleric, from soul to soul (the theme of *Le Crucifix*), and, through a new sacrifice, the individual soul that rejoins the soul of the Church, of humanity, of the col- lective ascent toward God; except that all this symbolic gran- deur, this epic and mystic substance of *Jocelyn,* is hardly more visible externally in the poem than the soul is in the body. The poet does not move us, does not seek to move us, otherwise than through individual living bodies, the people whom he depicts, the story that he tells, the tragedy in which he takes part. Jocelyn, in a letter to his sister, compares himself rather clumsily with Faust. The passage does not ring true, but the idea survives. The poem of *Jocelyn,* which Lamartine con- ceived as the conclusion and the final episode of [a] cyclical epic, does indeed include a Faustian conjecture on the nature and the destiny of man. But none of this Faustian conjecture violates the framework, the body, the feeling, the intimacy of a french *Hermann und Dorothea* [by Johann Wolfgang von Goethe]. Lamartine achieved this balance without a trace of obviousness in his scheme, of exaggeration in his effort. "I never think," he used to say; "my ideas think for me." In *Jocelyn* he felt for an idea, and an idea thought for him.

Jocelyn was to conclude [Lamartine's] human epic; *La Chute d'un ange* would be its beginning. The fate of this poem was remarkable. It was the only complete failure of Lamartine's poetry among his contemporaries, a Tarpeian rock two years after the Capitoline of *Jocelyn.* He himself, who was the first to extol *Jocelyn* . . . , called his *Chute d'un ange* abominable, offering the excuse that it was necessary to the following ep- isodes, in which one would see what was to be seen. Later the poem found admirers, who virtually discovered it, pre-eminent among them the leader of the anti-Lamartine reaction, Leconte de Lisle, who regarded it as the poet's masterpiece. (pp. 118-19)

One must admire the grandeur of the myth, the force and the importance of the ideas. Cédar, the angel who owes his fall to love but who, like the theologian, could say, "My love is my significance," realizes an idea of man, the idea that runs through Lamartine's life and poetry and that it was essential for him to express once in its totality. He had considered this idea religiously only during his journey through the land that was the cradle of religions. Standing before the stones of Bal- bek, he enlarged it with the vision of a materialistic humanity, the master of the forces of nature, which man uses only in order to oppress and to enjoy. A few persecuted men of worth, the keepers of the fragments of a revealed book, preserve a kingdom of God in hiding. These fragments of the *Livre primitif* are a masterpiece of gnomic poetry, strong, simple, classic, with a purity and a substance, a perfection of style unequaled elsewhere by Lamartine. But the famous chorus of the cedars of Lebanon is only a *Harmonie,* and inferior to the others.

La Chute, not [François René de Chateaubriand's] *Les Martyrs,* is the epic specifically prepared for and announced by *Le Génie du christianisme.* The theme is that of the religiosity of the romantics, the battle against the spirit of the eighteenth century in its double aspect: encyclopedism and sensuality. Ency- clopedism: man's domination of nature without a correspond- ing mastery over his own nature can lead only to a monstrous culture, and as early as 1838 the myth of *La Chute* had posed the anguishing problems with which Europe was wrestling a hundred years later. Sensuality: it is astounding what a facti- tious, ingenuous, and monster-ridden picture Lamartine drew of the lustful lives of these lords of nature. He simply copied it from the *cloaca maxima* in which the sensuality of the eigh- teenth century culminated, from the Marquis de Sade himself, whose works, read at the age of twenty by Lamartine with his friend, Guichard de Bienassis, terrified both young men.

Obviously one must not seek in *La Chute d'un ange* what is offered in *Jocelyn*—living humanity and individuals. Its people live only symbolically. But, whatever may be said of it, its poetic style is generally of a more consistent quality than that of *Jocelyn.* It is the style of an orator-poet. For four years Lamartine had been demonstrating his mastery of the art of the spoken word in the Chamber of Deputies. It shows in his poetry.

That mastery is revealed not only in the epic, which, unfor- tunately, he abandoned at this point, but in a lyric poetry that, more unusual than before, gained in harmony, in breadth, in substance, and that swelled and surged in the poems of *Les Recueillements,* written after 1830. The *Cantique sur la mort de la duchesse de Broglie* endowed the tomb of Albertine de Staël with the same sacraments that Bossuet provided for the grave of Henrietta of England. The odes to Wasp, to Guille- mardet, the tribute *A l'Académie de Marseille, Gethsémani* opened the idealized home of family and parents to the tides of politics. The lyric masterpieces of Lamartine in this time were his great political odes. With *A Némésis, Le Toast des gallois et des bretons, Utopie, Les Révolutions, La Marseillaise de la paix* the

A caricature of Lamartine by Nadar, a member of the extreme left, who accused Lamartine of attempting to prevent a socialist revolution in 1848.

flag of his parliamentary eloquence was flung out under the sky.

Lyric poetry in Lamartine had always matched a precarious state of grace. For a long time he thought that after *Les Méditations*, the fruit of his springtime, and *Les Harmonies*, the harvest of his summer, he would find the lyric sources of his autumn in *Psaumes*—that is, dialogues between the soul and God, closer to the Bible than those that Victor Hugo would conduct for several years on Guernsey but like Hugo's the testament of a way of thought that was always religious. The forced labors of journalism and the automatism of prose prevented him from writing them, except one day during the grape harvest at Milly in 1857, when, outside the house of his childhood, he wrote *La Vigne et la maison, Psaumes de l'ame*, the last warm golden cluster from the stripped trellis. No poet has been able to equal this poetry written at the age of sixty-seven. It is on the level of *Le Crucifix*. And, furthermore, opening the twenty-eight volumes of the *Cours familier de littérature* at random is enough to show that, if the poetic spring no longer pours forth, it survives under ground. (pp. 119-21)

In effect, Lamartine's function from 1820 on was to sustain poetry in France as an essence and as a climate. He was not so much a force of nature as a presence of nature, not so much a date as a season. In 1820, catching fallen poetry by the hand, he gave it a kingdom over a heart, over many hearts, and then over all the rest, over politics, over history, over criticism. (p. 121)

Albert Thibaudet, "Lamartine," in his French Literature from 1795 to Our Era, *translated by Charles Lam Markmann, Funk & Wagnalls, 1968, pp. 110-21.*

HERBERT J. HUNT   (essay date 1941)

[*Hunt studies* Les visions, *Lamartine's projected epic, within the context of nineteenth-century French epic poetry. After tracing Lamartine's changing plans for* Les visions, *Hunt discusses* Jocelyn *and* La chute d'un ange, *the only completed portions. Although Hunt praises the skillful narration, lyrical prose, and psychological insight of* Jocelyn *and* La chute d'un ange, *he faults the works' anachronistic and melodramatic traits. He also suggests that Lamartine was influenced by the French philosopher Pierre-Simon Ballanche's theories of universal religion and reincarnation. Hunt concludes that Lamartine was unable to complete* Les visions *because he could not create a plausible hero.*]

It is not an uncommon thing for men to be discontented with their lot, however pleasant. One is none the less surprised to learn that a man like Alphonse de Lamartine, awarded the palm of glory above all his contemporaries for the limpid spontaneity and intimacy of his lyric compositions, regarded himself as having missed his poetic destiny. The overwhelming success of *les Méditations poétiques* astonished him as much as the work itself enchanted the reading public of his time; and he was not the man to scorn the incense which was burnt so generously before the idol of his own popularity. Yet the *Méditations* doomed him to a rôle which he did not willingly accept, and as one volume after the other of his poems was offered to the world, his admirers either hailed the reappearance or lamented the absence of the 'Lamartine ignorant qui ne sait que son âme,' of the 'amant d'Elvire' to whose plaintively musical accents they had grown accustomed.

Lamartine had a vastly different conception of the poet's personality and function. From first to last his real model was a Homer, a Dante, a Milton, and he was fired with the ambition to write that great predestined poem of the nineteenth century which was to explain man to himself, by throwing on to the poetic screen the birth, the growth, the vicissitudes and the destinies of the human race. . . . Unable to recognize either lyric or dramatic poetry as the characteristic form of his age, refusing also to grace that form with the title 'epic,' too narrow a one to embrace its ample scope, he nevertheless makes it plain that his actual purpose in life is to create a humanitarian epic akin to those dreamed of and attempted by Ballanche and Edgar Quinet. (pp. 153-54)

Like Ballanche, and probably not altogether independently of Ballanche, Lamartine had a palingenetic notion of his era. 'L'esprit humain, plus plein que jamais de l'esprit de Dieu qui le remue, n'est-il pas en travail de quelque grand enfantement religieux?' And, long before the poet published his violent repudiation of his earlier 'manner' in the poem *À Félix Guillemardet,* he had ardently wished to be worthy of his times and attune his lyre to the superb harmonies of which he felt himself capable. (pp. 154-55)

It would be entirely wrong to imagine that such an ambition only came to Lamartine in his maturity, and that his nourishment of such humanitarian visions dates only from a tardy conversion due to the rapid evolution of French political, social and religious thought determined by the July Revolution and the crisis which followed it. Certainly works such as that of M. Citoleux reveal almost to a startling degree the development which Lamartine's outlook in all spheres underwent from the period of *le Désespoir* and *l'Immortalité* onwards. But he was never an egotist cloistered in the intimate experiences of his own daily life; and M. Henri Guillemin, in two remarkably thorough studies, first of *Jocelyn,* then of *les Visions,* has illustrated to the full the persistence of the epic dream in Lamartine's life. From 1813 to 1820 he was busy projecting a *Clovis,* a hackneyed subject in all conscience, but one he evidently had no intention of treating in the orthodox manner. Only a fragment of this subsists [*L'Ange, fragment épique* in *Nouvelles Méditations*], a scene in which Ithuriel, the guardian angel of the Frankish conqueror, is summoned to the Divine Throne and instructed to visit Clovis in the latter's dreams. As is frequent in these detached portions of Lamartine's projected poems, the comic and the sublime involuntarily rub shoulders. Comic for instance is the scene where the cherubim, spurred on by an infantile curiosity, flock round to overhear God's instructions to Ithuriel, but find that all communication is cut off; charming is the description of that fairy-land of nocturnal dreams presided over by 'l'astre au front changeant.'

In 1821 a decisive inspiration came to the poet, and he began to elaborate plans for his life-work: *les Visions.* Constant interruptions occurred, and the Muse proved discouragingly restive, but again and again Lamartine returned to his project until 1829. Despondency and even more serious distractions took his mind off it for a further period of years, but he did not entirely cease his efforts. His well-known poems *Jocelyn* and *la Chute d'un Ange* are salvages from the wreck of his youthful enterprise. (pp. 155-56)

From 1821 especially he was evidently anxious to avoid the absurdities, the tediousness and the banality which rendered [the ephemeral contemporary] epics scarcely readable, and, even at this early stage, it is the mantle of the prophet rather than the laurel wreath of a poetic technician that he is busy fashioning for himself. As M. Guillemin indicates, it is an open question how far Lamartine was at this time susceptible to theosophist influences, but his first idea for *les Visions* seems to betray a certain colouring of illuminist notions. The plan of 1821 shows a view of the universe based on a doctrine of emanation, and the mystery of life and creation is explained on the basis of 'l'épreuve.' The conception of a scale of beings descending from God, of trial and purification through metempsychosis, may of course as well be Pythagorean or Platonic as illuminist, and Lamartine was a votary of Plato; but it is sufficient to note that his philosophy was cast in that prevalent mould of the times. Briefly, this first poem was to relate the long pilgrimage, through a prodigious succession of lives, of twin-souls destined eventually to find eternal union in a happy consummation of the Divine purpose by whose means what we know as evil would be finally expunged from the universe. Revealed on a cosmic scale, the basic idea appears to have been the same as the one we find expressed later, and in more familiar terms, in *Jocelyn*. . . . (pp. 156-57)

The Platonic theory of soul-mates apart, the scheme, though elaborated before Ballanche was well-known and before the latter's most characteristic works were published, has definitely an 'Orphic' ring. There is, however, danger in building any seductive theories on this project, since we are indebted to a much older Lamartine, the author of the **Cours Familier de Littérature,** for our scanty knowledge of it, and it is quite on the cards that he was crediting the young dreamer of 1821 with notions gleaned in later readings.

In December 1823 a new and very different inspiration came to Lamartine. . . . [Though] Lamartine was continually revising his scheme and devising new details, we are able to form a very good idea of the shape the work would have assumed. There are three plans extant, the first of which is revealed in a letter to Virieu of the 12th December, 1823, while the sec-

ond . . . [is] dated the 24th December, 1823, and the third, composed after July 1824. . . . (pp. 157-58)

In the conception of 1823 no strong illuminist tendencies are perceptible. The idea of *épreuve,* in which the element of guilt is inconspicuous, has receded into the background since 1821, and that of *expiation* is much more to the fore. The poem would, in fact, have stood firm on the biblical doctrine of a Fall and Expiation expressed in the guise of a picturesque fable. For his fiction, however, Lamartine takes little from the Genesis narrative. . . .[To the stock of works based on the Genesis story] Lamartine grafted a fiction borrowed from Grainville's *Dernier Homme:* beginning his poem with scenes describing the last phases of life on this terrestrial globe prior to the Day of Judgment, the poet intended to evoke the picture of a fallen angel who had, by virtue of the doom meted out to him for his weakness in loving a mortal woman, witnessed all the important epochs of human history, and whose fate was that he should survive until the end of the world, only by repeated sufferings and renunciations attaining that forgiveness which would at the same time reconcile him with his Maker and fulfil his personality by final union with the woman he had worshipped.

The three Plans differ in important details, but the theme and the moral it contains are essentially the same throughout, and they may conveniently be resumed in the famous line from *l'Homme,* in the **Premières Méditations:**

L'homme est un dieu tombé qui se souvient des cieux.

(p. 158)

It is not surprising that little of the projected work was accomplished, and those portions which did actually come to light, either in published fragments or in manuscript relics, are not such as to convince us that Lamartine was capable of achieving his life-ambition. Among the survivals are: an **Invocation;** portions of a **First Vision** in which the scene was laid and the narrative begun; a few lines presenting the dilemma of the Thebaid ascetics and the motives which drove them to their useless self-sacrifice; a fairly large fragment, inspired by Tasso, Creuzé de Lesser, Marchangy, Walter Scott and probably Victor d'Arlincourt, recounting the passion and separation of a medieval page Tristan and his master's daughter Hermine, and intended as a prelude to crusading scenes culminating in the struggle between two women, Hermine and Charismé, for the possession of the hero; and, lastly, the **Chant lyrique du Jugement Dernier,** partly printed in **les Harmonies poétiques et religieuses.** M. Guillemin has suggested various reasons for Lamartine's abandonment of his poem: his realization that, without having as yet travelled in the East, he was in need of local colour for the oriental scenes; the evolution of his religious ideas, involving a growing conviction of the anachronistic nature of his fiction, based in the last resort on Catholic mythology and a Catholic interpretation of life; and above all, perhaps, the enormous difficulty the repetitive nature of *les Visions* would create in the avoidance of monotony. In each of his incarnations [the main character] Éloïm was doomed to pass through a similar series of vicissitudes and experiences, especially with regard to the love of women, and though the 'stuffing' of the poem—Lamartine's views on religion and philosophy and his interpretation of the march of time—might have provided considerable scope for variety, the fable itself would have necessarily proved wearisome in the long run.

Yet, in the poet's mind, the project was only interrupted, and not entirely abandoned. **Jocelyn** and **la Chute d'un Ange** are built on very much the same model, and utilize the same material. Moreover, the poet seems also to have dallied later with the plan of another Vision—les Pêcheurs, announced in the preface to la Chute d'un Ange as an episode to follow. Critics are not agreed as to whether les Pêcheurs was really intended to celebrate a primitive epoch of patriarchal simplicity or to have been in Lamartine's scheme what les Pauvres Gens was to be in Hugo's. At any rate there only remains to consider the two long poems which, though but reluctantly detached by the Poet from the proposed master-work, must necessarily be judged by themselves as specimens of nineteenth-century epic narration. (pp. 160-61)

In the Third Plan of les Visions Lamartine had proposed to include the French Revolution as occupying an important place in the providential scheme. . . . (p. 161)

It is a far cry from this to Jocelyn, Épisode, Journal trouvé chez un curé de village. From 1824 to 1836 Lamartine's views on the purport of the Revolution suffered a considerable modification. By the time he came to compose Jocelyn the poet recognized the predestined nature of the Revolution, and his opinion of it as a necessary experience of human history finds expression in the new work. Although he is revolted by the cruelty of the popular outbursts, he apologizes for the great upheaval as being indispensable to the march of progress, and with a calm impartiality he accords equal blame to both sides for atrocities committed. However, reserving for l'Histoire des Girondins his general judgment on the Revolution, he seems to be peculiarly preoccupied, in Jocelyn, with the problem: during great social cataclysms what principles are to guide the normal private person faced with the necessity of rebuilding a broken universe within the limitations of his own restricted sphere of action? (p. 162)

In an age when the necessity or the wisdom of enforcing celibacy on Catholic priests was a vexed question among sociologists, novelists and dramatists alike, when the memory of innumerable sacerdotal irregularities, and notably that of Lamartine's own friend and mentor the Abbé Dumont, was still fresh, it is not surprising that the author of Jocelyn saw in the theme of involuntary abstinence one of the critical issues of the Revolutionary epoch looked at from the view-point of the private individual. Hence Jocelyn is little concerned with the vast political and social problems evoked by the Revolutionary crisis. (pp. 162-63)

[Let us] consider the poem as it stands, since the poet never tried later to work it into the mosaic of a larger conception. It must be admitted that it contains little of the flavour of standard epic, or indeed of the humanitarian epic then in process of evolution at the hands of contemporary visionaries, even though, in its more purely narrative parts, it reveals Lamartine as a skilful and convincing raconteur, allowing for minor defects such as carelessness about points of detail. The arrival of the two refugees in the mountains, the separation of Jocelyn and Lawrence in the storm which leads to the discovery of the latter's true sex, the harrowing scene in the prison at Grenoble, Jocelyn's return to Lawrence in company with the dead bishop's sister, the death of Lawrence and the funeral procession to the Grotte des Aigles: all is superbly related. But throughout the poem a personal and intimate, rather than the epic note, predominates. Jocelyn is above all a lyrical outpouring, and not only in those passages which are most deservedly famous for their descriptive and meditative beauty, as for instance the religious duet between Jocelyn and Lawrence in the Quatrième Époque, which is far superior to many of the Harmonies, the

curé's lesson to his parishioners' children, the notable episode of les Laboureurs, etc. The whole work, a masterpiece of contemplative, almost of unctuous suavity, in spite of the outbursts of anguish and revolt which punctuate it, is the revelation of a human soul. Primarily of course it is the revelation of the poet himself, for it represents one of those many earnest efforts of Lamartine to crystallize his ever-evolving and always elusive religious convictions: it is in verse what the Profession de Foi du Vicaire savoyard [by Rousseau], to which it is greatly indebted, is in prose—the outpourings of a sensitive soul for whom religion is a necessity, but in whom a persistent strain of rationalism continually conquers the yearning for that peace and mental stability which the unquestioning acceptance of orthodox formulas can afford. And in this fact, rather than in the strange unsaintly rôle attributed to the condemned prelate, lies the explanation of that pious dismay which the poem evoked in the minds of submissive Catholics.

The poem is also the analysis, endowed with considerable psychological subtlety and truth and rendered in a language of truly Racinian musicality, of a real and permanent human dilemma, that which confronts any high-minded mortal who, as sometimes occurs, sees the problem of a choice between selfish happiness and self-immolation to immutable principles presented to him in a peculiarly sensational form. (pp. 165-66)

[La Chute d'un ange] marks a much more definite return than Jocelyn to Lamartine's inspiration of 1823. . . . (p. 167)

La Chute d'un Ange can perhaps only prove completely interesting to readers who are students of the mentality of Lamartine's epoch, and who are acquainted with what has gone before and what is to follow in this series of attempts to create an original type of epic poem. The quest of sources would be a facile diversion in studying this text, but from the point of view of these present researches the most striking fact in la Chute is the omnipresence of reminiscences from Ballanche. Lamartine admits having known the visionary of Lyon from 1829 onwards: until 1834 he was on familiar terms with him; and there seems no doubt that, even if we concede the greater rationalism of Lamartine's inspiration, his conception of primitive society, above all the symbolic fictions and the philosophy of religious progress which enrich this fantastic story, are largely culled from Orphée and the Essais de Palingénésie sociale. Lamartine, like Ballanche, is seized with the mania for making austere old sages the mouthpieces of pregnant utterance. The rôle of the hermit who leads the Poet to Lebanon, though a scanty one, recalls that of Thamyris in Orphée, while Adonaï is a veritable 'initiator' who, in the Sixth, Seventh and Eighth Visions, teaches his visitors the primitive arts of society—the cultivation of wheat and vegetables, the making of bread, the grafting of fruit-trees; like Orphée himself, he 'reveals' to his astonished listeners the blessings of property, marriage and legislation. Ballanche's idea of the march of civilization, the gradual laying-open of these boons to the uninitiated, the 'lesser breeds without the law,' was surely present in Lamartine's memory when he distinguished between the superior caste of 'giants' at Babel, and the race of slaves for whom marriage, property and religion were a closed book. (p. 171)

Many other 'palingenetic' notions, though somewhat diluted and melted into the mould of Lamartine's own thought, are also to be discerned in the poem. The basic idea of 'épreuve' and 'expiation' provides of course the central theme of la Chute, just as it had been destined to furnish that of les Visions. Other mystic conceptions gleaned by Ballanche from illuminist writings are those of the continuous 'échelle des êtres,' of the divine purpose by which all atoms of created matter are destined in their turn to contain the spark of animate life. (pp. 171-72)

Yet it would be going too far to make Lamartine a conscious imitator or disciple of Ballanche and the theosophist following. We must allow for the fact that he was exercising his undoubted right as a poet to incorporate such notions into his work only as a means of poetic embellishment, and even as a picturesque method of rendering concrete and visible his own spiritual philosophy. Metempsychosis is, for instance, a useful 'machine' capable of replacing the outworn figments favoured by imitative epicists; and, however wonderful the visions Lamartine permitted himself of the blissful harmony of universal creation before sin had darkened the horizon, his use of the language of mysticism is only a prelude to repeated assertions that human reason is after all the sole mediator between man and God. . . . [Throughout] the poem Lamartine remains clear and comprehensible; his language is the language of parable, not of apocalyptic vision. The obscurity of Ballanche's symbolism is entirely absent throughout the work. Herein, in fact, in my opinion, lies the true interest of this surprising composition. Lamartine has seized on the most suggestive material his age could offer him and transmuted it into the precious metal of his own view of life, often hesitant but always clear and rational, and at bottom attractively Christian.

From a technical point of view there are many features in the work capable of both arresting and astounding the reader. There is no doubt, to begin with, that the narrative in *la Chute* is much more *alive* than that of *Jocelyn*. This is not to say that passages of captivating lyrical beauty do not as usual abound, from the Chorus of the Cedars to the wooing and wedding scenes and to the cleverly suggestive musical description of the noises of Babel which, at the end of the Eighth Vision, reach the ears of the captives in their aerial vessel. The action is almost static in *Jocelyn;* it moves swiftly in *la Chute,* and in fact in this respect Lamartine has almost gone to the other extreme: his fable fringes on the romanesque and even the melodramatic. The thrilling rescues effected by Cédar are in the best popular tradition, and certain episodes in which he and his emigrant family figure recall at once the Swiss Family Robinson and the more modern Tarzan of the Apes. Occasionally incidents occur which border on the ridiculous, as when, in the darkness of night, Cédar engages in Herculean conflict with a supposed lion, stifles it and discovers he has killed his favourite dog. Moreover, the poet displays a talent for grim and even sadistic description which surprised and shocked many of his admirers. Cédar's combats with his enemies are atrocious in the extreme: in the Second Vision, as an example to Éviradnus, he uses the corpse of a slain adversary as a club against the rest; and the struggle to the death between the hero and Djezyd, the last survivor among Daïdha's ravishers, is related with gusto down to the last detail. The poet seems to have lashed his imagination to a state of fury, as if to rival the worst brutalities of the extravagant Romantics of the 'twenties and 'thirties; he even shows the tyrants of Babel, in search of dramatic relaxation, gloating over the sufferings of a pair of imprisoned lovers, Isnel and Ichmé, with whom their executioners play as a cat with a mouse. But he reaches the limit perhaps in his description of the mortal combat between Cédar and Asrafiel in the Fifteenth Vision, in which nail and tooth serve as weapons, and the struggle is concluded by Cédar's biting the heart out of his foe! (pp. 172-74)

[No doubt Lamartine] has classical models for . . . [the] atrocities he purveys throughout the work. Homer and Virgil scarcely

mince matters when it comes to the shedding of blood; but Lamartine proffers his work as 'une épopée métaphysique,' and must therefore bow to the judgment which finds in *la Chute* an excessive exploitation of the merely physical side of things.

After *la Chute d'un Ange* Lamartine had nothing more to offer in the epic line. Although he got further than Vigny in his attempt to realize his dreams of epic, his work must be considered a failure, unless we detach *Jocelyn* entirely from the rest, and admit *la Chute* as a daring and striking experiment which has not quite succeeded. . . . Certainly flagrant anachronisms are to be found in the epic work of . . . [Lamartine]. We find it in Lamartine when he attributes to an antediluvian sage a semi-rationalist, semi-evangelical 'religion naturelle' saturated with nineteenth century humanitarianism. . . . Lamartine's attempt to give picturesque concreteness, by means of vivid melodrama, to his philosophy of history, is . . . vitiated by his failure to create a convincing hero: one who, by his mental and moral reactions, should in some way reflect the soul of the two civilizations—the nomadic and the civic—through which he passes. . . . [The weak spot in Lamartine's conception is] the inability to combine a general idea with a living character who exists, not only as a personification of that idea, but is also of, as well as in the age the poem evokes, and yet subsists by virtue of his own humanity. (pp. 175-76)

> *Herbert J. Hunt, "Verse Epics of the Romantic Period," in his* The Epic in Nineteenth-Century France: A Study in Heroic and Humanitarian Poetry from *"Les Martyrs" to "Les Siècles Morts," Basil Blackwell, 1941, pp. 144-99.**

MILTON G. HARDIMAN (essay date 1957)

[*Focusing on Lamartine's concept of the poet as social reformer, Hardiman outlines Lamartine's philosophy as expressed in the essay "Contre la peine de mort" and in the poems* Jocelyn, La chute d'un ange, *and "La Marseillaise de la paix."*]

Lamartine idealized all of his adventures, all of his loves—his love of God, country, humanity, and his personal loves. And his greatest medium for the expression of all this sentiment, this inner exploration of the soul . . . was the medium of poetry. Lamartine was essentially a poet of nature, especially as it related to his own reminiscences, but some of us today, younger, supposedly sophisticated, amid the mechanization and modernization of life, have some difficulty, probably, in understanding or rather feeling the depths of his poetry because the sounds evoked from the country and other bucolic places are so different from our urban life of today. Although one of the best prose writers of his day and certainly placed high on the list of all time greats in French literature, poetry was natural for him—who, as he said, became a poet by accident. . . . And though he includes in his work that which is most intimate in the heart and most divine in the soul and thought, he was always aware of the realities of life in the midst of his taste for the ideal and mingled his *poésie* with the truth in a charming manner.

Lamartine was thirty-three when he wrote *Nouvelles Méditations,* which did not have the success of the *Méditations Poétiques*. What happened? The new volume included poetry more philosophical than that in the previous work. Could it be that now having girded himself with more mature age, he was beginning to by-pass the more romantic elements and become philosophic? Did the public repudiate his philosophy or did the public want the romantic in preference to the philosophic? With maturing years, he was also ambitious to become a public servant in the diplomatic service and later a political figure. Does he have these things in mind when he writes his poetry at this time?

Most of his adventures of the heart were now behind him—including his soul-stirring romance with Mme. Charles, a creole from Santo Domingo. Subsequent episodes in his life—his happy marriage to his English wife and the deaths of his son in England at the age of two and his daughter in Beyrouth at the age of ten—had helped to sober him.

Lamartine now became the poet-politician in France—or at least he tried to, like many of her *literati*—waxing eloquent in his emotion and his common sense appeals as a member of the *député* and later of the provisionary government. . . . (pp. 75-6)

Hugo, perhaps, was the most blatant and vociferous among the romantics in proclaiming the role of the poet as leader of the people, but a close study of Lamartine reveals that, though he was not as successful as his illustrious compatriot, he was nonetheless a believer that the fate of the nation lay as much—perhaps more—in the lap of the poet as in that of any other social leader, including the lawyer and/or politician.

Lamartine stated his ideas relative to the social mission of the poet for the first time perhaps in the preface which he wrote for the 1831 edition of the *Méditations* and which he called, *Les Destinées de la poésie*. In the preface he states the need of seeing poetry in a new light. A new poetry must be created which will be in harmony with the times just as the older forms of poetry were in harmony with the younger world. . . . (pp. 77-8)

Gone now are the days of the *Méditations* and the *Nouvelles Méditations*. The poetry of Lamartine is destined more and more to become a thesis-poetry as did that of Hugo. From singing for the sheer joy of singing, from "art for art's sake," Lamartine mounts the *Cathedra* and sets himself up as interpreter and pedagogue. Henceforth his poems are "lessons."

In *Joycelyn* [*sic*] Lamartine has given us a lesson in humility and self-effacement which is one of the most beautiful—in purpose at least—that the world has ever seen. We say this, even though we are cognizant of many of the defects of *Joycelyn* and many of the protestations raised against certain passages in it. These, however, do not detract one iota from the purpose of the poem, which, we believe, is lofty and really sincere. *Joycelyn* is a story of sacrifice, and of the resultant elevation of the soul. In order to assure his sister's dowry that she might marry in a fitting manner, Joycelyn gives up his claim to his heritage and enters a seminary. In order to confess an old priest, condemned by the terror, he gives up a beautiful and romantic love, the only happiness in his life, that he might be ordained a priest in order to shrive the older man. A priest in a village buried in the snow, he labors indefatigably and unselfishly for the parishioners. From beginning to end, the story is intended to show man that only by true unselfishness and unstinting abnegation can he justify himself before God and purge himself of the stigma of the original sin. (p. 79)

It is in the eighth vision of *Chute d'un Ange* . . . that Lamartine has given us his most definite ideas on society in general. In fact we have the outline of a social state as in Rousseau's *Contrat Social,* while the religious ideas there expressed would make an interesting comparison with those of Rousseau in his *Professions de foi du vicaire savoyard,* or with Diderot's *Lettre sur les Aveugles.* While the period of real skepticism had passed,

An engraving of Lamartine in 1848, at the height of his political popularity.

thanks to Chateaubriand, and to a natural rebellion which always forces the social pendulum to swing the other way, Lamartine felt, however, that there still was too little faith, that true religion had been smothered under too much form and too many doctrines. He counsels, therefore, a return to the simple, pantheistic, or, perhaps it would be better to say, omnipresent ideas of the fathers. There had grown up the belief that God existed in the temples only. This idea was brought about no doubt by too much stressing by the clergy of the necessity of church-going, and of the danger of staying away. This necessarily led to the idea that God was in holy temples only. Lamartine warns us, however, that our vision is being clouded by this erroneous idea, and that our children will come to feel that God is confined only to the temple. (p. 81)

Lamartine then rises in protest against those who seek to depict God in images of stone and canvas; who pretend to have the power of the prophets and saints of old. By faith and meditation within oneself can one come to see and to know God. Herein Lamartine sets himself up as an iconoclast, a Moses chastising the people whom he had saved from their idolatry in setting up and worshipping the golden calf. Here it seems that Lamartine is dangerously unorthodox, and violent in his denunciation of the wealth as well as the preposterous claims of the church. . . . (pp. 81-2)

[In *Chute d'un Ange,*] as in his *Marseillaise de la Paix* and in his *Contre la Peine de Mort,* Lamartine condemns capital punishment and the spilling of blood, human or animal. . . . Also Lamartine, like so many others, protested against the rapid urbanization of the country. Like Verhaeren in his *Villes Ten-*

taculaires he saw the city like a giant octopus reaching its tentacles out in all directions, sucking the life blood of the country. . . . And with the same idealism and humanitarianism that runs through all of his later poetry, he pleads for love and sympathy for the animals. . . . We feel, however, that his idealism carries him a little too far when he discounts the need of judges or courts on earth. (pp. 82-3)

It seems a little unfair to accuse Lamartine of wishing to found a state on anarchical lines. If the advice and exhortations of Lamartine are followed out there will be no need of judges or courts. The general desire for peace and well-doing which will animate man will be a sufficient deterrent for crime. Each one will feel responsible for peace and happiness of the community, and will therefore repress any untoward tendencies, whereas if courts and judges are established, the tendency will be to cast upon them the responsibility for the peace of the community. . . .

From the foregoing summary sketch of the ideas of Lamartine, as expressed in his poems . . . , it is apparent that Lamartine felt very deeply his role of pastor to the people, and, although a little less vociferous than Hugo, was just as sincere and confirmed in the belief of the sacredness of this rôle. (p. 84)

> Milton G. Hardiman, "The Role of Poetry in France according to Lamartine's Social Mission," in CLA Journal, Vol. I, No. 1, November, 1957, pp. 75-84.

J. C. IRESON (essay date 1969)

[*In this excerpt from his survey of Lamartine's verse, Ireson discusses such themes as the past, dispossession, and erotic and platonic love. He also comments on Lamartine's technique, particularly his use of symbols and images, and points out similarities between Lamartine's verse and that of other French poets, including Charles Baudelaire and Stéphane Mallarmé.*]

[Qualities] of fluidity and depth are discernible in the themes of Lamartine's writings. Over the years, no doubt because of the enduring influence of the neo-classical notions of rhetoric under which he wrote, the themes of his work have been handled according to intellectual categories, religion, nature, subjective experience, and so on. They have also been closely locked in the poet's autobiography, too closely locked for their peculiar quality and value to emerge. (p. 38)

It seems to me that Lamartine's poetry springs from a great unifying theme, the theme of dispossession, of disinheritance. I use both words in the first instance in their literal sense, of being cut off from an inheritance, of being prevented 'from coming into possession of a property or right which in the ordinary course would devolve upon him as his'. This theme ramifies into multiple aspects, each one a key to Lamartine's poetic impulse: the disinheritance, through the act of individuation, of the spirit from its natural abode, this 'pur séjour où l'esprit seul s'envole' constantly hymned by this poet; the disinheritance of the poet from the poetic universe which by choice he would inhabit—this universe becomes available at privileged moments of meditative or aesthetic enjoyment or communion with another person; the dispossession of the past, the recall of which, as Professor Poulet has recently suggested, places Lamartine in a tradition running through Rousseau, Chateaubriand and Nerval; disinheritance from the personal landscape—by a remarkable compensatory movement, Lamartine frequently restores with exactitude in his verse the rural background of his formative years; probably the most important of

all, the disinheritance from what is sensed as the chief birthright, full communion with another being through sexual love.

In their turn, these directive impulses resolve themselves into numerous *motifs,* through which they are conveyed and which provide the variations and changing substance of the verse: the quest for light through clouds, flight into the ether, a suggested goal or presence behind changing effects of atmosphere, a flow of images seen through a screen, images of fluidity, change, half-light, night, and all that these convey about the poignant evanescence of experience, the range and inclusiveness of thought, the cosmic context of human life.

These are the accompaniments of the original theme. The general direction in which they lead is towards solitude and depression. This solitude is, however, often pierced by an illumination, or enlightened by a certitude. Such an illumination is afforded, within the limits of the sensibility of the age, by experiences of the kind represented in *Apparition* of the *Nouvelles Méditations poétiques,* where moonlight on a tomb and the apparition of the dead mistress lead the poet towards an overwhelming revelation of after-life, even though the ultimate word which he craves 'crossing the barrier that separates two universes' is not spoken. A kind of certitude is found in the Platonic conviction of the poem *Invocation,* in the first *Méditations poétiques.* Taken in the context of the French poetic tradition and loosened from the tight biographical noose that criticism has placed round such pieces, this poem already captures the style of a century and a half of poets who have taken sexual exaltation up into the range of experiences near the limits of expression, who have used memory and imagination to raise woman into an ambiguous region where the real merges into the ideal, and who play deliberately on the border territories between dream and real perception. . . . (pp. 38-9)

[Moments] of illumination and certitude lead towards the other main impulse of Lamartine's inspiration, the reaction, the sense of praeternatural well-being, of moments of vigour when the spirit seems capable of leading the whole entity of a person back into possession of a plenitude of experience similar to that of the Psalmist noting reassuring signs of the presence of his God. . . . (p. 41)

Lamartine's obsession with the past is undeniably an enormous factor in the kind of art he produces. Just as the natural world offers a choice of symbols of an invisible reality, so the invisible past can be inspected by means of the focus of memory. Though much of the elegiac flavour of his verse comes from the intuition that memory is almost exclusively a human phenomenon, he tries to find signs of a similar focus of recall in the natural world, or to impose such signs on it. In one way, I suppose that this can be considered as indulgence in the pathetic fallacy; and if pathetic fallacy can be equated with anything as fundamental as Lamartine's *idéalisme pansymboliste,* this view may no doubt hold. The appeal, in *Le Lac,* to the objects of the scene to retain the memory of the famous boating expedition with Julie Charles is more than a figure of rhetoric. In a universe filled with the 'miracles' of the presence of a divine intelligence, the recreation of time is presumably, as Lamartine himself has said, the prerogative 'd'un Dieu'. . . . The idea of a place, an abode of things past, is then a Lamartinian theme. . . . (pp. 44-5)

The situation of his perception of time in the general context of his idealism is a question that needs detailed study over the whole of Lamartine's writings, and particularly the flow of time past into a *milieu divin*—the sense of which can be obtained through experiences that rouse or liberate the imagination.

Where the bitterest sense of loss and dispossession is involved is, of course, in the disappearance of beings whose existence seems to complete our own, bringing a sense of unity to the incomplete and striving individual life. I propose, within the limits of this paper, to develop this theme, the theme of the human couple, a little beyond the formal limits that traditional criticism has ascribed to it. Lamartine himself has never confronted, in an explicit and developed fashion, the problem of discovery and loss at the limits of human relationship. It becomes, in his personal poetry, the subject of endless allusion. *Le Lac* is a very obvious example, and I wonder what we should have made of this poem without the industrious glosses that have turned it into a kind of insert in a narrative sequence. Stripped of the embroidery, the poem reads as an ode on the fugacity of experience and shows itself more truly as a piece marking a step forward in the French lyrical tradition, relatively free from artificial development, proceeding by strong transitions, achieving variety. (pp. 45-6)

In the semi-autobiographical prose works (*Graziella, Raphaël*), the needs of morality throw the author on the defensive and cause him, happily perhaps, to use the techniques of fiction which vivify and strengthen the subject, whatever the cost to absolute sincerity may be. Lamartine is never very entertaining in his *Confidences,* nor particularly impressive, except perhaps where the descriptive afflatus takes him close to his authentic poetic manner. In his lyrical poetry, I think that on the love theme he is probably at his best in the meditative sections of the mature works, for instance in *Novissima Verba* of the *Harmonies poétiques et religieuses,* where he writes of the enchantment of love from the perspective of a disenchanted maturity. Elsewhere, although poems like *Souvenir* are interesting from a technical point of view, the lyrical and celebrative verse uses the sentimental experience as a means of impulsion towards elegy or enthusiasm, as we see in pieces like *L'Immortalité, Le Crucifix,* and *Le Premier regret.* Such poems further increase the notion of Lamartine as a decorous and chaste poet, filtering generous doses of experience through an archaic type of sensibility. Like most generalities of criticism, this is only partly true. It is quite obvious, from a reading of *Jocelyn,* that Lamartine is also deeply concerned with the complex and powerful forces released in sexual involvement. And the whole aspect of the amatory theme in Lamartine changes when we look more closely.

We can usefully start off from the belief in the existence of the soul-mate, the *âme soeur,* discovery of which is the most powerful motive and highest privilege of the individuated spirit. This belief is very strong and very personal in Lamartine and is all the stronger for being based on his own experience and not derived purely from bedside books such as the *Imitation of Jesus Christ* or Plato's *Dialogues.* His lyrical poetry is informed by this theme. *Jocelyn* and, to some extent, *La Chute d'un Ange* are based on it. *Raphaël* is based on it. So is *Fior d'Aliza.* (pp. 46-7)

Yet inevitably the soul-mates inhabit different bodies. Hence, in various of Lamartine's writings, we witness either the growth by imperceptible degrees of a unity fraught with explosive possibilities, or the emotional impact of two beings at their first encounter. The development of the relationship of Jocelyn and Laurence is an example of the first, as is also the intertwining of personalities and destinies in the case of Fior d'Aliza and her cousin, brought up as stepbrother and sister. The first

meeting of Raphaël and Julie is an example of the second, so to a lesser degree is that between Lamartine and Graziella as recounted in the work of that name. In *Raphaël,* the imaginative exaltation of the protagonist's speculations on Julie is comparable to the opening passage of Nerval's *Sylvie,* though a name which should also be mentioned in this context is that of the other Raphaël, in whom Lamartine notes elsewhere the talent for raising to the divine level female beauty of the remote and virginal type.

Even for soul-mates the exercise of discovery is a protracted business. . . . The mysteries presented by each other's nature are often associated with barriers not immediately in the control of the individuals. With Graziella there are barriers of class and age; with Julie those of marriage and age. Both Graziella and Julie are brought to the point of recognizing the intractability of these problems. The soul-mates in *Jocelyn* are separated by the sternest of forces, the vows taken by the priest. Mystery, forces of division and separation, small wonder that the strains undergone by the couples who strive to achieve a supreme unity produce restraints and ambiguities at every turn. The author himself imposes further restraints, of a literary kind, so that it is difficult to know whether the ambiguities in the depiction of personal relationships are those inherent in the sexual problem itself, or whether they are part of Lamartine's own nature.

There are crucial moments in the narratives, prose and verse, where the first physical contact occurs between the hero and heroine. These are moments that no doubt in the lyrical poetry would produce passages of elevated commentary without clear reference to their immediate origin. In the narratives, the episode is set down, dramatic, symbolical, with its implications left to be involved in the development. Thus Raphaël first makes contact with the body of Julie when she is unconscious after the boating mishap. . . . The young Lamartine approaches the sexual encounter with Graziella through a communal reading of *Paul et Virginie* [by Jacques Henri Bernardin de Saint-Pierre]. . . . The central scene in *Jocelyn,* the point of crisis of the whole narrative is, of course, the moment of discovery, the revelation of the true sex of the companion. This is the moment of contact with Laurence's wounded and unconscious body: the teeth of the male friend tearing the garment to expose the wound, the female breast revealed, blood—on these elements alone a psychoanalyst could start business straightway.

Ultimately the erotic theme in Lamartine is almost as complicated as in Baudelaire, and certainly more so than in the case of Hugo, Vigny, Leconte de Lisle or Mallarmé. The symbol of hair, for example, *la chevelure,* . . . is an important Lamartinian *motif.* Life, female beauty, the stirrings of sexual attraction in the tremor of long tresses caught by the wind or falling unheeded in a moment of emotion, femininity (at several points in Lamartine's writings—in *Graziella,* in *Fior d'Aliza,* in *La Chute d'un Ange*—the cropping of female hair corresponds to a pivotal moment, psychologically, dramatically, symbolically), Lamartine's creative writings weave a series of variations round this central image.

At all points there is a suggestive or equivocal quality in Lamartine's treatment of the love theme. In the lyrical poetry, the heroine, a composite figure of the same type as Vigny's Eva, is swept up into a kind of mid-heaven. Even the relatively precise recollections of *Le Premier regret,* which is about Graziella, are set within the formality of an elegiac piece with a wistful refrain. And the pieces showing a developed sensuous perception, not given prominence by the poet himself, pieces such as *A une jeune Arabe,* composed during his travels in the Middle East, harp more on the poetic suggestions of his subject than the sensual power of woman. . . . Elsewhere, the Lamartinian heroine is characterized by an aptitude for playing boys' roles. This is the case with the Italian singer in *Raphaël,* with Fior d'Aliza and with Laurence. So we are often faced with a familiar sexual ambiguity, the *travesti* as in Shakespeare, the theme taken up in another aspect by Gautier in the *Contralto* of *Emaux et Camées.* The ambiguity extends further into the field of sexual relationships themselves. Julie insists on the fraternal character of her relationship with Raphaël: her first words spoken in private in Raphaël's presence ('O mon Dieu, je vous remercie, j'ai donc un frère!') show the primary aspect of a relationship which also included some quality of maternal attachment. Certainly, in the actual relationship between Lamartine and Julie Charles, the maternal element is strongly stressed by her, as her letters to the poet show. To what extent do these elements complicate a passion already bearing the character of adultery? Does, in Lamartine's view, the touch of death in Julie redress in some way the ambiguous or adulterous nature of the passion? The relationship between Fior d'Aliza and Hyeronimo, which the author steadfastly characterizes as innocent, is also puzzling when viewed from any but a very simplified sexual perspective. In another prose narrative, which I have not so far mentioned, *Antoniella,* Lamartine takes up the theme of good and simple women struggling to maintain the balance of natural maternal instincts against powers that contrive against them. These powers are backward social conventions and a poverty which threatens the survival of children. The issues against which the women run are prostitution and infanticide, both ambiguously presented by the narrator, so that prostitution does not ultimately tarnish virtue, while a line of suspense is drawn along a sequence of events which appear to plunge into infanticide, but are shown in the end not to do so.

In the end the sexual drive sweeps, in all Lamartine's creative writing, through the conventional categories of morality and joins the cosmic flux, the force that through the green fuse drives the flower, the force that, consciously or not, the poet sets out to imitate, or to recapture, or to re-echo.

Such partial perspectives as I have opened here on Lamartine run the risk of falsifying the appearance of the poetic structure he has left. Because of the formality of his poetry we lose sight of the underlying forces which ultimately determine it. It might from this point of view be salutary to look at the organization of one of the lyrical collections, the volume of *Harmonies,* for example, since this is where, despite the poet's disclaimer in a preface, the attention to a kind of architecture is most apparent. The inspiration of the work is the counterpoise of doubt and faith and the attempt to set down verbal forms of certitude which will overwhelm doubt, as the last stanzas of *La Providence à l'homme* are designed to overwhelm the scepticism of *Le Désespoir* in the first *Méditations poétiques.* In the collection of 1830, where the high point of Lamartine's personal poetry is reached, each of the four books into which the poet divides his work has its purpose, either religious and philosophical, or aesthetic. Thus Book 1 is concerned with the quest for images, symbols and poetic forms to express faith. After the *Invocation* and two solar hymns, one to night and one to morning, the poet presents effective symbols of God: the lamp in the sanctuary (*La Lampe du temple*), and remote solitary places (*Bénédiction de Dieu*). An alternation of the theme of doubt and persecution (*Aux Chrétiens*) with that of simple faith (*Hymne de l'enfant; Hymne dans le temple*) follows, with a final se-

quence of symbols (tears, the moon, silent mountain landscape) offering reassuring meditation. Book 2, the longest, is constructed on the eternal macrocosm-microcosm theme. On the one hand the poet includes pieces on the creation and the Creator in which he suggests avenues of contact with the individual being (*Pensée des morts, L'Occident*) and, on the other, pieces dealing with the intuitions of personal life, such as doubt and grief (*Hymne à la douleur*), time (*La Source dans les bois*), reminiscence (*Souvenir d'enfance*). The book is founded on four powerful odes (*Jéhovah, Le Chêne, L'Humanité, L'Idée de Dieu*) which are intended to sweep away doubt by the affirmation of a universal religious sense, by presenting symbols of the life process, by the praise of man and by an evangelism of a deistic kind. It is this tetralogy which dominates Book 2 and gives it its centre round which the variations on the personal theme are grouped. Book 3 again takes a major religious subject as its centre, this time a meditation on the significance of Christ (*Hymne au Christ*). Round this are grouped various pieces based on the personal life of the poet, so that the general theme of the Book is inspired by the poet's own experience, the religious problem on the one hand, and various episodes or aspects of private life on the other. Already at the end of Book 3 we see the emergence of a more complex and varied form (*Cantate pour les enfants d'une Maison de Charité*). In Book 4 we see this tendency towards experiment developed, particularly in the later editions. In the first instance we have an opening hymn on the subject of survival (*Hymne de la Mort*) and a strong reflective conclusion, with the magnificently sustained *Novissima Verba* and a canticle (*A l'Esprit saint*), to which is subsequently added, in 1832, *Les Révolutions.* For the rest, Lamartine experiments with shorter pieces on the familiar themes of doubt, unease, elegiac recollection, achieving a more trenchant expression of doubt (*Sur l'Image du Christ écrasant le mal*) and attempting a new expression of faith through a developed melisma. . . . The poetry is guided into regular waterways; the current, however, as we have seen is a new one. (pp. 47-53)

The spread of inspiration in Lamartine ultimately blurs the categories of form. This writer, who has often been castigated for carelessness and indifference at the technical level, seems to me to have been instinctively drawn to a form outside the codified patterns. His prose, at its highest, is superb poetry, and I should be inclined to think that if ever a representative selection of Lamartine's poetic writing is made, prose no less than verse should figure there.

It is true, of course, that Lamartine's habits of composition, fortified by his notions about the didactic function of poetry, involve the expansion of an idea or theme into units which are normally the fullest possible stretch of the powers of development and variation of the author. If for Lamartine the interpretative function of the poet is the same as for Baudelaire, the author of *Harmonies* does not believe in the superlative virtues of *sorcellerie évocatoire* or in the unremitting quest for marvellous combinations of language. Lamartine does not attempt to create verse where the linguistic elements exist at such a pitch of tension that a change of one element would flaw the whole fabric. This is already enough for him to become vaguely suspect, particularly at a time when an ambitious aesthetic based on rigorous choice and the attenuation of the immediate sense of a poem has captured much of the attention of commentators in recent years.

In his verse, Lamartine accepts almost completely the conventions in force at the beginning of his career, which are concerned with elegance and correctness as well as with the production of given effects by adherence to accepted figures and devices. I think that his individual manipulation of the verse medium of the early nineteenth century has still to be studied, and such a study will include an assessment of the personal *sorcellerie* which he undeniably brought to his art. However, on the face of it, he is a poet squarely in the French rhetorical tradition. By passing the eye over the printed text of *Le Lac,* I find the following devices used: apostrophe, rhetorical questions, periphrasis, hyperbole, personification, poetic imperatives, invocation, accumulation of similar clauses. The poetry, the Lamartinian quality, must obviously lie elsewhere.

Lamartine's work is cumulative. He was a born orator, as the texts of his 'improvised' political discourses show; and the gift of continuity and development is an orator's gift, all the more impressive in Lamartine's case because it is linked to an inexhaustible power of inventing runs of illustrative metaphors and images. (pp. 54-5)

[Readers] of Lamartine's verse do not commonly realize how varied his verse production is in terms of types of poem: ode, epistle, elegy, hymn, canticle, rhapsody, dithyramb, idyll, epic, narrative, the list promises to be as long as Polonius's catalogue of types of play.

A further source of richness is the use of symbols. Lamartine, given the difficulties involved in the use of the word 'Romantic', could well be characterized as a symbolist poet.... We find in his poetry the two main kinds of symbol employed later by writers who represent a more orthodox moment of the Symbolist period. A great part of Lamartine's poetic effort is concerned with finding correspondences of the 'vertical' kind, between the visible and the invisible world, and in this respect his work has a distinctly Baudelairian appearance.... There is also a decorative symbolism of the type favoured by the disciples of Mallarmé and exploited by him as the basis of subtle poetic commentary on great themes. Swans, lakes, flight, and their inferences for idealism and elegy, are also present in Lamartine.... [With *Le Premier regret,* the] nameless and seasonless lake, the use of water as a symbol of translucency and transformation, and also as a substance mirroring and supporting a creature—we are already, in 1830, in a Mallarmean universe, and become still more involved in the Mallarmean world with the two senses given to the swan, the magnificent bird suspended on the calm lake with the reflected stars, and the creature trying to escape and rousing with the commotion of its wings impressions of agony and death. Mallarmean, too, is the lake-mirror analogy, and particularly the mirror reflecting the night sky; so is the preoccupation with images of purity which are transformed into images of distress and loss of brightness; so is the essential vocabulary: *eau, lac, cygne, miroir, vol, ailes, azur;* so is the allegorical sense of the whole passage, which in its context in Lamartine's poem refers, it is true, directly to the predicament of Graziella, losing thereby the value of Mallarmé's mystery and ambiguity.

The imagery of Lamartine has not yet been studied in anything like the depth and detail that it merits, particularly the emergence of this imagery from the neo-classical period and the anticipation of the neo-Romantic period of the eighteen-eighties and nineties.

Needless to say, before Lamartine's arrival as a poet, others had seen the need to reinvigorate French verse by a widened choice of images.... But Lamartine is the first to suggest, by the practice of his art, a poetry the movement of which is determined by the variety and interaction of images more clearly than by the imposition of a rhetorical structure. The final achievement of such poetry will be the reward of later writers. Lamartine's position can clearly be seen if we compare pieces written by him and, for example, by Millevoye, on related themes. Thus, in *Le Poète mourant* by Millevoye, we find a development in three carefully controlled parts: first an introductory section equating the poet's life with a flickering lamp; secondly, the death song of the poet of which the substance is the recognition of four painful truths, the rapidity of life, the illusory nature of sentimental love, the inefficacy of personal inspiration, the brevity of reputation; thirdly, the conclusion, equating the extinction of the lamp with the extinction of the poet's life. So the movement of the poem is closely connected with the outward ordering of ideas. The images, few in number, all conventional, are in each case fixed to a determinative element which limits their power of evocation. By contrast, Lamartine's *Le Poète mourant* begins to move out of the conventional range of effect of the neo-classical elegy by renewing old images through unexpected juxtapositions and variations. It is true that these variations are quite often the notation of examples. But the images have new qualities, one deriving from their diversity and number, the other from the author's ability to involve them, in a powerful and inexplicit fashion, in his own identity and experience.... (pp. 55-8)

The ultimate Lamartinian image would be the equivalent of Mallarmé's ideal art, which could focus the universe. Lamartine's poets aspire to the discovery of the image of infinity.... (p. 59)

At a level of perception where the divine mirror is shattered into fragments, Lamartine concentrates on combining disparate reflections. I have already mentioned his talent for expressing his affective life through a flow of images, a flow which, though it suggests the spontaneity and immediacy that will come later in French poetry, is nevertheless affected by the conventions which it tends to submerge. Where he is content to present a developed sequence of images of the natural world (for instance, in *Poésie, ou Paysage dans le golfe de Gênes* of the *Harmonies poétiques et religieuses*), the sequence is aesthetically as well as rhetorically purposeful, the poet's eye interpreting imaginatively and his mind extending the inter-

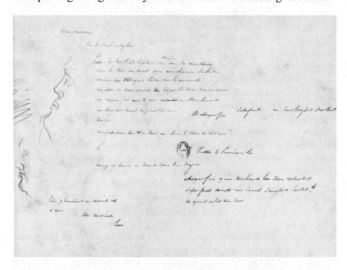

The first draft of a portion of Jocelyn. *Lamartine often sketched the masculine profile seen in the left margin.*

pretation by association and intuition. In Lamartine's narrative poetry, where the same struggle between easily accepted conventions and imaginative inventiveness is apparent, superb passages emerge in which outwardly discovered images are given depth and force by the related human feelings that are set running amongst them by secondary or associated images; sometimes, in the epic verse, the human feelings are replaced by carefully contrived suggestions of supernatural power.

Lamartine's personal handling of imagery prepares the way for Baudelaire and Mallarmé. He looks forward further, to the work of the generation of 1886. The cosmic sensibility of Laforgue is Lamartinian. . . . The early intimate lyricism of Kahn is in the Lamartine tradition, as is his later cult of the ode. The first stages of Verhaeren's poetic career show Lamartine's influence. At the other extreme, the 'vaporous' poet of *Le Lac* is on occasion a close observer of the fine detail of nature, adept at the notation of atmosphere and the living elements of a scene. *Jocelyn* has a number of such passages, which recall on the one hand the work of some eighteenth-century poets of nature—Cowper, perhaps, and James Thomson in our own literature—and on the other Sainte-Beuve, some of the Parnassians and the *musa pedestris* of minor *fin de siècle* writers like André Theuriet.

Another aspect of Lamartine's technique which I am sure will repay further investigation is the structure of his lyrical poetry. Valuable work has already been done on the persistence of classical style and forms in his verse; but one question among others that it would be rewarding to try to answer at this remove from the nineteenth century is how far Lamartine modified the rhetorical movement of the lyrical poem, for his own time and, if at all, for the future. For example, if we compare *Le Passé* by Lamartine with Baudelaire's *Le Voyage,* two meditative pieces on the same general theme of human experience (though employing different stanza units), we find a similar structure in each, if by structure we mean the arrangement of the elements which compose the developed theme. I do not think that questions of merit and details of procedure need be relevant here—the two poems are certainly unequal in merit—but as allegories of life, representing by indirect means the inevitable movement of human experience, they each follow the same stages. A preparatory section presents varied perspectives on experience, a central passage treats the theme of disillusionment out of past enchantment, and there is a conclusion of a transcendental order, built on the hope of renewal and survival. Adherence in each case to an old tradition? An attempt to find a fresh development of old themes? . . . [Lamartine] suggests new ways for the extended handling of spiritual themes, and ultimately the conveying of such themes by musicality and a minimum of architecture. (pp. 59-62)

Harmony, rhythm, rhyme, control and variation of stanza forms, all need evaluation in the poetry of Lamartine, and it is possible that more may be said about the solecisms than that they are reprehensible deviations. . . . Few poets have mastered the symphonic construction of poems of varied form and tone as Lamartine did in the lyrical work of his maturity. Few poets have shown such range and inventiveness in the creation and handling of stanza forms.

A writer who causes the notation of common experience to change from one manner to another is usually granted a long-term respect. A writer who focuses in his person the sudden sensibility of a new age without the accompaniment of a recognisably new diction becomes in the long run reduced and codified. Lamartine, the French lake poet of 1820, is in this

second category. But Lamartine is also a poet too new and too great for the forms of verse he accepts. He is the first writer in France to give expression in commanding verse to the nineteenth-century outlook. Yet French poetry does not crash from one gear to another with the *Méditations poétiques.* It settles into top and cruises deceptively. In doing so it finds an increased range, an increased capacity for covering distances. When these distances are considered they are found to be immense. They are the distances of the Romantic vision. The eyes of our contemporaries scan them with some indifference, looking for distances of other kinds, distances that separate particular psyches, the deserts between them. Lamartine, whose poetry moves over the summits of human experience, is too reassuring, too macrocosmic, too sublime about human dignity to appeal much to the present age. But it may well be when the sharply etched and interesting psyches that litter our present books are finally laid to rest, that Lamartine, in his poetry, will continue to live a long life. (pp. 63-4)

> *J. C. Ireson, in his* Lamartine: A Revaluation, *University of Hull, 1969, 66 p.*

ROBERT T. DENOMMÉ   (essay date 1969)

[*Denommé discusses the Neoclassical and Romantic elements in Lamartine's poetry, commenting on his lyricism, his concept of the social mission of the poet, and his importance as a transitional figure between the two movements.*]

The enthusiastic reception accorded the collection of twenty-four poems known as the *Méditations poétiques (Poetic Meditations)* in 1820, constitutes the most telling revelation on the nature of Lamartine's early lyricism. The freshness of inspration and the delicately-sustained elegiac tone elicited the enthusiasm of the advocates of change and the defenders of traditionalism alike. The younger readers reacted positively to the undeniable sincerity of expression so manifest in the poetry, while their conservative counterparts were reassured by the poet's unmistakable allegiance to neo-classical forms and techniques. Whatever literary innovations may have been contained in the poems of 1820, they were not immediately apparent at least to those readers who were anxious to recognize some adherence to the accepted methodology. The themes of love, anguish, despair, melancholy, and death in the *Méditations poétiques* could scarcely be regarded as revolutionary in French poetry, and the frequent appearances of worn metaphors, periphrases, biblical terms, and mythological allusions were devices that pointed rather to the direction of eighteenth-century strophic lyricism. Yet the spontaneity of emotion and sentiment joined in an effusive and melodious language heartened the young readers of 1820 who had been so avidly seeking out the articulation of their own feelings and experiences in literature. The ironic fact of the matter was that Lamartine's collection of poems owed no debt to either the neo-Classicists or the Romanticists. The poet avoided any scrupulous observance of neo-Classical techniques for fear that they would distort his sense of personal urgency. Nor could the young Romanticists speak convincingly of Lamartine's purported allegiance to their cause in 1820. Whatever remnants of classical method or hints at romantic innovation may have been discernible in Lamartine's early verse, they were more likely the result of the poet's unconscious adaptation of the most prevalent writing styles or his personal reaction to certain life experiences.

The feeling of sadness and resignation that dominates the *Méditations poétiques* constitutes their central theme and motif.

Each poem evolves from the poet's direct confrontation with some experience; his search for peace and contentment has led him away from the society of men to the bosom of a seemingly more sympathetic and benevolent nature. The love lyrics are inspired by Lamartine's early love for two women: Graziella, a teen-aged Neapolitan whom he knew during a trip to Italy in 1811, and the matronly Julie Charles with whom he had become acquainted in the summer of 1816. Although the poems celebrating Lamartine's feelings for Graziella are among the most frequently ignored in the collection, such poems as **"L'Adieu"** (**"The Farewell"**) and **"Le Golfe de Baïa"** are filled with the same kind of spontaneous sincerity and feeling of melancholia that characterizes the poems of the so-called Julie cycle. Lamartine's adroitness at transposition of his experiences into his poems probably accounts for the degree of pleasure with which they provided neo-classical traditionalists and radical innovators. There can be no mistaking Lamartine's intense lyricism in such poems as **"Le Lac"** (**"The Lake"**) and **"L'Isolement"** (**"The Isolation"**), for example, despite the fact that such lyricism is often camouflaged by the use of language that is both discreet and objective. The inspiration of such poems, however rooted in Lamartine's love episode with Madame Charles at the Lake Bourget, transfigures the personal experience in order to suggest more directly man's destiny and human predicament. Lamartine purposely refrains from any specific mention of Graziella and Julie Charles by name; they are referred to simply as "Elle" ("She") and "Elvire," an obvious idealization of woman. The conspicuous absence of any appreciable amount of concrete detail contributes in giving the majority of the poems in the *Méditations poétiques* their somewhat abstract and universalized effect. Lamartine's apt generalizations and transfigurations of his particular love experiences enable the reader to identify more directly with the sentiments and the emotions expressed. Thus, the poems often achieve the level of individual meditations on human destiny while retaining their basic lyrical qualities.

By so ably transforming his love experiences into tragic idylls, Lamartine succeeded in joining his own problems to the more general problems confronting man. The use of vague, ethereal, and semi-abstract language in most of the *Méditations poétiques* strips the poems of their suggestiveness and permits them to emerge as idealized love lyrics of purity and innocence. The poems in the "Julie cycle," for instance, are effective evocations of the ill-starred lover whose sorrow has become transfigured by the recollection of a time gone-by. With the adroit aid of his memory and imagination, Lamartine has managed to recreate his experience with Julie with an appropriate amount of personal intensity. In thus pleading with nature to safeguard the memory of his transitory moments of happiness, the poet invites the reader to meditate on man's fate by underscoring the pain and anguish that he now experiences. But it is principally the poet's intensely experienced anguish such as is expressed in the poems that causes their transformation into meditations on human destiny without their loss of any lyrical quality. The essentially lyrical tone that pervades the meditations accounts for their being considered romantic innovations.

The spirit of sadness that pervades the love poems in recollection of Graziella and Madame Charles provides a logical springboard for the more philosophical and religious verse that concludes the *Méditations poétiques*. Yet in his melancholy, Lamartine points to the harmony that exists between nature and the feelings of man. Nature plays the role of comforter to man, reflecting as it does for the poet the grandeur of God through its own beauties. The contemplation of nature leads the poet to make an eventual declaration of faith, which in turn allows him to experience a sense of peaceful resignation to life. Whatever doubt the poet may have entertained concerning the seeming indifference of a haughty nature proves to be momentary, and the majority of the poems end with a note of exhaltation and hope. The state of a bittersweet melancholy and a quiet resignation to his plight as a man marks the poet's ultimate fulfillment in the *Méditations poétiques*. Despite a heavy insistence upon imagery that conveys a sense of loss and near-despair in such poems as **"L'Isolement," "Le Vallon"** (**"The Dale"**), and **"L'Automne"** (**"The Autumn"**), for instance, the closing stanzas always carry forth constructive statements on human life. Whatever uncertainty may betray certain verses of the love poems, such concluding poems as **"L'Homme"** (**"Man"**), **"Le Désespoir"** (**"Despair"**), **"La Foi"** (**"Faith"**), and **"L'Immortalité"** (**"Immortality"**) counteract such an impression with their blunt and moral assertions on the existence of an afterlife. Yet even these exhortations for man to resign himself to the will of God emerge more as a personal appeal than as overbearing moral preachments. The reader cannot help but remember the personal anguish in the poet's words and recall his sense of personal loss even in these somewhat more pretentious poems. Thus, despite the sadness that permeates the *Méditations poétiques,* they are the poet's personal affirmation of hope and faith.

Despite their outward conventional appearance, these lyrics represented an important stage in the development of French lyricism. Whatever awkwardness in neo-classical technique remained was more than counterbalanced by the overall songfulness of the poems themselves. To understand the effect these poems had on the readers of 1820 requires perhaps a temporary abandonment of our twentieth-century critical sense. Whatever else, Lamartine's verse was a marriage of words with mood and emotion that constituted the kind of language unseen and unheard in France since the sixteenth century. To the readers of the *Méditations poétiques* in the early 1820's, what mattered most was the unadorned directness of communication achieved in the majority of the poems. The predictable yet delightfully musical strain of Lamartine's verse spoke an intuitive language that made itself understood to the readers without the usual recourse to the humdrum conventions of a complex exterior world. The union of the poet's feelings and emotions with nature scenes succeeded in conveying the poet's uncertainties with such intense urgency to an audience largely in sympathy with such a mood and such an attitude. The greatest single virtue of the *Méditations poétiques* resides in their ability to suggest a twofold vision: the first one emanating from the private world of the poet, and the second one projecting from the recognizable world of everyday realities. The total effect of the poems is one of intimacy and sincerity; the messages conveyed are only second in importance to the manner in which they are conveyed. (pp. 42-6)

Lamartine's lyrical sense does not always achieve the sense of balance and restraint throughout the *Méditations poétiques*. The relatively general and semi-abstract terms employed in such a poem as **"Le Lac,"** for example, enable the poem to obtain its quasi-objective effect despite its discernible lyric quality. The so-called romantic or personal elements in such a pessimistically-inspired poem as **"L'Isolement"** upsets the kind of balance obtained in **"Le Lac."** Written several months after Madame Charles' death in 1817, **"L'Isolement"** bespeaks the poet's inability to attain any kind of consolation in this world. Only the thought of rejoining his beloved in the afterlife prevents the poet from despairing. Composed at his home in Milly,

"**L'Isolement**" expresses Lamartine's attempt to regain his lost equilibrium. His picturesque description of nature betrays the wildness of his imagination in this particular instance more than a plausible respect for fact. (p. 48)

Lamartine's popularity among both the traditionalist and the revolutionary factions during the 1820's may be partially explained by his somewhat transitional position between these two groups. His religious and political views, for instance, such as are discernible in his publications, strike us as moderately liberal ones for his time. Cautiously avoiding the extremism of such radical reformers as Lamennais and Pierre Leroux, Lamartine preferred to strive for more gradual changes within the established structure and order of the day. If the conservatives were attracted to him, it was perhaps because they saw in him a reliable advocate of moderation and the status quo. The fact was that his political philosophy appeared to an extent determined by his religious convictions. Outwardly, he always paid lip service to Catholicism. Yet his religious position may be only described as an unorthodox one; it rejected the principle of revelation and consequently a majority of the Church's dogmas. Politically, Lamartine took a dim view of the association of Catholicism and the Crown, and he shared Lamennais' view that the whole of Christianity was in urgent need of reform through a critical re-examination of the spirit of the New Testament. However uncomfortable he may have felt in the Church, Lamartine avoided any outward break with it, a fact that no doubt reassured his more conservative audience. For the more discerning readers, however, his poetic expression betrayed his participation with other Romanticists in a movement to redefine and recast accepted theological conceptions to make them fit the needs of the time. Such modernization, of course, entailed the kind of doctrinal transformations that stripped religious belief of its orthodoxy and caused it to reflect, rather, the personal views and interpretations of the authors in question. Most of Lamartine's poetry reflected such a tendency.

The second collection of poems . . . , *Nouvelles Méditations poétiques (New Poetic Meditations),* did not meet with the same popular success enjoyed by Lamartine's earlier volume. Although the general tenor of the poems translates the poet's happier mood—such poems as "**Ischia**" and the "**Chant d'a-mour**" ("**Song of Love**"), for example, echo the joyous experience of living—the lingering yet admittedly faded memory of Julie Charles prompts Lamartine to render her one last homage with his poem, "**Le Crucifix.**" Largely inspired by the sight of the crucifix that Madame Charles was alleged to have clutched and embraced with her dying lips, "**Le Crucifix**" contains large draughts of the type of religious sentimentality that eventually became associated with Romanticism. (pp. 51-2)

The peace and serenity which Lamartine enjoyed during his long stay in Italy in 1827 inspired the codification of his personal and religious philosophy in the collection of poems published in 1830 under the title, *Harmonies poétiques et religieuses (Poetic and Religious Harmonies).* By and large, the poems are a fusion of the poet's lingering sense of melancholia produced by vivid reminders of death with an almost overstated expression of confidence in the existence of an afterlife. The harmony which the poet sees and hears is the wordless hymn that emerges from the beauties of the whole of creation in praise of God the maker. Like Chateaubriand before him, Lamartine conceives the unity of outer and inner reality in terms that are purely emotional and aesthetic. The pantheism frequently suggested in such poems as "**Hymne du matin**" ("**Morning Hymn**") and

"**Jéhovah ou l'idée de Dieu**" ("**Jehovah or the Idea of God**") betrays an appeal that is perhaps more poetic than religious. (pp. 53-4)

The Recueillements poétiques (Poetic Contemplations) of 1839 mark the poet's evolution from the almost exclusively elegiac and lyrical strains of his earlier collections to the adoption of a more visible attitude of social humanitarianism. Lamartine's social and political preoccupations, destined to articulate themselves by his candidacy for election to the presidency of the Second Republic in 1848, were in part motivated by the profound sense of grief that overwhelmed him when his only daughter, Julia, died during a trip to the Holy Land in 1832. Despite a diplomatic career begun in 1825 and such manifestations of his political involvement as in the "**Ode contre la peine de mort**" ("**Ode against Capital Punishment**") of 1830, and in the famous "**Ode sur les Révolutions**" ("**Ode concerning Revolutions**") of 1831 which announced his evolved liberalism, Lamartine appears to have waited until 1833 to enter the political arena with any real sense of dedication. Henceforth, both his writings and his political career underscore his greatest personal mission: the enlightenment and emancipation of the masses. The inspiration and the intuition that characterized his more personally effusive poetry up until this time give way to the social preachments made after 1834. . . . The epic, as a poetic form, unquestionably exerted a strong appeal to the majority of the French Romanticists. The ambitious challenge of the epic, its purported claims to narrate the beginnings and the destinies of the national and the universal human character, held a particular attraction for the most articulate social Romanticists who conceived of themselves as the responsible directors of the French conscience. The complex structure of the epic form, with its leisurely pace and its allowance for elaborate developments, provided just the kind of opportunity desired by poets who had ambitious humanitarian messages to impart. The two fragments of Lamartine's unfinished epic, *Les Visions,* were conceived as early as 1823 as a long series of related narratives and "epochs" meant to evoke the efforts of the human mind throughout the centuries to achieve its highest and noblest destiny. The philosophy underlying the idea of *Les Visions* is perhaps more revealing of the poet's Romanticism than the two fragments published in partial realization of the epic. Like Victor Hugo, Lamartine begins with an intuitive reassurance that his interpretation of the history of mankind embraces the most comprehensive view. His conviction stems from his own emotions and sentiments—his personal response to internal and external reality. The published fragments of *Les Visions* constitute a variegated blend of narratives, philosophical discourses, parables, idyllic, and elegiac poems. Despite their respective publication dates, *Jocelyn* in 1836, and *La Chute d'un ange (The Fall of an Angel)* in 1838, *La Chute d'un ange* was initially meant to precede *Jocelyn,* which Lamartine intended to serve as a conclusion to *Les Visions.* Jocelyn's abnegation and renunciation would redeem the fallen angel, Cédar, from his sin.

Published under the full title, *Jocelyn, Journal trouvé chez un curé de village (Jocelyn, A Journal Found in the Library of a Village Priest),* the ten thousand lines that make up this fragment contain a prologue followed by nine epochs and an epilogue. (pp. 55-7)

Despite its unusual length, *Jocelyn* maintains its essential unity; everything in the prologue, the nine epochs and the epilogue centers around Jocelyn, the principal hero of the fragment. The secondary episodes and moral developments are attached to the central story. Lamartine's theme or thesis is spelled out in unmistakably clear terms: the necessity of sacrifice, suffering, and abnegation to achieve one's spiritual destiny. *Jocelyn* symbolizes by his attitudes the struggle which the individual soul can expect to encounter in the quest for God. The social thesis discernible in *Jocelyn* is clearly subordinated to the spiritual theme that pervades the entire epic. The poet's romantic temperament dominates most of the fragment; its most glaring manifestations account for whatever implausibility mars the reading of *Jocelyn.* Lamartine's narration frequently betrays a somewhat blunt disregard for fact and external reality. The bishop, for instance, displays a blatant ignorance of Catholic theology and tradition. Jocelyn himself exhibits a curious aloofness as the village priest supposedly concerned with the spiritual administration of his flock. Yet despite such inaccuracies and blemishes in portraiture, the fragment is illuminated by the touching lyricism that graces a significant number of pages. The ninth epoch of *Jocelyn,* by far the most satisfying portion of the fragment, contains the touching episode of **"Les Laboureurs"** (**"The Tillers"**) in which Lamartine unfolds his social doctrine. It has been suggested that the entire section bears a striking resemblance in inspiration to the two paintings by Millet, *The Reaper* and *The Sower.* The poet issues an appeal for wider appreciation of the simple and good life as led by the French peasantry, and betrays his personal nostalgia for the ancestral land. Lamartine's celebration of country life captures the bucolic scene with particular vividness at times. Yet the characters that inhabit his idyllic poetry are almost completely divested of any real sense of individuality; they emerge more as symbolic representations of the ideal peasant type than real people. Such romantic symbolization fitted neatly into the pattern of Lamartine's humanitarian vision; he reveals a tendency to relegate his characters and his nature settings into the background in order to spell out his moral and social messages. (pp. 58-9)

The simplicity and the lyrical tenor so much in evidence in *Jocelyn* was doubtlessly responsible for the enthusiastic reception which it received in 1836. Despite an annoying desultoriness in presentation, certain glaring syntactical errors, and inconsistencies of style, Lamartine's fragment bespoke the breath of inspiration which elicited the kind of emotional response that he wished from his readers. The general success enjoyed by such publications as *Jocelyn* bore eloquent testimony to the type of literary evolution that had overtaken France since the Revolution of 1789.

La Chute d'un ange, originally intended as the initial episode of the unfinished *Visions,* is divided into fifteen "visions," all of which center upon the eighth vision which formulates Lamartine's poetic and philosophical creed. Lamartine's epic about the fallen angel, Cédar, prior to the great flood recalls Lord Byron's similar concern with the plight of angels in his mystery drama, *Heaven and Earth.* The Romanticists' obsession with the acquisition of an all-encompassing knowledge and vision excited their fascination for angels such as Lucifer who had been punished for their pride and presumption. For poets such as Lamartine and Hugo, convinced of the authentic voice behind their inspiration and eager to think of themselves as reflections of the divine, the position of the fallen angel piqued both their imagination and their curiosity. (p. 60)

La Chute d'un ange underscores the plight of primitive man not yet endowed with the moral sense of human suffering. The theme of revolt against suffering is often conveyed with striking effect thanks to Lamartine's dramatic imagination. Whatever

talent Lamartine may have demonstrated in *La Chute d'un ange* as an adept psychologist in the more dramatic and epic portions, the fragment failed to win the approval of readers and critics alike. The ambitious conception of *La Chute d'un ange* was overshadowed by its partial and unsatisfactory realization.

The most accessible of the French Romantic poets during the 1830's and 1840's, Lamartine's verse from the *Méditations poétiques* to the lengthy **"La Vigne et la maison"** (**"The House and the Vineyard"**) bears the stamp of spontaneity and directness of expression. Most of his poems display his dexterity in manipulating the imagination to speak so unassumingly to the emotions of his readers. The seemingly effortless ease with which he managed to crystallize his personal inspiration in poetry with a simplicity of form that appealed to all types of readers accounted for his influence and popularity among traditionalists and innovators alike. His publications betray the kind of cautious evolution from social and political moderation to liberalism that was susceptible of enlisting the support of both factions at once. Lamartine's poetic and political expression stemmed directly from his personal and emotional response to experience. His ability to adapt and adjust his form and his ideas to the shifting moods of a difficult era explains why his writing gave the impression of being dictated by a lingering sense of neo-Classicism and a vibrant conception of Romanticism. (pp. 61-2)

Robert T. Denommé, "Alphonse de Lamartine and the Neo-Classical Inheritance," in his Nineteenth-Century French Romantic Poets, *Southern Illinois University Press, 1969, pp. 42-62.*

A caricature of Lamartine soliciting subscribers to Le conseiller du peuple, *a journal he edited.*

WILLIAM CALIN (essay date 1983)

[In this excerpt from his collection of essays on the history of the French epic, Calin analyzes Jocelyn, *treating setting, plot, symbolism, themes, imagery, and characterization.]*

What an outrageous phenomenon [*Jocelyn*] is, from the perspective of Ronsard or Boileau! The protagonist is a poor country priest, the narrative is his own story, told by himself, a 'Journal trouvé chez un curé de village.' The peripetias are of the most down-to-earth, unheroic kind. Deciding to sacrifice his worldly heritage in order that his sister may marry, a boy enters the seminary. He escapes from the Terror by fleeing to the mountains where he falls in love with Laurence, the daughter of another refugee. Their idyll is broken when Jocelyn accepts ordination. The remainder of the poem recounts the young man's experiences as a priest in a mountain village, a trip to Paris accompanying his sister (where he beholds Laurence), and his administering the last rites to his mother, Laurence, and a weaver, the latter a victim of the plague. Like Wordsworth, Lamartine is concerned with the life of a private individual; the characters in his rustic, bourgeois tale are a widow, a country priest, a servant, peasants, and urban workers. He writes for all men but about simple, everyday things in the lives of little people, events treated in both the sentimental and tragic modes. By taking the life of his protagonist seriously, Lamartine makes the destiny of the individual meaningful, but by idealizing him and his surroundings, he avoids the critical realism we find in the novels of Balzac and Stendhal. (p. 302)

Jocelyn and Laurence are one of the great tragic couples in French literature, on a par with Tristan and Iseut, Lancelot and Guinevere, des Grieux and Manon, Saint-Preux and Julie, and Marcel and Albertine. In *Jocelyn,* as in *La Chute d'un Ange,* his novels, and so many of his finest lyrics, Lamartine adheres to the conventions of *fin' amor.* The woman is a figure of light, an angel to be adored, her eyes and hair shining upon her suitor's darkness. . . . Even though his love is menaced by obstacles and the inevitable passing of time, it is the most deeply satisfying condition to which a man can aspire. The discovery of one's anima, one's *âme-soeur* . . . is an extraordinary privilege, and the love of such a woman makes one a better person and raises one's soul to God. Since an Elvire, a Julie (in *Raphaël*), or a Laurence serves as an intercessor, a religious *mediatrix,* one attains immortality by being joined to her in heaven. Indeed, as a result of earthly separation, the beloved is metamorphosed into a purely spiritual force. Fulfillment is attained through renunciation and regeneration, a *Liebestod* transformed into art. Lamartine departs from the tradition, however, in that his characters never indulge in fornication or adultery. Laurence and Jocelyn avoid physical intimacies; the latter remains a virgin for his entire lifetime. Furthermore, their passion is doomed because it cannot achieve fruition in marriage and the birth of children; or, perhaps on the contrary, Lamartine condemns it because it does not result in wedlock and issue. In contrast, the happy couples in *Jocelyn,* whose loves serve as foils to the main intrigue—the protagonist's father and mother, his sister and brother-in-law, shepherds, farmers, weavers—all appear in a family situation. Lamartine's social ideal is clearly the rural family working together. And it is the atmosphere of the home—the world of *La Vigne et la Maison*—that gives *Jocelyn* much of its charm.

For the most part, the action takes place in the Alps, a mountainous setting which had become fashionable in the late eighteenth and early nineteenth centuries, largely owing to the influence of Rousseau, Senancour, Delille, and Byron. Nonetheless, such a décor, with its discreet yet explicit local color, is new to the French epic. In *Jocelyn* the Alps, far from the madding crowd, separated from corrupt cities both horizontally and vertically, provide solitude. The author's treatment of the mountain paradise is unusually complex, containing a variety of conventions and motifs. One of them is the *locus amoenus,* the idyllic garden spot conducive to the flowering of love, a paradise or Arcadia inhabited by amorous shepherds: here Lamartine was most directly influenced by Tasso, Fénelon, Bernardin de Saint-Pierre, and Chateaubriand. Another is the erotic grotto, hidden from the outside world, defended by a triple barrier: this Grotte des Aigles adheres to a more immediate epic tradition, in the line of Homer, Virgil, and the masters of the Renaissance. The grotto especially, associated with dripping water and a mountain lake (images of purity, baptism, and secular grace), evokes a maternal refuge, an Eden constructed by God in nature, which becomes a home for lonely people thrust into exile. In the second half of the poem these two motifs are undermined by, yet also synthesized in, Jocelyn's mountain presbytery at Valneige. There, in a celibate state, he nonetheless dines on the same bread, wine, milk, honey, fruit, and grapes as Daphnis and Chloe or, for that matter, Saint-Amant's Elisaph and Marie, and finds the same protection from a cruel world, the same womb-like refuge, as in the Grotte des Aigles. Indeed, this pervasiveness of nature contributes greatly to the 'message' of Lamartine's poem. God's true temple stands in the open air, where all is sparkle, light, bursting, and blowing, in an animistic, naturally fecund universe. We can even say that, in nature, man is initiated, attains an 'I-Thou' relationship with other people and with God, in an otherwise 'I-It' world.

The reality of Paris and of nearby provincial cities and the presence of forces from outside that impinge upon Lamartine's happy lovers remind us that an idyll is idyllic only in contrast to, and in contact with, the 'real world.' The pastoral mode takes shape as an imagined refuge, a wish-fulfillment décor for lovers or poets who seek happiness, innocence, wisdom, and good love, all without nagging responsibilities—far from urban centers, which in fact do not permit Eden to remain inviolate. Although natural disasters can also undermine the bucolic, the conflicts that corrode Lamartine's universe are of human origin, the result of people congregating in society. First of all, as with Jean de Meun, mankind suffers from gold, from a money economy in which prestige and even happiness are based upon possessions. Not only this, but exploitation gives rise to violence, war, and civil strife. Because of the French Revolution Jocelyn is chased from the seminary, his bishop is executed, and Laurence's father is murdered by soldiers. Although, but for the Terror, Laurence and Jocelyn would never have met, it also brings about their separation and the death of two fine men; the Revolutionary-Bonapartist mentality is partly responsible for the degradation of Paris, which becomes an armed camp, a forest of muskets, a city where people are metamorphosed into algae, and for the moral degradation of Laurence, who dwells there as a kept woman. Like so many writers of his and the previous century (Rousseau, Vigny, Baudelaire, and others), Lamartine envisages the capital as a place of alienation, an inferno, yet a place where the future of mankind will be determined. He assimilates Paris to decadent Biblical cities such as Sodom, Babel, and Babylon (cf. the demonic metropolis in *La Chute d'un Ange*), yet he also rejects preromantic Arcadian pastoral in favor of a more modern, true-to-life vision of the countryside as a region with roots based upon concrete traditions (as do Wordsworth, Balzac, Goethe, and Turgenev). *Jocelyn* manifests a tragic modern sense of reality in which events concerning humble people are based upon contemporary or near-contemporary history and treated in the most serious manner: an innovation in literature and a hallmark of the romantic period.

The city versus the country, revolution and military strife versus love and the family—these are the issues of conflict. On the one hand, a masculine realm of commerce and war, of urban society; on the other, a feminine world of home, of idyllic love in a natural refuge graced by a lake and a grotto. The tension between these opposing forces gives rise to melodrama, to extraordinary events that would normally be out of place in the lives of quiet, humble folk.

As a result, Jocelyn's private career corresponds . . . to the life of all heroes, and his adventures can be considered a low-mimetic version of the archetypal quest pattern. . . . Forced by circumstances beyond his control, he quits everyday existence in favor of a life of adventure in exile, a road of trials. Accepting the aid of an older guide, a creature of nature, he traverses a series of mountain barriers into a sort of Other World far from the eyes of mortal man. There, in this return to the womb, at the point of epiphany, in paradise, he encounters a maiden whom he worships as an angel or goddess. At his moment of greatest happiness, however, life takes another turn: like Aeneas, like Yvain, like Rinaldo, like Télémaque, the youth discovers existence to be hollow. Through an act of ascetic renunciation, he abandons the maiden (metamorphosed into a temptress), accepts guidance from a supremely powerful father-figure who also serves as his antagonist, and proceeds to embark upon a new series of adventures. He again climbs past mountain barriers, expiates sin through a series of ordeals, this time resists the woman's temptation, and learns to love, serve, and guide his people. Now his life is directed in accordance with the dictates of society. In the end he becomes a spiritual father, a teacher and sage; he dies in an aura of sanctity, having attained apotheosis in heaven, master of both worlds. In his career he has crossed more than one threshold and undergone more than one rite of passage: separation from family, love, ordination, and death.

Of particular significance is the fact that, for the first time since Chrétien de Troyes and Guillaume de Lorris, an epic hero's quest takes place within: his combat is spiritual rather than physical in nature. We find the typically romantic sequence of ordeal, expiation, and initiation (Ballanche, Quinet, Laprade, Hugo). Jocelyn twice sacrifices erotic happiness, in the process learning to devote himself to his fellow men and to God. The moment of initiation—the sacrament of ordination—occurs in the very center of the poem, Epoch 5, separating the realms of secular and sacred love, and marking the principal stage in Jocelyn's pilgrimage. Although he progresses from the outer world to an inner realm, paradoxically the *homo viator* finds fulfillment in a modern, realistic, and authentic rural setting (the *vita activa*) before arriving at a *unio mystica* with Laurence and God. To some extent, his quest conforms to the pattern of the Orphic poet-seer, the fundamental archetypal personage in the romantic period.

A major concern in medieval and baroque epic, religion is no less central to works composed by Chateaubriand, Ballanche, Quinet, Soumet, Laprade, Hugo, and, of course, the author of *Harmonies Poétiques et Religieuses. Jocelyn,* however, turns out to be the only major epic in French in which the protagonist is an ordained priest. Christian faith not only plays its usual role of recalling a warrior to duty, away from dalliance with

a temptress; as in *La Chanson de Roland* and *Les Tragiques* [by Agrippa d'Aubigné], it is central to the plot and to the poem's doctrinal line. Throughout the poem individuals are assimilated to Christ, become Christ-figures imitating his Passion. Jocelyn especially drinks from the Messiah's cup, teaches his flock by parables, and, accompanied by shepherds, retreats into solitude (his desert, his Mount of Olives), then returns to the city where he offers the ultimate sacrifice to God. . . . Sacrifice and regeneration through suffering is a favorite theme of Chateaubriand, Ballanche, and Lamartine himself, in all his novels: *Graziella, Raphaël, Geneviève, Le Tailleur de pierres de Saint-Point, Fior d'Aliza,* and *Antoniella.* Having fallen from a formerly privileged state, having been separated from a happy childhood, a rural home, the love of woman, only by imitating Christ can Lamartine's characters hope to recover their lost paradise and be reintegrated into a world of joy. What can be more heroic than to follow in the footsteps of the God-man who, like Moses, Theseus, and Hercules, came from obscure beginnings, underwent exile, temptation and humiliation, was martyred but then won rebirth, salvation, apotheosis with the Father, and epiphany?

To imitate Christ, one must learn to bear his Cross. A weaver bears his wife's coffin on his back for three days, seeking a priest to perform the last rites, then Jocelyn and the man transport it up into the Alps; this is the weaver's and, presumably, Jocelyn's Calvary. Significantly, the widower constructed the coffin from his own bed-boards, an act of charity anticipated by Jocelyn under other circumstances. And the latter's mother fainted away on the bed in which her husband died. Thus, Lamartine assimilates the bed, the coffin, and the cross; the womb and the tomb; birth, death, and rebirth. It is also true that Jocelyn's faith has been upheld by a real crucifix—one which received a kiss from the mouth of his dying father, which he shared with Laurence in the mountains, which was bathed in the dying bishop's blood, which hangs on the wall of his cottage at Valneige, and which, after his death, is bequeathed to the Narrator along with the diary that constitutes the poem *Jocelyn.* No less symbolic are the five rocks arranged in the shape of a cross by the protagonist over Laurence's father's grave at la Grotte des Aigles, where the lovers will also one day be buried. This site constitutes a sanction and a covenant governing their lives. Where man lives and loves he will die, and where he takes his daily rest he will ultimately repose; for death can lead to eternal redemption.

Finally, Jocelyn himself is a living rood, a tree of life. In the 'Epilogue' the Narrator refers to him as a splendid oak who grew to maturity, in spite of suffering, in spite of an axe that penetrated the bark to his inner heart. Similarly, a bush rises into the roof of Jocelyn's home; it cannot be separated from the cottage without the structure crumbling and the plant being killed. This imagery, which reinforces Lamartine's conception of benevolent nature, can be assimilated to Christian motifs of the Tree of Life, the Tree of Jesse, and, of course, the Holy Rood. Jocelyn as a tree provides sustenance, protection, and hope to his flock, while he himself benefits from Christian doctrine. He bears a cross and is a cross, imitates Christ and becomes Christ, for the sake of his parishioners (as a priest) and for his own salvation.

The nuptial cup of the Song of Songs has been metamorphosed into Christ's chalice of blood and bile. Jocelyn, the bishop, and the weaver all imitate Christ by drinking from his cup. Furthermore, during the Revolution much blood is shed, and people weep bitter tears. Water plays a special role in *Jocelyn* in terms of Christian ritual. For with the holy water of baptism, the wine of the Mass, the anointing of ordination and of extreme unction, the Christian dies and is reborn, a *homo novus* in Christ. In addition to the usual death-rebirth experiences, one pattern especially stands out: on the very same day that the bishop takes the Eucharist, that is, perishes spiritually and is reborn in Christ, Jocelyn is ordained a priest, that is, he dies to the world and is resuscitated as Christ's deputy in the Church; the bishop is literally dismembered only to relive in heaven; and finally France is resurrected from the tomb of Revolution, its joy restored thanks to the sacrifice of this holy scapegoat.

Most critics have assumed *Jocelyn* to be a profoundly religious poem that glorifies a country priest who keeps his faith and even succeeds in redeeming the Fallen Woman, his temptress. From this vantage-point, it narrates the slow progresion toward sainthood of a highly sensitive devout young man, his evolution from romantic love to the maturity of a clerical calling. In addition, on a symbolic level, the protagonist represents the modern Church that must make sacrifices for the good of society, and, as we have seen, Christ himself, for each and every vicar of Christ, a Christ-figure serving Mass, must forsake individual love (*concupiscentia*) for the love of many (*caritas*), one soul for the collective soul of the Church to be led back to God. . . . Such indeed is an appropriate lesson from a writer who devoted his lifetime *ad majorem Dei gloriam,* who, for most of his public, was the official, consecrated Catholic poet.

However, if in 1836 eight out of ten readers assumed that *Jocelyn* was a Catholic poem, they and subsequent generations were moved above all by a sentimental love story, by a melodrama in which two ideally mated young people are separated forever by circumstances beyond their control. We must not allow neat literary-historical assertions to convince us that all romantic epics preach optimism and progress. Furthermore, it is a literary-historical fact that *Jocelyn* was placed on the *Index librorum prohibitorum* (22 September 1836) and that many influential Catholics were scandalized by the poem, as they were by *Le Voyage en Orient* . . . and *La Chute d'un Ange* . . . , also placed on the *Index.* Although Lamartine sought God all his life, by December 1832 he ceased to be a believing, submissive Catholic, and his religion resembles the Deism of Voltaire, Rousseau, Bernardin de Saint-Pierre, and Swedenborg. It is from this perspective that we can appreciate certain romantic and pre-romantic anti-Catholic motifs, such as the evil bishop and the seminarist in love, and the central increment of the plot: the pathos of a sensitive young man, predestined to love and marriage yet forced to abandon life's dearest delights by the interference of a bishop and his Church, perhaps by God—for at one time or another, even the divinity is reproached for the misery inflicted on Jocelyn and his beloved. The rights of the heart to love and happiness, as opposed to the social or religious code, is a great theme in early nineteenth-century literature. . . . (pp. 302-09)

[The] problem is not whether Lamartine favors religion over love or love over religion. This is Jocelyn's story (he is the title figure), recounted in his voice from his point of view, whether as a protagonist or witness, the lone exceptions a **'Prologue'** and **'Epilogue'** ascribed to a young disciple, a Narrator who loves the priest and manipulates the reader on his behalf. Because of the diary format chosen by Lamartine, the protagonist expresses all the lyricism and passion of which his soul is capable, on the spot, without time for reflection or distancing. Indeed, the seeming authenticity of his voice is guaranteed by the fact that he does not write for a public, that these pages of a diary are tossed into the attic. We are moved by his ardor; he is participant, sufferer, visionary, and poet all in one. Therefore, the implied reader identifies with his amorous longings and with his religious commitment, each in turn. How can he be expected to choose between them? Does not the author himself refuse to take sides? . . .

Lamartine's sense of ambiguity extends to Jocelyn himself, that, in spite of the immediacy of the narrative mode, we are expected, while sympathizing and even identifying with the young man, also to judge him. No doubts are permitted of his success as a priest; but the youth's attainments as a lover and a man are another question altogether. Jocelyn is, in many respects, a typical romantic hero. Subject to melancholia and paralysis of the will, hypersensitive, egocentric, introspective, often withdrawn into himself, yet capable of the greatest leaps of passion and self-sacrifice, he embodies *le mal du siècle;* he is a younger brother to Saint-Preux, Paul, René, Obermann, Adolphe, Joseph Delorme, and Antony, as well as to the heroes created by Byron, Shelley, and Keats. (p. 309)

Standing back from Jocelyn, we observe that one of his most notable traits is an incapacity to make active decisions that will change his destiny. This passivity is accompanied by a propensity to witness life instead of living it, to be a spectator to others' happiness instead of an actor of his own. Thus (to note but the most significant examples), the young man silently spies on his mother and Julie talking of dowries, on Laurence reacting to the news of his ordination, on Laurence in Paris, on Laurence on her deathbed, and on the affectionate intimacy of three couples: Julie and her husband, two shepherds, and two farm laborers.

Along with his passivity and an inclination to voyeurism, we find that, brought up without a father, the youth has an almost pathological attachment to his mother, his alter ego whom he adores like a goddess. And he sacrifices all hope for natural, socially acceptable love with a woman for the sake of his sister, Julie. Mother, sister, and beloved are closely associated in his thoughts, and the youth wallows in tenderness for all three of them. Finally, he administers extreme unction to his mother and to Laurence, in the same terms and with identically passionate tenderness.

I consider it significant that Jocelyn also projects his affection for women onto the land, onto geographical locations associated with the women he loves. Forced to leave home, he embraces the earth more even than his mother and collects moss and soil to take with him. During the Terror he falls into a rage upon hearing that his mother has been exiled and his house burned. . . . And later, when informed that the family home now belongs to another, this disciple of Christ assimilates his anguish to that of a husband discovering he has lost his wife to another man. Jocelyn also loves his mountain grotto in the same terms as Laurence, and, as an alternative to his mother's home, finds satisfaction in the dark, silent, womb-like refuge of the seminary.

Finally, it is a fact that the youth's most sincere, most authentic and passionate love is nourished for a full fourteen months during which he believes Laurence to be a boy. There is no overt homosexual behavior on Jocelyn's part, far from it; but under the socially acceptable category of friendship, he does adore his companion like an angel; his affection for her is as deep as one human being's can possibly be for another, and he is quite aware of her physical beauty. . . . This forbidden, seemingly homosexual passion was one manifestation of romantic sensibility that Lamartine introduced into his epic to please the public. Disguise and subsequent change of sex had a long tradition in romantic literature, in authors read and loved by Lamartine—d'Urté, Prévost, Ossian, Goethe, and Byron—and he was to exploit the theme in *Raphaël* and *Fior d'Aliza*, as well as in *Jocelyn.*

The result of all this is a series of erotic situations in which the protagonist loves his mother, his sister, Laurence as a boy, Laurence as a girl, his old home, his grotto in the mountains—and on each occasion desire is thwarted, obstacles oppose its consummation. And well they might, considering that Jocelyn's passion so consistently takes on the form of tabu, whether it be the Oedipal stage, incest, homosexuality, or the breaking of priestly vows. Since the young cleric always becomes involved in forbidden relationships, is he therefore incapable of playing a more active, virile role when the possibility of a mature libido transferal presents itself? Or is it because he is a passive individual, a spectator and not an actor in life, that he unconsciously chooses love-objects he is doomed to lose? Whatever the answer, Jocelyn's relationship with Laurence definitely corresponds to the pattern of his life as a whole: he envisages her in the same terms as his mother and sister and, therefore, feels guilt and remorse as if his love for her were a form of incest. Indeed, his desire to enjoy freedom and love outside the law, to place spontaneous passion over reason, ends in disaster. Although the young man acts like a father to Laurence, calling her his child, she proves to be more mature and

A photograph by Nadar of Lamartine in his sixties.

authentic than he, more virile than her feminized suitor. As if to prove the point, at a key moment in the narrative the bishop sends for one of his 'children,' and Jocelyn, who in the poem has never had a living father, comes running. Acting with the wrath of a jealous God, of God the Father, the prelate castigates the seminarist's sinful passion for a weaker vessel, a mere woman, and drums it out of him. . . . Jocelyn was guilty of forbidden curiosity when he gazed upon Laurence's naked breasts in the mountains. Now the rebellious Oedipal son is punished for his sin by symbolic mutilation or impotence and condemned to abstinence for the rest of his life. And, like so many other epic heroes, he accepts the dictates of the Father-figure, the superego principle of reason and law, thrusting away the Mother-Temptress. He takes the Father's side against the Mother and against himself, repudiating those feminine, sensuous, emotion-oriented aspects of his psyche that he now, as a defense mechanism, represses or projects onto the Mother. Although this paternal surrogate acts with all the rage of a shadow-figure, a demon adversary, the hero masochistically yields to him and accepts his values. Indeed, the seminarist has found a double, who conveniently embodies his own latent rejection of woman and provides the sanction for abandoning her, and on whom he can blame his own failings. It will come as no surprise that the bishop's insults turn out to be prophetic, that the virgin girl is metamorphosed into a courtesan, whom Jocelyn then can virtuously pity and redeem. In his consciousness as in the story (the record of his consciousness), she has never been a woman, only a tabu maiden and whore. In this poem, as in so many other works, Lamartine compensates for the protagonist's sense of tabu by having him either indulge in narcissistic contemplation or retaliate by projecting onto the beloved his own guilt and punishing her, making her suffer and wallowing in her suffering. Jocelyn chooses Jupiter over the Titans but pays a terrible price for it.

From this perspective, we can perhaps account for certain patterns of imagery in *Jocelyn,* spatial patterns especially. Erotic passion is associated with light, fresh air, joy, and radiant self-fulfillment in the Alps, whereas Jocelyn's priestly vocation and his encounter with the Father are located in seminaries, ecclesiastical retreats, and prisons—demonic temples, cold, dark, damp, with the moral as well as physical characteristics of stone. Paradoxically, it is in the mountains, with Laurence, far from the seminary, that Jocelyn experiences an evanescent, dissolving space. For this is truly a 'high place,' sacred like Mount Sinai or the Mount of Olives in the Bible, a point of Epiphany between heaven and earth. The two are fused, and space radiates with divine force; in the Alps Jocelyn's spirit soars to God, free from gross material cares. He undergoes spiritual flight, conscious of God and the cosmos, in a state of ecstasy. Here also he experiences a sense of pulsation, in time and space, all joy and song, his inner being responding to God's harmony, the universe vibrating in unison with his soul. . . . Indifferent to the physical décor that surrounds him, Jocelyn experiences a *räumliche Expansionserlebnis,* a prenatal *ozeanisches Gefühl* that permits his soul to yearn for the Almighty and ultimately to partake of a divine, absolute *nunc stans.* However, since he cannot grasp God or does so only for tiny instants, he abandons infinite space and time for more concrete settings, for protection in an intimate, enclosed, narrow, shady décor, a refuge such as la Grotte des Aigles or a mountain valley. Hence also the ultimate return to the womb and to imagery of death, associated with the paternal superego. And it is here that the young hero perhaps comes closest to God: by delving into himself, into his deepest inner receptacle, his unconscious, he is enabled paradoxically to expand his soul and rise from within to the divinity, to know true love and the life-in-death of the spirit.

To arrive at such states of spiritual communion, Jocelyn is separated from his fellow men—from family, Laurence, his bishop, his parishioners—and reduced to solitude, a loneliness harder to endure than Adam's after the Fall. Some of the loveliest passages in the epic concern the young priest's affection for his dog, the only friend (except, later on, the Narrator) God permits him to keep. . . . Lamartine proclaims that suffering and isolation are the necessary prerequisites for spiritual visionary power. As in Wordsworth, all the major characters are solitaries, including the protagonist. However, Jocelyn is not permitted to remain in any one place for long. Indeed, as a questing hero . . . , he moves back and forth throughout the poem. The wanderer or *homo viator* as hero and the life of man as a voyage or pilgrimage are universal literary archetypes revived in the romantic period by the author of *Childe Harold*. For Lamartine, as for Byron, man is born to the Eden of heaven or an earthly childhood but then exiled to the reality of our mortal life, and he spends the rest of his days wandering to and fro seeking vainly to return home (**'Milly ou la Terre natale,' 'Le Retour,'** *La Vigne et la Maison*), to recover his lost paradise. Similarly, mankind travels through history like a caravan, in accordance with God's will. Jocelyn will eventually find contentment in his grotto, but in the afterworld, in death not life, in a realm of pure light where space and time cease to exist.

No less complex, no less ambivalent is Lamartine's attitude toward poetry, language, and the act of verbal communication. Jocelyn is a relatively literate country priest, who has been moved by Ossian and Bernardin de Saint-Pierre in addition to Thomas à Kempis and the Bible. Yet, during the two most happy, fulfilling periods in his life, he reads nothing, is proud to exist far from the world of letters. In the seminary he has not written in his diary for six years; his life is quiet and contented; he holds God's hand, not a pen. . . . And in the Alps he peruses no books, only the face and soul of Laurence, finer reading matter than any other. . . . [Still,] he and Laurence become poets, spontaneously singing hymns to God. And Lamartine's protagonist does find the time to write letters to his mother and sister, to compose two poems, 'Stances à Laurence' and a lyrical defense of the Church, and, above all, to keep his diary. We must not forget that, but for the **'Prologue'** and **'Epilogue,'** the entire epic is ascribed to the priest, is alleged to be a transcription of the diary he bequeathed, along with his Bible, to the Narrator. These pages, beaten by wind and rain, gnawed by rats or torn to kindle fires, are the outpouring of a sensitive soul. They also stand as an intense, powerful work of art. Because of them Jocelyn as a literary character has the right to be considered an author, an example of the romantic myth of the poet: a writer who is also an honest human being, his opus the spontaneous, artless projection of his soul. Jocelyn creates as well as acts, is a poet as well as a lover; indeed it is as a writer (and priest and lover) that he appeals to our sympathy: as *sacer vates*, a solitary visionary and leader, misunderstood by society but able to see beyond other men, worthy of initiation into the divine mysteries. Thus *Jocelyn* joins other works by Lamartine, such as *La Mort de Socrate, Les Chevaliers, Raphaël,* **'À Némésis,' 'Le Génie dans l'obscurité,'** in defense of art and the artist or in which the protagonist is a poet. And, because he is an ordained priest, Jocelyn the poetical diarist provides an example of the *sacerdoce poétique* typical of the romantic period, for he is a Catholic martyr of the Terror who yearns for both Laurence and God,

for secular and sacred love, in much the same terms, and who, as priest, lover, and diarist, embodies the best of mankind.

From Jocelyn's point of view, his deepest, most valid esthetic experiences occur not when he writes his diary but during moments of spiritual ecstasy. The universe throbs with poetry, God's soul and his own pulsating together. The young man's prayer is both verse and music, and his truest poetry the yearning of his soul for God. A secondary process involves his transferal of the divine 'harmonies' to others. He teaches Laurence, the peasants and shepherds in his village, children, and the most gifted of these, the youth from outside who is to become the Narrator, his literary heir and the editor of his diary. As a teacher of children, Jocelyn resembles his spiritual brothers depicted in *Graziella* and *Raphaël;* as a guide to his people, he resembles Ballanche's Orpheus, Lamartine's Socrates and Adonaï, and Hugo's Victor Hugo. The modern epic hero makes men better by teaching; he does for his contemporaries what Hercules and Theseus did for the Ancients, but through words—that is, he becomes a creator and civilizer without arms.

Paradoxically, however, the priest-poet fails to communicate verbally with Laurence. At their first encounter, the girl's dying father places their relationship under the sign of silence and mystery. . . . Needless to say, on several occasions verbal exchange between them is hindered or, if it does take place, leads to misunderstanding. Significantly, such failures occur after the first mystery is resolved, after Jocelyn has discovered that his companion is a girl and therefore that their relationship is a sexual one with overtones of sin and tabu. And when they meet in Paris, after Laurence has become a 'fallen woman,' not one word is exchanged. On the contrary, from the beginning their finest communication, before and after the fall, occurs on a totally different level, one which corresponds to the technique of *sous-conversation* in the French New Novel. Jocelyn tells us that no speech is necessary between Laurence and himself, for theirs is a perfect wedding of souls, and indeed they communicate with eye contact, posture, facial expression, gestures, and the flow of tears. Such body language is a standard trait in French Romanticism, especially in the work of Lamartine, and is to be found in *La Chute d'un Ange, Raphaël, Graziella,* and the lyrics, where it is shown to be the mark of soul mates in love. It may also correspond to the ineffable muteness in contemporary melodrama, the notion that truly virtuous and innocent people have recourse to a code less coarse than speech, truly a primal language. In sum, Jocelyn's greatness as a poet, priest, and lover resides not in verbal dexterity but in his soul, in sympathetic vibrations from his heart. (pp. 309-15)

> William Calin, ''Lamartine,'' in his A Muse for Heroes: Nine Centuries of the Epic in France, *University of Toronto Press, 1983, pp. 298-317.*

ADDITIONAL BIBLIOGRAPHY

Ages, Arnold. ''Lamartine and the *Philosophes.*'' In *Literature and History in the Age of Ideas: Essays on the French Enlightenment Presented to George R. Havens,* edited by Charles G.S. Williams, pp. 321-40. Columbus: Ohio State University Press, 1975.*
   Studies the influence of the French philosophers Voltaire and Jean Jacques Rousseau on Lamartine's thought and work.

Bassan, Fernande. "Chateaubriand, Lamartine, Nerval, and Flaubert in Palestine." *University of Toronto Quarterly* XXXIII, No. 2 (January 1964): 142-63.*

> Contrasts the travel memoirs of Palestine by François René de Chateaubriand, Gérard de Nerval, Gustave Flaubert, and Lamartine.

Birkett, Mary Ellen. *Lamartine and the Poetics of Landscape.* French Forum Monographs, edited by R. C. La Charité and V. A. La Charité, no. 38. Lexington, Ky.: French Forum, Publishers, 1982, 150 p.

> Focuses on Lamartine's contribution to French landscape poetry. Birkett maintains that Lamartine considered the creative process and poetic diction more important than the actual landscape depicted. In addition, the critic contends that Lamartine anticipated surrealist diction in his emphasis on the musical evocativeness of words rather than on their descriptive power.

George, Albert Joseph. *Lamartine and Romantic Unanimism.* New York: Columbia University Press, 1940, 200 p.

> Explores Lamartine's thought and works in light of unanimism, a twentieth-century poetic movement based on the premise that the poet's role is to show how the personality of an individual can merge with the collective soul of a group.

——. "Lamartine and a 'Literature for the People'." *Symposium: A Journal Devoted to Modern Foreign Languages and Literatures* III, No. 2 (November 1949): 245-60.

> Discusses Lamartine's view of the writer as reformer and its effect on his prose works.

Goddard, Eunice R. "Color in Lamartine's *Jocelyn.*" *Modern Language Notes* XXXVI, No. 4 (April 1921): 221-25.

> An analysis of Lamartine's use of color in *Jocelyn.*

Gosse, Edmund. "Lamartine and the English Poets." In his *More Books on the Table,* pp. 315-23. New York: Charles Scribner's Sons, 1923.*

> Suggests that Lamartine was influenced by the works of eighteenth- and nineteenth-century English poets, particularly Lord Byron, Thomas Gray, and Edward Young.

Harms, Alvin. "Lamartine and the Problem of the Ineffable." *Romanistisches Jahrbuch* XXIII (1972): 130-36.

> A discussion of Lamartine's aesthetic theories.

Hastings, Hester. "Man and Beast: Lamartine's Contribution to French Animal Literature." *PMLA* LXI, No. 4 (December 1946): 1109-25.

> A study of Lamartine's attitude toward animals and their representation in his works, particularly in *Harmonies poétiques et religieuses* and *Jocelyn.*

Lombard, C. M. "The Influence of Saint-Martin on Lamartine." *Modern Language Notes* LXX, No. 1 (January 1955): 42-4.*

> Describes the influence of the leading eighteenth-century French philosopher Louis-Claude de Saint-Martin on Lamartine's verse, especially as evidenced in *The Poetical Meditations.*

——. "Anglo-American Protestantism and Lamartine." *Revue de littérature comparée* XXXVII, No. 4 (October-December 1963): 540-49.

> A bibliographic survey of criticism on Lamartine by American and English Protestants.

Pirazzini, Agide. *The Influence of Italy on the Literary Career of Alphonse de Lamartine.* New York: Columbia University Press, 1917, 160 p.

> A biographical and critical study tracing the influence of Italian literature and culture on Lamartine's works.

Porter, Laurence M. "Appeal and Response in Lamartine's Elegies." In his *The Renaissance of the Lyric in French Romanticism: Elegy, "Poëme," and Ode,* pp. 19-46. French Forum Monographs, edited by R. C. La Charité and V. A. La Charité, no. 10. Lexington, Ky.: French Forum, Publishers, 1978.*

> Discusses Lamartine's verse within the context of the elegy in nineteenth-century French poetry. Porter concentrates on Lamartine's use of such poetic devices as mirror imagery, personification, and apostrophe.

Pugh, Anthony R. "On Analysing Poetry: 'Le Lac'." *Modern Languages* LI, No. 1 (March 1970): 20-4.

> A detailed interpretation of the poem "Le lac" from *The Poetical Meditations.*

Shields, John. "Three Elegies." *Studies in Philology* XL, No. 4 (October 1943): 576-82.*

> Compares Lamartine's "Le lac" with the poems "Tristesse d'Olympio" by Victor Hugo and "Souvenir" by Alfred de Musset.

Smith, Maxwell Austin. "The Intimate Poetry of Lamartine and Sainte-Beuve: A Contrast." In *Studies by Members of the Department of Romance Languages,* pp. 152-62. University of Wisconsin Studies in Language and Literature, no. 20. Madison: University of Wisconsin, 1924.*

> Contrasts the *poésie intime,* verse representing the joys of everyday life, of Charles Augustin Sainte-Beuve and Lamartine.

Tilley, A. "Lamartine's *Méditations Poétiques.*" *Modern Language Review* XXVI, No. 3 (July 1931): 288-314.

> A survey of *The Poetical Meditations.* Tilley describes the genesis of these poems and provides brief interpretations of each.

Whitehouse, Henry Remsen. *The Life of Lamartine.* 2 vols. Select Bibliographies Reprint Series. 1918. Reprint. Freeport, N.Y.: Books for Libraries Press, 1969.

> The standard English-language biography.

Matthew Gregory Lewis

1775-1818

English novelist, dramatist, diarist, short story writer, and poet.

Lewis is best known as the author of *The Monk,* a notorious eighteenth-century novel of horror that is considered one of the greatest examples of English Gothic fiction. Unlike Horace Walpole and Ann Radcliffe, his predecessors in the Gothic school who created genteel novels of suspense, Lewis emphasized the graphic and the sensational. *The Monk*'s blend of overt sexuality and terror created a scandal in England, and its author, branded licentious and perverse, came to be known solely as "Monk" Lewis. While the lurid elements of Lewis's work are still controversial, twentieth-century critics acknowledge his talent as an innovative writer of prose and verse who contributed to the development of the English Romantic movement.

Lewis was born into a wealthy and socially prominent London family. His mother and father separated while he was young, and his attempts to remain on good terms with both parents created an emotional strain that endured throughout his life. Some biographers contend, in fact, that this stress resulted in an emotional immaturity that manifested itself in Lewis's work. Although Lewis displayed a talent for writing at an early age and was encouraged by his mother, his father urged him to pursue a diplomatic career instead. After graduation from Oxford in 1794, he became an attaché to the British Embassy in Holland, an assignment he despised. Out of boredom, Lewis wrote *The Monk* in the span of ten weeks.

The notoriety that accompanied the novel's publication two years later made Lewis a financially successful, if infamous, author. Led by Samuel Taylor Coleridge, contemporary critics labeled Lewis's tale of Ambrosio, the wayward monk, immoral and obscene. Lewis had recently been elected to the House of Commons, and *The Monk* proved so controversial that, in order to retain his position, he was required to issue an expurgated edition. Shortly thereafter, Lewis left politics and began writing drama. Of his plays, the best known is *The Castle Spectre,* a Gothic creation that met the current demand for melodrama, spectacle, and two-dimensional characterization. Although it helped establish Lewis as one of the era's most popular playwrights, *The Castle Spectre* is largely overlooked today.

In 1801, Lewis published *Tales of Wonder,* a collection of poems dealing with the supernatural that also includes works by Sir Walter Scott and Robert Southey. Another anthology, *Tales of Terror,* had been published anonymously in 1801, and was ascribed to Lewis for many years; modern scholars, however, concur that it was probably written to satirize his work. Lewis also composed poetry that he included in his plays and later published, as well as two novels that never enjoyed the success or notoriety of *The Monk.* He ceased writing fiction in 1812, when his father died and left him a great deal of money.

In the years before his death, Lewis spent most of his time on the Jamaican estates he had inherited, which were maintained by slaves. By all accounts, Lewis was a compassionate man who advocated the abolition of slavery and retained his plantations solely at the request of his slaves, who feared the fi-

nancial responsibility of freedom. His posthumous *Journal of a West Indian Proprietor, Kept during a Residence in the Island of Jamaica* recounts his voyages to Jamaica, inspections of the plantations, and plans for change. Written in lively prose, the *Journal* reveals Lewis as a sensitive and perceptive observer of the natural world. Though it is seldom read today, critics who have studied the work consider it one of Lewis's greatest achievements. Even his early detractor, Coleridge, termed the *Journal* "by far his best work."

During his final trip to Jamaica, Lewis tried desperately to improve the living conditions of his slaves. Despite his efforts, he was able to implement little change and, despondent, decided to return home. By the time Lewis boarded a ship for England, he had already developed yellow fever. He died several days later. His crew prepared to bury him at sea, but as they lowered the casket, its shroud caught in the wind and the coffin sailed slowly back to Jamaica.

With the exception of the *Journal,* Lewis's works were ignored from the time of his death until the twentieth century, when critics began to recognize Lewis's influence on the Romantic movement. Although most commentators now agree that *The Monk* represents a successful synthesis of the techniques and materials used by both Gothic and horror writers, they provide widely varied interpretations of the work. Perhaps the most influential analysis of *The Monk* was offered by John Berryman, who praised its insightful characterization and poetic elements as significant contributions to English literature. Later studies have probed the conflict between sexuality and religion and the juxtaposition of violence and passion within the novel. In a recent essay, David Morse echoed the thoughts of the Marquis de Sade, who wrote in 1800 that *The Monk* was a product of the revolutionary atmosphere of late eighteenth-century Europe. The number of different readings accorded Lewis's work reveals the changing reputation of an author who has shed notoriety for critical acceptance.

PRINCIPAL WORKS

The Monk (novel) 1796
The Castle Spectre (drama) 1797
Adelmorn, the Outlaw (drama) 1801
Tales of Wonder [with Robert Southey and Sir Walter Scott]
    (poetry) 1801
Alfonso, King of Castile (drama) 1802
The Bravo of Venice (novel) 1805
Feudal Tyrants; or, The Counts of Carlsheim and Sargans
    (novel) 1806
Adelgitha; or, The Fruits of a Single Error (drama) 1807
Romantic Tales (short stories) 1808
Venoni; or, The Novice of St. Mark's (drama) 1808
Timour the Tartar (drama) 1811
Poems (poetry) 1812
*Journal of a West Indian Proprietor, Kept during a
    Residence in the Island of Jamaica* (journal) 1834

THE BRITISH CRITIC (essay date 1796)

[*The following excerpt is a negative assessment of* The Monk.]

[*The Monk, a Romance* is composed of] lust, murder, incest, and every atrocity that can disgrace human nature, brought together, without the apology of probability, or even possibility, for their introduction. To make amends, the moral is general and *very practical*; it is, "not to deal in witchcraft and magic, because the devil will have you at last!!" We are sorry to observe that good talents have been misapplied in the production of this monster.

A review of "The Monk, a Romance," in The British Critic, *Vol. VII, June, 1796, p. 677.*

[SAMUEL TAYLOR COLERIDGE] (essay date 1797)

[*An English poet and critic, Coleridge was central to the English Romantic movement and is considered one of the greatest literary critics in the English language. Besides his poetry, his most important contributions include his formulation of Romantic theory, his introduction of the ideas of the German Romantics to England, and his Shakespearean criticism, which overthrew the last remnants of the Neoclassical approach to William Shakespeare and focused on Shakespeare as a masterful portrayer of human character. Coleridge's review of* The Monk, *from which the following section is excerpted, is considered one of the most significant essays on Lewis. Although he acknowledges Lewis's genius, Coleridge objects to* The Monk's *indecency, immorality, and irreligious air. This essay is later discussed by Richard Harter Fogle*

(1972). For additional commentary by Coleridge, see the excerpts dated 1798 and 1834.]

[Cheaply] as we estimate romances in general, we acknowledge, [*The Monk: a Romance*], the offspring of no common genius. . . . Ambrosio, a monk, surnamed the Man of Holiness, proud of his own undeviating rectitude, and severe to the faults of others, is successfully assailed by the tempter of mankind, and seduced to the perpetration of rape and murder, and finally precipitated into a contract in which he consigns his soul to everlasting perdition.

The larger part of the three volumes is occupied by the underplot, which, however, is skilfully and closely connected with the main story, and is subservient to its development. The tale of the bleeding nun is truly terrific; and we could not easily recollect a bolder or more happy conception than that of the burning cross on the forehead of the wandering Jew. . . . But the character of Matilda, the chief agent in the seduction of Antonio, appears to us to be the author's master-piece. It is, indeed, exquisitely imagined, and as exquisitely supported. The whole work is distinguished by the variety and impressiveness of its incidents; and the author every-where discovers an imagination rich, powerful, and fervid. Such are the excellencies;—the errors and defects are more numerous, and (we are sorry to add) of greater importance.

All events are levelled into one common mass, and become almost equally probable, where the order of nature may be changed whenever the author's purposes demand it. No address is requisite to the accomplishment of any design; and no pleasure therefore can be received from the perception of *difficulty surmounted*. The writer may make us wonder, but he cannot surprise us. For the same reasons a romance is incapable of exemplifying a moral truth. . . . As far, therefore, as the story is concerned, the praise which a romance can claim, is simply that of having given pleasure during its perusal; and so many are the calamities of life, that he who has done this, has not written uselessly. The children of sickness and of solitude shall thank him.—To this praise, however, our author has not entitled himself. The sufferings which he describes are so frightful and intolerable, that we break with abruptness from the delusion, and indignantly suspect the man of a species of brutality, who could find a pleasure in wantonly imagining them; and the abominations which he pourtrays with no hurrying pencil, are such as the observation of character by no means demanded, such as 'no observation of character can justify, because no good man would willingly suffer them to pass, however transiently, through his own mind.' The merit of a novelist is in proportion (not simply to the effect, but) to the *pleasurable* effect which he produces. Situations of torment, and images of naked horror, are easily conceived; and a writer in whose works they abound, deserves our gratitude almost equally with him who should drag us by way of sport through a military hospital, or force us to sit at the dissecting-table of a natural philosopher. . . . Figures that shock the imagination, and narratives that mangle the feelings, rarely discover *genius*, and always betray a low and vulgar taste. Nor has our author indicated less ignorance of the human heart in the management of the principal character. The wisdom and goodness of providence have ordered that the tendency of vicious actions to deprave the heart of the perpetrator, should diminish in proportion to the greatness of his temptations. Now, in addition to constitutional warmth and irresistible opportunity, the monk is impelled to incontinence by friendship, by compassion, by gratitude, by all that is amiable, and all that is estimable; yet in a few weeks after his first frailty, the man who had been described as possessing much general humanity, a keen and vigorous understanding with habits of the most exalted piety, degenerates into an uglier fiend than the gloomy imagination of Danté would have ventured to picture. Again, the monk is described as feeling and acting under the influence of an appetite which could not co-exist with his other emotions. The romance-writer possesses an unlimited power over situations; but he must scrupulously make his characters act in congruity with them. Let him work *physical* wonders only, and we will be content to *dream* with him for a while; but the first *moral* miracle which he attempts, he disgusts and awakens us. Thus our judgment remains unoffended, when, announced by thunders and earthquakes, the spirit appears to Ambrosio involved in blue fires that increase the cold of the cavern; and we acquiesce in the power of the silver myrtle which made gates and doors fly open at its touch, and charmed every eye into sleep. But when a mortal, fresh from the impression of that terrible appearance, and in the act of evincing for the first time the witching force of this myrtle is represented as being at the same moment agitated by so fleeting an appetite as that of lust, our own feelings convince us that this is not improbable, but impossible; not preternatural, but contrary to nature. The extent of the powers that may exist, we can never ascertain; and therefore we feel no great difficulty in yielding a temporary belief to any, the strangest, situation of *things*. But that situation once conceived, how beings like ourselves would feel and act in it, our own feelings sufficiently instruct us; and we instantly reject the clumsy fiction that does not harmonise with them. These are the two *principal* mistakes in judgment, which the author has fallen into; but we cannot wholly pass over the frequent incongruity of his style with his subjects. It is gaudy where it should have been severely simple; and too often the mind is offended by phrases the most trite and colloquial, when it demands and had expected a sterness and solemnity of diction.

A more grievous fault remains,—a fault for which no literary excellence can atone,—a fault which all other excellence does but aggravate, as adding subtlety to a poison by the elegance of its preparation. Mildness of censure would here be criminally misplaced, and silence would make us accomplices. Not without reluctance then, but in full conviction that we are performing a duty, we declare it to be our opinion, that *The Monk* is a romance, which if a parent saw in the hands of a son or daughter, he might reasonably turn pale. The temptations of Ambrosio are described with a libidinous minuteness, which, we sincerely hope, will receive its best and only adequate censure from the offended conscience of the author himself. The shameless harlotry of Matilda, and the trembling innocence of Antonia, are seized with equal avidity, as vehicles of the most voluptuous images; and though the tale is indeed a tale of horror, yet the most painful impression which the work left on our minds was that of great acquirements and splendid genius employed to furnish a *mormo* for children, a poison for youth, and a provocative for the debauchee. Tales of enchantments and witchcraft can never be *useful*: our author has contrived to make them *pernicious,* by blending, with an irreverent negligence, all that is most awfully true in religion with all that is most ridiculously absurd in superstition. He takes frequent occasion, indeed, to manifest his sovereign contempt for the latter, both in his own person, and (most incongruously) in that of his principal characters; and that his respect for the *former* is not excessive, we are forced to conclude from the treatment which its inspired writings receive from him. (pp. 194-97)

If it be possible that the author of these blasphemies is a Christian, should he not have reflected that the only passage in the scriptures [Ezekiel, Chap. xxiii], which could give a *shadow* of plausiblity to the *weakest* of these expressions, is represented as being spoken by the Almighty himself? But if he be an infidel, he has acted consistently enough with that character, in his endeavours first to inflame the fleshly appetites, and then to pour contempt on the only book which would be adequate to the task of recalming them. We believe it not absolutely impossible that a mind may be so deeply depraved by the habit of reading lewd and voluptuous tales, as to use even the Bible in conjuring up the spirit of uncleanness. The most innocent expressions might become the first link in the chain of association, when a man's soul had been so poisoned; and we believe it not absolutely impossible that he might extract pollution from the word of purity and, in a literal sense, *turn the grace of God into wantonness*.

We have been induced to pay particular attention to this work from the unusual success which it has experienced. It certainly possesses much real merit, in addition to its meretricious attractions. Nor must it be forgotten that the author is a man of rank and fortune.—Yes! the author of *The Monk* signs himself a Legislator!—We stare and tremble.

The poetry interspersed through the volumes is, in general, far above mediocrity. (p. 198)

> [*Samuel Taylor Coleridge*], *in a review of "The Monk: A Romance," in* The Critical Review, *n.s. Vol. XIX, February, 1797, pp. 194-200.*

THE EUROPEAN MAGAZINE, AND LONDON REVIEW (essay date 1797)

[*In the following excerpt from a largely negative appraisal of* The Monk, *the critic reserves praise for the verse interspersed throughout the novel.*]

[*The Monk: A Romance,* a] singular composition, which has neither *originality, morals,* nor *probability* to recommend it, has excited, and will still continue to excite, the curiosity of the public. Such is the irresistible energy of genius. (p. 111)

Neither *morals* nor *religion* will acknowledge themselves benefited by a work, whose great scope and purport it is to shew, that the fairest face and semblance of virtue is commonly a cloak to the most horrible crimes; and unless all the other sources of *improbability* and *wonder* must be considered as completely exhausted, it is difficult to assign a reason for the revival of the exploded mysteries of *sorcery,* and the *spirits of darkness.* If it was our Author's intention, which we would not willingly suppose, to attack religious orders, and, of course, religion itself, by exhibiting the extreme depravity of its most eminent disciples, he will, in the opinion of all sound judges, be considered not only as having failed of his intention, but as having paid an honourable tribute, the more valuable for being *undersigned,* to *ecclesiastical establishments.* The *Monk* yields not to the first, nor to the second efforts even of *bellish assailants;* he resists blandishments which no mortals unsupported could have been able to repel; and becomes at last the unhappy victim of lust from excess of gratitude and attachment. His progress afterwards into the abyss of crimes is rapid and inexcuseable; and in this part of his work, our author has shewn considerable skill and dexterity; but even here, to inflame the atrocity of his character, the culprit sometimes is made to commit gratuitous and improbable enormities.

The poetry interspersed through this work would have given popularity to a composition much inferior to this both in matter and in style. Where Mr. L. has attempted to imitate the manner of the ancient ballad, he is eminently successful; retaining all its simplicity and pathos, without the vulgarity or the incorrectness; and there are few modern elegies that surpass the *Exile* either in elegance or imagery. Indeed, the chief excellence of Mr. L.'s prose consists in this latter attribute of the *muse;* all the scenes on which any care has been bestowed exhibiting both the truth of nature and the animation of genius.

If the reader wishes to be instructed in the secret of raising up spirits from the *vasty deep,* various specimens of that *recondite lore* may be collected from this singular performance; and one by a veteran and experienced artist, no less a personage than the *Wandering Jew himself.* (p. 112)

> *R.R., in a review of "The Monk: A Romance," in* The European Magazine, and London Review, *Vol. XXXI, February, 1797, pp. 111-15.*

S. T. COLERIDGE   (letter date 1798)

[*In the following excerpt from a letter written to his close friend the English poet William Wordsworth, Coleridge details the defects and merits of* The Castle Spectre. *The defects, according to Coleridge, include awkward language, poor characterization, and an unrealistic rendering of emotion. However, he does praise Lewis's ability to create dramatic situations as well as his composition of ballads for the play. Although he calls it "a mere patchwork of plagiarisms," he concludes that* The Castle Spectre *does succeed as a piece for the stage. For additional commentary by Coleridge, see the excerpts dated 1797 and 1834.*]

I have just read the **"Castle Spectre,"** and shall bring it home with me. I will begin with its defects, in order that my "But" may have a charitable transition. 1. Language; 2. Character; 3. Passion; 4. Sentiment; 5. Conduct. (1.) Of styles, some are pleasing durably and on reflection, some only in transition, and some are not pleasing at all; and to this latter class belongs the **"Castle Spectre."** There are no felicities in the humorous passages; and in the serious ones it is Schiller Lewis-ized, that is, a flat, flabby, unimaginative bombast oddly sprinkled with colloquialisms. (2.) No character at all. The author in a postscript lays claim to *novelty* in *one* of his characters, that of Hassan. Now Hassan is a negro, who *had* a warm and benevolent heart; but having been kidnapped from his country and barbarously used by the Christians, becomes a misanthrope. This is all!! (3.) Passion—horror! agonizing pangs of conscience! Dreams full of hell, serpents, and skeletons; starts and attempted murders, etc., but positively, not *one* line that marks even a superficial knowledge of human feelings could I discover. (4.) Sentiments are moral and humorous. There is a book called the "Frisky Songster," at the end of which are two chapters: the first containing *frisky* toasts and sentiments, the second, "*Moral* Toasts," and from these chapters I suspect Mr. Lewis has stolen all his sentimentality, moral and humorous. A very fat friar, renowned for gluttony and lubricity, furnishes abundance of jokes (all of them abdominal *vel si quid infra*), jokes that would have stunk, had they been fresh, and alas! they have the very *saeva mephitis* of *antiquity* on them. *But* (5.) the Conduct of the Piece is, I think, *good;* except that the first act is *wholly* taken up with explanation and narration. This play proves how accurately you conjectured concerning *theatric* merit. The merit of the **"Castle Spectre"** consists wholly in its *situations.* These are all borrowed and all absolutely *pantomimical;* but they are admirably managed for stage

effect. There is not much bustle, but *situations* for ever. The whole plot, machinery, and incident are borrowed. The play is a mere patchwork of plagiarisms; but they are very well worked up, and for stage effect make an excellent *whole.* There is a pretty little ballad-song introduced, and Lewis, I think has great and peculiar excellence in these compositions. The simplicity and naturalness is his own, and not imitated; for it is made to subsist in congruity with a language perfectly modern, the language of his own times. . . . This, I think, a rare merit: at least, I find, *I* cannot attain this innocent nakedness, except by *assumption.* . . . This play struck me with utter hopelessness. It would [be easy] to produce these situations, but not in a play so [constructed] as to admit the permanent and closest beauties of style, passion, and character. To admit pantomimic tricks, the plot itself must be pantomimic. Harlequin cannot be had unaccompanied by the Fool. (pp. 236-38)

> *S. T. Coleridge, in a letter to William Wordsworth in January, 1798, in his* Letters of Samuel Taylor Coleridge, *Vol. I, edited by Ernest Hartley Coleridge, William Heinemann, 1895, pp. 234-38.**

THE BRITISH CRITIC   (essay date 1798)

[*The following excerpt is drawn from a negative assessment of* The Castle Spectre.]

Youth courts the praise of wit, and despises that of morality. The time will come when Mr. Lewis will wish to find some better distinction, than that of author of a work [**The Monk**], which degrades him in the mind of every man who has one genuine feeling of morality or religion. Nor will he seek, we conceive, to be distinguished even as the author of [**The Castle Spectre**]; which, with all its popularity, has no other merit than that of keeping up, for once, a kind of nonsensical curiosity about the grossest improbabilities, and amusing the eye with pantomimical display. The spectre, from which it is named, instead of being necessary, contributes not a tittle to the plot of the drama, and might be omitted without any change, except the show. Even her last appearance, when, from the danger of being too late, it is rendered truly ludicrous, is not more requisite than the first; as a dagger will kill without the aid of a ghost. It is unnecessary for us to give any specimens of a drama so well known, on and off the stage. The prologue is highly poetical. To the play the author has subjoined notes, which prove at least the respect he has for his own notions. (pp. 436-37)

> *A review of "The Castle Spectre: A Drama," in* The British Critic, *Vol. XI, April, 1798, pp. 436-37.*

THE ANALYTICAL REVIEW   (essay date 1798)

[*The following excerpt is from a negative review of* The Castle Spectre. *The critic maintains that it should "be thrown into the class of subordinate productions . . . for it's dearth of originality in it's incidents, characters, and sentiments;—for it's want, in short, of power to elevate or shake us."*]

When we reviewed Mr. L.'s former publication of the '**Monk**,' we gave it an ample share of our commendation. We thought, indeed, that some of it's [*sic*] passages betrayed rather too strongly the juvenility of it's author; and we could discover, from the variety of sources from which it's materials were drawn, that Mr. L.'s acquaintance with the fictions of romance and the legends of superstition was of a more than common extent: but with all it's imperfections, and without much nov-

An illustration from Tales of Wonder.

elty in it's incidents, the **'Monk'** struck us a production, which seemed to ascertain the existence of considerable powers in it's writer; and to prove him equal to the accomplishment of greater enterprizes. When [**'The Castle Spectre'**], therefore, was announced from his pen, our expectations were raised to welcome it; and we pleased ourselves with the hope of being gratified with something of a higher order than those dramatic vanities, which had of late years abused our patience, and dishonoured our theatres. . . . [We] assured ourselves, that he would present us, in his drama, with good poetry, interesting dialogue, strongly marked and well-sustained characters, affecting and striking situations;—with scenes, in short, which, if they could not satisfy our judgment with their regularity, would fasten on our attention, and agitate our feelings with their power. But the perusal of the piece in question, for we have not been present at it's representation, has evinced the fallacy of our preconceptions in it's favour, and has compelled us to acknowledge with concern, that our hopes in this instance, with the fate usually attached to human hopes, have terminated in severe and utter disappointment. (pp. 179-80)

On the subject of the language of this dramatic piece, we must regret that it is prose, and still more that it is that rigid and stilted prose, which seems as if it would be verse if it could; which, wanting the melody and elevation of numbers, wants also the ease and propriety of unmeasured diction, and which, hard and laboured as it may seem, can be written perhaps with more facility than it can be read. As the primary object of the drama is to please, and as it has been conceived that this object could not be fully attained without the aid of metrical language, the tragic muse has always borrowed it's beauty for the vehicle of her sentiments. On the grecian, the roman, the italian, the french, and, excepting in a few instances unworthy of notice, on the english stage, has she invariably addressed herself to the passions with the charm and energy of verse. Our blank verse, varied with dissyllable and trissyllable terminations, which is our proper and discriminated dramatic measure, has been found to be admirably adapted to the purposes of the theatre, as it reconciles, in as great a degree perhaps as the ancient iambic, the harmony and graces of poetry with the flow and familiarity of dialogue. The dramatist, therefore, who indolently foregoes this advantage or is unable to attain it, must be regarded as an object of our censure or our pity: assured that an example which indulges indolence, and covers incapacity, will readily be followed, we feel it as a duty to enter our strongest protest against this precedent of a tragedy in prose,—a precedent which, if established, would prove most fatally injurious to our serious drama, and would contribute to keep it on that low level where it is now found,—prostrate, and fallen from those sublime heights, which it once proudly occupied. (p. 190)

[**'The Castle Spectre'**] must, indeed, as we feel no hesitation to affirm, be thrown into the class of subordinate productions, not principally for the deficiencies of it's plan, which are neither few nor trivial, but for the general poverty of it's execution;—for it's dearth of originality in it's incidents, characters, and sentiments;—for it's want, in short, of power to elevate or shake us; to make us merry or to make us sad. . . . (pp. 190-91)

> *A review of "The Castle Spectre: A Drama in Five Acts," in* The Analytical Review, *Vol. XXVIII, No. II, August, 1798, pp. 179-91.*

THE BRITISH CRITIC   (essay date 1800)

[*In the following excerpt from a negative review of* Tales of Wonder, *the critic terms the work "trifling, puerile, and unfair."*]

We do but express the feelings of the reading world in general, when we say that we consider [*Tales of Wonder*] a very daring imposition on the public; nor can we forbear expressing our astonishment, that an individual in so distinguished a situation as a member of the British Parliament, should lend his name to so palpable and mean a trick. A guinea is charged for two thin volumes, which might, and which ought, to have been comprised in one; and not a third of the contents will be found to be original composition. The reader who has not seen the volumes, will be surprised when we inform him, that these *Tales of Wonder* are made up of . . . pieces which have been published and republished in a thousand different forms, and make a part of almost every selection. Among those which are professedly original, there are some tales which we think exceedingly stupid. . . . The best are those by Mr. Walter Scot [*sic*]. We do not think it necessary to give any specimen of this trifling, puerile, and unfair publication. . . .

> *A review of "Tales of Wonder," in* The British Critic, *Vol. XVI, December, 1800, p. 681.*

MARQUIS DE SADE   (essay date 1800)

[*The Marquis de Sade was a notorious French novelist of the late eighteenth century whose erotic and licentious writings lent his name to the concept of sadism. He is also considered by some critics to be a forerunner of Romanticism and a precursor of Freudian psychology. Unlike other authors of the Enlightenment, Sade rejected the concept that reason and rational behavior should be the goals of humankind and advocated complete anarchy. The essay from which the following excerpt was drawn originally appeared in French in 1800 as* Idée sur les romans. *Sade interprets* The Monk *as a product of the tumultuous political climate in Europe at the time of its composition.*]

[Perhaps] we ought to analyze . . . new novels in which sorcery and phantasmagoria constitute practically the entire merit: foremost among them I would place *The Monk,* which is superior in all respects to the strange flights of Mrs. Radcliffe's brilliant imagination. But that would take us too far afield. Let us concur that this kind of fiction, whatever one may think of it, is assuredly not without merit: 'twas the inevitable result of the revolutionary shocks which all of Europe has suffered. For anyone familiar with the full range of misfortunes wherewith evildoers can beset mankind, the novel became as difficult to write as monotonous to read. There was not a man alive who had not experiencd in the short span of four or five years more misfortunes than the most celebrated novelist could portray in a century. Thus, to compose works of interest, one had to call upon the aid of hell itself, and to find in the world of make-believe things wherewith one was fully familiar merely by delving into man's daily life in this age of iron. Ah! but how many disadvantages there are in this manner of writing! The author of *The Monk* has avoided them no more than has Mrs. Radcliffe. Here, there are perforce two possibilties: either one resorts increasingly to wizardry—in which case the reader's interest soon flags—or one maintains a veil of secrecy, which leads to a frightful lack of verisimilitude. Should this school of fiction produce a work excellent enough to attain its goal without foundering upon one or the other of these two reefs, then we, far from denigrating its methods, will be pleased to offer it as a model. (pp. 108-09)

> *Marquis de Sade, "Reflections on the Novel," in his* The Marquis de Sade: The 120 Days of Sodom and Other Writings, *edited and translated by Austryn Wainhouse and Richard Seaver, Grove Press, Inc., 1966, pp. 91-116.**

THE CRITICAL REVIEW   (essay date 1802)

[*The following excerpt is from a largely negative review of* Adelmorn the Outlaw.]

Had the author of [*Adelmorn the Outlaw*] been content to have framed a farce from his story of Adelmorn, he might without any trouble have made it interesting;—nay, with the proper exercise of that genius which he certainly possesses, and which we are always willing to allow him, he might have even worked it into a regular drama, demanding more praise than is due to a number of the pieces now in the routine of performance. But Mr. Lewis was not satisfied with success in the beaten track; he introduces, as is usual with himself, preternatural agents; what is worse, he introduces them uselessly too—and a useless ghost and vision have damned the Outlaw. In a preface of some merit our author appears to be almost convinced that this mode of writing is culpable. It would give us great pleasure to see him not only *almost,* but *altogether* satisfied of it. One of his conclusions in this preface is assuredly a strange one. 'I firmly believe it possible to write extremely ill, yet be a very worthy member of society; and shall not feel much mortified at being known to scribble bad plays, till convinced that a dull author can never be a benevolent man.' We will take the liberty to put this position into other words, and ask Mr. Lewis what he thinks of it. 'I firmly believe it possible to know nothing of drugs, yet be a very good attorney; and shall not feel much mortified at being known to poison half the neighbourhood, till convinced that a man unskilful as an apothecary can never be an eminent lawyer.' . . . We beg leave, however, to assure Mr. Lewis, that we by no means look on him as a dull writer. As a mistaken one we certainly regard him. But if he would attend half so much to classical study and chaste drama as he has unfortunately done to German absurdity, instead of a stupid fellow (as he words it) there is no doubt of his proving a very clever one. We shall be happy when he gives us occasion to speak of him as a *genuine* English dramatist. (pp. 231-32)

> *A review of "Adelmorn, the Outlaw: A Romantic Drama, in Three Acts," in* The Critical Review, *n.s. Vol. XXXIV, February, 1802, pp. 231-32.*

SIR WALTER SCOTT   (essay date 1802)

[*Scott was a Scottish novelist, poet, historian, biographer, and critic of the Romantic period who is best known for his historical novels, which were great popular successes. A close friend of Lewis, Scott contributed, with Robert Southey, to* Tales of Wonder. *The essay from which the following portion was excerpted originally appeared in 1802. Scott here expresses his respect and admiration for Lewis.*]

[*The Monk*] has now passed from recollection among the changes of literary taste; but many may remember as well as I do the effect produced by the beautiful ballad of *Durandarte,* which had the good fortune to be adapted to an air of great sweetness and pathos; by the ghost tale of *Alonzo and Imogine;* and by several other pieces of legendary poetry which addressed themselves in all the charms of novelty and of simplicity to a public who had for a long time been unused to any regale of the kind. In his poetry as well as his prose Mr Lewis had been a successful imitator of the Germans, both in his attachment to the ancient ballad and in the tone of superstition which they willingly mingle with it. New arrangements of the stanza and a varied construction of verses were also adopted, and welcomed as an addition of a new string to the British harp. In this respect the stanza in which *Alonzo the Brave* is written was greatly admired, and received as an improvement worthy of adoption into English poetry.

In short, Lewis's works were admired, and the author became famous not merely through his own merit, though that was of no mean quality, but because he had in some measure taken the public by surprise by using a style of composition which, like national melodies, is so congenial to the general taste that, though it palls by being much hackneyed, it has only to be for a short time forgotten in order to recover its original popularity. (pp. 553-54)

Sir Walter Scott, "Essay on Imitations of the Ancient Ballad," in his Minstrelsy of the Scottish Border, *edited by Thomas Henderson, Thomas Y. Crowell Company Publishers, 1931, pp. 535-62.**

THE CRITICAL REVIEW   (essay date 1805)

[*In the following excerpt, the critic praises* The Bravo of Venice *for its vivid language and intriguing plot. However, the critic also suggests that Lewis should select a more original subject for subsequent work.*]

The history of *The Bravo of Venice* is interesting, the language glows with animation, and the *denouement* is rapid and surprising. It would not be fair to enter into an analysis of the story, as the mysteries of the tale would thereby be developed, and the reader would be deprived of the pleasure which results from astonishment. (pp. 252-53)

The taste and sentiments of our riper years are frequently the result of early associations, which cannot be traced to their source; but in some remarkable instances, the origin of a particular bias has been accurately ascertained. Reynolds became fond of painting from an early perusal of Richardson's treatise on the art: the genius of Chatterton received its peculiar direction from his being taught to read in a *black letter* bible; and we verily believe that Mr. Lewis was initiated into learning by one of those histories of harlequin, where the *turn up* and *turn down* of every leaf introduces the hero in a new situation, and creates fresh matter for surprise and wonder. Perhaps the nursery of our author was ornamented with those pictures of the gentleman and the lady, where half of each figure is in full dress, while the other half of each is a naked skeleton; and this may account for his perpetual introduction of characters, which are creatures partly of this world and party of another.

Novels have commonly been divided into the pathetic, the sentimental, and the humourous; but the writers of the German school have introduced a new class, which may be called the *electric.* Every chapter contains a shock; and the reader not only stares, but starts, at the close of every paragraph; so that we cannot think the wit of a brother-critic far-fetched, when he compared that shelf in his library, on which the *Tales of Wonder,* the Venetian Bravo, and other similar productions were piled, to a galvanic battery.

Mr. Lewis possesses a fertile imagination and considerable genius: we would therefore advise him to quit the beaten track of imitation.... We have had enough of ghastly visages, crawling worms, death's heads and cross bones. (pp. 254-55)

A review of "The Bravo of Venice, a Romance," in The Critical Review, *n.s. Vol. V, No. III, July, 1805, pp. 252-56.*

THE CRITICAL REVIEW   (essay date 1807)

[*In the following excerpt, the critic faults the excessive violence in Lewis's* Feudal Tyrants; or, the Counts of Carlsheim and Sargans *and asserts that the novel "displays a most melancholy inferiority to his former compositions."*]

The Monk is in some respects considerably the best of the works of [Mr. Lewis]. It has more merit and less morality than any of his other productions, though it has faults enough even in a literary point of view. Mr. Lewis seems to have improved himself in his knowledge of shew and stage trick, but we cannot congratulate him or his admirers upon any other species of improvement. Sober reason is disgusted at the endless display of ghosts, murders, conflagrations, and crimes. They are the instruments with which children may be governed or frightened, and by which grown people are liable to be affected exactly in proportion as they resemble children. A poet has said that men are but children of a larger growth, an assertion which Mr. Lewis has adopted as an axiom. But as the learned, the able, the ingenious, and the distinguished among the human race for mental accomplishments are less like children than the ignorant, the foolish, and the pert, so that gentleman must expect the applause bestowed upon his terrific tales of devils and bad men to arise more from the latter than the former description of persons. But the praise of the mob is not without its attractions, and if the qualities which obtain it do not always shine in the eyes of posterity with the most distinguished lustre, they afford some compensation in the extraordinary though temporary baze with which they dazzle the sight of the present beholders. (pp. 273-74)

Of blood, vengeance, and misfortunes Mr. Lewis has indeed woven a formidable web [in *Feudal Tyrants, or the Counts of Carlsheim and Sargans*], but not a ghost flits along the corner of a ruined hall or draws the curtain at the dead of night to delight the old or to terrify the timid fair. We cannot account for this moderation: we even humbly venture to doubt of the prudence of the proceeding. To take ghosts and devils from Mr. Lewis's tales is to endanger their very existence. By such a subtraction we expose ourselves to the risk of bearing what the mathematicians call a negative quantity, something less than nothing, which may only remind us of the former existence of a substance to support the baseless fabric.

These four volumes are of a more miscellaneous nature than Mr. Lewis's former productions. We have a series of tales connected by nothing very obvious, introduced in a very improbable and unnatural manner, and agreeing only in repetitions of stories of the tyranny of German or Helvetian barons during times of feudal violence. Mr. Lewis's imagination has certainly been in a languishing way when it has been unable to invent a story more interesting and terrible than any of these. We confess our patience to have been frequently on the point of exhaustion during the perusal of these doleful ditties, and we are greatly at a loss to assign any plausible reason for the author ransacking the repositories of German literature to produce nothing better than this. It is the labour of the mountain, and *Monk Lewis* has produced his mouse neither larger nor finer than has issued from the pen of many a teeming maiden in the sanctuaries of the Minerva press. (p. 274)

If we examine the general merits of this production with a critical eye, we shall find that they cannot be classed very high. It was formerly the aim of novelists to catch the manners living as they rise, and to present us with a portraiture of human nature where we do not readily discern the resemblance to the original. The excellence of such performances was estimated by the degree of likeness, and the merit of the successful artist was justly regarded as high. But Mr. Lewis's efforts are not of this description. His overcharged and horrific pictures have no resemblance to the life, and for whatever we praise them, it cannot be for a correct imitation of nature.

Other authors have contented themselves with qualifications of less difficult attainment, though still of unquestionable merit. Pursuing in prose the tract of the ancient satirists, their aim has been to shoot folly as it flies, and to hold up vice and absurdity to ridicule when they could, but at all events to excite the merriment of their readers. Such writers have seldom been very happy or exceedingly careful in the delineation of character; but they have great merit in their way, and afford us the means of a most agreeable and innocent relaxation. With this class Mr. Lewis cannot be arranged: his stern gravity, engaged in the contemplation of murderous deeds, seldom condescends to relax itself into a smile.

Some novelists who have found their abilities inadequate to cope with either of these classes, who have neither possessed the rare art to delineate characters with exquisite justness, or to ridicule the weaknesses of men with happy humour, have had recourse to other means of attracting our attention; abandoning the pursuits of art, they have cultivated the simplicity of nature. They have considered the effect of the whole rather than that of part. By exciting our interest, our compassion, our sorrow, or our indignation by the recital of unmerited misfortunes, of cruel oppression, of tales of love and of friendship, they have justly merited our applause. Perhaps no department of novel writing is more pleasing than this, and hardly any has been cultivated with more success of late years. These simple pictures of unadorned events, when decorated with the charms of pathetic eloquence, possess irresistible attraction, and are preferred by many to all the correct painting of men and the most biting ridicule in the world. But Mr. Lewis has no claim to a place in this class. Simplicity is a term of which he knows not the value, and hardly understands the meaning. The crowing of a cock is not more dangerous to a ghost than is a ruined hall, a midnight journey through vaulted passages, or a spectre in chains to that amiable quality.

The German school of blood and murder has, we presume, arisen from the following circumstances. Many excellent writers in various languages had painted the more remarkable characters which appear on the stage of human life with a degree of force and brightness which might terrify ordinary imitators. These latter were aware that the public would turn with disgust from more feeble efforts, and judge of their merits by a scale

with which they feared to be measured. Exquisite ridicule is no less difficult of acquirement, and the success of a few had no less engendered a fastidious taste fatal to subordinate attempts. Simplicity, on the other hand, is perhaps more hard of attainment than either of the others, and there attends the attempts to reach it this inconvenience, that when unsuccessful they become utterly vapid and ludicrous. The author having divested himself of every cover, is exposed naked to the pelting of the storm. Instead of all these plans so beset with obstructions, it was natural enough to propose one, the source of which could never fail. When a writer began to get dull, he had only to set a house on fire, and scorch a few damsels out of bed and into the arms of knights heaven-sent to relieve them: a death's head is an infallible antidote to the sleep of a reader; and when these expedients threaten to grow stale, we have store left of daggers, bowls, murders and ghosts sufficient to terrify the weak imaginations of many of the students of novels. But the strongest stimuli at last lose their effect, and the stomach loaths the repeated dose. Mr. Lewis's general plan has our decided disapprobation. For his particular execution of it in the instances before us we have only to observe, that without being more rational than most performances of a similar description, it is considerably more tiresome than many of them, and displays a most melancholy inferiority to his former compositions. (pp. 277-78)

A review of "Feudal Tyrants; or, The Counts of Carlsheim and Sargans," in The Critical Review, *n.s. Vol. XI, No. III, July, 1807, pp. 273-78.*

WILLIAM HAZLITT   (essay date 1819)

[*Hazlitt was one of the most important English critics and journalists of the Romantic age. The essay from which the following excerpt was drawn originally appeared in 1819 and reflects Hazlitt's admiration for Lewis's prose and verse. Hazlitt here also refers to Tobias Smollett's novel* The Adventures of Ferdinand Count Fathom.]

After Mrs. Radcliffe, Monk Lewis was the greatest master of the art of freezing the blood. The robber-scene in the *Monk* is only inferior to that in Count Fathom, and perfectly new in the circumstances and cast of the characters. Some of his descriptions are chargeable with unpardonable grossness, but the pieces of poetry interspersed in this far-famed novel, such as the *Fight of Ronscevalles* and the *Exile,* in particular, have a romantic and delightful harmony, such as might be chaunted by the moonlight pilgrim, or might lull the dreaming mariner on summer-seas. (p. 127)

William Hazlitt, "On the English Novelists," in his Lectures on the English Comic Writers with Miscellaneous Essays, *E. P. Dutton & Co., 1910, pp. 106-32.*

LORD BYRON   (journal date 1821)

[*Byron was an English poet and dramatist who is now considered one of the most important poets of the nineteenth century. Because of the satiric nature of much of his work, Byron is difficult to place within the Romantic movement. His most notable contribution to Romanticism is the Byronic hero: a melancholy man, often with a dark past, who eschews societal and religious strictures and seeks truth and happiness in an apparently meaningless universe. A friend of Lewis's, he respected Lewis's writing a great deal. However, in the following excerpt from his journal, written after Lewis's death, Byron comments on Lewis's personal weaknesses.*]

Lewis was a good man, a clever man, but a bore, a damned bore, one may say. My only revenge or consolation used to be, setting him by the ears with some vivacious person who hated Bores, especially Me. de Stael, or Hobhouse, for example. But I liked Lewis: he was a Jewel of a Man had he been better set. I don't mean *personally,* but less *tiresome; for* he was tedious, as well as contradictory, to every thing and every body.

Being short-sighted, when we used to ride out together near the Brenta in the twilight in Summer, he made me go *before* to pilot him. I am absent at times, especially towards evening; and the consequence of this pilotage was some narrow escapes to the Monk on horseback. Once I led him *into* a ditch, over which I had passed as usual forgetting to warn my convoy. Once I led him nearly into the river, instead of *on the moveable* bridge which *in*commodes passengers: and twice did we both run against the diligence, which, being heavy and slow, did communicate less damage than it received in its leaders, who were *terrassé'*d by the charge. Thrice did I lose him in the gray of the Gloaming, and was obliged to bring to his distant signals of distance and distress. All the time he went on talking without intermission, for he was a man of many words.

Poor fellow, he died, a martyr to his new riches, of a second visit to Jamaica—

> "I'll give the lands of Deloraine
> Dark Musgrave were alive again!"
> [From Scott's *Lay of the Last Minstrel*]

that is

I would give many a Sugar Cane
Monk Lewis were alive again!

> *Lord Byron, in a journal entry of October 15, 1821, in his* The Works of Lord Byron: Letters and Journals, Vol. V, *edited by Rowland E. Prothero, John Murray, 1901, p. 418.*

[JOHN GIBSON LOCKHART]   (essay date 1834)

[*Although Lockhart wrote several novels, his fame rests on his biography of Sir Walter Scott and his critical contributions to* Blackwood's Edinburgh Magazine *and the* Quarterly Review. *From 1817 to 1825, he was a principal contributor to* Blackwood's, *a Tory periodical that was founded to counter the influential Whig journal, the* Edinburgh Review. *His trenchant wit contributed to the early success of the magazine and earned him the nickname of "The Scorpion." He is regarded as a versatile, if somewhat severe, critic whose opinions of his contemporaries, though lacking depth, are generally considered accurate when not distorted by political animosities. In the following excerpt, Lockhart offers a positive assessment of Lewis's* Journal of a West Indian Proprietor. *He also discusses the long poem entitled "The Isle of Devils" that was included in the* Journal. *Lockhart concludes that Lewis possessed "a slender command either of imagery or of passion" and that his prose is better than his poetry.*]

[*Journal of a West India Proprietor*] is in many respects, indeed, a curiosity: it is a posthumous production of the author of *The Monk,* and we are inclined to say, the best of all the creatures of his pen. Why it has been kept lying *perdu,* during the fifteen years that have elapsed since Mr. Lewis's death, we are not told; but sure we are, the delay has been extremely injurious not only to the reputation of the author, but to what is (or was)

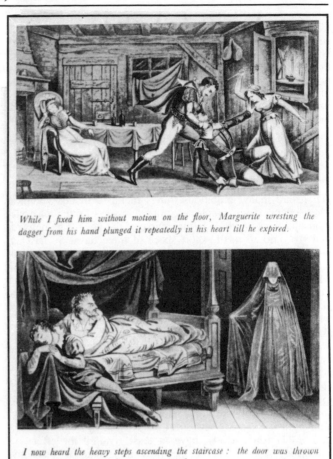

While I fixed him without motion on the floor, Marguerite wresting the dagger from his hand plunged it repeatedly in his heart till he expired.

I now heard the heavy steps ascending the staircase : the door was thrown open and again the bleeding nun stood before me.

Two illustrations from the 1826 edition of The Monk.

of much higher consequence, the cause of the body he belonged to—the West India proprietors. Had this book been published in 1818, or 1819, it might have turned many an enemy of the colonists into a friend. Now . . . it comes too late to be of any use in that point of view; but it does not come too late to vindicate the talents of Mr. Lewis from the oblivious disparagement into which, from various circumstances, . . . they had been allowed to fall. (p. 374)

[These] *Journals,* of themselves, would take good care of the author's reputation, as to many of the most important parts of a human character. In them the kindly, gentle, warmly-benevolent disposition of the man is manifest everywhere; together with a shrewd common sense and sagacity, which few might have looked for in one so devoted to the veriest 'cloudland' of imagination—and, moreover, not a little of that practical *tact* in the details of business, for which the evening life of a London diner-out would, in general, be considerd as poor a preparation as the morning reveries of a Germanized romancer. As to the literary merits of the posthumous book, we have already expressed our high notion of them—and, indeed, on that point, there can, we think, be little differencc of opinion. The graphic power displayed, whether in sketching scenery, manners, or incidents, appears to us not only high but first-rate. . . . The quiet humour, and the plain sterling English of these pages, are equally delightful.

The narrative of the Monk's first voyage to the West Indies is in itself a charming performance. Familiar as we are with

Captain Hall's 'Fragments,' . . . it is easy even for us to detect some inaccuracies in his use of sea-terms; but this is a trifle. Nay, perhaps, perfect accuracy would have rather diminished than improved the pleasure of the reader. His very blunders help to keep before us the idea of a fondled little dandy-lion of forty, fresh from his own luxurious chambers in the Albany,—the brilliant talk of Melbourne-House dinners,—and the sarcastic tittle-tattle of Lydia White's *soirées*. (pp. 377-78)

The *Journal* is every now and then enlivened with a snatch of rhyme—and not a few of the little pieces thus introduced will, we are sure, be made prize of forthwith by the musical composers. (p. 380)

[There are many] ambitious things included in this volume. There occurs, for example, a complete poem of more than one thousand lines—written in the course of the voyage homeward in 1816, and all in the short space of three days. So hasty a production may be expected to show abundance of errors and inaccuracies; yet **'The Isle of Devils'** appears to us, on the whole, the best poem, of any considerable length, that Mr. Lewis ever wrote. And what is his *best*? Why, certainly, in poetry, not very much:—pretty conceits airily tricked out in what are called songs; in his more elaborate efforts melodious, skilfully-varied versification, and here and there a line of such happy ease in construction, that it is sure to linger on the ear; but a slender command either of imagery or of passion. As a poet, Lewis is to a Byron what a scene-painter is to a Hobbima. He produces a startling grotesque of outline, and some grand massy contrasts of light and shade; but he has no notion of working in detail—no atmosphere, no middle-tints to satisfy a daylight spectator. The subject of **'The Isle of Devils'** would, in Lord Byron's hands, have at least rivalled the effect of 'Manfred;' from Lewis it comes only in the shape of a sketchy extravaganza, in which no feeling is seriously grappled with, and a score of magnificent situations are, to all intents and purposes, except that of filling the ear with a succession of delicious sounds, thrown away. The truth is, that . . . it was only in his very first flights that he ever was able to maintain a really enthusiastic elevation—and he did so more successfully in the prose of *The Monk* than in the best of his early verses. That vein was a thin one, and soon worked out. Had he lived, in all likelihood, he would have turned in earnest to prose composition; and we think no reader of his *West India Journals* can doubt that, if he had undertaken a novel of manners in mature age, he would have cast immeasurably into the shade even the happiest efforts of his boyish romance. (pp. 398-99)

> [*John Gibson Lockhart*], *in a review of "Journal of a West India Proprietor," in* The Quarterly Review, *Vol. L, No. C, January, 1834, pp. 374-99.*

SAMUEL TAYLOR COLERIDGE   (conversation date 1834)

[*The following excerpt is from a conversation dated March 20, 1834 that was published in Coleridge's* Table Talk. *Coleridge here praises Lewis's* Journal of a West Indian Proprietor *as "by far his best work."*]

Lewis's **"Jamaica Journal"** is delightful; it is almost the only unaffected book of travels or touring I have read of late years. You have the man himself, and not an inconsiderble man,—certainly a much finer mind than I supposed before from the perusal of his romances, &c. It is by far his best work, and will live and be popular. Those verses on the Hours are very pretty; but the **"Isle of Devils"** is, like his romances,—a fever dream—horrible, without point or terror. (p. 280)

> *Samuel Taylor Coleridge, "Lord Byron and H. Walpole's 'Mysterious Mother', Lewis's 'Jamaica Journal'," in his* The Table Talk and Omniana of Samuel Taylor Coleridge, *edited by T. Ashe, G. Bell and Sons, Ltd., 1923, pp. 279-80.*

ANTHONY TROLLOPE   (essay date 1869)

[*A major Victorian novelist, Trollope is best known for his "Barsetshire Chronicles," a series of novels that realistically and humorously depicts English provincial life. Trollope wrote the following disparaging comments on* The Monk *in his copy of the novel in 1869.*]

[*The Monk*] is so bad, that nothing ever could have been worse:—and yet the book had a great success! There is no feeling of poetry in it. Everything is pretended, made up, and cold. We are obliged to suppose that its charm consisted in its indecency,—which in itself would not have been much; but is enhanced by being the indecency of a monk.

> *Anthony Trollope, "Notes and Queries: Trollope on 'The Monk'," in* Nineteenth-Century Fiction, *Vol. IV, No. 2, September, 1949, p. 167.*

LAFCADIO HEARN   (lecture date 1899)

[*Considered one of America's leading impressionistic critics of the late nineteenth century, Hearn produced a large body of work that testifies to his love of the exotic and the beautiful. His sketches, short stories, and novellas demonstrate a vision of evil and the supernatural reminiscent of Edgar Allan Poe and Charles Baudelaire. In addition, Hearn's writings about Japan sparked international interest in that nation's cultural life. His lectures on American and European literature are exceptional for their divergence from the conventions of Victorian criticism. Because Hearn made no written record of these presentations, his lectures were reconstructed from students' notes. His comments on Lewis were delivered in a lecture at the University of Tokyo in 1899. In the following excerpt, Hearn briefly assesses Lewis as a figure of historical rather than literary interest.*]

As for Lewis's own work there was really very little of merit to be found in it. His prose works were stories and dramas about madness, ghosts, grave-yards, and monstrous crimes—including incest—the whole of these fancies being so mixed together as to give the reader a combination of lust and murder, horror and pity, after the style of Webster and Ford in the old English drama, but much more atrocious, and much less artistic. It was a curious fact that this man who probably never did an ignoble or a cruel thing in his life should have written the most abominable stories written in the 19th century. His poetry was not much better than his prose, either as to tone or workmanship. But both prose and poetry supplied the English public with the certain coarse pleasure of a very novel kind. To-day we can only laugh at what seemed to Lewis very horrible; and it is good proof that the English mind has made a good deal of progress within the last fifty or sixty years. Skulls and bones and blood and lustful monsters do not frighten anybody to-day; they simply disgust. But when I was a boy people still were learning the horrible poems of Lewis by heart, and declaiming them upon certain occasions. I remember particularly the popularity of the famous ballad **"Alonzo the Brave and the Fair Imogene."** What a primitive conception of ghosts people must have had who could be pleased with such verses as these!—I cite the closing stanza:—

While they drink out of skulls newly torn from the
  grave,
Dancing round them the spectres are seen;
Their liquor is blood, and this horrible stave
They howl: 'To the health of Alonzo the Brave,
  And his consort, the fair Imogene!'

Our notions of the supernatural have quite changed since the days of Lewis. It was not his literary but his personal influence rather that makes him a noble figure. (pp. 79-80)

> *Lafcadio Hearn, " 'Monk Lewis', and the School of
> Horror and Mystery," in his* Some Strange English
> Literary Figures of the Eighteenth and Nineteenth
> Centuries, *edited by R. Tanabé, 1927. Reprint by
> Books for Libraries, Inc., 1965, pp. 74-89.*

EDITH BIRKHEAD (essay date 1921)

[*Birkhead's* The Tale of Terror, *from which the following excerpt is drawn, is considered one of the first significant studies of the Gothic movement. Here, Birkhead discusses the melodramatic elements of Lewis's writings.*]

To pass from the work of Mrs. Radcliffe to that of Matthew Gregory Lewis is to leave "the novel of suspense," which depends for part of its effect on the human instinct of curiosity, for "the novel of terror," which works almost entirely on the even stronger and more primitive instinct of fear. Those who find Mrs. Radcliffe's unruffled pace leisurely beyond endurance, or who dislike her coldly reasonable methods of accounting for what is only apparently supernatural, or who sometimes feel stifled by the oppressive air of gentility that broods over her romantic world, will find ample reparation in the melodramatic pages of "Monk" Lewis. Here, indeed, may those who will and dare sup full with horrors. Lewis, in reckless abandonment, throws to the winds all restraint, both moral and artistic, that had bound his predecessor. The incidents, which follow one another in kaleidoscopic variety, are like the disjointed phases of a delirium or nightmare, from which there is no escape. We are conscious that his story is unreal or even ludicrous, yet Lewis has a certain dogged power of driving us unrelentingly through it, regardless of our own will. Literary historians have tended to over-emphasise the connection between Mrs. Radcliffe and Lewis. Their purposes and achievement are so different that it is hardly accurate to speak of them as belonging to the same school. It is true that in one of his letters Lewis asserts that he was induced to go on with his romance, *The Monk,* by reading *The Mysteries of Udolpho,* "one of the most interesting books that has (sic) ever been written," and that he was struck by the resemblance of his own character to that of Montoni; but his literary debt to Mrs. Radcliffe is comparatively insignficant. His depredations on German literature are much more serious and extensive. Lewis, indeed, . . . seizes his booty where he will in a high-handed and somewhat unscrupulous fashion, but for many of Mrs. Radcliffe's treasures he could find no use. Her picturesque backgrounds, her ingenious explanations of the uncanny, her uneventful interludes and long deferred but happy endings were outside his province. The moments in her novels which Lewis admired and strove to emulate were those during which the reader with quickened pulse breathlessly awaits some startling development. Of these moments, there are, it must be frankly owned, few in Mrs. Radcliffe's novels. Lewis's mistake lay in trying to induce a more rapid palpitation, and to prolong it almost uninterruptedly throughout his novel. By attempting a physical and mental impossibility he courts disaster. Mrs. Rad-

cliffe's skeletons are decently concealed in the family cupboard, Lewis's stalk abroad in shameless publicity. In Mrs. Radcliffe's stories, the shadow fades and disappears just when we think we are close upon the substance; for, after we have long been groping in the twilight of fearful imaginings, she suddenly jerks back the shutter to admit the clear light of reason. In Lewis's wonder-world there are no elusive shadows; he hurls us without preparation or initiation into a daylight orgy of horrors. (pp. 63-4)

The Monk, despite its cleverness, is essentially immature, yet it is not a childish work. It is much less youthful, for instance, than Shelley's *Zastrozzi* and *St. Irvyne.* The inflamed imagination, the violent exaggeration of emotion and of character, the jeering cynicism and lack of tolerance, the incoherent formlessness, are all indications of adolescence. In ***The Monk*** there are two distinct stories, loosely related. The story of Raymond and Agnes, into which the legends of the bleeding nun and Wandering Jew are woven with considerable skill, was published more than once as a detached and separate work. It is concerned with the fate of two unhappy lovers, who are parted by the tyranny of their parents and of the church, and who endure manifold agonies. The physical torture of Agnes is described in revolting detail, for Lewis has no scruple in carrying the ugly far beyond the limits within which it is artistic. The happy ending of their harrowing story is incredible. By making Ambrosio, on the verge of his hideous crimes, harshly condemn Agnes for a sin of the same nature as that which he is about to commit, Lewis forges a link between the two stories. But the connection is superficial, and the novel suffers through the distraction of our interest. In the story of Ambrosio, Antonia plays no part in her own downfall. She is as helpless as a plaster statue demolished by an earthquake. The figure of Matilda has more vitality, though Lewis changes his mind about her character during the course of the book, and fails to make her early history consistent with the ending of his story. She is certainly not in league with the devil, when, in a passionate soliloquy, she cries to Ambrosio, whom she believes to be asleep: "The time will come when you will be convinced that my passion is pure and disinterested. Then you will pity me and feel the whole weight of my sorrows." But when the devil appears, he declares to Ambrosio: "I saw that you were virtuous from vanity, not principle, and I seized the fit moment for your seduction. I observed your blind idolatry of the Madonna's picture. I bade a subordinate but crafty spirit assume a similar form, and you eagerly yielded to the blandishments of Matilda." The discrepancy is obvious, but this blemish is immaterial, for the whole story is unnatural. The deterioration in Ambrosio's character—though Lewis uses all his energy in striving to make it appear probable by discussing the effect of environment—is too swift.

Lewis is at his best when he lets his youthful, high spirits have full play. His boyish exaggeration makes Leonella, Antonia's aunt, seem like a pantomime character, who has inadvertently stepped into a melodrama, but the caricature is amusing by its very crudity. She writes in red ink to express "the blushes of her cheek," when she sends a message of encouragement to the Conde d'Ossori. This and other puerile jests are more tolerable than Lewis's attempts to depict passion or describe character. Bold, flaunting splashes of colour, strongly marked, passionate faces, exaggerated gestures start from every page, and his style is as extravagant as his imagery. Sometimes he uses a short, staccato sentence to enforce his point, but more often we are engulfed in a swirling welter of words. He delights in the declamatory language of the stage, and all his characters speak as if they were behind the footlights, shouting to the gallery. (pp. 66-8)

He revelled in the horrific school of melodrama. He delighted in the kind of German romance parodied by Meredith in *Farina*, where Aunt Lisbeth tells Margarita of spectres, smelling of murder and the charnel-breath of midnight, who "uttered noises that wintered the blood and revealed sights that stiffened hair three feet long; ay, and kept it stiff." (p. 70)

In **Blanche and Osbright, or Mistrust** . . . , Lewis depicts an even more revolting portrait than that of Abellino in his bravo's disguise. He adds detail after detail without considering the final effect on the eye: "Every muscle in his gigantic form seemed convulsed by some horrible sensation; the deepest gloom darkened every feature; the wind from the unclosed window agitated his raven locks, and every hair appeared to writhe itself. His eyeballs glared, his teeth chattered, his lips trembled; and yet a smile of satisfied vengeance played horribly around them. His complexion seemed suddenly to be changed to the dark tincture of an African; the expression of his countenance was dreadful, was diabolical. Magdalena, as she gazed upon his face, thought that she gazed upon a demon." Here, to quote the Lady Hysterica Belamour, we have surely the "horrid, horrible, horridest horror." But in **Königsmark the Robber, or The Terror of Bohemia** . . . , Lewis's caste includes an enormous yellow-eyed spider, a wolf who changes into a peasant and disappears amid a cloud of sulphur, and a ghost who sheds three ominous drops of boiling blood. (p. 71)

Edith Birkhead, "The Novel of Terror: Lewis and Maturin," in her The Tale of Terror: A Study of the Gothic Romance, E. P. Dutton & Company Publishers, 1921, pp. 63-93.*

H. P. LOVECRAFT (essay date 1927)

[*Lovecraft is considered one of the foremost modern authors of supernatural horror fiction. As is evident from his own fiction, Lovecraft was well versed in the history of Gothic writing, and his* Supernatural Horror in Literature *(1927), from which the following excerpt is drawn, is one of the earliest and most comprehensive studies of this genre. Here, Lovecraft maintains that* The Monk *played an important role in the development of the Gothic novel, but contends that it is, nonetheless, "too long and too diffuse."*]

Horror in literature attains a new malignity in the work of Matthew Gregory Lewis. . . . This young author, educated in Germany and saturated with a body of wild Teuton lore unknown to Mrs. Radcliffe, turned to terror in forms more violent than his gentle predecessor had ever dared to think of; and produced as a result [*The Monk*,] a masterpiece of active nightmare whose general Gothic cast is spiced with added stores of ghoulishness. . . . The novel contains some appalling descriptions such as the incantation in the vaults beneath the convent cemetery, the burning of the convent, and the final end of the wretched abbot. In the sub-plot where the Marquis de las Cisternas meets the spectre of his erring ancestress, The Bleeding Nun, there are many enormously potent strokes; notably the visit of the animated corpse to the Marquis's bedside, and the cabbalistic ritual whereby the Wandering Jew helps him to fathom and banish his dead tormentor. Nevertheless *The Monk* drags sadly when read as a whole. It is too long and too diffuse, and much of its potency is marred by flippancy and by an awkwardly excessive reaction against those canons of decorum which Lewis at first despised as prudish. One great thing may

be said of the author; that he never ruined his ghostly visions with a natural explanation. He succeeded in breaking up the Radcliffian tradition and expanding the field of the Gothic novel. (pp. 359-60)

H. P. Lovecraft, "Supernatural Horror in Literature," in his Dagon and Other Macabre Tales, edited by August Derleth, Arkham House Publishers, Inc., 1965, pp. 347-413.*

EINO RAILO (essay date 1927)

[*In his* The Haunted Castle, *from which the following excerpt is drawn, Railo analyzes the various elements of English Romanticism found in Gothic literature. Here, Railo discusses the settings Lewis uses in his writings, such as haunted houses, dungeons, and graves, and examines how Lewis creates an effective atmosphere of terror.*]

[In Lewis's picture of the haunted castle,] we find a kind of general setting of terror, created partly by an expansion of different features of the haunted castle, partly by the additions and alterations necessitated in this stage by new themes of terror. Disintegration is apparent already in **The Monk**.

In the above-ground portion of its stage-setting—a monastery in Madrid—where the action takes place mostly in the daytime, a comparison with the haunted castle already familiar to us reveals nothing new; we are compelled, indeed, to admit that the clarity and matter-of-factness of Lewis's realistically-inclined descriptions cause it to lose in romantic atmosphere when compared with the work of his predecessors. In contrast, the Castle of Lindenberg which appears in the book is a faithful rendering of the haunted castle. "The night was calm and beautiful; the moonbeams fell upon the ancient towers of the castle, and shed upon their summits a silver light. All was still around me; nothing was to be heard except the night-breeze sighing among the leaves, the distant barking of village dogs, or the owl who had established herself in a nook of the deserted eastern turret. I heard her melancholy shriek, and looked upwards; she sat upon the ridge of a window, which I recognized to be that of the haunted room." Lindenberg Castle has its own bell that proclaims midnight and the hour of ghosts; it has creaking, heavy doors and shutters, narrow passages and big, moss-grown gates. Seen in the moonlight it is both "awful" and "picturesque": "Its ponderous walls, tinged by the moon with solemn brightness; its old and partly ruined towers, lifting themselves into the clouds, and seeming to frown on the plains around them; its lofty battlements, overgrown with ivy, and folding gates, expanding in honour of the visionary inhabitant; made me sensible of a sad and reverential horror." In his description of Lindenberg Castle, Lewis is clearly influenced by impressions gathered from Mrs. Radcliffe.

This traditional type of haunted castle survives unaltered in **The Castle Spectre,** the setting of which, Conway Castle in Wales, reveals all the characteristic features of the type. It has a haunted tower, a great hall with its own ghost, a chapel and gloomy subterranean dungeons. In this play Lewis brought the haunted castle on to the stage, and similar castles form the setting of most of his plays, such as **Adelmorn** and **Alfonso**. They appear also in his ballads, in **Alonzo the Brave** and in several of the **Tales of Wonder,** now powerfully, now vaguely delineated. In his ballad **The Stranger,** for example, we note the "deep-sounding bell," "the slow monks moving through the cloister's thick gloom," the "deep-vaulted tomb," the "moon-silvered battlements frowning over the glade"; in **The

Wanderer of the Wold "the crackling old staircase of Ethelbert's tower," "the castle dismantled by time," "the bells that chime from the abbey," "the old castle falling to decay," "his father's old castle with dark ivy spread," "the owl's screeching note," "the ivy spreading wide over a huge heap of stones," etc. In *The House upon the Heath,* . . . the following effective features are given:

> Fast by the moor a lonely mansion stood;
> Cheerless it stood! a melancholy shade
> Its mouldering front, and rifted walls arrayed;
> Barred were the gates, the shattered casements closed,
> And brooding horror on its site reposed;
> No tree o'erhung the uncultivated ground,
> No trace of labour, nor of life around.
>
> (pp. 136-37)

As for the other settings created by Lewis, I regard them as being so far related to the picture of the haunted castle that their origin must be sought within its precincts. The haunted castle has two actual sources of terror at command—its supernatural element and its dungeons. Finding himself unable to endow the above-ground portion of his monastery with the necessary romantic half-light, in conformance with the cabbalistic nature of certain of his themes Lewis dived into its subterranean storeys, where all the horrors of funeral vaults and secret dungeons were at his beck. In exploiting these he appears as a ruthless and undeterred exponent of terror-romantic realism, rioting in horrors to an extent hardly to be found elsewhere than in some of Shakespeare's most pungent scenes and, later, in Maturin's work. This side of his literary talent brought from Byron the epithet of "Apollo's sexton." The following is a brief expositon of Lewis's charnel-house material [taken from *The Monk:*]

> The subterranean portion of his monastery possesses vast and dark vaults, illumined only by a ceaselessly-flickering grave-lamp, whose faint, wan rays reveal the mighty pillars which bear up the roof, but are unable to combat the deep gloom in which the vaulted arches are hidden. Growing gradually accustomed to the darkness, the eye sees nothing but the most repulsive objects; skulls, bones, graves and effigies of saints that seem to stare in horror and amaze. Still deeper lie the hidden dungeons of the monastery, the entrance to the passage leading to these being cunningly concealed. Fettered in one of these secret cells, cut off from light and human society, their only support the consolation provided by religion, the hapless captives of the monastery linger through the final chapter of their existence. No one hears their voices, no friendly word comes in reply to their speech, only a deep, unbroken silence wraps them round. In their vicinity there may be a human head which worms are devouring and which can be recognized as the head of some lately dead monk or nun.
>
> Terrible is the fate of the fallen nun sentenced to such imprisonment. The air is raw and moist, the walls green with mould and the wretched straw pallet lonely and inhospitable. She is bound to the wall by fetters and horrid reptiles of every kind that swarm around terrify her until her brain can no longer stand the strain. A repul-

sively-swollen and slimy toad clambers across her breast, a cold and agile lizard darts over her head, entangling itself in her hair, and on awakening she will find, coiled round her fingers like rings, the same long worms which feast on the rotting corpse of her child.

(pp. 137-38)

In such descriptions of places and objects intended to evoke horror and disgust, it would be difficult to find the equal of this pitiless and tastelessly detailed realism. It was something totally different from the innocent attempts at horrors, the bygone murders and skeletons discovered in fetters, of Lewis's predecessors, something new and strange in English romanticism. (p. 139)

This atmosphere of dungeons and graves expands in Lewis's later work, notably in his ballads, into a general romanticism of the graveyard, into a kind of dance of death in spectral moonlight. Typical of this side of his work is the ballad *Grim, King of the Ghosts; or, the Dance of Death,* styled by its writer "a churchyard tale," which has as motto a line from *Othello*— "On horror's head, horrors accumulate." The dignitary referred to in the title takes the grave-digger's daughter to his "charnel-house palace," where a ball and rout of skeletons takes place; in depicting the subsequent horrors, piled up to the verge of caricature, Lewis displays the power of his realism. Chiefly in his ballads, German and original, Lewis gradually withdraws farther and farther from the confines of the actual haunted castle, taking for his settings the snows of Lapland, the madhouse, the rivers and mountains of Scotland, and romantic enchanted forests, renewing in the last the romantic settings of Percy's and Herder's ballads.

The part played by nature in Lewis's settings is neither as extensive nor as finely-calculated as in Mrs. Radcliffe's works, but though nature as seen by Lewis contributes little to the general development of this side of romanticism, it is yet worth reviewing briefly. His scanty descriptions of landscape are derived from Mrs. Radcliffe, a fact evident in the passage wherein he depicts the site of Ambrosio's death: "The disorder of his imagination was increased by the wildness of the surrounding scenery—by the gloomy caverns and steep rocks, rising above each other, and dividing the passing clouds; solitary clusters of trees, scattered here and there, among whose thick-twined branches the wind of night sighed hoarsely and mournfully; the shrill cry of mountain eagles, who had built their nests among these lonely deserts; the stunning roar of torrents, as swelled by late rains they rushed violently down tremendous precipices, and the dark waters of a silent sluggish stream, which faintly reflected the moonbeams, and bathed the rock's base on which Ambrosio stood. The abbot cast round him a look of terror." This is pure Radcliffe, fortified by a deeper gloom. As the quotation concerning Lindenberg Castle revealed, Lewis makes use of moonlight, the night-wind and the owl; add to these thunder, lightning and storm, and the inventory of his arsenal of natural effects is complete. (pp. 139-40)

Of the furnishings of the haunted castle, the one that seems to have taken Lewis's fancy most is the clock, which . . . has its own romantic task. "Scarcely had the abbey-bell tolled for five minutes, and already was the church of the Capuchins thronged with auditors," is the opening sentence of his romance, in which the clock regularly ushers in the hour of ghosts. It appears in nearly every one of his ballads, usually to proclaim the advent of the dark hour of midnight. "For whom tolls the

A depiction of the temptation of Ambrosio from The Monk.

deep-sounding bell, why move the slow monks through the cloisters' thick gloom?'' (pp. 140-41)

> Eino Railo, *''Later Developments of the Picture of the Haunted Castle,''* in his The Haunted Castle: A Study of the Elements of English Romanticism, E. P. Dutton & Co., 1927, pp. 135-72.*

BERTRAND EVANS (essay date 1947)

[*An important Shakespearean critic, Evans argues that Lewis was the most significant and influential figure in Gothic drama. Briefly considering each of his plays as prototypes of that genre, Evans concludes that Lewis's plays ''represent better than any others a composite of the traditional, native materials and the foreign and new ones.''*]

The name of Matthew Gregory Lewis is perhaps the most important in the history of Gothic drama. Lewis wrote many plays which exploited the familiar paraphernalia, added new tricks to the art of terrifying, and reached a wide audience over a period of many years. He reached maturity precisely in time to inherit the combined properties of English and German subliterary materials, and to use the so-called new melodrama introduced from France. Better than any other, he represents the juncture of the native and foreign streams. Further, his influence on Byron and Shelley was more immediate than that of any other confirmed Gothicist, and that fact contributes much to his significance. . . .

[*The Castle Spectre*] is one of the most remarkable Gothic plays. In it Lewis exploited the combined materials of his predecessors and contemporaries, English and German, and out-Gothicized them all. [It provides] the best evidence of the state of Gothic drama after almost thirty years of development. . . . (p. 132)

The manner of Lewis is . . . generally distinguished from that of Walpole, Mrs. Radcliffe, and Maturin, the other principal figures in Gothic literature, all of whom seem to become absorbed in their own painting of unrelieved gloom and terror; it is always obvious that Lewis relished his profession and his reputation as terrifier. (p. 138)

From the early nineteenth century to the present, the play has passed as a notorious specimen of German drama. Undeniably there is as much reason to call it German as there is so to describe any other Gothic play. But let us examine the facts to see just how strong this reason is.

The main character types—villain, hero, heroine, and unknown—, the atmosphere, the techniques, the motifs, the settings, and the machinery, when viewed against a background of Gothic tradition, blend with that background and are indistinguishable from it. . . . [This] tradition was well established in England before any subliterary materials were borrowed from Germany. Furthermore, English sources are indicated in the facts that Lewis began work on the prose romance which later became *The Castle Spectre* after reading *Otranto* and before he visited Germany, and that he resumed work on his subject after reading *Udolpho*. The influences of Walpole and Mrs. Radcliffe predominate in the completed play.

This is not to say that there are no German elements in it. There are several, but they are limited to a single passage. . . . (p. 144)

[Lewis' other] plays illustrate at once the continuation of the familiar Gothic trappings which had accumulated since Walpole, and the introduction of new excesses which tended to obscure the Gothic origins. Castles, convents, and caverns, agonized tyrants and persecuted maidens, sliding panels and underground passages, midnight bells and supernatural manifestations, and the past event—all these abound, along with an admixture of new elements which, whether they emanated from Lewis' own mind or from German tales, were brought firmly into line with the traditional Gothic purpose. . . .

Adelmorn, an amazing collection of claptrap, shows as well as any play upon what evil days drama had fallen. It is nevertheless important in the history of Gothic drama and in the history of English literature. It is a link—and a particularly valuable one—between the crude and monstrous elements of the Gothic school and the finer romantic ones, for example, of Shelley's *Prometheus Unbound* and Byron's *Manfred*. It is the kind of vital link that studies in the Gothic novel have failed to reveal. (p. 146)

In this play, as in *The Castle Spectre*, Lewis contrived to exhibit virtually the whole contents of the Gothic treasury. The usual castle, convent, and cavern settings abound, and there are dungeons with grated windows, winding staircases, galleries, vaults, underground passages, bells, forests by moonlight, sliding panels, and violent scenes of nature in thunder, lightning, and rain. But these seem overshadowed by the spectacular arrangements for the three appearances of the ghost.

The first "real" manifestation of the supernatural occurs when Adelmorn, chained in a gloomy dungeon to await execution, falls asleep. Whether or not what follows is to represent a dream the author leaves unexplained. The dungeon, with its grated windows, chains, and flickering light, might have been a sufficient source of terror for any earlier playwright, but not for Lewis. As Adelmorn sleeps, there is a "Chorus of Invisible Spirits," and then [an] elaborate and amazing spectacle is pictured. . . . The scene is crude and creaking, lurid with blood, daggers, and a red moon; yet we have not found a Gothic spectacle quite like it before. The very process of transmutation is exposed in its blending of Gothic monstrosities and the ethereal machinery of high romanticism. It shows that groping beyond and above the baser materials of castles, convents, and caverns by which dramatists, not novelists, opened the way to Byron and Shelley. The walls that here draw apart to disclose a blasted heath and a red moon needed but to be changed to clouds that would roll back to show Alpine or Earth spirits, or other creations of a higher poetic conception than Lewis' two "daemons" who pinion the arms of Ulric. Surely, to knock the rough edges off this Gothic spectacle was to discover the "romantic" scenes of *Manfred* and even the sublimer ones of *Prometheus Unbound*. Nothing so mysterious as a sea change was required to complete the transformation. Needed were a refining by more delicate hands than those of the vulgar Lewis, a shaping by a more subtle chisel, and a raising by a rarer poetic spirit.

This scene from *Adelmorn* was an inevitable result of the process of accumulation which had begun a generation earlier around a nucleus of a medieval ruin. We have seen the paraphernalia grow outward from the castle ruin to the convent and the cavern; from the cavern to forests and "romantic rocks"; from these to moonlight and precipices: eventually the stretching for materials was certain to touch and finally to embrace the metaphysical world, where the possibilities for exploitation of demons and airy spirits were unlimited. The Gothic urge, requiring ever greater applications of ever more potent kind, compelled an expansion beyond the ordinary properties and forces of earth. We have seen the original tyrant, a gross object of terror equipped with personal physical authority, grow in stature and in power; as a member of the Secret Tribunal or the Inquisition, he became more formidable than he had been; as a magician, and then as one who could call up devils, he was to become mightier still. Thus, through extension into another world, both the machinery and the protagonist of crude dramatists mounted toward such a creation as *Manfred*.

The evolution of the hero in this play is as significant as that of the machinery. Adelmorn is composed in part of qualities which had earlier characterized the villain. He is therefore more impressive than the hero had been in any earlier Gothic play.

Because he believes himself the assassin of his uncle, Adelmorn endures a villain's agony of remorse. His conscience is stung by the scorpions that had earlier tormented villains alone. It is the hero, for the first time, whose sense of guilt causes him to hear the supernatural voice of the murdered man and to endure an unearthly vision. . . . For the first time, a Gothic hero was attractive. Adelmorn escapes the insipidness of his forbears by assuming a villain's pain.

The Wood Daemon further illustrates Lewis' tendency to expand the Gothic paraphernalia to include properties of another world. (pp. 147-50)

In the cast, besides the wood demon, are other supernatural or preternatural creatures: wood spirits, a giant, zephyrs, and fu-

ries. No such figures had ever before appeared in a Gothic play. But in the hands of so confirmed a Gothicist as Lewis, they served to expand, not to erase or even to distort, the conventional pattern. The basic purpose to arouse mystery, gloom, and terror remained just as it was in Walpole, Jephson, Boaden, and the rest. The settings, too, emphatically assert the heritage and denote the essential kind of play that *The Wood Daemon* is: "A Gothic Hall, with large painted window"; "A marble staircase winding up towards two doors above"; "A Cavern, with a burning lamp. In the background is a grated door, with steps; above is a gallery, etc." Various elements of the elaborate machinery can be set in motion. There is a bed, for instance, which sinks through the floor when a secret spring is touched; by leaping on this bed and touching the spring, Hardyknute carries Leolyn to the cavern. (pp. 151-52)

Thus settings and machinery are predominantly traditional, but certain magic properties have been added. Similarly, Hardyknute is essentially a Gothic villain, whose stature as an object of terror has been heightened through his acquisition of magic powers. Like earlier tyrants, he stalks through the castle and the dungeons, one moment sunk in gloom, the next exhilarated by a sudden thought of evil. . . . [To] the conventional Gothic machinery, settings, character types, and theme of persecution, Lewis grafted a good deal that may perhaps be described best as necromancy. His villain retains the usual marks, but has acquired new powers: he carries an enchanted key and waves a magic wand; Una is under his magic spell. The Gothic settings are familiar, but they are moved by a new machinery of enchantment. The castle is typically Gothic, but zephyrs and wood spirits—creatures of quite another world than that which had originally surrounded the medieval ruin—fly about it. Perhaps, in concluding, a single striking incident will serve to characterize the entire mixing of familiar and alien materials: on this occasion, the wood demon flies through an open Gothic window in "a car, surrounded by four dragons." (pp. 152-54)

The "tragedy" of *Alfonso,* unquestionably the best play Lewis wrote, is the least Gothic. Devoid of the claptrap of *Adelmorn* and *The Castle Spectre,* it has a restraint rare in Lewis. In blank verse, it is his only dignified play. (p. 154)

Venoni and *Raymond and Agnes* represent a continuation of Gothic tradition with less intrusion of foreign material than we have found in Lewis's other plays. *The Harper's Daughter,* an adaptation of Schiller's *Kabale und Liebe,* is a story of violent sentimentalism rather than violent terror, and is one of the less Gothic plays by Lewis. Gothic elements are included, but it is they which appear out of place, and obviously they entered the non-Gothic subject only because the author was so steeped in Gothic dye that he could not handle other materials without staining them. *Rugantino* is a version of a popular German and French tale of "Abällino," a figure who started a vogue which compared with that of Karl Moor.

Adelgitha is for one particular reason . . . a remarkable specimen of Gothic tragedy at the turn of the century. . . . Lewis named Gibbon as the source, and the preface to the printed edition makes clear how much history meant to Gothicists whose chief aim was to dispense thrills. . . . Gothic dramatists, unlike Shakespeare, did not merely alter history to fit dramatic need: they designed a plot and a set of characters and then sought a place in history for them. In *Adelgitha* are materials which in earlier plays are to be found associated indiscriminately with Italy, Greece, France, Spain, Germany, and England, and with times ranging from the eighth to the eighteenth century. (pp. 155-56)

The epilogue to *Adelgitha* critically surveys the theatrical fare and the taste of the times, and sheds light on the widening gap between literary and acting plays:

> When all is full around—above—below,
> And eager crowds sit jammed in every row,
> Ask for what cause they crowd and push and stew.
> For Shakespeare? Otway? no! the play is *new*!

> • • • • •

> But oh! too oft does Otway's lute complain
> And Shakespeare wave his magic wand in vain.
> While Young or Congreve, Sheridan or Rowe
> Scarce at one house attract a decent show.

> Too oft some *novelty,* all glaze and pother,
> With gaping gazers deluges the other.
> Too oft does Romeo feel his deepest woes
> Spring not from Juliet's death—but vacant rows.

> • • • • •

> Yet why blame novelty? Where ere mine eyes
> I turn, fresh tokens of her powers arise!
> 'Tis her command make Lydia Languish stop
> Daily her sky-blue coach at Hookham's shop.
> Some strange hob-goblin story meets her view,
> She's seized with rapture! why? the book is *new*!
> In vain Cecilia's leaves their charms unfold.
> "Cecilia"—lisps the nymph—"That book is *old*!
> The characters are drawn from life, 'tis said.
> Give me a work which draws them from the dead!"
> So cramm'd with mysteries that the more it has on't,
> The less the reader makes, or tails or heads on't.
> With ghosts, and tapers, and robbers so alarming,
> One's *terrified to death*—and then that's *charming*!

This account of a dismal chapter in the history of English taste by the foremost purveyor of theatrical monstrosities and "new" claptrap perhaps explains the success of such a play as *Timour the Tartar,* one of Lewis' most excessive spectacles. . . . Perhaps it was *Timour* which initiated a series of animal plays. Horses soon appeared in other plays, and not only horses, but dogs and magpies. Magpies assumed roles of greater consequence than had customarily been given heroes in Gothic plays.

The craze for novelty tolerated no limitation of excesses, and in these excesses the conventional Gothic elements, somewhat "old" and relatively dignified, were often overwhelmed. . . . In the early nineteenth century, lightning struck castles and caverns, demolishing everything except hero and heroine. The pursuit of the novel often led to spectacles which bore no apparent relation to the Gothic quest for objects of mystery, gloom, and terror, though actually it had been that quest which started the exploitation of objects and events ever farther afield from the conventional castles, convents, and caverns. It grew "old" to blow up a castle: A burning forest, a rampaging flood, or a falling bridge provided the "new" sensation. Searching for the spectacular, some playwrights themselves forgot the Gothic Revival which had long ago given the impulse toward this very search. (pp. 157-59)

Lewis's claim to a place of first importance in the history of the Gothic novel is contested by Walpole, Mrs. Radcliffe, and Maturin. His preëminence in Gothic drama is almost uncontested. The number of Gothic plays from his pen equals that of any other playwright, and his novel was adapted several times. His influence upon his contemporaries and successors,

both greater and lesser than himself, perhaps exceeded even that of Mrs. Radcliffe. Furthermore, he stood between the two centuries and was most instrumental in passing the Gothic collection over to the romantics. His plays represent better than any others a composite of the traditional, native materials and the foreign and new ones. (p. 160)

> Bertrand Evans, *"Lewis and Gothic Drama,"* in his Gothic Drama from Walpole to Shelley, *University of California Press, 1947, pp. 132-61.*

JOHN BERRYMAN   (essay date 1952)

[*Berryman is one of the most important, and certainly one of the most widely read, modern American poets. His own work developed from objective, classically controlled poetry into an esoteric, eclectic, and highly emotional type of literature. In the following excerpt from his introduction to* The Monk, *Berryman is critical of the Gothic novel as a whole and maintains that* The Monk *deserves to be considered outside the Gothic genre because of its insightful characterization and poetic elements.*]

The Monk is one of the authentic prodigies of English fiction, a book in spite of various crudenesses so good that even after a century and a half it is possible to consider it unhistorically; and yet it has never quite become a standard novel. Several reasons for this must be its intermittent unavailability, its reputation for eroticism, its not being reinforced by excellence in Lewis's other imaginative work, so that it has had to stand alone. But the chief reason must be that it has long suffered from a prejudice against the 'Gothic' novel in general, which I am anxious not to combat except as it affects our experience of *The Monk.* Deservedly forgotten—all but two or three exemplars—save by enthusiasts and specialists, this grotesque school helped usher in the English Romantic movement and debauched taste without ever really participating in the glories of the movement unless in the book before us. Here we might take refuge in the notion that *The Monk* is only incidentally a Gothic novel, and owes its excellence to other qualities; that it is good in spite of being to some extent a Gothic novel. But I don't think this is true. *The Monk* seems to me exactly a Gothic novel, in a sense to be elucidated. What I propose is to consider the book critically, without making any allowances whatever for it. . . . But though nothing could recommend itself less obviously to current critical taste than Lewis's masterpiece, it is clear that in certain respects we are better placed with regard to it than his contemporaries were. (pp. 11-12)

Somehow *The Monk* ought not to have been good at all. Its author was a witty diplomat aged nineteen, its locale the Spain of the Inquisition and romantic Germany, its mode the Gothic mode that had been originated, unpromisingly, by Horace Walpole's *The Castle of Otranto* thirty years before and appeared to have just reached its highest development in Mrs. Radcliffe's *The Mysteries of Udolpho.* This lachrymose, spineless, more or less insufferable romance Lewis much admired and aspired to imitate. Well, we read at once of 'hurry and expedition,' and to the end of his novel a 'loud and audible' youthful diffuseness will recur. The author's immediate, artless, extensive revelations of precedent action do not promise much by way of address. The aunt who fancies herself admired is tiresome. Even Ambrosio does not begin well. We probably resent the secret of his character's having been delivered up to us at once in the initial epigraph given by Lewis, which is about Angelo's apparent character in *Measure for Measure.* In Chapter Two, when we come on him alone, the note of spiritual pride is struck so emphatically that his hypocrisy seems almost laughable. Shakespeare at least—we say to ourselves—had the instinct to make his paradigm a truly virtuous man up to a point. Now our conception of what Lewis is up to is quite wrong, in the event, and this second chapter, occupied with the Monk and 'Rosario' up to his fall, gradually becomes impressive. But the two long chapters that follow, devoted to Raymond's adventures with the robbers and his and Agnes' story, though they are very well, are perhaps less impressive; and so with the fifth, which resumes the Lorenzo-Antonia story and conducts Raymond and Agnes to her 'burial.' I have scarcely ever read an excellent novel which for so long fails to declare its quality. Up to the sixth chapter, or halfway through the book, it is charming and interesting in varying degrees, eminently readable, but hardly remarkable. Then it becomes, with great suddenness, passionate and astonishing.

Ambrosio has been so long neglected that one has almost forgotten him, in the Bleeding Nun and other events. Now he emerges dead-centre again, and upon his direct satiation with Matilda we realize that we are not dealing with Shakespearian pastiche at all; the development is a novelist's, it has more in common with one strain in *Anna Karenina*. An inexperienced author has been learning as he proceeded. The ambitious, complex pages that follow, generalizing Ambrosio's character as it has issued from his powers and weakness in the governing monastic environment, are a product of genius. They cite Angelo again, but it was solely Angelo's temptation and fall that interested Shakespeare, who besides had other fates at heart in that strange comedy. Lewis is interested in the *progress* of Ambrosio. His enlargement takes over Antonia from Lorenzo, the Raymond-Agnes story dwindles to her miseries under the nuns (as these counterpoint the monkish corruption of Ambrosio's progress), and henceforward he dominates the book. Matilda too is an engrossing character, and the alterations of the two in Chapter Six might be studied with advantage by a modern chronicler of passion. But Ambrosio is the point; the point is to conduct a remarkable man utterly to damnation. It is surprising, after all, how *long* it takes—how *difficult* it is—to be certain of damnation. This was Lewis's main insight, fully embodied in his narrative, and I confess that such a work as Thomas Mann's *Doctor Faustus* seems to me frivolous by comparison. (pp. 12-13)

Discriminating thus its principal intellectual and spiritual substance, it must be acknowledged that we hardly have behind us the authority of Coleridge. Coleridge thought *The Monk* an 'offspring of no common genius' and allowed it to possess 'much real merit' [see excerpt dated 1797]; the tale of the Bleeding Nun was 'truly terrific'; but the book contained 'abominations.' It violated equally nature and morality. One of his objections, concerning Ambrosio's pursuit of Antonia, is too curious to be neglected. It is 'contrary to nature,' the great critic asserts, for a mortal, fresh from his impression of the Devil's presence and employing for the first time the witching myrtle, to be 'at the same moment agitated by so fleeting an appetite as that of lust.' I am less confident about this than Coleridge; but the question being not altogether a literary one, the reader must seek his own counsel. It seems to me that it is just in the presentment of the Monk's flickering affections and lusts that Lewis is most steadily natural. Very striking is the turn of motive that he first *loves* Antonia. Coleridge himself found the character of Matilda, in whom the same problems occur, 'exquisitely imagined, and as exquisitely supported.' (p. 14)

[On] the whole, especially with Ambrosio, [Lewis] contrives with the strange to deepen interest while maintaining the nat-

ural. Since the passions are his motor subject, it is necessary that they should be realistic; this 'impassioned realism' is what distinguishes radically *The Monk* . . . from Mrs. Radcliffe's work, even from *The Italian*, which shows his influence; and so his book was bound to give offence. (p. 16)

[*The Monk*'s] supernatural elements are more likely to trouble the reader now; not, I think, very likely. They are strongly done, for one thing. But the book is poetic, for another. I allude not only to the far from contemptible poems irregularly introduced, though these help to determine its character. I mean the general colouring of its inspiration. Lewis mistook and misrepresented, for example, the procedure of the Spanish Inquisition, but he pursues Ambrosio to the wall and behind the wall to the next wall and beyond that to the abyss. At the same time, he is as alive to the inconstancy of human purpose as he is to its obsessive character, and some of his highest effects are simple indeed, as when the monk, eager to damn himself by reading a certain passage in the Bible backward—the Inquisition's officers are at his cell-door—can't find the page. (pp. 16-17)

Lewis's work, good and bad, exerted a considerable influence over the writing of several countries during the first half of the century. Even his verse has a monument in that graveyard, literary history. (p. 26)

[It] is clear that Lewis's real importance in the extraordinary pageant of the novel in English is symbolic. He helped to recover poetry—I say recover, because the Elizabethan novel was poetic. The school in which he laboured deserved Miss Austen's ridicule, but Lewis did not. Most of our critical admiration (just now) is devoted to her line, the prose line, but there is another line, and Lewis reopened it. Perhaps, in a more concrete way too, he helped the century to two of its greatest masterpieces in the other line. Of Emily Bronte's reading not much is known, but Mrs. Gaskell gives us one glimpse of her making bread in the kitchen with a German book open before her standing against the edge of the kneading trough, and it is almost certain that she knew Hoffmann, who had learned from Lewis and whose "Die Majorat" her plot resembles. And it was his reading of *Wuthering Heights* that exploded Hawthorne's spirit for *The Scarlet Letter*. Little enough of the criminal monk survives in the Rev. Arthur Dimmesdale, but something though, and in his hypocritical physician (oddly) more. To have played a part in the long, strange process that made possible these works is Lewis's honourable final claim.

What essentially distinguishes these greater novels from *The Monk*—wherein their immense superiority consists—is a nice question. Decidedly, it is not style. Emily Bronte and Hawthorne wrote better than Lewis did. . . . [If] you have not read *Wuthering Heights* lately (but that would be a pity), what you remember as the book is only the first half of the book, and even so Mr. Lockwood is a notorious bore. As for Hawthorne's echolalic allegorizing, no sensible reader has ever pretended that there is not much too much of it. Lewis's uncertainty and unevenness do not register his place. The difference is one of weight, size, drive of conception. We really cannot say much about what deeply matters in stories, novels. They had stronger minds than Lewis, tougher hearts, a superior intuition of necessity—the 'dark necessity' invoked by Chillingworth when he refuses to pardon. Lewis had this intuition too, but in a form less terrifying and affecting; but then he had it. (pp. 27-8)

John Berryman, in an introduction to The Monk *by Matthew G. Lewis, edited by Louis F. Peck, Grove Press, 1952, pp. 11-28.*

A portrait of Lewis.

LOWRY NELSON, JR.   (essay date 1962)

[*Nelson discusses Ambrosio as a prototype of the Gothic hero and concludes that he "is close to becoming a true villain-hero."*]

In narrow summary *The Monk* might seem trite: the saintliest man in Madrid revealed as the grossest sinner. It could superficially be dismissed as a Protestant's cautionary tale of Roman Catholic hypocrisy. Though the charges of triteness and naïveté cannot wholly be avoided, there are good reasons for seeing the book as an importantly symptomatic novel. The monk Ambrosio is not a monster of vice to begin with. By his own ambition and the adulation of the faithful, he is elevated to an impossible pinnacle of perfection. When the devil's temptations surround him he finds himself drawn into contradictory behavior: since he falls short of his ideal he must be damned; since he is led into debauchery he must be unredeemable; since he has sinned he must continue to be wicked to insure his damnation. His downfall is the handsome little novice who devotedly follows him about the monastery and soon reveals that he is really the lovestricken Matilda. By arousing Ambrosio's pity and thereby his senses, she seduces him and he becomes a slave to passion. (pp. 239-40)

The final paragraph is the local masterpiece of gothic novel writing. In it are described the terrible six days of suffering Ambrosio underwent before he died and the rain-swollen river carried away his corpse. In an obverse way it is quite as violent and yet rhetorically finished as Pushkin's poem "The Prophet," which it strangely resembles. Somehow it manages to be more than a final condemnation of monasticism. For once we encounter in the gothic novel a seemingly preposterous character whose motivation is carefully, if awkwardly, delineated. To

create successfully such a violently self-contradictory character was perhaps impossible in Lewis's day. That he half-succeeded would seem to portend the later success of Dostoevsky. Ambrosio is not simply evil masquerading as good; he is not the stock hypocrite. In one sense it would be proper to characterize him as an instance of what may happen when normal impulses are unnaturally thwarted. In another, historically more important, sense, it would be proper to see in him a heightened model of the universal good-bad conflict in human nature. By implication, whoever is capable of great good is also capable of great evil. The archetype, of course, would be Lucifer himself. In ordinary people good and evil seem to dilute each other with their small quantities. In unusual people, either extreme continuously dominates the other or the two violently alternate in ascendancy. Such would be the superficial view, and the psychology of *The Monk* often stays on the surface. It is surprising, though, how close Ambrosio's outward struggles can come to a presentation of the subconscious drama of the mind. Not that *The Monk* is significantly pre-Freud or that Freud is significantly post-Lewis. But it is important to note that *The Monk,* with other novels of the school, presented under the license of sensationalism significant and basic traits of human nature that elsewhere, in "polite" fiction, went unexpressed. Lewis takes his characterization of Ambrosio seriously enough not to intrude a pat moral at the end. He leaves us with the impression that it may be once again possible to create a character like Edmund or like Claudius or like Macbeth.

Though he minimizes it, Lewis does not dispense with the supernatural claptrap of the gothic mode: there is the fortune-teller's prophecy, the magic mirror in which the lusting Ambrosio is made to see Antonia undressing, and the actual appearance of Lucifer and Matilda, the devil's handmaiden. (pp. 242-43)

With *The Monk* . . . we find that the claptrap has begun to take on symbolic resonance. Ambrosio's descent into the tombs is a descent into evil. His rape of Antonia in those surroundings prompts him to say, "This sepulchre seems to me Love's bower," thus reviving the old mythic and Shakespearean theme of the sepulchral marriage bed. (p. 248)

The gothic hero easily shades into what is commonly called the romantic hero; or, perhaps to put it better, both are members of the same genus. Both share an essential loneliness and feeling of incommunicability; both are generally scapegoats or guilt-haunted wanderers. Without attempting a perhaps futile contrast between the two, we may provisionally confine ourselves to describing the gothic cousin. Characteristically he harbors a nameless guilt. He is haunted by an acute feeling of the discrepancy between good and evil. Indeed, both qualities are present in him in heightened form. He possesses some extraordinary virtue (scientific genius, strength, sanctity) which is transformed somehow into an extraordinary vice. Finally, he is in touch with nether forces, originally demonic but later inside the mind. . . . Lewis, though he makes his survivors happy at the end of his novel, rejected the simplist notion that virtue is always rewarded or, indeed, that anyone has a monopoly of virtue. Ambrosio is close to becoming a true villain-hero. (p. 249)

> Lowry Nelson, Jr., "Night Thoughts on the Gothic Novel," in The Yale Review, Vol. LII, No. 2, December, 1962, pp. 236-57.*

HARRISON R. STEEVES   (essay date 1965)

[*Steeves briefly assesses* The Monk *and maintains that Lewis attempted "to raise sexual violence to the level of tragic significance" in the novel.*]

What Lewis attempted to do in *The Monk,* and with no small success, was to raise sexual violence to the level of tragic significance. Yet the story is tainted with juvenility; for Lewis was not yet twenty when he wrote it, although it is supposed to have undergone substantial revision before it was published.

The monk Ambrosio's story is a fall from seeming spiritual strength and grace to Satanic evil and final damnation, and the cause of his fall is his vainglorious confidence in his spiritual invulnerability—a modern case of the Greek tragic *"hubris."* The vehicle of his fall is a sexuality latent under fanatic monasticism, which is brought forward at the very opening of the story in his cruel exposure of a girl who has for a moment strayed from virtue with the young man to whom she regards herself as betrothed. She has entered a nunnery as an act of expiation, only to find after she has taken the veil that she is to bear a child. The future of this erring nun and her lover moves along intermittently with the story of the monk himself. These episodes include in turn a digression on her lover's personal history, which in itself contains an all but completely irrelevant piece, the legend of a bleeding nun who haunts a castle far from the essential scene of the story. The romance is therefore involved and interrupted, and scarcely begins to show interest until it is nearly a third completed. (pp. 265-66)

The Monk is by no stretch of the term great literature. It fell within that period of little more than a decade when many readers could lend a willing ear to poppycock. Lewis's management of his medium was equal to the demands of his situations and his characters; that is all. Apart from his central theme of the apostate monk, which was not unfamiliar, he taps traditional sources for other matters of legend. The wandering Jew, the haunted castle, the demon lover, the wayside inn as a cover for a shambles, all have a part in the continuity of *The Monk.* Yet stale themes are blended into something effective in its own way.

There is no need to deride the extravagance of the story. If one is to introduce the Devil in person, he need not, like Mrs. Radcliffe, set up compromises with reality, or, like Walpole, apologize for the effects he has been at the pains to create. Today the story calls for a well-disposed reader, free from twentieth-century inhibitions, and not worried by blatant irrationality. If there are such readers left, then Lewis's bold tale may appeal to them. (pp. 270-71)

> Harrison R. Steeves, *"The Gothic Romance,"* in his Before Jane Austen: The Shaping of the English Novel in the Eighteenth Century, *Holt, Rinehart and Winston, 1965, pp. 243-71.**

RICHARD HARTER FOGLE   (essay date 1972)

[*Fogle interprets Ambrosio as an "Aristotelian tragic hero" and contends that, like Oedipus, Ambrosio is unaware of his identity and is subsequently an unwitting participant in patricide and incest. Further, he argues that* The Monk *is, in the tradition of Aristotle's dramas, a tragic tale of doomed passion. In addition, Fogle discusses Samuel Taylor Coleridge's comments on* The Monk *(see excerpt dated 1797), disputing Coleridge's contention that the plot is well constructed and effective. Fogle maintains, instead, that the novel is too complicated and its actions too far-fetched. While Fogle finds much to admire in* The Monk, *including Lewis's use of supernatural and Gothic elements, he concludes that Lewis "has given himself and his readers too much to keep up with."*]

[I am concerned here] primarily with Coleridge's praises of *The Monk,* and above all with his admiration of its plot structure. Critics have almost invariably been struck with Lewis's conception of his chief character Ambrosio, but have been less impressed by the novel as a whole. Coleridge is in fact too generous to the "underplot"; this is an amiable foible, however, and also most suggestive. Both the Ambrosio story and the underplot are conducted with care and skill, and as Coleridge says the two are very nicely connected. Nevertheless, there is simply too much of the latter; it is an intrigue-plot, ingenious rather than imaginative, a masterly job of carpentry by a master joiner.

Ambrosio himself can fairly be considered an Aristotelian tragic hero. (Inevitably, I am more interested in finding resemblances than differences, although I shall try to preserve due discriminations.) In the first place, he is like Oedipus a foundling, a circumstance that involves eventually the plot elements of reversal and recognition. His is the tragedy of a family or "house," which Aristotle says is the best kind because of its potentiality for interesting complications. Ambrosio's ignorance of his identity leads him, like Oedipus, unwittingly into incest and parricide. One has to add here the element of Elizabethan villainy and positive evil: Ambrosio knows perfectly well that he is committing murder and rape, although he is unaware that the victims, Elvira and Antonia, are his mother and sister. Lewis arranges his plot with great care, from the first mention of the circumstances in Leonella's story . . . to the fiend's ultimate revelation at the end. . . . (p. 37)

Ambrosio is a man of outstanding talents, and as abbot and preacher a leader in his society of Catholic Madrid, as is the Reverend Mr. Dimmesdale in the theocracy of Puritan Salem. As Coleridge mentions, he is generally called the Man of Holiness. . . . Apparently the ideal representative of his society, Ambrosio is of course too good to be true. His humility is false, and his disastrous fault is pride. Yet he is at the beginning truly unaware of his own defects. He genuinely aspires to goodness, and is thus a true tragic character. (pp. 37-8)

The "thought" or message of *The Monk* is sincere and sustained, though not particularly impressive. It is simply that repression of the natural man is wrong, and the anti-Catholicism, anti-monasticism, and hereditary hatred and fear of Spanish institutions that Lewis could expect of his English audience would make this message easy to swallow, like an artfully sweetened pill. "Superstition" and repression are objects of attack throughout the novel. Yet deeper, however, is the agency and the tragedy of the passions, principally sexual, by which all action in *The Monk* is motivated, and from which all misfortune arises. (p. 39)

[Passion in *The Monk*] has something of the dignity of fate, an element not to be repressed or avoided. And in the conduct of Ambrosio's downfall the movement of his passions is realized with great artfulness and symmetry. Despite the large problem that Lewis gives himself of conveying significant emphasis in a book where all is emphatic, the relentless downward course of Ambrosio has life, development, and progression. Each episode is consistent with his "thought" about Ambrosio . . . but with enough flexibility to maintain the interest. The monk is always offered a moral choice, he always hesitates, then chooses wrong—and we always sympathize and understand his erring. At worst, Lewis is an amazingly successful *advocatus Diaboli.* John Berryman complains that he tells us too much at the beginning: "We probably resent the secret of his character's having been delivered up to us at once in the initial epigraph given by Lewis, which is about Angelo's apparent character in *Measure for Measure*. In Chapter Two, when we come upon him [Ambrosio] alone, the note of spiritual pride is struck so emphatically that his hypocrisy seems almost laughable'' [see excerpt dated 1952]. The objection has force, and in any event it occurs in an appreciative and profitable discussion of Lewis's skill as a novelist. It is, however, unrealistic, as regards the possibility of any writer of fiction of the English eighteenth or nineteenth century, including Richardson, Fielding, Smollett, Scott, Dickens, Thackeray, George Eliot, and Trollope, either achieving or in any way desiring the twentieth-century art of gradual revelation of character. Their forte was to establish it firmly. Ambrosio is thus from the beginning boldly outlined, though the outline is not the complete picture.

His characteristic movement is inevitably downward, but rather oscillating than rigidly linear. Thus he finally yields to Matilda's seductions, influenced by love and gratitude as well as sexual passion. "The burst of transport was past: Ambrosio's lust was satisfied." . . . Incidentally, if one yields to lawless speculation, this transport has lasted 118 pages. It was commenced on page 109 ("'Thine, ever thine,' murmured the friar, and sunk upon her bosom"), and has been suspended during the entire interim, consisting mainly of the "History of Don Raymond, Marquis de las Cisternas." Ambrosio suffers a violent reaction, and reproaches his seductress and himself: "'What atonement can purchase the pardon of my crime? Wretched Matilda, you have destroyed my quiet forever!'" He is, however, won over by her arguments: "'Unnatural were your vows of celibacy; man was not created for such a state: and were love a crime, God never would have made it so sweet, so irresistible! Then banish those clouds from your brow, my Ambrosio.'"

One further instance of this basic movement, more complex and horrific, may stand for the rest. Ambrosio, now almost at the end of his progress toward damnation, has ravished the angelic Antonia in the gloomy vaults of St. Clare. Considering its content *The Monk* is remarkably free of perversity, but in this instance "even the gloom of the vault, the surrounding silence, and the resistance which he expected from her, seemed to give a fresh edge to his fierce and unbridled desires." . . . (pp. 40-2)

Coleridge condemns the supernatural machinery of *The Monk*: "where the order of nature may be changed whenever the author's purposes demand it. . . . No address is requisite to the accomplishment of any design. . . . The writer may make us wonder, but he cannot surprise us." (p. 42)

Now to the fundamental questions raised by this great critic about Lewis's use of the supernatural: one would first concede that Lewis cannot compare with Coleridge himself in *The Ancient Mariner* and *Christabel;* his spiritual beings are relatively superficial, merely material and spectacular. But, as John Berryman well says, "the point is to conduct a remarkable man utterly to damnation. It is surprising, after all, how *long* it takes—how *difficult* it is—to be certain of damnation. This was Lewis's main insight, fully embodied in his narrative. . . ". There is great fascination in the entrapment itself, and its progress is managed by Lewis with marvellous ingenuity and resourcefulness. . . . Further, once he has selected his terms, Lewis carries them out with the utmost boldness and consistency. He sticks to his guns: Ambrosio is to be damned, and damned he is; correspondingly, having elected the supernatural, he does not betray it with naturalistic explanations, like

Mrs. Radcliffe, or Charles Brockden Brown. . . . The fantastic conclusion of *The Monk* is a triumph of sheer pertinacity. Driven to the last extremity, Ambrosio tries to pray. At this the devil, "darting his talons into the monk's shaven crown," flies away with him. . . . Lewis all but carries Ambrosio to Hell himself.

He manages a genuinely tragic dilemma by holding to the notion of an omnipotent deity, in Ambrosio's imagination both vengeful and loving. Ambrosio holds to his faith in God's infinite mercy almost to the end—to make him utterly despair is the devil's final triumph. Coleridge, condemning Lewis's psychology, at the same time testifies to his success. "Now, in addition to constitutional warmth and irresistible opportunity, the monk is impelled to incontinence by friendship, by compassion, by gratitude, by all that is amiable, and all that is estimable; yet in a few weeks after his first frailty, the man . . . degenerates into an uglier fiend than the gloomy imagination of Dante would have ventured to picture." Ambrosio, however, is a fiend only at the end, and Coleridge has failed to perceive the many regular steps that bring him to damnation.

As regards Coleridge's chief contention—that *The Monk* falsifies human nature by motivating Ambrosio with "lust"—plainly few moderns would agree with him. This, however, is not the point, which is that Lewis clearly felt otherwise about the matter, and that *The Monk* is consistently a tragedy of passion, sexual and otherwise. One would argue, too, for the dramatic appropriateness of Ambrosio's desires. He is a *monk*, sworn to chastity, and he places great weight on the sin of breaking his vow. It symbolizes the defeat of the spirit by the flesh. Rationally, repression of the natural man brings great and dreadful consequences. Further, as Coleridge himself implicitly acknowledges, what Ambrosio feels is a good deal more complicated than lust. He is led into his disastrous connection with Matilda by affection and gratitude, and his unhallowed longings for the unhappy Antonia are mingled with reverence for her archetypal innocence.

Indeed, Ambrosio's disastrous mixture of sacred and profane love has extremely interesting effects. He worships a picture of the Madonna, which turns out to be a portrait of Matilda, whose face he has never seen till she reveals herself by apparent accident. (pp. 43-5)

[His] feelings about Antonia are complex, and so are Antonia's feelings about Ambrosio. The unobtrusive resemblance of their names is a nice touch. At first sight she is instinctively attracted to him. Hearing him preach, "'till this moment I had no idea of the powers of eloquence. But when he spoke, his voice inspired me with such interest, such esteem, I might almost say such affection for him, that I am myself astonished at the acuteness of my feelings'." . . . The possibility exists, then, that Antonia's instinctive affinity for her brother Ambrosio is sexual and incestuous. It is only a possibility, an overtone—if it were more it would wreck the plot—but as a mere suggestion it enlivens the design appreciably.

Returning for the moment to *The Monk*'s resemblance to Aristotelian tragedy, one would have to relegate it to Aristotle's second and inferior class, the double action with poetic justice, where the wicked are punished and the virtuous are—at long last—rewarded. The good receive a due measure of happiness in the penultimate Chapter XI, leaving the conclusion to fix Ambrosio in eternal misery. The terms of happiness are significant beyond the characters they concern:

The remaining years of Raymond and Agnes, of Lorenzo and Virginia, were happy as can be those allotted to mortals, born to be the prey of grief, and sport of disappointment. The exquisite sorrows with which they had been afflicted, made them think lightly of every succeeding woe. They had felt the sharpest darts in misfortune's quiver. Those which remained, appeared blunt in comparison. Having weathered fate's heaviest storms, they looked calmly upon its terrors: or, if ever they felt affliction's casual gales, they seemed to them gentle as zephyrs which breathe over summer-seas. . . .

This too is the tragedy of passion, with something of the settled resignation of a Greek ending. Poor Antonia, the beloved of Lorenzo, has of course perished, and the beautiful Virginia de Villa-Franca is a moderately satisfactory substitute for her.

This subplot of Raymond-Agnes and Lorenzo-Antonia-Virginia functions as a mask and as counterpoint for the Ambrosio story. It is expansive, leisurely, and varied, whereas the latter is concentrated, swift, and direct, but is enveloped and half-concealed within the larger narrative. As was remarked by Coleridge, the longer subplot is skilfully joined to the Ambrosio story, and perhaps its effect in turning us back to Ambrosio is premeditated. . . . The subplot is worked out with commendable care and skill. Lewis leaves no loose ends among the many strands of story and motif that he has set himself to weave together, and he prepares his grounds admirably in his opening chapter. It is in the subplot, for the most part, that his virtuosity in handling the largest possible number of Gothic elements chiefly appears. Nevertheless, in relative terms this plot is not finally an artistic and imaginative success.

Despite Lewis's conscientiousness he has given himself and his reader too much to keep up with. The story reads as if he had prepared an extremely careful and elaborate outline, then found that he had notwithstanding to fill in with afterthoughts. Singularly bold in his conduct of the supernatural, he is unhappily fussy about detail, like the wicked who flee where no man pursueth. Thus, in Raymond's "History," the hero overhears outlaws plotting against him outside his window. Now, it is a bitterly cold night, as is mentioned on several occasions, so it is carefully specified that "I drew near the window, which, as the room had been long shut up, was left open in spite of the cold." . . . When we find out a few moments later that "He spoke in a low voice; but as he was just below my window, I had no difficulty to distinguish his words" . . . , our response is likely to be, "Oh, yeah?" Further on, Raymond instantaneously overpowers one of the brigands. "I sprang from my seat, darted suddenly upon Baptiste, and, clasping my hands round his throat, pressed it so forcibly as to prevent his uttering a single cry." This is a considerable feat, and so the author evidently finds it, for Raymond immediately explains: "You may remember, that I was remarkable at Salamanca for the power of my arm." . . . Later, the same Don Raymond finds it necessary to masquerade as a gardener, "Disguised in a common habit, and a black patch covering one of my eyes. . . ." He is obliged to carry out his role: "I immediately entered upon my employment. Botany having been a favorite study with me, I was by no means at a loss in my new station." . . . Part of the science-requirement at Salamanca, no doubt. (pp. 45-7)

Lewis threads his way admirably through all this circumstance, but his methods could hardly be called economical. (pp. 48-9)

The **"History of Don Raymond"** contains within it the interpolated stories of Marguerite, the Bleeding Nun, and, more briefly, the Wandering Jew; and there are ten songs and ballads in *The Monk,* extremely competent in versification and in their time much admired. Lewis's talents were many, and tended to jostle. His episodes are frequently constructed like theatrical scenes, to achieve a single striking effect, or a series of effects, both visual and oral. The main plot of Ambrosio usually subsumes these in its intensity, but not always. Thus Antonia, grieving for the death of Elvira and in general filled with thoroughly justified unease, picks up for diversion "a volume of old Spanish ballads" and reads **"Alonzo the Brave and Fair Imogine,"** which is reproduced in its entirety. In its horrendous climax Alonzo comes back from the dead to claim the faithless Imogine, at her wedding to "A Baron all covered with jewels and gold."

> The lady is silent: the stranger complies.
>   His vizor he slowly unclosed:
> Oh! God! what a sight met Fair Imogine's eyes!
> What words can express her dismay and surprise,
>   When a skeleton's head was exposed!
> All present then uttered a terrified shout,
>   All turned with disgust from the scene.
> The worms they crept in, and the worms they crept out,
> And sported his eyes and his temples about,
>   While the spectre addressed Imogine.

It is remarked that "The perusal of this story was ill calculated to dispel Antonia's melancholy" . . . , which is highly understandable. With us, however, the case is different; as Oscar Wilde said in a similar situation, "One must have a heart of stone to read the death of Little Nell without laughing." (p. 49)

Richard Harter Fogle, "The Passions of Ambrosio,"
in The Classic British Novel, *edited by Howard M. Harper, Jr. and Charles Edge, The University of Georgia Press, 1972, pp. 36-50.*

ROBERT KIELY (essay date 1972)

[*Kiely outlines the weaknesses of* The Monk, *which he contends derive not from its didactic message, but rather from its emotional tone. According to Kiely, the excessively emotive language of the novel overwhelms Lewis's story. Further, he argues that* The Monk *is an intensely artificial work dominated by the depiction of characters whose relationships are defined by subjugation.*]

Like most fiction of the [Romantic] period, the novel of terror nearly always made claims, especially on final pages, of high moral intention. Man's inhumanity to man, the dangers of excess, the fate of pride, were all paraded for inspection in the last chapter so that any reader of bad conscience and little discrimination could close the volume content that he had been given a stern lesson. What makes the didactic protestations in **The Monk** ring slightly hollow is the tone rather than the narrative context of the whole book. There is no reason to assume that Lewis set out to write an immoral novel or that his didactic intrusions are mere cynical compromises with public taste. The fact is that his novel does show the dangers of excess and the fate of pride, but the power and originality with which he treats the physical, emotional, and psychological elements of the story tend to obscure the moral assertions even when they do not contradict them. Lewis's vocabulary of violent emotions was part imitation and part artistic creation, but his moral terminology was an inherited rhetoric which lacked the energy of belief or discovery.

The monk Ambrosio is a Faustian protagonist who sells himself to the devil for the sake of temporary pleasure, but there is little space given to rational analysis, theological dispute, or metaphysical speculation. Plot and the conventional implications of chronology and causal relationships are relegated to a position of unobtrusive significance. The author concentrates not on how things come about but on how they look and feel. The main narrative is repeatedly interrupted by the details of a subplot and, at one point, by a long digressive tale. Nevertheless, *The Monk* does have a unique structure which derives from an accumulation of strikingly realized scenes rather than from a logical knitting together of events. More than any fiction which preceded it, the novel of terror is picturesque. It appeals first to the eye and only secondarily to reason and conscience.

Lewis sought to reproduce an intensely private vision of a character in extreme circumstances, an institutional man suddenly at war with every kind of convention. Given the novel's roots in social convention and common speech, it would seem that he was attempting the impossible. (pp. 101-02)

Seeking out the novel for its apparent capaciousness, Lewis nonetheless found himself struggling against inherited formulas of situation and expression, and using the genre as a medium for debate between strict form and freedom in life as well as in art. . . .

The limits of the prison and "the weight of too much liberty" are the major themes of *The Monk*. The mood is one of constant and agonizing struggle between two equally undesirable alternatives, both of which seem to tempt and betray the author along with his characters. There are, on one hand, the victims, innocent and noble, whose beauty shines all the brighter for being shut up in a cell, cloaked in a monk's habit or stretched upon the rack. On the other hand, there are the free spirits who have escaped the bonds of convention, but who, in doing so, have escaped distinct identity as well and have disappeared into a timeless, spaceless limbo where all distinctions are prison walls seen from the outside. (p. 102)

It is not surprising that the Marquis de Sade put *The Monk* at the top of his list of favorite contemporary novels [see excerpt dated 1800]. Its brutal episodes seemed to him to reflect the mood of an age of bloodshed and rebellion and to be the only means by which a writer could hope to move readers accustomed to calamity. . . .

Sade's argument is an important one, and it should not be shrugged off as the self-justification of an isolated mind. Much of the "madness" of the *roman noir* imitates and caters to the madness of an unstable society. Despite the theatricality and superficial contrivance of a book like *The Monk,* there is a sense in which it may be called realistic. Moreover, Sade's stress on the need to "move" readers is a common romantic preoccupation and one which poses a particular problem for the artist living in a period when human sensibilities are repeatedly overstimulated. (p. 103)

In his characterization of the monk Ambrosio, Lewis goes well beyond the simplistic psychology of Sade in exploring the dual nature of man. Despite his theoretical allowance for great diversity in human nature, Sade's fiction is populated by characters whose "true" selves are invariably the clear reverse of what they seem to be in public. Thus, the chaste virgin is a whore at heart, the pious hermit a debaucher, the brave soldier a coward, the kindly matron a murderess and so on through an almost infinite monotony of predictable opposites. Lewis begins his novel in much the same vein, showing a contrast

between appearance and reality with an ease which even he must laugh at. For the first hundred pages, the novel wavers between melodrama and burlesque; and when the pious young monk Rosario throws himself before Ambrosio, confessing, "Father, I am a woman," burlesque seems to have gained the day. Lewis is too taken by the absurdity of the situation to insist upon reaching for a tragic note. After Rosario/Matilda, threatening to stab herself, exposes the "dazzling whiteness" of her bosom, the grave superior muses, "I have never seen her face; yet certainly that face must be lovely, and her person beautiful, to judge by her—by what I have seen."

If *The Monk* had continued in this vein it would have been a psychologically slight and ultimately silly book. But even from the beginning, in the midst of the formulaic contrasts and "shocking" reversals, there are signs that the familiar Gothic devices are being manipulated by an artist who never fully trusts the "unconventional" conventions which he has adopted. The dagger against the bared breast cannot be taken seriously because the author himself sees it as a bit of theatrics, even as, later on, the rape in the charnel house, though externally more detailed and grotesque, seems a stage pantomime in comparison to the successfully realized horror of the rape of Clarissa. Unlike Sade, Lewis recognized the frustration of meeting one cliché with another opposite one. To substitute a knife for a fan, a lie for a promise, a murder for a marriage, can become, despite its initial shock value, another routine, another formula, another language without sufficient range to suggest the complexity of life. (pp. 105-06)

[Lewis] appears to have adopted a literary form not altogether worthy of his imagination. *The Monk* derives much of its interest from the curious division between a narrative voice which seems wittier, subtler, and more human than the narrative framework to which it has committed itself. One often has the feeling in reading *The Monk* that it is about to become a much funnier or sadder book than it is. A new Rabelais or Marlowe seems always about to be revealed, but then the stock devices—the Gothic properties and the melodramatic reversals—intrude and bring us back to a world of artifice and infuriating limitation. Of particular importance is the fact that Lewis, as revealed in his tendency to burlesque or treat with perfunctory interest certain episodes in the narrative, felt this disparity himself. (p. 106)

If *The Monk* is a morbid and disturbing book, it is also one which seems to flaunt its own artificiality. (pp. 106-07)

For him, the artist, no less than the priest or the member of Parliament, was a role player who affected a costume, a voice, even a kind of behavior, which could never fully represent the changeable and complex being of the total man. Unlike Sade, he does not try to show human character stripped down to its supposed animal essence because, for him, to play the brute was still to act out only a part of the self. The proper metaphor for personality was not, therefore, one of depth, but of surfaces. The closest the artist or any man would come to a realization of his "whole" self was to take into account the variety of roles he could imagine himself playing.

In the context of Freudian psychology, this sounds naïve and superficial. But then, despite patterns which correspond to Freudian theory, *The Monk* is not interesting primarily as a precursor of early twentieth-century psychology. It is not sufficiently optimistic, mechanistic, or deep. Too many modern critics have tried to rescue it from the rubbish heap by claiming profundity for it, but this is doing no favor to Lewis, who knew rubbish when he saw it. (p. 107)

The Monk is not an early account of an identity crisis, but an exploration of imposture and the chaos which it so imperfectly conceals.

Ambrosio is not simply the holy man who eventually yields to temptation; he is the hero too large for any of the roles which society or nature provides for him. Until the age of thirty, given to study, prayer, and the mortification of the flesh, he is a model priest at the expense of the passionate side of his nature. But when he finally succumbs to the charms of Matilda, the young monk who is not a monk, he is not released into a state of full self-realization, but only harnessed by a different and even more limiting role. Lewis's concern was not with the psychological damage caused by a conventual life—hardly a problem in the England of 1796—but with the dilemma of an ego unwilling to accept a life of moderation and unable to find fulfillment in extremes. Ambrosio's tragedy is not so much that he "falls" from a state of pious chastity into an obsessive lust, but that, in either case, he is forced to be something less than his true self. Neither sexual abandon nor ascetic mortification answers the real longings of Ambrosio's heart. Both force him into a kind of servitude, both close out other areas of experience, both turn into mechanical rituals, and both are finally false and temporary diversions from the infinite possibility which he seeks.

Like the artist superior to his art, Ambrosio is the priest superior to his religion and the male superior to his gender. His ego is a vast universe of which society and nature can give only imperfect representations. That the scenes of sexual possession in *The Monk* are as elaborately and artificially staged as the liturgical ceremonies is perfectly appropriate since they bear the same peculiarly detached relationship to Ambrosio's potential life. All choice of mind or body, insofar as it limits and subdues the self with relation to an external object, is a sign of defeat or dishonesty. Man's professions of faith, whether to a god or a mistress, are, at best, fragments of a temporary reality and, at worst, outright lies. The world of *The Monk* is theatrical, a world of performers and spectators, because every word and act is a work of art, and every work of art a pretense. (p. 108)

In a sense, each stage of the novel's plot repeats the peculiar creative act of the author and shows it to be a form of self-indulgence. Lewis conjures up Ambrosio, who conjures up Matilda, who conjures up the devil, who conjures up Antonia. Lewis's artist is creator, audience, and critic. He fashions, enjoys, and, ultimately, distrusts his own pleasures. What force his art has derives from the individual will, not from a correspondence to external reality. Writing at the end of the eighteenth century, Lewis could not expect to convince many of his readers that Matilda had raised the devil. He could expect to convince them that Ambrosio wanted his way enough to believe, temporarily, whatever appeared to give it to him.

Art, as conceived by Lewis, is the lie which makes human longing, whether for an ideal or material goal, appear capable of fulfillment. Ambrosio's descent from his monastery cell to the magic circle drawn by Matilda is a movement from one deception to another rather than a conventional fall from grace. Like all Gothic novelists, Lewis uses Roman Catholicism primarily for the show of it—and for his Protestant readers, the obviously empty show of it. Imperfectly concealed by the orderly processions, the chants, and the purple reflections from stain-glass windows are wretched, ambitious, and doubt-ridden souls. The convent of St. Claire is built above a particularly gruesome sepulcher, and the famous statue of the patron saint conceals a black pit where insubordinate nuns are put to meditate on their sins among the bones of their predecessors. The arts of sex are no more substantial or genuine than the arts of religion: Matilda's portrait, her harp-playing, and her incantations in the charnel house produce temporary illusions, but they do not long keep Ambrosio from experiencing satiety and disgust. Hardly a week has passed before he tires of Matilda and her harp.

The moral, it would seem, is obvious—so much so that it hardly carries any force at all when Lewis states it. Ambrosio's sin is pride which eventually leads him to the excesses of lust and wrath. A moral (and sensible) man would be humbler, avoid extremes in all things, and distrust the snares of art. Yet, *The Monk* is not finally a drama of moral alternatives. Indeed, like a great many later romantic heroes, Ambrosio is a being for whom reform and salvation are unthinkable. He has most of the attributes of a conventional hero—beauty, strength, intelligence—but they are inhibited by the circumstances of his life, by the monastery cell, the forbidden bedchamber, the magic circle. What assumes central importance in the novel is the spectacle of energy imprisoned, given hope of escape, and then disappointed. In Ambrosio's case, moral culpability is admitted, but the fact that nearly all the characters in the novel—innocent and guilty alike—suffer the same fate casts some doubt on its relevance.

All who reach out for a life beyond their own—even by means of unselfish love—are greeted by a nightmare and thrust into confinement, darker and more isolated than the prison they had originally sought to escape. Thus, in the subplot of Raymond and Agnes, though the young lovers are guilty of no crime other than their desire to be together, they encounter supernatural as well as mundane obstacles of the most gruesome sort. (pp. 110-11)

Whereas Raymond and Agnes are primarily victims of circumstance, Ambrosio is both victim and victimizer. He embraces a body which becomes a corpse on his first visit to the lovely Antonia's bedchamber, though this is no spectre but Elvira, the girl's mother, whom he murders when she discovers him about to rape her daughter. Ambrosio arrives in the room imagining Antonia's youthful beauty and suddenly, as in a nightmare, finds himself wrestling with an aged demon: "He dragged her towards the bed . . . and pressing his knees upon her stomach . . . witnessed without mercy the convulsive trembling of her limbs beneath him . . . Her face was covered with a frightful blackness . . . her hands were stiff and frozen." Ambrosio's reaction is much like Raymond's. He is not sufficiently sadistic to be stimulated by his crime, but, on the contrary, suffers from it almost as though he had been his own victim. . . . (p. 112)

Two patterns are woven through the different accounts of these strange embraces. One is the reversal of the medieval tale of the "loathly lady" in which the courage and fidelity of a young knight married to an old hag are rewarded when the bride turns into a beautiful damsel. True beauty is seen not only as the prize of virtue but as a durable quality which may be veiled but not defeated by ugliness. The union of the real and the ideal is possible. In *The Monk,* beauty, physical and spiritual, is a deception, an apparition as unattainable and incredible as a stock Gothic ghost. The only reality outside the self is seen in the second pattern, in which the sexual drive ends in an act of murder. Sex, no more than religion, can provide the self with a route to transcendence. The reality beyond the sex act, like that beneath the church floor, is a tomb.

All of the encounters with female corpses are, in addition to their intrinsic unpleasantness, stylistically striking. Lewis's touch is nearly always lighter and surer than Mrs. Radcliffe's, but for the most part he shows a similar reliance on Latinate abstractions, circumlocutions, euphemism, and a connotative rather than denotative vocabulary. Nearly every page contains such sentences as, "Her distress was beyond the power of description" or "Excessive was the universal grief at hearing this decision." Yet in the scenes where a desirable sexual partner is replaced by a dead body, irony and euphemism vanish, and a sudden specificity of language brings the scene into shocking focus. (pp. 112-13)

It is Ambrosio and his surrogate Raymond in the subplot who give credence to what they see. The reaction to the vision of death is a trance in which the human witness becomes like the thing he sees. But Lewis takes his protagonist beyond the ephemeral confusion of Walpole's heroes or the hysterical paralysis of Mrs. Radcliffe's heroines. True, Ambrosio is a confused hero, subject to contradictory impulses, desirous of obtaining incompatible goals, but his solution to complexity is violence. Strangely enough, despite his reputed intelligence and emotional strength, Ambrosio is a character who seems to have almost no capacity to assimilate change. Every new and unexpected idea or event makes him flutter and reel. (p. 113)

In a novel in which so much is theatrical and ornamentally grotesque, [the] scenes of violence possess an energy and realism for which the reader is not fully prepared. The abbess

A portrait of Lewis by H. W. Pickersgill.

is without question presented as a wicked woman, but, like Elvira in the role of interfering parent, she is an uninteresting caricature *except* at the moment of her terrifying death when she becomes for a brief time the vivid image of a tormented human being. It is almost as though Lewis had played an unfair trick on the reader by endowing his Gothic stereotypes with life at unexpected and fatal moments.

When we speak of "realism" or truth to life in a novel like *The Monk,* it is not a Defoe-like accumulation of detail that is meant, but a contrast between static and stylistically formal scenes and short episodes of concrete action, presented in relatively straightforward language. The murder of Elvira follows the long, elaborate, and ritualistic conjuring scene in the sepulcher; the mutilation of the abbess interrupts a slow, stately procession described with almost Spenserian solemnity. Lewis displays a detachment and control over his mode, first, by means of the amusing ironical aside and, increasingly and more effectively, by means of the pathetic aside, the quick glimpse at pain as inflicted and felt. From one point of view, conventional Gothic cruelty is too preposterously exaggerated, and therefore laughable. From the other, it does not go nearly far enough; it is only a weak charade when compared with human brutality and suffering as they really are.

What seems to have held Lewis's imagination more than institutional despotism was the more intimate and essentially psychological subjugation of one individual by another. Unlike Walpole's caricatures, his characters do relate to one another, but primarily as slaves to masters or victims to tormentors. The conventional pairs of lovers, Raymond and Agnes, Lorenzo and Antonia, are kept apart during most of the narrative, whereas emphasis is given to Ambrosio's contact with Matilda, Elvira, and Antonia, all of whom he presumes to overpower while, in another sense, he is himself being overpowered.

It is precisely this question of power—the conditions under which it increases and those under which it is transferred from one individual to another—which seems to have fascinated Lewis and led him to the rigidities and excesses of Gothic fiction. He appears to have recognized that the one could not exist without the other; that excess of any kind could not tolerate contradiction or complexity, and that excess of individual freedom thrives on the potential subjugation of everything but the self. The combination of the extreme gesture of release from convention, on one hand, and the imposition of an absurdly rigid reductionism, on the other, defines a human predicament as well as a peculiar stage in the history of the novel.

It is often said that in Gothic fiction there are either no believable characters at all or else there is one so monstrously absorbent as to make the form seem a kind of obscene exhibitionism. There is nothing between the cipher and the creature of gargantuan potency in an empty world. If this is not true of *The Monk* from the beginning, it becomes true in time. As Ambrosio casts off old roles, he deserts simplicity, bypasses complexity, and finds contradiction and confusion the corollaries of uninhibited power. The history of his personality is not one of growth, but one of painful constriction alternating with disastrous expansion. (pp. 114-16)

The nightmare of this novel is the spectacle of a creature whose nature dilutes and immobilizes itself. Where is a hero, a man in control of his own power, in a world of mannish women, effeminate men, servile masters, commanding slaves, where the dead often seem more animated than the impotent, rigid, terrified living? How does one wake up from the double nightmare of a realm of excessive and inhibiting classificaiton which gives way to one of vanishing distinctions? Though Lewis's symbolism is largely sexual and sepulchral, the questions have obvious political, social, philosophical, and aesthetic applicability. (pp. 116-17)

Lewis's final vision is of a chaos which neither man nor art has the capacity to control or avoid. Indeed, uncontrollable energy would seem to be the only energy there is in the world of *The Monk.* The artist, like the monk who seeks liberation from lifeless conventions, is apt to find himself unexpectedly on the side of the flood. (p. 117)

> Robert Kiely, "'The Monk'," *in his* The Romantic Novel in England, *Cambridge, Mass.: Harvard University Press, 1972, pp. 98-117.*

HOWARD ANDERSON (essay date 1973)

[*Anderson contends that the action of* The Monk *progresses "toward the discovery of the infinite danger within or beneath what had seemed familiar and safe." According to Anderson, the novel's plot is defined by the protagonist's insatiable, self-destructive quest for fulfillment.*]

The action of *The Monk* follows a direction quintessentially Gothic: not only Ambrosio's story, but the subsidiary narratives as well, move toward the discovery of the infinite danger within or beneath what had seemed familiar and safe. It is the accomplishment of the most powerful Gothic fiction to lead the reader to participate in this discovery, rather than merely to observe it; it is the accomplishment of *The Monk* to involve both characters and readers in awareness sufficiently disturbing for the book to survive as a masterpiece of a genre that has explored and captured our imaginations for the last two hundred years.

Certainly the scene of the novel's opening chapter, Madrid in the days of the Inquisition, seems to pose no threat to either the Monk or the reader. Ambrosio is not only at home in this world, he is on top of it: the abbot of a prestigious monastery, idolized as a 'man of holiness', he believes himself to be supremely in command of his own considerable powers and those of the great city that flocks to hear his sermon. As for the reader, while the epigraph from *Measure for Measure* may lead him to doubt the solidity of the Monk's virtue, Inquisitional Spain seems too remote to be taken seriously as a setting for anything touching actual experience, whether in the eighteenth century or the twentieth. And the satiric stance we are invited to take toward the well-lighted scene at the Capuchin Cathedral, where 'one half of Madrid was brought ... by expecting to meet the other half', appears to provide a secure perspective from which to look on whatever ensues with equanimity and rational objectivity. The reader seems no more in danger of being impinged upon by whatever may happen to validate the comparison of Ambrosio to Shakespeare's Angelo than by the vain and comic crowd that has assembled with so little dignity to hear him speak.

The darkness that follows suddenly upon the departure of the noisy congregation, however, turning the Cathedral into a suitable setting for Lorenzo's dream, though introduced with clumsy melodrama, indicates the way in which, throughout the novel, places of safety are transformed into places of danger and commonsensical assumptions about human nature and human behaviour are forced to give way before a recognition of the power of darkness and the irrational. In the story of Ambrosio's

dissolution, closely interwoven with the account of the unhappy love affair of Lorenzo and Antonia, and in the tangentially related adventure of Raymond and Agnes, the situation of the characters is revealed as more problematic than they had themselves originally assumed. As everywhere in the Gothic novel, sexual passion is the locus of danger. In the world of *The Monk,* it constitutes such a threat that its innocent expression by Raymond and Agnes is enough to summon up a bloody ghost and to induce the sadism of the convent's superior. And in the case of the Monk himself, sexual repression has been so great that innocent expression is impossible; sexuality provides the medium for the violent assertion of his individual will, which ultimately expresses itself in murder, rape, and incest. Agnes finds herself buried alive in the vaults beneath the beautiful convent garden where she and Raymond had made love, and Ambrosio is even more effectively trapped in the psychological and moral deformations imposed upon him by his early education in the monastery. In both cases, the dangerous unknown reveals itself in the encounter between individual sexual licence and irreconcilable forces from the past.

The story of Raymond and Agnes, which interrupts that of the Monk through a long early section of the novel, thus provides a variation of its theme: the attempt of the two highly rational and 'modern' young lovers to run away and get married is baffled first by the appearance of a ghost and then by the vindictive mother superior of Agnes's convent. (pp. ix-xi)

The supernatural forces from the past, aroused by the young lovers' youthful attempt to elope together, have their parallel in the ancient code of the convent which the vicious superior enforces to punish Agnes's later sexual transgression. The perilousness and fragility of their circumstances, borne in on them so powerfully as soon as they attempt to act on their personal sexual impulses, are evoked by Agnes's recollection of her feelings as she lay chained in the burial vaults beneath the convent in the heart of Madrid, the putrefying body of her illegitimate child in her arms. . . . The suddenness of the change, its sexual causation, captivity beneath and within the place that had seemed to exist for her personal and social comfort, transformations so quick and terrifying that they cannot be believed *or* denied—these are all essentials of the Gothic vision. . . . And they are as vital to Lewis's portrait of the Monk as to the subsidiary story of Raymond and Agnes.

Like Agnes, Ambrosio finds his fall hard to believe: its bewildering suddenness is often in his mind. And if Ambrosio's disintegration possesses all the constituents of the dream (or nightmare) vision of human possibility characteristic of the Gothic, it also provides important suggestions about the reasons for the urgency and frequency with which just these dreams have recurred in popular fiction from Lewis's time to our own.

'Presumption', we later learn, 'formed the groundwork of his character', and when Ambrosio passes from the public scene in the Cathedral where he has been introduced to us at the brilliant height of his powers, we observe his self-congratulation on the extraordinary virtue that has enabled him to rise to such distinction at the age of thirty. But with all his abilities, Ambrosio is unfortunately unaware of the strength of his own sexuality and of how badly his past has equipped him to deal with this. These are the characteristics that will combine to destroy this impressive human being, and their manifestation in Ambrosio is powerful enough, and the problems to which they give rise sufficiently complex in their implications, to impress not only the characters themselves but the reader as well. Ambrosio's initial seduction by Matilda is composed of a series of discoveries—beginning with the revelation of Matilda's true sexual identity (she has gained entrance to the monastery as a novice) and culminating in that of his own—which are more striking to Ambrosio than they are to us. But when we return to the two lovers in the monastic cell after our long excursion to the Castle of Lindenberg with Raymond and Agnes, it is to find Ambrosio already possessed by ennui, and to watch those masculine urges, which we had found natural and sympathetic, beginning to form themselves into a megalomaniac quest for means of making his environment totally subservient to his personal, and specifically his sexual, will.

Lewis himself appears to be of two minds about where the blame should fall for this explosion in the Monk's personality. In a long passage he carefully details the corrupting influence of Ambrosio's education, and in numerous shorter ones he adds further evidence of the responsiblity of the Church in general, and monastic life in particular, for the perversion of his splendid natural qualities. But he also suggests again and again that while his hero is not to be held strictly accountable for his first transgressions, he is guilty of the complex horrors that ensue. The ironic trap that Lewis arranges for Ambrosio in the end, and the ghastly punishment that concludes the novel and his life are retribution upon a will that, once set free, could not be accommodated even by its author.

Lewis contributed an important example to the developing tradition of the Gothic hero-villain in making Ambrosio's character one in which splendid potential is twisted and defeated by destructive conflicting qualities. . . . When we realize that all [Ambrosio's] ruin has resulted from his desertion by his parents, it is hard to resist the conclusion that Lewis, however consciously, found some ironic justice in Ambrosio's (unknowing) murder of his own mother—who had, we are told rather off-handedly, 'in the abruptness of her flight' from a father-in-law angry at his son's improvident marriage, been forced to leave her son behind. It is similarly tempting to attribute Lewis's inclusion of a situation that makes this ghastly deed possible (like the even more horrible punishment of the mother superior of the convent) to the author's ambiguous feelings toward his own mother following her elopement with a music master. The fusion of sexuality with violence, and specifically with revenge, in the novel undoubtedly has its origins in Lewis's own problematic personality. But more important, it is grounded in his perception of the implications of conflict between the individual sexual will and the forces inhibiting and prohibiting its expression.

The destructive effect of Ambrosio's upbringing centres in his inability to do without the support of the very institutions that oppose his individual desires. The social reformist tendencies that one senses in many parts of the novel result from Lewis's awareness that society's most dangerous weapon against the self is its seductive appeal to the human need for the regard of others. (His own pleasure and pride in dining with duchesses equipped him admirably for such an awareness.) The Monk is unable even to think of simply leaving the monastery when his vows become onerous: elopement is even less possible for him than for Raymond and Agnes. In fact we are told several times that his concern for his reputation becomes greater in direct proportion to his loss of virtue. His hypocrisy, then, is more than an old-fashioned vice: it is a name for the ultimately inadequate defence that Ambrosio builds to enable him to live in a new world of unrestricted individual freedom without sacrificing the old esteem and concern of society. This inability either to accept old values or to break completely with them

is typified in his reluctance to sell his soul to the devil. A deal with the devil, in this novel . . . , constitutes a total commitment to the life of this world and a rejection simultaneously of the possibilities of the next and of the regard of a society that limits individual fulfilment here in favour of the hereafter.

Ambrosio is torn between these alternatives, which he tries to reconcile by recourse to the supernatural. The devil does serve him, in a limited way, with magical devices bearing remarkable similarities to those developed by twentieth-century technology to help human beings master the world. As in Milton, the woman is the agent through whom the devil works; but there is less doubt in Ambrosio than in Adam that the impulse toward self-assertion originates in the man's own heart. It is only furthered and encouraged by the devices it calls to its aid: when the Monk looks into his magic mirror (as if into a closed-circuit television set) to observe the young girl who has attracted him as his passion for Matilda cooled, his lust is sufficiently enflamed to push him to find the one further magical device that seems required for its fulfilment.

Lewis makes clear that the demonic is necessary precisely because it is impossible for him openly to express and act upon his desires. The need for secrecy leads him to use magic to enter Antonia's room at night, and to put her to sleep so that he can enjoy her in solitary pleasure. It leads to his murder of her mother when she discovers and threatens to expose him; and it leads, finally, to his abduction of Antonia (drugged like Juliet) and his rape of her. That rape takes place, appropriately, in the vaults where Agnes is also imprisoned, and in the midst of the rotting corpses of recently-dead nuns. But while Lewis has all along written sympathetically of the man prevented from normal enjoyment of his sexuality, he has also revealed increasing ambiguity in his attitude toward the behaviour this repression gives rise to. Early on, in the dream sequence that heavily foreshadows the ensuing horror, he had alluded to a scene in Richardson's *Clarissa*, a novel which is concerned only in a less sensational way with many of the problems that preoccupy M. G. Lewis, and which contains, in Lovelace, one of the great embodiments of the dangers of the individual will. Like Richardson, Lewis finds it necessary to stop the career of his hero-villain, and he does so with tortures whose prolonged description constitutes the brilliantly horrific conclusion of the novel. In a final ironic variation on its central theme, Ambrosio finds himself once again in a place very different from what he had expected; his long quest for individual fulfilment at last impales him on a barren peak.

It is as if Lewis gradually became aware of disastrous human potential in excess of that which can be accounted for by environmental misfortunes. Rape—incestuous rape—murder of mother and sister: how far can the past, parents, society, and institutions be held responsible? What if the *self* is insatiable? These are questions the Monk's story implies, and it is not surprising if his nineteen-year-old creator stopped short of answering them. (pp. xii-xviii)

> *Howard Anderson, in an introduction to* The Monk:
> A Romance *by Matthew Lewis, edited by Howard
> Anderson, Oxford University Press, London, 1973,
> pp. vii-xix.*

PETER BROOKS   (essay date 1973)

[*Brooks contends that* The Monk *dramatizes the passage from the Age of Reason into the Romantic era. According to Brooks,* The Monk *is a reaction against the rationalism of the Enlightenment period as well as a denial of religious, or Sacred, power. He thus concludes that the novel ultimately communicates "an ethics of terror."*]

Matthew Gregory Lewis' *The Monk* is not only the aberrant masterpiece of the Gothic novel. It is also one of those works of literature that demonstrate a remarkable understanding of their own historical situation, of the epistemological moment to which they belong and to which they contribute. Published four years before the close of the eighteenth century, at the intersection of revolution and reaction, *The Monk* contains an important dramatization, an acting out of the passage into a new world—modern, frightening, our own—of moral transvaluations in which, at the dead end of the Age of Reason, the Sacred has reasserted its claim to attention, but in the most primitive possible manifestations, as taboo and interdiction, and ethics has implicitly come to be founded on terror rather than virtue. The novel can in fact be read as one of the first and most lucid contextualizations of life in a world where reason has lost its prestige, yet the Godhead has lost its otherness; where the Sacred has been reacknowledged but atomized, and its ethical imperatives psychologized.

The precondition of the ethical universe explored by Lewis is Enlightenment secularism, the decision that man should be understood in terms of mankind alone. The Gothic novel, as its best historians and critics have recognized, stands in reaction to the pretensions of rationalism. It reasserts the presence in the world of forces which cannot be accounted for by the daylight self and the self-sufficient mind. . . . [*The Monk* strikingly demonstrates that] the Sacred in its traditional Christian form, even in the more purely ethical version elaborated by Christian humanism, is no longer operative. (pp. 249-50)

The problem of the Sacred in *The Monk* comes to crisis in its ethical relation, in the problem of guilt and its definition. The question is articulated in acute terms when the Monk's temptress, Matilda, proposes to call upon diabolical aid in the seduction of Antonia, so ardently desired by Ambrosio. Ambrosio at first refuses this momentous step: if he has sinned grievously, he is nonetheless unwilling to renounce all hope of eventual salvation: "No, no, Matilda, I will not ally myself with God's enemy." In reply, Matilda shows herself a fierce logician:

> Are you then God's friend at present? Have you not broken your engagements with him, renounced his service, and abandoned yourself to the impulse of your passions? Are you not planning the destruction of innocence, the ruin of a creature whom he formed in the mould of angels? If not of daemons, whose aid would you invoke to forward this laudable design? Will the seraphims protect it, conduct Antonia to your arms, and sanction with their ministry your illicit pleasures? Absurd! But I am not deceived, Ambrosio! It is not virtue which makes you reject my offer; you *would* accept it, but you *dare* not. 'Tis not the crime which holds your hand, but the punishment; 'tis not respect for God which restrains you, but the terror of his vengeance! Fain would you offend him in secret, but you tremble to profess yourself his foe. Now shame on the coward soul, which wants the courage either to be a firm friend, or an open enemy!

The argumentation here—as so often in Lewis's nightmare world—is rigorously demonstrative. It is a logic of the excluded middle, typical of melodrama, which tends to resolve life into large polarized gestures, symbolically extreme moral commitments. If Ambrosio is no longer friend to God, whose aid shall he invoke if not that of God's enemies? For Matilda the lines are clearly drawn: the seraphim have their appointed task, which is surely not to abet the seduction of the innocent. It is the daemons who are relevant here. If recognition of the Holy means, on the psychological plane, a feeling of dependence . . . and a sense that one is "covered" by the numinous, Matilda understands that Ambrosio has moved out from under this cover, that a new relationship of dependency has been established, and must be acknowledged. Her exclamation—"Absurd!"—points to the logical inconsequence of Ambrosio's position, his failure to understand this shift in relationships and allegiances. If he can advance so illogical an argument, it is because he retains a vestigial belief in the Christian paradox of salvation. He is unclear about the premises of morality in the post-sacred universe in which he has chosen to live. These Matilda proceeds to elucidate: Ambrosio's refusal is motivated not by virtue but by fear; he no longer respects God, he is in terror of his vengeance.

The essential point here is the passage from virtue to terror so accurately described by Matilda. Her statement images a world in which God exists still, but no longer as holy mystery and as moral principle eliciting love, worship, and respect. No longer the source and guarantee of ethics, "God" has become rather an interdiction, a primitive force within nature that strikes fear into men's hearts but does not move them to allegiance and worship. God as experienced by Matilda is no longer symbol and incarnation of the Sacred, but rather of the nature of a taboo. The way in which she brings him to bear on the situation—and it is a way that Ambrosio will accept—suggests a world where there is no longer an operable idea of the Sacred or Holy, but rather a set of supernatural forces in the universe which must be acknowledged, combatted, propitiated, conjured with. "God" is simply one figure in a manichaeistic daemonology. (pp. 250-51)

From the outset of the novel, Lewis takes pains to make his fictional world accommodating to the dramatization of the numinous by consciously exploding both an excessively rationalist world view and the traditional eighteenth-century novel's framework of "manners." *The Monk,* like many other novels aware of their newness and importance, contains indications of the principles to be used in its explication, and within its own frame deliberately dramatizes the coming to life of the supernatural forces with which man must deal. Lewis carefully and progressively makes his world receptive to the solicitations of the supernatural; the first half of the novel moves toward creation of an imaginative framework within which these forces can have a real existence.

This movement is evident from the start, in the play of false appearances and dark realities, in the use of dreams as premonitions and, more, as discoveries about the true nature of things. But the most decisive representation of passage into a realm where the rational and social self must renounce its claims to the mastery and interpretation of life comes in the episode of the Bleeding Nun, in the narrative told by Don Raymond to Lorenzo. This narrative begins at the moment of the novel's first major crisis, when Ambrosio has succumbed to Matilda's seductions and spent his first riotous night in her arms, and the reader at first reacts with some annoyance to the intercalation of nearly one hundred pages which initially appear tangential to the main plot. Yet it eventually becomes apparent that the narrative has an indispensable functional role in the novel, and that through the subplot (Raymond and Agnes) Lewis is transforming the universe in which all the characters will move. By the end of Don Raymond's narrative, all is changed utterly.

The narrative begins by situating us explicitly in a world where the proper study of mankind is man: Don Raymond is charged by his father to undertake a grand tour for the observation of manners and instruction in the varying ways of the world.

"Examine the manners and customs of the multitude," his father specifically commands, "enter into the cottages; and, by observing how the vassals of foreigners are treated, learn to diminish the burthens, and augment the comforts, of your own." . . . This charge to observe the habits of the humble motivates Don Raymond's acceptance of shelter with the woodcutter Baptiste, in the forest near Strasbourg, an incident which then quickly leads us from the observation of social conditions into nightmare. Baptiste is a bandit who with his two loutish sons kills rich and unwary travellers who traverse the Alsatian woods, and Don Raymond, along with the Baroness Lindenberg, barely escapes the bloodbath. When his rescue of the Baroness, Donna Rodolpha, procures Raymond an invitation to Lindenberg Castle, we seem momentarily to return to the world of social manners, and to the tone of social comedy: when Donna Rodolpha mistakes the object of Don Raymond's affections, and flatters herself to be the occasion of tender addresses in fact directed to her niece Agnes, we seem to be moving in the medium of a Sheridan comedy. But the grandiose intensity of Donna Rodolpha's resentment quickly transforms this, and reorients things definitively toward nightmare. Agnes proposes to elope with Raymond under the disguise of the Bleeding Nun—a legendary figure in whose existence she and Raymond disbelieve, but whose machinery of terror will be a useful safe-conduct out of the castle: the servants once a year leave the gates open for the ramblings of the restless ghost. Thus Raymond and Agnes assume the posture of mockery toward the world of spirits. And as happens more than once in *The Monk,* the forces which we deny, mock, put down, are precisely those that assert their reality and smite us (a situation familiar to Euripides: for instance, in the *Hippolytus* and *The Bacchae*). Agnes is supplanted by the real Bleeding Nun, who receives Raymond's marriage pledge and drives off in the nuptial coach.

It is in fact possible to specify within this episode the point of intersection of the natural world and the supernatural, the moment at which the natural yields, cedes, gives way to the imperative solicitations of the supernatural. The moment of passage comes as Raymond waits for the stroke of one o'clock and the appearance of what he expects to be Agnes, and will in fact be the ghost. . . . The passage exploits the Gothic emotion—a delectation in chiaroscuro, in the experience of ruin, mystery, awe—in order to imply the capacity and aptitude of the natural world to receive and produce the supernatural. Nature is primed, readied to produce things beyond its phenomenological appearances. With the entry of the Bleeding Nun into Raymond's coach begins a wild ride which quickly becomes the stuff of diabolism: "Uttering a loud shriek, the drivers were hurled upon the ground. Immediately clouds obscured the sky: the winds howled around us, the lightning flashed, and the thunder roared tremendously." . . . The natural world has given birth to something else; and after this point,

the rest of Raymond's adventures—the nightly visitations of the Nun, the revelation of her bloody history, the exorcisms of the Wandering Jew, the mystic rites to lay the Nun's bones to rest—follow with perfect appropriateness and plausibility. And not only Raymond's adventures: when we return to the main plot, to Ambrosio, Matilda and Antonia, we move with ease into the evocation of diabolical agents, the use of magic mirrors and magic myrtle branches and subtle opiates.

The intercalated narrative of Don Raymond, then, is not simply a vestigial intrusion from the *roman à tiroirs,* with its successive narrators and tales, but a necessary breakthrough within the novel itself, from a world which has, despite dreams and grandiose passions, up to this point been largely natural and social. After the Bleeding Nun episode, the world has expanded to accommodate itself to shadows from without this world, and the consciousness of both characters and reader must expand to encompass this new dimension of experience. Lewis has managed a demonstration on stage that we do live in a world charged with forces beyond our rational grasp, that our gestures do unwittingly call spirits from the vasty deep. By showing within the frame of the novel itself the generation, the production of the supernatural, its imposition on characters who have professed incredulity, and its congruence to the natural world rightly conceived, Lewis has fictionally "proved" the terms of the rest of his novel, and prepared us for the continuation of the tale to be played out amidst forces which are both beyond man's control (as they are beyond natural explanation) and yet inhabiting within man, as they inhabit within nature.

The status of these forces and the method of their generation is important to what we have been saying about the degeneration and transmutation of the Sacred. The Bleeding Nun is a ghost, a supernatural presence who refers us not to the *mysterium* but to the *tremendum:* to the complex of omens, interdictions, taboos which must be acknowledged if man is to survive. Genealogically, she is the product of an ancient familial crime which links, centuries back, the families of Agnes and Raymond in a tale of criminal passion. Hence she must stand in opposition to their love until her bones are recovered from Lindenberg Hole and given proper burial, and her vexed spirit laid to rest. She can most immediately be read as a *product* of their love, an interdiction created by the very excess of their passion and their insistence upon its satisfaction, their claim to erotic fulfillment. Throughout the novel the state of exacerbated passion—nearly always erotic passion—is what leads to the production and intercession of the supernatural. . . . In *The Monk,* the forces of the supernatural enter the realm of human experience in response to man's excessive erotic drives, as a representation of the forces within himself which he must recognize and struggle with. (pp. 253-57)

[*The Monk*] makes it clear that the world of the supernatural which it has evoked, from the Bleeding Nun to Matilda's satanic satraps, is interpretable as a world within the characters themselves, and that Ambrosio's drama is in fact the story of his relationship to the imperatives of desire. His tale is one of Eros denied, only to reassert itself with the force of vengeance, to smite him—in the manner of folktale and Greek tragedy— through and in his very claims to superiority, which are in fact denials, repressions, psychic disequilibrium. Matilda, disguised as the innocent and adoring young novice Rosario, makes her first approach to Ambrosio precisely through his piety and loathing for the impurity of the secular world, and works his downfall through his confidence in his own purity, his failure to recognize the repressions that it represents. The narcissism of his proud chastity will lead to—lead back to—the erotic narcissism which is incest. Matilda's masterstroke is to have her own portrait painted in the disguise of the Madonna: underneath Ambrosio's passionate adoration of the sacred icon there will be, unbeknownst to him, a latent erotic component, which Matilda will need only to make explicit. The painting of the Madonna/Matilda is in fact a kind of witty conceit demonstrating why God can no longer be for Ambrosio the representative of the Sacred: spirituality has a latent daemonic content; the daemonic underlies the seemingly Holy. And the daemons represent, not a wholly other, but a complex of interdicted erotic desires within us. (pp. 257-58)

It is notable that toward the end of the novel, all the major characters are impelled to descend into the catacombs of the Convent of St. Clare, and that it is deep in this multi-layered sepulchre that the climaxes of all the different plots in the novel will be played out: here Agnes has been imprisoned by the Domina, here Ambrosio has sequestered Antonia in order to rape her, and here the nuns of St. Clare retreat as the incensed mob sacks and fires their convent. The sepulchre, into which the Domina descends for her sadistic punishments, and Matilda for her diabolical conjurations, has come in the course of the novel to represent the interdicted regions of the soul, the area of the mind where our deepest and least avowable impulses lie, and at the novel's climax the characters are driven uncon-

sciously, but all the more powerfully, to go to confront their destinies in the sepulchre. (p. 258)

The erotic implications of the sepulchre and its labyrinth are patent, for it is here, down below the daylight world, that Lewis can indulge the richest, and most sadistic, urgings of his decidedly perverse imagination. The descriptions of Agnes's attachment to the putrified corpse of her baby become almost unbearable. But Lewis's exploitation of sepulchre and labyrinth also confirms our sense of his intuitive understanding of his psycho-historical moment. It is easy to document that there was a veritable explosion of "claustral" literature at this period, especially in France from the onset of the Revolution. . . . Part of the epistemological moment to which *The Monk* belongs, and which it best represents, is this opening up of sepulchral depths, the fascination with what may lie hidden in the lower dungeons of institutions and mental constraints ostensibly devoted to discipline and chastity. What does lie hidden there is always the product of erotic drives gone berserk, perverted and deviated through denial, a figuration of the price of repression.

Lewis's psychic architecture, then, offers further confirmation of what we have suggested about the nature of the supernatural in the novel, and the transformation of the Sacred into taboo. Ambrosio's story is most centrally a drama of conquest by a desire made terrific by its freight of repression. Its liberation

Facsimile of a letter from Lewis to his mother discussing the failure of one of his dramas.

will have to be equally terrific: unconsciously and inexorably he will be led to commit both matricide and incest. That is, through the play of repression, erotic pleasure has been necessarily tied to the idea of transgression, violation of taboo; and Ambrosio, once he has given himself over wholly to his erotic drive, will manage to transgress the most basic of them. Particularly, Ambrosio with growing urgency discovers the need to violate, defile, to soil and profane the being who has come to represent for him the summum of erotic pleasure precisely because she is most clothed in the aura of the Sacred, and most protected by taboo. (pp. 258-59)

[The word "disgust" recurs] with remarkable frequency throughout the novel every time an imperious desire has been satisfied. Typically, desire blocked and frustrated becomes "phrensy," out of which desire is satisfied in a moment of violence, which then leads to disgust. A notable moment is the murder of Elvira (Ambrosio's and Antonia's mother), a moment of frenetic passion which culminates: "Ambrosio beheld before him that once noble and majestic form, now become a corse, cold, senseless, and disgusting" . . .—and the object which he sought to gain by the murder, Antonia's possession, now equally appears to him "an object of disgust." . . .

One notes here Lewis's typical laying-on of horrors. Excess in horror, leading to revulsion and disgust, does not, however, seem gratuitous. It points to an attitude toward the dialectic of desire and satisfaction found in that master of the horrific, Sade. It is clear that Sade is obsessed by extreme outrage because he is obsessed by the indifference and impassibility of nature: its lack of ethical content and transcendent value, and man's utter impotence to make his mark upon it. . . . The only principle inherent in nature is in fact destruction, and desire is both inflamed and frustrated by the recurrent discovery that its logical outcome is destruction. Desire, that is, follows a logic which discovers the inevitable destruction of everything it depends upon, its own inherent destructiveness and self-destructiveness. This is what Ambrosio, too, discovers deep in the sepulchre amidst the decomposing corpses, in the morbid nuptial bower where he rapes Antonia. . . . (p. 260)

This outcome of the most imperious desire in the novel suggests that "nature" is profoundly a source of despair, for in its mirror we ultimately discover only our own death and decomposition. Antonia raped images the impossibility of the existence of purity, incorruption, immutability. Her dishonor sums up the inevitable pollution and destruction of the world, and fixes the desirer, Ambrosio himself, in the damned identity of pollutor. (p. 261)

The climactic confrontation of Ambrosio and Antonia—brother and sister, though they don't know it, who share a common obsession with purity—gives the novel's final definition of what guilt means in this world. Guilt is essentially pollution, impurity, violation of the taboo of untouchability. This is of course a very "primitive" conception of guilt. On the one hand, it makes guilt reside in the transgression of taboos, in the profanation of idols. On the other hand, since such pollution is inevitably bound up with the very condition of mortality, it makes guilt incorporate with the very definition of life and of man. As the story of Oedipus the riddle-solver suggests, the sin which must be so terribly expiated is finally that of being a man, the creature whose upright presence on the earth can never be justified.

In pursuing the question of Ambrosio's guilt, we discover finally an ethics of terror. *The Monk* on the one hand tends to

assert that the world is inhabited by irrational and supernatural forces which act upon man, are implicated and brought into play by man's actions and gestures, whether he consciously acknowledge them or not, and on the other hand suggests that these forces do not derive, or no longer derive, from a traditional conception of the Sacred. What has in fact been left after the desacralization of the world is not its rationalization—man's capacity to understand and to manage everything in terms of a rational epistemology and a humanistic ethics—but rather a terrifying and essentially uncontrollable network of violent primitive forces and taboos which are summoned into play by the dialectics of man's desire. Without any operable idea of the Sacred to refer himself to, yet surrounded by supernatural forces with which he must reckon, Ambrosio is at last constrained to see himself, by the process of his desiring, as a man trapped in this network of forces which he can neither control nor deny, which he cannot worship but must sacrifice to.

The Monk, then, seems to give an especially clear and forceful symbolic representation of passage into a world—the Romantic and post-Romantic world, our world—in which the confident rationalism of the Enlightenment has been called into question, yet recognition of the force of the irrational is not accompanied. . . . Ethically, this universe is one where the support of morals in the Sacred is gone, and the definition of guilt and innocence has to do rather with a primitive and irreducible opposition of purity and pollution. There is no guarantee that in his struggle with his inner daemons man will succeed in asserting his innocence. On the contrary, Matilda's logic looks forward to that of Ivan Karamazov [from Dostoevski's *The Brothers Karamazov*], to the posing of the damned question of whether in a world where there is no Sacred, everything is not permitted. In the sense that there is no respect due to a "wholly other," everything *is* permitted. But if virtue need not be acknowledged, there is nonetheless Terror, which has been shown to inhabit nature, and nature's creature, man. (pp. 261-63)

> Peter Brooks, "Virtue and Terror: 'The Monk'," in ELH, *Vol. 40, No. 2, Summer, 1973, pp. 249-63.*

CORAL ANN HOWELLS (essay date 1978)

[*In her book-length study,* Love, Mystery, and Misery, *Howells analyzes the literary craftsmanship of Gothic writers and their presentation of emotion in the novel. In the following excerpt, Howells discusses* The Monk *within the context of Gothic literature and examines its sexual and religious elements. According to Howells,* The Monk *is more "shocking and subversive" than other Gothic works because of its graphic depiction of the relationship between sex and violence. She concludes that "Lewis's storytelling in* The Monk *consciously exploits the secret appeal of Gothic fiction, whose deliberate mode is to separate passion and instinct from everyday life."*]

The Monk is the most daring, the most shocking and the most Gothic of eighteenth-century English Gothic romances. It is daring in its treatment of sexual fantasy and violence; it is shocking in the luridly sensational sense as well as in its radical insights into criminal psychology; and it is Gothic in its presentation of a dark subterranean world filled with supernatural terrors and the odours of death. The areas of feeling with which *The Monk* is concerned go far deeper than the confines of Radcliffian sensibility; they plunge into the murkier regions of Gothic neurosis, especially the dangerous and violent excesses of the erotic imagination which Mrs Radcliffe had scrupulously repressed. It is a fantasy of the buried life of passion and instinct, where the wanderings of unreason are contained and concealed within the Gothic cadre of ecclesiastical architecture. Monastic cells, burial vaults and underground passages provide a frighteningly extensive area for the tortuous exploration into forbidden feelings, making the daylight world look pallid and mediocre. The looming figures in the narrative all belong to the subterranean world, against which the forces of reason and humanity are totally ineffectual. *The Monk* comes close to being a Gothic nightmare but curiously it is not one; instead, it is a Gothic entertainment. What saves *The Monk* from giving us an attack of the horrors is its presentation as pure fantasy for it is a tale of exaggeratedly Gothic dimensions told with immense narrative energy and a gusto which both embellishes the conventions of horror and at the same time subverts them by ridicule. The authorial voice ranges restlessly and wittily over Gothic conventions, engendering in the reader a kind of radical insecurity about the limits of nightmare and reality, but finally denying any connection between the fictive world of the novel and the real world outside it. *The Monk* has the double appeal of allowing us to indulge in extravagances of feeling while protecting us from their consequences by locating such extravagances quite specifically in the remote reaches of fantasy. (pp. 62-3)

With *The Monk* we have for the first time a novel by an English writer which has the German emphasis on fantasies of sexual brutality and on the horrors of physical corruption. This corrupt fleshliness is really very un-English: the main influence on Gothic fiction before Lewis was arguably Shakespearean and Jacobean drama and indeed the influence of Shakespeare is pervasive in *The Monk* as well; there were plenty of murders and ghosts in the English dramatic tradition but not the emphasis on sensual horror or the combination of sexuality and diabolism which Lewis introduced. *The Monk* is much more overtly concerned with suffering and horror than anything produced in the English novel before and the critical question that it raises for us is how the author manages to mediate and control these painful feelings through his literary art.

Lewis is a highly self-conscious storyteller working within a recognisable literary tradition to which he constantly alludes. The resonance of English and German Gothic romance is strongly felt throughout the novel, as he plays with certain predictable responses in his readers, sometimes exploiting Gothic conventions when he wants sensationalism and horrific effects and sometimes drawing attention to their artificiality through comic burlesque. His literary range extends beyond contemporary Gothic to include the folkloric world of ballads and older romances whose titles and characters are woven into the texture of his narrative. . . . Lewis had ample opportunity to play with a wide range of responses in his readers but the responses he evokes are always those appropriate to fantasy rather than to a direct confrontation with the pressures of real life.

The narrative itself hardly encourages us to see it as the imitation of real life; it is highly sensational and unlikely from beginning to end. . . . (pp. 63-4)

Certainly male sexual fantasy seems to be the informing principle of *The Monk* and the pornographic stimulus is clearly there in the thrill of illicit sex; but the sustaining interest is a narrative one, for the novel deftly weaves several subplots in and out of the main one concerning the Monk to contrive a whole range of variations on the theme of sexual disaster. By weaving in the literary strands of ghost stories, German robber stories, ballad narratives of demon lovers and tales of monastic

tyranny, Lewis gives his narrative a resonance beyond that of sexual nightmare. Indeed the narrative interest extends beyond the tale to the teller, into the contemplation of authorship as an activity, a subject which is handled humorously and compassionately in the case of the poetry-writing young page Theodore who is caught up in the 'mania of authorship'. (pp. 65-6)

The Monk was daring in its treatment of sexual fantasy, for it dares to be explicit about desire as it speculates on the dangerous connections between the erotic imagination and the darker instinctual urges towards violence, destruction and death. Like *The Mysteries of Udolpho*, *The Monk* was a response to an oppressive social milieu, but it is much more aggressive than *Udolpho* with striking extensions into criminal pathology as Lewis explores male sexual guilts rather than female sexual fears. Lewis did not write sentimental fiction illustrating the triumph of female virtue but a savage story about the forces of destruction. While treating that conflict between reason, conscience and feeling which is so characteristically Gothic, he turns the conventional moral structure on its head, presenting us with the disturbing possibility that the forces of passion and instinct are stronger than the forces of reason and conscience. All his emphasis is on the power of passion over judgement so that the novel registers a keen sense of moral shock—not only on the part of his characters but on the author's part too—at the revelations of the destructive potential contained within the self. What makes the fantasy so sombre and terrifying is the claustrophobic sense of imprisonment; in a world which Lewis sees as 'base, perfidious and depraved' passion can find no safe place where tenderness and sexuality could flourish and produce life; instead, the sexual instincts have to be kept secret, hidden underground in monastic cells or furtively concealed beneath flowing ecclesiastical robes where they flourish into a bizarrely destructive existence, asserting their power in ways attended by the torments of remorse, guilt and misery. *The Monk* is about sexual obsession but it is not erotic: in no other novel is sex presented more forlornly, as Lewis catches the syndrome of desire, consummation and its aftermath in all its incessant repetitiveness and frustration.

It is in the figure of the Capuchin abbot Ambrosio that sexual desire is imaged most frighteningly. Certainly it was no frivolous choice on the author's part to make his main character a monk, for monkishness with its rigid polarisation of sex and religion and its contempt for the desires of the flesh strikes exactly the right note for dark erotic fantasy. Clearly *The Monk* is anti-Catholic (as most English Gothic fiction was) but hostility to the tyranny and repressiveness of monastic institutions is here directed specifically against their denial of the emotional imperatives of the individual, and it is the vow of chastity that comes in for special attack. Lewis, like Milton, cannot praise a fugitive and cloistered virtue; he criticises as false the virtue of sexual purity when it is only the result of ignorance and lack of contact with the world. Indeed, the simplest part of the narrative shows the destruction of this kind of innocence—as Ambrosio is seduced by a novice in the monastery who turns out to be a woman! The author is certainly keen to persuade his readers of the erotic appeal of illicit sex in a monastic cell by moonlight as the cowls are flung back but Ambrosio's indulgence carries more serious overtones as well. Not only does it falsify his public image of sanctity but it also destroys his fragile self-image, torturing him with guilt and fear till he actually becomes the hypocritical monster that the monks of anti-clerical fiction so often are. From being a worshipper of the Virgin Mary's ideal image, Ambrosio is initiated into the mysteries of sex by the disguised novice who is really a female demon with the Virgin's face, then by tormented stages he gradually becomes a criminal psychopath who rapes and murders an innocent girl after strangling her mother. What is so terrifying to the reader of this lurid history is that we watch Ambrosio degenerating, totally blinded to the inevitability of his crises of feeling, consistently shocked by his own criminal propensities yet powerless to escape from his guilt-ridden obsession. To claim that it is finally not 'obsession' but demonic 'possession' as the author does is, I think, to dodge the issue about the monk's compulsive behaviour which is expressive of repressed desires and fears; but then Lewis was no analyst of feeling like Maturin—he rejects emotional complexity for the shock value of dramatic scenarios.

Ambrosio looms over the novel as a dark tormented figure. Kiely sees him as the type of the Romantic rebel fighting against the forces of repression to seek fulfilment of the infinite possibilities within himself, a being for whom reform and salvation are unthinkable as he pursues his reckless course [see excerpt dated 1972]. But in Ambrosio we also have the spectacle of a crippled hero, whose energies have been so constricted by his monastic upbringing that they have turned inwards, creating the self-imprisonment of obsession. The architectural structures that Ambrosio inhabits become in the course of the novel images of his own tortuous psychology; instead of being places of retreat they turn into places of death and imprisonment as his course leads him out of the cathedral and the monastic cell into the funeral vaults and finally to the prisons of the Inquisition. Through it all, Lewis traces the course of frustrated sexual desire, perverted by monkish repression from its romantic yearnings and imaginative idealisation into a dark destructive lust for power. For Ambrosio, the sexual impulse has been so contaminated by deception and guilt from the beginning that it is productive of nothing but an inveterate hostility towards women as the betrayers and humiliators of men. This in turn encourages the dreadful complicity between him and his first mistress, who is a *femme fatale* in the literal sense. Their partnership is much more evil than its mechanics of diabolism suggest for it consistently denies and betrays natural human feeling. The real shock to the reader is not the thrill of monkish sexuality but the revelation of Ambrosio's potential for cruelty and violence. In him desire can only find its consummation in rape and murder in the funeral vaults of a convent, a terrible image of sexuality dehumanised but not deprived of its instinctual energy.

Behind his sanctified public image Ambrosio is remarkably unstable, for human character as Lewis reveals it is not something fixed, as most Gothic novelists pretended to believe. . . . For Lewis inconsistency and instability are part of the nature of things, not only of human beings and feelings but of the whole contingent world. *The Monk* is organised on this principle, not on the static notion that appearances and reality are different but that reality itself is a very shifty concept and at any time we are likely to be confronted by something entirely outside our expectations and which undermines all our assumptions about the way things ought to be. The narrative forces on us these shocks of confrontation in its incidents, its revelations about feeling and motive and in its changes of tone, striking through our accustomed responses into new apprehensions of insecurity.

A startling instance of the subversive nature of Lewis's fiction occurs in a ghost story, one of the sub-plots in *The Monk,* about two lovers Raymond and Agnes who plan to elope from a German castle together with Agnes disguised as the ghost of

a nun. The narrative context deliberately parodies Gothic romance, mocking the legend of the ghostly nun with Agnes's own 'burlesqued gravity' and joking about romances like *Tristan and Iseult,* 'those unmerciful volumes' as Raymond calls them. The lovers' adventure promises to be played out as high farce, with Agnes calmly walking past the superstitious inhabitants of the castle in her disguise; everything looks like a comic exploitation of Gothic and the lovers drive away in their carriage. Only then does the tone change: the carriage begins to fly away at breakneck speed . . . and when it is smashed to pieces in a storm Raymond is struck senseless by a piece of flying flint. It is not till he recovers that the bizarre truth of his adventure begins to dawn on him: it is not his beloved Agnes with whom he has eloped but the Bleeding Nun herself! His terrible realisation is recorded as a Gothic nightmare. (pp. 66-70)

[Lewis traces Raymond's sensations] in the behaviouristic detail of a theatrical performance, with the 'sudden chillness' of premonitory dread, the 'shuddering' and the hair 'bristling with alarm'. Then the ghost herself appears, impassive and slow-moving as befits the animated corpse that she is, and we have the nightmare description of the demon lover who is commonly portrayed as a ghost or a corpse or a vampire. The figure whom Raymond and the reader had assumed to be part of legend suddenly leaps out into a different kind of existence. Lewis insists on keeping close to physical notation as we watch Raymond transformed by sheer terror into the mirror image of the ghost herself: his 'stillness', 'the blood frozen in his veins' and his 'nerves bound up in impotence' convert him into a death image too. (p. 71)

It is typical of Lewis to create a grotesque Gothic entertainment like this, filled with the clichés of dread and horror and amusingly amplified by the ghost's own words singing a silly rhyme in a 'sepulchral voice'. . . . For Lewis there are no limits to fantasy but fantasy becomes a way of plumbing the psyche to the area of those forces which lie below rational comprehension and whose images are available only through nightmare. What is so shocking about the supernatural nun, for Raymond and for us, is the way she corresponds to a vision of sexuality as being something dangerous to life. (p. 72)

The history of the Bleeding Nun provides a kind of warning to the reader about Ambrosio's career with its furtive monastic sexuality. Once the Monk has been awakened to the possibilities of sex through his seduction in the monastery, he is caught up in a web of guilt-ridden erotic fantasy from which he cannot escape, and when the young girl Antonia comes to him begging for a confessor for her dying mother he sees her, whose 'affliction seemed to add new lustre to her charms' . . . , as the perfect victim. Though her feeling for her begins as the most conventional romantic fantasy, the impossiblity of a love relationship with her rapidly transforms tenderness into desperate lust; to fulfil his ambitions in such repressive conditions he has to resort to diabolical arts. (pp. 72-3)

The rape of Antonia reads like a demonic distortion of the final scene of *Romeo and Juliet,* with Antonia drugged and buried in the funeral vaults of the convent and 'resurrected' by Ambrosio. Lewis knew that he could rely on his readers' literary expectations to respond to the gloomy horror of echoing vaults, funeral trappings and dimly receding architectural perspectives, just as he could exploit the common Gothic situation of a beautiful heroine persecuted by a lustful villain. What shocked his readers out of their comfortable literary horrors was that he went far beyond conventional Gothic fears to the ultimate assault of rape, showing both its physical brutality and its dimensions of nightmare fantasy. (p. 73)

As an account of sexual outrage [the rape of Antonia] comes very close to pornography, with its excited insistence on the illicit thrills of monkish sensuality and its attempts to shock us by the display of physical cruelty. Ambrosio and Antonia are reduced to the level of rapist and victim, stripped of any other feelings but those directly related to this act of violation: Ambrosio's tormented rhapsody of the flesh only acts as a stimulus to his brutal assault, while Antonia like a true victim can do nothing but aggravate his lust by her 'evident disgust' and 'incessant opposition'. There is no question of gratification or delight on anybody's part—the characters' or the readers'—but there is for us the voyeuristic fascination of watching how far conventional limits can be transgressed, as the Monk dares to proceed along ways that are forbidden until the rape is accomplished. The authorial language of moral opprobrium at the end merely underlines the shockingness of the rape.

Even after the rape there is no release from the dark fantasy world for Ambrosio's frenzies of self-recrimination flower into his nightmarish project to keep Antonia as a prisoner in the vaults so that he can secretly come to do penance to her in yet another convolution of his deranged and perverted idealism. There is deadlock between them, until suddenly voices from the outside world break in and Antonia attempts to escape. However, Ambrosio catches her by her streaming hair and stabs her twice as she clings to a pillar crying out for help. This stabbing is the only possible ending to such a nightmare, where sexual desire has been perverted from a life-giving to a death-dealing force: orgasmic destruction is the appropriate consummation. . . . Obsessed as it was with sexual feeling as a forbidden but fascinating area of speculation, Gothic fiction always leans towards pornography; Lewisian Gothic takes the further step of making the connection between sex, guilt and death quite explicit.

The final movement of the novel is also towards death as it pushes through a labyrinth of Gothic terrors to Ambrosio's destruction. After his unmasking he is thrown into the prison of the Inquisition, that place of mysterious persecution which fascinated not only Lewis but Gothic novelists from Mrs Radcliffe to Maturin. Totally cut off from the outside world, Ambrosio moves through his nightmare of damnation, tormented in body by the Inquisition and tempted by Matilda on the plea of their 'mutual guilt and danger' to sell his soul to the Devil for release. He signs the Faustian pact at the very moment that the guards enter to take him away to be ceremonially burned as a heretic and the conventional Gothic machinery of sensationalism and diabolism once more stifle any exploration of the psychological drama. . . . By totally alienating Ambrosio from society, the author seems concerned to deny any connection between his tormented career and real-life problems. In his last-minute revelation that Ambrosio had been the victim of diabolical stratagems from the beginning, he implies that nothing in the Monk's history relates to sexual or religious oppression but that it is all demonic. He actually identifies the irrational with the supernatural, a shocking instance of authorial bad faith when we consider that the stuff of the novel has been the exploration of the buried life of passion and instinct. (pp. 75-7)

Lewis's rhetoric of sensationalism with its 'tortures most exquisite and insupportable' almost obscures Ambrosio's genuine moral anguish, for he does achieve some knowledge in his commerce with the devil, an insight into human fallibility which confirms his despair. The horrors are so extreme that they mask any understanding of his suffering; the language is not the notation of real life but entirely literary in its resonance. It links Ambrosio's suffering with that of other great sinners of Christian and pagan myth, from the echoes of Satan in the debased Miltonic of 'Headlong fell the Monk through the airy waste' to the torments of Prometheus and Tantalus. The exaggerated claims made for the Titanic proportions of Ambrosio's sin and its punishment culminate in his death on the seventh day presented as a savage inversion of the Creation. After such a grandiose display we are left in a state of shock as the 'despairing Monk' and all his concerns are swept off the face of the earth. A kind of catharsis has been achieved in the liberation of violent feelings within Gothic horror fantasy.

Lewis is shocking and subversive in a way that Mrs Radcliffe never was in his exploration of the dark irrational hinterland of the human mind whose glooms and terrors find an appropriate image in the labyrinthine Gothic underworld. Far from restricting his imagination, the rhetoric of Gothic fantasy gives him the freedom to explore an extensive range of hidden feelings with the escapist world of romance. It may even be argued that Lewis's storytelling in *The Monk* consciously exploits the secret appeal of Gothic fiction, whose deliberate mode is to separate passion and instinct from everyday life, so allowing their indulgence and effectively controlling the threat of the irrational by forcing it back into the realms of fantasy. (pp. 78-9)

Coral Ann Howells, "M. G. Lewis, 'The Monk'," in her Love, Mystery, and Misery: Feeling in Gothic Fiction, *The Athlone Press, 1978, pp. 62-79.*

DAVID MORSE   (essay date 1982)

[*Morse interprets* The Monk *as a reflection of the political upheaval following the French Revolution and the subsequent degeneration of traditional morals. In addition, Morse discusses the conflict between sexuality and religion in the novel.*]

The publication of *The Monk* by Matthew Lewis in 1796 marked a decisive turning-point in the development of Gothic. Other writers of the 1790s, such as Radcliffe, Bage and Holcroft, had taken over a genteel literary tradition and attempted to open it up by broaching within its parameters themes of personal and political liberation. Since their paramount value was reason, they felt obliged to maintain a consistent moral perspective in their work. Oddly, *The Monk* too is written from a rationalistic point of view and there is much in it that is consistent with the radical temper of the times, but it is marked off from its predecessors by its unequivocal character as a work of popular literature, by its frank espousal and even exultation in the erotic, in violence, in the horrors of the supernatural. Where Mrs Radcliffe presented mysterious happenings and then explained them away, Lewis presented the satanic as real; where she hinted at illicit sensuality and gestured towards obscure crimes, Lewis openly presented and described. What made the book all the more disturbing was the equivocal attitude which Lewis took towards his subject: behind a genteel deploring of such nefarious goings-on can be discerned a humanistic point of view, similar to that of Diderot, which sees the religious and ascetic life as unnatural because it contradicts the essential nature of man; but at the back of that is the implication that man is most truly himself when most utterly perverse: that is to say, when he follows deep and unexplained impulses within him. *The Monk* reflects the intellectual ferment and confusion in the aftermath of the French Revolution: its clearest message is the disintegration of all traditional moral values and one which the Gothic iconography is able to present with the utmost force.

Virtually all the paradoxes of *The Monk* are linked with its pretensions to be a polemic against the Catholic Church. Lewis can write about Catholicism with confidence, secure in the knowledge that his Protestant readers will be only too ready to concur in his condemnation, without examining too closely the standpoint from which the condemnation is made. Lewis alternates between an indictment characteristic of the Reformation period, in which the church is seen as a decadent and morally corrupt institution, propagating mystifying doctrines to deceive the people while licensing practices that are morally abhorrent, and a more contemporary view in which the church is seen as violating man's natural instincts. . . . There is also much in Lewis's criticism of the church that is consonant with the views of Godwin and other radical contemporaries. The novel points to the dangers of absolute and irresponsible use of power, so that the prioress can commit murder (or contemplate it) without fear of retribution and can even deny a papal bull. Hypocrisy and lack of openness are identified as the gravest of moral crimes. The dangers associated with closed institutions and the excessive practice of secrecy are insisted upon. Like Godwin, Lewis also shows that justice or the lack of it is bound up with one's position in society: Agnes can have the severest punishments inflicted upon her, while Ambrosio and the prioress can act with complete impunity. The irrational is displayed as the means by which arbitrary power is masked and veiled. For Lewis everything that is connected with the institutional is false; it is therefore fitting that the novel should reach its climax with the destruction of the convent of St Clare. Since many religious institutions were similarly invaded during the French Revolution, it is difficult not to see Lewis as associating himself with the destruction of an irrational and oppressive past—its replacement by a society based more securely on the principles of human nature.

Critical discussions of *The Monk* tend to focus obsessively on the character of Ambrosio; yet it is crucial to any understanding of the novel to recognise both its polycentric character and the intricacy of its construction. In particular it is clear that the story of the Bleeding Nun, or the History of Don Raymond, as it is known, is not an exotic interpolation but is the motif that underlies everything else, as it is subjected to various permutations. Lewis took the theme of the Bleeding Nun from traditional German literature, but there can be little doubt but that Lewis clearly understood its erotic signficance—the repression of female sexuality. For Lewis's purpose it was necessary to show that convents, as much as monasteries, were unnatural places and that the confinement of women within them involved the denial of their libidinal instincts as well as their capacity for bearing children. The myth of the Bleeding Nun is built around a structural opposition between the fact that the nun is veiled and the fact that she is bleeding. The veil stands for the traditional chastity ascribed to women, the fact that their charms are traditionally covered, the belief that sex does not and need not concern them. The symbol of the veil is contradicted by the symbol of blood, which implies both the defloration of the virgin and the menstrual flow, which is a perpetual sign of a woman's capacity to have children. (pp. 50-3)

Thematic doubling is a notable feature of literature of the Romantic period and *The Monk* is no exception. Lewis lays great stress on the idea of the erotic woman, and all the female characters in the novel are shown to be highly sexed—in fact, the women characteristically take the initiative. Baroness Lindenberg presses her attentions on Don Raymond in a way that he finds embarrassing. Marguerite, who aids him when he is in danger from brigands, describes her nature as being 'licentious and warm'. When it is suggested that Agnes be confined within a convent, Lewis refers to this as 'a fate so contrary to her inclinations'. Ambrosio is initiated into the delights of sex by Matilda in a way that strongly recalls the corruption of Adam by Eve. Even the beautiful Virginia de Villa Franca is induced to give up the veil by the fact that Lorenzo's 'person pleased her'. . . . The whole novel can be seen as a struggle between those who conceal or deny the nature of feminine sexuality and those who seek to bring it out into the open. For this reason it is symbolically appropriate that Agnes after her terrible sufferings should finally be freed from the convent of St Clare and enabled to marry Don Raymond; for Agnes has become identified with the Bleeding Nun and her liberation signifies the ending of the nightmare induced by the false and unnatural ideal of chastity.

The motif of the veil that conceals feminine sexuality is doubled and paralleled by the mask of sanctity that covers the uncontrollable desires of Ambrosio. This symmetrical relation is apparent form the opening scene in the church of the Capuchins: Antonia is introduced as the veiled woman, Ambrosio as 'the man of holiness'—a transparent disguise, since as soon as he is alone he 'gave free loose to the indulgence of his vanity'; humility is only a 'semblance', pride the reality. This first chapter announces, in the manner of an overture, the principle themes of the novel: Antonia's reluctance to unveil, even in church as is customary, can be seen as symbolically contradicting the assumption that there is nothing to offend a woman's modesty in church, while both Lorenzo's dream and the gypsy's prophecy suggest that in a future confrontation between Ambrosio and Antonia all such cultural concealments of the nature of sexuality will be thrown aside. Indeed, the theme of the picture strongly suggests that Ambrosio's religious fervour is a deflection from the path of normal profane love. (pp. 53-5)

Ambrosio's progress through the novel is not from sensuality to spirituality, but from the spiritual to the sensual; but, what is still more important, Lewis suggests that Ambrosio as a model of religious piety, as a man who does not even know the difference between the sexes, can only be bogus; when erotically obsessed, he is most completely genuine. Moreover, Lewis is perfectly clear that it is culture that prevents the free expression and fulfilment of his desires: 'The danger of discovery, the fear of being repulsed, the loss of reputation—all these considerations counselled him to stifle his desires'. Nevertheless, Lewis suggests that because of his education within religious institutions Ambrosio's sexuality has become warped. His heart has been corrupted by a thoroughgoing Catholic education, so that it is no longer possible for him to respond in a completely spontaneous and authentic manner. . . . The position that Lewis adopts is one very characteristic of the Enlightenment. Since man's natural inclinations are good, it is only necessary to give them scope for expression; in contact with others and with the opposite sex, in an expanded commerce with the ordinary world, his benevolence and sympathy for others can expand and flourish. The passions, when acknowledged and given latitude, can also be directed and controlled. A religious education, on the other hand, denies a man's essential nature, cuts him off from his fellow men, develops irrational prejudices and partial sympathies. *The Monk* is a lesson in the catastrophic consequences of such an education: desires that under other circumstances would be natural in Ambrosio become perverse and are deflected from their appropriate forms of expression: erotic tenderness is transformed into sadistic negativity and violence.

That Ambrosio represents the working out in a perverse form of normal human desires is clearly demonstrated by a counter-plot of Don Raymond and Agnes: just as Matilda/Rosario pursues Ambrosio into the monastery and attempts to awaken his natural impulses, so Don Raymond follows Agnes and attempts to secure her release from the convent. Don Raymond's disguise as a gardener's assistant repeats Matilda's disguise as a religous novice. However, there is a very crucial difference between the two cases: Ambrosio has been so long cut off from a pattern of normal relations between the sexes that his desires, when awakened, can find no adequate object; it is his tragedy that his self-discovery necessarily leads him on a downward path of self-destruction.

The conflict between *eros* and the Catholic Church in *The Monk* also has the form of a conflict between life and death. The church is associated with rottenness, putrescence, decay: the transformation of life into death. Indeed this, for Lewis, is precisely the function fulfilled by the monastery or convent. The church is unnatural, for, instead of acknowledging that the living and the dead are mutually exclusive categories, in its preoccupation with the dead and in its denial of life, it represents the means whereby the world of the living is invaded by the world of the dead. That the church is an institution which contradicts human nature is emphasised by Lewis in the opening lines of the novel: 'The audience now assembled in the Capuchin church was collected by various causes, but all of them were foreign to the ostensible motive. The women came to show themselves—the men, to see the women'. Sexual attraction, not religiosity, is the real motive for the gathering; but, while normal human instincts can express themselves through the forms prescribed by religious convention, the church also has a sinister significance: as a mechanism whereby the living are transformed into the dead. Ambrosio, by a process of religious instruction, is made into a monster of virtue, a man made unnatural as well as hypocritical by the pretence that he is not touched by human feeling. Significantly, his sexual awakening is also associated with revival from death: it is only after Matilda has sucked the venom from a deadly snake bite and after he is restored to consciousness that he also becomes aware of her nature as a woman and his initiation into the erotic takes place. The struggle between *eros* and death is also worked out in the theme of the Bleeding Nun and through its relation to Agnes. The denial of *eros* in the case of Beatrice with catastrophic consequences is nearly repeated with Agnes, who is thwarted in her attempt to escape with Don Raymond, her lover, through the fact that her own impersonation of the Bleeding Nun is inverted, when the spectre of the Bleeding Nun is thought by Don Raymond to be Agnes. The appearance of the Bleeding Nun—herself a symbol of the cultural repression of female sexuality—represents an invasion of the world of the living by the world of the dead. . . . [The] state of being between life and death is paralleled by Ambrosio and Antonia. The multiple symbolic deaths of Agnes also befall Antonia: first rendered insensible by mysterious powers, then buried in a state of suspended consciousness, from which she revives only to be slain by Ambrosio. Although Antonia is the most modest and virtuous feminine character in the book, her death figures symbolically as a punishment both of Lorenzo, her lover, and herself for their denial of *eros*. (pp. 55-8)

Nevertheless, Lewis is not an unqualified sexual libertarian. Lewis recognised that a free and spontaneous sexuality necessarily implied the acknowledgement of feminine sexuality, and he saw the harm caused by its denial; but when it came down to it he was as fearful of opening this Pandora's box as anyone else. Indeed, *The Monk* can also be read as an allegory of the rejection of female sexuality by Monk/Lewis! . . . The demonic conclusion of *The Monk* has a certain psychological truth, if Lewis himself is far from the moral pietism which it notionally invokes: the dream of freedom and fulfilment has turned into a nightmare.

Although Lewis sealed Ambrosio's fate with terrifying retribution and punishment, he nevertheless did write *The Monk* very much from the point of view of his demonic hero—so much so that there can be little doubt that the longing for erotic liberation, and the anxiety which the prospect induces, is Lewis's own. Lewis ostensibly deplored the duplicity and sensuality of Ambrosio, but his manner of exhibiting Ambrosio's awakening has powerfully amoral overtones. For Ambrosio could only be moral as long as he was not acquainted with his own erotic drives, and, if his consciousness of them left him no alternative but to follow them, there could only be one conclusion: that the appearance of morality could only be hypocritical and inauthentic, that the strength of a man's impulses becomes for him at once truth and nemesis. *The Monk*, for contemporary readers, was shocking simply in the garishness of its surface details, but it also disconcerted at this deeper level. For, although Lewis had retained damnation, he had nevertheless very effectively disposed of morality! (pp. 60-1)

> *David Morse, ''The Transposition of Gothic,'' in his* Romanticism: A Structural Analysis, *Barnes & Noble Books, 1982, pp. 50-103.*

ADDITIONAL BIBLIOGRAPHY

B[aker], E. A. Introduction to *The Monk: A Romance*, by M. G. Lewis, edited by E. A. Baker, pp. vii-xvi. London: George Routledge & Sons, 1929.
> Contends that *The Monk* ''has little claim to perpetuation on its own merits,'' but underscores the novel's historical significance as ''the most notorious exemplar of the 'Gothic' school of romance.''

[Baron-Wilson, Mrs. Cornwell]. *The Life and Correspondence of M. G. Lewis*. 2 vols. London: Henry Colburn, Publisher, 1839.
> The first biography of Lewis. Though now considered inaccurate, Baron-Wilson's work is notable for its extensive collection of Lewis's letters as well as for the inclusion of previously unpublished poems.

Church, Elizabeth. ''A Bibliographical Myth.'' *Modern Philology* XIX, No. 3 (February 1922): 307-14.
> Argues that Lewis was not the author of *Tales of Terror*, a work commonly attributed to him that was published anonymously in 1801.

Conger, Syndy M. ''An Analysis of *The Monk* and Its German Sources.'' In her *Romantic Reassessment: Matthew G. Lewis, Charles Robert Maturin and the Germans, an Interpretative Study of the Influence of German Literature on Two Gothic Novels*, edited by James Hogg, pp. 12-125. Salzburg Studies in English Literature, edited by Erwin A. Stürzl, no. 67. Salzburg: Universität Salzburg, 1977.
> Explores the nature and extent of Lewis's reliance on German sources in writing *The Monk*.

Emerson, Oliver F. "'Monk' Lewis and the *Tales of Terror*." *Modern Language Notes* XXXVIII, No. 3 (March 1923): 154-57.
> Discusses the authorship of *Tales of Terror*. Emerson contends that the volume, rather than being Lewis's own work, is in fact a parody of his style.

Irwin, Joseph James. *M. G. "Monk" Lewis*. Twayne's English Authors Series, no. 198. Boston: G. K. Hall & Co., Twayne Publishers, 1976, 176 p.
> An overview of Lewis's life and works. Irwin's focus is biographical rather than critical.

Lewis, Paul. "Fearful Lessons: The Didacticism of the Early Gothic Novel." *CLA Journal* XXIII, No. 4 (June 1980): 470-84.*
> A discussion of the didactic elements in the works of Ann Radcliffe and Lewis.

Lydenberg, Robin. "Ghostly Rhetoric: Ambivalence in M. G. Lewis's *The Monk*." *Ariel: A Review of International English Literature* 10, No. 2 (April 1979): 65-79.
> Suggests that Lewis's ambivalent attitude toward the sexual and fantastic elements in *The Monk* indicates his uncertainty about his role as a writer.

McNutt, Dan J. "Matthew Gregory Lewis (1775-1818)." In his *The Eighteenth-Century Gothic Novel: An Annotated Bibliography of Criticism and Selected Texts*, pp. 226-64. New York: Garland, 1975.
> An annotated bibliography of writings about Lewis from 1796 to the mid-twentieth century. McNutt also provides a listing of Lewis's principle works.

Parreaux, André. *The Publication of "The Monk": A Literary Event, 1796-1798*. Paris: Librairie Marcel Didier, 1960, 202 p.
> Examines the reception of *The Monk* following its first publication.

Peck, Louis F. "Southey and *Tales of Wonder*." *Modern Language Notes* L, No. 8 (December 1935): 513-14.*
> A discussion of Robert Southey's contribution to *Tales of Wonder*.

———. "*The Monk* and *Le diable amoureux*." *Modern Language Notes* LXVIII, No. 6 (June 1953): 406-08.*
> Analyzes the similarities between *The Monk* and Jacques Cazotte's novel *Le diable amoureux*.

———. *A Life of Matthew G. Lewis*. Cambridge: Harvard University Press, 1961, 331 p.
> The definitive biography by the foremost Lewis scholar. Peck provides the first comprehensive account of the author's life and corrects a number of errors in earlier biographical studies. A large portion of the book is composed of Lewis's correspondence, much of it previously unpublished.

Praz, Mario. "La belle dame sans merci." In his *The Romantic Agony*, 2d ed., translated by Angus Davidson, pp. 197-300. London: Oxford University Press, 1970.*
> Surveys the theme of the "Fatal Woman" in Romantic literature. Praz cites Matilda, the witch in *The Monk*, as an example of this type of "arrogant and cruel" female character.

Quennell, Peter. "The Moon Stood Still on Strawberry Hill." *Horizon* XI, No. 2 (Summer 1969): 113-17.*
> A brief history of the Gothic novel from Horace Walpole's *The Castle of Otranto* up to Jane Austen's *Northanger Abbey*.

Summers, Montague. "Matthew Gregory Lewis." In his *The Gothic Quest: A History of the Gothic Novel*, pp. 202-308. London: Fortune Press, 1938.
> An analysis of many of Lewis's works from one of the most thorough studies of the Gothic movement. The chapter also contains a general summary of the author's life and literary career.

———. "Lewis, Matthew Gregory (1775-1818)." In his *A Gothic Bibliography*, pp. 96-9. London: Fortune Press, 1947.
> Bibliography of Lewis's writings that contains information regarding the performances of his dramas.

Thomas, William. "They Called Him 'Monk'." *The Personalist* XLVII, No. 1 (Winter 1966): 81-90.
> A general introduction to Lewis's life and writings.

Varma, Devendra P. "Schauer-Romantik: or Chambers of Horror." In his *The Gothic Flame: Being a History of the Gothic Novel in England, Its Origins, Efflorescence, Disintegration, and Residuary Influences*, pp. 129-72. London: Arthur Barker, 1957.*
> Discusses Lewis as an exponent of the Schauer-Romantik phase of the Gothic novel, which was characterized by violence, sensationalism, and horror.

John Stuart Mill

1806-1873

English philosopher, economist, autobiographer, essayist, and critic.

Mill is considered the greatest English philosopher of the nineteenth century. In addition, critics regard his essay *On Liberty* as one of the seminal works in the development of English liberalism. Mill's theories are admired for their exceptional probity and for their ability to transcend the conventional boundaries of philosophy, sociology, history, and politics. Enhanced by his powerful, lucid, and accessible prose style, Mill's writings on government, economics, and logic suggest a model for society that remains compelling and relevant.

Mill was born in London, the eldest of the nine children of James and Harriet Mill. His father, trained as a minister but employed as a free-lance journalist, was a devout follower of his friend Jeremy Bentham's radical brand of utilitarianism. Benthamite utilitarianism stressed pragmatism, agnosticism, and "the greatest good for the greatest number" as its philosophical ideals; in addition, Benthamites were guided solely by the question "Is it useful?" in all matters from government policy to religion and art. As an educational theory, utilitarianism called for rigorous training with particular emphasis on logic and analysis. The elder Mill, anxious to raise his son in accordance with the strictest utilitarian principles, soon embarked on a training project that he dubbed the "Great Experiment." His education completely overseen by his father, young Mill was reading Greek at the age of three and by the age of eight had completed a university-level course of study. Constant, grueling mental drilling formed Mill into a child prodigy, but it also left him emotionally and socially underdeveloped. This "Great Experiment" later caused Thomas Carlyle to label Mill a "logic-chopping machine," and the statesman William Gladstone to refer to Mill as the "saint of rationalism."

To Mill's father, the experiment had proved a success. By the age of sixteen, his son had mastered French, psychology, law, and political economy, and had founded the Utilitarian Society. In addition to handling the affairs of the society, Mill became embroiled in political debate over the merits of utilitarianism, writing prolifically for such periodicals as the *Traveller,* the *Morning Chronicle,* and the *Westminster Review.* He defended Bentham's ideas, argued for their application, and supported Robert Malthus's theory of population growth. Because his father wanted Mill to shun politics, he advised his son to begin working with him at the East India Company, a foreign trade concern. Mill did so in 1823, and remained at the company until his retirement thirty-five years later.

In 1825, as he participated in the Speculative Society debate series, Mill began to question his former beliefs, feeling that he was perceived as a "manufactured man" and that his utilitarian creed and way of life could never bring him true personal satisfaction. As he later recounted in his *Autobiography,* in 1826 Mill suffered a "mental crisis" that caused him to doubt all of his values and precipitated several months of depression. He realized that his early training had deprived him of an emotional life, friendship, and the ability to feel joy; he longed

for a variety of experiences and wrote that he felt "stranded at the commencement of [his] voyage with a well-equipped ship and rudder, but no sail." Seeking to broaden his spectrum of knowledge and range of sympathies, Mill began to read the works of Auguste Comte, Carlyle, Samuel Taylor Coleridge, and William Wordsworth and became particularly enchanted with Wordsworth's Romantic mysticism and Carlyle's passion for social reform. In addition, in 1830 Mill met Harriet Taylor, a wealthy and educated married woman, and the two soon formed what he described as a "perfect friendship." Taylor's husband acknowledged and approved of their platonic relationship, although it scandalized their friends. After corresponding and meeting publicly for twenty years, they married in 1851, two years after the death of Taylor's husband. Following their marriage, they became virtual recluses as they worked together in their villa in St. Véran, France. Mill credited Taylor with coauthoring almost all his works, particularly *The Subjection of Women.* Though critics acknowledge Taylor's influence, some also believe that Mill's evaluation of her intellectual capabilities was exaggerated and that he allowed her to exercise too much control over his writings—for example, she excised whole sections of the *Autobiography.* To the end of his life, Mill viewed his character as a curious mixture of the intellectual capabilities imparted by his father and the greater emotional expressiveness nurtured by his wife.

Taylor's death in 1858 devastated Mill, and he gradually sought new activities to hold his interest: he served in the House of Commons from 1865 to 1867 and was then elected to the honorary position of rector of St. Andrew's University. He continued to write prolifically and was at work on an essay on socialism when he died in Avignon, France.

Mill distinguished himself in many different fields throughout his life. His public prominence as a political theorist and philosopher was first established in the 1820s with the publication of his early essays and continued to grow while he served as editor of the *London and Westminster Review* from 1835 to 1840; his reputation was further enhanced by the publication, in 1843, of his first major book, *A System of Logic, Ratiocinative and Inductive*. Sympathetic critics eagerly received the work, and some compared him to the great English philosopher John Locke. An argument in favor of empiricism, *A System of Logic* spiritedly defended the superiority of inductive reasoning and, in particular, the validity of the syllogism. In addition, Mill differentiated between the connotation and the denotation of syllogistic terms and devised a system for classifying logical propositions as either analytic or synthetic. Critics cite his development of a method for proving conclusions in ethics and social science as one of Mill's chief contributions as a logician.

In 1848, Mill published *Principles of Political Economy*, in which he studied the interrelationship between capital, labor, and production. Influenced by the English economist David Ricardo, Mill focused on the ramifications of the growth of the working class in England, including the need for redistribution of wealth. Mill showed how the wage system perpetuated poverty in England and Ireland and advocated a system of peasant-proprietorships as an alternative to land ownership.

One of Mill's most important works, often considered his masterpiece, *On Liberty* appeared in 1859 to both widespread praise and censure. In this work, Mill delineated his concepts of liberty and liberalism, stressing the importance of education and freedom from convention. Upholding the supremacy of individual rights in society, he formulated his notorious proclamation that "the state exists for man, and hence the only warrantable imposition upon personal liberty is self-protection."

Mill's *Utilitarianism*, which originally appeared in 1861 as a series of articles in *Fraser's* magazine, represents a revision of his views on Bentham's philosophy. Critiquing Bentham's notion that the "calculus of pleasure and pain" is the main motivating force in human behavior, Mill described altruism as the impetus for action and differentiated between gradations of pleasure. He was especially concerned to correct any misconceptions of his ethical theory based on Benthamite utilitarianism, emphasizing his later acceptance of the imagination and emotions as factors in evaluating human wants and needs.

Published in 1869, Mill's revolutionary treatise *The Subjection of Women* remains one of the seminal documents of the women's liberation movement. By exploring such issues as the psychology of the sexes, social conditioning, women's education, and marriage laws, Mill argued for full equality and voting rights for women. Critics consider his analysis of the domestic and social forces that account for differences between the sexes to be one of Mill's main achievements in this work.

His *Autobiography*, published posthumously, forms the basis for Mill's consideration as a literary figure. He achieves his stated purpose—relating the Benthamite experiment that shaped his extraordinary education and early life—through a detailed account of the various stages of his emotional and intellectual growth. In what critics assess as an admirably direct and perceptive prose style, Mill also discusses the causes and effects of his 1826 "mental crisis" and the evolution of his political, economic, and ethical philosophies.

Although his works were greeted with mixed reviews upon publication, most of them came to be recognized as classics in their fields. Mill's death and the subsequent publication of his *Autobiography* were followed by a resurgence of critical interest in his works. His early theoretical books, *A System of Logic* and *Principles of Political Economy*, have served as standard university textbooks since their appearance, and his other works, especially *On Liberty* and the *Autobiography*, have been widely discussed by both nineteenth- and twentieth-century commentators. While many critics have praised Mill's elegant exposition and ability to explain complex ideas in clear terms, they regard his extensive knowledge, eclectic approach, and philosophical theories as his most outstanding contributions. Scholars admire his complex, intricately argued positions, yet point out that they are vulnerable to criticism. For example, R. W. Church, James Fitzjames Stephen, Bernard Bosanquet, and Malcolm Cowley have examined what they consider the inherent inconsistencies and inadequacies of Mill's defense of individuality in *On Liberty*. Moreover, such critics as Noel Annan and J. B. Schneewind have explored the question of the originality of his theories. Modern critics, including M. H. Abrams, Edward Alexander, F. Parvin Sharpless, and Thomas Woods, have also assessed Mill's theories of and relation to literature. Other commentators, among them Georg Brandes, Kate Millett, Wendell Robert Carr, and Susan Moller Okin, have delved into the strengths and weaknesses of Mill's position on women's rights.

The diversity of Mill's social concerns and the breadth of his knowledge continue to impress readers. By contributing to the systematization of logic and political economy, expanding the domain of the social theorist, and championing the cause of women's suffrage, Mill has earned a distinguished place among English philosophers. As Marshall Cohen has written, Mill was "the last philosopher of any nationality to cover the whole range of philosophical problems with comparable distinction."

PRINCIPAL WORKS

A System of Logic, Ratiocinative and Inductive: Being a Connected View of the Principles of Evidence and the Methods of Scientific Investigation (essay) 1843
Essays on Some Unsettled Questions of Political Economy (essays) 1844
Principles of Political Economy, with Some of Their Applications to Social Philosophy (essay) 1848
*Dissertations and Discussions: Political, Philosophical, and Historical. 4 vols. (essays) 1859-75
On Liberty (essay) 1859
Utilitarianism (essay) 1863
Auguste Comte and Positivism (criticism) 1865
An Examination of Sir William Hamilton's Philosophy and of the Principal Philosophical Questions Discussed in His Writings (criticism) 1865
The Subjection of Women (essay) 1869
Autobiography (autobiography) 1873
**Nature, the Utility of Religion, and Theism (essays) 1874

Collected Works of John Stuart Mill. 21 vols.
    (autobiography, essays, criticism, and letters)   1963-84

*This work includes the essays "Bentham" and "Coleridge."

**This work is commonly referred to as *Three Essays on Religion.*

ALEXIS DE TOCQUEVILLE (letter date 1835)

[*Tocqueville was a French essayist, historian, and memoir and travel writer. His* De la démocratie en Amerique (Democracy in America) *ranks as one of the greatest political, social, and cultural investigations ever written. In the following excerpt from a letter to Mill, Tocqueville expresses his admiration for Mill as a reviewer. Greatly influenced by Tocqueville's theories, Mill had critiqued the first part of* Democracy in America *in the* Westminster Review *in 1835.*]

Your article on me is so flattering that it surpasses even an author's appetite. Whatever be the amount of vanity with which Heaven has endowed me, and you know that authors are in general liberally provided, there is in your article one thing that I must say pleases me even more than your praise. Of all my reviewers you are, perhaps, the only one who has thoroughly understood me; who has taken a general bird's-eye view of my ideas; who sees their ulterior aim, and yet has preserved a clear perception of the details. The profession of an author would be too delightful if one met with many such readers! Your article, therefore, gave me intense pleasure. I keep it carefully, to prove to myself that it really is possible to understand me. I wanted this testimony to console me for all the false conclusions that are drawn from my book. I am constantly meeting people who want to persuade me of opinions that I proclaim, or who pretend to share with me opinions that I do not hold.

To return to your article. I repeat that I have read nothing so good on my book. You enter into my conception more than any one; and as you see the whole, you are capable of administering praise and blame. Believe that I do not exaggerate, when I say that your unfavorable criticisms gratified me as much as those that are favorable. The friend may always be seen through the critic. They instruct, therefore, and never wound me. I wish that I could discuss every one of your objections, my dear Mill; but I should send you a volume instead of a letter. (pp. 28-9)

> *Alexis de Tocqueville, in a letter to John Stuart Mill on December 3, 1835, in his* Memoirs, Letters and Remains of Alexis de Tocqueville, Vol. II, *edited by M.C.M Simpson, Ticknor and Fields, 1862, pp. 28-9.*

[ALEXANDER BAIN] (essay date 1843)

[*Bain, a student, friend, and biographer of Mill, extols the clarity and simplicity of Mill's style in* A System of Logic. *While commending Mill's stylistic restraint, Bain also emphasizes the potential moral influence of the work. For additional commentary by Bain, see the excerpt dated 1882.*]

[*A* System of Logic, Ratiocinative and Inductive] is far from being the first that has pretended to construct the ultimate or final philosophy of truth,—that has proposed to lay down the universal characters of knowledge and evidence, in a manner applicable to everything that can be believed by the human mind. But it is, so far as we are aware, the first which, in our own country and in this age, has attempted to construct such a philosophy by a systematic generalization of the methods and processes of modern positive science.

The name Logic does not and cannot convey to the reader any notion of the contents of Mr Mill's book, because they are such as no reader has seen under this or any other title. In comparing it with common manuals of logic we may say, that it contains everything about the discovery and proving of truth, excepting the part handled in those manuals. He has not come forward to drive Whately from the throne, but refers his readers to Whately for all that is there taught. He occupies himself with laying down principles that comprehend, and put in its proper place, the syllogistic logic of the schools, and along with it other departments of still higher import. (pp. 413-14)

The introduction is occupied with defining, according to the author's view, the province of logic. Truths are known to us in two ways, by *intuition* or immediate consciousness, and by *inference*. Truths known by intuition need no proof, and admit of no questioning; if they are not true, truth is unattainable. Those known by inference are known because of a known connexion with some known thing. (p. 414)

The science of logic, . . . according to Mr Mill, is that which investigates the evidence of all propositions which are inferred from others—finds what connexion of the seen with the unseen justifies belief in the latter. It is, in short, the science of Evidence, or Proof. It is not strictly the science of invention or discovery, but it walks side by side with these processes, and cannot be severed from them. Hence the author feels himself called on, and we think most imperatively, to characterize and discuss the various methods in which truths are sought, that those methods may be tried by the laws of evidence, which laws, in fact, determine what the methods ought to be. In the introductory chapter the reader will find the view which we have stated of the object of the work considerably expanded, and accompanied with illustration, proof, and the necessary discriminations, in a style of great clearness. (p. 415)

[Of the style of Mr Mill's *A System of Logic,* we may] venture to say that simplicity, clearness, and the utter absence of all affectation, are joined with a considerable command of the resources of the English language in as far as they are applicable to presenting philosophical truths easily, precisely, and strongly to the mind. The words never say more nor less than is intended; and the structure and arrangement is so simple and natural, that the meaning evolves itself with astonishing readiness. The language instantaneously yields up the thought, and draws no attention upon itself. There is no stammering and tripping between the natural order of the ideas and the order into which the language throws them. The author makes no display of profuse expression, but he clothes every meaning with an appropriate dress. Of ornament, indeed, or flowers of fancy, there is none. To deck truth with beauty, to gratify taste while enriching reason, to exemplify his principles with lovely and touching pictures as well as apposite facts, to make his pages sparkle with classic allusions, the author has no tendency whatever. He never stirs an emotion alien to his subject. The philosophy of Dugald Stewart, so often shallow and unsatisfactory, may be read as beautiful and classic writing; Mr Mill has renounced the excitement of extraneous though pleasing emotions, and is content with giving plain and forcible expression to profound and important truths. And if he declines the assistance of the beautiful, he is still more indisposed to humour or the ludicrous, with which writers often relieve their graver instructions, protected by the never-dying apology of Horace.

His felicitous clearness, brevity, and point, make him spirited and even fascinating, but he rather avoids than seeks to be either witty or imaginative. He has, no doubt, followed the tendency of his nature, and the dictates of his judgment in this particular, and each one will decide upon it according to taste; but we need not hesitate to say that the primary end of the book will be the more effectually fulfilled, that the appeals to understanding and reason are undisturbed by emotions which may distract attention from the truths as well as stimulate it towards them, but cannot improve their evidence.

We must not overlook a great moral efficacy possessed by this book. As a philosophy of evidence, it will naturally tend to invigorate that Faith in Evidence, which is the most essential active accompaniment of man's reasoning faculties. Without faith in proof, without the irresistible determination to cling to everything that has been proved, in spite of adverse beliefs, habits, prejudices, authorities, and the fear of consequences, reason is but a wise monarch with a nominal sceptre. The effect upon the reader of so lengthened a discussion of the sufficiency of evidence, with so many examples both of sufficient and insufficient reasonings, must be to loosen the roots of prejudices and increase the active power of truth. But in addition to the tendencies of the subject, the character of the writer is eminently favourable to the impression of this great moral lesson. He is a teacher by example. Throughout all his writings there is manifest a purity and intensity of devotion to truth, a susceptibility to every breath of reason, that have a most refreshing and delightful effect upon the reader. He is a preacher of the highest faith of the human mind. It need not be said how immensely important, to any mind or to any age, it is to be strong in this faith. Evidence is the only security of our proceeding and acting upon the truth of things; the habit of deferring to evidence in defiance of all other motives is essential to the adequate support of the conclusions of reason. And in this as well as every other virtue, we derive much from great examples. (pp. 455-56)

> [*Alexander Bain*], *in a review of "A System of Logic, Ratiocinative and Inductive," in* The Westminster Review, *Vol. XXXIX, No. II, May, 1843, pp. 412-56.*

THE ECLECTIC REVIEW   (essay date 1844)

[*The author of this detailed review of* A System of Logic *posits that Mill's advocacy of deductive reasoning is too extreme and that in general his evidence fails to prove his theory. Nevertheless, the reviewer grants "that his speculations are those not merely of a bold intellect, but of an acute, sagacious, and comprehensive one."*]

[Mr. Mill's *A System of Logic, Ratiocinative and Inductive* affords] encouraging indication of the revival which is taking place in the study of mental science, and are eminently fitted to conduce to its progress. 'In the existing state of the cultivation of the sciences,' Mr. Mill judiciously remarks, 'there would be a very strong presumption against any one who should imagine that he had effected a revolution in the theory of the investigation of truth, or added any fundamentally new process to the practice of it.' The time appears to have gone by, when every Columbus in philosophy might expect a new world to reward his search, and the adventurous and observant explorer of the domain of mental science might strike into untrodden paths in every direction, and stumble on new or forgotten truths almost at every turn. Very much, however, yet remains for us to accomplish in this, as well as other departments of philosophy,—in laying down correct maps (if we may be allowed to

carry on the metaphor) of the broad regions which our predecessors had the honour of first exploring, in opening roads from point to point, removing the tangled thickets with which large tracts are still overspread, and increasing by careful labour the fertility of the soil. 'To cement together the detached fragments of a subject, never yet treated as a whole; to harmonize the true portions of discordant theories, by supplying the links of thought necessary to connect them, and by disentangling them from the errors with which they are always more or less interwoven,' is a task of no mean importance, which to perform well demands powers of profound and original thought, as well as patient and judicious investigation, of a very uncommon order. It is a task of this kind which Mr. Mill has proposed to himself; and if it shall be thought that his success is not in all respects complete, it will be admitted, we think, that he has displayed very distinguished abilities in its performance, and produced a work worthy of taking a permanent and high rank among the standard treatises on mental philosophy.

The limits to which this article is necessarily restricted would not allow of a detailed examination of the whole work. Our investigations, therefore, will chiefly relate to two or three of what we deem the more important points.

That which seems first to claim attention is, the extent which Mr. Mill assigns to the science of logic. Everybody knows how loose and variable the use of the term has been, as employed by writers of different schools. It is not, however, as might at first sight appear, a mere verbal question. The question is not merely—what meaning, or how many meanings, shall we assign to the word 'logic;' but, (since all applications of the term have some reference, more or less determinate, to processes and rules of *reasoning*,) what are those mental processes, concerned in the investigation of results, which are so connected, that they ought properly to be regarded as objects of a single science. This question is evidently one of real, not merely verbal importance. In answer to it, we cannot but think, that Mr. Mill's view of the extent of the science is more philosophical than that of those writers who use the term in a more restricted, or in a baser sense. (pp. 268-69)

[In Book II., 'Of Reasoning,'] we meet with what is to our mind the least satisfactory part of Mr. Mill's work: viz., his account of deduction, or, as he prefers to call it, (though without giving any reason for such a restricted use of the term,) ratiocination; the scientific form of which is syllogism. We must be content to intimate, rather than fully to develope our objections, which chiefly relate to these two positions:—1st, 'that all inference is from particulars to particulars' . . . ; and 2ndly, that the syllogism, according to the established way of regarding it, is 'not a process of inference,' *i.e.,* 'that nothing ever was or can be proved by syllogism, which was not known, or assumed to be known before.' . . . Connected with this is the assertion . . . , that 'it must be granted, that in every syllogism, considered as an argument to prove the conclusion, there is a *petitio principii*.' We must premise that we fully agree with the Author, that the *dictum de omni,* as he explains it, (and as it is to be found explained in Archbishop Whateley's 'Analytical Outline,') is an insufficient substratum for the syllogism, and in fact, merely authorises *verbal transformations*. But we should be glad to know on what passage of Aristotle's works either Mr. Mill or Archbishop Whateley grounds this view of the 'dictum.' The view proceeds, if we understand it, on a peculiar theory of propositions, of which we think Mr. Mill has sufficiently exposed the erroneous character. [Book I., ch. 5, & 3.] But in fact, a different explanation of the 'dictum' is given by Whateley himself in his 'Synthetical Compendium;' and, Mr. Mill seems not to be aware that his two 'principles' . . . almost exactly correspond to Whateley's two 'axioms or canons,' . . . on which the latter founds the rules of syllogism. Yet, as we think it will appear, it is only on this view of the syllogism that Mr. Mill's objections can be sustained. Before proceeding, however, it may be as well just to revert to the distinction between induction and deduction. If preceding writers on logic have erred in making induction a species of syllogism, Mr. Mill surely errs in going to the opposite extreme. Aristotle's account of the relation between these two processes appears to us both more perspicuous and more philosophical than the one under consideration. According to that philosopher, there are two grand processes by which we infer the truth of propositions. The first of these is when from particulars we ascend to general propositions. This he calls, (though the term is not indeed restricted by him to this sense,) epagogè, *anglicè,* induction. The second is when from general propositions we infer less general, or at least not more general ones. This he calls apodeixis, to which the English term 'demonstration' corresponds in etymology as well as in application. These processes are perfectly distinct. The greater part, indeed, of the universal propositions from which our demonstrations start, (Mr. Mill would even include mathematical axioms,) are obtained by induction; but this makes no difference in the process of deduction (or demonstration) itself. *That* would proceed in precisely the same manner, if all these universal propositions were known by intuition, without the use of induction at all. Now Mr. Mill is not content with these two old-fashioned methods. He contends, as already stated, that, in reality, we reason *from particulars to particulars,* without passing through general propositions; that this is the essential process in syllogistic reasoning; and, that the general propositions which appear as the premises, are only a contrivance for *'registering'* our particular propositions, so as to be used even after they are individually forgotten. We cannot but deem this one of those false apparent simplifications which in reality confuse a subject. Somewhat as though a person should think to *simplify* musical notation by disusing the distinction of clefs, and writing all the parts on one stave of eleven lines. It is evident that, although this might seem at first sight the simpler plan, it would in fact produce inextricable confusion. It would be scarcely possible to read music written on such a system. In the same way, admitting Mr. Mill's account of the process of reasoning to be a correct representation, (as the stave without clefs would be of the succession of musical sounds,) yet it would be necessary to make the division commonly made, in order to [emphasize] any certain or intelligible rules being given or applied. Even admitting that *in fact* we reason frequently from particular to particular, without the intervention of any general principle, yet (as Mr. Mill admits,) our conclusion *supposes* the truth of the general proposition, *i.e.,* if the latter be not true, the conclusion cannot be true; but on the other hand, it is certain that we often do reason with an explicit reference to the general proposition, and our conclusion is then formally as well as really correct, since it does not take anything for granted, which is not expressed. This being the case, what conceivable advantage is gained by regarding the unscientific process, the truth or fallacy of which depends on something not expressed, as the type of reasoning in general?

We should, however, demur to the fact itself, considered as a statement of what generally takes place. Mr. Mill's examples by no means appear to establish his point; and we venture to think he has been led astray by not sufficiently bearing in mind, (what yet so practised a thinker must be perfectly acquainted with,) that the operations of the mind are often so rapid and subtile, that, the mind itself fails to take notice of them. How many unobserved links, for example, must intervene between our looking at a printed page, and receiving the meaning of the author! Or, to take a yet stronger instance, how paradoxical the assertion at first appears, that we do not *see* distance, but infer it by an exercise of judgment! Much in the same way, the mind may feel the force of a general principle, and deduce the conclusion so rapidly, that the inference will appear to be made immediately, 'from particular to particular,' without the aid of any general proposition. (pp. 270-73)

But we must hasten to glance at the second point referred to, the claim of the syllogism to the name of reasoning, and the *petitio principii* which is charged upon it, founded on the well-known rule, that a syllogism is vicious if any thing more is contained in the conclusion, than was assumed in the premises. We must allow, that, if such an argument as, 'All men are mortal; Socrates is a man; *therefore* Socrates is mortal,'—be admitted as a fair type of syllogism, then Mr. Mill's objections would have weight. But, at the peril perhaps of being reckoned as great heretics almost as Mr. Mill, we boldly deny that this is a syllogism at all, or anything more than a verbal imitation of one. For the proper name, 'Socrates,' is nothing but another (and more convenient) expression for 'this man.' What appears as the minor premise is, therefore, merely equivalent to the trifling proposition, that 'this man is a man;' and in no way contributes to the conclusion. The particular proposition, 'this man is mortal,' follows immediately from the general one, 'all men,' & c., being necessarily implied in it. It is not a case of *reasoning* at all, but a mere verbal transformation, effected (in logical phrase) by limiting the quantity of the proposition. If, indeed, there were any doubt whether the being called Socrates were a man or not, (*e.g.* if he might be an angel), then the minor would be a *real* premise, requiring independent *proof;* and the whole would be a real syllogism. But, in this case, Mr. Mill's objections would not apply. For here we come upon what appears to be the root of the erroneous views (as we cannot avoid considering them) adopted by this able writer. The rule of the syllogism, as above stated, is, that the conclusion must contain nothing but what is contained in the *premises;* but, in the example adduced as a fair specimen of syllogism, the conclusion is in fact contained in *one* premise; and, therefore, considered as an argument, it is, as Mr. Mill justly regards it, a mere begging of the question, and no 'process of inference' at all; unless we consider changing the quantity, from general to particular, a process of inference. (pp. 273-74)

In a real syllogism, . . . the conclusion depends not on either premise alone, but on the union of the two. It is not a mere verbal transformation, but a real process of inference. There is no begging the question, for the thing to be proved, is not assumed in either premise. The conclusion is like the bag of gold which was to be delivered, 'not to one, nor to two, but to the three,' and which none of the three separately could claim as his own. Whether the premises be obtained by induction, or by intuition, or be assumed as mere baseless hypotheses, makes no difference in the process itself: grant the premises, *and put them together,* and the conclusion follows of necessity. And to deny the name of reasoning to this process, appears to us a perversion of language. (pp. 274-75)

[The fourth and fifth chapters of Book IV.] are especially deserving of perusal, and would alone be sufficient to indicate an original and truly philosophic mind. Book V. treats 'Of Fallacies.' Under this head Mr. Mill repeatedly refers to Archbishop Whateley's work, and bestows well-merited eulogy on the manner in which the subject is there handled; but Mr. Mill's own enumeration naturally takes a wider range than Whateley's, in accordance with the general system of the present treatise. Fallacies are divided into five classes: *à priori* fallacies; fallacies of induction, which are either fallacies of observation, or fallacies of generalization; fallacies of deduction; and fallacies of confusion. The examples are, as usual, very happily chosen, and this book will be found by no means the least valuable part of the work.

The VIth and concluding book, is a kind of supplement, devoted to 'the logic of the moral sciences.' Under this head are included the science of mind, the science of the formation of character, and the science of society. In these branches of inquiry, if we except that portion of social science called political economy, any thing deserving the name of science has yet to be created. Here, therefore, if anywhere, we may look for a beneficial application of the logical principles to the elucidation of which the present work is devoted. It will easily be supposed, that in this wide field of discussion there is much that tempts comment. But we refrain. Perhaps Mr. Mill may err in over-estimating the power of the human mind in respect to subjects like these; but, at all events, it must be owned, that his speculations are those not merely of a bold intellect, but of an acute, sagacious, and comprehensive one. (pp. 279-80)

There are some other points on which we have been tempted to break a lance with Mr. Mill; but even supposing ourselves (as reviewers are bound to do) in the right, this would not detract from our high estimate of his treatise as a whole. It is a work which perhaps no other philosophic school, nor any age previous to our own, could have produced; to which no one would have been competent who did not possess, in addition to the qualifications usually deemed essential to a logician, a mind trained to methods of scientific inquiry, and familiar with the principles and results of those investigations by which philosophers, from Newton to Liebig, have won from nature so many of her secrets, and rendered the present so pre-eminently the age of science. A work of this character can hardly be expected to become speedily or extensively popular; but, if it aids in forming the minds of the few thinkers by whom the future progress of knowledge will be guided, the Author will find in this his noblest success and reward. An inaptitude to judge of the value of evidence, it has been most truly remarked, lies at the root of the most opposite errors: of unreasonable unbelief, as well as of too easy credulity. It is a striking characteristic, not merely of those who professedly exalt blind faith above reason, but of many who call themselves 'rationalists' *par excellence*. Let us have men well trained to the appreciation of evidence in the school of Archbishop Whateley and Mr. Mill, and we shall be provided with one of the best safe-guards, alike against German scepticism or mysticism, and Oxford popery. (pp. 280-81)

> "*Mill's System of Logic,*" in The Eclectic Review, n.s. Vol. XVI, August, 1844, pp. 268-81.

THE BRITISH QUARTERLY REVIEW (essay date 1846)

[*Pointing out inconsistencies, generalizations, and inaccuracies in* A System of Logic, *this reviewer contends that Mill "has totally failed" in realizing his goal in the work; despite that judgment, the critic deems Mill's essay an original and competent production.*]

[Mr. Mill's '**A System of Logic, Ratiocinative and Inductive**'] is a treatise which deserves, and will repay, the most attentive study. No one who intelligently examines it can fail to perceive the vigour, clearness, and originality, by which it is in great part characterized. Yet we must express our conviction, that the clearness and depth which the author has so frequently shown, by no means distinguish every portion of his work. As we read it, Mr. Mill often seemed to us like a man so confident in the quickness and penetration of his sight, as sometimes to consider it scarcely worth while to keep his eyes wide open; unless, indeed, we are to suppose that motes and beams do sometimes find their way even into eyes the most clear and piercing. Either supposition will account for the fact, that discussions and analyses of great accuracy and depth alternate with strange oversights and inconsistencies which occasionally amount to contradictions. Mr. Mill must not take it amiss that we measure the faults of his book in a great degree by its pretensions. It is an elaborate attempt to reduce to a consistent system the entire body of the laws of inference; 'to cement together,' as he himself says, 'the detached fragments of a subject never yet treated as a whole; to harmonize the true portions of discordant theories, by supplying the links of thought necessary to connect them, and by disentangling them from the errors with which they are always more or less interwoven.' . . . Our opinion is, that in respect to his object as thus stated, Mr. Mill has totally failed; that unsoundness marks not merely the system as a whole, but very many of the subordinate parts; and that, while the author may claim a large measure of approbation for his originality, patience, and labour, and for much that is discriminating, sound, and profitable in the treatise which it is our purpose to examine, he is not destined, by means of this work at least, to be the founder of a new era in the science of logic. (pp. 1-2)

To the conclusions at which Mr. Mill has arrived on [general inference] we can by no means assent; they appear to us pregnant with misconception and confusion. To the *general* account which he gives of inference we have no objection to make. 'To infer,' says he, 'a proposition from a previous proposition or propositions; to give credence to it, or claim credence for it, as a conclusion from something else, is to *reason* in the more extensive sense of the term.' He then proceeds, quite rightly, to deny the applicability of the term *inference* to certain cases, where there is no advance from known to unknown truths, but the mere statement of the same truth in a different form. (p. 17)

Mr. Mill agrees with those who assert that the syllogism unavoidably involves a *petitio principii;* but he does not agree with them in rejecting it as useless on that account. Its utility he holds to consist in its being a convenient and safe mode of translating the conclusions arrived at by induction, and applying them to particular cases. He remarks that Inference is popularly said to be of two kinds: reasoning from particulars to generals, and reasoning from generals to particulars; the former being called Induction, the latter Ratiocination or Syllogism. So that Induction is inferring a proposition from propositions less general than itself, Ratiocination is inferring a proposition from propositions equally or more general. 'When from a general proposition, not alone, but by combining it with other propositions, we infer a proposition of the same degree of generality with itself, or a less general proposition, the process is ratiocination.' (p. 18)

These our author holds to be connected in the following manner. Every syllogism has for its major premiss a general proposition. All general propositions are arrived at by a process of induction from the observation of particular instances, and are records, not merely of observed cases, but of all that we infer from our observations, thus giving us only one proposition to remember or communicate instead of an infinite number; but they are merely registers; in themselves they add nothing to the evidence which we possess. In forming any decision with respect to a new instance, we can do nothing more than decide upon the evidence which we possess; and the individual cases which we have observed *are all the evidence which we can possess*. . . . Hence, in any new case the evidence which is sufficient to establish the general proposition is sufficient to establish its truth in the particular instance before us, and is in fact the only evidence on which it rests; and as the general proposition adds nothing to its force, it may safely be dispensed with. All inference, therefore, is ultimately from particulars to particulars; general propositions are merely registers of such inferences already made, and short formulae for making more. When, therefore, as in a syllogism, we avail ourselves of these registers, the conclusion is drawn, not *from* the formula, but *according to it;* the real logical premises being the particular facts from which the general proposition was collected by induction. But it is essential that we should read the record correctly, and the rules of the syllogism are a set of precautions to ensure our doing so. . . . The only advantage derivable from using these intermediate general propositions is, partly that they save trouble, partly that our induction is more likely to be conducted carefully, and, if insufficient, to have its insufficiency detected, when we do not confine ourselves to one particular instance, but include in our inference all to which it can apply. Mr. Mill does not scruple to apply these principles to the case of laws, and announcements received as matters of revelation. (pp. 18-19)

The sum and result of all which is, that an induction leading to a general proposition, and a syllogism interpreting that proposition with reference to the case in hand, is a form into which we always *may* throw our reasoning, but it is by no means essential to its validity that this form should be adopted. If adopted, it is merely for the sake of precaution. Hence the universal type of the reasoning process is not the syllogism, but consists of the following elements: certain individuals have a certain attribute; an individual, or individuals, resemble the former in certain other attributes; therefore they resemble the former in the given attribute. 'The validity of this depends, not upon its form, but upon *other considerations.*' . . .

This view is ingenious and plausible, but it will not stand examination. On what grounds is it asserted that the syllogism involves a *petitio principii*,—that 'nothing ever was or can be proved by syllogism, which was not known, or assumed to be known before?' (p. 19)

What Mr. Mill really intends to substitute for the syllogism, as the general type of the reasoning process, it is not easy to say, as his statements are not quite consistent with each other. (p. 23)

Meantime, Mr. Mill, in accordance with the doctrine which he has laid down, proceeds to say, that the definitions, as they are called, are generalizations concerning those natural objects; that they are not exactly true, but so nearly, that no error of any importance in practice will be incurred by feigning them to be exactly true. 'So long as there exists no practical necessity for attending to any of the properties of the object except its geometrical properties, or to any of the natural irregularities in those, *it is convenient to neglect the consideration of the other properties and of the irregularities, and to reason as if they did not exist.*' . . . Does Mr. Mill forget that he has main-

tained that all our reasoning is induction from actual experience? If we have no experience of facts relating to lines without breadth and perfect circles, we cannot possibly have experience except with relation to lines possessing breadth, to imperfect circles, &c. But as things cannot divest themselves of any of their properties, we can only have experience of things *as they are.* Experience is not an arbitrary act of the mind. We have no control over experience; we must take it exactly as it presents itself. As experience, therefore, cannot present us with phaenomena divested of any features which are inseparable in actual fact from the phaenomena, and we reason, according to our author, entirely upon experience, if we attempt to reason with respect to things, feigning them to be divested of some of their properties, we reason apart from experience; that is, we do what we never do. Will Mr. Mill explain the contradiction? (pp. 29-30)

Though we differ widely from Mr. Mill in the view which we take of Induction, especially with regard to its basis, and think that he has made several great mistakes in the way in which he applies even his own principles, we yet gladly bear our testimony to the great ability by which most of the chapters in the Third Book are marked. Very few persons have made such progress in science and logic as to dispense with a careful study of them without loss. Nevertheless, we still think that the *logic* of induction has yet to be written.

The Fourth Book treats of operations subsidiary to Induction, Observation, Description, Abstraction, Naming, &c. It is a masterly exhibition of a profound knowledge of the subject. The Fifth Book, On Fallacies, merits scarcely less praise. The Sixth Book, On the Logic of the Moral Sciences, though it professes to do little more than indicate the manner in which investigations in this department are to be carried on, contains much that is most valuable and suggestive. Nine out of ten of our writers and speakers on politics and political economy would be much the better for a careful perusal of it. The discussion in the second chapter, on Liberty and Necessity as connected with the Will, seems to us to leave the matter very much as it finds it. Mr. Mill believes that the will is subject to the laws of causation, that it is determined in each case by the motives present to the mind. But he seems to make moral freedom consist in the fact, that these motives are to some extent under our control. But motives in any way under our control cannot be present to the mind without an act of volition. That volition must be determined by other motives. These motives, again, if we have any control over them, pre-suppose an act of volition, and so on *ad infinitum.* How we are to escape from this bewilderment, Mr. Mill does not tell us. (pp. 37-8)

The nature of the work of which we have reviewed a portion, seemed to require that we should point out its defects rather than its merits; but we cannot conclude without expressing our thanks to Mr. Mill for the pleasure and profit which the study of his work has afforded us: with all its defects, it is one of the ablest treatises on Logic which have yet made their appearance. (p. 38)

"Mill's System of Logic," in The British Quarterly Review, *Vol. IV, No. VII, August 1, 1846, pp. 1-38.*

THE NORTH AMERICAN REVIEW   (essay date 1848)

[*While censuring Mill's Malthusian tendencies and his negative opinion of the American character, the author of the following review of Mill's* Principles of Political Economy *praises the work as "the most comprehensive and the most satisfactory exposition of the whole science of political economy since the days of Adam Smith."*]

Political Economy is not quite so thorny and unpromising a topic as Logic, and in this age, indeed, more perhaps than in any other, we might suppose that it would be a favorite subject of study. Unluckily, it treats of wealth only in the abstract, and while it lays bare many of the causes of national grandeur and decline, it affords to individuals very little aid in what is to them the most important of all enterprises, that of making their fortunes. It is the science, but not the art, of money-making; and, as frequently happens in the other sciences, its general principles often seem to conflict very seriously with the practical rules—*axiomata media*, as Lord Bacon calls them—which common men draw immediately from their own experience in the counting-room and the stock-market. There is a common prejudice, therefore, against the reasoning and the conclusions of the political economists, a prejudice which is much increased by the dissensions and disputes which prevail among the economists themselves. Who shall decide when doctors disagree? is the question that is triumphantly asked, both by the booby merchant who has blundered into a fortune, and by the booby, if not dishonest legislator, who passes laws without any consideration of their ultimate effects on the material interests of the community, though he very carefully estimates the bearing which they will have on his own popularity with his constituents. There is no subject pretending to the rank of a science, of which American legislators, merchants, and manufacturers are so profoundly and wilfully ignorant, as that of political economy; though there is none which it more concerns them to be acquainted with, whenever they would look beyond the present moment, either for their own interests, or for those of the public. We rejoice that they may now have the services of so competent a teacher as Mr. Mill, whose admirably pure and lucid style, correct method, copious illustrations, and stringent reasoning [in his ***Principles of Political Economy***], carry light and conviction to some of the darkest problems and most vexed questions of the science, so as to remove the prejudices of the misinformed, and give understanding even to the simple. (pp. 370-71)

[Mr. Mill] has gained for himself the opportunity of considering the great social problems of the day, the practical solution of which is even now convulsing a great part of the civilized world. A most valuable portion of his book is the clear and decisive refutation that it affords of the theories of the Saint Simonians, the Fourierites, the Communists, and other half-insane speculators, who have reduced France to her present degradation and misery, and have found too many proselytes even on this side of the Atlantic.

But our author is no blind conservative; in England, indeed, he must be considered as belonging to "the extreme left" among the writers on politics, economical science, and social philosophy. His doctrines respecting the ownership of land, the descent of property, the regulation of the currency, and other matters, go certainly to the verge, as most persons will think, of sweeping and hazardous innovation. (p. 372)

Mr. Mill does not acknowledge either the justice or the expediency of favoring the concentration of riches, and leaving the bulk of the community destitute or dependent. He recognizes the great truth, that "property is only a means to an end, not itself the end"; and consequently, even if capital when in large masses should be a more effective agent of production than when distributed more evenly, the legislature ought not

to favor its aggregation, if it should appear that this enlarged production was not a sure means of promoting the general welfare and the highest interests of the community. Here is the vice of that narrow definition of political economy . . . , that, by restricting the inquiry to the means of increasing wealth, writers upon this science have been led to advocate measures which tend to diminish the sum of human happiness, and which are repelled alike by the sense of justice and the feelings of common humanity. (p. 388)

Mr. Mill goes on to expound his opinion as to the mode in which succession to property vacant by death should be regulated, so as to insure the proper diffusion of wealth and the equality of chances for all classes and members of society. He would take away the right of inheritance, as distinguished from bequest, altogether; the property of intestates, whether of land or movables, should escheat to the state, to be distributed anew among its members, yet always with some regard to the expectations naturally created in the children of the deceased by the style of life in which they have been brought up. After making due provision for them, which in no case should exceed that which is considered as a moderate competency in the class of society in which they had moved, the remainder of the property should be added to the common stock. (pp. 389-90)

The scheme for the division of property in its passage from one generation to another . . . is not proposed by its author with direct reference, as it seems, to the immediate effect which it would have in improving the condition of the majority of the English and Irish people. It is rather a speculative sketch of what Mr. Mill considers as just in itself, and desirable for its economical consequences and its effects on the constitution of society at large, than a plan to alleviate or remove the present sufferings of the laboring classes. Mr. Mill, we are sorry to see, reasons after the old fashion of the English economists upon this great and perplexing subject; in his opinion, the whole evil consists in low wages, and the only remedy, the only means of raising the rate of wages, is to check the growth of the population. He is a follower of Malthus to the full extent, and therefore almost a fatalist in his view of the evils which now afflict society, and of the inevitable aggravation of them, if the opinions and conduct of the poor in relation to marriage and the increase of their kind do not undergo a total change. (p. 393)

The great and palpable error of the Malthusians consists in assuming, without a particle of evidence, without condescending even to argue the matter, that the time has already come, that population has reached its limits, and that there is even now a deficiency of food, so that the only mode of increasing the happiness of the lower classes is to lessen their numbers. When asked to furnish proof of this assertion, they immediately begin to talk of something else,—of low wages, starving Irish, insufficient employment, and the like, and invariably end by appealing to the rapid and immense effects of increase in a geometrical progression, and so concluding that, if the time has not yet come, *it will be here very shortly, which amounts to the same thing.* (p. 397)

Mr. Mill and his brother economists make the great mistake of confounding the undue relative number of a class with a general excess of the population. The former evil might be corrected by portioning out society anew, through the gradual influence of altered laws, so that the divisions or castes which are too thin in number might be recruited from those which are in excess, and the proper balance be thus restored without the necessity of adopting any measures which would affect the bulk of the people. The latter difficulty, if it ever really existed, could be removed only by war, pestilence, famine, or a general adoption of the doctrines of Malthus. (p. 401)

That riches are not the only good, however, and that the constant strain of the faculties, the restlessness, the feverish anxiety to get on, which are seen in the eager pursuit of them, are not the most desirable habits or traits of character, nor the most conducive to the real welfare either of the individual or of society, we are quite as ready as Mr. Mill to admit. But the following lively picture, which he draws, of this aspect of American life, though true in some respects, is overcharged in others, and is unfaithful because incomplete.

> I confess I am not charmed with the ideal of life held out by those who think that the normal state of human beings is that of struggling to get on; that the trampling, crushing, elbowing, and treading on each other's heels, which form the existing type of social life, are the most desirable lot of human kind, or any thing but the disagreeable symptoms of one of the phases of industrial progress. The Northern and Middle States of America are a specimen of this stage of civilization in very favorable circumstances; having, apparently, got rid of all social injustices and inequalities that affect persons of Caucasian race and of the male sex, while the proportion of population to capital and land is such as to insure abundance to every able-bodied member of the community who does not forfeit it by misconduct. They have the six points of Chartism, and they have no poverty: and all that these advantages do for them is that the life of the whole of one sex is devoted to dollar-hunting, and of the other to breeding dollar-hunters.
>
> (p. 412)

No, Mr. Mill, it is not all. The energies which are first awakened in the pursuit of wealth soon find other objects on which to expend themselves, and the gratifications of the taste and the intellect are as eagerly sought here as in the Old World. Hereditary fortunes unquestionably give more spare time to their possessors; but abundance of leisure is not the only requisite for the attainment of the higher graces of life. Activity of mind is at least equally essential, and those who are born to vast estates and high social position are more apt to allow their faculties to rust from disuse, or to turn them in search of trivial or gross amusement, than those who are obliged first to achieve these advantages by their own efforts. Letters, science, and the arts find ardent votaries even in this paradise of dollar-hunters; the progress of invention in the elegant as well as the useful arts is probably more rapid here than in Great Britain. (pp. 412-13)

Though we cannot agree with [Mr. Mill] in all his speculations, and object particularly to his uncompromising defence and broad application of the theory of Malthus, we gladly acknowledge our obligations to him for much instruction on this particular subject, and for what is, on the whole, unquestionably the ablest, the most comprehensive, and the most satisfactory exposition of the whole science of political economy that has appeared since the days of Adam Smith. His book ought to take its place by the side of *The Wealth of Nations* in the library of every well-informed man, both in the Old and the New World. (p. 419)

"Mill's 'Political Economy: Population and Property'," in The North American Review, *Vol. LXVII, No. CXL, July, 1848, pp. 370-419.*

[W. E. HICKSON] (essay date 1848)

[*In the following brief excerpt from his review of* Principles of Political Economy, *Hickson focuses on Mill's careful scholarship and the application of his theory. This review appeared in the* Westminster and Foreign Quarterly Review, *the organ of utilitarian thought; Mill had been the journal's editor from 1835 to 1840.*]

[Mr. Mill applies political economy] to the practical business of the day. This is the great characteristic of the present work; the one in which it differs the most essentially from the treatises of nearly all the author's predecessors. It is something to be able to say of such a book that it is not a Jeremiad. Mr. Mill is not content to explain and deplore the evils which afflict society, but fairly grapples with them for their correction; and without discarding Malthus, he speaks hopefully to the masses who, with no *malice prepense,* have committed the crime of getting born into the world, as of an offence which may yet be forgotten and forgiven, and its fatal consequences by possibility averted.

The work is a careful and pains-taking summary of all the principles of the science as laid down by Adam Smith, Turgot, Jean Baptiste Say, Ricardo, &c., with those modifications and amendments to which later discussions have led; presented in a more systematized form than any in which they have hitherto appeared, and separately considered in their application to social philosophy. (pp. 291-92)

[*Principles of Political Economy*] is a book of all others the most required for the present time; certain to be recognised by all as the production of a master mind; pregnant with thought in every line, and perhaps unrivalled in modern literature for the comprehensiveness of its philosophical survey of the highest subjects of human interest. (p. 314)

[*W. E. Hickson*], *in a review of "Principles of Political Economy,"* in The Westminster and Foreign Quarterly Review, *Vol. XLIX, No. II, July, 1848, pp. 289-314.*

FRASER'S MAGAZINE (essay date 1848)

[*Emphasizing Mill's humanitarian spirit and blending of theory and practical advice, this reviewer hails* Principles of Political Economy *as a major philosophical work. However, the critic differs with Mill on the questions of aid for Irish laborers and land ownership for English workers.*]

[Since it] is destined to dissipate many of the errors which are linked with the very name of political economy, . . . we hail with sincere and fervent gratitude the opportune appearance of Mr. Mill's [*Principles of Political Economy*]. For, great as will be the benefits conferred on the science itself by this masterly exposition of its principles, this comprehensive, profound, and thoroughly catholic description of its limits and its aims, far greater, we conceive, will be the good effected by the *spirit* in which the whole is composed and all its disquisitions conducted. Here is no indifference to human suffering, no inordinate estimation of wealth, no sordid and grovelling morality; every page evinces the warm sympathies of the writer with the joys and sorrows of his fellow-men. The happiness of mankind is ever before him as the object of inquiry; though no mawkish sentimentality blinds his judgment or prevents his exposing, with unflinching courage, the errors of those for whom he labours, nor from stating, without hesitation or ambiguity, the circumstances upon which the happiness of the immense majority of mankind, viz. that of the labouring classes, ultimately depends. (p. 247)

The Euclid of Political Economy has not yet appeared. Mr. Mill professes not to restrain himself within the comparatively narrow bounds of the abstract science; but at the outset, in his Preface, describes his work as one intended to embrace a wider field than the limits of the abstract science afford. In the present state of opinion respecting the science, we believe that his labours will prove more widely and immediately useful by being thus bestowed upon considerations of direct and practical application, than if they had been directed merely to a severe exposition of the whole abstract science. Yet we regret that his work does not include a synoptic and formal view of the whole subject, by which the various and often opposing assumptions upon which its abstract principles rest would be brought at once into view, and the minds of those who desire thoroughly to master the subject be enabled to frame, with Mr. Mill's direct aid, a systematic scheme of all its separate parts.

Mr. Mill, indeed, seems anxious to divest his work of all such *formal* appearance. . . . (p. 248)

His varied knowledge and his truly catholic spirit peculiarly fitted him for the task; and the grand characteristic excellence of his work is the combination, in every instance, of a simple yet severely accurate exposition of the abstract doctrine (the *pure* political economy), with an inquiry into the modifications to which the doctrine is subject, when applied to any given and really existing condition of things. . . . Mr. Mill has united the office of the abstract philosopher with that of the practical expositor; and as he in this latter character evinces throughout an anxious interest in the well-being of mankind—as he brings to bear upon every proposed application of economic science the dictates of a comprehensive and exalted morality—as in the pursuit of the means for the attainment of happiness he never loses sight of the end, viz. happiness itself,—all that in some instances of the purely speculative economists has appeared harsh, unfeeling, and thereby repulsive, entirely disappears; and political economy stands forth under his guidance such as it really is, and ought to be considered, viz. a branch of knowledge absolutely necessary for those to whom, as legislators or teachers, the destinies of the human family are in any way confided.

But is Mr. Mill justified in thus speaking of political economy as a science? Can it be said—supposing this first question answered in the affirmative—can it be said, that of the facts relating to this economical science a sufficient number have been so accurately observed as to justify such generalisation as will prove the expression of a law? And are any of these laws, supposing them to exist, of any real practical importance?

Those who are sincerely desirous of attaining the truth on this important subject will see, that upon the answers which can be given to these inquiries the whole question really depends; and they will, without being swayed by preconceived opinions, or influenced by mere violence and abuse, be in their minds determined by the reply which the works of economists give to the queries here propounded. The work before us affords a full, thoroughly complete, and satisfactory answer to every one of them. A wider and more careful induction can hardly be conceived than that by which Mr. Mill has been led to his

several conclusions. The whole field of inquiry has been surveyed—each part minutely investigated; while the varied illustrations, the exquisitely simple and lucid style employed throughout the intricate and profound discussions, with which the whole work abounds, lure us over what are usually deemed the arid paths of economical philosophy, and make us forget the labour of the inquiry in the charms which attend it. (pp. 248-49)

[We find ourselves in disagreement] with respect to one opinion strenuously maintained by Mr. Mill, and the opposite of which is also as strenuously maintained by others, whose opinion is of great weight and authority. The position relates to that important branch of political science which we have been now considering, viz. the mode in which, in future, the condition of the labouring classes generally, and specifically those of Ireland, may be permanently ameliorated, and that misery which now—as, indeed, it has ever done—enthrals their minds and bodies, debases and degrades the one and almost destroys the other, can be *permanently* removed. We reiterate the word permanently, because in that lies the chief difficulty. By a great effort, and by a new distribution of the means of subsistence,—of wealth, and land, in short,—we might, possibly, for a few years relieve this misery. But as the causes of distress are permanent, this temporary alleviation would, in the end, prove only an extension of the mischief. We should find that we had brought all to the one dead level of wretchedness, and that having taken no precaution by which the active causes of man's distress might be coerced and rendered ineffective, we had simply, by our great effort of benevolence, increased the ills against which our efforts were directed.

Coinciding with Mr. Mill entirely in his exposition of the theory of wages—believing that the amount of wages depends upon the relation existing between capital and the number of the labouring class to be maintained by it; and believing that this number is ever tending to increase indefinitely, while on the contrary the amount of subsistence which the land can produce is, after a certain point, continually growing less, in return *to equal quantities of labour expended on it*,—we, nevertheless, do not agree with him in supposing that we establish a more effective check to the too rapid increase of numbers among the labouring class, by making them small proprietors of the soil in place of being servants employed by the possessors of capital, and paid by wages. . . . (p. 254)

With the exception of these two instances, we have found little in this extensive and profound exposition of the ***Principles of Political Economy*** from which we dissent; but from every part, even from those expositions with which we have been unable to agree, we have derived most important instruction; and we would solicit the attention of all who have any doubts respecting the value of the whole science to the fifth and concluding book of the treatise, which treats of the functions of government— a masterly discussion, stretching beyond the mere limits of political economy, and reaching the very apices of philosophic inquiry. They who complain of the narrow views of the economic school, may here find a reason for modifying their unfavourable opinion. (p. 259)

The mode in which this class of questions is discussed; the manner in which the discoveries of modern science, whether in moral or physical philosophy, are brought to bear upon the doctrines of political economy, and its practical application in legislation, in the social relations of life, and even to private transactions, in so far as they regard production and its concomitants, constitutes the great and distinguishing excellence

From a miniature of Harriet Taylor.

of Mr. Mill's labours. His work forms an epoch in the science, by collecting, arranging, and explaining with perfect clearness, and the ease which power confers, all that other inquirers have discovered and established with respect to its general principles. Every special treatise upon all the separate questions which have occupied the attention of the various labourers in this field has been carefully studied; and the admirable candour with which Mr. Mill entertains a new idea, no matter how opposed to his own previous conceptions, must win the confidence, respect, and regard even, of all honest labourers in the cause of truth. The *repose* we find in this truly philosophic exposition, after all the storms and turmoil which in every department of inquiry we perceive now raging, creates in us a pleasure analogous to that which we receive from contemplating a quiet, serene landscape by Claude, or a Madonna by Perugino, after tasking our aching eyes with the melodramatic extravagance—the lampblack and lightning of modern art. Mr. Mill seems to lay no claim to the merit of discovery; he takes the science, and all its separate, scattered, and apparently disjointed parts, connects and frames them into one comprehensive whole, modifying the abstract doctrines throughout by a consideration of the manner in which they would be effected by all the contemporaneous events to which they are to be applied. In this application his merit is often equal to, if it be not, indeed, that of a discoverer. And to him who is commencing a study of political economy, as well as to him who has wearied himself with all the various controversial works with which the press has of late years teemed respecting it, this general yet minute explanation of the whole science, and all the separate and distinct questions belonging to it, will prove of equal advantage. The first will find himself prepared by its aid to grapple with, and understand, every difficulty as it arises hereafter, and to *place* each newly acquired portion of knowledge in his mind as it is attained; while the second will have

his ideas and opinions, which by desultory discussion and multifarious reasonings have been confused, scattered, and confounded, all brought together into one harmonious system; discrepancies removed, difficulties overcome, doubts solved. Viewing from afar off, and as from a vantage ground, each independent thinker and his works—seeing them all in his mind's eye at one and the same moment—Mr. Mill has been able to consider, and almost to create, that harmony in all the different results of separate inquiries which to the inquirers themselves would have been impossible; and could Turgot, and Ricardo, and Malthus, and the great father of the author, see this grand combination of their thoughts and labours in the thorny regions of economic science, they would accept his labours as the worthy complement of their own, and hail him as one deserving to be placed in the same rank with themselves. (p. 260)

"Mill's Political Economy," in Fraser's Magazine, *Vol. XXXVIII, No. CCXXV, September, 1848, pp. 245-60.*

[WILLIAM HENRY SMITH]   (essay date 1848)

[*Smith expresses his admiration for the exhaustiveness and, in parts, "thrilling eloquence" of Mill's* Principles of Political Economy. *Maintaining that Mill's treatment of capital is the most complete study available in his time, Smith also points out that Mill's discussion of "unproductive consumption" is somewhat flawed. Smith's overall estimate of* Principles of Political Economy, *however, is that it ranks "amongst the sterling literature of our country."*]

[In Mr Mill's *Principles of Political Economy*,] the science of political economy has received its latest and most complete exposition. Nor, as the title itself will inform us, is the work limited to a formal enunciation of abstract principles, . . . but it proceeds to apply those principles to the discussion of some of the most vital and momentous questions with which public opinion is at present occupied. There are things in these volumes, as may easily be conceived, in which we do not concur—views are supported, on some subjects, to which we have been long and notoriously opposed; but there is, in the exposition of its tenets, so accurate a statement, so severe and lucid a reasoning, and, withal, so genuine and manly an interest in the great cause of humanity, that we cannot hesitate a moment in awarding to it a high rank amongst the sterling literature of our country. . . . [*Principles of Political Economy* is of more general interest than Mr Mill's *System of Logic*,] yet it has the same severe character. In this, as in his logic, the author has sacrificed nothing deemed by him essential to his task, to the desire of being popular, or the fear of being pronounced *dry*— the word of most complete condemnation in the present day. Dry, however, no person who takes an interest in the actual condition and prospects of society, can possibly find the greater portion of this work. For, as we have already intimated, that which honourably distinguishes it from other professed treatises of political economy is the perpetual, earnest, never-forgotten interest, which accompanies the writer throughout, in the great questions at present mooted with respect to the social condition of man. Mr Mill very wisely refused to limit himself to the mere abstract principles of his science; he descends from them, sometimes as from a vantage ground, into the discussions which most concern and agitate the public mind at the present day; and, if his conclusions are not always, or even generally, such as we can wholly coincide with, there is so penetrating an intelligence in his remarks, and so grave and serious a philanthropy pervading his book, that it would be impossible for the most complete opponent of the work not to rise a gainer from its perusal. From what else can we gain, if not from intercourse with a keen, and full, and sincere mind, whether we have to struggle with it, or to acquiesce in its guidance? There are passages in this work, didactic as its style generally is, which have had on us all the effect of the most thrilling eloquence, from the fine admixture of severe reasoning and earnestness of feeling. (pp. 411-12)

Political economists have some of them wasted much time, and produced no little ennui, by unprofitable discussions on the definition of terms. These Mr Mill wisely spares us: an accurate writer, by a cautious use of ordinary expressions, will make his meaning more evident and precise than he will be able to do by any laboured definitions, or the introduction of purely technical terms. Such have been the discussions on the strict limits of the science of political economy, and the propriety of the title it has so long borne; whether intellectual efforts shall be classed amongst productive or unproductive labour, and the precise and invariable meaning to be given to such terms as *wealth, value,* and the like. These will generally be found to be unprofitable controversies, tending more to confusion of ideas than to precision of language. Let a writer think steadily and clearly upon his subject, and ordinary language will be faithful to him; distinctions between the several meanings of the same term will be made as they are wanted. He who *begins* by making such distinctions is only laying a snare for his own feet; he will hamper himself and perplex his reader. And with regard especially to the range of topics which an author thinks fit to embrace in his treatise upon this science, surely he may permit himself some liberty of choice, without resolving to mete out new boundaries to which all who follow him are to conform. (p. 415)

But there is another class of discussions which, although to the general reader, who is mostly an impatient one, they will appear at first sight to be of a purely technical character, must not be so hastily dismissed. These will be often found to have a direct bearing on the most important questions that can occupy the mind of the statesman. They are in fact explanatory of that great machine, a commercial society, upon which he has to practise—which he has to keep in order, or to learn to leave alone—and therefore as necessary a branch of knowledge to him as anatomy or physiology to one who undertakes to medicine the body. Such are some of the intricate discussions which concern the nature of *capital*—a subject to which we shall in the first place and at once turn our attention. It is a subject which Mr Mill has treated throughout in a most masterly manner. We may safely say, that there is now no other work to which a student could be properly directed for obtaining a complete insight into all the intricacies of this great branch of political economy. The exposition lies scattered, indeed, through the two volumes; he must read the entire work to obtain it. This scattering of the several parts of a subject is inevitable in treating such a science as political economy, where every topic has to be discussed in relation to every other topic. We do not think that Mr Mill has been particularly happy in his arrangement of topics, but, aware as we are of the extreme difficulty, under such circumstances, of making *any arrangement at all,* we forbear from any criticism. A man must write himself out the best way he can; and the reader, after obtaining all the materials put at his disposition, may pack them up in what bundles may best suit his own convenience.

We must premise that on this subject—the nature and employment of capital—there appears to be in one part of Mr

Mill's exposition—not an error—but a temporary forgetfulness of an old and familiar truth, which ought to have found its place there. Its very familiarity has occasioned it to be overlooked, in the keen inquiry after truth of a more recondite nature. The part which the economists call "unproductive consumption," the self-indulgent luxurious expenditure of the rich—the part this plays in a system of society based on individual effort and individual possession, is not fully stated.

He who spends his money, and lives to do little else, however idle he may be himself, has always had the consolation that he was, at least, setting other people to work. Mr Mill *seems* to deny him utterly this species of consolation; for in contending against a statement, made by political economists as well as others, that unproductive consumption is necessary, in a strictly *economical* sense, to the employment of the workmen, and as the indispensable relative to productive consumption, or capital spent in industrial pursuits, he has overlooked that *moral* necessity there is, in the present system of things, that there should be those who spend to enjoy, as well as those who lay out their money for profit. "What supports and employs productive labour," says Mr Mill, . . . "is the capital expended in setting it to work, and not the demand of purchases for the produce of the labour when completed. Demand for commodities is not demand for labour. The demand for commodities determines in what particular branch of production the labour and capital shall be employed; it determines the *direction* of the labour, but not the more or less of the labour itself, or of the maintenance and payment of the labour. That depends on the amount of the capital, or other funds directly devoted to the sustenance and remuneration of labour." Now, without a doubt, the man who purchases an article of luxury when it is manufactured, does not employ labour in the same sense as the manufacturer, who spends his wealth in supporting the artisan, and finding him the requisites of his art, and who, after selling the products of this industry, continues to spend the capital returned to him, together with the profit he has made, in the further sustenance of workmen. But it has been always understood, and the truth appears to be almost too trite to insist on, that unless the unproductive consumer were there to purchase, the capitalist would have had no motive to employ his wealth in this manner; and, what is of equal importance to bear in mind, unless the capitalist also calculated on being, some future day, an unproductive consumer himself, he would have no motive, by saving and toiling, to increase his wealth. (pp. 415-16)

Any of our readers into whose hands the work of Mr Mill has already fallen, will be aware of the numerous topics on which it must excite controversy or provoke discussion. . . . His observations upon [the limits and province of government] are so temperate and judicious, and conceived throughout in so liberal and enlightened a spirit, that although there must always be a *shade* of difference between such a writer and ourselves, we should have little hesitation in adopting almost the whole of the chapter. He draws a very necessary distinction between the authoritative interference of government, controlling and interdicting, and that kind of intervention where a government, "leaving individuals free to use their own means of pursuing any object of general interest, but not trusting the object solely to their care, establishes, side by side with their arrangements, an agency of its own for a like purpose. Thus it is one thing to maintain a church establishment, and another to refuse toleration to other religions, or to persons professing no religion. It is one thing to provide schools or colleges, and another to require that no person shall act as an instructor of youth without a government license.'' (pp. 426-27)

[Among the subjects we wish we had room to discuss are Mr Mill's] views, rather hinted at than explained, on the position which the female sex ought to take in society. . . . Speaking of the Americans, he says they have ''apparently got rid of all social injustices and inequalities that affect persons of Caucasian race *and of the male sex;*'' leaving it to be inferred, that even in America there still remain certain social injustices and inequalities affecting *the female sex*. There are many inuendos scattered throughout the book of the same description, but we nowhere gather a distinct view of the sort of reformation that is called for. In a writer of another character these expressions would be encountered only with ridicule; coming from Mr Mill, they excite our surprise, and, in some measure, our curiosity. (p. 428)

[William Henry Smith], ''Political Economy, by J. S. Mill,'' in Blackwood's Edinburgh Magazine, *Vol. LXIV, No. CCCXCVI, October, 1848, pp. 407-28.*

[WALTER BAGEHOT]   (essay date 1850)

[*Bagehot is regarded as one of the most versatile and influential authors of mid-Victorian England. In addition to literary criticism, he wrote several pioneering works in the fields of politics, sociology, and economics. As editor of the London* Economist, *he was instrumental in shaping the financial policy of his generation. Despite their diverse subject matter, Bagehot's works are unified by his emphasis on factual information and his interest in the personalities of literary figures, politicians, and economists. His works also reflect his belief that ''the knack in style is to write like a human being.'' Many modern commentators contend that it is partially because of the ''readable'' quality of his prose that Bagehot's writings, which were primarily composed as journalistic pieces, are still enjoyed today. In this critique of Mill's theory of inference, Bagehot attacks his insistence on reasoning from observation rather than from belief. According to Bagehot, Mill's unswerving dedication to logic implies a rigidity of mind and ''seems to us rather to create than deduce its conclusions.'' For further commentary on Mill by Bagehot, see the excerpt dated 1873.*]

[Mr. Mill's intellect] is one subtle enough in analysis, and that delights in deductive inference, but which can yield no belief to anything that is not capable either of direct perception, or of stringent deduction from facts of direct perception. He is inclined, therefore, to attribute any degree of influence to *known* causes, i.e. to facts capable of direct observation, rather than to assume any, even the slightest, cause, not capable of such perception, however perfectly it may account for the facts, and however disproportionate those facts may be to the hitherto observed results of any observed antecedents; in short, his tendency is rather to ascribe the very greatest degrees of influence to perceived causes, than the very smallest to those which are only assumed. Of this characteristic tendency in Mr. Mill's mind, his rejection of all *a priori* truth, his utilitarian creed in morals, his strong leaning to the doctrine that men's minds differ, *not* from different original constitution, but from the various influences to which they are subjected, and his remarks on Hypotheses, are perhaps sufficient indications. (p. 80)

The theory of inference . . . adopted by Mr. Mill, states that the mind is *carried on* in thought from the evidence, to the thing evidenced, that this is the whole and only operation: that if the mind be thus irresistibly carried on, the inference is certain; if only prominently, so that it remain partially open to

different successions in its place, the inference is only probable; and that these different degrees of mental connection correspond to different numbers of repetitions in past experiences. What becomes then of Mr. Mill's lofty and reiterated censure of those who ''adduce as evidence of the truth of fact in external nature any necessity that the human mind may be conceived to be under of believing it?'' The law of association is simply and purely a necessity of the human mind, in reproducing and forcing upon it again, conjunctions which have once or oftener taken place within its observation, and any belief which rests upon this law, which expects *a,* after seeing A, because A and *a* have been previously connected in observation, does not ''adapt itself to the realities of things,'' but only to its own inward necessity. Mr. Mill entirely fails to point out any distinction between the law of association and any other laws of mind (proved to be such) justifying us in accepting the one as more *objective* than any other. A casual reader would be led to suppose, from his mode of writing in [*A System of Logic*] and other places, that Mr. Mill had really dispensed with so ungrounded an hypothesis as laws of *mind* altogether, and had succeeded in identifying his mind, in every respect, with the outward world and its laws.—He might perhaps reply that the superior safety of the law of association lies *not* in its always ruling its expectations by past facts (which obviously need not necessarily be a good guide to the future), but in its self-verification in generally *coming out* right. But this must be the case with any law of evidence that could be shown to be even plausible, much more true; there is no question about inventing an imaginary law of evidence, but only about determining the true nature of the existing law: whatever it is, or has been, it must agree with the facts of human inference; and the point now at issue is *not* whether the associative law or any other law most accurately corresponds with the *facts* of human belief, but what reason Mr. Mill has for asserting that a law which *compels* us to expect the future to resemble the past, is, *per se,* in the least less liable to the charge of adducing subjective necessity as evidence for the truth of an objective fact, than any other law of mind whatever, whether *a priori* or otherwise. We are not at present arguing against the actual law assumed by Mr. Mill, but only against the unfair attempt to establish it, not by showing its more perfect agreement with the facts of belief, but by arbitrarily asserting, that it alone, of all laws, does not bring any internal necessity as evidence of an external truth. The attempt, so often made, to disclaim any law of belief different from those of external occurrence, could only come to disclaiming any possibility of belief not warranted by actual *observation;* so that no belief at all could be possible *before* an event: if the expectation of future facts is to be formed upon the experience of past facts, then this is, in itself, a law of mind, and of mind *only,* which brings as evidence of an outward fact ''a necessity which the human mind is believed to be under, of believing it,'' and is therefore protested against by Mr. Mill.

We think then that we have proved that we may, or rather *must,* put faith in the laws of our own mind, whatever these may be, if we are to believe anything about future events at all, even of those of external nature; and that if Mr. Mill's protest is worth anything, it is directed against his own theory of evidence, quite as strongly as against any other. The next remark we have to make upon this rationale of the process of evidence, is, that its whole basis, viz. that every change has (to a moral certainty) an invariable and unconditional antecedent, i.e. one which will, in every case, be followed by the same change, is obviously founded on the theory of probabilities, and is, in truth, simply an application of that theory to a particular case. We have heard it asked why Mr. Mill has not put his chapter on Chances *before* his chapter on the ground of Induction; and certainly we found it on consideration quite impossible to explain. He would obviously have given much greater unity to his book by so doing, and would have relieved his readers of much of the mystification which we felt, when we were suddenly introduced to the law of universal causation, without a word of explanation about its evidence, except that it was a truth grounded on familiar observation. This of course assumes that observations of the past are (according to their degree of universality and familiarity) grounds of presumption for the future; but nowhere does Mr. Mill explain why this is the case, or even refer it explicitly to the law of association (except incidentally in a chapter of the Fourth Book quoted above, on operations subsidiary to Induction, when all the theory of the process itself is completed), nor does he explicitly refer his doctrine of probabilities to the same law, but only, in general terms, grounds them both on experience (or the absence of all experience).—Surely he ought to have considered and classed together our inferences from *uniform* or nearly uniform experience (moral certainty), and from occasional experience (moral probability); the law of causation, he says, rests on the one, and we therefore expect an invariable unconditional antecedent for every change with perfect confidence; but that does not alter the *principle* of our expectation, which is identical with that of a probable guess; and no one who considers the question for a moment, will deny that Mr. Mill ought to have prefixed to his book on Induction, an analysis of the principle of expectation, and then immediately grounded upon this his doctrine of probability, of analogy, and of certainty; and so made us to understand *why* he considers the axiom of universal causation to be morally certain. Assuredly to have done so, would materially have altered the whole of his book on Induction. Let him once have stated clearly, that the association of A with *a*, in fact, is the only ground for our expecting its association in similar cases, and that the strength of such past association is a *minimum* measure of its probability in *every* case (though of course no *sufficient* measure where A can be shown to be related to *a*, as cause to effect, because then the special probability reaches the same certainty as the general truth that every change is preceded by some invariable and unconditional antecedent), and we should not have had the confusion, of founding the whole doctrine of chances and of causation upon analogy, and then making analogy to depend entirely upon causation. Certainly when we found Mr. Mill stating as the ultimate principle of all inference that because an individual resembles certain other individuals in some one or more ways, therefore it will resemble them also in other ways (which is the principle of analogy), we were not prepared to find him asserting that analogy is worthless, unless we have reason to suspect that the inferred resemblance is connected *by causation* with the perceived resemblance. Lest our readers should doubt that so clear-headed a writer could have so slighted and reversed his own theory, we quote his own words: he says,—

> We conclude that a fact *m,* known to be true of A, is more likely to be true of B, if B agrees with A in some of its properties (even though no connection is known to exist between *m* and these properties), than if no resemblance at all could be traced between B and any other thing known to possess the attribute *m.* To this argument it is of course [!] requisite, that the properties common to A with B shall be merely not known to be connected with *m;* they must not be properties known to be unconnected with

it. If, either by processes of elimination, or by deduction from previous knowledge of the laws of the property in question, it can be concluded that they have nothing to do with *m,* the argument of analogy is put out of court. The supposition must be that *m* is an effect really dependent upon some property of A, but we know not upon which. . . .

(pp. 91-5)

In other words, the argument from analogy is good to prove the law of causation, to make us believe that, because we see the same consequents always following the same antecedents, it will be so in other cases also; but for any other purpose it must not be used for a moment. The association of phenomena is good ground for anticipating their association, while we keep within the sphere of causation; but once go beyond, and then the same association which was set up as a presumption for *all* unknown cases, loses its function, and becomes simply worthless. That which is Mr. Mill's ground for the doctrine of chances, upon which really the whole fabric of his system is built, ceases to be his ground directly he has got rid of the difficulty of establishing a fixed point from which to reason; and the old friend who relieved him, when in need, by lending him the whole of his logical capital, is cut directly he has provided himself with richer resources, and even talked of as a poor dependent. Surely Mr. Mill means to assert that constant experience in the past, is moral certainty for the future; and that frequent experience is moral probability, and that too, antecedent to *all* doctrine about causation (which is only established upon it). If this be the case, what right can he have to say subsequently, that such experience is no criterion whatever, *unless* there be reason to suspect causation? There *was* no reason to suspect causation in that mythical period (where does Mr. Mill place it? before the historical period? or even so late as the revival of learning?) of which he speaks when there was no conclusive reason to believe in causes at all; cause was an idea not then established, and as he says, all expectation must then have been formed from the induction *per enumerationem simplicem* merely, i.e. "because it does happen so in some cases, it will happen so in similar cases;" and this was the reason first for suspecting, then for expecting, lastly for believing, that all events would have invariable antecedents; surely this expectation was *rational* expectation?

Why Mr. Mill calls it "unreasoning" . . . when it has helped him to such a truth, we cannot understand; for reason to be founded on unreason, is most paradoxical: and it seems to us sheer ingratitude to revile a principle to which he owes his logic itself. If this principle aided us before any proof of invariable laws at all, why then may it not guide us now, whenever those laws fail to help us? The doctrine of probability is entirely based on this principle, according to Mr. Mill. . . . There he is more consistent, not attributing, in words at least, our expectation to any guess at causes, but simply to an instinct that experience on the whole is uniform; why he should reject the same principle in the exactly similar case of analogy we are at a loss to say, except indeed on the hypothesis, that his doctrine of causation contains radical errors, which confuse him at every turn. The truth seems to be that Mr. Mill (like many other able reasoners, who so rejoice in their power of both analysis and deduction that they can never be at peace if they are asked to take anything as ultimate, and simply to have faith in it) is rather well pleased, we imagine, than otherwise, at the shadowy *basis* which he gives us for Inductive science. To use one of his own terms, he has more fitness for the

Dynamics than for the Statics of philosophy, and delighting in *Inference,* feels the more at ease the further he can travel from the [archi] of his science. He congratulates himself that, while it has served his turn, it is quite useless for any other purpose, and is decidedly glad to be able to warn his readers against the loose habit of unscientific inference, to which he and all of us are, according to him, nevertheless indebted for the possibility of scientific rules. He evidently hates any unproved assumption as belonging to the sphere of transcendental metaphysics, a region which he regards with mingled dread and asperity, as a kind of scientific purgatory, that must be passed in order to reach the paradise of Reasoning; but to be shut out as soon as possible from the memory. Yet as he is too clear-sighted to think *all* can be proved, and nothing assumed, he trusts an original propensity of our nature for a while, only that he may dispense with it altogether, and thenceforth evidently owes it a grudge for ever having been necessary to him at all. We think, however, that this tendency of Mr. Mill to make the argument, from analogy (or what should be, with him, probable evidence), depend wholly on causation, is not without foundation, though, in him, it is certainly inconsistent. (pp. 95-7)

It is a somewhat presumptuous, and not an easy task, to criticise so able a thinker as Mr. Mill, especially when his writings appear to have quite subdued the not very independent spirit of English philosophy. The prolonged silence with which his book has been received by English critics seems to imply a surrender without terms; and in fact the qualities of Mr. Mill's mind are eminently calculated to impress and frighten our countrymen into silence, even when unconvinced. The dread of mysticism in this country, or even of the mere imputation of assuming anything that is not capable of proof, is almost morbid, and Mr. Mill's quiet contempt for any superfluity of belief is likely enough to intimidate, even where his arguments do not overwhelm. And in truth even the extreme of incredulity is more tolerable in philosophy than the tendency to admit without the strictest examination, as foreign philosophers so often do, that any psychological fact is ultimate. Still the theoretical results of the incredulous school are often more astonishing, and this, by far the ablest statement of what may be called the *multum-in-parvo* school of philosophy, constantly seems to us rather to create than deduce its conclusions. Valuable as Mr. Mill's book is, we do not think that even the Logic of Induction (by far its most important and, in our estimation, its least erroneous part) has received from him a really permanent form, since the principles of symmetric arrangement seldom or never reveal themselves, while the fundamental assumptions of a science remain erroneous or unfixed. (pp. 110-11)

> [*Walter Bagehot*], *"Mill and Whewell on the Logic of Induction,"* in The Prospective Review, *Vol. VI, No. XXI, 1850, pp. 77-111.**

THE SOUTHERN QUARTERLY REVIEW   (essay date 1856)

[*The author of the following excerpt maintains that Mill, in A* System of Logic, *created a set of principles that ignores the "higher faculties of the mind." Mill, according to this critic, misinterprets the philosophy of Francis Bacon and proves inconsistent in his own writings, so that "the best refutation is to leave him in the entanglement of his own contradictions."*]

Mr. John S. Mill, in his *Logic, Ratiocinative and Inductive,* dragged down logic into the very mire of empiricism. Taking Brown, who, we have seen, makes consciousness convertible with feeling, as his guide in the philosophy of the mind, he constructed a system of logic in which the higher faculties of the mind are ignored. While Whately, with some show of reason, resolved induction into deduction or syllogism proper, Mill most preposterously resolved all deduction into induction; and thereby consummated the degradation of logic. Mr. Mill repudiates entirely all necessary truths; consequently ignores the formal laws of thought, of which pure logic is the science, and reduces all thought to the uncertainty of the empirical conditions of observation. He ignores all distinction between the apodictic and the hypothetical exercise of the understanding. He seems never to consider, that the determinations of the understanding are often effected solely by the relation in which intelligence stands to itself in thought. He maintains that deduction is but an extension of induction, and from the beginning to the end of his exposition confounds *inference* with *deduction.* The intrusion of matter between the premises and the conclusion of a syllogism, which is the cardinal error to be guarded against in logic, is the very thing which Mr. Mill strives to effect as the great end and consummation of correct reasoning. The syllogism is founded upon matter which it passively receives. It does not even develope potential knowledge into actual, but merely evolves implicit knowledge into explicit. The conclusion is already known before the syllogism is formed. Ratiocination is determined by the relations into which intelligence puts itself to itself in regard to some object-matter. Such being the nature of ratiocination, its very form in the syllogism excludes everything intrusive between the premises and the conclusion. In a word, Mr. Mill does not discriminate pure logic, wherein the mental determinations are effected by the formal laws of thought, from concrete or modified logic, wherein the mental determinations are effected under the laws of thought, modified by the empirical circumstances under which we exert our faculties. But even in concrete or modified logic, thought is not considered as applied to any particular matter, but the necessary are considered in conjunction with the contingent conditions under which thought is actually exerted. Mr. Mill does not even discriminate pure from applied logic, formal from material illation, but confounds even these.

It may be said, in answer to these strictures, that Mr. Mill defines in the beginning of his treatise what scope he intends to give it, and that the objection we make is one merely of the meaning of words. This mode of answering our objection, while it has the air of looking at the subject from a more comprehensive point of view, is a sheer evasion. Mr. Mill has not the right to confuse the boundaries of a science. Logic is found by reflective analysis as well as by the indications of its history to be confined to the formal laws of thought as its adequate object-matter; else all the material sciences must be intruded into it. Mr. Mill, therefore, by taking into logic so much foreign matter, is like a geographer who should take into the map of America, the continent of Europe. But Mr. Mill's is not merely an error of boundary: it is a blunder in all the fundamental doctrines of logic, leading him to repeat, with emphasis, the stale misapprehension, that Bacon's method is one-sided, excluding deduction altogether as a process of investigation. Playfair, in his celebrated *Dissertation on the Progress of the Mathematical and Physical Sciences,* pronounced the same judgment, and disparaged Bacon's method as Mr. Mill does, by saying that it ignored the process which in the advanced stage of the sciences becomes the most important and effective. Whereas, what Mr. Mill and his forerunners in the error call deduction, is not deduction, a demonstrative process, at all, but is what Bacon means by the descending scale of induction, being in fact a hypothetical and not an apodictic process, and is sometimes, as we have already shown, called the synthetical process of induction. The blunder of Mr. Mill is thus a double one; first, in supposing the process to be deduction when it is not; secondly, in supposing that Bacon excluded it from his method. The truth is, Bacon strode with such colossal steps along the paths of philosophy, that but few have been able to step in his exact footprints, and of these few Mr. Mill is not one, as his numerous misapprehensions of Bacon's method show.

But the most mischievous error which derationalizes Mr. Mill's logic, is the notion, that "Deduction is the great scientific work of the present and future ages;" and that "a revolution is peaceably and progressively effecting itself in philosophy, the reverse of that to which Bacon has attached his name." This doctrine, assuming as it does, that the highest generalities have been reached, evinces a narrowness of comprehension, which of itself would put Mr. Mill below any very high elevation as a thinker; but when it is also a broad contradiction of the fundamental doctrine of his system of logic, which resolves deduction into induction, Mr. Mill stands revealed as a thinker who does not understand himself, but crosses his own path in his exposition of doctrines; and the best refutation is to leave him in the entanglement of his own contradictions. (pp. 256-58)

> *"History of Philosophy," in* The Southern Quarterly Review, *Vol. II, No. 1, November, 1856, pp. 256-60.**

JOHN STUART MILL (essay date 1859)

[*In this excerpt from his introduction to* On Liberty, *first published in 1859, Mill makes his controversial claim that "the only purpose for which power can be rightfully exercised over any member of a civilized community . . . is to prevent harm to others." He then elucidates the limitations and conditions necessary for genuine individual liberty.*]

The object of this Essay is to assert one very simple principle, as entitled to govern absolutely the dealings of society with the individual in the way of compulsion and control, whether the means used be physical force in the form of legal penalties, or the moral coercion of public opinion. That principle is, that the sole end for which mankind are warranted, individually or collectively, in interfering with the liberty of action of any of their number, is self-protection. That the only purpose for which power can be rightfully exercised over any member of a civilized community, against his will, is to prevent harm to others. His own good, either physical or moral, is not a sufficient warrant. He cannot rightfully be compelled to do or forbear because it will be better for him to do so, because it will make him happier, because, in the opinions of others, to do so would be wise, or even right. These are good reasons for remonstrating with him, or reasoning with him, or persuading him, or entreating him, but not for compelling him, or visiting him with any evil in case he do otherwise. To justify that, the conduct from which it is desired to deter him, must be calculated to produce evil to some one else. The only part of the conduct of any one, for which he is amenable to society, is that which concerns others. In the part which merely concerns himself, his independence is, of right, absolute. Over himself, over his own body and mind, the individual is sovereign.

It is, perhaps, hardly necessary to say that this doctrine is meant to apply only to human beings in the maturity of their faculties. We are not speaking of children, or of young persons below the age which the law may fix as that of manhood or womanhood. Those who are still in a state to require being taken care of by others, must be protected against their own actions as well as against external injury. For the same reason, we may leave out of consideration those backward states of society in which the race itself may be considered as in its nonage. The early difficulties in the way of spontaneous progress are so great, that there is seldom any choice of means for overcoming them; and a ruler full of the spirit of improvement is warranted in the use of any expedients that will attain an end, perhaps otherwise unattainable. Despotism is a legitimate mode of government in dealing with barbarians, provided the end be their improvement, and the means justified by actually effecting that end. Liberty, as a principle, has no application to any state of things anterior to the time when mankind have become capable of being improved by free and equal discussion. Until then, there is nothing for them but implicit obedience to an Akbar or a Charlemagne, if they are so fortunate as to find one. But as soon as mankind have attained the capacity of being guided to their own improvement by conviction or persuasion (a period long since reached in all nations with whom we need here concern ourselves), compulsion, either in the direct form or in that of pains and penalties for non-compliance, is no longer admissible as a means to their own good, and justifiable only for the security of others.

It is proper to state that I forego any advantage which could be derived to my argument from the idea of abstract right, as a thing independent of utility. I regard utility as the ultimate appeal on all ethical questions; but it must be utility in the largest sense, grounded on the permanent interests of man as a progressive being. Those interests, I contend, authorize the subjection of individual spontaneity to external control, only in respect to those actions of each, which concern the interest of other people. If any one does an act hurtful to others, there is a *primâ facie* case for punishing him, by law, or, where legal penalties are not safely applicable, by general disapprobation. There are also many positive acts for the benefit of others, which he may rightfully be compelled to perform; such as, to give evidence in a court of justice; to bear his fair share in the common defence, or in any other joint work necessary to the interest of the society of which he enjoys the protection; and to perform certain acts of individual beneficence, such as saving a fellow-creature's life, or interposing to protect the defenceless against ill-usage, things which whenever it is obviously a man's duty to do, he may rightfully be made responsible to society for not doing. A person may cause evil to others not only by his actions but by his inaction, and in either case he is justly accountable to them for the injury. The latter case, it is true, requires a much more cautious exercise of compulsion than the former. To make any one answerable for doing evil to others, is the rule; to make him answerable for not preventing evil, is, comparatively speaking, the exception. Yet there are many cases clear enough and grave enough to justify that exception. In all things which regard the external relations of the individual, he is *de jure* amenable to those whose interests are concerned, and if need be, to society as their protector. There are often good reasons for not holding him to the responsibility; but these reasons must arise from the special expediencies of the case: either because it is a kind of case in which he is on the whole likely to act better, when left to his own discretion, than when controlled in any way in which society have it in their power to control him; or because the attempt to exercise control would produce other evils, greater than those which it would prevent. When such reasons as these preclude the enforcement of responsibility, the conscience of the agent himself should step into the vacant judgment seat, and protect those interests of others which have no external protection; judging himself all the more rigidly, because the case does not admit of his being made accountable to the judgment of his fellow-creatures.

But there is a sphere of action in which society, as distinguished from the individual, has, if any, only an indirect interest; comprehending all that portion of a person's life and conduct which affects only himself, or if it also affects others, only with their free, voluntary, and undeceived consent and participation. When I say only himself, I mean directly, and in the first instance: for whatever affects himself, may affect others through himself; and the objection which may be grounded on this contingency, will receive consideration in the sequel. This, then, is the appropriate region of human liberty. It comprises, first, the inward domain of consciousness; demanding liberty of conscience, in the most comprehensive sense; liberty of thought and feeling; absolute freedom of opinion and sentiment on all subjects, practical or speculative, scientific, moral, or theological. The liberty of expressing and publishing opinions may seem to fall under a different principle, since it belongs to that part of the conduct of an individual which concerns other people; but, being almost of as much importance as the liberty of thought itself, and resting in great part on the same reasons, is practically inseparable from it. Secondly, the principle requires liberty of tastes and pursuits; of framing the plan of our life to suit our own character; of doing as we like, subject to such consequences as may follow: without impediment from our fellow-creatures, so long as what we do does not harm them, even though they should think our conduct foolish, perverse, or wrong. Thirdly, from this liberty of each individual, follows the liberty, within the same limits, of combination among individuals; freedom to unite, for any purpose not involving harm to others: the persons combining being supposed to be of full age, and not forced or deceived.

No society in which these liberties are not, on the whole, respected, is free, whatever may be its form of government; and none is completely free in which they do not exist absolute and unqualified. The only freedom which deserves the name, is that of pursuing our own good in our own way, so long as we do not attempt to deprive others of theirs, or impede their efforts to obtain it. Each is the proper guardian of his own health, whether bodily, or mental and spiritual. Mankind are greater gainers by suffering each other to live as seems good to themselves, than by compelling each to live as seems good to the rest.

Though this doctrine is anything but new, and, to some persons, may have the air of a truism, there is no doctrine which stands more directly opposed to the general tendency of existing opinion and practice. Society has expended fully as much effort in the attempt (according to its lights) to compel people to conform to its notions of personal, as of social excellence. The ancient commonwealths thought themselves entitled to practise, and the ancient philosophers countenanced, the regulation of every part of private conduct by public authority, on the ground that the State had a deep interest in the whole bodily and mental discipline of every one of its citizens; a mode of thinking which may have been admissible in small republics surrounded by powerful enemies, in constant peril of being subverted by foreign attack or internal commotion, and to which even a short interval of relaxed energy and self-command might so easily be fatal, that they could not afford to wait for the salutary permanent effects of freedom. In the modern world, the greater size of political communities, and above all, the separation between spiritual and temporal authority (which placed the direction of men's consciences in other hands than those which

controlled their worldly affairs), prevented so great an interference by law in the details of private life; but the engines of moral repression have been wielded more strenuously against divergence from the reigning opinion in self-regarding, than even in social matters; religion, the most powerful of the elements which have entered into the formation of moral feeling, having almost always been governed either by the ambition of a hierarchy, seeking control over every department of human conduct, or by the spirit of Puritanism. And some of those modern reformers who have placed themselves in strongest opposition to the religions of the past, have been noway behind either churches or sects in their assertion of the right of spiritual domination: M. Comte, in particular, whose social system, as unfolded in his *Système de Politique Positive*, aims at establishing (though by moral more than by legal appliances) a despotism of society over the individual, surpassing anything contemplated in the political ideal of the most rigid disciplinarian among the ancient philosophers.

Apart from the peculiar tenets of individual thinkers, there is also in the world at large an increasing inclination to stretch unduly the powers of society over the individual, both by the force of opinion and even by that of legislation: and as the tendency of all the changes taking place in the world is to strengthen society, and diminish the power of the individual, this encroachment is not one of the evils which tend spontaneously to disappear, but, on the contrary, to grow more and more formidable. The disposition of mankind, whether as rulers or as fellow-citizens, to impose their own opinions and inclinations as a rule of conduct on others, is so energetically supported by some of the best and by some of the worst feelings incident to human nature, that it is hardly ever kept under restraint by anything but want of power; and as the power is not declining, but growing, unless a strong barrier of moral conviction can be raised against the mischief, we must expect, in the present circumstances of the world, to see it increase. (pp. 223-27)

> *John Stuart Mill, in an introduction to "On Liberty,"*
> *in his* Essays on Politics and Society, *edited by J. M.*
> *Robson, University of Toronto Press, 1977, pp.*
> *213-310.*

[R. W. CHURCH]   (essay date 1860)

[*Evaluating Mill's* On Liberty *in this important early review, Church raises many of the fundamental criticisms reiterated by later Mill scholars. He commends "the distinctness, the daring, the vigour" of Mill's essay, but points out that his model of society is only partially valid. Church contends that custom, though it can impinge on personal liberty, is also necessary for social cohesiveness; though some individuals are capable of exercising free choice, others need to be guided by social consensus and tradition. Mill's greatest error in the essay, according to Church, is that he fails to consider the individual "as a link in the network of society, necessarily acting as others, and acted on by them."*]

[The value of Mr. Mill's **'On Liberty'**] is not to be measured simply by the conclusions arrived at. A man must be very sanguine who should expect to see a question, which he must have found for ever recurring in human history and pervading his own experience, closed and settled, even by a thinker like Mr. Mill. Only very young speculators, who, in their earliest attempts at thought, turn in their simplicity to logic, or to Locke on the 'Conduct of the Understanding,' for an infallible specific which shall insure their thinking and reasoning right, believe that such final solutions are anywhere to be looked for. At any rate, only those who are very easily satisfied, or are very servile admirers, will admit that it has been arrived at in Mr. Mill's Essay. The gain is in the treatment of such a subject at all by one so competent to handle it. The distinctness, the daring, the vigour of the discussion, the novelty which it throws round what is old and trite, the reality into which it quickens what is inert and torpid, even the peril and menace which it not obscurely discloses to convictions which may be matters of life and death to us, act as a tonic to the mind, and awaken, exercise, and brace it, even if they do not, as they well may, elevate the heart and widen the range of its ordinary contemplations. The reading of a book like this ought to be an event in a man's mental history. It is a challenge to him to analyze much that is vague and confused in his thoughts and current notions; and it is at the same time a help and guide in the process, by presenting the problem itself as conceived by a mind of greater than average reach and clearness. The discussion is important, too, in other ways, whether or not we are convinced by its argument, or even whether we can get any satisfactory and consistent answer to the question at all; for it shows us the term to which difficulty and inquiry have reached on the subject, on what scale the debate has to be carried on, and under what conditions; and, possibly, within what limits an approximately sufficient truth may be hoped for at present. It is both interesting and important as a measure of the grasp and strength of one of the foremost thinkers of his time. And perhaps its use is not the least, if it teaches us something more vividly of the real power or inability of the human mind to penetrate and master the complicated elements of our social state, and of its success in bringing them into a harmony, which we can feel to be both philosophically complete and also answering to the fact.

The subject of social liberty may be said to belong by special appropriateness to Mr. Mill, and to have a natural claim on him for a thorough sifting. Mr. Mill, as every one knows, regards democracy as the inevitable and beneficial result to which society is everywhere tending. In this he is not singular; but he differs from the majority of those who think with him, in the great clearness with which he discerns the probability, and in the extreme uneasiness with which he regards it, that as the dangers of political oppression of the many by the few disappear, the dangers of social oppression of the few by the many will increase. The foresight of this result does not, indeed, in any degree shake his full faith in the democratic principle; but it presents a serious abatement to the benefit which he hopes from it, and he loses no opportunity to show his ever-present sense of the danger, and of the necessity of providing means to counteract it. . . . One who hopes everything from popular ascendancy also fears it, and tries beforehand to establish in the opinion of society some well-recognized line round private life and private freedom, before the foreseen power of democracy arrives, to invade and confound all limits by blind usurpations to which there can be no resistance, and by a wayward but inexorable interference from which there will be no escape.

But Mr. Mill's aim is not wholly prospective. He thinks that the control of society over individual opinion and action is at present far too stringent; that it is illegitimate and exorbitant in its pretensions and mischievous in its effects. And as he is markedly distinguished from the common run of representatives of liberal doctrines in another point besides the one just alluded to, that is, in thinking very meanly of the men, the society, and the opinions of this generation, and in holding cheap the measure of improvement to which it has reached,

he finds the yoke all the more intolerable. His Essay is directed not only to provide against anticipated dangers, but to abate what he feels to be an existing evil. Having but little respect for the opinions which hold sway over present society, and which it sanctions and arms with its influence, he is anxious at once to cut from under them the ground on which their power over the separate units of society rests. The path of thought and truth and individual development is, he holds, miserably encumbered with ignoble entanglements, with maiming and crippling snares, with arbitrary and cruel restrictions, arising out of the interferences of society and the deference or the fear which it inspires. It is the purpose of his Essay to reduce within much narrower limits these customary and hitherto recognized rights of interference, as he finds them exercised now; and to lay down a rule for the jurisdiction of society over the individual, grounded on a clear and definite principle; lightening the weight with which society presses on its members, and destroying the prerogative by which its accidentally prevailing opinions impose themselves with irritating or degrading peremptoriness on those who wish to have, or ought to have, opinions of their own.

His claim for individual liberty is of the very broadest, and involves serious consequences. Adopting William Von Humboldt's maxim, that the great purpose of government and society is the completest development of the individual, according to his own proper nature and tendencies, he demands for the individual every liberty compatible with the same liberty in others, and with the preservation of that society which alone makes any real liberty possible. (pp. 434-37)

In his view, society as it now exists, and by the maxims on which it acts, crushes and dwarfs the individual. There was a time when the individual was too strong for society, and by his lawlessness, self-will, or merely by the excessive accumulation of power in his hands, set at nought its fair influence, and hindered its healthy growth. But that time, in England at least, is long past. Society for many centuries has been slowly and surely gaining on the individual, till it has come at last to be, not merely his protector but his taskmaster, pedagogue, and even Pope. It has established a hold on his thoughts, opinions, and belief, justifiable only on a claim to infallibility. It has formed a number of moulds for his character and plan of life, and of some one or other of these it compels him to make his choice, as the shape into which he is to force and squeeze his whole nature. The individual, according to the received understanding as to its rights and its claims to submission, has no chance with society. Neither has he any escape from it. It is everywhere: it surrounds him: it penetrates into his own retirement, cows his reason, unnerves his own self-reliance, discredits and shakes his faith in his own clearest convictions, intimidates his purest purposes. Conscious of its invisible presence, he dares not think, he dares not like, as he would. Society 'executes its own mandates;' and its penalties, as they are more elastic and comprehensive than those of law, so are they more exquisitely adapted to their end, for they reach the soul and subjugate the will. Mr. Mill does not stint the strength of his words in characterizing the effect of this despotism of society. If we did not remember that he writes in view of a very high ideal, we should find it hard to resist the continual impression that his language, though it might be very well in a satire, a sermon, or a novel, is singularly unmeasured for a grave discussion of one of the most complicated questions of human life. It is the sort of view which recommends itself to a mind with a twist in it, or with a humour of its own, a view which we bear with as being its humour, not as if it were even meant to be taken as true. We might almost fancy, at times, that we were reading a description of some debased or declining condition of society, such as is popularly supposed to have been in the later ages of Rome or of the Greek empire. . . . (pp. 438-39)

But we can ascertain something positive of what is going on round us; and on this ground it seems to us that we recognize in Mr. Mill's picture but a partially true representation of what is. Custom is very powerful, but not omnipotent. The current which runs through society is neither so uniform nor so irresistible as he makes it. On the contrary, the face of society appears seamed and traversed in all directions by a vast number of currents, different in their course, strength, and tendencies, pressing on one another or violently conflicting; accelerating, diverting, retarding, with endlessly varying results from day to day; and, as in the sea and the atmosphere, each strong current infallibly provoking its balancing counter-current. Such a state of things is consistent with much respect for custom, but it is inconceivable without also a large amount of activity of mind and resistance to custom. . . . Mr. Mill must have lived long enough to have seen his contemporaries, not indeed turned into Benthamites, but distinctly and forcibly impressed by much of what Bentham said. The degree of readiness at the present time to canvass on their merits and to accept new doctrines, must be a matter of opinion. The characteristic cry of modern thought, in art as in literature, for the unconventional, the real, the true, the strong, may be a deception. We may be mistaken in thinking that there has been no lack of as bold experiment in writing, if not in life, as in any age. But we find it difficult to reconcile the aspect which society presents to our eyes with the sweeping statement of its slavery to custom, and indifference or indisposition to what is spontaneous and original, on which Mr. Mill's Essay is founded.

But however this may be, Mr. Mill's estimate of society as it is forms the pressing reason with him for calling attention to principles, which, true as he thinks them, at all times, are especially necessary now. They are needed, he maintains, for practical and immediate relief. Society actually presents hindrances to the individual development which is the end of life, and so, to that perfection of the race, which can only be with that of that individual; and these hindrances must be met by a strong and clear assertion of the principle of liberty. And what is that principle? It is that in everything relating to themselves as individuals, and to their own interests, men ought, without any interference from society or other men, from authority or from custom, to think and speak as they like, to act as they like, and to combine among themselves as they like. The only limit to this absolute liberty is, in other individuals the same liberty; in society the right of self-preservation. With respect to the liberty of thought, as it can in itself, in Mr. Mill's view, infringe on no other rights, it does not require limitation; and with it, is to be joined the liberty of expressing thought, which, though not standing exactly on the same ground, must practically go with it. . . . He argues for unrestricted liberty of action, on the ground that unless men are allowed to desire, choose, and act for themselves, there is no possibility of individual development and character; that experiment, in life and conduct, is necessary as a test between good and bad; and that even if customs are good ones, resistance to custom, *as such,* is necessary, to prevent society from becoming stationary. But liberty of action is liable, in a way that liberty of thought is not, to come into conflict with the wills, the interest, the welfare of others. It must have limits; and these limits are, that in all cases directly affecting society or others, society

may step in, by law or by opinion, to restrain liberty, or punish it if abused; but that in what relates, first, to acts of individuals regarding self, and next, to habits and dispositions, as such, society may not step in at all by law, and only partially by opinion, to control them. If men choose to ruin themselves by folly and excess, all that naturally results from our not liking them or despising them, they must be content to bear; but for these, which Mr. Mill will not call immoralities, direct and intentional social punishment is illegitimate. Against vices which directly threaten the interest of others, such as envy or avarice, we may deliberately direct our disapprobation and abhorrence, though we cannot make laws against them. To the objection that, in the long run, these private vices, though primarily only hurtful to the individual, do mischief to others and to society, by example and otherwise, he replies, that even so, it is a greater good, in the long run, to maintain liberty; that society has no business to be hard on what it could and ought to prevent by education; and that there is the enormous probability, that if it interferes, it will interfere wrongly. On the liberty of combination, which flows from the preceding positions, he only touches, in speaking of some of the practical applications of his doctrine.

The argument itself, both for liberty of thought and liberty of action, is nothing new. Its main points are common to all writers of the liberal school; what is remarkable in it is the vigour with which the chief reasons of this philosophy are condensed and brought to an edge, the formidable consistency and uncompromising completeness with which they are unfolded and connected with their consequences, and still more, perhaps, the moral colouring and earnestness which pervade the whole statement. Whether, even in Mr. Mill's hands, the liberal philosophy exhausts the facts and meets all the difficulties in human affairs, is doubtful. The perplexing jar of liberty and authority, of the uncertainty of knowledge and the necessity of action, still remains, even after Mr. Mill's trenchant method of settling it, a harsh and importunate discord, in human speculation as much as in human practice and society.

No one can undervalue the strength and clearness with which Mr. Mill has stated the argument for liberty of thought in its largest sense. If it leads to the unpleasant consequence, that society may do and is doing too much for what we hold to be truth in religion and morality, its ground, at least, in the fallibility of man is but too undeniable to any one who reflects either on himself or others. Opinions, says Mr. Mill, must neither be proscribed nor protected, because we none of us can be certain for others, however we may practically be for ourselves, that we are right: opinions must be left to find their level, persons must be left to make them out for themselves, because there is no public and universal test of certainty to which men can appeal against their opponents; and each man can but fall back, as the last resort, on his own reason. (pp. 441-45)

It seems to us as inconceivable that all men should think out their opinions, as that the world should ever improve if none did; as absurd to require even in theory, that all should know enough, and have time and intelligence enough to stand on their own ground, as to bind those who can to foregone conclusions. And if so, what is to become of those whose independent reason and judgment will not serve them to find their place in the world? The wise and thoughtful may claim liberty for themselves, but what liberty are the mass to have among themselves, and what liberty is to do for them? We said that Mr. Mill presupposes, in one part of his argument, that the thinkers represent mankind, as they are to be regarded in a question of this kind; but his practical estimate of the majority is of a very different kind, and it lies at the foundation of his appeal for immunity from all accountableness to their judgment on behalf of those who do use their reason. 'That miscellaneous collection of a few wise and many foolish individuals called the public,' how are they to get on in the strife of opinions which they cannot master, and among reasons about which they are totally incapable of judging? (pp. 446-47)

If liberty be claimed for those who can use it by having the power to think for themselves, we should have thought that at this moment they have it in most ample measure, as far as is compatible with their living at all in a society of most various and complicated relations; and that they have it in a daily-increasing degree. If the same conditions of liberty, extending to the very foundations of belief and morality, are required to pervade the whole body of society, and to be realized among the masses of common men, it seems to us that this is as impossible as it is undesirable. By that liberty is understood, in Mr. Mill's book, not merely absence of the restraints of law, but much more, the absence of the restraints, more subtle but as efficacious, of social opinion. Society in the mass, the society of active life and intercourse, the society of those who have little time for thought, must take many things, and many things of the utmost importance, for granted, and take them for granted as the exclusive truth. Men in general cannot be expected to be, at the same time, examining things and admitting the possibility of their being false and wrong, and acting upon them. How many, indeed, of those whose training is of a higher kind, can face the fact of a principle being open to question, and yet act earnestly upon it as if it were true? To preserve this true balance between thought and choice, is the fruit of the highest education of the whole man, in the highest sense of the word. And common men want beliefs, principles, rules of action, and supports of life, as well as those who can think them out for themselves; and where are common men to get them, except from the common stock, which has its warrant from the society in which they live? Unless they are to pass their lives drifting to and fro on a sea of doubt among the conflicts of opinion and argument, helpless navigators and hopeless of ever acquiring the art, they must stick on to something: they may, no doubt, choose to stick on to a stronger mind; but if they may do this, they may at least as legitimately stick on to the current beliefs and ideas sanctioned by public and general agreement around them. (pp. 448-49)

Of course, society may be wrong, or may take wrong modes of imposing its opinions and enforcing its social principles. It may be corrupt or misled; and it may be oppressive. Its beliefs and usages are shaped and consolidated not only by the wise and good, but by the foolish, and yet even more, by the half-wise and the half-good. Everybody knows how often society has wanted reform and renovation before, and may well believe that it may need it in his own time: and, doubtless, when men, singly or in crowds, have made up their minds decisively and feel strongly, they are apt to persecute. But there is a natural counterpoise for this stringency of social authority, a natural remedy for its stagnation or degeneracy, a natural antagonist to its overzeal. It is the liberty, intellectual and moral, not of all, whether they can use it or not, but of those who *can* use it: not a chimerical and impossible liberty, proposed in theory to those who, if they would, cannot by the nature of things live in society and really use it, but a liberty, proportionate to and coextensive with each man's power to examine, to judge, to form his own opinions. That which is the salt of society,

that which is the source of all improvement in it, and the antidote to the stiffness and hardness which grow out of belief and usage left too long to themselves, is the play and collision of minds, thinking their own thoughts and standing on ground of their own choosing or making. Society has been kept alive, and saved when on the brink of perishing, by an independence and originality, which were the opposites to its own habits of thinking in masses, and of taking for granted the authoritative and traditional. For such thinkers liberty may be claimed—claimed in as full measure as Mr. Mill makes the claim. As little as we can see what the preaching of such liberty as the paramount idea in society at large, could do, except make its present confusions worse confounded, so strongly do we feel the force of Mr. Mill's arguments for liberty among those who have earned their right to it. (p. 450)

[Mr. Mill] is quite alive to the necessity, in the state, of something settled, accepted, permanent, and not to be questioned—'something which men agree in holding sacred'—open to improvement, of course, but having some fixed point, without which nothing can be improved, but only destroyed, to make way for something else. He quite admits the idea that society is in some sense the guardian of certain principles and a certain spirit, which belong to its very essence and constitution. Can, then, the opinions and sentiments belonging to such a state of things fail to frown down those which are at variance with and destructive of it? Will public feeling in a democracy look tamely on, content with bare unimpassioned argument, at the insidious encroachment of an adverse opinion? Can it be expected, that social force will not put forth its power against doctrines, which imperil what is permanent, and invade 'what all agree in holding sacred?' Will not society—we do not say necessarily stifle and silence the discussion of them—but, from the instinct of self-preservation, inevitably present to their free course those formidable barriers of disapproval or condemnation, which are quite compatible with leaving individuals unmolested to think and speak as they please? Rightly or wrongly it may be; we only say that it is natural to society to have certain characteristic principles, and, as long as it cares about them, to protect them by a social ban on their opposites. And our objection to Mr. Mill's way of putting the argument for liberty of opinion is, that he puts forward the individual only, and takes no account of society; that he draws no line between questions which are open to the schools, and those which society must close, or go to pieces; that, on his theory, there can be no closed questions whatever; and that on that theory it is hard to see how society has any right to resent and reprobate—at least without each time giving, or, at any rate, seeing all its reasons—a defence of lying, of selfishness, of cowardice, or of bigotry. (pp. 456-57)

In attempting, then, to simplify and generalize the doctrine of liberty, and to lay down a principle which should decide without difficulty the 'endless jar' between society and individual liberty, and cut away with a clean sweep the usurpations of the former, Mr. Mill seems to us to have given too little weight to considerations which make the application of his principles far from simple. The points which chiefly strike us as overlooked by him are two. First, the way in which the mass of the people *must* depend more or less on society for their opinions. . . . The second point is, that the interests of society and of others seem to us far too closely interwoven and entangled with those of individuals to allow of that clean division which Mr. Mill's theory requires. (pp. 462-63)

We cannot entirely pass over a grave subject, which must be met with in an inquiry of this kind. With broad statements like those of Mr. Mill's Essay, on the exclusive claims of liberty, there always presents itself, as their inseparable correlative and anxious attendant, their bearing on the possibility of a religion. There would be nothing specially difficult in the question, if the world were made up of philosophers, or if only the religion of those who can examine and think were concerned. But religion is for the poor and weak. Religion must be a joint thing and a thing of faith. Men must believe together, and believe without doubt; be united in a common hope, and be united in full dependence on it, for those sympathies and harmonies to be developed among them by which they are supported themselves and support one another, in the darkness and disappointments of life, on a trust which goes beyond it. No one can look at the documents of Christianity and doubt that this religion was meant to produce the same ordinarily unquestioning faith as that, for example, of our family affections: and without that entire faith it cannot be the religion which we read of in the New Testament. If there is not faith, it may be philosophy, but not religion; and if there is faith, then, at some period or other, doubt of its truth must be cast behind. How such a state of mind is possible, either in the individual, who, on the ground of the fallibility of man and the infinite revolutions of opinion, keeps himself on continual guard against the too certain persuasion of what he holds, or in society, in which it is the normal and perpetual condition, that every conviction and belief is for ever held to be on its trial, and where public opinion, neutral about conclusions, discourages nothing but slackness of debate and the disposition to feel too positive, is a question—we are very far from saying, unanswerable, but which deserves an answer. Mr. Mill does not help us to one, or even as to whether one is to be hoped for. But throughout the discussion, we feel that it is, however latently, on uneven ground. (pp. 467-68)

We close Mr. Mill's book, not without great admiration for much clearly and nobly said, but yet with disappointment. Nowhere has the obligation been more strongly urged, on those who are responsible for truth in society, of giving a fair hearing to opposite opinions; nowhere the advantage more forcibly set forth, to opinion and belief, of collision with real opposition. . . . But we cannot find in it the clear line drawn, which it was written to draw, between liberty and the claims of society. It seems to us that, after all, our philosophical view of liberty is but slightly improved: that we must still work out its problems by experience, and find their limits by mere rule of thumb, and by taking out of the scales, as each case arises for settlement, first from one side and then from the other, till the balance hangs even, as we do when measuring sugar against pound weights.

The value of a philosophical doctrine depends on the completeness with which it meets various and opposite difficulties of the case. It is not enough, that it states clearly and impressively the facts of one side, or that it wraps up and contains in itself a vast amount of important truth. If it does not lay this out in order and unravel it distinctly, so that the limits of each expression of truth are truly and clearly given—so that we are not obliged to take the truth in a lump with a whole tangle of possible ambiguities and misunderstandings hanging around it, it so far fails in its claim and utility as a philosophical doctrine. . . . (pp. 471-72)

And we cannot but feel that, with much that is true and admirable, this is the case with Mr. Mill's Essay. It is vitiated by the principle on which, according to it, the jurisdiction of society is to be regulated. That principle seems to us to leave

A Punch *cartoon portraying the parliamentary battle between William Gladstone and Benjamin Disraeli. Mill, depicted on a hobby horse, is on the lower left.*

out one great side of human nature, which is as clearly to be taken into account as the one on which Mr. Mill's theory lays stress,—the way, namely, in which by natural and inevitable laws, we *do* take account of the good of others, and feel ourselves bound to look after it and promote it, even in cases where they are indifferent or hostile to it. By the only conditions of human life and society with which we are as yet acquainted, we are invested with influence over others, over one another, of which we cannot divest ourselves, which we cannot help feeling, and cannot help using, ill or well. Mr. Mill is the last man to take mere abstract views of society. He must take things as he finds them, as they really exist—not as they would be under other imaginable circumstances, or as it might be supposed that they ought to be, under the supposition of man being a reasonable and responsible being. If he had stated the limits between the two principles, which often come into conflict,—the right of the individual to look after his own good, and the right and duty of others and of society to do so too,—he would have done good service; but to leave one out in theory is not to abolish it in nature, and to make a theory with one only, omitting the other as having no existence, is not to give us a sufficient philosophy. A theory of freedom, without also a theory of mutual action and influence, is but a theory of part of the social relations of men. He has told us a great deal about man, conceived as moving among others alone as an individual: he has not told us about man as a link in the network of society, necessarily acting as others, and acted on by them. People who are content with a vigorous, one-sided statement about liberty, may think that Mr. Mill has done enough. People who think that there is another side to the matter, besides individual liberty, will wish that it had been fairly dealt with by so powerful a mind, and will be of opinion that there is something still to be said and cleared up on the subject. We want those whose love of liberty is beyond suspicion to tell us the limits and benefits of custom and control; as we want those who do not undervalue authority to speak honestly and heartily of the claims and necessity of liberty. (pp. 472-73)

[R. W. Church], "Mill on Liberty," in Bentley's Quarterly Review, *Vol. II, No. IV, January, 1860, pp. 434-73.*

JAMES M'COSH (essay date 1866)

[*An early Mill scholar, M'Cosh offers in the following excerpt a balanced evaluation of Mill's characteristics and stature. He writes that the circumstances of Mill's education account both for his originality and for his often "exclusive and angular" thinking. This education, M'Cosh asserts, also predisposed him toward change and practical goals. After comparing Mill's philosophy with those of Auguste Comte and John Locke, M'Cosh attributes the acceptance of Mill's theories to their "delusive simplicity."]*

[Mr. Mill] is well acquainted with the various departments of physical science; . . . he is extensively read in all historical and social questions; and . . . he is competently conversant with the opinions of philosophers and logicians in different ages. His thinking has many of the qualities of a self-educated man: that is, it is fresh and independent, but, at the same time, it is often exclusive and angular, in consequence of its not being rubbed and polished and adjusted by being placed alongside of the philosophic and religious wisdom of the great and good men of the past. Taught to think for himself from his boyhood, he has prepared opinions on all subjects. . . . (pp. 12-13)

In historical speculation he was early seized with an admiration of the general principles of the philosophy of M. Auguste Comte, who was becoming known to a select few at the time when the character of the young Englishman was being formed. . . . Not that he has followed the founder of the Positive School in every respect; in particular, he has been prevented by his adherence to his father's metaphysics from following M. Comte in his denunciations of all attempts to study the human mind by consciousness. But he was led by the influence of this teacher to regard it as impossible for the mind to rise to first or final causes, or to know the nature of things; and to adopt his favorite method of procedure, which is by deduction from an hypothesis, which he endeavors to show explains all the phenomena. Though a fairly informed man in the history of philosophy, he has attached himself to a school which thinks it has entirely outstripped the past; and so he has no sympathy with, and no appreciation of, the profound thoughts of the men of former times: these are supposed to belong to the theological or metaphysical ages, which have forever passed away in favor of the positive era which has now dawned upon our world. Bred thus in a revolutionary school of opinion, his predilections are in all things in favor of those who are given to change, and against those who think that there is immutable truth, or who imagine that they have discovered it. His expressed admiration of Coleridge may seem to contradict this statement, but it does so only in appearance, for he has no partiality for any of the favorite principles of that defender of transcendental reason; it is clear that he delights in him chiefly because his speculations have been acting as a solvent to melt down the crystallized philosophical and theological opinions of England. The school of Comte has hitherto had no analyst of the mind (the founder of it was a phrenologist, and studied the mind through the brain); and Mr. Mill may be regarded as, for the present, the recognized metaphysician of the school, and will hold this place till he is superseded by the more comprehensive system, and the bolder speculative grasp of Mr. Herbert Spencer.

With an original clearness of intellectual apprehension, his whole training has disposed him towards distinct enunciations and practical results. Engaged for many years in a public office, he has acquired habits which enable him to understand the business of life and the condition of society. He is particularly fitted to excel in the exposition of those *media axiomata* upon which, according to Bacon, "depend the business and fortune of mankind." With an English love of the concrete, he has a French skill in reducing a complex subject into simple ele-

ments, and a French clearness of expression. He is ever able to bring out his views in admirable order, and his thoughts lie in his style like pebbles at the bottom of a transparent stream, so that we see their shape and color without noticing the medium through which we view them. I have to add, that in his love of the clear, and his desire to translate the abstract into the concrete, he often misses the deepest properties of the objects examined by him; and he seems to me far better fitted to co-ordinate the facts of social science than to deal with the first principles of fundamental philosophy. As to his spirit, there are evidences of a keen fire, of enthusiasm, perhaps of passion, burning within, but the surface is ever still and ever green. (pp. 14-16)

Some of his admirers claim for Mr. Mill, that he is the genuine philosophical descendant of Locke. I acknowledge that in some respects he resembles our great English metaphysician. He is like him in his clearness of thought and diction. Both are careful to avoid, as far as possible, abstruse arguments and technical phrases. Both have a name in other departments as well as mental philosophy,—Locke having thought profoundly on political questions, and Mr. Mill having given us one of the best works we have on political economy. Both have written on toleration or liberty, and defended views in advance of those generally entertained in their own times. I am inclined further to admit that Mr. Mill has quite as much influence in our day in England as Locke had in his. But with these points of likeness there are important points of difference. Locke had an originality, a shrewdness, a sagacity, and a high-principled wisdom and caution which have not been equalled by the later speculator. Locke avows extreme enough views in opposing the doctrines of professed metaphysicians, but he is saved by his crowning sense, and his religious convictions, acquired in Puritan times, from taking up positions adverse to the sound sense of mankind. Vehement enough in opposing a doctrine of innate ideas supposed to be held by philosophers, and laboring in vain to derive all our ideas from sensation and reflection, we do not find him falling back on such extreme positions as those of Mr. Mill, when he endeavors to draw our higher ideas out of sensation by means of association, and maintains that we can know nothing of mind except that it is a series of sensations, aware of itself, or of matter, except that it is a possibility of sensations. I believe that Locke abandoned, without knowing it, some important fundamental truths; but he resolutely held by many others, as that man has high faculties working on the original materials, and that in particular he has an intuitive knowledge "which is irresistible, and, like bright sunshine, forces itself immediately to be perceived, as soon as ever the mind turns its view that way, and leaves no room for hesitation, doubt, or examination, but the mind is presently filled with the clear light of it." . . . Mr. J. S. Mill is the successor and the living representative of an important British school, but it is that of Hobbes, of Hartley, of Priestley, of David Hume, and of James Mill. . . . But even on the supposition that Mr. Mill is the Locke of the nineteenth century, it would be necessary to examine and correct his views. For while the *Essay on the Human Understanding* evolved much truth, and exercised, upon the whole, a healthy influence, it contained very grave defects and errors, which issued in very serious consequences both in France and in this country; in the former landing speculation in a miserable sensationalism, and in the latter originating the wire-drawn attempts to fashion all our ideas out of one or two primitive sources by means of association. I have already intimated that I believe the errors of Mr. Mill to be far more numerous and fundamental than those of Locke; and should his sensational and nescient system come to be adopted, it will be followed, both in theory and in practice, with far more fatal results than any that ensued from the combined idealistic and realistic philosophy expounded in Locke's great work. (pp. 26-8)

I certainly do not look on Mr. Mill as a superficial writer. On the contrary, on subjects on which he has not been led to follow Mr. James Mill or M. Comte, his thoughts are commonly as solid and weighty as they are clearly expressed. But, speaking exclusively of his philosophy of first principles, I believe he is getting so ready an acceptance among many for his metaphysical theories, mainly because, like Hobbes and Condillac, he possesses a delusive simplicity which does not account for, but simply overlooks, the distinguishing properties of our mental nature. (p. 30)

> James M'Cosh, in his An Examination of Mr. J. S.
> Mill's Philosophy: Being a Defence of Fundamental
> Truth, *Robert Carter & Brothers, 1866, 434 p.*

THE NATION   (essay date 1869)

[*In the following excerpt from a review of* The Subjection of Women, *the critic discusses Mill's argument as a whole and concludes that its chief weakness is its failure to consider "the fact of sex." Mill pleads for the equal rights of women, the critic posits, without taking into consideration the ways in which women by nature are different from men. This reviewer also suggests that "the tinge of passion" that characterizes Mill's style in* The Subjection of Women *will add to its popularity.*]

The case of the advocates of women's rights has never been so ably stated as in [Mr. Mill's *The Subjection of Women*], and probably nearly everything they will say hereafter will be said simply in amplification or illustration of Mr. Mill's arguments. His first chapter is devoted to showing that woman's position in society is conventional and not natural; that her subjection to man is simply one of the few remaining results of the régime of brute force by which the world was once governed. The relations of men with one another, he maintains, have been gradually based on abstract justice and equality, but the relations of the sexes are still governed by rules established when superiority of physical force constituted the only recognized title to authority. The continuance of this state of subjection on the part of women, their failure to follow the example of all other subject classes, and rise against their oppressors and throw off their yoke, he ascribes to the elaborate pains which the masters have taken to enslave their minds as well as their bodies by their mode of education; to the natural attraction between the opposite sexes; to the wife's entire dependence on the husband for every principal object of human pursuit, consideration and all objects of social ambition being only attainable through him. This great means of influence over the minds of women an instinct of selfishness has made men avail themselves of to keep women in subjection, by teaching them that meekness, submissiveness, and resignation are an essential part of sexual attractiveness. Had similar machinery, he thinks, been brought to bear on the education of young plebeians and serfs, by way of fixing their relations to the patricians and seigneurs, their emancipation would never have taken place. In fact, Mr. Mill asks boldly whether, had this been done, "patricians and plebeians, seigneurs and serfs, would not be as broadly distinguished at this day as men and women are," "and would not all but a thinker here and there have believed the distinction to be a fundamental and unalterable fact of human nature?"

In order to make this question a "poser," however, we have to admit that sex has in no way affected the relations of men and women, either by way of increasing women's readiness to be subjected, or men's disposition to subject them. Unless Mr. Mill can fairly say that the patrician would have found in the young serf precisely the same material on which to try his educational prowess as man has found in woman, he can hardly ask anybody to admit that it would have produced the same startling effect on the one as on the other; and in this question we find what we consider the source of whatever weakness there may be in Mr. Mill's whole argument. Is there such a thing as sex? and does sex influence character, and to what extent? are questions which must be answered fully and fairly before the ground can be considered cleared for a complete discussion of the extent to which woman's subjection is artificial. If sex does influence character, all comparisons of woman's position and that of other subject classes must have a serious flaw in it. Mr. Mill admits that the natural attraction between the sexes has rendered it all the easier for the men to keep the women in subordination, but what we need to know is whether this has been its only effect. Is anybody quite sure it has had no other? Is it fair to assume, as Mr. Mill does, that it has had no other?

Coming to the question whether the nature of the two sexes adapts them to their present functions and position, Mr. Mill denies that anybody knows the nature of the two sexes, as long as they have only been seen in their present relation to each other. Consequently, he denies also that men *know* women; the nature of women, or what passes by that name now, he says, is "an eminently artificial thing, the result of forced repression in some things, of unnatural stimulation in others." The only way, he says, of getting at a knowledge of the natural difference between the two sexes is by means "of an analytic study of the laws of the influence of circumstances on character"—a work which is in its very nature almost impossible of accomplishment, as Mr. Mill has himself shown in his **"Logic."** The whole of the circumstances by which character is influenced are never in any individual case within any investigator's reach, nor can he calculate the exact force of any one of them, so that, no matter how much care he took, his conclusions would be little better than guesses. If we cannot know woman from an examination of her as we find her—that is, as a member of society—neither can we know men. The character of men is also highly artificial. The natural man, or man in the abstract, uninfluenced by the circumstances which surround him as a member of human society, none of us have ever seen or will ever see. So that, if we refrained on this account from forming any judgment about his rights and duties, and acting on it in legislation and usage, we should bring the social machine to a dead-lock. In assigning a man his position in society, we do not take into account what he might have been if he had had a different father or mother, or been differently brought up, or had been born in a different church or in a different civilization. All this would furnish interesting matter for speculation, but for practical purposes—for the purpose of deciding whether we shall or shall not make him a judge, or a legislator, or a teacher, or the captain of a seventy-four—we have to consider him just as he stands—the product of a thousand agencies, known and unknown, which we did not create and cannot modify.

We may say the same thing of woman. If all that Mr. Mill wishes to deduce from his denial that we know her, is that no restriction should be placed on the play of her faculties by legislation, he will carry most persons with him; but if he wishes to base on it a positive assertion of her equality with man in capacity, we do not well see how he is to carry anybody with him. We are willing to study woman *in vacuo*—but how is the vacuum to be obtained? (p. 72)

Thus far Mr. Mill has been talking of woman's right to equality in the family. In his third chapter he discusses her admissibility to all the functions and employments hitherto claimed as a monopoly by the stronger sex; and he expresses his belief that the disabilities here are only clung to in order to maintain her subordination in domestic life. Here he argues simply from observations of woman in domestic life, and has comparatively easy work; but he marks out her right to the suffrage as a right entirely independent of any question which may be raised concerning her faculties; and her competency to exercise it he deduces *à fortiori* from the fact that law and usage already admit her competency to choose her husband, who is to govern her to the end of her life. As regards fitness of women for office, he is willing to leave that to be decided by experiment. If women are not fit for various callings, they will not succeed in them and will soon cease to follow them; and there is therefore no need for, and may be great injustice and great waste of power in, legislation excluding them from such. His analysis of woman's faculties, as revealed by history and everyday experience, is of course masterly and interesting, though the effect of the argument is somewhat weakened by the extent to which his eagerness diminishes the candor which is one of the great charms of his writing. For instance, by way of accounting for the fact that, though a great number of women are taught music, there have been no great female composers, he says: "Women are taught music, but not for the purpose of composing—only of executing it; and, accordingly, it is only as composers that men in music are superior to women." Now surely this is not a fair statement of the case. Women are not taught music for the purpose solely of executing it any more than men. Both are taught music in the hope of a result of some kind—money, fame, or pleasure. If, amongst the thousands of children who learn it, the teacher should light on a genius, that child becomes a composer, no matter what the intentions of the teacher may be; and that many such geniuses have presented themselves amongst the comparatively few men who are taught music, and none amongst the many women who are taught, is surely a fact worth serious consideration. To be sure, Mr. Mill seeks to account for this by the circumstance that the great male composers have all appeared in Germany and Italy, where the women are in a low state of culture; and this circumstance is no doubt worth consideration also; but he urges it with an air of eagerness to make the most of it which is not characteristic of him.

The book will probably be read by everybody who reads at all; and it is, therefore, needless to attempt anything like a condensation of his whole argument. It displays the dialectical skill, the mastery of style, the breadth and force of thinking, which have won Mr. Mill his high position both as a social and mental philosopher; and the tinge of passion which runs through it, though it has in places somewhat damaged the work for the philosopher, will increase its attraction to the general reader. We have endeavored simply to point out what are, it seems to us, two serious defects in the very basis of the argument. No discussion of the woman question will ever satisfy the public mind, or settle woman's position on a new basis, in which the fact of sex is ignored, or its influence on character and on social and domestic life left out of consideration, and treated lightly; and yet to the charge of doing both these things every leading advocate of woman's rights (Mr. Mill included)

is more or less open. As long as woman's case is argued as if she were simply a small and weak man, we shall not get much nearer to a final solution of the great problem of her condition. Everybody knows, as a matter of fact, that not only is sexual attraction one of the strongest of all the social forces, but that its apparently excessive strength is at once one of the greatest puzzles of the world and one of the greatest sources of human misery; and that the question of controlling it or diminishing its force, without affecting injuriously either health or morals or population, has been in every age the question that went deepest down towards the foundations of order and duty—which is simply another mode of saying that marriage is the most important feature of human society; and in marriage woman plays the principal part. Any discussion of her rights, therefore, which treats her relation to marriage as but a subordinate and secondary incident in her career, must be incomplete. We say this in the spirit of an enquirer. Of the evils of her present position we are profoundly sensible; all attempts to improve it have our cordial sympathy; but it cannot be really and permanently improved without treating her maternal function as her principal and highest one, while making ample provision for the happiness and activity of all those who are prevented, by either inclination or fortune, from undertaking it, or who are conscious of the possession of gifts which can be made of more value to society and the owner in other departments than that of rearing or educating children. (pp. 72-3)

> *"Mr. Mill's Plea for Women," in* The Nation, *Vol. IX, No. 212, July 22, 1869, pp. 72-3.*

[WALTER BAGEHOT]   (essay date 1873)

[*Briefly assessing Mill's career, Bagehot singles out his lucid style, analytical prowess, and "rare kind of contagious enthusiasm" as his most impressive traits. For Bagehot's earlier commentary on Mill, see the excerpt dated 1850.*]

To treatises such as Mr Mill's **"Logic"** and his **"Political Economy,"** it is not usually easy to give important praise which no one will deny. The subjects with which they deal, the "logic" particularly, are too full of doubts and too fertile in animosities. But no one, we think, will deny that hardly ever, perhaps never, in the history of philosophy, have two books so finished and so ample been written by a man who had only his leisure moments to give to them, and who had a day's work to do besides. (p. 588)

The great merit of Mr Mill, we think, was the merit of intellectual combination. Many philosophers—several contemporaries even—were much more eminent for absolute originality. But no one comes near Mr Mill in the art—the invaluable art when, as now, philosophy is at once rich and fragmentary—of piecing together. In Mr Mill's great works theories are placed in just juxtaposition which were wide apart before, and thirteen are named in the same sentence, where one would have hardly comprehended how they could be coupled together. (pp. 588-89)

[A book on logic], it will at once be seen, requires a most delicate art of exposition. For these comparisons, the style of a writer must describe not only "meanings" but shades of meaning—not large ideas in the rough, but nice ideas with nice finish. And for this Mr Mill was well fitted both by genius and by culture. He inherited a philosophical acumen from his father (and, we suspect, from a long line of Scotch and argumentative ancestors), and an education in France had given him the French gift of precise and graceful explanation. That he also caught a little, though only a little, of the tendency to diffuseness of modern French philosophers must, we admit, be acknowledged; but he also gained the literary talents most useful to a comprehensive philosopher—their extreme clearness and their wonderful readability.

In Political Economy there was an eminent field for Mr Mill's peculiar powers of comparison. There is little which is absolutely original in his great work ["**Political Economy**"]; and much of that little is not, we think, of the highest value. The subject had been discussed in detail by several minds of great acuteness and originality, but no writer before Mr Mill had ever surveyed it as a whole with anything like equal ability; no one had shown with the same fulness the relation which the different parts of the science bore to each other; still less had any one so well explained the relation of this science to other sciences, and to knowledge in general. Since Mr Mill wrote, there is no excuse for a political economist if his teaching is narrow-minded or pedantic; though, perhaps, from the isolated state of the science, there may have been some before. . . .

Mr Mill's two great treatises have had a unique and immense influence. In Political Economy the writer of these lines has long been in the habit of calling himself the last man of the ante-Mill period. He was just old enough to have acquired a certain knowledge of Ricardo and the other principal writers on Political Economy before Mr Mill's work was published; and the effect of it has certainly been most remarkable. All students since begin with Mill and go back to all previous writers fresh from the study of him. They see the whole subject with Mr Mill's eyes. They see in Ricardo and Adam Smith what he told them to see, and it is not easy to induce them to see anything else. Whether it has been altogether good for Political Economy that a single writer should have so monarchical an influence may be argued, but no testimony can be greater to the ability of that writer and his preeminence over his contemporaries. In a wider field the effect of the "**Logic**" has also been enormous. Half the minds of the younger generation of Englishmen have been greatly coloured by it, and would have been sensibly different if they had not been influenced by it. And there is no other book of English philosophy of which the same can be said, even with a pretext of truth.

A complete estimate of Mr Mill would include an account of his career in Parliament, and also an account of some peculiarities of his mind, which gave him, considering the dry nature of most of his pursuits and studies, a most singular influence. To very many younger minds he was not so much a political economist as a prophet, not so much a logician as a seer. He had, besides his rare power of arguing and analysing, an equally rare kind of contagious enthusiasm, which influenced a multitude of minds, and made them believe as he did. (p. 589)

> [*Walter Bagehot*], "*The Late Mr Mill*," *in* The Economist, *Vol. XXXI, No. 1551, May 17, 1873, pp. 588-89.*

THE SPECTATOR   (essay date 1873)

[*In the following excerpt from an unfavorable review of the* Autobiography, *the author focuses on Mill's natural reserve and "monotonous joylessness"—qualities that make the* Autobiography "*a dreary one*."]

On the whole, [Mr. Mill's *Autobiography*] will be found, we think, even by Mr. Mill's most strenuous disciples, a dreary one. It shows that in spite of all Mr. Mill's genuine and generous compassion for human misery and his keen desire to alleviate it, his relation to concrete humanity was of a very confined and reserved kind,—one brightened by few personal ties, and those few not, except in about two cases, really hearty ones. The multitude was to him an object of compassion and of genuine beneficence, but he had no pleasure in men, no delight in actual intercourse with this strange, various, homely world of motley faults and virtues. His nature was composed of a few very fine threads, but wanted a certain strength of basis, and the general effect, though one of high and even enthusiastic disinterestedness, is meagre and pallid. His tastes were refined, but there was a want of homeliness about his hopes. He was too strenuously didactic to be in sympathy with man, and too incessantly analytic to throw his burden upon God. There was something overstrained in all that was noblest in him, this excess seeming to be by way of compensation, as it were, for the number of regions of life in which he found little or nothing where other men find so much. He was strangely deficient in humour, which, perhaps, we ought not to regret, for had he had it, his best work would in all probability have been greatly hampered by such a gift. Unique in intellectual ardour and moral disinterestedness, of tender heart and fastidious tastes, though narrow in his range of practical sympathies, his name will long be famous as that of the most wide-minded and generous of political economists, the most disinterested of Utilitarian moralists, and the most accomplished and impartial of empirical philosophers. But as a man, there was in him a certain poverty of nature, in spite of the nobleness in him,—a monotonous joylessness, in spite of the hectic sanguineness of his theoretic creed,—a want of genial trust, which spurred on into an almost artificial zeal his ardour for philosophic reconstruction; and these are qualities which will probably put a well-marked limit on the future propagation of an influence such as few writers on such subjects have ever before attained within the period of their own life-time. (p. 1339)

> "*Mr. John Stuart Mill's 'Autobiography*'," *in* The Spectator, *Vol. 46, No. 2365, October 25, 1873, pp. 1337-39.*

THOMAS CARLYLE   (letter date 1873)

[*A noted nineteenth-century essayist, historian, critic, and social commentator, Carlyle was a central figure of the Victorian age in England and Scotland. In his writings, Carlyle advocated a Christian work ethic and stressed the importance of order, piety, and spiritual fulfillment. Known to his contemporaries as the "Sage of Chelsea," Carlyle exerted a powerful moral influence in an era of rapidly shifting values. Though he and Mill were friends, in this excerpt from a letter to his father Carlyle characterizes Mill as a "logic-chopping engine." Carlyle also refers to Mill's* Autobiography *as "a mournful psychical curiosity."*]

You have lost nothing by missing the autobiography of Mill. I have never read a more uninteresting book, nor I should say a sillier, by a man of sense, integrity, and seriousness of mind. The penny a-liners were very busy with it, I believe, for a week or two, but were evidently pausing in doubt and difficulty by the time the second edition came out. It is wholly the life of a logic-chopping engine, little more of human in it than if it had been done by a thing of mechanized iron. Autobiography of a steam-engine, perhaps, you may sometimes read it. As a mournful psychical curiosity, but in no other point of view, can it interest anybody. I suppose it will deliver us henceforth from the cock-a-leerie crow about 'the Great Thinker of his Age.' Welcome, though inconsiderable! The thought of poor

Mill altogether, and of his life and history in this poor muddy world, gives me real pain and sorrow.

> *Thomas Carlyle, in a letter to John Carlyle on November 5, 1873, in* Thomas Carlyle: A History of His Life in London, 1834-1881, Vol. II *by James Anthony Froude, Longmans, Green, and Co., 1884, p. 420.*

JAMES FITZJAMES STEPHEN   (essay date 1873)

[*Considered one of Mill's most important and convincing opponents, Stephen challenges Mill's concept of liberty in the excerpt below. He starts with the assertion that Mill presents little proof for his theory and goes on to characterize it as paradoxical and contrary to human nature.*]

The object of this work is to examine the doctrines which are rather hinted at than expressed by the phrase 'Liberty, Equality, Fraternity.' This phrase has been the motto of more than one Republic. It is indeed something more than a motto. It is the creed of a religion, less definite than any one of the forms of Christianity, which are in part its rivals, in part its antagonists, and in part its associates, but not on that account the less powerful. (p. 52)

No better statement of the popular view—I might, perhaps, say of the religious dogma of liberty—is to be found than that which is contained in Mr Mill's essay on the subject. His works on Utilitarianism and the Subjection of Women afford excellent illustrations of the forms of the doctrines of equality and fraternity to which I object. Nothing is further from my wishes than to make a captious attack upon the writings of a great man to whom I am in every way deeply indebted; but in stating the grounds of one's dissent from wide-spread and influential opinions it is absolutely necessary to take some definite statement of those opinions as a starting point, and it is natural to take the ablest, the most reasonable, and the clearest. (p. 54)

There is hardly anything in [*On Liberty*] which can properly be called proof as distinguished from enunciation or assertion of the general principles quoted. I think, however, that it will not be difficult to show that the principle stands in much need of proof. In order to make this clear it will be desirable in the first place to point out the meaning of the word liberty according to principles which I think are common to Mr Mill and to myself. I do not think Mr Mill would have disputed the following statement of the theory of human actions. All voluntary acts are caused by motives. All motives may be placed in one of two categories—hope and fear, pleasure and pain. Voluntary acts of which hope is the motive are said to be free. Voluntary acts of which fear is the motive are said to be done under compulsion, or omitted under restraint. A woman marries. This in every case is a voluntary action. If she regards the marriage with the ordinary feelings and acts from the ordinary motives, she is said to act freely. If she regards it as a necessity, to which she submits in order to avoid greater evil, she is said to act under compulsion and not freely.

If this is the true theory of liberty—and, though many persons would deny this, I think they would have been accepted by Mr Mill—the propositions already stated will in a condensed form amount to this: 'No one is ever justified in trying to affect any one's conduct by exciting his fears, except for the sake of self-protection;' or, making another substitution which he would also approve—'It can never promote the general happiness of mankind that the conduct of any persons should be affected by an appeal to their fears, except in the cases excepted.'

Surely these are not assertions which can be regarded as self-evident, or even as otherwise than paradoxical. What is all morality, and what are all existing religions in so far as they aim at affecting human conduct, except an appeal either to hope or fear, and to fear far more commonly and far more emphatically than to hope? (pp. 56-7)

The only moral system which would comply with the principle stated by Mr Mill would be one capable of being summed up as follows: 'Let every man please himself without hurting his neighbour;' and every moral system which aimed at more than this, either to obtain benefits for society at large other than protection against injury or to do good to the persons affected, would be wrong in principle. This would condemn every existing system of morals. Positive morality is nothing but a body of principles and rules more or less vaguely expressed, and more or less left to be understood, by which certain lines of conduct are forbidden under the penalty of general disapprobation, and that quite irrespectively of self-protection. Mr Mill himself admits this to a certain extent. In the early part of his fourth chapter he says that a man grossly deficient in the qualities which conduce to his own good is 'necessarily and properly a subject of distaste, or in extreme cases even of contempt,' and he enumerates various inconveniences to which this would expose such a person. He adds, however: 'The inconveniences which are strictly inseparable from the unfavourable judgment of others are the only ones to which a person should ever be subjected for that portion of his conduct and character which concerns his own good, but which does not affect the interests of others in their relation with him.' This no doubt weakens the effect of the admission; but be this how it may, the fact still remains that morality is and must be a prohibitive system, one of the main objects of which is to impose upon every one a standard of conduct and of sentiment to which few persons would conform if it were not for the constraint thus put upon them. In nearly every instance the effects of such a system reach far beyond anything that can be described as the purposes of self-protection.

Mr Mill's system is violated not only by every system of theology which concerns itself with morals, and by every known system of positive morality, but by the constitution of human nature itself. There is hardly a habit which men in general regard as good which is not acquired by a series of more or less painful and laborious acts. The condition of human life is such that we must of necessity be restrained and compelled by circumstances in nearly every action of our lives. Why, then, is liberty, defined as Mr Mill defines it, to be regarded as so precious? What, after all, is done by the legislator or by the person who sets public opinion in motion to control conduct of which he disapproves—or, if the expression is preferred, which he dislikes—which is not done for us all at every instant of our lives by circumstances? The laws which punish murder or theft are substitutes for private vengeance, which, in the absence of law, would punish those crimes more severely, though in a less regular manner. If there were laws which punished incontinence, gluttony, or drunkenness, the same might be said of them. Mr Mill admits in so many words that there are 'inconveniences which are strictly inseparable from the unfavourable judgment of others.' What is the distinction in principle between such inconveniences and similar ones organized, defined, and inflicted upon proof that the circumstances which call for their infliction exist? This organization, definition, and procedure make all the difference between the restraints which Mr Mill would permit and the restraints to which he objects. I cannot see on what the distinction rests. I cannot understand why it must always be wrong to punish habitual drunkenness by fine, imprisonment, or deprivation of civil rights, and always be right to punish it by the infliction of those consequences which are 'strictly inseparable from the unfavourable judgment of others.' It may be said that these consequences follow, not because we think them desirable, but in the common order of nature. This answer only suggests the further question, whether nature is in this instance to be regarded as a friend or as an enemy? Every reasonable man would answer that the restraint which the fear of the disapprobation of others imposes on our conduct is the part of the constitution of nature which we could least afford to dispense with. But if this is so, why draw the line where Mr Mill draws it? Why treat the penal consequences of disapprobation as things to be minimized and restrained within the narrowest limits? What 'inconvenience,' after all, is 'strictly inseparable from the unfavourable judgment of others'? If society at large adopted fully Mr Mill's theory of liberty, it would be easy to diminish very greatly the inconveniences in question. Strenuously preach and rigorously practise the doctrine that our neighbour's private character is nothing to us, and the number of unfavourable judgments formed, and therefore the number of inconveniences inflicted by them, can be reduced as much as we please, and the province of liberty can be enlarged in a corresponding ratio. Does any reasonable man wish for this? Could any one desire gross licentiousness, monstrous extravagance, ridiculous vanity, or the like, to be unnoticed, or, being known, to inflict no inconveniences which can possibly be avoided?

If, however, the restraints on immorality are the main safeguards of society against influences which might be fatal to it, why treat them as if they were bad? Why draw so strongly marked a line between social and legal penalties? Mr Mill asserts the existence of the distinction in every form of speech. He makes his meaning perfectly clear. Yet from one end of his essay to the other I find no proof and no attempt to give the proper and appropriate proof of it. His doctrine could have been proved if it had been true. It was not proved because it was not true. (pp. 58-60)

> *James Fitzjames Stephen, "The Doctrine of Liberty in General," in his* Liberty, Equality, Fraternity, *1873. Reprint by Cambridge at the University Press, 1967, pp. 52-73.*

[HENRY REEVE]   (essay date 1874)

[In the following survey of Mill's career, Reeve outlines the paradoxes of Mill's philosophy and concludes that "as a guide, no thinker was more unsafe." The reviewer also denigrates Mill's veneration for Harriet Taylor, argues that his philosophy should have "condescended to touch the earth," and ends by stating that Mill's noble traits were "crushed by a cruel education, a false philosophy, and an evil fate."]

The life of John Stuart Mill was so uneventful, secluded, and even obscure, with the exception of the three years during which he sate in the House of Commons, that few men who have produced a powerful effect upon the world have been so little known by their contemporaries. But his death . . . seemed suddenly to awaken the curiosity of the public to know more of the character, the habits, and the early education of so remarkable and courageous a thinker. His merits and his mistakes were canvassed with unusual vivacity, although, except within the very limited circle of his personal friends, neither of them were sufficiently known to be correctly appreciated. His candour, his boldness, his vast intellectual strength, his

simplicity, his genuine devotion to great public interests and to the cause of truth, caused him to be almost deified by his admirers, but their enthusiasm led them to overlook his paradoxes, his delusions, and some acts of his life which savoured of grave moral error. With a power of analytical reasoning unsurpassed by the wisest philosophers, he combined an infirmity of judgment which not unfrequently led him to mistake Utopian dreams for established truths; so that a course of argument sustained with inimitable subtlety and art, landed him at last in conclusions which the common sense of a child would have rejected. As a guide no thinker was more unsafe, for he was perpetually exploring devious paths, which led him into regions where neither certainty nor truth could be found. What spectacle can be more melancholy than that of a seeker after truth of vast powers and of unbounded attainments, whose existence was spent in an ineffectual struggle, and who died leaving all that it most concerns a man to know and to believe undiscovered and unsolved? In thinking of Mill, the words of an authority he did not acknowledge involuntarily recur to the mind, for he was pre-eminently one 'ever learning and never able to come to a knowledge of the truth.' Thus, to quote one or two of his paradoxes, he contended in the House of Commons, at the time of the Cattle Plague, that the farmers, whose cattle had been killed by order of the Government, were sufficiently indemnified by the increased value of cattle to those persons whose stock had not suffered. Cheshire was ruined, Dorset had rather gained than otherwise, therefore Cheshire was indemnified. Again, he held that the unearned increment of the value of land, caused by external causes, ought not to belong to the owner of the land. But why of land alone? All trade, all commercial enterprise, is based on the hope of increment. Why is real property to be treated differently from a work of art or the public securities? In truth this is the denial of property itself. Mill defended capital punishment in Parliament on the ground that the lives of great criminals were of very little value, and that their maintenance in prison is a serious burden to the community. We have ourselves heard him argue against the severity of penal servitude for life as compared with capital punishment, and his conclusion was that it would be well to supply men undergoing penal servitude with the means of self-destruction. All these instances denote a failure of correct judgment, to be traced to the absence of sound principle. The conclusions are absurd because the basis is false. According to what Mill terms 'common morality,' to supply the means of self-destruction to a man likely to use them is an act not very remote from murder; but Mill's morality was very uncommon, not from wickedness, but from a false standard of right and wrong.

No one but himself could have afforded an explanation of so singular and perplexing a phenomenon. No other hand but his own could have recorded the extraordinary peculiarities of his early education and the gradual evolution of his mind. Fortunately he seems to have thought that the tale deserved to be told; and casting aside that modesty which causes most men to hide their secret thoughts, he completed his philosophical labours by this dissection of his own mind, to be published soon after his death, and he has thus left us [his **'Autobiography,'**] one of the most curious and instructive volumes which exist in all literature. The only works to which we can compare it are the 'Confessions' of St. Augustine and the 'Confessions' of Rousseau: for although Mill was as remote from the religious enthusiasm of the one as he was from the sensualism and depravity of the other, there was something of both of them in his nature, and he felt the same resolute determination to leave a record of his life, which is a cast rather than a statue, a photograph rather than a picture. (pp. 91-3)

[One] of the distinctive peculiarities of John Mill was what, for want of a simpler term, we must call his *receptivity*. Seldom has so powerful a thinker been so subject to the unconscious influence of others: but in him sympathy was more powerful than individuality—he had more of the feminine principle that receives, than the masculine power which imparts, an impression. Hence through life, whenever his sympathies and affections were excited, his opinions followed. Originally a Benthamite among all Benthamites (for he knew no other society), we have seen him modified, by the touch of poetry and friendship, into something not far remote from Sterling and Maurice. So he passed successively under the influence of the St. Simonians, the Positivists, and the Socialists, each of whom might be identified with some individual acquaintance, and from each of whom, with sceptical impartiality, he took something and rejected the remainder of their opinions. He was ever prone to form an exaggerated estimate of those he liked: his own intense self-consciousness and self-confidence were flattered and soothed by those who reflected his own doctrines; and he would, in perfect good faith, describe as men of the highest eminence persons of very secondary merit (it would be invidious to name them), who had in truth no better recommendation than that of being his own acolytes. Of the persons most nearly connected with himself, his father and his wife, he speaks in the language of extravagant panegyric. His father left 'no equal among men, and but one among women,' and so on. A man must have a very imperfect view of society and mankind to be so imposed upon by the magnitude of objects, because they are near him. The world abounds with people of considerable force of character and ability; but we distrust the transcendent genius men discover in their nearest connexions. The same amiable tendency was fatal to his judicial impartiality as a critic. Most of his literary criticisms were suggested by the desire to make known the merits of a friend, and his personal predilections are manifest in all of them; much more manifest, we hasten to add, than his antipathies, for he was singularly free from malice, and in controversy he was a noble and generous opponent.

It is the old story—the struggle to decipher the enigmas of life, written in a character you have not learned to read—the effort to open a lock with a key that does not fit it. From the dawn of philosophy—from the sophists of Greece down to the magician of the middle ages—whether truth was sought behind the veil of Isis or in the schools of Oxford—the result has been the same on the mind of the disappointed seeker, who turns, like Faust, from these phantoms of the brain, to the worship of nature, or by a sensual impulse to coarser indulgences. The great Poet of Germany [Johann Wolfgang von Goethe] has traced with a master's hand the cycle of this eternal drama, which might be compared, scene by scene, with the pages and incidents of Mill's **'Autobiography.'** There is the same weariness of accumulated knowledge, the same visionary glow of sympathy with the future destinies of mankind—sinking at last into what might be called a vulgar passion, were it not that such a passion has an incredible power of glorifying the object of it. Mephistopheles exclaims when he sees his victim launched in pursuit of the butterfly, which is to perish in his grasp, that a man in such a condition of mind thinks every woman a Helen. . . . Mill was, we believe, the subject of a similar hallucination: but it lasted for the remainder of his life; forty years did not exhaust it, marriage did not abate it, death did not interrupt it, and he has left behind him in these pages a memorial of her in whom his affections were concentrated, of which we shall only venture to say, that, if true, it would place her above all the men and women who have ever existed on the earth. Henceforth his life is a romance, and fiction itself would hardly venture upon so bold a creation of the brain. (pp. 117-19)

Mill never lived in what may be called society at all; and this was one of the misfortunes of his life. His manners were shy and awkward. His powers of conversation, though remarkable enough in argument, were wholly didactic and controversial. He had no humour, no 'talk,' and indeed no interest in the minor concerns of life. He had been bred in a small *coterie* of people of extreme opinions, whom he regarded as superior beings, and he seemed to shrink from all contact with ordinary mortals. In later life he affected something of the life of a prophet, surrounded by admiring votaries, who ministered to him largely that incense in which prophets delight. He had neither the wit and readiness which adorn the higher circles of the world, nor the geniality and desire to oblige which impart a charm to the lower. To the virtue of humility he was, as is evident from his book, a total stranger. Concentrated in speculation on abstract truths or fallacies, confining his affections within the narrowest limits, mankind itself was to him an abstraction rather than a reality. He knew nothing of the world, and very little of the play and elasticity of human nature. It would have been of incalculable value to his philosophy if he had condescended to touch the earth, and to live with men and women as they are; but that was a lesson he had never learned, a book he had never opened. Moreover, the natural tendency of his nature to seclusion was heightened by the circumstances in which he had unfortunately placed himself. (p. 121)

John Stuart Mill has undoubtedly made a very considerable impression on his age. His books are read, in popular editions, to a degree which is really astonishing, for works treating of the most difficult and abstruse subjects in a singularly hard, though lucid style: and it is an interesting subject of inquiry what will be their ultimate effect. Will they be thrown aside like the writings of Godwin and Tom Paine in the last century, or will they survive to kindle a conflagration in society like the 'Contrat Social' and the 'Émile'? We incline to think that although Mill laid himself out from his earliest years to be a regenerator of society, he has not accomplished his object, and that his writings will not accomplish it after his death. In truth if the whole work of his life be examined, it will be found to be eminently destructive but not to contain one practical constructive idea. He may have helped to blow up some old buildings and sweep away some rubbish, but he has not added one atom or one contrivance to the real efficient mechanism of society and good government in this country: and if he had been invested with absolute power, the world would have obtained at his hands nothing but checks to population and agrarian laws. The French Encyclopédistes of the 18th century encountered all the abuses of pre-revolutionary France, and they had a great destructive work to do: Mill and his friends have only headed an irregular corps in the victorious army of liberal reform. They have sometimes done good service as skirmishers, for which we feel indebted to them; but they may rely upon it, they would not have effected any real good at all if they had not had the main body of the Whig party behind them. We deplore the influence of Mill on philosophy, properly so called, for it has contributed to the reaction against all we hold to be spiritual truth, and to the strong materialist tendency of modern science, by teaching that all knowledge is derived exclusively from the senses, and that all character is formed by circumstances. To him religion was a dream; morals, a code of utility; law, as administered in this country, a farrago of obsolete technicalities; society in England insipid, and most of the objects of life contemptible. We cannot, therefore, suppose that any large number of our countrymen in the next generation, any more than in the present, will be eager to adopt so unattractive and negative a creed. And if anything can deter them from it, it will be the record of his own life. But with all his errors and failures, there were in him the elements of a noble nature—a genuine love of truth, an invincible courage and perseverance in pursuit of it, a cordial desire for the improvement and enlightenment of mankind, and latent gifts of imagination and sensibility which would have made him a better and a happier man if they had not been crushed by a cruel education, a false philosophy, and an evil fate. (pp. 128-29)

[*Henry Reeve*], *"Autobiography of John Stuart Mill," in* The Edinburgh Review, *Vol. CXXXIX, No. 283, January, 1874, pp. 91-129.*

[JOHN MORLEY] (essay date 1874)

[*Morley, a student and friend of Mill, stresses his "singular neutrality," self-effacement, and scholarly earnestness in this excerpt from a review of the* Autobiography. *Morley also challenges those critics who find Mill's philosophy lacking because of his self-imposed social isolation. For additional commentary by Morley, see the excerpt dated 1906.*]

Those of us who dislike literary hysteria as much as we dislike the coarseness that mistakes itself for force, may well be glad to follow [in Mr. Mill's *Autobiography*] the mental history of a man who knew how to move and grow without . . . reactions and leaps on the one hand, or . . . overdone realism on the other, which may all make a more striking picture, but which do assuredly more often than not mark the ruin of a mind and the nullification of a career. If we are now and then conscious in the book of a certain want of spacing, of changing perspectives and long vistas; if we have perhaps a sense of being too narrowly enclosed; if we miss the relish of humour or the occasional relief of irony; we ought to remember that we are busy not with a work of imagination or art, but with the practical record of the formation of an eminent thinker's mental habits and the succession of his mental attitudes; and the formation of such mental habits is not a romance, but the most arduous of real concerns. If we are led up to none of the enkindled summits of the soul, and plunged into none of its abysses, that is no reason why we should fail to be struck by the pale flame of strenuous self-possession, or touched by the ingenuousness and simplicity of the speaker's accents. A generation continually excited by vehement sterile narratives of storm and stress and spiritual shipwreck, might do well, if it knew the things that pertained to its peace, to ponder the unvarnished history of a man who though not one of the picturesque victims of the wasteful torments of an uneasy spiritual self-consciousness, yet laboured so patiently after the gifts of intellectual strength, and did so much permanently to widen the judgments of the world.

If Mr. Mill's autobiography has no literary grandeur, nor artistic variety, it has the rarer merit of presenting for our contemplation a character that was infested by none of the small passions, and warped by none of the more unintelligent attitudes of the human mind; and we have to remember that it is exactly these, the smaller passions on the one hand, and slovenliness of intelligence on the other, which are even worse agencies in spoiling the worth of life and the advance of society than the more imposing vices either of thought or sentiment. Many have told the tale of a life of much external eventfulness. There is a rarer instructiveness in the quiet career of one whose life was an incessant education, a persistent strengthening of the mental habit of "never accepting half-solutions of difficulties as complete; never abandoning a puzzle, but again and again returning to it until it was cleared up; never allowing obscure corners of a subject to remain unexplored, because they did not appear important; never thinking that I perfectly understood any part of a subject until I understood the whole.". . . It is true that this mental habit is not so singular in itself, for it is the common and indispensable merit of every truly scientific thinker. Mr. Mill's distinction lay in the deliberate intention and the systematic patience with which he brought it to the consideration of moral and religious and social subjects, where hitherto, for reasons that are not difficult to seek, the empire of prejudice and passion has been so much stronger, so much harder to resist, than in the field of physical science. (pp. 3-4)

[The] *Autobiography* shows us the picture of a man uniting profound self-respect with a singular neutrality where his own claims are concerned, a singular self-mastery and justice of mind, in matters where with most men the sense of their own personality is wont to be so exacting and so easily irritated. The history of intellectual eminence is too often a history of immoderate egoism. It has perhaps hardly ever been given to any one who exerted such influence as Mr. Mill did over his contemporaries, to view his own share in it with such discriminativeness and equity as marks every page of his book, and as used to mark every word of his conversation. Knowing as we all do the last infirmity of even noble minds, and how deep the desire to erect himself Pope and Sir Oracle lies in the spirit of a man with strong convictions, we may value the more highly as well for its rarity as for its intrinsic worth Mr. Mill's quality of self-effacement, and his steadfast care to look anywhere rather than in his own personal merits for the source of any of those excellences which he was never led by false modesty to dissemble. (pp. 7-8)

In more than one remarkable place the *Autobiography* shows us distinctly what all careful students of Mr. Mill's books supposed, that with him the social aim, the repayment of the services of the past by devotion to the services of present and future, was predominant over any merely speculative curiosity or abstract interest. His preference for deeply reserved ways of expressing even his strongest feelings prevented him from making any expansive show of this governing sentiment. Though no man was ever more free from any taint of that bad habit of us English, of denying or palliating an abuse or a wrong, unless we are prepared with an instant remedy for it, yet he had a strong aversion to mere socialistic declamation. Perhaps, if one may say so without presumption, he was not indulgent enough in this respect. . . .

It is [his] devotion to the substantial good of the many, though practised without the noisy or ostentatious professions of more egoistic thinkers, which binds together all the parts of his work, from the *System of Logic* down to his last speech on the Land Question. (p. 9)

[With] Mr. Mill, no less than with Comte, the ultimate object was to bring people to extend positive modes of thinking to the master subjects of morals, politics, and religion. Mr. Mill, however, with a wisdom which Comte unfortunately did not share, refrained from any rash and premature attempt to decide what would be the results of this much-needed extension. He knew that we were as yet only just coming in sight of the stage where these most complex of all phenomena can be fruitfully studied . . . [using] positive methods, and he was content with doing as much as he could to expel other methods from men's minds, and to engender the positive spirit and temper. Comte, on the other hand, presumed at once to draw up a minute plan of social reconstruction, which contains some ideas of great beauty and power, some of extreme absurdity, and some which would be very mischievous if there were the smallest chance of their ever being realised. "His book stands," Mr. Mill truly says of the *Système de Politique Positive,* "a monumental warning to thinkers on society and politics of what happens when once men lose sight in their speculations of the value of Liberty and Individuality." . . . (pp. 11-12)

It was his own sense of the value of Liberty which led to the production of the little tractate [*On Liberty*] which Mr. Mill himself thought likely to survive longer than anything else that he had written, "with the possible exception of the *Logic,*" as being "a kind of philosophic text-book of a single truth, which the changes progressively taking place in modern society tend to bring out into ever stronger relief; the importance to man and society, of a large variety in types of character, and of giving full freedom to human nature to expand itself in innumerable and conflicting directions." . . . It seems to us, however, that Mr. Mill's plea for Liberty in the abstract, invaluable as it is, still is less important than the memorable application of this plea and of all the arguments supporting it to that half of the human race whose individuality has hitherto been blindly and most wastefully repressed. The little book on the *Subjection of Women,* though not a capital performance like the *Logic,* was the capital illustration of the modes of reasoning about human character set forth in his *Logic* applied to the case in which the old metaphysical notion of innate and indelible differences is still nearly as strong as ever it was, and in which its moral and social consequences are so inexpressibly disastrous, so superlatively powerful in keeping the ordinary level of the aims and achievements of life low and meagre. The accurate and unanswerable reasoning no less than the noble elevation of this great argument; the sagacity of a hundred of its maxims on individual conduct and character no less than the combined rationality and beauty of its aspirations for the improvement of collective social life, make this piece probably the best illustration of all the best and richest qualities of its author's mind, and it is fortunate that a subject of such incomparable importance should have been first effectively presented for discussion in so worthy and pregnant a form. (pp. 12-13)

Mr. Mill has been ungenerously ridiculed for the eagerness and enthusiasm of his contemplation of a new and better state of human society. Yet we have always been taught to consider it the mark of the loftiest and most spiritual character, for one to be capable of rapturous contemplation of a new and better state in a future life. Why do you not recognise the loftiness and spirituality of those who make their heaven in the thought of the wider light and purer happiness that in the immensity of the ages may be brought to new generations of men by long force of vision and endeavour? What great element is wanting in a life guided by such a hope? Is it not disinterested, and magnanimous, and purifying, and elevating? . . .

Then Mr. Mill's life as disclosed to us in [his *Autobiography*] has been called joyless by that sect of religious partisans whose peculiarity is to mistake boisterousness for unction. Was the life of Christ himself, then, so particularly joyful? Can the life of any man be joyful who sees and feels the tragic miseries and hardly less tragic follies of the earth? (p. 16)

Much has been said against Mr. Mill's strictures on society, and his withdrawal from it. If we realise the full force of all that he says of his own purpose in life, it is hard to see how either his opinion or his practice could have been different. He ceased to be content with "seconding the superficial improvements" in common ways of thinking, and saw the necessity of working at a fundamental re-constitution of accepted modes of thought. This in itself implies a condemnation of a social intercourse that rests on the base of conventional ways of looking at things. The better kind of society, it is true, appears to contain two classes; not only the class that will hear nothing said hostile to the greater social conventions, the popular theology among them, but also another class who will tolerate or even encourage attack on the greater social conventions, and a certain mild discussion of improvements in them—provided only neither attack nor discussion be conducted in too serious a vein. . . . Perhaps there is nothing wiser among the wise things written in the *Autobiography* than the remarks on the fact that persons of any mental superiority who greatly frequent society are greatly deteriorated by it. "Not to mention loss of time, the tone of their feelings is lowered: they become less in earnest about those of their opinions respecting which they must remain silent in the society they frequent: they come to look on their most elevated objects as unpractical, or at least too remote from realisation to be more than a vision or a theory: and if, more fortunate than most, they retain their higher principles unimpaired, yet with respect to the persons and affairs of their own day, they insensibly adopt the modes of feeling and judgment in which they can hope for sympathy from the company they keep." . . . That a man loses something, nay, that he loses much, by being deprived of animating intercourse with other men, Mr. Mill would probably have been the first to admit. Where that intercourse can be had, nothing is more fit to make the judgment robust, nothing more fit to freshen and revive our interests, and clothe them with reality. Even second-rate companionship has some clear advantages. The question is whether these advantages outweigh the equally clear disadvantages. Mr. Mill was persuaded that they do not.

Those whom disgust at the aimlessness and insignificance of most of our social intercourse may dispose to withdrawal from it—and their number will probably increase as the reaction against intellectual flippancy goes on—will do well to remember that Mr. Mill's retirement and his vindication of it sprang for no moral valetudinarianism. He did not retire to gratify any self-indulgent whim, but only in order to work the more uninterruptedly and definitely. The *Autobiography* tells us what pains he took to keep himself informed of all that was going on in every part of the world . . . , and those who knew him will perhaps agree that he was more widely and precisely informed of the transactions of the day in every department of activity all over the world, than any other person of their acquaintance. (pp. 19-20)

[*John Morley*], *"Mr. Mill's 'Autobiography',"* in The Fortnightly Review, n.s. Vol. XV, No. LXXXV, January 1, 1874, pp. 1-20.

THE NATION   (essay date 1874)

[*Unlike most critics, the author of the following review of the* Autobiography *defends the manner in which Mill was educated by his father. Though this education was not faultless, the anonymous critic writes, Mill "towered among his companions" as a result of it.*]

Mill has described his ['**Autobiography**'] with characteristic precision. It is "the record of an education which was unusual and remarkable." It is further the history of the "successive phases" of a "mind which was always pressing forward, equally ready to learn or to unlearn, either from its own thoughts or from those of others." Such a book has not the charms of a full and complete biography like the life of Scott or of Johnson. Nor can it possess the peculiar interest of the "confessions" in which men of genius have occasionally unveiled the inmost secrets of their nature to the world. Of this Mr. Mill was well aware. "The reader," he writes, "whom these things do not interest, has only himself to blame if he reads further, and I do not desire any other indulgence from him than that of bearing in mind that for him these pages were not written." The neglect of this warning has given rise to a mass of irrelevant and misleading criticism or conjecture. It is vain, for example, to ask why Mr. Mill has not told us much more than he has done of his relations and of his friends. It is even more vain to attempt to read between the lines and discover facts which it was not his purpose to disclose. It is most futile of all to contradict, on the imperfect information provided by the '**Autobiography**,' the direct assertions of its author, and, as we have heard done, confidently argue that Mr. Mill's childhood must have been miserable, in the face of his own direct statement that it was happy. It is open to a critic to argue that Mill attempted an impossible task when he sat down to give a history of his intellectual growth apart from the record of all those numerous facts, feelings, or influences which make up a life. But no critic, whether approving or disapproving of the scheme on which the '**Autobiography**' is written, can criticise with any real effect unless he is willing to recognize its true nature as a mere history of intellectual training and development. (pp. 26-7)

Mill was educated by a philosopher, and was educated on a system. To impart to him the benefits of the highest philosophical views was the object, or one of the main objects, of James Mill's energetic and laborious life. Other parents have occasionally labored with the same assiduity in the education of their children, but we doubt whether any man ever achieved as great a measure of success as was attained by the elder Mill. It is easy to point out blemishes in the teaching which he gave his son. Those who do not hold the tenets of the school to which the Mills belonged will feel that John Mill suffered by being imbued with erroneous moral and philosophical doctrines. But no fair judge can deny that James Mill's rare force of character, hard sense, and power of influencing others achieved in no department a greater triumph than in training up his son to be the head of the school of politicians and philosophers of which the elder Mill was one of the founders. Any one can perceive at a glance that the scheme of training through which John Mill's powers were developed was unusual and remarkable. But it is not so easy as it may at first sight appear, to answer the enquiry wherein the essential peculiarity of this education consists. An obvious reply is, that James Mill perceived the truth, and acted upon it, that it is possible, under favorable circumstances and under the guidance of a philosophical teacher, to impart in mere childhood an amount and kind of knowledge which most persons acquire, if at all, in early manhood. The reply is true as far as it goes. James Mill undoubtedly proved "how much more than is commonly supposed may be taught, and well taught, in those early years which in the common modes of what is called instruction are little better than wasted." And his son acquired an amount of information which, to those who have not reflected on the utterly unsystematic nature of ordinary teaching, and upon the

influence which a man of great mental power can bring to bear on an intelligent pupil, may appear almost incredible. . . . [We do not] for a moment suppose that merely to increase his son's information or erudition was the real object or the main effect of James Mill's scheme of education. To understand the essential features of that plan it is necessary to look deeper than the mere mass of knowledge acquired by the younger Mill. What James Mill really achieved for the benefit of his son was to teach him the full use of his understanding, and to bring him up under the full influence of a system of belief. . . .

Whatever other faults can be laid to the charge of John Mill, no one can deny that, from the time he came forth from his father's training to the day of his death, he exhibited, whether in writing or in speaking, the skill of a trained logical athlete. A good deal was due to natural gifts, yet it would be grossly unfair to deny that Mill's argumentative capacity, his readiness in performing what may be termed the mechanical part of thinking, were due in great measure to James Mill's intellectual drill.

The elder philosopher did, however, much more for the intellect of his son than merely to practise him in the use of his understanding. He brought him up as a firm believer in a definite philosophical creed. . . . And to whatever extent John Mill may in later days have deviated from the belief of his father, he was admittedly throughout his early manhood his father's zealous disciple; and, moreover, started in life care-

PUNCH, OR THE LONDON CHARIVARI.—June 1, 1867.

THE LADIES' ADVOCATE.

Mrs. Bull. "LOR, Mr. Mill! WHAT A LOVELY SPEECH YOU *DID* MAKE. I DO DECLARE I HADN'T THE SLIGHTEST NOTION WE WERE SUCH MISERABLE CREATURES. NO ONE CAN SAY IT WAS *YOUR* FAULT THAT THE CASE BROKE DOWN."

A Punch *cartoon occasioned by Mill's failed attempt to amend the Reform Bill of 1867 to include voting rights for women.*

fully preserved from any beliefs or prejudices which might come into contradiction with his father's views of "the truth." . . . That Mill was educated to believe in as definite a form of doctrine as that in which any religious zealot ever educated his son, cannot be disputed by any one who reads the **'Autobiography'** and studies James Mill's works. But those who do not agree with James Mill's philosophy will question the intellectual gain to his son of being educated under a definite, and to their minds false, philosophical creed. (p. 27)

It has been said that, at a certain stage of civilization, a nation gains from the possession of any law whatever, be that law good or bad. It may with the same truth be said that, at a certain stage of education, a man gains intellectually from the honest belief in any philosophical or religious system. This gain James Mill conferred on his son. John Mill started in life supplied with Benthamism for a creed, and armed with every logical weapon for the defence of his faith. The creed may have been defective; but at the beginning of the century it aroused the enthusiasm of some of the noblest minds in England. The weapons may not have been faultless, but John Mill's career proved that they were arms of great power. John Mill's early success, at any rate, was derived from his training and from his faith. He towered among his companions not so much from his knowledge as from the fact that he came forth the trained soldier of a cause, to do battle against men who, whatever their powers, had received nothing like his discipline. (p. 28)

"Mill's Autobiography," in The Nation, *Vol. XVIII, No. 445, January 8, 1874, pp. 26-8.*

THE SPECTATOR (essay date 1874)

[*In the following excerpt from a review of* Nature, the Utility of Religion, and Theism, *the author speculates on the evolution of Mill's philosophy and critiques his argument that "either* [God] *is not omnipotent, or he is not perfectly good." The reviewer concludes that these essays are characterized by "feebleness of thought and execution."*]

It is a little hard on Mr. John Stuart Mill that the school which once treated him as an oracle, now turns round on him, because he has in many respects transgressed its very narrow limits, and speaks of him as little better than a crack-brained fanatic. . . . The wider and wider flights which he indulged in round the centre of his hereditary philosophy [Utilitarianism],—a philosophy never really deserted, though he circled so far beyond its customary boundaries that his brethren in the craft almost looked upon him as a renegade and an adventurer,—never had the effect of convincing any fresh class of minds that he was of their kith and kin, though these excursions had the effect of exciting suspicion, jealousy, and contempt amongst his colleagues of the empirical school. And the result is that he has to some extent fallen between the two stools. The Millites of fifteen years ago know him no more. The believers in an Ethics that are something more than utility in disguise, and in a Religion which is something beyond a naked induction from the facts of human life, are disposed to claim him rather as an instance of a mind too great for the philosophy on which he was nourished, than as one great enough to throw off the trammels of its origin and grasp at the higher truth beyond. And no doubt this is the natural reward of Mr. Mill's candour, and of that expansion of his intellectual apprehensions which his candour betrayed. . . . [The most striking discrepancy in *Nature, the Utility of Religion, and Theism*] is not one between anything in the first essay and the third, but one between

a passage in the second essay and the third,—*i.e.*, between the essay on the **"Utility of Religion"** and that on **"Theism."** In the former of these, Mr. Mill expressly declares that an ideal religion,— *i.e.*, a religion without any personal *object*, which consists solely in the cultivation of a particular class of ideal admirations and hopes in relation to humanity, is not only capable of fulfilling "every important function of religion, but would fulfil them better than any form whatever of supernaturalism. It is not only entitled to be called a religion, it is a better religion than any of those which are ordinarily called by that title." It is true that even in the course of the same essay, he makes a great exception to this assertion. He admits that to give up the hope of reunion in another world with those who have gone before us in this, is a loss "neither to be denied nor extenuated. In many cases, it is beyond the reach of comparison or estimate." But there Mr. Mill is speaking of a loss to the human heart, more than of one to the religious affections properly so called. In the final essay on **"Theism,"** he goes far beyond this, and deals a blow at the relative influence of mere religious idealisms of all kinds, as compared with that of religious supernaturalism properly so called. "It cannot be questioned," he says, "that the undoubting belief of the real existence of a Being who realises our own best ideas of perfection, and of our being in the hands of that Being as the ruler of the universe, gives an increase of power to these feelings [aspirations towards goodness] beyond what they can receive from reference to a merely ideal conception." That seems to us in direct contradiction of the assertion that the idealisation of human life is not only a religion, but a better religion than any which supernaturalism is capable of affording us. In fact, it is evident that this progress of his mind from religious idealism towards religious realism, no less than its progress from something like pure indifference to Christianity to a genuine enthusiasm for Christ, shows Mr. Mill to have been unconsciously working his way out of the philosophical system in which he was *cast*, and so earning for himself the agreeable reputation of presenting to the world fruit "sour and cankered with a worm at its wasted core." For our own parts, Mr. Mill's progress from a narrow and barren set of word-bound notions into a true religion of what he himself calls "hope,"—though it was nothing more,—seems to show that he had a nature far richer than his intellect, and even an intellect capable of discerning in what direction the growth of his life was breaking down the barrier of his preconceived thoughts.

Still, though these essays contain ample evidence of a growing mind, it would be impossible to say that the great subjects treated in them are treated with the fullness and care exhibited in Mr. Mill's earlier works. They are rather outlines than dissertations, outlines which require filling up to produce their full effect on the reader. There are writers, as there are artists, with whom the rough sketch is even more than the finished work,—whose first designs are more fruitful of impression and suggestion than the elaborately executed picture. But Mr. Mill was never one of that class. Execution and elaboration were his forte; he exerted half his influence through the fidelity of his detail, and essays like these, which are mere rough outlines, do not produce the characteristic effect of painstaking exhaustiveness which we find in his **"Logic,"** or his **"Examination of Sir William Hamilton."** . . . Mr. Mill has assumed that Omnipotence is a perfectly intelligible conception to finite minds, the absence of which, or else the absence of perfect goodness, it is perfectly possible for us to prove, by merely producing evidence of pain or evil, and reasoning that if God were both perfectly good in the human sense, and could have removed such pain or evil, he must have done so;—therefore, either he is not omnipotent, or he is not perfectly good. But this seems to us to be mere groping in the dark. No doubt, goodness must mean, in an infinite being, the same *quality* which it means in a finite one, or it can mean nothing at all to us. But it does not in the least follow that because it must mean the same quality, it must involve, to an omniscient Creator, the same actions. . . . Mr. Mill lays it down very peremptorily that an Omnipotent Being who permits the existence of a moral imperfection or a sensitive pain, cannot be a perfect Being. But what if the very idea of the maximum of moral being, positively includes, as it well may, the existence of relations between moral perfection and moral progression (which last implies, of course, moral imperfection)? What if a universe consisting exclusively of perfect beings would be a smaller and poorer moral universe than one consisting both of perfect and of imperfect beings, with a real relation between the two? What if the world of pain, as treated by God, includes secrets of moral glory and beauty, of which a world without pain would be incapable? Mr. Mill would apparently reply,—"That only means that God is not Omnipotent. If he were, he could do as much without pain, which is in itself an evil, as with it. And if he cannot, he works under conditions which exclude Omnipotence." . . . The truth is, Mr. Mill evidently never gave himself the trouble to compare relative degrees of power, or he would have seen at once that a universe containing absolute perfection in an infinite variety of relations with imperfection is a universe which would at once impress us as one of larger scope and power, than one containing only the former. And this is really all man can do towards judging of Omnipotence. We are utterly unable to conceive the absolute attribute. But we are able to say whether a power that has created, and is always creating, all shades and degrees and varieties of progressive life, as well as perfect life, is greater or less than one which produces and sustains perfection only. It seems to us perfectly obvious that though moral goodness in man and in God must be of the same kind, it is childish to say that *actions* which are wicked in man, in whom they imply one kind of motive, must be evil in God, who sees the whole scope of what he is doing, and in whom they may imply a totally different kind of motive. You might much more reasonably identify capital punishment with murder, than identify, as Mr. Mill does, the infliction of death by the imposition of natural laws, with murder. Yet this confusion between the moral evil involved in the rash actions of ignorant and finite beings, and the same when proceeding from utterly different motives in an omniscient Being, pervades the whole of Mr. Mill's essay on **"Nature."**

Such is a characteristic specimen of the feebleness of thought and execution visible in these Essays. . . . Mr. Mill has signally failed in his attempt to prove that if God were both perfect morally and also omnipotent, the state of the world could not be what it is. . . . On the whole, Mr. Mill's chief endeavour,—his attempt to prove that God, if he exists,—which, as we understand him (though his language wavers), Mr. Mill thought more probable than not,—is either a being of considerable, but very limited power, or not a good being, appears to collapse utterly. But Mr. Mill was precluded by his philosophy from taking note at all of the attestation of God's goodness by the human conscience, and on this side also his essays seem to us deplorably defective for the purpose to which he intended them to contribute. (pp. 1366-67)

"Mr. Mill's Essays on Religion," in The Spectator, *Vol. 47, No. 2418, October 31, 1874, pp. 1366-67.*

GEORG BRANDES (essay date 1879)

[*Brandes, a Danish literary critic and biographer, was the principal leader of the intellectual movement that helped to bring an end to Scandinavian cultural isolation. He believed that literature reflects the spirit and problems of its time and that it must be understood within its social and aesthetic context. Brandes's major critical work,* Hovedstrømninger i det 19de aarhundredes litteratur (Main Currents in Nineteenth-Century Literature), *won him admiration for his ability to view literary movements within the broader context of all of European literature. Brandes, an acquaintance of Mill, here briefly discusses his attitude toward women's emancipation and general character. This essay was first published in 1879.*]

[Mill had once] designated the woman question as "in his eyes the most important of all political questions of the present day." At all events, it was one of those which during the last years of his life personally occupied him the most.

He did not hesitate, either in his written or in his spoken words, to use the strongest expressions in order to place in the right light his conception of the unnaturalness of women's state of dependence. Indeed, he had not been afraid to challenge universal laughter through his vehement assertion, that, as we had never seen woman in freedom, we did know nothing whatever until now of her nature; as though Raphael's Sistine Madonna, Shakespeare's young maidens, all the literature about women, in fact, had taught us nothing of the feminine character. On this point he was almost fanatical. He, who in all the relations between man and woman was refinement and delicacy itself, allowed himself to be positively insulting in his expressions when an opinion differing from his own on his favorite topic was uttered in his presence. (p. 191)

The peculiarity of Mill's standpoint in [the women's] emancipation question was, that it was based solely and entirely on a Socratic ignorance. He refused to see in the accumulated experience of ages any proof in regard to the boundaries of the so long enthralled feminine mind, and insisted that *à priori* we knew nothing at all about woman. He proceeded from no doctrinal view of especial feminine faculties, resting content with the simple proposition that man had no right to deny woman any occupation to which she felt attracted; and he declared everything like guardianship to be utterly useless as well as unjust, since free competition would of itself exclude woman from every occupation for which she was incapacitated, or in which man decidedly surpassed her. He has repelled many people by immediately deducing the final logical consequences of his theory the first time the question was brought forward, and by advocating the immediate participation of women in the affairs of government; but, as an Englishman, he had a too matter-of-fact mind not to limit the practical agitation to a single point. (p. 192)

It is of considerable importance in grasping the character of an author to learn in what relation the impression of his human disposition stands to that of his disposition as an author. I have never known a great man in whom these two impressions were so thoroughly harmonious as in Mill. I have never discovered any quality in him as an author that I have not rediscovered in my personal intercourse with him, and I have found his different characteristics in both spheres exalted above and subordinated to one another in precisely the same order and manner. There are authors in whose writings some definite quality—for instance, philanthropy, or wit, or dignity—plays a more prominent rôle than in their lives; others whose writings display not a trace of those qualities, such as humor or free humanity, which render them amiable in their private lives. Most authors are far inferior to their books. In Stuart Mill no such inequality existed, for he was the very incarnation of truthfulness. (pp. 202-03)

In daily life, too, Mill bore that invisible nimbus of exalted love of truth. His whole being radiated with purity of character. It is needful to look back to the most sublime philosophic characters of antiquity, to Marcus Aurelius and his peers, if peers he has, to find a parallel to Mill. He was equally true and equally great, whether he addressed his maturely considered thought in some renowned work to a circle of readers spread over the whole globe, or whether, in his own home, without any assumption of superiority, he dropped an accidental remark to a chance visitor. (pp. 203-04)

> Georg Brandes, "John Stuart Mill," in his Creative Spirits of the Nineteenth Century, translated by Rasmus B. Anderson, Thomas Y. Crowell Company, 1923, pp. 184-204.

ALEXANDER BAIN (essay date 1882)

[Upon examining Mill's writings and speeches, Bain argues that his style was generally deficient in "strength, energy, or momentum." He adds that despite this failing, Mill's works greatly influenced his generation. For additional commentary by Bain, see the excerpt dated 1843.]

[Mill's language faculty] was merely ordinary. Great cultivation had given him a good command of expression for all his purposes, but nothing could have made him a Macaulay. To begin with his vocabulary—including in that, not simply the words of the English dictionary, but the stock of phrases coined by our literary predecessors for expressing single ideas—we cannot say that in this he was more than a good average among men of intelligence and culture. He was greatly inferior to Bentham in the copiousness, the variety of his primary stock of language elements. He was surpassed, if I mistake not, by both the Austins, by Grote and by Roebuck. Had he been required to express the same idea in ten different forms, all good, he would have come to a standstill sooner than any of those.

His grammar is oftener defective than we should expect in any one so carefully disciplined as he was from the first. In some of the points that would be deemed objectionable, he probably had theories of his own. (p. 174)

Critically examined, his style is wanting in delicate attention to the placing of qualifying words generally. He had apparently never thought of this matter farther than to satisfy himself that his sentences were intelligible.

Another peculiarity of grammar tending to make his style not unfrequently heavy, and sometimes a little obscure, was the excess of relatives, and especially of the heavy relatives "which" and "who". (pp. 175-76)

Of arts of the rhetorical kind in the structure of his sentences, he was by no means wanting. He could be short and pithy, which goes a great way. He had likewise caught up, probably in a good measure from the French writers, his peculiar epigrammatic smartness, which he practised also in conversation. (p. 176)

He was not deficient in the power of illustration by metaphor and allusion, although he could not in this respect compare with men whose strength consists mainly in the power of ex-

pression. Moreover, as expository style requires that illustrations should be apposite, their employment is limited with precise writers.

As a whole, I should say that Mill was wanting in strength, energy, or momentum. His happiest strokes were of the nature of a coruscation—a lightning flash, rather than effects of impetus or mass in motion. His sentences and paragraphs are apt to be diffuse; not because of unnecessary circumstances, but from a want of steady endeavour after emphasis by good collocation and condensation. Every now and then, one of his pithy sentences comes across us, with inexpressible welcome. He is himself conscious when he is becoming too involved, and usually endeavours to relieve us by a terse summary at the close of the paragraph. (p. 177)

He knew how to introduce a generality, how to state it clearly, and what amount of exemplification was needed for the ordinary reader. He could occasionally provide very good illustrations as distinct from examples, that is to say, figurative comparisons, or similes. In the strict forms of exposition, logical power comes in aid; the logician is well accustomed to see the one in the many, and the many in the one—the generality in the particulars, and the particulars supporting the generality.

There are far more trying situations, however, than the statement and exemplification of one single truth. A principle has often to be qualified by another principle; and both may need to be elucidated together. A different form of complication is brought out, when a subject has not one predicate but several, all requiring to be attended to. Very often what has to be expounded is a highly complex idea, whose defining particulars have to be separately illustrated. These are a few of the testing forms of the expository art. Such matters cannot be despatched currente calamo—with the pen of a ready writer. They need careful retouching to find for each particular the best possible place. Mill has often such topics to handle, and certainly does not fall below the average of ordinary writers; yet he does not rise above being passable. (pp. 178-79)

The power of persuasion was with him not much a matter of mere style; it lay more in his command of thoughts, and in his tact in discerning what would suit the persons addressed. When he set himself to argue a point, his information and command of principles usually enabled him to exhaust his case. His political writing is enough to show this.

It was seldom that he was deficient in knowledge of his audience. If he ever failed here, it was in matters of religion, where he was necessarily little informed, and on the women question, where his feelings carried him too far.

Not only could he shape arguments to the reason, properly so called, he could also address the feelings. The *Liberty* and the *Subjection of Women,* as well as his political writing generally, exemplify what might be called impassioned oratory; they leave nothing unsaid that could enlist the strongest feelings of the readers. His best Parliamentary speeches appealed to the understanding and to the feelings alike, and he seldom, so far as I can judge, lost ground for want of suiting himself to a most difficult assembly. Although he could not clothe his feelings with the richness of poetry, he could warm with his subject, and work by the force of sympathy.

All this . . . had to do with knowledge and thinking power, more than with style. In the oratory of rhetoric, he was entirely wanting. He could appeal to men's feelings by suitable circumstances plainly and even forcibly stated; but that luxuriance of verbal display, whereby the emotions can be roused with a hurricane's might, was not a part of his equipment. He could not be an orator in the same sense as the two Pitts, Burke, Canning, Brougham, Macaulay, D'Israeli, or any of our rhetorical writers; although I am not sure that he might not often have rivalled such men in acutal effect, by the gifts that were peculiarly his own.

The powerful adjunct of Wit was hardly within his reach, any more than rhetorical display in general. He had the sense of humour, but not a sufficient creative power to embody it in writing; and he was careful not to attempt what he could not do well. (pp. 184-85)

Although in order to [secure] a permanent reputation, it is necessary to produce a work great in itself and of exclusive authorship, yet this is not the only way that original power manifests itself. A multitude of small impressions may have the accumulated effect of a mighty whole. Who shall sum up Mill's collective influence as an instructor in Politics, Ethics, Logic, and Metaphysics? No calculus can integrate the innumerable little pulses of knowledge and of thought that he has made to vibrate in the minds of his generation. (p. 195)

> *Alexander Bain, in his* John Stuart Mill: A Criticism, with Personal Recollections, *Longmans, Green, and Co., 1882, 201 p.*

JOHN M. ROBERTSON   (essay date 1891)

[*Focusing in particular on the essays "Bentham" and "Coleridge" and on Mill's philosophy of religion as evidenced in his essay* Theism, *Robertson maintains that "salient intellectual shortcomings" exist throughout Mill's writings. Yet Robertson attributes them mostly to Mill's altruism, asserting that even when the shortcomings are unextenuated, they are tempered by Mill's earnestness and openness to criticism.*]

[On freshly surveying Mill's] life and work, one becomes conscious of a certain sympathetic waywardness which every now and then took him a little to one or other side of truth, sometimes in pessimism, sometimes in optimism, sometimes in hostility, sometimes in eulogy, oftenest and furthest in the latter direction indeed, but always in a pure and high-minded way, and hardly ever from a small motive. Take for instance his critical treatment [in **"Bentham"** and **"Coleridge"**] of the school in which he was trained, that of Bentham, and the school which most opposed it, that of the transcendentalists, represented in England by Coleridge. Certainly no man then could be trusted to deal out a more nearly even-handed justice to two such opposite schools; and yet, as he himself admits in his ***Autobiography***, he has to some extent strained matters against Bentham and in favour of Coleridge. He explains characteristically that, writing as he did for an audience of Utilitarians, he saw fit to lay special stress on the flaws of Benthamism, and on the strong points of Coleridge's school, both things which that audience would be specially prone to overlook; and that the two sorts of stress in question were rectified by his other writings. But one doubts whether this is either just or politic. Surely one has no more right to press hardly on one's own side than to press hardly on the other; and surely Mill forgot that the special praise you give to an enemy, and the special blame you pass on a friend, are equally likely to be made too much of in the enemy's interest. In that case, too, it was certainly not the transcendental cause that most needed helping in England. Indeed, ... whatever be the full explanation in terms

of heredity, he really had a certain constitutional bias to traditional supernaturalist views of life which his father's more firmly logical intelligence had outgrown. We are in fact led to feel that but for the training and indoctrination of his father, Mill would have been very much nearer supernaturalism throughout his whole life. Certainly he is most uncritical of Coleridge's glaring intellectual frailties, while laborious and, as I think, in part misleading, in his insistence on the errors of Bentham; and his praise of Bentham on other points is certainly no warmer than his praise of Coleridge. Reading the strictures on Bentham, and feeling that in some respects they are well grounded, I cannot but feel also that in some highly essential qualities Bentham was nearer a scientific attitude or temper in morals than his critic. His science was incomplete; it could not but be, pioneer as he was, even if he had been more ready to learn from others; but he has a gift of dispassionateness which Mill never quite attains. Bentham was a most remarkable combination, as Mill justly points out, of a powerful moral inspiration with a faculty for the cool analysis of moral questions. All scientific history goes to show that moral science, to be sound, must be gone about in as passionless a temper as that of the chemist over his crucible. While you actively either love good or hate evil you may be doing the most valuable moral work, but you are not philosophising. Now, Mill is wonderfully philosophic in temper, compared with the average man; but his very enthusiasm of humanity kept him short of absolutely scientific method. Bentham again was indeed unscientific in the sense of leaving out whole classes of data in some of his reasonings—notably those on the treatment of criminals—but there is a fine colourlessness about his mental atmosphere, a fine north light, so to say, in his studio. And while Mill had been fitted by his training to appreciate this, you feel that on the other hand he had a certain temperamental readiness to do justice to the poetic colour in Coleridge's thinking, and to be tolerant of the mirage in which it so often ended. (pp. 65-7)

Mill seems to me to have been singularly weak in his handling of a set of questions which some people would call abstract, namely, those discussed under the head of religion. I will call these concrete problems to be settled on logical principles; and my contention is that in handling them Mill's logical resources (so apparently wide when he discusses the forms and laws of logic) seem to be of the slenderest description, the work being really done for the most part by his sympathies, feebly chaperoned, as it were, by a reasoning faculty grown elderly and languid, though remaining always conscientious. It is remarkable, indeed, how the habit of judicial reasoning clings to Mill under all circumstances.

Take first his main line of reasoning on the subject of Theism. He makes a good show of treating judicially the doctrines of a First Cause, and of miracles, and of natural tendencies of belief; and duly shows that the ordinary First Cause argument destroys itself; that miracles are as good as incredible, philosophically speaking; and that natural tendencies of belief prove either nothing or too much. But not only does he introduce a flagrant fallacy in his partial defence of the theory of miracles, but he maintains continuously a position which is untenable from the very commencement of the argument—that, namely, of a good deity of limited powers. This notion had a strange attraction for him, since it is not merely elaborated in the essay on Theism but laid down in the previous essay on the Utility of Religion. There he says that

> One only form of belief in the supernatural—
> one only theory respecting the origin and gov-

ernment of the universe—stands wholly clear both of intellectual contradiction and of moral obliquity. It is that which, resigning irrevocably the idea of an omnipotent creator, regards Nature and Life not as the expression throughout of the moral character and purpose of the Deity, but as the product of a struggle between contriving goodness and an intractable material, as was believed by Plato, or a Principle of Evil, as was the doctrine of the Manicheans. A creed like this, which I have known to be devoutly held by at least one cultivated and conscientious person of our own day, allows it to be believed that all the mass of evil which exists was undesigned by and exists not by the appointment of, but in spite of, the Being whom we are called upon to worship.

Such a passage forcibly arouses that perplexity that is sometimes excited by exhibitions of glaring fallacy from thinkers who have specialised in logic. . . . And no reasoner of standing ever made a more obvious oversight than is here made by Mill in undertaking to set forth as an explanation or theory of the *origin* of the universe the doctrine of a deity of limited power, struggling with an intractable material. On the very face of the case, this is no theory of the origin of the universe at all, but one which sets the problem of origin aside; and just as little is it a theory of deity or the supernatural, since the very purpose of such a theory is to formulate the universe in terms of will and administration, while Mill's formula presents a subaltern God, the victim of circumstances, struggling with a universe which is too much for him, and either taking a hopelessly pessimistic view of it as a mystery he cannot make out, or figuring to himself in turn another and bigger superior God who is either incorrigibly bad or is in turn the victim of circumstances. That is what limited-liability Theism logically comes to. It is amazing that a man of philosophical training should have been capable of writing down such a childish restatement of one of the most naïve conceptions of antiquity. We are told that the essay on Theism had not been finally revised; but this passage occurs in an essay written long before; and the essay on Theism elaborates the proposition. It is the most futile suggestion towards a philosophy of the universe to be found in modern literature of the better class; and I can only account for its existence by Mill's own remark that "the scepticism of the understanding does not necessarily exclude the Theism of the imagination and feelings." In this case the Theism of the feelings had got so far the upper hand that it claimed to sit in the chair of the understanding, declaring that its dream was "wholly clear of intellectual contradiction;" and the only demur that Mill's reason was able to murmur was that the "evidence" for the proposition of his feelings was "too shadowy and unsubstantial . . . to admit of its being a permanent substitute for the religion of humanity." Evidence, forsooth, for a contradiction in terms! Unsubstantial is not the word. And in the very act of making this nugatory admission, Mill proceeds to urge, as he urged at the close of the essay on Theism, that apart from all belief men should cherish religious hopes which were agreeable to them. . . . According to Mill the appropriate culture of the imagination is to fancy that the reason may be mistaken. One is fain to remember his own remark that the subject of the proper means of culture for the imagination has not hitherto attracted the serious attention of philosophers. Certainly his view of the subject is the crudest and most primitive that could well be conceived, dividing as it does the imagination from the reason, as if there were no reason in

imagination and no imagination in reason. He does say, indeed, that imagination is to "make life pleasant and lovely inside the castle, in reliance on the fortifications raised and maintained by reason round the outward bounds;" but the whole effect of his argument is to prescribe to imagination a holiday on the loose, out of sight of the castle, every time, so to speak, that the horses are disengaged. Surely men are prone enough to put guess and inclination above science without being thus strangely encouraged to it in the name of science itself. Every purpose that Mill professed to have in view could be met by the cherishing of hopes of an ideal future for humanity in this world; and he gratuitously, nay, treasonably, gave away that motive power in the professed service of humanity.

And if he is illogical in his general scheme of philosophical culture for the feelings, he is worse than illogical, he is inexcusably heedless, in his treatment of the claims of the religion which in his own community professes both to train the feelings and inform the reason. His eulogy of the Jesus of the Gospels, and his unwarrantable and fallacious defence of the historic actuality of that figure, have been picked out of the mass of rhetorical empiricism that makes up the essay on Theism, and brandished in the faces of rationalists as a complete admission that Jesus lived and spoke as he is said to have done; that Jesus was perfect; that nobody else had such ideas; and that he really may have had a special message from God—for to this extremity of unreasoning hypothesis Mill actually proceeds, though for some unexplained reason he will not accept the doctrine of the Incarnation. The whole exposition is arbitrary and illogical to the last degree. Professing to argue the question whether Jesus existed, and to show that he must have done, Mill contends that this is clear because *nobody else could* have said the things he says in the synoptics. It is the most scandalous case of begging the question that I can remember. You ask: Is the teaching Jesus of the Gospels a true historical figure, or are not his professed teachings a compilation of many current at that and a later period? Answer, No: because we know that Jesus existed and taught such things, and nobody else was capable of inventing them. That is the thing to be proved is taken for granted.

If Mill had ever paid the least critical attention to New Testament criticism, however fallaciously he might continue to reason, he could scarcely have played fast and loose with the matter to the extent he did. (pp. 80-4)

Of these salient intellectual shortcomings we can only say that they give staggering proof of the laxity of Mill's mind in the application of his own logical principles to the discovery of turth in regard to the constitution of the universe and the history of religion. But if we are right in saying that these intellectual weaknesses were correlative with his sympathetic qualities, they finally serve to give us a more vivid idea of the strength of the element of benevolent feeling in his character. These unhappy reasonings on Theism, that headlong deliverance as to the character and actuality of the Jesus of the Gospels, were on this view partly the outcome of his wish to preserve for his fellows every possible comfort and consolation from their old religious beliefs, every vestige of their old devotions, that seemed tenable without injury to good morals. If he miscalculated on the last head, at least the aim was good. And at worst, even if we attribute his fallacy not wholly to pure altruism but partly to intellectual infirmity, hereditary or acquired, in himself, still no one who has studied him ever harboured a doubt as to his integrity in debate, or his readiness to listen to criticism when it came. (p. 85)

John M. Robertson, "John Stuart Mill," in his Modern Humanists: Sociological Studies of Carlyle, Mill, Emerson, Arnold, Ruskin, and Spencer, *Swan Sonnenschein & Co., 1891, pp. 62-111.*

BERNARD BOSANQUET   (essay date 1899)

[*A noted English Hegelian philosopher and aesthetician, Bosanquet was also an anti-empiricist and the author of books on political theory and logic. Here he analyzes Mill's* On Liberty, *noting his prejudices and inconsistencies in reasoning. Bosanquet points out that because Mill was influenced by the Benthamite bias against regulatory law, his theory of liberty confuses "inner morality and outer action" and incorporates the logically questionable distinction between personal freedom and the needs of society. This essay was first published in 1899.*]

[What is instructive in Mill's position in **"Liberty"**] is that, having so deep a sense, as he has, of social solidarity, he nevertheless treats the central life of the individual as something to be carefully fenced round against the impact of social forces.

i. Mill's idea of Individuality is plainly biassed by the Benthamite tradition that law is an evil. It is to be remembered that Anarchism of a speculative kind, the inevitable complement of a hide-bound Conservatism, was current in the beginning of this century, as in Godwin and Shelley. Thus we find concentrated in a few pages of the **"Liberty"** all those ideas on the nature of Individuality, Originality, and Eccentricity which are most opposed to the teaching derived by later generations in England from the revival of philosophy and criticism. . . . That the individuality, or genius, the fulness of life and completeness of development which Mill so justly appreciates, is not nourished and evoked by the varied play of relations and obligations in society, but lies in a sort of inner self, to be cherished by enclosing it, as it were, in an impervious globe, is a notion which neither modern logic nor modern art criticism will admit. In the same way, the connection of originality and eccentricity, on which Mill insists, appears to us to-day to be a fallacious track of thought; and in general, in all these matters, we tend to accept the principle that, in order to go beyond a point of progress, it is necessary to have reached it; and in order to destroy a law, it is necessary to have fulfilled it. Here, however, is the heart of the point on which we are insisting. If individuality and originality mean or depend upon the absence of law and of obligation; if eccentricity is the type of the fully developed self, and if the community, penetrated by a sense of universal relations, is therefore a prey to monotony and uniformity, then it needs no further words to show that law is a curtailment of human nature, the necessity of which remains inexplicable, so that self-government is a contradiction in terms.

ii. How then does Mill bring the two terms into relation? How does he represent the phenomenon that, in the life of every society, the factors of self and of government have to be reconciled, or at any rate to coexist?

To find the answer to this question, the whole of the chapter, "Of the limits of the authority of society over the individual," should be carefully studied. (pp. 56-8)

Every one who lives in society . . . is bound not to interfere with certain interests of others (explicitly or implicitly constituted as "rights"), and is bound to take his fair share of the sacrifices incurred for the defence of society and its members. These conditions society may enforce, at all costs to recalcitrants. Further, it may punish by opinion, though not by law, acts hurtful to others, but not going so far as to violate their rights. But acts which affect only the agent, or need not affect others unless they like, may be punished, we are given to understand, neither by law nor by opinion. Mill expects his conclusion to be disputed, and the following is the conclusion of the passage in which he explains and reaffirms it: ". . . when a person disables himself, by conduct purely self-regarding, from the performance of some definite duty incumbent on him to the public, he is guilty of a social offence. No person ought to be punished simply for being drunk; but a soldier or policeman should be punished for being drunk on duty. Wherever, in short, there is a definite damage, or a definite risk of damage either to an individual or to the public, *the case is taken out of the province of liberty, and placed in that of morality or law.*"

It will probably occur at once to the reader that, considered as a practical rule, the view here maintained would by no means curtail unduly the province of social interference. We should rather anticipate that it would leave an easy opening for a transition from administrative nihilism to administrative absolutism; and some such transition seems to have taken place in Mill's later views. This tendency to a complete *bouleversement* is the characteristic of all conceptions which proceed by assigning different areas to the several factors of an inseparable whole, which then reasserts itself in its wholeness within the area of either factor to which we may happen to attend. Indeed, even in the passage before us, the defence of individuality has already well-nigh turned round into its annihilation. Every act that carries a definite damage to any other person belongs to the sphere of law, and every act that can be supposed likely to cause such a damage, to that of morality; and individuality has what is left. The extraordinary demarcation between the sphere of morality and that of liberty is to be accounted for, no doubt, by the Benthamite tradition which identified the moral and social sanctions; so that in this usage the sphere of morality means much the same as what, in the first passage referred to, was indicated as the sphere of opinion.

Now, it is obvious that the distinction which Mill is attempting to describe and explain is one practially recognised by every society. The question is whether it can be rightly described and explained by a demarcation which, if strictly pressed, excludes individuality from every act of life that has an important social bearing; while, owing to the two-sided nature of all action, it becomes perfectly arbitrary in its practical working as a criterion. For every act of mine affects both myself and others; and it is a matter of mood and momentary urgency which aspect may be pronounced characteristic and essential. It may safely be said that no demarcation between self-regarding and other-regarding action can possibly hold good. What may hold good, and what Mill's examples show to be present to his mind, is a distinction between the moral and the "external" aspects of action on the ground of their respective accessibility to the means of coercion which are at the disposal of society. The peculiar sense in which the term "external" is here employed will explain itself below.

For our present purpose, however, what we have to observe is merely that the demarcation between individuality and society, contrived in defence of the former, has pretty nearly annihilated it. And thus we see once more how overwhelming is the *prima facie* appearance that, in the idea of self-government, the factors of self and government are alien and opposed; and yet how hopeless it remains to explain the part played by these factors in actual society, so long as we aim at a demarcation between them as opposites, rather than at a relative distinction between them as manifestations of the same principle in different media.

iii. A few words may here be said on the applications by which Mill illustrates his doctrine, in order to point out what confusion results from relying on a demarcation which cannot strictly be made.

It will be noted in the first place that he objects altogether to the attempt to prevent by punishment either immorality or irreligion as such. This objection a sound social theory must uphold. But if we look at Mill's reason for it, we find it simply to be that such an attempt infringes liberty, by interfering with action which is purely self-regarding. Without entering further upon the endless argument whether this or any action is indeed purely self-regarding, we may observe that by taking such ground, Mill causes the above objection, which is substantially sound, to appear as on all fours with others which are at any rate very much more doubtful. Such is the objection on principle to all restrictions imposed upon trade with a distinct view to protecting the consumer, not from fraud, but from opportunities of consumption injurious to himself. The regulation or prohibition of the traffic in alcoholic liquors is of course the main question here at issue; and it may be admitted that Mill's discussion, with the many distinctions which he lays down, is full of shrewdness and suggestiveness. But the ultimate ground which he takes . . . is quite different from the genuine reasons which exist against attempting to enforce morality by law and penalty, and introduces confusion into the whole question of State interference by ranking the two objections together. Closely analogous are his objections to the statutes respecting unlawful games, which, whether wise or unwise, are quite a different thing from an attempt to punish personal immorality as such. And lastly, the same principle is illustrated by his whole attitude to the strong feeling and the various legal obligations which determine and support the monogamous family. In maintaining the general indissolubility of marriage, and supporting the parental power, the State is interfering, for him, with the freedom of parties to a contract, and conferring power over individuals, the children, who have a right to be separately considered. Such interference is for him *ipso facto* of a suspected nature. It is an interference hostile to liberty; and whether it is or is not an external condition of good life, which the State is able effectively to maintain, is a question which he does not discuss. Throughout all these objections to authoritative interference we trace the peculiar prejudice that the criterion of its justifiability lies in the boundary line between self and others, rather than in the nature of what coercive authority is and is not able to do towards the promotion of good life. On many points indeed, when the simple protection of "others" is concerned, Mill's doctrine leads to sound conclusions. (pp. 58-62)

But yet a strange nemesis attaches to grounds alleged with insufficient discrimination. Just as, by ranking inner morality and outer action alike under the name of freedom, Mill is led to object to interference which may be perfectly justified and effectual; so by the same confusion he is led to advocate coercive treatment in impossibly stringent forms, and in cases where it runs extreme risk of thwarting a true moral development. We are amazed when he strongly implies, in respect to the education of children and the prospect of supporting a family, that the existence of a moral obligation to an act is a sufficient ground for enforcing the act by law. The proposal of universal State-enacted examinations by way of enforcing the parental duty of educating children, to the exclusion of the task of providing education by public authority, in which Mill sees danger to individuality, opens a prospect of a Chinese type of society, from which, happily, the good sense of Englishmen has recoiled. And just the reverse of his proposal has come to pass under the influence of the logic of experience. The State has taken care that the external conditions of an elementary education are provided, and, while doing this, has no doubt exercised compulsion, in order that these conditions may be a reality. But the individual inquisition by examination is tending to drop out of the system; and the practical working of the public education is more and more coming to be that the State sees to it that certain conditions are maintained, of which the parents' interest and public spirit leads them to take advantage. Sheer compulsion is not the way to enforce a moral obligation.

Still more startling is the suggestion that it might be just to interdict marriage to those unable to show the means of supporting a family, on the ground of possible evil both to the children themselves through poverty, and to others through over-population. This is a case in which authoritative interference (except on account of very definite physical or mental defects) must inevitably defeat its object. No foresight of others can gauge the latent powers to meet and deal with a future indefinite responsibility; and the result of scrupulous timidity, in view of such responsibilities, is seen in the tendency to depopulation which affects that very country from which Mill probably drew his argument. To leave the responsibility as fully as possible where it has been assumed is the best that law can do, and appeals to a spring of energy deeper than compulsion can reach.

Thus we have seen that by discriminating the spheres of non-interference and interference, according to a supposed demarcation between the sphere of "self" and of "others," a hopelessly confused classification has been introduced. Sometimes the maintenance of external conditions of good life, well within the power of the State, is forbidden on the same grounds as the direct promotion of morality, which is impossible to it. In other cases the enforcement of moral obligations is taken to lie within the functions of the State, although not only is the enforcement of moral obligations *per se* a contradiction in terms, but almost always, as in the cases in question, the attempt to effect it is sure to frustrate itself, by destroying the springs on which moral action depends.

It is worth noticing, in conclusion, that in two examples, the one trivial, the other that of slavery, both theoretically and practically very important, Mill recognises a principle wholly at variance with his own. Here he is aware that it may be right, according to the principle of liberty, to restrain a man, for reasons affecting himself alone, from doing what at the moment he proposes to do. For we are entitled to argue from the essential nature of freedom to what freedom really demands, as opposed to what the man momentarily seems to wish. "It is not freedom to be allowed to alienate his freedom," as it is not freedom to be allowed to walk over a bridge which is certain to break down and cause his death. Here we have in germ the doctrine of the "real" will, and a conception analogous to that of Rousseau when he speaks of a man "being forced to be free." (pp. 62-5)

Bernard Bosanquet, "The Paradox of Political Obligation: Self-Government," in his The Philosophical Theory of the State, *fourth edition, Macmillan and Co., Limited, 1923, pp. 50-73.**

LESLIE STEPHEN (essay date 1900)

[*Stephen is considered one of the most important literary critics of the late Victorian and early Edwardian era. In his criticism, which was often moral in tone, Stephen argues that all literature is nothing more than an imaginative rendering, in concrete terms, of a writer's philosophy or beliefs. It is the role of criticism, he contends, to translate into intellectual terms what the writer has told the reader through character, symbol, and plot. Stephen's analyses often include biographical judgments of the writer as well as the work. As Stephen once observed: "The whole art of criticism consists in learning to know the human being who is partially revealed to us in his spoken or his written words." In the following excerpt, Stephen discusses Mill's treatment of Jeremy Bentham's theory of motivation in order to trace Mill's ambivalent attitude toward Benthamism as a whole.*]

The omissions with which [Bentham's] greatest disciple charges him are certainly significant. We find, says Mill, no reference to 'Conscience,' 'Principle,' 'Moral Rectitude,' or 'Moral Duty' among the 'springs of action,' unless among the synonyms of a 'love of reputation,' or in so far as 'Conscience' and 'Principle' are sometimes synonymous with the 'religious' motive or the motive of 'sympathy.' So the sense of 'honour,' the love of beauty, and of order, of power (except in the narrow sense of power over our fellows) and of action in general are all omitted. We may conjecture what reply Bentham would have made to this criticism. The omission of the love of beauty and æsthetic pleasures may surprise us when we remember that Bentham loved music, if he cared nothing for poetry. But he apparently regarded these as 'complex pleasures,' and therefore not admissible into his table, if it be understood as an analysis into the simple pleasures alone. The pleasures of action are deliberately omitted, for Bentham pointedly gives the 'pains' of labour as a class without corresponding pleasure; and this, though indicative, I think, of a very serious error, is characteristic rather of his method of analysis than of his real estimate of pleasure. Nobody could have found more pleasure than Bentham in intellectual labour, but he separated the pleasure from the labour. He therefore thought 'labour,' as such, a pure evil, and classified the pleasure as a pleasure of 'curiosity.' But the main criticism is more remarkable. Mill certainly held himself to be a sound Utilitarian; and yet he seems to be condemning Bentham for consistent Utilitarianism. Bentham, by admitting the 'conscience' into his simple springs of action, would have fallen into the very circle from which he was struggling to emerge. If, in fact, the pleasures of conscience are simple pleasures, we have the objectionable 'moral sense' intruded as an ultimate factor of human nature. To get rid of that 'fictitious entity' is precisely Bentham's aim. The moral judgment is to be precisely equivalent to the judgment: 'this or that kind of conduct increases or diminishes the sum of human pains or pleasures.' Once allow that among the pains and pleasures themselves is an ultimate conscience—a faculty not constructed out of independent pains and pleasures—and the system becomes a vicious circle. Conscience on any really Utilitarian scheme must be a derivative, not an ultimate, faculty. If, as Mill seems to say, the omission is a blunder, Bentham's Utilitarianism at least must be an erroneous system. (pp. 252-54)

> Leslie Stephen, "Bentham's Doctrine," in his The English Utilitarians, G. P. Putnam's Sons, 1900, pp. 235-318.*

JOHN MORLEY   (essay date 1906)

[*In this eulogistic overview of Mill's career as a philosopher, Morley discusses the influence of Mill's writings. Morley concludes that Mill's most memorable contribution was his plea for*

the emancipation of women. For additional commentary by Morley, see the excerpt dated 1874.]

Nobody who claims to deal as a matter of history with the intellectual fermentation between 1840 and 1870 or a little longer, whatever value the historian may choose to set upon its products, can fail to assign a leading influence to Mill. (p. 3)

[The] writings of Mill set the problems and defined the channels for people with a taste for political thinking and thinking deeper than political. He opened all the ground, touched all the issues, posed all the questions in the spheres where the intellects of men must be most active. (p. 4)

The failure of what he regarded as an expiring theology made [his] exaltation of social feeling a necessity. One profound master sentiment with Mill was passionate hatred for either coarse or subtle abuse of power. Hatred of oppression in all its forms burned deep in his inmost being. It inspired those fierce pages against the maleficence of Nature (in the **"Three Essays on Religion"**), his almost vindictive indictment of Nature's immorality—immoral because "the course of natural phenomena is replete with everything that when committed by human beings is most worthy of abhorrence; so that any one who endeavored in his actions to imitate the natural course of things would be universally seen and acknowledged to be the wickedest of men." This poignant piece is perhaps the only chapter to be found in his writings where he throws aside his ordinary measure of reserve, and allows himself the stern relief of vehement and exalted declamation. The same wrath that blazes in him when he is asked to use glozing words about the moral atrocities of Nature to man, breaks out unabated when he recounts the tyrannical brutalities of man to woman. Nor even did the flame of his indignation burn low, when he thought of the callous recklessness of men and women to helpless animals—our humble friends and ministers whose power of loyalty, attachment, patience, fidelity so often seems to deserve as good a word as human or a better. . . .

[In] Mill pity and wrath at the wrong and the stupidities of the world nerved him to steadfast work and thought in definite channels. His postulate of a decided predominance of the active over the passive meant devotion of thought to practical ends. His life was not stimulated by mere intellectual curiosity, but by the resolute purpose of furthering human improvement. (p. 6)

The **"Logic"** was an elaborate attempt to perform the practical task of dislodging intuitive philosophy, as a step towards sounder thinking about society and institutions; as a step, in other words, towards Liberalism. (p. 8)

[Even those who do not place Mill among the greatest philosophers] agree that at least he raised the true points, put the sharpest questions, and swept away the most tiresome cobwebs. If the metaphysical controversy has not always been good-natured, perhaps it is because *on ne se passionne que pour ce qui est obscur.*

In point of literary style—a thing on which many coxcombries have sprung up since Mill's day—although both his topics and his temperament denied him a place among the greatest masters, yet his writing had for the younger men of his generation a grave power well fitted for the noble task of making men love truth and search for it. There is no ambition in his style. He never forced his praise. Even when anger moves him, the ground does not tremble under him, as when Bossuet or Burke exhorts, denounces, wrestles, menaces, and thunders. He has none of the incomparably winning graces by which Newman made mere siren style do duty for exact, penetrating, and coherent thought. . . . Mill's journey from Bentham, Malthus, Ricardo, to Coleridge, Wordsworth, Comte, and then on at last to some of those Manichean speculations that so perplexed or scandalized his disciples, was almost as striking, though not so picturesquely described, as Newman's journey from Evangelicalism to Rome. These graces were none of Mill's gifts, nor could he have coveted them. He did not impose; he drew, he led, he quickened with a living force and fire the commonplace that truth is a really serious and rather difficult affair, worth persistently pursuing in every path where duty beckons. He made people feel, with a kind of eagerness evidently springing from internal inspiration, that the true dignity of man is mind. (p. 9)

If it be true that very often more depends upon the temper and spirit in which men hold their opinions than upon the opinions themselves, Mill was indeed our benefactor. From beginning to end of his career he was forced into the polemical attitude over the whole field; into an incessant and manful wrestle for what he thought true and right against what he regarded as false or wrong. One of his merits was the way in which he fought these battles—the pains he took to find out the strength of an opposing argument; the modesty that made him treat the opponent as an equal; an entire freedom from pedagogue's arrogance. . . . He really succeeded in procuring a sort of popular halo round the dismal and derided name of philosopher, and his books on political theory and sociological laws went into cheap popular editions. Like Locke and Hobbes, he propounded general ideas for particular occasions, and built dykes and ramparts on rational principles for movements that had their source not so much in reasoning as in passions and interests, sectarian or material, and in the confused and turbid rush of intractable events.

Among all the changes of social ordinance in Mill's day and generation, none is more remarkable, and it may by-and-by be found that none cuts deeper, than the successive stages of the emancipation of women. And to this no thinker or writer of his time contributed so powerfully as Mill. Much of the ground has now been won, but the mark made by his little tract on the **"Subjection of Women"** upon people of better minds among us was profound, and a book touching so impressively the most penetrating of all our human relations with one another is slow to go quite out of date.

In political economy . . . he is admitted, by critics not at all disposed to put his pretensions too high, to have exercised without doubt a greater influence than any other writer since Ricardo, and as an exposition of the principles on which the emancipating work between 1820 and 1860 was done, his book still holds its ground. (pp. 10-11)

Measure the permanence of his contribution to thought or social action as we will, he will long deserve to be commemorated as the personification of some of the noblest and most fruitful qualities within the reach and compass of mankind. (p. 12)

> *John Morley, "John Stuart Mill," in* The Living
> Age, *Vol. CCXLX, No. 3235, July 7, 1906, pp. 3-12.*

JAMES BONAR   (essay date 1911)

[*Bonar analyzes the far-reaching implications of Mill's* Principles of Political Economy *and offers a balanced assessment of his style in that work.*]

[Mill's *Political Economy*] was at once successful and passed through seven editions in Mill's lifetime. In England at least, it superseded the earlier [economics] textbooks. It became a new point of departure; and this alone might show that its author was not . . . a mere formulator. If he is now in his turn superseded, there is small wonder after sixty years. That his fame is less in later generations is partly from a reaction against the overestimates of his contemporaries. But in any event more has been left of John Stuart Mill the economist than of John Stuart Mill the philosopher.

Certain broad features were impressed by him on political economy with every chance of permanence. He not only taught the necessity of abstractions, but the necessity of our continually remembering that they are abstractions, that they are not the whole of the concrete world, and that even the economic man wears the clothes of a particular society. (p. 720)

For good or for mischief he has widened the range of economic study among English-speaking folk. He has served economics too by his style and temper. This does not (though it easily might) refer to his careful English, but to his manner of handling discussions, even of burning questions. He seldom speaks (except in the *Autobiography*) in the tone of a superior being; he recognizes that he is but a man; he acknowledges his debts to great and small writers; he states his opponent's case at its best, which often means better than the opponent can state it; he is the model of a fair controversialist.

But like all "epoch-making" books his *Political Economy* is hardly in all respects a safe model for writers of a later epoch. From his announced resolution of being nothing if not practical, the topics of the day and the topics suggested by his own personal experience fill too much of his space. . . . The long illustrations quoted verbatim from other books seem to us a little tedious now. In some cases our experience has widened. We have the phases of socialism over two generations to occupy us. Mill had before him what there was of it in 1848, and his posthumous papers on the subject show his difficulty in grasping the "scientific" sort. (pp. 721-22)

There are many details of economic doctrine [in his *Political Economy*] in respect of which Mill has probably few followers now. Occasionally his positions, instead of being solemnly refuted, are quietly dropped as purely Ricardian. Many of the pages devoted to wages and profits are so treated. His particular form of Malthusianism has gone out of doors into the hands of an energetic sect of reformers. Without adopting the sweepingly adverse verdict of Jevons, we may admit that there is at once too much and too little in Mill's *Political Economy* for most of us now. We should not confine wealth to exchange value, or believe that nothing remained to be added to the theory of value. We should not say that without competition there is no economics. We should not say so broadly that industry is limited by capital. We should not make so much of the distinction between productive and unproductive labor or try to prove that a demand for goods can never in any sound sense be a demand for labor. We cannot be induced to rank land, labor, and capital as co-ordinate factors in production, or to adopt Senior's view that abstinence is rewarded in interest. We should probe further into the cause of interest. We might ratify the general principle of Malthus without making all progress turn on the practical recognition of it. We should be more chary than Mill in the use of the word "laws." We should not, all of us, admit that the "laws" of production were purely physical and the "laws" of distribution "of human institution solely." Mill was probably aware that the abandonment by him in 1869 of the wages fund carried consequences reaching into the heart of his arguments on profits and wages reducing them largely to useless dialectic. When he says, "The results are not ripe for incorporation in a general treatise," he probably means that he is disinclined at his age to recast his own treatise.

It is remarkable that a man, otherwise so little academic, should adopt so conspicuously a plan of exposition better suited for a lecturer than for a writer of books, the initial exaggeration of a doctrine followed by qualifications of it. In his case the qualifications often come near to destroying its generality altogether. The most frequent examples are perhaps in the discussions on money, though there is no lack of others. But we need to remember that, unlike Comte, Mill had no mind to make a system. (pp. 722-23)

*James Bonar, "The Economics of John Stuart Mill,"
in* The Journal of Political Economy, *Vol. 19, No.
9, November, 1911, pp. 717-25.*

HAROLD J. LASKI (essay date 1924)

[*An English political scientist and economist, Laski was a Marxist critic who wrote extensively on American government, politics, and history. In this excerpt from his introduction to Mill's* Autobiography, *Laski ranks the work as "a document of the first importance in the intellectual history of the nineteenth century."*]

Sir Leslie Stephen has complained that Mill's **Autobiography** is almost wholly lacking in the qualities which give charm to that class of literature. Certainly it is far more completely an intellectual exercise than any comparable work. Save for the few pages which deal with his wife, there is almost no reference to the human emotions of love or friendship. Even his most intimate friends are judged much as a writer would judge a person whose obituary estimate he had been charged to compile. The Mill who was a tender and lovable human being, anxious, as in the case of Lord Morley, to do all he could to further the prospects of a young man on the threshold of a career, hardly emerges in these pages. The book is essentially a record of the development of convictions. It has nothing of that magic which makes Newman's *cri de cœur* so irresistible. It is not, like Gibbon's *Autobiography,* a living picture of its

In this 1867 Punch *cartoon denigrating women's suffrage, Mill is saying to John Bull, "Pray clear the way, there, for these—a—persons."*

creator. It does not, like Trollope's portrait of himself, move us more than we care to admit by its humble simplicity.

But Mill's *Autobiography* is, nevertheless, a document of the first importance in the intellectual history of the nineteenth century. It is, in the first place, a careful record, by the subject himself, of a great educational experiment; and though, to most, the experiment will read like a record of medieval torture, no one can deny the value of its details. It is, in the second place, an account of the influence and creed of the Benthamite School by one who, Bentham himself apart, was probably its most distinguished member. It explains better than any other record why Benthamism failed to satisfy the England of the later nineteenth century, and why, after 1870, T. H. Green took the place of Mill as the most influential writer on matters of social philosophy. It paints a convincing, and, I think, a not unattractive picture of the way in which a body of ardent young men set out to convert a dubious generation to the acceptance of ideas which are only commonplaces now because they were occupied, with full minds and full hearts, in making them commonplaces. It reveals a devotion to the public good which is, it may be urged, without parallel in English history when the width of its achievement and the period of its effort are taken into account. It shows how that life on the heights which Plato commended can be combined with essential happiness. It displays a catholicity of outlook which is, I think, rarely achieved by men engaged in the promotion of a particular doctrine. It lacks, obviously, that power of self-analysis which makes the great autobiography, above all, for instance, the *Confessions* of Saint Augustine, a part of the essential literature of the world. But no man can afford to neglect it, who desires to understand the forces which make for the success of great movements. (pp. ix-x)

The ultimate thing for which [Mill] was concerned was the elevation of the mind of man. That was, at bottom, the root of all he wrote. It lends a quiet passion to his economic discussion as to his examination of the foundations of logic. It was the explanation alike of his zeal for popular education and of his defence of femininism. It was the motive behind his every attack upon injustice, whether of the American slave or the Irish peasant. Indignant pity, indeed, was with Mill, as with Burke, one of the noblest elements in his composition. That quality, with the power to be optimistic even when progress was heartbreakingly slow, informed all that he said and wrote. It lends, in the aftermath of fifty years, something of a prophetic quality to much of his speculation. It serves almost as much to encourage as to warn. It meant, as he once somewhere remarked, that if you can inform the passion of the multitude against the self-interest of a few, you have the right to await the outcome with confidence. But it meant also that the outcome is not a matter of some single person's lifetime. The great changes of history are the result of a gradual and imperceptible accumulation of minute changes; and the adjustment of man's nature to new demands is, in matters of ultimate social constitution, the slowest of all efforts. But the adjustment can be made; and it was therein that Mill discovered our right to hope.

He is not the author of a system. His mind, unlike that of his father or Bentham, responded too quickly to new ideas to acquire the vigour of outline that system-making demands. (pp. xv-xvi)

No one, on any final estimate, can doubt that Mill, as no other figure of his time, raised the moral stature of his generation. He ceaselessly directed its attention to the problems that are fundamental; he always made those problems intelligible and interesting. The *Autobiography,* in the end the most imperishable of his writings, is a record as noble as any in our literature of consistent devotion to the public good. Whatever he touched he did not fail to clarify. Few men have been more rigorous in their standards, and no man more zealous in the pursuit of justice. Certain defects, of course, he had; beside Rousseau, for instance, the fires of his emotion seem pallid and thin. But where Rousseau appealed to men's hearts, Mills elevated their minds. He held as high as any man the lamp of reason, and it burned the more brightly because he lived. There are men in the record of English thought, like Hobbes and Hume, whose work has been more universal; there have been men also, like Bentham, whose immediate influence has been more profound. But there are few who have better illuminated the tradition of their age, and none whose contribution was more honourable or more nearly stainless. (p. xx)

> *Harold J. Laski, in an introduction to* Autobiography *by John Stuart Mill, Oxford University Press, London, 1924, pp. ix-xx.*

MALCOLM COWLEY (essay date 1939)

[*An American critic, editor, poet, translator, and historian, Cowley has made valuable contributions to contemporary letters with his editions of the works of such American authors as Nathaniel Hawthorne, Walt Whitman, and Ernest Hemingway, his writings as a literary critic for the* New Republic, *and his chronicles and criticism of modern American literature. Acknowledging the importance of Mill's* On Liberty, *Cowley writes that it nevertheless embodies "a false or at least an oversimplified notion of the mechanics of social change." Cowley also suggests that Mill's concept of "Reasoning Man," which later thinkers found limiting, contributed to the decline of his importance.*]

John Stuart Mill's great essay **"On Liberty"** was published in 1859, that is, in the same year as [Darwin's] ''The Origin of Species.'' Since then its influence has been felt in every country that had or hoped to have a middle-class constitutional government. Reading it today, one cannot fail to be impressed by a tone of high conviction that is seldom found in the writing of our own times. One cannot fail to admire the consistency and coherence of its arguments, or to accept its guiding principle, ''That the only purpose for which power can be rightfully exercised over any member of a civilized community, against his will, is to prevent harm to others.'' Indeed, this plea for individual freedom has such a power of persuasion that one cannot help wondering whether harm to others might not be prevented if the officials of every autocratic government were forced, against their wills, to learn whole chapters of the book by heart. At the same time, one feels that its background is pre-Marxian and pre-Darwinian. There is a curious simplicity, not so much in its arguments or conclusions, as in its unspoken assumptions about men in society. (pp. 238-39)

There is, first of all, the assumption that progress is the normal state of affairs, ''that the tendency of things, on the whole, is toward improvement.'' . . .

[A] second assumption was that progress depended wholly on the intellect, and resulted from the ''preponderance among mankind of rational opinions and rational conduct.'' . . .

[A] third assumption . . . [was] that progress was due entirely to individuals. Society was not so much an organism as the arithmetical sum of its members. (p. 239)

A fourth and last assumption concerned the nature of knowledge. Mill believed that those with sufficient aptitude might develop it by cultivating the virtues of humility and open-mindedness. The superior few, of whom he often spoke, were never instinctive or impulsive or intuitive; they never jumped to conclusions. Instead they went about improving themselves and others by looking at all sides of a case, by listening to all the arguments and comparing them, by rejecting the false and accepting the true—''No wise man ever acquired his wisdom in any way but this.''

To readers of our own time, it seems that Mill wrote his great essay on a false or at least an oversimplified notion of the mechanics of social change, of the part played in it by the intellect, of the relation between the individual and society, of the nature of knowledge and the methods by which it is normally acquired. It seems to us, moreover, that behind all his other assumptions lay the picture of an idealized creature that might be called the Reasoning Man. This was not the same as the Economic Man often mentioned in college courses, since all living persons are economic in the sense of being consumers, if not always producers, whereas Mill believed that only one out of a hundred was even comparatively rational. Yet this hundredth person was responsible for the whole of human knowledge and human progress. He was a creature outside of history as we know it; he had no acquired prejudices, no family or class or national loyalties; he was never ruled by animal instincts or sexual neuroses; he performed no reflexive or purely habitual actions. Except for his bondage to reason, he was free. Indeed, he was almost a god, almost the Unmoved Mover of medieval theology, since he contributed everything to society at large while receiving almost nothing in return.

The Reasoning Man was of course an abstraction, yet Mill seems to have believed that such a creature existed in the world about him. He believed, moreover, that this being, this entity, was strong enough to drive barbarism backwards, step by step, using no weapon but the pure force of its reason. He believed that he was himself a Reasoning Man and was writing for an audience composed of other Reasoning Men. He believed in his own impartiality and independence, never stopping to think that much of what he said revealed *unconscious* motivations (the word is of our own day), or was the result of previous *conditioning,* or represented the *attitudes* and *frame of reference* proper to his own *class* of highly trained administrators selected from the British bourgeoisie. In those days the bourgeoisie was triumphant, could see no end to its rule, so reason too was triumphant, and progress, always peaceful, stretched out into the future like the two safe rails of the trunk line from Manchester to London. (p. 240)

. . . . .

The history of thought for the last eighty years might be centered around the attack on the abstract conception of the Reasoning Man as the basis of social philosophy. That attack was a slow and complicated process, and could be described in its details only by someone familiar with all the scientific and historical problems involved in it. (p. 264)

[The result] was the utter destruction of the Reasoning Man. John Stuart Mill had portrayed him as possessing certain attributes: he was rational, he was civilized, he was morally free, he was an individual. Now, one by one, these attributes had been stripped away from him. He was not rational; on the contrary, most of his actions were conditioned reflexes and many of them were the acting out in symbolic forms of suppressed desires; his psychology could best be understood by studying that of animals or children. He was not civilized; on the contrary, his social behavior was full of concealed survivals from barbarism and was capable of reverting at the least excuse to forthright savagery. He was not morally free, except within a limited sphere; on the contrary he was subject to his biological nature, to his physical environment, to his class loyalties, to a whole series of laws the existence of which had not even been suspected in the early nineteenth century. And finally he was not even an individual, in the sense that Mill had used the word, since his life as a human being was inseparable from his social life. Unless he belonged to a community, he was deprived of his human heritage, he was a beast among beasts.

In other words, the Reasoning Man was exactly as real as Milton's angels.... Years ago when I studied zoölogy, my professor used to say that he did not know whether angels existed, but in any case they had six limbs—counting their wings—and therefore could not be mammals. In the same fashion we might say of the Reasoning Man that if he does exist, in some corner of the world, his qualities are different from those of the living men around us; he does not belong to the human species. (p. 265)

> *Malcolm Cowley, "The End of the Reasoning Man" and "The End of the Reasoning Man: II," in* The New Republic, *Vol. C, Nos. 1296 and 1297, October 4 and October 11, 1939, pp. 237-40; 264-67.**

FREDERICK A. von HAYEK (essay date 1942)

[*In this excerpt from his introduction to a collection of Mill's essays, Hayek discusses the impact of foreign writers on Mill's philosophy in the early 1830s, the period when he began to rebel against Jeremy Bentham and utilitarianism. Hayek focuses on the influence of August Comte, the Sainte-Simonians, and the German philosophers as evidenced in Mill's essay "The Spirit of the Age."*]

John Stuart Mill may not have been an original thinker of the very first rank. But he was certainly not, as is now sometimes suggested, merely a late representative of a once powerful school whose thought he summarized at the height of its popular influence. Any suggestion of this sort completely misjudges Mill the mature thinker and confuses him with the boy writer who had been the mere expositor of the ideas of his elders. Mill the man was less than most men the exponent of the views of any school or sect or country. There was little that was typical of anything about the man who has been well described as "an alien among men of his own class in English society" and whose catholicity of mind enabled him to draw from the widest possible range of sources. It would indeed be less unjust to call him an eclectic than to regard him as the representative of any one school. And he is representative of his age only because his rare capacity of absorbing new ideas made him a kind of focus in which most of the significant changes of thought of his time combined. Though he built on the foundation of a strong English tradition, the new structure that he erected upon it added more that derived from foreign than from native sources. In fact, if one may speak of prejudices of so singularly candid a mind, there can be little doubt that Mill had acquired something like prejudice and even contempt not only for English society, which he little knew, but also for contemporary development of English thought and especially of English political economy, which he neglected to a surprising extent.

This character of the mature work of one whose unique education had been designed, and for a period had succeeded, in steeping him exclusively in the doctrines of one school makes the period in which this young but fully trained mind discovered entirely new intellectual worlds an unusually fascinating chapter of biography. The young Mill in the years when he had just broken away from the inherited views and in the enthusiasm of his discoveries went much further than sober reflection would allow him to remain is in many ways a more attractive figure than the zealous sectarian of his early days or the austere and balanced philosopher of mature years. The essay on **"The Spirit of the Age"** derives its peculiar interest from the fact that it shows Mill almost at the height of his reaction against his earlier views. (pp. vi-viii)

[In the essay,] Mill takes from Comte and the Saint-Simonians his leading idea and several details, but he uses them for his own ends. What he takes are characteristic aspects of their philosophy of history which probably appealed to him the more for its obvious resemblance to certain German strands of thought with which he had recently become acquainted. The conception of his age as an age of transition, the central theme of the essay, pervades the whole of the work of the Saint-Simonians. The idea of the "necessary stage in the process of civilisation," the description of the existing "intellectual anarchy," and the discussion of the significance of the "exercise of private judgement," with its emphasis on the different role of private judgment in the natural sciences as compared with the discussion of social problems, are taken straight from Comte. Mill's contrast between the "natural" and the "transitional" states of society is the same as that between the "organic" and "critical" phases of social evolution in the philosophy of Comte and the Saint-Simonians. Obvious also is the influence of the Saint-Simonian discussion of the relations between the spiritual and the temporal powers in the different stages of evolution, which occupies much space in their discussions. But beyond this there is not much resemblance in the detail of the argument, however similar the phraseology. It is significant that, beyond a strong awareness of what in the *Autobiography* Mill was to call "the very limited and temporary value of the old political economy, which assumes private property and inheritance as indefeasible facts, and freedom of production and exchange as the *dernier mot* of social improvement," there is nothing in the essay of the concrete socialist proposals for reform. Mill indeed, while sympathizing with the ultimate aims of socialism, disagreed to the end with the concrete suggestions for the abolition of private property, and particularly never ceased, as he put it in the *Political Economy,* "utterly [to] dissent from the most conspicuous and vehement part of their teaching, their declamations against competition."

His argument leads him to an interesting distinction, which I believe in this form is his own, between "the two states of society, that in which capacity raises men to power, and that in which power calls forth their capacity." From time to time, in ages of transition like his own, it happens, however, that "power and fitness for power have altogether ceased to correspond." The aristocracy is no longer fit to exercise the power which it still possesses, and the crisis can be resolved only by admitting to power the classes which in the new circumstances are best qualified to govern. Thus the argument is made directly to apply to the burning question of the reform of parliamentary representation. (pp. xxvii-xxxi)

Mill himself did not regard the essay on **"The Spirit of the Age"** as part of his mature work.... But the importance of the essay lies not in its style or in any permanent contribution to knowledge but in the light it throws on one of the most interesting phases in the development of a great figure of the past century. As such it deserves to be rescued from the oblivion in which it has rested for over a hundred years. (pp. xxxii-xxxiii)

Frederick A. von Hayek, "John Stuart Mill at the Age of Twenty-Five," in The Spirit of the Age *by John Stuart Mill, The University of Chicago Press, 1942, pp. v-xxxiii.*

F. R. LEAVIS (essay date 1949)

[*Leavis was an influential contemporary English critic. His methodology combines close textual criticism with predominantly moral and social concerns; however, Leavis is not interested in the individual writer per se, but rather with the usefulness of his or her art in the scheme of civilization. Leavis considers Mill's essays on Bentham and Coleridge significant not only for what they convey about those two figures, but also for what they reveal about Mill as a critic. He praises Mill's perceptive style and terms him "a great representative figure in Victorian intellectual history."*]

[The due status of Mill's **'Bentham'** and **'Coleridge'**] as key documents is indisputable. To begin with, the two subjects are the key figures that Mill so convincingly exhibits them as being. (p. 107)

But Bentham and Coleridge are not only, in actual history, the key and complementary powers by reference to which we can organize into significance so much of the field to be charted; even if they had had no great influence they would still have been the classical examples they are of two great opposing types of mind. . . . (pp. 107-08)

And as we follow Mill's analysis, exposition and evaluation of this pair of opposites we are at the same time, we realize, forming a close acquaintance with a mind different from either—the mind that appreciates both and sees them as both necessary. . . . (p. 108)

Mill's is itself, as these essays sufficiently evidence, a very distinguished mind. To read them with close attention is an educative experience. This is true as it is not true, for example, of *Biographica Literaria,* that academic classic which is habitually prescribed for study as an initiating and enlightening document. Mill's essays deserve to be called classical for their intrinsic quality; they are models of method and manner. Coleridge was a genius, but his writings cannot be said to be products of a disciplined mind. Mill's pre-eminently are, and they have an intellectual distinction that is at the same time a distinction of character. And the rigorous training that issues in such apparently easy mastery doesn't mean narrowness or dryness. The desiccating rigours and narrownesses of Mill's own education are, of course, notorious; he describes them himself in the *Autobiography.* But, as the describing shows, he derived from them a kind of profit that had not entered into the intention behind them, so that when he defines Bentham's limitations his phrases represent something more than the 'vague generalities' of vaguely general recognition. . . . [Mill], for all the restrictive rigours of his father's educational experiment shows that he has a sensitive intelligence, informed by introspective subtlety, wide perceptions and a lively historical sense. The pupil of James Mill, and the self-styled Utilitarian, can write the classical appreciation of Coleridge and of the kind of reaction he stands for against that eighteenth century which is

characterized with such admirable trenchancy in the Coleridge essay. . . . (pp. 108-09)

The thinker who could write [the] complementary appreciations of the two great opposites might call himself Utilitarian, and avow that in respect of the philosophical issue he stands with Locke as against the transcendentalists, but he was clearly no unqualified Benthamite. In fact, as we know, he spent his life in a strenuous endeavour, pursued with magnificent integrity, to justify his contention that the Benthams and the Coleridges, 'these two sorts of men, who seem to be, and believe themselves to be, enemies, are in reality allies': the side from which he inevitably worked having been determined by his upbringing, he worked indefatigably to correct and complete Utilitarianism by incorporating into it the measure of truth attained by the other side. And here we come to a third main point, for our purpose, about these essays of Mill's: the essayist is not merely a distinguished mind of a different type from Bentham or Coleridge; he is a great representative figure in Victorian intellectual history, and the essays lead on to the *Autobiography.*

Mill's *Autobiography* is a classic that every cultivated person should have read. . . . It is certainly a main document for us. The account of the young Mill's early training (and the consequent spiritual crisis) for which it is best known—a *locus classicus* of great significance in any case—has itself a direct bearing on the central themes of the essays and what should be central themes in any study of the Victorian age. The account of his intellectual life that forms the body of the book is an immediately relevant piece of Victorian history that, by reason of the contacts and connexions it records, lends itself peculiarly to the business of educing significant organization in the whole complex field. (p. 110)

F. R. Leavis, "Mill, Beatrice Webb and the 'English School': Preface to an Unprinted Volume, in Scrutiny, *Vol. XVI, No. 2, June, 1949, pp. 104-26.**

A. D. LINDSAY (essay date 1950)

[*In this excerpt from his introduction to* Utilitarianism, *Lindsay explores the ways in which Mill both adopted and moderated the utilitarian philosophy he inherited from his father and Jeremy Bentham. According to Lindsay, Mill's most notable modifications are the distinction between pleasure and happiness and the emphasis on liberty.*]

His eclecticism is both the strength and the weakness of Mill's writings—the strength because their very great popularity was largely due to the wideness of their appeal and their evident sympathy with what was best in opposing schools; the weakness because of the inconsistency and lack of real clearness of thought which so often goes with a sympathetic mind. Mill had a very great reverence for his father and for Bentham, and hardly realised how very different was the tenor of his mind from theirs. When he found that he had sympathies which they did not share, he did his best to minimise the differences. Where his reverence and loyalty were not thus engaged, he could admire and yet criticise freely. Comte, for example, exercised a great influence upon him, but Mill was always very conscious of where he and Comte differed. Could he have examined his father's and Bentham's principle as candidly, his own position would have been very differently expressed; but it was not in his nature.

In consequence we find him in all his books enunciating with firmness the Utilitarian principles, then compelled by his fairness and openness of mind to admit exceptions and insert qualifications which the older Utilitarianism, complete but narrow, had never recognised. The resultant picture is much fairer to the facts, but presents much less of a consistent doctrine, and the critical reader is always wondering why, if Mill admits this or that, he persists in maintaining general principles with which the facts admitted are clearly inconsistent. The truth is that Mill's open-mindedness was too large for the system he inherited; his power of system-making too small for him to construct a new one. Had Mill possessed Bentham's saving irreverence, he would have broken away from Benthamism altogether, and tried to construct a system truer to the facts which he recognised. He was both too loyal and too little systematic, and preferred, like many others in a similar case, to make the principles to which he was loyal as elastic as possible, not troubling very much whether he stretched them beyond what they could bear. This procedure had certainly its temporary advantages, as such procedure always has. The open and candid character of Mill's writings won many adherents to the system; but it has had in time a prejudicial effect on Mill's reputation as a philosopher. For there are two ways of interpreting his writings. The first and the more natural is to take him on his own profession as a Utilitarian in the sense in which Bentham and the older Mill were Utilitarians. If we begin in that way, Mill's very open-mindedness works his downfall. For every admission and qualification becomes an excuse to recall him relentlessly to his professed creed, and to make him an unwilling witness to its inadequacy and falsehood. Such a method has its value as a logical exercise and in an examination of the historical development of Hedonism, but it misses the real value of Mill's writings. On the other hand, if we recognise that, just because of his historical position, we cannot look for a complete systematic exposition, we may take his writings rather as pointing the way to a new philosophy than as constituting one in themselves. Philosophy may suffer as much from narrowness as from inconsistency, and it is a great mistake to undervalue those writers who, by their receptive sympathy, ensure that philosophic problems shall be stated as widely and broadly as possible. At the same time, we must not minimise the debt Mill owed to his Utilitarian predecessors or regard his professed adherence to their principles as only a mistake to be regretted. He owed to Bentham and his father a love of clearness and precision, and a distrust of vague generalities and what he called mysticism, which were of great service in his work. In all study of human activity, whether in ethics, politics, or economics, the data with which we have to deal are so manifold and complicated that we are apt either to fix upon principles which shall be clear and simple and allow the facts to shift for themselves—that had been the mistake of Bentham in politics and of the older economists in political economy—or, when we recognise that the facts are too big for these simple theories, to give up principles altogether and take refuge in suggestive but vague words which cloud as much as they reveal, or to advocate an empiricism which shall somehow describe the facts without discerning in them any principles whatsoever. Mill keeps firmly before himself and his readers the double necessity of clear thinking and unprejudiced observation.

Whether he achieved that clearness of thought to which he attached such importance is a question on which opinions vary. Consistency and lucidity can never be far apart, and behind the immediate clearness of Mill's style there often lurks a confusing ambiguity of thought. In this he resembles his great predecessor Locke. Locke had the same openness of mind, the same unprejudiced willingness to admit facts. Both achieved popularity by the apparent ease of their writing, and both have suffered from the same repeated charges of inconsistency. . . . [Their] desire for precision and their dread of anything that savoured of intuition made them reluctant to follow up the full consequences of their admissions. Locke seems the simplest of writers in a cursory reading: try to work out the implications of his thought, insist that he shall always mean the same thing by the same words, and you find his system riddled with ambiguities. It is the same with Mill. The truth is that, while words which Mill disliked, such as organism and intuition, may in some cases cover confused and cloudy thinking, they need not do so, and without these conceptions no true view of society or of knowledge is possible. We constantly find Mill being led by the facts towards an organic view of society and then pulling himself back lest he should fall into ambiguity. The only way of escape was to go right on and think out a conception of society which should be clear because really philosophic. That he never achieved though he pointed the way.

These characteristics of Mill's writings are illustrated nowhere better than in the short treatise on Utilitarianism. It was published later than *Liberty,* but, as its scope is wider, a general sketch of Utilitarianism as a system, it deserves prior consideration. In the chapter on the meaning of Utilitarianism, Mill begins by a statement of what was practically the position of Bentham. ''The creed which accepts as the foundation of morals utility, or the greatest happiness principle, holds that actions are right in proportion as they tend to promote happiness, wrong as they tend to produce the reverse of happiness. By happiness is intended pleasure and the absence of pain: by unhappiness, pain and the privation of pleasure.'' To the first part of this statement Mill adheres throughout, and it is the main principle which this treatise advocates; but to the second he appends so many qualifications and exceptions that its presence is only confusing. For Bentham the second part was all-important. For his system was founded on a psychological assumption, as simple as it is unwarrantable, that pleasure or relief from pain is the sole possible object of desire or will. That implies that there is no sense in saying that you *ought* to desire pleasure. Every one, as a matter of psychological necessity, acts in that way which he thinks will give him most pleasure. This is the essential fact of human nature, the inherent selfishness of mankind, with which the legislator must reckon. To this was added the all-important assumption that pleasure is calculable: that there is meaning in talking of a sum or calculus of pleasures. That involves that all pleasure is qualitatively the same, for pleasures of different qualities cannot be summed. Pleasure, therefore, is an object of desire, which can be regarded in complete abstraction from the objects which produce it (pushpin is as good as poetry) and from those who feel it (each to count as one and no one to count as more than one). It is not too much to say that all those assumptions are clearly untrue. For desire is not for pleasure but for objects. We only feel pleasure when we get what we want. We must therefore want something first. That in its turn involves that we cannot separate pleasure from the objects which produce it. Only a crude psychology could suppose that pleasures were statable in ''amounts'' of each other. There is no meaning in talking of two sums of pleasure being the same, although the pleasures making up the two sums are entirely different. There is as little in assuming that the pleasures of different persons can be quantitatively compared: that we can regard society as an aggregate of individuals each of whom the wise and successful legislator would see to possess or enjoy an equal *lot* of pleasure. Now none of these three assumptions are really essential to John Stuart Mill's position. The second he explicitly denies in his well-known statement of the qualitative distinction of pleasures, which immediately follows the preliminary definition we have quoted. The third is denied in the statement, . . . "Better to be Socrates dissatisfied than a fool satisfied." The first is thrown over in Mill's statement of the paradox of Hedonism that, "the conscious ability to do without happiness gives the best prospect of realising such happiness as is attainable." . . . Within thirteen pages there is nothing left of the main principles of Benthamism. For the calculus of pleasures and self-interest are the very essence of Bentham's Utilitarianism. His is a philosophy for the legislator who is to deal with men as units capable equally of pleasure, which he, the legislator, is to put within their grasp. If the law is to be impartial, it cannot afford to deal with fine shades of qualitative difference. Its only concern is to ask whether each individual has the chance of an equal amount of pleasure; of what kind his pleasures may be is not the law's concern, provided always that the enjoyment of them does not interfere with other people. This determined narrowness and heroic simplification of the problem was a strength in a system whose object was mainly to destroy "sinister interests" and to remedy abuses. When it had to face the problem of construction its weaknesses were more apparent, and . . . John Stuart Mill came at a time when the destructive work was mainly done, and the difficulties of constructive work were beginning to reveal themselves.

If Benthamism then is given up, what is left, or what has taken its place? This will best be seen if we examine more closely Mill's qualification of pleasures and his treatment of the relation of the individual's pleasure to that of other people. Pleasures, Mill asserts, are so different in kind that any question of quantity may be disregarded. "A being of higher faculties requires more to make him happy, is capable probably of more acute suffering, and is certainly accessible to it at more points than one of an inferior type; but in spite of these liabilities, he can never really wish to sink into what he feels to be a lower grade of existence." Pleasure, then, as such, is not the good; men do not as a matter of fact simply desire pleasure. The motive that determines them to seek one pleasure rather than another is not statable in amounts of pleasure. A man will be happier in one way with less pleasure than he would be in another way with more. This is asserting a distinction between happiness and pleasure. (pp. viii-xiv)

His treatment of the problem of the relation of the happiness of the individual to the happiness of other people has the same features. He gives up Bentham's notion of the happiness of society being built up of the irremediably selfish interests of the individuals who compose it, a paradoxical combination of an unshaken optimism as regards social law, and a most pessimistic view of individual character. He admits that in the imperfect state of the world the happiness of others may best be served by the absolute sacrifice of the happiness of the individual. Instead of looking forward cheerfully to every one being selfish, he insists that the power of doing without happiness is a necessary social virtue. But that involves the existence of motives quite other than the universal desire for pleasure which Bentham postulated. This Mill freely admits, and, except in the grotesque argument at the beginning of chapter iv., bases his Utilitarianism on social motives. The firm foundation of the Utilitarian morality is, he says, "the social feelings of mankind: the desire to be in unity with our fellow creatures." "The social state," he says, "is at once so natural, so necessary, and so habitual to man, that, except in some unusual circumstances or by an effort of voluntary abstraction, he never conceives himself otherwise than as a member of a body." This doctrine that man is by nature a social being means that society cannot be regarded as an aggregate of individuals, moved only by self-seeking motives. It involves an organic view of society. Here again Mill's real thought seems to point to profounder principles than he will himself recognise. His nominal adherence to his inherited system makes him obscure those principles by his use of the doctrine of sanctions, a doctrine only in place in a Hedonistic system, and the abstract distinction between motive and intention, and patch up any incoherence by the theory of indissoluble association, that mysterious maid-of-all-work of Utilitarianism. But these are excrescences. His real teaching has little to do with the mechanism of sanctions or association.

The force of Mill's doctrine is understood best in contrast with the theories to which he was most opposed. Throughout the *Utilitarianism* he refers to the intuitive school as providing to his own position an alternative which is clearly wrong. It is the great merit of Mill's work that he insists on those elements in morality of which intuitionism is unappreciative. He has no mercy for that way of thinking which prefers to leave things uncriticised, and does so by calling them mysteries. Utilitarianism for him is primarily an insistence that all moral acts shall conduce to one end, and that an end recognised and attainable in life. A great deal of his argument is really a contention on behalf of reason, a demand that all human life should be seen as having a rational purpose, a demand inspired by an optimistic conviction that the clear recognition of that purpose is a long step towards its attainment. Yet Mill does not make the mistake of supposing that you may demand a reason for everything. That ultimate principles cannot be proved he asserts as strongly as any intuitionist, but contends at the same time that this does not mean that they are unintelligible and cannot be reflected upon. He is able to conceive of the moral life as a slow growth, as having its origin in something that would not be recognised as distinctively moral, and yet to see that the absolute validity of moral laws is in no way affected by their history. He is afraid of an *à priori* which would do without experience or an intuition which would save the trouble of thinking; but his own position, if its implications are properly understood, affirms a moral experience involving ultimate principles for which in the end he claims intuitive assent. No rationalist system of morals can afford to ignore the importance of the empirical element in ethics, so well brought out in his analysis of conscience or his admirable account of justice in the last chapter.

That last chapter ends with the assertion of a principle of much importance for Mill's political doctrine. The belief that utility is the ultimate standard of all value is quite compatible with holding that there are "certain social utilities which are vastly more important and therefore more absolute and imperative than any others are as a class (though not more so than others may be in particular instances), and which, therefore, ought to be, as well as naturally are, guarded by a sentiment not only different in degree but in kind." The greatest of these in Mill's eyes was liberty. While Utilitarianism seems to demand that everything ought to yield to the demands of social happiness and that we can lay down no absolute principles as to what constitutes that happiness, but must follow the guidings of experience, his treatise on Liberty is an eloquent assertion of one principle which is so truly the foundation of all social happiness that any experiment which encroaches on it is foredoomed. (pp. xv-xviii)

A. D. Lindsay, in an introduction to Utilitarianism, Liberty, and Representative Government *by John*

Stuart Mill, E. P. Dutton and Company, Inc., 1950, pp. vii-xxix.

M. H. ABRAMS (essay date 1953)

[*Abrams is an American critic best known for his writings on English Romanticism. In* The Mirror and the Lamp: Romantic Theory and the Critical Tradition, *from which the following excerpt is drawn, he elaborates on the images of "the mirror" as a metaphor for the classical conception that art must imitate reality and "the lamp" as representative of the Romantic belief that artists should express personal perceptions through their creations. Using these symbols, Abrams traces the development of Romantic critical theory. Here, Abrams briefly outlines Mill's theory of poetry, discussing it in the context of expressive philosophies of literature.*]

[Whatever] Mill's empirical pretensions, his initial assumption about the essential nature of poetry remains continuously though silently effective in selecting, interpreting, and ordering the facts to be explained.

The primitive proposition of Mill's theory is: Poetry is 'the expression or uttering forth of feeling.' Exploration of the data of aesthetics from this starting point leads, among other things, to the following drastic alterations in the great commonplaces of the critical tradition:

(1) *The poetic kinds.* Mill reinterprets and inverts the neo-classic ranking of the poetic kinds. As the purest expression of feeling, lyric poetry is 'more eminently and peculiarly poetry than any other . . .' Other forms are all alloyed by non-poetic elements, whether descriptive, didactic, or narrative, which serve merely as convenient occasions for the poetic utterances of feeling either by the poet or by one of his invented characters. To Aristotle, tragedy had been the highest form of poetry, and the plot, representing the action being imitated, had been its 'soul'; while most neo-classic critics had agreed that, whether judged by greatness of subject matter or of effect, epic and tragedy are the king and queen of poetic forms. It serves as an index to the revolution in critical norms to notice that to Mill, plot becomes a kind of necessary evil. An epic poem 'in so far as it is epic (i.e. narrative) . . . is not poetry at all,' but only a suitable frame for the greatest diversity of genuinely poetic passages; while the interest in plot and story 'merely as a story' characterizes rude stages of society, children, and the 'shallowest and emptiest' of civilized adults. Similarly with the other arts; in music, painting, sculpture, and architecture Mill distinguishes between that which is 'simple imitation or description' and that which 'expresses human feeling' and is, therefore, poetry.

(2) *Spontaneity as criterion.* Mill accepts the venerable assumption that a man's emotional susceptibility is innate, but his knowledge and skill—his art—are acquired. On this basis, he distinguishes poets into two classes: poets who are born and poets who are made, or those who are poets 'by nature,' and those who are poets 'by culture.' Natural poetry is identifiable because it 'is Feeling itself, employing Thought only as the medium of its utterance'; on the other hand, the poetry of 'a cultivated but not naturally poetic mind,' is written with 'a distinct aim,' and in it the thought remains the conspicuous object, however surrounded by 'a halo of feeling.' Natural poetry, it turns out, is 'poetry in a far higher sense, than any other; since . . . that which constitutes poetry, human feeling, enters far more largely into this than into the poetry of culture.' Among the moderns, Shelley represents the poet born and

Wordsworth the poet made; and with unconscious irony Mill turns Wordsworth's own criterion, 'the spontaneous overflow of feeling,' against its sponsor. Wordsworth's poetry 'has little even of the appearance of spontaneousness: the well is never so full that it overflows.'

(3) *The external world.* In so far as a literary product simply imitates objects, it is not poetry at all. As a result, reference of poetry to the external universe disappears from Mill's theory, except to the extent that sensible objects may serve as a stimulus or 'occasion for the generation of poetry,' and then, 'the poetry is not in the object itself,' but 'in the state of mind' in which it is contemplated. When a poet describes a lion he 'is describing the lion professedly, but the state of excitement of the spectator really,' and the poetry must be true not to the object, but to 'the human emotion.' Thus severed from the external world, the objects signified by a poem tend to be regarded as no more than a projected equivalent—an extended and articulated symbol—for the poet's inner state of mind. Poetry, said Mill, in a phrasing which anticipates T. E. Hulme and lays the theoretical groundwork for the practice of symbolists from Baudelaire through T. S. Eliot, embodies 'itself in symbols, which are the nearest possible representations of the feeling in the exact shape in which it exists in the poet's mind.' Tennyson, Mill wrote in a review of that poet's early poems, excels in 'scene-painting, in the higher sense of the term'; and this is

> not the mere power of producing that rather vapid species of composition usually termed descriptive poetry . . . but the power of *creating* scenery, in keeping with some state of human feeling; so fitted to it as to be the embodied symbol of it, and to summon up the state of feeling itself, with a force not to be surpassed by anything but reality.

And as an indication of the degree to which the innovations of the romantics persist as the commonplaces of modern critics—even of those who purport to found their theory on anti-romantic principles—notice how striking is the parallel between the passage above and a famous comment by T. S. Eliot:

> The only way of expressing emotion in the form of art is by finding an 'objective correlative'; in other words, a set of objects, a situation, a chain of events which shall be the formula of that *particular* emotion; such that when the external facts, which must terminate in sensory experience, are given, the emotion is immediately evoked.

(4) *The audience.* No less drastic is the fate of the audience. According to Mill, 'Poetry is feeling, confessing itself to itself in moments of solitude . . .' The poet's audience is reduced to a single member, consisting of the poet himself. 'All poetry,' as Mill puts it, 'is of the nature of soliloquy.' The purpose of producing effects upon other men, which for centuries had been the defining character of the art of poetry, now serves precisely the opposite function: it disqualifies a poem by proving it to be rhetoric instead. When the poet's

> act of utterance is not itself the end, but a means to an end—viz. by the feelings he himself expresses, to work upon the feelings, or upon the belief, or the will, of another,—when the expression of his emotions . . . is tinged also by that purpose, by that desire of making an

impression upon another mind, then it ceases
to be poetry, and becomes eloquence.

(pp. 23-5)

*M. H. Abrams, "Introduction: Orientation of Crit-
ical Theories," in his* The Mirror and the Lamp:
Romantic Theory and the Critical Tradition, *1953.
Reprint by Oxford University Press, 1971, pp. 3-29.**

CURRIN V. SHIELDS (essay date 1956)

[*In his introduction to* On Liberty, *which he terms "a parcel of
logical difficulties," Shields evaluates Mill's effort to resolve the
problem of preserving personal freedom while condoning governmental action for safeguarding society. He then examines Mill's
theory that individual liberty will lead to social progress, concluding that it, too, is an inadequate guide to practical government.*]

It has been said that political theories are of two sorts: some
are logical, others are useful. To accommodate Mill's theory
of liberty, a third category must be added.

The argument of the essay in its separate parts seems rather
clear, but the argument as a whole is far from clear. In fact,
Mill's theory is a parcel of logical difficulties. These chiefly
result from confusion on Mill's part about his purpose, or
purposes, in the essay. Mill often leaves an impression that he
is discussing one issue, when actually he is discussing, in a
misleading way, an entirely different issue. This confusion is
enhanced by Mill's failure to draw with precision and maintain
with consistency three crucial distinctions he at least tacitly
assumes: (1) between thought and action; (2) between social
convention and governmental control; and (3) between self-
regarding and other-regarding conduct.

On Liberty has been praised as a classic statement of the case
for individual liberty from governmental control. Such praise
misses the mark. Mill does caution against certain *excesses* of
governmental intervention in private affairs, and does plead
for what he calls "individuality." But the sort of liberty that
Mill is anxious to preserve does not directly concern government. His plea is definitely not an injunction against governmental control over individual action where other members of
society have an interest. In fact, in the last chapters of his
essay, Mill advances a cogent argument for governmental intervention in individual affairs. Using the principle Mill en-
dorses, most any governmental restraint on individual conduct
can be readily justified.

The impression that Mill is advocating liberty from governmental control is given in part by his remarks about freedom
of thought. Much of Mill's argument in defense of liberty
pertains only to freedom of thought and is not relevant to any
relation between individual action and governmental authority.
Mill contends that freedom of thought is socially valuable in
searching out truth and in cultivating the mental and moral
character of the individual, thus fostering social progress. It is
Mill's phrase "the expression of opinion" which obscures the
difficulty. What a person thinks has no social consequences,
unless he expresses his opinion. The expression of an opinion
is for Mill an action which may affect other members of society.
On the question of limiting liberty of opinion, Mill's argument
about freedom of individual action has direct bearing. This is
significant because Mill's principal concern in the essay is
about human conduct in society.

On the matter of freedom of opinion, Mill's plea is directed
against interference by "the collective authority of public opinion" in the affairs of individuals which are of no interest to
the other members of society. (pp. xix-xx)

In the essay Mill's purpose in part is, then, to show the social
value which accrues from the full and rich cultivation of individual characters. In behalf of this purpose Mill argues that
in developing his mental and moral nature an individual should
not be restrained by social conventions. Mill advocates the
greatest possible amount of individual liberty from collective
authority—compatible with living in a society.

This suggests another difficulty in Mill's theory. It was Mill's
purpose, again in part, to promote the acceptance of a moral
principle which could, he believed, satisfactorily guide the
conduct of members of society. Mill's position is that an individual should be free to act, provided his actions adversely
affect no one else. He argues that an individual should not be
interfered with when other members of society have no interest
in his conduct. This sort of conduct Mill calls "self-regarding." But Mill is not particularly concerned about conduct
which does not affect other people, since it involves no problem
of social ethics. Mill holds the position that society has jurisdiction over conduct where the members of society have an
interest. To protect the general interest, he argues, society is
entitled to intervene in what he calls "other-regarding" conduct. (pp. xxi-xxii)

The problem of social ethics for Mill was to separate the legitimate sphere of individual liberty from that of collective
authority. The key to Mill's solution is "social progress." Mill
does not value the freedom of other-regarding conduct as an
end in itself. He stresses the value of liberty and urges its
recognition, but he makes no claim that any liberty is absolute.
Individual freedom is justified, according to Mill, by a contribution to the general interest. Liberty is a valuable means to
the more highly valued end of progress, in which every member
of society has an interest. Mill believed that his principle supplies a practical criterion for distinguishing those actions which
advance progress from those which hamper it. The former
actions should be encouraged in practice, while the latter could
be restrained. Thus Mill believed he solved the problem of the
relation between liberty and authority.

In his belief about the practicality of his "very simple principle," Mill was plainly mistaken. Implicit in his formulation
of the problem is a practical question: Who should decide which
actions are contrary to the general interest and should be restrained? This question Mill never really answers. He does say
that the individual has jurisdiction over his "self-regarding"
conduct, while society has jurisdiction over "other-regarding"
conduct. But this is no help, because the problem in practice
is to determine which actions adversely affect other people.
When persons disagree about this, who should make the binding decision? The individual? Or society? Mill gives no forthright answer to this question; he shrinks from the two logical
alternatives his theory implies. Mill cannot accept the view
that the individual should decide because he believes that few
people are capable of making reasoned decisions. The alternative, that society should decide, Mill finds unpalatable, too;
after all, part of his message is to caution against the tyranny
of common opinion. What Mill tacitly assumes, apparently, is
that "reason" can reveal to an exceptional few the correct
answer. But doubts about this assumption are suggested by the
inability of the "saint of rationalism" himself to decide whether
or not certain individual actions should be restrained in the

general interest. As a practical matter, Mill's principle offers no guidance whatsoever in determining the morality of "other-regarding" conduct. (pp. xxii-xxiii)

> *Currin V. Shields, in an introduction to* On Liberty *by John Stuart Mill, edited by Currin V. Shields, The Bobbs-Merrill Company, Inc., 1956, pp. vii-xxvi.*

BERTRAND RUSSELL (essay date 1956)

[*Russell was an English philosopher and fiction writer who won the Nobel Prize for literature in 1950; he was also Mill's godson. In this excerpt, he assesses Mill's importance as a philosopher, pointing out his strengths and weaknesses and asserting that Mill's "intellectual integrity was impeccable."*]

It it not easy to assess the importance of John Stuart Mill in nineteenth-century England. What he achieved depended more upon his moral elevation and his just estimate of the ends of life than upon any purely intellectual merits.

His influence in politics and in forming opinion on moral issues was very great and, to my mind, wholly good. Like other eminent Victorians he combined intellectual distinction with a very admirable character. This intellectual distinction gave weight to his opinions, and was thought at the time to be greater than it appears in retrospect. There are various modern trends which are adverse also to his ethical and moral theories, but in these respects I cannot feel that the world has made any advance since his day.

Intellectually, he was unfortunate in the date of his birth. His predecessors were pioneers in one direction and his successors in another. The substructure of his opinions remained always that which had been laid down for him in youth by the dominating personality of his father, but the theories which he built upon this substructure were very largely such as it could not support. (p. 122)

Mill's first important book was his *Logic,* which no doubt presented itself in his mind as a plea for experimental rather than a priori methods, and, as such, it was useful though not very original. . . . Everything that Mill has to say in his *Logic* about matters other than inductive inference is perfunctory and conventional. (p. 123)

Mill, although he knew a certain amount of mathematics, never learned to think in a mathematical way. His law of causation is not one which is employed in mathematical physics. It is a practical maxim employed by savages and philosophers in the conduct of daily life, but not employed in physics by anyone acquainted with the calculus. The laws of physics never state, as Mill's causal laws do, that A is always followed by B. They assert only that when A is present, there will be certain directions of change; since A also changes, the directions of change are themselves continually changing. The notion that causal laws are of the form "A causes B" is altogether too atomic, and could never have been entertained by anybody who had imaginatively apprehended the continuity of change. (p. 125)

Apart from the pronouncements on Socialism and Communism, Mill's *Political Economy* is not important. Its main principles are derived from his orthodox predecessors with only minor modifications. Ricardo's theory of value, with which on the whole he is in agreement, was superseded by Jevon's introduction of the concept of marginal utility, which represented an important theoretical improvement. As in his *Logic,*

Mill is too ready to acquiesce in a traditional doctrine provided he is not aware of any practical evil resulting from it.

Much more important than Mill's longer treatises were his two short books *On the Subjection of Women* and *On Liberty.* In regard to the first of these, the world has gone completely as he would have wished. In regard to the second, there has been an exactly opposite movement. (p. 131)

Mill deserved the eminence which he enjoyed in his own day, not by his intellect but by his intellectual virtues. He was not a great philosopher, like Descartes or Hume. In the realm of philosophy, he derived his ideas from Hume and Bentham and his father. But he blended the harshness of the Philosophical Radicals with something of the Romantic Movement, derived first from Coleridge and Carlyle and then from his wife. What he took over, he made rational in assimilating it. The follies and violences of some Romantics made no impression upon him. His intellectual integrity was impeccable. When he engaged in controversy, he did so with the most minutely scrupulous fairness. The people against whom his controversies were directed deserved almost always the urbanely worded strictures which he passed upon them.

In spite of his purely intellectual deficiencies, his influence was very great and very beneficent. He made rationalism and Socialism respectable, though his Socialism was of the pre-Marxist sort which did not involve an increase in the powers of the State. His advocacy of equality for women in the end won almost world-wide acceptance. His book *On Liberty* remains a classic: although it is easy to point out theoretical defects, its value increases as the world travels farther and farther from his teaching. The present world would both astonish and horrify him; but it would be better than it is, if his ethical principles were more respected. (pp. 143-44)

This Max Beerbohm cartoon depicts John Morley (center) introducing Mill (r.) to Dante Gabriel Rossetti (l.) in 1869.

Bertrand Russell, "John Stuart Mill," in his Portraits from Memory and Other Essays, *Simon & Schuster*, 1956, pp. 122-44.

NOEL ANNAN   (essay date 1964)

[*Annan explains why a student of English literature should study Mill. Discussing Mill as a social philosopher, Annan faults the "feebleness and timidity" and the lack of originality of his theories. Yet, he maintains that Mill contributed greatly to the theory of rationalism and singles out truth, intellectual freedom, and the idea of an intellectual elite as Mill's seminal concepts.*]

Why should those who love and study English literature read Mill? It is not quite enough to say that everyone who is moved by Victorian poetry and novels and who tries to criticize them should enlarge his understanding of the age by becoming acquainted with its philosophers. It is not even enough to point out that literature is concerned among other things with morality and society, and that Mill . . . wrote about both. But what did he write that compels a critic or a student to study him? (p. 219)

His writings, in particular *The System of Logic* during the fifties and sixties, captured the minds of a strong minority among the young men of those decades, and when he died one of them canonized him as the 'saint of rationalism'. But does the saint still work miracles? His treatise on logic, the great counterblast against Whewell's intuitionism, was less revolutionary than it seemed at first sight. . . . His inquiry into the methods of the natural sciences was certainly more original once he had set aside his argument about causation and had seen that tests, prediction and probability theory were the important concepts in the logic of the natural sciences. But the greater part of his work was connected with the social sciences, and here he added little. His *Political Economy* ran into many editions, but it made no contribution of importance to any part of economics. He did not appreciate the part that mathematics or statistics were to play in economics or in social inquiry. In common with most contemporary social philosophers, including Marx, he thought his task to be the discovery of the laws that governed human behaviour and the progress of society. He admitted that, in order to be significant, *a priori* deductions from abstract principles must be checked against empirical data obtained by observing history. But he realized neither how detailed and statistical such observations had to be if they related to the present, nor how boldly and powerfully they had to be analysed if they were extracted from the past. His *a priori* studies derived, as we have seen, from the positivist theory that all social events are ultimately the product of human motives, and the analysis that he made of history was feeble in comparison with that of Marx, Hegel or even the utopian socialists or Comte.

There is indeed a feebleness and timidity in Mill. He has not the same courage as his predecessors in the positivist tradition. He has not their assurance that even when they were criticizing the tradition in which they worked they were enhancing it. Nor has he their political confidence that reforms which were to give reality to popular rights, such as the right to vote, would not destroy order and prosperity. . . . Although Mill was often trying to see through the formulae of radicalism to discover what would make government not more democratic but better, and although he deplored individuals pursuing their own personal or class interests, he never understood the play of social forces. If his essays had been really searching criticisms of the styles of life in his times, surely one of them would have been concerned with urbanization and industrialization and their ap-

palling problems? He applied Tocqueville's analysis of democracy in America to England, oblivious for the instant of the immense strength of aristocratic and upper-middle-class power. He could not imagine that for the next hundred years the intellectual minority, which he was so concerned to protect, was in danger not of being stifled by the masses but of being gelded by the upper classes.

Imagination! *That* has never been the quality that comes first to mind when one reads the rationalist philosophers. There is no need to tell again the failings of the middle-class liberal thinkers. They did not understand that their political reforms would in practice have the effect of transferring power from an aristocracy to a plutocracy. They ignored the destruction by the cash nexus of whatever gains had been made by political action in achieving equality. Their non-historical and dehumanized creed could not take account of the new historiography of dynamic history and daemonic man. Their reform programme of mechanized devices and governmental adjustments was inadequate to meet the new formulations of power politics and revolution. Finally, in psychology they neglected the startling notion of the Unconscious whether it operated in individuals or in the mass. Beside the German Idealists or the utopian socialists, or the Marxists or the historians, Mill seems deplorably unoriginal and uninventive, staid and sedate. He seems to be fiddling with small methodological points or constitutional and financial reforms. (pp. 227-29)

[Mill] was a social philosopher—which is something more and something less than a critic of culture. His flat undistinguished tone of voice was quite distinct from the peculiar powers of persuasion that the Victorian sages exercised. Arnold quite rightly claimed for the critic an autonomous mode of discourse. He was for ever wringing his hands at his own lack of erudition, his deplorable incompetence in abstract argument, his inability to be precise or to be a good party man or to grasp the principles of science or theology; and we know, of course, as his good humour bubbles over, that he is delighted to have imposed upon his readers a style of thinking that does not rely for its power on erudition, scientific principle, precision or orthodoxy. So much so that when F. H. Bradley used the techniques of philosophy to dissect Arnold's concepts, we feel that, despite his shrewd blows, he was not moving on the same plane and the brilliant exhibition leaves Arnold untouched. Just so with Mill. The philosopher and political reformer does not have to be a critic of culture. On that score he is immeasurably inferior to Arnold and even to Carlyle. But, in representing the strain of rationalism, he made several notable contributions to the culture of his own times that still echo in ours. (p. 231)

[Of Mill's social theory,] three notions ought to live for the critic and student of literature: Mill's call to truth, his passion for intellectual freedom and his belief in the clerisy.

Truth for Mill was almost a tangible entity. You feel that for him it was composed of hard, gritty particles which needed to be poured into a centrifuge in order to be redistributed correctly. (pp. 232-33)

Mill's insistence on the sacredness of truth had the force of a religious commandment; and it had an immense influence not only upon his rationalist followers but throughout the Victorian clerisy. It forced people to consider the grounds for their beliefs, it compelled them to give reasons for these beliefs where formerly they had not needed to do so, it put a premium upon intellectual honesty and scrupulousness. A literary critic may object that Mill's criteria for establishing truth are excessively scientific; and his criteria, no less than those of Arnold, have of course dated. So, perhaps, has Mill's hunger for truth. There are in every academic discipline or activity in life today innumerable accommodations that enable men to treat other qualities such as goodness or scepticism as more important. But during the nineteenth century the notion that truth was tangible and in some degree, however small, attainable was an element in culture. (pp. 233-34)

The essay *On Liberty* . . . is often referred to as a classic defence of individual freedom, yet very few of its arguments stand up to criticism. Only one of them is utilitarian, the others are assertions that a man must always be responsible to himself for his actions—which is a religious notion. Time and again we can think of instances which contradict Mill's reasons—for instance, those who care most deeply about the truth are often those most ardent in suppressing it, because they mistakenly believe that they, and they alone, have attained it. Time and again, to justify freedom today, we would use arguments that Mill would have disliked, such as the argument that good ends conflict, or that diversity of opinions and of moral standards are good in themselves. Time and again we have seen political situations arise that justify the suppression of certain freedoms that Mill thought should never be suppressed. Mill did not appreciate how greatly social factors determined freedom: how freedom in Britain, for instance, rested on the supremacy of the mid-Victorian Royal Navy, and the absence of any internal subversive movement willing to aid an external enemy.

And yet Mill's essay continues to exist as a monument to belief in intellectual liberty. It is a solemn reminder how important it is to keep alive the idea of *negative* liberty, that is to say the right to allow people to go their own way even if it is to hell. For although Mill thought that it was of importance not only what men do but what manner of men they are that do it, he also thought that individual spontaneity had a value in itself and he was not prepared to coerce men to realize their better selves. The Essay burnt itself into the conciousness of each succeeding generation of liberals: whatever else they discarded from mid-Victorian radicalism, they retained the Essay—it troubled the conscience of converted Marxists and mellowed the convictions of British socialists. Its spirit was one of the challenges to the prudery and podsnappery that Thackeray complained hamstrung the novel in England. It still provides some of the standard arguments against censorship and the burning of books, because it insists that the onus of proving that a book or some poisonous opinions will cause irreparable social harm must fall on the prosecution. (pp. 234-35)

Mill's third contribution to culture was his notion of an intellectual élite, which he developed from Coleridge's woolly concept of a national clerisy. (p. 236)

There have always been many ready to analyse and reform social evils: if they do not share Mill's faith in the perfectibility of man in its pristine form, they act as if it might be true. Indeed a double portion of his spirit falls on a few, they inherit Mill's moral temperament and, in a new form, his religion of humanity. . . . But the student of literature, as he reflects on the writers of importance during the past hundred years, will come to a melancholy conclusion. They have loathed and rejected Mill's vision of life. Whether it is Tolstoy or Dostoievsky, Flaubert or Proust, Yeats or Joyce, Nietzsche or Rilke, Henry James, Lawrence or T. S. Eliot, none has any love for this abstract description of human behaviour and prediction of moral and material improvement. The only novel of any merit

I know which realizes in fictive form some of Mill's emotion is Gorki's *A Confession:* the only outstanding figure whose criticism of progressive humanitarianism shows how much of it an artist in the liberal tradition has to reject is Forster. Nor has the gospel of progress gripped any writer of importance today.

There are many reasons, some of them highly complex, why this should be so. Perhaps something not entirely pleasant, which artists are quick to sense, emanates from high-minded and dedicated human beings such as Mill. . . . There is a censorious, waspish tone of voice, a lack of sympathy and humour, a contempt for living foolish human beings (as distinct from humanity), an inability to see people except as material to be moulded and exploited, a mind which, if at first open to arguments and facts, closes like a rat-trap once it has digested them—a temperament which in fact is at variance with their creed. . . . Creative writers, moreover, may also recognize in the social scientists' description of human behaviour something that is a genuine challenge to their art. In Mill's time the method was still crude, but with the revolution in sociology at the beginning of this century their description of human behaviour is more penetrating. As sociologists no longer tried to discover grandiloquent social laws in the style of Mill or Marx, and as they explored how family, class, age-group, occupation and a maze of other social institutions conditioned human behaviour and moulded the morality of society, so a new and no less inimical way of depersonalizing life and discarding the living individual in favour of the group acquired prestige. Yet although sociology abstracts and categorizes life, it also sometimes brings to life the way in which living people describe their style of life and the institutions through which they live. . . . Whereas once artists were confident that their vision of life was a whole vision which did not have to break up life into a spectrum as the social scientist did, now their vision is partly focussed by the findings of the social scientists: the Coleridge of today is panting after Bentham. One thing only is certain. We know little about the relation of art to society and practically nothing about the reasons why it flourishes or declines. Dogmatic assertions about the superiority of 'organic' communities are as fanciful as the sketches that Mill's contemporaries made of the Middle Ages. If we see in Mill the ominous portent of a method of looking at society which at the moment coincides with a decline in the arts, we must admit that this method seems the most likely to explain why this decline has occurred. (pp. 238-39)

Noel Annan, "John Stuart Mill," in The English Mind: Studies in the English Moralists Presented to Basil Whilley, *edited by Hugh Sykes Davies and George Watson, Cambridge at the University Press, 1964, pp. 219-39.*

A.O.J. COCKSHUT   (essay date 1964)

[*Cockshut is considered a major critic of Victorian literature. In this analysis of Mill's writings on religion, particularly in the essay "Theism," Cockshut explores the discrepancy between Mill's emotional disposition and his "bleak rationalism," which resulted from the contradictory influences of Benthamism and Christianity. Tracing Mill's shifting stance, Cockshut warns against the danger of oversimplifying his philosophy of religion.*]

Mill is fascinating because almost every crux and conflict in the agnostic thought of his time can be tracked down somewhere in his work, and because of his fine powers of reasoning. It is especially fascinating to follow the long, unfinished battle conducted in his mind and spirit by two traditions, the tradition of Bentham and the tradition of Christianity. And this contest acquires a particular interest from the fact that the normal order of these two great influences was reversed. The modern utilitarian fairy brooded over his infancy and the ancient influence of Christianity, forgotten by his father, haunted his manhood.

But Mill's work, in his time as to-day, was admired more than it was enjoyed; a sentence of Mill has no overtones, and at first sight it may seem that his work has no emotional content at all. But I hope to show that this impression is mistaken. Whatever may be the truth about that, it is certainly depressing to find that in one of his most Wordsworthian passages, horses are called quadrupeds. And this heaviness of language is by common consent characteristic of all his writings. (p. 19)

The coolness, the almost dispiriting lucidity of Mill's writings in detail is like the deliberate gentleness of Hercules. The unconscious humour, as in [his] comparison of Harriet Taylor to Shelley, springs, as often as not, from a heroic determination to explain a feeling of deep and nervous reverence in terms appropriate to a follower of Bentham and to his father's son. Take, for instance, his comment on the structure of the human body from his essay on *Theism:* "The human body, for example, is one of the most striking instances of artful and ingenious contrivance which nature offers, but we may well ask whether so complicated a machine could not have been made to last longer, and not to get so frequently out of order."

This passage was written apparently, between 1868 and 1870, near the end of Mill's life. It is not only funny, it is extraordinarily old-fashioned. It sounds like an attempt to answer Paley. If we had this passage on its own, and knew its date but not its author, we might surmise that he was culpably out of touch with the thought of his time. But this is certainly not true of Mill. Perhaps we should see it rather as a valiant attempt to suppress his abundant Victorian emotionalism, and thrust the argument back into "rational" eighteenth century terms.

Similarly, what depths of religious sensibility, and agonising doubt lie hidden behind the unconscious bathos of this passage in the same essay: "When this pre-eminent genius of [Christ] is combined with the qualities of probably the greatest moral reformer, and martyr to that mission, who ever existed upon earth, religion *cannot be said to have made a bad choice* in pitching on this man. . . ." (My italics.)

In these two quotations as in the speculations about the remediability of life, which are scattered through his writings, we see how misleading his influence could be. For Mill himself the remediability of life is a tremulous wish for what is believed half-impossible. His own autobiography by itself is enough to prove that you cannot make people happy by the application of utilitarian principles. But a hypothetical reader who agreed with Mill, who nodded his head sagely as Christ was called "not a bad choice," a reader who did not notice the traces of strong suppressed feelings, and the neuroses so courageously borne, might well be what Mill emphatically was not, a presumptuous ass. Indeed, few men of such distinguished intellect have been so modest. He was perfectly sincere when he wrote in praise of the system on which he was educated: "If I had been by nature extremely quick of apprehension, or had possessed a very accurate and retentive memory, or were of a remarkably active and energetic character, the trial would not be conclusive; but in all these natural gifts I am rather below than above par; what I could do could assuredly be done by any boy or girl of average capacity and healthy physical con-

stitution." Now this is, of course, the merest nonsense, but one has a greater respect than ever for the man who could write and mean it. Once again we notice the misleading impression made on us by Mill's usual style of writing. He often sounds like a man who over-confidently tried to solve every problem in simple terms; in reality, he was so modest that he never even attempted anything subtle. (pp. 24-5)

It is impossible to read a paragraph of Mill without being at once absolutely clear about what he meant. But the general tendency and inner meaning of his works is enigmatic, and perhaps even contradictory. His *Utilitarianism,* for instance, ostensibly designed to show that the finest moral sensibilities and attainments can spring from utilitarian principles, may well be judged to show the opposite. It is not merely that Mill, like so many writers, may fail to convince us; it is rather that he does not seem able to convince himself. And what should be his triumphant summary, "In the golden rule of Jesus of Nazareth we read the complete spirit of the ethics of utility" has in the context a hollow ring. If we are right in seeing Mill as a deeply emotional man, who attempted in vain to exclude the consequences of emotion from his writings, this lack of inner harmony is not surprising. The magnificent lucidity of his detailed statements only serves to make it more obvious.

Mill's most interesting works on religious questions were published posthumously—*The Utility of Religion* and the *Essay on Theism.* But the former had been in existence unpublished for more than fifteen years before the author's death in 1873. Lucid as ever in detail, they are very puzzling works. *The Utility of Religion* is ostensibly an attack both on the practical usefulness of religion, and on the vicious principle of judging religious questions by usefulness instead of by truth. But it ends, nevertheless, by tacitly admitting that religion is useful in making people happier and morally better; and then at the end quite vaguely for no more than a page or so, it speaks of the Religion of Humanity, which might in the future do the work better. To some extent, this may be justified as being an appeal to the future. Mill, it could be argued, was compelled to be vague here because the Religion of Humanity remained only an aspiration, and could not be discussed in detail. But when we recall that Mill wrote a devastating attack in his *Auguste Comte and Positivism* on the only existing scheme for a Religion of Humanity, it must seem odd that he neglected even a rough idea of the form he wished his substitute for traditional religious practice to take. In the circumstances, the reader is bound to conclude that Mill's hopes of any effective new system are slight, and that the traditional method of preserving moral sanctions by Christianity is indispensable as far as he can foresee.

The essay on *Theism,* a later production, which reveals several new developments in Mill's thought, is even more notable for this mixture of perfect lucidity in detail, leading to a set of enigmatic conclusions. (pp. 25-7)

In all his doubts and hesitations during all his protracted, painful approach to the borderlands of theism, one conviction, shared with so many of his contemporaries of all schools of thought, remained unchallenged in Mill's mind. It was the idea that we know for certain without argument what is good. But this belief in instinct or conscience or inspiration was precisely the one that Bentham set out to destroy. And though Mill came to feel that there was some inadequacy in Bentham's view of the world, he continued to accept Bentham's fundamental ethical conception, that moral truths are to be discovered by reason. But this principle, which he thought he held so strongly, and for which he argued so powerfully, seems to have had little influence on his actual moral judgments. They breathe the spirit of Sinai.

When he comes to judge the moral content of Christianity, it is this instinctive, interior standard that he always applies. Speaking of what he calls the "authentic" sayings of Jesus of Nazareth he says, "these are sufficiently in harmony with the intellect and feelings of every good man or woman, to be in no danger of being let go, after having been once acknowledged as the creed of the best and foremost of our species." The word "good" here is not the good of the philosophers, or the sociologists or the utilitarians. It is a self-justifying absolute. That Mill, so eager as a rule to define and distinguish his terms, makes no comment on its meaning is very significant. And there is another ambiguity in the word "authentic." One would suppose that it referred to some canon of textual criticism. In fact it introduces an unconscious confusion between authentic—correctly reported—and authentic—morally satisfying to the conscience of the nineteenth century. By means of this confusion, which, I repeat, is quite unconscious, Mill is enabled to use the "historic" Christ to rebuke Christianity without ever making any inquiry of his own into the nature of the historical Christ. Thus he says elsewhere, (in the essay on *Nature*) "According to the creed of most denominations of Christians (though assuredly not of Christ) man is by nature wicked." How is this Christ known to the devout agnostic? He is known not by history, but by faith. Mill's moral doctrine, in fact, turns out to have a remarkable similarity to the idea of inspiration from the Holy Spirit, although the existence of God remained an open question. The saint of rationalism possessed in the depths of his mind the fiery conscience of a covenanter.

But in the end the movement back towards religion took only a dubious and tentative form. At the end of his life, in the essay on *Theism,* he wrote, "To the conception of the rational sceptic, it remains a possibility that Christ actually was what he supposed himself to be . . . a man charged with a special, express and unique commission from God to lead mankind to truth and virtue."

It is difficult to interpret all this. Does it lead forward or back? Does Mill's sense of an interior knowledge of Christ's purposes spring from a half-forgotten religious tradition, which influenced so many agnostics when overt faith was gone? Or do his shadowy hints about Christ's divine mission show that Mill's thought was really tending towards the acceptance of Christianity itself?

If the essay on *Theism* really springs from an old religious tradition, then it is a strange case of atavism. For the evidence of the autobiography is clear: "I am thus one of the very few examples, in this country, of one who has, not thrown off religious belief, but never had it: I grew up in a negative state with regard to it. I looked upon the modern exactly as I did upon the ancient religion, as something that in no way concerned me. It did not seem to me more strange that English people should believe what I did not, than that the men I read of in Herodotus should have done so."

Moreover, the approach to Christianity remains purely intellectual; there is no trace in the later works of religious sensibility. A bleak rationalism predominates.

If I am right in finding Mill a very emotional man, one of two conclusions follows. Either Mill experienced some religious emotion, of which there is no record, (an unsafe hypothesis), or else his personality was divided in his last years in a new way, but a way comparable to the old way so poignantly described in the autobiography. Then it had been a division between the Benthamite training and Wordsworthian sensibilities. Now it was a division between a half-Christian intellect and emotional agnostic loyalties.

Mon coeur est rationaliste, mais ma raison s'y oppose.

It would seem that for Mill nostalgia worked in favour of Benthamism. This should not surprise us, if we remember his abiding reverence for his father. In those early days when his hands had been scarcely strong enough to lift the Greek lexicon all religious questionings had been excluded. Mill presents us with a perfect mirror-image of the more usual kind of Victorian doubt, where nostalgia is felt for the religious comforts of childhood. His case is a valuable warning against an over-neat assessment either of belief or unbelief as being purely rational or purely emotional. (pp. 28-30)

> A.O.J. Cockshut, "John Stuart Mill: The Half-Circle," in his The Unbelievers: English Agnostic Thought, 1840-1890, Collins, 1964, pp. 19-30.

J. B. SCHNEEWIND   (essay date 1965)

[*A major Mill scholar, Schneewind analyzes Mill's theory of historical change and its effect on his ethical precepts. Influenced by the theories of St. Simon, Mill interpreted history as a process of alternating periods, the organic and the critical, a theory he presented in its most complete form in* Utilitarianism. *Schneewind outlines the way in which Mill transformed Bentham's utilitarian doctrine into a wider philosophy of life capable of accommodating his theory of history.*]

Underlying Mill's manifold interests, shaping his aims, and influencing the ways in which he worked to achieve them, is a theory of historical change and of the conditions for stability in society. Mill was not the originator of the theory of history which he used—he learned it from the St. Simonian writers in France—but he accepted it early in his career, and some knowledge of it is important for an understanding of his writings on ethics.

According to this view, history proceeds in a series of alternating periods. Although the details of the events within each period are unique, there are nonetheless only two kinds of period: organic and critical. In an organic period, society is stable and well-organized; it is run by those who have ability and is united by a widely accepted set of opinions. Those who make and modify public opinion are a small and cohesive body—Mill is thinking here of the clergy in the Middle Ages—whose views, accepted by the mass of men as issuing from an authoritative source, provide a framework within which particular disputes can be carried on and particular problems solved. In a critical period, by contrast, the men in power are not the men with ability, and the men who form public opinion are not agreed among themselves. Consequently the old bonds of social cohesion slowly dissolve. Men begin to think for themselves and refuse to accept guidance from those wiser or more learned than themselves, the framework of beliefs is lost, and society splits with increasing rapidity into factions and parties not united by any common concern or shared viewpoint. Only with the gradual growth of a new framework of accepted beliefs can a stable society emerge again. (pp. 13-14)

The importance of having a consensus on basic moral beliefs is . . . enormous, on Mill's view, and to obtain it sound moral philosophy is indispensable. The point is all the more vital because, with [his] analysis of the role of opinion in history, Mill couples the view that his own period is a critical period. His task, as he sees it, is to aid his times to make the transition to an organic period, not by attempting to go back to some supposedly golden past, but by absorbing the lessons of the period of criticism and progressing on to a new state of society based on a new set of beliefs. If the critical spirit were allowed to continue unchecked, it might well, Mill fears, lead to the sort of chaos and wanton destructiveness that characterized the last phases of the French Revolution. But though a renewal of agreement on these points is desirable, it will not be easy to bring it about. A thinker who lives during an organic period can propound his views directly and fully to the opinion-forming group. If they agree with him, he can be sure that the public will eventually come to agree as well, while disagreement will at least not cause fierce divisions in society. This is not true in a critical period. Public opinion being already splintered, new theories are apt to act as further sources of disunity and disagreement; they will at most serve as party slogans, not as comprehensive views. And there is in addition the problem of the peculiar temperament of the English people, who distrust general theories as such. It would be worse than useless to try to propagate a whole system among them. (p. 15)

Mill's view of history, then, posed two problems for him. (i) Whatever theory he might construct, there would be the difficulty of gaining acceptance for it during a critical period. In solving this problem, Mill applied a lesson his father had taught him. James Mill had made him read, at an early age, the orations of Demosthenes, and had pointed out particularly "how everything important to his purpose was said at the exact moment when he had brought the minds of his audience into the state most fitted to receive it; how he made steal into their minds, gradually and by insinuation, thoughts which, if expressed in a more direct manner, would have aroused their opposition. Most of these reflections," Mill comments, "were beyond my capacity of full comprehension at the time; but they left seed behind, which germinated in due season." Thus, in putting his moral views before the public, he did not at first publish a systematic treatise. Instead he suggested his opinions in numerous essays on a variety of topics; he applied them constantly in his writings on current social and political issues; he outlined or defended an aspect or a part of them in a critical essay here and there, or he used them in the course of illustrating points in the *Logic*. It was not until quite late in his career that he presented, in *Utilitarianism,* anything like a complete exposition of his theory—and by then he had come to think that the state of the public mind was somewhat improved. (ii) The second problem Mill faced was, of course, that of formulating a moral theory that would be adequate for the purpose which, on his view, such a theory must serve. In working out a solution Mill never abandoned the basic Utilitarianism which he had been taught as a child. He did not go in search of a new first principle. His aim was rather to transform the old, narrow Utilitarianism from a party ideology into a comprehensive view, and to show that it need not be a divisive slogan but could serve as a unifying philosophy of life.

Discussion of three main aspects of Mill's thought will suggest some of the ways in which he tries to make Utilitarianism more comprehensive and more widely acceptable than it was previously.

(A) Because the Benthamites accepted the view that all men necessarily seek their own pleasure in voluntary action, they were accused of teaching that men are brutish and selfish;

because they held that pleasure and the absence of pain are the ultimate good, they were thought to be propagating a low, debasing view. Mill tries to eliminate these objections by (1) slightly modifying, and formulating more carefully, the Benthamite psychology of action, (2) emphasizing a point about its view of happiness which had not been made prominent before, and (3) revising its concept of pleasure.

(1) Mill holds that Bentham's formulation of the doctrine of psychological egoism is misleading. Granted that in some sense of "pleasure" and "pain" all voluntary actions are done for the sake of obtaining pleasure or avoiding pain for the agent, it is still erroneous to conclude from this that men are all selfish. Some men voluntarily do deeds which would normally be thought of as totally unselfish, and psychology has nothing to object to this view of them. The sense in which the psychologist uses "pleasure" and "pain" is broad enough to allow him to include among his list of motives the pleasure of altruistic action and the pain of callousness which would be felt by a virtuous man. If Bentham speaks as though this were not so, it is because he confuses this broad sense of his key terms with the narrower, and more ordinary, sense in which it would be said, for instance, that the self-sacrificing crusader gives up a life of pleasure for a life of devotion to a cause. It is simply not true that in the narrow sense men seek their own pleasure in all their actions, nor, Mill insists, is it an implication of the psychology of Utilitarianism. A more serious mistake is made by Bentham, Mill thinks, in holding that men act for the sake of pleasures which they *foresee* will be consequences of their actions. Bentham overlooks the fact that the present thought of a particular act may be pleasant enough to lead to the doing of it without any further thought about the consequences that will result from it. Indeed the point of moral education—as we shall see later—is precisely to ensure that the thought of certain actions is so pleasant as to lead the agent to do them without worrying about their consequences, while the thought of others is painful enough to prevent them from being done. In this sort of situation no calculation at all, let alone "selfish" calculation, is involved.

(2) The fact that certain actions and states of mind may be felt to be pleasant in themselves is important for Mill's broadened understanding of the Utilitarian goal. It had seemed shocking to many people to make virtuous action simply a means to a goal beyond itself, and virtuous character not the highest good but only the best available tool for bringing into existence what is intrinsically good. The older Utilitarian vocabulary seemed to force this view upon its adherents, for it allowed only pleasure and the absence of pain to be ends in themselves and consequently made all else into mere means. But Mill points out that we can speak of certain activities and states of mind as being themselves *parts* of happiness, in the sense that they are actions or states in which we can directly take pleasure and which therefore are good for themselves and not for their consequences. (pp. 16-18)

(3) A far more radical change in orthodox Benthamism is made by Mill in attempting to show why Utilitarianism is not an ignoble philosophy fit only for pigs. The Benthamites had recognized only one basic feature of pleasure and pain as relevant to moral choice: the *amount*. . . . This proved offensive to many people, and Mill tries to alter the Utilitarian theory so as to remove the source of offense. He introduces a distinction between *kinds* of pleasures (or pains)—a qualitative distinction, a distinction between "higher" and "lower" pleasures, which, he thinks, will enable him to say that a large quantity of a lower pleasure may fail to be more valuable than

even a small quantity of a higher pleasure. Though fewer people enjoy looking at paintings than at television, still, if the former is a higher pleasure, it may be more valuable; though the pleasures of drug addiction seem to be particularly intense, and the pleasures of intelligent conversation may not be so, still the latter may be more valuable than the former. The test here is *preference:* if those who have tried both prefer one to the other, quite regardless of quantity, then the pleasure that is preferred must be the higher one. (pp. 19-20)

(B) The Benthamites were accused of being entirely too *a priori* in their ethics, of ignoring, despite their loud boast that they were the only remaining champions of the Philosophy of Experience, all that experience had to teach about morality. They denied the claims of the accepted morality of the people as contemptuously as they threw out the belief that the wisdom of the ages was embodied in the political institutions of the country, and they treated those who defended either of these as probably motivated by sinister self-interest. Against this, Mill argues that, in the traditions, customs, and commonsense morality of a people, as expressed in sayings and aphorisms handed down from generation to generation, there is to be found a source of guidance which is indispensable even to the reforming Utilitarian. We must (1) note briefly his reasons for holding this view and (2) indicate its importance for his philosophical position in ethics.

(1) Mill's attitude toward commonsense morality is supported by his analysis of the problems involved in obtaining sociological knowledge and the methods properly employed for this purpose. It is clear that, if we accept the fundamental Utilitarian imperative, we shall need much information about the consequences that actions will have on individuals and groups. Although the basic laws of psychology are known, Mill holds, they are by themselves too abstract to be useful for obtaining detailed answers to questions of the sort we shall have to answer, and indeed the number of factors involved in social interaction is too great even to permit the direct deduction of sociological laws from them. Experiment, which is the tool of the physical sciences for complex situations, is, for obvious reasons, also impossible. Our only resource is to gather as many generalizations as we can about the tendencies of humans to act or respond in various ways under various circumstances, and then see whether we can arrange these systematically by connecting them with fundamental laws of human nature and human character. All of us have observed a certain amount of human life and formed from our experience and reading a number of generalizations, about friends, about groups we are members of, about our countrymen, perhaps about people in general. But personal observation has one formidable defect—and here we touch a basic theme in Mill's thought—in that it tends to be *one-sided.* . . . Mill holds that, in the commonsense morality of a people, as in its proverbs and aphorisms, we have a vast fund of information of the sort needed by the social sciences, gathered from and passed through ages of experience and millions of lives, and therefore one of the best available correctives to the narrowness in theory that results from lack of factual knowledge. (pp. 20-1)

(2) While Mill's attitude toward commonsense morality has an important bearing on his tactics for aiding progress, it is at least as important for the way he handles the chief philosophical position opposed to Utilitarianism, the position he labels "Intuitionism." The Intuitionists interpret commonsense morality quite differently from the way Mill interprets it. They hold that each man is in some way able to "see" or "intuit" the absolute truth of a number of moral principles and rules, and that what one intuits in this way cannot be wrong. The propositions grasped by intuition are eternally true, as the axioms of geometry are eternally true; consequently, morality is immutable, not open to improvement and refinement as our sociological knowledge increases. Mill thinks that there are three main arguments in support of Intuitionism. First, the feeling accompanying moral judgments is unique, and therefore it must have a unique source, viz., the intuited moral truth. Second, moral judgments are not in fact generally arrived at by a process of reasoning; they come with the rapidity of sense perception, and Intuitionism alone accounts for this. Third, the moral principles and judgments even of the plain man have a degree of authority or weight which is inexplicable except on Intuitionist grounds, for the plain man's opinions on the consequences of actions are not usually as authoritative as his moral judgments. To each of these arguments Mill has a reply. By giving alternative psychological explanations of the peculiarity of moral feelings and the rapidity of moral judgment, explanations which remove the alleged need for the Intuitionist account of these features of moral thought, he undercuts the first two. And his reply to the third argument is, simply, that a Utilitarian account of the authority of commonsense morality and the moral opinions of the plain man is quite possible. We have already seen the grounds on which he holds that commonsense morality is to be respected: the plain man, heir to the whole tradition of the people, is aided in judging by what he has learned from the past.

There is therefore, Mill thinks, no compelling reason to accept Intuitionism, and on general epistemological grounds he is opposed to it. He thinks, moreover, that Utilitarianism has one very considerable advantage over Intuitionism within the domain of morality. On the Intuitionist view moral disputes must come down, since intuition is supposed to be infallible, to a war of assertion and counter-assertion. A denial of an alleged intuition can be treated only in the way that a denial (say) that this page is white with lines of black on it can be treated: by charges either of blindness or of disingenuousness. And this is hardly a pleasant position for a moralist to be in, especially in an age when old opinions are changing rapidly, when there are many diverse groups with divergent interests within the community, and when old authority is being challenged. The Utilitarian, however, is not faced with this problem, for he holds that, while commonsense morality undoubtedly conveys much valuable knowledge, it is far from being infallible. Mixed with its insights there is faulty inference, mixed with its information there is superstition, mixed with sympathy and love there are prejudice and group interest, and all these sources of error must eventually be detected and eliminated. There is no easy or automatic way to do this, but at least it can be done rationally, by using the methods of the social sciences to help answer the question of what actions tend to make people happy. In his emphasis on the way in which Utilitarianism appeals to empirical science and rejects any claim to absolute infallibility or complete immunity to criticism, Mill is in agreement with one of the deepest and most important strains in Bentham's thought. No matter how far he may go in seeking to appreciate the wisdom of the ages and the good that lies in established institutions, he never abandons the belief that the Utilitarian principle provides a rational basis for their evaluation and points to the ways in which they may be improved.

(C) Nowhere is Mill's desire to learn from his opponents and to minimize points of disagreement more prominent than in his view of the importance of individual character and in his presentation of that view. The Benthamites were generally thought to have placed their hopes for progress wholly on impersonal economic, legal, and political arrangements, which would improve the way men live and act without altering what men are. Almost the whole range of vocal opinion during much of Mill's lifetime was united against this approach. The reasons for such unanimity of sentiment are complex. In large part, of course, the Christian emphasis on the individual soul is responsible, even among those who had come to doubt or disbelieve the Christian religious teaching, while the strength and pride of the newly powerful middle class, self-reliant and self-made, is another potent factor. Whatever the reasons, the belief that the state of one's soul or the condition of one's moral character was the most important thing in the world could very easily have seemed to Mill to be one of those truths that philosophy is not called on to prove but may justly be required to account for. Mill presented this view so forcefully that he has been frequently accused of the radical inconsistency of teaching on the one hand that perfection of character is the only intrinsic good and, on the other, that happiness is the only intrinsic good. There is, however, no such contradiction in Mill's thought. He holds, as might be expected, that the development and perfection of character is "the highest utility." (pp. 22-4)

Mill believes the advent of some form of mass rule or popular government to be inevitable in any country which has come to the stage reached, he holds, by the England of his times. The ruling group will never again be the small privileged elite that it was formerly, and there is no use trying to restore unity to the nation by setting up such a group. Increasingly, from now on, the rulers will be in reality the great mass of the people. The number and importance of their votes will swell their influence in politics, and the majority opinion is all too likely to gain an overwhelming and terrifying weight. It is consequently more important than ever before that the people be educated, both intellectually and morally. Society at this point may, as we have seen, move in either of two directions: it may become increasingly fragmented, filled with conflicting groups and detached individuals, devoid of any but the most limited loyalties, or it may begin to reorganize, to become increasingly cohesive, to develop into a society which attracts the loyalties of more and more of its members, finding them ever more willing to identify themselves with the society and to find their happiness in its well-being. Which way will it go? The answer, Mill thinks, depends on what we do. Those of us who have come to understand the situation and who are sympathetic enough to want to help others can, through educating feelings as well as minds—in other words, through building character—in the populace, help bring about a better society. If we succeed, we can hope to create a public which, when it finally gets the right to vote (which it did not have, to any very great extent in England, until 1867), will be able to select the best of the candidates, and willing to do so even at the expense of their own immediate interests, because their feelings and sympathies will have bound them to the welfare of society and made that more precious to them than their own material well-being. If we fail, we can only look forward to an increasingly tyrannical and unenlightened mobocracy.

Thus a political forecast is the second reason behind Mill's belief in the importance of moral character. Unlike the Benthamites, he is not willing to trust an external "Duty-and-Interest-Juncture-Producing-Principle." It is rather within each man that he hopes to produce that identity of individual and

social interest which is so essential for the greatest happiness of the greatest number. (pp. 26-7)

It is a commonplace to say that Mill lived at a time when disaffection with Christianity was becoming more general and more widespread than it had ever been before. Affecting not only the cultivated upper classes but the middle and often illiterate working classes as well, it came not as a minor hesitation about this or that point of faith, but as a major change of view. Doubts about religion were no longer merely circulated clandestinely but publicly expressed by many of the most prominent leaders of thought; where there were no doubts about religion, it was often because there was no concern with it at all. With both these states of mind there came, among those who thought, much reflection about morality. In many cases, a rejection of Christianity meant primarily a denial or abandonment of the supernatural part of its doctrines, and left the moral part more or less untouched. But the official teaching had stressed the dependence of the moral code on religious revelation, and one of the most influential of religious groups, the Evangelicals, had insistently preached not only that without religion there could be no knowledge of morality, but that without religious motivation no one could be a really good man. What was one to think about these matters once one gave up one's religion?

Attempts to formulate a comprehensive alternative to the Christian view were made by many writers, but few if any of the results were as thoroughgoing and as carefully worked out as Mill's philosophy. He succeeded, moreover, to a considerable extent in his aim of constructing a view that would introduce new ideas without offending old habits of thought, for his broad Utilitarianism was a view that could be accepted by those who, having lost their religious beliefs, still adhered in large part to the morality that had been taught with it. At the same time, Utilitarianism would not leave the original religious morality untouched. It might not give its adherents a principle with which they could easily reach decisions on all disputed or difficult questions (nor, of course, did Mill think it would do so: "It is given to no human being," he wrote, "to stereotype a set of truths, and walk safely by their guidance with his mind's eye closed"). But placing one's detailed moral beliefs in the Utilitarian framework would lead one to see them in a new light. Utilitarianism forces one to relate morality not to God's will, the soul's salvation, and blessedness in another life, but to man's desires, human happiness, and increasing satisfactoriness of life on earth. The feeling that moral principles and rules are awesome and imposing dictates from on high, to be neither challenged nor changed by reason but simply accepted and obeyed, is replaced by an attitude which takes them as one of the many devices that men construct, as they work together for the general welfare. Morality is felt to be an instrument in our hands, to be used by us and for us, to be changed or not as the facts demand and we see fit. This attitude toward morality is in essence the Benthamite attitude. It leads us to ask of every rule or prohibition, as Bentham asked of every law and institution, "What is the use of it?", and to conclude that what cannot be justified in terms of resultant happiness ought to be abandoned. And it is precisely because Utilitarianism fosters this liberal humanistic attitude that Mill hoped to see it become the replacement for what he took to be the rapidly decaying Christian framework.

Whatever the reasons—and they are complex—the humanistic moral attitude has become increasingly widespread since Mill's time. Although it may take many different forms, it received its most influential philosophical articulation during the nine-teenth century from Mill, and his ethical writings repay study now for the help they can give us in coming to a fuller un-derstanding of its problems and its enduring strength. (pp. 37-9)

> *J. B. Schneewind, in an introduction to* Mill's Ethical
> Writings *by John Stuart Mill, edited by J. B. Schnee-*
> *wind, Collier Books, 1965, pp. 7-39.*

SHIRLEY ROBIN LETWIN   (essay date 1965)

[*Letwin characterizes Mill's philosophy as revolutionary because he expanded the province of the economist to include both political and moral concerns. In her commentary on* On Liberty, *Letwin focuses on the "profound division within Mill," which she sees reflected in the flawed logic and inherent contradictions in the essay.*]

[Mill had] made a revolution, not by what he said about eco-nomics or economic organization, but by what he implied about the role of the social scientist in politics. What he had said in the **Logic** suggested that the economist should only sparingly, if at all, abstract from the complex realities of actual life, that he should deal with men as they really are, moved by diverse motives and influenced by the actual conditions of their society. In the **Political Economy,** Mill did draw a clear line between the scientific and practical part of economics, in order to dis-sociate economics from some of the policies his former col-leagues had advocated. But at the same time, he encouraged the notion, developed on the Continent more than in England, that the economist *qua* economist must not merely analyse the motives and effects of economic activity, but must also weigh and compare the moral merits of different economic policies. The economist was not only given leave but obliged to discuss the effects on justice and morality as well as the economic aspects of the production and distribution of wealth. He had to set forth an idea of economic development, keeping in view the intellectual and moral, as well as the material ends of life, and to discuss the ways and means—such as strengthening right motives, spreading sound customs and habits in industrial life, direct intervention by the State—of achieving that ideal.

By requiring the economist as such to speak on political and moral issues, Mill suggested that there was a connection be-tween his competence as an economist and as a moralist and politician. Unlike Adam Smith, Mill never distinguished be-tween 'What is properly called political economy', a science that 'treats of the nature and causes of the wealth of nations', and the tasks of civil government. Mill was an economist more nearly like the Physiocrats whom Smith had rebuked for failing to make this distinction. What was even more radical for Ben-tham's heir was the implication that as moral and political questions were within the province of the economist, they were not properly in the realm of common sense or political wisdom to decide. They became instead the business of the expert and beyond the ordinary man, matters of science, not prudence. (p. 287)

[Mill's **On Liberty**] is carefully reasoned, and in some ways admirably lucid, yet its central message is by no means per-fectly clear. So subtly is it woven, that the pattern almost escapes detection. Not that Mill meant to write an esoteric essay, for what he made most evident was, as he expected, most offensive to his contemporaries. The intricacies of *On Liberty* simply reflect the complexity of Mill's own thought, which had by then taken in, altered, and created more than he himself realized.

But on the surface, **On Liberty** is simply an ardent and per-suasive argument for the most unhindered individualism. While the problem of political liberty, that is, freedom from the tyr-anny of government, was no longer an issue in England, Mill declared, the yoke of opinion was even heavier than in other countries. This might in time lead again to political tyranny as well, when the majority learned to think of government as its own. But for the moment the pressing problem was the tyranny of public opinion, imposed through custom, enforcing the ideas and practices of the majority on all. The purpose of the essay was therefore to assert that, 'There is a limit to the legitimate interference of collective opinion with individual indepen-dence . . .' and to help stem the tide that was inclined to 'stretch unduly the powers of society over the individual'. (p. 297)

The purpose of **On Liberty** was not to insist on the priority of liberty over morality, but on the priority of the higher over the lower morality: 'All the difficulties of morality in any of its brands, grow out of the conflict which continually arises be-tween the highest morality and even the best popular morality which the degree of development yet achieved by average hu-man nature will allow to exist'. The best popular morality is that which pacifies as many natures as possible, and so it must be much inferior to what higher natures want and require. As popular morality is essentially a compromise between the low-est and the highest, the best people lose most; they are

> the greatest, indeed the only real, sufferers by
> the compromise; for *they* are called upon to
> give up what would really make them happy;
> while others are commonly required only to
> restrain desires, the gratification of which would
> bring no real happiness. In the adjustment,
> moreover, of the compromise, the higher na-
> tures count only in proportion to their number,
> how small! while the conditions of the com-
> promise weigh heavily upon them in the states
> of their greater capacity of happiness. . . .

If the leadership of the superior few were permitted, all human beings would ultimately become noble, more given to high thoughts and elevated feelings. Then there would be no ob-jection to being bound closely to the race, because the race would be more worth belonging to. In the meantime, however, one had to free the superior few from the vulgar many. But Mill so thoroughly merged his plea for liberating the minority of ideal individuals from the common herd with his vision of progress toward a race of ideal individuals, that his chief pur-pose was easily overlooked. Had it been recognized, his rule for distinguishing public from private interests would not have seemed so ambiguous and inadequate. For if there is a clear notion of what 'good' private interests are and a definite goal ahead for society, if there are men who can judge where hap-piness lies, which pleasure or life should be preferred, then it is not so difficult to decide in most cases whether public or private interests should prevail. It is only when individuality can take widely different forms, when there is no one goal to be reached, that Mill's rule is useless in those cases where the conflict is most serious. For then the 'public' interest is just one among many interests and there is no scale on which to measure any.

The ambiguity in **On Liberty** did not arise from careless or faulty reasoning. It reflected a profound division within Mill. He had after all been educated as Bentham's heir, and with part of him believed ardently that human dignity required the freedom of each man to go his own way. But he had also inherited from his Calvinist father a conviction, reinforced by his later experiences, that there were superior beings who should guide the rest. Of course, neither Hume nor Bentham would have denied that some men were in some ways superior to others, or that the average man would do best to look for a superior model to follow. But they did not believe there was a clearly defined class of superior beings. And they did not think it was easy to put everything into words. Besides, they were not trying to formulate a complete creed. Hume was content to let customary ways regulate deference without harping on the subject. Bentham, who believed the deference had gone too far in some areas, set out to destroy it there. Neither tried to include all good things in their political recommendations. But Mill could leave nothing unsaid—he even felt obliged to write a contract guaranteeing his recognition of Harriet's equality. He could not allow himself or society to achieve any good thing without deliberately aiming at it. As he insisted on including everything within one system, neither could he, as Hume and Bentham did, give priority to one object for the purposes of social policy alone. He would have liked society self-consciously to pursue two incompatible ends. The dilemma was not made obvious because Mill's plea for freeing the superior few from the inferior mass was so sweetly enclosed in general arguments for liberty and individuality that it could be accepted somehow by all sorts of individualists.

On Liberty is consequently a classic statement of late Victorian and twentieth century liberalism. For it enables the liberal to feel assured of his tolerance, and at the same time to feel it is right, even obligatory, to impose his own views on the less fortunate mass of people in want of uplifting. Thus he can pay homage to both liberty and progress without having to acknowledge any conflict between them. Mill had poured his new learning—that there was perfection ahead—into the old mould—that it was indecent to prevent any adult from choosing his way of life. He himself managed to remain devoted to both aspects of his creed at once. But he made it easy for his successors to discard the mould. He provided a justification for withholding personal liberty from any claimant unable to demonstrate that he was pursuing the 'right' ideal and was possessed of sufficient will power to pursue it steadily and energetically. (p. 308)

> Shirley Robin Letwin, *"John Stuart Mill: From Puritanism to Sociology,"* in her The Pursuit of Certainty: David Hume, Jeremy Bentham, John Stuart Mill, Beatrice Webb, *Cambridge at the University Press, 1965, pp. 191-318.*

EDWARD ALEXANDER   (essay date 1967)

[*Alexander discusses Mill's conception of literature in relation to his sociopolitical views. According to Alexander, because Mill believed that poetry had the function of "purifying and elevating . . . emotions" and therefore encouraging proper behavior in society, his aesthetic theory helps to illuminate his social and political philosophy.*]

How does Mill's view of literature serve his belief in a democratic culture? How does his definition of the nature and function of literature give it a vital role in providing democratic societies with a high and noble ideal of individual perfection?

In his attempts to define poetry, and in most of his discussions of individual poets, Mill scrupulously separates poetry from rhetoric and oratory. In the essay **"What is Poetry?"** and in his review of Carlyle's *The French Revolution*, he refuses the

title of poet to any writer who has designs upon his audience, who wishes to inculcate certain doctrines or urge certain actions. The poet's primary task, Mill in effect says, is to be sincere, to give a truthful picture of his own feelings and state of mind.

Such a view of poetry hardly seems the prelude to an exposition of the view that poetry serves a particular social and even political function. If the poet must do nothing more than be true to himself, of what possible use can his poetry be to others? Had not the great critics of the previous century given to the practice of poetry a moral justification which assumed that the poet addressed himself to the social world and used the tools of rhetoric to persuade his audience of moral truths?

Mill was aware of the moral objections that might be made to so "inner-directed" a view of art. But he was aware too that the conditions of the nineteenth century made it impossible for poetry to perform its moral function in the old way. The eighteenth-century poet, if he urged certain moral or political or philosophical doctrines upon his audience, could take it for granted that most of his audience would readily assent to these doctrines (even if it never acted on them). His audience was relatively small and homogeneous, and held many beliefs in common. The nineteenth-century writer, as Mill noted with dismay in his speech **"On the Present State of Literature,"** had a potentially larger, but also more heterogeneous and less cultivated, audience. He had to address a society fiercely sectarian in religion and politics, and divided into factions on most other issues. In such an atmosphere the prudent author with high moral intentions must seek to gain influence by means other than didacticism. George Eliot, Mill's great contemporary who referred to herself as an aesthetic rather than a doctrinal teacher, wrote:

> If Art does not enlarge men's sympathies, it does nothing morally. I have had heart-cutting experience that opinions are a poor cement between human souls; and the only effect I ardently long to produce by my writings, is that those who read them should be better able to *imagine* and to *feel* the pains and the joys of those who differ from themselves in everything but the broad fact of being struggling erring human creatures.

George Eliot's ideal of imaginative sympathy was also espoused by Mill. For Mill believed as firmly as Dr. Johnson that literature should perform a moral function. In his review of Tennyson, which appeared in 1835, just two years after his essays in definition, he declared that the higher end of poetry is "that of acting upon the desires and characters of mankind through their emotions, to raise them towards the perfection of their nature." Poetry, that is, performs its moral function directly, not by urging men to think or to act differently, but by purifying and elevating their emotions so that they will become more receptive to true doctrines and more inclined to good conduct. Poetry is able to work upon the emotions precisely because it does not *try* to do so, but instead retains its artistic integrity.

Mill's aesthetic theory always stresses the need for imagination and sympathetic identification. In the essay on Bentham he calls imagination "the power by which one human being enters into the mind and circumstances of another." It is a power characteristic of the poet and one that he cultivates in his reader, who is in effect asked temporarily to suspend his own rhythm of existence and to experience that rhythm which is the essence of a particular poem. Without such imaginative identification, Mill insists, a human being can have no knowledge of the inner life of his fellow men.

Poetry, then, provides a kind of emotional knowledge; and Mill believed that only such knowledge could lead to genuine morality. In one of his articles on Plato, he said that arguments in favor of virtue, never persuaded anyone to *be* virtuous. Knowledge becomes virtue, he argued, only when it takes hold of the feelings—only, that is, when it is the kind of knowledge supplied by poetry. (pp. xxiii-xxiv)

The role that his conception of poetry plays in Mill's social and political philosophy may be understood by considering his argument for the feasibility of a Utilitarian morality in *Utilitarianism.* ... In the course of this argument, contained in Chapter Three of *Utilitarianism,* Mill transfers the pattern of his mental crisis and recovery to the solution of a general problem of moral philosophy. He first argues that the moral faculty of man may be developed, without doing violence to human nature, in any one of a number of different ways. Nearly any system of morality, or set of principles, may be inculcated in such a way as to make it speak to the individual with what appears to be the voice of conscience. Yet moral associations of an artificial kind will not take permanent hold unless they appeal to some essential principle of human nature: "Moral associations which are wholly of artificial creation, when intellectual culture goes on, yield by degrees to the dissolving force of analysis." The force of analysis had, as has been shown, nearly dissolved the young Mill's Utilitarian principles. On the basis of his own experience, Mill now warns that if the Utilitarian morality continues to make a purely intellectual appeal, it will indeed be doomed, even if the whole educational system of a country were used to enforce it. Fortunately, however, Mill continues, there exists a foundation for the Utilitarian social philosophy in the "social feelings of mankind." The task of the Utilitarian reformer was no longer simply to articulate and to teach the Utilitarian social philosophy, as Bentham and James Mill had done; the task was to educate those emotions and sympathies that could make men take pleasure in doing good as defined by Utilitarianism:

> Not only does all strengthening of social ties, and all healthy growth of society, give to each individual a stronger personal interest in practically consulting the welfare of others; it also leads him to identify his *feelings* more and more with their good. ...

Throughout *Utilitarianism* Mill is warning that a social philosophy which does not take into account all that part of life which is unconnected with action or morality will be incomplete and therefore incapable of commanding the full conviction of its supposed adherents. Such incompleteness and such ineffectuality are the penalties meted out to "Utilitarians who have cultivated their moral feelings, but not their sympathies nor their artistic perceptions."

Six years after *Utilitarianism* appeared, Mill recommended poetry as the best means for cultivating the sympathetic and social feelings upon which the Utilitarian ethos was founded. Poetry, he says in the Inaugural Address of 1867 [delivered at St. Andrews University], not only makes men love virtue and eschew selfishness, but it also—

> brings home to us all those aspects of life which take hold of our nature on its unselfish side,

and lead us to identify our joy and grief with the good or ill of the system of which we form a part; and all those solemn or pensive feelings, which, without having any direct application to conduct, incline us to take life seriously, and predispose us to the reception of anything which comes before us in the shape of duty.

Thus poetry transforms our duty into our pleasure and makes possible the "disinterested love of virtue" that is recommended, surprising as it may seem to readers unacquainted with that work, in *Utilitarianism.* The unleavened Utilitarian pursues virtue because it is conducive to pleasure; the Utilitarian leavened by poetry and its habitual enforcement of the association between virtue and pleasure comes to regard virtue as a good in itself. Poetry, as defined in the Inaugural Address, thus provides the motive power for the Utilitarian morality set forth in the earlier work.

Yet, in the same Inaugural Address that judges poetry by its social utility, Mill has much to say about the power of poetry to elevate the individual. For Mill believed that poetry performs its moral function not only democratically, by extending sympathies, but also aristocratically, by elevating them. Because he was aware that democracy could not supply the distinctively aristocratic virtues of heroism, nobility, and style, he hoped that literature would. (pp. xxvi-xxviii)

In the Inaugural Address Mill combines his two definitions of poetry's power of moral inspiration. Only poetry, he argues, can cause us to sympathize with elevated ideals, but it is not only loftiness or heroic feelings that poetry cultivates. "Its power is as great in calming the soul as in elevating it—in fostering the milder emotions, as the more exalted."

Mill's definition of poetry's moral function as its power to arouse imaginative sympathy is the link between his theory of literature and his idea of a democratic culture. By widening the sympathies of men and extending them to more objects, poetry re-enforces the peculiar power of democratic society; by elevating the sympathies of men, poetry brings to democratic society precisely those aristocratic qualities that it lacks. For these reasons Mill came to believe that "upon the existence of the capacity for sympathy rests the possibility of any cultivation of goodness and nobleness and the hope of their ultimate entire ascendancy." (p. xxix)

> *Edward Alexander, in an introduction to* Literary Essays *by John Stuart Mill, edited by Edward Alexander, The Bobbs-Merrill Company, Inc., 1967, pp. xiii-xxix.*

F. PARVIN SHARPLESS (essay date 1967)

[*Sharpless here explores Mill's ideas regarding the role of literature. He states that Mill's literary criticism reveals his lifelong search "for a person who could fulfill the role of the philosopher-poet." He draws on the text of Mill's St. Andrew's Address, a speech delivered at his inauguration as rector there in 1867.*]

Viewed in its entirety, from the earliest pieces in the *Westminster* to the broad liberality of his mature statements, Mill's literary criticism represents an unceasing search for the philosopher-poet, an attempt to discover the ideal man who inspires admiration both for what he is, *and* for what he says, a man whose work and life reconcile the opposites of fact and feeling, of intuition and reason, and who thus solves finally the contradictions which grew directly out of the mental crisis, and continued to figure in almost all of Mill's work. But the praise. . .of the ideal man as man and not as philosopher, for what he is, and not for what he writes, becomes an admission on the part of Mill that the quest was a vain one. The admiration of the poet has always been qualified by criticism of his ideas, of the hero with criticism of his politics.

The failure to find any such perfect resolution, either in the past or the present, requires a new confrontation of the basic assumptions of his work and life, and produces a new, final development in Mill's thinking, which is liberal and humane in tone, and which gives literature a higher and more crucial place than it had ever had in his earlier writing. (p. 220)

All of Mill's assertions about the value of aesthetic cultivation emphasize the utility of placing before the mind higher and better objects and ideas than those which occur in the everyday lives of ordinary men. Literature, when it does this, contributes to the progressive improvement of the soul, and cultivation of the spirit. The difference between this view and the view of Mill's utilitarian predecessors is considerable. (p. 236)

The full measure of Mill's distance from the views of his father and of Bentham is found in his consideration of the values of art and literature. Mill finds clear utility in activities which the Enlightenment had dismissed as irrelevant to serious concerns of social and moral reform. In the concluding pages of the St. Andrew's Address, Mill talks about the close relation between aesthetic philosophy and moral philosophy, and the fact that they both serve the progressive march of men and institutions. The Beautiful, says Mill, is a special and exalted form of the Good.

> There is / . . . / a natural affinity between good-
> ness and the cultivation of the Beautiful, when
> it is real cultivation, and not a mere unguided
> instinct. He who has learned what beauty is, if
> he be of a virtuous character will desire to re-
> alize it in his own life—will keep before him-
> self a type of perfect beauty in human character,
> to light his attempts at self-culture.

Beauty is "the Good made perfect, and fitted with all the collateral perfections which make it a finished and completed thing". It is, in other words, another way of describing the "ideal", the noble and elevating but unrealized level of life and achievement which men must have as an inspiration for the struggle onward and upward. Beauty is, in short, a moral quality, directly tied to the social and moral improvement of society and of the individual. Beauty embodies that perfection or "sense of perfection, which would make us demand from every creation of man the very utmost that it ought to give, and render us intolerant of the smallest fault in ourselves or in anything we do." In this sense then, the moral and ethical ideal finds its most effective representation in works of "pure Art".

> No other human productions come so near to
> perfection as works of pure Art. In all other
> things, we are, and may reasonably be, satisfied
> if the degree of excellence is as great as the
> object immediately in view seems to us to be
> worth: but in Art, the perfection is itself the
> object. If I were to define Art, I should be
> inclined to call it, the endeavor after perfection
> in execution. . . . Art, when really cultivated,
> and not merely practised empirically, main-

tains, what it first gave the conception of, an ideal Beauty, to be eternally aimed at, though surpassing what can be actually attained; and by this idea it trains us never to be completely satisfied with imperfection in what we ourselves do and are: to idealize, as much as possible, every work we do, and most of all, our own characters and lives.

This statement specifically brings together the Beautiful and the Good; it reconciles art and morality, the real and the ideal; it joins aesthetic and moral philosophy. In another way too, it represents the synthesis of Mill as a philosopher—as an intellectual analyzer, and Mill as a man, as a being of emotion and feeling.

The validity of this position may, it is true, be questioned. It may, for example, be said that this idealized perfection was merely a consolation to Mill for his realization that the confidence of the Enlightenment was unfounded and that the possibilities of fulfilling this ideal were small. But again there are two considerations which support Mill's view. In the first place, the validity of this idealization of goodness and beauty is not to be found in any absolutist philosophy, but, in a pragmatic view, that this view serves the greatest happiness. And secondly, Mill engages in hypotheses of this kind only after he has exhausted the possibilities of rational analysis. Mill was neither a visionary nor a dreamer. He knew that the solution of the specific problems to which he devoted much of his life would only uncover new ones. He speaks of the unceasing fight between Good and Evil and "the ever new problems which the changing course of human nature and human society

A portrait of Mill at sixty-seven.

present to be resolved.'' But, in a time when men of intelligence and sensitivity were falling into pessimism and despair, Mill was not dismayed. Human nature was neither corrupt nor perfect, but was like a neutral ground where, to use his own favorite figure, beneficent plants may be grown as easily as weeds. Therefore, the struggle must avail something. Just as we are to admire the hero not for what he says but for what he is, so, in the struggle for social and moral improvement we must look not so much to the improvements the struggle accomplishes, but to the way in which the struggle is carried on.

Mill sought throughout his life for a person who could fulfill the role of the philosopher-poet, who could reconcile in an acceptable fashion fact and feeling. It may be that Mill himself fulfills this description as well as anyone. His obvious claim to the title of philosopher, however, has obscured the measure and depth of his interest in feelings and poetry and his support of them. Where these have been noticed they have too often been considered as a lamentable lapse. But Mill would not have accepted this objection. In fact, as we admit the limitations of his philosophy in meeting modern conditions and modern knowledge (as Mill certainly would have been willing to do) it may be that the poetic qualities of Mill's character become more and more those which catch the imagination and move the feelings. We may feel about Mill as Mill did about Plato, that his own strong feelings toward virtue, make us capable of the same feelings; that the courage of Socrates on behalf of virtue and truth in the face of hostility and contempt, is repeated in John Mill, while Mill's courage produces in us the same admiration for him, which he felt for Socrates. These qualities are not dimmed by time nor historical relativity. They are immutable poetic qualities which carry on in spite of the obsolescence of sectarian doctrine. In the flux of history only poetic qualities remain. But the final justification of the poet is found in the terrible inadequacy of experience as a basis for truth. ''Human existence'', says Mill, ''is girt round with mystery: the narrow region of our experience is a small island in the midst of a boundless sea, which at once awes our feelings and stimulates our imagination by its vastness and its obscurity''. Only as a poet can a man pass beyond these confining shores. (pp. 238-41)

> *F. Parvin Sharpless, in his* The Literary Criticism of John Stuart Mill, *Mouton, 1967, 246 p.*

JOHN M. ROBSON   (essay date 1968)

[*In this excerpt from his full-length study of Mill's early and mature theories, Robson outlines Mill's philosophical method, stressing his insistence on the interplay between science and art.*]

In his general approach to the theory of reform Mill is clearly in the mainstream of British empiricism. He wished to introduce into the study of human behaviour the scientific approach that had demonstrated its fruitfulness elsewhere. Like Huxley, for example, he was convinced, and worked to convince others that, properly considered, the law of cause and effect is exhibited in individual and social behaviour. The panorama of history and of contemporary society can and should be studied in an attempt to discover causal sequences, with the ultimate aim of prediction and control through understanding. Such a belief can, of course, lead to an abandonment of moral imperatives, but it should be unnecessary to say that Mill agreed with Emerson and Arnold that there is a law for man and a law for thing. To recognize this distinction, however, is not to deny that man is subject to the law of nature as well as

moral law. The ''Scientist'' does not make normative decisions, but his findings enable the ''Artist'' to avoid futile and foolish proposals. Mill's purpose was the amelioration of mankind's lot through the Artist's application of the Scientist's findings.

This purpose should be borne in mind throughout the following discussion, for not the similarities, but the differences, between Mill's view and that of, say, Comte, are the hallmarks of his sociological thought. In spite of his enthusiasm, in spite of the glorious possibilities he saw in the distant future, in spite of his faith in science to reveal useful laws, he is sceptical. Man cannot penetrate beyond the phenomenal level; his inductions can never be complete; his generalizations can never be fully proved. Investigations into human nature produce at best empirical laws, mere graspings after a description of phenomenal relations, not at all explanatory. Even when connected by deduction with previously established and more basic ''laws'' they are of uncertain validity, to be recognized as approximations to the order of an unknowable and perhaps non-existent substratum. The mind of man abstracts and selects; reason can formulate ''natural laws,'' but cannot comprehend nature; a law does not correspond to a process. As Mill points out, sciences can be ''exact,'' that is, deal in ''real laws'' rather than ''approximate generalizations,'' only by treating ''tendencies'' and not ''facts.'' The scientist, and particularly the Moral Scientist, who is deprived of the experimental and observational techniques of his brother scientists, must not expect to find more than provisional truths, and if he thinks he is finding absolute truths he must not be allowed to persuade society of his omniscience. Mill is no worshipper of science; he sees it as a good servant but a ruinous master. Passages could easily be collected from his *Logic* to show that the Moral Scientist cannot unconditionally predict the future. Without certainty, complete faith must not be placed in the would-be controller. Science is, however—and here Mill is insistent— useful in the moral area, since knowledge insufficient for prediction is valuable for guidance. Men aware of the limitations of scientific knowledge are best prepared to use science's findings to promote utility.

This view, as much as anything else, prevented Mill from outlining a complete sociology. Compared to Comte's, his hierarchy of sciences is fragmentary and inconclusive, for he did not know enough, and felt he could not know enough, to fix finally its shape. He described limits and interconnections, but did not attempt to force organization on provisional materials. Here, it may be said, is his failure as a theorist, but the failure itself refutes any attempt to characterize him as a pure ideologue. His humility arises from the inductive basis of his theory of knowledge, and his awareness of the complexity of human affairs. Ratiocination, the great weapon of the dogmatist, cannot in his view discover new truths, being bound in its own closed system. The syllogism is a shorthand expression of thought, a tool useful for understanding, expression, and conviction, but not for revelation. Formal logic merely shuffles the cards given in experience. Since induction is always uncertain, the dogmatic social scientist is an unnatural hybrid not to be entrusted with political power. Science, it must be asserted again, is not normative; it needs Art's directional commands. (pp. 160-62)

> *John M. Robson, in his* The Improvement of Mankind: The Social and Political Thought of John Stuart Mill, *University of Toronto Press, 1968, 292 p.*

WENDELL ROBERT CARR   (essay date 1970)

[Carr maintains that Mill's The Subjection of Women *is an important historical document that "stands unchallenged as the most distinguished intellectual monument the cause has yet produced." In his exploration of women's psychology and abilities, Carr writes, Mill was unparalleled in his time. However, Carr also concedes that even in his own time Mill's views were "commonplace" within the women's rights movement and that his "old-fashioned" approach to history and psychology have limited the work's appeal to later writers.]*

John Stuart Mill's *The Subjection of Women* is unquestionably the most eloquent, the most ambitious, and at the same time among the most heartfelt pleas in the English language for the perfect equality of the sexes. . . . What *The Wealth of Nations* is for classical liberalism and *Das Kapital* for socialism, *The Subjection of Women* is for the century-old agitation for women's rights. It provided the movement with a philosophic rationale of cosmic proportions and, more than a century after its publication, stands unchallenged as the most distinguished intellectual monument the cause has yet produced. The present-day Women's Liberation movement is not soon likely to surpass it. (p. v)

The *Subjection of Women* appeared at the very moment the status of women was beginning to undergo its greatest revolution in modern history. The work unmistakably identified Mill as the herald of one of the most controversial and influential reform movements of modern times. (p. vi)

In his concrete proposals Mill differed little from a host of other writers spawned by the women's rights movement. Similarly, most of the grounds on which he based his recommendations had been staples of advanced liberal thought for most of the nineteenth century. What distinguished *The Subjection of Women* was its typically "Millian" combination of deep passion and high philosophy; its relentless concern with questions about human nature, the formation of character, and the psychology of the sexes; its pervasive uncertainty about whether masculine and feminine character were essentially different; and its insistence on the inseparable connection between women's rights and one of the overriding aims of all Mill's mature thought—the moral reformation of mankind. This distinctive combination of qualities serves at once to define the place of *The Subjection of Women* in the voluminous literature on women's rights, to identify it unmistakably with Mill's more general social philosophy, and to account for its peculiar fate during the century since its publication. (pp. vii-viii)

In addition to basing his critique of existing institutions on principles of human nature, Mill also recognized that the whole debate over women's rights ultimately turned on a crucial point of psychology: whether "masculine" and "feminine" natures differed from one another in any fundamental way. Discussions of women's rights had long been marked by claims and counterclaims about the nature of woman. . . .

Among all the proponents—as well as the opponents—of women's rights in late nineteenth-century England, Mill alone confronted the question of woman's nature and abilities head on. Virtually every chapter of *The Subjection of Women* bore witness to the conviction . . . that it was "thoroughly time to bring the question of women's capacities into the front rank of the discussion."

Though working in a psychological tradition that provided little help in resolving the issue, Mill carried out the inquiry according to his highest standards of intellectual rigor. (p. xviii)

[Convinced] that uncertainty "does not forbid conjecture," Mill went on to broach even the question he had pronounced insoluble—what "natural character" of women would be revealed if all "artificial causes of difference were withdrawn." And despite the inadequacies of his psychological theory, in defining a way to solve the problem Mill displayed his usual acumen. Given the impossibility of isolating human beings from their surroundings, the only way to discover what part of feminine character might be "natural," Mill said, was to trace "the mental consequences of external influences" and to consider whether the circumstances in which a person has been placed were sufficient to account for "what he is." (pp. xix-xx)

Mill's conclusions were of course predictable. Taking up what appeared to him "the only marked case . . . of apparent inferiority of women to men," that women had produced no work of "philosophy, science, or art, entitled to the first rank," Mill asserted after a long and careful argument that the domestic and social circumstances in which women lived sufficiently explained almost all "the apparent differences between women and men, including the whole of those which imply any inferiority." As for current sentimentalities about the moral superiority of women, and the somewhat contradictory allegation of their tendency toward moral bias, Mill dismissed both as the product of blindness to the fact that women's moral character, like their intellectual proclivities, resulted from the circumstances in which they had been placed. (p. xx)

For all its painstaking—if sometimes fallacious—logic, *The Subjection of Women* was more than a philosophical treatise. It was also an impassioned secular sermon. For behind Mill's philosophic method, his critique of unrestrained power, and his theories of human nature lay an encompassing moral vision—a vision as characteristic of Mill as the concept of culture was of Matthew Arnold. On a superficial level Mill's ideal of human existence differed little from that of many other English liberals. It consisted in part of a passionate celebration of freedom in the great English tradition of Milton, Adam Smith, and Herbert Spencer. In questions of women's rights, as in economics, the only adequate principle, Mill proclaimed, was "that things in which the individual is the person directly interested, never go right but as they are left to his own discretion; and that any regulation of them by authority, except to protect the rights of others, is sure to be mischievous." "The anxiety of mankind to interfere in behalf of nature, for fear lest nature should not succeed in effecting its purpose," was, he declared, an "altogether unnecessary solicitude."

Yet Mill did not regard liberty merely as a principle of social organization. Drawing once more on his belief in the power of society to mold human nature, he ultimately justified freedom on the grounds that it alone could accomplish his overriding moral aim: the reformation of human character. Not content merely with a negative argument against male superiority, Mill acknowledged in the final chapter of *The Subjection of Women* that many persons, though convinced of the necessity to reform the laws of marriage and willing to concede the invalidity of all the major arguments against equality, might still want to know what "express advantage would be obtained" by removing women's social and political disabilities. In reply, Mill cited as the primary gain "the advantage of having the most universal and pervading of all human relations regulated by justice instead of injustice." And if justice, he continued, prevailed in the relationship between men and women, "all the selfish propensities, the self-worship, the unjust self-preference, which exist among mankind" would be permanently rooted out. "The child," Mill hoped, "would really, for the first time in man's existence on earth, be trained in the way he should go, and when he was old there would be a chance that he would not depart from it."

To be sure, Mill also noted that to give women the "free use of their faculties" would double "the mass of mental faculties available for the higher service of humanity." But after only a brief discussion Mill abandoned that argument and turned once more to the moral effects of female equality, pointing out as yet another advantage of freedom that it would give to the opinion of women a "more beneficial . . . influence upon the general mass of human belief and sentiment. (pp. xxii-xxiii)

The Subjection of Women has continued to be quoted occasionally even up to our own day. But besides the comparative infrequency of the quotations, the work is almost always cited merely on a specific point and is seldom accorded any special authority. It is not, as it legitimately might be, praised as the overarching philosophic rationale for the equality of women; nor is Mill's name used to give added weight to controversial assertions. *The Subjection of Women*, in short, is generally treated as one work among many, not as a sacred text embodying a unique revelation. (p. xxvi)

Viewed from the broadest perspective, the fate of *The Subjection of Women* was no doubt merely one example of the general decline in Mill's reputation as a thinker which began in the two decades after his death and from which he is only now beginning to recover. The old-fashioned way in which *The Subjection of Women* approached history and psychology, moreover, clearly precluded its being an important source for such later writers on the history of the family and the psychology of the sexes as Havelock Ellis, who unfailingly made use of the latest available research. Equally important, by the time *The Subjection of Women* was published in 1869, Mill's arguments were already commonplace among those involved in the women's rights movement. (pp. xxvii)

> Wendell Robert Carr, in an introduction to The Subjection of Women *by John Stuart Mill,* The M.I.T. Press, *1970, pp. v-xxix.*

KATE MILLETT   (essay date 1970)

[*A prominent feminist and the author of* Sexual Politics, *Millett praises Mill's understanding of women's oppression in* The Subjection of Women. *Millett asserts that unlike other nineteenth-century writers, Mill recognized that "the system of sexual dominance is the very prototype of other abuses of power and other forms of egotism."*]

[Mill's] *The Subjection of Women* is a reasoned and eloquent statement of the actual position of women through history as well as an attack on the conditions of legal bondage, debilitating education, and the stifling ethic of "wifely subjection" within the Victorian period. It is argued as powerfully as the essay *On Liberty* and is as full of Mill's splendidly controlled humanist outrage as any of his statements on slavery or serfdom, to which he draws frequent parallels.

A political realist, Mill was quite aware of the revolutionary character of his thesis:

> That the principle which regulates the existing social relations between the two sexes—the legal subordination of one sex to the other—is wrong in itself, and now one of the chief hindrances to human improvement; and that it ought

to be replaced by a principle of perfect equality, admitting no power or privilege on the one side, nor disability on the other.

This was a drastic recommendation to make then, just as it is now. Mill was fully awake to the resistance he would meet, the appalled uproar, the noisy irrationality of the old school, chauvinist or chivalrous, neither dreaming of producing any real evidence for their assertion that things were quite as they should be between man and woman. Mill even predicts the uncritical bigotry of the opposition: "In every respect the burden is hard on those who attack an almost universal opinion. They must be very fortunate as well as unusually capable if they obtain a hearing at all." For all his extraordinary capability, Mill was scarcely fortunate before a male audience: the reaction in the reviews was disastrous; he was denounced as mad or immoral, often as both. (pp. 65-6)

Mill realizes that what is commonly regarded as feminine character is but the predictable outcome of a highly artificial system of cultivation, or to adopt his own metaphor, society's female is a plant grown half in a steam bath and half in the snow. Mill is optimistic that an idolatrous attitude toward the myth of nature is bound to disintegrate before a "sound psychology." Deplorably, such assistance has yet to appear. In the meantime one may do well to rely on Mill's own, for its psychological contribution is the book's great achievement. In fact, Mill's psychology is grounded in a more lucid distinction between prescription and description than one encounters for example, in Freud, and a more intelligent grasp of the effects of environment and circumstance. Mill is also sensitive to the mechanisms by which conservative thought construes the status quo as the inevitable, a fine trait in a social psychologist. Until we undertake "an analytic study of the most important departments of psychology, the laws of the influence of circumstances on character," we are, Mill observes, unlikely to be able to know anything about the innate differences in male and female personality, for "the most elementary knowledge of the circumstances in which they have been placed clearly points out the causes that have made them what they are." Meanwhile, since nothing is known, it is presumption in man to "lay down the law to women as to what is, or is not, their vocation."

Because he understands how conditioning produces a sexual temperament appropriate to sexual role, Mill is in an excellent position to understand how woman is the product of the system which oppresses her: how all her education, formal and informal, is dedicated to perpetuating it. He also believes "the mental differences supposed to exist between women and men are but the natural effects of the differences in their education and circumstances, and indicate no radical differences, far less radical inferiority of nature." (pp. 69-70)

In Mill's analysis, the system of sexual dominance is the very prototype of other abuses of power and other forms of egotism. Just as Engels came to see in sexual supremacy and subordination a model for later hierarchies of rank, class, and wealth, Mill has discovered in it the psychological foundations of other species of oppression. "All the selfish propensities, the self-worship, the unjust self-preference, which exist among mankind, have their source and root in, and derive their principal nourishment from, the present constitution of the relation of men and women." (p. 77)

[Mill's conclusion is rational and] full of a new and promising vigor. He urges the complete emancipation of women not only for the sake of the "unspeakable gain in happiness to the liberated half of the species, the difference to them between a life of subjection to the will of others and a life of rational freedom," but also for the enormous benefit this would confer on both sexes and on humanity: "We have had the morality of submission and the morality of chivalry and generosity; the time is now come" for "the most fundamental of the social relations" to be "placed under the rule of equal justice." In Mill's tones one hears the energy and cry of revolution. . . . (pp. 80-1)

> Kate Millett, "The Debate over Women: Ruskin Versus Mill," in Victorian Studies, Vol. XIV, No. 1, September, 1970, pp. 63-82.*

H. J. McCLOSKEY (essay date 1971)

[*In this excerpt from his full-length work on Mill's life and philosophy, McCloskey critiques Mill's metaphysics as evidenced in his essay* An Examination of Sir William Hamilton's Philosophy. *Concluding that his "account of matter is a reductionist one," McCloskey argues that Mill's theory was overly concerned with sensations and not enough with "matter, substance, qualities."*]

Mill nowhere set out a systematic statement of his metaphysical theories. However, his *An Examination of Sir William Hamilton's Philosophy* contains discussions of problems in metaphysics, philosophical psychology and logic. It is predominantly expository and polemical in character, Mill's main concern being to expose the inadequacies of Hamilton's, Mansel's and others' arguments and theories; he advanced his own theories as more satisfactory alternatives, but without detailed development. . . .

Mill's view was that all reality is mental, that matter and material objects, if conceived of as things distinct from mental phenomena, were philosophers' and theologians' illusions, the belief in which could be explained in terms of the psychological tendency to 'mistake mental abstractions, even negative ones, for substantive realities'. The sources of his inspiration were Hartley's *Observations on Man* . . . which set out the Associationist psychology, and Berkeley's idealist writings. (p. 142)

The commonsense view is that the things we perceive, chairs, tables, houses, cars, other people, are real and external to us, and not dependent on us for their existence, and that our knowledge of them springs from our sense perceptions. We see, touch, feel, hear or taste them. There are obvious grounds for questioning these commonsense beliefs. Our senses may mislead us, such that things cannot always be as they appear; the straight stick, in water, appears bent, parallel lines appear to meet in the distance, we see mirages, people experience hallucinations. Further, science suggests that the colour and other features of objects are not qualities inherent in the things perceived but the results of interactions between things and observers. There would therefore seem to be a real problem concerning the nature and our knowledge of the external world. Yet this is not quite how the problem arose for Mill. His approach consisted rather in examining the origins of our beliefs, and what is necessary to explain them.

Mill rejected the realist theory that we directly intuit material objects, and the more qualified view of Hamilton, that we know directly the so-called primary qualities (extension, solidity, figure, etc.). His grounds were various. Part of his case for rejecting direct realism of any kind consisted in his detailed account of how we come to gain knowledge of the qualities of objects. *Hamilton,* chap. 13, contains a careful, detailed

discussion of the origin and basis of our belief in the primary qualities. Equally important is the claim that 'it is impossible to doubt a fact of internal consciousness', that 'to feel, and not to know that we feel is an impossibility' . . . , and that we can fully explain our belief in the external world by reference to these indubitable sense experiences (sensations) and the laws of the mind. There is no systematic exploration of the direct realist contention that we have direct awareness of the real world (illusory perceptions can be explained as errors, and much done to render the theory more plausible than Mill represented it as being), and similarly, while Mill noted and commented on a number of causal theories such as the representative theory of perception, Kantian phenomena—noumena theories (if they can accurately be characterised as causal theories), he engaged in no systematic examination of them, instead resting his rejection of them on two main considerations, namely, that it is possible to explain the external world without reference to these unknowable causes of sensations, and that on a correct understanding of causality there can be no grounds for postulating such unknowable causes.

Mill sought to explain the belief in the external world in terms of sensations, possible sensations and psychological laws, including the law that we are capable of expectation (and memory) of possible (actual) sensations, and the various laws of association that 'similar phenomena tend to be thought together', 'Phenomena which have either been experienced or conceived in close contiguity to one another, tend to be thought together—the kinds of contiguity being simultaneity and immediate succession', 'Associations produced by contiguity become more certain and rapid by repetition, this leading to inseparable and indissoluble association', Mill here observing that when an association acquires this character of inseparability, the facts or phenomena answering to those ideas come at last to seem inseparable in existence; 'things we are unable to conceive apart appear incapable of existing apart'. Mill therefore stated the Psychological Theory which he explained as maintaining 'that there are associations naturally and even necessarily generated by the order of our sensations and of our reminiscences of sensation, which, supposing no intuition of the external world to have existed in consciousness, would inevitably generate the belief, and cause it to be regarded as an intuition.' . . . In this way Mill sought to show that all that is meant by 'material object' (matter) can be explained in terms of actual or possible sensations, that there is no need to postulate anything over and above sensations and possible sensations, ordered and grouped in certain ways, to explain what ordinary people and philosophers mean when they speak of material objects. Mill's so-called Psychological Theory is now seen as one of the early statements of Phenomenalism. (pp. 143-45)

[According to Mill,] when we believe in the existence of material objects, what we believe in are actual and possible sensations, or simply possible sensations, where the sensations are thought of as coming in groups, in such a way that, as a result of association of ideas, some are symbols or signs of others. Thus, when we observe a horse, i.e. have visual-type horse sensations, we, in believing it to be a real horse, a material object, believe that we should experience the other material object horse sensations if we touched, felt, smelt it. This Mill expressed by saying that some possibilities are conditional certainties and, less accurately, that they are permanent possibilities, and potentialities. In asserting that material objects exist, for example that there is a cat in the next room, I am concerned to assert the existence of things which have *public, independent* and, in some sense, *continuing* existence, where the contrast is with purely private sensations such as a pain, hallucination, sensations as of mirages (which may be shared but not be independent of observers), purely imagined objects, and mere fleeting phenomena such as a flash of lightning. In believing the cat to be a material object, we believe that it is public, observable in principle, and usually in practice, by other observers; that its existence is independent of our perceptions, such that it continues to exist (unless changed or destroyed) when not observed; and that its existence is a continuing one in that it has temporal duration. Mill sought to accommodate these features in his slogan statement 'Matter is a permanent possibility of sensation'.

Even though this statement is often quoted with approval, it is an inaccurate, misleading summary of Mill's thesis. Mill used it to express a number of claims. He wished to note the enduring connections between the sensations within each group of material object sensations, stones, horses, trees, by explaining the possibility of experiencing some after experiencing other of the sensations as *permanent*. This is an intelligible but less illuminating description than other possible ones: it is the connection between the actual and the possible, or some and other possible sensations, rather than the possibilities, which are permanent. Mill also wished to note that objects, e.g. prehistoric plants and animals, may exist independently of all observation. Mill's summary statement explains their existence as of there being permanent, indefinitely lasting possibilities of sensations of these now non-existent entities. Here he seems to use 'permanent' in its ordinary sense. He also sought to explain the continuing existence of things after we cease to observe them. This we often express by observing that while the table is permanent, our perceptions of it are not. This too he sought to note by speaking of the possibilities as permanent. In fact, material objects are not permanent in the sense of lasting indefinitely; hence the possibilities of observing them, e.g. by re-entering the room, ought to be no more permanent than the material objects the belief in the existence of which is being explained. It could be argued that 'permanent' has a legitimate use in all these contexts, namely, that all the so-called permanent possibilities, if expressed in terms of hypothetical propositions, claim permanent truth. Thus it is claimed to be permanently true that some sensations are signs of others, e.g. that certain this-horse sensations are signs of other this-horse sensations; that sensations consequent on change of the observer's position would/will occur; that had an observer been present (none could be), certain sensations would have been experienced. Mill did seem to view these as permanent hypothetical truths, but this sense of 'permanent' would not exhaust his meaning or be adequate for the purpose of his theory. Further, the first hypothetical is not a permanent truth; deception, where some sensations are wrongly taken as signs of others, occurs.... [What] is important is that Mill attempted to express in summary form what can only accurately be expressed in longer, more qualified statements.

Mill's account of matter is a reductionist one. He sought to explain the world in terms of sensations, certain orders or arrangements of sensations and possible sensations, without reference to matter, substance, qualities. However, he neither represented nor advanced it as such, but rather as a translation of ordinary material object statements. He claimed simply to explain what we mean by matter, that we assert no more than a permanent possibility of sensations when we assert that matter exists. (He did concede that some philosophers and theologians invoked some other concept or concepts of matter, and he noted the strength of the human tendency to mistake mental abstractions for substantive realities; hence he did not completely rule out the reductionist aspect of his account.) (pp. 146-49)

H. J. McCloskey, in his John Stuart Mill: A Critical Study, *Macmillan, 1971, 186 p.*

R. J. HALLIDAY   (essay date 1976)

[*In the following excerpt, Halliday briefly summarizes Mill's traits as a philosopher. He traces Mill's disillusionment with the ideas of the English romantics and the French positivists and his belief in consensus and rejection of dogmatism.*]

Mill was a cautious and uncertain pessimist, with an extraordinarily acute sense of the dangers of first principles and grand theories. He was always likely to retreat into a disenchanted pragmatism and, more often than not, was to be found shaking his head in a mixture of disbelief and disillusion. Partly this was a question of personal morale. The hopes he derived from the English romantics and the French positivists, after the resolution of his nervous breakdown in 1826, proved to be flimsy and insubstantial when confronted with the press of illiterate and intemperate proletarians upon the institutions of national politics. The growth of the English working class as a consciously separate political force filled him with fear; he was convinced that their grubby materialism would finally issue into a despotism. His observation of the aristocracy and middle classes confirmed the worst of his forebodings. It was also partly a question of intention. Mill designed his political theory with few terminal points; he was more interested in conducting a continuous holding operation than in arriving at a particular destination. In this way, each extreme could be resisted as it appeared, and each bitter controversy could be gently encouraged to fade into comfortable agreement. This was the whole point of Mill's eclecticism and his most enduring commitment as a political thinker. Consensus was indeed his basic value.

But his commitment to consensus was not absolute and all-consuming. The agreement Mill so earnestly sought rested upon the self-conscious and critical choices of all those individuals concerned to understand the difficulties of politics and the dilemmas of moral living. Their agreement could neither be bought nor forced; and without the activities of self-culture and all of the convictions arising from those activities, agreement would either be totally spurious or completely intolerant. This was the lesson that Mill had learned at the feet of the romantics. People should think for themselves and try experiments for themselves, constantly seeking a quality of experience that was unique; only in this way could the conduct of human beings approach responsibility. Like all other activities, morals and politics had to be learnt. As a sceptic prone to disenchantment, Mill was inclined to believe that on the whole people learned slowly and rather badly. There is nothing sinister or reprehensible in this belief: Mill still remained committed to free inquiry and to liberty of conscience and pursuits. And he may well have been right in thinking that when improvement comes, it comes only very slowly, emerging piecemeal here and there: the view is as plausible as any other.

Indeed, despite his emphasis on the methods of observation, analysis and induction and his continuing reputation as a philosopher of science, in politics at least, Mill was most impressed by the limitations of time, place and circumstance. He recognised that skills had only a very local application and that knowledge, like experience itself, could never be complete. In his view, the art of judgement could not be separated from the limitations inherent in particular situations; and while politics was not merely the pursuit of whatever appeared from day to day, the practitioner was forced to proceed pragmatically, case by case, issue by issue, with whatever certainty was to hand. This helps to explain the great range and variety of causes to which Mill was able to commit himself. His firm belief was that, in politics, now one theory was right, now another; one was bound to use whatever was to hand at a particular time. Consequently, dogmatism was always his enemy, and his cautious and uncertain pessimism was matched by a determination to keep his mind open. So while Mill was frequently likely to be grumbling, he was also prepared to learn. This is what made him a serious political thinker. (pp. 142-43)

> *R. J. Halliday, in his* John Stuart Mill, *George Allen & Unwin Ltd., 1976, 151 p.*

SUSAN MOLLER OKIN (essay date 1979)

[*Unlike most twentieth-century critics, Okin is critical of* The Subjection of Women. *She faults Mill for restricting his comments to middle- and upper-class women and for advocating "the traditional division of labor within the family." Sections of this essay originally appeared in* The New Zealand Journal of History, *1973,* Philosophy and Public Affairs, *1977, and* The Journal of Politics, *1979.*]

The unjust treatment of women has, Mill argues in *The Subjection of Women,* the detrimental effect that they attempt to gain influence in subversive ways, and to use it for selfish purposes, as happens in other cases in which legitimate access to power is denied. Under existing conditions within the family, he argues, women are forced to resort to cunning and underhand tactics in order to have their wishes fulfilled, when they and their husbands disagree. There exists no motivation to discuss such issues openly and rationally, since the husband is legally constituted as the family's decision-maker. As far as women's political influence is concerned, Mill is sure that the indirect influence they exert, through their pressure on their enfranchised husbands, is bound to be unconcerned with the welfare of anyone beyond their own immediate families. Thus he, unlike Rousseau, recognizes that the outside world has no hope of winning over the family in the conflict of loyalties that unenfranchised women face. For "their social position allows them no scope for any feelings beyond the family except personal likings & dislikes, & it is assumed that they would be governed entirely by these in their judgment & feeling in political matters." But if they were themselves enfranchised, and thereby given their own legitimate means of influencing the political process, Mill argues, they would in the course of time become far more likely to use these means responsibly and in a more humanitarian spirit. (pp. 224-25)

Mill argues, too, that the abolition of the legal inequality of husband and wife would have immeasurable effects on the value of the family as an educative institution. Since he believes that "society in equality is its normal state," and moreover that "the only school of genuine moral sentiment is society between equals," he considers that the everyday assumption by men of their superiority over women constantly detracts from the value of their own lives as well as those of their wives, and has very harmful effects on their children. There can be nothing approaching the highest potential of human companionship between two human beings, one of whom is convinced a priori of his greater capacities and value, and of the justice of his always taking precedence over the other. What hope, Mill asks, is there for the moral advancement of society,

so long as the domestic atmosphere in which all its members receive their earliest moral education is based on such an unjust distribution of rights and powers? Only when marriage were to become recognized by law and society as a cooperative partnership between equals, might the family at last become, for the children, "a school of sympathy in equality, of living together in love, without power on one side and obedience on the other." Only then could children be prepared for what he regards as the "true virtue of human beings," that is, "fitness to live together as equals."

In spite of these protestations about equality within the family, however, it is in fact because of John Stuart Mill's assumptions and convictions about the family and its traditional roles that his feminism falls short of advocating true equality and freedom for married women. Mill's feminist writings are, implicitly, concerned only with middle- and upper-class women, and it is the bourgeois family that is his model. Though he rejects the legalized inequalities of its patriarchal form, he regards the family itself as "essential for humanity," and is concerned to reassure his readers that family life has nothing to fear, but rather much to gain, from the complete political and civil equality of the sexes. Though presently "a school of despotism," once justly constituted, it would be "the real school of the virtues of freedom."

Moreover, Mill argues in favor of the traditional division of labor within the family. While he asserts that women should have a real choice of a career or marriage, he assumes that the majority of women are likely to continue to prefer marriage, and that this choice is equivalent to choosing a career. He states:

> Like a man when he chooses a profession, so, when a woman marries, it may in general be understood that she makes choice of the management of a household, and the bringing up of a family, as the first call upon her exertions, during as many years of her life as may be required for the purpose; and that she renounces, not all other objects and occupations, but all which are not consistent with the requirements of this.

In keeping with this mode of thinking, Mill asserts that there is an "infinitely closer relationship of a child to its mother than to its father," and that "nothing can replace the mother for the education of children." He does not pause to reflect that the qualities of motherhood, just as much as any of the other existing differences between the sexes, might be at least partly due to environmental factors, most particularly to the conditioning that resulted from customary modes of socialization. Again, in spite of his general rejection of the pressures of opinion, he calmly accepts that the sexual division of duties within the family is "already made by consent, or at all events not by law, but by general custom," and he defends it as "the most suitable division of labour between the two persons." (pp. 225-27)

Mill's acceptance of traditional sex roles within the family places serious limitations on the extent to which he can apply the principles of freedom and equality to married women. First, though he argues in favor of equal property *rights* for married women, these are rights to property inherited or earned by the woman herself, not rights to equal shares in the family income. "The rule," Mill says, "is simple: whatever would be the husband's or wife's if they were not married, should be under their exclusive control during marriage.'' Clearly, then, the income of the male earner is his, as much after marriage as before, and Mill does not recognize the anomaly that women's work in the home is unpaid labor. Only in *The Enfranchisement of Women* do we find the assertion that it is not only necessary for married women to be able to earn their own subsistence, but that their position in the family would improve significantly ''if women both earned, and had the right to possess, a part of the income of the family.'' Although in *The Subjection of Women* Mill agrees that married women must be able to support themselves, he explicitly rejects the idea that they should actually do so, regarding such a practice as liable to lead to the neglect of the household and children. (pp. 228-29)

Second, Mill's defense of traditional sex roles within the family amounts to a denial of freedom of opportunity and individual expression of talents to that majority of women whom he assumes would always choose to marry. Though he is so much aware that the care of a household is an incessantly preoccupying duty that he cites it as a major reason for women's comparative lack of achievement in many artistic fields, he in fact condones the continuance of this barrier for most women. His refusal to concede that the tiresome details of domestic life should be shared by both sexes, and his failure to question the social institutions that made such sharing practically impossible are striking in the light of the fact that he recognizes that the principal means by which women would come to be recognized as equals was via success in fields formerly monopolized by men. (p. 229)

John Stuart Mill tried fervently to apply the principles of liberalism to women. He eschewed patriarchy within the family, and the legal and political subordination of women, as anachronisms in the modern age and as gross violations of liberty and justice. However, although a very forward-looking feminist in many respects, he in no way perceived the injustice involved in institutions and practices which allowed a man to have a career and economic independence, *and* a home life and children, but which forced a woman to choose between the two. His refusal to question the traditional family and its demands on women set the limits of his liberal feminism. (p. 230)

> *Susan Moller Okin, ''John Stuart Mill, Liberal Feminist,'' in her* Women in Western Political Thought, *Princeton University Press, 1979, pp. 197-230.*

PETER GLASSMAN (essay date 1982)

[*In the following excerpt, Glassman offers a psychoanalytic interpretation of Mill's* Autobiography. *The style and structure of the work, Glassman argues, is determined primarily by Mill's ''strategy of simultaneously expressing and denying his most subversive instincts.''*]

[In his *Autobiography*] Mill comments: ''Whoever, either now or hereafter, may think of me and the work I have done, must never forget that it is the product not of one intellect and conscience but of three, the least considerable of whom, and above all the least original, is the one whose name is attached to it.'' The sentence is so disconcerting that we scarcely know how to read it. This calm acceptance of tripartition, this quiet acknowledgment of inconsiderableness and unoriginality perplexes and frightens us. Mill's conviction that his personality and experience have evolved as ''the product'' solely of ''intellect and conscience'' seems unthinkable. His belief that his sensibility and ''work'' have occurred directly in response to

other persons' ''intellect and conscience'' seems absurd and abhorrent. We feel as disturbed by Mill's use of language as by his perceptions and judgments. We notice, for example, that he refuses to employ the personal pronoun. ''Me'' and ''I'' reduce themselves to ''it'' and ''the one whose name is attached to [the text].'' We observe that the sentence's energy and motion emanate from the writer's deprecations of himself. We remark that the prose derives its order and strength from the author's ascriptions of powerlessness and prosaicness to himself. The writing is fascinating. But it is fascinating primarily because of its power to bewilder and to horrify.

This sentence and its attitudes are characteristic of Mill's work in the *Autobiography*. Throughout the book he testifies to his lack of substance. He repeatedly indicates that he is inadequate, unimaginative, and somehow impersonal or nonauthoritative in his own life and ''work.'' This is particularly true of the opening paragraph of the *Autobiography*. Mill begins what he calls his ''biographical sketch'' of himself by declaring that his history and his ways of describing it cannot in themselves seem compelling or even ''interesting.'' ''I do not for a moment imagine,'' he remarks, ''that any part of what I have to relate, can be interesting to the public as a narrative, or as being connected with myself.'' . . . He finds it necessary to legitimize his existence and his art. He believes, he tells us, that he must make ''some mention of the reasons which have made me think it desirable that I should leave behind me such a memorial of so uneventful a life as mine.'' . . . (pp. 193-94)

The opening paragraph of the *Autobiography* defines a man who has been both created and destroyed by a set of circumstances which appear to have been too strong and too active for the ''mind'' which they engendered and then abandoned. The brilliant but bizarre paragraph describes a person whose history has made him at once knowable and undiscoverable, conspicuous and undiscernible.

This is Mill's crucial problem in the *Autobiography*. He wants and apparently needs to ''think of [himself] and the work [he has] done.'' But he does not know how to locate or to speak about himself. He solves this problem, I believe, by circumventing it. Because he does not know how to define his character and consciousness, he describes his ''intellectual and moral development'' and the ''other persons'' who determined it. Because he cannot identify the attitudes and emotions which might have made him tangible, he tries to discuss the evolution or the etiology of his intangibleness. The problem and its resolution are almost insuperably complex. In order to characterize himself, Mill must acknowledge and represent himself as his lack of character. In order to write about his own substance, he must write about ''the successive phases'' of his reactions to other, more obviously substantive people.

The person who most significantly affected Mill's ''development'' was his father. It is for this reason, I believe, that the narrative portion of the *Autobiography* opens in the peculiar way it does. Mill declares: ''I was born in London, on the 20th of May 1806, and was the eldest son of James Mill, the author of the History of British India.'' . . . He goes on to write a ''biographical sketch'' not of himself but of James Mill. He discusses not his own but his parent's history and accomplishments. He can approach the fact of himself, it seems, only by engaging and celebrating the fact of his progenitor.

This tactic is intelligible. A man who believes himself to have been psychically determined by his father will wish to think and to write about his father before he thinks and writes about himself. And yet, however intelligible it may be, the stratagem is extremely confusing as the beginning of an autobiography. For it conceals from us the nature of the text and the identity of the author. As we read the work's opening paragraphs we feel perplexed and estranged. Is this, we wonder, a biography or an autobiography? Who is the subject? Who is the writer? Whose life will give the book its issues, events, and energies? Whose personality will give the book its ideas, ideologies, and voice?

Our questions are soon answered. We quickly discover that, no matter how puzzling it may be to ourselves, the opening is entirely appropriate to its subject matter. For we learn that the *Autobiography* is principally concerned with the tragic circumstance that Mill does not know how to distinguish himself from his parent. We learn that the work is chiefly about the sad and startling fact that Mill can imagine and discuss his own existence only by imagining, discussing, and trying to participate in his father's existence. The beginning of the *Autobiography* disorients and vexes us. But it ingeniously reports Mill's own disorientation and anger. It sincerely confesses, indeed, that confusion and rage are the theme and, as it were, the author of the *Autobiography*. The paragraph acquaints us with the fact that as we read the *Autobiography* we shall encounter a hugely bewildered man who is trying to trace "the successive phases" and relieve the incapacitating pains of his terrible persuasion that he is an unidentifiable and unworthy person—that he is, in particular, a much less actual and much less excellent person than his imposing father. (pp. 194-96)

Mill orders the entire *Autobiography* upon [the] mechanism or strategy of simultaneously expressing and denying his most subversive instincts. Describing himself as a man who could at once experience and suppress everything volatile in his psychology seems to have given him a pleasing sense of authority over both his history and his imagination. This consoling idea gradually dominates the processes and structures of his self-portraiture. It became one of Mill's principal purposes in the *Autobiography* to characterize himself as a creature who had no untoward, unruly, or ungovernable impulses. He represents himself in the book not as a personality replying to irresistible passions and percepts, but as an intelligence answering to disinterested wisdoms. He tries to describe himself as an essentially affectless and disembodied mind: an instrument for detached and formal speculation rather than an emotive individual who somewhat chaotically responds to unique and fractious desires, drives, and demands. In effect and probably in subconscious intention, Mill fulfilled the mandate of his childhood in the *Autobiography*. He defines himself in the work as the minimally responsive, perfectly controlled, purely intellective human being whom his father had insisted that he become. (p. 203)

I have described the *Autobiography* as an extraordinarily self-effacing memoir. I have suggested that in his "biographical sketch" Mill unconsciously felt extremely reluctant to identify and to praise himself. This also became an important quality or trait of his conscious thought. In both his public and his private discourse he repeatedly proclaimed that excessive self-involvement (by which he often seems to have meant virtually any self-involvement) is reprehensible and ridiculous. (p. 207)

And yet, despite Mill's conscious and unconscious campaigns against egotism, and despite his many motives for depersonalizing himself in his own work, the *Autobiography* frequently assumes an aggressively self-assured and self-assertive tone. As we read the work we often encounter what seems to be a

congratulation or a celebration of self. The narrative is layered with passages which may strike us as especially egregious exhibitions of "the constant unceasing unsleeping elastic pressure of human egotism." What is startling and intriguing about these passages is the fact that they aggrandize not Mill himself, but his father and his wife. To our amusement—and, I think, to our sorrow and horror—we discover that in the *Autobiography*, as so often in his life, Mill manifests a sensibility which focused an inordinate amount of attention and regard upon not his own but two other persons' egos. (pp. 207-08)

Many people find Mill's literature deficient in its feelings and sparse in its excitements. The *Autobiography* seems to some readers the least engaging of the major modernist autobiographical works. It seems to me, though, that the *Autobiography* is a profoundly moving and a profoundly important achievement. Sometimes Mill's writing seems stiff and contorted. Often it may appear to be cold. But the emotions which the *Autobiography* expresses and resolves are extraordinarily interesting, and of volcanic intensity. No doubt Mill's cognitions and beliefs are less striking than, say, Wordsworth's. Certainly Mill was less ardently involved with and less clairvoyantly aware of himself than Rousseau. The *Autobiography* seems to me, however, fully as inventive and fully as significant a creation as *The Prelude* or *The Confessions*. For Mill shares, I believe, Wordsworth and Rousseau's great impulse: the impulse to claim an identification; the impulse to locate and to seize a definitive, durable, and describable sensibility. (p. 213)

Peter Glassman, "'Who Made Me?': The 'Auto-biography' of John Stuart Mill," in Prose Studies, *Vol. 5, No. 2, September, 1982, pp. 193-213.*

ADDITIONAL BIBLIOGRAPHY

Aiken, Susan Hardy. "Scripture and Poetic Discourse in *The Subjection of Women.*" *PMLA* 98, No. 3 (May 1983): 353-73.
　　Examines Mill's use of biblical narrative as "a poetic subtext" in *The Subjection of Women*. Aiken also analyzes the relationship between the essay's poetic structure and its historical context.

Albee, Ernest. "John Stuart Mill." In his *A History of English Utilitarianism*, pp. 191-267. London: Swan Sonnenschein & Co., 1902.
　　A discussion of Mill's life and works, focusing on his utilitarian philosophy and his contribution to theoretical ethics.

Anschutz, R. P. *The Philosophy of J. S. Mill*. Oxford: Clarendon Press, 1953, 184 p.
　　A detailed examination of Mill's philosophy. Anschutz analyzes his attitude toward democracy and his theories of logic, epistemology, and induction.

Britton, Karl. *John Stuart Mill*. 2d ed. New York: Dover Publications, 1969, 224 p.
　　Surveys Mill's life and works. Britton includes chapters on Mill's political beliefs and his theories of ethics, deduction, induction, and reality.

Courtney, W. L. *The Metaphysics of John Stuart Mill*. London: C. Kegan Paul & Co., 1879, 156 p.
　　An evaluation of Mill's treatment of metaphysical problems intended for the non-specialist. Courtney assesses Mill's handling of such topics as consciousness and the nature of the body, the mind, and matter.

Cowling, Maurice. *Mill and Liberalism*. Cambridge: Cambridge University Press, 1963, 161 p.

Analyzes Mill's doctrine of liberalism. Cowling concludes that Mill's ideological acceptance of this doctrine was achieved "at the price of fundamental sociological self-deception."

Cumming, Ian. *A Manufactured Man: The Education of John Stuart Mill.* Auckland, New Zealand: University of Auckland, 1960, 35 p.
  Documents Mill's early life and details the Benthamite educational experiment that his father conducted on him.

Ellery, John B. *John Stuart Mill.* Twayne's English Authors Series, edited by Sylvia E. Bowman, no. 5. New York: Twayne Publishers, 1964, 134 p.
  A brief introduction to Mill's life and works.

Friedrich, Carl J., ed. *Nomos IV: Liberty.* New York: Atherton Press; London: Prentice-Hall International, 1962, 333 p.
  A collection of essays commemorating the one-hundredth anniversary of the publication of *On Liberty*. Critics represented include William Ebenstein, Henry D. Aiken, David Spitz, and Mark De Wolfe Howe.

Garforth, F. W. *Educative Democracy: John Stuart Mill on Education in Society.* Oxford: Oxford University Press, 1980, 256 p.
  Examines Mill's ideas on elitism, individuality, and the separation of church and state as they relate to his theory of education. Garforth emphasizes that Mill believed education was "an indispensible means to social reform."

Griffiths, A. Phillips, ed. *Of Liberty.* Royal Institute of Philosophy Lecture Series, no. 15. Cambridge: Cambridge University Press, 1983, 233 p.
  A collection of essays on various aspects of Mill's *On Liberty* by such critics as J. P. Day, Jack Lively, David E. Cooper, and Alan Ryan.

Halévy, Elie. *The Growth of Philosophic Radicalism.* Translated by Mary Morris. 1934. Reprint. New York: Augustus M. Kelley, 1965, 554 p.*
  The standard history of utilitarianism. Halévy focuses on Jeremy Bentham's life, his philosophical ideas, and his followers.

Hamburger, Joseph. *Intellectuals in Politics: John Stuart Mill and the Philosophic Radicals.* Yale Studies in Political Science, no. 14. New Haven: Yale University Press, 1965, 308 p.
  Reviews Mill's political opinions and career in the light of Philosophic Radicalism. Hamburger also discusses Mill's interactions with the Philosophic Radicals George Grote, John Arthur Roebuck, Charles Buller, Joseph Hume, and Sir William Molesworth.

Hayek, F. A. *John Stuart Mill and Harriet Taylor: Their Correspondence and Subsequent Marriage.* Chicago: University of Chicago Press, 1951, 320 p.*
  The fullest account of Mill's courtship of and marriage to Harriet Taylor. Hayek reprints their correspondence, discusses their literary collaboration, and provides an appendix of Taylor's writings.

Himmelfarb, Gertrude. *On Liberty and Liberalism: The Case of John Stuart Mill.* New York: Alfred A. Knopf, 1974, 345 p.
  Discusses the leading characteristics and evolution of the theory advanced in *On Liberty*. Himmelfarb describes Mill's notion of liberty as riddled with "ambiguities and ambivalences" and emphasizes the contradictions inherent in his thought.

Jackson, Reginald. *An Examination of the Deductive Logic of John Stuart Mill.* Oxford Classical & Philosophical Monographs. London: Humphrey Milford, 1941, 193 p.
  An in-depth analysis of Mill's theory of deductive logic. Jackson describes its origin and development and reliance on syllogistic reasoning. He asserts that "while Mill discovered no new *species* of deduction, he did advance a new view about the *genus*."

Kubitz, Oskar Alfred. *Development of John Stuart Mill's "System of Logic."* Urbana: University of Illinois, 1932, 310 p.
  A thorough study of Mill's system of logic. Kubitz explores Mill's theories of psychology as well as his inductive and deductive methodology.

Laine, Michael. *Bibliography of Works on John Stuart Mill.* Toronto: University of Toronto Press, 1982, 173 p.
  An annotated bibliography covering criticism of Mill through 1978. Laine also lists cartoon and portrait representations of Mill as well as poems in which he is mentioned.

Levi, A. W. "The 'Mental Crisis' of John Stuart Mill." *Psychoanalytic Review* 32, No. 1 (January 1945): 86-101.
  The seminal account of Mill's mental crisis in 1826. Levi traces the causes, symptoms, and progress of the episode, which permanently changed Mill's life.

MacCunn, John. "The Utilitarian Optimism of John Stuart Mill." In his *Six Radical Thinkers: Bentham, J. S. Mill, Cobden, Carlyle, Mazzini, T. H. Green,* pp. 39-87. London: Edward Arnold, 1910.
  A comprehensive assessment of Mill's philosophy and writings.

MacMinn, Ney; Hainds, J. R.; and McCrimmon, James McNab. *Bibliography of the Published Writings of John Stuart Mill.* Northwestern University Studies in the Humanities, edited by J. W. Spargo, no. 12. Evanston: Northwestern University, 1945, 101 p.
  A complete and annotated listing of Mill's works published between 1822 and 1873.

The Mill News Letter. Toronto: University of Toronto Press, 1965-.
  A biannually published journal devoted to Mill criticism.

Nesbitt, George L. *Benthamite Reviewing: The First Twelve Years of the "Westminster Review," 1824-1836.* Columbia University Studies in English and Comparative Literature, no. 118. New York: Columbia University Press, 1934, 208 p.*
  A study of the reviewers who wrote for the *Westminster Review,* the main organ of the Benthamites, between 1824 and 1836. Nesbitt includes a section in which he identifies the authors of anonymously and pseudonymously published essays.

Packe, Michael St. John. *The Life of John Stuart Mill.* London: Secker and Warburg, 1954, 567 p.
  The standard biography.

Radcliff, Peter, ed. *Limits of Liberty: Studies of Mill's "On Liberty."* Wadsworth Studies in Philosophical Criticism, edited by Alexander Sesonske. Belmont, Calif.: Wadsworth Publishing Co., 1966, 118 p.
  A collection of essays on *On Liberty* by such critics as Albert William Levi, Willmoore Kendall, and Isaiah Berlin.

Robson, John M. "John Stuart Mill." In *Victorian Prose: A Guide to Research,* edited by David J. DeLaura, pp. 185-218. New York: Modern Language Association of America, 1973.
  An annotated research guide to works on Mill's life and career. Robson surveys bibliographic, critical, and biographic studies of Mill and includes individual sections listing criticism of his writings on philosophy, economics, and literature.

Ryan, Alan. *John Stuart Mill.* New York: Random House, Pantheon Books, 1970, 268 p.
  An in-depth study of Mill's philosophical system of "inductivism." Ryan discusses Mill's attempt "to link scientific rationality and moral rationality on the basis of an empiricist . . . metaphysics."

Schneewind, J. B., ed. *Mill: A Collection of Critical Essays.* Modern Studies in Philosophy. Garden City, N.Y.: Doubleday & Co., Anchor Books, 1968, 455 p.
  An important collection of essays on Mill by such critics as Reginald Jackson, J. O. Urmson, J. D. Mabbott, Jean Austin, R. J. Halliday, and Richard B. Friedman.

Schwartz, Pedro. *The New Political Economy of J. S. Mill.* Translated by Mrs. B. Leblanc and Pedro Schwartz. Durham, N.C.: Duke University Press, 1972, 341 p.
  Discusses Mill's philosophy of political economy and its rise and decline in acceptance.

Seth, James. "The Nineteenth Century: The English Development of Hume's Empiricism." In his *English Philosophers and Schools of Philosophy,* pp. 240-97. The Channels of English Literature, edited by Oliphant Smeaton. London: J. M. Dent & Sons, 1912.*

Treats Mill as a transitional figure who transformed Benthamism into a broader version of utilitarianism. Seth also provides an overview of Mill's writings and the various influences on his philosophy.

Spitz, David, ed. *"On Liberty": Annotated Text, Sources and Background, Criticism,* by John Stuart Mill and others. New York: W.W. Norton & Co., 1975, 260 p.

An annotated text of *On Liberty*. Smith appends several seminal essays on the sources and background of the work as well as on Mill's concept of liberty.

Stillinger, Jack. Introduction to *The Early Draft of John Stuart Mill's "Autobiography,"* by John Stuart Mill, pp. 1-33. Urbana: University of Illinois Press, 1961.

A complete account of the successive revisions of Mill's *Autobiography*. Stillinger discusses Mill's original and final drafts as well as the first published edition of the work, which reflected changes made by his wife and step-daughter. Stillinger argues that the various stages of the *Autobiography* demonstrate a progression from a personal to a public tone.

————. Introduction to *"Autobiography" and Other Writings,* by John Stuart Mill, edited by Jack Stillinger, pp. vii-xxi. Boston: Houghton Mifflin Co., 1969.

Compares Mill's *Autobiography* with William Wordsworth's *The Prelude*. Stillinger also describes the various manuscripts of Mill's work.

Thompson, Dennis F. *John Stuart Mill and Representative Government*. Princeton: Princeton University Press, 1976, 241 p.

Examines Mill's theory of government.

Whewell, William. "Mr. Mill's Logic." In his *On the Philosophy of Discovery: Chapters Historical and Critical,* pp. 238-99. London: John W. Parker and Son, 1860.

A notorious refutation of Mill's views on inductive logic by a noted philosopher and contemporary of Mill.

Willey, Basil. "John Stuart Mill." In his *Nineteenth Century Studies: Coleridge to Matthew Arnold,* pp. 141-86. New York: Columbia University Press, 1949.

An overview of Mill's most famous published works, with a critique of his ideas. Willey considers *On Liberty* Mill's most lasting contribution to social philosophy.

Woods, Thomas. *Poetry and Philosophy: A Study in the Thought of John Stuart Mill*. London: Hutchinson & Co., 1961, 207 p.

Documents the influence of William Wordsworth and his poetry on Mill's thought.

Nikolai Alekseevich Nekrasov

1821-1878

(Also transliterated as Nikolaĭ, Nikolaj, Nicholas, Nikolay; also Alekseevič, Alekseyevich, Alexeivitch, Alexeyevich; also Nekrasoff, Nekrásoff, N'ekràsov, Nekrassov) Russian poet, journalist, critic, editor, novelist, dramatist, and short story writer.

One of the most important poets of mid-nineteenth-century Russia, Nekrasov brought social realism, topical relevance, and bitter indignation to Russian verse at a time when the country's liberal writers and intellectuals had begun to play an important part in the movement for political and cultural reform. The poet described his muse as one of "vengeance and sorrow," and his works offer a harshly satirical perspective on the sources of oppression and injustice in Russian society. In such poems as *Moroz krasni nos (Red-nosed Frost)*, *Korobeyniki (The Pedlars)*, and *Komu na Rusi zhit khorosho (Who Can Be Happy and Free in Russia?)*, he portrays the life of Russian peasants with profound understanding; his sympathetic depiction of their hardships earned him the sobriquet "poet of the people's sufferings."

Born in the village of Nemirov in the Podolia region of southwestern Russia, Nekrasov was the son of a military officer and a Polish noblewoman. In 1824, his father retired from the army and the family moved to an ancestral estate in the village of Greshnevo. The household was an unhappy one: Nekrasov's father was a brutal drunkard who mistreated his wife and serfs and openly engaged in affairs with serf women. In contrast, Nekrasov's mother was a gentle, well-educated woman who bore her husband's cruelty and dissipation in silence. The poet's interest in literature and his intellectual development are often ascribed to the influence of his mother, whose sympathy for the lot of the Russian peasant he inherited. Following five years in a local secondary school, Nekrasov was sent by his father to St. Petersburg in 1838 to become a military cadet. The boy's ambition was to enter the university, however, and after refusing to attend military school he was cut off and left penniless in the city. For the next several years Nekrasov lived in a state of near starvation, supporting himself by whatever literary hackwork he could find.

In 1840, he published his first volume of poems, *Mechti i zvuki*, known in English as *Dreams and Sounds*. Contemporary reviewers were nearly unanimous in their unfavorable opinion of this work, which they considered juvenile and derivative. The influential critic Vissarion Belinski declared the poems full of "all the familiar and worn-out emotions, banalities, slick verses." Despite this negative appraisal, however, Belinski was favorably impressed by several reviews Nekrasov had published in the periodical *Otechestvennye zapiski*, known as *Notes of the Fatherland*. The two entered into a close friendship that had an enormous impact on the poet's artistic development. As the foremost Russian critic of the nineteenth century, Belinski championed the idea that contemporary literature should concern itself with the reality of life in Russia and serve as a force for progressive social reform. Nekrasov adopted these principles wholeheartedly, and during the 1840s he edited several collections of progressive poetry and prose featuring works by such authors as Ivan Turgenev, Aleksandr Herzen,

and Fedor Dostoevski alongside his own contributions. In 1847, Nekrasov became coeditor of the periodical *Sovremennik*, known as *The Contemporary*, and under his leadership the journal became the primary outlet for radical thought in Russia. Despite heavy censorship and constant surveillance by the secret police, Nekrasov turned *The Contemporary* into an important forum of intellectual and artistic expression and a financial success, gaining in the process the reputation of a shrewd, even grasping, businessman.

In 1856, with the publication of his second volume of poetry, *Stikhotvorenia*, known as *Verses*, Nekrasov became the most popular poet in Russia. In style and content, *Verses* bore little resemblance to *Dreams and Sounds*; the work exhibited a powerful mastery of realistic detail and a complete and ruthlessly honest portrait of the conditions of peasant life under the system of serfdom. The unsentimental candor of Nekrasov's colorful but often pathetic descriptions of life in a backward and oppressive society struck a responsive chord in the Russian people, and *Verses* was an overwhelming success. In his next volume, *The Pedlars*, Nekrasov more closely integrated idioms borrowed from Russian folklore into his poems about the peasantry. His use of popular proverbs and the rhythms characteristic of Russian folk songs lent authenticity and immediacy to the tale of two pedlars murdered for their money by an impoverished woodsman. Implicit in the story was Nekrasov's suggestion that the government, not the peasants, was responsible for the conditions under which such crimes occurred. Written immediately after the emancipation of the serfs by decree of Czar Alexander II, *The Pedlars* also reveals the poet's firm belief that the situation of the peasants had not been materially improved by their liberation. The poem proved immensely popular, and Nekrasov printed an inexpensive edition so that it might find a wider audience. Many of its verses were subsequently taken up by the people and turned into folk songs.

Nekrasov continued his innovative use of folk materials in *Red-nosed Frost,* which was published in 1864 in *The Contemporary.* The first of his works to be translated into English, it is considered by many critics to be Nekrasov's most fully realized study of peasant life. The poem concerns a woman who is frozen to death by Red-nosed Frost—the personification of the Russian winter—after venturing into the forest to cut firewood. Nekrasov borrowed the figure of Red-nosed Frost from Russian folklore and combined it with his own comprehensive knowledge of peasant customs, superstitions, and religion to create an intimate picture of human dignity and struggle under adverse circumstances. Critics praised in particular Nekrasov's descriptions of nature, his characterization, and his remarkable sensitivity to the hardships of peasant life. In Russia, where its lines have been committed to memory by generations of schoolchildren, *Red-nosed Frost* has achieved the status of a popular folk myth.

In 1866, Nekrasov published the first part of his long poem, *Who Can Be Happy and Free in Russia?* This work, often described as Nekrasov's masterpiece, appeared in a series of installments over the next decade, but was left unfinished when the poet died. *Who Can Be Happy and Free in Russia?* centers on a group of peasants engaged in a dispute over who in their country is happy with their lot in life. Each of the peasants argues for a different class of society, from that of the lowest peasant to that of the Czar. Eventually they decide to travel throughout Russia to discover for themselves whether Russians are happy. In this fashion, Nekrasov planned to survey the entire panorama of Russian society, commenting, through the observations of the peasants, on the political, social, and economic conditions of the country. As the travelers journey to different regions, it becomes clear that few, if any, of the people are satisfied—or even free from hardship and despair. This discovery reinforced Nekrasov's longtime contention that the situation of the peasant could only improve through education and a more equal distribution of wealth and power. Throughout *Who Can Be Happy and Free in Russia?* Nekrasov employs a virtuosic mixture of peasant dialect, folk songs, and local color to give verisimilitude to his diverse array of characters and locales. Critics point out that the poet's skill in working with folk materials had progressed to the stage where his borrowings from folklore blended seamlessly with his own inventions. Unlike many of his contemporaries, Nekrasov was actually writing and thinking in the language of the peasants, not merely imitating it. For this reason, and for the encyclopedic knowledge of Russian society that it displays, *Who Can Be Happy and Free in Russia?* is one of the most important Russian poems written in the nineteenth century.

During the decade before his death, Nekrasov also published the important poem *Russkie zhenshchini (Russian Women).* The poem recounts the story of two princesses who traveled to Siberia to join their husbands, who were exiled for taking part in the 1825 Decembrist uprising against Czar Nicholas I. The political implications of the heroic story of the two women were obvious to Nekrasov's readers, for whom the princesses symbolized individual courage in the face of political oppression. The poet managed to complete a final collection of his verse, *Posliednia piesni,* known as *Last Songs,* before he died of cancer in 1878. His funeral drew an immense crowd from every level of Russian society.

Nekrasov's conviction that literature should serve a social purpose and his rejection of the concept of "art for art's sake" are reflected in the frankly utilitarian aspect of most of his work. As a result, during his lifetime commentary on his poetry was often sharply divided according to the political sympathies of the individual critic. Readers frequently focused on Nekrasov's political stance, its place in his works, and whether his writings could be considered true poetry or merely "rhymed journalism." To many writers and critics, Nekrasov's works lack the aesthetic qualities of good poetry; he himself believed that his verse lacked fluency and artistic refinement. To advocates of "pure poetry," the didacticism and topicality of his verse were anathema, while for many radical critics he was the epitome of the socially responsible, progressive poet. Toward the end of his life, however, even his harshest critics acknowledged the emotional power and expressive imagery of such works as *Red-nosed Frost.* Following the poet's death, commentators began to perceive that Nekrasov had made a conscious decision to abandon the more polished and elegant style of his predecessors. He was considered an innovator who had created his own appropriate voice for poetic expression, rather than a mere violator of established standards. A number of critics noted that Nekrasov was fully capable of writing according to accepted notions of taste and style, but that such an approach was entirely at odds with both the subject matter of his works and the popular audience he hoped to reach. In the twentieth century, Nekrasov has enjoyed official approval and wide popularity in the Soviet Union. While the emphasis of Soviet scholars on the ideological aspects of Nekrasov's works has tended, in the view of some Western critics, to obscure the nature of the poet's aesthetic achievement, he remains an author whose political and sociological message is inseparable from his art. In the poem "Poèt i grazhdanin," known as "Poet and Citizen," Nekrasov declared in defense of his artistic outlook that "You do not have to be a poet, / A citizen though you're obliged to be." Modern critics have vindicated Nekrasov's artistic practices, and he is now recognized both for the social content of his poems and for his accomplishments in matters of form, including his innovative use of Russian folk rhythms within the metrical structure of his works. Though overshadowed for Western readers by his predecessors Alexander Pushkin and Mikhail Lermontov, Nekrasov remains a highly influential and popular figure in Russian literature.

*PRINCIPAL WORKS

Mechti i zvuki   (poetry)   1840
Stikhotvorenia   (poetry)   1856
Korobeyniki   (poetry)   1861
   [*The Pedlars* published in *Poems by Nicholas Nekrasov,* 1929]
Russkie zhenshchini   (poetry)   1871-72; published in journal *Otechestvennye zapiski*
   [*Russian Women* published in *Poems by Nicholas Nekrasov,* 1929]

Moroz krasni nos   (poetry)   1872
   [*Red-nosed Frost*, 1886]
Posliednia piesni   (poetry)   1877
Komu na Rusi zhit khorosho   (unfinished poem)   1880
   [*Who Can Be Happy and Free in Russia?*, 1917]
Poems by Nicholas Nekrasov   (poetry)   1929
Polnoe sobranie sochineni i pisem. 12 vols.   (poetry,
   novels, short stories, letters, criticism, and dramas)
   1948-53

*Most of Nekrasov's works were originally published in periodicals.

NIKOLAJ SOLOV'EV   (essay date 1840)

[*The following excerpt, translated from an 1840 review of* Dreams and Sounds *in the Russian periodical* Severnaya pcela, *reflects the consensus of opinion among contemporary critics. Solov'ev contends that although Nekrasov's poems showed promise, they were written in an overly romantic and highly derivative style.*]

We have undertaken to read **Dreams and Sounds**, the poems of N. N. The author's name is entirely unknown to us; it seems to appear in our literature for the first time. For this same reason, it gives us even greater pleasure to point out a few poems that clearly hint at the author's giftedness. But this very mark of talent forces us to express our opinion frankly. The author, evidently, is much attached to the previous poetic school which thought there was no poetry outside the feelings of sadness, hopelessness, and despair. This tendency, unfortunately, has been reflected quite strongly in the poems of Mr. N. N. Moreover, his close reading of our best poets has also left traces that are too obvious to be disregarded. . . .

> *Nikolaj Solov'ev, in an extract, translated by Sigmund S. Birkenmayer, in* Nikolaj Nekrasov: His Life and Poetic Art *by Sigmund S. Birkenmayer, Mouton, 1968, p. 62.*

IVAN SERGEEVICH TURGENEV   (letter date 1868)

[*Turgenev was a prominent nineteenth-century Russian novelist. Best known for his insightful portrayal of the political and social problems of mid-century Russia in such works as* Fathers and Children, *he also reveals in his novels a profound psychological understanding of different character types. In the following excerpt from a letter to the poet Iakov Petrovich Polonski, Turgenev harshly attacks Nekrasov's poetry.*]

Mr. Nekrasov, is a poet of strainings and tricks; I tried to read his collected poems again a few days ago. . . . No! Poetry did not even spend a night there—and I threw that chewed-up papier-mâché with its strong vodka sauce into the corner. (p. 173)

> *Ivan Sergeevich Turgenev, in an extract from a letter to Iakov Petrovich Polonski on January 13, 1868, in his* Turgenev's Letters: A Selection, *edited and translated by Edgar H. Lehrman, Alfred A. Knopf, 1961, pp. 172-73.*

F. M. DOSTOIEVSKY   (journal date 1877)

[*One of Russia's best-known novelists, Dostoievsky is considered one of the most outstanding and influential writers of modern literature. His greatness as a fiction writer lies in the depth and range of his vision, his acute psychological insight, his profound philosophical thought, and his brilliant prose style. While best known for his novels* Prestuplenye i nakazanye (Crime and Punishment) *and* Brat'ya Karamazovy (The Brothers Karamazov), *his critical writings reveal his insight into the artistic process. In the following excerpt from his* Dvevnik Pisatelya (The Diary of a Writer), *Dostoievsky discusses Nekrasov's ability to empathize with the sufferings of the Russian people as one of the great strengths of his work. The critic believes that the poet's understanding of the "people's truth" grew out of grief over his own experiences and that his personal shortcomings were redeemed by his love of the masses.*]

[It is his] worship of the people's truth that I perceive (alas, perhaps, I alone among all his admirers) in Nekrasov, in his best creations. I treasure—very much so—the fact that he was "the commiserator for the people's sorrow"; that he spoke so much and so passionately about the people's grief. But still dearer to me is the fact that in the great, painful and ecstatic moments of his life—despite all the opposing influences and even his own personal convictions—he bowed before the people's truth with all his being, a fact to which his loftiest creations bear full witness. (pp. 942-43)

[As for any comparison of Nekrasov with Pushkin,] I am not measuring with a yardstick who is taller and who is shorter, since here there can be no comparison, nor even a question of comparison. By the grandeur and depth of his Russian genius Pushkin up to this day shines like a sun over our whole Russian intelligent world outlook. He is a great prophet who is still not understood. Compared with him, Nekrasov is but a tiny dot, a small planet which, however, emerged from that great sun. And leaving aside all measurements—who is taller or shorter—immortality, fully deserved immortality, belongs to Nekrasov, . . . for his worship of the people's truth which, in him, was not a result of some kind of imitation, nor even of a fully conscious process—it was an urge, an irresistible impulse. And in Nekrasov this was all the more remarkable as all his life he had been under the influence of people who, perhaps, very sincerely loved and pitied the people but who never acknowledged any truth in them, and who always placed European enlightenment far above the truth of the people's spirit. (p. 944)

Despite his remarkable and extraordinarily keen intellect, Nekrasov, however, lacked serious education; at least it was limited. All his life he was unable to rid himself of certain influences—he had no strength to do so. Yet he possessed an original psychic power of his own which never left him, a genuine, passionate—and what is most important—direct love of the people. With all his soul he commiserated with their suffering, perceiving in them not merely an image degraded by slavery—a bestial image—but through the force of his love he was able to grasp almost unconsciously the beauty of the people, their strength and intellect, their suffering humility, and partly even to believe in their future predestination. Oh, intellectually, Nekrasov could be mistaken in many a thing. In an impromptu, recently published for the first time, contemplating with alarmed reproach the people liberated from serfdom, he found it possible to exclaim:

> . . . But are the people happy?

The great instinct of his heart revealed to him the people's sorrow, but if he had been asked: "What should one wish for the people? How can it be done?"—he might have given a quite erroneous, perhaps even detrimental answer. And, of course, he could not be blamed: in Russia there is still extremely little political sense, while Nekrasov, I repeat, was all his life under alien influences. But with his heart, with his great poetic inspiration, in some of his grand poems, irresistibly he merged with the very essence of the people. In this sense he was a popular poet. Everyone descending from the people, even with a minimum of education, will understand much in Nekrasov, provided, however, he is educated. The question whether the Russian people as a whole can understand him is obviously a senseless one. What will the "common people" understand in his masterpieces: *The Knight for an Hour, Silence, Russian Women*? Even in his great *Vlas*, which might be intelligible to the people (but which in no way would inspire them, since this poetry has long been divorced from life itself) they would unfailingly discern two or three false traits. What would the people make out of one of his mightiest and most appealing poems—*On the Volga*? This is Byron's genuine spirit and tone.

Nay, as yet, Nekrasov is merely a poet of the Russian intelligentsia who spoke with love and passion to the same Russian intelligentsia about the people and their suffering. I am not speaking of the future: in the future the people will take notice of Nekrasov. Then they will understand that once upon a time there lived a kind Russian nobleman who shed lamenting tears over their popular grief, and who could find nothing better, when running away from his wealth and from the sinful temptations of his nobleman's life, in his very distressful moments, than to come to the people, and, in his irresistible love of them, cleanse his tormented heart, since Nekrasov's love of the people was but *an outlet of his personal sorrow about himself.* (pp. 944-46)

[To] me it is clear why Nekrasov loved the people so much; why he was so attracted to them in the difficult moments of his life; why he went to them and what he found in them. It is because—as I stated above—in Nekrasov love of the people was, as it were, *an outcome of his own sorrow for himself.* Once you suppose and admit this, the whole Nekrasov—both as a poet and a citizen—will be intelligible to you. In the service of the people with his heart and talent he perceived his self-purification. The people were his inner need not only for the sake of poetry. In his love of them he found his own exculpation. By his sentiments for the people he elevated his own spirit. But still more important is the fact that among the people who surrounded him he failed to find an object of love, nor did he find it in the fact that these people respected and worshipped him. Moreover: he detached himself from them and went to the insulted, to the suffering, to the naïve and humiliated—in those minutes when he was seized with disgust with that life to which, at times, he yielded faint-heartedly and viciously: he beat himself against the slabs of his own poor village church, and he was healed. He would not have chosen such a solution *had he not believed in it.* In the love of the people he felt something steady, a firm and sacred outcome of everything that tormented him. He knew of nothing holier, steadier and more truthful which he could worship. Indeed, he could not have perceived his whole self-exculpation in mere verses about the people. And further, this being the case, he worshipped *the people's truth.* If, in his whole life, he found nothing worthier of love than the people, this means that he did recognize *both the people's truth and truth in the people,* and also that truth does exist and is preserved in the people. If he did not quite consciously or rationally recognize this, with this heart he accepted this irresistibly and absolutely. In that vicious peasant, whose humiliated and humiliating image tormented him so strongly, he thus perceived something genuine and sacred which he could not help esteeming, to which he could not help responding with all his heart.

It is in this sense that, speaking above of Nekrasov's literary significance, I classed him among those who recognized the people's truth. And his eternal quest for that truth, his unceasing striving for it, obviously bear witness to the fact—this I repeat—that he was attracted to the people by an inner and supreme urge, and that, therefore, this craving must indicate that perpetual inner anguish which could not be quenched with any crafty arguments of temptation, with any paradoxes or practical exculpations. If so, he must have suffered all his life.... In this case, what kind of judges are we?—Even if we be judges, we are not accusers.

Nekrasov is a Russian historical type,—one of the great examples of the extent of contradictions and bifurcations in the realm of morality and rational convictions which a Russian can reach in our sad transitional epoch. But this man stays in our hearts. His impulses of love so often were sincere, pure and naïve! His longing for the people was so lofty that it places him as a poet in a superior station. As for the man, the citizen, by his suffering for them, he exculpated himself and he redeemed much if actually there was anything to redeem.... (pp. 952-53)

> *F. M. Dostoievsky, in a diary entry in December, 1877, in his* The Diary of a Writer, *edited and translated by Boris Brasol, George Braziller, 1954, pp. 913-58.*

CHARLES EDWARD TURNER (essay date 1881)

[*In the following excerpt, Turner focuses on Nekrasov as the poet of the Russian peasant's life and sorrows, asserting that the melancholy atmosphere of much of his poetry accurately reflects the sad reality of peasant life. Commenting on the topical relevance of Nekrasov's writings, Turner concludes: "More than any other poet, he has taught the present generation what the work is they have to accomplish."*]

In order to understand the position which Nekrasoff occupies in contemporary Russian literature, we should remember that whilst one class of writers, chiefly represented by Polonski, the poet, and Count Tolstoi, the dramatist, have maintained the Poushkin conception of poetry, and are artistic idealists, another and far more numerous group, composed of writers like Goncharoff, Tourgenieff, Dostoevski, and Tolstoi, the novelist, are the immediate followers of Gogol in their portrayal of humanity as it is, and in the pictures they give of common daily life. They have brought poetry down from heaven, and made it the echo, not of the fantastical, but of the real. "The real hero of my tales," writes Tolstoi, "is truth;" and the same may be said of Nekrasoff, who is essentially the poet of the people. The life of the peasant, his toil, vexations, distresses, faults, weaknesses, and rare joys, form the theme of his best poems. They describe to us the vice and misery which he himself had witnessed and partly felt in his youth, and they are completely free from those "tinsel trappings" of style poets generally employ to adorn and set off their pictures. His poetry is of this world, unmixed with the purely ideal or imaginary, and his music, to use his own expression, is "the fellow-friend of the wretched poor born to strife, suffering, and toil." In these words we have the crowning characteristic of Nekrasoff's poetry. Others had before him, from time to time, denounced serfdom, condescendingly pitied the hard fate of the *moujik,* and even prophesied the day "when slavery should disappear at the nod of the Tsar;" but their verse lacks too often that touch of reality which nothing but actual experience can give; they write as outsiders, and occupy towards the people much the same position as the actor in *Hamlet* does to Hecuba, whose woes he none the less so passionately declaims. Nekrasoff, on the contrary, is of, not above, the people; he does not write about them, but he feels with them, and their belief, hopes, and griefs are his own. It is this dominant trait which has gained for his poems such a marvellous popularity; nor need we find any difficulty in attaching credit to the story related by his biographer, how one of the speeches delivered on the day of his funeral, in which a comparison was drawn between Nekrasoff and Poushkin, was interrupted by loud cries of "Greater! greater!" Of course no comparison can really be made between the two; but the anecdote well explains the origin of the strong hold which Nekrasoff has secured on the mind and sympathy of the youth of Russia.

Some of Nekrasoff's critics have been pleased to censure his poems for their tone of monotonous gloom. But is not this rather the highest tribute that can be paid to the truthfulness with which they reflect the unrelieved gloom of that life of serfdom to which, for so many generations, the peasantry of Russia were pitilessly condemned? And when these critics proceed to contrast Nekrasoff with poets like Burns, we can only urge that such comparisons are idle and inappropriate. The conditions of life surrounding them were radically different, and it is only natural if the outcome of their experiences, the impressions produced on them by all they felt and witnessed, should be equally opposed. The gaiety of a Burns would be strangely misplaced in pictures of a life whose lightest songs are coloured with a tinge of melancholy. To a foreigner, and to one ignorant of the actual condition of the Russian peasant prior to his emancipation, there may seem something exaggerated and affected in the sombre tone of Nekrasoff's poems; but, in reality, which of us has ever listened to the wailing, plaintive songs chanted by the labourer at his work, without recalling those lines in which the poet has so sadly seized on their true signification—

> I am on the Volga: what groan echoes
> O'er the waters of the great Russian river?
> That groan with us is called a song.

In one of his most characteristic poems, Nekrasoff has given us a portrait, "drawn at full length as in a picture," of the typical Ivan, as he stands before his master, unwashed, silent, and unkempt, everlastingly half drunk, with tattered clothes, and boots innocent of blacking and down at heel, his favourite pipe and greasy tobacco-pouch leering out of his pocket. Neither he nor any of his forefathers have ever boasted of a home of their own; nor has he been brought up to any one particular trade, but "is sempstress, cook, and carpenter all in one," and does any job to which he is set, or if he fails is sworn at and well beaten. One day Ivan is nowhere to be found, having sneaked off to pass a merry night with his friend the publican, who was "also a secret purloiner of the squire's turkeys and fowls." Careless of what may come, Ivan gives himself up heart and soul that night to the dance, so that "every limb and joint and the very ring in his right ear danced madly for joy," and he became for a few hours completely oblivious of the ills of life.

> In the morning he is called before his lord:
> Where have you been skulking since yesterday?
> I? nowhere: before God: it is true,
> I have been standing at the gate.
> What, all night long? And then came rude
>   equivocations,

Stupid, manifest, and patent lies.
> If he had teeth,—one or two were knocked down his
>   throat;
> If he had none,—his ears half twisted off.
> Pardon, pardon! cries with whining voice Ivan.
> Go, idiot, and roast a goose for dinner,
> And see the cabbage-soup is well prepared!

And then, another day, poor Ivan is again summoned before his master. In his drunken fear, his mind is dazed as to what new offence is going to be brought up against him, but to his surprise "liberty had come," and he is allowed to go whither he likes:—

> And lost among the enfranchised people
> Our Ivan suddenly disappears:
> How dost thou live in thy new-won liberty?
> Where are thou? Eh? Ivan?

"How dost thou live in thy new-won liberty?" is a question most of us have asked, and I think there is to be found in the poems written by Nekrasoff subsequently to the year 1861 an answer, which recommends itself the more because unfounded on the wild dreams of enthusiasts who imagined that, once the edict of emancipation was signed, the work of reform was finally accomplished. "To redress the wrongs of centuries," he warns us, "is no easy task;" and there is a wise moderation in the joy he feels at the thought that henceforth the peasant is free to choose his work and lot in life:—

> If thou wilt—remain a *moujik* all thy life,
> If thou canst—soar to heaven with an eagle's flight!
> Many of our fondest hopes will be deceived:
> The mind of man is cunning and inventive,
> I know: and in the place of slavery chains
> Men will easily forge a hundred others:
> So be it: but the people shall have strength to break
>   them
> And my muse with hope salutes the dawn of liberty.

> (pp. 503-06)

In one of his latest poems, written but a few weeks before his death, Nekrasoff speaks of his muse as being weak in tone and powerless to move, and proudly anticipates the advent of the true poet, the two heroes of whose song shall be the Tsar, destroyer of the inequalities of centuries, and the peasant, in whom the nation shall recognise the source and guardian of imperial power. This unity of interest and tie of mutual responsibility between ruler and ruled forms the central idea of Nekrasoff's poetry. More than any other poet, he has taught the present generation what the work is they have to accomplish; and it is for this reason that his writings possess such a peculiar worth to the student of contemporary Russian life. (p. 512)

Charles Edward Turner, "Nicholas Alexeivitch Nekrasoff," in The Fortnightly Review, *n.s. Vol. XXX, No. CLXXVIII, October 1, 1881, pp. 499-512.*

P. KROPOTKIN (essay date 1901)

[*Kropotkin was a Russian sociologist, philosopher, geographer, essayist, and critic. Born of an aristocratic family, Kropotkin became an anarchist in the 1870s and later fled to Europe, where he composed several of his best-known works. Chief among these is his* Memoirs of a Revolutionist, *which is considered a monumental autobiographical treatment of the revolutionary movement in Russia. Kropotkin also composed several literary histories, including* Russian Literature, *which was drawn from a series of lectures he gave in the United States in March, 1901, and later published as* Ideals and Realities in Russian Literature. *In the following excerpt from that work, Kropotkin examines the importance of content rather than artistic form in determining Nekrasov's poetic achievement. The critic concedes that his use of rhyme is often awkward, but counters with the suggestion that his imagery is consistently powerful and poignant. Kropotkin concludes his observations by contrasting the popularity of Nekrasov's poetry with the more artistically refined but less accessible verse of Alexander Pushkin.*]

[Shortly after his death there] began the passionate discussion which has never ended, about the merits of Nekrásoff as a poet. While speaking over his grave, Dostoyévskiy put Nekrásoff by the side of Púshkin and Lérmontoff ("higher still than Púshkin and Lérmontoff," exclaimed some young enthusiast in the crowd), and the question, "Is Nekrásoff a great poet, like Púshkin and Lérmontoff?" has been discussed ever since. (pp. 171-72)

Some people repudiate such a comparison. He was not a poet, they say, because he always wrote with a purpose. However, this reasoning, which is often defended by the pure aesthetics, is evidently incorrect. Shelley also had a purpose, which did not prevent him from being a great poet; Browning has a purpose in a number of his poems, and this did not prevent him from being a great poet. Every great poet has a purpose in most of his poems, and the question is only whether he has found a beautiful form for expressing this purpose, or not. The poet who shall succeed in combining a really beautiful form, *i.e.*, impressive images and sonorous verses, with a grand purpose, will be the greatest poet.

Now, one certainly feels, on reading Nekrásoff, that he had difficulty in writing his verses. There is nothing in his poetry similar to the easiness with which Púshkin used the forms of versification for expressing his thoughts, nor is there any approach to the musical harmony of Lérmontoff's verse or A. K. Tolstóy's. Even in his best poems there are lines which are not agreeable to the ear on account of their wooden and clumsy form; but you feel that these unhappy verses could be improved by the change of a few words, without the beauty of the images in which the feelings are expressed being altered by that. One certainly feels that Nekrásoff was not master enough of his words and his rhymes; but there is not one single poetical image which does not suit the whole idea of the poem, or which strikes the reader as a dissonance, or is not beautiful; while in some of his verses Nekrásoff has certainly succeeded in combining a very high degree of poetical inspiration with great beauty of form. It must not be forgotten that the *Yambs* of Barbier, and the *Châtiments* of Victor Hugo also leave, here and there, much to be desired as regards form.

Nekrásoff was a most unequal writer, but one of [his] . . . critics has pointed out that even amidst his most unpoetical "poem"—the one in which he describes in very poor verses the printing office of a newspaper—the moment that he touches upon the sufferings of the workingman there come in twelve lines which for the beauty of poetical images and musicalness, connected with their inner force, have few equals in the whole of Russian literature.

When we estimate a poet, there is something general in his poetry which we either love or pass by indifferently, and to reduce literary criticism exclusively to the analysis of the beauty of the poet's verses or to the correspondence between "idea and form" is surely to immensely reduce its value. Everyone

will recognise that Tennyson possessed a wonderful beauty of form, and yet he cannot be considered as superior to Shelley, for the simple reason that the general tenor of the latter's ideas was so much superior to the general tenor of Tennyson's. It is on the general contents of his poetry that Nekrásoff's superiority rests.

We have had in Russia several poets who also wrote upon social subjects or the duties of a citizen—I need only mention Pleschéeff and Mináyeff—and they attained sometimes, from the versifier's point of view, a higher beauty of form than Nekrásoff. But in whatever Nekrásoff wrote there is an inner force which you do not find in either of these poets, and this force suggests to him images which are rightly considered as pearls of Russian poetry.

Nekrásoff called his Muse, "A Muse of Vengeance and of Sadness," and this Muse, indeed, never entered into compromise with injustice. Nekrásoff is a pessimist, but his pessimism, as Venguéroff remarks, has an original character. Although his poetry contains so many depressing pictures representing the misery of the Russian masses, nevertheless the fundamental impression which it leaves upon the reader is an elevating feeling. The poet does not bow his head before the sad reality: he enters into a struggle with it, and he is sure of victory. The reading of Nekrásoff wakes up that discontent which bears in itself the seeds of recovery.

The mass of the Russian people, the peasants and their sufferings, are the main themes of our poet's verses. His love to the people passes as a red thread through all his works; he remained true to it all his life. In his younger years that love saved him from squandering his talent in the sort of life which so many of his contemporaries have led; later on it inspired him in his struggle against serfdom; and when serfdom was abolished he did not consider his work terminated, as so many of his friends did: he became the poet of the dark masses oppressed by the economical and political yoke; and towards the end of his life he did not say: "Well, I have done what I could," but till his last breath his verses were a complaint about not having been enough of a fighter. He wrote: "Struggle stood in the way of my becoming a poet, and songs prevented me from becoming a fighter," and again: "Only he who is serviceable to the aims of his time, and gives all his life to the struggle for his brother men—only he will live longer than his life."

Sometimes he sounds a note of despair; however, such a note is not frequent in Nekrásoff. His Russian peasant is not a man who only sheds tears. He is serene, sometimes humourous, and sometimes an extremely gay worker. Very seldom does Nekrásoff idealise the peasant: for the most part he takes him just as he is, from life itself; and the poet's faith in the forces of that Russian peasant is deep and vigorous. "A little more freedom to breathe—he says—and Russia will shew that she has men, and that she has a future." This is an idea which frequently recurs in his poetry.

The best poem of Nekrásoff is *Red-nosed Frost*. It is the apotheosis of the Russian peasant woman. The poem has nothing sentimental in it. It is written, on the contrary, in a sort of elevated epic style, and the second part, where Frost personified passes on his way through the wood, and where the peasant woman is slowly freezing to death, while bright pictures of past happiness pass through her brain—all this is admirable, even from the point of view of the most aesthetic critics, because it is written in good verses and in a succession of beautiful images and pictures.

The Peasant Children is a charming village idyll. The "Muse of Vengeance and Sadness"—one of our critics remarks—becomes wonderfully mild and gentle as soon as she begins to speak of women and children. In fact, none of the Russian poets has ever done so much for the apotheosis of women, and especially of the mother-woman, as this supposedly severe poet of Vengeance and Sadness. As soon as Nekrásoff begins to speak of a mother he grows powerful; and the strophes he devoted to his own mother—a woman lost in a squire's house, amidst men thinking only of hunting, drinking, and exercising their powers as slave owners in their full brutality—these strophes are real pearls in the poetry of all nations.

His poem devoted to the exiles in Siberia and to the Russian women—that is, to the wives of the Decembrists—in exile, is excellent and contains really beautiful passages, but it is inferior to either his poems dealing with the peasants or to his pretty poem, *Sasha*, in which he describes, contemporaneously with Turguéneff, the very same types as Rúdin and Natásha.

It is quite true that Nekrásoff's verses often bear traces of a painful struggle with rhyme, and that there are lines in his poems which are decidedly inferior; but he is certainly one of our most popular poets amidst the masses of the people. Part of his poetry has already become the inheritance of all the Russian nation. He is immensely read—not only by the educated classes, but by the poorest peasants as well. In fact, as has been remarked by one of our critics, to understand Púshkin a certain more or less artificial literary development is required; while to understand Nekrásoff it is sufficient for the peasant simply to know reading; and it is difficult to imagine, without having seen it, the delight with which Russian children in the poorest village schools are now reading Nekrásoff and learning full pages from his verses by heart. (pp. 172-76)

> P. Kropotkin, "Gontcharoff, Dostoyevskiy, Nekrásoff," in his Russian Literature, 1905. Reprint by Benjamin Blom, 1967, pp. 151-90.*

ROSA NEWMARCH (essay date 1907)

[In the following excerpt, Newmarch comments on a wide range of issues relevant to Nekrasov's poetry, including the indignation and bitterness that pervades his work, the rough quality of his versification, his approach to realism, and his fascination with the lives of the Russian people. Among the poems discussed are Red-nosed Frost, Russian Women, and Who Can Be Happy and Free in Russia?]

"I am sick of love songs," said Shelley to Leigh Hunt; "will no one give us a hate song?" In Nekrassov we have a poet whose entire work—according to some of his critics—may be described as an implacable "hate song." Among our own poets, not a few owe their greatest moments to the quality of being "good haters." But I do not think in all our literature we shall find an instance of a writer—unless it be Swift—who frankly admits that his whole inspiration is rooted in bitterness and indignation. It needed the harsh school of Russian social and political life, as it existed under Nicholas I, to force such an abnormal growth, such an accumulation of the *saeva indignatio.* "More than thirty thousand verses shot forth in a single jet of gall," says M. de Voguë. And if we entirely trust the judgment of this distinguished writer, the spring, poisoned at the source, resisted all the defecating processes of time, and ran bitter and troubled to the last.

I think it is Hazlitt who has observed that "spleen is the soul of patriotism and of public good"; and undoubtedly Nekrassov's splenetic genius was a powerful weapon in the hands of the radical party in Russia. Some critics have endeavoured to excuse his bitterness on the ground that such rancour was the outcome of an excessive love for the people and an almost morbid sympathy for the sorrows of his race. This excuse—if indeed any excuse is needful—does not seem in conformity with what we know of Nekrassov's character. His irreconcilable bitterness and pessimism were, I think, partly due to the atmosphere in which his genius developed, but still more to the peculiarities of his temperament, which showed throughout a harsh, unbending fibre. I am not one of those who can see in the poems of Nekrassov much trace of that pent-up love for humanity to which, in milder moments, he himself attributes his inspiration. He certainly had not Dostoievsky's mystical tenderness, nor his passion of charity; still less can I discern the broad smile of indulgent humour characteristic of so many of his compatriots. A powerful dissolvent he is of the old systems, of serfdom, of spiritual oppression and narrowness of view; but undoubtedly what Matthew Arnold calls "an acrid dissolvent."

The childhood of a poet frequently colours his whole after-life. As in Wordsworth's case, it may appear as the luminous point in his existence, to which he can look back in times of doubt and difficulty, the reflection from which, cast along the whole path of life, will not leave him altogether in unrelenting darkness. Nekrassov never possessed this reserve of gladness. Listen to Wordsworth in the opening pages of "The Prelude":—

> Fair seed-time had my soul, and I grew up
> Fostered alike by beauty and by fear,
> Much favoured in my birthplace.

Contrast these lines with the harshly ironical poem "My Birthplace," in which Nekrassov evokes the memories of childhood: "Lo, there it stands, the ancestral home.—'Twas there I learnt to suffer and to hate!—Days of my youth, days we so falsely call precious and wonderful,—Pass before me in all your beauty!—Here is the dark and gloomy garden,—Down yonder path what face is that which flits among the sad and livid shadows?—I know what makes you weep, Mother!—Who ruined all your life? I know, I know!—But the thought of rebellion filled you with horror—You bore your fate with the silence of a slave."

Here we have the respective key-notes of two poets who, united in their choice of subjects—the cares and sufferings of the humble classes—have, as regards temperament, scarcely anything in common. Although they employed the same themes, it was invariably in different tonalities. Realism and optimism have been accepted as the poetical ideal of Wordsworth: realism and pessimism are the chief components of Nekrassov's work. But it is precisely to the latter element, so acceptable to a generation awaking from Utopian dreams of progress to intolerable disillusionment, and standing on the verge of the abyss of nihilism, that Nekrassov owes a popularity far exceeding anything that has fallen to the share of the saner English poet. Nekrassov is probably more widely read than any other writer in Russia. One learns the lesson of his popularity within a week of visiting that country, where the large octavo which represents the popular edition of his poems meets one at every turn of life. (pp. 153-56)

I do not know what inscription may be found upon Nekrassov's tomb, but surely there could be none more fitting than that which Swift chose for his own epitaph:—

Where bitter indignation cannot lacerate the heart.

If I seem to have drawn a somewhat negative and unlovable picture of Nekrassov, I must appeal in justification to such of his poems as have impressed me most. By these I have judged him, and it is generally acknowledged that his poems constitute the truest biography of this original but warped genius. Yet it is precisely against this method of judgment that one of his greatest admirers, A. M. Skabichevsky, has protested in his *History of Modern Russian Literature*. In Nekrassov's poetry there are, he says, two principal elements, and in judging from individual examples of his work we must be careful that we do not altogether overlook one or the other of these leading constituents. The one most constantly present in his earlier poems, is the reflective pessimistic spirit of the forties; the other is of later growth, and is defined by Skabichevsky as a passionate enthusiasm for the people, and a fervent faith in their ultimate victory over darkness and oppression. The secret of Nekrassov's extraordinary popularity, according to that writer, lies in the fact that he is "the universal singer of his country and his age." I do not deny Nekrassov's variety of theme, nor his wide outlook upon contemporary life, far from it; it is only the light in which he views things which seems to me to a certain extent both false and monotonous. A coloured-glass window will show as wide an expanse of the outer world as a clear one; yet be the tint rose-coloured or smoked, those who look through it cannot pretend that they have seen nature as it really exists. But if he is monotonous in mood, Nekrassov certainly commands a varied range of subjects. He has represented all the strata of Russian society, from the drawing-rooms of the capital to the garrets and cellars of the proletariat, from the houses of the country gentle-folk to the dilapidated hut of old Aunt Nelina. He is the poet of every class in turn, and his verses, as he himself has said, are "the living witnesses of tears which I have shed for all."

And not only does Nekrassov paint the external life of his fellow-countrymen, but he reflects the spirit of the transition period in which he lived. The poet started his career under the influence of that subjective pessimism which was the characteristic temper of the forties, when the conscience of the intelligent classes was awakening to new ideals, but also to a bitter sense of their inability to realise them. Hence the spirit of profound weariness which breathes in so many of his early works. In this mood he created the hero of his poem "Sasha," that type of Russian youth whose "powers of action have been eaten up by thought." Noble-minded, accessible to all lofty ideals, but lacking in passion and will-power; who, when he thinks himself in love, is yet conscious that it is his brain which is excited—not his blood. Sasha is own brother to Tourgeniev's Roudin, and both in their turn are the direct descendants of Hamlet. But, as time went on, Nekrassov's poetry began to show the presence of a second influence, altogether new in the poetry of Russia, though already noticeable in the fiction—that enthusiasm for the common people and interest in their lot which inspired all his best work. In his well-known poem "The Schoolboy" he first shows this change of mood. Here we have the nearest approach to an optimistic view of life which can be found in all Nekrassov's works: "Not unendowed is that nature,—Not yet lost is that land,—Which sprang from such a people—So glorious—aye so good and noble.—There we find strong and loving spirits,—Amid the weak, the indif-

ferent, and the selfish." It seemed as though the poet had discovered a cure for the malady of his age. Had Nekrassov himself possessed a more robust faith in his new ideal "the people," and a greater share of the uplifting spirit of hope, he might indeed have been the saviour of his generation and those to come. But who believes in a remedy which the physician himself seems half to doubt? Too often he relapses from this ideal view of the people and shows them up with merciless realism, as in his last great poem, half-civilised, given up to superstition, "in the depths of night, without a notion of God or of truth," moving as in "subterranean darkness without a torch."

Nekrassov, though he has analysed love from several points of view, has left no love lyrics in the ordinary sense of the word. This was not because, like Crabbe, he was merely an objective writer, the realistic painter of rural life. An intensely subjective note is frequently heard in Nekrassov's poetry. Nor was it altogether because, like Wordsworth, his emotions were diffused over wider areas of human sympathy. The real reason seems to be that the part which sexual love played in his life did not tend to awaken sweet or tender harmonies. His passions appear to have run in the same rugged and bitter channels as all his other sentiments. Even Swift can drop the lash of savage scorn with which he flagellates humanity at large, can grow gentle and have recourse to his "little language," when he addresses Stella. Nekrassov has no "little language"; he cannot soften, even to the woman he seems to have loved best. In his poem **"The Unhappy"**—generally believed to have some biographical significance—he speaks of the love-episode of his life in a tone which suggests as much hatred as tenderness. . . . (pp. 161-66)

Rarely does [his] . . . harsh mood give place to a more tender sentiment, the short poem **"I visited thy tomb"** being an exquisite exception. This attitude towards the other sex, compounded of fierce passion and fiercer remorse, deprives Nekrassov of one charm common to nearly all the great Russian writers: we shall search his poems in vain for such a sympathetic and noble type of womanhood as Poushkin created in Tatiana; or for such instances of subtle and delicate feminine psychology as Tourgeniev and Tolstoi have given us in later years. For it is impossible to agree with Skabichevsky, who sees in the histrionic figures of the princesses in *Russian Women* real creatures of warm and palpitating flesh and blood. These embodiments of all the antique virtues, who are suddenly transformed from fashionable women of the world into Roman matrons, do not greatly appeal to me; nor am I moved by all their sufferings, which take place in a very scenic Siberia. Of all his heroines, the most touching and real seems to me the peasant Daria in *Red-nosed Frost*.

And if Nekrassov lacks the tenderness and delicate insight which could enable him to create a beautiful and convincing feminine type, he occasionally falls short in another quality which belongs essentially to the traditions of Russian literature and art—I mean the quality of absolute sincerity. There are passages—intended to be the most impressive—in Nekrassov's poems which bring us a sudden sense of disillusionment. We become aware that the poet is forcing the note, and it rings false in consequence. A breath of exaggeration, a suspicion of special pleading—and the "palpable design" stands revealed before us. The poet is posing as the mouthpiece of a party, and our sympathies suffer an instantaneous collapse. These highly wrought pictures of human suffering, such as we have in the very popular poem of rural life **"Orina, the Soldier's**

Mother,'' are they indeed realistic art, or something touched up to look larger and more lurid than actual life? Like ''Uncle Tom's Cabin,'' ''Oliver Twist,'' or ''The Ticket of Leave Man,'' their excuse may be that they have done good service in rousing an apathetic public to redress special evils, but does not their emphasis obscure a portion of the truth? And is not truth more important than all else?

This pose of ''emphasis'' and ''purpose'' gradually grows upon Nekrassov, until in his last long poem, *Who lives happily in Russia?* we find little beside it. The poet is lost in the pamphleteer. . . . There are some vigorous descriptive moments in the work, but the general effect is tedious and depressing. (pp. 166-68)

The subject [of *Who lives happily in Russia?*] might have been as effectively handled in prose, especially from the pulpit or the platform. As poetry the work is more oppressive than ''The Excursion,'' and moves with more unrelenting slowness than Crabbe's ''Parish Register.''

It is not, however, in any of the works enumerated that Nekrassov's verse is most strenuous and profoundly pathetic, but rather in those poems of popular life which appealed most successfully to his objective realism, and in which he is so carried away by the subject that he forgets for a time to pose as the ''Träger der Zeit-Idee.'' If it is difficult to classify Nekrassov by such poems as **''The Unhappy''** and *Russian Women,* when we come to the crown of his work—his great national epic, *Red-nosed Frost*—we recognise him at once as belonging to the main current of modern Russian literature, the naturalistic school, the origin of which is usually ascribed to Gogol. In that chain of prose writers who caught up the essential spirit of the nation and uttered it in fiction—Gogol, Dostoievsky, Tourgeniev, Tolstoi, and others—Nekrassov, although he employs poetry as a medium of expression, is undoubtedly a connecting link. In *Red-nosed Frost* he deals once more with ''the moving common-places of the human lot''; but here he uses his powers at once with more freedom and more self-control than in many of his poems. He subdues on the one hand the violence of diction which mars much of his intimate verse; and on the other he rises above the flatness and dullness of dialect by which he sometimes reminds us of Wordsworth at his worst. (pp. 169-71)

[Daria, the heroine of *Red-nosed Frost,* belongs to a type of peasantry] as far as possible removed from those examples ''stamped with dull apathy and ceaseless fear'' which the poet has created in his pessimistic vein. Daria is a sympathetic and arresting figure: a true epic heroine, fighting to her last breath against an inexorable destiny. In the first part of this great national picture, Nekrassov has chosen to employ the subdued colours and sober lights that recall some masterpiece of Millet's. There are wonderful realism and true pathos in the scenes from rural life, which succeed each other rapidly, naturally, and without any of the verbosity of *Who lives happily in Russia?* (pp. 171-72)

In this poem Nekrassov shows throughout an imaginative power and a passionate observation of nature which raise him for the time being to the level of the greatest poets—not of Russia only, but of all the world.

Coming to the question of style, we observe that, either because the subject of his verse absorbed him to the exclusion of technical consideration, or because he was naturally deficient in a fine sense for form, beauty of utterance takes a secondary place in Nekrassov's work. In this respect he owes nothing to the great singers, Poushkin and Lermontov, who preceded him and left traditions of a stately and perfected art. Nekrassov has not the sustained afflatus of the author of *Eugene Oniegin,* nor the glowing colour and passionate abandonment of Lermontov; neither has he the lyric lilt and rapture of Koltsov. Of his poetry one can rarely say: *Ça coule de source.* His verses—he himself admitted it—are ''rough and uncouth without creative art.'' But their dissonance and want of spontaneity are forgotten in their vigour and striking originality. His manner—or lack of it—is his own. His imagery is new and forcible. He carries his bluntness to the verge of uncouthness, and his frankness over the border-line of cynicism. He aimed at being a great didactic poet, and undoubtedly possessed some of the necessary qualities for the part. His convictions were sincere, though he sometimes expressed them with exaggerated eloquence. Against the tyranny and obscurantism of the world in which he lived his irony was unsparing. But his teaching, though impressive, was one-sided and untrustworthy. Nekrassov had not the balanced mind that ''sees life steadily and sees it whole.'' To him the world must often have appeared in an atmosphere made tremulous by the heat of his own fury. Temperamentally he was unable to see any but the dark places of life into which no light of joy or hope could penetrate for long. Nekrassov's liturgy of life was comminatory. It contained the *Miserere,* but no *Jubilate Deo.* Looking back to the circumstances of his career, we understand and pardon the unquenchable fires of indignation which consumed the tenderness of his nature. But seeing the widespread influence of his poetry, it is impossible to disregard his potency as a teacher; and we cannot but confess that in that capacity it is a message of bitterness and revolt, rather than of hope and self-control, which his work hands on to successive generations of Young Russia. (pp. 173-75)

Rosa Newmarch, ''The Popular Poets—Nekrassov,'' in her Poetry and Progress in Russia, *John Lane Company, 1907, pp. 153-75.*

N. JARINTZOV (essay date 1917)

[In the excerpt below, Jarintzov discusses the timeliness of Nekrasov's contribution to Russian literature, stressing the importance of his sympathetic and realistic treatment of important social issues.]

A translation in prose, phrase by phrase, of all N'ekràsov's poetry (two bulky volumes) would be like unfolding beneath the eyes of a Westerner a map or a picture of the Russian land, showing innumerable details of the life of the proletariat and officialdom, of village toil and town vanity. This picture would be sore to one's eyes. N'ekràsov was the poet of suffering in general, and of Russian woman's suffering in particular; but, oh, how far from any sentimentality! Quite as far from it as Russian reality is. The picture would abound in sharp, cutting shapes and colours, for he was the prophet of denouncement.

He came at the time of the omnipotent bloom of bureaucracy (before the Crimean War), hovering over the murk of serfdom, when the strain under the oppression was so great that ''something had to happen.'' And he was the first to mould that lurking, engendering flow of civic thought which was harking to the people's suffering and preparing to lay the road for the emancipation—only just harking, and lurking, and preparing: because there was not such a thing as a pronounced progressive society in the beginning of the fifties. Therefore N'ekràsov was not following a general current, but chose an individual way for his sober mind and honest heart. The immense success of his first volume . . . , which overshadowed even Gogol's, showed that he spoke out that Something which was fermenting in the minds of many, but at that time had no way of public self-expression. That Something was an *idealistic longing for a realistic and civic substance* in literature. N'ekràsov picked up the threads of naturalism dropped by Gogol' and B'elìnski, and thus blended with the engendering To-the-People movement of the younger generation. Certainly, that generation did not cherish any luxuries of art for art's sake, and it welcomed whole-heartedly his versified but real life-stories of cabmen, carters, gardeners, printers, sweating journalists, soldiers, hawkers, prostitutes, convicts, and peasants, illuminating all possible aspects of their hardships; descriptions of street scenes, fires, funerals, or tragic weddings, cruel dissipations, vulgarity and platitudes of town life, corruption of officialdom, etc.— all this appeared for the first time in the annals of Russian poetry.

It was for that very reason that some Russians called N'ekràsov (and some of them still call him) "not a poet, but a newspaper reporter"; the question still rises from time to time: "Was N'ekràsov a poet, or was he not?" But his admirers love him for that very element of his writings which makes him a "civic" poet.

The fact is that the substance of N'ekràsov's poetry overweighs its technical value and overshadows its occasional rays of pure lyric beauty. His realism as a thinker and publicist has certainly never reached that realism which turned Pùshkin's sketches into pearls of creation. Nevertheless, N'ekràsov's deepest suffering caused by deepest love for the people, the clearness and honesty of his observations, and his essentially Russian speech, are national treasures to most people of our land.

Very Russian, too, is the vein of bitter satire interwoven into his work. He calls his Muse "the Muse of sorrow and vengeance"; and when it comes to characteristic touches of Russian bureaucracy, the last days of convinced serf-owners, silly philanthropy, the degeneration of the rich, etc., N'ekràsov's lines are as pointed as arrows. His sarcasm is never abstract in wit either, but always rooted in facts, facts, facts—reminiscent of the exactness of photography. He and Dostoyèvski are the two men whose passionate love for Russia was to them unbearable suffering at the same time; only, Dostoyèvski is ever throbbing, and this makes him unconsciously intensify Russian reality by culminating too many extreme features in one character, while with N'ekràsov every detail of Russian life remains a separate haut-relief, full of meaning in its own place.

Sound knowledge and doubtless sincerity of this poet account for his power over the minds of the masses of Russian population. Everyone understands him; there is nothing in his poetry that requires wondering over its meaning; nor is there any of that elegant mentality about him which makes T'ùtchev's and Fet's creations a kind of refined delight for the epicureans of literary art. N'ekràsov knew this very well, but the starting-point of his poetry was different from theirs altogether:

> Be at one with my Muse of distress:
> I have no other lilt in possession.
> He who lives without wrath or depression
> Love of Motherland does not possess.

(pp. 257-60)

N. Jarintzov, "N. N'ekràsov," in her Russian Poets and Poems: Classics, *Vol. I, B. H. Blackwell, 1917, pp. 257-88.*

D. S. MIRSKY   (essay date 1927)

[*Mirsky was a Russian prince who fled his country after the Bolshevik Revolution and settled in London. While in England, he wrote two important and comprehensive histories of Russian literature,* A History of Russian Literature *and* Contemporary Russian Literature. *These works were later combined and portions were published in 1949 as* A History of Russian Literature. *In 1932, having reconciled himself to the Soviet regime, Mirsky returned to the U.S.S.R. He continued to write literary criticism, but his work eventually ran afoul of Soviet censors and he was exiled to Siberia. He disappeared in 1937. In the following excerpt, Mirsky surveys Nekrasov's poetry, discussing his identification with the sufferings of the Russian people, his lack of aesthetic refinement, and his originality. The critic divides the poet's verse into two categories: poems that take their form from previous works and those whose form is derived from elements of the Russian folk song. Discussing the latter category of works in his conclusion, Mirsky asserts that* Who Can Be Happy and Free in Russia? is *"Nekrasov's greatest achievement in the folk-song style, and perhaps his greatest achievement altogether." The essay from which the following excerpt was drawn was first published in 1927 in* A History of Russian Literature from the Earliest Times to the Death of Dostoevsky (1881).]

In spite of his enormous popularity among the radicals, in spite of the tribute given to him as a poet by enemies like Grigóriev and Dostoyévsky, Nekrásov can hardly be said to have had his due during his lifetime. Even his admirers admired the matter of his poetry rather than its manner, and many of them believed that Nekrásov was a great poet only because matter mattered more than form, and in spite of his having written inartistically. To the aesthetes he was frankly unpalatable. According to Turgénev, "Poetry never so much as spent a night in his verse" [see excerpt dated 1868]. Perhaps Grigóriev, with his profound intuition of values, was alone capable of really gauging the greatness of Nekrásov. After Nekrásov's death his poetry continued to be judged along party lines, rejected en bloc by the right wing and praised in spite of its inadequate form by the left. Only in relatively recent times has he come into his own, and his great originality and newness been fully appreciated. This has been owing, first of all, to our increased ability to understand "non-poetic" poetry. It is also owing to the displacement of Nekrásov the legendary radical saint (which he most certainly was not, in the sense in which Belínsky, Chernyshévsky, Dobrolyúbov, Gleb Uspénsky were) by a better-known and more real Nekrásov, a complex, not always edifying, but profoundly human and original, personality.

So different in most respects from his contemporaries, Nekrásov shared with them a lack of conscious craftsmanship and of artistic culture. He only dimly and subconsciously knew what he was after, and, though an excellent critic of other people's verse, he had no judgment of his own. He wasted much of his creative energy on ungrateful subjects that were not really congenial to him. He had a dangerous verse-writing facility that he had developed during his years of hack work in writing vaudevilles and rhymed *feuilletons*. He was essentially a rebel against all the stock in trade of "poetic" poetry, and the essence of his best work is precisely the bold creation of a new poetry unfettered by traditional standards of taste. But his own creative taste was not always unerring, and though he came very near creating a new and self-justified style (especially in his great satiric poem *Who Is Happy?*), he never obtained a secure command of it. But the inspiration, the sheer poetic energy of many of even his most questionable poems, is so great that one has to accept the occasional bathos as an ingredient of the whole. For originality and for energy Nekrásov holds one of the very first places among Russian poets and need not fear a comparison with Derzhávin.

The main subject of Nekrásov's poetry was, in his own phrase, "the sufferings of the people." But his inspiration is subjective and individual rather than social. Except in those of his poems in which he approaches nearest to the spirit of folk song and thus frees himself from the all too personal, his poetry is always personal, never group poetry. The social wrongs of contemporary Russia are for Nekrásov not so much an objective fact as a torturing subjective experience. One can speak of a "social compassion" complex in Nekrásov. It is precisely compassion (suffering with the other), not pity (condescending to the other's suffering), that animates the poetry of Nekrásov. For all the political seriousness and sincerity of Nekrásov's democratic feelings, psychologically speaking, "the sufferings of the people" were to him an emanation, a symbol of his own sufferings—from poverty, from illness, from gloom, from the pangs of conscience. He had an unusual power of idealization, and the need to create gods was the most profound of his needs. The Russian people was the principal of these gods; next to it stood the equally idealized and subjectively conditioned myths of his mother and of Belínsky. His idealized conception of the people of course tended towards sentimentality, and he did not always avoid this pitfall, but at his (frequent) best all suspicion of sentimentality is purged by the red heat of his poetic energy and poetic sincerity. Questions of taste and good form are supremely idle and irrelevant in the presence of such elemental creative processes as produced, for instance, the realistic myth poem of *Frost the Red-Nosed.* But Nekrásov's people were not only an object of compassion and worship. He could sympathize with their humor and their laughter as well as their sufferings, and of all Russian poets of the nineteenth century, he was the only one who was genuinely and creatively akin to the spirit of popular songs; he did not imitate it—he simply had in him the soul of a popular singer.

All Nekrásov's work may be divided into two sections: that in which he uses forms conditioned (though often only negatively conditioned) by the preceding development of literary poetry, and that in which he worked in a spirit of folk song. It may be generally said that in the former he is subjective; in the latter, objective and impersonal. The two aspects of Nekrásov are very different, but it is the combination of the two that makes his unique personality. On the whole the traditionally literary part of his work is much the more uneven of the two. Its lower strata merge in the absolutely inartistic and mechanical verse mongery in which he engaged in the early forties and which he never abandoned. Much of that which was particularly highly praised by his contemporaries for its civic and humanistic contents today seems rather a negative item in the legacy of Nekrásov. On the other hand, his ironic and satirical poems probably find more response in us than they did in our fathers and grandfathers. The biting and bilious, tersely concentrated sarcasm of such a condensed masterpiece as *The Thief* is enough to place Nekrásov in the front rank of the world's greatest satirists. And in most cases his poems of rhetorical invective have won from the action of time more than the lesser Nekrásov has lost. Personally I think that such a poem as the elegy *Home* is one of the highest pinnacles of Russian poetry, and leaves most of the poetical invective of Lérmontov simply nowhere. Another group of Nekrásov's poems that have won by the lapse of time are his love lyrics—remarkably original in their unsweetened, unsentimental, poignantly passionate, and tragic accounts of a love that brings more pain than joy to both parties. Lastly, among his very earliest poems (1846)

there is that veritably immortal poem which so many people (Grigóriev, among others, and Rózanov) have felt and experienced as something more than poetry, that poem of tragic love on the brink of starvation and moral degradation which begins: "Whether I am driving in the night down a dark street" (*"Édu li nóchiu po úlitse tëmnoy"*). The same intensity is often present in the poems written during his last illness (*Last Songs*).

Of his objective and narrative poems, *Sásha* . . . , which he was accused of plagiarizing from Turgénev's *Rúdin,* is an attempt at a problem story in verse and, though it contains some beautiful passages, compares very poorly with the novels of Turgénev. Much more interesting are the numerous chiefly short and dramatic narrative poems of peasant life. Among the most famous is *Vlas* . . . , one of those poems in which Nekrásov gave proof of his sympathy, not only with the people's sufferings, but also with their religious ideals. The most ambitious of his poems not in folk-song style is the majestic and statuesque *Frost the Red-Nosed* . . . , with its almost mythological idealization of the Russian peasant woman and the grand pictures of the silent and frozen forest.

In his folk-song poetry Nekrásov transcends his *moi haïssable,* frees himself from his torturing obsessions of suffering, and becomes the poet of more than individual expression. This is already noticeable in the poems for children, especially in the delightful *General Toptýgin* (where a performing bear is taken by a terrorized postmaster for an angry general). But it is especially apparent in the most singing of all Nekrásov's poems, *The Pedlars* . . . , a story ultimately of tragic content but told in a lusty and vigorous major key. The opening of the poem in particular has been appropriated by the people as a folk song. It is perhaps the most genuinely popular snatch of song in the whole range of Russian literary poetry. A very different note is struck in the same poem by the weirdly effective *Song of the Wanderer,* one of the most powerful and purely original ever written by Nekrásov. It is one of those poems which are human because (in Synge's phrase, so often applicable to Nekrásov) they are brutal.

Nekrásov's greatest achievement in the folk-song style, and perhaps his greatest achievement altogether, is the vast, realistic satire *Who Is Happy in Russia?* at which he worked in the seventies. The poem relates how seven peasants, to settle the question as to who lives happily in Russia, set out on foot to walk the round of the country. They meet representatives of various classes of society, the Squire, the Parson, the Peasant Woman, and so on. They are told tales of extraordinary moral achievements, heroism, and crime, and the poem ends on a note of joyful confidence in the future of the people with the help of the new democratic intelligentsia. The style is full of originality, wonderfully racy and vigorous. The poet never lets himself fall into his usual subjective lamentations, but conducts the story in a tone of keen and often good-humored, shrewd satire, in a popular style, with frequent scenes of strong and simple realism, and occasionally a heroic note when speaking of the virtues of the strong Russian peasant. Full of remarkable verbal expressiveness, vigor, and inventiveness, the poem is one of the most original productions of nineteenth-century Russian poetry. (pp. 239-43)

D. S. Mirsky, "The Age of Realism: Journalists, Poets, and Playwrights," in his A History of Russian Literature from Its Beginnings to 1900, *edited by Francis J. Whitfield, Vintage Books, 1958, pp. 215-55.**

LASCELLES ABERCROMBIE   (essay date 1929)

[*Abercrombie was an English poet, critic, and dramatist who played a prominent role in the Georgian movement in English poetry in the early years of the twentieth century. His collections of verse include* Interludes and Poems *and* Emblems of Love, *but he is best known today for such works of literary criticism as* The Theory of Poetry *and* Romanticism. *In the following excerpt, Abercrombie affirms the universality of Nekrasov's poetry, despite its thoroughly Russian subject matter and theme.*]

Of all Russian poets [Nekrassov] is perhaps the most distinctively Russian; of all modern poets, it might possibly be said, he is the most national. Outside Russia, his reputation as a poet could only await the chance of an adequate translation.

Russians, we are told, find in Nekrassov something analogous to that which we may suppose the ancient Greeks found in Homer. The analogy, at first sight, might seem injudicious. But the suggestion is not that *Who can be happy in Russia* compares, or was ever meant to compare, with the splendour of the Homeric art or the grandeur of the Homeric theme. It is simply that in Nekrassov, as in Homer, a nation recognizes, typified once for all, and rendered into a shapely comprehension, its own peculiar manner of being conscious of its own peculiar life, as history, geography, ethnology, and a hundred other factors, have determined it. Nekrassov's critics, I understand, even his Russian critics, accuse him of being ridden—perhaps hag-ridden—by a single idea. The accusation refers, apparently, to what we may roughly call his political attitude; and will certainly be ignored by those who are to decide whether translations from Nekrassov are worth making—whether, in fact, he shall take his place among the great poets of Europe as well as of Russia. For that, he will simply be judged as a poet; the judges will have no knowledge of and no concern with Russian politics, past or present. We may share his indignation against the censorship, because the mutilations it inflicted on his poetry are injuries to us as well as to him. But what does it matter, for Nekrassov's poetic reputation outside Russia, what the politician in him thought about serfdom? As little as it matters, for Shakespeare's poetic reputation, what he thought about the monarchy. Nevertheless, that Nekrassov was, as a poet, ridden by a single idea is the most obvious truth about him; and that idea was Russia. We are not to expect in him those ideas which bear the unmistakable stamp of international currency, like the ideas of Goethe, Shelley, or Leopardi. His theme is simply Russia: what life in Russia is, and means; and even if it is what life in Russia wants, the want is as Russian as the fact from which it seeks to escape. (pp. xviii-xx)

If Russia is Nekrassov's gift to us, who can value the gift but those who already know something about it? Must not the value of it lie in its truth? And how can the ignorant judge of that? But poetry is nothing if it does not transmute the local and temporary into the universal and permanent; every time a poet expresses his experience in his art, he effects that, whatever his experience may have been. . . . Everything that is circumstantial in Nekrassov—the climate, the scene, the manners, the social structure, the average mentality—everything, that is to say, that must seem to a Russian entirely homely and familiar, has on us an effect clean contrary; it strikes us as wholly strange and outlandish. But it is not my business to speculate what Nekrassov may mean to his countrymen; I am merely trying to suggest, judging from myself, how a translation of Nekrassov is likely to appeal to the intelligent ignorant, to whom the whole notion of Russia is foreign. What will be the result of this sense of the strange and outlandish in the setting of his poetry? Will it be the annoyance, or perhaps the fascination, of the incomprehensible? I am sure it will be neither. About anything that can be brought under the heading of that disastrous word 'psychology', nonsense is sure to be talked. A great deal of nonsense has been talked about 'Russian psychology'; by which is simply meant the behaviour of Russian temperament under Russian conditions. This is certainly, to us, strange enough; but, I believe, only superficially; and I doubt whether it is any more incomprehensible than the behaviour of Elizabethan temperament under Elizabethan conditions.

Now the effect of this outlandish setting and circumstance of Nekrassov's poetry seems to be just this: it throws into unusual imaginative isolation its essential humanity; so that every gesture it mentions, every movement in it of thought and feeling, take on an air of important emphasis, and seem somehow vivid with significance. That is how it appeals to us; but it is the mark of great poetry that it can adapt its appeal to all sorts of readers. The final result, however, is no doubt the same for all. Nekrassov's poetry can no more appeal to Englishmen in the same way as it does to Russians, than *Paradise Lost* (which is, or was, popular in Russia) can appeal to Russians in the same way as it does to Englishmen. But in each case, the difference of appeal will doubtless be found to lead to the same conclusion. In Nekrassov, by whatever means his poetry makes its effect on us, it is plain that we have a poet who is entirely content to abide by the reality of things; and reality, for him, is humanity. But his artistic contentment with reality proceeds from his extraordinary capacity not merely for seeing it but for seeing into it. In the lucid, lively movement of his art, we seem to have before us the very passage of reality, with its infinite pathos strangely complicated with infinite humour; and we watch this poetic reality with a clairvoyance which makes the familiar reality of everyday things seem, by comparison, a mist of baffling illusion. Let *Red-Nose Frost,* that masterpiece of a kind that cannot be paralleled in any other poet, typify what Nekrassov has to say, whether to Russian or to Englishman, whether by means of entirely national or by means of entirely foreign circumstance. There is astonishing penetration here into the inmost nature of humanity; there is an equally astonishing faithfulness to the harsh simplicity of mere fact. And by whatever means the appeal has been made, what comes home is a unique moment of understanding what an inexplicable world this is, and what an inexhaustible miracle in it human nature is. (pp. xxi-xxiv)

> *Lascelles Abercrombie, in an introduction to* Poems *by Nicholas Nekrassov, translated by Juliet M. Soskice, 1929. Reprint by Scholarly Resources Inc., 1974, pp. xvii-xxiv.*

MARC SLONIM   (essay date 1950)

[*Slonim was a Russian-born American critic who wrote extensively on Russian literature. In the following excerpt, he provides a broad overview of Nekrasov's poetic persona and literary achievement, discussing the sympathy he felt for the Russian people, the topicality of his verse, and the contradiction between his extravagant mode of life and the egalitarian outlook of his works.*]

[Nekrassov's] contemporaries regarded him as primarily 'the poet of the people' and, more precisely, the poet of the people's 'grief and sufferings'—and so he is regarded even today. Both before and after the Emancipation he portrayed a good many peasant types: some idyllic, like Grandfather Mazai, but for the most part tragic, like old Vlas, a rapacious man who repents after a sudden illness and goes around as a pilgrim, collecting money for building churches; or Orina, the poor mother whose stalwart son is ruined and done to death by the rigors of military service; or Daria, the comely widow who is frozen to death, and the heroine of his epic poem **'Jack Frost,'** with its wonderful description of the Russian winter. In several poems he pictured the fate of peasant women, crushed by slavery, hard work, the cruelty of their masters, and the coarseness of their own mates. Shorter poems, such as **'The Unreaped Row,' 'The Forgotten Village,' 'The Funeral,'** and many others are expressive in their melancholy, almost despondent mood. But the height of pathos and his humane sympathy for the misery and grief of millions of his countrymen is attained in a few lyrical pieces. In his famous **'Reflections Before a Mansion Doorway'** he wrote lines which were memorized afterwards by generations of reflective Russians. . . . (p. 234)

After the abolition of serfdom Nekrassov asked: 'The people are freed—but are they happy?'—and his answer in the negative expressed the feelings of educated society. Never before, in the history of Russian literature had the cause of the peasants found such an impassioned pleader. He assumed the role of spokesman for these illiterate multitudes, and his poems have the genuine quality of folk songs, as, for example, **'Who Finds Life Good in Russia?'** . . . . This treasury of popular life is an unrhymed epic, dealing with the adventures of seven peasants who meet with all sorts of people—merchants, priests, artisans, farmers—while trying to find out who lives in happiness, peace, honor, and prosperity in 'wretched and abundant, oppressed and powerful, weak and mighty Mother Russia.'

Nekrassov's peasant poems were as popular as his other short and long pieces, which reflected the yearning for freedom and the fighting spirit of the radical youth. They appealed to the imagination and aroused people to action like martial music, often formulating the aspirations of educated society . . . or expressing admiration for those who had fought and suffered in the past. **'Russian Women'** . . . deals with the Princess Trubetskaya and Volkonskaya, who had followed their Decembrist husbands into Siberian exile. The same exaltation of courage and idealism runs through **'The Bear-Hunt,'** in which the admirable portrait of Belinsky, as the Teacher, is a blending of pathos and delicacy.

Nekrassov's poetry covered many topics but it was in the main devoted to eulogizing those who had given their lives for their people and for liberty. 'Nothing comes free,' he said. 'Fate demands expiatory victims. The cause of Freedom can be firm only if cemented with blood.' He refused to sing of 'the beauty of valleys, skies, and sea, or of the caresses of the beloved, in these days of woe.' The word 'woe' was often used by Nekrassov to indicate social slavery and political oppression—and the censors, as well as the readers, did not mistake the real meaning of his melancholic stanzas.

Long before the Marxists he declared that poetry ought to have a message and that artists ought to be aware of social conditions. 'You may not be a poet, but you must be a citizen'—this slogan, taken for granted in the 'sixties and 'seventies, expressed his personal feelings. As a poet-citizen Nekrassov had his own symbolism from which he drew his strength and which furnished the themes of his poetry. One aspect of it was the Fatherland and the 'wide, clear road' that lay ahead of it. This faith in Russia was closely related to the symbol of the people, who represented the country, the soil, the virtues of simplicity and patience, and the sources of native greatness.

Both themes merged in an apotheosis of radical nationalism. Unlike many of the poets of his own times, Apollon Maikov, Nicholas Shcherbina, *et al.*, who looked for inspiration to Greece, Rome, or the Renaissance, or who dealt with abstract concepts, Nekrassov was an eminently national poet, intent on portraying and interpreting the domestic scene, the Russian landscape, and Russian men and women. (pp. 235-36)

Nevertheless this poet, who claimed to have chosen to sing 'thy sufferings, O people of astonishing patience,' this bard of his people's sorrows, was a nobleman and an intellectual. The day he dreamt of, when the peasant would be buying the works of Belinsky and Gogol at country fairs, had not yet come; and the poems of Nekrassov were read and admired by educated society, mostly by men and women who were well off and who therefore felt the same moral obligations toward the underprivileged as did Nekrassov himself. There was a contradiction between Nekrassov's life and his work, between the shrewd businessman and the sensitive, bitterly despondent, suffering poet. Ashamed of his wealth and influence, of the many things he possessed and loved, he was perpetually conscience-stricken. (pp. 236-37)

Caught between the regime that threatened his publications, his work, his position, his influence, and his fortune, and the high moral standards of the intelligentsia, who wanted him to be a Knight *sans peur et sans reproche*, Nekrassov always proclaimed his guilt and was ready to wear sackcloth and ashes. Hence his inner torment and his repentance during the visitations of conscience, hence his public confessions, his cry of *Peccavi!* in so many verses, his constant self-accusations, invariably followed by a pathetic self-defense. Whether this was a myth or a situation of real life, this theme of guilt, remorse, and self-redemption constituted one of the most striking trends in his poetry.

In one of his last poems he again tried to explain the main contradiction of his existence:

> Soon I shall die, leaving thee but a poor heritage, O my country! A fatal yoke oppressed my childhood, a painful struggle marred my youth. If brief, a tempest strengthens us; if long, it makes the soul accustomed to taciturnity . . . I did not offer my lyre for sale, yet there were times when its notes jarred . . . O Fatherland, forgive me all for the drop of blood I had in common with my people.

In another poem he makes the confession: 'The fight kept me from being a poet; the poems kept me from being a fighter.'

In spite of his self-contradiction, repentance is one of the main themes of Nekrassov's poetry, to which it bestows a distinctly moral character. His restlessness and penance are expressed in a pathetic manner, with grief and sincerity. Ibsen's definition of artistic creation as a perpetual trial of one's own self may be fully applied to Nekrassov. He acted both as prosecutor and defender, and he himself described his muse in aphoristic sentences, which were repeated by critics and readers: 'Muse of vengeance and of sorrow . . . This wan Muse, flogged and covered with blood; none but a Russian could behold her with love.'

His love lyrics also are stamped with despondency and contrition. Some of them are unforgettably melancholy, as is his classic **'If I Drive at Night through the Dark Street,'** or they are highly emotional: 'I like not your irony: leave it to those who have outlived themselves, or have not lived at all.' After Pushkin and Lermontov only Nekrassov ever rose to such intensity of feeling, to such directness of self-expression.

This atheistic and materialistic man, enamored of reality, was a hypochondriac: all his poetry sounds like a requiem. He mourns over the sufferings of others as well as his own; this constituted his main aim in poetry. According to some critics, in this he struck a truly national note: the melancholy of the Russian landscape, the grief of generations who slaved, suffered, and died in the immensity of the Russian land correspond to the *andante lacrimoso* of his songs. 'He wept more effectively and beautifully than any other Russian poet,' remarked Chukovsky; he sobbed over the sad fate of the peasants and over his own 'broken life,' over his mother, over Belinsky, over the wives of the Decembrists. His mellifluous verse, drawling with dactylic endings and prolonged vowels, sounds like a solo in a choir—a slow, mournful voice repeating his complaint, which other voices pick up in a collective moan. It is not chamber poetry or a stage recitation; in its oratoric sweep it has a definite aim: to move and stir the audience, and to make the individual join in the chorus and feel a part of a whole. In addition to the fact that many of Nekrassov's poems have the people rather than an individual as their hero, their choral, collective aspect is obvious and has a strong social impact. Their appeal, however, is to a limited group, not to the multitude and this again makes them different from both Derzhavin and Mayakovsky.

The problems confronting Nekrassov are always of a moral nature. In Lermontov, man faces God and Nature; his own passions have roots in the hostile elements of the universe. In Nekrassov man faces men, and his emotions derive from the activity of humanity in the aggregate—society, state, party. Lermontov is concerned with the individual acting in a world of solitude, evil, and pride. Nekrassov is concerned over man's behavior in the world of his fellow men, all conditioned by their work, social environment, or political struggles. Where Lermontov expressed himself in Romantic terms of rebellion, challenge, and abstract ideas, Nekrassov tried to bring his poetry down to earth and used a simple, almost pedestrian form. He dealt with concrete, contemporary material, such as railroads, banks, prisons, the sweat of peasants, lack of money, or shabby clothes. The reunion of poetry and life proclaimed by Pushkin becomes in Nekrassov the reunion of poetry and actuality—in both content and style. Consequently he seemed vulgar, graceless, and journalistic to those of his contemporaries who felt horrified by this invasion of *muzhiks*, rustic shouts, city slang, and newspaper lingo, into the sanctuary of Apollo.

The social and political purpose of his poems offended the esthetes to the same extent as his style shocked all the lovers of sweet melodies and poetic smoothness. They did not understand that Nekrassov was a Realist—mainly a peasant Realist—and that his advent, anticipated by Koltzov and the group of peasant poets of the 'forties, corresponded to the entire trend of native Russian literature. A product of his times, he carried through the same reform in poetry that Gogol was supposed to have accomplished in prose: the triumph of realistic understatement over the stilted and inflated Romanticism. This Realism was combined with an affirmation of the popular tradition. Drawing upon peasant songs, using formalistic preambles, deliberate repetitions, parallels, negative similes, and other devices of folklore, Nekrassov built all his poetry on the rhythms and structural peculiarities of the ballads—the recitative and oral heritage of Central Russia.

It is true that Nekrassov is extremely uneven. Writing was for him like a fever, tormenting and exhausting. He was afraid of moments of inspiration and tried to avoid them. Whatever he wrote, yielding to this 'sacred illness,' was genuine and beautiful; when he simply used his ability as a versifier his poems sounded like the work of a scribbler. Some of them—dealing with railroads, engineers, moneylenders, censorship, and other modern topics—are simply editorials in rhyme. Of course, they had their value in counteracting the so-called 'esthetic poetry' and they were an instructive novelty to his readers. Resuming the traditions of Radishchev, Ryleyev, and Pushkin, he broadened and perfected Russian civic poetry. He thus became the forerunner and master of all the poets of political struggle, popular feelings, and revolution, who flourished until the end of the century. He did create an actual school, but his influence went beyond the limitations of any group: not only social awareness but also the civic aspiration and the moral anxiety of a repentant nobleman helped to form Nekrassov's legacy to his successors.

This warped and twisted man came to an atrocious end: he suffered from cancer of the rectum, and his agony lasted two years. He died in 1877, his last poem dealing with the old theme of repentance and justification:

> O Muse, I am at Death's door. Even if I am guilty of much, even if the malice of men will exaggerate a hundredfold my faults—pray, weep thou not. Our lot is an enviable one—for long wilt thou maintain the living blood-tie between myself and honest hearts.

No poet provoked such violent discussions, and probably no poet with the single exception of Pushkin, was so admired and revered as Nekrassov. In the 'seventies and 'eighties he was the bard of the Populists and the radical intellectuals. Revolutionaries adopted his lines as slogans, liberals quoted them in newspapers—and this tradition has continued uninterrupted until the present. In the Soviet Union he is officially recognized as 'a democratic poet with revolutionary tendencies' and an example of 'civic poetry of social utility.' Today Nekrassov's dream has been fulfilled; he has become the poet of large popular masses, the herald of the agrarian revolution.

Even in his time he was strongly attacked by the representatives of 'pure poetry.' They reproached him for the coarseness of his images, the 'low level' of his poems, the prosaic ring of his lines, his heavily specific subject matter. Turgenev [see excerpt dated 1868] rejected his poetry with revulsion. Many contemporaries criticized his use of dissonances, his rhetoric, exaggeration, love of melodrama. Nekrassov himself qualified his verse as uncouth and rugged, and had many doubts about the value of his own work. Of course, the supporters of civic poetry praised him extravagantly, while a few writers, such as Dostoevsky [see excerpt dated 1877], valued him highly. In his speech at the poet's funeral Dostoevsky declared that Nekrassov was second only to Pushkin and Lermontov.

It is curious that it was the Symbolists, the disciples of art for art's sake, who pointed out in the 'nineties the true nature of Nekrassov's style. They claimed that all his poetry was that of the folk song occasionally interrupted by 'conversational verses.' Most of Nekrassov's poems are narratives with a definite topic, occasionally with a plot; yet these tales in verse cannot be spoken—they must be sung. His long poems are distinctly operatic, his diction is that of a ballad-singer, and the sobbing melody, which is the main motif of Nekrassov's

Nekrasov in middle age.

poetry, has the genuine ring of popular music, of couplets sung at village reunions, of the *lento* of work-songs, of the sentimental ballads chanted by peasant girls. Much later Blok remarked that Nekrassov expressed the very essence of Russian character through his 'triumphantly sad tunes, borne by a blizzard.' As an evidence of this truly national character of his poetry the amazing fate of some of his songs is usually cited: they were taken over by the people and were adopted in villages and factories, where the name of their author was unknown. **'The Peddlers'** (a dramatic ballad of love and crime) or the lyric **'There Goes, There Drones the Green Noise, the Noise of Spring'** have become favorites, as have his **'Lullabies'** and other incisive poems, which form an indispensable part of the entertainment wherever and whenever Russian youth foregathers. (pp. 237-42)

> Marc Slonim, "Nekrassov, Tiutchev, and the Minor Poets," in his The Epic of Russian Literature: From Its Origins through Tolstoy, *Oxford University Press, New York, 1950, pp. 231-49.**

RENATO POGGIOLI   (essay date 1960)

[*Poggioli was an Italian-born American critic and translator. Much of his critical writing is concerned with Russian literature, including* The Poets of Russia, 1890-1930, *which is one of the most important examinations of this literary era. In the following excerpt from that work, Poggioli offers a general overview of Nekrasov's career and importance, noting in particular the influence of the famous Russian critic Vissarion Belinski upon Nekrasov's work. The poet "basically subordinated his own creation to an extra-aesthetic purpose," asserts Poggioli. Yet despite Nekrasov's strict adherence to the tenets of didactic realism, Poggioli*

nevertheless acknowledges that the poet's imaginative achievement often transcends his topical approach.]

Throughout his life, as a writer even more than as an editor, Nekrasov remained loyal to the literary preachings of Belinskij. He basically subordinated his own creation to an extra-aesthetic purpose. The cause he chose to serve had been predetermined by a programmatic criticism, committed to shaping literature rather than to appraising it. Critical leadership aimed at imposing on each writer the single-minded endeavor of satisfying social demands which the critic felt should be voiced on behalf of an audience at once captive and mute. Almost all the great Russian writers freed themselves, at least in part, from such influences and premises, especially from the rigorous tyranny of Pisarev and his followers, who wanted to reduce literature to the drab handmaid of a trivial and coarse utilitarianism. Yet Nekrasov felt always duty-bound to sacrifice his artistic calling to this missionary task. The doctrine which Nekrasov preached in words and deed was not new: it had already been stated in verse by Kondratij Ryleev (1795-1826), a lesser Romantic whose celebrity was mainly due to the martyrdom he underwent in the cause of freedom, when he was hanged for the part he had taken in the Decembrist revolt. Nekrasov rephrased Ryleev's creed in two lines no less ugly than famous: "You may be allowed not to be a poet, but you cannot avoid being a citizen."

All the main writers of Nekrasov's age claimed to be realists, and he was the only poet who fully accepted their creed. Nekrasov's realism was all too often pathetic and topical, yet not infrequently it raised itself to the level of a visionary insight. Far more than many of his fellow prose writers, Nekrasov kept faith with the realistic ideal as understood by Belinskij. The latter had stated that ideal in the formula of "natural school," by which he traced not only the current trends, but even the future course, of Russian fiction. The task of that school was for Belinskij the representation of Russian life in its inner and outer truth, as well as the transformation of that life into a better existence. The instruments of such transformation were to be not only love and pity, but also indignation and scorn. In brief, realism should be shaped by both compassion and protest. In their reforming bent, both Belinskij and Nekrasov pushed compassion and protest far beyond the limits Gogol' had marked in his motto of "laughter through tears." In Nekrasov the laughter becomes a sneer, while the tears dry up, embittering rather than relieving the heart. Nekrasov's soul seems indeed to heed solely, in the poet's words, "the muse of grief and wrath." Such tension often had adverse effects on his art, producing jarring notes that spoil even the purest music with sounds which Merezhkovskij described as "scratchings of glass."

Nekrasov's inspiration found its outlet not only in versified eloquence, but also in the poetic equivalents of genre painting and the comedy of manners, such as sermons and apologues, true stories and fables with an all-too-obvious moral. Yet his imagination was frequently able to transcend such forms and materials, ascending to the sphere of prophecy and vision, of legend and myth. The old saying *facit indignatio versum* is rarely as well suited to anyone as to him; yet his wrathful zeal is so extreme and intense that it prevents his poetry from calming down into the skeptical smile of worldly sarcasm. The ethos and pathos of his poetry are not satirical, but lyrical in temper. Thus they find their most natural avenues in the invective and the complaint; their most congenial vehicles in the elegy and the iamb. Ultimately Nekrasov's passion reaches its own catharsis in a tragic and yet serene contemplation of the elemental existence of the Russian peasantry, slowly unfolding within the fixed cycle of the seasons, with their recurring labors and hardships, ruled by malady and death. Thus this ideological poet becomes a mythmaker: breaking from the confines of description and narration, from the bane of propaganda and rhetoric, his poetry enters freely and boldly into the unknown realms of the primeval and the fabulous. When this happens, Nekrasov turns even his popular fancies into vivid allegories, at once national and universal in scope, as in the poem *Vlas* . . . , where the poor farmer by that name becomes the eternal archetype of the peasant, singing in choral notes the plight of the Russian Everyman; or even better in the polyphonic suite *Red-Nosed Frost* . . . , which is at once a naïve fairy tale of Russian winter and a cosmic vision of the sorcery and magic of nature, of its secret and sacred witchcraft. It was such compositions that led Rozanov to claim that in Nekrasov's poetry "there is more national spirit than in the whole of Tolstoj. . . . A fifth or so of his poems are an everlasting treasure of Russian letters, and will never die. . . . Nekrasov knew how to find novel strains in both rhythm and speech. . . ." It is the legendary and visionary quality of his imagination, as well as the strange novelty of his dissonant music, that saved Nekrasov's literary heritage from that neglect to which it seemed natural that the new poetic generations should condemn it. (pp. 41-3)

> *Renato Poggioli, "The Masters of the Past," in his*
> The Poets of Russia: 1890-1930, *Cambridge, Mass.:*
> *Harvard University Press, 1960, pp. 1-45.**

SIGMUND S. BIRKENMAYER (essay date 1967)

[*Birkenmayer is a Polish-born American educator and author who specializes in the study of Slavic languages and literature. In the following excerpt, he discusses Nekrasov's poems written about the Russian peasant, emphasizing the poet's close familiarity with the lives of the people and his compassionate understanding of their sufferings. The critic explores how Nekrasov used the language of the peasants and elements borrowed from Russian folklore to make his portraits of peasant life both authentic and poignant. Birkenmayer concludes, "Few knew as much as he about the Russian peasant, and still fewer could express the truth so laconically and yet so powerfully and poetically." For additional commentary by Birkenmayer, see excerpt dated 1968.*]

[Nekrasov] may be called the singer *par excellence* of the Russian peasant. He was born and raised on a country estate and knew the muzhik at first hand. His concern over the peasant's lot found artistic expression for the first time in the poem *V doroge* . . . , which tells in dramatic fashion an apparently common story in the Russia of the 1840's: a peasant girl, having attracted the landowner's eye, is taken to his mansion (ostensibly to be his daughter's companion), lives there with him for a number of years, and, after the old master's death, is sent back to her village (by the new master, whom she failed to please) and forced to marry an illiterate muzhik. This story is told by the woman's husband to a nobleman whose coach he is driving, and the peasant sums up his feelings in a statement containing pointed social criticism: "Pogubili ee gospoda, a byla by babenka lixaja!" (She's been ruined by the masters, and what a fine wife she would have made!) The form of the poem is balanced and polished; the reader has the impression of being carried along the road at a fast pace from beginning to end. The swinging rhythm of the anapaest line—so typical of many of Nekrasov's poems—is well suited to the motion of the carriage and to the earthy peasant language.

Nekrasov wrote many poems about the Russian peasant in the years 1845-1875, but not all of them could be called peasant poems. Only in some did the poet use the style and diction of the muzhik while at the same time setting them to his unique metrical patterns, which often resembled those of Russian folk songs. He frequently made his peasant heroes tell their stories in their own language, thus employing the Russian folk-tale device of indirect narrative known as *skaz*. A typical example is *Ogorodnik* . . . , which begins: "Ne guljal s kistenem ja v dremučem lesu, / Ne lezal ja vo rvu v neprogljadnuju noč',— / Ja svoj vek zagubil za devicu-krasu, / Za devicu-krasu, za dvorjanskuju doč'." . . . The negative comparisons here (*Ne guljal . . . Ne ležal*) and the repetition of a phrase (*za devicu-krasu*) both are well-known mannerisms of folk poetry. In this respect, *Ogorodnik* is a typical peasant poem, and it differs sharply from several other poems Nekrasov wrote in 1846: *Trojka, Rodina,* and *Psovaja oxota* are emotional, subjective outpourings of the poet's grief over the fate of the Russian peasant. The easily discernible tone of self-accusation, the guilt complex so typical of a "repentant nobleman" (especially in the elegy *Rodina*), the involvement of the author in the narrative, and, finally, his alternate use of colloquialisms and literary words make it difficult to classify the three poems as "peasant" poems.

Between 1847 and 1854, when he was carrying on a tempestuous love affair with Avdot'ja Panaeva, Nekrasov wrote many love lyrics, but few peasant poems. A remarkable exception is the poem *Vino*, whose main character, a luckless peasant lad, tells in unvarnished language why he is always drunk: "Ne vodis'-ka na svete vina, / Tošen byl by mne svet. / I, požaluj,—silen satana!— / Natvoril by ja bed." . . . This folk song-like quatrain precedes each of the three episodes of the poem. In the final episode, we see the muzhik again drowning in alcohol his thoughts of murder and vengeance. . . . Just as in *Ogorodnik,* the device of *skaz* is used, the hero narrating in his inimitable peasant dialect, in vivid primitive style. The poem was written in 1848, that remarkable year in which freedom movements were flaring up throughout Europe, with the exception of Russia, where the government's oppression weighed heavily on the peasantry. The muzhiks drank to forget their miseries, and the main character of *Vino* expresses this idea poignantly and forcefully.

Three highly successful peasant poems were written by Nekrasov in the years 1854-1855: *Nešžataja polosa, Vlas,* and *Zabytaja derevnja.*

Nešžataja polosa is a very interesting poem. Its main theme is the plight of a peasant who is too weak or too ill to harvest his strip of grain. But there is more to the poem than that. Nekrasov wrote it in a tone of half fantasy, half reality, in a style resembling that of a ballad or a folk song. He achieved his peculiar effect by endowing the wheatfield and the wind in the poem with speech and emotion, and by introducing an element of sadness from the very beginning. The opening lines set the mood of the poem: "Pozdnjaja osen'. Grači uleteli, / Les obnažilsja, polja opusteli, / Tol'ko ne sžata poloska odna . . . / Grustnuju dumu navodit ona." (I, 100.) And then we hear the ears of grain whisper to one another. . . . The wind, which has been listening to their conversation, answers them sadly: Vašemu paxarju močen'ki net. . . . Ne po silam rabotu zatejal. Ploxo bednjage—ne est i ne p'et, červ' emu serdce bol'noe soset. . . ." (I, 101.) This is a poetic presentation of what in real life was often a stark tragedy for a peasant, since everybody else was too busy with his own work to help the one who was too ill to harvest his grain.

The peasant never actually appears in *Nesžataja polosa,* but he is spoken of by the wheatfield and the wind in direct and intimate fashion.... The artistic effect of the poem is heightened through Nekrasov's skill in using a favorite poetic device of animization of nature (the grain and the wind). The poet's imagination has been given a free rein, and his verses are set to a haunting tune composed in dactylic feet (as so often used in Russian folk laments) in order to enhance the mood of gloom and hopelessness which pervades *Nesžataja polosa* from beginning to end.

The poem *Vlas* . . . may be regarded as one of Nekrasov's first attempts at a dramatic presentation of a special peasant type. Vlas is a thoroughly Russian figure, a repentant sinner who "wanders tirelessly, alms for holy church to seek, shod in rags, and hung with fetters, with a scar upon his cheek." What were his sins? Being the richest peasant in his village, he lent money to his needy neighbors at a high interest rate; he abetted crime when he saw profit in it; he treated his family with extreme cruelty. But then came the retribution: Vlas fell ill and was growing worse every day despite his halfhearted promise to build a church if he recovered. One night he had a terrible vision in which he saw sinners being tormented in hell. The vision so terrified him that he at last repented of his evil deeds and became a new man.... Mirsky [see excerpt dated 1927] calls *Vlas* "one of those poems in which Nekrasov gave proof of his sympathy, not only with the people's sufferings, but also with their religious ideals." Vlas is indeed a kind of peasant *jurodivyj* 'God's fool'; but, at the same time, his is a typical peasant mentality: he gives little thought to God's commandments or to man-made laws until bodily pain and fear of eternal punishment make him turn from his evil ways.

A new and different theme, that of the absentee landowner's neglect of his estate and his peasants, was first presented by Nekrasov in *Zabytaja derevnja.* . . . The poem is short, but its five stanzas are so replete with dry irony that their combined impact far surpasses that of *Vlas,* for example. The story of the forgotten village is told simply and effectively, with no comment on the poet's part, so that the conclusion is left up to the reader.... [All] the peasants in the village cling to the hope that some day the landowner will come and settle all their problems.... But when the master does finally come, he comes in a coffin, and the new landowner, his son, stays in the village only long enough to attend his father's funeral before going back to Petersburg: "Starogo otpeli, novyj slezy vyter, / Sel v svoju karetu—i uexal v Piter."

Nekrasov's understatement in *Zabytaja derevnja* makes the poem more effective than *Vlas.* The plight of forgotten human beings is described in simple words which are peasant vocabulary part and parcel. A conscious attempt to imitate the language of the muzhik was truly one of the most prominent traits of Nekrasov's "village realism," as Lavrin aptly observes [in an essay first published in 1954 and revised in 1973 (see excerpt below)]: "Through his peculiar assimilation of the folk style . . . he enlarged the scope and the area of Russian poetry. . . . It is the genuine folk flavor that makes a number of his poems (including *The Pedlars, The Green Rustle,* and the whole of his epic, *Who Is Happy in Russia?*) untranslatable. . . ." *Zabytaja derevnja,* short as it is, has all the characteristics of a ballad or a folk song: its tone is impersonal and objective, a recurrent motif ("Vot priedet barin") unites the separate sections of the poem, the details are few but vivid, carefully selected, and charged with emotional appeal.

In 1861 Nekrasov wrote *Korobejniki (The Pedlars),* regarded by some critics as the best example of his ability to compose poetry in the spirit and style of Russian folklore. This long poem is really a series of poems or "songs" about traveling peasant vendors. It is written in the typical four-line stanza of a folk song and in deliberately simple language. (pp. 159-63)

Much has been written about the essentially lyric character of *Korobejniki,* as revealed in its various songs. The lyricism is heightened by the author's introduction of two motifs typical of folk poetry: love followed by separation, and nature warning the heroes of danger that threatens them. The second motif was allegedly first used in *Slovo o polku Igoreve,* and is traditional in Slavic folk poetry. The two lyrical lovers in the poem are young and colorfully attractive. Katja, with her depth of feeling and feminine patience, strikes one as perhaps a variant of Dar'ja, the heroine of *Moroz-Krasnyj Nos.* . . . Her song in part five of the poem, expressing her love for Van'ka, is simple, earthy, but finely wrought. Generally speaking, the imagery in *Korobejniki* is so permeated by lyricism that even narrative passages are tinged with it.

The poem contains some glimpses of the seamy side of peasant life, but even these are parts of the local color whose faithful reproduction is Nekrasov's primary concern. The romance of travel is also a prominent feature. The artistic device of a real or imaginary journey proved so effective in *Korobejniki* that Nekrasov used it again in his peasant "epic," *Komu na Rusi žit' xorošo.*

Nekrasov's longest poem about the peasantry, *Komu na Rusi žit' xorošo,* was begun as early as 1863 and was nearing completion when its author died in 1878. Conceived as a poetic encyclopedia of Russian rural life in the period immediately following the abolition of serfdom, it is actually a poetized folk tale narrating the odyssey of seven muzhiks wandering the length and breadth of Russia in search of a happy man. It could also be called a peasant travelogue similar to *Korobejniki. Komu na Rusi žit' xorošo* is written in the country people's style and language and contains numerous folk songs and proverbs as well as assorted bits of peasant wisdom. Scattered throughout it are all kinds of sociological, economic, and political observations, almost invariably made from the standpoint of the muzhik. The author's personality remains in the background, which gives the poem an appearance of objectivity. The reader has a feeling that Nekrasov sympathizes deeply with the Russian peasants, whose lot improved but slightly after the "reform" of 1861. But the author studiously avoids bewailing the peasant's fate and even manages to communicate some of his own idealism and optimism to his readers while entertaining and amusing them with vivid and even racy accounts. Nekrasov, like Gogol', is a master of the "laughter through tears" technique: lighthearted humor and profound reflection constantly intermingle in his *magnum opus.*

Whether in narrative or descriptive passages, Nekrasov's poetic power is revealed time and again. . . . Nekrasov does not merely describe the northern countryside; his love for it shines through, as does his concern over the poverty of its inhabitants. His appeal is to the heart, as well as the senses and the imagination.

Many of Nekrasov's nature descriptions sing in images full of the unpretentious suggestiveness of a Russian folk song. (pp. 164-65)

Portrayals of groups of people, as well as of individuals, are vivid and skilfully done. In Chapters 2 and 3 of Part I, e.g., he describes a country fair and the night of revelry following it. He is probably at his best when describing the behavior of drunken peasants (in Ch. 3). The reader sees only the shadowy figures of both sleeping and reeling muzhiks, and hears fragments of conversation that are often highly amusing, as when a half-tipsy village lad complains to his girl in the dark: "But where are you off to, / Olenushka? Wait now— / I've still got some cakes. / You're like a black flea, girl, / You eat all you want to / And hop away quickly / Before one can stroke you!" In the same chapter there is the famous passage in which a tipsy peasant stands up and, in a fiery speech, justifies the peasants' drinking as their only means of momentarily escaping from trouble and sorrow. The idea here is similar to the one expressed by Nekrasov in his early poem, *Vino* . . . , but is clothed with a fine poetic language, showing what a long way the poet had come in terms of artistic perfection.

Many Russian literary critics are of the opinion that Nekrasov drew very heavily on folklore materials when writing *Komu na Rusi žit' xorošo*. They also point out, however, that the poet never copied or adapted these materials mechanically but used them in accordance with his artistic design. As the critic Tverdoxlebov aptly remarks, "The poet made frequent use of oral folk literature not for the sake of poetic ornamentation or falsely understood beauty, but to achieve maximum expression of his artistic concepts and ideas."

The element of folklore permeates the style of Nekrasov's long poem, with the notable exception of some chapters of Part IV. Even the main topic of *Komu na Rusi žit' xorošo*, the search for a happy man, was taken from Russian folklore. Consequently, the form and style of a Russian fairy tale would seem eminently suited to his narrative and were actually used by him in the prologue to Part I. In Part II, the element of folklore is manifest in riddles or sayings, often incorporated by the author into peasant dialogue to enhance its stylistic effectiveness. The examples of Nekrasov's use of folklore are especially numerous in Part III, which is actually a story within a story: a peasant woman's tale of woe is interrupted or accompanied by lyrical songs about family life, by traditional wedding and funeral laments, and so on. The "folk" style is still evident in Part IV, but only through Chapter 3, after which it is displaced by Nekrasov's "civic" style, used whenever the author wishes to make a social point. In this closing part of *Komu na Rusi žit' xorošo*, however, even the folklore material is utilized by Nekrasov to depict the evils of serfdom, officially abolished in 1861.

Among Nekrasov's works, *Komu na Rusi žit' xorošo* stands out as a poetic but realistic portrayal of Russian life in the post-Reform period, besides being a veritable treasury of Russian folklore, a cornucopia of folk songs, tales, beliefs, customs, sayings, and proverbs. While one could argue that most of these are not Nekrasov's original creations but adaptations of folklore material, it was the poet that gave them artistic form in harmony with his folk "epic." His use of the authentic language of the peasant was unerring and therefore taken for granted. By its artistic subtlety it enhances the folk-tale atmosphere.

Nekrasov did not succeed in creating a school of his own; no "peasant" poets of any stature came in his wake. But he, more than any other Russian poet, made his contemporaries aware of the existence of the muzhik and his problems. To be sure, he did point out the evils of serfdom prior to 1861 and the shortcomings of the Emancipation after 1861; but he rendered his most valuable service to his country in general, and to Russian literature in particular, by the artistry with which he

did it. Few poets could sing of the beauty of the Russian countryside as Nekrasov did, and few knew as much as he about the Russian peasant, and still fewer could express the truth so laconically and yet so powerfully and poetically.

The muzhik, in spite of his humble social status, his poverty, and his human faults, seemed to be able to find (or at least it appeared so to Nekrasov) a certain spiritual peace in his philosophical attitude toward life. The poet, perhaps a trifle wistfully, stressed this quality of the peasant character more than once in his poetry. But the one poem in which he brought all the traits of the peasant into focus is *Komu na Rusi žit' xorošo*. (pp. 165-67)

> Sigmund S. Birkenmayer, "The Peasant Poems of Nikolaj Nekrasov," in Slavic and East-European Journal, *Vol. XI, No. 2, Summer, 1967, pp. 159-67.*

M. B. PEPPARD (essay date 1967)

[*Peppard was an American educator and essayist who specialized in German and Russian literature. In the following excerpt, he closely discusses two of Nekrasov's major poems—*Russian Women *and* Who Can Be Happy and Free in Russia?—*and provides a broad perspective on the poet's place in Russian literature. His commentary on the poems is both historical and biographical, and he locates each within the context of Nekrasov's overall career. In his assessment of the poet's contribution to Russian letters, Peppard cites such innovations as Nekrasov's use of precise detail in his depiction of the natural world, his novel approach to various aspects of versification, and his memorable depictions of Russian women. Peppard concludes with the assertion that* "Nekrasov is the greatest poet of the mid-century in Russia and has a claim to world fame far beyond that which he has enjoyed up to now."]

From the beginning to the end of his career Nekrasov was attracted to the fate of political exiles and prisoners. . . . The role of women in society, at a less heroic level, of course, than the princesses who were wives of Decembrists, occupied many pages of the *Notes of the Fatherland* during the late 1860's and 1870's. Articles on women's rights appeared frequently in its pages. In literature too novels and stories had already begun to take the emancipated woman seriously. . . . It should be remembered, however, that the heroines of Nekrasov's **"Russian Women"** belong to the 1820's; interesting also is the fact that neither Princess Trubetskaya nor Princess Volkonskaya took any part in the actual revolt or in the revolutionary activities of their husbands. But their trip to Siberia in voluntary exile in order to join their husbands was a political act of the highest order. (p. 135)

This political factor in the story of the two princesses appealed to Nekrasov, who saw an opportunity to present a view of the Decembrist revolt from a new perspective. But of course he was interested in more than merely giving new interpretations to historical data; he was fascinated by the people involved, for themselves and not just for their symbolic or historical value. This is clear not only from the warmth and sympathy with which they are portrayed, but also from the fact that Sasha from the poem of that name and Dar'ia of **"Red-nosed Frost"** live again in the aristocratic ladies of **"Russian Women."** He describes the princesses with the same words as those used for Sasha and Dar'ia: blonde curls, tall stature, firm gait, and pretty face. These are patently conventional and standing epithets to a large degree, and lead us back to folk poetry and its ornamental, undifferentiated epithets. The form of description is deliberate, however, since Nekrasov is able thereby to suggest the typical Russianness of the princesses and artfully imply their common heritage with the peasant women to whom he had set a monument in the earlier poems. The impression of solidarity with the common people is strengthened by the actions of the princesses as well as by the responses of sympathy and support of the *narod*. On the other hand, the poet stressed the coldness of the officials with whom the ladies came in contact.

Individual characterization is achieved by emphasizing a certain trait and singling it out for special use. . . . In addition to the scenes of dialogue in direct confrontation, a further dramatic quality is lent to the poem by the fact that Nekrasov allows the women to reveal their character in word and deed. The variant readings of the poem illustrate eloquently the efforts the poet made in order to characterize by direct speech and action rather than to describe or narrate from the author's perspective.

The poem is written with many purposes in mind. It is not merely the struggle with an autocratic regime that Nekrasov wishes to portray, but the relationship of the revolutionaries to the *narod*. In stressing the positive and close nature of both sides of this relationship, the poet is to a degree idealizing and drawing a picture somewhat colored by wishful thinking. But in the documents and memoirs which Nekrasov studied so carefully there is also evidence of the warmth of the relationship, and expressions of sympathy for the fate of the revolutionaries occur in the poet's source material, a fact which attracted him from the first. A third aspect of the material with which he was working also finds expression in the poem, namely, the rights of the women to their own lives. The right to decide the course of one's own life and dedicate it to a cause is a major theme of the poems about the two princesses. For this reason the poet devotes so much space to Princess Volkonskaya's struggle with her family. Her moral courage is shown in her conflict with her father, who is also a man of great will and determination. Her reasons for joining her husband in Siberia, like those of Princess Trubetskaya, are at first personal and reflect her profound love for her husband, for whom she is willing to sacrifice everything. Only gradually does the poet unobtrusively suggest the political implications of the women's decisions; only gradually do both become aware of the ideological import of their actions and grow to be sharers in the ideals and idealism of their husbands. Through this new awareness they are able to bear the hardships of exile, buoyed up not only by unselfish love but by the profound conviction of the rightness of the cause. The heroines' gradual moral growth is shown in harmony with the popular sympathy for their fate. (pp. 135-37)

"Russian Women" is the finest epic work that Nekrasov created. It has remained a favorite with the reading public since it was first printed. As a monument to the splendid heroines of the Decembrist revolt it has no peers in Russian literature. The poet wrote this masterpiece at the height of his powers. The language achieves a wide range of effects, dramatic, descriptive, evocative, with brilliantly concise narration of historical events. Yet critics, notably other poets and writers, have often been reserved in their judgments. The reason for this is difficult to discover, for close reading reveals excellence in nearly every line. There are dreams revealed in interior monologue, great flights of fancy, wonderful vignettes of the Russians and the Russian scene in the early and middle century, and all this is artistically interwoven with a narrative that gains in momentum from the contrastive flashbacks which serve to highlight it. And above all the emotions of the heroines are communicated with convincing intensity. The poem remains as fresh and rewarding today as when first published. As a work of art, combining epic, lyric, and dramatic qualities, it is unsurpassed among Nekrasov's poems.

During the time of its composition, however, the poet had already started an even larger project. The long epic poem **"Who Can Be Happy in Russia?"** occupied the poet's attention from 1863, when it was first planned, until his death fourteen years later. (p. 142)

To enumerate the folkloristic elements in the poem would be tantamount to retelling most of it. The *bylina* "How the Birds Live in Russia," from Rybnikov's collection of folk tales published in 1862, may have suggested the title, and several other parallels with tales from the collection have been identified by folklorists. But many songs and proverbs that seem to be drawn from an oral folk tradition are actually Nekrasov's own inventions. To this folkloristic basis Nekrasov added the basic, grandiose irony that it is seven peasants who will resolve the question of who is happy in Russia. They are the judges of the whole country, the arbiters who will decide the question, introduced at first half-playfully, but gradually assuming monumental proportions. From a humorous variation on a folk tale to the climax in the vision of Dobrosklonov, the poem grows in depth and breadth until it seems to span the fate of all Russia. Of all of Russia that is important, it should be noted, since Nekrasov does not deal with the government, the high officials, or the ruling classes, except for some isolated minor aristocrats who are satirized. What is important is the *narod;* its fate is seen as the determining factor for the future.

Present in the poem are idealization and grandeur of prophetic vision, but there is also much homely realism and good-natured irony. Not all peasants are heroes. The village elder, Gleb, is an example of a peasant who rejects his status as peasant and goes over to the side of the landowners. A more subtle scene is that in which the peasant Luka, pondering the priest's answer to their key question, also thinks in materialistic terms. The poet wishes to show that the task of enlightenment has barely begun. One can hardly demand of the peasants that they think in higher terms than those of the people supposedly their betters. Nekrasov maintains a humorous distance from his peasants, describing their excesses, especially in drinking, along with their positive virtues. But their vices are seen with tolerance and without anger, whereas their virtues, namely their strength, their ability to work hard, and their courage, are portrayed with fondness and admiration. There is also some humor in the portraits of the negative characters, who are usually characterized by stressing humorous details.

The last part of the poem no longer keeps to the perspective of the peasants but is told largely in the author's voice. At the same time the style changes to a more pathetic, high style, and the simple similes taken from popular speech give way to extended metaphors, except of course, in the many interpolated songs. The critic T. A. Besedina has counted one hundred lines of similes in the poem. Twenty of these are made up of proverbs and riddles. The poet made such generous use of proverbs for the sake of their laconic brevity and compactness as well as to illustrate popular speech. Even so he often shortened them and made them more concise, although most proverbs are naturally aphoristic. When using folk riddles Nekrasov often turned them about and partially resolved them, taking up into the simile the implied answer to the riddle. Few proverbs were taken over directly, since he often changed the proverb to fit a different context, thereby giving the original saying a totally new meaning. Sometimes the proverb is kept intact but presented in such a different context that it comes to serve a very different function. In one case words traditionally spoken by the bride were assigned by Nekrasov to the mother.

Since brevity and compression of the original into fewer words is the chief method Nekrasov used in weaving proverbs and riddles into his verse, the end result may be only an allusive hint. This is a delight to folklorists, but it is quite possible for an innocent reader to be baffled. One obvious effect of such uses of folk similes and sayings is to give a popular, folksy tone to the poetry. Another is the impression of concision and condensation, although at times this kind of shorthand use of simile may result in exaggeration, as for example in the prologue to the section **"A Peasant Woman,"** where Matrëna Timofeyevna is introduced as "a cow, not a woman." This is intended as a compliment, for the same verses describe her as peerless in her village, but the comparison is a dubious one. Of all the similes noted by Besedina, only a few are actually based on true folk proverbs; those that are original with Nekrasov sound so much like popular sayings that only an expert can distinguish them. The poet was original and creative in this field, and his ability to coin folk sayings with a genuine tone is equaled only by his skill in adapting or composing original folk songs.

Metrical variations are frequent throughout the poem. The basic form, modulated to give different rhythms and tonal effects, is that of iambic trimeter with two final unaccented syllables. The rhyme scheme shifts from section to section in order to avoid monotony in the short lines; there are frequent internal rhymes, some in the full lines, some also in the interspersed two-beat lines. Often the poet saves the grammatical object for the end of the sentence, or sometimes for different emphasis the verb appears in final position. The end of the line or strophe, as the place of highest emphasis, usually contains the key word of the sentence. For stress at the beginning of a line he often uses an exclamation. Caesura is more frequent in this poem than in Nekrasov's other poems; the caesura is not generally an important feature of his verse, which normally flows in even cadences, but whenever he wishes to make the rhythm of the poem more emphatic he interrupts the line with the caesura. The lexical level of the poem is deliberately kept low, since the poet's intention is to make poetry out of everyday language. Nekrasov always found delight in the common people's language, in its inventiveness, and in its turns of phrase. In addition to the many proverbs, riddles, and folk songs which Nekrasov employed, there are also his own aphoristic lines of social criticism:

> You work alone,
> When work is done,
> There stand the three you owe:
> Our God, the Czar, the master. . . .

Similar lines are scattered through the poem, but without rendering it didactic in tone, since most are kept within the basic tonality of folk songs and speech. The poem contains a vast store of information on folk customs, rituals, and forms of rustic living. For this and for its portraits of folk-heroes it can still be read with pleasure. But it is, in spite of its wealth of forms and virtuosity in versification, not on an artistic level of achievement with **"Red-nosed Frost"** or **"Russian Women."** The Soviet critic Egolin calls it Nekrasov's "most powerful work," an opinion other Soviet critics would not dispute. Although it has passages of great power and beauty, its interest

for the modern reader is more historical and folkloristic than esthetic. (pp. 145-48)

Much of the failure to see Nekrasov's greatness and to appreciate his position as the great continuer of the poetic tradition founded by Pushkin and Lermontov is because of a misunderstanding of his style and choice of lexical levels. Even modern critics are bemused by his prosaisms, his use of popular speech, and even vulgarisms in his satiric verses. It is easy and traditional to overemphasize these features of his poetry. It is true, however, that he was an innovator in the use of the language of business, with words like career, credit, series, or bank note and benefits, all of which appear in "Contemporaries." The conversational tones in his narrative diction, sometimes spiced with journalistic phrases, have led critics to speak of his "lowering" the level of poetic language and using an "inferior" style. The changes in style and tonality within the same poem have brought the reproach of impurity of genre in his verses. His constant protesting has been a stumbling block for those who believe that such tendencies are by nature unpoetic, and we must admit that some poems have an overemphasis in this respect.

Overlooked in such assessments is a basic fact which forms the core of Chukovsky's excellent study of Nekrasov, namely that the poet always used that specific style which was uniquely appropriate to the subject matter and the intent of the particular poem. Shifts in style and lexical level are possible where the dominant tone of a poem is capable of blending such changes into the whole. And it is in this skill of blending that Nekrasov is unexcelled; those transitions which are still felt as breaks in style are deliberate and mark off sections of a particular poem and a shift either of subject or of attitude toward it. The reader may test this for himself in a poem like **"The Railroad,"** where there is a neutral, narrative style, the voice of a child, ecstatic vision, ironized tones from the general, satiric effects in the description of the petty exploiters, humor, pathos, subtle counterpoint and careful composition, and all this wide range is balanced and woven together into an artistic whole. Changes in style and tone are not necessarily defects; they may serve to enrich a poem with variations and nuances in diction as well as in such formal aspects as rhyme and meter. Nekrasov's use of changes in formal respects such as length of line and change of meter may be observed in all their subtlety and skill in poems like **"Red-nosed Frost,"** where, for example, the emphatic short line often precedes a shift in the narrative perspective. If we admit the possibility of a mixed genre in which narration, description, and dialogue with dramatic scenes are all permissible, then we may conclude that Nekrasov mastered this form in his longer poems.

But it is not only in his longer, narrative poems that we find traits which are either innovations or continuations of that part of the Pushkin legacy overlooked or rejected by his contemporaries. As a poet of nature Nekrasov has few equals. The special quality of those passages in his poems which conjure up the Russian landscape is due to several factors. Most of his descriptions are remarkable for their specific, sharply observed details. The primacy of people over objects, however, is always present as a compositional principle, so that these details never exist for themselves, but only as the precise setting for human beings with their joys and sorrows. The poem **"Knight for an Hour"** is one of the striking examples of this feature of his poetry. In this poem the attention to nature and the descriptions of intimate details are used to organize the poet's mixed feelings, and the descriptions accompany the waverings of his emotions as he tries to escape his emotional urges or overcome them, or yields to the melancholy of memory. But of course the feelings of sorrow and self-reproach are not the only ones associated with the pictures of nature. In **"The Green Sound"** the harmony of life and its connection with the changing seasons, especially the joy of springtime, are a cause for rejoicing and enjoyment. The sights and sounds of nature are for man's pleasure and spiritual comfort. Closest to nature is the peasant who tills the soil; the favorite figure from peasant life is for Nekrasov the plowman. Peasants who worked in the fields seemed to the poet to have a "natural" growth and health in consonance with nature, and in this he delighted. He took pleasure in natural beauty for its own sake, but more often and typically he used the beauties of nature as a contrast to the sorry condition of mankind. One of his most striking uses of nature for this purpose is to be found in the opening lines of **"The Railroad."**

A large part of the poet's enduring fame rests on his famous portraits of women. Here better than in any other respect he may be easily set apart from his contemporaries, none of whom equaled him. He continued the tradition of *Eugene Onegin* in making his feminine figures at once both representative and individual. He rarely wrote in the abstract about womankind, or generalized about some undefined and unvisualizable beloved, but created contoured figures with recognizable traits and personality. The economy of effort with which he produced these figures was unparalleled in his time. The concision and compactness with which he is able to make even minor figures come alive in his verses is brilliantly illustrated in **"Russian Women."** Even when a general type is the subject of the poem, as is the case in **"At the Height of the Harvest,"** in which any peasant woman might be meant, intimate details and close observation make the total picture vivid. Dramatic effects in scenes that could easily be acted out recur in his poems frequently; dramatic dialogues were developed far beyond anything since *Eugene Onegin*.

Not only in his famous portraits of Russian women, but in all his verse there is a constant tension between two complementary forces. On the one hand Nekrasov sought to suggest, particularly in his portraits of people, the broadest representative qualities. He endowed his figures with individual traits, but at the same time gave them a setting and function that was typified. On the other hand, especially in his descriptions of nature and of objects, he strove for the most precise details. These two strivings reinforce each other. Sometimes the urge to achieve the specific detail leads to prosiness, as for example in the use of exact numbers which are often startling in their unexpected context. These prosaisms were unusual and disconcerting for his contemporaries. A poem that begins "Yesterday at six o'clock" suggests a reporter's narrative, not a poem of pity and pathos. But in his striving for typical qualities, especially in drawing his emblematic heroes, he did not hesitate to achieve a generalizing effect by the use of abstract language. He spoke, when he considered it apposite, of Love, Faith, Hope, Work, Truth, Freedom, and Service, capitalizing the nouns for emphasis. His broad range of tones included the language of high rhetoric as well as the turns of popular speech or the jargon of journalism. He was careful to fit his language to the person speaking or being spoken of; his characterization by the use of language is often very subtle. In his serious poems, but not in his satire, he frequently indicated the social level of the speaker and assigned personal speech forms by the use of varying syntactical constructions rather than by a choice of vocabulary. There are notable exceptions to this general

rule, and in those passages where he speaks as author-narrator the lexical choice covers the full range from near-dialect to solemnly archaic words of Church Slavonic form. And again and again he returned to condensation and concision as the means of lending emphasis to his message. It is not surprising then that the most famous quotations from his poems are largely aphoristic.

The path of an innovator is seldom smooth. The difficulty in assessing Nekrasov's proper worth arose from a misunderstanding of very personal developments which are innovations only to the extent that the emphasis and personal tone color was new. As we have pointed out in our discussion of Nekrasov's relations to his predecessors, a precedent can be found for almost everything which Nekrasov undertook. But it was difficult for his contemporaries to see those basic aspects of his work which represent a consistent continuation of the classic tradition, and their misunderstandings have survived over the years and have been repeated often enough to become clichés of criticism. Madame Jarintsov [see excerpt dated 1917], seeking to characterize briefly his poetic production, mentions his poems about cabmen, carters, gardeners, printers, soldiers, hawkers, prostitutes, convicts, and peasants, and his descriptions of street scenes, fires, funerals, tragic weddings, cruel dissipation, the vulgarities and platitudes of town life, and the corruption of officialdom. If one lists his subjects in this bald fashion, it seems obvious enough that Nekrasov does not stand in the Olympian tradition. He provided Russian verse with a new melody, broadening the scope of what was acceptable as "poetic" and enlarging the horizons of literary verse. Nekrasov was the boldest of his period in creating new genres, mixtures of genres, combining political verses with confessional lyrics, satirical chronicles with revolutionary poems with a historical base, and vignettes of mixed dramatic and lyric effects. The synthesis of the social and the intimately personal in his verse meant an enrichment of the possibilities of poetry. In prosody too he had a great influence. Until his time, with the exception of Koltsov, the folk-meters, trochaic rhythm with dactyls at the end of the metric line, were infrequently used in literary verse. Nekrasov's success with these meters marks an enrichment of the accepted forms in Russian versification. (pp. 166-70)

Nekrasov was primarily a practitioner; he never developed a theory of poetry, nor did he seek to buttress his writing with philosophical speculations. As a poet he was an innovator who seemed to overturn the old esthetic canons of poetry, but as a theorist he never established a poetics nor made any attempt to formulate his ideas on poetry in essayistic fashion. He was not an abstract thinker but a poet most at ease with visual images. His letters contain the scattered fragments of a poetics, and from the reviews and the poems themselves we can deduce some of his esthetic beliefs. But in a way it would seem that he never really accepted his own poetry in the light of a firm philosophical and theoretical position. In part his severe and hypercritical self-depreciation accounts for this seeming paradox. Even up to his last days he felt that he had failed as person and as poet.

His sense of failure was not shared by the reading public. And it was not shared either by many poets who became, in some degree, his successors and the continuers of the tradition he had established. Among those who show a good deal of affinity with Nekrasov we may mention A. N. Pleshcheyev (1825-93), I. S. Nikitin, and M. L. Mikhailov. Especially in the case of the last-named poet it is debatable to what degree he was influenced by Nekrasov; it is more likely that he was a congenial product of the *Zeitgeist*. Nekrasov's influence on like-minded writers can easily be exaggerated, especially if one forgets that much of what Nekrasov was doing was in the popular current of his times that swept along others as well. The radical intelligentsia consisted of differentiated individuals with common concerns. Since Nekrasov is the greatest poet of the group it is easy to assign to him what was in fact common property. His distinctive contribution is to be sought in his art, not in his ideology. (pp. 172-73)

Nekrasov is the greatest poet of the mid-century in Russia and has a claim to world fame far beyond that which he has enjoyed up to now. (p. 176)

> *M. B. Peppard, in his* Nikolai Nekrasov, *Twayne Publishers, Inc., 1967, 192 p.*

SIGMUND S. BIRKENMAYER   (essay date 1968)

[*In the following excerpt, Birkenmayer offers a general appraisal of Nekrasov's poetic skill and outlook, focusing on the poems he wrote about his mother. For additional commentary by Birkenmayer, see excerpt dated 1967.*]

Nekrasov's life was in a sense a drama in which he was the chief actor, and the stage for that drama was Russia itself. His family heritage and his emotional and intellectual development shaped his poetic temper and determined his choice of topics to write on. The best of his poems actually dealt with but two recurrent themes: 1. his recollections of his mother, 2. the life of the Russian peasant. It is in such poems that his empathy and his proneness to grieve over human suffering strike us as genuine and artistically convincing. On the other hand, one cannot deny that in many of his contemporary satires (and even in his long narrative poem, **"Russian Women"**) Nekrasov seems to assume an altogether hypocritical attitude, paying lip service to artistic perfection and being concerned primarily about the salability of his literary production. The poet himself admitted (in his poem, **"To an Unknown Friend"**) that at times his lyre "was clearly out of tune". His poetry could not—and never did—appeal to all strata of contemporary Russian society; and those to whom it did appeal, often interpreted it in terms of ideas rather than art. It was Černyševskij, after all, who cast Nekrasov in the role of a radical saint. Yet the poet was no social reformer any more than Puškin and Gogol had been; it was his essential humaneness that prompted him to devote his talent to the cause of social betterment. Nekrasov's lifetime dream was to be remembered after his death by the Russian peasantry, whom he had portrayed so lovingly in his long narrative poem, *Who is Happy in Russia*. Since he identified himself with his people and his country, Russia looms large in his poetry as in his life.

Nekrasov has been called by some "a poet of vengeance and grief", and his own words could be cited as proof that such an apellation was at least partly justified:

> Be at one with my Muse of distress:
> I have no other lilt in my possession.
> He who lives without wrath or depression
> Love of Motherland does not possess.

Nekrasov's "Muse", however, seems to have been at her best in purely lyrical poems. He was primarily a lyrical poet and only secondarily a social satirist. The figure of Nekrasov-the-artist overshadows the social prophet. The gap between his world and ours can be bridged only through appreciation of his poetic art, of which his own personal life and the life of

his Russian homeland were the matrix. Nekrasov, "a poet of vengeance and sorrow", and a first-rate lyricist, cannot be seen in his true perspective if considered apart from the times and the society in which he lived. His poetry, taken in its entirety, not only provides the key to the understanding of his complex personality but also reflects all the important political and social changes that occurred in Russia between 1845 and 1875. But it is the lyricist, not the satirist, that appeals to us as we read Nekrasov's poems. The "anger and grief" in Nekrasov's poetry have long since ebbed away, but his art remains. (pp. 7-8)

There are several reasons why Nekrasov's mother, who died in 1841, occupies a prominent place in his poetry. First of all, her love for him was the only bright reminiscence of his otherwise unhappy and gloomy childhood. She was his only friend and best teacher in those years: she read to him, encouraged him to write poetry, shielded him from his father's anger, and—contrary to the latter's wishes—urged her son to obtain a university education. And it was she who opened his eyes to human suffering around him and, by her own example, taught him to love his fellow human beings and feel compassion for them. Her romanticism and idealism, her capacity for emotion and tender passion, were the traits that Nekrasov inherited from her and, in turn, embodied in his poetry. Secondly, as some critics surmise, it was only after her death that the poet began to realize how much she had loved him and what she had done for him. Perfectly normal feelings of guilt and remorse undoubtedly entered into his poetic idealization of his mother throughout the rest of his life. To her he dedicated many of his lyrics, some of which are extremely moving, like **"A Knight for an Hour"**. It might perhaps be interesting to examine these poems in chronological order, so as to see how different Nekrasov's portrayal of his mother is in each of them.

In his strongly autobiographical **"Homeland"** (**"Rodina"**), written in 1846, the poet's mother appears to him as a helpless but patient victim of her husband's cruelty. . . . She dies, like Christian martyrs did, after forgiving him who caused her death. The contrast between the father he hated and the mother he worshiped must have been firmly engraved on Nekrasov's mind, for he used it again as a theme in 1856 in his poem, **"The Unfortunates"** (**"Nesčastnye"**). The passage which is most characteristic here is the one in which the poet speaks of himself as a little boy who, hiding in a corner with his mother, is a witness to the drunken carousing of his father and the latter's companions, whom he mistrusts and hates. . . . The boy's devotion to his mother shows clearly in his refusal to obey the wish of one of his father's friends. He clings to her, seeking comfort in her love for him, trying to forget his frightening experience. Such experiences must have been fairly common in the poet's childhood, for he refers to them in the same poem as a "depressing dream" (*tjaželyj son*).

In **"A Knight for an Hour"** (**"Rycar' na čas"**), written in the year 1860, Nekrasov combined his idealization of his mother with an expression of his feeling of failure and his fear of death. The poem begins with a description of the poet taking a walk in the country at night. Vainly striving to overcome his melancholy and pensive mood, he walks through fields and meadows, finally succumbing to a deep sadness. . . . In his thoughts, Nekrasov sees the country church where his mother is buried; and, in his half-waking and half-dreaming state, he hears the bells of the church strike midnight. He can almost see his dead mother, whom he addresses as if she were still alive. . . . In the lines that follow, Nekrasov speaks of his urge to unburden himself to his mother of his ''grief of many years'', as if he were still her child. It is for her, he says, that he will sing his ''last bitter song''. He begs her forgiveness for making her suffer again instead of comforting her, but he has no choice; she is the only one who can save him from spiritual death. . . . He bewails his spiritual deterioration, the result of passion and greed. Even his mother's prayers, which so often kept him from tumbling into the abyss, could not prevent his ultimate downfall. He has sunk into ''the filthy mire of petty thoughts and passions''. . . . [The poem] ends not with the radiant picture of Nekrasov's mother but with the melancholy image of the ''superfluous man'' whose traits are unmistakable to anyone familiar with Russia's history of the time. Written in 1860, on the eve of the Emancipation, **''A Knight for an Hour''** is a poignant expression of the poet's pessimism and his inability to rid himself of a deep sense of guilt. Morbid though its moods may be, it remains one of the best lyrical poems by Nekrasov.

A very interesting poem is **''Mother''** (**''Mat'''**), written in 1868. It is said that Nekrasov explained the subject with a marginal note: ''I think it is obvious; the wife of a political exile or prisoner.'' Others believe that it contains at least an indirect description of Nekrasov's mother.

> Within her heart o'erflowing care was preying,
> And while her sons in noisy frolics vie,
> Three children round their mother gaily playing,
> Her lips in pensive tone made whisper, saying:
> ''My hapless sons, why were you born, o why?
> However straight your way of life—o hearken,
> Escape is none from your appointed fate.''

The ''fate'' to which the woman in the poem refers is apparently that of orphans of an executed political prisoner. It is also possible to extend the meaning of the Russian word *sud'ba* (fate or destiny) to the general unhappiness of the Russian people at the time. In the second part of the poem, Nekrasov addresses the grieving mother directly and gives her advice and comfort:

> With anxious care do not their pleasure darken,
> O martyr-mother, cease, thy tears abate,
> And let their tender youth from thee be learning,
> That times there are of ageless nights and morns
> In which we deem the goal of dearest yearning,
> The fairest gift on earth—a crown of thorns. . . .

This is a far cry from **''A Knight for an Hour''**, where Nekrasov represented himself as his mother's ''lost son'' in dire need of her love and comfort. In **''Mother''**, in a sudden outburst of spiritual strength, he seems to be giving advice (in a somewhat sententious manner) to a grief-stricken woman who bears some resemblance to his mother. The poem lacks the sincerity of feeling that is so manifest in **''A Knight for an Hour''**.

The most ample reference to Nekrasov's mother is found in his **''Excerpts from the Poem *Mother*''** (**''Otryvki iz poèmy *Mat'*''**), published in his last collection of poems. . . . In it, she is portrayed as her son still remembers her: a loving parent, a gentle teacher, a shining example of Christian virtue to be admired and imitated. Nekrasov is not afraid or ashamed of placing his mother on a pedestal. . . . [At one point early in the poem,] the poet begins to have misgivings about disturbing his mother's eternal rest, and he begs her forgiveness for doing so again. But his excuse is, he points out, the need to have the world know of a woman's cross. . . . This lyrical introduction (I) is followed by Part II, in which the poet goes back

to his childhood and evokes long-forgotten sights and events on his family estate. Thus, for example, the linden trees remind him of his mother's fondness for walking in their shade; and the tombstone on her grave makes him recall what he would rather forget: that she died just before he came back from Petersburg. . . . At this point there is a gap in the poem, the reason for which is unknown. Then Nekrasov recalls a letter that he found among his mother's papers, and again a train of recollections comes to his mind. In his imagination, he goes into the garden half-expecting his mother to appear. She does appear to him—walking in the moonlight, a letter in her hand. . . . Here follows Part III, which opens with an apparently authentic letter written to Elena Andreevna (Nekrasov's mother) by her Polish mother. The letter is replete with a mother's sorrow over her daughter's running away and becoming ''a slave to a hated Muscovite'' (Nekrasov's father); it ends with a final plea for Elena to return to Poland—a plea which, as we already know, went unheeded. Suddenly the vision disappears, the voice fades, and the poet finds himself alone in a moonlit garden, clutching the letter in his hand.

Another fragment follows, in which Nekrasov leafs through the books that his mother brought with her ''from a faraway land'' (i.e., Poland). He reads the chance remarks she put in the margins, and comments in a tone of deep conviction: ''A searching, penetrating mind is evident in these.'' Suddenly he feels compelled to read the fateful letter once more—and, as he does it, a poetic image of his mother again appears before his eyes. . . . In the subsequent stanzas, full of autobiographical reminiscences, Nekrasov tells how his mother awakened his interest in literature by telling him stories ''about knights, monks, and kings'' when he was a little boy. . . . Here Nekrasov's thoughts turn once more to his early childhood, when his mother was to him ''a nurse and a guardian angel''. He speaks with compassion of the suffering brought upon her by her decision to leave her country and to marry a stranger. . . . Then he recalls another incident from his childhood, that of his mother playing the piano in one of her sad moods. However, she tried to appear ''poised and cheerful'' to others, including her son. And when comparing her own lot with that of the people of Russia, she thought that she was perhaps the less unfortunate. . . . At this point, the poet begins to realize that he has become enmeshed in a bewildering maze of disconnected recollections; his poem is turning into a chaos. Nevertheless, he has to make one final effort to accomplish the task he set before himself—that of enshrining his mother in people's memory. He hopes that his poetic art, inspired by his filial love, will not fail him this time. . . . In the last section of the poem, which artistically seems to be the best, Nekrasov portrays his mother as a woman of great spiritual strength. To him she is a heroine, who ''dragged her chains with her'' for twenty years until she died. In death she achieved her ultimate moral victory over those who had wronged her; her love conquered them in the end. . . . Nekrasov recognizes his mother's spiritual greatness (''Your soul glows like a diamond . . .'') as revealed by the way in which she lived and died. He speaks with admiration of her loving and kind attitude toward the peasants. In spite of her limited powers, she brought hope, comfort and sometimes inspiration to many a household serf in Grešnevo. . . . The last two stanzas of the poem are extremely interesting, for it is in these that Nekrasov openly acknowledges his mother's influence on his mature attitudes. . . . **''Excerpts from the Poem *Mother*''** was written less than a year before the poet's death. It ends on a far more optimistic note than, for example, **''A Knight for an Hour''**. Nekrasov indeed believes that he, at long last, has been able to express how much his mother meant to him, and to render to her the kind of tribute that can only come from a grateful and loving son. Even if he exalts his mother's Christian virtues, he does not make a deliberate effort to set her up as an example for others. He does it inobtrusively through his poetry which immortalizes his mother in this unique and most personal poem.

"Lullaby" ("Bajuški-baju"), also written in the year 1877 (on March 3), is the very last poem that Nekrasov dedicated to his mother. In it the poet, already on his deathbed, sees her and hears her comforting voice. . . . In the last stanza of the poem, the image of his mother seems to assume a superhuman proportion, that of "Mother Russia", who brings a final message of comfort and hope to her loving son. . . . And so, in an extremely moving lyric written shortly before his death, Nekrasov's love for his Polish mother and his Russian motherland became as one. (pp. 189-99)

In our present-day assessment of Nekrasov it is well to keep in mind that he was, first and foremost, a lyrical poet singing his feelings. The best among his poems are the subjective ones, in which he suffers with others or accuses contemporary society both directly and by implication. Here belong many of his poems written in the years 1845-1865: **"On the Road"**, **"Homeland"**, **"Reflections at the Grand Entrance"**, **"On the Volga"**, **"The Peddlers"**, and **"Red-Nose Frost"**. His poetic preoccupation with the Russian peasant shows clearly in all of them, but it reaches its apogee in his folk "epic", *Who is Happy in Russia*. But there is another group of poems, just as subjective and lyrical, addressed to his mother, to whom he devoted his personal lyrics, **"A Knight for an Hour"** and **"Excerpts from the Poem *Mother*"**. Directness of feeling transmuted into lyrical singing, sometimes rough-hewn in form but often exquisite, characterizes Nekrasov's best poems. Wherever these elements are lacking, his poetry becomes a combination of bathos with rhymed journalism (which Turgenev was quick to observe).

Nekrasov did not succeed in creating a school of his own: no "peasant" poets came in his wake. But he, more than any other Russian poet, made his contemporaries aware of the existence of the muzhik and his problems. To be sure, he did point out the evils of Tsarist serfdom prior to 1861 and the shortcomings of the Emancipation after 1861; but he rendered his most valuable service to his country in general, and to Russian literature in particular, by the artistry with which he did it. Few poets could sing of the beauty of the Russian countryside as Nekrasov did, and few knew as much as he about the Russian peasant, and still fewer could express the truth so laconically and yet so powerfully and poetically. (p. 201)

Sigmund S. Birkenmayer, in his Nikolaj Nekrasov: His Life and Poetic Art, *Mouton, 1968, 204 p.*

JANKO LAVRIN   (essay date 1973)

[*Lavrin is an Austrian-born British critic, essayist, and biographer. He is best known for his studies of nineteenth- and twentieth-century Russian literature. In such works as* An Introduction to the Russian Novel, *Lavrin employs an approach that combines literary criticism with an exploration into the psychological and philosophical background of an author. In the following excerpt, Lavrin surveys various aspects of Nekrasov's poetry, including his use of folk song melodies, realism, and sympathetic portrayal of peasant life.*]

Nekrasov found his own poetic voice rather late—towards the end of the 1850s and in the first half of the 1860s. As for the

general trend of this poetry, it had a number of themes some of which had their sources in his experience at home and in Petersburg. In boyhood he witnessed the cruel treatment meted out to the serfs, as well as to his own mother (a Polish woman of some education and refinement), by his uncouth father. In Petersburg again he saw the very depths of misery bred by a big city. His opposition to everything that was connected with serfdom and autocracy made him write civic poetry, whereas his sympathy with the oppressed serfs drove him towards the people and was responsible for the voice of a 'repentant nobleman', with a strong guilt-complex, in most of his work. To this the realism of his 'big city' poems, dealing with the Petersburg he had learned to know, should be added. In one of them, beginning with the line, 'When I drive at night in a darkened street', he describes with haunting directness a starving couple whose baby has just died. Both of them have been reduced to such straits in their garret as to be unable to buy even the coffin in which to bury their child. In the end the young mother is compelled to go out on the streets whence, later on, she returns—her eyes full of shame and despair—with money for the coffin. The extremes of such misery appealed to Nekrasov the poet as much as they did to Dostoevsky the novelist. And he was among the first to introduce the 'big city' motif to Russian poetry. His *Street Scenes* and pictures of Petersburg outcasts were further enlarged by social satires, by caustic scenes from bureaucracy and high life. These border, however, on his civic poems proper. Much of his civic and political verses can be dismissed as rhymed pamphleteering. If we want to find Nekrasov at his best and most original, we must look for him in the poems he wrote about the toiling people and frequently also in the manner of the people. (p. 119)

Whatever one may think of Nekrasov's civic and political-didactic verses, there can be no doubt of the power and the melody he so often extracted from the folksong. Elements of such creative *rapprochement* with the people can be found before him—in Pushkin, Lermontov, and especially in Kol'tsov, but none of them went farther in this direction than Nekrasov. It may have been partly for this reason that the populist Chernyshevsky (not a reliable judge of poetry) put Nekrasov higher than Pushkin and Lermontov.

Nekrasov's flair for the melody of the folksong (with its peculiar rhythms and verbal instrumentation) was exceptionally strong. It was he, too, who cultivated on a large scale the dactylic endings typical of the *bylíny* and many other Russian folksongs. Through his peculiar blend of anapaests and iambics with dactylic rhymes he enlarged the scope and the melodiousness of Russian poetry, thus building a bridge between literature and the people. Having turned, on many occasions, against the accepted canons, he made the next step and tried to depoetise literary poetry by introducing all sorts of unpoetic and peasanty words. Yet it is the genuine folk-flavour that makes a number of his poems, including *The Pedlars (Korobéiniki)*, *The Green Rustle (Zelyóny shum)* and the whole of his epic *Who can be Happy and Free in Russia? (Komú ná Rusi zhit' khoroshó?)*, almost untranslatable. Even the best rendering of the contents does not do justice to such poems unless one catches all the peculiarities of Nekrasov's inflection, rhythm and melody, and these are inseparable from the Russian language. So much for Nekrasov's technique. Another strong point of his work is its village realism which also deserves to be mentioned.

Nekrasov's 'big city' motifs were largely connected with his civic poetry and owed a great deal to the 'natural school,' advocated by Belinsky. The same holds good of his poems directed against his own class—the poems of a nobleman who, for moral as well as humanitarian reasons, became a defender of the peasant and the village. One of such examples is his **Home**. It makes one think of Lermontov's indictments and of Pushkin's poem, *In the Country,* with the difference, though, that Nekrasov openly accuses himself, his ancestors and particularly his own father. (pp. 120-21)

In the end the poet—a descendant of serf-owners—experienced something like a moral satisfaction when seeing his ancestral home almost ruined. On the whole, the virulence of his indictment was always in direct ratio to his own repentance. Repentance, or rather a mood of ever-recurring moral masochism and self-castigation, may well have been needed by him even as a creative stimulus. This alone would be enough to throw some light on the quality of his behaviour during his years of prosperity; on the one hand the sumptuous living typical of a squire, and on the other his self-reproaches—turned into poetry. And the more he hated the remnants of the squire in him, the more acutely he felt also the people's tragedy and the people's cause, with which he was anxious to identify himself in his verses. After all, he called his Muse 'the people's sister'.

Nekrasov's realism of the countryside does not entirely concentrate on the negative and tragic side of village life. There are bright moments as well. What could be more delightful than the realism of his poem, **Peasant Children (Krestyánskie déti),** in which he describes a bevy of little village urchins clandestinely looking at him through a chink and making comments of their own! (p. 122)

Equally delightful are some of his other poems—humorous, descriptive, didactic—dedicated to Russian children: **Uncle Jack,** for instance; or **General Toptýgin,** in which the frightened peasants mistake a run-away bear for an angry General; or **Grandad Mazáy,** who during a spring flood rescues a boatful of hares and would not touch the bewildered creatures. (pp. 122-23)

Yet in the majority of his peasant or village poems the sad and gloomy disposition prevails. Nekrasov's verses about the people's woe always strike the right note and are particularly moving when he sings of the hard lot of the Russian peasant woman. The account in **Orína—a Soldier's Mother** of how a peasant woman's only son, a healthy young giant, had been forcibly conscripted, and after a few years returned home a complete wreck only in order to die of tuberculosis, is heart-rending in its tone and simplicity. Then there are the suffering toilers on the Volga and elsewhere, whom the poet asks at the end of his famous **Meditation at a Porch,** whether the only thing they have given to the world is their 'song resembling a groan', after which they are perhaps doomed to disappear for ever. Nekrasov himself may have wavered in his answer, but not for long. Behind the people's tragedy he felt also the people's vitality, as well as that broad, generous goodness which comes only from latent strength. And his admiration for them is testified by a number of his best poems, such as **The Green Rustle, The Pedlars, Vlas, The Red-Nosed Frost** and **Who Can be Happy and Free in Russia?** It was in these poetic creations that Nekrasov identified himself with the very soul of the people in a more distinctive way than any other Russian poet of that period.

Take such a lyrical drama in miniature as **The Green Rustle.** The bracing rhythm of the opening verses is itself suggestive of the arrival of the spring. The manner, the accent and the imagery are those of the peasants. Even the blossoming trees are white as if someone had 'poured milk over them'. And then we listen to the monologue of a peasant who, on his return home from Petersburg (where he had been working), learned that his wife had been unfaithful to him. All through the Winter he had brooded resentfully and in the end sharpened a knife with which he intended to kill her. Suddenly the Spring arrived and drove all evil thoughts out of his mind. As though spellbound, his heart could not resist the wave of generosity and forgiveness brought along by so much beauty. (p. 123)

The Pedlars again is a series of poems about two enterprising Yaroslavl' peasants, peddling their wares in the countryside:

> Making profit with each mile;
> Everything they chance to meet with
> Serves the journey to beguile.

In this series Nekrasov came so near to the accent and the spirit of the people that its opening verses have actually become a folksong:

> Oy! How full, how full my basket!
> Calicoes, brocades, a stack,
> Come, my sweeting, make it lighter,
> Ease the doughty fellow's back.
> Steal into the ryefields yonder,
> There till night-fall I'll delay,
> When I see thy black eyes shining
> All my treasures I'll display.

There follow the pedlars' jokes, arguments and adventures with the village folk. As a contrast to their carefree gaiety the *Song of a Poor Pilgrim* is interpolated, but the wailing tune and rhythm of its Russian words can hardly be rendered in any translation. . . .

The whole of the unhappy, exploited peasant Russia is . . . reviewed, and each line ends with the refrain of either 'cold' or 'hungry', the slow repetition of which in Russian (*khólodno, gólodno*) suggests the moaning of the wind or the howling of beasts. The motif of desolation in these lines also prepares the reader for the tragic end of the cycle. (p. 124)

Red-Nosed Frost (Moróz-Krásny nos . . .) is another gem of Nekrasov's poetry. Although written in conventional metres, it is a perfect blending of poetic realism, peasant-mentality and folklore. The theme is simple. . . . There remains Nekrasov's central work **Who can be Happy and Free in Russia?** . . . This epic is unique of its kind and occupies in his writings a position similar to that of *Onégin* in the work of Pushkin. If *Onégin* combines and completes, as it were, all the ingredients of Pushkin's poetry, **Who can be Happy and Free in Russia?** shows all the main features of Nekrasov the poet. Its aim was to give a picture of the whole of Russia after the abolition of serfdom in 1861, but it is written in the people's spirit, style and language. The loom on which it is woven is that of a folk-tale, which does not prevent the poet from displaying plenty of realism, indictment, satire, boisterous humour, as well as the implied didactic purpose within the frame of the epic. (pp. 125-26)

Russia passes before us in a variety of aspects, and whatever her trials, she has enough vigour and vitality to overcome them all. So the epic, although unfinished, contains a note of faith and hope. An ambitious youth, Grisha, from among the commoners, sees in his poetic dreams what is in store for his country and people; dreams which are enough to chase away despondency and pessimism from the reader's mind.

> His bosom was burning;
> What beautiful strains
> In his ears began chiming;
> How blissfully sang he
> The wonderful anthem
> Which tells of the freedom
> And peace of the people.

Such was the apotheosis of Nekrasov's populism in poetry while this trend was still being followed by the majority of the intelligentsia as well. (p. 127)

And what of Nekrasov's place in literature? Turgenev [see excerpt dated 1868] once said that the Muse of poetry had not spent a single night in Nekrasov's verse. With all respect for Turgenev's aesthetic sense, such a verdict no longer holds good. By turning against accepted canons, Nekrasov opened up new possibilities with regard both to contents and technique. By introducing a number of 'unpoetic' themes in a purposely depoetised language, he divested his verse of solemnity on the one hand and of 'prettiness' on the other. As a result, his directness made him accessible to a wider circle of readers. Even his journalistic verses performed a useful task in so far as they awakened and kept alive an interest in poetry among those readers who otherwise had little mental equipment for it.

This was why Nekrasov found so many ardent admirers among those commoners whose cultural background was smaller than that of the members of the intelligentsia. One of his recent critics, Kornei Chukovsky, is therefore justified in saying that Nekrasov wrote for a new type of political and social consciousness. His work served as a literary link between the intelligentsia and the masses.

Nekrasov failed to create a definite school of his own. Nevertheless, his attitude towards the village, the people and the folk-poetry acted as an inspiration for several poets who came—even long after him—from the people (the best known of them being Sergey Esenin). His attempt at marrying poetry to topical journalism may not have augured a happy union, but it had a strong following in Soviet Russia, where Mayakovsky and his group made—after 1917—a series of further experiments of this kind. Nekrasov's technical devices, too, have drawn considerable attention of late. We may no longer think (as some of his contemporaries did) that he is greater than Pushkin. Yet with all his faults and virtues, he occupies one of the important places in the Russian Parnassus. (pp. 128-29)

> *Janko Lavrin, "Nekrasov," in his* A Panorama of Russian Literature, *Barnes & Noble Books, 1973, pp. 117-29.*

THOMAS GAITON MARULLO   (essay date 1980)

[*In the following excerpt, Marullo studies Nekrasov's critical attitudes toward poetry as reflected in two articles written for the journal* The Contemporary, *disputing the notion that Nekrasov judged poetry solely on the basis of its political and social content.*]

The advent of literary realism in Russia reflected a general European trend in which writers rejected conventional poetic genres and experimented with new prose forms. In Russia this trend was championed by the critic V. G. Belinskii who insisted

that prose better suited the new "democratic" spirit of the times. Intoxicated with the heady demands for reform, the writers of the new realism agreed that the less rigid forms of the novel and *povest'* provided them with maximum flexibility for aesthetic innovation and for statements of social indignation. Poetry, they thought, lacked the creative plasticity necessary for either. (p. 247)

In 1847, the journal *Otechestvennye zapiski* attacked the standard poetic genres viciously; and, by the following year, most of the major journals had followed suit. Prominent editors let it be known that prose was the preferred item for publication, and that readers who abandoned poetry for more "serious" reading were ideologically mature. The staff of N. A. Nekrasov's journal, *Sovremennik*, as self-styled leaders of the realistic avant-garde, joined the attack. By means of a series of vicious parodies, Nekrasov, I. Panaev and N. Gaevskii, under the collective name of "Novyi Poet," insisted that writing sonorous verse had become a mechanical task. Predictably, such a verbal onslaught diminished the publication of good lyrical pieces until, beginning in 1848, Nekrasov could not find a single poem worthy of inclusion in his journal. In fact, at this time and for a period of three years, Nekrasov refused to publish even his own lyrical works.

As both editor of a progressive journal and a promising poet in his own right, Nekrasov temporarily found it difficult to reconcile his support of the new realism with his personal love for the poetic form. The deepening crisis proved crucial to Nekrasov's dual development as poet and critic; that is, he responded to the increasing rejection of verse by acknowledging his own native affinity for poetry and by re-evaluating the quality of contemporary lyrics. Between 1849 and 1854, therefore, Nekrasov was almost exclusively preoccupied with the analysis of verse form. As was often to be the case in his almost forty-year literary career, he stood alone; but he was influential both in damning the fashionable ridicule of verse and in encouraging the revitalization of the Russian poetic tradition.

A careful scrutiny of Nekrasov's critical pronouncements during this period overturns four traditional evaluations of his literary career: namely, that Nekrasov's fostering of poetry at this time was the result of the "dark censorship terror" which prohibited prose expressions of "civic" realism; that he was primarily a practitioner of art and was thus alien to poetics or theories of poetry *per se;* that he was unable to formulate his ideas on poetic art in logical essays; and that since Nekrasov was convinced of the exclusively social purpose of art, his world view was materialistic in scope and was allied strictly with the utilitarian outlook of Belinskii and the "radical" critics, N. G. Chernyshevskii and N. A. Dobroliubov.

Two critical pieces written by Nekrasov at this time provide essential evidence for a fresh and radically different appraisal of his literary stance. In his article, **"Russkie vtorostepennye poety,"** written in 1849, and in his review of *Damskii al'bom,* published in 1854, Nekrasov did, in fact, articulate a personal *ars poetica.* In this he sought to revive the reader's interest in verse and to restore poetry to a position of importance in the national literature. In both articles, Nekrasov specifically identified those obstacles which were hindering poetic growth; tempered current negativism with an objective defence of what was good in Russian verse; strove to create a supportive atmosphere for novice poets; rescued the writer Fedor Tiutchev from what may well have been eternal oblivion; and finally, praised many of the so-called "aesthetic" poets, in particular,

A. A. Fet, A. N. Maikov and I. P. Polonskii, for the formal aspects of their craftsmanship. A re-examination of Nekrasov's aesthetic position also points out the speciousness of such generalizations as "aesthetic" and "radical" criticism. What emerges from this re-examination is not the image of an inflexible Nekrasov, intent on the purely utilitarian or revolutionary aspects of art; rather, it is one of a sincerely dedicated artist seeking to restore respect and tolerance for all legitimate forms of literary art and for all artists who embody eternal beauty in the written word.

From the very beginning of **"Russkie vtorostepennye poety,"** Nekrasov displayed a sensitive awareness of those obstacles which were preventing a poetic renewal. In his view, the commercial profits of prose, the hostility of both journalists and critics toward verse, and the indifference of the public to poetry had gradually smothered poetic talent. (pp. 248-50)

The burning issue for Nekrasov, however, was the disproportionate emphasis on poetic form alone. In this, he shared Belinskii's belief that the decay in verse had resulted from its sterile content and from the use of poetic techniques which had become studied imitations of a once productive Pushkin-Lermontov standard. That is, he believed that form and content both helped to create a sense of remoteness from reality and allowed for little surprise or enjoyment from the reader. Since poetic diction had become the hallmark of the poetic piece, however, the writer's individual message counted for little and inhibited the graceful adaptation of form to content. . . . Nekrasov claimed, therefore, that it was precisely the mannered style characterized by smoothness and euphony which had smothered content. Moreover, stylistic devices and poetic diction had come to be used so blatantly that, in Nekrasov's opinion, formerly "sacred" verse was now conceivably within the competence of the most average poet. . . . Nekrasov recognized that, given the public's disdainful attitude toward verse, the novice poet was unwilling, if not fearful, to develop his aesthetic gifts. In fact, the anticipation of ridicule had already taken its toll: Nekrasov's youthful contemporaries were foregoing verse for a variety of popular, prose genres. (p. 251)

Though Nekrasov understood the material advantages of writing prose, his own poetic sensibilities would not let him allow the decline of verse to continue. Apparently, it would have been only with reservation that Nekrasov would have accepted Belinskii's dictum that prose was the one adequate means for the further development of the national literature. Nekrasov foresaw, rather, that a continued neglect of poetry, the disruption of its tradition, and the loss of acquired competence in verse would cause irreparable loss to Russian literature. In the second part **"Russkie vtorostepennye poety,"** therefore, Nekrasov strove to create a supportive atmosphere for novice poets who displayed independent talent. Nekrasov's rationale for this program was his confident belief that public preference for good poetic pieces was still active and that, as long as this force was vital, journalists and poets must respond to it as to every public need and demand. Despite the supposedly utilitarian spirit of the age, Nekrasov sensed that the human soul still clamoured for beauty. . . . Nekrasov's insistence on public demand was a clever strategy in that it awakened the readers' interest in poetry and sought to involve them in the national search for new talent. Nekrasov tempered his initial enthusiasm with the realization that the Golden Age of Russian verse was indeed over, and that the talents of contemporary poets were, at best, "minor" . . . : yet, he saw the undeniable necessity of fostering new and positive circumstances in which truly

exceptional talents could develop. Thus, Nekrasov's call was to balance past negativism with a more objective view; and, to this end, he struck out against the caustic nature of past criticism. (p. 252)

Nekrasov published a variety of contemporary verse in his review, thereby showing both his readers and his fellow critics evidence for his assertions. Those writers whom "he has extracted from the gloom of oblivion" are, with one or two notable exceptions, of minor importance. The names, N. Spiglazov, V. A. Solonitsyn, and D. Fon Lizander are long-since forgotten; N. P. Ogarev and I. S. Turgenev (under the pseudonym, T. L. or Turgenev-Lutovinov) are of more interest. Most important, however, was Nekrasov's discovery of a then unknown poet, "F. T."—subsequently known as Fedor Tiutchev. (p. 253)

In the absence of the critical tolerance Nekrasov was advocating, much of the contemporary poetic writing seemed unsuccessful, even vacuous. Careful examination, however, revealed to truly discerning readers that the poems, collectively, maintained a striking unity in tone, style and motivation and were notably devoid of the abrasive aspects of romanticism which Nekrasov so abhorred. The poets were tapping their sober personal reflections as the source of their creativity and the resultant works employ a wealth of sensual impressions and pale colours to generate wistful sadness or even, at times, an elegiac tone. Since the poet had crafted an expression of an authentic experience, the poetic devices were correlated with the content and the reader could perceive the message with empathy, with the feeling that he, too, has shared these emotions, this loss or this quiet. Nekrasov's ideas, then, led to more objective appraisals and to deepened aesthetic satisfaction.

The validity of Nekrasov's critical sensitivity becomes even more apparent in his discovery of the poet Tiutchev. (pp. 253-54)

Nekrasov was the first critic to point out the excellence of Tiutchev's art and, in particular, his creative adherence to the poetic tradition of Pushkin and Lermontov . . . ; he thereby rescued the poet from the devastating effects of public indifference. Predicting that Tiutchev would become one of the great talents in Russian literature . . . , Nekrasov took continual pleasure in seeing his prophecy fulfilled. Moreover, in his analysis of Tiutchev's verse, Nekrasov unconsciously projected his own image as a poet, that is, much of what he approved of in Tiutchev's art can also be said of his own. The twenty or so of Tiutchev's poems which Nekrasov was considering were taken from an early collection entitled "Stikhotvorenniia, prislannye iz Germanii." These pieces, taken together with Nekrasov's insightful commentary, embodied a coherent statement on the nature of the poetic art. The basis of Nekrasov's appraisal was his belief that sincere verse must maintain an inherent delicacy, that is, poetry should capture "thought, originality and charm of expression." . . . The notion of "delicacy" implied that art and thought enter into an organic union in which profound content energizes the beauties of aesthetic structures while the latter assimilates the message into life-giving forms. Nekrasov believed that it was this successful fusion of poetic phenomena with the author's thought and emotion that aroused a reader's response. Thus, in Nekrasov's view, the writer, the reader and the poem itself contributed to an interaction of creative response. Such results, he believed, were attained through the merger of independent creativity and a strongly national flavour which "bore the imprint of the

Russian mind and soul.'' . . . Above all, however, Nekrasov argued that if the poetic piece were to be successful, it must express a true and self-contained message; that is, it must be a creation in which "every word was to be precise, weighty and pliable in its nuances." . . . (pp. 254-55)

Essentially, Nekrasov understood Tiutchev's work as exemplifying these critical ideas. In his analysis, Nekrasov correctly discerned two central themes of Tiutchev's writing: first, Tiutchev's spiritual empathy with nature; and second, his disaffection with the lot of mankind. Nekrasov paid singular tribute to the poet's ability to capture the elusive essence of nature. . . . In Nekrasov's view, Tiutchev's fusion of art and thought was successful; for example, he believed that the poet's rendition of a spring day generated sufficient energy to infect the reader with exhilaration. . . . Moreover, Nekrasov accurately sensed Tiutchev's predilection for themes of order and chaos. Throughout the published pieces, the poet delicately balanced motifs of light and dark to reflect the Manichaen struggle of good and evil forces; and he posed rays of light against an eerie twilight and the onrushing chaos of night. Nekrasov also appreciated Tiutchev's ability to relate seasonal changes to man's spiritual condition. In the cited lyrics, the poet, often and with a tone of oratorical pathos, identified the darkness of a wintry night with a depressed world, burdened with human loss and exhaustion, while the charm of a burgeoning spring would for him symbolize hope for the spiritual renewal for all creation. Tiutchev's love of nature and his rich use of nature symbols were, of course, close to Nekrasov's own technique; and since Nekrasov also viewed nature as a primary source of life-experience, his approval of such themes is understandable. Finally, it is noteworthy that Nekrasov was the first to have intuitive insight into the gentle irony of Tiutchev's world view; and, in a second group of poems also published at this time, he called attention to the poet's ironic touch in dealing with themes of isolation, death and treacherous love. . . . (pp. 255-56)

In writing **"Russkie vtorostepennye poety,"** Nekrasov's ostensible goal was to rescue poets from public indifference. Upon closer analysis, it can be seen that he also achieved a variety of other important aesthetic goals. His call for critical moderation, his program for a valid critical method, and his conception of an organic poetic system were not only interesting in themselves, they were also influential in restoring interest in Russian verse. Nekrasov realized, however, that remarks of theoretical import had to be grounded in a firm promise of support to the novice writer, so, toward the end of the article, he wrote the following:

> Poetry is often sent to the staff of *Sovremennik* as well as the staff of other journals. But, if the authors do not see their works in print, they think that we consider them without talent. We hasten to set their minds at ease. In certain pieces which are sent to us, there are undoubtedly signs of talent; we do not print them because such pieces are few, and almost every one of them lacks independence. This must not prevent the poet from writing, since, in perfecting his talent, he can attain independence. Often, a business-like journal obstructs his efforts. We, however, are prepared and with pleasure, to note all that is good, and we will . . . put forth poems which have quality . . . and warrant their inclusion and thus give us hope

for something better from them in the future. . . .

(pp. 256-57)

This stirring defence of Russian poetry soon became a basic tenet of Nekrasov's critical program and, from time to time, he reiterated his poetic goals. Thus in his review of *Dam'skii al'bom* . . . , written in 1854, he issued a type of progress report on the status of the national art. Using the device of a letter supposedly received from one Mr. Starozhil (or "Mr. Old Fashioned"), Nekrasov repeated many of his earlier objectives: the plea for sincere verse, the appeal for a new attitude, the promise of support for the beginning writer, and so forth. In the guise of "Starozhil," Nekrasov acknowledged his affinity for verse and his belief that poetry provided for both the expression of the spirit and for its liberation from the confines of earthly matter. . . . Nekrasov believed that the Russian's innate love for poetry resulted in a national demand which was far more sophisticated than that of western European readers. To Nekrasov, this was cause for great hope; a more exciting sign of progress, however, was his ability to cite a number of new Russian poets who, in his opinion, had attained critical independence. Particularly in his review of *Damskii al'bom* but also in other articles written between 1851 and 1856, Nekrasov warmly endorsed the writings of Fet, Maikov, K. Pavlova, I. Polonskii, A. M. Zhemchuzhnikov, N. Shcherbina and L. A. Mey—in effect, poets who have been traditionally associated with the so-called "aesthetic" school of nineteenth-century Russian poetry. (pp. 257-58)

What is more unexpected but very significant is that those verse pieces which Nekrasov published as models of good poetry in his review, though impressive aesthetically, dealt exclusively with the intimate and personal, and were completely devoid of social comment. Included among the works to which Nekrasov gave approval were discourses on impressionistic dreams, scenes of fairy-like nature, and panegyrics to mysterious maidens and goddesses. In a reassessment of Nekrasov's achievement as a critic, one can see that those inclusions were innovative and hardly the choices of a critic who was reputed to adhere exclusively to the exposure of social ills.

Soviet scholars have explained Nekrasov's departures from the sacred principles of sociological criticism primarily as his sincere though futile attempt to promote coöperation between the mutually hostile liberal and radical camps of *Sovremennik*. This analysis, however, fails to take into account that Nekrasov was, supremely, a true poet whose flexibility and aesthetic intuitions left him open to the subtle beauty of poetic forms. He could understand a fellow poet's creative delight even when it was expressed in a highly personal manner. Thus, though Nekrasov generally abhorred poetic albums for their outworn romantic, if not sentimental outlook, he could sincerely praise *Damskii al'bom* for providing several moments of genuine aesthetic pleasure.

Both **"Russkie vtorostepennye poety"** and the review of *Damskii al'bom* yielded positive results. Though both articles did, in fact, represent a lone voice midst the demands for either utilitarian or "civic" realism, they had an echo in a whole series of positive appraisals of unknown poets, and were instrumental in bringing about a poetic revival in Russia in 1854 and 1855. . . . More importantly, both essays stimulated a reassessment of the traditional evaluations of Nekrasov's literary activity. While it is true, of course, that Nekrasov geared his own art primarily to discussing the political and social fate of his nation, he nonetheless insisted that all aspects of the new

Russian literature—his own included—be aesthetically viable. Conventional assertions which stress Nekrasov's exclusively materialistic orientation or his unquestioning adherence to the "radical" school of nineteenth-century Russian literary criticism have been shown to be unilateral and inadequate. If anything, it was Nekrasov's wrestling with the failing aesthetic qualities of verse which gradually forced him to recognize and avow his own poetic gifts, and to formulate, with convincing and logical directness, a new *ars poetica* from which the revival of Russian verse could issue forth. (pp. 258-59)

> *Thomas Gaiton Marullo, "Reviving Interest in Verse: The Critical Efforts of Nikolai Nekrasov, 1848-54," in* Canadian Slavonic Papers, *Vol. XXII, No. 2, June, 1980, pp. 247-59.*

ADDITIONAL BIBLIOGRAPHY

Chukovsky, Kornei. *Masterstvo Nekrasova.* 4th ed. Moscow: Gosizidat, 1962, 727 p.
  A seminal study, in Russian, of Nekrasov's writings. Chukovsky explores the poet's style, the major influences on his work, and his methods of composition.

————. *The Poet and the Hangman (Nekrasov and Muravyov).* Translated by R. W. Rotsel. Ann Arbor, Mich.: Ardis, 1977, 95 p.
  A detailed biographical and historical investigation of the circumstances surrounding the composition of Nekrasov's ode to Mikhail Nikolaevich Muravyov, a widely feared government official known as "the hangman of Wilno" because of his ruthless repression of the 1863 Polish uprising in the Lithuanian provinces.

Evgen'ev-Maksimov, V. E. *Zhizn' i deiatel'nost N. A. Nekrasova.* 3 vols. Moscow: Goslitizdat, 1947-52.
  The most thorough biography in Russian.

Gregg, Richard. "A Brackish Hippocrene: Nekrasov, Panaeva, and the 'Prose in Love'." *Slavic Review* 34, No. 4 (December 1975): 731-51.
  Examines the series of poems Nekrasov addressed to his mistress, Avdotia Panaeva. Gregg discusses the biographical and psychological background of the poems and speculates upon early experiences in Nekrasov's life that may have shaped his attitudes toward women.

Lojkine, A. K. "Nekrasov's Anapaests." *Melbourne Slavonic Studies,* Nos. 9-10 (1975): 54-63.
  A technical discussion of Nekrasov's innovative use of anapestic meter.

Margaret (Oliphant Wilson) Oliphant

1828-1897

(Born Margaret Oliphant Wilson) Scottish novelist, biographer, short story writer, translator, and critic.

A prolific writer who was extremely popular in her day, Oliphant is now remembered primarily for her novels depicting English and Scottish provincial life, her inventive narrative style, and her independent and resourceful female characters. Of her large body of works, the *Chronicles of Carlingford*, a series of five novels that records life in a small English town, is perhaps her best known.

Born in Wallyford, Scotland to a customs officer and his wife, Oliphant was the youngest of three children. Her father was a shy, retiring man, so her mother became the dominant figure in the Wilson household, intervening in family conflicts and supervising the education of her children. She taught Margaret to read and write and instilled in her an appreciation for Scottish lore that is evident in many of Oliphant's early works. Her later writings often reflect the contrasting personalities of her parents: her female characters are strong and determined, while many of her male characters are weak and indecisive.

In 1849, Oliphant and her brother William Wilson moved to London, where she anonymously published her first work, *Passages in the Life of Mrs. Margaret Maitland of Sunnyside*. The novel's popular success prompted the publication of two additional novels, *Caleb Field: A Tale of the Puritans* and *Merkland: A Story of Scottish Life*. All three portray early nineteenth-century Scottish history, provincial life, and culture, and all were immensely popular. In 1852, she married her cousin Francis Oliphant, a prominent artist.

The early years of Oliphant's marriage were clouded with misfortune. She nursed her mother during a fatal illness, and two of her children died in early infancy. Her husband's stained-glass designs, once in demand, became less profitable, and his business faltered. In 1859, he contracted tuberculosis and, in a futile attempt to forestall the disease, moved his family to Rome, where he died within several months. Oliphant, the mother of two young children and pregnant with a third, waited until the birth of her child and then, already heavily in debt, borrowed money from her publisher, William Blackwood, for her return to England.

In the early years of her marriage and during her stay in Italy, Oliphant wrote prolifically, contributing historical, biographical, and critical essays to *Blackwood's Edinburgh Magazine*. Upon her return to England, however, she found that much of her work was rejected by the periodical. Struggling to support her family and repay Blackwood for advances on her unwritten work, Oliphant conceived the plan for the *Chronicles of Carlingford*. The series was a popular and financial success, yet Oliphant's lifestyle was extravagant, and her expenses continued to exceed her income. She returned to Italy in 1864, where her only daughter died. That same year, her widower brother and his three children moved in with her, and Oliphant assumed responsibility for their support. She continued to write despite continuing personal tragedy, including the deaths of her two sons and nephew. In the last years of her life, Oliphant began writing stories that dealt with the supernatural, a subject she

was drawn to following the deaths of her children. Among the most popular of these works were *A Beleagured City* and *A Little Pilgrim in the Unseen*. Oliphant also produced several historical studies, including *The Literary History of England in the End of the Eighteenth and Beginning of the Nineteenth Century* and *Annals of a Publishing House: William Blackwood and His Sons, Their Magazine and Friends*. These works, though significant in her lifetime, are today considered less important than her fiction. In a preface to her last work, *The Ways of Life: Two Stories*, Oliphant commented that she had lost much of her early enthusiasm and had little interest in presenting a positive, romantic view of life to her readers. Although she continued to write prolifically until her death in 1897, her last works, which reflect this change in outlook, are not considered among her best productions.

As the author of numerous contributions to nineteenth-century periodicals and nearly one hundred novels, Oliphant enjoyed popular success throughout her career. Today, she is remembered primarily for her novels, which are noted for their realistic characters, imaginative depiction of Scottish life, and blend of humour and pathos. *Mrs. Margaret Maitland, Katie Stewart*, and *Kirsteen: A Story of a Scottish Family Seventy Years Ago*, perhaps the best examples of Oliphant's Scottish stories, are especially praised for their female characters, who are resourceful, intelligent, and determined. The main character in *Kirsteen* typifies the Oliphant heroine: driven from home by her domineering father, the young girl successfully establishes herself in a profitable and independent career. While the *Chronicles of Carlingford*, Oliphant's best-known works, also contain resourceful female characters, they are noted for more than strong characterization. In the first two novels of the series, *The Rector and the Doctor's Family* and *Salem Chapel*, Oliphant creates many of the characters and themes that recur throughout the *Chronicles of Carlingford* as a whole. In these novels, Oliphant sympathetically portrays the nine-teenth-century conflict between the Protestant Church of England and the reemerging Roman Catholic Church. In the first two novels, she examined the internal conflicts of Carlingford's young clergy, while in the final two volumes of the series, *Miss Marjoribanks* and *Phoebe, Junior: A Last Chronicle of Carlingford*, Oliphant concentrated more extensively on the townspeople.

Oliphant's reputation has diminished dramatically since the initial publication of her works. Despite her wide popularity in the nineteenth century, many critics suggest that the rapid production and sheer volume of Oliphant's writings prevented her from composing any work of lasting literary distinction. While her works have been praised by modern critics for their realistic and memorable characters, none of her novels have achieved the enduring recognition enjoyed by the works of such other nineteenth-century English novelists as Jane Austen, George Eliot, or Anthony Trollope. Today, Oliphant remains a minor figure in Victorian literature who is recognized for her skill in storytelling and for her memorable portraits of strong, capable women.

(See also *Dictionary of Literary Biography*, Vol. 18: *Victorian Novelists After 1885*.)

*PRINCIPAL WORKS

Passages in the Life of Mrs. Margaret Maitland of Sunnyside (novel) 1849
Caleb Field: A Tale of the Puritans (novel) 1851
Merkland: A Story of Scottish Life (novel) 1851
Katie Stewart (novel) 1853
Lilliesleaf: Being a Concluding Series of Passages in the Life of Mrs. Margaret Maitland (novel) 1855
The Days of My Life (autobiography) 1857
The Life of Edward Irving, Minister of the National Scotch Church (biography) 1862
**The Rector and the Doctor's Family* (novel) 1863
**Salem Chapel* (novel) 1863
**The Perpetual Curate* (novel) 1864
**Miss Marjoribanks* (novel) 1866
Madonna Mary (novel) 1867
Francis of Assisi (biography) 1868
Historical Sketches of the Reign of George Second (biography) 1869
The Minister's Wife (novel) 1869
Memoir of Count de Montalembert (biography) 1872
**Phoebe, Junior: A Last Chronicle of Carlingford* (novel) 1876
A Beleagured City (novel) 1879
The Literary History of England in the End of the Eighteenth and Beginning of the Nineteenth Century (history and criticism) 1882
A Little Pilgrim in the Unseen (novel) 1882
The Wizard's Son (novel) 1883

Kirsteen: A Story of a Scottish Family Seventy Years Ago (novel) 1890
Memoir of the Life of Laurence Oliphant and of Alice Oliphant, His Wife (biography) 1891
The Victorian Age of English Literature [with Francis Roman Oliphant] (history) 1892
***Annals of a Publishing House: William Blackwood and His Sons, Their Magazine and Friends*. 2 vols. (history) 1897
The Ways of Life: Two Stories (short stories) 1897
The Autobiography and Letters of Mrs. M.O.W. Oliphant (autobiography and letters) 1899

*Many of Oliphant's works were first published serially in periodicals.

**These works are collectively referred to as the *Chronicles of Carlingford*.

***The third and final volume of this work was completed by Mary Porter in 1898.

F[RANCIS] JEFFREY   (letter date 1850)

[*Jeffrey was a founder and editor of the* Edinburgh Review, *one of the most influential magazines in early nineteenth-century England. A liberal Whig, Jeffrey often allowed his political beliefs to color his critical opinions. Oliphant sent a copy of the anon-ymously published novel* Mrs. Margaret Maitland *to Jeffrey for review. Here, in a letter forwarded to the unidentified novelist by her publisher, Jeffrey expresses admiration for the novel. He favorably compares Oliphant's work to John Galt's* Annals of the Parish, *but notes that* Mrs. Margaret Maitland *is "purer and deeper" than Galt's* Annals. *Jeffrey also addresses Oliphant's anonymity and challenges her decision to remain unknown to the public*.]

I was captivated by '**Margaret Maitland**' before the author came to *bribe* me by the gift of a copy and a too flattering letter—which I am now taking the chance of answering—though not trusted either with the name or address of the person to whom I must express my gratitude and admiration! Nothing half so true or so touching (in the delineation of Scottish character) has appeared since Galt published his 'Annals of the Parish'—and this is purer and deeper than Galt, and even more absolutely and simply true. It would have been better though and made a stronger impression if it had copied Galt's brevity, and is sensibly injured by the indifferent matter which has been admitted to bring it up to the standard of three volumes. All about the Lectures and Jo Whang, and almost all about Reuben and the ladies at the Castle, is worse than superfluous; and even the youthful Poet and his allegory, though the creation of no ordinary mind, is out of place and *de trop*.

The charm is in Grace and Margaret Maitland, and they and their immediate connections ought to have had the scene mostly to themselves. It is debased and polluted by the intrusion of so many ordinary characters. The conception of Grace, so original and yet so true to nature and to Scottish nature, is far beyond anything that Galt could reach; and the sweet thought-fulness and pure, gracious, idiomatic Scotch of Margaret, with her subdued sensibilities and genial sympathy with all innocent enjoyments, her ardent but indulgent piety, and the modest dignity of her sentiments and deportment, make a picture that does equal credit to the class from which it is taken and to the right feeling and power of observation of the painter. Claud perhaps is scarcely made thoroughly deserving of Grace, though it certainly must not have been easy to finish a *male* character either so highly or so softly as these two delightful females—and Mary, especially in the later scenes, is nearly as good as they are.

When I first read the book I settled it with myself that it was the work of a *woman*—and though there are *pronouns* in the letter of the author now before me which seem to exclude that supposition, I am so unwilling to be disabused of this first impression that I still venture to hope that it was not erroneous, and that these words were introduced only to preserve the *incognito* which the author (though I am sure I cannot guess for what reason) seems still anxious to maintain.

I have no wish certainly, as I have no right, to violate the *incognito*, but write now merely to return my humble and cordial thanks for the honour the author has done me, and to express the deep and most pleasing sense I have of the great merit of his (if it must be *his*) *personnel*, and with all good wishes transcribe myself the said author's very grateful and sincere humble servant. . . . (pp. 153-55)

> F[rancis] Jeffrey, *in a letter to Margaret Oliphant on January 5, 1850, in* Autobiography and Letters of Mrs Margaret Oliphant *by Margaret Oliphant, edited by Mrs Harry Coghill, Leicester University Press, 1974, pp. 153-55.*

LITTELL'S LIVING AGE   (essay date 1852)

[*The following excerpt provides an assessment of Oliphant's anonymously published early novels. The critic considers* Mrs. Margaret Maitland *her most enjoyable work, but concedes that some readers will prefer the carefully constructed plot of* Merkland. *In a more mixed evaluation of* Caleb Field *and* Adam Graeme, *the critic predicts that the subject matter and characterization of these novels will do little to enhance the author's reputation.*]

The author of "**Mrs. Margaret Maitland**" is not to be dismissed wth disrespect as a mere tenth-rate planet, even by those who hesitate to worship her as a fixed star. . . . She has probably less of the poetry of pathos and passion than her fair countrywoman who has given us the fortunes of the "**Ogilvies,**" and the heart-struggles of the "**Head of the Family**" [the critic unwittingly refers here to Oliphant, who published these works anonymously]. But there is more of subdued wisdom, of mellowed art, of equable manner, of quiet reflectiveness, and of unobtrusive sagacity, in the subject of our present sketch. And but that she has evinced something of a disposition to overwrite herself—or at least to be content with repeating herself "with a difference"—we might augur very promising things in her behalf, and a reputation which shall survive a reäction. We are disappointed if she has yet done her best.

Truth to nature—the harvest of a quiet eye, which sees somewhat deeply, if not very widely—an unexaggerated manner, together with a well-defined national individuality . . .—in these lies the charm of the now celebrated "**Passages in the Life of Mrs. Margaret Maitland, of Sunnyside.**" They open admirably; nothing of the kind can be better than the good spinster's reminscences of early years, when she lay on the grass in the garden of her father's manse, looking at the white clouds sailing upon the sky, and thinking no mortal could be happier if she could but have abode there; or drawn thence into more stirring idleness by her brother Claud, "it being little in the nature of a blithe boy to bide quiet and look at the sky—that I should speak of him so! that is a man with gray hairs upon his head,

and a father in the kirk; but the years steal by us fast, and folk forget.'' If our interest in these life-passages flags by the way, it is because they, with all their linked sweetness, are *too* long drawn out. Not, indeed, that they are passages which lead to nothing; but they are a roundabout way of reaching the proposed something. . . . When matter which should find ample room and verge enough in one volume is ambitious of the rule of three, we are apt to "weary" before the quotient is worked out, and (a thing unknown elsewhere) to murmur at the largeness of the dividend. Thus it is possible to be delighted with a first volume, to yawn over a second, and to "play a loud solo on a wind instrument" (a periphrasis of the verb "to snore") over the third. We do not say that we committed either of these two enormities n the perusal of the Sunnyside chronicles; nevertheless, we had, at intervals, a depressing suspicion that the excellent annalist was trenching on the border-land of—twaddle. Perhaps, however, this very circumstance aids rather than injures the effect of the book as a whole; just as Richardson's illimitable details are thought to be the secret of his success. Mrs. Maitland would not, perhaps, be herself in one volume; she might cease to handle the pen of a ready writer, if she tried to be a terse and restrained one. And, therefore, we gladly and gratefully take her as we find her—and that is, as a generous, warm, and pure-hearted Scottish gentlewoman of the old school. . . . Throughout the biographical excerpts her character is sustained with a beautiful unity. (pp. 488-89)

Those who desiderate a plot, a mystery, a dramatic evolution of events in the construction of a novel, will find "**Merkland**" more to their taste than the simple passages in the life of the Sunnyside spinster. A murder—the force and the results of circumstantial evidence, implicating an innocent man—the sorrows and magnanimity of the wrongly accused—the cowardice and remorse of the real homicide—the heroic devotion of both their sisters—and the moral adjustment of the seemingly chaotic elements of retributive justice—these topics form the substratum for a fiction of considerable inventive art, clever portraiture, and natural pathos. Faults it has, but they are such as pertain to the author's novitiate. The story covers too large a surface; it introduces more characters than can justify their *entrée*, whether by relationship to the unity of action, or by individuality and personal pretensions; it is often desultory, fragmentary, and (are we coining a word?) platitudinary. The clue to the mystery, retailed charily bit by bit, is doled out more in accordance with the exigencies of novel-craft than with the probabilities of actual life. . . . The author is fond of getting up a surprise; but it is not always that it succeeds; instead of doing execution, there is often a mere flash in the pan, which startles none but raw recruits. But taking it altogether, the interest of "**Merkland**" is well sustained, and frequently reaches a high standard. Passages in abundance of power and pathos reward the reader. (p. 489)

Among such a crowd of characters as have their exits and their entrances in "**Merkland**," it is quite reasonable that two or three should but indifferently please us. We are sorry to put Lillie, Norman's pretty daughter, on the list, because the author has taken pains on the outfit, and readers generally accept her as a little darling; whereas we confess to a disrelish for her rather hackneyed and melo-dramatic dialect—her mystic vocables—her too sophisticated infantine-cy, and her habit . . . of using the third for the first person singular. Of the leading male characters, hardly one is to our fancy, to say nothing of the tiresome Mr. Fitzherbert, and the plastic Giles Sympelton; we stumble a little at the quick and perfect conversion of Archibald

Sutherland, nor is there that probability in the prolonged secrecy of Patrick Lillie, which Mr. Hawthorne has so powerfully
contrived in the case of Arthur Dimmesdale; it is surely on the
author's behoof that Patrick, being such as she depicts him,
endures such a burden of shame and sorrow for eighteen weary
years. Lewis Ross we should like to forbid the house had *we*
a little sister Alice; and the mention of her name induces us
forthwith to turn from captiousness to panegyric. If the men
of **"Merkland,"** as we have complained, are wanting . . . ,
and suggest a female hand as their originator, the women,
young and old, are rich in faith and good works, and are for
the most part clear-headed and lead-hearted, tender and true.
Alice Aytoun is a sweet picture of a girl just emerging from
the child's mirth and unrestrained gayety into those sensitive,
imaginative years, which form the threshold of graver life—

> Standing with reluctant feet
> Where the brook and river meet,
> Womanhood and childhood sweet;

and a touching chapter in her history is that wherein she is told
that Lewis—*her* Lewis—is the brother of her father's assassin,
when, with a long, low cry of pain, involuntary and unconscious, she turns from Mrs. Catherine's lap, feeling that there
is nothing more to say or to hope, and the mist and film of
her first sorrow blinds and stills the girlish heart, till now so
gay and high in its beatings, and she wanders up-stairs to her
own room, and thinks it *so* dim, and cheerless and cold, and
hides her sad white face in the pillow, and silently weeps.
"The girlish light heart sank down under its sudden burden,
without another struggle. '*I am not strong,*' murmured little
Alice, '*and there is no one with me.*'" A more beautiful sketch
of gentle maidenly dependence one seldom meets withal. *The*
character of the novel, however, is, or is meant to be, the Lady
of the Tower, Mrs. Catherine Douglas. She belongs to the
Scottish family, of which we have eminent types in the redoubtable presence of Mrs. Violet M'Shake, in one of Miss
Ferrier's capital tales, and of Galt's Leddy Grippy, which, in
Byron's opinion, was surpassed by no female character since
the days of Shakspeare for truth, nature, and individuality. But
Mrs. Catherine is their superior [and yet their peeress] . . . ;
albeit, on the whole, there may be a lack of freshness and a
slight air of effort about her. Still she commands respect and
unstinted love. (p. 490)

One salient objection meets the story of **"Caleb Field"** *in
limine;* and that is, the incompatibility of its subject—a narrative of the great Plague—with the assumed province of art.
The horrible, it is contended, is foreign to that province, and
cannot, ought not, to be naturalized. . . . The opinion of some,
that we have too much of pain and evil in actual life; and,
therefore, may shun them in fiction, has been not unjustly
controverted on the ground that this is to make art a mere
"amusement (*i.e.,* an escape from the Muse), and to look on
the terrible realities of life only as things to be endured," thus
refusing to connect them with the "ideals of God, with the
visions and ambitions of the soul." Our author is not the one
to omit this religious element in any story of her weaving, least
of all in one where God moves in so mysterious a way, and
where the reader is called upon to stand between the living and
the dead, and to behold a thousand fall beside him, and ten
thousand at his right hand, victims of the pestilence that des-
troyeth at noon-day—which fanaticism personifies as a dreadful form with out-stretched sword "gleaming like a diamond-
stone," and his eyes "like fire gazing over the city, and his
face terrible, and yet so fair, and his garments like a wondrous

mist, with the sunshine below." Edith Field is the bright presence, with something of angelic light, amid the blackness of
darkness; and the part she plays, and the tone given to the tale
by her pervading spirit, distinguish it from previous fictions
on the same theme. . . .

We are not so sure as some of our "irritable race" that **"Adam
Greene"** has enhanced and will enhance its author's reputation;
though we acknowledge the beauty of holiness, the truthfulness
and pathos, the faithful presentment of Scottish life and manners, and the secret struggles of human suffering, which here,
as in all her writings, impress, interest, and instruct. Tenderness and simplicity are here, with ample power to chasten and
subdue; passing into our "purer mind, with tranquil restoration," and breathing there the "still, sad music of humanity."
This we are "well pleased to recognize." But, on the other
hand, it is neither very carefully nor completely written, and
it reveals little novelty of character or incident. Probably it was
written too fast—at any rate, with too much faith in the writer's
hold on the public. A firm and kindly hold she has, and sorry
we should be to see the grasp relaxed. (p. 491)

> *"The Author of 'Margaret Maitland',"* in Littell's
> Living Age, *Vol. XXXV, No. 447, December 11,*
> *1852, pp. 488-91.*

THE SATURDAY REVIEW, LONDON (essay date 1863)

[*The following excerpt is from a positive review of* Salem Chapel.]

Rumour—we do not know how correctly—attributes this remarkable work [*Chronicles of Carlingford: Salem Chapel*] to
the pen of the authoress of the *Life of Irving.* At any rate, this
story, full of grace and originality, has many of the same merits
that characterized the biography. There is also a general resemblance between the career of the hero and that of Irving,
which can scarcely be accidental. . . . The pictures of the minister and his friends . . . are so vivid, and sketched with so
much humour, and so keen a sense both of the ludicrous and
the pathetic, that the early part of the story, at least, might be
considered quite worthy of the authoress of *Adam Bede.* The
tale falls off very much towards its close, and the latter half
is almost wearisome; but no faults of detail can permit us for
a moment to forget the power and originality of many of the
scenes. It is a tale without a plot, and the subsidiary plot which
is thrown in to give it zest is as ill-contrived as a plot well
could be. An idiotic girl has literally to be presented, in the
last two pages, with half a headful of sense, in order that the
hero may have some one to marry. It is, therefore, a work
which readers must expect to enjoy because it depicts character,
rather than because it interests and amuses as a story. . . .

We prize these *Chronicles of Carlingford* because they open to
us new ground, and take us among people who have every
appearance of being life-like but who are quite new to us.
(p. 210)

There is a good deal besides Salem in the book, but what there
is cannot be compared to the Salem part. But this part is itself
very much improved, and its effect heightened, by the introduction of Vincent's mother, who is brought by circumstances
to be with him at the period of his trouble, and whose character
is drawn with admirable skill and freshness. . . . There is a
masterly description of the way in which, when her tender
heart is sinking with fear for her daughter's fate, she can yet
trim the lamp and scold the maid for trimming it badly, in
order that the maid may not be able to go out gossiping and

announce that the minister and his mother are in a terrible state of misery about something. Vincent and his mother are both studies of character worthy of the best writers of modern fiction, and there is throughout the book the same delicacy, refinement, and facility of expression which lent so great a charm to the *Life of Irving*. There is, too, the same spirit of justice and of toleration; and no one could have discharged better than the authoress the difficult task of depicting the weak and ludicrous side of Dissent without ever passing into an arrogant assumption of superiority, or sneering with idle bitterness at the creed of shopkeepers and the illusions of Homerton. (p. 211)

> *A review of "Chronicles of Carlingford: Salem Chapel," in* The Saturday Review, *London, Vol. 15, No. 381, February 14, 1863, pp. 210-11.*

THE NATIONAL REVIEW, LONDON (essay date 1863)

[*In the following discussion of* Salem Chapel, *which Oliphant published anonymously, the critic faults the novel for its digressions yet praises its skillful delineation of Carlingford's distinct social classes.*]

[We] shall venture to assume that no one but a woman could have written *Salem Chapel*. Its merits and its faults are not easily explicable on any other ground. The delicate observation and subtle analysis of character, no less than the incapacity for broad effects, are alike feminine. A man could hardly have painted men so ill, or women so well. Nevertheless we start from this assumption chiefly to vindicate our right of calling the novelist *"she"* by hypothesis. . . . What we have to say concerns rather the substance of the book than the individuality of its author.

Salem Chapel consists of two different and incongruous parts,—the plot of a sensation novel, and a series of descriptions of the inner life of a dissenting congregation. The plot may be dismissed summarily as not only bad but unnecessary. It assumes a young girl of puritan education and high character going off on a most improbable story with her lover, who, unknown to her, is a married man; it rescues her by the intervention of the lover's wife, who shoots her husband in his room at an inn, a few hours only after she has traced him there, and with so much ingenuity as to defy discovery; and it represents the authorities as desisting from all inquiry on the simple statement of the wounded man, that he exonerates one person who has been wrongfully apprehended, and that he will give no further particulars. The worst of it all is, that these improbabilities, and many pages of horrors piled upon horrors, terror, despair, and suspense to the innocent victims of Colonel Mildmay's crime, only divert the reader from the main purpose of the book. For its purpose, which the plot rather impairs than strengthens, is to show the weakness of enthusiasm, refinement, and mere well-meaning, in contact with the vulgar realities of every-day life. (pp. 350-51)

[The] under-current of theological purpose has a little impaired the unity of the book, while it has probably heightened its interest. It is a palpable fault that Vincent is made too much a gentleman for his position, in order that the sharp contrasts of refinement and vulgarity may be better brought out. Men equally sensitive to interference are no doubt born in every section of society; but such men would be gratified and conciliated by much of the vulgar kindness that stifles Vincent. It is surely a little overstrained, when the minister thrills "with offence and indignation" because pretty Miss Phoebe Tozer brings him round, soon after his arrival, a shape of jelly "that

was over supper last night." A more genial man would probably take the whole affair in the spirit of simple good-nature that prompted the gift; and it is scarcely fair to mix up the deficiencies of an over-sensitive temperament with the faults of the Voluntary system. . . . Vincent's nature is throughout over-wrought, and it is sometimes difficult to distinguish whether the author means him to be laughed at or admired. His innocent entanglement in the draught-net of Lady Western's admirers; the curious interweaving of his convictions and his little social annoyances; his hysterical fits of passion, and helplessness when the time for action comes,—are all true to the life of a weak, and in some respects a ridiculous, man only. He is always giving a subdued groan, or straying into the clerical counterfeit of an oath, or grasping hands "in an overflow of gratitude and compunction." There is something positively revolting and most unmanly in the scenes where he threatens Mrs. Hilyard with denouncing her to the police, not from any stern sense of duty or any urgent need of clearing his sister's fame, but rather from an impulse to satisfy himself by doing something, and latterly even from a certain hardness of mood that would like a victim. Yet we hold, on the whole, that the author intended Vincent's as the type of a high character. As a woman, she perhaps overrates the interest that his power of loving genuinely lends him in the eyes of half the world; but, as an artist, she was right in giving consistency to his character by at least one strong sentiment. Not that his religious feelings are insincere, but they are loose colours, and will not stand the test of rough weather. The man is unable to pray or preach out of himself; and his troubles are not disturbing, but controlling, elements in his speculation. All this makes him the more genuine and effective, but the less real. . . . In the fact that he is not self-poised or self-contained, lies all that makes him distasteful to common men, and his peculiar charm for the author of *Salem Chapel*. She seems to be at once attracted and repelled by enthusiasm; to recognise something godlike in every man who acts fearlessly upon honest impulses, and yet, from invincible good sense or artistic instinct, to see clearly the foibles and follies of the enthusiastic temperament. Probably to a great extent her pencil is truer than her purpose, and she draws honestly what she has analysed subtly and grouped well, without regard to her own philosophy of art. Probably also her experience of life, a little depreciatory it may be, has yet taught her that there is infinite good mixed up with the infinite littlenesses of human nature and society. She is unconscious of the force of her own satire, because she knows so clearly what large allowances she has made.

In strict keeping with the unheroic hero are his surroundings and friends. We pass over for the moment the inimitable deacons and their families, who are not of the stuff of which romance is made. Colonel Mildmay, the shadowy debauched villain, and Mr. Fordham, the shadowy well-meaning gentleman, like the curate of St. Roque and Dr. Rider, are rather lay-figures than flesh and blood. When all are summed up, and the separate feeling for each analysed, the reader will probably be surprised to find how largely contempt, good-natured genial contempt at best, makes up his estimate. And if this be true of the men, . . . the same, or even worse, may be said of the women. . . . The restlessness, the energy, the desperate unreasoning love, are all admirably given in their way; but the one fatal vice of sensation novels, the necessity for stage-effects, has driven the author upon attempting something more. We disbelieve in the midnight conversation with Colonel Mildmay, precisely because a woman who announces her intention to murder with so much calmness, and rallies her husband on a fastidious feeling about the gallows, can hardly be compact of good to the extent Mrs. Hilyard is meant to be. It is true that the mind may easily grow familiar with the thought of a great crime by long brooding over it, so that when temptation and opportunity offer, the passage from inaction to guilt is almost imperceptible. But here there has been no real occasion for such devilish casuistry. . . . There are other smaller traits in Mrs. Hilyard's character which strike us as inconsistent with herself. She is meant to be a lady of high breeding, who, from oddness, self-assertion, and carelessness of the world's opinion, permits herself to say rude things pretty much at random among her friends. The character is not exactly uncommon; but, in a woman of shrewd observation and real good-nature, social tact at least would determine the sphere of action within very definite limits. (pp. 351-54)

On the other hand, the characters of Lady Western and of Mrs. Vincent are thoroughly of a piece, and are so excellent in their conception as to be originals. It may seem a little harsh to compare the minister's mother to Mrs. Nickleby, yet the difference is chiefly in the far more exquisite workmanship which softens and refines the traits of the Lonsdale widow. Through out Mrs. Vincent is a lady at heart and a good mother, and is therefore recommended by all the enhancements of refinement and tenderness; and yet these are not the qualities by which any one reading the book remembers her. The absolute want of judgment and will which make her a cipher in her daughter's emergency are so perfectly contrasted with her tact of manner and address in handlng her son's congregation and in baffling awkward questioners, that she not only lives herself in the pages of *Salem Chapel,* but is the occasion of life to others. It is not a high characteristic this double-natured pliancy, which bows to circumstances and adapts itself to persons; it is rather an instinct of the lower animals, who hide and whine during a storm, but divine in a moment if the stranger near them be a friend or an enemy. The whole question is, whether the type be not fairly conceived and essentially feminine. . . . It is a great tribute to the skill with which the character has been drawn, that [her] little insincerities scarcely strike the reader as an immoral element in it. It requires some reflection to see that Mrs. Vincent's goodness is that of a shallow nature and a prosperous life, and that its very existence is secondary to her excellence as a social strategist and her instinct of motherhood.

As perfect in its way is the conception of Lady Western. The graceful radiant creature, all sweetness and sunniness, who plays with her lover's feelings in utter unconsciousness that they can be deeper than her own, and because she likes to see him happy and to be admired herself, is so inimitably reproduced, that her gestures, the very tones of her voice, seem present to us. (pp. 354-56)

It is a great descent in the social scale when we pass from Lady Western to the deacons of Salem Chapel. But, setting aside charm of manner and refinement of language, the vestry is not much more vulgar than the Hall. The unsympathetic isolation of most characters in the book, from the hero and from one another, is in fact the secret of much of their interest. (p. 357)

[In the last thirty years,] the novel of home-life has gradually become the accredited type of romance; domestic virtues have been the staple of interest; and the decalogue of creative art is summed up in the commands, to be genteel, and marry at the end of the third volume. . . . The weak side of the school is exposed in such a book as *Salem Chapel,* not because it is not a consummate work of art, but because its author is more fearless than most in her portraitures. She has pushed the theory to its climax of logical absurdity. Her women in Mr. Thackeray's hands would be as dull as Amelia or Laura Pendennis [characters, respectively, in *Vanity Fair* and the Pendennis novels], and we should pass them quietly by as failures. In *Salem Chapel* we are riveted by the artist's skill, and see the meanness of the type all the better, because of the keen scalpel which has dissected it. The obvious answer is, that the actual has its peculiar charm and claims to be eternalised precisely because it is the actual. Herein lies, we believe, the essential fallacy. That there is in every life, however trivial, a latent something which might have been great; and that every nature, however dull, may be lighted up with a casual gleam of beauty, is happily so true as to be beyond dispute. But the artist's concern is like Mary's, with the spiritual guest, not like Martha's, with the platters and household serving. It is at his peril if he bring the tables of the money-changers and voices of the street into the House Beautiful.

Our censure may seem exaggerated. We are not pleading, however, against miniature sketches of grotesque life, but against their absolute substitution for ideal art. We incline to believe that there is a craving in the mind for something beyond meals, dress, and small-talk, which demands satisfaction, as imperiously in its way as the lower appetites. Nay more, the monotony of common things, after a point easily reached, becomes unnatural. . . . With the author of *Salem Chapel* it is different. Her power of character-sketching is so perfect up to a certain level, that she might almost have written the under-plot for a Shakespearian drama. Dogberry and Verges would have come out under her hands a little less simple in effect, but yet exquisitely felt and rendered. Her weakness—and she seems conscious of it—is, that her sympathy is less appreciative than her satire. She has learned to disbelieve in all singleness of motive and grandeur of life, and the feeling comes out painfully in all she writes. In default of this, she tries to crowd her pages with startling incident. She can believe in great crime and extravagant folly, if she distrusts absolute virtue. All this appears to us to be full of evil augury for her future success. She cannot write up to her own mark without conviction, and she cannot have appropriate figures with a dash of moral excellence sketched-in for her by an artist of the ideal. Her rare talent, to which we willingly do homage, will be crippled by the one-sidedness of her perceptions. (pp. 360-62)

A review of "Chronicles of Carlingford: Salem Chapel," in The National Review, *London, Vol. XVI, No. XXXII, April, 1863, pp. 350-62.*

THE BRITISH QUARTERLY REVIEW (essay date 1869)

[*The following excerpt is from a brief survey of Oliphant's early novels.*]

[The] first work of Mrs. Oliphant, **'Passages from the Life of Mrs. Margaret Maitland of Sunnyside, written by Herself,'** [is] a book that charmed and soothed us when we were young, and which we can read over still on summer days and winter nights with undiminished satisfaction. Mrs. Margaret Maitland is no echo and no wraith, but a real living woman, set in the midst of the loving, hoping, fearing, stirring little world of a Scotch rural parish. The place in our regard that dear old lady of Sunnyside originally achieved she keeps, and we think of her always as a person whom we have known. Her story is very simple, but her way of telling it is delightful; and when, after the lapse of a few years, she takes up the thread of it again, and in **'Lilliesleaf'** relates the married trials of 'the dear bairns' whose early days are the brightest passages in her own life, we take it up with her, and listen to the story as if it concerned personal friends of our own from whom we have been severed for awhile.

It is a great merit in a writer when she can thus compel us to realize her characters, and it is a power that Mrs. Oliphant possesses in a very high degree. These two books, **'Mrs. Margaret Maitland'** and **'Lilliesleaf,'** should be read consecutively. The personal experiences of Mrs. Margaret Maitland are not told in detail until she is 'an eldern person,' left alone in the quiet, pretty cottage of Sunnyside, to which she and her mother have betaken themselves on the death of the minister, her father. She has had her griefs of heart, but they are over, and God has comforted her; we get occasional glimpses of them, and very bitter they are, but the main story is that of her brother's children, Claud and Mary, at the manse of Pasture Lands, and of Grace, a little lassie whom she brings up at Sunnyside in simple, pious ways, quite unwitting that her charge is a rich heiress. (pp. 305-06)

Mrs. Oliphant is far too voluminous a writer to permit us to treat all her works in detail. We must in the majority of cases content ourselves with a passing allusion, and devote our space to the consideration of those novels by which her fame is, we trust, secured beyond this generation. **'Merkland'** was her second story, and the scenery is Scotch again, as it is also in **'Harry Muir,' 'The Laird of Norlaw,'** and **'Adam Graeme of Mossgray';** but in **'The House on the Moor'** she has crossed the Border, and written a story as eerie and dreary as a sunless day on the fells in November. It is not a pleasant book. The bad people fill far more than their fair share of the stage, and they are dismal and uninteresting, and the misery amongst them is as all-pervading as an east-wind. . . . We shall not transcribe any of its scenes; it is a good *situation* wasted, which might have been put to excellent profit, if the authoress had but taken it up in her sweeter vein, and shown the victims . . . resisting the devil with the natural affection and confidence of their kinship, instead of giving place to him at his first assault; and it would have been, so far as our judgment goes, a truer story, and certainly a pleasanter and more healthy story to study.

It is, however, by **'The Chronicles of Carlingford'** that Mrs. Oliphant will most probably live and amuse her grandchildren to the third and fourth generation. . . . They are capital studies of country-town life in our own times; and Carlingford has by their means become a much more real place to hundreds of readers than half the chief cities and celebrated places on the railway map. (pp. 308-09)

"Works by Mrs. Oliphant," in The British Quarterly Review, *Vol. XLIX, No. XCVIII, March 1, 1869, pp. 301-29.*

THE SATURDAY REVIEW, LONDON (essay date 1869)

[*In the following excerpt, the critic discusses the major characters of* The Minister's Wife.]

The West Coast of Scotland is eminently adapted for the purposes of novelists, its scenery being everything that could be desired for their picturesque passages, and its inhabitants readily falling into artistic attitudes. . . . And so, in such a county as the Lochshire in which Mrs. Oliphant has laid the scene of [*The Minister's Wife*], it is as easy to find characters as landscapes which, even when transferred to paper with photographic exactness, retain an air of romance about them, and

which require but a few artistic touches in order to become capable of satisfying the requirements of even an exceptionally critical sentimentalist. Of these natural advantages Mrs. Oliphant has made excellent use, and the result is a story which, like the country it describes, is rich in pictures that are pleasant to see, scenes on which the eye gladly lingers, and which, like the people it portrays, is subtle in its reasonings and shrewd and canny in its opinions, eloquent in its outbursts of feeling, very tender in its natural and unstrained pathos, and genuinely, though somewhat grimly, humorous in its unfrequent and subdued jocosity.

The description of the Revival in the parish of Loch Diarmid is excellent, and there is great vigour in the sketches of the meetings which take place there at night, when the cottagers gather together under the impression that the end of all things is at hand, that the Lord is shortly to appear among his people, and that they themselves, poor men and women as they are, may be on the point of becoming the reformers of the world. Especially good is the account of the meeting at which the heroine for the first time hears the voice of one speaking in an "unknown tongue," and feels the full effect produced by its utterance amid the darkness which the few faint lights fail to dissipate in the building to which the enthusiasts have resorted. No character in the book is more interesting than that of the speaker on this occasion—the young girl, Ailie Macfarlane, with her mystical blue eyes, her delicate, half-hectic colour, and her wealth of golden hair, who has suddenly risen from what was supposed to be her deathbed, and has taken upon herself in all good faith the task of converting a sinful world. Her full, unhesitating belief, her wild enthusiasm and her noble capacity for self-sacrifice, are rendered into words with great vigour and feeling, full justice beng done to all the nobler side of what is generally looked upon as a merely ridiculous delusion. Only an essentially tolerant and sympathetic writer could have dealt with such a subject as Mrs. Oliphant has treated it, especially in the passages which describe the terrible struggle through which Ailie has to pass when a brother enthusiast suddenly claims her, in the name of the Lord, as his bride.

John Diarmid, her strange lover, forms the subject of a very powerful sketch. Mrs. Oliphant emphatically declares in her preface that the personages of her story are "entirely fictitious," and of course we believe her; but those who are intimate with the religious life of Scotland will be apt to imagine that they have long known John Diarmid, the man who "had lived a wicked, sensual, evil life," and who afterwards "rushed into religion as he had rushed into dissipation, from the same passionate thirst for excitement." . . . It is not easy to depict the visions which sweep across the mental eye of one whose brain religious enthusiasm has almost crazed, without rendering them ludicrous, but there is unmixed pathos in the picture which Mrs. Oliphant has drawn of this poor Lowland maiden as she knelt before open Bible on her bed, and remained there lost "in one long trance of prayer and reverie, while the short autumn day came to an end, and the twilight closed around her," collecting her energies in order that she might submit to the marriage which she dreaded far more than she would have feared the scaffold or the stake. Only by thorough sympathy and great artistic power could such a character placed in such a position be not merely rendered interesting, but even invested with a kind of saintly glory. And, moreover, a humorous perception of the latent absurdity of the position was necessary on the part of the artist, together with a complete suppression of anything like humorous comment. . . . In the analysis of poor Ailie's feelings on the eve of the decision which was to affect her whole life, Mrs. Oliphant has succeeded in giving an air of dignity and grandeur to delusions which might have provoked a smile had she not been herself keenly alive to the dangerous proximity to the ludicrous in which her prophetess stood. Ailie's is by far the most striking character in the story, although she is not its principal heroine. Isabel Diarmid, whose marriage with Mr. Lothian, the minister of the parish, gives the book its title, is very charmingly described, but she does not greatly differ from many of her predecessors in fiction; whereas Ailie is completely new and original. Isabel's sister Margaret forms the subject of a very delightful sketch, but she soon fades out of the scene. Isabel's first lover and second husband, the frivolous and selfish Horace Stapylton, is an unsatisfactory production. We absolutely refuse to believe that he ever existed. What men would have looked like if they had figured in pictures painted by lions it is difficult to say; but they are, as a general rule, sufficiently caricatured when their portraits are attempted by lady-novelists—that is to say, whenever an attempt is made to depict those of their number who rejoice in youth and beauty. For it is only in portraying the young and outwardly attractive Horace Stapylton that Mrs. Oliphant has not met with full success. Mr. Lothian, the elderly but well-preserved minister, is capitally painted; and the grim old dominie, his friend, is excellently sketched; while the village blacksmith and his gossips are hit off with thorough truth, their different characteristics being brought out in strong relief by a few sure, rapid touches.

The weakest point of the story seems to be the murder which suddenly, and as it were wantonly, drags a ghastly corpse upon the quiet stage. It is something like the conventional flash of lightning which is so often to be seen in the corner of an engraving, utterly at variance with the rest of the composition, and to be accounted for by no theory of electrical disturbance. Throughout the quieter scenes of her story, Mrs. Oliphant displays an amount of skill which deserves the highest praise. We have few artists who could have brought a Kirk Session, for instance, so vividly before our eyes as she has done in the first volume, or who could surpass the vigour and pathos of the scene in which Ailie expostulates with Isabel and Stapylton when she meets them on the hillside, and her heart thrills with warm zeal for their conversion, or that in which John Diarmid visits the deathbed of the woman whom he had loved in the wild days which preceded his conversion. But a murder is easily represented, and a master's hand is not required to depict the "something all covered over with a great grey plaid" which casts a gloomy horror over the close of the second volume, or the "cold mouth of iron" which touches Isabel's cheek towards the end of the third. The introduction of such agents as these in the story will probably add to its popularity with the many, but they may detract from its effect as a work of art upon the few. It must not be forgotten, however, that, after all, it is for the many that novels are written. (pp. 25-6)

> *A review of "The Minister's Wife,"* in The Saturday Review, *London, Vol. 28, No. 714, July 3, 1869, pp. 25-6.*

THE SATURDAY REVIEW, LONDON   (essay date 1869)

[*The following excerpt is from a largely positive assessment of Oliphant's* Historical Sketches of the Reign of George Second.]

Mrs. Oliphant's style is always charming, and it would be difficult to find pleasanter reading than her [*Historical Sketches of the Reign of George the Second*]. She makes no pretence of being an independent historical investigator. She has unearthed no new documents. She has not revolutionized the popular conception of any well-known personage. Her reading shows no traces of having extended beyond the range of the most ordinary and accessible authorities. Her aim has simply been, by means of judicious selection and careful and sympathetic painting, to form a portrait-gallery which shall illustrate the characteristics of a given age.

We think that she has on the whole been very successful. The period which she has chosen is one which is eminently suited for biographical treatment. The public history of England during the reign of George II. is not of a kind to which we can look back with satisfaction, or which we can study with pleasure. Its foreign policy is made up of ignoble, confused, and aimless bickerings, its domestic policy of a series of selfish struggles for place. No great reforms, no heroic contests, no brilliant feats of arms illustrate the dull rule of Walpole and the Pelhams, and we wade through their tedious and eventless annals with *ennui* and disgust. But the result is widely different if we turn from politics to society. Here the scene is full of life, variety, and movement. It is true that the principal actors are not, for the most part, troubled with any very high thoughts or complex feelings; but just for that reason they have laid bare their characters, for the benefit of their correspondents and of posterity, with a sincerity and completeness which is impossible to a more serious or impassioned generation. (p. 709)

Mrs. Oliphant has written so pleasantly that we are not disposed to be angry with her for talking nonsense about a subject which she does not understand. Her book is a thorough woman's book, feminine in its merits and its defects, and the former far outbalance the latter. She is a little too much given to gushing—a fault natural to a novelist, especially a female novelist. And we doubt if her powers of analysis would be equal to the resolution of the more complex problems which humanity sometimes presents. . . . [Given] a character or a situation which excites her sympathy, she is excellent. Her quick instinct divines where a man's more ponderous intellect would often go astray. And, lastly, if her light is seldom dry, so also is her style. Her mode of treatment makes her sometimes extravagant and sometimes unfair, but always readable. (p. 710)

> *"Mrs. Oliphant's Historical Sketches," in* The Saturday Review, *London, Vol. 28, No. 735, November 27, 1869, pp. 709-10.*

THE SATURDAY REVIEW, LONDON   (essay date 1871)

[*The following excerpt is from a positive review of Oliphant's biography* Francis of Assisi.]

We must confess to having opened Mrs. Oliphant's [*Francis of Assisi*], not indeed with any fear of offences against good taste—of which there was little danger—but with some uneasy suspicion, especially as the work appears in the *Sunday Library*, that we might on the one hand be annoyed with indiscriminate hero-worship, such as is conspicuous in her *Life of Irving,* and on the other hand with tedious cautions against the theological errors of the saint, and the miracle-mongering credulity of his hagiographers. But we have been pleasantly disappointed. Few, if any, of St. Francis's many biographers, Catholic or Protestant, have told the exquisite tale of his life and work with more quiet grace and appreciative sympathy. The miraculous element which is so prominent in it is rather described than criticized; but as regards one marked speciality, the extraordinary power over the lower animals ascribed to

Francis in all the accounts we have of him, and which cannot be wholly fabulous, the authoress observes that such a gift has certainly been possessed by many who laid no claim to supernatural powers, and is asserted in our day to be heriditary in her family by a personage so little like him as the famous novelist George Sand. On the culminating miracle of his life, the impression of the mysterious "Stigmata" on Monte Alverno, she dwells at considerable length, pointing out that, unlike many mediaeval miracles, it rests on a weight of consentient and independent contemporary testimony which, in the case of any ordinary event, would be considerd conclusive, while she abstains from pronouncing any definitive judgment, except that "the evidence altogether is of a kind which it is almost equally difficult to accept or to reject." . . . [Mrs. Oliphant's] account of the period, and of the place occupied by St. Francis in the history of the Church, is substantially correct. (pp. 740-41)

> "Mrs. Oliphant's Life of St. Francis," in The Saturday Review, *London, Vol. 31, No. 815, June 10, 1871, pp. 740-42.*

THE SATURDAY REVIEW, LONDON   (essay date 1872)

[*The following excerpt is from a negative review of Oliphant's biography* Memoir of Count de Montalembert.]

[In] the fervour of her hero-worship [in *Memoir of Count de Montalembert,* Mrs. Oliphant] offers to us a panorama where we should have preferred an analysis of Montalembert. Every successive chapter is intended to embody some phase of his chequered life; but in each case the first thought has too obviously been to pose the model in a picturesque attitude, and then the historical background has been filled in to suit the posture; it is not therefore to be wondered at that an unsatisfactory atmosphere of unreality should float round the whole production. As we read Mrs. Oliphant's volumes we miss Montalembert as his friends knew him—astute, impetuous, sarcastic; quick to get into his opinions, and very slow to get out of them again; with a Gladstonian power of making the whole world for the time being run upon one consideration, and a power of ready speech Gladstonian in its volume, but not in its epigram, and (as suited the son of a Frenchman and an Englishwoman) equally ready in both languages to prove that this one thing was the whole world; but, behind all these salient manifestations, possessed of a unity of purpose which sooner or later was sure to fix the more volatile attributes of the external man. . . .

We fully admit that it would have been a most unlikely piece of posthumous good fortune if [Montalembert] had found a biographer who had personally sought—we do not say won—distinction in these various pursuits, or who would personally have felt an equal and sustained interest in their several details. But that consciousness of the differences between self and subject which a biographer ought at the very outset of his task to work out should lead him to begin by mapping out the life of his hero, lest his own differences of taste or deficiencies in information should tempt him to overlook or to depreciate marked phases of character or important fields of labour. Of this analytic quality we can find no trace in Mrs. Oliphant's Memoir; while she heads her chapters with mildly sensational titles, such as "Downfall," "Catholic Submission," "The Wander-Year—St. Elizabeth." To enable her readers to estimate Montalembert as an author, his biographer might easily have devoted a few pages or an appendix to the list of his

various writings. No such catalogue, however, appears, while the various notices of his larger writings are so scattered through the volumes as to fail in giving any complete picture even of his larger publications. (p. 763)

> "Mrs. Oliphant's Memoir of Montalembert," in The Saturday Review, *London, Vol. 34, No. 894, December 14, 1872, pp. 763-64.*

THE SATURDAY REVIEW, LONDON   (essay date 1873)

[*In the following excerpt, the critic discusses the central characters of* May.]

We should be sorry to place any limits to industry, and we know that the amount of productive power varies in each individual writer; that some minds are like the elephant, capable of only rare efforts, while others are like rabbits, that bring forth young at all seasons and in large numbers. . . . George Eliot is a slow worker, while the Ouidas, the Woods, and the Cudlips are prolific. We are sorry to add also Mrs. Oliphant to the list, whom yet we are far from placing in the same category with her feebler sisters. We would rather bracket her with a steadygoing worker like Mr. Trollope. . . . One thing, however, we can say of Mrs. Oliphant—fresh or weary, she is always original. Her books have a certain stamp of their own, an individuality of character and an unhackneyed plan of story that go far to redeem some of the faults which time and use and haste only deepen. Whatever she does, she does with all the strength she possesses at the moment; she is thoroughly honest, however exhausted; and her heart is never cold to her labour, though her brain may be tired and her hand heavy. And it is this quality of honesty that raises her work above the ordinary standard of that which is done at too great speed and without taking time enough to rest between whiles.

The gem of this novel, *May,* is the character of May or Marjory herself. She is essentially feminine and natural, loveable and tender, but planned on a nobler scale than is usually assigned to the marriageable young ladies of novels. She is a woman of three-and-twenty, with a young half-sister clinging to her like her child; which also is a relief from the rosebud and bread-and-butter inanities of seventeen and eighteen, so dear to the hearts of many authors. Here we have a woman still young and beautiful and fresh and fair, but with a fine matured dignity and common sense that enrich the story with possibilities of action denied to callow innocence. Consequently she becomes the heroine, not so much by the arbitrary will of the author as by natural and logical necessity. . . . She is a grand creature, and we congratulate Mrs. Oliphant on the beauty and harmony of her character. (pp. 594-95)

[None of the characters] are very prominent, save May; and none of them are so purely beautiful. Fanshawe, with whom she has so much to do, gains his chief importance through his association with her and hers; Uncle Charles is hazy; and the Laird her father dies before the core of the struggle is reached. We see the elder brother Tom only on his death-bed, which, though well described, tells us nothing beyond the fact that he has been wild and something worse, and that he dies with a secret undivulged. The other brother, Charlie, is a mere name; and his wife and sister-in-law are rather caricatures than anything else. Women are often painfully silly, we admit, and some are to be found as selfish, vain, and vulgar as Matilda; a few also are as clever as Verna Bassett; but we do not like the portrait of either, and we think that in them Mrs. Oliphant has overstepped the line which separates realism from triviality, and has condescended to something very like spite. A good deal might have been made out of the situation, and the broad characteristics of the two sisters might have been kept; but it would have been a higher kind of art to have toned down the episode into more quietness than our author has allowed; and the drawing would have been stronger had its uglier details been less elaborated. We do not say that it is not natural; it is only too much so. . . .

The love affair between May and Fanshawe is very prettily described. It is of the gradual, unimpassioned, and sensible kind which is so like reality and so unlike love-making in novels in general. They do not soliloquize to the moon, nor kiss franticly in the woods, nor have brain fevers because things go cross, nor give up all their social chances in life for the sake of a few months' earlier marriage, nor do anything of the mad and mischievous kind; but they drift quietly from indifference to pleasure in each other's society, from pleasure to doubt, from doubt to resolve, and from resolve to certainty; the stages interspersed with the little starts and flights which belong to the devious road on which they are travelling, and which give life and colour by the way. And there always comes in the golden head and clinging fondness of little Milly, to add that half-matronly purity and responsibliity which does so much for Marjory's character. There has seldom been a more successful portrait of a child than this of Milly. She is nothing wonderful in any way; just a "bonnie bit bairn" of ten or so, who rides about the country with her sister, and follows ever after her like her shadow, who has long bright golden hair that streams in a mane behind her, who cries copiously for vague sympathy and vaguer "dool" when their troubles come on the family and "my May" is distressed, and her father estranged. She says her prayers, and reads heavy Sunday books as the right thing to do when they are all in grief and mourning; and when Fanshawe makes her laugh right out, she feels conscience-stricken, as if she had committed an impiety. She is probably not very clever, not very promising, not very anything; but her presence in the story is one of the prettiest things in it; and Mrs. Oliphant has proved herself a master of the art in this sweet and lifelike child's portrait. If novel-writers would only go more to nature for their models, and trust less to their own sickly fancies, we should have better work than we have now. . . . [We] accept with gratitude such work as Mrs. Oliphant's, even though in this, her latest production, she has given signs that she would be all the better for a rest, and a spell of playtime void of pen and paper. (p. 595)

> *A review of "May," in* The Saturday Review, *London, Vol. 35, No. 914, May 3, 1873, pp. 594-95.*

MRS. OLIPHANT (essay date 1882)

[*In her preface to the first edition of* The Literary History of England, *Oliphant apologizes in advance for any inaccuracies or deletions she may have made. These alleged flaws are addressed in an August 1882 review in the* Spectator *(see excerpt below).*]

It is with diffidence that the Author of the following volumes offers them to the public. The subject is a great one, and so manifold in its details that it is impossible not to have made omissions in various quarters: and especially in those on which she can pretend to least knowledge, in the graver literature of Science and Philosophy. It was intended originally that the work should extend farther, and come down to the elder figures even of our own times, the poets who are now regnant in England, and the many eminent writers who have but just

departed; but the period before our own, which has formed them and us, and which reaches into our own by so many survivals, was found too rich and ample to allow of further additions. The aim of the Author has been throughout rather to give, as fully as she was able, a history of the new departures, in poetry above all, in criticism, in fiction, and, to the extent of her ability, to indicate those which have occurred in history and philosophy—than to undertake an absolute commentary upon every individual writer. She is prepared to be told that she has passed too lightly over some important names; and if some lesser ones have escaped her altogether, to receive with humility any strictures which may be pronounced upon her on this account. Her aim has been to set forth the remarkable outburst of new and noble genius by which the end of last century and the beginning of our own was distinguished, and made into a great and individual age in literature. It is hard to cut the line clear across all those intertwinings of human life and influence by which one generation links itself to another; and consequently the story will be found to overlap the boundaries on both sides, now going too far back, now reaching too far forward. The kind and sympathetic reader will see how this comes about, and how the uneven lines of life—some cut so sadly short, some holding on their course up to old age—cannot fail to leave an irregular outline. For all faults of omission or redundancy, she makes her apology beforehand, with the hope of being able to amend them at some future time. (pp. ix-x)

> *Mrs. Oliphant, in a preface to her* The Literary History of England in the End of the Eighteenth and Beginning of the Nineteenth Century, Vol. I, *1882. Reprint by Macmillan and Co., 1886, pp. ix-x.*

THE SPECTATOR (essay date 1882)

[*The critic praises the style of Oliphant's* The Literary History of England, *but suggests that the volumes are composed with "irregular ability." Oliphant is secure in her assessment of Scottish writers, the critic claims, but is less credible when discussing Irish or English authors. Oliphant addressed the topics raised in this review in the preface to the second edition of the work (see excerpt below).*]

[Mrs. Oliphant's *The Literary History of England, in the End of the Eighteenth Century and Beginning of the Nineteenth Century*] is a very difficult book to estimate. At once brilliant and uncertain, now containing as bright and true a criticism as combined genius and sympathy could produce, now dashing off a paradoxical condemnation which seems to come in part of haste and carelessness, and in part of self-will, Mrs. Oliphant's three volumes contain much more that is fine and true than any book of the kind that is so little trustworthy, and much more that is arbitrary and capricious, than any book so full of admirable passages. If Mrs. Oliphant had limited herself to essays on her own favourite authors of this period, we should have liked her book much better, though even then we should, we suppose, have been compelled to read the strangely inadequate estimate of Wordsworth, who is more praised for his weaker work and less for his greatest work than we should have thought it possible for a warm admirer of Wordsworth to achieve. She is, by the way, often inaccurate about Wordsworth, a sure sign of not really liking him as well as she herself fancies. She quotes, for instance, with just condemnation, an expression which she herself has made worse than it actually is in the process of passing it through her own memory, namely, "the very pulse of the machine," which Mrs. Oliphant renders, "the very heart of the machine." Either expression is prosaic enough, but the latter is much the worse. A steam-engine, with its throb, might, perhaps, be conceived as pulsating, but the "heart" of a machine is a monstrous conception. (p. 1111)

The essay on Cowper is among the most brilliant and satisfactory of all Mrs. Oliphant's estimates. It seems to us, as a literary estimate, quite perfect,—as a personal estimate, somewhat less so, for in the ridicule which she gently pours over Cowper's self-indulgent indolence and unwillingness to take upon himself family cares, she forgets, we think, that the taint of insanity in him ought to have had, and probably had, very much to do with this reluctance. . . . It would be hard to find a more effective, and brilliant, and faithful description of any poet and man to whom English literature has been indebted for a great and critical revolution. Even, however, in the criticism of Cowper, we cannot always agree with Mrs. Oliphant. She appears to place, for instance, the lines to his mother's picture and the lines to "My Mary" far above "The Castaway;" but it seems to us that no "profound and morbid study of a despairing soul" ever was more vivid than that which ends in the magnificent lines which she herself quotes:—

> No voice divine the storm allayed,
>   No light propitious shone,
> When, snatched from all effectual aid,
>   We perished, each alone;
> But I, beneath a rougher sea,
> And whelmed in deeper gulphs than he.

That was Cowper's epitaph on himself, and a more memorable one was never written.

Mrs. Oliphant is always strong when she is on Scotch ground (though she overpraises Wilson, and some others of that group), but often much less so on Irish and English ground,—which makes us admire all the more her brilliant chapters on Cowper. Nothing can be more wilfully inadequate than her notice of Moore, whose greatest strength of all, his extraordinary wit and satirical brilliancy, actually receives no shadow of notice; while even his lyrical power is greatly under-rated, and represented by one of the feeblest specimens of his melodies, and one so incorrectly printed as to injure both the rhythm and the effect of the first verse. But even in her criticism of the figures of the greater English poets, Byron and Shelley, Mrs. Oliphant seems to us often capricious. Thus she lays little stress on the supreme wit of Byron, whose *Vision of Judgment,* as well as much of his *Don Juan,* seems to us to show Byron at the very height of his power. She, however, regards *Childe Harold* as the greatest effort of his genius. In this estimate, and that of Byron's letters, which Mrs. Oliphant treats as on the whole poor affairs, we find ourselves entirely unable to agree. (pp. 1111-12)

Of the minor sketches, the least just, or perhaps we ought to say the most unjust, is that of Hazlitt, to whom Mrs. Oliphant gives but seven pages, while to the tedious and pedantic Godwin and his surroundings she gives nearly sixty. We confess that we cannot understand this in a writer of Mrs. Oliphant's keenness and brilliancy. What she says of Hazlitt's obsoleteness, too, is, so far as we can judge, simply erroneous. . . . Among the caprices of Mrs. Oliphant's judgment, we find none odder than her notion of the obsoleteness of Hazlitt, unless it be the notion that Goethe's *Goetz von Berlichingen* is a poor affair. . . .

It will be seen that we find Mrs. Oliphant's book one of very irregular ability. Some parts of it are as good, and some as inadequate, as it is possible for criticisms to be; but the style

of the whole is delightful, and it is certainly the most interesting literary production of the present year. If Mrs. Oliphant had attempted less,—if she had made her book not a history, but a criticism of selected authors, and had wasted less of her power on authors in whom she felt a very slender interest, she would, we think, have produced a book as uniformly delightful as she has certainly produced one that is uniformly interesting and lively. (p. 1113)

"Mrs. Oliphant's Literary History of England, 1790-1825," in The Spectator, *Vol. 55, No. 2826, August 26, 1882, pp. 1111-13.*

M.O.W.O. [MARGARET OLIPHANT WILSON OLIPHANT]
(essay date 1882)

[*The following preface first appeared in the second edition of* The Literary History of England. *Here, Oliphant responds to a mixed review of the work's first edition that appeared in the* Spectator *(see excerpt above, 1882). She defends, in particular, her treatment of William Wordsworth.*]

I am glad to take the opportunity thus given me to answer one or two of the more important remarks that have been made by critics upon [*The Literary History of England in the End of the Eighteenth and Beginning of the Nineteenth Century*]. In the first place, as it is most easily to be done, I have to express my great regret for the mistake by which all mention of Lockhart's spirited and admirable *Spanish Ballads* were left out of the notice of his works. (p. v)

It is, however, in respect to Wordsworth that there is most to say. Brought up in his worship and service, I find myself treated as a publican and an infidel by those who consider themselves his expositors in the present generation; and learn, with astonishment, that the instances of his power which I have chosen please them little more than the exceptions which I have taken. In one particular—that of his Sonnets—I have nothing more to do than to own a personal deficiency which no doubt impairs my judgment, but which it is more honest to confess than to attempt to ignore. A sonnet may be a work of supreme and exquisite art—but it may be, at the same time, almost more than any other form of poetical composition, a strained and artificial medium. And I think the mental faculty is rare which can keep its ear clear and its soul alive as it takes its way through the linked sweetness long drawn out of series after series of such compositions. I am glad that there are so many critics who are capable of this high appreciation, but I am not myself one of them. The severity of the art and its monotony are above my level. I recognize the perfection of a few—but I cannot go farther. It is an individual disability which I can only deplore.

A word more seems to be necessary as to one quotation made, at which various of my critics have taken exception, the little poem about the child and the weathercock, which it seems now has puzzled more, even of the most genuine Wordsworthians, than it has edified. It appears to me to belong to a section of Wordsworth's poems in which he is almost, if not altogether, unrivalled—Victor Hugo's amazing realizations of infantine qualities and gifts being the only others that occur to me as fit to be spoken of in the same breath—with this difference, however, that the great Frenchman's conceptions are individual, and those of Wordsworth abstract. The great *Ode on the Intimations of Immortality* is the centre of this infantile revelation. It is not, perhaps, for this that it is chiefly prized: but when we separate the little figure in the midst of all these immortalities from the high reflections and suggestions that open heaven and earth about him, we can scarcely help recognizing that our poet has left us no more complete (if any such complete) impersonation. (pp. v.-vii)

One further and much smaller piece of self-defence. One of my critics has accused me of so much carelessness as not even to have quoted Wordsworth right. It is an accusation to which, in common, I suppose with most people in whom the crispness of youthful memory has become blunted, I am not unlikely to be open—indeed, I acknowledge, with confusion, a misprint of a verse of Shelley's which has escaped revision; but in the case of the Wordsworth quotations the censure is without foundation, as I find by careful comparison. There are occasional differences, no doubt, in different editions. The quotations were all corrected from a "complete popular edition." . . . (p. viii)

> M.O.W.O. [Margaret Oliphant Wilson Oliphant], "Preface to the New Issue," in her The Literary History of England in the End of the Eighteenth and Beginning of the Nineteenth Century, Vol. I, 1882. Reprint by Macmillan and Co., 1886, pp. v-viii.

THE SPECTATOR (essay date 1882)

[The following excerpt is from a review of the second edition of Oliphant's The Literary History of England. The critic reiterates several charges made in a review of the work's first edition that appeared in the Spectator (see excerpt above, 1882) and specifically challenges Oliphant's assessment of William Wordsworth. Still, according to this reviewer, The Literary History of England represents a "great critical achievement."]

As Mrs. Oliphant has done us the honour to add to her new issue of her unequal, but often brilliant, book on the **Literary History of England between 1790 and 1825** a new preface, in which she replies to some of our criticisms upon her estimate of Wordsworth [see excerpt above by Oliphant, 1882], and as we are sensible that, in spite of our cordial appreciation of her treatment of Cowper, Lamb, Scott, Campbell, and others of the writers of this period, we, in our very grave differences from Mrs. Oliphant on the subject of Wordsworth, have hardly said enough of the merits of many portions of a book which it would have been a great credit for a writer without any of Mrs. Oliphant's imaginative pre-engagements of mind to have produced, we return for a few minutes to the new issue of her book, in order to supplement what we have already written. Mrs. Oliphant says of herself, in her new preface:—"It is, however, in respect to Wordsworth that there is most to say. Brought up in his worship and service, I find myself treated as a publican and an infidel by those who consider themselves his expositors in the present generation; and learn with astonishment that the instances of his power which I have chosen, please them little more than the exceptions which I have taken." We need hardly say that it would never have occurred to us to treat Mrs. Oliphant's judgment on any literary subject whatever de haut en bas, still less as that of "a publican and an infidel." But we thought that she carefully assumed the character of an exceedingly discriminating, not to say a somewhat patronising, admirer of Wordsworth, who found the bulk of his writings dull, and wished to mark her decided preference for Coleridge. . . . Mrs. Oliphant admits but a dozen of Wordsworth's sonnets to "the highest rank" . . . , and frankly declares herself unable to appreciate the rest. She passes, on the whole, a very depreciating judgment on "The Excursion" and "The Prelude," and with the exception of the great "Ode on the Inti-

mations of Immortality" and "The Daffodils," she has hardly signalised one of the poems by which Wordsworth lives in the hearts of those who love him. No wonder she has not represented adequately the view of Wordsworth taken by those who have grown up in "his worship and service." To them, she seems to have picked out one noble ode, and, in addition, two or three pretty pieces, of which one, at least (the "Anecdote for Fathers," which all Mrs. Oliphant's subtlety and eloquence cannot persuade us to regard as truly characteristic of Wordsworth's genius), might have suited better the genius of Cowper, while she has turned the cold shoulder to that unique genius in the poet which has made Wordsworth to many of us not so much a potent intellectual interest as the revealer of new spiritual powers in man.

At the same time, we are well aware that Wordsworth does not, and cannot, appear to every man of genius in the same light; and we are far from wishing to harp on our difference from Mrs. Oliphant on the subject of Wordsworth, as if this were the great feature of her book. Perhaps in our first review we may have done less than justice to other parts of that book, though we tried to express fully our profound admiration for the criticism of Cowper, as well as for much of the criticisms of Scott, Byron, Shelley, and other great writers of the period. We ought to have spoken with especial admiration of her criticism of Burns, especially of Burns the man, who is most skilfully and subtly treated, though we differ to some extent from Mrs. Oliphant's criticism of the poems, where she accords, in our opinion, too much admiration to the pathetic English poems, and too little to the broadly humorous and even coarse Scotch poems. Still, no one living could have written a more striking chapter on Burns than Mrs. Oliphant has given us. And great as seem to us the defects of her book, especially in relation to Wordsworth, to Moore, to Hazlitt, and several other minor names, we should be sorry to speak of these three remarkable volumes, except as a great critical achievement by one who has proved that, in her hands at least, criticism is not the dernier ressort . . . of a writer who had failed in higher imaginative efforts. (pp. 1656-57)

> "Mrs. Oliphant's Literary History of England, 1790-1825," in The Spectator, Vol. 55, No. 2843, December 23, 1882, pp. 1656-57.

[JOHN SKELTON] (essay date 1883)

[In the following excerpt, Skelton praises Oliphant's skill as a storyteller and critic. Characterizing Oliphant's writings as "perfectly sweet and clean and wholesome," the critic suggests that if Oliphant had concentrated her powers, she might have written like George Eliot or Charlotte Brontë, but with "the soft gracious and winning charm of mature and happy womanhood."]

Don't bear malice,—there's a good fellow. I know perfectly what you are going to say; and every word is true—that's the worst of it. It is the simple truth that one of the most delightful books on English literature [**The Literary History of England from 1790 to 1825**'] that has been written for some years, has been lying on my table for six months, not unread indeed—for it is a book that one reads without break or pause, the interest is so skilfully sustained, and the characters are treated with such living sympathy—but without eliciting those words of welcome which Maga [Blackwood's Edinburgh Magazine] delights to use when one of her favourite children enters the crowded lists, and carries off the big prize, or one of the big prizes, of the day. And of all living men or women, who deserves better of Maga than Mrs Oliphant? (p. 73)

I do not suppose that Mrs Oliphant is one of the writers who consciously entertain or profess, what is called in the jargon of the day, "high views of the literary *calling;*" but it may certainly be said of her that she has never written a page which she would wish unwritten, and which is not perfectly sweet and clean and wholesome. The *nastiness* of some of our female novelists is simply amazing; it sins against art as much as against good morals and good manners; it leaves a bad taste in the mouth for weeks afterwards; yet the most prolific and the most brilliant of the Sisterhood, who has had the widest experience and shows the clearest insight, never once fails to preserve her womanly reticence, never hurts the most shrinking modesty, never violates the finest code of honour. (pp. 76-7)

Mrs Oliphant is of course specifically a story-teller,—as Walter Scott and the Homer who wrote the Odyssey were story-tellers. There is an air of almost garrulous ease about her best work which is highly characteristic. She is not a "painful" preacher— she does not care overmuch for that curious felicity in the construction of sentences to which the Thackerays and the Matthew Arnolds attain—she does not polish her periods till they shine like old silver. We are told nowadays that Scott was no poet, and that his prose style was abominably ungrammatical. Mrs Oliphant is never so slovenly as Scott can be when he likes; but we learn when we read her books, as we do when we read his, that there is something better than style. . . . Mrs Oliphant's style at its best has something of . . . [an] outdoor charm. It belongs to the conservatory and the hothouse as little as Sir Walter's. It does not surprise us therefore that in particular her description of natural scenery should be brightly picturesque. She does not know much of our brilliant West, with its orange and purple sunsets, across the wide Atlantic; but the bleak charm of the east of Scotland, of breezy headlands and level links, is dwelt upon and emphasised with the true artist feeling. (p. 77)

[In] the essential elements of her craft, Mrs Oliphant has few rivals. When we remember that, for at least thirty years, not a summer has passed without its romance in three volumes, its thrilling ghost-story, its sea-side ramble, we get some measure of the amazing fertility of her invention. And take them all in all, how good they are! There may be no Uncle Toby or Jonathan Oldbuck among the characters; but what variety, what delicate discrimination, what a keen sense of the subtler lights and shades of human nature! She treats the male sex, it must be admitted, with habitual tolerant good-humoured contempt,—these big unwieldy awkward creatures, who are so much in the way, who don't know what to do with themselves of a wet morning, but stand about with their hands in their pockets before the fire and yawn in your face, are apt to provoke a soft breezy laughter, that after all has no malice in it,—but the girls are invariably attractive. The estimable Miss Marjoribanks (why not spell it Marchbanks at once?) who is so resolved to do her duty to her dear papa, is in many ways, to be sure, little better than a man, and is therefore regarded at first with a certain implicit suspicion; but Mrs Oliphant cannot harden her heart for long against a woman, and even Miss Marjoribanks is ultimately allowed to escape. They are none of them by any means faultless; they practice the engaging ruses, and are not superior to the charming foibles of their sex; but yet with infinite diversity of superficial trait, how tender and gracious and womanly they are. Mrs Oliphant's ideal of English girlhood, kept constantly before us for so long, has done a world of good to our girls, who begin to see that to be loud and fast and *risqué* is essentially bad style. And the *talk*— how unaffected and natural it is—no one saying what he ought

not to say, but just the right thing—never strained or rhetorical, though often nervous and sparkling, and rising at a tragic crisis to an almost monumental simplicity. There are whole passages of dialogue in the more intense and dramatic situations which for close sustained excellence of mere writing could hardly be surpassed.

Love must always be, as it has always been . . . , the main theme of the story-teller. . . . It must be admitted that Love with her, even at its slightest, is always a fine and noble pastime. It is never materialised into mere animal instinct,—never made cynical sport of, as even a Thackeray could make cynical sport of it. It may be fooling; but it is tender and gracious fooling—such as befits pure maidens and wholesome lads. For none of her works appeal to the moody satirist or the cynic whose text is *Vanitas!* or only to the very gentlest of the craft; they are addressed to a simpler audience—*virginibus puerisque!*

But a story-teller who cannot invent a good story cannot after all be said to be a good story-teller. Wherein consists the excellence of a good story? That it should proceed in its development in strict obedience to natural laws—unfolding itself in the sure instinctive inevitable way in which the lily or the rose unfolds itself—is, I should fancy, the main condition of excellence. The Greek tragedians, it is supposed, rightly or wrongly, were supreme in this difficult art. The definition assumes of course that nothing abnormal, nothing extraneous, is to be introduced, and so does not cover what may be called the "grotesque" in story-telling—'Don Quixote,' and 'Tristram Shandy,' and 'Pantagruel,' which are as discursive as they are whimsical. But with this exception the definition may be accepted as tolerably comprehensive; and judged by this standard, Mrs Oliphant is, upon the whole, a firstrate story-teller. Homer sometimes nods; and so does Mrs Oliphant. The **'Chronicles of Carlingford'** mark in various keys the highest level she has reached; nowhere else has she given us such close and strenuous work; the picture of the reticent high-strung youthful Nonconformist divine, surrounded by the vulgar Tozers and Pigeons of the dissenting sheepfold, is humorous as well as pathetic in the highest sense; but as stories they are by no means faultless. A not inconsiderable amount of irrelevant incident is introduced, which tends to spoil the simplicity of the interest. The sensational needlewoman, and all her connections, male and female, have no business in a quiet place like Carlingford. They belong distinctly to a quite different class of fable, and the entanglements and complications they give rise to interrupt the orderly development of the relations between Vincent and his flock, and, as factors in the inevitable rupture, mar an otherwise almost perfect design.

It may be the system indeed—not Mrs Oliphant—that is to blame. That a story cannot be told except in three octavo volumes is surely a monstrous and degrading superstition. Of this malignant fetish of the book trade Mrs Oliphant (in common with many others) has been the victim. . . . It must be sorrowfully confessed that Mrs Oliphant sometimes gets the least little bit weary of her sweetest heroines; and then perhaps she is apt to communicate a shade of her own weariness to the reader. But it is simply marvellous, all things considered, how seldom this happens,—on the contrary, from the first page to the last, what spirit! what animation! what *verve!*

While I cheerfully recognise that the imaginative force of Charlotte Brontë and George Eliot is in certain respects inimitable, I am often inclined to maintain that Mrs Oliphant is the most remarkable woman of her time. . . . Each of these great romance writers concentrated all her faculties for months (I might say for years) upon a single work. Mrs Oliphant has never had leisure for this absorbing devotion, this almost fierce concentration. Many a year she has written three or four novels at least, to say nothing of Essay, History, and Criticism—the mere trifles of an unfrequent holiday. . . . Had Mrs. Oliphant concentrated her powers, what might she not have done? We might have had another Charlotte Brontë or another George Eliot, with something added which neither of them quite attained,—the soft gracious and winning charm of mature and happy womanhood. And this leads me to say that the pitiless and searching anatomy of 'Adam Bede' and 'Romola'—of Hetty in the one, and Tito in the other—is not so much beyond Mrs Oliphant's power, as outside her inclination. We feel that she might try it—not without fair hope of success; but that she does not care to try it. I hesitate to affirm that this modest restraint—the womanly reticence and delicacy which refuses to probe the festering sores of humanity—is, even from the exclusively artistic point of view, an error to be condemned, though in the serene impartiality of a Goethe or a Shakespeare, there is, I suppose, something of the moral insensibility of the great surgeon who does not shrink from vivisection. The artist, however, who seeks his subjects in the pest-house and prison incurs serious risk,—the imaginative realism of a Balzac or a Hugo being apt to degenerate into the brutal indecorum of a Zola. There is, no doubt, as wide a gulf between the anatomy of 'Adam Bede' and the anatomy of dismal Comedy of Human life, as there is between Balzac and Zola; still they are on the same plane, and are capable of being pushed to the same conclusions by a vile and vulgar imagination. Mrs Oliphant never incurs this risk; she keeps resolutely aloof from the criminal classes—detected or undetected. From the earliest to the latest, from **'Katie Stewart'** to **'The Ladies Lindores,'** her books smack of the bracing and wholesome air which blows across the heather and the sea.

The sustained and serious interest of **'The Chronicles of Carlingford'** entitles them to a foremost place in the long catalogue of Mrs Oliphant's writings; but considered simply as the story-teller, she is at her best, I think, in her shorter tales,—in **'Katie Stewart,' 'A Rose in June,' 'The Beleaguered City,' 'The Curate in Charge.'** The readers of Maga are familiar with more than one of her weird and gruesome excursions into that unseen world which is so remote and yet so real. The conditions of the spiritual life have been apprehended by Mrs Oliphant with really startling vividness; and the pathetic loneliness of the unclothed soul—separated by an invisible but impregnable barrier from all that it loves—has seldom been more sympathetically portrayed. **'The Curate in Charge'** is one of the simplest but most perfect of these shorter pieces. There is only the slightest scrap of narrative; but how fresh, how tender, how true to nature it is—a village idyl, in which the simple English life and the simple English landscape are touched with a softly pathetic light. It is a distinct conception—absolutely graceful because absolutely simple—like a soap-bubble or a Greek play or a Raphael. There is nothing by the way or out of the way; nothing that does not lend itself to the progressive development of the history. If life could record itself as on a photographer's glass we know that this is the record which it would leave; there is the unambitious exactness, the homely sincerity, the inevitableness. And yet there is something more,—there is the imagination which realises the immense pathos of human life,—of life, that is to say, into which no special adventure or misadventure enters, but which simply as *life* is so fundamentally sad, so intrinsically a tragedy. *For what is your life? It is even*

a vapour that appeareth for a little time, and then vanisheth away. (pp. 77-81)

[Mrs Oliphant] is not a story-teller only,—she is a critic, a biographer, a historian. **'The Makers of Florence,'** the **'Life of Edward Irving,'** her **'Cervantes,'** her **'Molière,'** her **'Dante,'** are brilliant contributions to literary and artistic criticism. Her sound and admirable common-sense is seldom at fault; and in her animated narrative the forgotten writers of past times become real and credible to us again. Her latest and most elaborate work in this department—**'The Literary History of England from 1790 to 1825'**—is also in some respects her best. It is more complete, more thorough, consistent, and sustained; and by it, I fancy, she would wish to be judged. (pp. 81-2)

Her narrative of the lives of the great men to whom the larger share of her canvas is devoted, as distinct from her criticism of their writings, is extremely vivid: as *biography,* in fact, nothing could be better than her Burns, her Cowper, her Wordsworth, her Coleridge, her Byron, her Scott. We feel that here at least the genius of the creative artist has been at work. Whether exactly accurate or not, she has formed in each case a vital conception of the character and surroundings of the man, and she brings him before us in his habit as he lived. The book is admirably arranged. Mrs Oliphant disposes her forces like a skilful general, and groups them with the eye of an artist. And when we remember that among a host of smaller men she has to introduce us to Burns, Byron, Campbell, Coleridge, Cowper, Crabbe, De Quincey, Hazlitt, Jeffrey, Keats, Landor, Moore, Scott, Shelley, Southey, Wilson, Wordsworth (all the letters of the alphabet, in fact), it will be obvious at once how much this "genius for order" conduces to the comfort of the reader. It may be added that her criticism of Wordsworth and Coleridge among poets, and of Jane Austen and Susan Ferrier among prose writers, leaves little to be desired,—is adequate as well as appreciative. I do not know where we can find anything better in its way than her rapid and brilliant sketch of the great Lake Poets. . . . (p. 82)

There are one or two points, however, on which I am rather inclined to try conclusions with Mrs Oliphant,—her disparaging estimate of the Eighteenth Century, for instance, as well as the precise significance of that renewal of the poetical spirit, the earliest manifestations of which it is thought are to be found in the poetry of Cowper and Burns. (p. 83)

> [*John Skelton*], *"A Little Chat about Mrs Oliphant,"* in Blackwood's Edinburgh Magazine, *Vol. CXXXIII, No. DCCCVII, January, 1883, pp. 73-91.*

THE SATURDAY REVIEW, LONDON   (essay date 1883)

[*The following excerpt is from a mixed review of* It Was a Lover and His Lass.]

It was a Lover and his Lass is a book towards which, from the moment of seeing the first page of it, the reader feels amiably disposed. It is very satisfactory to find Mrs. Oliphant once more writing about Scotch scenery and character; and it is (if she and still more a recent well-intentioned defender of hers in *Blackwood* will forgive us) [see excerpt by John Skelton dated 1883] still more satisfactory not to have her writing about English literature. It is true that, as with all Mrs. Oliphant's later novel work, the reader must not be unreasonable. He must not expect more story, or more character, or more description than is necessary to carry him smoothly from the first page of Volume I. to the last page of Volume III., and he must not

An illustration from the 1907 edition of Salem Chapel.

lose his temper if the motive power sometimes seems to flag a very little. But he will find less of this extreme economy of material and workmanship in *It was a Lover and his Lass* than in most of its author's recent books. Indeed there is a very fair supply of minor characters and a kind of adumbration of a second plot. The sole real fault which can be found with *It was a Lover and his Lass* as a novel, not of extraordinary genius, but of workmanlike talent a long way above the average, is one which has to be found so often with English novels that the critic is almost weary of noticing it. Almost the whole of the second volume might with advantage have been boiled down into a couple of chapters or thereabouts and put into the first and third. But apparently the public or the publishers, or something and somebody powerful and stupid, will have it so. . . .

The plot of *It was a Lover and his Lass,* if not entirely novel, has nevertheless a fair appearance of novelty. . . . Mrs. Oliphant may be congratulated on Lewis Grantley, who is a successful character as he is, and who only just comes short of being a remarkably successful one. His English nature and his Continental education combine, with a happier result than that of a similar combination recorded in the old story of the wise and ugly knight and the beautiful but foolish girl. He has the simplicity, the freedom from snobbishness, the natural and unconstrained manners and impulses, which are theoretically supposed to belong to the best type of "foreigner," together with the sincerity and the moral cleanliness which we Englishmen are good enough to attribute to ourselves at our best. At the same time Mrs. Oliphant has not committed the fault of making him a faultless monster. He is merely a very amiable, natural, and extremely unconventional young man. (p. 316)

[There] is something of an underplot, out of which Mrs. Oliphant contrives to get another contrast of situation in a skilful enough fashion, but which does not, on the whole, please us. . . . Mrs. Stormont herself is good; though Mrs. Oliphant has rather shown her claws (if it may be permitted to hint that a lady has claws) in drawing her; and Katie, a lively, coquettish, good-natured, but somewhat egotistical and light-minded, Scotch girl, is also a capital picture. . . . The conversation of the Murrays, Setons, and Stormonts is perhaps better than anything the author has done since the days of *The Chronicles of Carlingford,* when it is at its best; but it is not always at its best, and there is decidedly too much of it. With fear and trembling, but from some actual observation, a Southern critic may perhaps hint a doubt whether Mrs. Oliphant has not peppered her countrywomen's talk somewhat too heavily with "justs." That expletive is an acknowledged feature of Scotch talk, but it is, we think, unusual for ladies of the rank of the Miss Murrays to use it in every sentence or nearly so. Some of the social satire in the London part is also decidedly conventional, an unfortunate defect which is frequently observable in social satire, especially in that of lady novelists. The scene is laid at an uncertain period "before photographs were common." But did men use the phrase "bad form" before photographs were common? Our memory inclines us to think not. This, however, is hardly a heinous shortcoming, and indeed none of the shortcomings of *It was a Lover and his Lass* are heinous, while its merits are sufficiently decided. (p. 317)

A review of "It Was a Lover and His Lass," in The Saturday Review, *London, Vol. 55, No. 1428, March 10, 1883, pp. 316-17.*

THE SATURDAY REVIEW, LONDON   (essay date 1883)

[This excerpt is from a positive assessment of The Ladies Lindores.]

Mrs. Oliphant as a rule never shows more advantage than in the Scotch novels by which she originally made her reputation. If *It was a Lover and his Lass,* which seems to have appeared only the other day, was comparatively uninteresting for want of a backbone, *The Ladies Lindores* is in every respect excellent. There is an enchanting provincial colouring about those local scenes which are laid in one of the Scottish north-eastern counties; some of the quaint Scottish types are especially good, and the local dialogue is given to perfection. But at the same time the author shows her knowledge of life by embracing a wide variety of characters. We hardly know whether the old family butler of the Erskines of Dalrulzian, who, until he had some reason to believe that his end was approaching, had never gone further than the neighbouring borough, or the accomplished and eccentric young Marquis of Millefleurs, who had wandered over the greater part of the world, is the better man in his way. It is true that the butler is apparently but a faithful piece of portrait-painting, where the individuality is made absolutely unmistakable; while the Marquis is a more fanciful study, for which the author must have drawn on her imagination. But then the study of the Marquis, notwithstanding his many eccentricities, which often surprise though they never shock us, shows a shrewder and deeper insight into human nature. Indeed in this story Mrs. Oliphant indulges more freely than usual in keen though unobtrusive psychological analysis; yet, if we see a good deal of the baser aspects of human nature, we have much that is engaging by way of relief. In so far as we remember, she has never yet written a book which has not left a more or less agreeable impression behind it, altogether irrespectively of the nature of the *dénouement.* There are two girls at least in *The Ladies Lindores* who might make the fortune of any novel, being deliciously feminine and natural, though with very unmistakable strength of will. With no strikingly sensational plot, although there is one sufficiently dramatic incident, the scheme of the story is happily devised for the illustration of the various persons concerned. (p. 675)

The undercurrents of feeling and passion beneath the lives of the Lindores family are ingeniously directed and powerfully indicated; but Scotch readers will certainly find more entertainment in the admirable studies of genuine Scottish character. Young Erskine of Dalrulzian, who is supposed to be the hero of the tale, like the heroes of Scott as of many inferior novelists, possibly turns out more commonplace than the author meant him to be. . . . In short, Mrs. Oliphant's latest novel is one proof the more that her extreme fertility is not incompatible with freshness. (pp. 675-76)

A review of "The Ladies Lindores," in The Saturday Review, *London, Vol. 55, No. 1439, May 26, 1883, pp. 675-76.*

THE SPECTATOR   (essay date 1883)

[The following excerpt is from a positive review of Hester. Although the work was not as successful as Oliphant's other novels, this critic praises its characterization and discusses how Catherine Vernon differs from the author's other strong female characters. The novel's flaw, the critic notes, is its weak story line.]

Hester is hardly one of the best of Mrs. Oliphant's novels. It wants more compression, especially in the first volume, more incident, a little more of what art critics used to call "pyramidal form." The story is too level, too like actual life, with its trivial incidents which are yet so important, and its personages who have so little that is dramatic in them, yet are always making up scenes, and its catastrophes so cruel yet so ordinary, and so easily foreseen. And yet the narrative is far superior in interest to the ordinary run of novels. Throughout, Mrs. Oliphant has such a perfect comprehension of her charcters, of what they will and will not do, of their true springs of action, and of the way in which they would meet unexpected or menacing circumstances, that her personal scenery is as real to the reader as if he stood among the group. The central figure is, as usual with Mrs. Oliphant, a woman, and, as usual, too, an elderly, unmarried woman, with wealth and brains and a will, a "woman of character" so strong that she ought to have been Scotch. When we first lighted on Catherine Vernon, the capable woman who saved a bank and managed it, and gave herself to benevolent despotism, and reigned in Redborough feared yet worshipped by half its people, we felt as if we had once more seen an old friend, and said, "Ah! here is Catherine Douglas, Millicent Mortimer, or Sarah in *Whiteladies,* or Phoebe Junior, grown old and resting from her labours, and placed in novel circumstances!" Mrs. Oliphant loves that kind of strong, half-masculine, clear-sighted woman, blind to nothing, not even to her own foibles, and loves, too, to place her in the position of a man, and show how much better she can control both circumstances and people than a man—who with her is essentially a feeble and impulsive creature, or else vaguely strong but shadowy—would, if so situated, be likely to do. The impression, however, soon disappears. Catherine Vernon is herself strong, like her predecessors, and healthy and competent to do man's work, but a separate being, is, in fact, that rare character, a female cynic, a woman full of benevolence and active kindness, but *au fond* sardonic, expecting little in return, aware that gratitude is infrequent, seeing through all the pettinesses, and spites, and falsehoods of her protégés, but tolerating all, and deriving from all an amusement which in a man would have been saturnine. In her cynicism, too, she becomes a little base, rules her dependents too hardly, is too apt to believe that their motive must be bad, and to tread her subjects down with a contempt which is not altogether unconscious, for she sometimes gives it voice. She has filled a great house with dependent relatives, to whom she is all kindness, but whom when she entertains them she grossly neglects; whom she snubs when needful remorselessly; and whose consequent dislike she regards with a large-hearted yet contemptuous understanding. Nevertheless, she is, of course, taken in, that being, in Mrs. Oliphant's theory, more or less women's destiny. She has adopted one of the Vernons, placed him at the head of the bank, and made him her son, and he, outwardly all deference, in reality despises and almost hates her, fretting under the restraint of her affection, deeming her watchful care espionage, and believing her loving control to come from a desire to govern,—which is partly true as regards all but himself,—from which his only passionate impulse is to be free. Her large, yet spoiled nature . . . is drawn with the firm, free hand which tells of perfect comprehension, and in her ability and her weakness, is as real as any character in history. We never tire of her and her ways and her acts, unpleasant as the latter often are, and never for an instant fail to see in her the largeness of nature, force of character, and mental insight which forbid all around, even when she is doing or saying small things, ever to think her small. She is the true heroine of the story, and her relation to her adopted son, whom she trusts implicitly, but who all the while is secretly speculating with her money, not out of roguery, or malice, or avarice, but in an ungovernable desire to be independent of her, and to rule his life for himself, is described with almost tragic power. Mrs. Oliphant does not succeed in this son quite so well as in Catherine, failing always, as she usually does, to give the impression of manliness, which must have been in the real man, but the woman's side of the story is wonderfully told, and culminates in this new form of tragedy. (pp. 1660-61)

The heroine, Hester, is not quite so good. She is intended throughout to be, and is, a repetition of Catherine herself, though without the cynical humour, which, of course, only experience, and experience of a peculiar kind, can develop, and placed in far different circumstances. She is as competent as Catherine, but has nothing to do with her competence, being wretchedly poor, and surrounded by feeble people,—her mother, who is a washed-out creature, originally a lady and a beauty; a cousin Emma, pretty, stupid, and mercilessly frank in her avowals that she is husband-hunting, and "ought to have her chance;" the spiteful or very old inmates of the genteel almshouse, the Vernonry, as the neighbours call it; a suitor, Harry Vernon, who is good, kindly, and faithul, but a fool; a second suitor, who hardly comes forward; and a third, the Edward Vernon, Catherine Vernon's adopted son. He wins, of course; and it is in the relation between the two that we have the only sense of disappointment in the book. We do not know why he wins, and do not believe he would have won. Pride of a sound and healthy kind is the strongest feeling in Hester, and we can hardly believe that she would have borne Edward's calculated neglect whenever he meets his love in his adopted mother's company, or his silence towards his adopted mother,—unless, indeed, Hester's love had been stronger still, strong enough to defy all things and induce her to cling to Edward when he asks her to elope, even though she is aware of, as she has long half supsected, his guilt. He dominates Hester, with her quick brain and strong character, far too completely, yet incompletely; and neither success nor failure is satisfactorily accounted for. The truth is, Mrs. Oliphant sees no necessity for explanation. Girls of fine nature are always giving themselves to the unworthy, just as wise men are always marrying fools, and her own explanation of the fact in her heart is that men are mostly fools, and that women have not yet completely found them out. We cannot recall among all her books one picture of a thoroughly competent man who is also good, or one—unless it be Tom in *Miss Marjoribanks,* who is the slightest of sketches—whom a male reader thoroughly likes. As, however, she does not wish to press this theory too strongly, she leaves explanation out, sometimes, as in this case, to her readers' bewilderment and annoyance. The facts granted, however, the situations are clear and exciting, and Mrs. Oliphant's power of writing bright and interesting dialogue, dialogue with thought and purpose in it, never fails her any more than her power of creating side figures. This time the book is full of them,—Captain Morgan, the old officer, whose life has been one long benevolence, but who, in extreme age, has come to the conclusion that altruism may be pushed too far, and holds, as a theory often breaking down, that every man should have a life of his own beyond destruction or spoiling by others; Mrs. Morgan, the gentle, old wife, who against this theory is immovable; Emma Ashton, their grandchild, a really wonderful sketch, the girl who has nothing bad in her, is, indeed, simple, and truthful, and unmalicious, but has in her an incurable coarseness of fibre, a Zolaish realism which has the effect of badness; Ellen Merridew, the spirited, active, vain butterfly, without evil in her composition, but a ruinous wife to own; Roland Ashton, the self-conscious, vain, young stockbroker, who flirted by instinct with all accessible women, yet had sense and heart somewhere about him; and Harry Vernon, the good man, who has a certain strength derived from principle and feeling alone, but is always conscious that when brain is required he is "out of it;" there is a whole gallery of such people, all sketched successfully and apparently without pains. Among them all, the reader loves Hester, the proud, able, pure girl, who protects her mother, and defies Catherine Vernon, and would protect her lover if only he would be protected, yet hardly follows her impulse when she gives herself away to such a man, one who, though full of intelligence and capacity of various kinds, is still essentially a mere hypocrite. That, after all, is the true defect of the book. The adopting mother would not have detected the hypocrite element in Edward, for adopting mothers never do, but Hester would have done, and would have despised it. That she does not, gives the reader pain, not because of Hester, who, he feels certain, will be rescued at last, but because it creates an impression of a defect in art.

We have said nothing of the plot of the story, because there is practically none, except the catastrophe produced by Edward Vernon's hunger to be free, and because we cannot consider Mrs. Oliphant from the point of view of the story-teller. She has risen far beyond that, though she has not reached her true level yet, and never will till she determines to put all the wealth of imagination at her disposal into some one book. She still beats out her gold, thinking the clever scenes she makes up so easily good enoguh for Mudie. So they are,—too good; but they are not good enough for her own reputation, if she is ever to be recognised for what she is,—at least the second female novelist of our time. (pp. 1661-62)

*A review of "Hester: A Story of Contemporary Life,"
in* The Spectator, *Vol. 56, No. 2895, December 22,
1883, pp. 1660-62.*

THE SPECTATOR   (essay date 1884)

[*This reviewer considers* The Wizard's Son *one of Oliphant's best novels, despite its numerous flaws. The plot is exciting, the critic maintains, even though the author falters in her treatment of the supernatural.*]

[*The Wizard's Son*] is a difficult story to review, on account of the strange way in which its merits and demerits are mixed throughout. Considered simply as a novel, it is one of the very best that Mrs. Oliphant has produced—or, in other words, one of the best novels in the language. The heroine, Oona Forrester, is ideally charming; the hero, Lord Erradeen—though injured by that trace of feebleness, of self-will, unregulated either by principle or intellect, which Mrs. Oliphant sees in every man— is carefully studied, and is alive; and the minor characters are, as usual, admirable. We do not know where to look for a sketch more perfect than that of Mrs. Forrester, the vain, shallow-brained old beauty of Loch Houran, with her kindly heart and perfect breeding, and deep love for all who belong to herself; while Katie Williamson, the millionaire's pretty daughter, so conscious of wealth, and so little befooled by it, with her bright sense and clear eyes, and utter directness, and simplicity which is not simple, is, so far as we know, quite new. No one surpasses Mrs. Oliphant in describing, what is so constantly seen in real life and so seldom in literature, earthiness which has no taint in it, a girl who wants to win the best from life, and to obtain promotion, and to enjoy herself every day, and yet is as completely without badness in her nature as without silliness in her brain. The honest, undecided factor; the worthy old minister, with his gentle tolerance; the old servant, who is filled with superstition, yet fearless in his fears,—all these are admirably drawn amidst a scene, the waters and banks of Loch Houran, of which it is a pleasure only to read. Scott could not make *locale* more real to his reader than Mrs. Oliphant does in her latest book. Nor could a difficult and painful, yet natural and frequent relation, between mother and son be better sketched than is the relation between Mrs. Methven and her son: she all love, yet driving him half crazy with her tactless interference and inability to understand his moods; he full of love too, yet fuller of half-sullen resolution to be free. The plot, too, is exciting; and though the end is clear from the first, curiosity to know how that end will be secured holds the reader enchained from the first page to the last. We have read *The Wizard's Son* twice, once in snippets and once as a whole, and our interest has never flagged.

It is not thus, however, that this novel must be judged. That Mrs. Oliphant can write a charming story, rising in chapters to something much higher, and occasionally to a display of true literary genius of a kind which we at least rank high, all who have studied her work know well. But she has here attempted something demanding yet loftier powers,—the use of machinery avowedly supernatural, the introduction of a being who in many essential points is human, yet not human, who does things, for example, that man as we know him could not do, who is gifted with the serenity we attribute to the immortals, and who governs, or tries to govern, not only the fates, but the wills of all to whom he stands in the relation of progenitor. The true hero of *The Wizard's Son* is the Wizard, the ancestor of the Methvens of the Loch, who, centuries ago, first built the greatness of the house, who has won from science the secret of deathlessness, the secret of thought-reading, even at a distance, the secret of movement by volition like Homer's Gods, and the secret of invisibility,—and who uses all these powers to play the part of Mephistophiles, and induce his descendants by a mixture of advice and threat, to aggrandise steadily the fortunes of his race. . . . When an author offers to the world so audacious a conception as this, she must be judged by her failure or success in working the conception out; and it is with regret and reluctance that we say . . . that her success in this effort has not been perfect. The figure of the Warlock Lord is, indeed, splendidly conceived. He is no vulgar wizard, but a grand and gracious gentleman, who has lived on, whose mind has grown with its vast knowledge and vaster experience, till even when it counsels evil, it is from a wider perception than that of man, a perception as to the material results of given action akin to that of Providence. He recommends, for example, cruel evictions which would be ruinous to the *morale* of the man who sanctioned them, but sees that in those evictions would be the germ of happiness for the families evicted. He wishes no evil for evil's sake; prefers, when there is a choice, that his descendant should be good, for goodness removes half the difficulties of life; is in no respect a devil, or the slave of a devil, but only a man in whom width of intelligence, unaccompanied by any spiritual gain, or rather accompanied by spiritual decay, has killed out the perception of right and wrong,

except as differences like red and blue. He is not without consciousness that there is a loftier ideal than his own, or a faint shame within himself, such as he feels and half confesses when, only once in the story, he resorts to a device of the lower magic, influencing Lord Erradeen through power brought to bear upon his *picture;* but he deliberately keeps this consciousness down:—

> 'You are taking (he says to his reluctant victim), I hope, a less highflown view of the circumstances altogether. The absolute does not exist in this world. We must all be content with advantages which are comparative. I always regret,' he continued, 'resorting to heroic measures. To have to do with some one who will hear and see reason, is a great relief. I follow the course of your thoughts with interest. They are all perfectly just; and the conclusion is one which most wise men have arrived at. Men in general are fools. As a rule you are incapable of guiding yourselves; but only the wise among you know it.'—'I have no pretension to be wise.'—'You are modest—all at once. So long as you are reasonable that will do. Adapt your life now to a new plan. The ideal is beyond your reach. By no fault of circumstances, but by your own, you have forfeited a great deal that is very captivating to the mind of youth, but very empty if you had it all to-morrow. You must now rearrange your conceptions and find yourself very well off with the second best.'

Lord Erradeen resists furiously, but only excites his companion's cynicism:—

> 'When you have taken my advice (as you will do presently) and have come down from your pinnacle and accepted what is the ordinary lot of mankind, you will find no longer any difficulty in living—as long as is possible; you will not wish to shorten your life by a day.'— 'And what is the ordinary lot of mankind?' cried Walter, feeling himself once more beaten down, humiliated, irritated by an ascendency which he could not resist.—'I have told you— the second best. In your case a wife with a great deal of wealth, and many other qualities, who will jar upon your imagination (an imagination which has hitherto entertained itself so nobly!) and exasperate your temper perhaps, and leave your being what you call incomplete: but who will give you a great acquisition of importance, and set you at peace with me. That alone will tell for much in your comfort; and gradually your mind will be brought into conformity. You will consider subjects in general as I do—from a point of view which will not be individual. You will not balance the interests of the few miserable people who choose to think their comfort impaired, but will act largely for the continued benefit of your heirs and your property. You will avail yourself of my perceptions, which are more extended than your own, and gradually become the greatest landowner, the greatest personage of your district; able to acquire the highest honours if you please,

to wield the greatest influence. Come, you have found the other position untenable according to your own confession. Accept the practicable. I do not hurry you. Examine for yourself into the issues of your ideal—now that we have become friends, and understand each other so thoroughly—'—'I am no friend of yours. I understand no one, not even myself.'—'You are my son,' said the other, with a laugh. 'You are of my nature; as you grow older you will resemble me more and more. You will speak to your sons as I speak to you. You will point out these duties to them, as I do to you.'—'In everything you say,' cried Walter, 'I perceive that you acknowledge a better way. Your plans are the second best—you say so. Is it worth living so long only to know that you are embracing mediocrity after all, that you have nothing to rise to? and yet you acknowledge it,' he said.—The stranger looked at him with a curious gaze. He who had never shown the smallest emotion before grew slightly paler at this question: but he laughed before he replied. 'You are acute,' he said. 'You can hit the blot. But the question in hand is not my character, but your practical career.'

That is a new Mephistophiles,—a most original conception, thoroughly well worked out; and yet it fails. The man with these grand powers, and this separate life, uses both like some small Jew tradesman. Mrs. Oliphant has made the mistake of giving this being a purpose so inconceivably small, that it appears by the side of his powers ridiculous. An intelligence like his, versed in all men's natures, full of all experiences, swelling with triumphs in the field of science, could not have striven through the ages only to give a Scottish laird a little more money. The end is too petty—so petty, that the reader's power of belief, which it is indispensable to evoke, fails at every page. If the Methvens, once owners of all Scotland, were to do something grand with their ownership, bad or good,—but there is no such hint; they are only to grow bigger, and richer, and grander, in the most vulgar sense, with every generation. That is an impossible end for a Mephistophiles to seek,—

> In Heaven ambition cannot dwell,
> Nor avarice in the vaults of Hell,
> Earthly those passions of the Earth;

and the reader would even begin to ridicule, but for his appreciation of the means taken to defeat the Warlock Lord. There Mrs. Oliphant, who has lost her perception of character for a moment—having perhaps studied the life of Scott till she fancies that Scott's poor end could have continued to be his end even had he acquired the wisdom of twenty men and the experience of hundreds—at once recovers her powers, and fights her Mephistophiles with a brain as subtle as his own. Her inner conception of him—forgotten for a moment in that earthy hint about the lamp and the picture—is that he can work only by mental influence upon a single mind linked with his own by the mystical, not understood but very real, tie of descent. How then will it be if the mind to be subdued is strengthened by the strength of another mind . . .? It is in love that Lord Erradeen finds the needful aid, and Mrs. Oliphant the opportunity for a love-story as beautiful and as original as has ever been painted, a story not spoiled by the fact that the natural relation

of the sexes is inverted, and that no man can study Lord Erradeen without a faint contempt for his feminine clingingness to the stronger character. That is Mrs. Oliphant's permanent idea of the facts of the world; and false as it is, it is so permanent that it causes no more disturbance than any other mannerism in a great writer. We accept it. . . . No one can read of Oona without admiration and sympathy for that mixed passion of pity and devotion and true love which at the supreme moment gives her the courage that enables her to quell the Warlock Lord, and drive him, serene and grand still, but defeated, from the scene. His defeat has incidents in it far too theatric for our taste, and we protest once more against the mystic lamp and its incendiary powers; but still, the impelling force which drives Oona is a spiritual one, and it is because Lord Erradeen's mind has escaped, not because the lamp is broken, that the baffled wizard retires,—not, we fear, with much regret that he must suspend for a few years his supernatural endeavours to make Loch Houran a still more "rapidly improving" property. (pp. 713-14)

> *A review of "The Wizard's Son," in* The Spectator, *Vol. 57, No. 2918, May 31, 1884, pp. 713-14.*

M.O.W.O. [MARGARET OLIPHANT WILSON OLIPHANT] (essay date 1892)

[*In the following excerpt from her preface to* The Heir Presumptive and the Heir Apparent, *Oliphant comments on the rapid composition of her works.*]

The conditions of literary work, especially in fiction, have so much altered since the time when a book came solidly before the world in one issue, that I think it right to say a word in explanation of the rapidity with which one work of mine has recently, within a few months, followed another. The fact is, that a writer of fiction is now so much drawn into the easy way of serial publication that he, or she, not unfrequently loses command of the times and seasons once so carefully studied. (p. v)

It has been my fate in a long life of production to be credited chiefly with the equivocal virtue of industry, a quality so excellent in morals, so little satisfactory in art. How it is that to bear so virtuous and commendable a character should be unpleasing, is one of those whimsicalities of nature which none of us are without. I should prefer to disclaim that excellence if I might; but at all events so old a friend of the public as myself, who has always found so much moderate and kind friendliness of reception if seldom any enthusiasm, may be allowed to disclaim the corresponding vice of hurry in composition, which is alike disrespectful to the common patron, and derogatory to one's self. (pp. vii-viii)

> *M.O.W.O.* [*Margaret Oliphant Wilson Oliphant*], *in a preface to her* The Heir Presumptive and the Heir Apparent, *Vol. I, Macmillan & Co., 1892, pp. v-viii.*

MARGARET OLIPHANT   (essay date 1894?)

[*In this excerpt from* Autobiography and Letters of Mrs Margaret Oliphant, *Oliphant comments briefly on her writings and reputation. The* Autobiography and Letters *was first published in 1899, although all the autobiographical entries were written by 1894.*]

I don't suppose my powers are equal to [Charlotte Brontë's]— my work to myself looks perfectly pale and colourless beside hers—but yet I have had far more experience and, I think, a fuller conception of life. I have learned to take perhaps more a man's view of mortal affairs,—to feel that the love between men and women, the marrying and giving in marriage, occupy in fact so small a portion of either existence or thought. When I die I know what people will say of me: they will give me credit for courage (which I almost think is not courage but insensibility), and for honesty and honourable dealing; they will say I did my duty with a kind of steadiness, not knowing how I have rebelled and groaned under the rod. Scarcely anybody who cares to speculate further will know what to say of my working power and my own conception of it; for, except one or two, even my friends will scarcely believe how little possessed I am with any thought of it all,—how little credit I feel due to me, how accidental most things have been, and how entirely a matter of daily labour, congenial work, sometimes now and then the expression of my own heart, almost always the work most pleasant to me, this has been. (p. 67)

Margaret Oliphant, in her Autobiography and Letters of Mrs Margaret Oliphant, *edited by Mrs Harry Coghill, Leicester University Press, 1974, 464 p.*

THE ATHENAEUM   (essay date 1897)

[*The following excerpt is from a balanced assessment of Oliphant's writings. Unlike many other commentators, the critic suggests that her rapid production was not responsible for the defects in her writings, but rather that the flaws resulted from Oliphant's inability to criticize her own work. The reviewer concludes that Oliphant holds a secure place as a novelist of the "second rank."*]

[Oliphant was] probably the most industrious woman who ever followed the profession of letters in this country. . . . It was impossible that people who realized how prodigious was the quantity of work, and really excellent work, she turned out should not sometimes regret that she did not produce less and try to achieve some masterpiece of fiction that would secure her an undisputed place among the immortals. This feeling was especially general after the appearance of **'The Chronicles of Carlingford,'** the wit and humour of which delighted numbers of people to whom **'Passages in the Life of Mrs. Margaret Maitland'** had remained unknown because of its Scottish dialect. And yet we greatly doubt if, had she devoted years to one book, she would have produced anything of higher quality than she achieved. Mrs. Oliphant was a good critic of other people's books, as her articles in *Blackwood* often showed; but she was no critic of her own. Like Scott, she never knew whether what she had written was good or bad, and had to wait till she got another person's verdict. No doubt her novels did occasionally show the effects of constant production—she would have been more than mortal had they not. They sometimes failed to keep up the bright promise of the opening, became languid, and concluded ineffectively. This may have been in part due to fatigue, but it was also due in part to other causes. She had singular fertility of invention, unusual adroitness and felicity in observing and depicting character; in short, she had a wonderful brain; but the genius that builds up a great work of imagination complete in all its parts, the architectonic faculty, was denied her. She could not dwell on any one theme for a long space of time. It apparently oppressed her, and, to gain relief she must pass on to another subject. Another great drawback was that she was deficient in passion. The kindly Scottish lady, whose bright face and pleasant manner made her a favourite with all who knew her, was sagacious, humorous, and a quick critic of the foibles and the heroisms of humanity,

but she had not the *diable au corps*. She could not have written a book like 'Jane Eyre' or 'The Tenant of Wildfell Hall.' But allowing all this, how much wholesome and true pleasure has she not afforded her contemporaries! It gives us some idea of the decadence of the novel when we compare **'Mrs. Margaret Maitland'** and **'Adam Graeme'** with the much lauded works of Mr. Crockett and Ian Maclaren or even with Mr. Barrie's. In construction, in knowledge of human nature, and in acquaintance with Scottish life—even in so comparatively secondary a matter as dialect—Mrs. Oliphant's early stories are immeasurably superior to any of the productions of the kailyard school. And if she was not a novelist of the first rank, her place in the second rank is high.

As a biographer she was somewhat uncertain. When she got hold of a theme that interested her, as in her life of Edward Irving, she produced admirable work. The romance of the great preacher's life and the pathos of his end fascinated her, and she made her readers feel the fascination. But in many of the works she compiled for the booksellers she was much less successful, because they were simply hackwork, and she had not the learning, and, what was worse, she had not the training, necessary for writing about **'The Makers of Florence'** or **'St. Francis of Assisi.'** In books of this sort she is seen at a disadvantage. Her very worst peformance was her biography of Sheridan.

A word may be said regarding the tales in which she dealt with the supernatural. They were certainly remarkable *tours de force*, far superior to what one would have predicted they would prove had one known she was writing them. At the same time they were certainly overrated by a section of her admirers. **'The Beleaguered City'** was the ablest of them, and a very powerful piece of work it is; but it has a moral, and a moral is fatal in literature of this kind. (pp. 35-6)

"Mrs. Oliphant," in The Athenaeum, *Vol. 2, No. 3636, July 3, 1897, pp. 35-6.*

THE SPECTATOR   (essay date 1897)

[*In the following general discussion of Oliphant's works, the critic first addresses the unevenness of her writings and then compares her works with those of Jane Austen and Walter Scott.*]

Mrs. Oliphant's marvellous industry impeded the public recognition of her still more marvellous gifts. . . . Naturally the public refused to believe that a writer so prolific could be a great genius, while critics regretted that her work, pursued under all manner of conditions and personal trials, was sometimes unequal and sometimes excited the suspicion, not, we think, wholly untrue, that she was beating out the gold of her brain, of which she could not have been unconscious, a little thin. It even happened occasionally, as in the marked case of **"Salem Chapel,"** that the last half of a book was ordinary, well-written stuff while the first half was flashing with genius and humour. So extraordinary, indeed, were the occasional inequalities in her work—just compare **"Lucy Crofton"** with **"The Ladies Lindores"**—that the present writer, one of her devoted admirers, who, like Kinglake, felt that life was happier when one of her novels had appeared, once asked Mr. Blackwood at Strathtyrum whether he had ever suspected Mrs. Oliphant of employing a ghost. "Yes," was the unexpected reply of that most acute of born critics, "but the suspicion was unfounded. The hills and plains are all in her mind." There were hills and plains, but the hills reached to a wonderful height. Mrs. Oliphant, whom, in spite of the great merit of her biographies, especially the **"Life of Irving,"** and the still greater merit of many occasional essays, we refuse to consider except as a novelist, produced stories of three absolutely distinct kinds,—in one, the novel of religious mystery, she stood absolutely alone without rival or fellow; in another, the novel of description, the only reasonable comparison is with Sir Walter Scott; and in the third, the novel of modern society, she rivals, both in humour and the subtle delineation of ordinary character, Jane Austen. There is nothing in English literature of its kind like **"The Beleaguered City,"** the account of the invasion of the city of Sens by an army of ghosts, so audacious, so weird in its effect, yet so intensely softening and spiritual. We know of nothing like the painting of the different personages in that book,—of the honest Mayor, his *bourgeoise* mother, and his angel wife; of the earthly priest, who yet longs to be a true priest; of the old aristocrat; and of the mystic Lecamus, the feeble man for whom alone God has opened his inner eyes,—all so exquisitely natural while surrounded, engulfed, lost in an overwhelming mystery which, though it is like nothing ever recorded or even imagined before, the reader feels as he advances and slowly drinks in an impression which thenceforward never leaves him, might have happened. The atmosphere of the story is the atmosphere of another world permitted for a moment to supersede the atmosphere of this one, but in it moves figures of this one, in all of whom, without exception, their special characteristics are brought out softly, yet sharply, by the very fog, which yet is not a fog but a haze let down from heaven, in which they are enveloped. Only a genius of the loftiest order could have produced that book, which never had a predecessor and will, we think, never have a successor, the most wonderful example in literature of the range of woman's imagination. It is the more wonderful because Mrs. Oliphant, though she tried two or three times, could never do the same thing again, and in spite of the exquisite style and painting of the first part of **"Old Lady Mary,"** her other excursions into the spiritual world were distinctly failures.

We have said that in some of her novels the true comparison for her powers is with Scott, and Scott alone, and this is true in a special degree of **"Young Musgrave," "The Minister's Wife," "The Son of the Soil," "Katie Stewart," "The Ladies Lindores," "May," "The Wizard's Son," "The Last of the Mortimers,"** and parts, at least, of **"Whiteladies."** There is the same breeziness, the same healthy realism, the same power of story-telling, the same perception of originality and force in ordinary or inferior characters. There are chapters in **"Young Musgrave,"** especially the one in which the old gipsy-woman appears in Court to hear for the first time that one son has guiltlessly murdered another, of which, in their restrained force and passion, Scott would have been proud, as he would have been of the revivalist scenes in **"The Minister's Wife,"** so like in their power the best chapters of "Old Mortality," and of the character of Rolls the butler in **"The Ladies Lindores."** The irresistibleness of the comparison with Scott is the more striking because Mrs. Oliphant's central figures were always women. There is perceptible through all her stories a faint contempt for men, as unaccountable, uncomfortable works of God, whom she understood best when they were most ordinary, like the slightly thick-witted and entirely loveable hero of **"Harry Joscelyn,"** or most foolish, like Paul in **"He Who Will Not When He May."** It was women she loved to depict, but they are the women Scott would have drawn under the very circumstances he would have created, had his genius taken him that way. This fancy for studying women comes out in all her stories, and especially in some of those of which the scene is laid in Carlingford—**"Miss Marjoribanks," "Phoebe Ju-**

nior," "The Perpetual Curate"—stories in which Jane Austen would have recognised a humourist as great as herself, though of a different kind. Mrs. Oliphant entirely lacked Miss Austen's power of painting the inherent vulgarity in some women who yet are ladies, and though, like Miss Austen, she never made of crime a *motif*—there is a partial exception in **"Whiteladies"**—and never condescended to what is now called the sex question, yet her social situations are stronger and more interesting, and she could conceive of a woman, like Lady Car as she appears both in **"The Ladies Lindores"** and in the sequel called by her own name, who was wholly beyond the limits of Miss Austen's range. We say nothing of **"Mrs. Margaret Maitland,"** for that is not a novel but a sketch drawn most lovingly from life, and the original neither came nor could have come in Jane Austen's way. Add that Mrs. Oliphant had in the most unusual degree the faculty of pleasant story-telling, so that her novels gave acute pleasure to many different minds, and were waited for by men like the late Mr. Kinglake through life with eager expectation, and we have a novelist who in our day was inferior to George Eliot alone. Mrs. Oliphant's humour, though of a subtly pleasant kind, was not mordant like George Eliot's, nor could she have drawn either Maggie Tulliver or Dorothea [heroines, respectively, in "The Mill on the Floss" and "Middlemarch"]; but her stories had a healthy breeziness in them as of the Scotch scenery she loved, which it was not in George Eliot's powerful imagination to infuse into her tales.

We believe that as time advances there will be more, and not less, appreciation of Mrs. Oliphant, and we trust that Messrs. Blackwood, who through two generations regarded her as a dear friend, will see their way to an edition of some twenty of her best novels. . . . To publish a collection of all her novels is to do her injustice,—even **"Hester,"** for example, in spite of the delicious character of the heroine, has in it some quality of tediousness, as if a tired writer were recollecting what passed,—and we see no sense in printing the works of imagination and the works of labour together. The latter contain many fine things, but with the exception of the **"Life of Irving"** they bear little trace of the original genius which most unquestionably dwelt behind those humorous, watchful eyes, which saw and comprehended everything except, indeed, the man who is at once able and good. In all the vast array of her stories there is not one such man, though she thought of one in Russell, in **"The Poor Gentleman,"** and even him she was obliged to make a do-nothing who knew himself. (pp. 12-13)

"Mrs. Oliphant," in The Spectator, *Vol. 79, No. 3601, July 3, 1897, pp. 12-13.*

[J. H. MILLAR]   (essay date 1897)

[*In the following excerpt, Millar praises Oliphant's popular fiction, noting "sympathetic and masterly delineation of character" and "vivid presentation" of atmosphere as the two most important features of her works. Oliphant is at her best, the critic maintains, when she depicts scenes from Scottish life. For additional commentary by Millar, see excerpt dated 1899.*]

[In] confining our attention to the fiction that came from her pen, we are very far from meaning to disparage the vast body of work which Mrs Oliphant produced in other departments of literature. Few are so richly endowed as she was with the enviable faculty of assimilating historical or other information and imparting it to the public in an agreeable manner. Still fewer have so thoroughly learned the secret of the biographer's art. Her **'Life of Edward Irving'**—to name but one of her performances in this kind—is little less than a masterpiece. Copious, yet not diffuse; bristling with detail, yet coherent and orderly; fed from innumerable sources through countless channels of information, yet consistent and well-digested—it is not unworthy to be ranked with Lockhart's Life of Burns or Southey's of Wesley. Neither are the readers of 'Maga' likely soon to forget the ripe and sagacious criticism, often brilliant, ever shrewd and ever kindly, which she contributed to these pages over a tract of many years. Yet we believe that in fiction Mrs Oliphant's genius found its truest and most adequate expression, and that the qualities which characterise her historical, biographical, and critical writings are there displayed in even greater intensity. (p. 306)

Into some descriptions of character, it is true, Mrs Oliphant seems to have been unable to enter, or at all events she was unable to reproduce them with distinctness and effect. What we may call the "actress" or "adventuress" type of woman, for example (a specimen of which may be found in **'A Poor Gentleman'**), had doubtless not come within her own immediate observation; and her attempt to depict it suggests many reminiscences of other people's novels. Adventuresses after all are kittle cattle, and few are the writers who have "made an 'it" with them, to borrow Mr Beecher's phrase from **'Salem Chapel.'** Similarly Mrs Oliphant's heart seems to fail her in the portrayal of villains. Jack Wentworth and the Miss Wodehouse's brother in **'The Perpetual Curate'** are not the real thing, and the raffish Underwood in **'The Wizard's Son'** does not abound in vitality. For precisely the opposite reason she is equally unsuccessful with her millionaires and parvenus, who are painted in the most repulsive colours. Mr Penrose, in **'Madonna Mary,'** who seems really to have had no more serious fault than that of being a sharp and prosperous man of business, is shaken and *worried,* so to speak, much in the same way as any character whom she particularly dislikes is dealt with by Miss Ferrier. Mr Copperhead, in **'Phoebe, Junior,'** comes off even worse; while Pat Torrance, in **'The Ladies Lindores,'** is revolting in his brutality, and is so overdrawn as to throw the whole picture out of keeping. We wish indeed that the same severity of treatment had been applied to Oswald Meredith in **'Carita'**—a most finished young snob and cad, whom Mrs Oliphant "lets down" all too gently for his deserts, out of fondness, we suspect, for his affectionate mother.

Even if this enumeration does not exhaust Mrs Oliphant's failures, and we do not pretend that it does, the successes remain in a vast majority. There is that rabid evangelical Mrs Kirkman in **'Madonna Mary,'** worthy to hobnob with old Lady Southdown; and there is Winnie Percival, spoilt and *incomprise,* in the same book.... Among men, there is Kirsteen's father, Douglas of Drumcarro, old West Indian slave-driver and West Highland laird; there is Lord Lindores (a portrait which strikes us as particularly true to nature), whose easy-going amiability is transformed into inexorable worldliness by unexpected accession to a title and a landed estate; there is his son, Rintoul, "rampant" in his ingenuous worldly wisdom, and as firmly set himself upon marrying a penniless beauty as he is upon his sister marrying riches and position; there is the father of the **"Rose in June,"** Mr Damerel, the embodiment of refined epicureanism and self-indulgence; and there is Dr Marjoribanks, the hard-headed parent of the incomparable Lucilla. Our list has been compiled, so to say, at random; it contains no character of more than secondary importance; and we have left the rich treasures of the Scottish stories and of the Carlingford series practically undrawn upon. Yet, such as it is, it may

satisfy the most sceptical of the wide extent and diversified nature of Mrs Oliphant's domain. Her talent was *borné* only if it be *borné* for an author to keep his head, to refuse either to clamour for the burning down of ninety-nine persons' houses in order that the hundredth may have a meal of roast-pig, or to join in the shrill and importunate pleading of the socially mutilated fox in favour of tails being generally dispensed with.

The most conclusive proof, however, of Mrs Oliphant's keen susceptibility to impressions is the remarkable vividness with which she could convey them. There is no more prominent feature in her art than the combined precision and delicacy with which the physical and social surroundings of her characters are indicated. Her novels are rich in "atmosphere"; the setting of the gem is a subject of anxious care; the background of the picture is not left to take care of itself; nor are the *dramatis personae* permitted to wander about seeking for a lost *milieu,* or a *monde* which once was theirs. Even the weakest of her books begins well. There is no beating about the bush. Miss Austen herself scarcely enjoyed more fully the gift of putting the reader *au fait* of the situation, or of mapping out in a few bold and sweeping strokes a serviceable *carte du pays.* The pity is that, in Mrs Oliphant's case, her hand often seems to tire so soon, and that as the work proceeds the lines become somewhat vague and blurred. To us, in truth, it seems the merest paradox to pretend that she would not have written better had she written less. But take her at her best, and dissatisfaction vanishes. Every street in Carlingford seems familiar to us. If we put up for a night or two at the Blue Boar, we should need no guide to take us round the town.... Our only fear would be that the temptation to greet that portly shopkeeper or yonder ascetic-looking clergyman on the strength of old acquaintance might prove overwhelming. And it is the same with quite different scenes. Miss Rhoda Broughton in **'Joan'** has gone very far to make us realise or remember what summer may mean in poky quarters bounded by a dusty highroad. But we mop our foreheads even harder as we pant and groan with worthy Mrs Burchell up the steep hill which leads to Miss Charity Beresford's delightful house in the neighbourhood of Windsor, and, once arrived at our goal, are transported by the delicious coolness, the undisturbed repose, and the exquisite fragrance of the garden with its innumerable roses. What an acute perception Mrs Oliphant had of the little matters that make all the difference between comfort and discomfort in externals! Again and again she reverts to the *res angusta domi,* contrasting it with the results of opulence; and the large family living on narrow means is one of her favourite topics. (pp. 309-11)

In none of her stories is the effect of "atmosphere" more triumphantly attained than in those where the scene is situated in Scotland; for Mrs Oliphant knew her native country, and she knew its people. And if we may discriminate where all is excellence, she seems to reach her very highest level when she sets foot in the Kingdom of Fife. **'Katie Stewart,'** one of her most beautiful productions, and the first of a long series of stories to adorn the pages of 'Maga'; **'John Rintoul,'** a simple yet affecting tale of life in a fishing village; and the **'Romance of Ladybank,'** a slight but singularly graceful sketch—are all very different in kind from one another. Yet they have this in common, that each of them transplanted from the soil of Fife would forfeit the greater part of its peculiar charm and virtue. (p. 311)

It is indeed in delineating the ordinary domestic relations and in recording the emotions to which they give rise that Mrs Oliphant excels any novelist of her generation. The particular relation which seems to have interested her most was not the conjugal, though that was frequently her theme, and Dr and Mrs Morgan, for example, in **'The Perpetual Curate,'** are a couple whom Balzac need not have been ashamed to call his own. The relationship on which she dwells with most insistence, and to which she constantly reverts, is that of parent and child. This proposition scarcely stands in need of illustration; but an excellent specimen of her treatment of the topic will be found in **'The Wizard's Son,'** where Walter Methven and his mother live in a state of perpetual friction. Walter is leading an idle and useless life, with which, in his better moments, he is disgusted, but to which his mother's petulant and injudicious remonstrances always drive him back. (pp. 313-14)

Mrs Oliphant seems somewhat to have distrusted her own power of doing anything like justice to scenes and circumstances which had not come within the range of her own direct observation and experience. There is a modest disclaimer, for instance, in **'Madonna Mary,'** of any attempt to describe life in India: a disclaimer which forcibly reminds us who it is that rush in where persons like Mrs Oliphant fear to tread. . . . [We] prefer Mrs Oliphant's habit of frankly avowing ''ignorance, pure ignorance,'' and believe that she was well advised in her diffidence. With all her knowledge of history, at all events, and all her attachment to the past, the strictly historical novel was a *genre* in which she was wholly unsuccessful. **'Magdalen Hepburn,'** if it be readable, is nothing more.

What then, it may be asked, of the region which Mrs Oliphant made peculiarly her own—the region believed by most people to be wholly beyond the scope of the senses, the region of the ''unseen,'' of the supernatural? Mrs Oliphant manifestly had a strong predilection for topics transcending the limits of ordinary human experience, and we believe that in yielding to it she at once gratified the taste and stimulated the interest of an immense section of the public. We should rather conjecture, indeed, that she shared the illogical though widespread opinion that every well-attested case of a ghostly apparition is, somehow or other, an additional testimony to the truth of revealed religion. Whether such a belief contributes to the effective telling of a ghost-story may, however, very well be doubted; and Mrs Oliphant's ghost-stories, though workmanlike and dexterous (for she never relapsed into the amateurish), are neither very favourable specimens of her powers nor comparable to the efforts of others who were perhaps less inclined to believe than she. She is even more disappointing when she employs the supernatural in a long story. The mysterious stranger in **'The Wizard's Son'** is excellent up to a certain point; but how is a being to be held in awe whose very existence (as we are told) comes to be doubted by the persons whose lives he has powerfully influenced? A spectre who is merely the means of conveying moral lessons, and who once incurs the suspicion of representing nothing more imposing than some great moral or immoral principle, has lost his true occupation. (pp. 314-15)

In **'A Little Pilgrim'** Mrs Oliphant of course approaches the unseen on a much more serious and solemn side—a side on which no thinking man would willingly cast ridicule or contempt. We trust we are fully conscious of the simple and unaffected pathos, and of the deep and heartfelt reverence, with which the subject of the next world is treated; and we are sure that the pages of that little volume have carried consolation and refreshment to many a sorrowful and penitent heart. If the thing must be done, it could by no possibility be done better. (p. 315)

An indescribable sense of futility seems to be left behind by [Mrs Oliphant's] excursions into the supernatural. Granted that the city of Semur, in the Haute Bourgogne, was seized upon for three days by ''les morts'' in clouds and darkness, what is the ultimate result of their occupation? Nothing. When the inhabitants are permitted to return to their homes, everything resumes its former course. No one's character is permanently altered for better or for worse; and the only tangible outcome of the terrible visitation is that wonderful visions are attributed by the Sisters of Mercy to Pierre Plastron, who had remained behind in the town and seen nothing—as happy a flash of insight that into human character as can be found in all Mrs Oliphant's writings. We heartily agree with those who think **'A Beleaguered City'** a great book. But its interest lies not in the supernatural, but in the human; not in the doings of the ghostly invaders, but in the conduct of the men and women whom they drive outside the walls. The wife and the mother of the Maire are admirably characterised and discriminated. But it is Martin Dupin, the Maire himself—fussy, consequential, half-sceptical, half-credulous, affectionate, and stubborn—who dominates the book, and, in truth, he is one of Mrs Oliphant's greatest triumphs. Once more, too, we notice the astonishing ease, accuracy, and skill with which the ''atmosphere'' of life in a French provincial town is diffused over the work.

These, then, are two of the main qualities that mark Mrs Oliphant's writings—the sympathetic and masterly delineation of character, and the vivid presentation both of external scenes and of the circumstances in which the action of her personages takes place. When these excellences co-exist—which they by no means always do—little room is left for plot; nor was plot one of Mrs Oliphant's strong points. Not that she dealt in wild improbabilities, or inconceivable complications, or impossible disentanglements. Tact she never failed in. We can picture to ourselves how a writer of coarser fibre and more vulgar instincts would have revelled in marrying Mr Vincent to Lady Western, or how one of a more sarcastic and fiery temperament would have made him abandon in disgust the errors of dissent and embrace ''those of'' the Church. Mrs Oliphant knew better than either. Thus she kept well within the bounds of good sense and accuracy, and paid her readers the compliment of assuming that their intelligence was at least not below the average. (p. 316)

[In] reading Mrs Oliphant's novels one does not stop to think of the fable. One may sometimes look back and admire the ingenuity which brings about unexpected combinations of the pieces on the board, as in **'Phoebe, Junior,'** where the least likely thing in the world would seem to be the close friendship of Tozer's granddaughter, and Mr Northcote, the dissenting firebrand, with the family of so excellent a churchman as Mr May. But in nine cases out of ten the question one asks is not, What will the next conjuncture be? but, Given a certain conjuncture, how will the various characters comport themselves? When melodrama is introduced it is ineffective: the mysterious Mrs Hilyard is the one blot on **'Salem Chapel.'** Probably Mrs Oliphant's most successful attempt in the tragic vein is **'The Minister's Wife':** an impressive and powerful story, for all its inordinate length. (p. 317)

Differences of opinion must necessarily exist as to which of Mrs Oliphant's novels is the best, and we should not be disposed to quarrel with anyone who awarded the palm to **'Margaret Maitland.'** Modelled obviously upon Galt, it is a work of extraordinary finish and maturity for a young girl to have produced. The very idiom in which it is written is peculiarly attractive, and harmonises perfectly with the subject and scope of the tale. No genuine Scot can surely fail to be grateful to Mrs Oliphant for her pictures of his compatriots. Her Scottish servants—her Marg'ts, and Baubies, and Rollses—are perhaps a little conventional. . . . But all the rest of Mrs Oliphant's Scots characters come fresh from the mint, and bear the stamp of nature. (pp. 317-18)

With all respect and admiration for **'Margaret Maitland,'** however, our own view is that Mrs Oliphant reached the zenith of her art in the Carlingford series. What judicious selection of material! What dexterity of handling! What lightness of touch! It was a happy thought to group the characters round Church and Chapel, and it would be hard to say of which division the idiosyncrasies are most happily touched off. Perhaps, if anything, the dissenters are superior in execution. Or is it only that they are a little more amusing, and afford a more promising subject for humour to play about? Comparison with Trollope is, of course, irresistibly suggested; and we are not prepared to say that in 'Barchester Towers' he did not reach as high a level as Mrs Oliphant. . . . The future social historian, at all events, will find much matter in the **'Chronicles of Carlingford.'** . . . It is needless to run over the familiar characters who fit so admirably into the picture as a whole. But we must own to an exceptional regard and liking for Mr Tozer. The scene at the meeting in the chapel where he takes up the cudgels for Mr Vincent is one not easily forgotten. We have already indicated the opinion that **'Miss Marjoribanks'** is unrivalled as a study of female character. **'Salem Chapel'** has perhaps more bloom and freshness, yet we know of no substantial ground on which either should be preferred to **'The Perpetual Curate.'** We decline, accordingly, to draw invidious distinctions, and beg leave to bracket the three at the very top of the first class. (pp. 318-19)

> *[J. H. Millar], "Mrs. Oliphant as a Novelist," in* Blackwood's Edinburgh Magazine, *Vol. CLXII, No. DCCCCLXXXIII, September, 1897, pp. 305-19.*

GERTRUDE SLATER (essay date 1897)

[*Slater finds Oliphant's characterizations realistic and free of sentimentality and sensationalism.*]

Mrs. Oliphant is so exactly truthful that she has hardly had full praise given her for her truthfulness; her men and women are so absolutely the men and women of real life that it almost seems as if no art need have gone to their making: they are so very real that we have forgotten to call their creator a realist. Yet if by realism we mean, not a particular mannerism nor the acceptance of any particular catchword, but what it ought to mean, the habit of depicting men and women exactly as they are—a sight free from illusion, a hand inapt at exaggeration or suppression, and a disposition to use these gifts freely and simply—then there has never been a more uncompromising realist than Mrs. Oliphant.

No one is further than is she from making, or from trying to make, a flattering picture of life. She does not underline her sombre passages, or draw her readers' attention to the fact that in this or that personage she has ventured to draw an undilutedly bad character; but she is equally far from obeying the dictates of those very pessimistic readers who require their authors to look through frankly optimistic spectacles, paying human nature the very bad compliment of holding that it must be falsified to be made endurable. Mrs. Oliphant has never denied the shadows, and has introduced them into her pictures in due

proportion; and when, now and then, she is in the mood to draw a bad character, how relentlessly truthful she can be! In all our fiction there is scarcely a more odious picture of unlovely old age than is given in **Old Mr. Tredgold,** published last year; and it is not the physical or mental weaknesses, the accidents of senility, that disgusts us, but the utter sordidness of the man's soul. And who, except Mrs. Oliphant, would have ventured on such a conclusion to this story, a conclusion so entirely at variance with the requirements of poetic justice? (pp. 682-83)

No one is so kindly a critic as Mrs. Oliphant of the weaknesses of our poor humanity, or quicker to see how often they are entwined with its good; direct vice she rarely admits into her plots, but the heroic aspects of life figure there as seldom. Her characters are seldom cast in a grand mould, and this, it is to be feared, will be something of a hindrance to her future reputation, for nothing is a greater help to the public memory than the close association of an author's name with his principal characters. The mention of her name does not immediately call into mind certain of her creations, as George Eliot's name recalls Maggie Tulliver, or Thackeray's Becky Sharp. Her temperament leads her to give us in a novel a number of characters equally worked up, rather than one or two striking figures. Yet there are many instances that show that she had the poetic feeling that is necessary for the conception of a grand character. Who that has ever read their story could forget Diarmid and Ailie in **The Minister's Wife,** or Meredith in the **Son of the Soil,** or Drumcarro, Kirsteen's tempestuous father, the old giant who neglects and tyrannises over his daughters, but promptly throws Lord John over the cliff the moment he suspects him of trifling with one of them, and then dies of the excitement, though not in the least of compunction for the deed?

Mrs. Oliphant's religious studies are always marked by fine insight, and she can sometimes venture on the supernatural with marked success; her **Beleaguered City** is a book apart, and, on a lower level, **The Wizard's Son** is a wonderfully happy introduction of the marvellous, yet these books yield us no single striking character. That much-cultivated department of the novelist's province, romance, is little cultivated by her; hardly one of her books can, in the proper sense of the word, be called a love-story, **Kirsteen** being perhaps the nearest to one, for in that book, though one of the lovers is out of the story almost from the beginning, we are made to feel that it does really matter a great deal to the two young people's happiness whether they are brought together again or no. (pp. 686-87)

The sorrows of middle age, so much more poignant than the passionate griefs of the calf-love period, are Mrs. Oliphant's peculiar property. Lady Car's story stands for so many tragedies in real life—the disillusionment which comes to her from the husband who was to have been her hero, the foreknown bitterness of watching the son develop into a likeness of his father. More common, so common and ordained of nature that the sufferers themselves do not ask for pity, is the mother's sorrow in **Harry Joscelyn**—"She saw her children now and then, and they were all happy and in no need of her. What could any woman want more?" . . . Mrs. Oliphant reverses the novelist's natural bias in favour of youth; her older men are more likeable than her boys, and some of her most attaching women characters, such as Lady Car and Evelyn in **The Railway Man and His Children,** have left their youth behind them.

It is very characteristic of Mrs. Oliphant that when, as very rarely happens, there is something of the sensational in her plot, it is on very unexpected persons that the sensation centres.

Sensational in spirit and treatment she cannot be, but the few occasions on which she approaches the sensational in theme markedly illustrate her unconventionality. **Madonna Mary** is the story of a most esteemed and beloved lady who lives for years on the brink of a precipice, knowing that at any moment her elder children may be branded with the unjust stain of illegitimacy; and at last it is her own son who brings the accusation against her. In **Madam** we have suspicion attaching itself to a matron equally honoured and loved, of apparently still firmer position socially. (p. 688)

What a wonderfully full portrait-gallery hers is! If there are few portraits in it of very exceptional physiognomy, it embraces every variety of our every-day folk in their ordinary habit, and no artist has given these with more fidelity and minuteness. It might have been thought that this art, so unflinchingly truthful, yet so completely free from the spice of truth, satire, would not be sufficiently appreciated; but Mrs. Oliphant's early recognition by the reading public and her enduring popularity are happy tokens, and prove again, if further proof were necessary, that nothing in literature is so sure of success as honesty of workmanship. Mrs. Oliphant has followed the natural bent of her talent, making no concessions to the supposed demands of the public either on the point of sensation or of sentiment, and the result has shown her wisdom. Whether many generations will continue to hold her in remembrance, and, better still, to read her, is a matter on which it is idle to speculate; we ourselves allow so many novelists of so varied talent to lie forgotten on their shelves. But here again there seems to be no better merit in which to trust than this one of truthfulness. Where anything of the false has been allowed to creep in, though an author's contemporaries may like him the better for it, the flaw is bound to show in time; and it is just on these two sides, of sensation and of sentiment, that the novelist is likely to be led into falsity. Dickens' wonderful exaggerations, full of genius as they are, already are turning that enchanted country of his into too much of a fairyland; and how unreadable is the stale sentiment of a Lytton! To put too much of even absolutely genuine sentiment into a book is a somewhat dangerous proceeding, and there are many fine passages in George Eliot's novels which one is half inclined to wish away for that reason. But Mrs. Oliphant has steered very clear of these two dangers; and while people continue to be interested in reading about men and women there seems to be no reason why they should not continue to read the books in which her men and women are so well described. (pp. 689-90)

Gertrude Slater, "Mrs. Oliphant as a Realist," in The Westminster Review, *Vol. CXLVIII, No. 6, December, 1897, pp. 682-90.*

HENRY JAMES   (essay date 1897)

[*James was an American-born English novelist, short story writer, critic, and essayist of the late nineteenth and early twentieth centuries. Regarded as one of the greatest novelists of the English language, James is also admired as a lucid and insightful critic. In the following excerpt from an essay written in 1897, James commends Oliphant's "extraordinary fecundity" and storytelling ability, proclaiming her a "great* improvisatrice.*"*]

[Mrs. Oliphant's] success had been in its day as great as her activity, yet it was always present to me that her singular gift was less recognised, or at any rate less reflected, less reported upon, than it deserved: unless indeed she may have been one of those difficult cases for criticism, an energy of which the spirit and the form, straggling apart, never join hands with that

effect of union which in literature more than anywhere else is strength.

Criticism, among us all, has come to the pass of being shy of difficult cases, and no one, for that matter, practised it more in the hit-or-miss fashion and on happy-go-lucky lines than Mrs. Oliphant herself. She practised it, as she practised everything, on such an inordinate scale that her biographer, if there is to be one, will have no small task in the mere drafting of lists of her contributions to magazines and journals in general and to "Blackwood" in particular. She wrought in "Blackwood" for years, anonymously and profusely; no writer of the day found a *porte-voix* nearer to hand or used it with an easier personal latitude and comfort. (p. 452)

The explanation of her extraordinary fecundity was a rare original equipment, an imperturbability of courage, health and brain, to which was added the fortune or the merit of her having had to tune her instrument at the earliest age. That instrument was essentially a Scotch one; her stream flowed long and full without losing its primary colour. To say that she was organised highly for literature would be to make too light of too many hazards and conditions; but few writers of our time have been so organised for liberal, for—one may almost put it—heroic production. One of the interesting things in big persons is that they leave us plenty of questions, if only about themselves; and precisely one of those that Mrs. Oliphant suggests is the wonder and mystery of a love of letters that could be so great without ever, on a single occasion even, being greater. It was of course not a matter of mere love; it was a part of her volume and abundance that she understood life itself in a fine free-handed manner and, I imagine, seldom refused to risk a push at a subject, however it might have given pause, that would help to turn her wide wheel. She worked largely from obligation—to meet the necessities and charges and pleasures and sorrows of which she had a plentiful share. She showed in it all a sort of sedentary dash—an acceptance of the day's task and an abstention from the plaintive note from which I confess I could never withhold my admiration. (p. 453)

She had small patience with new-fangled attitudes or with a finical conscience. What was good enough for Sir Walter was good enough for her, and I make no doubt that her shrewd unfiltered easy flow, fed after all by an immensity of reading as well as of observation and humour, would have been good enough for Sir Walter. If this had been the case with her abounding history, biography and criticism, it would have been still more the case with her uncontrolled flood of fiction. She was really a great *improvisatrice*, a night-working spinner of long, loose, vivid yarns, numberless, pauseless, admirable, repeatedly, for their full, pleasant, reckless rustle over depths and difficulties—admirable indeed, in any case of Scotch elements, for many a close engagement with these. She showed in no literary relation more acuteness than in the relation—so profitable a one as it has always been—to the inexhaustible little country which has given so much, yet has ever so much more to give, and all the romance and reality of which she had at the end of her pen. Her Scotch folk have a wealth of life, and I think no Scotch talk in fiction less of a strain to the patience of the profane. It may be less austerely veracious than some—but these are esoteric matters. (p. 454)

[Reading **"Kirsteen"**] I was, though beguiled, not too much beguiled to be struck afresh with that elusive fact on which I just touched, the mixture in the whole thing. Such a product as **"Kirsteen"** has life—is full of life, but the critic is infinitely baffled. It may of course be said to him that he has nothing to do with compositions of this order—with such wares altogether as Mrs. Oliphant dealt in. But he can accept that retort only with a renunciation of some of his liveliest anxieties. Let him take some early day for getting behind, as it were, the complexion of a talent that could care to handle a thing to the tune of so many pages and yet not care more to "do" it. There is a fascination in the mere spectacle of so serene an instinct for the middle way, so visible a conviction that to reflect is to be lost.

Mrs. Oliphant was never lost, but she too often saved herself at the expense of her subject. I have no space to insist, but so much of the essence of the situation in **"Kirsteen"** strikes me as missed, dropped out without a thought, that the wonder is all the greater of the fact that in spite of it the book does in a manner scramble over its course and throw up a fresh strong air. This was certainly the most that the author would have pretended, and from her scorn of precautions springs a gleam of impertinence quite in place in her sharp and handsome physiognomy, that of a person whose eggs are not all in one basket, nor all her imagination in service at once. There is scant enough question of "art" in the matter, but there is a friendly way for us to feel about so much cleverness, courage and humanity. We meet the case in wishing that the timed talents were a little more like her and the bold ones a little less. (pp. 454-55)

Henry James, *"London Notes, August 1897," in his* Notes on Novelists, with Some Other Notes, *Charles Scribner's Sons, 1914, pp. 446-55.**

[J. H. MILLAR]   (essay date 1899)

[*In the following excerpt from a posthumous tribute to Oliphant, Millar reviews her* Autobiography and Letters *and discusses her contributions to* Blackwood's Edinburgh Magazine. *For additional commentary by Millar, see excerpt dated 1897.*]

Whatever merits or defects this remarkable volume [**'The Autobiography and Letters of Mrs M. O. W. Oliphant'**] may possess, no one can deny its absolute straightforwardness. You feel instinctively that the writer is in good faith; and, whether you approve or disapprove, whether you censure or applaud, you cannot help acknowledging the frankness of the record. Not one line is written for mere effect; not one sentence but is stamped with the unmistakable hall-mark of the writer's mind and heart. (p. 895)

It is difficult to believe that the narrative could have been more free from affectation and pretence, more open and more intimate. . . . We will not call this book a human document; we will not say that it echoes with the true *cri du coeur*. Such phraseology would have moved Mrs Oliphant to just indignation and disgust. She detested all cant, and none more than that of introspection—the jargon of the *"psychologues."* But here is, no question, that combination of qualities which those slang terms so inadequately express. He who seeks an elaborate exposition of changes of belief—a pompous recital of how a first reading of Hegel made the writer think this, and a prolonged study of Mr Herbert Spencer made her think that—will, indeed, go empty away. Those who care for complacent whimperings over the loss of a creed never seriously held, or who love the lucubrations of such as brood, with a self-pitying, self-satisfied melancholy, upon the ruins of a faith which has yielded to the "pressure of the German historical movement" (Mesopotamic phrase!)—such persons may be directed to go elsewhere. To them this must needs appear the eminently "prosaic little narrative" which Mrs Oliphant avows it to be. But over

the more ordinary members of the human race, who have little taste for reasoning high on such matters, it will cast an irresistible spell. Its power and attraction are not to be gauged by mere extracts. It must be read as a whole—the correspondence . . . illustrating Mrs Oliphant's own story; and, so read, it cannot, we should imagine, appeal in vain to any save the most stolid or the most supercilious of mankind. (pp. 895-96)

No other contributor [to 'Maga'], except Aytoun, approached her versatility and diligence. . . . With the exception of purely political subjects, there was almost no topic on which she was not prepared to write. Old-fashioned in her ideas, she preferred the system of anonymous to that of signed articles; but she held out vigorously for her own views when they were not in harmony with the Editor's, as the correspondence sufficiently testifies. She was extremely plain-spoken in her comments on the Magazine upon occasion, and in writing to the Editor did not hesitate to stigmatise any article as "dreadful nonsense" if she thought it so. As a critic she was fair and open-minded: not averse from "a little slashing" when that operation seemed necessary, and well able to apply the rod to serious delinquents. Her opinions were strongly held, and sometimes, perhaps, prevented her from catching the true drift of ideas with which she was unfamiliar. Yet she had no "fads" or eccentricities, no logs to roll, no axes to grind; and in the great majority of cases her views were both sensible and sound. Long practice had endowed her with a species of instinct for discovering the salient points of a book at a mere glance and on the first turning over of the leaves. The knack of what is called "journalism" she possessed in an unusual degree. Her "copy," particularly in the case of her more important articles, was often delayed till the last possible moment, but never longer. She was extraordinarily apt and ready at taking up a hint, and at working into her articles any new line of thought or argument suggested to her, provided always that it did not conflict with her own prejudices or convictions. In that case she was tenacious to the point of obstinacy; nor did she face the task of recasting a completed work with any more equanimity than her neighbours. Yet, when the first shock of annoyance was past, she was often wise enough to profit by distasteful advice; and **'The Beleaguered City'** is a striking instance of judicious, though at the time, perhaps, reluctant, deference to the counsel of another. She wrote *currente calamo*. It was impossible to foretell what length her articles would "run to": she herself had probably little notion when she took up her pen. Hence a slight readjustment of balance or proportion might sometimes have effected a perceptible improvement. But these shortcomings were trivial indeed in comparison with her abounding merits. No periodical was ever better or more loyally served by a contributor: not the 'Quarterly' by Croker, not the 'Saturday Review' by Venables, scarce even 'Maga' herself by John Wilson or Professor Aytoun. (pp. 902-03)

We believe that the judgment of the public upon Mrs Oliphant's life and character will be conceived in terms infinitely more favourable than she . . . anticipated. But what, after all, does the verdict of her contemporaries or of posterity matter? She has passed to the bar of a Tribunal whose Justice and whose Mercy are infinite; and, in so far as it is permissible to mortals to attempt to penetrate within the veil, we may rest assured that she is reaping the reward allotted, by the express promise of the Almighty, to all those who in their day and generation have been good and faithful servants. (p. 904)

[*J. H. Millar*], *"The Record of a Life," in* Blackwood's Edinburgh Magazine, *Vol. CLXV, No. MIII, May, 1899, pp. 895-904.*

[H. W. PRESTON] (essay date 1899)

[*The following excerpt is from a positive review of* Autobiography and Letters.]

Such as it is, the record [*Autobiography and Letters of Mrs. Oliphant*] is a welcome one. It has not much of the interest which one usually expects from such a life. Mrs. Oliphant's existence was singularly retired, and such literary personages as she mixed with were mostly of the second rank. Only here and there do we get a glimpse of a Carlyle, a Kinglake, or a Tennyson. She esteemed herself a bad observer; and here, certainly, she does not show the gift of setting a personality on paper or recording characteristic touches. The interest of the book lies elsewhere—in its unaffected portrayal of a typical English gentlewoman's life during the middle century, peacefully absorbed in children and husband. It is a little epic of the domesticities. (p. 553)

> [*H. W. Preston*], "*The Autobiography of Mrs. Oliphant,*" *in* The Academy, *Vol. 56, No. 1411, May 20, 1899, pp. 553-54.*

STEPHEN GWYNN (essay date 1929)

[*In the following excerpt, Gwynn assesses Oliphant's place in literature. While commending her simple and natural technique, Gwynn asserts that Oliphant will not "continue to hold a place in literature for the sake of her style." Instead, she will be remembered for her stories of the unseen world and for her depiction of the bond between mother and child. According to Gwynn, the overall quality, content, and production of Oliphant's work were determined by her roles as a woman and a mother. Her preoccupation with her children and her daily responsibilities prevented her from devoting time to more serious writing. Thus, Gwynn concludes, motherhood was, for Oliphant, both "the hindrance to high achievement in the way of the novelist's art" and "the inspiration of the wisest and most beautiful things that she wrote."*]

[Mrs. Oliphant's] fragmentary Autobiography—even such pages as are merely reminiscences—shows the woman as she was: a creature in whom intensity of feeling was matched with incisive intellect, prone to analysis, stripping off all illusions and going to the very heart of things, finding bitterness enough, but never losing hope; strong to act, strong to think, strong to endure, and strong to believe; womanly in everything, keen with a woman's keenness, and strong with a woman's strength. Such a temper and faculties in one endowed with a rare gift of expression cannot but have left something that will last, and the best service that can be done to her memory is to disencumber the vital parts in her achievement. Work that means little to its author can never mean much to the world, and it is easy to see from the Autobiography, and from stray passages in the letters, when Mrs. Oliphant wrote because there was a thing in her that demanded to be uttered. We may dismiss at once all the history, biography, and the rest, as hackwork, yet need not for a moment allow that by doing this work she in any way disqualified herself for doing better. All Goldsmith's drudgery—and he wrote, as he said himself pathetically, a volume a month—never harmed *The Vicar of Wakefield;* rather, it went to give that ease of the much practised hand which is half the charm of his masterpiece. And knowledge is never amiss, and the variety of Mrs. Oliphant's enforced reading gave a richness to her writing. It does not keep one on the stretch with continual expectation of the unexpected word: it is never contorted or tormented, never emphatic, never affected. The words flow simply and smoothly, like the utterance of a perfectly well-bred woman, talking sometimes eagerly, sometimes with a grave earnestness, but more often with a delicate undercurrent of laughter in the tone; and the style answers by a sort of instinct to each inflection of the voice. She is thinking more about what she has to say than about the way in which she is to say it; and Mrs. Oliphant was one of the fortunate who had none of the vehemences and eccentricities of temperament which make it difficult for the writer to arrive at a harmonious manner of expression; nor was she obliged to hide mediocrity under a solemn vesture of language. She knew instinctively the mode of expression suited to her talent, and she was delighted to make the most of it. She had the artist's pleasure "in small technical successes" that Stevenson writes of, and was, by her own avowal, "ever more really satisfied by some little conscious felicity of words than by anything else." (pp. 224-26)

[Although] Mrs. Oliphant is not Goldsmith, she is far nearer to the best English than nine-tenths of the later writers whom it is the fashion to praise for excellence in style. She wrote sometimes worse, sometimes better, always with a certain looseness of texture in the sentence; but from her earliest beginnings to the latest of her work there was never a period in which one could not pick out from her writings passages of rare beauty and charm. *Miss Marjoribanks,* perhaps the best written of all her novels, is a model of refined irony—the most difficult of all qualities to achieve—and the conscious pleasure of workmanship is apparent in the neatly turned sentences which round off each chapter cleanly, as if with the crack of a whip, while the laugh hides itself behind a studied decorum of phrase. But for the best of Mrs. Oliphant's writing we should go to the evening of her life—to the period when according to a certain cant of criticism her whole faculty must have been blunted and worn down by her lifelong disregard of the minuter delicacies of language. The melody in it is simple and not greatly varied; yet there are few pieces of English writing more musical than the *Little Pilgrim in the Unseen.*

It could not, however, be plausibly asserted that Mrs. Oliphant will continue to hold a place in literature for the sake of her style. The versatility of her mind, the variety and extent of her work may secure her a place in the dictionaries, but will not keep her memory alive. If she survives at all it must be in some sort or other as a writer of fiction; and the stories which have a chance to live must be those in which she herself was most interested—into which, consciously or unconsciously, she put most of herself. Without the Autobiography one could guess readily enough: with it we ought to be able to know. It is a little difficult, however, because Mrs. Oliphant, as she says, never took herself or her work very seriously.

> I have written because it gave me pleasure,
> because it came natural to me, because it was
> like talking or breathing, besides the big fact
> that it was necessary for me to work for my
> children.

That passage illustrates at once the strength and the weakness of her gift. She wrote simply from a pleasure in the occupation, to pass away long hours by her mother's bedside. Her family were sympathetic, and made an audience to whom she read out her early attempts; they delighted at her success, but they never talked to her of genius, or encouraged her to spell art with a capital A. Her gift was encouraged and applauded, "but always with a hidden sense that it was an admirable joke." She did her writing at a corner of the family table, joining in whatever talk was going just as if she "had been making a shirt instead of writing a book." . . . Mrs. Oliphant never lived in the life of her characters, as Trollope, for instance, describes himself to have done, and that is why Trollope, in many respects so inferior to her, is, nevertheless, a greater novelist. Mrs. Oliphant's characters were to her—it is her own illustration—no more than people in a book; and the reason is not far to seek. There were always other things far more engrossing to occupy her mind. Womanlike, she lived her life chiefly in the interests of those about her, and those concerns were always of a nature to leave her no breathing space "to labour with an artist's fervour and concentration to produce a masterpiece." (pp.227-30)

[Mrs. Oliphant's best work] cannot be placed higher than in the second rank of fiction; lower certainly than Trollope's best work. Yet Mrs. Oliphant had gifts denied to Trollope; she had eloquence, charm of style, grace and ease where he is heavy and clumsy; above all, she had the power to construct a story full of high-strung situations, yet in no way sinning against common sense; and her insight into feminine character and her skill to depict it at least rival his mastery over men. Why with all these advantages does she get no further? What is it that sets the dividing line between her and George Eliot, or Charlotte Brontë? (p. 237)

It is what may be called force or sincerity: the result of the artist's passionate absorption in his work. Mrs. Oliphant complains in her Autobiography that she spoiled her fortunes by making light to others of her own work. In reality she made light of it to herself. It did not mean much to her. . . . Mrs. Oliphant was a woman and a mother, and the innermost preoccupation of her mind—the point to which her fluctuating thoughts would always swing back—was her children. The women who have been great artists have been childless women. (pp. 238-39)

The art of the poet indeed may incorporate with itself any emotion; and Mrs. Oliphant revealed the best of her in work that is essentially poetry. But happiness seldom needs to find a voice; and in the days when the first *Carlingford* tales were being written, Mrs. Oliphant was thoroughly happy. It was not for long. (p. 239)

[Following the deaths of her daughter and nephew, Mrs. Oliphant] wrote the first of her stories of the Unseen—*The Beleaguered City*—which relates how in the city of Semur the dead by reason of the impiety of the living came back, and for a little while ousted the sinners from their homes; and how during those days the men encamped round about the town, which was enveloped in a thick darkness, but were at every point repulsed from it by an invisible and impassable barrier. Mrs. Oliphant possessed that art of circumstantial invention in which Swift, Defoe and Bunyan are the great masters. Like them she obtains a credibility for her narrative by presenting vividly through the narrative the character of the narrator. There is no other man known to us in her books so distinctly as the Mayor of Semur, who draws up, as if officially, the *procès-verbal* of the whole affair: just a good type of the French *bourgeois*—brave, homely, kindly, full of a sense of duty and of law's majesty, especially as incorporated in his own official person; Voltairian by temper and training, yet respectful to the amiable beliefs of others. He begins and ends the story of the exodus and the return. But in the meanwhile other narratives are included: the story told by Lecamus, the visionary, a living man, yet more at home among the dead than the living, to whom it was permitted to stay in the town and at last to come with a message from the dead to those who would not be convinced; and, chiefly, the narrative of Agnès Dupin, the Mayor's wife, one of those more spiritually-minded women

who saw as well as felt when the invisible hands pushed the population out of the gates. She saw what no man saw, what only some among the women could see—she saw her dead child.

There you have the key to it all. To certain men perhaps the dead are not dead; the wife of Lecamus comes back to him, and for a moment they have the joy of each other's presence: Mrs. Oliphant writes of this as if she believed it. But that the dead are to many mothers truly living is more than a belief with her; it is a kind of revelation. What she writes of again and again in all these fancies of the Unseen is the meeting and greeting between mother and child. The only blessedness that she can conceive of is something like the highest blessedness that she knew in this world, but perfected and completed. (pp. 244-46)

And because she was an artist this strong central preoccupation [with the unseen world] took shape in form of art. *The Beleaguered City,* which is, properly speaking, not a story but a poem, though it is pitched studiously in the key of prose, and touched often with a delicate humour, was the first work of her life which she wrote neither for amusement nor to make money, but because she was possessed by it. . . . And to the end of her life stories of the unseen she could only write—as she expresses it herself—when they came to her; they were not written to order or for money. (pp. 247-48)

Motherhood was the soul of Mrs. Oliphant's life; it was the hindrance to high achievement in the way of the novelist's art; it was also the inspiration of the wisest and most beautiful things that she wrote. (p. 256)

Stephen Gwynn, "A Mother," in his Saints & Scholars, *Thorton Butterworth, Limited, 1929, pp. 221-56.*

MARION LOCHHEAD   (essay date 1961)

[*Lochhead discusses Oliphant's use of sin, mystery, and comedy. In her best work, according to Lochhead, Oliphant concentrates exclusively on mystery and sin or on comedic situations. When all three of these elements are combined, however, her works are less successful.*]

A sense of sin is an excellent thing in a novelist, besides being conducive to repentance in general. It is evident in most Victorian fiction but too rare in that of to-day, unless in detective novels. When along with this awareness go charity and understanding, the result is a singularly agreeable personality; with more than a dash of irony and cynicism added, the mixture is piquant. All these are found in that unjustly neglected novelist Mrs. Oliphant. For the neglect she is partly herself to blame; she wrote, as she admitted, too copiously and too fast, because she had the capacity, and was driven by necessity. She was as matter-of-fact as Trollope about her work, and her cynicism extended to her own talent. (p. 300)

Mrs. Oliphant used sin, and her own vivid sense of sin, to add colour to her narratives: a splash of vermilion on the canvas, a flamboyant trimming on a discreet dress. Jane Austen's cynicism is transmuted into perfect art; Mrs. Oliphant's sense of sin could become an artistic flaw. She can hurl her characters into crime, as actors or as victims, for the excitement of it. Sin itself she deplores, showing clearly its tragic consequences, but the 'certain soft despair of any one human creature ever doing good to another' which she found in Jane Austen is often apparent in her own novels, especially as regards her men. Women now and then do something real and valuable; a woman may indeed save a man, as Oonah, in *The Wizard's Son,* saves Walter. But for men, on the whole, this valiant woman had only a modified use. (pp. 308-09)

Her sense of sin and her cynicism together produced quantities of sensation. It can be entertaining, but it is not always good art, not always credible, nor are her villains.

There is a fearful scoundrel in *Salem Chapel,* so frightful that his wife, one of the few incredibles, not only leaves him but tries to murder him; what, precisely, he has done we are not told. Novels being intended for family reading, must not be too explicit, and sex must have its head kept down. Walter Methuen in *The Wizard's Son* is led wildly astray by the 'Wizard' who haunts his family, but we are given no details of his scarlet sins. (p. 309)

In an earlier day, or with less education and no need to write, she would, like her mother, have been an inspired story-teller. The conventions of her time circumscribed her; and she was as lavish in her plots as in her spending. Sensation was popular, so she bestowed it largely. *Salem Chapel* could have been a masterpiece of comedy, but she 'farced' it (in the culinary sense) with incredible crime. The best of Carlingfords is probably *Miss Marjoribanks;* it is pure comedy of character, and the heroine, who is a pale reflection of Emma, but also a personage in her own right, would have delighted [the author of *Emma,*] Jane Austen. *Phoebe Junior* has the same astringency; sensation intrudes again, though not so much as in *Salem Chapel.* Neither of these young women is the conventional, ideal heroine; they are both clever, managing, Miss Marjoribanks prone to error, Phoebe admirably adroit. Neither is cold-hearted, and both win our amused affection.

When Mrs. Oliphant concentrates either on mystery and sin or on comedy, she is at her best. In the one class *Merkland* and *The Wizard's Son* are admirable, in the other *Miss Marjoribanks, Phoebe Junior, The Sorceress,* and *The Richest Heiress in England.* These last two are extremely entertaining, delightfully ironical, gently mocking. It is when she mixes her two elements that she is at her weakest. With an excellent cellar of wine, she too often dispensed cocktails. There is also the third class—her tales of the unseen in which she comes near poetry. *The Open Door* has the poignancy of a ballad; *The Beleagured City* is a moving parable, compassionate, yet with that 'soft despair,' for its text is: 'Neither will they be persuaded though one rose from the dead.'

She by no means lacked humour; but she kept it too carefully in control. It gleams out from time to time in her novels, and in her reviews and criticism. There is a sudden flash in her review of Trollope's *Last Chronicle of Barsetshire.* Having expressed the disbelief of all right-minded people in the death of Mrs. Proudie, she amplifies her assertion. That redoubtable woman did not, as her author vainly declared, suffer from any heart-disease. If she died, it was by murder or at least manslaughter. And it was the Bishop 'who done it.'

A great and beautiful thought! The mind that conceived it could have given us much more entertainment. . . . Mrs. Oliphant too often drew a cloak and veil over her daftness, her *gaminerie,* as she did over her knowledge of evil, over her liking for Bohemia and all its wayward citizens.

Had she lived to-day, how would she have developed? There is the possibility that she would have become a mediocre best-seller, pouring out the same stream of serials, enlarged further by the scope of television and radio. But there is the alternative

that having absorbed the modern technique she would have disciplined the form of her work, giving us fewer books but more masterpieces. Her humour, her realism, would have had more freedom. It is possible, too, even probable, that she would have written in two separate *genres:* the novel of romance and comedy; and the detective story. In the latter, strict discipline of form would have been essential; but she had it in her to produce a first-class whodunit.

Whatever might have been, she remains a story-teller, an entertainer of high rank, who should not be neglected. (pp. 309-10)

> Marion Lochhead, "Margaret Oliphant: A Half-Forgotten Victorian," in The Quarterly Review, *Vol. 299, July, 1961, pp. 300-10.*

VINETA COLBY AND ROBERT A. COLBY (essay date 1966)

[*In the only twentieth-century book-length study of Oliphant, the Colbys examine Oliphant's life and works, focusing on the personal factors that influenced her literary career. In the following excerpt, they discuss each of the novels that form the* Chronicles of Carlingford *and maintain that the excessive length of the novels, as well as Oliphant's intent to popularize the works by means of intricate plots and melodrama, have undermined the series' lasting success.*]

Mrs. Oliphant's Carlingford, like [Trollope's Barchester and George Eliot's Middlemarch], is a country of the mind. It lacks the breadth and depth of Middlemarch and the minute particularity of Barchester. On the one hand it is not, as is George Eliot's imagined community, a microcosm, a universalization of the whole pattern of Victorian provincial life. On the other, neither does it have a local habitation, as Trollope's community had in Salisbury, nor its precise geographical detail. It would be impossible to draw a map of Carlingford and difficult to illustrate the scenes and characters of the Carlingford novels. Yet the scenes are described with sufficient vividness so that Carlingford emerges as a place with an identity of its own. It is a pleasant, sleepy little town, far enough from London to be free of its pressures yet close enough for its inhabitants to run up in a short rail journey whenever the plot demands it. (pp. 41-2)

Seven works of fiction comprise the **"Chronicles of Carlingford."** Three, *The Executor, The Rector,* and *The Doctor's Family,* are long short stories. Indeed, *The Executor* and *The Doctor's Family* may claim to be part of the series only because they are set in Carlingford, but they form no real part of the Carlingford scheme. The longer novels are two which center mainly on clerical life, *Salem Chapel* [and *The Perpetual Curate*] . . . with clergymen as their leading characters, and two which center mainly on social life in the community, *Miss Marjoribanks* [and *Phoebe, Junior*] . . . , with young women as their leading characters. (p. 43)

The major theme which unites the three principal religious stories of the series is vocation for the priesthood. It is a subject so serious that one wonders at Mrs. Oliphant's daring to treat it at all. On closer examination one finds she was peculiarly well suited by background and by sympathy for the subject. Because of the popular success of *Salem Chapel* and the relative obscurity into which the other novels fell soon after their publication, it is generally assumed that the Carlingford series was about Dissenters and the Dissenting Church only. Mrs. Oliphant was not a Dissenter herself. Only *Salem Chapel* and *Phoebe, Junior* actually treat of the Dissenting movement. The Rector, in the story of that name, is a staunch member of the

Church of England, as is the hero of *The Perpetual Curate;* and while some Low Church members figure amusingly in the latter novel, Dissent has no place in it. Indeed, it is the question of how High a man may go short of conversion to Roman Catholicism which is central in this work.

Still it is true that her picture of the Dissenting congregation of Salem Chapel was the great attraction of that novel for Victorian readers. This gave the book its ring of truth and of originality—an inside view of an independent congregation presented with candor and humor and with just enough snobbish condescension to appeal to a predominantly Church of England reading public for whom the popular image of the Dissenter was still a vulgar, hymn-singing tradesman. (pp. 45-6)

The Rector, the shortest of the Carlingford series and a fine story in its own right, is an excellent illustration of . . . self-analysis on the part of a clergyman. Mr. Morley Proctor, a gentle, middle-aged bachelor, comes to his post in Carlingford after fifteen quiet years as a Fellow of All Souls. Faced with the practical demands of a congregation, he soon begins to doubt his fitness for the office. He is socially awkward and shy. When called to minister at the deathbed of a parishioner, he is helpless and tongue-tied. In contrast, his poised young curate Wentworth ("not half nor a quarter part so learned as he, but a world further on in that profession which they shared—the art of winning souls") knows how to say and do all the right things, leaving the older man painfully aware of his own inadequacies. The Rector preaches his sober, learned sermons to "a crowd of unsympathetic, uninterested faces." Defeated, not by an action of his congregation but by his own conscience, he resigns his post and returns to the academic life. Here, however, he is now curiously dissatisfied, remembering not only his failures but the parallel situation of the aging spinster Miss Wodehouse. . . . Yet the story does not end on this gloomy note. Almost as an afterthought Mrs. Oliphant adds a hopeful last paragraph suggesting that Proctor will marry Miss Wodehouse (as he does in *The Perpetual Curate*) and return to the world.

In one sense *Salem Chapel* is an expansion of the theme treated so delicately and charmingly in *The Rector.* Mr. Vincent, many years younger and far more gifted for clerical life than Mr. Proctor, has nevertheless the same problem. He too comes to doubt his fitness for the office, at least as it is administered in his church, and in the end he too resigns with a keen sense of personal failure. Had Mrs. Oliphant explored and developed the idea at leisure, she would certainly have produced a better book. Unfortunately, she set out to write a best seller. More unfortunately, from the point of view of her literary reputation, she succeeded. Artistically it is a failure. Her interesting young hero becomes enmeshed in a crudely melodramatic plot almost totally obscuring the important issues of the book. (pp. 48-9)

There can be no doubt that the intrigue of *Salem Chapel* was devised with *The Woman in White* in mind. No element of the fantastic enters into it, although the coincidences and improbabilities are so gross as to be almost fantastic. As in Collins' novel, the villainy for all its horrible threats comes to nothing. No one is killed—though there is attempted murder, abduction (with threats of seduction), concealed identities, and two victimized young women, one who is driven nearly mad, the other who is feeble-minded. But where Collins' plot holds the reader in breathless suspense, Mrs. Oliphant's simply confuses. (pp. 50-1)

Salem Chapel is not the only example in Mrs. Oliphant's work of a potentially good novel which is almost wrecked by the author's efforts to make it a best seller, but it is a particularly unfortunate example because there is so much in it both promising and original. Vincent, the hero, is finely conceived. He is the "unheroic" intellectual hero—self-centered, arrogant, insecure. Outside his pulpit and his study he is weak and ineffectual. He goes dashing off on well meaning but futile efforts to rescue his sister. He is forever five minutes too late or miles off in the wrong direction. Instead of being a comfort and support to his widowed mother—a typical Oliphant mother, weak and genteel but where her children are concerned a giantess of energy and strength—he withdraws into his own problems and ignores her. In matters of romance he also behaves foolishly and unheroically, falling madly in love with a woman socially superior but spiritually unworthy of him and suffering agonies of what he knows is hopeless passion.

The really valid issue of the novel is the character of this young man, "well educated and enlightened according to his fashion . . . yet so entirely unacquainted with any world but that contracted one in which he had been brought up" . . . , and the gradual discovery he makes of his unfitness for his chosen profession. (pp. 52-3)

The Perpetual Curate did not sell as well as its predecessor. It is, however, a far better novel. Whether at [her publisher] Blackwood's urging or in response to her own good taste, she avoided melodrama and the sensational. The story concerns the struggles of an upright young clergyman, Frank Wentworth, of rather "High" persuasion, to find a secure living in which he will not have to compromise his principles. The obstacles in his way are the community itself, full of gossip and misunderstanding, the enmity of his hot-tempered rector, Dr. Morgan, and his own rather divided and confused family. Mrs. Oliphant introduces a subplot which is potentially lurid (a mysterious bearded stranger, the disappearance of a young girl, for which the hero is blamed) but which actually proves to be comic. The bearded stranger is a disreputable but harmless scapegrace brother; the abducted girl is a silly young thing who fully deserves and enjoys the scandal she causes. This is the first of the Carlingford novels in which the parallel to the Barsetshire series is noticeable, although Mrs. Oliphant was not indebted to Trollope for specific details. Yet the novel has the happy insularity that is so characteristic of Trollope's clerical novels—the self-contained, snug world of the Established Church and the squirearchy: stubborn, outspoken older clergymen and their patient wives, strong-minded spinsters, oily and unctuous curates, stalwart but rather unworldly heroes, and dewy-eyed but common-sensical heroines. Into this mild and pleasant atmosphere, however, Mrs. Oliphant introduces one far more serious issue—a clergyman who becomes converted to Catholicism. She treats the subject with delicacy and sympathy. While it may seem at first glance a jarring note in the otherwise smooth harmony of the book, it in fact gives the novel greater depth and interest. The weakness of *The Perpetual Curate* is a characteristic failing in Mrs. Oliphant's fiction. It is too long. There is simply not enough incident to support its length. Where *Salem Chapel* suffered from an excess of incident, *The Perpetual Curate* suffers from a deficiency. But the fact that she manages to sustain the reader's interest even when nothing important is happening is a tribute to her skill. Making bricks without straw was becoming a habit with her. (pp. 56-7)

There is a good deal of fairly serious religious matter in *The Perpetual Curate* including a theological discussion between the two brothers which is a simplified but not oversimplified debate on the Oxford Movement—with Gerald clinging desperately to the ''rock of authority'' which Rome offers him, and Frank accepting the mysteries of existence, his own doubts and perplexities, as part of his fundamental faith. But Mrs. Oliphant carefully keeps the balance between religion and social comedy. Unlike *Salem Chapel, The Perpetual Curate* moves smoothly from one plane to another, its material thoroughly integrated. (pp. 60-1)

Mrs. Oliphant's comedy in *The Perpetual Curate* is gentle and her satire mild. Even while she laughs at her characters and holds their weaknesses up to mockery, she treats them with sympathy. (p. 61)

The gentle humor of *The Perpetual Curate,* the sympathy and compassion for human weakness, turn into chilling satire in *Miss Marjoribanks.* There are traces of the old tenderness now and then—for example, a sketch of a devoted elderly couple who, in spite of their devotion, get on each other's nerves: ''thus the two old people kept watch upon each other, and noted, with a curious mixture of vexation and sympathy, each other's declining strength''; or in her admirably restrained but moving account of the death of gruff old Dr. Marjoribanks. But for the most part the satire is bitter and the feeling cold. (p. 63)

Miss Marjoribanks was thus a disappointment to its publisher and consequently to its author. Its Victorian readers too were disappointed, for the smug, self-centered, self-righteous heroine was not appealing or attractive enough to hold their interest through three volumes. The charms of the Carlingford series— those ''inside'' glimpses of church and home life—are lacking. In their place we find a relentlessly satirical character sketch of a female egoist. There is very little ''charm'' in the novel and almost none in its heroine. The satire wears thin when stretched to three volumes. There is, properly speaking, no plot, and only the most minimal character development. Yet the sharpness, the malice, the wit of the book are remarkable. In *Miss Marjoribanks* for the first time in her fiction the sophisticated, anti-sentimental, hard core of Mrs. Oliphant's personality asserts itself. Lucilla Marjoribanks is the spiritual granddaughter of Jane Austen's Emma Woodhouse. She is a ''managing'' woman, running her widower father's household and the lives of all who come into her orbit. Like Emma, she tries to mould and manipulate people—with results that sometimes come perilously close to disaster for them. Like Emma, she is absolutely convinced of the rightness of her actions. The comparison ends there. Miss Marjoribanks lacks Emma's intelligence and sensitivity. Although she has her moments of self-doubt, she never comes to any real self-knowledge. She grows older and stouter in the ten-year span of the novel, but she never grows spiritually. At the end of the book she is the same person she was at the beginning. This is the essential humor of the book, but it is also its principal limitation.

The comic conception of the novel is clever and ambitious. The form that Mrs. Oliphant was attempting here was mock domestic epic. (p. 65)

It is certainly in epic terms that Mrs. Oliphant tells her story. . . . When one of her suitors, Mr. Cavendish, is suspected of flirting with another girl and enters a room full of Miss Marjoribanks' loyal friends—''The Balaclava charge itself, in the face of all the guns, could have been nothing to the sensation of walking through that horrible naked space, through a crowd of reproachful men who were waiting for dinner.'' Or when Miss Marjoribanks herself makes a dramatic entrance before her guests: ''Fifty eyes were upon Lucilla watching her conduct

at that critical moment—fifty ears were on the strain to divine her sentiments in her voice, and to catch some intonation at least which should betray her consciousness of what was going on.'' And finally, when the news of her marriage to her cousin is announced in Grange Lane:

> there was first a dead pause of incredulity and amazement, and then such a commotion as could be compared to nothing except a sudden squall at sea. People who had been going peaceably on their way at one moment, thinking of nothing, were to be seen the next buffeted by the wind of Rumour and tossed about on the waves, of Astonishment. To speak less metaphorically (but there are moments of emotion so overwhelming and unprecedented that they can be dealt with only in the language of metaphor), every household in Grange Lane, and at least half of the humbler houses in Grove Street, and a large portion of the other dwellings in Carlingford, were nearly as much agitated about Lucilla's marriage as if it had been a daughter of their own.

Miss Marjoribanks too has the ingenuousness and self-confidence of epic heroes. In her there is none of that modesty and self-questioning characteristic of weaker mortals. . . . (pp. 66-7)

The portrait of Miss Marjoribanks has wit, freshness, and originality, but it lacks humanity. In 1876, when Mrs. Oliphant returned to Carlingford, she brought back with her a heroine who is Lucilla Marjoribanks reduced to human dimensions. This is Phoebe Junior, the blooming daughter of Phoebe Tozer who, back in *Salem Chapel,* had married the Dissenting minister Mr. Beecher (or Beecham, as he becomes in the later novel). She is the same self-possessed, marvellously assured and capable young woman, but she has been softened down and humanized into a thoroughly charming and believable character. *Miss Marjoribanks* was a broad joke which lost most of its effectiveness through exaggeration and repetition; *Phoebe, Junior* is a quiet witticism, delivered with subtlety and economy. Technically it is by far the best of the Carlingford novels. It has a well-constructed though by no means original plot. The action is swift. The characters are lively and interesting, and one at least, the Reverend Mr. May, is fairly complex. The intrigue is kept to a minimum, but what there is is handled skillfully. The novel, written a decade later than its predecessors in the Carlingford series, shows on every page the author's increased mastery of her craft. (pp. 67-8)

In giving the new novel the subtitle **''A Last Chronicle of Carlingford,''** she was deliberately echoing Trollope's *The Last Chronicle of Barset.* . . . And there are more than mere echoes of Trollope in *Phoebe, Junior.* One whole episode is lifted out of *The Warden.* . . . Young Reginald May, fresh from Oxford, with the dimmest economic prospects, is offered and under family pressure accepts a sinecure as chaplain to the Carlingford College, an ancient foundation which supports a few indigent old men. The post comes under sharp attack from the Dissenting minister, Mr. Northcote, who immediately seeks to make a great issue out of it—all of which of course harks back to Mr. Harding's difficulties with Tom Towes and the press. A less overt case, but certainly an example of unconscious, if not conscious, borrowing, is the main dramatic incident of the book—the curate Mr. May's poverty and his forging of Tozer's name to a promissory note—which recalls the charges, in this case unwarranted, against the much put upon Reverend Josiah Crawley in Trollope's *Last Chronicle*.

These borrowings concern only secondary issues in the novel, however. The lively social comedy is Mrs. Oliphant's creation exclusively. Into the narrow provincial world of Carlingford she introduces a breath of fresh London air with young Phoebe, who comes to visit her grandparents, the Tozers. . . . (pp. 68-9)

Phoebe, Junior concludes the Carlingford series with a slightly mocking laugh at Dissent. It is not a "religious novel" in the sense that **The Rector, Salem Chapel,** and **The Perpetual Curate** are religious novels, having clergymen and their spiritual problems at their centers. Instead, it reduces sectarianism to social comedy. What interested Mrs. Oliphant, and her readers, in **Phoebe, Junior** is no matter of church doctrine but of human behavior. If Mrs. Oliphant sees Dissent with cynical eyes, it is only because she is looking at society in the same way. And Carlingford, in its modest way, has made its contribution to the Victorian human comedy. (p. 74)

> *Vineta Colby and Robert A. Colby, in their* The Equivocal Virtue: Mrs. Oliphant and the Victorian Literary Market Place, *Archon Books, Hamden, CT, 1966, 281 p.*

Q. D. LEAVIS (essay date 1969)

[*Leavis was a twentieth-century English critic, essayist, and editor. Her professional alliance with her husband, F. R. Leavis, resulted in several literary collaborations, including the successful quarterly periodical* Scrutiny, *in which she published many critical essays. Leavis's critical philosophy, as professed in her work for* Scrutiny, *stressed that "literary criticism is not a mystic rapture but a process of the intelligence." Furthermore, Leavis assigned to the critic the duty of remaining objective. She suggested that a responsible critic should ignore impressionistic responses to a work and, most importantly, asserted that a work should be judged on the basis of its moral value. In her introduction to* Miss Marjoribanks, *excerpted below, Leavis compares the work with those of Oliphant's contemporaries, particularly Jane Austen and George Eliot. Calling it a "tour de force," Leavis states that* Miss Marjoribanks *is a "wise and witty novel in which every sentence is exactly right and every word apt and adroitly placed." For Leavis's general assessment of the* Chronicles of Carlingford, *see excerpt dated 1974.*]

I think most of us have felt at some time that there must have been somebody who bridged the gap between Jane Austen and George Eliot—the aspect of course of George Eliot that had grown out of Jane Austen—and not been satisfied by such inward reminders as that Trollope in the Barchester series has frequently the air of being a Victorianised, minor Jane Austen, or that most of *Coningsby* would surely have delighted Jane Austen, or that in *Little Dorrit* Dickens presents a serious comedy of manners in the scenes between the Meagleses and Mrs Gowan that is decidedly in the Austen tradition. . . . [I suggest *Miss Marjoribanks*] and its author, Mrs Oliphant, for that missing link. Her Lucilla has long seemed to me a triumphant intermediary between Emma and Dorothea, and, incidentally, more entertaining, more impressive and more likable than either.

That this novel is, in its consistent ironic comedy, probably unique in Mrs Oliphant's *oeuvre* (I do not claim to have read the lot, nor does anyone else I imagine) does not mean that she hasn't a continuous "Miss Marjoribanks" vein running through most of her work, a vein which constantly surfaces and which the connoisseur will soon learn to recognise and

look out for; in her short stories it is more frequently dominant. Tough-mindedness did not disappear for the rest of the century with Jane Austen and *Coningsby*. . . . [*Miss Marjoribanks*] is something that Jane Austen might almost have created and written herself (though it would have been in fewer words) if she had not died prematurely, for it brings to bear on Victorian provincial-town and county society the same acute and unsentimental critical mind that had produced *Emma* in the Regency period: the technique and style as well as the language of our novel is essentially witty from start to finish. The opening is as anti-sentimental as the author of *Northanger Abbey* could have desired, though of course not directed at her targets but at Victorian conventional sentiment—e.g. in the course of the novel Rose Lake says of her sister: "But I am sorry to say she has not a strong sense of duty" and "'I have always been brought up to believe that duty was happiness', said Miss Marjoribanks with some severity"—authorial jokes inconceivable in *Middlemarch*. Lucilla is a Victorian anti-heroine, large, strong, unsentimental, insubordinate to men and with a hearty appetite.

Who else in 1865 could habitually write thus?—

> Lucilla had a great deal too much sense to upbraid anyone with ingratitude, or even to make any claim upon that slippery quality.

> 'He will never learn that he is old', she said in Lucilla's ear; and thus the two old people kept watch upon each other, and noted, with a curious mixture of vexation and sympathy, each other's declining strength.

> . . . nor had she the ordinary amount of indifference to other people, or confidence in herself, which stands in the place of self-control with many people.

> . . . hurriedly clasping together a pair of helpless hands as if they could find a little strength in union.

> 'We must leave that to Providence,' said Miss Marjoribanks, with a sense of paying a compliment to Providence in entrusting it with such a responsibility.

> (pp. 1-2)

In *Miss Marjoribanks,* where the mode is social comedy, Mrs. Oliphant can be seen to be aware of her tendency to extend to men in general her experience with the men of her own family: it is here made fun of as one aspect of her heroine's massive conviction of superiority. Yet in Lucilla's mild and patient contempt for Them there is also some endorsement from the novelist. (pp. 3-4)

Though over-production and also over-extension (into the necessary three volumes) prevented any other of her novels than [*Miss Marjoribanks*] from being outstanding, a number of them are worth looking at twice and especially some of the Scottish ones, such as *Kirsteen*. . . . In these, and in the many admirable short stories with a Scotch setting, we find her continuing Sir Walter Scott's investigation into what it meant to be Scottish. She plays the English off against the natives to the constant disadvantage of the former while registering the grimmer characteristics of her fellow-countrymen; she must have been the first novelist to notice and pay attention to the disconcerting results of educating young Scots of the land-owning class at English Public-schools. . . . [Henry James] pays Mrs Oliphant an obituary tribute in which he chiefly complains that, with so many gifts as a novelist, she did not have more art, specifying *Kirsteen* in illustration [see excerpt dated 1897]. Yet what one remembers about *Kirsteen* is the powerful picture of an unimaginable form of life it imprints—the poor proud violent Douglas laird, his weak wife with a 'bairntime' of fourteen children, the sons each in turn launched early on the world with only an outfit, the daughters with no future unless they fight for it or break with their fearsome father. There is no softening with humours or sentiment as so often in Scott, for even where her Scottishness is concerned Mrs Oliphant is hardheaded; her interest there is chiefly of the sociological and psychological kind, leaving the art of the novel to take care of itself.

It will be noticed that *Miss Marjoribanks* is also part of this inquiry, an illustration of the impact of Scottish capacity on English provincial life in its contemporary (mid-Victorian) phase of civilisation, the limitations and ridiculous aspects of which she thus dexterously shows up. Dr Marjoribanks with "the well-worn cordage of his countenance" who "had a respect for 'talent' in every development, as is natural to his nation", with his complete absence of tenderness or conventional sentiment in the relation of husband and father and his grim enjoyment of his daughter's difficulties as well as his appreciation of her "capabilities", is yet another of Mrs Oliphant's studies of her own nation. Lucilla, with her large Scotch bones and her moral solidity, her literal-mindedness, and that characteristic Scotch complacency, based on the consciousness of undeniable superiority, which makes her able to ignore other people's so-called sense of humour—thus disabling the mimic Mrs Woodburn—while yet having all her wits about her and a canny tongue of her own, is evidently of a different make from the Carlingford folk who naturally have no chance against her. (pp. 5-6)

Though for some time it seems that it is Lucilla who is to be the subject for ironic examination, it is in fact the nature of the society she operates in that becomes the main object of irony. The progress of the novel is to take the reader through the father's phases too, and though we may start with the fear that Lucilla is so limited that she will bore us, this is presently seen to be far from being so, since it is soon apparent that she hands out her stock phrases, the acceptable clichés of the age, as passwords, camouflaging herself in conventional clothing to conceal her originality and get her own way. Nor is the joke, as at first seems probable, a matter of repeating a pattern, for though Lucilla's suitors, with one exception, really never come up to scratch, they are all very different cases and are never predictable. In fact, a series of surprises is sprung on us right up to the end, with Lucilla able always to rise to each fresh occasion, and each is increasingly a challenge to her ingenuity and powers. With the death of the old doctor and the advent of the new one (who has, of course, once been one of the gentlemen expected to marry Lucilla) she soars away into County society with an unlimited sphere of usefulness in view. Imperceptibly Lucilla grows ever more interesting and endeared to us as ten years pass before our eyes. Her realisation that the man whom she is "fond of" is, socially speaking, fraudulent (though no one else at Carlingford knows this), and must therefore be permitted to aspire no higher in marriage than the drawing-master's daughter—whom in fact he has always preferred—may be comedy, but with her father's death, and the jolt this gives her, deeper and more complex feelings come into sight, as well as more admirable ones, and Lucilla faces poverty with dignity and fortitude. We are therefore not

surprised, nor incredulous, as her father would have been, at her volunteering to the lawyer with regard to the new doctor who had slighted her, that she had never been deceived, having perceived (as so often had been the case with the gentlemen who had "paid her attentions") that he was in love elsewhere: "'And I am rather fond of men that are in love—it shows they have some good in them'". Which prepares us for the grand and exciting scene of Lucilla's being unable to bring herself to accept the one eligible suitor who actually makes her an offer and of her succumbing instead to the only genuine lover she has ever had and who—though always snubbed—turns out to be the right man for the demanding position of husband to a Lucilla. And this, though still comedy, is yet genuinely moving, a convincing love-scene. (Mrs Oliphant is rare among Victorian novelists in being one who accepts and can establish the existence of passion and the miseries of the thwarted.) Lucilla's future happiness is shown to be at least as likely as Emma Knightley's and a great deal more convincing than Mrs Ladislaw's. (pp. 6-7)

Mrs Oliphant's irony is maintained to the end, when it is seen that, as Miss Bury's Evangelical faith assured her, everything is for the best; Lucilla's trust in Providence was justified; everyone benefits, even Barbara gets her dream-husband (though both of them are by now much the worse for wear)—except poor Rose Lake who, having to give up her Career for a daughter's duties, has even lost her belief in the value of art (except, of course, High Art). . . . The mode of the novel has not proved restrictive. The range from the broadly comic opening and such irresistibly funny scenes as Miss Bury being outraged by the irreverence of the young barristers at Lucilla's table, to Lucilla's surrender to "honest love", and the moving history of Dr Marjoribanks's death (than which I know nothing finer of its kind in all Victorian fiction), is really greater than in an Austen novel or many more pretentious Victorian novels. Mrs Oliphant had had rougher experience of life than George Eliot (who, she remarked, had been kept in "a mental greenhouse") and knew what men were like when not in the presence of ladies. Her gentlemen are particularly good—though "good" does not perhaps convey the right idea. *Miss Marjoribanks* is really nearer in sensibilty and tone to *Coningsby* than to either *Emma* or *Middlemarch,* and connoisseurs of Disraeli's brilliant novel will appreciate the sly reference to its Lord Monmouth in Ch. XVIII here. The death of the old Doctor is an outstanding artistic achievement: full of feeling as that is, it is kept successfully within the mode of the novel (anti-sentimental and ironic) by her treatment of Carlingford's reaction to it, and by the author's unresentful acceptance of the lack of idealism in real life—a very un-Victorian trait. A more than technical triumph is the inclusion of a systematic humourist whose line is "taking off" her acquaintances but who is seen to be a weak woman without resources or morale when trouble looms, thus justifying Lucilla's contempt for mere humour as an end in itself.

One can go on frequenting *Miss Marjoribanks,* noticing fresh subtleties and getting ever more enjoyment. As Henry James said in another connexion, all novelists of manners "are historians, even when they least don the uniform", and one aspect of the value of this novel is as social history—the kind that, in default of the novelist, no historian could supply. Mrs Oliphant shows us what it would have felt like to be living then and there. (pp. 8-9)

Though *Miss Marjoribanks* enjoyed some success as entertainment, and subsequently got into [a] cheap pocket edition accordingly (in which I myself first made its acquaintance), it was the inferior *Salem Chapel* that made a hit and got taken into "Everyman" as Mrs Oliphant's classic. It was *Miss Marjoribanks* that, she wrote "cost me an infinite deal of trouble", but neither Barrie nor Henry James mentions it in his obituary, nor is it selected for praise in the [*Dictionary of National Biography*] article on her. Mrs Oliphant had reason to be exasperated at being relegated to inferior status even in her own hey-day.... Her disadvantage was, that ... the Oliphant tone was calculated to grate on Victorian sensibility. If the public of the mid-sixties had signified enthusiasm for *Miss Marjoribanks,* no doubt she might have continued to produce interesting fiction that satisfied her own critical judgment.... As it is, *Miss Marjoribanks* stands alone as a *tour-de-force.* The reading-public then had become accustomed to take its domestic fiction straight and in an infusion of warm feeling. Mrs Oliphant had plenty of feeling, but it is not simple-minded or self-indulgent, and she had neither the Victorian sentimentality nor even the necessary reticence and sense of propriety. (pp. 22-3)

Miss Marjoribanks obliges adjustment to an individual scale as well as tone. The scale of *Emma* and *Cranford* is too minute for it, that of *Middlemarch* and *Barchester Towers* too large. One has also to get into step with the movement and be prepared for its being very slow at first and highly repetitive in phrasing (to get into the mentality of Carlingford). Then it gets brisker and gathers speed with the death of the member for Carlingford, slows down again as if to grind to a halt with the old Doctor's death, and then picks up pace to gallop home with the lover whose return in the nick of time—perhaps a satirical cliché—is heralded by Lucilla's panic at the peal of her dead father's disused night-bell which decides her fate at last. The plotting is faultless and, on top of everything else, we have one of the best elections in Victorian fiction, rich in them as that is.

This novel is full of wit, surprises and intrigue, its heroine a classic addition to the English Comic Characters, sub-division female. Lucilla belongs in the company of Lady Catherine de Burgh, Lady Bracknell, Mrs Proudie, Mrs Poyser, Emma Woodhouse and the rest—all women of ability and presence. One would have expected it to have been kept in print with a loyal following over the years, seeing that its insipid contemporary, *Wives and Daughters,* has. Perhaps our age will at last do justice to this wise and witty novel in which every sentence is exactly right and every word apt and adroitly placed.... Lady Ritchie, Thackeray's daughter and her dear friend, wrote ... perceptively: "She was one of those people whose presence is even more than a *pleasure,* it was a stimulus; she was kindly, sympathetic, and yet answering with that chord of intelligent antagonism which is so suggestive and makes for such good talk." I think this most acurately indicates the quality that stamps her work. We can imagine Jane Austen reading *Miss Marjoribanks* with enjoyment and approval in the Elysian Fields. (pp. 23-4)

Q. D. Leavis, in an introduction to Miss Marjoribanks *by Mrs. Oliphant, The Zodiac Press, 1969, pp. 1-24.*

Q. D. LEAVIS (essay date 1974)

[*In her introduction to* Autobiography and Letters, *Leavis appraises Oliphant as an autobiographer, woman of letters, and literary critic. In the following excerpt from that introduction, Leavis discusses Oliphant as a novelist, dividing her works into three categories: novels of Scottish characters and setting, the* Chronicles of Carlingford, *and novels with supernatural, romantic, or social themes. According to Leavis, Oliphant's reputation as a novelist rests on the* Chronicles of Carlingford *and other stories of English life, and she thus concentrates on these works in her discussion. For Leavis's discussion of* Miss Marjoribanks, *see excerpt dated 1969.*]

Mrs Oliphant's output as a novelist can best be considered as three phases, overlapping but distinct. The first starts even before her early marriage, the regional novels of Scottish setting and characters; but they are inferior to her later Scottish novels and the short stories she wrote when more mature, and are not of much account.... [During the second phase,] she launched a series, the "**Carlingford Chronicles**", with a short story in "Maga" for May 1861, "**The Executor**". No doubt the success of novelists in the previous decade with Cranford, Barchester and Milby had suggested to her an English provincial setting with its opportunities for satiric insights into contemporary social and religious institutions, but her wit and analysis are her own and in no way parasitic. Two excellent *nouvelles,* "**The Rector**" and "**The Doctor's Family**", followed, then, rapidly, *Salem Chapel, The Perpetual Curate* and—the high-water mark—*Miss Marjoribanks,* altogether an amazing flood of creative power while she was also producing an incessant flow of periodical essays, literary criticism, inferior novels of other kinds, and biographical works.... [With] *Phoebe, Junior: A Last Chronicle of Carlingford* she ended an impressive series—*Miss Marjoribanks* indeed has claims to be considered the wisest and wittiest of Victorian novels. It is so beautifully "done" that its ironic comedy is unique outside Jane Austen's works for consistency of tone and maturity of criticism of a closed society. The third phase is miscellaneous, containing more and better Scottish-based fiction that is thoroughly realistic, anti-romantic novels and tales of English social life which are essentially studies of a changing society, and, as a literary curiosity, beginning with *A Beleaguered City* ..., a group of tales of supernatural experiences with a *frisson* of a spiritual or professedly mystical nature, which seem to me to have been over-rated then and since. Though Mrs Oliphant valued them highly herself and some have Dantean overtones, they represent a self-indulgence, the complement of her hard-headed professional self which required some nondogmatic vaguely religious sustenance. Yet they are not so much literary curiosities as specimens of that special variety of thriller, the supernatural, of which there are so many examples by respectable writers in the Late Victorian and Edwardian periods—a genre containing "The Turn of the Screw". Mrs Oliphant in fact tried her hand, deliberately or instinctively, at every literary form known to her, even verse and drama. (pp. 21-2)

[The "**Carlingford Chronicles**"] rival Trollope's Barchester series in several respects and contain material much more valuable as sociology and social criticism than anything in his. Owing to the popularity of *Salem Chapel,* Mrs Oliphant has the reputation of being a novelist who was merely an authority on Dissent, but even so *Salem Chapel* must be supplemented by *Phoebe, Junior,* a sort of sequel and far better. It is true that Mrs Oliphant thoroughly understood the dissidence of Dissent.... In fact, the truth to life of Mrs Oliphant's rendition of provincial Dissent is borne out by the experiences of it recorded by "Mark Rutherford" and others later in the century as well as by Crabb Robinson, a contemporry Dissenter.

That Mrs Oliphant does not merely make easy play with irony is proved by her sympathetic appreciation of the difficulties, even sufferings, of the rising generation of the better educated

Nonconformists and of the really superior members of the old-established Dissenting communities of northern cities who were still socially non-existent. The masterly charting of the rise of the Beechams, from Salem Chapel in Carlingford to a "final apotheosis in a handsome chapel near Regent's Park", with a corresponding change in their attitude to the Established Church as "social elevation modified their sectarian zeal", is not unkind, even though we are told of Phoebe's father: "He had not, perhaps, much power of thought, but it is easy to make up for such a secondary want when the gift of expression is so strong". But we are also shown types more worth attention:

> Horace Northcote was not of Mr Beecham's class. He was not well-to-do and genial, bent upon keeping up his congregation and his popularity, and trying to ignore as much as he could the social superiority of the Church without making himself in any way offensive to her. He was a political Non-conformist, a vigorous champion of the Dis-establishment Society, more successful on the platform than in the pulpit, and strenuously of opinion in his heart of hearts that the Church was the great drawback to all progress in England, an incubus of which the nation would gladly be rid.

Phoebe Beecham, lovely, clever and unshakeably sensible, is the granddaughter of the prosperous but socially impossible Carlingford grocer; she cannot reconcile her superior education and social life in London with the vulgarity of her parents' origins; and though she is heroic in her determination to act rightly by her grandparents, her position when at Carlingford is shown to be painful. She says thoughtfully to Northcote:

> "Which is best; for everyone to continue in the position he was born in, or for an honest shop-keeper to educate his children and push them up higher, until they come to feel themselves members of a different class, and to be ashamed of him? Either way, you know, it is hard."

Northcote himself is a minister with no sense of perplexity, being well-off, well educated abroad ("2 or 3 years at Jena studying philosophy"), and whose relatives are all "Manchester people with two or three generations of wealth behind them, relatives of whom nobody need be ashamed". Mrs Oliphant as a Scot was free of Victorian class-feeling but she thoroughly comprehended its nature and was interested in the problems of social change that were affected by it. Where she saw it to be based on something genuine she did not treat it ironically, as where the really superior children suffer from the narrow outlook, the meanness of mind and the blatant money-values of the Salem congregation. But she was equally appreciative of the Church as a comic spectacle, and more inclined to treat ironically (as richer and worthier material for her satiric powers) the Victorian ecclesiastical establishment—Low, High-and-Dry, Anglo-Catholic, Broad, and Catholic conversion—even than the Nonconformists. (pp. 23-5)

[In *The Perpetual Curate*] something more than the idiom of the Victorian Anglican movement is being satirized. The author's irony is distributed equally between a confident aestheticism which is disgusted by a fine eighteenth-century parish church but gratified by a Victorian Gothic *pastiche,* and the confusion between aesthetic taste (shown to be merely fashionble cant) and religion.

In *Miss Marjoribanks* we meet a totally ironic dissection of the mid-Victorian culture. The Carlingford doctor and his daughter are Scots, their environment being English is unworthy of them; though they both daunt it and elicit respectful admiration, the society is inadequate to Lucilla's needs and provides little scope for her "capabilities", which are immense, so powerful indeed that the comedy consists largely in the camouflage she must give them in order to operate without alarming her friends and neighbours. The novel is witty and high spirited yet on a serious basis. (pp. 25-6)

[There] is about all her work a real distinction, an identifiable Oliphant manner and attitude and tone, more suited to a later age than the ones she lived through. It inheres in her honesty and unflinching realism and her recognition—without cynicism or resentment—of the lack of idealism in ordinary life (a very unVictorian trait). This did not in that age make for popularity, of course. A characteristic observation in her novels is that "Next to happiness, perhaps enmity is the most healthful stimulant of the human mind." There is something disturbing in even her liveliest fictions and just as Trollope's novels always contain unhappy people and that is where his real strength lies, so Mrs Oliphant's concentrate on painful situations of all kinds. She wrote about life as she knew it and made her characters—often faulty or unattractive people—face and cope with, or come to terms with, the dilemmas, the disillusions, the mental sufferings, she herself had survived. But there is no self-pity in her work, as in Hardy's tragic novels, nor any idealization or self-transfiguration, as in George Eliot's. She was the opposite, too, of the bestseller novel-writer who peddles day-dreams and wish-fulfilment. It is typical of her that she wrote that "a 'happy ending' is simply a contemptible expedient" and this no doubt explains her inability to obtain from Victorian publishers, those shrewd judges of the market values, high enough prices for even her best novels.

She investigates by dramatizing the relations of husband and wife and parent and child, and the position of women in a man-dominated society; and here she is genuinely original. She was making studies of masculine arrogance and insensitiveness to the capacities and legitimate claims of wives and daughters and sisters before George Eliot and Meredith, illustrating what she had noted as the "inherent contempt for women which is a settled principle in the minds of so many men." Her novels don't end characteristically with happy marriages, sometimes they end with the tragic breakdown of a marriage, or with no marriage at all for the heroine, for her gaze was fixed on the nature of marriage itself—its shortcomings and disasters, the clash of wills, the inability to preserve a balance or make a lasting compromise, and the difficulty of facing and then either cutting losses or accepting them. *A Country Gentleman and His Family* shows a marriage of love hastily contracted between a young widow and a younger man and then breaking down because of the man's obstinate self-assertion in demands for masterhood, and his jealousy of her boy to whom she is more attached than to himself. The consequences of the separation that ensues, for husband, wife and children, are fully investigated in a sequel, *A House Divided Against Itself.* . . . A repeated theme throughout all the phases of her fiction is that of the wife who suffers disillusionment as to her husband or whose apparently happy married life has actually been a bondage or imprisonment. . . . (pp. 27-8)

She had had a great deal of experience of life as a struggle and an exposure to all kinds of hardship and disenchantment, and she seems to have realized that this was an asset to a creative writer for she doubts that she would have done better if, like George Eliot, she "had been kept in a mental greenhouse and taken care of". The conception of a heroine in her novels is correspondingly original for a Victorian. Her admirable women are clever, efficient, vital, highly articulate, practical-minded, superior and managing—but magnanimous and tolerant enough of the shortcomings and failings natural to men, whom they often see mainly as means to an end. And most original of all, the Oliphant heroine *works,* a condition otherwise almost unknown in Victorian novels outside *Jane Eyre* and *Villette.* Lucilla, Phoebe, Patty Hewatt, Maisie Rowland, Kirsteen and the rest see what needs doing or saying undaunted by the obstacles men and circumstances set up against them. Lucilla, having reorganized the social life of Carlingford and got her chosen candidate elected for Parliament on a slogan invented by herself, tells her betrothed: "What we both want is someting to do" and has him buy a run-down estate in a squalid village so that "You can improve the land, you know, and the people you could leave to me. *We* could make it pay". *Hester* shows woman in banking; Kirsteen, a laird's daughter, runs away from an intolerable home to make a career for herself as a Court dressmaker; Patty, the socially ambitious daughter of a village innkeeper, succeeds in eloping with the feeble-minded son of the great house and by her vulgar arts and unscrupulous tactics ousts and supersedes the well-bred but helpless heirs-at-law in *The Cuckoo in the Nest:* the daughters of *The Curate in Charge,* left penniless on the death of their high-minded father, refuse to fall back on relatives or charity: one resigns herself to the loss of caste by becoming the village schoolmistress (Mrs Oliphant explores the situation with relish, showing that the gentry are embarrassed and drop the girl), the other, who is artistically gifted, trains to become a book illustrator. These are only a few specimens of a rich crop. Her girls paint seriously, play Bach and Beethoven "scientifically", study the Classics, despise their mothers' merely social lives and insist on working in Whitechapel and the London hospitals; young widows manage their sons' estates and wives like Phoebe and Lucilla write their husbands' speeches. But most remarkable is the working out of the theme in *The Railway Man and His Children,* where the Ruskinian theory about woman's place and the Victorian gospel of work are both logically examined and routed, and "the new girl" of the age voices her creed (less than twenty years after Dorothea Brooke). (pp. 28-9)

How did [Mrs Oliphant] arrive at this degree of originality? We have seen one of her assets—her experience of life. It would be untrue to say that she deliberately drew on this for her novels, but what we see was the truly creative process of her feeding the problems she had encountered and the sufferings she had endured into dramatic arrangements of life where these could be analysed and discussed and seen in a true light. (p. 32)

Her honesty and disenchanted insight into human relations are assets, . . . and this maturity was what made her write that though Charlotte and Emily Brontë's novels "are vivid, original and striking in the highest degree", "Their philosophy of life is that of a school girl, their knowledge of the world is almost *nil,* their conclusions confused by the haste and passion of a mind self-centred and working in the narrowest orbit". Comparing herself with Charlotte Brontë she writes: "I have had far more experience and, I think, a fuller conception of life. I have learned to take perhaps more a man's view of mortal affairs. . . ." Another such asset as her Scottish conditioning was that she had been an artist's wife and lived both in London and in Italy in a mildly Bohemian atmosphere. This certainly emancipated her for ever from the drawing-room point of view and from social conformism; Victorian conventions of feeling and behaviour are always a subject for ironic exposure in her novels. We can see that her knowledge of the artist's life gave her a positive position from which to criticize the snobbery and stupidities of Victorian good society. Before du Maurier and Henry James had made their separate but not unrelated attacks on it from the studio point of view, Mrs Oliphant had, for instance in *Miss Marjoribanks,* used that as a standard of judgment as well as to provide ironic jokes. It must have given her pleasure to make the Colonel's wife say: "For my part I never like to have anything to do with those artist kind of people—they are all adventurers", and to give Lucilla's objection to *professional* singing, and to show Carlingford's relegation to social obscurity of a poor but talented family of professional artists. Her style is the natural expression of such a character. It is witty, but the apt epithet, the adroit sentence, the telling phrase, the lively conversational manner, are never sought after or strained, as she herself puts it: "I have always had my sing-song, guided by no sort of law, but by my ear, which was in its way fastidious to the cadence and measure that pleased me; but it is bewildering to me in my perfectly artless art, if I may use the word at all, to hear of the elaborate ways of forming and enhancing style, and all the studies for that end". (pp. 32-3)

> *Q. D. Leavis, in an introduction to* Autobiography and Letters of Mrs Margaret Oliphant *by Margaret Oliphant, edited by Mrs Harry Coghill, Leicester University Press, 1974, pp. 9-34.*

JOHN STOCK CLARKE   (essay date 1979)

[*This excerpt is from a survey of Oliphant's writings in which the critic calls for a reappraisal of her work. According to Clarke, although Oliphant's works appear to conform to Victorian stereotypes, the novels actually demonstrate the author's ambivalence toward the conventions of Victorian fiction. In fact, Clarke contends, Oliphant's works often reflect anti-romantic views of life and challenge "orthodox views . . . of romantic love, and the ideal hero." Clarke also discusses Oliphant's character analysis and narrative technique.*]

There may be some excuse for the neglect of Mrs. Oliphant; she was probably the most prolific novelist of the nineteenth century, publishing about ninety-six works of fiction besides many uncollected shorter stories; and to make a serious study of such a writer must seem an act of mere masochism. Could anybody who wrote so much maintain any literary standards at all? In fact Mrs. Oliphant does fully warrant close study; she did maintain high standards throughout her career, and in spite of what critics have said of her she never degenerated into a hack writer. She is very much within the great tradition of the nineteenth-century novel, and when she is in the right vein she handles this tradition—in particular, the tradition of ironic social observation inherited from Jane Austen—with intelligence, accepting and yet modifying it, as important writers always do. (p. 123)

On a superficial survey Mrs. Oliphant may seem to be merely the stereotype of the Victorian lady novelist, with naive love scenes, over-ingenious mystery themes, harrowing vigils in the sick room, emotional death scenes, noble-hearted heroes and heroines and a ruthless stress on the most innocent domestic virtues. Under the stress of over-production she often did write like that; but a closer examination of her novels—even the less successful ones—will show that her attitudes to the conventions of Victorian fiction are always (or almost always) ambivalent.

She accepts the conventions in one part of the book; but the pattern or plot-development of the book will suggest a very different view. For example, she accepts the convention that every novel must end in a marriage for the heroine (or at least the sub-heroine) and that a happy marriage solves all problems a heroine may meet. But in *The Curate in Charge* . . . , where the heroine, Cicely St. John, reduced to a humiliating loss of caste by accepting the position of parish schoolmistress, could be 'saved' by marrying Mr. Mildmay, Mrs. Oliphant protests:

> To change all her circumstances at a stroke, making her noble intention unnecessary, and resolving this tremendous work of hers into a gentle domestic necessity, with the 'hey presto!' of the commonplace magician, by means of a marriage, is simply a contemptible expedient. But, alas! it is one which there can be no doubt is much preferred by most people to the more legitimate conclusion; and, what is more, he would be justified by knowing the accidental way is, perhaps, on the whole, the most likely one, since marriages occur every day which are perfectly improbable and out of character, mere tours de force, despicable as expedients, showing the poorest invention, a disgrace to any romancist or dramatist, if they were not absolute matters of fact and true.

The book ends with a discreetly ambiguous conversation which may or may not imply (according to the reader's wishes) that Cicely accepts Mr. Mildmay.

This quotation subtly illustrates Mrs. Oliphant's remarkable attitude to the role of women in Victorian life. Cicely St. John, she feels, would be better advised to refuse marriage and devote herself to work which would give her a sense of fulfilment; and indeed this is Cicely's own view. In many of Mrs. Oliphant's books there is a similar stress on the need for women to find work. And yet when she chose to express overt opinions she did not favour any change in the position of women. She contributed two articles on the Condition of Women to *Blackwood's Magazine* in 1856 and 1858 in which she firmly rejects all radical feminist views. Yet her experience of life (where first her father, then her two brothers and her husband, then both her sons, showed moral or physical weakness, leaving her to carry alone the task of supporting her family) led her to take a coolly ironic view of men, and of the uselessly decorative role of many women in middle class Victorian life. She knew all about

> that pitiful endurance of the meanness of the men belonging to them, and the anxious endeavours to give it the best possible aspect to the world, which some women are obliged to bear. . . .

[In *Cousin Mary*] she points out:

> Women have a great deal to bear in this world. Their lot is in many respects harder than that of men, and neither higher education, nor the suffrage, nor anything else can mend it.

And when she chooses she can describe unhappy marriages in which a woman finds frustration and disillusion, a theme which she can handle as impressively as George Eliot and Trollope. Indeed she is far less likely to over-dramatize this theme than Trollope. (pp. 124-26)

When Mrs. Oliphant chooses to voice an opinion she expresses orthodox Victorian views; but when we turn to the action and characterization of her novels she seems to express a far more ironic or disillusioned view. Her heroines constantly suffer from frustration or disillusion, or crave the chance to engage in satisfying work. If they cannot find paid work of their own, they will (like Phoebe Beecham, heroine of *Phoebe Junior*) marry a man of weak character by whose means they can, in all but name, find a career. Miss Marjoribanks, craving for an outlet for her superabundant energies, can find no other use for them than to become a sort of one-woman Arts Council for the provincial town of Carlingford; and like Phoebe Beecham she marries to find a vicarious career through her husband.

Equally remarkable is her treatment of Love. Like any good Victorian, she is in favour of it and can seem to be very severe on those who enter upon marriage without it. Yet she knows it often leads to disillusion. In *A Country Gentleman and His Family* she follows Dick Cavendish and Charlotte Warrender, characters in the sub-plot, through to an apparently idyllic conclusion; but we meet them again many years later in *A House Divided Against Itself* . . . and Charlotte is now lonely and neglected. (p. 127)

There is always a great affection in [Mrs. Oliphant's] view of English society, of which in her later books she shows a shrewd and accurate understanding; but the tone is usually that of an ironic observer, especially when she writes of the new aristocracy of money, trade and industry. Many of her books are set partly or wholly in Scotland and these are notable for their zest and their authenticity (especially in the dialogue); but they are not usually her best books, being too inclined to self-indulgence, full of descriptions of scenery aimed seemingly at the tourist market. Her series of novels set in English provincial life, starting with the Carlingford series . . . , constitute her main claim to fame—a fame which she has so far notably failed to achieve.

The best Oliphant novels have a distinctive pattern and 'flavour' of their own. She worked to no theory of the novel and made no conscious innovations, and when at the end of her life theories—such as those of Henry James—about the novel began to appear in print she was doubtful of their value, though very respectful. Yet in the Carlingford novels she used a method of interlocking the characters of the various books resembling Trollope's method in the Barchester and Palliser novels; but much more sophisticated. Indeed in a rudimentary way she anticipated Bennett's use of parallel actions in *Clayhanger* and *Hilda Lessways*. She experimented with the first-person narrator—and very strikingly in *The Days of My Life* . . . she chose a narrator meant to seem insufferably arrogant and egotistical. But this book is not a complete success, being written before she was ready for such ironic objectivity. She adopted the Victorian system of serializing novels in literary periodicals . . . and this tended to favour the traditional 'strong' plot line with mysteries, coincidences, surprises and prolonged tension. Indeed her worst weakness was a disastrous taste for melodramatic characters and situations which she was unable to handle imaginatively. But elsewhere her tone is coolly ironic and her characterization remarkably free from stereotypes. (pp. 129-30)

Mrs. Oliphant has a particular gift for the analysis of motivation, often complex and ambivalent motivation. She understands the perverse thought-processes of the self-deceiver, and the dishonesty that may underlie the best of intentions. Though she does tend to sentimentalize the soft-hearted young and (a special weakness, this) the affectionate elderly spinster, she softens the impact of her characters (at least in her best work) far less often than Trollope, who is also noted for his analysis of self-deception. This is because in spite of her willingness to supply on occasion the obligatory 'happy ending' she was temperamentally inclined to an anti-romantic view of life, which led her to challenge orthodox views, for example, of romantic love, and the ideal hero. (p. 131)

Apart from *Miss Marjoribanks* and the *Autobiography and Letters* and a couple of ghost stories, nothing by Mrs. Oliphant has survived into print in our times. . . . *Salem Chapel,* one of the Carlingford series, and *A Beleaguered City,* a **'Tale of the Seen and Unseen',** have retained a sort of reputation. But her best work has remained utterly unknown, scarcely recognized in its own time for what it was, and in consequence not rediscovered until recently. . . . Perhaps Mrs. Oliphant can be called the most neglected novelist of all time; certainly it is my belief that she warrants the closest examination, and to be given a place entirely out of reach of Mrs. Henry Wood, Mrs. Craik and all the other queens of the circulating libraries. (pp. 132-33)

> John Stock Clarke, "Mrs. Oliphant: A Case for Reconsideration," in English, Vol. XXVIII, No. 131, Summer, 1979, pp. 123-33.

ADDITIONAL BIBLIOGRAPHY

Barrie, J. M. "Unveiling of Memorial to Mrs. Oliphant." In his *M'Connachie and J. M. B.: Speeches by J. M. Barrie,* pp. 21-5. New York: Charles Scribner's Sons, 1939.
    A speech delivered at the dedication of an Edinburgh memorial to Oliphant. Barrie calls her "the most distinguished Scotswoman of her time."

Clarke, Isabel C. "Margaret Wilson Oliphant, 1828-1897." In her *Six Portraits,* pp. 193-230. London: Hutchinson & Co., 1935.
    A brief overview of Oliphant's life and career.

Colby, Vineta. "William Wilson, Novelist." *Notes and Queries* n.s. 13, No. 2 (February 1966): 60-6.*
    Reiterates Sara Keith's assertion (see annotation below) that Oliphant was the author of several novels that are commonly attributed to her brother William Wilson.

Hart, Francis Russell. "Mid-Victorians: Oliphant, MacDonald, Tytler." In his *The Scottish Novel: From Smollett to Spark,* pp. 93-113. Cambridge: Harvard University Press, 1978.*

A discussion of Oliphant's novels in relation to the writings of George MacDonald and Sarah Tytler.

Johnson, R. Brimley. "*Jane Eyre* to *Scenes of Clerical Life:* Writers from 1847-1858." In his *The Women Novelists,* pp. 179-203. New York: Charles Scribner's Sons, 1919.*
    Compares Oliphant's writings with those of other women writers of the same era. According to Johnson, unlike those of her female contemporaries, Oliphant's novels possess an "almost masculine insight."

Keith, Sara. "Margaret Oliphant." *Notes and Queries* CC (March 1955): 126-27.
    Suggests that Oliphant wrote all of the novels that have been attributed to her brother William Wilson.

Peterson, Linda H. "Audience and the Autobiographer's Art: An Approach to the *Autobiography* of Mrs. M.O.W. Oliphant." In *Approaches to Victorian Autobiography,* edited by George P. Landow, pp. 158-74. Athens: Ohio University Press, 1979.
    Maintains that Oliphant's autobiography is unsuccessful as an artistic work. Peterson contends that Oliphant's overwhelming sense of duty prompted her to interpret incidents from a "maternal rather than an artistic point of view."

Porter, Mrs. Gerald. "Mrs. Oliphant and New Recruits." In her *Annals of a Publishing House, William Blackwood and His Sons, Their Magazine and Friends: John Blackwood,* Vol. III, pp. 335-74. Edinburgh: William Blackwood and Sons, 1898.*
    The last volume of a three-part study of the publishing firm of William Blackwood and Sons; the first two volumes were written by Oliphant. Porter chronicles Oliphant's involvement with the Blackwood family and reprints correspondence pertaining to her career with the company.

Stebbins, Lucy Poate. "Margaret Oliphant." In her *A Victorian Album: Some Lady Novelists of the Period,* pp. 155-91. New York: Columbia University Press, 1946.
    Discusses characterization in many of Oliphant's novels. Stebbins contends that members of Oliphant's family served as models for her characters.

Terry, R. C. "Queen of Popular Fiction: Mrs. Oliphant and the *Chronicles of Carlingford.*" In his *Victorian Popular Fiction, 1860-80,* pp. 68-101. London: Macmillan Press, 1983.
    Analyzes Oliphant's success with the Victorian public, which Terry attributes to her believable characters and settings.

Watson, Kathleen. "George Eliot and Mrs. Oliphant: A Comparison in Social Attitudes." *Essays in Criticism* XIX, No. 4 (October 1969): 410-19.*
    Compares the religious and social values portrayed in the works of Oliphant and George Eliot. Watson concludes that Oliphant's writings are "unusual" in their comprehensive exploration of problems common to Victorian society.

Appendix

The following is a listing of all sources used in Volume 11 of *Nineteenth-Century Literature Criticism*. Included in this list are all copyright and reprint rights and acknowledgments for those essays for which permission was obtained. Every effort has been made to trace copyright, but if omissions have been made, please let us know.

THE EXCERPTS IN NCLC, VOLUME 11, WERE REPRINTED FROM THE FOLLOWING PERIODICALS:

The Academy, v. V, February 21, 1874; v. LVI, May 20, 1899.

American Quarterly Review, v. XVII, March, 1835; v. XVIII, December, 1835.

The American-Scandinavian Review, v. XII, November, 1924.

The Analytical Review, v. XXVIII, August, 1798.

Appleton's Journal, v. XV, June 24, 1876.

The Athenaeum, n. 1353, October 1, 1853; n. 1898, March 12, 1864; n. 3636, July 3, 1897.

The Atlantic Monthly, v. IX, January, 1862; v. XXXI, February, 1873.

Bentley's Miscellany, v. XXXVI, 1854.

Bentley's Quarterly Review, v. II, January, 1860.

Blackwood's Edinburgh Magazine, v. LIII, May, 1843; v. LXIV, October, 1848; v. CXIV, July, 1873; v. CXIX, February, 1876; v. CXXXIII, January, 1883; v. CLXII, September, 1897; v. CLXV, May, 1899.

The Bookman, New York, v. XV, July, 1902.

Boston University Studies in English, v. II, Autumn, 1956.

The British and Foreign Review, v. IX, July, 1839.

The British Critic, v. VII, June, 1796; v. XI, April, 1798; v. XVI, December, 1800.

The British Quarterly Review, v. IV, August 1, 1846; v. VII, February, 1848; v. VIII, August 1, 1848; v. XLIX, March 1, 1869.

Bulletin of The John Rylands Library, v. 38, September, 1955.

The Journal of Political Economy, v. 19, November, 1911.

The Knickerbocker, v. III, March, 1834.

Littell's Living Age, v. XXIII, December 15, 1849; v. XXXV, December 11, 1852.

The Living Age, v. XXXV, December 25, 1852; v. CCXLX, July 7, 1906.

The London and Westminster Review, v. XXVI, October, 1836.

The London Magazine, v. IV, September, 1821; n.s. v. II, May, 1825; n.s. v. II, July, 1825.

Macmillan's Magazine, v. LXX, September, 1894; v. LXXIX, February, 1899.

Middlesex Standard, August 1, 1844.

Modern Drama, v. 2, December, 1959. Copyright *Modern Drama,* University of Toronto. Reprinted by permission.

Monatshefte, v. LII, April-May, 1960. Copyright © 1960 by The Board of Regents of the University of Wisconsin System. Reprinted by permission.

The Monthly Magazine, London, v. 10, November 1, 1800 and January 1, 1801.

The Monthly Review, London, v. CIII, April, 1824; v. CVII, August, 1825.

The Nation, v. IX, July 22, 1869; v. XVIII, January 8, 1874.

The National Review, London, v. XVI, April, 1863.

The New England Quarterly, v. XXXVIII, June, 1965 for "Fredrika Bremer's 'Spirit of the New World'" by Carl L. Anderson. Copyright 1965 by *The New England Quarterly.* Reprinted by permission of the publisher and the author.

The New Republic, v. C, October 4 and October 11, 1939 for "The End of the Reasoning Man" and "The End of the Reasoning Man: II" by Malcolm Cowley. © 1939 The New Republic, Inc. Renewed 1966 by Malcolm Cowley. Both reprinted by permission of the author./ v. 191, November 5, 1984. © 1984 The New Republic, Inc. Reprinted by permission of *The New Republic.*

The New York Review, v. II. April, 1838.

The New York Times, February 20, 1948. Copyright © 1948 by The New York Times Company. Reprinted by permission.

The New York Times Book Review, November 23, 1924. Copyright © 1924 by The New York Times Company. Reprinted by permission.

The Nineteenth Century, v. XXXV, February, 1894.

Nineteenth-Century Fiction, v. IV, September, 1949. © 1949, renewed 1977 by The Regents of the University of California. Reprinted by permission of The Regents.

The North American Review, v. XLVIII, April, 1839; v. LVI, January, 1843; v. LVI, April, 1843; v. LVIII, April, 1844; v. LXVII, July, 1848; v. LXXVIII, April, 1854; v. LXXXIII, October, 1856; v. 244, Winter, 1937-38.

The North British Review, v. IX, May, 1848.

Overland Monthly, n.s. v. I, April, 1883.

PMLA 67, v. LXVII, September, 1952.

Proceedings of the American Philosophical Society, v. 87, July, 1943.

Prose Studies, v. 5, September, 1982. © Frank Cass & Co. Ltd. 1982. Reprinted by permission of Frank Cass & Co. Ltd.

The Prospective Review, v. VI, 1850.

Putnam's Monthly, v. II, December, 1853.

THE EXCERPTS IN NCLC, VOLUME 11, WERE REPRINTED FROM THE FOLLOWING BOOKS:

Abercrombie, Lascelles. From an introduction to *Poems*. By Nicholas Nekrassov, translated by Juliet M. Soskice. Oxford University Press, London, 1929.

Abrams, M. H. From "Introduction: Orientation of Critical Theories," in *The Mirror and the Lamp: Romantic Theory and the Critical Tradition*. By M. H. Abrams. Oxford University Press, 1953. Copyright 1953 by Oxford University Press, Inc. Renewed 1981 by Meyer Howard Abrams. Reprinted by permission of the publisher.

Adams, John. From an extract of a letter to Timothy Pickering on August 6, 1822, in *The Works of John Adams, Vol. II*. By John Adams, edited by Charles Francis Adams. Charles C. Little and James Brown, 1850.

Alexander, Edward. From an introduction to *Literary Essays*. By John Stuart Mill, edited by Edward Alexander. Bobbs-Merrill, 1967. Copyright © 1967 by Macmillan Publishing Company. Reprinted with permission of Macmillan Publishing Company.

Amiel, Henri Frederic. From a journal entry of April 25, 1862, in *The Private Journal of Henri Frederic Amiel*. By Henri Frederic Amiel, translated by Van Wyck Brooks and Charles Van Wyck Brooks. Revised edition. Macmillan, 1935. Copyright 1935 by Macmillan Publishing Company. Renewed 1962 by Van Wyck Brooks and Charles Van Wyck Brooks. Reprinted with permission of Macmillan Publishing Company.

Anderson, Howard. From an introduction to *The Monk: A Romance*. By Matthew Lewis, edited by Howard Anderson. Oxford University Press, London, 1973. Introduction, notes, bibliography, and chronology © Oxford University Press 1973. All rights reserved. Reprinted by permission of Oxford University Press.

Annan, Noel. From "John Stuart Mill," in *The English Mind: Studies in the English Moralists Presented to Basil Willey*. Edited by Hugh Sykes Davies and George Watson. Cambridge at the University Press, 1964. © Cambridge University Press 1964. Reprinted by permission.

Aptheker, Herbert. From *The American Revolution, 1763-1783: A History of the American People*. International Publishers, 1960. © International Publishers Co., 1960. Reprinted by permission of International Publishers Co., Inc.

Bain, Alexander. From *John Stuart Mill: A Criticism, with Personal Recollections*. Longmans, Green, and Co., 1882.

Becker, Carl. From *The Declaration of Independence: A Study in the History of Political Ideas*. Harcourt, Brace and Company, 1922.

Benger, Elizabeth Ogilvie. From an introduction to *Klopstock and His Friends: A Series of Familiar Letters Written between the Years 1750 and 1803*. Translated by Elizabeth Ogilvie Benger. Henry Colburn, 1814.

Benson, Adolph B. From an introduction to *America of the Fifties: Letters of Fredrika Bremer*. By Fredrika Bremer, edited by Adolph B. Benson. American-Scandinavian Foundation, 1924. Copyright, 1924, renewed 1952, by The American-Scandinavian Foundation. Reprinted by permission.

Berryman, John. From an introduction to *The Monk*. By Matthew G. Lewis, edited by Louis F. Peck. Grove Press, 1952.

Birkenmayer, Sigmund S. From *Nikolaj Nekrasov: His Life and Poetic Art*. Mouton, 1968. © copyright 1968 Mouton & Co., Publishers. Reprinted by permission of Mouton Publishers, a Division of Walter de Gruyter & Co.

Birkhead, Edith. From *The Tale of Terror: A Study of the Gothic Romance*. E. P. Dutton & Co., 1921.

Bosanquet, Bernard. From *The Philosophical Theory of the State*. The Macmillan Company, 1899.

Brandes, Georg. From *Eminent Authors of the Nineteenth Century: Literary Portraits*. Translated by Rasmus B. Anderson. Thomas Y. Crowell & Co., 1886.

Brandes, George. From *Main Currents in Nineteenth Century Literature: The Reaction in France, Vol. III*. Translated by Mary Morison. William Heinemann, 1903.

Brandes, George. From *Main Currents in Nineteenth Century Literature: The Romantic School in France, Vol. V*. Translated by Diana White and Mary Morison. William Heinemann, 1904.

Britt, Albert. From *The Great Biographers*. McGraw-Hill Book Company, Inc., 1936.

Bryan, William Jennings. From "The Statute for Establishing Religious Freedom," in *The Writings of Thomas Jefferson, Vol. VIII*. By Thomas Jefferson, edited by Andrew A. Lipscomb. The Thomas Jefferson Memorial Association of the United States, 1903.

Bulwer, Henry Lytton. From *France: Social, Literary, Political, Vol. II*. Harper & Brothers, 1834.

Byron, Lord. From a journal entry of October 15, 1821, in *The Works of Lord Byron: Letters and Journals, Vol. V*. By Lord Byron, edited by Rowland E. Prothero. John Murray, 1901.

Calhoun, John C. From a speech on the Oregon Bill given on June 27, 1848, in *Appendix to the Congressional Globe*. Blair & Rives, 1848.

Calin, William. From *A Muse for Heroes: Nine Centuries of the Epic in France*. University of Toronto Press, 1983. © University of Toronto Press 1983. Reprinted by permission.

Carlyle, Thomas. From a letter to John Carlyle on November 5, 1873, in *Thomas Carlyle: A History of His Life in London, 1834-1881, Vol. II*. By James Anthony Froude. Longmans, Green, and Co., 1884.

Carlyle, Thomas. From a letter to John Forster on November 18, 1847, in *New Letters of Thomas Carlyle, Vol. II*. By Thomas Carlyle, edited by Alexander Carlyle. John Lane/The Bodley Head, 1904.

Carr, Wendell Robert. From an introduction to *The Subjection of Women*. By John Stuart Mill. M.I.T. Press, 1970. Introduction copyright © 1970 by The Massachusetts Institute of Technology. Reprinted by permission of Wendell Robert Carr.

Chesterton, G. K. From an introduction to *The Life of Charles Dickens*. By John Forster. E. P. Dutton & Co., 1927.

Closs, A. From *The Genius of the German Lyric: An Historic Survey of Its Formal and Metaphysical Values*. George Allen & Unwin Ltd, 1938.

Cockshut, A.O.J. From *The Unbelievers: English Agnostic Thought, 1840-1890*. Collins, 1964. © A.O.J. Cockshut, 1964. Reprinted by permission of the author.

Colby, Vineta and Robert A. Colby. From *The Equivocal Virtue: Mrs. Oliphant and the Victorian Literary Market Place*. Archon Books, Hamden, CT, 1966. © copyright 1966 Vineta and Robert A. Colby. Reprinted by permission of the authors.

Coleridge, S. T. From a letter to William Wordsworth in January, 1798, in *Letters of Samuel Taylor Coleridge, Vol. I*. By Samuel Taylor Coleridge, edited by Ernest Hartley Coleridge. William Heinemann, 1895.

Coleridge, Samuel Taylor. From a conversation of March 20, 1834, in *Specimens of the Table Talk of the Late Samuel Taylor Coleridge*. By Samuel Taylor Coleridge, edited by Henry Nelson Coleridge. John Murray, 1835.

Collyer, Joseph. From a preface to *The Messiah, Vol. 1*. By Friedrich Gottlieb Klopstock, translated by Joseph Collyer. R. and J. Dodsley, 1763.

Cox, Stephen D. From "The Literary Aesthetic of Thomas Jefferson," in *Essays in Early Virginia Literature Honoring Richard Beale Davis*. Edited by J. A. Leo Lamay. Franklin, 1977. © 1977 Burt Franklin & Co., Inc. All rights reserved. Reprinted by permission of Stephen D. Cox.

Davies, James A. From *John Forster: A Literary Life*. Barnes & Noble, 1983. Copyright © Barnes & Noble 1983. All rights reserved. Reprinted by permission of Barnes & Noble Books, a Division of Littlefield, Adams & Co., Inc.

Denommé, Robert T. From *Nineteenth-Century French Romantic Poets*. Southern Illinois University Press, 1969. Copyright © 1969 by Southern Illinois University Press. All rights reserved. Reprinted by permission of the publisher.

Dickens, Charles. From a letter to John Forster on April 22, 1848, in *The Letters of Charles Dickens: 1833 to 1856, Vol. I*. By Charles Dickens, edited by Mamie Dickens and Georgina Hogarth. Charles Scribner's Sons, 1879.

Dostoievsky, F. M. From a diary entry in December, 1877, in *The Diary of a Writer*. By F. M. Dostoievsky, edited and translated by Boris Brasol. Charles Scribner's Sons, 1949. Copyright 1949 Charles Scribner's Sons. Copyright renewed © 1976 James Maxwell Fassett, executor of the Estate of Boris Brasol. All rights reserved. Reprinted with the permission of Charles Scribner's Sons.

Douglass, Elisha P. From *Rebels and Democrats: The Struggle for Equal Political Rights and Majority Rule during the American Revolution*. University of North Carolina Press, 1955. © 1955 by The University of North Carolina Press. Renewed 1983 by Elisha Peairs Douglass. Reprinted by permission.

Elwin, Malcolm. From *Victorian Wallflowers: A Panoramic Survey of the Popular Literary Periodicals*. Jonathan Cape, 1934.

Evans, Bertrand. From *Gothic Drama from Walpole to Shelley*. University of California Press, 1947.

Fenstermaker, John J. From *John Forster*. Twayne, 1984. Copyright 1984 by Twayne Publishers. All rights reserved. Reprinted with the permission of Twayne Publishers, a division of G. K. Hall & Co., Boston.

Fitzgerald, Percy. From *Life and Adventures of Alexander Dumas, Vol. I.* Tinsley Brothers, 1873.

From an extract from a review of "Antony," translated by Percy Fitzgerald, in *Life and Adventures of Alexander Dumas, Vol. I.* By Percy Fitzgerald. Tinsley Brothers, 1873.

Fogle, Richard Harter. From "The Passions of Ambrosio," in *The Classic British Novel.* Edited by Howard M. Harper, Jr. and Charles Edge. University of Georgia Press, 1972. Copyright © 1972 by the University of Georgia Press. All rights reserved. Reprinted by permission of The University of Georgia Press.

Ford, George H. From *Dickens and His Readers: Aspects of Novel-Criticism Since 1836.* Princeton University Press, 1955. Copyright 1955, © 1983 renewed by Princeton University Press. Excerpts reprinted with permission of Princeton University Press.

Ford, Paul Leicester. From an introduction to *The Writings of Thomas Jefferson, Vol. I.* By Thomas Jefferson, edited by P. L. Ford. G. P. Putnam's Sons, 1892.

Forster, John. From *The Life and Times of Oliver Goldsmith, Vol. I.* Second edition. Bradbury and Evans, 1854.

Forster, John. From *The Life of Charles Dickens: 1852-1870, Vol. III.* J. B. Lippincott & Co., 1874.

Francke, Kuno. From *Social Forces in German Literature: A Study in the History of Civilization.* Henry Holt and Company, 1896.

Galsworthy, John. From *Candelabra: Selected Essays and Addresses.* Charles Scribner's Sons, 1933. Copyright 1932 John Galsworthy. Copyright renewed © 1960 A.J.P. Sellar & R. H. Sauter. Reprinted with the permission of Charles Scribner's Sons.

Gautier, Théophile. From *The Complete Works of Théophile Gautier: The Romance of a Mummy, Portraits of the Day, Vol. III.* Edited and translated by F. C. DeSumichrast. G. D. Sproul, 1901.

Ginsberg, Robert. From "The Declaration as Rhetoric," in *A Casebook on The Declaration of Independence.* Edited by Robert Ginsberg. Thomas Y. Crowell Co., Inc., 1967. Copyright © 1967 by Harper & Row, Publishers, Inc. All rights reserved. Reprinted by permission of Harper & Row, Publishers.

Griswold, Rufus Wilmot. From *The Prose Writers of America.* Revised edition. A. Hart, 1852.

Gwynn, Stephen. From *Saints & Scholars.* Thorton Butterworth, Limited, 1929.

Halliday, R. J. From *John Stuart Mill.* Allen & Unwin, 1976. © George Allen & Unwin (Publishers) Ltd. 1976. All rights reserved. Reprinted by permission.

Hayek, Frederick A. von. From "John Stuart Mill at the Age of Twenty-Five," in *The Spirit of the Age.* By John Stuart Mill. University of Chicago Press, 1942. Copyright 1942 by The University of Chicago. Renewed 1970 by Frederick A. von Hayek. All rights reserved. Reprinted by permission of The University of Chicago Press.

Hazlitt, William. From *Lectures on the English Comic Writers.* Taylor and Hessey, 1819.

Hearn, Lafcadio. From *Some Strange English Literary Figures of the Eighteenth and Nineteenth Centuries.* Edited by R. Tanabé. N.p., 1927.

Hemmings, F.W.J. From *Alexandre Dumas: The King of Romance.* Charles Scribner's Sons, 1979. Copyright © 1979 F.W.J. Hemmings. All rights reserved. Reprinted by permission of the author.

Herder, Johann Gottfried von. From an extract from *Herder and Klopstock: A Comparative Study.* By Frederick Henry Adler. G. E. Stechert and Company, Publishers, 1914.

Howells, Coral Ann. From *Love, Mystery, and Misery: Feeling in Gothic Fiction.* The Athlone Press, 1978. © Coral Ann Howells 1978. Reprinted by permission.

Howitt, Mary. From a preface to *The Neighbours: A Story of Every-Day Life.* By Frederika Bremer, translated by Mary Howitt. Longman & Co., 1842.

Hunt, Herbert J. From *The Epic in Nineteenth-Century France: A Study in Heroic and Humanitarian Poetry from "Les Martyrs" to "Les Siècles Morts."* Basil Blackwell, 1941.

Hutchinson, Thomas. From *Strictures upon the Declaration of the Congress at Philadelphia: In a Letter to a Noble Lord, &c.* N.p., 1776.

Ireson, J. C. From *Lamartine: A Revaluation*. University of Hull, 1969. © The University of Hull 1969. Reprinted by permission of the publisher and the author.

James, Henry. From *Notes on Novelists, with Some Other Notes*. Charles Scribner's Sons, 1914. Copyright 1914 Charles Scribner's Sons. Copyright renewed 1942 Henry James. Reprinted with the permission of Charles Scribner's Sons.

Jarintzov, N. From *Russian Poets and Poems: Classics, Vol. I*. B. H. Blackwell, 1917.

Jefferson, Thomas. From an inaugural address given on March 4, 1801, in *The Writings of Thomas Jefferson: Being His Autobiography, Correspondence, Reports, Messages, Addresses, and Other Writings, Official and Private, Vol. VIII*. Edited by H. A. Washington, J. C. Riker, 1856.

Jefferson, Thomas. From a letter to Henry Lee on May 8, 1825, in *The Writings of Thomas Jefferson: 1816-1826, Vol. X*. By Thomas Jefferson, edited by Paul Leicester Ford. G. P. Putnam's Sons, 1899.

Jefferson, Thomas. From a letter to James Madison on August 30, 1823, in *The Writings of Thomas Jefferson: 1816-1826, Vol. X*. By Thomas Jefferson, edited by Paul Leicester Ford. G. P. Putnam's Sons, 1899.

Jeffrey, Francis. From a letter to Margaret Oliphant on January 5, 1850, in *The Autobiography and Letters of Mrs. M.O.W. Oliphant*. By Margaret Oliphant, edited by Mrs Harry Coghill. William Blackwood and Sons, 1899.

Kiely, Robert. From *The Romantic Novel in England*. Cambridge, Mass.: Harvard University Press, 1972. Copyright © 1972 by the President and Fellows of Harvard College. All rights reserved. Excerpted by permission.

Kropotkin, P. From *Russian Literature*. McClure, Phillips & Co., 1905.

Landor, Walter Savage. From *The Works of Walter Savage Landor*. E. Moxon, 1846.

Lang, Andrew. From *Essays in Little*. Charles Scribner's Sons, 1891.

Laski, Harold J. From an introduction to *Autobiography*. By John Stuart Mill. Oxford University Press, London, 1924.

Lavrin, Janko. From *A Panorama of Russian Literature*. Barnes & Noble, 1973. Copyright © 1973 by J. Lavrin. All rights reserved. By permission of Barnes & Noble Books, a Division of Littlefield, Adams & Co., Inc.

Leavis, Q. D. From an introduction to *Miss Marjoribanks*. By. Mrs. Oliphant. The Zodiac Press, 1969. Introduction © Q. D. Leavis 1969. Reprinted by permission of Q. D. Leavis and Chatto & Windus.

Leavis, Q. D. From an introduction to *Autobiography and Letters of Mrs Margaret Oliphant*. By Margaret Oliphant, edited by Mrs Harry Coghill. Leicester University Press, 1974. Introduction copyright © Q. D. Leavis 1974. Reprinted by permission.

Letwin, Shirley Robin. From *The Pursuit of Certainty: David Hume, Jeremy Bentham, John Stuart Mill, Beatrice Webb*. Cambridge at the University Press, 1965. Reprinted by permission.

Levy, Leonard W. From *Jefferson & Civil Liberties: The Darker Side*. Cambridge, Mass.: Belknap Press, 1963. Copyright © 1963 by the President and Fellows of Harvard College. All rights reserved. Reprinted by permission of the author.

Ley, J.W.T. From an introduction to *The Life of Charles Dickens*. By John Forster, edited by J.W.T. Ley. Cecil Palmer, 1928.

Lincoln, Abraham. From a letter to H. L. Pierce and others on April 6, 1859, in *The Writings of Thomas Jefferson, Vol. I*. By Thomas Jefferson, edited by Andrew A. Lipscomb. The Thomas Jefferson Memorial Association of the United States, 1903.

Lincoln, Abraham, and Stephen Arnold Douglas. From speeches delivered from June 10, 1858 through October 7, 1858, in *The Illinois Political Campaign of 1858: A Facsimile of the Printer's Copy of His Debates with Senator Stephen Arnold Douglas as Edited and Prepared for Press by Abraham Lincoln*. The Library of Congress, 1958.

Lind, John. From *An Answer to the Declaration of the American Congress*. Fifth edition. T. Cadell, 1776.

Lindsay, A. D. From an introduction to *Utilitarianism, Liberty, and Representative Government*. By John Stuart Mill. E. P. Dutton and Company, Inc., 1950.

Lovecraft, H. P. From *Dagon and Other Macabre Tales*. Edited by August Derleth. Arkham House, 1965. Copyright 1965, by August Derleth. Reprinted by permission of Arkham House Publishers, Inc.

Madison, James. From a letter to Thomas Jefferson on September 6, 1823, in *Letters and Other Writings of James Madison, Fourth President of the United States, 1816-1828, Vol. III*. By James Madison. J. B. Lippincott & Co., 1865.

Matthews, J. Brander. From *French Dramatists of the 19th Century*. Charles Scribner's Sons, 1881.

Maurois, André. From *The Titans: A Three-generation Biography of the Dumas*. Translated by Gerard Hopkins. Harper & Brothers Publishers, 1957. Copyright © 1957 by André Maurois. All rights reserved. Reprinted by permission of the author and the author's agents, Scott Meredith Literary Agency, Inc., 845 Third Avenue, New York, NY 10022 and Georges Borchardt, Inc.

McCloskey, H. J. From *John Stuart Mill: A Critical Study*. Macmillan, 1971. © H. J. McCloskey 1971. All rights reserved. Reprinted by permission of Macmillan, London and Basingstoke.

M'Cosh, James. From *An Examination of Mr. J. S. Mill's Philosophy: Being a Defence of Fundamental Truth*. Robert Carter & Brothers, 1866.

Menhennet, Alan. From *Order and Freedom: Literature and Society in Germany from 1720 to 1805*. Weidenfeld and Nicolson, 1973. © Alan Menhennet 1973. All rights reserved. Reprinted by permission.

Merriam, Charles Edward. From *A History of American Political Theories*. The Macmillan Company, 1903.

Mill, John Stuart. From an introduction to *On Liberty*. By John Stuart Mill. Parker, 1859.

Mirabeau, Comte de. From "The Declaration in France: Mirabeau," in *A Casebook on The Declaration of Independence*. Edited by Robert Ginsberg. Thomas Y. Crowell Co., Inc., 1967. Copyright © 1967 by Harper & Row, Publishers, Inc. All rights reserved. Reprinted by permission of Harper & Row, Publishers, Inc.

Mirsky, D. S. From *A History of Russian Literature from the Earliest Times to the Death of Dostoyevsky (1881)*. Alfred A. Knopf, Inc., 1927.

Monod, Sylvère. From "John Forster's 'Life of Dickens' and Literary Criticism," in *English Studies Today, fourth series*. Edited by Ilva Cellini and Giorgio Melchiori. Edizioni di Storia e Letteratura, 1966. All rights reserved. Reprinted by permission of the publisher and Sylvère Monod.

Morley, John. From *Edmund Burke: A Historical Study*. Macmillan and Co., 1867.

Morse, David. From *Romanticism: A Structural Analysis*. Barnes & Noble, 1982. © David Morse 1982. All rights reserved. By permission of Barnes & Noble Books, a Division of Littlefield, Adams & Co., Inc.

Musset, Alfred de. From *The Complete Writings of Alfred de Musset: Poems, Vol. II*. Translated by Marie Agathe Clarke. Edwin C. Hill Company, 1905.

Newmarch, Rosa. From *Poetry and Progress in Russia*. John Lane Company, 1907.

Okin, Susan Moller. From *Women in Western Political Thought*. Princeton University Press, 1979. Copyright © 1979 by Princeton University Press. All rights reserved. Excerpts reprinted with permission of Princeton University Press.

Oliphant, Margaret. From *The Autobiography and Letters of Mrs M.O.W. Oliphant*. Edited by Mrs Harry Coghill. William Blackwood and Sons, 1899.

Oliphant, Margaret Oliphant Wilson. From "Preface to the New Issue," in *The Literary History of England in the End of the Eighteenth and Beginning of the Nineteenth Century, Vol. I*. By Mrs. Oliphant. Macmillan and Co., 1882.

Oliphant, Margaret Oliphant Wilson. From a preface to *The Heir Presumptive and the Heir Apparent, Vol. I*. By Mrs. Oliphant. Macmillan & Co., 1892.

Oliphant, Mrs. From a preface to *The Literary History of England in the End of the Eighteenth and Beginning of the Nineteenth Century, Vol. I*. By Mrs. Oliphant. Macmillan and Co., 1882.

Oncken, Wilhelm. From "The Strategy of Composition," translated by Robert Ginsberg, in *A Casebook on The Declaration of Independence*. Edited by Robert Ginsberg. Thomas Y. Crowell Co., Inc., 1967. Copyright © 1967 by Harper & Row, Publishers, Inc. All rights reserved. Reprinted by permission of Harper & Row, Publishers, Inc.

Parigot, Hippolyte. From an extract in *The Titans: A Three-generation Biography of the Dumas*. By André Maurois, translated by Gerard Hopkins. Harper & Brothers Publishers, 1957. Copyright © 1957 by André Maurois. All rights reserved. Reprinted by permission of the author and the author's agents, Scott Meredith Literary Agency, Inc., 845 Third Avenue, New York, NY 10022 and Georges Borchardt, Inc.

Cumulative Index to Authors

This index lists all author entries in the Gale Literary Criticism Series and includes cross-references to other Gale sources. References in the index are identified as follows:

AITN: *Authors in the News*, Volumes 1-2
CAAS: *Contemporary Authors Autobiography Series*, Volumes 1-2
CA: *Contemporary Authors* (original series), Volumes 1-116
CANR: *Contemporary Authors New Revision Series*, Volumes 1-16
CAP: *Contemporary Authors Permanent Series*, Volumes 1-2
CA-R: *Contemporary Authors* (revised editions), Volumes 1-44
CLC: *Contemporary Literary Criticism*, Volumes 1-36
CLR: *Children's Literature Review*, Volumes 1-9
DLB: *Dictionary of Literary Biography*, Volumes 1-42
DLB-DS: *Dictionary of Literary Biography Documentary Series*, Volumes 1-4
DLB-Y: *Dictionary of Literary Biography Yearbook*, Volumes 1980-1984
LC: *Literature Criticism from 1400 to 1800*, Volumes 1-2
NCLC: *Nineteenth-Century Literature Criticism*, Volumes 1-11
SATA: *Something about the Author*, Volumes 1-41
TCLC: *Twentieth-Century Literary Criticism*, Volumes 1-19
YABC: *Yesterday's Authors of Books for Children*, Volumes 1-2

Author Index

Author Index

Author Index

Author Index

Author Index

Kiely, Benedict 1919- ....CLC 23
See also CANR 2
See also CA 1-4R
See also DLB 15

Kienzle, William X(avier)
1928- ....CLC 25
See also CAAS 1
See also CANR 9
See also CA 93-96

Killens, John Oliver 1916-.........CLC 10
See also CAAS 2
See also CA 77-80
See also DLB 33

King, Francis (Henry) 1923- ....CLC 8
See also CANR 1
See also CA 1-4R
See also DLB 15

King, Stephen (Edwin)
1947- .... CLC 12, 26
See also CANR 1
See also CA 61-64
See also SATA 9
See also DLB-Y 80

Kingman, (Mary) Lee 1919- ....CLC 17
See also Natti, (Mary) Lee
See also CA 5-8R
See also SATA 1

Kingston, Maxine Hong
1940-................... CLC 12, 19
See also CANR 13
See also CA 69-72
See also DLB-Y 80

Kinnell, Galway
1927-.......... CLC 1, 2, 3, 5, 13, 29
See also CANR 10
See also CA 9-12R
See also DLB 5

Kinsella, Thomas 1928- .... CLC 4, 19
See also CA 17-20R
See also DLB 27

Kinsella, W(illiam) P(atrick)
1935-........................CLC 27
See also CA 97-100

Kipling, (Joseph) Rudyard
1865-1936........... TCLC 8, 17
See also CA 105
See also YABC 2
See also DLB 19, 34

Kirkup, James 1927-...............CLC 1
See also CANR 2
See also CA 1-4R
See also SATA 12
See also DLB 27

Kirkwood, James 1930- ....CLC 9
See also CANR 6
See also CA 1-4R
See also AITN 2

Kizer, Carolyn (Ashley) 1925-......CLC 15
See also CA 65-68
See also DLB 5

Klausner, Amos 1939-
See Oz, Amos

Klein, A(braham) M(oses)
1909-1972....................CLC 19
See also CA 101
See also obituary CA 37-40R

Klein, Norma 1938-...............CLC 30
See also CLR 2
See also CANR 15
See also CA 41-44R
See also SATA 7

Klein, T.E.D. 19??-...............CLC 34

Kleist, Heinrich von
1777-1811.................. NCLC 2

Klimentev, Andrei Platonovich 1899-1951
See Platonov, Andrei (Platonovich)
See also CA 108

Klinger, Friedrich Maximilian von
1752-1831................... NCLC 1

Klopstock, Friedrich Gottlieb
1724-1803................. NCLC 11

Knebel, Fletcher 1911-............CLC 14
See also CANR 1
See also CA 1-4R
See also SATA 36
See also AITN 1

Knowles, John 1926-......CLC 1, 4, 10, 26
See also CA 17-20R
Scc also SATA 8
See also DLB 6

Koch, Kenneth 1925- .... CLC 5, 8
See also CANR 6
See also CA 1-4R
See also DLB 5

Koestler, Arthur
1905-1983....... CLC 1, 3, 6, 8, 15, 33
See also CANR 1
See also CA 1-4R
See also obituary CA 109
See also DLB-Y 83

Kohout, Pavel 1928- ....CLC 13
See also CANR 3
See also CA 45-48

Konrád, György 1933- .... CLC 4, 10
See also CA 85-88

Konwicki, Tadeusz 1926-....... CLC 8, 28
See also CA 101

Kopit, Arthur (Lee)
1937-................. CLC 1, 18, 33
See also CA 81-84
See also DLB 7
See also AITN 1

Kops, Bernard 1926-...............CLC 4
See also CA 5-8R
See also DLB 13

Kornbluth, C(yril) M.
1923-1958.................. TCLC 8
See also CA 105
See also DLB 8

Kosinski, Jerzy (Nikodem)
1933-.......... CLC 1, 2, 3, 6, 10, 15
See also CANR 9
See also CA 17-20R
See also DLB 2
See also DLB-Y 82

Kostelanetz, Richard (Cory)
1940-.......................CLC 28
See also CA 13-16R

Kostrowitzki, Wilhelm Apollinaris de
1880-1918
See Apollinaire, Guillaume
See also CA 104

Kotlowitz, Robert 1924-............CLC 4
See also CA 33-36R

Kotzwinkle, William
1938-............... CLC 5, 14, 35
See also CLR 6
See also CANR 3
See also CA 45-48
See also SATA 24

Kozol, Jonathan 1936- ....CLC 17
See also CANR 16
See also CA 61-64

Kozoll, Michael 1940?-
See Bochco, Steven and Kozoll, Michael

Kramer, Kathryn 19??- ....CLC 34

Krasicki, Ignacy 1735-1801 ...... NCLC 8

Krasiński, Zygmunt
1812-1859................... NCLC 4

Kraus, Karl 1874-1936........... TCLC 5
See also CA 104

Kristofferson, Kris 1936- ....CLC 26
See also CA 104

Krleža, Miroslav 1893-1981........CLC 8
See also CA 97-100
See also obituary CA 105

Kroetsch, Robert 1927-......... CLC 5, 23
See also CANR 8
See also CA 17-20R

Krotkov, Yuri 1917-...............CLC 19
See also CA 102

Krumgold, Joseph (Quincy)
1908-1980...................CLC 12
See also CANR 7
See also CA 9-12R
See also obituary CA 101
See also SATA 1
See also obituary SATA 23

Krutch, Joseph Wood
1893-1970...................CLC 24
See also CANR 4
See also CA 1-4R
See also obituary CA 25-28R

Krylov, Ivan Andreevich
1768?-1844................. NCLC 1

Kubrick, Stanley 1928-............CLC 16
See also CA 81-84
See also DLB 26

Kumin, Maxine (Winokur)
1925-................. CLC 5, 13, 28
See also CANR 1
See also CA 1-4R
See also SATA 12
See also DLB 5
See also AITN 2

Kundera, Milan
1929-................CLC 4, 9, 19, 32
See also CA 85-88

Kunitz, Stanley J(asspon)
1905-................ CLC 6, 11, 14
See also CA 41-44R

Kunze, Reiner 1933-..............CLC 10
See also CA 93-96

Kuprin, Aleksandr (Ivanovich)
1870-1938................. TCLC 5
See also CA 104

Kurosawa, Akira 1910-............CLC 16
See also CA 101

Lelchuk, Alan 1938- ....CLC 5
 See also CANR 1
 See also CA 45-48

Lem, Stanislaw 1921- ....CLC 8, 15
 See also CAAS 1
 See also CA 105

L'Engle, Madeleine 1918-..........CLC 12
 See also CLR 1
 See also CANR 3
 See also CA 1-4R
 See also SATA 1, 27
 See also AITN 2

Lennon, John (Ono)
   1940-1980....................CLC 35
 See also Lennon, John (Ono) and
   McCartney, Paul
 See also CA 102

Lennon, John (Ono) 1940-1980 and
   McCartney, Paul 1942- ....CLC 12

Lennon, John Winston 1940-1980
 See Lennon, John (Ono)

Lentricchia, Frank (Jr.) 1940-......CLC 34
 See also CA 25-28R

Lenz, Siegfried 1926- ....CLC 27
 See also CA 89-92

Leonard, Elmore 1925-........ CLC 28, 34
 See also CANR 12
 See also CA 81-84
 See also AITN 1

Leonard, Hugh 1926- ....CLC 19
 See also Byrne, John Keyes
 See also DLB 13

Lerman, Eleanor 1952-.............CLC 9
 See also CA 85-88

Lermontov, Mikhail Yuryevich
   1814-1841...................NCLC 5

Lesage, Alain-René 1668-1747.......LC 2

Lessing, Doris (May)
   1919-.......CLC 1, 2, 3, 6, 10, 15, 22
 See also CA 9-12R
 See also DLB 15

Lester, Richard 1932-.............CLC 20

Leverson, Ada 1865-1936........ TCLC 18

Levertov, Denise
   1923-........CLC 1, 2, 3, 5, 8, 15, 28
 See also CANR 3
 See also CA 1-4R
 See also DLB 5

Levin, Ira 1929-................ CLC 3, 6
 See also CA 21-24R

Levin, Meyer 1905-1981............CLC 7
 See also CANR 15
 See also CA 9-12R
 See also obituary CA 104
 See also SATA 21
 See also obituary SATA 27
 See also DLB 9, 28
 See also DLB-Y 81
 See also AITN 1

Levine, Philip
   1928-.......... CLC 2, 4, 5, 9, 14, 33
 See also CANR 9
 See also CA 9-12R
 See also DLB 5

Levitin, Sonia 1934- ....CLC 17
 See also CA 29-32R
 See also SATA 4

Lewis, Alun 1915-1944.......... TCLC 3
 See also CA 104
 See also DLB 20

Lewis, C(ecil) Day 1904-1972
 See Day Lewis, C(ecil)

Lewis, C(live) S(taples)
   1898-1963........ CLC 1, 3, 6, 14, 27
 See also CLR 3
 See also CA 81-84
 See also SATA 13
 See also DLB 15

Lewis, (Harry) Sinclair
   1885-1951................ TCLC 4, 13
 See also CA 104
 See also DLB 9
 See also DLB-DS 1

Lewis, Matthew Gregory
   1775-1818..................NCLC 11
 See also DLB 39

Lewis, (Percy) Wyndham
   1882?-1957................ TCLC 2, 9
 See also CA 104
 See also DLB 15

Lewisohn, Ludwig 1883-1955 .... TCLC 19
 See also CA 107
 See also DLB 4, 9, 28

Lezama Lima, José
   1910-1976............... CLC 4, 10
 See also CA 77-80

Li Fei-kan 1904-
 See Pa Chin
 See also CA 105

Lie, Jonas (Lauritz Idemil)
   1833-1908.................. TCLC 5

Lieber, Joel 1936-1971.............CLC 6
 See also CA 73-76
 See also obituary CA 29-32R

Lieber, Stanley Martin 1922-
 See Lee, Stan

Lieberman, Laurence (James)
   1935-..................... CLC 4, 36
 See also CANR 8
 See also CA 17-20R

Lightfoot, Gordon (Meredith)
   1938-........................CLC 26
 See also CA 109

Liliencron, Detlev von
   1844-1909.................. TCLC 18

Lima, José Lezama 1910-1976
 See Lezama Lima, José

Lind, Jakov 1927-.........CLC 1, 2, 4, 27
 See also Landwirth, Heinz
 See also CA 9-12R

Lindsay, David 1876-1945 ...... TCLC 15
 See also CA 113

Lindsay, (Nicholas) Vachel
   1879-1931.................. TCLC 17
 See also CA 114
 See also SATA 40

Lipsyte, Robert (Michael)
   1938-........................CLC 21
 See also CANR 8
 See also CA 17-20R
 See also SATA 5

Liu E 1857-1909 .... TCLC 15
 See also CA 115

Lively, Penelope 1933- ....CLC 32
 See also CLR 7
 See also CA 41-44R
 See also SATA 7
 See also DLB 14

Livesay, Dorothy 1909-......... CLC 4, 15
 See also CA 25-28R
 See also AITN 2

Llewellyn, Richard 1906-1983.......CLC 7
 See also Llewellyn Lloyd, Richard (Dafydd
   Vyvyan)
 See also DLB 15

Llewellyn Lloyd, Richard (Dafydd Vyvyan)
   1906-1983
 See Llewellyn, Richard
 See also CANR 7
 See also CA 53-56
 See also obituary CA 111
 See also SATA 11

Llosa, Mario Vargas 1936-
 See Vargas Llosa, Mario

Lloyd, Richard Llewellyn 1906-
 See Llewellyn, Richard

Lockhart, John Gibson
   1794-1854................... NCLC 6

Lodge, David (John) 1935-........CLC 36
 See also CA 17-20R
 See also DLB 14

Logan, John 1923-.................CLC 5
 See also CA 77-80
 See also DLB 5

Lombino, S. A. 1926-
 See Hunter, Evan

London, Jack 1876-1916 ...... TCLC 9, 15
 See also London, John Griffith
 See also SATA 18
 See also DLB 8, 12
 See also AITN 2

London, John Griffith 1876-1916
 See London, Jack
 See also CA 110

Long, Emmett 1925-
 See Leonard, Elmore

Longfellow, Henry Wadsworth
   1807-1882................... NCLC 2
 See also SATA 19
 See also DLB 1

Longley, Michael 1939-............CLC 29
 See also CA 102
 See also DLB 40

Lopate, Phillip 1943-..............CLC 29
 See also CA 97-100
 See also DLB-Y 80

López y Fuentes, Gregorio
   1897-1966...................CLC 32

Lord, Bette Bao 1938-.............CLC 23
 See also CA 107

Lorde, Audre (Geraldine)
   1934-........................CLC 18
 See also CANR 16
 See also CA 25-28R
 See also DLB 41

Loti, Pierre 1850-1923 .... TCLC 11
 See also Viaud, (Louis Marie) Julien

Lovecraft, H(oward) P(hillips)
   1890-1937................... TCLC 4
 See also CA 104

Mull, Martin 1943- . . . . CLC 17
See also CA 105

Munro, Alice 1931- . . . . CLC 6, 10, 19
See also CA 33-36R
See also SATA 29
See also AITN 2

Munro, H(ector) H(ugh) 1870-1916
See Saki
See also CA 104
See also DLB 34

Murdoch, (Jean) Iris
1919- . . . . . . CLC 1, 2, 3, 4, 6, 8, 11, 15,
22, 31
See also CANR 8
See also CA 13-16R
See also DLB 14

Murphy, Sylvia 19??- . . . . CLC 34

Murry, John Middleton
1889-1957 . . . . TCLC 16

Musgrave, Susan 1951- . . . . CLC 13
See also CA 69-72

Musil, Robert (Edler von)
1880-1942 . . . . TCLC 12
See also CA 109

Musset, (Louis Charles) Alfred de
1810-1857 . . . . NCLC 7

Myers, Walter Dean 1937- . . . . CLC 35
See also CLR 4
See also CA 33-36R
See also SATA 27, 41
See also DLB 33

Nabokov, Vladimir (Vladimirovich)
1899-1977 . . . . . . CLC 1, 2, 3, 6, 8, 11,
15, 23
See also CA 5-8R
See also obituary CA 69-72
See also DLB 2
See also DLB-Y 80
See also DLB-DS 3

Nagy, László 1925-1978 . . . . CLC 7
See also obituary CA 112

Naipaul, Shiva 1945-1985 . . . . CLC 32
See also CA 110, 112
See also obituary CA 116

Naipaul, V(idiadhar) S(urajprasad)
1932- . . . . CLC 4, 7, 9, 13, 18
See also CANR 1
See also CA 1-4R

Nakos, Ioulia 1899?-
See Nakos, Lilika

Nakos, Lilika 1899?- . . . . CLC 29

Nakou, Lilika 1899?-
See Nakos, Lilika

Narayan, R(asipuram) K(rishnaswami)
1906- . . . . CLC 7, 28
See also CA 81-84

Nash, (Frediric) Ogden
1902-1971 . . . . CLC 23
See also CAP 1
See also CA 13-14
See also obituary CA 29-32R
See also SATA 2
See also DLB 11

Nathan, George Jean
1882-1958 . . . . TCLC 18
See also CA 114

Natsume, Kinnosuke 1867-1916
See Natsume, Sōseki
See also CA 104

Natsume, Sōseki
1867-1916 . . . . TCLC 2, 10
See also Natsume, Kinnosuke

Natti, (Mary) Lee 1919-
See Kingman, (Mary) Lee
See also CANR 2

Naylor, Gloria 1950- . . . . CLC 28
See also CA 107

Neihardt, John G(neisenau)
1881-1973 . . . . CLC 32
See also CAP 1
See also CA 13-14
See also DLB 9

Nekrasov, Nikolai Alekseevich
1821-1878 . . . . NCLC 11

Nelligan, Émile 1879-1941 . . . . TCLC 14
See also CA 114

Nelson, Willie 1933- . . . . CLC 17
See also CA 107

Nemerov, Howard
1920- . . . . CLC 2, 6, 9, 36
See also CANR 1
See also CA 1-4R
See also DLB 5, 6
See also DLB-Y 83

Neruda, Pablo
1904-1973 . . . . CLC 1, 2, 5, 7, 9, 28
See also CAP 2
See also CA 19-20
See also obituary CA 45-48

Nerval, Gérard de 1808-1855 . . . . . NCLC 1

Nervo, (José) Amado (Ruiz de)
1870-1919 . . . . TCLC 11
See also CA 109

Neufeld, John (Arthur) 1938- . . . . . . CLC 17
See also CANR 11
See also CA 25-28R
See also SATA 6

Neville, Emily Cheney 1919- . . . . CLC 12
See also CANR 3
See also CA 5-8R
See also SATA 1

Newbound, Bernard Slade 1930-
See Slade, Bernard
See also CA 81-84

Newby, P(ercy) H(oward)
1918- . . . . CLC 2, 13
See also CA 5-8R
See also DLB 15

Newlove, Donald 1928- . . . . CLC 6
See also CA 29-32R

Newlove, John (Herbert) 1938- . . . . . CLC 14
See also CANR 9
See also CA 21-24R

Newman, Charles 1938- . . . . CLC 2, 8
See also CA 21-24R

Newman, Edwin (Harold)
1919- . . . . CLC 14
See also CANR 5
See also CA 69-72
See also AITN 1

Newton, Suzanne 1936- . . . . CLC 35
See also CANR 14
See also CA 41-44R
See also SATA 5

Ngugi, James (Thiong'o)
1938- . . . . CLC 3, 7, 13, 36
See also Ngugi wa Thiong'o
See also Wa Thiong'o, Ngugi
See also CA 81-84

Ngugi wa Thiong'o
1938- . . . . CLC 3, 7, 13, 36
See also Ngugi, James (Thiong'o)
See also Wa Thiong'o, Ngugi

Nichol, B(arne) P(hillip) 1944- . . . . . . CLC 18
See also CA 53-56

Nichols, Peter 1927- . . . . CLC 5, 36
See also CA 104
See also DLB 13

Niedecker, Lorine 1903-1970 . . . . CLC 10
See also CAP 2
See also CA 25-28

Nietzsche, Friedrich (Wilhelm)
1844-1900 . . . . TCLC 10, 18
See also CA 107

Nightingale, Anne Redmon 1943-
See Redmon (Nightingale), Anne
See also CA 103

Nin, Anaïs
1903-1977 . . . . CLC 1, 4, 8, 11, 14
See also CA 13-16R
See also obituary CA 69-72
See also DLB 2, 4
See also AITN 2

Nissenson, Hugh 1933- . . . . CLC 4, 9
See also CA 17-20R
See also DLB 28

Niven, Larry 1938- . . . . CLC 8
See also Niven, Laurence Van Cott
See also DLB 8

Niven, Laurence Van Cott 1938-
See Niven, Larry
See also CANR 14
See also CA 21-24R

Nixon, Agnes Eckhardt 1927- . . . . . . CLC 21
See also CA 110

Norman, Marsha 1947- . . . . CLC 28
See also CA 105
See also DLB-Y 84

Norris, Leslie 1921- . . . . CLC 14
See also CANR 14
See also CAP 1
See also CA 11-12
See also DLB 27

North, Andrew 1912-
See Norton, Andre

North, Christopher 1785-1854
See Wilson, John

Norton, Alice Mary 1912-
See Norton, Andre
See also CANR 2
See also CA 1-4R
See also SATA 1

Norton, Andre 1912- . . . . CLC 12
See also Norton, Mary Alice
See also DLB 8

Norway, Nevil Shute 1899-1960
  See Shute (Norway), Nevil
  See also CA 102
  See also obituary CA 93-96

Nossack, Hans Erich 1901-1978 . . . . . **CLC 6**
  See also CA 93-96
  See also obituary CA 85-88

Nova, Craig 1945- . . . . **CLC 7, 31**
  See also CANR 2
  See also CA 45-48

Nowlan, Alden (Albert) 1933- . . . . . .**CLC 15**
  See also CANR 5
  See also CA 9-12R

Noyes, Alfred 1880-1958 . . . . **TCLC 7**
  See also CA 104
  See also DLB 20

Nunn, Kem 19??- . . . .**CLC 34**

Nye, Robert 1939- . . . .**CLC 13**
  See also CA 33-36R
  See also SATA 6
  See also DLB 14

Nyro, Laura 1947- . . . .**CLC 17**

Oates, Joyce Carol
  1938- . . . . .**CLC 1, 2, 3, 6, 9, 11, 15, 19, 33**
  See also CA 5-8R
  See also DLB 2, 5
  See also DLB-Y 81
  See also AITN 1

O'Brien, Darcy 1939- . . . .**CLC 11**
  See also CANR 8
  See also CA 21-24R

O'Brien, Edna
  1932- . . . . **CLC 3, 5, 8, 13, 36**
  See also CANR 6
  See also CA 1-4R
  See also DLB 14

O'Brien, Flann
  1911-1966 . . . . **CLC 1, 4, 5, 7, 10**
  See also O Nuallain, Brian

O'Brien, Richard 19??- . . . .**CLC 17**

O'Brien, Tim 1946- . . . . **CLC 7, 19**
  See also CA 85-88
  See also DLB-Y 80

O'Casey, Sean
  1880-1964 . . . . **CLC 1, 5, 9, 11, 15**
  See also CA 89-92
  See also DLB 10

Ochs, Phil 1940-1976 . . . .**CLC 17**
  See also obituary CA 65-68

O'Connor, Edwin (Greene)
  1918-1968 . . . .**CLC 14**
  See also CA 93-96
  See also obituary CA 25-28R

O'Connor, (Mary) Flannery
  1925-1964 . . . . . . **CLC 1, 2, 3, 6, 10, 13, 15, 21**
  See also CANR 3
  See also CA 1-4R
  See also DLB 2
  See also DLB-Y 80

O'Connor, Frank
  1903-1966 . . . . **CLC 14, 23**
  See also O'Donovan, Michael (John)

O'Dell, Scott 1903- . . . .**CLC 30**
  See also CLR 1
  See also CANR 12
  See also CA 61-64
  See also SATA 12

Odets, Clifford 1906-1963 . . . . . . **CLC 2, 28**
  See also CA 85-88
  See also DLB 7, 26

O'Donovan, Michael (John) 1903-1966
  See O'Connor, Frank
  See also CA 93-96

Ōe, Kenzaburō 1935- . . . . **CLC 10, 36**
  See also CA 97-100

O'Faolain, Julia 1932- . . . . **CLC 6, 19**
  See also CAAS 2
  See also CANR 12
  See also CA 81-84
  See also DLB 14

O'Faoláin, Seán
  1900- . . . .**CLC 1, 7, 14, 32**
  See also CANR 12
  See also CA 61-64
  See also DLB 15

O'Flaherty, Liam
  1896-1984 . . . . **CLC 5, 34**
  See also CA 101
  See also obituary CA 113
  See also DLB 36
  See also DLB-Y 84

O'Grady, Standish (James)
  1846-1928 . . . . **TCLC 5**
  See also CA 104

O'Hara, Frank
  1926-1966 . . . .**CLC 2, 5, 13**
  See also CA 9-12R
  See also obituary CA 25-28R
  See also DLB 5, 16

O'Hara, John (Henry)
  1905-1970 . . . . **CLC 1, 2, 3, 6, 11**
  See also CA 5-8R
  See also obituary CA 25-28R
  See also DLB 9
  See also DLB-DS 2

Okigbo, Christopher (Ifenayichukwu)
  1932-1967 . . . .**CLC 25**
  See also CA 77-80

Olds, Sharon 1942- . . . .**CLC 32**
  See also CA 101

Olesha, Yuri (Karlovich)
  1899-1960 . . . .**CLC 8**
  See also CA 85-88

Oliphant, Margaret (Oliphant Wilson)
  1828-1897 . . . . **NCLC 11**
  See also DLB 18

Oliver, Mary 1935- . . . . **CLC 19, 34**
  See also CANR 9
  See also CA 21-24R
  See also DLB 5

Olivier, (Baron) Laurence (Kerr)
  1907- . . . .**CLC 20**
  See also CA 111

Olsen, Tillie 1913- . . . . **CLC 4, 13**
  See also CANR 1
  See also CA 1-4R
  See also DLB 28
  See also DLB-Y 80

Olson, Charles (John)
  1910-1970 . . . . . . **CLC 1, 2, 5, 6, 9, 11, 29**
  See also CAP 1
  See also CA 15-16
  See also obituary CA 25-28R
  See also DLB 5, 16

Olson, Theodore 1937-
  See Olson, Toby

Olson, Toby 1937- . . . .**CLC 28**
  See also CANR 9
  See also CA 65-68

Ondaatje, (Philip) Michael
  1943- . . . . **CLC 14, 29**
  See also CA 77-80

Oneal, Elizabeth 1934-
  See Oneal, Zibby
  See also CA 106
  See also SATA 30

Oneal, Zibby 1934- . . . .**CLC 30**
  See also Oneal, Elizabeth

O'Neill, Eugene (Gladstone)
  1888-1953 . . . . **TCLC 1, 6**
  See also CA 110
  See also AITN 1
  See also DLB 7

Onetti, Juan Carlos 1909- . . . . . . **CLC 7, 10**
  See also CA 85-88

O'Nolan, Brian 1911-1966
  See O'Brien, Flann

O Nuallain, Brian 1911-1966
  See O'Brien, Flann
  See also CAP 2
  See also CA 21-22
  See also obituary CA 25-28R

Oppen, George
  1908-1984 . . . .**CLC 7, 13, 34**
  See also CANR 8
  See also CA 13-16R
  See also obituary CA 113
  See also DLB 5

Orlovitz, Gil 1918-1973 . . . .**CLC 22**
  See also CA 77-80
  See also obituary CA 45-48
  See also DLB 2, 5

Ortega y Gasset, José
  1883-1955 . . . .**TCLC 9**
  See also CA 106

Orton, Joe 1933?-1967 . . . . **CLC 4, 13**
  See also Orton, John Kingsley
  See also DLB 13

Orton, John Kingsley 1933?-1967
  See Orton, Joe
  See also CA 85-88

Orwell, George
  1903-1950 . . . .**TCLC 2, 6, 15**
  See also Blair, Eric Arthur
  See also DLB 15

Osborne, John (James)
  1929- . . . .**CLC 1, 2, 5, 11**
  See also CA 13-16R
  See also DLB 13

Osceola 1885-1962
  See Dinesen, Isak
  See also Blixen, Karen (Christentze Dinesen)

Author Index

Sauser-Hall, Frédéric-Louis 1887-1961
  See Cendrars, Blaise
  See also obituary CA 93-96

Sayers, Dorothy L(eigh)
    1893-1957 . . . . TCLC 2, 15
  See also CA 104
  See also DLB 10, 36

Sayles, John (Thomas)
    1950- . . . . CLC 7, 10, 14
  See also CA 57-60

Scammell, Michael 19??- . . . . CLC 34

Schaeffer, Susan Fromberg
    1941- . . . . CLC 6, 11, 22
  See also CA 49-52
  See also SATA 22
  See also DLB 28

Schell, Jonathan 1943- . . . . CLC 35
  See also CANR 12
  See also CA 73-76

Scherer, Jean-Marie Maurice 1920-
  See Rohmer, Eric
  See also CA 110

Schevill, James (Erwin) 1920- . . . . CLC 7
  See also CA 5-8R

Schisgal, Murray (Joseph)
    1926- . . . . CLC 6
  See also CA 21-24R

Schlee, Ann 1934- . . . . CLC 35
  See also CA 101
  See also SATA 36

Schmitz, Ettore 1861-1928
  See Svevo, Italo
  See also CA 104

Schneider, Leonard Alfred 1925-1966
  See Bruce, Lenny
  See also CA 89-92

Schnitzler, Arthur 1862-1931 . . . . . TCLC 4
  See also CA 104

Schorer, Mark 1908-1977 . . . . CLC 9
  See also CANR 7
  See also CA 5-8R
  See also obituary CA 73-76

Schrader, Paul (Joseph) 1946- . . . . . . CLC 26
  See also CA 37-40R

**Schreiner (Cronwright), Olive (Emilie
    Albertina)** 1855-1920 . . . . TCLC 9
  See also CA 105
  See also DLB 18

Schulberg, Budd (Wilson) 1914- . . . . . CLC 7
  See also CA 25-28R
  See also DLB 6, 26, 28
  See also DLB-Y 81

Schulz, Bruno 1892-1942 . . . . TCLC 5
  See also CA 115

Schulz, Charles M(onroe)
    1922- . . . . CLC 12
  See also CANR 6
  See also CA 9-12R
  See also SATA 10

Schuyler, James (Marcus)
    1923- . . . . CLC 5, 23
  See also CA 101
  See also DLB 5

Schwartz, Delmore
    1913-1966 . . . . CLC 2, 4, 10
  See also CAP 2
  See also CA 17-18
  See also obituary CA 25-28R
  See also DLB 28

Schwartz, Lynne Sharon 1939- . . . . . CLC 31
  See also CA 103

Schwarz-Bart, André 1928- . . . . . . CLC 2, 4
  See also CA 89-92

Schwarz-Bart, Simone 1938- . . . . CLC 7
  See also CA 97-100

Sciascia, Leonardo 1921- . . . . CLC 8, 9
  See also CA 85-88

Scoppettone, Sandra 1936- . . . . CLC 26
  See also CA 5-8R
  See also SATA 9

Scorsese, Martin 1942- . . . . CLC 20
  See also CA 110, 114

Scotland, Jay 1932-
  See Jakes, John (William)

Scott, Duncan Campbell
    1862-1947 . . . . TCLC 6
  See also CA 104

Scott, F(rancis) R(eginald)
    1899-1985 . . . . CLC 22
  See also CA 101
  See also obituary CA 114

Scott, Paul (Mark) 1920-1978 . . . . CLC 9
  See also CA 81-84
  See also obituary CA 77-80
  See also DLB 14

Scudéry, Madeleine de 1607-1701 . . . . . LC 2

Seare, Nicholas 1925-
  See Trevanian
  See also Whitaker, Rodney

Sebestyen, Igen 1924-
  See Sebestyen, Ouida

Sebestyen, Ouida 1924- . . . . CLC 30
  See also CA 107
  See also SATA 39

Seelye, John 1931- . . . . CLC 7
  See also CA 97-100

Seferiades, Giorgos Stylianou 1900-1971
  See Seferis, George
  See also CANR 5
  See also CA 5-8R
  See also obituary CA 33-36R

Seferis, George 1900-1971 . . . . . . CLC 5, 11
  See also Seferiades, Giorgos Stylianou

Segal, Erich (Wolf) 1937- . . . . CLC 3, 10
  See also CA 25-28R

Seger, Bob 1945- . . . . CLC 35

Seger, Robert Clark 1945-
  See Seger, Bob

Seghers, Anna 1900- . . . . CLC 7
  See Radvanyi, Netty

Seidel, Frederick (Lewis) 1936- . . . . . CLC 18
  See also CANR 8
  See also CA 13-16R
  See also DLB-Y 84

Seifert, Jaroslav 1901- . . . . CLC 34

Selby, Hubert, Jr.
    1928- . . . . CLC 1, 2, 4, 8
  See also CA 13-16R
  See also DLB 2

Sender, Ramón (José)
    1902-1982 . . . . CLC 8
  See also CANR 8
  See also CA 5-8R
  See also obituary CA 105

Serling, (Edward) Rod(man) 1924-1975
  See also CA 65-68
  See also obituary CA 57-60
  See also DLB 26
  See also AITN 1

Serpières 1907-
  See Guillevic, (Eugène)

Service, Robert W(illiam)
    1874-1958 . . . . TCLC 15
  See also CA 115
  See also SATA 20

Seton, Cynthia Propper
    1926-1982 . . . . CLC 27
  See also CANR-7
  See also CA 5-8R
  See also obituary CA 108

Settle, Mary Lee 1918- . . . . CLC 19
  See also CAAS 1
  See also CA 89-92
  See also DLB 6

Sexton, Anne (Harvey)
    1928-1974 . . . . . . CLC 2, 4, 6, 8, 10, 15
  See also CANR 3
  See also CA 1-4R
  See also obituary CA 53-56
  See also SATA 10
  See also DLB 5

Shaara, Michael (Joseph)
    1929- . . . . CLC 15
  See also CA 102
  See also DLB-Y 83
  See also AITN 1

Shaffer, Anthony 1926- . . . . CLC 19
  See also CA 110
  See also CA 116
  See also DLB 13

Shaffer, Peter (Levin)
    1926- . . . . CLC 5, 14, 18
  See also CA 25-28R
  See also DLB 13

Shalamov, Varlam (Tikhonovich)
    1907?-1982 . . . . CLC 18
  See also obituary CA 105

Shamlu, Ahmad 1925- . . . . CLC 10

Shange, Ntozake 1948- . . . . CLC 8, 25
  See also CA 85-88
  See also DLB 38

Shapiro, Karl (Jay) 1913- . . . . . CLC 4, 8, 15
  See also CANR 1
  See also CA 1-4R

Sharpe, Tom 1928- . . . . CLC 36
  See also CA 114
  See also DLB 14

Shaw, (George) Bernard
    1856-1950 . . . . TCLC 3, 9
  See also CA 104, 109
  See also DLB 10

Shaw, Irwin 1913-1984 . . . . . . CLC 7, 23, 34
  See also CA 13-16R
  See also obituary CA 112
  See also DLB 6
  See also DLB-Y 84
  See also AITN 1

Sutro, Alfred 1863-1933.......... **TCLC 6**
See also CA 105
See also DLB 10

Sutton, Henry 1935-
See Slavitt, David (R.)

Svevo, Italo 1861-1928 .... **TCLC 2**
See also Schmitz, Ettore

Swados, Elizabeth 1951-..........**CLC 12**
See also CA 97-100

Swados, Harvey 1920-1972 ....**CLC 5**
See also CANR 6
See also CA 5-8R
See also obituary CA 37-40R
See also DLB 2

Swarthout, Glendon (Fred)
1918-.......................**CLC 35**
See also CANR 1
See also CA 1-4R
See also SATA 26

Swenson, May 1919-.......... **CLC 4, 14**
See also CA 5-8R
See also SATA 15
See also DLB 5

Swift, Jonathan 1667-1745........... **LC 1**
See also SATA 19
See also DLB 39

Swinburne, Algernon Charles
1837-1909.................. **TCLC 8**
See also CA 105
See also DLB 35

Swinfen, Ann 19??-................**CLC 34**

Swinnerton, Frank (Arthur)
1884-1982....................**CLC 31**
See also obituary CA 108
See also DLB 34

Symons, Arthur (William)
1865-1945.................. **TCLC 11**
See also CA 107
See also DLB 19

Symons, Julian (Gustave)
1912-................. **CLC 2, 14, 32**
See also CANR 3
See also CA 49-52

Synge, (Edmund) John Millington
1871-1909.................. **TCLC 6**
See also CA 104
See also DLB 10, 19

Syruc, J. 1911-
See Miłosz, Czesław

Tabori, George 1914- ....**CLC 19**
See also CANR 4
See also CA 49-52

Tagore, (Sir) Rabindranath
1861-1941.................. **TCLC 3**
See also Thakura, Ravindranatha

Tamayo y Baus, Manuel
1829-1898.................. **NCLC 1**

Tanizaki, Jun'ichirō
1886-1965.............. **CLC 8, 14, 28**
See also CA 93-96
See also obituary CA 25-28R

Tarkington, (Newton) Booth
1869-1946.................. **TCLC 9**
See also CA 110
See also SATA 17
See also DLB 9

Tate, (John Orley) Allen
1899-1979...... **CLC 2, 4, 6, 9, 11, 14, 24**
See also CA 5-8R
See also obituary CA 85-88
See also DLB 4

Tate, James 1943-........... **CLC 2, 6, 25**
See also CA 21-24R
See also DLB 5

Tavel, Ronald 1940- ....**CLC 6**
See also CA 21-24R

Taylor, C(ecil) P(hillip)
1929-1981....................**CLC 27**
See also CA 25-28R
See also obituary CA 105

Taylor, Eleanor Ross 1920- ....**CLC 5**
See also CA 81-84

Taylor, Elizabeth
1912-1975............... **CLC 2, 4, 29**
See also CANR 9
See also CA 13-16R
See also SATA 13

Taylor, Kamala (Purnaiya) 1924-
See Markandaya, Kamala (Purnaiya)
See also CA 77-80

Taylor, Mildred D(elois) ....**CLC 21**
See also CA 85-88
See also SATA 15, 41

Taylor, Peter (Hillsman)
1917-...................... **CLC 1, 4, 18**
See also CANR 9
See also CA 13-16R
See also DLB-Y 81

Taylor, Robert Lewis 1912-........**CLC 14**
See also CANR 3
See also CA 1-4R
See also SATA 10

Teasdale, Sara 1884-1933........ **TCLC 4**
See also CA 104
See also SATA 32

Tegnér, Esaias 1782-1846........ **NCLC 2**

Teilhard de Chardin, (Marie Joseph) Pierre
1881-1955................... **TCLC 9**
See also CA 105

Tennant, Emma 1937- ....**CLC 13**
See also CANR 10
See also CA 65-68
See also DLB 14

Teran, Lisa St. Aubin de 19??-.....**CLC 36**

Terry, Megan 1932- ....**CLC 19**
See also CA 77-80
See also DLB 7

Tertz, Abram 1925-
See Sinyavsky, Andrei (Donatevich)

Teternikov, Fyodor Kuzmich 1863-1927
See Sologub, Fyodor
See also CA 104

Tey, Josephine 1897-1952 .... **TCLC 14**
See also Mackintosh, Elizabeth

Thackeray, William Makepeace
1811-1863................... **NCLC 5**
See also SATA 23
See also DLB 21

Thakura, Ravindranatha 1861-1941
See Tagore, (Sir) Rabindranath
See also CA 104

Thelwell, Michael (Miles)
1939-........................**CLC 22**
See also CA 101

Theroux, Alexander (Louis)
1939-..................... **CLC 2, 25**
See also CA 85-88

Theroux, Paul
1941-............. **CLC 5, 8, 11, 15, 28**
See also CA 33-36R
See also DLB 2

Thibault, Jacques Anatole Francois
1844-1924
See France, Anatole
See also CA 106

Thiele, Colin (Milton) 1920-........**CLC 17**
See also CANR 12
See also CA 29-32R
See also SATA 14

Thomas, Audrey (Callahan)
1935-...................... **CLC 7, 13**
See also CA 21-24R
See also AITN 2

Thomas, D(onald) M(ichael)
1935-................. **CLC 13, 22, 31**
See also CA 61-64
See also DLB 40

Thomas, Dylan (Marlais)
1914-1953................. **TCLC 1, 8**
See also CA 104
See also DLB 13, 20

Thomas, Edward (Philip)
1878-1917.................. **TCLC 10**
See also CA 106
See also DLB 19

Thomas, John Peter 1928-
See Thomas, Piri

Thomas, Joyce Carol 1938-........**CLC 35**
See also CA 113, 116
See also SATA 40
See also DLB 33

Thomas, Lewis 1913-................**CLC 35**
See also CA 85-88

Thomas, Piri 1928-...............**CLC 17**
See also CA 73-76

Thomas, R(onald) S(tuart)
1913-...................... **CLC 6, 13**
See also CA 89-92
See also DLB 27

Thompson, Francis (Joseph)
1859-1907.................. **TCLC 4**
See also CA 104
See also DLB 19

Thompson, Hunter S(tockton)
1939-..................... **CLC 9, 17**
See also CA 17-20R

Thoreau, Henry David
1817-1862.................. **NCLC 7**
See also DLB 1

Thurber, James (Grover)
1894-1961...........**CLC 5, 11, 25**
See also CA 73-76
See also SATA 13
See also DLB 4, 11, 22

Thurman, Wallace 1902-1934 ..... **TCLC 6**
See also CA 104

Tieck, (Johann) Ludwig
1773-1853................... **NCLC 5**

Van Doren, Mark
1894-1972................ CLC 6, 10
See also CANR 3
See also CA 1-4R
See also obituary CA 37-40R

Van Druten, John (William)
1901-1957.................. TCLC 2
See also CA 104
See also DLB 10

Van Duyn, Mona 1921- .... CLC 3, 7
See also CANR 7
See also CA 9-12R
See also DLB 5

Van Itallie, Jean-Claude 1936- ......CLC 3
See also CAAS 2
See also CANR 1
See also CA 45-48
See also DLB 7

Van Peebles, Melvin 1932-...... CLC 2, 20
See also CA 85-88

Van Vechten, Carl 1880-1964 ......CLC 33
See also obituary CA 89-92
See also DLB 4, 9

Van Vogt, A(lfred) E(lton)
1912-..........................CLC 1
See also CA 21-24R
See also SATA 14
See also DLB 8

Varda, Agnès 1928-...............CLC 16
See also CA 116

Vargas Llosa, (Jorge) Mario (Pedro)
1936-.......... CLC 3, 6, 9, 10, 15, 31
See also CA 73-76

Vassilikos, Vassilis 1933- .... CLC 4, 8
See also CA 81-84

Verga, Giovanni 1840-1922 .... TCLC 3
See also CA 104

Verhaeren, Émile (Adolphe Gustave)
1855-1916.................. TCLC 12
See also CA 109

Verlaine, Paul (Marie)
1844-1896.................. NCLC 2

Verne, Jules (Gabriel)
1828-1905.................. TCLC 6
See also CA 110
See also SATA 21

Very, Jones 1813-1880 .... NCLC 9
See also DLB 1

Vian, Boris 1920-1959 .... TCLC 9
See also CA 106

Viaud, (Louis Marie) Julien 1850-1923
See Loti, Pierre
See also CA 107

Vicker, Angus 1916-
See Felsen, Henry Gregor

Vidal, Eugene Luther, Jr. 1925-
See Vidal, Gore

Vidal, Gore
1925-........CLC 2, 4, 6, 8, 10, 22, 33
See also CANR 13
See also CA 5-8R
See also DLB 6
See also AITN 1

Viereck, Peter (Robert Edwin)
1916-..........................CLC 4
See also CANR 1
See also CA 1-4R
See also DLB 5

Vigny, Alfred (Victor) de
1797-1863................... NCLC 7

Villiers de l'Isle Adam, Jean Marie Mathias Philippe Auguste, Comte de,
1838-1889.................. NCLC 3

Vinge, Joan (Carol) D(ennison)
1948-..........................CLC 30
See also CA 93-96
See also SATA 36

Visconti, Luchino 1906-1976 ....CLC 16
See also CA 81-84
See also obituary CA 65-68

Vittorini, Elio 1908-1966 ..... CLC 6, 9, 14
See also obituary CA 25-28R

Vliet, R(ussell) G. 1929-...........CLC 22
See also CA 37-40R

Voigt, Cynthia 1942-..............CLC 30
See also CA 106
See also SATA 33

Voinovich, Vladimir (Nikolaevich)
1932-..........................CLC 10
See also CA 81-84

Von Daeniken, Erich 1935-
See Von Däniken, Erich
See also CA 37-40R
See also AITN 1

Von Däniken, Erich 1935- ....CLC 30
See also Von Daeniken, Erich

Vonnegut, Kurt, Jr.
1922-...... CLC 1, 2, 3, 4, 5, 8, 12, 22
See also CANR 1
See also CA 1-4R
See also DLB 2, 8
See also DLB-Y 80
See also DLB-DS 3
See also AITN 1

Vorster, Gordon 1924-............CLC 34

Voznesensky, Andrei 1933- ..... CLC 1, 15
See also CA 89-92

Waddington, Miriam 1917-........CLC 28
See also CANR 12
See also CA 21-24R

Wagman, Fredrica 1937-...........CLC 7
See also CA 97-100

Wagner, Richard 1813-1883 ...... NCLC 9

Wagoner, David (Russell)
1926-...................CLC 3, 5, 15
See also CANR 2
See also CA 1-4R
See also SATA 14
See also DLB 5

Wahlöö, Per 1926-1975 ....CLC 7
See also CA 61-64

Wahlöö, Peter 1926-1975
See Wahlöö, Per

Wain, John (Barrington)
1925-................... CLC 2, 11, 15
See also CA 5-8R
See also DLB 15, 27

Wajda, Andrzej 1926-.............CLC 16
See also CA 102

Wakefield, Dan 1932-..............CLC 7
See also CA 21-24R

Wakoski, Diane
1937-.............. CLC 2, 4, 7, 9, 11
See also CAAS 1
See also CANR 9
See also CA 13-16R
See also DLB 5

Walcott, Derek (Alton)
1930-............. CLC 2, 4, 9, 14, 25
See also CA 89-92
See also DLB-Y 81

Waldman, Anne 1945- ....CLC 7
See also CA 37-40R
See also DLB 16

Waldo, Edward Hamilton 1918-
See Sturgeon, Theodore (Hamilton)

Walker, Alice
1944-.............. CLC 5, 6, 9, 19, 27
See also CANR 9
See also CA 37-40R
See also SATA 31
See also DLB 6, 33

Walker, David Harry 1911-........CLC 14
See also CANR 1
See also CA 1-4R
See also SATA 8

Walker, Edward Joseph 1934-
See Walker, Ted
See also CA 21-24R

Walker, Joseph A. 1935- ....CLC 19
See also CA 89-92
See also DLB 38

Walker, Margaret (Abigail)
1915-...................... CLC 1, 6
See also CA 73-76

Walker, Ted 1934-...............CLC 13
See also Walker, Edward Joseph
See also DLB 40

Wallace, Irving 1916- .... CLC 7, 13
See also CAAS 1
See also CANR 1
See also CA 1-4R
See also AITN 1

Wallant, Edward Lewis
1926-1962................. CLC 5, 10
See also CA 1-4R
See also DLB 2, 28

Walpole, Horace 1717-1797.......... LC 2
See also DLB 39

Walpole, (Sir) Hugh (Seymour)
1884-1941.................. TCLC 5
See also CA 104
See also DLB 34

Walser, Martin 1927-..............CLC 27
See also CANR 8
See also CA 57-60

Walser, Robert 1878-1956 .... TCLC 18

Walsh, Gillian Paton 1939-
See Walsh, Jill Paton
See also CA 37-40R
See also SATA 4

Walsh, Jill Paton 1939-............CLC 35
See also CLR 2

White, E(lwyn) B(rooks)
1899-1985 . . . . CLC 10, 34
See also CLR 1
See also CANR 16
See also CA 13-16R
See also obituary CA 116
See also SATA 2, 29
See also DLB 11, 22
See also AITN 2

White, Edmund III 1940- . . . . .CLC 27
See also CANR 3
See also CA 45-48

White, Patrick (Victor Martindale)
1912- . . . . CLC 3, 4, 5, 7, 9, 18
See also CA 81-84

White, T(erence) H(anbury)
1906-1964 . . . . .CLC 30
See also CA 73-76
See also SATA 12

White, Walter (Francis)
1893-1955 . . . . TCLC 15
See also CA 115

Whitehead, E(dward) A(nthony)
1933- .CLC 5
See also CA 65-68

Whitman, Walt 1819-1892 . . . . NCLC 4
See also SATA 20
See also DLB 3

Whittemore, (Edward) Reed (Jr.)
1919- .CLC 4
See also CANR 4
See also CA 9-12R
See also DLB 5

Whittier, John Greenleaf
1807-1892 . . . . NCLC 8
See also DLB 1

Wicker, Thomas Grey 1926-
See Wicker, Tom
See also CA 65-68

Wicker, Tom 1926- . . . . .CLC 7
See also Wicker, Thomas Grey

Wideman, John Edgar
1941- . . . . CLC 5, 34, 36
See also CANR 14
See also CA 85-88
See also DLB 33

Wiebe, Rudy (H.) 1934- . . . . . CLC 6, 11, 14
See also CA 37-40R

Wieners, John 1934- . . . . .CLC 7
See also CA 13-16R
See also DLB 16

Wiesel, Elie(zer) 1928- . . . . CLC 3, 5, 11
See also CANR 8
See also CA 5-8R
See also AITN 1

Wight, James Alfred 1916-
See Herriot, James
See also CA 77-80

Wilbur, Richard (Purdy)
1921- . . . . .CLC 3, 6, 9, 14
See also CANR 2
See also CA 1-4R
See also SATA 9
See also DLB 5

Wild, Peter 1940- . . . . .CLC 14
See also CA 37-40R
See also DLB 5

Wilde, Oscar (Fingal O'Flahertie Wills)
1854-1900 . . . . TCLC 1, 8
See also CA 104
See also SATA 24
See also DLB 10, 19, 34

Wilder, Billy 1906- . . . . .CLC 20
See also Wilder, Samuel
See also DLB 26

Wilder, Samuel 1906-
See Wilder, Billy
See also CA 89-92

Wilder, Thornton (Niven)
1897-1975 . . . . . . CLC 1, 5, 6, 10, 15, 35
See also CA 13-16R
See also obituary CA 61-64
See also DLB 4, 7, 9
See also AITN 2

Wilhelm, Kate 1928- . . . . .CLC 7
See also CA 37-40R
See also DLB 8

Willard, Nancy 1936- . . . . .CLC 7
See also CLR 5
See also CANR 10
See also CA 89-92
See also SATA 30, 37
See also DLB 5

Williams, C(harles) K(enneth)
1936- .CLC 33
See also CA 37-40R
See also DLB 5

Williams, Charles (Walter Stansby)
1886-1945 . . . . TCLC 1, 11
See also CA 104

Williams, (George) Emlyn
1905- .CLC 15
See also CA 104
See also DLB 10

Williams, John A(lfred)
1925- . . . . CLC 5, 13
See also CANR 6
See also CA 53-56
See also DLB 2, 33

Williams, Jonathan (Chamberlain)
1929- .CLC 13
See also CANR 8
See also CA 9-12R
See also DLB 5

Williams, Joy 1944- . . . . .CLC 31
See also CA 41-44R

Williams, Paulette 1948-
See Shange, Ntozake

Williams, Tennessee
1911-1983 . . . . CLC 1, 2, 5, 7, 8, 11,
                                          15, 19, 30
See also CA 5-8R
See also obituary CA 108
See also DLB 7
See also DLB-Y 83
See also DLB-DS 4
See also AITN 1, 2

Williams, Thomas (Alonzo)
1926- .CLC 14
See also CANR 2
See also CA 1-4R

Williams, Thomas Lanier 1911-1983
See Williams, Tennessee

Williams, William Carlos
1883-1963 . . . . . . CLC 1, 2, 5, 9, 13, 22
See also CA 89-92
See also DLB 4, 16

Williamson, Jack 1908- . . . . .CLC 29
See also Williamson, John Stewart
See also DLB 8

Williamson, John Stewart 1908-
See Williamson, Jack
See also CA 17-20R

Willingham, Calder (Baynard, Jr.)
1922- .CLC 5
See also CANR 3
See also CA 5-8R
See also DLB 2

Wilson, A(ndrew) N(orman)
1950- .CLC 33
See also CA 112
See also DLB 14

Wilson, Andrew 1948-
See Wilson, Snoo

Wilson, Angus (Frank Johnstone)
1913- . . . . CLC 2, 3, 5, 25, 34
See also CA 5-8R
See also DLB 15

Wilson, Brian 1942- . . . . .CLC 12

Wilson, Colin 1931- . . . . CLC 3, 14
See also CANR 1
See also CA 1-4R
See also DLB 14

Wilson, Edmund
1895-1972 . . . . CLC 1, 2, 3, 8, 24
See also CANR 1
See also CA 1-4R
See also obituary CA 37-40R

Wilson, Ethel Davis (Bryant)
1888-1980 . . . . .CLC 13
See also CA 102

Wilson, John 1785-1854 . . . . NCLC 5

Wilson, John (Anthony) Burgess 1917-
See Burgess, Anthony
See also CANR 2
See also CA 1-4R

Wilson, Lanford 1937- . . . . . . CLC 7, 14, 36
See also CA 17-20R
See also DLB 7

Wilson, Robert (M.) 1944- . . . . CLC 7, 9
See also CANR 2
See also CA 49-52

Wilson, Sloan 1920- . . . . .CLC 32
See also CANR 1
See also CA 1-4R

Wilson, Snoo 1948- . . . . .CLC 33
See also CA 69-72

Winters, (Arthur) Yvor
1900-1968 . . . . CLC 4, 8, 32
See also CAP 1
See also CA 11-12
See also obituary CA 25-28R

Wiseman, Frederick 1930- . . . . .CLC 20

Witkiewicz, Stanislaw Ignacy
1885-1939 . . . . TCLC 8
See also CA 105

Wittig, Monique 1935?- . . . . .CLC 22
See also CA 116

Cumulative Index to Nationalities

AMERICAN

Alcott, Amos Bronson **1**
Alcott, Louisa May **6**
Alger, Jr., Horatio **8**
Allston, Washington **2**
Bellamy, Edward **4**
Bird, Robert Montgomery **1**
Brackenridge, Hugh Henry **7**
Brown, William Wells **2**
Bryant, William Cullen **6**
Child, Lydia Maria **6**
Cooke, John Esten **5**
Cooper, James Fenimore **1**
Crockett, David **8**
Douglass, Frederick **7**
Dunlap, William **2**
Emerson, Ralph Waldo **1**
Field, Eugene **3**
Frederic, Harold **10**
Freneau, Philip Morin **1**
Fuller, Margaret **5**
Hammon, Jupiter **5**
Hawthorne, Nathaniel **2, 10**
Irving, Washington **2**
Jefferson, Thomas **11**
Kennedy, John Pendleton **2**
Lanier, Sidney **6**
Lazarus, Emma **8**
Longfellow, Henry
  Wadsworth **2**
Lowell, James Russell **2**
Melville, Herman **3**
Paulding, James Kirke **2**
Poe, Edgar Allan **1**
Rowson, Susanna Haswell **5**
Simms, William Gilmore **3**
Stowe, Harriet Beecher **3**
Thoreau, Henry David **7**
Tyler, Royall **3**

Very, Jones **9**
Whitman, Walt **4**
Whittier, John Greenleaf **8**

AUSTRIAN

Grillparzer, Franz **1**

DANISH

Andersen, Hans Christian **7**
Grundtvig, Nicolai Frederik
  Severin **1**

ENGLISH

Arnold, Matthew **6**
Austen, Jane **1**
Bagehot, Walter **10**
Beardsley, Aubrey **6**
Beddoes, Thomas Lovell **3**
Borrow, George **9**
Brontë, Anne **4**
Brontë, Charlotte **3, 8**
Browning, Elizabeth Barrett **1**
Bulwer-Lytton, Edward **1**
Byron, George Gordon, Lord
  Byron **2**
Carroll, Lewis **2**
Clare, John **9**
Coleridge, Samuel Taylor **9**
Collins, Wilkie **1**
Cowper, William **8**
De Quincey, Thomas **4**
Dickens, Charles **3, 8**
Disraeli, Benjamin **2**
Eden, Emily **10**
Eliot, George **4**
FitzGerald, Edward **9**

Forster, John **11**
Gaskell, Elizabeth Cleghorn **5**
Hunt, Leigh **1**
Jerrold, Douglas **2**
Keats, John **8**
Lamb, Charles **10**
Lear, Edward **3**
Lewis, Matthew Gregory **11**
Marryat, Frederick **3**
Mill, John Stuart **11**
Mitford, Mary Russell **4**
Montagu, Elizabeth **7**
Morris, William **4**
Pater, Walter **7**
Patmore, Coventry Kersey
  Dighton **9**
Radcliffe, Ann **6**
Reade, Charles **2**
Rossetti, Christina Georgina **2**
Rossetti, Dante Gabriel **4**
Southey, Robert **8**
Thackeray, William
  Makepeace **5**
Trollope, Anthony **6**

FRENCH

Balzac, Honoré de **5**
Banville, Théodore de **9**
Barbey d'Aurevilly, Jules
  Amédée **1**
Baudelaire, Charles **6**
Becque, Henri **3**
Chateaubriand, François René
  de **3**
Constant, Benjamin **6**
Daudet, Alphonse **1**
Dumas, Alexandre (père) **11**
Dumas, Alexandre (fils) **9**

Flaubert, Gustave **2, 10**
Fromentin, Eugène **10**
Gautier, Théophile **1**
Goncourt, Edmond de **7**
Goncourt, Jules de **7**
Hugo, Victor Marie **3, 10**
Joubert, Joseph **9**
Laclos, Pierre Ambroise
  François Choderlos de **4**
Laforgue, Jules **5**
Lamartine, Alphonse de **11**
Mallarmé, Stéphane **4**
Maupassant, Guy de **1**
Mérimée, Prosper **6**
Musset, Alfred de **7**
Nerval, Gérard de **1**
Rimbaud, Arthur **4**
Sade, Donatien Alphonse
  François, Comte de **3**
Sainte-Beuve, Charles
  Augustin **5**
Sand, George **2**
Staël-Holstein, Anne Louise
  Germaine Necker, Baronne
  de **3**
Sue, Eugène **1**
Tocqueville, Alexis de **7**
Verlaine, Paul **2**
Vigny, Alfred de **7**
Villiers de l'Isle Adam, Jean
  Marie Mathias Philippe
  Auguste, Comte de **3**

GERMAN

Arnim, Achim von **5**
Brentano, Clemens **1**
Droste-Hülshoff, Annette Freiin
  von **3**

529

Eichendorff, Joseph Freiherr
  von 8
Fouqué, Friedrich de La
  Motte 2
Goethe, Johann Wolfgang
  von 4
Grabbe, Christian Dietrich 2
Grimm, Jakob Ludwig Karl 3
Grimm, Wilhelm Karl 3
Heine, Heinrich 4
Herder, Johann Gottfried
  von 8
Hoffmann, Ernst Theodor
  Amadeus 2
Immermann, Karl 4
Jean Paul 7
Kleist, Heinrich von 2
Klinger, Friedrich Maximilian
  von 1
Klopstock, Friedrich 11
Ludwig, Otto 4
Mörike, Eduard 10
Storm, Theodor 1
Tieck, Ludwig 5
Wagner, Richard 9

IRISH
Carleton, William 3
Croker, John Wilson 10
Darley, George 2
Edgeworth, Maria 1
Griffin, Gerald 7
Le Fanu, Joseph Sheridan 9
Maginn, William 8
Maturin, Charles Robert 6
Moore, Thomas 6
Sheridan, Richard Brinsley 5

ITALIAN
Foscolo, Ugo 8

NORWEGIAN
Wergeland, Henrik Arnold 5

POLISH
Fredro, Aleksander 8
Krasicki, Ignacy 8
Krasiński, Zygmunt 4
Mickiewicz, Adam 3

RUSSIAN
Aksakov, Sergei
  Timofeyvich 2

Belinski, Vissarion
  Grigoryevich 5
Chernyshevsky, Nikolay
  Gavrilovich 1
Dobrolyubov, Nikolai
  Alexandrovich· 5
Dostoevski, Fedor
  Mikhailovich 2, 7
Gogol, Nikolai 5
Goncharov, Ivan
  Alexandrovich 1
Herzen, Aleksandr
  Ivanovich 10
Karamzin, Nikolai
  Mikhailovich 3
Krylov, Ivan Andreevich 1
Lermontov, Mikhail
  Yuryevich 5
Nekrasov, Nikolai 11
Pushkin, Alexander 3

SCOTTISH
Baillie, Joanna 2
Ferrier, Susan 8
Galt, John 1

Hogg, James 4
Lockhart, John Gibson 6
Oliphant, Margaret 11
Stevenson, Robert Louis 5
Wilson, John 5

SPANISH
Alarcón, Pedro Antonio de 1
Caballero, Fernán 10
Castro, Rosalía de 3
Tamayo y Baus, Manuel 1
Zorrilla y Moral, José 6

SWEDISH
Bremer, Fredrika 11
Tegnér, Esias 2

SWISS
Amiel, Henri Frédéric 4
Keller, Gottfried 2
Wyss, Johann David 10

Cumulative Index to Critics

Critic Index

Day, Robert A.
Eugene Field 3:212

De Bellis, Jack
Sidney Lanier 6:274

De la Mare, Walter
Lewis Carroll 2:111
Wilkie Collins 1:184
Christina Georgina Rossetti
2:568

DeLaura, David J.
Walter Pater 7:334

Delille, Edward
Guy de Maupassant 1:449
Paul Verlaine 2:617

Demorest, D. L.
Gustave Flaubert 10:127

Deneke, H. C.
Jean Paul 7:235

Dennett, J. R.
James Russell Lowell 2:508
Harriet Beecher Stowe 3:553

Dennie, Joseph
Philip Morin Freneau 1:313

Dennis, Carl
Jones Very 9:389

Denny, Norman
Victor Marie Hugo 10:377

Denommé, Robert T.
Théodore de Banville 9:27
Alphonse de Lamartine 11:281
Alfred de Vigny 7:480

De Quincey, Thomas
John Clare 9:80
Samuel Taylor Coleridge 9:148
Thomas De Quincey 4:62
John Forster 11:96
Johann Wolfgang von Goethe
4:170
Johann Gottfried von Herder
8:296
Jean Paul 7:224
Charles Lamb 10:395, 396
Ludwig Tieck 5:511
John Wilson 5:553

De Selincourt, Basil
Walt Whitman 4:561

De Sélincourt, E.
John Keats 8:342

Dessaix, Robert
Guy de Maupassant 1:477

De Vere, Aubrey
Coventry Kersey Dighton
Patmore 9:331

Dewey, Horace W.
Nikolai Mikhailovich Karamzin
3:282

Diaconoff, Suellen
Pierre Ambroise François
Choderlos de Laclos 4:340

Dicey, A. V.
Walter Bagehot 10:22
Alexis de Tocqueville 7:427

Dickens, Charles
Wilkie Collins 1:174
George Eliot 4:92
John Forster 11:95
Douglas Jerrold 2:395
Harriet Beecher Stowe 3:537
William Makepeace Thackeray
5:462

Dickey, James
Matthew Arnold 6:73

Dickson, Keith A.
Otto Ludwig 4:361, 363

Dilke, Charles Wentworth
George Darley 2:124

Dillon, E. J.
Adam Mickiewicz 3:391

Dobrée, Bonamy
Charles Lamb 10:423

**Dobrolyubov, Nikolai
Aleksandrovich**
Vissarion Grigoryevich Belinski
5:93
Fedor Mikhailovich Dostoevski
2:157
Ivan Alexandrovich Goncharov
1:359

Dobrzycki, Stanislaw
Ignacy Krasicki 8:398

Dodds, John W.
William Makepeace Thackeray
5:481

Donaghy, J. Lyle
William Maginn 8:441

Donne, William Bodham
George Borrow 9:41

Donner, H. W.
Thomas Lovell Beddoes 3:38

Donoghue, Denis
Walt Whitman 4:600

Donovan, Robert Alan
Charles Dickens 8:188

Dostoevski, Fedor Mikhailovich
Fedor Mikhailovich Dostoevski
2:158; 7:69
Ernst Theodor Amadeus
Hoffmann 2:340
Alexander Pushkin 3:424
George Sand 2:594

Dostoievsky, F. M.
See also **Dostoevski, Fedor
Mikhailovich**
Vissarion Grigoryevich Belinski
5:95
Aleksandr Ivanovich Herzen
10:326
Nikolai Alekseevich Nekrasov
11:399

Doubleday, Neal Frank
Mary Russell Mitford 4:407

Douglas, Ann
Margaret Fuller 5:168

Douglas, George
Susan Ferrier 8:243
John Galt 1:333
John Wilson 5:561

Douglas, Malcolm
Horatio Alger, Jr. 8:17

Douglas, Stephen Arnold
Thomas Jefferson 11:155

Douglass, Elisha P.
Thomas Jefferson 11:191

Douglass, Frederick
Frederick Douglass 7:123

Doumic, René
George Sand 2:602

Dowden, Edward
William Cowper 8:115
George Eliot 4:105
Heinrich Heine 4:244
Victor Hugo 3:266
Dante Gabriel Rossetti 4:499
Robert Southey 8:468
Walt Whitman 4:547

Dowling, Linda C.
Aubrey Beardsley 6:152

Doyle, Arthur Conan
George Borrow 9:52
Robert Louis Stevenson 5:408

Drinkwater, John
William Morris 4:431

Driver, C. H.
Walter Bagehot 10:36

Driver, Tom F.
Richard Wagner 9:471

Dubruck, Alfred
Gérard de Nerval 1:483

Duclaux, Madame
Victor Marie Hugo 10:368

**Dudevant, Amandine Aurore
Lucile Dupin**
See **Sand, George**

Duff, J. D.
Sergei Timofeyvich Aksakov
2:12

Dugan, John Raymond
Guy de Maupassant 1:469

Duganne, Augustine J. H.
John Greenleaf Whittier 8:490

Dukes, Ashley
Henri Becque 3:15

Dumas, Alexandre
Alexandre Dumas (*père*) 11:41,
60

Dumesnil, René
Gustave Flaubert 2:247

Dunbar, Paul Laurence
Frederick Douglass 7:127

Dunham, T. C.
Franz Grillparzer 1:387

**Dunin-Borkowski, Alexander
(Leszek)**
Aleksander Fredro 8:283

Dunlap, William
William Dunlap 2:209
Royall Tyler 3:571

Dunn, John J.
Coventry Kersey Dighton
Patmore 9:362, 363

Durant, David
Ann Radcliffe 6:443

Durant, Will
Gustave Flaubert 2:243

Dustin, John E.
Anthony Trollope 6:499

Duthie, Enid L.
Elizabeth Cleghorn Gaskell
5:203

Duyckinck, Evert A.
Nathaniel Hawthorne 10:269
Washington Irving 2:374
Herman Melville 3:328, 330

Dyboski, Roman
Aleksander Fredro 8:284
Zygmunt Krasiński 4:307

Dyson, A. E.
Matthew Arnold 6:65
Samuel Taylor Coleridge 9:210
William Makepeace Thackeray
5:493

Dyson, H.V.D.
Charles Lamb 10:422

Eagle, Solomon
See also **Squire, J. C.**
Johann David Wyss 10:469

Eagleton, Terry
Anne Brontë 4:54

Easson, Angus
Douglas Jerrold 2:408

Eccles, F. Y.
Harold Frederic 10:185

Eckford, Henry
Eugène Fromentin 10:228

Eckstrom, Fanny Hardy
Henry David Thoreau 7:368

Eco, Umberto
Eugène Sue 1:561

Eddings, Dennis W.
Edgar Allan Poe 1:526

Edel, Leon
Henry David Thoreau 7:405

Eden, Anthony
Emily Eden 10:106, 107

Eden, Emily
Emily Eden 10:103

Edgell, David P.
Amos Bronson Alcott 1:26

Edgeworth, Maria
Elizabeth Cleghorn Gaskell
5:176

Edwards, P. D.
Anthony Trollope 6:511

Eells, John Shepard, Jr.
Matthew Arnold 6:62

Eggert, Carl Edgar
Heinrich Heine 4:247

Ehre, Milton
Ivan Alexandrovich Goncharov
1:375

Eichelberger, Clayton L.
Harold Frederic 10:206

Ekeblad, Inga-Stina
Anne Brontë 4:47

Critic Index

Critic Index

Critic Index

Critic Index

Critic Index

Critic Index

Critic Index

Critic Index

Critic Index